CURRENT
BIOGRAPHY

CURRENT
BIOGRAPHY

WHO'S NEWS AND WHY

1946

EDITED BY

Anna Rothe

THE H. W. WILSON COMPANY
NEW YORK, N. Y.

SEVENTH ANNUAL CUMULATION—1946

PRINTED IN THE UNITED STATES OF AMERICA

Copyright 1947
by
THE H. W. WILSON COMPANY

Preface

International affairs of great moment held the attention of the world press during 1946. That many of these events centered about United Nations personages is reflected in CURRENT BIOGRAPHY's 1946 Yearbook. Other important figures—heads of new governments, and new Cabinet members both in the United States and abroad—came into the news. In the United States, too, the second year of the Truman Administration is represented by a number of Presidential appointees. The 1946 scene was also occupied by men and women prominent in the social sciences, education, business, labor, and the arts—to name a few of the groups listed in the "Classification by Profession" at the back of this volume.

All the biographies which have appeared in CURRENT BIOGRAPHY during seven years are recorded in the "Cumulated Index—1940-1946," which begins on page 696. Users of this Yearbook should therefore consult that index if this annual does not contain the biographies they wish to read. The index will show, for example, that the biographies of the present Secretary of War, Robert P. Patterson, and scientist Harold C. Urey appear in the 1941 Yearbook; and that General Eisenhower's biography is contained in the 1942 volume. Reference librarians will find the seven-year index of particular value: it includes references to the monthly issues as well as to the Yearbooks published since 1940.

Like the volumes of the past six years, 1946 CURRENT BIOGRAPHY Yearbook is a one-alphabet cumulation of the biographical articles and obituary notices that appeared in the year's monthly issues. However, before the articles were reprinted in the Yearbook, they were revised, when necessary, to include events that occurred in 1946 after the publication of those articles in the monthly numbers. While many biographies were thus rounded out as of December 31, 1946, that deadline of necessity left some matters pending at the close of the year.

The assembling of material for these biographies entails thorough-going research. Files of clippings are drawn upon when a name is selected for inclusion in CURRENT BIOGRAPHY. Indexes to magazine articles and books guide writers to a mass of information which is culled for biographical and background facts. Various "Who's Whos," encyclopedias, and other reference works contribute data. Information is also obtained from government offices and a variety of commercial and educational organizations. Whenever it is possible to get in touch with the subjects of the biographies, they are asked to confirm or correct facts; it should be pointed out, however, that these are not authorized biographies. The biographees, too, may send their own photographs, although a number of the prints are procured from photographers, who are given due credit. The Press Association, Inc., 50 Rockefeller Plaza, New York, is the source of those photographs not supplied by biographees or photographers.

The following members of CURRENT BIOGRAPHY's present staff of writers shared with the editor in the preparation of this Yearbook: Helen Alperin, Constance Elioplos, Edith Faigman, Patricia Healy, Ruth Mann, Corinne Posner, Marian Prince, and Dana Rush. Other writers and revisers who assisted are Selma Cohen, Lorraine Goverman, Joan Kaufman, Katharine Ryder, and Frances Wallace.

A. R.

Contents

Explanations

Authorities for biographees' full names, with few exceptions, are the bibliographical publications of The Wilson Company. When a biographee prefers a certain name form, that is indicated in the heading of the article. For example, "Nelson, (John) Byron (Jr.)" means that Nelson prefers to be called Byron Nelson; and when a professional name like "Pickford, Mary" is used in the heading, the real name—in her case Gladys Mary Smith—appears in the article itself.

The heading of each article includes the pronunciation of the name if it is difficult, date of birth (if obtainable), and occupation. The article is supplemented by a list of references to sources of biographical information, in two alphabets: (1) newspapers and periodicals, (2) books. Space limitation requires that these bibliographies be kept short, but an effort is made to include the most useful references.

References to newspapers and periodicals are listed in abbreviated form; for example, "Sat Eve Post 217:14-15 S 30 '44 por" means *Saturday Evening Post*, volume 217, pages 14-15, for September 30, 1944, with portrait. (See the section "Periodicals and Newspapers Consulted" for full names of the publications.) The books given as references are limited to those of a biographical nature, including such reference works as *Who's Who in America, Living Musicians*, etc. (See the section "Biographical References Consulted" for complete list.) Each obituary notice includes full dates when that information is available, and the reference is to the New York *Times*. When a name in the body of an article is followed by '40, '41, '42, '43, '44, '45, or '46, the reference is to the CURRENT BIOGRAPHY Yearbook in which a biography of that person appears.

As indicated in the table of contents, this volume contains three name indexes, the purposes of which are self-evident. The all-inclusive index—the cumulated index to the biographies and obituary notices in the seven volumes of CURRENT BIOGRAPHY published thus far—includes references to monthly issues as well as to Yearbooks.

Key to Pronunciation
(Based on Webster's Guide to Pronunciation *)

ā	āle	N	Not pronounced, but indicates the nasal tone of the preceding vowel, as in the French *bon* (bôN).	û	cūbe
â	câre			û	ûrn; French eu, as in *jeu* (zhû); German ö, oe, as in *schön* (chûn), *Goethe* (gû′tĕ).
ă	ădd				
ȧ	loyȧl				
ä	ärm				
à	àsk				
ạ	sofạ			ŭ	tŭb
ē	ēve	ō	ōld	ü	Pronounced approximately as ē, with rounded lips: French u, as in *menu* (mē-nü′); German ü, as in *grün*.
ĕ	ĕnd	ô	ôrb		
ē	makēr	ŏ	ŏdd		
		oi	oil		
g	go	ōō	ōōze		
		ŏŏ	fŏŏt		
ī	īce	ou	out		
ĭ	ĭll			zh	azure
ᴋ	German ch as in *ich* (ĭᴋ)	*th*	then	′ = main accent
		th	thin	″ = secondary accent

(* Exceptions: *th* in then; main and secondary accents.)

KEY TO ABBREVIATIONS

AAA — Agricultural Adjustment Administration
A.A.A.A. — Amateur Athletic Association of America
AAF — Army Air Forces
A.A.U. — Amateur Athletic Union
A.A.U.W. — American Association of University Women
ABC — American Broadcasting Company
A.C.L.U. — American Civil Liberties Union
ADA — Americans for Democratic Action
AEC — Atomic Energy Commission
AEF — American Expeditionary Force
A.F. of L. — American Federation of Labor
Ag — August
A.L.A. — American Library Association
A.M.A. — American Medical Association
AMG — Allied Military Government
ANT — American Negro Theatre
Ap — April
A.P. — Associated Press
ASCAP — American Society of Composers, Authors and Publishers
ASF — Army Service Forces
ASNE — American Society of Newspaper Editors
ATC — Air Transport Command
AVC — American Veterans Committee
AWVS — American Women's Voluntary Services
AYC — American Youth Congress
b. — business address
B.A. — Bachelor of Arts
BBC — British Broadcasting Corporation
B.D. — Bachelor of Divinity
BEF — British Expeditionary Force
B.L.S. — Bachelor of Library Science
B.S. — Bachelor of Science
C.B. — Companion of the Bath
C.B.E. — Commander of (the Order of) the British Empire
CBS — Columbia Broadcasting System
CCC — Civilian Conservation Corps
C.E. — Civil Engineer
C.E.D. — Committee for Economic Development
CIO — Congress of Industrial Organizations
C.M.G. — Companion of (the Order of) St. Michael and St. George
Com. — Commodore
C.P.A. — Certified Public Accountant
C.S.C. — Congregatio Sanctae Crucis (Congregation of the Holy Cross)
CWA — Civil Works Administration
CWS — Chemical Warfare Service
D — December
D.A.R. — Daughters of the American Revolution
D.C.L. — Doctor of Civil Law
D.D. — Doctor of Divinity
D.Eng. — Doctor of Engineering
D.F.C. — Distinguished Flying Cross
D.J. — Doctor of Jurisprudence
D.Lit. — Doctor of Literature
D.Mus. — Doctor of Music
D, Pol. Sc. — Doctor of Political Science
Dr. — Doctor
D.Sc. — Doctor of Science
D.S.C. — Distinguished Service Cross
D.S.M. — Distinguished Service Medal
D.S.O. — Distinguished Service Order
EDB — Economic Defense Board
F — February
FAO — Food and Agriculture Organization
FBI — Federal Bureau of Investigation
FCA — Farm Credit Administration
FCC — Federal Communications Commission

FEPC — Fair Employment Practice Committee
FERA — Federal Emergency Relief Administration
F.F.I. — French Forces of the Interior
FHA — Federal Housing Administration
FSA — Farm Security Administration
FTC — Federal Trade Commission
G.B.E. — Knight or Dame Grand Cross Order of the British Empire
G.C.B. — Knight Grand Cross of the Bath
G.C.V.O. — Knight Grand Cross of Royal Victorian Order
GHQ — General Headquarters
GSO — General Staff Officer
h. — home address
H.M. — His Majesty
HOLC — Home Owners' Loan Corporation
ICC — Interstate Commerce Commission
I.F.T.U. — International Federation of Trade Unions
I.L.A. — International Longshoremen's Association
I.L.G.W.U. — International Ladies' Garment Workers' Union
I.L.O. — International Labor Office
I.L.P. — Independent Labour Party
INS — International News Service
I.W.W. — Industrial Workers of the World
J — Journal
Ja — January
J.C.B. — Juris Canonici Bachelor
J.D. — Doctor of Jurisprudence
Je — June
Jl — July
K.B.E. — Knight of (the Order of) the British Empire
K.C. — King's Council
K.C.B. — Knight Commander of the Bath
L.H.D. — Doctor of Humanities
Litt.D. — Doctor of Letters
LL.B. — Bachelor of Laws
LL.D. — Doctor of Laws
LL.M. — Master of Laws
M.A. — Master of Arts
mag — magazine
M.B.A. — Master of Business Administration
MBS — Mutual Broadcasting System
M.C. — Military Cross
M.C.E. — Master of Civil Engineering
M.Com. — Master of Commerce
M.D. — Doctor of Medicine
M.E. — Master of Engineering
MGM — Metro-Goldwyn-Mayer
Mgr. — Monsignor, Monseigneur
M.Lit. — Master of Literature
M.P. — Member of Parliament
M.P.P.D.A. — Motion Picture Producers and Distributors of America
Mr — March
MRP — Mouvement Républicain Populaire
M.Sc. — Master of Science
MVA — Missouri Valley Authority
My — May
N — November
NAACP — National Association for the Advancement of Colored People
NAB — National Association of Broadcasters
NAM — National Association of Manufacturers
NBC — National Broadcasting Company
N.E.A. — National Education Association
NFTW — National Federation of Telephone Workers
NLRB — National Labor Relations Board
N.M.U. — National Maritime Union
NRA — National Recovery Administration
NRPB — National Resources Planning Board

ns — new series
NYA — National Youth Administration
O — October
OCD — Office of Civilian Defense
ODT — Office of Defense Transportation
OPA — Office of Price Administration
OPM — Office of Production Management
OWI — Office of War Information
OWMR — Office of War Mobilization and Reconversion
PAC — Political Action Committee
P.C. — Privy Councilor
PCA — Progressive Citizens of America
P.E.N. — Poets, Playwrights, Editors, Essayists and Novelists (International Association)
PGA — Professional Golfers Association
Ph.B. — Bachelor of Philosophy
Ph.D. — Doctor of Philosophy
por — portrait, -s
POW — Prisoner of War
PWA — Public Works Administration
RAF — Royal Air Force
RCA — Radio Corporation of America
REA — Rural Electrification Administration
RFC — Reconstruction Finance Corporation
RKO — Radio Keith Orpheum
RRA — Retraining and Reemployment Administration
S — September
SEC — Securities and Exchange Commission
SHAEF — Supreme Headquarters, Allied Expeditionary Force
S.J.D. — Doctor of Juridical Science
SPA — Surplus Property Administration
SPAB — Supply Priorities and Allocation Board
SSB — Social Security Board
S.T.B. — Bachelor of Sacred Theology
S.T.D. — Doctor of Sacred Theology
S.W.O.C. — Steel Workers' Organizing Committee
SWPC — Smaller War Plants Corporation
TERA — Temporary Emergency Relief Administration
TNEC — Temporary National Economic Committee translator
TVA — Tennessee Valley Authority
TWA — Transcontinental and Western Air, Inc
TWUA — Textile Workers Union of America
U.A.W.A. — United Auto Workers of America
U.M.W.A. — United Mine Workers of America
U.N. — United Nations
UNESCO — United Nations Educational, Scientific, and Cultural Organization
UNRRA — United Nations Relief and Rehabilitation Administration
U.P. — United Press
USO — United Service Organizations
U.S.S.R. — Union of Socialist Soviet Republics
VA — Veterans Administration
V.F.W. — Veterans of Foreign Wars
WAA — War Assets Administration
W.C.T.U. — Woman's Christian Temperance Union
WFA — War Food Administration
WLA — Women's Land Army
WLB — War Labor Board
WMC — War Manpower Commission
WPA — Work Projects Administration
WPB — War Production Board

ABERCROMBIE, SIR (LESLIE) PAT-RICK 1879- British architect and town planner

Address: b. London University College, Gower St., London

The plan for the re-creation of London after the devastation caused by enemy bombardment in World War II is the work of Sir Patrick Abercrombie. His proposals for the London of tomorrow, to be achieved in the course of fifty years, involve more than ten million people, twenty-seven hundred square miles, the moving of more than one million individuals to new homes, and the building of ten new "satellite" towns separated from Greater London by a green belt of countryside. Also serving as chief consultant for the replanning and re-building of many other British cities and towns, Abercrombie has achieved "architectural miracles" which have been compared to those wrought by Sir Christopher Wren in the seventeenth century.

Leslie Patrick Abercrombie was born at Ashton-upon-Mersey in 1879, one of nine children of a Manchester stockbroker. His father, William Abercrombie, who had come originally from Fifeshire, was a devotee of William Morris. Patrick Abercrombie was thus reared in an atmosphere of literature and good design, and does not remember that he ever thought of being anything but an architect.

After receiving his schooling at Locker's Park and Uppingham, Abercrombie entered upon six years of practical experience in the offices of Manchester and Liverpool architects, where he became expert in the essentials of civic planning. Possessed of a literary faculty, he wrote many articles for the early numbers of *Town Planning Review,* of which he became the first editor. At this time Dublin was inviting architects of all nations to submit plans for the planning of the city. In collaboration with a friend (Sydney Kelly), Abercrombie entered the competition and was declared the winner in 1913. Two years later he became professor of civic design in the School of Architecture at Liverpool University. Since this was a new subject for university study, the architect sought to fuse academic knowledge with practical study. A traveling fellowship enabled him to go to the Continent every year to study the cities of Berlin, Brussels, Paris, and Vienna. From his application of the new art and science of town planning came the many projects he developed, with others, for English towns and areas. Among them were places like Bristol, Bath, Sheffield, East Kent,

British Official Photo.

SIR PATRICK ABERCROMBIE

Cumberland, and Plymouth; Abercrombie took special pride in his Doncaster plan, which, conceived on the satellite principle, was the first regional report to be published in England. In 1923 he was selected with his brother Lascelles, the poet, to report upon the preservation of Stratford-on-Avon, for which his interest in the theater was an added asset.

In 1935 the architect was invited by London University to become the professor of town planning at University College. Among the projects he planned during the first years in London were camps and homes for English miners and the plan for the University of Ceylon (with A. C. Holliday). Within four years, however, the outbreak of war in 1939 and the subsequent destruction brought to many British towns by Nazi bombs thrust new tasks upon the architect. He had previously planned a new center for the naval port of Plymouth; after the great damage inflicted upon it by the Luftwaffe, Abercrombie was assigned the task of providing a new layout for the town. He undertook also the replanning of blitzed areas such as Bournemouth and Hull, which had undergone constant and heavy bombing, and the restoration of Bath and Clydeside. Of much greater scope than any of these, however, was his work upon the London Plan, in which he

ABERCROMBIE, SIR PATRICK—*Cont.*

was assisted by the London County Council architect and a staff of experts.

The master plan, which took two years to evolve, attempts to eliminate the four major defects of London: traffic congestion, inadequate housing, the maldistribution of open spaces, and the indiscriminate jumble of houses and industry. London proper is to be composed of a number of distinct communities, each of which will have its own community shopping, business, cafe, and entertainment sections. The development of the city as a single area would cease: satellite towns are planned to grow in carefully selected places, with efficient transportation facilities connecting them; factories are to be grouped in relation to the homes of the workers rather than remain situated along the main exits from the metropolis. In essence, the plan "thus provides for an orderly decentralization of population to replace the uncontrolled sprawl which occurred between the two World Wars." Proposing this resettlement of millions of people over a period of fifty years, Abercrombie believes that a sufficient number of people must leave London so that those who remain may live happily and work under decent conditions. His plan would tend to provide adequate housing since the average population density would be reduced to one hundred and thirty-six persons in a residential acre. The *London Economist* has offered one criticism of this aspect, observing that under this proposal, only one-third to one-half of the people are to live in houses, whereas "a family of any size requires a house, not a flat, and large families are a national necessity."

To lessen "indeterminate zoning," small new self-sufficient units of from six to ten thousand people will be established within the large community—the city proper. The design will tend to separate the industrial and residential sections of the neighborhood, leaving each accessible to the other by new city-wide arterial roads. This, one observer commented, will be perfect in shortening the long trip to work which is the bane of the Londoner's existence. Despite the "vast revolutionary upheavals," however, London itself will be preserved. "The task," Abercrombie stated, "is to make the old structure workable." The historic landmarks of London and of the Empire will be protected as will the ancient villages which were absorbed as London expanded but which retain traces of traditional distinctions. "To ignore or scrap these communities," the architect continued, "would be both academic and too drastic; the plan might look well on paper, but it would not be London."

In attempting to restrain the overgrowth of London and to achieve a more balanced distribution of population throughout Britain, approximately one million Londoners and a related quota of industries are to be relocated in new homes beyond the green belt of surrounding suburbs. To aid decentralization and resettlement, they are to live and work in satellite towns—compact settlements surrounded by open country. This proposal is the focal point of all postwar rebuilding in England, since the population of Greater London is more than one-fifth of that of Great Britain. As Lord President of the Privy Council Herbert Morrison observed, "The County of London project has a pervasive national importance."

One of the founders and present chairman of the Council for the Preservation of Rural England, Abercrombie is also a member of the Royal Commission on the Location of Industry and the Miners' Welfare Commission and National Camps Corporation. Formerly president of the Town Planning Institute, he is at present chairman of the Housing Centre. An ardent supporter of both the Repertory Theatre and the Philharmonic Orchestra, Abercrombie's interest in culture led him to join the Royal Fine Art Commission and the Union Club. He has been honored twice by the King: he was created a Knight Bachelor in 1945, and upon the recommendation of the Royal Institute of British Architects (of which he is a member), was awarded the Royal Medal for 1946.

The architect, who is a widower, has a son and daughter. One writer has described Sir Patrick as a slim, vivid, highly articulate man who is as expressive with his voice as with his pencil, and who has the gift of swiftly turning his mind from one plan to another. He is usually monocled in society, spectacled in the office, and has "the vivacity of spirit which his staccato speech, fluent wit, and unquenchable enthusiasm suggest." The London *Sunday Observer* has added that "when he decides, he is ruthlessly loyal to his own decisions and to those who agree and cooperate."

References

N Y Sun p18 N 14 '44
Who's Who, 1946

ADAIR, FRANK E(ARL) (à-dâr') Apr. 9, 1887- Surgeon

Address: b. 75 E. 71st St., New York; h. 791 Park Ave., New York; "Sherwood," East Hampton, N.Y.

That cancer is curable, if recognized in time and approached intelligently, is the message that Dr. Frank E. Adair has been working to bring to ever-increasing numbers of people through the American Cancer Society. President of the American Cancer Society since 1944 and a noted specialist in mammary diseases, he is director of the Breast Cancer Service at New York's Memorial Hospital.

Of Scotch-English ancestry, the son of country doctor Samuel Graham Adair and the former Ella Florence Patterson, Frank Earl Adair was born on April 9, 1887, in Beverly, Ohio, to which his parents had come from New England. Because his father's bills were generally paid in corn, hay, potatoes, and other food products, young Adair had to work for his education, earning his tuition first by selling newspapers and later by teaching at a country school—a position which necessitated a four-mile daily walk and paid him thirty-five dollars a month. Also, he sold aluminum ware during summer vacations. In 1905-06 he attended Marietta Academy in the near-by Ohio city and the next year matriculated at Marietta

College, from which he received his B.A. in 1910. Five years later, in 1915, Adair received his M.D. from Johns Hopkins University, having been a student surgical interne during the last year of his medical course. Then, on July 1, 1915, the young doctor became an interne in surgery at New York Hospital. Soon he was promoted to house surgeon. But by this time (July 1917) the United States had entered World War I, and Adair joined the United States Army Medical Corps as a staff surgeon with the New York Hospital Unit at Base Hospital, No. 9. He served, too, as assistant to Dr. Joseph A. Blake, commanding officer and surgeon-in-chief of American Red Cross Military Hospital, No. 2, in Paris and as a surgeon at the front during the second battle of the Marne, the Battle of Cambrai, and the Meuse-Argonne offensive. He had risen from the rank of first lieutenant to that of captain.

After his discharge from the Army in 1919, Adair joined the staff of the Hospital for the Ruptured and Crippled in New York City. where he served as assistant surgeon until 1930. In addition, in 1920, having become interested in the problems of cancer control, he obtained a similar position with New York's Memorial Hospital for Cancer and Allied Diseases. His specialty during his subsequent close and continued association with Memorial has been mammary diseases, particularly cancer, on which he is a recognized authority. In this field he is the originator of the preoperative irradiation method of treatment, in which irradiation with radium and x-rays is combined with "total eradication by a wide, careful, and radical extirpation of the cancer, its surrounding tissue, and its drainage basins." His theory, which has been generally accepted, gives the cause of this type of cancer as "faulty drainage and the malfunction of the ovarian hormones." In 1923, together with Dr. Burton Lee, Adair established the Breast Cancer Service at the hospital, today the second largest of Memorial's special departments, of which he is the director. In 1926 he was promoted to associate surgeon on Memorial's staff; in 1929, to full attending surgeon; and since 1935 he has also been an executive officer of the institution.

Since 1920, when Adair first became associated with it, Memorial, through its biological, chemical and physical research and its refinement of diagnostic and therapy methods, has grown into "a cancer institute of national significance. . . .[and] has taken on the role of a leader of thought in the international field of cancer." Early physical growth was slow, however, despite such projects as the Breast Cancer Service, and it was not until 1926 that Memorial received its first sizable donation— $250,000 from Edward S. Harkness. "Up to that time," pointed out Dr. James Ewing, Memorial's "grand old man of oncology" and its director for more than twenty-five years, "the hospital had enjoyed the studied neglect of the public, while the medical profession had let us severely alone." Then, in 1939 a grant of three million dollars from the General Education Board, a gift of a two-and-a-half-million-dollar site from John D. Rockefeller, Jr., and several smaller contributions enabled Memorial

FRANK E. ADAIR

to erect a new twelve-story modern hospital. By 1946 plans had been completed for "the largest and most modern cancer center in the world": to consist of the existing Memorial building—remodeled; a new three-hundred-bed hospital unit—to be erected and maintained by New York City; and the Sloan-Kettering Institute for Cancer Research—to be financed with a grant of four million dollars from the Alfred P. Sloan Foundation and organized by Charles F. Kettering in accordance with modern industrial research techniques; the remainder of the program to be financed by contributions totaling another four million dollars to be sought from the general public.

Second only to his work at Memorial has been Adair's activity in behalf of the American Society for the Control of Cancer, since 1945 known as the American Cancer Society. Variously a holder of all the society's offices since the early 1930's, Adair was elected president at its thirty-first annual meeting in March 1944 and re-elected to that post in the reorganized and newly incorporated American Cancer Society at the thirty-second, in April 1946. In 1944 the annual cancer funds drive had succeeded in bringing in a maximum of $850,000, or a scant 50 cents for each case of cancer. Two years later, in 1946, Adair was able to report that intensified drives, spearheaded by Eric A. Johnston [43], chairman of the society's executive committee and national drive chairman, and himself, had raised the sum of money collected for research, education of the public, and care of cancer patients from $850,000 to $12,000,000. By 1946 the number of cancer prevention clinics in the United States had also risen to four hundred, and the public was becoming aware of the need for preventive measures. But this, according to Adair and other cancer fighters, is only the beginning, for most cancer clinics are booked for appointments six months in advance and there are not

ADAIR, FRANK E.—*Continued*

yet nearly enough trained doctors, equipment, or hospitals to accommodate even the small number of people who are aware of the wisdom of frequent medical examinations.

For cancer, Adair has reiterated in numerous articles in popular magazines, is curable—if recognized in time. "Cancer should never be considered as an incurable disease," he wrote in the *American Mercury* for June 1946. "Diagnosed and treated in time, the chances of cure are high. The proof lies in the more than 40,000 cases of cured cancer on file with the American College of Surgeons, and the untold thousands more to be found in the files of surgeons and radiologists throughout the country." "If present knowledge alone is put to use to detect and treat cancer in its early stages," he had pointed out in *Look* of April 2, 1946, "nearly half the people now dying of cancer [estimated at twice the number killed in World War II] can be saved. . . .We have two weapons for the control of cancer," he continued, "ray therapy, and surgery—and we are getting increasingly good results from them. . . . These tools alone will cure early cancer. Know the warning signs of the disease and have them investigated medically. Cancer is not to be dreaded. It must be faced and fought with intelligence and courage."

Although he has been closely associated with Memorial Hospital since 1920, Adair also has a large private practice in New York. In addition, he has at various periods acted as a consultant in surgery to a number of other hospitals, including the United States Veterans Hospital, No. 81, Caledonian Hospital (Brooklyn), St. Joseph's Hospital (Far Rockaway), St. Luke's Hospital (Newburgh), Home for Incurables (New York), and Southampton Hospital. And while he terminated his association with the Hospital for the Ruptured and Crippled in 1930, in 1934 he became assistant professor of clinical surgery at Cornell University Medical College and is now associate professor. In 1938 he was named honorary chief of clinic by Tata Memorial Hospital in Bombay, India, and was consultant in cancer to the National Cancer Institute of the United States Public Health Service. In 1939 he was Bulkley lecturer of the New York Academy of Medicine, and one year later he delivered the annual oration of the California Academy of Medicine. He has been since 1934 the holder of an honorary D.Sc. degree from his alma mater, Marietta College, since 1937 one of its trustees, and is the donor of the Adair prize at the institution, given to the graduating student who has contributed most to the *esprit de corps* of the college "without regard to his standing as a student."

Holder of high positions on numerous medical and cancer bodies, the specialist is also a member of the Sons of the Revolution, of Delta Upsilon and Phi Chi, and of the University (New York) and Maidstone (East Hampton, Long Island) Clubs. Tall and gray-haired, he stands six feet one, weighs 200 pounds, has intensely blue eyes and a ready smile. In 1935 he was married to Marion Hopkinson, who is, to quote her husband, "a very beautiful and talented lady who blessed the home with two boys, Robert Ewing and Michael." For recreation Adair turns to golf or swimming, primarily at his country home, but he is, he says, the kind of a man who "promises too quickly to help out in good causes" and "tries to do too much in a day."

References

American Men of Science (1938)
National Cyclopædia of American Biography Current vol E p74
Who's Who in America, 1946-47

ADAMS, JOSEPH QUINCY Mar. 23, 1881—Nov. 10, 1946 Director of the Folger Shakespeare Library in Washington, D.C., from 1931 until his death; professor of English at Cornell University from 1919 until 1931; general editor of *The New Variorum Shakespeare*; author of *Shakespearean Playhouses* (1917), editor of *Chief Pre-Shakespearean Dramas* (1924), *The Adams Shakespeare* (1929), and many other books on the life and works of Shakespeare.

Obituary

N Y Times p27 N 11 '46

AGA KHAN, THE (AGA SULTAN SIR MAHOMED SHAH) (ä'gȧ κän' sōol-tän má-hŏm'ĕd shä) 1877- Religious leader

Address: Aga Hall, Bombay, India

The fabulously wealthy Moslem spiritual ruler, the Aga Khan, official leader of some eighty million Ismailian Moslems and the founder of the All-India Moslem League, possesses no political territories but is recognized as an important factor in Oriental politics and an influence in the lives of many factions of Islam not directly under his jurisdiction. At the same time he is known to the world at large as a sportsman and a man-about-Europe.

His Highness the Right Honorable Aga Sultan Sir Mahomed Shah Aga Khan was born Mahomed Shah in 1877 in a palace at Karachi, India. He is directly descended from Mohammed through the Prophet's daughter Fatima, which makes him a leader of the Shiah faction of Islam and a divinity to the rich Khoja subsect. His descent from the eighth-century Ismail, last Revealed or infallible Imam of the Ismailian sect, makes the Aga Khan the hereditary Unrevealed Imam or pope of the sect. The present Aga Khan's grandfather, Hasan Ali Shah, governor of a Persian province, had gone to India after a quarrel with the Shah of Persia. His services to the British there were rewarded with a large pension, decorations, and the title of "His Highness the Aga Khan." The first Aga Khan died in 1881, and his son, the second Aga Khan, in 1885, whereupon eight-year-old Prince Mahomed succeeded his father as Imam and Aga Khan.

An only son, little Mahomed was prepared for his role of spiritual ruler of millions with drills in the Koran and Moslem theology and in Persian and Indian history, literature, and philosophy. Later he was placed under the care of English tutors by his mother, the Princess Ali Shah, sister of King Nasr-ed-Din of Persia, to be taught Western civilization and languages. They were strict with their royal pupil, even administering corporal punishment with the approval of his mother, who is reported to have remarked on one occasion that she would rather see her son dead than ignorant. The young Aga Khan completed his education in England, at Eton and Cambridge. As a youth in his teens he had already lectured his followers on Ismailian theology, and, when a smallpox epidemic raged in western India, had saved lives by traveling about the stricken regions having himself publicly vaccinated at each stopping place and instructing his followers likewise to submit to vaccination. During the early years of his Imamate, state journeys took him to the scattered colonies of his eighty million followers in India, Afghanistan, Persia, Syria, Arabia, Morocco, Zanzibar, the East Indies, and other parts of Africa and the Orient. In 1900 he received his first foreign decoration, the Brilliant Star of Zanzibar, first class; in 1901 the Kaiser added the Prussian Order of the Royal Crown, after the twenty-four-year-old Imam had won valuable concessions for his followers in German East Africa.

At twenty-five the Ismailian leader was chosen by heads of the seventy-odd Moslem sects to preside over the all-Moslem Educational Conference. He is said to have shown no little courage at this time by criticizing such traditional Mohammedan practices as celebrating sectarian martyrdoms, segregating women (there was, he maintained, nothing in the Koran or in the early practices of Islam to justify it), and spending too much time in "meaningless prayers" and pilgrimages. He advocated that Moslem children be taught modern science as well as their faith, and favored universal compulsory education for both sexes. The Aga Khan is perhaps unique among leaders of Islam in his desire for such social reform, against which Moslem opposition has always been particularly bitter. Besides building some schools, hospitals, and recreational centers on his own authority, he has sought more and better schools from the British Government of India—and in this was partially successful during his term of service on the Viceroy's Council between 1902 and 1904. In 1910 he was responsible for raising the Moslem college at Aligarh to the status of a university, and it has remained one of his favorite projects. The Aga Khan has also made attempts to reconcile the different Islamic sects, and for this purpose visited the Caliph in Constantinople when a young man, an action compared to a visit of the Archbishop of Canterbury to the Vatican.

During and following World War I the Aga Khan has acted to quiet Moslem unrest and has been "a pillar of support to the British raj," believing that, without the British, India would fall into civil war and chaos. A gradualist, he withdrew his followers from Gandhi's passive resistance movement. In 1906 he was one of the founders of the All-India Moslem

THE AGA KHAN

League, the political organization created to speak for the Moslem Indian minority, which met for the first time in December of that year. Although the League later split into two factions, which were led respectively by Sir Muhammad Shafi and M. A. Jinnah '42, it reunited under the Aga Khan in 1928. While there is some question as to how much of the Moslem world looks to him for leadership, there seems to be no one qualified to speak for a greater portion of it, and he has on a number of occasions assumed the role of spokesman for all Mohammedans. As such, although he rallied Indian Moslems to the aid of Great Britain in World War I (thus winning him an eleven-gun-salute rank), he sought to ease the terms for Turkey, opposed the abolition of the Caliphate, and advocated a unified and independent Arabia. His *India in Transition,* published in 1918, is said to have been an important factor in bringing about the passage by Parliament of the Indian Act of 1919; and although the constitution which it granted provided less than he had asked, he took the position, then as later, that the British reforms, though not satisfactory, were acceptable. His efforts to secure peace in India also brought him a nomination for the Nobel Prize from the Indian Council of State. Of later years, however, it has been said that the advance of separatism among the Moslems has decreased the Aga Khan's influence.

"Interstitially," as one writer stated, the Imam worked at politics. He was chairman of the British Indian delegation to the Round Table Conference in London in 1930 and 1931, represented India at the World Disarmament Conference at Geneva in 1932, and led the Indian delegation to the League of Nations Assembly in 1932 and thereafter each year from 1934 to 1937. Of the fifty votes cast by the nations for President of the 1937 League Assembly, forty-nine were for the Aga Khan and one was blank. The Moslem leader is reported

AGA KHAN, THE—*Continued*

to have shown Oriental finesse in negotiation and skill in devising compromises; however, he later had cause to remark, "All my predictions have been utterly wrong." After the Munich pact, for example, the Aga Khan's much discussed article in the London *Times* (reprinted in the *Living Age* of December 1938), called "Faith in Hitler," set forth the views of the pro-Chamberlain conservatives: "We find no reason why the glorious victory for peace with honor won by the Prime Minister need degenerate into a truce. Reason, [Hitler's] self-interest, and conscience all point to peace."

But the Aga Khan is known to newspaper readers mainly as an international sportsman and *bon vivant*. His income is estimated at six hundred thousand to ten million dollars a year, but no one knows how much of it comes from his sect (2 per cent of all Ismailians' incomes, 10 per cent of all Khojas' incomes plus special levies, the fees for indulgences, and countless gifts), and how much from his shrewd investment of his inherited fortune. His profits as one of the big financiers of Europe (where he lives eight months of the year) are said to be several times his income as Imam. There is no agreement among commentators as to how much of his followers' donations goes to the expenses of the sect and to education, charity, and emergency relief work, and how much is appropriated to his own use. At any rate, the Aga Khan's scale of living is a fabulous one: the servants at his various palaces and estates are said to number about thirty-seven hundred, and his collection of jewels is described as fantastic, the rubies alone being estimated by an expert as worth more than two hundred million dollars. The twelve racing stables he maintained in England, Ireland, France, and India before World War II were the most valuable in the world, estimated at five million dollars in 1935, and his green and chocolate colors were carried to victory in the 1930, 1935, and 1936 English Derbies and in five St. Leger Stakes. He was the first Oriental admitted to the exclusive Jockey Club. During the war, however, the Aga Khan was in Switzerland, cut off from most of his revenues and occupying himself with the less expensive sport of mountain climbing, while the Hindu leader Gandhi was interned in the Imam's luxurious villa at Poona, India.

According to *Newsweek,* the Aga Khan's first marriage was to a cousin, a union he dissolved. In 1908 he was married to Teresa Magliano, an Italian who was received into his faith. She bore him a son, Prince Aly Shah Aly Khan, who is conspicuous in European society and who has served in the British forces. The second Begum died in late 1926, reportedly on the day her husband purchased the "unlucky" sixty-one-carat Golden Dawn diamond. He was married again in 1929, to Andrée-Joséphine Carron, a French candy-store clerk, whom he divorced in Geneva in 1943. (They have a son, Sadruddin.) Neither she nor Yvette Labrousse, the young Frenchwoman to whom the sixty-seven-year-old pontiff was married in 1944, professed Mohammedanism. The Imam explains that Moslem men are permitted to marry infidel women if the latter are Scripturaries, that is, believers in God.

In Bombay and later in Tanganyika on the occasion of his diamond jubilee in 1946, the tall, silver-haired, spectacled Aga Khan was balanced with 243½ pounds of diamonds, the cash value of which was to be spent by him for public works such as agricultural loans and education—augmented by a contribution of his own. (The Aga Khan had been presented with his weight in gold on his golden jubilee.) On such occasions he and his family wear magnificent oriental robes, but in general the Imam prefers the costume of an English gentleman. He is said to like best the tweeds appropriate to life on his Irish estate. The Aga Khan has taken part in a number of sports, including polo, tennis, boxing, and tiger shooting. He says that he considers it a duty to set his flock an example of physical exercise. For that reason he has donated athletic trophies and playing fields, and has given large money prizes for achievements in civil aviation by Indians; and to provide his fellow nationals with recreation, he has also sponsored the Indian moving picture industry. In Europe he was one of the backers of the Diaghilev Ballet.

The Aga Khan is described as meticulous in the performance of his religious duties. He keeps a learned Imam in his retinue to give him advice and discuss the Koran with him; prayers are said at the appointed times, and he is accessible at a definite hour each day to the humblest of his followers. There has, however, been criticism by Occidentals of his way of life, which hardly coincides with the conventional idea of a spiritual ruler. A writer for the British *New Statesman and Nation* once summed up the Aga Khan's outstanding qualities as "a genial cynicism of temper; an enormous appetite for life; a profound desire to show that he can do, and do well, all that the aristocratic children of this world can accomplish; a power to recollect on great occasions that he is, after all, something between a pope and a prince, with the title to a status that befits this mystery. . . .He is content to prove that, not less than Leo X, one may have the obligations of a papal office, and yet find them compatible with enjoyment."

References

Brooklyn Eagle Ja 19 '41
Cur Hist ns 42:591-7 S '35
Liv Age 349:327 D '35
N Y Sun p22 Mr 20 '46 por
Newsweek 7:43-4 Je 6 '36 por
Scholastic 31:20 O 2 '37 por
Gunther, J. Inside Asia (1942)
Who's Who, 1946

ALBANESE, LICIA (äl-bä-nä′sä lē′chä″) July 22, 1913- Opera singer
Address: b. c/o Columbia Concerts, Inc., 113 W. 57th St., New York

Among the younger singers of several years' experience with the Metropolitan Opera Association, Licia Albanese has proved herself an outstanding exponent of the Italian lyric style. The beauty of her voice and her convincing portrayals of Violetta, Micaela, and of Cio-Cio-San—the role in which she made her impromptu, formal, and Metropolitan debuts—have brought her a large public following.

One of six children of a musical Italian family, Licia Albanese was born July 22, 1913, in the city of Bari on the Adriatic, to Michele Albanese, a salesman for a chain grocery company, and Maria (Rugusa) Albanese. She received her general education in a convent school, but did not begin to think seriously about music, she says, until she was twelve years old. In fact, her first ambition at this time was to become a dancer, while it was her older sister Stella who was looked upon as the probable singer of the family. At the age of twelve Licia joined Stella in taking piano lessons from a local teacher. Sometimes she would sing while her sister played, and the teacher, approving the quality of her voice, suggested that she take singing lessons as well. Licia, then painfully shy, it is said, at first refused but was finally coaxed into preparing an aria from *Tosca* for her father's birthday. "At the family celebration," relates Innes Maccammond in *Collier's,* "she was so nervous and embarrassed that she had to do it with her back to the audience, [but] her father was delighted, convinced that she had a future." Despite her protests, he now found a teacher for his timid daughter in the retired tenor Emanuel De Rosa, and she began study in her native Bari.

Three years later her father, who had been ill, took Licia with him when he went to Naples to consult a specialist and while there obtained an audition for her with the conductor Mario Bellini (of the same family as the nineteenth-century composer of *Norma,* Vincenzo Bellini). Mario Bellini, who was then a chorus master and operatic coach, recommended that she continue her vocal studies in Naples; but the girl, knowing that the doctor's report had not been encouraging, refused, preferring to return to Bari to help care for her father. Before accepting her refusal, however, the elder Albanese exacted her promise that if it became necessary she would make singing her career, a promise of which he reminded his daughter just before he died three years later. Shortly after her father's death—she was then eighteen—Licia accepted a cousin's invitation to go to Milan, one of the great music centers of the world. There she was introduced to Giuseppina Baldassare-Tedeschi, a famous Italian soprano and noted interpreter of the title role of *Madama Butterfly* who had herself studied with Rosina Storchi, the creator of Puccini's tragic Cio-Cio-San. Thus in 1932 began Licia's final vocal preparation with Mme. Baldassare-Tedeschi in Milan. Two years later the young aspirant unexpectedly made her debut at the Teatro Lyrico in Milan as Cio-Cio-San. At the last moment the manager of the theater had been informed that his regular prima donna, who had insisted that she was well enough to go on, was too ill to sing. Someone suggested Miss Albanese who was in the audience and knew the role, and, as Miss Maccammond puts it, "Licia was

Bruno of Hollywood

LICIA ALBANESE

literally yanked from the audience into the leading part."

Nevertheless, the young singer went back to her studies for another year, refusing an invitation to audition at La Scala on the plea that she was not yet ready for the operatic stage. Even when her big opportunity came, in the form of a national contest sponsored by the Sindacato Stampa Propaganda, a Government-operated auditioning and booking bureau for musical talent, Miss Albanese almost let it pass by. She entered the local competition at the last moment and then left with her teacher for Cinecittà, the Italian film colony. Mme. Baldassare-Tedeschi saw her name as winner from Milan in a newspaper announcement, however, and with the help of Giuseppe (Gino) Marinuzzi, one of Italy's foremost conductors and principal judge of the competition, got her to Bologna for the contest finals. After four grueling nights, during which she competed against three hundred singers from all over Italy, she won not only one of the six silver medals given but first prize and an additional gold medal. As a result, her formal debut was made as Cio-Cio-San at the Teatro Reale in Parma on December 19, 1935.

This debut appearance at the age of twenty-two was followed by a season at the San Carlo Theatre in Naples. Soon afterward she became a regular member of the La Scala company in Milan but also made frequent guest appearances—with the Royal Opera in Rome, in Paris, Malta, Tunis, and Monte Carlo, and in other music centers in Italy, France, and Spain. She was chosen to sing at the inauguration of the Vatican City radio station and was decorated by Pope Pius XI. She gave a command performance before King Victor Emanuel, and in 1937 she participated in the Coronation Opera Season at Covent Garden in London. In 1939 she sang at a concert in honor of Sir Neville Chamberlain and Lord Halifax in

ALBANESE, LICIA—*Continued*

Rome. She also attracted the attention of the famous tenor Beniamino Gigli, with whom she made records of *La Bohème* in 1939, and it was through his recommendation that she was engaged by the Metropolitan Opera Association in New York. Her repertoire included, besides the roles of Violetta, Mimi, Cio-Cio-San, Marguerite, Micaela, and Nedda, which she generally sings at the Metropolitan, the title roles in Massenet's *Manon*, Puccini's *Manon Lescaut*, and Von Flotow's *Martha*, Zerlina in *Don Giovanni*, Antonia in *Tales of Hoffmann*, Norina in *Don Pasquale*, Liu in *Turandot*, Susanna in *The Marriage of Figaro*, Nanetta in *Falstaff*.

Licia Albanese made her Metropolitan debut on February 9, 1940, again as Butterfly, and very soon built up a loyal following. The critics consider her best roles to be Butterfly, Violetta, Nedda, and Micaela, and they believe her miscast as Marguerite and (except in this season's Toscanini radio *Bohème*) as Mimi. Reviewing her first appearance in *Traviata* at the Metropolitan on December 5, 1942, Virgil Thomson wrote in the *Herald Tribune*: "Miss Albanese began by looking beautiful but singing with a tremolo that was no doubt due to nervousness. . . .After fifteen minutes, the tremolo disappeared, leaving only beauty, both personal and vocal. She was as deeply touching in her gaiety as in her heartbreaks and in her tubercular agony. She used her limpid voice, her delicate person and her excellent musicianship to equal effect in creating the character, Violetta. I use the word *create* for her achievement because that is what she really did. She did not play or imitate or sketch. She created a complete personality that lived and loved and drank champagne and made decisions and died. She did this with skill, with art, with conviction, with beauty and with all loveliness. . . .One has heard many Violettas. Miss Albanese's is, I should think, one of the great ones, because, like all the great ones, it resembles no other yet is wholly convincing." Other critics have since borne him out. "Hers was a Violetta," noted Noel Straus of the *Times* at a subsequent performance, "captivating in its refinement, sincerity, and freedom from the slightest hint of overstatement, as well as deftly sung." "Always a distinguished interpretation from the purely vocal aspect," wrote Jerome D. Bohm of the *Herald Tribune* later, "Miss Albanese has developed her characterization in remarkable fashion so that it now tarries on the highest peaks of musical and dramatic accomplishment."

When the first *Madama Butterfly* since Pearl Harbor was performed on January 19, 1946, the critics were loud in their praise of its Cio-Cio-San. "I have shouted brava at Miss Albanese for so long," said Edward O'Gorman of the *Post*, "I find that I am almost too hoarse to give her Cio-Cio-San all it deserves." She "has so thoroughly mastered" the role, wrote Robert Bagar in the *World-Telegram*, "that no flaws whatever exist. . . .I doubt whether it has ever been done better. . . .Certainly she is mighty like a Duse in her spoken lines of Act III. A calm of finality has de-

scended upon her, as she says, 'With honor dies who cannot live with honor.' The coy little girl, the wife and the mother and, finally, the woman 'whom the gods may destroy, but not defeat,' these, in succession, she conveyed with the sharpest and most discerning intelligence." "Her characterization," Miles Kastendieck wrote in the *Christian Science Monitor*, "is outstanding from the human point of view. . . .[She gives] an illusion of living the part. It lies well for her voice, [too,] though she competed unsuccessfully at times with Puccini's orchestration and Pietro Cimara's conducting."

But Miss Albanese has received her share of bad notices—ranging from Virgil Thomson's "French music [in *Faust*] does not show off her pure Italian singing style to the best advantage" to Oscar Thompson's "Miss Albanese was just an every-day operatic heroine in a blonde wig and with a small voice that was used discreetly." Before February 1946 one of Virgil Thomson's comments might have been taken as typical concerning her Mimi: "The very reserve that makes her Micaela moving in *Carmen* and the moral dignity that makes her *Traviata* a great creation are what prevented her from being a pathetic figure as Mimi. Her dramatic qualities are as miscast in this weepy role as her vocal ones are above Puccini's insistent horns." Toscanini's anniversary radio presentation of *La Bohème* on February 3 and 10, however, changed the criticism as Miss Albanese, chosen by Toscanini to sing the leading role, with this performance finally fulfilled a desire—which contract difficulties had frustrated earlier at Salzburg—to sing under the direction of the great maestro. Olin Downes spoke of her "adorable simplicity and poignancy"; Miles Kastendieck of "strongly appealing singing" which was "unusually persuasive because of its understanding and its intimacy, especially in the final scene." The critic of the New York *Sun* wrote: "Licia Albanese realized with remarkable vocal skill and much warmth of feeling the kind of character Puccini invented and Toscanini sought to recreate. Heard at the broadcast end, there was complete illusion both in her singing of the music and the vocalizing of the spoken passages. Her Mimi will never be the same after this experience."

Miss Albanese was married on April 7, 1945, to Joseph A. Gimma, a stockbroker and native of Bari, whom she did not meet, until, however, she came to the United States with a letter of introduction from his sister. Eight months later, on December 10, 1945, she received her final United States citizenship papers. She is a woman of apparently boundless energy: her daily schedule consists of rehearsals, lessons, two or three hours of practice except on days when she is appearing at the Opera House, more rehearsals and fittings. During non-season months she appears in concerts and operatic performances throughout the United States and in Canada, and South America and Mexico would like to hear her. From fall through spring of each year she is the star of Mutual's *Treasure Hour of Song*. On her infrequent vacations she likes to swim and fish and, on occasion, to dig clams with her fingers. At first concerned over a feeling that Americans looked askance at her Italian "enemy" nationality, Miss Albanese returned to Italy in the late spring of 1940, but she soon came back to America, that "wonderfully happy and comforting place." Described as good-natured and cordial, she is on friendly terms with all her colleagues, but her circle of intimate friends does not include professional musicians, nor does she provide good copy for gossip writers. It has been remarked that she has a figure like the women in the old Italian paintings. Edward Johnson has said of her: "There are two qualities which great artists have, simplicity and sincerity. Albanese has both. And not only is she gifted with a very beautiful voice, but for opera she has an emotional intensity—a silvery quality that is very rare. Any publicity that comes to her is through merit alone."

Reference
Collier's 115:36+ Ap 14 '45

ALCAYAGA, LUCILA GODOY *See* Mistral, G.

ALEKHINE, ALEXANDER (ŭ-lyā′kyĭn)
Nov. 1, 1892—Mar. 24, 1946 Russian-born, French-naturalized chess player; became master in 1909, grand master in 1914, world champion, 1927-35, and from 1937; chess writer and annotator; held world record for concurrent blindfold games.

Obituary
N Y Times p25 Mr 25 '46 por

ALEMAN, MIGUEL (ä″lä-män′ mē-gĕl′)
1902- President of Mexico; lawyer
Address: Palacio Nacional, Mexico, D.F.

The new president of Mexico, Miguel Alemán, who assumed his position on the first of December 1946, has the distinction of being the first nonmilitary candidate ever to be elected to the office. The July 1946 election in Mexico, which ended a century of soldier-president tradition, is notable also for being the most democratic election in Mexico's history. Alemán, formerly Minister of Government in Camacho's '40 Cabinet, has pledged himself to the furthering of Mexico's growth in democratic institutions during his six-year term.

Miguel Alemán was born in 1902, of Spanish-Indian ancestry, in Sayula in the state of Veracruz, Mexico. He was the namesake of his father, Miguel Alemán, originally the keeper of the village store before his outspoken opposition to the thirty-year dictatorial regime of Porfirio Díaz, Mexico's president, obliged him to seek haven in the forests of Veracruz as the chief of a band of guerrillas. Later, Alemán's father became a famous general and took part in uprisings in various parts of the country and finally in the revolt, led by Francisco Madero, which brought about the abdication of Díaz in May 1911. Because of the complicated political situation which preceded and

followed this deposition and the subsequent assassination of Madero, Alemán's family had to move frequently. As a result, the youth, reared in the strictest Roman Catholic faith, was educated in schools in Acayucan, Coatzacoalcos, Orizaba, and Mexico City (Alemán had been denied access to the Sayula grade school because of his father's political convictions). This forced travel, coupled with Alemán's later varied occupations, is considered to be largely responsible for his acquaintance with Mexicans of many classes, a fact of value to him in his political career.

The Alemán family at length chose Mexico City as their permanent home. At school there young Miguel participated in student elections and helped his friends to form athletic teams and to begin a newspaper, *Eureka*, which proved good enough to be bought by the Minister of Education for school libraries. In 1925 Alemán entered the School of Jurisprudence of the National University of Mexico. In his spare time he worked so as to obtain money for his tuition, and during vacations he took jobs in mining companies and as a geologist's assistant in the oil fields. About this time Miguel's father once more rebelled, with fatal results, against a dictatorial general and former president who, contrary to Mexican constitutional law, wished to take office as president for a second term. Alemán graduated from law school with honors in 1928, having finished a five-year course in three years. His thesis was on protective laws for the workingman.

At the age of twenty-six, shortly after he received his law degree, Alemán was admitted to the Mexico City bar and set up practice in partnership with a close friend with whom he had solicited prospective clients even before his graduation. Alemán at first sought his clients among miners, many of whom suffered from silicosis, but who at that period could expect little compensation for this occupational disease. His law firm's handling of these cases was competent, and soon Alemán was representing labor unions as well as individuals. Two notable legal victories were scored by Alemán while he was engaged in the suits: he secured compensation for the dependents of railroad employees killed in revolutionary battles and indemnities for miners injured at work. The law business was so lucrative that both partners invested surplus profits in a mine, a cider plant, and about fifteen other money-wasting enterprises before they finally succeeded in real estate. During the two years' duration of his private law practice, Alemán held public office as attorney in the Ministry of Agriculture. About this time, also, Alemán was appointed to a federal board which decided upon the legality of all strikes.

In 1930 the young lawyer was advanced to the post of justice of the superior court of appeals for the federal district by President Pascual Ortiz Rubio, who selected Alemán at the request of the labor unions. His judicial career was unspectacular, and in Alemán's opinion, too sedentary; he resigned from the bench to take a more active role in the country's political affairs. Aleman's opportunity to enter politics came with his election to the Mexican Senate from his native state of Veracruz. Later,

MIGUEL ALEMAN

when the governor-elect of Veracruz was assassinated (1936), Alemán retired as senator to
fill his appointment to the governorship. From
the very beginning of his work in this position,
Alemán concerned himself with providing educational advantages for his constituents. "What
good is it to have political freedom," Alemán
asked, "if a man cannot read the ballot which he
is asked to mark?" He allotted half of the state
budget to education, and within two years the
number of students attending the state's schools
increased from ninety thousand to about one
hundred twenty-five thousand. During the four
years he served in this post, Alemán also instituted a number of penal reforms.

Alemán resigned as governor of Veracruz
in 1940, two years before his term expired, in
order to become campaign manager for General
Manuel Avila Camacho, the official candidate of
Mexico's strongest political organization, the
Party of the Mexican Revolution or P.R.M.,
for the office of president. General Juan
Andreu Almazán was Camacho's chief opponent.
Alemán's management was purportedly the determining factor which aligned Veracruz and
other southern states behind Camacho. When
Camacho gained the presidency, Alemán was
granted the post of Secretario de Gobernación
(translated variously as Secretary, also Minister of the Interior, and Minister of Government). This office in some respects is similar to that of the Vice-President of the United
States, since Alemán served as chief of the
Cabinet and was empowered to succeed the
president in the event of his death. The Government services under Alemán's jurisdiction as
Minister of Government were immigration,
tourism, radio, publicity, a secret service organization, all penal institutions, and police and
juvenile courts. Alemán's bureau also had
charge of the Government's relations with the
Roman Catholic Church, and acted as liaison

between the Government and the twenty-eight
states and two territories.

One of the first actions taken by Alemán
in his new work was to redefine official Mexican attitude on the expropriation, in Cárdenas'
administration, of oil property developed within
Mexico by outside interests, primarily British
and American. Alemán himself in 1938 had
urged all state governors to support expropriation. In February 1941 Alemán announced
that once a settlement had been reached with the
nations involved, foreign capital again would
be allowed to participate in oil operations but in
new enterprises only and through Mexican-
owned companies. His major domestic measures were the reforms he accomplished "in the
fields of penology and juvenile delinquency"
during his five-year service as Camacho's chief
associate.

Little more than a year after Alemán assumed office, he was confronted with new domestic and international responsibilities brought
on by the Japanese attack on Hawaii. Asserting in the latter part of December 1941 that
"the enemies of the United States are the
enemies of Mexico," Alemán in his official
capacity suppressed, within a few months, the
activities of Axis agents, completed the internment of German, Japanese, and Italian nationals, and kept under strict surveillance the
movements of the Spanish Falangists. In May
1942 Mexico declared war on the Axis and
allied itself with the United Nations. Alemán
helped to unify his nation in its defense measures as chairman of the Comisión Coordinadora
de la Propaganda Nacional, an information
committee designed to acquaint Mexicans with
the issues involved in World War II and with
the necessity of producing strategic supplies to
be exported to the members of the United
Nations. Alemán's commission promoted the
symbolic movement known as the Abanderados
de la Libertad (Standard-Bearers for Liberty),
similar to the "V for Victory" campaign of
other nations.

Minister of Government Alemán was instrumental, too, in effecting further rapprochement
between Mexico and other nations of the Western Hemisphere. In October 1943, Latin American and United States delegates of the Inter-
American Demographic Congress, founded by
Alemán, met in Mexico City to consider questions "pertaining to the regulation of postwar
immigration" to the American continents. Alemán maintained that although each republic
was entitled to decide, as protection for its nationals, the type and extent of immigration it
desired, it should abstain from discrimination.
To facilitate inter-American travel and communication, Alemán introduced new regulations
in the Mexican Immigration Service: he expe-
dited passport issuing, improved the conditions
of border immigration stations, and provided
arrangements whereby a North or South American tourist need only prove his nationality in
order to enter Mexico. Prior to this, Alemán
has assisted at meetings of presidents Franklin
D. Roosevelt and Avila Camacho in Monterey,
Mexico, and Corpus Christi, Texas, in April

1943 for discussion of matters common to the welfare of both republics.

In June 1945, with the presidential election in the offing for July of the following year, the Minister of Government began his campaign for the office of Mexico's chief executive. Some months later Alemán resigned from his Ministry post. January 1946 witnessed the conversion of the P.R.M. (in order to include many labor syndicates hitherto unconnected with it) into the Party of Revolutionary Institutions. Since Alemán was primarily responsible for this reorganization, he thus strengthened his standing in Mexico's largest political faction. In the same month, he was nominated as P.R.I.'s official candiate to become one of the major contenders for the presidency.

Alemán's leading opponent was Ezequiel Padilla '⁴², Foreign Minister in Camacho's Cabinet (1940-45) and head of the Mexican delegation to the United Nations Conference at San Francisco, who in July resigned from his posts and party affiliation to organize the new Mexican Democratic Party. Other candidates were Generals J. Agustín Castro and Enrique Calderón. In addition to support from the Government's bureaucratic organization (observers noted that especially in the Mexican provinces it was often employed unfairly to the detriment of the Padilla campaign), Alemán received the backing of many ideologically opposed groups— among them the Mexican peasants, the Mexican Confederation of Workers, (regarded by some as Communist-inspired) the conservative Sinarquistas (often suspected of Falangist sympathies), and businessmen who felt that Alemán sought no further drastic steps toward state socialization of industries. Padilla found his main advocates among certain industrialists and those who opposed graft and favoritism in the Government, but he was not very popular among many of his compatriots because they believed him to be the tool of foreign imperialisms. Padilla, for example, was known to be openly friendly toward the United States and had favored use of outside, especially United States, capital to industrialize Mexico.

Miguel Alemán was elected president of Mexico in July 1946, and took office in December. To insure a democratic election, the Camacho Government had passed the Federal Electoral Law of December 1945: all males over twenty-one fulfilling registration requirements were eligible to vote, and control of electoral mechanism was removed from the local bosses and was placed under the jurisdiction of the Federal Government. This new law was taken advantage of by over two million voters, an unprecedented event for Mexico, where previously not even half a million people had voted. Federal troops patrolled the polls to insure a fair ballot. When the returns came in, Padilla, fortified by reports from the provinces that Alemanistas had hindered the Padillistas from exercising the democratic right of suffrage and that ballot counting had been unjust, charged fraud, and insisted that he had actually been elected president. Although Ezequiel Padilla was reported to have dropped charges of electoral mismanagement and to have conceded the election to Alemán, he did not actually cease making his accu-

sations. In August 1946 the Mexican Government announced that it had uncovered a plot to assassinate Alemán but had acted quickly to suppress the conspirators. Mario Lasso, Padilla's nephew and head of the Federal District committee of the Mexican Democratic Party was arrested and imprisoned as perpetrator of what *Newsweek* (August 19) called a "tangled plot" involving complaints of duplicity on both sides.

At his inauguration in the capital's Palacio de Bellas Artes, an event which lasted six days and was attended by eminent representatives from thirty-nine nations, Alemán delivered a "cautious" inaugural address interpreted by some observers to signify a more Rightest Governmental policy for Mexico during Alemán's Administration. Observers commented on the fact, too, that Lázaro Cárdenas was not present at the officiation. (The new president had been described earlier as a "middle-of-the-roader" who intended "to give Mexico a moderately 'Leftist' Government" with "prolabor leanings.") The composition of the new Cabinet, announced by Alemán in his speech, is considered to be partial evidence of this trend. Referring briefly to the oil question, the Mexican chief executive stated that outside experts and technicians would be encouraged to employ their abilities for the progress of national industrialization. This is seen as a continuation of the policy permitting foreign nationals to aid in exploring and exploiting oil property but barring them from ownership. Alemán, as reported earlier in the fall, proposed to remedy the inefficiency of the oil industry management as operated by the Government bureau, Petróleos Mexicanos (Pemex), and the friction between workers and management by means of long-term contracts "covering hours and working conditions." In December, upon his taking office, he placed in the vacant directorship of Pemex a businessman, Antonio López Bermúdez, as successor to Efraín Buenrostro, a Cárdenas man.

Such programs as the construction of large irrigation projects and hydroelectric power plants and dams, increased exports, limited protective tariffs, and further industrialization of Mexico through the industries developed during wartime are measures, too, which the Alemán Government will undertake to provide greater self-sufficiency for the nation. Instead of instituting private ownership (subsidized by agricultural agencies) of small farms to replace the existing system of communal farming as was once expected, the president indicated that a new land resettlement program would be put into effect in order to counteract overpopulation in some regions of the country and to provide workers for new lands about to be opened. Government control of some public utilities, aside from oil industries, will continue. Mediatory settlement of labor disputes, the removal of all forms of graft, the curbing of inflation, promotion of Cárdenas' and Camacho's grade-school program and the campaign to obliterate illiteracy, and the attainment of complete women suffrage (the new president is sponsoring a bill to grant women the right to vote in municipal elections) are among other

ALEMAN, MIGUEL—*Continued*

Alemán projects. In the field of international relations Mexico is pledged by its president to "continental unity," the "doctrine of the good neighbor," and "international understanding."

The intensive application of Alemán to his work is well known. As Minister of Government he maintained a twelve-hour schedule, disregarding the siesta. Medium in height, verging on stockiness, Alemán has "keen, piercing black eyes" and black hair. Described as a modest, "reticent man, wary of flamboyancy" and a "diffident speaker," he possesses considerable charm and suavity. His English is fluent. One of the greatest influences in his life has been his father, General Alemán, whose portrait dominates the wall of his son's office and library. The books he prefers are those which concern Mexican statesmen and patriots from earliest times—the Aztec Cuauhtemoc, Juárez, and Morelos. As pastimes, Alemán enjoys listening to classical records and playing golf at the Cuernavaca Country Club, of which he is a member. In addition to his public work, Alemán has continued to derive income from small business enterprises. The well-tailored Mexican was married to the former Beatriz Velasco in the late 1920's while he was engaged in his private law practice. They and their two children, Beatriz and Miguel, resided at the elegant Alemán home in Cuernavaca before Alemán became president.

References

    Christian Sci Mon Mag p8+ Ap 10 '43;
      p3 Je 8 '46 por
    Collier's 118:26+ Jl 6 '46 por
    Inter-American 2:19-21 Mr '43 por
    N Y Herald Tribune II p2 Je 30 '46 por
    N Y Sun p18 O 15 '45
    N Y Times Mag p12 Jl 21 '46 por
    Time 47:38+ F 11 '46
    World Report 1:9-10, 32 Jl 25 '46 por
    Who's Who in Latin America; Part I,
      Mexico (1946)

ALLEN, GEORGE E(DWARD) Feb. 29, 1896- United States Government official

Address: b. c/o Reconstruction Finance Corporation, Washington, D.C.

President Truman's nomination and the Senate's approval of George E. Allen as director of the Reconstruction Finance Corporation gave rise to much discussion of the man whose wit and high spirits have amused Washingtonians since the 1930's. Often the object of his own barbs, he has been dubbed "court jester," while more serious pro and con comments have been directed at his important business connections, ability and shrewdness, and political judgment.

George Edward Allen observes his birthday every fourth year—he was born February 29, 1896, in Booneville, Mississippi, to Samuel P. and Mollie (Plaxico) Allen. Samuel Allen's brother, John Allen, who served as a private in the Confederate Army, was elected to Congress for eight terms—a point of heredity commentators see as one explanation for George Allen's abilities. In 1917 George Allen received

his LL.B. degree from Cumberland University, in Tennessee, from which he returned to his native state to be admitted that same year to the bar and to set up practice in Okolona. After a year as attorney for the town, Allen's law career was interrupted by World War I, in the course of which he served as a first lieutenant in a machine gun battalion in France. Upon his return to civilian life in 1918, he took up his law practice, only to give it up the following year. He was "not much of a lawyer," he has said of himself. He then accepted a position with the Indiana State Chamber of Commerce, but after a short time moved on to Chicago, where he managed one of the city's largest hotels.

The hotel business, which claimed Allen's interest until 1933, brought him to Washington in 1929. As head of several of Washington's big hotels he met many prominent people of the financial and political world who liked their host for his abundant geniality and well-told Southern stories. Pat Harrison, the Mississippi Senator, took Allen to the Democratic National Convention in 1932 and, after Franklin D. Roosevelt's first inauguration, was instrumental in securing for Allen one of the three commissionerships of the District of Columbia, an office he held from 1933 to 1938. The youngest commissioner on record, Allen, as reported by the *United States News* (February 1, 1946), "excelled at gladhanding visiting notables and making speeches, humorous or otherwise, on ceremonial occasions." He effected improved municipal services for Washington by putting through a District of Columbia income tax, which won him the applause of Washingtonians. Meanwhile, he became an aide to Harry Hopkins in the Government relief program—in the Emergency Relief Administration and the Works Progress Administration. Knowing little about the problems of the unemployed, Allen, dressed like one of the jobless, traveled through the Middle West. He slept in flophouses and tourist camps and tells that he unsuccessfully applied for thirty-six jobs.

In 1938, when his term as District commissioner expired, Allen became vice-president of the Home Insurance Company of New York. Other important industrial connections followed, among them directorships of Republic Steel Corporation, Consolidated Vultee, and Aviation Corporation. His interest in the political scene continued, however. Made secretary of the Democratic National Party in 1943, by the following year George Allen had become one of the "Truman for Vice-President" backers: he arranged the vice-presidential candidate's first public address in Detroit, met the nominee, and managed much of his campaign. When Truman succeeded Roosevelt in the White House, Allen became a frequent visitor. As a member of the President's "breakfast" or "kitchen" cabinet, he offered advice, reportedly helped in the preparation of Truman's speeches, and acted as liaison between the White House and Capitol Hill. Not the least of his contributions to Presidential conferences and cruises on the Potomac was his unfailing good humor.

In September 1945 Allen was given offices in the State Department when Truman asked him to survey existing war agencies and make recommendations for their liquidation. In his report Allen proposed that most war emergency offices be closed by June 30, 1946, in a "reconversion" that should be achieved in "a democratic and a decent manner" under an experienced governmental administrator. He recommended the retention of those agencies dealing with prices and other reconversion problems and of research bureaus "vital to our national welfare"; and he urged the appointment of specialists who would be assigned the duty of finding new employment for discharged employees; those unable to obtain employment should be provided with transportation to their homes or an equivalent distance.

In January 1946 President Truman nominated Allen to the important directorship of the fifteen-billion-dollar Reconstruction Finance Corporation. This agency, as is explained in the 1945 *Government Manual*, had been established fourteen years earlier for the primary purpose of extending financial assistance to agriculture, commerce, and industry. Since the beginning of World War II, however, its authority has been greatly increased by means of supplementary legislation and Executive orders and it has been designated by the Surplus Property Board as disposal agent for the Government's postwar surplus of capital and producers goods.

The reaction in Washington in a number of quarters was that the President, who had also named Edwin Pauley as Under Secretary of the Navy, was "passing jobs around." Some Republicans and opponents of big business found fault with the appointment, questioning Allen's administrative and banking ability and pointing to his parallel rise in business and influence in the White House. In the hearing before the Senate Committee on Banking and Currency, Allen met all questions with humor and frankness—his replies provoked much mirth—and the outcome was a 14-to-5 recommendation for Senate approval. Senator Robert A. Taft of Ohio stated he did not doubt Allen's integrity but rather his ability for the RFC post. Taft carried his opposition into the Senate Chamber but failed to prevent the Senators' voice vote of approval of Allen on February 18. The *United States News* saw Allen's influence on Truman as "conservative," of which one example is Allen's feeling that labor-management problems will solve themselves. (He favored the Case '46 antistrike bill.) On the other hand, a good friend of the President's has called Allen "a good liberal, a good business man." In accepting the office Allen resigned from the Home Insurance Company, from which he received $28,000 a year, while retaining, according to *Time*, other corporation posts from which he receives an estimated $50,000 annually.

In October 1946 the RFC director led a twelve-member economic mission to Germany. The group, which also included representatives of the State, Treasury, War, and Commerce Departments, had as its task to plan that country's economic revival in the American zone with a view to making it self-sufficient; to work out a joint plan with the British for providing German exports to cover German imports into

GEORGE E. ALLEN

American and British zones; to study export potentials of a peacefully industrialized postwar Germany; and to review American reparations rights and policy. One of the agreements reached in the American zone finances the procurement of raw materials (to be used in German industry for subsequent exports) through temporary loans extended Germany by the United States Commercial Corporation, an RFC subsidiary. After his return to the United States, in November 1946, Allen participated in Anglo-American negotiations to work out the economic unification of those two occupation zones in Germany. Before the end of the year he proposed an amendment to the RFC Act that would divest the depression-born agency of its wide war powers. Late in December Allen sent the President his resignation from his RFC post, to become effective in January 1947.

Allen's interests have led him outside the spheres of business and politics. For several years he was special assistant to the late Norman H. Davis, chairman of the American Red Cross, who in 1943 appointed Allen chairman of the newly created committee on American and United Nations prisoners of war. He has also devoted time to Warm Springs Foundation and its March of Dimes campaign, and the Boy Scouts of America, which organization awarded him the Silver Buffalo. Secretary of the Democratic National Committee, he is also president of the Franklin D. Roosevelt Memorial Foundation. Two other interests in Washington are a deaconship in the Negro Universal Church of God and a trusteeship of Columbia Hospital. In 1938 Cumberland University, his old college, bestowed an honorary LL.D. degree on him. Allen is a member of Kappa Sigma fraternity, and his clubs are in Louisville, Chicago, New York, and Washington.

Word pictures of George E. Allen usually include references to his generous girth and

ALLEN, GEORGE E.—*Continued*

grin. To this Delos W. Lovelace (New York *Sun*) adds "an Irvin Cobb chin," and Oliver Pilat (New York *Post*) the information that the six-foot 212-pound Allen likes detective stories. Other writers also mention his liking for an occasional game of poker and his two-dollar bets at the race track. Mrs. Allen is the former Mary Keane of Washington, to whom the RFC director was married in 1930, and whose humorous remarks Allen retells with relish.

References

Life 21:61+ S 9 '46 por
N Y Post p7 F 16 '46 por
N Y Sun p12 Ag 16 '45; p22 Ja 17 '46
N Y Times Mag p54-5 F 24 '46 por
Time 48:17 Ag 12 '46 por
U S News 20:66-7 F 1 '46 por
Who's Who in America, 1946-47

ALTMEYER, ARTHUR J(OSEPH) May 8, 1891- United States Government official

Address: b. c/o Federal Security Agency, Washington, D. C.; h. 4613 Rock Spring Rd., Arlington, Va.

Dr. Arthur J. Altmeyer, Commissioner for Social Security in the Federal Security Agency, directs the largest insurance system in the world—it has more than eighty-four million "customers" as of early 1946. Altmeyer has administered the Social Security Act since 1937, during most of the period as chairman of the Social Security Board, and he has therefore been responsible for the Federal programs of public employment service, and of old-age and survivors' insurance. In addition, social security includes, on a cooperative Federal-State basis: unemployment insurance; aid to dependent children, the needy aged, and the needy blind; health and welfare services, especially for children; and retraining of disabled workers.

Born in the small town of De Pere, Wisconsin, on May 8, 1891, Arthur Joseph Altmeyer is the son of John G. and Carrie (Smith) Altmeyer. Young Arthur attended the University of Wisconsin, where he was elected to the national scholastic honor society Phi Beta Kappa; and after receiving his B.A. in 1914 he became a high school teacher. Two years later he was a principal, and two years after that, in 1918, he left the field of education to accept appointment as statistician for the Wisconsin Tax Commission. (Altmeyer has published a study of the receipts and disbursements of civil divisions in Wisconsin.)

Transferred to the Wisconsin Industrial Commission in 1920, as chief statistician, Altmeyer obtained his Master's degree from the university the next year. He became secretary of the Industrial Commission in 1922 and held this office for eleven years, during which he wrote *The Industrial Commission of Wisconsin —A Case Study in Labor Law Administration* (1932) and received his Ph.D. (1931). Dr. Altmeyer's writings also include *General Accident Statistics for Wisconsin.*

When the National Recovery Administration was set up in 1933, the forty-two-year-old labor-law administrator moved to Washington to enter Federal service as head of the NRA Compliance Division. By the time NRA was pronounced unconstitutional in June 1935, however, Altmeyer had been Second Assistant Secretary of Labor for a year. He served concurrently on the interdepartmental technical board assisting the President's committee to study the question of economic security. In August 1935, when Assistant Secretary Altmeyer was appointed to the new three-man Social Security Board, *Business Week* described him thus: "Minor brain truster without the usual connotations. Studious type. A good administrative technician—some say he now runs the Labor Department while his superiors, Miss Perkins [40] and McGrady, settle strikes. Favors organized labor but without the shoulder chip."

Eight days before this appointment, the Wisconsinite had been named to the Interdepartmental Committee on Health and Welfare Activities of the United States Government, on which he was still serving in 1946. In 1935, while working with the two other board members to set up the national social security system, he served also on the NYA executive committee. After some time as acting chairman of the Social Security Board, Altmeyer was appointed chairman by President Roosevelt in February 1937, at which time the Supreme Court had not yet ruled on all the phases of the Act he was to administer. One of the new chairman's early actions was to appoint a committee to coordinate the Federal-State unemployment insurance program with the employment service.

"Social legislation requires the development of new [Governmental] techniques, calling for resourcefulness and imagination of a high order," Altmeyer wrote in 1937. "Its success lies entirely in its administration." "Regardless of how efficiently social legislation may be administered," he added, "the very fact that it affects so many people directly and continuously gives rise to administrative irritations. Orderly procedure is likely to be castigated as 'red tape,' and a trained personnel is likely to be attacked as a bureaucracy."

Reappointed to a six-year term in 1939 (after rumors of his impending elevation to head of the entire Federal Security Agency), Altmeyer presented the Social Security Board's recommendations to the Congressional committees hearing testimony on proposed amendments to the Social Security Act that year. Then and later, Altmeyer advocated extending the old-age and survivors' insurance system to cover permanent disability and adding insurance against temporary disability; lowering the retirement benefits age for women to sixty; extending coverage to several millions of persons exempted because they were domestic servants, maritime workers, agricultural labor, self-employed, or employees of religious and charitable institutions; and changing the unemployment insurance program from a Federal-State basis to a purely Federal one, for administrative reasons. (This last proposal he later modified.) Altmeyer recommended further that, while the Federal Government should continue to match the wealthier States dollar for dollar in the public-assistance and the health and welfare programs, the poorer States should be given more Federal money because their need was greater.

During the defense program expansion of 1940-41, while World War II was raging in Europe and Asia, Altmeyer rebuked those who suggested a temporary curtailment of social security work. "Defense has been regarded by some as a substitute for a working democracy at home," he charged as he warned against this "proposal to find steel for the turrets of the Ship of State by prying a few plates off the bottom." Later he told an inter-American conference: "It is through social security that great masses of the citizens of our countries can be assured decent food, clothing, and shelter and essential health services necessary to make them able and willing defenders of their country and their way of life." The United States Employment Service, taken over by the War Manpower Commission later, was under the SSB in 1941, when Southern Congressmen were roused to protest by the elimination of Jim Crow practices in the District of Columbia offices of the USES.

Arthur Altmeyer was a member of the Interdepartmental Advisory Council to coordinate health, welfare, and related defense activities; and five months after Pearl Harbor, in May 1942, he was made executive director of the new War Manpower Commission, under his superior, Federal Security Administrator Paul McNutt[40]. He served in that capacity until December, continuing afterwards as SSB representative on the nine-member commission. Meanwhile, in September, Altmeyer headed the delegation to the six-day first Inter-American Conference on Social Security at Santiago, Chile. There he was elected president of the new Permanent Inter-American Committee on Social Security. (Three years earlier, he had been chairman of another delegation, to the regional I.L.O. conference at Havana.) Later, addressing another meeting, Altmeyer urged that a world-wide charter of social security principles be worked out internationally, to serve as a basis for continuing cooperation in the field.

Before Altmeyer's reappointment by President Truman in July 1945, he was reported to be the choice of the remaining brain trusters to replace Veterans Administration head Hines[44]—the post which finally went to General Omar Bradley[43]. By February 1946, Altmeyer's board had charge of more than eighty-four million individual workers' accounts, which were administered at an average annual cost of seventeen cents each. About 1,300,000 persons were receiving monthly old-age and dependent-child benefits, a number expected to rise to two million by the end of the year. Various studies by the board had convinced Altmeyer that the benefit rates set in 1939 had been inadequate even then—and had become far more so with increased cost of living—and he therefore suggested a revised formula for computing them, and also advocated doubling the $14.99 monthly maximum which a beneficiary was

ARTHUR J. ALTMEYER

permitted to earn without losing his right to the benefits. He continued to urge enactment of the extensions and reforms he had presented without success in 1939, and in May he asked Congress to reduce the Federal unemployment insurance tax from 3 to 2 per cent, because of the size of existing reserves. Two months later, in a reorganization, the SSB functions were transferred to the FSA directly, with Altmeyer becoming Commissioner for Social Security, and his two fellow-members assigned to other posts.

In November 1946 Commissioner Altmeyer announced that the country's unemployment insurance fund stood at nearly seven billion dollars, and expressed the opinion that this "healthy accumulation of reserves" would prevent any really serious depression. At this time, the Commissioner was serving also as adviser to the United States representative on the U.N. Economic and Social Council. In December President Truman[45] appointed him to the Social Commission, a body of experts set up by the Economic and Social Council to report on social problems requiring immediate attention.

Scholarly, spectacled Arthur J. Altmeyer is described as an earnest man, not given greatly to humor. His church affiliation is Unitarian. A fourth academic degree from the University of Wisconsin, the LL.D., came to him in 1939. Altmeyer lives in Arlington, Virginia, near the capital. His wife is the former Ethel M. Thomas of Superior, Wisconsin, to whom he was married in July 1916.

References

N Y Sun p26 N 22 '46
Survey G 34:368+ S '45 por
Who's Who in America, 1946-47

ANANDA MAHIDOL (ä-nän-tä mä-hĕd-dōn) Sept. 20, 1925—June 9, 1946 King of Thailand from 1935 under regency on the abdi-

ANANDA MAHIDOL—*Continued*

cation of his uncle, King Prajadhipok; spent
little time in his own land; born in Germany,
educated in Thailand and in Switzerland; was
found dead of a bullet wound in the royal
palace.

Obituary

N Y Times p1+ Je 10 '46 por

ANDREWS, CHARLES O(SCAR) Mar.
7, 1877—Sept. 18, 1946 United States Demo-
ratic Senator from Florida from 1936 until his
death; worked for the elimination of the practice of attaching "unrelated riders" to proposed
legislation.

Obituary

N Y Times p31 S 19 '46 por

ANTONESCU, ION (än-tōn-ĕs-kōō′ ē-ōn′)
1882—June 1, 1946 Premier General of Rumania, 1940; became dictator after dissolving
Parliament and the constitution and forming totalitarian state; demanded abdication of King
Carol II, assumed command of Iron Guard;
took over four Cabinet posts; foreign policy
based on complete accord with Rome-Berlin
axis; regarded as anti-Semitic, anti-Soviet, pro-
British; executed for war crimes. See *Current
Biography* 1940 Yearbook.

Obituary

N Y Times p19 Je 2 '46

ARLISS, GEORGE Apr. 10, 1868—Feb. 5,
1946 English actor; appeared for sixty years
on the British and American stage and screen;
best known for his stage roles in *The Second
Mrs. Tanqueray, Paganini,* and *The Green Goddess,* and his biographical portrayals in the
films *Disraeli, The House of Rothschild, Alexander Hamilton, The Iron Duke,* and *Cardinal
Richelieu;* wrote or collaborated on six plays;
Up the Years from Bloomsbury (1927) and
My Ten Years in the Studios (1940) were his
autobiographical works.

Obituary

N Y Times p23 F 6 '46 por

ARMSTRONG, CHARLOTTE May 2,
1905- Author; playwright
Address: h. 604 Cavanagh Rd., Glendale, Calif.

Charlotte Armstrong, writer of mystery
stories, has a theory that accounts for the flood
of detective stories which appeared during the
war. "Nobody," she says, "could write realism
—and nobody wanted to read it, either. Everybody would have liked to read comedy, but who
could write it? A close-knit little private murder, with justice at the end, was the very thing.
Escape or something." Miss Armstrong found
her own escape in the writing of a trio of
"whodunits," leading up to her last book, *The
Unsuspected,* which appeared in the 1946 spring
publishing season.

Born in Vulcan, Michigan, on May 2, 1905,
Charlotte Armstrong is the daughter of Frank

CHARLOTTE ARMSTRONG

Hall and Clara (Pascoe) Armstrong. She grew
up in the iron-mining country of northern
Michigan where her father, who comes from a
long line of "covered-wagon" Yankees, was a
mining engineer and inventor. Her mother's
people were Cornish. After attending the Vulcan High School, she went to Ferry Hall, in
Lake Forest, Illinois, and then spent two years
at the University of Wisconsin. For her last
year of academic work, she went to Barnard
College, Columbia University, where she received her B.A. in 1925.

After leaving the university, Charlotte Armstrong found a position with the New York
Times, but it had nothing to do with writing:
she took classified advertisements over the telephone for a salary of eighteen dollars a week.
Following this she was a reporter for a buyer's
guide called the *Breath of the Avenue,* going
around from shop to shop noting fashion
trends. Then, for a while, she was an office
worker in a firm of certified public accountants
in the downtown district. Three years after
she had come out of college, in 1928 Miss Armstrong's business experiences were terminated
by her marriage to Jack Lewi, an advertising
man.

Since childhood Charlotte Armstrong has
been writing: first in school, then as editor
of the Ferry Hall magazine, and later as contributor of poems to the *New Yorker.* After
her marriage she became interested in the theater. Her first play, *The Happiest Days*
(1939), was produced on Broadway under the
direction of Marc Connelly. Though not generally well-received, the play did interest Brooks
Atkinson, drama critic for the New York
Times. "Out of a shattering tragedy," he
wrote, "Charlotte Armstrong has recovered a
few merciful strands of beauty. . . .She has
put a rueful tale on the stage with simplicity

and tenderness." Miss Armstrong's second play, *Ring Around Elizabeth,* produced on Broadway in November 1941, reaped a negative reaction in New York, although it did rather well in Philadelphia. The New York *Times* called the drama a "misguided comedy" and deplored the fact that so distinguished an actress as Jane Cowl should concern herself with such "fiddle-faddle." Miss Cowl, nevertheless, played her part "with the gusto of a woman who is having a grand time."

While *Ring Around Elizabeth* was in rehearsal Miss Armstrong sold her first mystery story, which was published in 1942 with the title *Lay On, Mac Duff.* Critics called it a "generally pleasing item," a "well-constructed and exciting baffler," and "refreshing." The author developed "the promise she exhibited in her first book" in a second mystery, *The Case of the Weird Sisters* (1943). This was followed by *The Innocent Flower* (1945), which Elizabeth Haxton Bullock described in the Chicago *Sun* as "on the mild side," but amply rewarding. A foreword states that all characters are synthetic, with the exception of three of the children, modeled after the author's own. Miss Armstrong's latest book, *The Unsuspected* (1946), is not a true mystery story, since the murderer is known from the start; nor is it, according to Howard Haycraft [41], a psychological study, but rather, an "extraordinarily exciting surface melodrama," distinguished by "tight writing and broad, colorful delineation of character and mood." While this suspense novel was being serialized in the *Saturday Evening Post,* many people telephoned the author to suggest a solution, advise about the plot, make a guess as to the ending. Miss Armstrong found this somewhat wearing at first, but then decided that some reader reaction would be helpful in the future. Before publication in book form, *The Unsuspected* was bought for the motion pictures. The author, accompanied by her family, went to Hollywood to supervise the filming.

Before going to California, Charlotte Armstrong, her husband, and their children, Jeremy Brett, Penny, and Peter, lived in New Rochelle, New York. As a hobby she ran a little theater with a troupe of twenty high school students in a stable in the back yard of her home. Other recreations included gardening and the reading of "quantities of mystery stories." A favorite book in another category is Stanislavski's *An Actor Prepares.* The author is of the Protestant faith, but has no particular political affiliation. Undaunted by the reception accorded to her first two plays, the slight, hazel-eyed, brown-haired Miss Armstrong expects to write others. She also contemplates doing a novel some day —an idea which frightens her, she says, because, unlike the drama or the mystery story, the novel has no rules and limitations. In 1946 the author was at work on a new suspense story, "The Better to Eat You!"

Reference

N Y World-Telegram p8 O 3 '45

ARTHUR, SIR GEORGE (COMPTON ARCHIBALD) Apr. 30, 1860—Jan. 14, 1946 British biographer, editor, translator; British Army officer, private secretary to Lord Kitchener, equerry of Duchess of Teck; his books include biographies of Kitchener, Sarah Bernhardt, King George V, the Queens Mary, Alexandra, and Victoria, and his friend Winston Churchill.

Obituary

N Y Times p23 Ja 15 '46 por

ASTON, FRANCIS WILLIAM Sept. 1, 1877—Nov. 21, 1945 British physicist; awarded the Nobel Prize for chemistry in 1922; renowned for his work with isotopes; developed the mass spectrograph; in early twenties warned against the danger of releasing of atomic energy.

Obituary

N Y Times p36 N 22 '45 por

ATCHESON, GEORGE, JR. Oct. 20, 1896- United States Government official

Address: b. c/o Department of State, Washington, D.C.

A career diplomat with more than twenty years of experience in Far Eastern affairs, George Atcheson, Jr., became the chairman of the four-power Allied Council for Japan after he was assigned to Tokyo as political adviser to General Douglas MacArthur [41], supreme Commander for the Allied Powers in Japan.

George Atcheson, Jr., sometimes confused with Under Secretary of State Dean Acheson [41], to whom he is related only by State Department ties, was born in Denver, Colorado, on October 20, 1896, to Dr. George and Effie A. (Moore) Atcheson. After graduation from Fremont High School in Oakland, California, he attended the University of California, where he received his B.A. degree in 1919. During World War I he served for a year (1918-19) in the United States Army as instructor at a school of military aeronautics and was a first lieutenant in the Officers' Reserve Corps. After about five years of work for various newspapers and magazines before and after the war (1915-20), Atcheson, at twenty-four, decided to enter the diplomatic corps, whereupon he was appointed student interpreter at the United States Legation in Peking in 1920. At the College of Chinese Studies there, from which he obtained his M.A. degree in 1924, he learned Chinese dialects and enriched his knowledge of the Asiatic country whose leaders were then preparing for the "Great Revolution" of 1925-27.

The young diplomat rose steadily in the United States Foreign Service. He was vice-consul, interpreter, and then consular assistant at Changsha in 1923-24; he served in the State Department at Washington for the next two years; and in 1926-27 he was stationed at North Bay, Ontario. In 1927, the year of Chiang Kai-shek's [40] split with the Communist Party, Atcheson, who was then formally com-

GEORGE ATCHESON, JR.

missioned in the Foreign Service, once more received an appointment in China, this time in Tientsin. He was appointed consul in that city in 1928, and had a temporary assignment at Foochow (August 1928 to February 1929). He was sent to Nanking in 1934, where he served both as consul and as second secretary of the legation. A year later he became the second secretary of the Nanking Embassy. Appointed second secretary at the Peiping Embassy in the spring of 1938, he served at the same time as consul at Tientsin. For about nine months he was also the president of the administrative commission of the diplomatic quarter in Peiping until he returned to the State Department in Washington in 1939. He held the position of assistant chief of the Division of Far Eastern Affairs in 1941-42 and became acting chief in December of 1942. That year he was a representative for the Department of State on the *Drottningholm,* the ship which carried exchanged nationals during World War II.

In May 1943, when China was waging a desperate fight against the Japanese invaders while clashes occurred between Chinese Government and Communist troops, Atcheson returned to the Orient. He was made counselor of the Embassy at Chungking, and for a period in 1943 as well as in 1944 was chargé d'affaires there. Atcheson was one of the foreign service officers whom General Patrick J. Hurley[44] charged with insubordination. In hearings before the Senate Foreign Relations Committee in December 1945, Hurley, who had been sent to China as President Roosevelt's special envoy to help unify China's factions, accused the diplomats of having sabotaged his efforts to uphold Chiang Kai-shek's Government. He charged that Atcheson, acting as chargé d'affaires in his absence, had sent a report to the State Department recommending Lend-Lease shipments to the Chinese Communists, a measure which Hurley maintained

would have led to the downfall of Chiang's Government. Secretary of State James Byrnes[41] stated before the committee that there was no proof that Atcheson or any of his colleagues had been guilty of the charge, that the wire dated February 28, 1945, which Atcheson had sent while acting as counselor of the Chunking Embassy in Hurley's absence "contained a broad and thoughtful analysis of the situation in China" and proposed a change in strategy for discussion with Generals Hurley and Albert Wedemeyer[45]. (Wedemeyer was the commanding general of the United States Army Forces in the China theater of war.)

In September 1945 Byrnes appointed Atcheson a political adviser to General Douglas MacArthur, Supreme Commander for the Allied Powers in Japan and commander in chief of the occupation forces. A New York *Herald Tribune* editorial commented that Atcheson, who had also been named as Minister to Siam but did not assume the post because of his duties in Japan, was stepping into a "lion's den." According to a subsequent newspaper account, and a statement by the diplomat himself while on a visit to the United States, he and the Supreme Commander for the Allied Powers worked well together. In April 1946 MacArthur appointed him the American member and chairman of the four-power Allied Council for Japan. The council, which had been set up in accordance with the provisions of the Moscow Communique of December 27, 1945, to act as an advisory body to General MacArthur, was in the opinion of newspapermen, "little more than a sounding board for criticism of SCAP [Supreme Commander for the Allied Powers] policies." It was expected that Atcheson, now ranked as an Ambassador, would bring peace to the council sessions which up to that time had been characterized by ill feeling and heated exchanges between the Russian and American delegates. These hopes, however, were not realized—discussions on such subjects as land reforms, labor legislation, and the expansion of Japanese fishing areas continued to turn into ideological disputes between the Russian representative, Lieutenant General Kuzma Derevyanko, and Atcheson. Some newspapermen criticized him for a "tendency to impugn the Soviet delegate and Russian policy" during council sessions.

When an unsigned petition adopted at a 1946 May Day meeting in Tokyo and claiming that the interests of laborers and farmers were not receiving adequate protection from Allied headquarters was discussed at a council meeting, Atcheson declared that the document contained the "sign marks of Communist propaganda." While approving the right of freedom of expression and action for all groups, he stressed that it was the duty of the council not to support "any one Japanese political party." He also added that "the United States [did] not favor communism in the United States or Japan," a statement quoted by anti-communistic members of the Japanese Diet and approved by the State Department.

Meetings of the council in the months that followed were the occasion of continued controversy over such issues as labor legislation, land reforms, a proposal for the confiscation of all Japanese literature of a fascist, militarist, or anti-Allied nature, and the repatriation of Japanese prisoners of war. According to Darrell Berrigan, the Far East editor of the New York *Post*, the council "served only to exacerbate Russian-American relations in Japan," which some commentators felt were strained by Soviet suspicions of designs by MacArthur to build up a conservative Japanese Government to serve as a future American military ally. At a special meeting on August 13, called to discuss procedural organization and to make suggestions for improving the council's work, Atcheson pointed to the supposition of some observers "rightly or wrongly, that there is resentment in the council that the United States, by dictate of circumstance, has taken a predominant role in the occupation." To overcome such an attitude, he set forth the proposal that representatives of the eleven Allied powers with missions in Tokyo be invited to contribute their views at council meetings in an unofficial capacity.

George Atcheson was awarded the United States Navy expeditionary medal in connection with the Japanese sinking in 1937 of the U.S.S. *Panay*. He is a member of several societies: the Winged Helmet, Skull and Keys, Golden Bear, Delta Upsilon. In 1922 the career diplomat was married to Mariquita de Laguna; they have one son, George 3d.

References

N Y Herald Tribune II p4 D 9 '45 por
N Y Sun p18 Ap 19 '46 por
Biographic Register of the Department of State, Sep 1, 1944

ATWILL, LIONEL Mar. 1, 1885—Apr. 22, 1946 British stage and screen actor; established himself in plays by Shaw and Ibsen; became one of the most famous of America's screen villains; among his stage plays are *The Walls of Jericho* (1905) and *The Little Minister* (1912); appeared with Lily Langtry, Nazimova, Katharine Cornell, and Helen Hayes; acted "horror" roles in *Mystery of the Wax Museum, Son of Frankenstein, Hound of the Baskervilles*, and other films.

Obituary

N Y Times p21 Ap 23 '46 por

AYRES, LEONARD PORTER Sept. 15, 1879—Oct. 29, 1946 Economist and statistician, known for his forecasts of financial trends; editor of the *Monthly Business Bulletin*, published by the Cleveland Trust Company, of which he was vice-president from 1920 until his death; chief statistical officer, War Department, in both world wars; economic adviser to Government commissions and private organizations; author of monographs on education and books on economics. See *Current Biography* 1940 Yearbook.

Obituary

N Y Times p29 O 30 '46 por

BADEN-POWELL, LADY (OLAVE ST. CLAIR) (bā'd'n-pō'ĕl) Feb. 22, 1889- Leader of the international Girl Scout movement

Address: h. Hampton Court Palace, East Molesey, Surrey, England

Lady Baden-Powell, who has been identified with the Girl Guides of England for many years, is Chief Guide of the World—of the British organization, the Girl Scouts of America, and similar groups throughout the world. Rose Kerr, in her history of Girl Guide and Girl Scout groups, states that it was Lady Baden-Powell who, "full of new ideas and enthusiasm . . . really created the *spirit* of the movement" in England. And, believing that international Scouting, by uniting the young people in all countries, can make a valuable contribution to world peace, she successfully continued to organize Girl Guides and Scouts on an international scale. Their number, according to Girl Scouts Headquarters in New York, has doubled within the past nine years to reach approximately three million.

A student of Norway's history, Harold Soames named his youngest child, Olave (the feminine of Olaf) St. Clair. She was born in Chesterfield, Derbyshire, England, on February 22, 1889, and grew up in the country. After her twelfth birthday, formal education for Olave was discontinued; she went on only with the study of the violin, for which she showed an aptitude. After her debut at the age of eighteen Miss Soames participated in the usual activities of a young lady of her social standing—going to parties, hunting, traveling with her father. It was a visit to the West Indies in 1912 that had an important bearing on the rest of her life, for it was on that trip that she met her future husband. In a letter to her mother written on the boat, she said: "The only interesting person on board is General Baden-Powell, the Scout man." In the fall of the same year Olave Soames and Sir Robert Baden-Powell, the founder of the Boy Scout movement and Chief Scout, were married. Ten years later Baden-Powell was made a baronet, and in 1929 was elevated to the peerage as the first Baron Baden-Powell of Gilwell. (The title is now borne by the Baden-Powells' son Arthur Robert Peter, an official of the Southern Rhodesian Government and an honorary officer of the local Boy Scouts.)

The next few years of Lady Baden-Powell's life were taken up with household and family duties in their Sussex home. Three children were born: Peter in 1913, Heather in 1915, and Betty in 1917. The young mother found time, however, to help her husband with his work in the rapidly expanding Scout movement; she also ran a YMCA canteen in Calais during World War I. In 1916 Lady Baden-Powell, who had thus far been concerned only with the Boy Scouts was asked by the Girl Guide Association to become Guide Commissioner of Sussex. Inspired by the Boy Scout movement, which had been founded in 1908, Girl Scout groups had sprung up here and there, and in 1909, when some of them attended a rally of ten thousand Boy Scouts at the Crystal Palace and asked to be inspected along with the boys

Paul Parker Photo.
LADY BADEN-POWELL

the Chief Scout, Baden-Powell, gave his consent. Realizing that the time had come to organize a Scout movement for girls also, but too busy to take charge himself, he at first entrusted the task to his sister, Miss Agnes Baden-Powell. The girl groups became known as Girl Guides.

As Commissioner of Sussex, Lady Baden-Powell proved herself to be an able organizer. Realizing the importance of publicizing the new movement (printed publicity was not available at headquarters in those days) and of getting more workers, she wrote letters to people whom she thought might be interested. Those who replied they did not have the time to help, she impressed with the fact that training girls to be good citizens was important war work. Using the Boy Scout organization as a model, she set up local committees in each town to encourage organization; in the various districts, commissioners were assigned to direct activities and to form a liaison with headquarters.

So successful was Lady Baden-Powell with her work in Sussex, that in 1917, upon the request of all the other county commissioners, she became Chief Commissioner. In this position she extended the network of organization which she had developed in Sussex to every county in Great Britain as well as to the British dominions and colonies overseas. The various units which had been working with only occasional contact with each other became a strong, united whole under her leadership. In order to share her experience as a commissioner and be of help to her fellow workers Lady Baden-Powell wrote a book entitled *Training Girls as Guides,* which was published in 1917. In it, while emphasizing the importance of organization as a "sound footing" for all, she cautioned that it must not have a stagnating effect, that it must be flexible enough to allow for progress and reform. Stressing

also that such principles as loyalty, sympathy, and consideration for others must give meaning to the machinery of organization, she suggested that commissioners maintain a personal contact with their companies and visit them often. She proposed, in addition, that they win the confidence and support of parents and other members of the community by holding meetings with them.

With the movement organized in Great Britain and the Empire, Lady Baden-Powell looked toward world organization. Before the outbreak of World War I there had been some contact with the Girl Guide and Girl Scout groups, which had been formed in other countries, through an interchange of visits. For example, Mrs. Juliette Low, who had founded the Girl Scouts of America in 1912, visited England every summer and was thus able to maintain contact with British headquarters. The war, however, put a stop even to these unorganized international connections.

After the Armistice, when travel once again became possible, Lady Baden-Powell, who had by this time been unanimously elected permanent Chief Guide by a large group of commissioners in 1918, began to make plans for the organization of an International Council. She envisoned such a body as an information center on the world Scouting movement and as a means of integrating the many groups; it would not be a governing body, however. In order to form such a group, it was necessary to enlist the cooperation of people in a position to get information about the Girl Guide groups abroad. Gradually Lady Baden-Powell assembled a group representing about twenty countries, and in February 1920 the International Council met for the first time. Thereafter meetings, presided over by the Chief Guide until 1926, were held quarterly in London.

As the first activity of the International Council, Lady Baden-Powell suggested that leaders from other countries be invited to a world conference to exchange ideas. In July 1920, at St. Hugh's College, Oxford, the first International Conference, attended by representatives from such countries as Belgium, Denmark, Italy, Poland, Sweden, the British dominions, the United States, and Switzerland, was held. The delegates felt the meeting was so valuable that it was decided to hold conferences biennially thereafter. Not only was this carried out but the international meeting of 1926 brought about the creation of a World Association with permanent headquarters and a staff. At the second International Conference the delegates honored Lady Baden-Powell for her work by presenting her with a gold chain bracelet of twenty-six links, each link a symbol for one of the twenty-six countries represented at the meeting. In 1930 she was chosen as Chief Guide of the World by all the member countries participating in that year's World Conference. Representatives attending the conference held in Poland in 1932 designated a special day in the year as "Thinking Day" for all Girl Guides and Girl Scouts; the day selected was February 22, which is the birthday of both the Chief Guide and the Chief Scout.

Another important development in the Girl Guide and Girl Scout movement was the establishment of international camps. In 1924, at Lady Baden-Powell's suggestion, eleven hundred Guides and Girl Scouts, more than five hundred from overseas, spent the summer camping at Foxlease, England. Those from foreign countries were distributed among thirty groups of English girls so as to allow all nationalities to mingle, and patrol duties brought together the young people who spoke different languages. Before 1924 international camps had been held in Switzerland and also at the Chateau d'Argeronne in Normandy.

Lord and Lady Baden-Powell were truly Chief Scout and Chief Guide of the World: In frequent world tours they visited Scout groups everywhere. They made such a trip in 1919, and in 1921 went to India to coordinate the Scout groups which had been formed there. During the thirties, they made two more trips around the world. While in Italy the two Chiefs had an audience with the Pope, who told them how much he approved of the work of the Guides and Scouts. They also saw to it that several hundred of the leaders in their organization had an opportunity to travel and observe the progress of the movement in other countries; in 1933 they led one group on a goodwill cruise of the Baltic ports, and in 1934 they took another party to the Mediterranean region. In *Travelogues* and *Guide Links*, which Lady Baden-Powell wrote in 1935 and 1936, respectively, those who stayed at home could share her journeys vicariously.

Because of the Chief Scout's failing health, he and his wife retired in 1938 to Kenya, East Africa, where he died three years later, and where Lady Baden-Powell continued to make her home until 1942. That year, when she was asked to return to England by those who felt her presence would be an incentive to British Girl Guides as well as to the World Bureau, which had headquarters in London, she came at once and resumed her work with the World Association. During World War II, Girl Guides and Scouts in Allied countries gave much of their time to helping on the home front. In addition to aiding in blood bank campaigns, collecting salvage, selling bonds, raising funds, and supplying clothes and food to the needy people of Europe, they served during the air raids and helped with the evacuation of children from cities. They also worked in hospitals, on farms, in day nurseries, and in canteens. Those in Nazi-occupied lands "were up to their necks in the resistance movement," said their Chief Guide.

When she visited America in 1946, Lady Baden-Powell stated that the international Scouting movement had gained by a "reinspired" growth since the end of the war, a growth which has spread to remote parts of Africa and even to such isolated places as Tristan da Cunha, a minute island in the South Atlantic about midway between Capetown and Buenos Aires. She also emphasized the significance of the movement to the growth of world fellowship and peace. In 1946, a year after the Nazi surrender, European Girl Guides visited each other's homelands once more, at-tending conferences and camps. The members of one American Girl Scouts troop, inspired by the World Guide, who had urged them not to postpone a trip to Britain, crossed the Atlantic to camp with English Girl Guides. It was the first United States Girl Scouts troop to visit a foreign country as a unit.

In 1932 Lady Baden-Powell was made a Dame of the Grand Cross of the Order of the British Empire. Dame Olave also holds the Order of the Jubilee of George the Fifth, and the Order of the Coronation of George the Sixth, as well as such foreign orders as the Order of Merit of Poland, a citation for her work in World War I, and the Order of the White Rose of Finland. In accordance with a custom affecting the widows of a certain number of famous Englishmen, she was given, by royal order, an apartment at Hampton Court Palace for her lifetime.

References

Baden-Powell, O. Training Girls as Guides (1917) ; Travelogues (1935)
Kerr, R. Story of a Million Girls (1937)
Reynolds, E. E. Baden-Powell (1943)

BAGLEY, WILLIAM CHANDLER Mar. 15, 1874—July 1, 1946 Educator, writer; professor of education at Teachers College, Columbia University, from 1908 to 1940; editor of *School and Society*, 1939-46; editor of the National Education Association *Journal* from 1920 to 1925, president of its national council of education, 1931-37; author of many texts, among them, *History of the American People* with C. A. Beard (1918), *Determinism in Education* (1925), *A Century of the Universal School* (1937).

Obituary

N Y Times p25 Jl 2 '46 por

BAILEY, THOMAS L. Jan. 6, 1888—Nov. 2, 1946 Governor of Mississippi from 1944 until his death; a member of the Mississippi legislature from 1916 until 1940, speaker of the State House of Representatives from 1924 to 1936; opposed measures of former Governor Theodore G. Bilbo.

Obituary

N Y Times p63 N 3 '46

BAILLIE, HUGH Oct. 23, 1890- Press association executive

Address: b. United Press Associations, 220 E. 42d St., New York; h. 450 E. 52d St., New York

With the end of World War II, the attention of both newsmen and world leaders is being increasingly directed toward the restitution and expansion of world-wide free news dissemination, particularly as a means toward keeping the peace. In the forefront of the movement is Hugh Baillie, president of the United Press Associations, a graduate from its ranks, and still a reporter whose "beat is the world."

A fourth generation newspaperman of Scottish ancestry, Hugh Baillie was born in Brook-

HUGH BAILLIE

lyn, New York, on October 23, 1890. His father, David Gemmell Baillie, was a prominent political correspondent for the New York *Tribune* and the New York *World*, and for a time was literary secretary to Andrew Carnegie; his mother was the former Fannie Mead Hays, daughter of John B. Hays, in his heyday the dean of New York's City Hall reporters. Young Baillie received his elementary education in Brooklyn, but midway in his high school career the Baillie family moved to California. His high school diploma consequently bears the seal of a Los Angeles school. From 1907 to 1910 he attended the University of Southern California, where his journalistic career began. He was, first, campus correspondent for the Los Angeles *Herald* and, after leaving the university, for a time sports reporter for the paper.

That same year (1910), however, he took a job with the Los Angeles *Record,* a Scripps paper, thus beginning his long association with the Scripps interests. In addition to reporting, the budding journalist wrote three columns for the *Record.* Under the pseudonym of Jim Frothingham he produced a summary of local news in rhyme; as The Reformed Office Boy, a Broadway column; and as John Danger, a vice exposé. The third was responsible not only for the doubling of the *Record*'s circulation (in reward for which Baillie received, among other things, a watch he still wears) but also for his having to leave town when the local gangsters learned his true identity. In 1912 came his first association with the United Press when the *Record* lent him to the news agency to cover the trial of Clarence Darrow on charges of bribing the jury in the McNamara-Los Angeles *Times* case in which Darrow had been lawyer for the defense the preceding year.

Baillie remained with the *Record* until 1915 and then joined the San Francisco bureau of the United Press. During the course of the next five years he directed, successively, the Los An-

geles, Portland (Oregon), New York, and Washington bureaus of the news agency. In 1921 he was promoted to the position of assistant general news manager of the United Press and a year later was named general news manager. Turning from the editorial to the business end of the enterprise in 1924, Baillie, newly appointed sales manager, organized a system under which each main section of the country was placed in charge of one man given responsibility for both news coverage and sales. By 1927 the young executive had risen to the position of general business manager and vice-president; by 1931, to general manager and executive vice-president. Since 1935 Hugh Baillie has been the U.P.'s president and general manager, having been nominated for the post by the retiring president Karl A. Bickel.

The United Press Associations had been founded in 1907 by the merger of the Scripps-McRae Press Association, the Scripps News Association (both controlled by Edward Wyllis Scripps), and Publishers' Press. Roy Wilson Howard [40] became New York manager of the new organization which was formed to fill the need for a source of foreign news independent both of the obviously biased subsidized news services of foreign governments and of the monopolistic, cartelized international news services which then controlled the field. Unlike the Associated Press, the U.P. was to be a profit-making organization; also, it was to be non-exclusive, independent, and impartial: undominated by any outside interest it would gather its own news for distribution to any responsible paper anywhere. From the outset it made a point of setting up its own foreign bureaus and of establishing the best and fastest media of communication. Slowly but steadily its staff of predominantly young men impressed the new service upon publishers at home and abroad. In 1916 it pioneered the first American news service to South American newspapers, especially the important *La Prensa.* After World War I it inaugurated the first direct service to European papers by an American agency. By September 1939 U.P. dispatches were being used by 251 newspapers in 22 European nations and similar expansion had been recorded in the U.P.'s service to Asia, the Pacific, and Latin America. The latest estimate (1946) notes service to 860 foreign papers. Within the United States contracts were concluded with all the leading dailies (986 in 1946), and in 1935, the year Baillie became president, U.P. pioneered news distribution for radio broadcasting, in which field it in 1946 supplies 588 stations in the United States and abroad and is the only service to reach every State in the union. In addition, the U.P. was the first to employ the signed news story and the first to add to its other services material for sports and women's pages, cartoons, comic strips, and human interest stories.

Always the reporter, Baillie has periodically taken time off from his managerial duties to cover important news at home and abroad, or has found ways to combine his two interests. Following the Armistice of 1918 he acted as U.P. correspondent on President Woodrow Wilson's tour of the United States on behalf of the League of Nations. In 1920 he was the only reporter allowed a typewriter in the press box at the Republican national convention—he used a noiseless one. In 1932 he obtained from Franz von Papen '41 in an historic interview the opinion that Germany's only way back to her former place in the sun lay in scrapping the Versailles Treaty, retrieving her lost colonies, and rearming. Just after he succeeded to the presidency of U.P. he went abroad for the first of a series of inspection trips designed to make certain that the U.P. communication system would function with maximum effectiveness if and when the strained diplomatic relations in Europe should actually give way. Thus *Look* was able to write of him in 1944 that whenever Baillie appears "big things happen," pointing out that he was in Rome in 1935 when Mussolini '42 attacked Ethiopia, in London in 1936 during the events leading up to the abdication of King Edward VIII, now Duke of Windsor '44, that he interviewed Chamberlain after Munich, and that he was in London when World War II broke out in September 1939. In addition, Baillie secured interviews with many of the statesmen involved in those events: with Hitler '42, Mussolini, Blum '40, Litvinov '41, Herriot '46, Laval '40, and others.

Between 1939 and 1943 administrative problems of war news coverage kept Baillie at his desk in the United Press New York headquarters. In the spring of 1943, however, he departed for North Africa to see how U.P. correspondents were "making out with censorship and communications." Before he was done he had personally covered the launching of the Sicilian campaign for the United Press in a series of vivid dispatches which were later compiled in book form under the title *Two Battlefronts* and sent out among U.P.'s correspondents as samples of the kind of writing he wanted. "Avoid heavy writing," he had told his men at the front; "the communiqués take care of that. We want our readers to see, hear, feel, even smell the war!" He also managed to relax censorship in Malta, he reported, and in one spot, where American dispatches were being delayed by motorcycle carriage, he was able to arrange for a plane ferrying service. A year later Baillie was covering the Western Front with equal energy and talking to the principal Allied commanders—Eisenhower '42, Montgomery '42, Bradley '43. In September-October 1945, on a two-month tour of the Pacific theater undertaken to restore U.P. service to peacetime stability, he was at one time a dinner guest of Generalissimo Chiang Kaishek '40, was one of the two United States newspapermen to obtain an interview with Emperor Hirohito '42 of Japan (Frank Kluckhohn of the New York *Times* beat him by six hours); and by persuading General MacArthur '41 that it might by clarifying his position serve to lessen domestic controversy over American policy in Japan, Baillie was able to obtain an important and exclusive interview with the Allied commander, which shortly afterward, during the debate on the nomination of Dean Acheson '41 as Under Secretary of State, was introduced into the *Congressional Record*.

In September 1946, in a telegram to General Joseph McNarney '44, American member of the Allied Control Council for Germany, he protested the exclusion of news reporters from the executions of Nazi war criminals sentenced to death at the Nuremberg trials. Baillie declared that secrecy in this case would be contrary to American principles of freedom of the press, and, further, that it might breed rumors that the executions were not carried out as planned. Newspapers in many parts of the United States supported Baillie's contentions. As a result, the council reversed its earlier decision to bar the press. In October he obtained answers to thirty-one questions telegraphed to Joseph Stalin '42 which the New York *Times* editorially called "the most important and most hopeful statement of Russian policy made since the war."

On his second warfront tour in 1944 Baillie also began a one-man campaign for world-wide freedom of news dissemination after the war—not necessarily, he made clear, world-wide freedom of the press as it is known in the United States, because that is as yet an impractical goal, but the "freest possible flow of news among nations." In person and by cable Baillie presented to the heads of European governments a four-point program which, he had told the Michigan Press Association when he announced it in January 1944, was "based on the principle of free and fair competition in news gathering and distribution for which the United Press has fought and campaigned in virtually every country of the world since the U.P. was founded in 1907." In it he advocated: "1) News sources, particularly official sources, competitively open to all. 2) Transmission facilities competitively available to all. 3) A minimum of official regulation of the flow of news itself. 4) All newspapers throughout the world to have access to all possible sources of news." Before the end of the year he was able to obtain assurance of agreement with his ideas from the Governments of Belgium, Czechoslovakia, France, the Netherlands, Norway, Sweden, the Union of South Africa, Canada, and Switzerland. The leading English publishers expressed their agreement, while the United States Congress passed a resolution expressing its "belief in the world-wide right of the exchange of news by news gathering and news distributing agencies, whether individual or associated, by any means, without discrimination as to sources, distribution, rates or charges; and that this right should be protected by international compact." Baillie's ideas on a free world press were, further, included in *Treasury for the Free World* (1946), edited by Ben Raeburn, which the publishers described as an anthology "in which the urgent problems of our age are explored and progressive solutions sought, written by some of the very men who are now actually helping to shape the future."

Early in 1946 the issue of a free press drew the president of the U.P. into a controversy with the United States Government. When on January 16 the Associated Press announced the discontinuance of its wartime service of news delivery to the OWI, the Office of Inter-American Affairs, and the State Department, because

BAILLIE, HUGH—*Continued*

it felt that "Government cannot engage in news-
casting without creating the fear of propaganda
which necessarily would reflect upon the objectivity of the news service from which such
newscasts were prepared," Hugh Baillie indicated that the U.P. would take similar action for
the same reasons. At that time he refrained from
voicing a final decision until further opportunity
for presenting the Government's case had been
given William Benton, Assistant Secretary of
State. At the end of the month, however, he
announced that U.P. service would be discontinued on February 16. "We have seen it
demonstrated," he explained, "that no government, no matter how scrupulously careful it may
be, can distribute news and not be suspected of
spreading propaganda. The great strength of
the American press associations has been that
they were not identified, even indirectly, with
government propaganda. Thus, the American
press associations have developed into vital national assets. If the State Department wants
to open an official American agency to distribute
news abroad that will be the concern of the
Congress and the American people. But our
participation in any such program would be an
historic step—backward."

The head of the United Press is also president
of United Feature Syndicate, United Radio
Shows, and Ocean Press, Inc., and is a director
of British United Press. He is an Episcopalian,
and he has memberships in the St. Andrew's
Society and in athletic clubs in New York, California and Florida. On July 14, 1916, he was
married to Constance Scott, a San Francisco
newspaperwoman; the couple are the parents of
Hugh Scott Baillie, in 1946 a San Francisco
Chronicle reporter. Associates describe the
blue-eyed, square-jawed executive, whose blond
hair is turning gray, with such adjectives as
dramatic, vigorous, direct, and decisive. "He
hasn't much patience with the think-stuff," one
of them told a *PM* reporter. "Some of us on
U.P. have been more concerned with the newer
kind of reporting that gets under the news,
analytical and interpretative. But give *him* a
good old-fashioned blood-and-guts story, with
physical combat . . . in it." In the words of
Jack Alexander in the *Saturday Evening Post*,
Baillie retains the "fiery stamp" of the "rip-
roaring individualistic era" of the U.P.'s
growth. "His attitude toward events is that
of an old-fashioned fire-engine-and-police-raid
reporter. He is an incurable seeker of the
spectacular and the human-interest angle."
Commented another U.P. official, "News is
news to Mr. Baillie as flour is flour to a baker,
and whether it's a report of a prize fight or
diplomatic negotiation, he strives for a story
that will give the reader the facts clearly right
away, without requiring study or any task of
interpretation on the reader's part."

References

Lit Digest 119:10 Ap 20 '35
Newsweek 5:16 Ap 20 '35
PM p13-15 Ap 21 '46 por
Sat Eve Post 218:9-10+ Je 1 '46 por;
  218:20+ Je 8 '46 por
Who's Who in America, 1946-47

BAKER, PHIL Aug. 24, 1898- Radio comedian; accordionist
Address: b. c/o Columbia Broadcasting System,
485 Madison Ave., New York

On the *Take It or Leave It* program, over
the CBS network, Phil Baker, master of ceremonies, quizzes contestants selected from the
studio audience, often helping them with broad
hints and drawing laughs with his "skillful ad
libbing." As the audience heckles "You'll be
sorry," he poses "the 64-dollar question," a
term which has come into wide popular use.
Comedian and accordionist, Baker appeared for
many years in vaudeville and musical comedy
before beginning his radio career.

Phil Baker was born in Philadelphia on August 24, 1898, and reared on New York's lower
East Side. He "early had attacks of wanderlust that resulted in his running away and being sent back." At fourteen, it is told, he
once ran away to Boston and there won fifty
cents, the first prize in an amateur vaudeville
contest at the Bowdoin Square Theater. To
earn some money the young boy gathered fire-
wood in New York's vacant lots for twenty-
five cents a week, ran errands for a doctor
after school, and sold newspapers on a Broadway corner. Later he found a job at six dollars a week as an office boy for Carl Laemmle,
who was then operating the old I.M.P. film
company. Phil had no love for school and left
it as soon as he could. But he loved music.
Unable to afford music lessons, he taught himself to play the harmonica and ocarina.

Baker's first job in show business was in a
neighborhood movie house, where he often went
to watch the pianist. "One night," wrote Jack
Gaver and Dave Stanley in their book, *There's
Laughter in the Air,* "she failed to show up,
and Phil, unable to resist the temptation an
unemployed piano always presented to him,
slipped down to the piano and began to play."
His repertoire consisted of about three tunes,
but by relying on "Hearts and Flowers" for
loves scenes and by imitating Indian war cries
and "trains rushing through the night," he managed to hold the audience. The result was a
regular job. Next he played the piano in a
vaudeville act with Ed Janis, a violinist, but,
except for the fact that it enabled Baker to
purchase a secondhand acccordion for a hundred dollars, the venture was not very successful. When the Baker-Janis team broke up,
the nineteen-year-old youth, after a period of
unemployment, found another partner, Ben
Bernie "[1]. They played in major theaters in
the larger cities of the country; before long
their violin-accordion performance became "one
of the top-notch vaudeville acts of the time."

Phil Baker's career in vaudeville was interrupted when he enlisted in the World War I
Navy, but was soon resumed after he was discharged. He now developed his own act, a
combination of singing, talking, and accordion-
playing with a comic twist, and was featured
at Ziegfeld's *Midnight Frolics* atop the New
Amsterdam Theater, Morris Gest's Century
Roof, and other night clubs. He found a valuable addition for the performances with which
he amused vaudeville audiences in the "stooge,"

a comic character whose discovery some writers credit him with: One evening in the early 1920's Jojo, an acquaintance of Baker's in the audience, interrupted his act by calling for a popular song which he wanted to hear. "When Baker tried to ignore the interruption," wrote Robert Eichberg in *Radio Stars of Today* (1937), "the plea was repeated—louder, and in more detail. The more embarrassed Baker became, the harder the audience laughed." Recognizing the value of this heckling, Baker decided to make Jojo a regular part of the act. (The stooge is essential to most comic shows today—his principal function is to "feed" lines to the chief comedian.)

During most of the 1920's and in the early 1930's Baker played in musical revues on Broadway. After appearing in *Greenwich Village Follies* and *The Passing Show*, the latter a Shubert production, he was given a six-year contract by the famous producers. Among his musical comedy successes were *Artists and Models, A Night in Spain, Pleasure Bound,* and Billy Rose's *Crazy Quilt*, in which Fannie Brice and Ted Healey were also starred. Another Broadway show was *Calling All Stars.* At about this time (1921) the comedian was married to Vivian Vernon, a *Follies* girl. A secret marriage because both their families disapproved, it was terminated by divorce three years later.

Baker began his career in radio in 1933, with a program for Armour and Company. For the next seven years he and his two "stooges" —Bottle, "the impeccable, oh-so-veddy-British butler" and Beetle, Baker's haunter, whose voice came through a loud speaker and was not seen by the studio audience—amused Sunday night radio listeners. Except for occasional changes in sponsor, cast, and format, the program, which had a high Hooper rating, changed but little. Following the 1939-40 broadcast season, Baker, tired of the show, left radio for almost two years. He did not return until December 1941 and then in an entirely different role, that of the easygoing quizmaster on Eversharp's *Take It or Leave It* program.

On this CBS program Baker has been posing questions for half an hour every Sunday night to the housewives, students, servicemen, clerks, and other types of contestants selected at random from the studio audience before the program begins. The questions, prepared by two researchers, are based on music, sports, science, history, and sixteen other categories, from among which the contestant selects one. The quizmaster candidly admits that he probably would not know many answers if the question-and-answer script were not handed to him immediately after a contestant states his choice. Baker also receives a card from the occupation file, which contains jokes about almost every kind of job. Should his usually ready ad lib or his memory's stock of jokes fail him, he can relieve the housewife's tension before the microphone by advising her to keep her hands smooth and lovely by putting "two things in the dishwater—your husband's hands."

Enlivened also by the studio audience, which is encouraged to heckle, and by the element of suspense involved when the contestant

PHIL BAKER

chooses to take the chance of doubling his money or winning nothing by going on to the next question, the program, according to Hooper, was in late 1946 the most popular American radio quiz show. Radio columnist Harriet Van Horne of the New York *World-Telegram,* however, has called it the "boorish" competitor of the Theatre Guild broadcast, which is on the air at the same time. According to Baker, 75 per cent of the show is prepared in advance (Hal Block is one of its gag writers) while "the remaining 25 per cent is ad libbed." "That 25 per cent," says the comedian, "sheds heavy pounds."

Baker is a good-natured questioner, often giving a hint of the answer to a nervous contestant. During World War II he was especially considerate of the servicemen who came before the microphone on his broadcast. Once, when a shy sailor from Nebraska chose "Rodgers and Hart tunes" as his category, Baker, sensing the subject had been selected more from bewilderment than wisdom, gave the sailor the script, saying, "Here, you ask me." And then, after having disposed of "the 64-dollar question," Baker gave him the prize money. His concern for servicemen went beyond that, however. After the end of the war Baker arranged to audition veterans desirous of becoming entertainers and planned to coach the qualified, whom he would help in getting jobs.

In 1944 Baker appeared in his radio role of quizmaster on the screen in the comedy film *Take It or Leave It.* He has also played in United Artists' *The Golden Follies* (1938) and in *The Gang's All Here* (1943) for Twentieth Century-Fox. The composer of a number of tunes, he collaborated on the songs for Columbia's *Start Cheering* (1938). In 1946 he was reported to be discussing with Twentieth Century-Fox the possibilities for a movie which would be based on his life. (According to an item in *Variety,* for which he has at times

BAKER, PHIL—*Continued*

written articles, he was also writing his autobiography.) Baker, part owner of the script for a musical extravaganza, *Holiday for Girls,* started planning the production of the show on Broadway in 1944, but a year and a half later decided to abandon it, returning the money invested in it to its backers. Gaver and Stanley wrote that the comedian really would like to return to the legitimate stage. Back in the late 1930's he toured successfully in Robert Sherwood's *Idiot's Delight* and then in *Charley's Aunt.*

In 1932 Baker was married a second time, to an English actress, Margaret Cartwright. They have four children: Margot Eleanor, Stuart Henry, Michael Conway, and Susan Carol. Divorced in 1941, Baker was married three years later, to Irmgard Erik, a dancer. For a while they lived in an elaborate four-story, fourteen-room house, which they later leased to Alexandre Parodi, the French delegate to the United Nations Security Council. Mrs. Baker praises her husband's cooking. He likes to invent "exotic sauces and strange cheese combinations" but must counteract the effects of his appetite for good food by attending a gymnasium, where he keeps his weight down to about one hundred and eighty pounds. A moderate drinker and smoker, he sleeps nine hours nightly. The comedian has been described as "a serious individual with a devout sense of social consciousness" and with "an intense interest in trying to find out what life is all about." His reading includes both "popular and unpopular" books. Although he now uses the accordion professionally only "to play the question" when a contestant on his radio program chooses the musical category, he is rated by musicians as "one of the best accordionists in the country." He practices on that instrument and the piano several hours each day, his parrot "Pete" playing the stooge by screeching "Stop it! Stop it!"

References

N Y Post p37 Ag 29 '45
N Y Times II p7 Mr 3 '46

Eichberg, R. Radio Stars of Today (1937) por
Gaver, J. and Stanley, D. There's Laughter in the Air! (1945)
International Motion Picture Almanac, 1943-44

BAKER, RAY STANNARD Apr. 17, 1870 —July 12, 1946 Author and historian; under the pseudonym of David Grayson wrote philosophical essays which were published in the series of books entitled *Adventures in Contentment* (1907), *Adventures in Friendship* (1910), *Adventures in Understanding* (1925), and *Adventures in Solitude* (1931); also wrote the novel *Hempfield*; won the Pulitzer Award for 1939 for his eight-volume biography of Woodrow Wilson; editor of *McClure's,* 1899-1905; his autobiographical works are *Native American* (1941) and *American Chronicle* (1945). See *Current Biography* 1940 Yearbook.

Obituary

N Y Times p14 Jl 13 '46 por

BALABAN, BARNEY (băl'a-băn) June 8, 1887- Motion picture executive

Address: b. c/o Paramount Pictures, Inc., 1501 Broadway, New York; h. Brevoort Lane, Greenhaven, Rye, N.Y.

Pioneer motion picture exhibitor Barney Balaban, whose first venture was a one-hundred-seat "nickelodeon" theater, became president of Paramount Pictures, Incorporated, on July 2, 1936, and six years later president of the Balaban and Katz Midwestern "theatrical empire" which he had helped to found about thirty years earlier.

Barney Balaban, eldest of the seven sons of Israel and Goldie (Manderbursky) Balaban, was born June 8, 1887, in Chicago, Illinois. His Russian-born father owned a small grocery store on Chicago's West Side, where Barney attended elementary school. That schooling ended when he began to work at the age of twelve as a messenger boy for Western Union. In 1903, after he had become an employee of the Western Cold Storage Company, young Balaban was attracted by the developing motion picture industry. Discouraged by friends, however, he remained with the cold storage company for another five years. It was his mother, he recalls, who gave him the needed "push." An article in *Forbes* described the incident: She came home dumbfounded from her first motion picture show, exclaiming, "Why, Barney, the customers pay before they even see what they're paying for! There'll be money in that business." Thus, at the age of twenty-one, Balaban entered motion picture exhibition in Chicago with his four brothers and five years later purchased the Kedzie theater, seating capacity one hundred. Their total capital was sixty-eight dollars and twenty cents.

Balaban's innovations within the industry began in 1910, when he built the Circle Theatre with a balcony, the first motion picture house to have one. By 1915, in association with Sam Katz, to whom his sister was marrried, he had made plans for a chain of theaters in the Middle West. The first, Chicago's Central Park, which was opened in 1917, is said to have contained the first air-cooling equipment in a theater, an idea credited to Balaban. Inspired by his earlier experience in the refrigeration field, he devised his first cooling apparatus—the biggest fan he could buy, set to blow against a pan of water. "Unfortunately," he reports, the fan not only sounded like a "truck parade," but also blew an occasional shower upon a woman's hat. Eventually an engineer friend designed satisfactory machinery—and crowds began to go to the cool theaters in the hot months. This made motion picture exhibition a year-round occupation and, perhaps, *Forbes* suggested, because of additional financial returns to producers and theater owners, speeded movie development a full twenty years.

The Balaban-Katz organization pioneered, too, in cutting dull pieces from newsreels and was, according to *Time,* the first to build "supercolossal" theaters. Of these, the Riviera, Tivoli, Chicago, and Uptown (all in Chicago) formed the nucleus of the chain which in 1946 operated forty-five theaters in that city alone, and which grossed in the 1930's an annual fifteen million dollars. Balaban and Katz was incorporated in 1923, and three years later Paramount obtained a controlling interest for about thirteen million dollars of Paramount stock. At this time Balaban was the largest Paramount stockholder, with the exception of Adolph Zukor, chairman of the board of directors of the film company. Until Warner Brothers '45 bought it in 1927, Balaban was also an owner of First National Productions. While Sam Katz, who had contributed "most of the showmanship" to their organization, went into Paramount Pictures proper, Balaban, who had done "the figuring," remained in the Midwest to run Balaban and Katz as a Paramount subsidiary. He became president of Balaban and Katz, Incorporated, in 1942.

After months of "sober head-scratching," in July 1936 the directors elected Barney Balaban president of Paramount Pictures, of which he had been chosen a director the month before. The selection, approved by Adolph Zukor, Balaban's old friend, was made because Paramount felt that Balaban was the most capable among the chain owners who remained one of the reorganized corporation's major strengths. *Fortune* reported in 1937 that as president and member of the executive committee, Balaban did not receive a salary; his total earnings for 1943, according to the *Hollywood Reporter*, were $141,451. In 1943 Balaban was allowed by stockholders to purchase two million dollars' worth of convertible notes in addition to the two thousand shares he already owned.

By consolidating various overlapping departments of Paramount, *Fortune* stated, and by cutting down home-office expenses by over eight hundred thousand dollars a year, Balaban helped the corporation to realize a profit of more than five million dollars for 1936. After the antitrust suit brought against Paramount and four other members of the industry had been settled by the signing of a consent decree on November 20, 1940, Balaban stated, "Paramount intends to make the decree work successfully in the interest of the public and of the motion picture industry. The decree requires among other things a different method of licensing film for exhibition in theaters . . . which in turn will necessitate increasing and realigning of our sales organization to meet the new requirements."

During World War II Paramount began "trimming its sails" in anticipation of a postwar decline in business. Balaban reported at the annual stockholders' meeting in 1944 that the company had a thirteen-million-dollar inventory of pictures on hand—"the best position the corporation ever held because none of the films is dependent on any particular war theme." He cited Paramount's subsidiary interest of 44 per cent in the Allen B. DuMont '46 Laboratories and a part ownership of Scophony, which give it a stake in wide-screen and arc-type projections, two major television developments pertaining to theaters. Paramount, Balaban announced, had developed a method whereby a televised story could be developed on film and projected on the screen almost immediately.

A. L. Whitey Schafer

BARNEY BALABAN

Balaban has emphasized that the industry has a responsibility "to explain America, its customs, and its people to the world," and that it must exercise care in the selection of pictures for export, sending abroad only those films that "accurately reflect our national life, even if this means lessening the profits of certain pictures which might create a distorted impression." Because he felt that *The Lost Weekend* had proved that a picture "doesn't necessarily have to be escapist to be good entertainment," Balaban asserted that the "screen must continue to pioneer new avenues of entertainment material. . . .We should not hesitate to experiment," he added, "even when such a course might involve a measure of financial risk."

The film executive has doubted whether a continuation of the Office of War Information informative film program under State Department auspices would be as successful as commercial plans. A picture endorsed by the Government, Balaban believes, is viewed abroad with suspicion. His tour of European war areas in the summer of 1945, with other industry executives, under the sponsorship of the Army and the State Department, resulted in Balaban's feeling an "urgent need for a worldwide program of theater building." The New York *Times* quotes his report that "Paramount plans to embark upon an international theater construction program in association with local interests and eventually hopes to have one such theater in every large city." Balaban defends his plan for foreign distribution: "The industry has been accused of draining money out of countries which can't afford to buy bread, but that is false. The truth is that the people have more money to spend than they have bread to buy. They want entertainment and we want a fair share of profit for the product we have to sell them and which they—the man in the street, that is—want to buy."

(Continued next page)

BALABAN, BARNEY—*Continued*

Balaban, who is a collector of Americana, presented the original manuscript of the Bill of Rights of the United States Constitution to the Library of Congress on February 21, 1945. The document (purchased from A. S. W. Rosenbach [46]), the only important one not already included in Government archives, was given by Balaban, the United States Treasury said, in "appreciation for the freedom which drew . . . [his] parents to this country from Europe." Archibald MacLeish [40], then Librarian of Congress, called the gift "an extraordinary act of generosity." A member of several philanthropic and religious associations, Balaban in 1929 headed the campaign for the erection of a library for Chicago's Hebrew Theological College. He is a trustee of the National Foundation for Infantile Paralysis, a vice-president of the Bill of Rights Commemorative Society, a member of the board of directors of the American Cancer Association, and of the National Committee on Post-War Immigration Policy. In July 1946 he was named national chairman of the motion picture division of the United Jewish Appeal for refugees, overseas needs, and Palestine, in its campaign for a hundred million dollars. His club is the Standard, of Chicago.

Barney Balaban was married to Tillie Urkov of Chicago in 1929, on Washington's Birthday. Their three children are Burton, Leonard, and Judith. Five feet nine and one half inches tall, he weighs 175 pounds and has hazel eyes and sandy-colored hair. He lists his favorite recreations as yachting, fishing, and riding.

References

Forbes 50 F 1 '45
Fortune 15:87, 96+ Mr 37 por
N Y Times II p3 Mr 24 '46
Time 28:64+ Jl 13 '36 por

Who's Who in America, 1946-47

BALDWIN, RAYMOND E(ARL) Aug. 31, 1893- Governor of Connecticut; United States Senator-elect

Address: b. State Capitol, Hartford, Conn.; h. 880 Judson Pl., Stratford, Conn.

Raymond E. Baldwin, serving his third term as Governor of Connecticut in 1946, ran for the United States Senate and was elected by a record plurality. The Senator-elect had long been identified with the internationalist thinking in Republican ranks, and with the belief that the private enterprise system, given the encouragement of a friendly Government, a balanced budget, and low taxes, could meet the nation's unemployment problem.

Like Wendell Willkie [40] whose "devoted follower" he became, Raymond Earl Baldwin was a successful lawyer before he entered politics. He was born in Rye, New York, on August 31, 1893, the son of Lucian Earl and Sarah Emily (Tyler) Baldwin. After schooling at Middletown High School in Connecticut, young Baldwin entered Middletown's Wesleyan University. He received his B.A. degree with the class of 1916. Commissioned an ensign in the United States Navy, Baldwin served during World War I on the destroyers U.S.S. *Talbot* and *Badger*. In September 1918 he was advanced to lieutenant (junior grade). After the war Baldwin entered the Yale Law School, in June 1921 received his LL.B. degree, and the same year was admitted to the Connecticut bar. Beginning as a clerk in the law office of McKinstry, Taylor and Patterson in New York, by the year 1922 he was associated with lawyer Philip Pond in New Haven. In 1924 he joined Pullman and Comley in Bridgeport, and four years later became a partner in that firm, remaining with them until he became Governor in 1939.

Baldwin's public career began with local offices in the judiciary: from 1927 to 1930 he was prosecutor for the town court of Stratford; from 1931 to 1933, a judge in that court. Elected in 1931 for a two-year term to the Connecticut House of Representatives (which meets biennially), in the 1933 session he was majority leader of the House and chairman of the judiciary committee. By virtue of a "dynamic campaign," in which he demanded a "cleanup" of the G.O.P. in Connecticut, in 1938 this forty-five-year-old newcomer to State politics won the Republican gubernatorial nomination. In 1938 "in Connecticut the Republican star was in the ascendancy." Robert R. Mullen later wrote in the *Christian Science Monitor Magazine*: "It was a party resurgent, new leaders, new candidates, new enthusiasm." The Republican nominee devoted much of his campaign to an attempt to bring young and independent voters into the Republican ranks. He also made, Mullen added, the "usual Republican promises about balanced budgets, economy, and the 'American Way.'"

Although Republican victories reached a high point all over New England in 1938, actually it was the popularity of the Socialists in Connecticut that won the election for Baldwin; Mayor Jaspar McLevy of Bridgeport, a perennial Socialist candidate for Governor, that year reached the peak of his popularity, polling 166,253 votes, most of them coming from the Democratic column. The Democratic candidate, Wilbur L. Cross, seeking re-election for the fifth consecutive term, garnered 227,549 votes while Baldwin got 230,237, thus "skimming into office" by a plurality of some three thousand.

According to Mullen, Republican leaders felt that Baldwin had a chance to provide a "G.O.P. preview" in Connecticut of what the Republican philosophy of government might accomplish if it replaced the New Deal in 1940. Said the new Governor: "We are going to be openly, militantly friendly to business and to private industry and to labor." Baldwin's first act was to slash drastically almost every item in the State's proposed budget; uncut, however, were allotments for individual relief, for the department which publicized the State, the flood-control commission, and the division concerned with labor problems and working conditions. The Governor also held down taxes. By 1940 Connecticut had wiped out a deficit of one and a half million, and had a one-million-dollar balance in the treasury.

An early, much-discussed program of the Governor's was the establishment in 1939 of a State industrial training plan. Based on a study of unemployment in Connecticut prepared by a commission under Carl A. Gray, the plan was the model for the later Federal plan for training workers for defense industries. With instructors provided by private industry, the State re-trained "skill-rusty" men and trained the unskilled for "the specific jobs their communities could offer." When Connecticut's armament industry boomed, through the use of a State-wide inventory of available manpower, some thirty-five thousand persons were placed where they were needed. As the defense orders poured in, the Connecticut Aeronautical Development Commission, established to determine what factories could be used for making planes and plane parts, was in a position to channel the orders to the proper plants. Meanwhile the State Development Commission extolled Connecticut as a location for residence, recreation, and industry. One hundred and sixty new plants opened in the State in 1940.

The Democratic sweep in 1940, a presidential election year, put Baldwin out of office, and brought in the Democratic candidate, Robert A. Hurley, with a plurality of thirteen thousand votes. Baldwin returned to the law firm he had left in 1939. In the next election (1942) he challenged Hurley, and won by more than twenty-five thousand votes. Running for a third term in 1944, Baldwin again was opposed by Hurley, and again defeated him, although the Democrats carried all other State offices, and took over the State Senate. Thus, while the Roosevelt ticket swept the State, Baldwin, it was pointed out, "demonstrated a personal popularity and a vote-getting ability" which his supporters believed might make him a national contender in 1948.

Connecticut's problems, as Baldwin became Governor again, were related to the State's rapid and tremendous industrial expansion in the face of a critical labor shortage. Its factories, the most diverse in the country, were shifted to war industries. The Governor set up a State war council to deal with situations threatening the tempo of production. After V-J Day, while some plants were able to turn, for example, from bomb fuses to alarm clocks, others were closing down, leaving thousands jobless. To facilitate reconversion, Baldwin planned the establishment of a Labor Management Advisory Council, the setting up of an information service to provide State-wide data on employment opportunities, the expansion of the State job-training program, and a testing program for veterans and war workers to determine what education and training would best suit them. The Governor also invited business delegates from Central and South America to tour Connecticut to see what its manufacturers had to offer and to examine its markets, with a view to trade pacts.

Good labor-management relations were maintained through the war years, but at the end of 1945 difficulties at the Yale and Towne Manufacturing Company developed into a bitter one-hundred-and-fifty-day strike. The Governor was criticized by labor groups when he assigned

RAYMOND E. BALDWIN

State troopers to the plant because strikers were not permitting management personnel to cross the picket lines. Clashes between the strikers and the State police followed. "I intend to be firm," said the Governor, "and will not tolerate unlawful picketing." The troopers remained at the plant to keep order, while Baldwin declared, "The union can maintain picket lines, but cannot use threats, force or intimidation—what we call mass picketing."

An early and influential supporter of Wendell Willkie, Baldwin, who headed the Connecticut delegation, was a Willkie floor-manager at the 1940 Republican national convention. In January of the next year, Willkie adherents boomed Baldwin to succeed Joseph Martin '40 as party chairman, but the move was unsuccessful. At Mackinac Island, where the Republican postwar advisory council met in September 1943 to evolve an election platform, Baldwin made sufficient impression to be added, said Turner Catledge of the New York *Times,* to the winter list of presidential possibilities for 1944. The Connecticut Republican led a "revolt" of Governors, who demanded that the council adopt a "positive nonpartisan stand on postwar international problems," and advanced proposals on international collaboration similar to those of Willkie. "We should promote a council of nations to eliminate those factors in international relationships which cause difference and provoke armed conflict, and a world court to decide justifiable disputes between nations," Baldwin declared. "We should advocate that the actions of this council and the decisions of this court be enforced by the collaboration of the military, naval, and air power of the nations of the world." He added: "On the home front we must return to the American system of increasing and expanding production through individual energy and initiative, so that jobs in private industry and commerce will furnish a living for our people

BALDWIN, RAYMOND E.—*Continued*
and an opportunity for the advancement of the
energetic, frugal and willing worker."

While some observers felt that the final Republican program was a compromise document
in which Baldwin's group had given ground
under pressure of greater numbers, others insisted that the Baldwin faction had "cracked the
shell" of Republican isolationism. Speculation
before the 1944 Republican convention placed
Baldwin as a likely "favorite son" candidate of
the Connecticut delegation; the State convention, however, though it passed a resolution
urging that Baldwin be considered for the
Presidential nomination, sent sixteen unin-
structed delegates to the convention. Connecticut
supported Governor Thomas E. Dewey '44, and
Baldwin spoke in his behalf in the election of
that year. It was at Governor Dewey's urging
that Baldwin, who had said he would refuse
renomination with the statement that no man
was "indispensable," agreed to run for Governor
a third time, in the interests of "the State and
the party." In June 1945, elected vice-president,
general counsel and a director of the Connecticut Mutual Life Insurance Company, Baldwin
announced that he would withdraw from political life at the expiration of his term in January
1947. Urged to run for the United States Senate, the fifty-two-year-old Governor in June
1946 reaffirmed his decision to return to private
life, but Representative Clare Boothe Luce '42
stated: "I still think there is a chance that
Governor Baldwin can be persuaded to run.
There could be no better candidate."

In August, unable to persuade Mrs. Luce to
run for the Senate, Baldwin announced that
he would yield to the insistence of his friends
and become a candidate himself. In the November elections the Republican Party swept
Connecticut, winning its greatest victory in the
State in twenty years. Baldwin led the winning ticket, defeating Democrat Joseph M.
Tone by 104,704 votes. Also defeating Democrat Wilbur L. Cross, Governor Baldwin likewise was elected to succeed Republican Senator Thomas C. Hart, his own appointee who
filled the vacancy caused by the death of Senator Francis T. Maloney. It was announced
that Baldwin would resign from the governorship late in December, when he will serve in
the Senate during the few days' interval between the expiration of Hart's term and assumption of the six-year Senatorial term.

In the *American Magazine* (November
1945) Governor Baldwin set forth his economic
philosophy in the article "We Need Job-Mak-
ers." "Our responsibility to the job-maker is to
reduce his risk as much as possible. We must
remove every impediment to his success, bring
to him the maximum of our local resources in
aid of his effort." He also said: "It is the
small fellow we must help and nurture so that
we may grow bigger. It is all very well for the
secretary of Commerce, Henry A. Wallace '40,
to plan his 'Magna Charta' for little business
through loans and other devices. But the home
town and the home State have an even greater
opportunity to help. They are a lot closer to the
little job-maker than anybody in Washington."

The Governor has also written for *Look*
("How Connecticut is Solving Unemployment,"
August 13, 1940), and for the New York *Times
Magazine* ("Jobs, Not a Dole, For the Veteran," May 28, 1944). On the international
scene Baldwin had the opportunity to lend his
aid toward the realization of world government;
when the United Nations chose territory cutting into Connecticut for the world capital,
Baldwin played host on a tour for the site-
hunting committee, "sought to restore calm to
the agitated citizenry" of Greenwich who
feared they would be dispossessed, appointed a
Connecticut advisory committee to aid the U.N.
headquarters commission, and gave "heartening assurances of assistance" during preliminary
discussions of the final choice in June 1946.

"Big, blond, and affable," the six-foot, two-
hundred-pound Governor lives in a two-story
stucco house in Stratford, with "a small neatly
kept lawn in front, and carefully clipped
shrubs about." Mrs. Baldwin, to whom he was
married on June 29, 1922, is the former Edith
Lindholm; their children are Lucian Earl, 2d,
Raymond Earl, Jr., and Tyler. According to
Delos Lovelace of the New York *Sun*, Baldwin
"has a sense of hospitality to fit his physiological proportions. He's a careful dresser . . .
talks like an eloquent lawyer, acts like a top-
flight executive, a Governor, for instance."

References

Christian Sci Mon Mag p3+ O 19 '40
    por
N Y Herald Tribune p18 Ja 7 '41 por;
    p22 Jl 17 '43
N Y Sun p22 Je 20 '46
Who's Who in America, 1946-47

BANKHEAD, JOHN H(OLLIS) July 8,
1872—June 12, 1946 United States Democratic
Senator from Alabama, 1930-46; while in Alabama legislature was author of the Alabama
Election Law, drawn to keep Negroes from
using the ballot; generally supported the New
Deal; opposed the Wagner-Costigan lynch
bill and ceiling price on cotton; in 1934 pushed
the cotton control bill through the Senate, an
act repealed in 1936; champion of the tenant
farmer. See *Current Biography* 1943 Yearbook.

Obituary

N Y Times p 27 Je 13 '46 por

BANTOCK, SIR GRANVILLE Aug. 7,
1868—Oct. 16, 1946 British composer, conductor, and teacher of music; principal of the
school of music at Birmingham and Midland Institute from 1900; professor of music at Birmingham University from 1908 until 1934;
composer of operas, symphonic poems, over-
tures, and songs.

Obituary

N Y Times p23 O 17 '46 por

BARCLAY, MCCLELLAND May 9,
1893—July 18, 1943 Artist; designed covers and illustrated fiction stories for the
Ladies' Home Journal, the *Saturday Eve-*

ning Post, and other magazines; drew numerous recruiting posters during both world wars; as a lieutenant commander in the United States Navy from 1940, he made paintings and sketches for a permanent historical record of the war; killed while on duty in the South Pacific. See *Current Biography* 1940 Yearbook.

Obituary

N Y Times p1+ Jl 25 '45 por

BARRY, WILLIAM BERNARD July 21, 1902—Oct. 20, 1946 Irish-born United States Democratic Representative from New York State from 1935 until his death; practiced law in New York City for some years after 1929; assistant New York district attorney, 1932-33; special United States attorney for the Department of Justice, 1933-35.

Obituary

N Y Times p31 O 21 '46 por

BARTLETT, ROBERT A(BRAM) Aug. 15, 1875—Apr. 28, 1946 Arctic explorer; commanded Peary's ship in the expedition which discovered the North Pole; accompanied Vilhjalmur Stefansson through the Bering Straits, 1913; when his ship was crushed by ice, with one Eskimo crossed to Siberia and returned with rescuing party, 1914; cruised annually for sixteen years to the Arctic; received the Peary Polar Expedition Medal.

Obituary

N Y Times p21 Ap 29 '46 por

BEGTRUP, BODIL (bä'trŏp bō-dēl) Nov. 12, 1903- United Nations delegate

Address: b. c/o United Nations, New York

When the United Nations Subcommission on the Status of Women in April 1946 elected Bodil Begtrup of Denmark as its chairman, it chose a woman who since early youth had dedicated herself to the improvement of women's lot not alone in Denmark but on the international scene. President of the National Council of Women in Denmark and Danish film censor, she was one of Denmark's delegates to both the London and New York convocations of the United Nations Assembly in 1946.

Bodil Begtrup, née Andreasen, was born in Nyborg, a seaport on the eastern coast of Fyn Island, in southern Denmark, on November 12, 1903. Her father was Judge Christian A. Andreasen; her mother, Carla Sigrid (Locher) Andreasen, descendant of a family of artists, poets, and musicians. "It was, I suppose," she says, "rather naturally assumed that I would follow in the family's footsteps," and at about the age of fourteen she had almost decided that she would specialize in artistic studies, possibly painting. One day, however, she came across a volume on the religion of citizenship written by the Chinese philosopher Ku Hung Ming. "It was strange," she commented reminiscently to interviewer Ann Foster of the *Christian*

Science Monitor, "how the philosophy and ideas of that man affected me.'"

Thoughts of a life devoted to art began to change to visions of service to her fellow countrymen, especially to the women of Denmark. During the next four years, as she attended secondary school in Aalborg, Jutland, the new half-formed goal remolded her interests, and in 1921, when she matriculated at the University of Copenhagen, she chose science and economics as the fields of her major endeavors. By her twenty-third year, she says, her mind had been irrevocably made up. "I found there was much work to be done in Denmark, and applied myself as earnestly and intelligently as I could—there were wide fields needing endeavor, both economic and cultural." In 1929 she was awarded the degree of Master of Economics by the University of Copenhagen. She had been active in student affairs, had participated in an international students' congress, and had won a scholarship for study in Geneva.

A member of the Danish National Council of Women, the young woman became a member of its board in 1930, vice-chairman of the board in 1931, and president in 1946. At the same time that she was bringing up a family of stepchildren and one child of her own—she had been married to Erik Begtrup, a physician, in February 1929—she was working continuously in the interests of Denmark and Danish women. In 1938 (two years after her divorce from Begtrup) she was a member of her country's delegation to the League of Nations Assembly at Geneva. A year later she was appointed to the Council for Maternal Health and made chairman of the Commission for Children's Health. Also in 1939, she became one of three Danish film censors, and in this capacity, wrote Joseph G. Harrison of the *Christian Science Monitor's* staff, "not only banned the worst of America's gangster films but during the war years prevented the showing of hundreds of German movies." In January 1946 she was one of Denmark's representatives to the first United Nations Assembly in London; that April she arrived in the United States to attend the meetings of the United Nations Subcommission on the Status of Women and was promptly elected chairman by unanimous vote.

The prospectus of the subcommission, which was a unit subordinate to the U.N. Commission on Human Rights headed by Mrs. Franklin D. Roosevelt, had set forth its concern with the "political, civil, and economic status and opportunity of women, with special reference to discrimination and limitations placed on them on account of their sex." Commented Mrs. Begtrup at the time of her election: "It is no longer a question of whether women shall participate in the affairs of the world. It is rather a question today of how to get their full cooperation in every nation." Then, quickly, the eight women members, led by Mrs. Begtrup, got to work. In two weeks they had prepared a two-thousand-word document covering details of policy, program, and composition for a permanent United Nations agency concerned with women's rights.

Expressing their faith in democracy as "the only social order in which women can enjoy

BODIL BEGTRUP

full rights as human beings," the women recommended surveys and polls to determine present conditions, an executive office on women's affairs as part of the U.N. Secretariat, and an international women's conference. As goals to be achieved they recommended equal rights and opportunities with men in all nations and all fields of human endeavor—political, civil, educational, social, and economic—including everything from the opportunity for "compulsory, free, and full education" and the right to hold public office to the abolition of prostitution and the right to obtain a divorce. Designedly they made their report comprehensive, because, Mrs. Begtrup was quoted as saying, the women of the world expected it. "We know [their] hopes and wishes. . . .They want us to do something. . . .As the field of discrimination is so vast our report has to be comprehensive; [in fact, we think] it's not comprehensive enough."

At first, when it was referred to the parent Commission on Human Rights—composed of nine men and Mrs. Roosevelt—the women's document caused consternation. The program was too ambitious; it might result in infringement of national sovereignties; in any case, the subcommission had not been expected to go into such detail—these were some of the comments. And despite Mrs. Begtrup's strong defense, the version which was finally transmitted to the Economic and Social Council, through which the report must pass before consideration by the General Assembly, was cut to a few summarizing paragraphs, with the original being appended merely because it demonstrated "the conscientious care and thoroughness" of the preparation. In the Economic and Social Council, however, the women's report met with a far different fate, for early in June the drafting committee unanimously approved the elevation of the Subcommission on the Status of Women to commission standing and a week later the eighteen-member council recorded its

assent. Said Sir Ramaswami Mudaliar of India, president of UNESCO, "I congratulate women on the first step they have achieved in raising their status to that of men."

That the fight to implement the objectives outlined by the Subcommission on the Status of Women will still be long and hard Bodil Begtrup is well aware. Once, asked by a reporter about her group's progress, she is said to have replied, "It will move very slowly. See me in a thousand years." For where the goal is "the final, international recognition, in common practice as well as theory, of the essential dignity of man," points out Ann Foster, the undertaking can only be described as "gigantic."

On the other hand, Bodil Begtrup understands also that it is equally the apparently insignificant matters which may spell doom or success for the project. "It is all very well for us," she has said, "to talk about raising the status of women; but so many of them live in homes so ill-equipped, kitchens so meagerly planned and furnished, that it is practically impossible for them to find time or energy to take any sort of part in public or community life. . . . If we want the women of the world to take an active part in the affairs of the world and of their communities, we must do more than give them equal status with men and urge them on to active public life—we must make it possible for them to accept their responsibilities as citizens, to freely, and without anxiety or strain, take their place with men in order to accomplish, jointly, with the men of the world, those great tasks that must be fulfilled if thinking and living on this earth are to transcend to any degree at all the thinking and living it has known so far!"

In addition to being chief Danish film censor, Mrs. Begtrup is a member of the Danish Board for Cultural Films and of the film committee of the International Women's Organization. Her favorite recreations are sailing, gardening, and embroidery. Described as "modest and engaging," she is striking in appearance—tall and slim, with brown hair and brown eyes. She has said "no" to honorary orders.

Reference

Christian Sci Mon p6 Je 6 '46

BEIRNE, J(OSEPH) A. (bûrn) Feb. 16, 1911-   Union official

Address: b. c/o National Federation of Telephone Workers, 1505 Maryland Ave., N.E., Washington, D.C., h. 420 McKinley St., Fairview, N.J.

J. A. Beirne, the president of the National Federation of Telephone Workers, an independent union, is a young man who is said to "use his power cautiously despite his embryo John L. Lewis eyebrows." During the strike crises of January, February, and March of 1946, Beirne's guidance led the union to observe the thirty-day strike notice of the Smith-Connally Act. His conduct of negotiations with the Labor Department won from Secretary Schwellenbach the tribute, "One of the best labor leaders I've known in keeping his promise," while Fulton Lewis, Jr., pronounced him "a young man with a future in labor circles." The NFTW, with a paid-up membership of 182,000 and representing 263,000 telephone workers, is a strategically powerful union. Though it does not embrace all telephone workers (the New York Telephone Company's 13,000 employees belong to four other unions), the interlocking system of this public utility gives it the power to tie up the nation's telephone service.

Born in Jersey City, New Jersey, on February 16, 1911, Joseph A. Beirne is the son of Michael Joseph and Annie T. (Giblin) Beirne, both of whom are natives of County Roscommon, Ireland. The labor leader's father is a member of the Brotherhood of Railroad Engineers. Joseph grew up in Jersey City, where he attended the Dickinson and the Accredited Evening High Schools. When he was seventeen years old, Beirne went to work as a stock clerk in the Kearney (New Jersey) plant of Western Electric Company. Before he resigned to devote all of his time to union work, he had worked as an assembler of relay coils, on a drill press, at repair work, and as a department clerk. His first important post in a labor organization was as a district union representative, and in 1937 he became president of the NFTW-affiliated National Association of Telephone Equipment Workers. In 1934, when he was twenty-three, Beirne entered the evening classes of St. Peter's College (Jersey City) where he continued to study until January 1937; he then transferred to New York University. However, by 1938 his heavy union duties forced him to give up his college courses. According to the New York *World-Telegram,* by 1946 Beirne had headed NFTW for about two and a half years.

The National Federation of Telephone Workers was formed in 1934, but their formal organization, as reported by the *Monthly Labor Review,* did not take place until June 1939. From thirteen affiliates with a total membership of 40,000, the federation in the last seven years has increased to fifty-one autonomous unions with a membership of 182,000, estimated to be about 71 per cent of all employees in the Bell System. Drawn from all branches of the industry—accounting, commercial, manufacturing, research, plant, and traffic—the affiliates range in size from the United Plant Telephone Workers of Delaware, with 150 members, to the Western Electric Employees Association, in Kearney, New Jersey, with 20,000 members. Unions within the federation carry on negotiations in local questions, assisted only when necessary by the parent organization. The most important achievement of NFTW has been the raising of wage scales. Before the unionization of the workers, telephone operators were paid a minimum of eleven dollars a week and a maximum, not reached for many years in some companies, of twenty to twenty-two dollars a week. The low wages were accompanied by close supervision, and in many localities, by speed-up methods.

Since the NFTW has always been independent of both CIO and A.F. of L., Beirne's announcement on February 3, 1946, that a com-

J. A. BEIRNE

mittee had been set up to confer with CIO and A.F. of L. leaders on possible affiliation, came as a surprise to some observers. As late as the previous October the NFTW had engaged in a four-hour work stoppage as a protest against such an affiliation. In July 1945, the CIO United Electric Radio and Machine Workers of America, as a test case, made the complaint to NLRB that the NFTW's largest affiliate, the WEEA, was "a company-dominated union." When an NLRB trial examiner ruled in the affirmative, although the case had to pass three other NLRB examiners before a final decision would be reached, Beirne announced that the federation had voted for a general stoppage as a protest. At the same time he requested that further hearings on the case be made open to the public.

Counsel for WEEA asked not only that the complaint be dismissed but also that the national association, NFTW, "be held to be of such a type as to require NLRB to place it on a parity with the A.F. of L., and the CIO." The WEEA attorney, reported the New York *Times,* had also argued that while company domination had once been present, there had been no such domination for seven years in the Western Electric case. The CIO's UERMW at the time announced plans to organize the Western Electric Company plants and denounced the federation's decision to strike as "another attempt to stop NLRB from carrying out the purpose of the Wagner Act." The work stoppage by the telephone workers which took place on October 5, 1945, although it lasted only four hours, demonstrated the power of NFTW to tie up the nation's telephone service. Two months later, with the final decision from NLRB on the company domination charge still pending, WEEA voted to strike when the Western Electric Company refused their demands for a 30 per cent raise.

(Continued next page)

BEIRNE, J. A.—*Continued*

On the announcement of the WEEA strike, Beirne requested a poll of the other affiliates on whether or not they wished to go out in a sympathy strike. He, at the same time, appealed to President Truman to intervene in the dispute between the Western Electric Company and its employees' association so as to avert the strike which had been scheduled for January 3, 1946. Although several of the affiliates voted against a sympathy strike, all federation members were—as Beirne put it—too union-conscious to cross a picket line. Picket lines were thrown around the telephone exchanges not only by WEEA but also by another affiliate, the Association of Communications Equipment Workers, whose 7,700 workers install and maintain telephone switchboards. The result was what the New York *Times* described as the worst communications tie-up in the nation's history. On the weekend of January 12-13, walkouts of telephone operators in scores of cities crippled or paralyzed local service and cut American Telephone and Telegraph Company long-distance Sunday traffic to 15 per cent of normal. The result of the poll on the sympathy strike which Beirne had requested from members of the affiliates was announced on January 14. The federation had voted to file a thirty-day strike notice, then called for negotiations for a two-dollar raise per day, a minimum wage of sixty-five cents per hour, and a forty-hour work week. Obedient to instructions from the parent union the affiliate ACEW called off the strike they had begun the week before. The seventeen thousand Western Electric production workers remained on strike but it was announced that there would be no further picketing of telephone exchanges, that is, "for the present."

A month later, when the executive board of the federation met in Memphis, a general strike was recommended to support the demand for the wage-scale revisions on which the company had offered an increase of only half of the amount requested. A heated controversy arose between two factions of the federation when Beirne insisted upon keeping a promise to the Labor Department not to set a date for the strike until after further conference between them. When further conferences failed to bring about an agreement between the union and the telephone company officials, the date of March 7 was set for the strike. In the event of a strike, it was reported that the Government would seize the public utility under the "unexpired powers of the War Labor Disputes Act." "This seizure would carry no penalty for any employee then on strike; but any worker who went on strike afterward, or anyone who attempted to interfere with a worker going to his job would be liable to a five thousand dollar fine and a year in jail." Although some union officials hinted that they would not work even with Government operation of the telephone companies, Beirne declared that they probably would not strike against the Government in event of Federal seizure. Contrary to the general belief, a strike of the telephone operators would not shut down radio networks and press association teletypes—the leased wires of these "involve only a little plug-pushing, and services can be maintained with a handful of men." The threatened strike came close to materializing on March 7. That it had been averted was announced early that morning by Beirne, following the negotiation of a pay-increase contract with the American Telephone and Telegraph Company (Western Electric and Bell System telephone companies are A.T.&T. subsidiaries) and his poll of officials of affiliated unions.

In April 1946 the president of the National Federation of Telephone Workers announced that his organization had prepared a "comprehensive program to bring 125,000 additional workers in the telephone industry within the NFTW fold." Another project of Beirne's later in 1946 was to "transform his loose federation of autonomous independent unions into a strong national telephone union." This "new integrated union" would admit all those employed (including telegraphers) in communications industries, even persons already members of other unions. Beirne's plan, which would prevent strikes by local unions unless such action was approved by national union leaders and which would give Beirne "unprecedented power in the telephone field," was submittted to the NFTW delegates at their November convention held in Denver (Colorado) and accepted by them. They voted also to become known as the Communications Workers of America as of June 1947 when their constitution was to be ratified. Although the CIO and the A.F. of L. are said to seek the affiliation of telephone workers with their respective organizations, they intend to "resist stiffly" all "raiding" of their unions, which "they fear is implicit in Beirne's plans" (*Newsweek*, October 7, 1946). Referring to the strike by Pittsburgh power-plant employees which paralyzed the city's industrial and commercial life, Beirne, in October, made a statement which resulted in his being described as "seeming to accept the idea of compulsory arbitration of utility disputes." He maintained that "utility workers must be allowed to strike unless the Government is to guarantee 'in some way,'" according to the *United States News* for October 11, 1946, "that wages and working conditions of utility employes are to be kept 'on a par with, or above,' those of other workers."

The young labor leader was married on July 2, 1933, to Anne Mary Abahaze; their three daughters are Carol, Maureen, and Bren. Beirne, who has brown eyes and hair, is five feet eight and a half inches tall and weighs 165 pounds. He is a Democrat and a member of the Roman Catholic Church. A member of the Elks and a councilman of the borough of Fairview, he has also served on the Board of War Communication in the United States. Favorite sports of the "mild-mannered" president of the NFTW are swimming and ice skating.

Reference

Who's Who in Labor (1946)

BELL, DANIEL W(AFENA) July 23, 1891- United States Government official; banker

Address: b. c/o Price Decontrol Board, 20th St. & Constitution Ave., N.W., Washington, D.C.; American Security and Trust Company, Washington, D.C.; h. 3816 Gramercy St., N.W., Washington, D.C.

Of the three members appointed to the Price Decontrol Board, Daniel W. Bell is the best known, having previously gained national attention as acting Director of the Bureau of the Budget and as the Under Secretary of the Treasury. After more than thirty-four years in Government service, Bell is also the president of the American Security and Trust Company of Washington, D.C. On the basis of his civil service status, he is considered as representing the public on the board.

Daniel Wafena Bell, one of six children, was born July 23, 1891, in Kinderhook, Illinois, to Daniel Morgan Bell, a carpenter and farmer. Young Bell's mother, Otis (Hardy) Bell gave him his Indian middle name "Wafena," the meaning of which has since been forgotten. The boy was reared on the Pike County farm, where he found he was more interested in arithmetic than in agriculture. After his elementary education in the grammar school of his native town and two years at the Kinderhook High School, Bell studied at the Gem City Business College in Quincy (Illinois) for seven months in 1910-11.

A high grade in a civil service examination brought Bell to Washington, D.C., in September 1911 as a seven-hundred-dollar-a-year stenographer-typist-bookkeeper-clerk in the United States Treasury Department. Early in the course of World War I, in October 1918, twenty-seven-year-old Bell enlisted in the United States Army as a private in the newly formed Tank Corps. He served in France from October 1918 to April 1919 with Company B of the 304th Battalion. After his discharge on May 14, 1919, Bell returned to the Treasury as an accountant in charge of foreign loans, where he remained for a year. His next promotion came on July 1, 1920, when he was appointed the executive assistant to the assistant secretary of the Treasury. Bell, who had attended college while working in Washington, received his LL.B. in June 1924 from the National University Law School and the degree of Bachelor of Commercial Science from Southeastern University three years later. By 1924 Bell had become assistant commissioner of accounts and deposits, serving in that capacity until 1931, when he became commissioner. After four years Bell's title was assistant to the Secretary of the Treasury on financial and accounting matters. He held this post from March 1935 until January 1940.

During the same period, from 1934 until early in March 1939, Bell was the acting director of the Bureau of the Budget, an independent branch of the Treasury Department responsible only to the President. (Bell had not taken a permanent budget directorship in order to preserve his civil service status.) Succeeding former Arizona Congressman Lewis

DANIEL W. BELL

W. Douglas in the "ungrateful job of bearing down on . . . expenses," Bell came to the "abruptly vacated" post in time to arrange an issuance of Treasury securities and submit a budget estimate to the next session of Congress. As "budget tamer," Bell worked with the House Appropriations Committee chairman and Secretary of the Treasury Henry Morganthau, Jr.[40], to prepare President Roosevelt's fiscal estimates, although Bell often disagreed with the spending policies that the budgets reflected. The Federal budget, adopted by the Harding administration in 1921, was perfected as an instrument of national "psychotherapy" by the Roosevelt Administration: although considered "gloomy" by fiscal conservatives, the maximum-expenditures-and-minimum-receipts budget was to stimulate business in time of slow activity. Bell also directed the Federal Farm Mortgage Corporation, an agency established to help finance lending operations of Federal land banks and of the land bank commissioner, dealing mainly with the farm debt refinancing program begun in 1933.

Bell held the post of Under Secretary of the Treasury from January 1, 1940, until December 31, 1945, his appointment by President Roosevelt having been confirmed by the Senate with the understanding that he would not lose his civil service standing and its retirement pension. John W. Hanes, Bell's predecessor, who resigned to re-enter business, proposed that Bell be made assistant secretary for life since the appointment had evoked such widespread approval. In that post Bell supervised the bureau of the currency comptroller, the division of research and statistics, and the fiscal services branch which covers the bureaus of finance, of accounts, of public debt, and the office of the Treasurer of the United States. Secretary of the Treasury Fred M. Vinson[43] told reporters, "It will be very difficult to replace Danny," when Bell, one of the few politically unspon-

BELL, DANIEL W.—*Continued*

sored civil service career men to reach "little cabinet" rank, left the Government for private enterprise. On January 15, 1946, the day of his election as a director of the company, Bell became president of the American Security and Trust Company, a large Washington bank, at a salary reported as more than twice what he received as Under Secretary.

Having been named by President Truman for the three-man Price Decontrol Board, Bell was approved as a member on July 29, 1946, by the Senate Banking Committee as well as by a Senatorial vote the same day (the usual interval between committee recommendation and voting had been waived). The Price Decontrol Board was given one of the "toughest" assignments of critical importance to the country; it was created by the June 1946 Office of Price Administration Extension Act as a final authority for the removal or restoration of price ceilings. Like chairman Roy L. Thompson '46 and George H. Mead '46, Bell had not previously been one of the OPA administrators. *Time* pointed out that while Bell "helped the New Deal by keeping its books," he "neither embraced nor repudiated New Deal measures for controls over business." The political independent was hailed by Republican Senator Kenneth S. Wherry '46 of Nebraska (a critic of the OPA) as a "good choice," and by Democratic Senator George L. Radcliffe of Maryland as "one of the most competent men" the President could have chosen.

Bell, Mead, and Thompson, regarded as representing the public, industry, and agricultural interests in that order, had as their first task the decision as to which commodities were to revert to price control on August 20, 1946. All interested groups and individuals were heard at legally prescribed open meetings of the board, reports from various Government agencies were received, and the board based its decision upon this evidence. On the ground that items had risen "unreasonably" in price since June 30, 1946, were of "short supply," were "practical and enforceable" in their recontrol, and were such that their regulation would be in the "public interest," livestock, meat, soybeans, cottonseed, flaxseed, and their by-products were placed again under OPA ceiling price control. These commodities were re-released from regulation when the price decontrol process was accelerated in October 1946; the Price Decontrol Board reduced its staff to a skeleton force in the same month.

Princeton University awarded Bell an honorary M.A. in June 1940. Treasurer of the American Red Cross when Under Secretary, a former member of the American Legion, Bell is now, in 1946, on the Brookings Institute board of trustees and on the Washington (D. C.) Board of Trade. He was married on June 22, 1921, to Washington-born Sarah Agnes Killeen, daughter of John F. Killeen, a contractor of that city; they have a daughter, Mary Kathleen. Bell is a member of the Methodist Church. An amateur baseball player in his youth, Bell now plays golf (his score is in the nineties) and likes to swim at the Man-

or Country Club in Norbeck, Maryland; his Washington (D.C.) club is the Metropolitan. Described as "the most inquisitive" member of the Decontrol Board, Bell is a man of cheerful disposition. He has brown eyes, "patent-leather" black hair, and stands five feet eight and one half inches tall. *Newsweek* once called him "a small, slightly corpulent edition of Clark Gable."

References

Time 48:22 Ag 5 '46 por
U S News 8:38 Ap 12 '40 por
National Cyclopædia of American Biography Current vol F p71
Who's Who in America, 1946-47
Who's Who in the Nation's Capital, 1938-39

BENCHLEY, ROBERT (CHARLES) Sept. 15, 1889—Nov. 21, 1945 American humorist, author, editor, critic, and actor; dramatic editor of *Life* (1920-29) and of the *New Yorker* (1929-40); appeared in motion pictures from 1935 until death and on radio programs from 1937; author of many works, including *The Early Worm* (1922), *The Treasurer's Report* (1930), *From Bed to Worse* (1934), *Benchley Beside Himself* (1943). See *Current Biography* 1941 Yearbook.

Obituary

N Y Times p35 N 22 '45 por

BENNETT, HUGH H(AMMOND) Apr. 15, 1881- United States Government official
Address: b. c/o Soil Conservation Service, United States Department of Agriculture, Washington, D.C.; h. Eight Oaks, R.F.D. 2, Falls Church, Va.

"One reason for the encouraging spread of sane farmer practices has been Dr. Bennett's successful hammering at the thesis that 'conservation pays,'" wrote the New York *Times* in October 1946 in describing the work of Hugh H. Bennett, chief of the United States Soil Conservation Service. A man who has devoted his life to the prevention of land wastage, Bennett has seen his ideas gradually become the means of saving much of his nation's farm and forest land.

A farm near Wadesboro, Anson County, in a badly eroded agricultural section of North Carolina, is the birthplace of Hugh Hammond Bennett. He was born April 15, 1881. His father, William Osborne Bennett, owned and farmed a plantation, and his mother, the former Rosa May Hammond, was a descendant of the largest exporter of cotton in the world before the Civil War. The land on which young Hugh helped his father (from whom "he learned a reverence for and love of dirt") had once been fertile, but the continual plantings of cotton and the clearing of trees had impoverished much of it. He want to Goulds Fork Academy and the McGregor School in Anson County. After graduation from the latter in 1896 he matriculated at the University of North Carolina. For a period he had to interrupt his college work in order to earn money to pay his expenses there; he relates that he cleared trees from a hillside to make way for cotton crops.

After Hugh Bennett received his degree in chemistry in 1903, he was employed by the Bureau of Soils in the United States Department of Agriculture as a laboratory assistant. He had not been there long when he and an associate were sent to Louisa County, Virginia, to discover why the soil in that area was poor. In that section, Bennett found that many sloping fields bordering arears of rich virgin woodland had lost their topsoil, by slow rainwash, and here discovered the principle of sheet erosion—the wearing away of layers of the soil by water erosion. In 1906 Bennett became a soil scientist with the Bureau of Soils and was placed in charge of the soil surveys of a number of counties in the South, East, and Midwest. In 1909 Bennett was given general supervision of the soil survey work in the Eastern and Southern states and portions of the Central and Southwestern divisions, a responsibility he held until 1928.

In connection with his work with the Department of Agriculture, Hugh Bennett was a member of a special commission to determine the agricultural possibilities of the Canal Zone in 1909. In 1914 he was in charge of an expedition which made similar investigations preparatory to the building of a railroad in Alaska, and in 1916 he was a member of the Alaskan Chugach National Forest Commission. During World War I Bennett was commissioned a first lieutenant in the Engineer Corps (he remained in the Officers' Reserve Corps as a captain until 1929). In 1919 he was a member of a special commission the State Department sent to Guatemala and Honduras in an unsuccessful attempt to mediate a boundary dispute between the two countries. The scientist again visited the Central and South Americas in 1923 and 1924 as a member of a commission to study the rubber-producing soils in these countries; and in 1925 and 1926 he conducted a reconnaissance soil survey in Cuba to discover possibilities of lowering the cost of sugar production and of increasing its efficiency. This work was done under the sponsorship of the Tropical Plant Research Foundation, which in 1928 was joined by the Cuba Sugar Club in assigning Bennett the task of classifying Cuban lands and reorganizing plantation procedure.

The planning and direction of the work at soil erosion stations throughout the United States and making detailed erosion surveys comprised Bennett's duty with the Bureau of Chemistry and Soils when he became senior soil scientist in charge of soil erosion investigations in 1928. The scientist, who since 1905 had been preaching soil conservation, was able to convince several Congressmen of the need for erosion control: in 1929 the Buchanan Amendment of the Agricultural Appropriations Bill assigned Federal funds for the purpose of studying erosion and installing methods of control. Experimental stations were set up in every major area in serious need of conservation work.

HUGH H. BENNETT

In 1933 erosion control was placed under the jurisdiction of the newly created Soil Erosion Service of the Department of the Interior, with Hugh Bennett as director. The group received an allotment from the Public Works Administration to set up practical demonstrations of the possibilities of erosion control. Of this work Bennett wrote that it was the "first attempt in the history of the country to put through large-scale, comprehensive erosion and flood-control projects." Not long after the establishment of the service, the great dust storms which swept across the Midwest gave proof of the desperate need of saving the soil of the United States. With the help of the Civilian Conservation Corps (whose permanent establishment Bennett later urged) in controlling erosion, by April 1935 the Soil Erosion Service had thirty-two erosion projects in thirty-one states.

Hugh Bennett, in *This Land We Defend* (1942), which he wrote in collaboration with William C. Pryor, describes the work of the Soil Conservation Service, successor to the Soil Erosion Service, which had been transferred in 1935 to the Department of Agriculture. Named chief of the new group, the scientist was given the direction of all conservation activity of the Federal Government. The demonstration projects, which usually comprised all the land within a watershed (the land lying within the drainage basin of a given stream), gradually evolved into soil conservation districts, formed after a referendum taken on the initiative of the farmers themselves. The procedure is defined by individual State laws. Once established as members of a Soil Conservation District, the farmers elect their own board of directors. The Federal Government's only part is the supplying of trained technicians to assist the farmers. Stress is laid on the fact that the government spends no money except for this work, and all facilities for conservation must be within the means of the

BENNETT, HUGH H.—*Continued*

farmer. Thus, for example, a man is taught how to terrace his land without machinery which he cannot afford to buy.

Disregarding the boundaries of individually owned tracts, the farmers learn about contour tillage (laying furrows to follow the slope of the land rather than in straight lines), about stubble mulch (the leaving of the stubble of wheat on the ground summer and winter to prevent winds from carrying loose soil away), about the varieties of soil-building legumes (some of which Bennett had introduced in the United States). They also discover that soil conservation is an integral part of flood control. But most important, they are shown the Soil Conservation Service maps which divide the whole of the United States into eight classifications, ranging from land which may be cultivated with no special treatment to that which should not be cultivated at all. By 1946 there were almost seventeen hundred Soil Conservation Districts in the United States, comprising almost two-thirds of the farms of the nation. Some farm incomes have increased from $2,500 to $3,000 as a result of conservation practice, and Herbert Corey in *Nation's Business* estimated, "Conservation will add at least one-fifth to our farm income."

Hugh Bennett has written numerous other books and articles devoted to the cause for which he has been working for over forty years. To prove that "throughout the world there is an acute need for a much better adjustment of agriculture to the physical environment, not only to gain a sorely needed increase in agricultural production, but also to maintain a healthful agricultural economy," he estimated that there are, in the world, only four billion acres of arable land to feed two billion people, and pointed out that some nutritionists assert that two and a half acres per person are essential. He has continually advocated education not only of farmers but also of urbanites to the need of conservation for the well-being of all. In 1946 he predicted that "farming will become an expert profession—the inexpert and inept will be forced off the land. It is not impossible that the prospective farmer will have to satisfy society that he is qualified by training and experience to take on the trusteeship of a piece of productive land." Bennett's articles may be found in the *Saturday Evening Post, Survey Graphic, New Republic,* and technical magazines. In addition to *This Land We Defend,* his books include *Soils of the United States* (1913); *Agricultural Possibilities of Alaska* (1916); *Soils and Agriculture of the Southern States* (1921); *Soils of Cuba,* with R. V. Allison (1928), and *Soil Conservation* (1939). His book "Elements of Soil Conservation" is scheduled for publication in 1947.

During the period that it has taken to build up the Soil Conservation Service, Hugh Bennett has also served on other Governmental groups that seek to prevent soil wastage. In 1936 he was a member of the President's National Drought Committee and of the Great Plains Drought Committee, which advised the Secretary of Agriculture on the ultimate solution of the erosion problems in plains lands. He helped to organize the Upstream Engineering Conference, and was a member of the National Resources Board committee on water resources which outlined a national water plan. He was asked by the Venezuelan Government to study erosion problems in that country, and in 1941 he led the North American Technical Mission to Venezuela. At the eighth American Scientific Congress he was named to serve on the Pan American Soil Conservation Committee, which is acting as the coordinator of conservation plans of the two American continents. At the request of the Government of the Union of South Africa, the scientist spent three months in 1944 in that country studying erosion problems and methods of control. A number of countries are now undertaking conservation projects patterned after the United States Soil Conservation Service, thirteen Central and South American countries alone having sent men to study under the conservation chief. In 1944 Bennett became a member of the staff of the War Food Administration. Governor R. Gregg Cherry of North Carolina declared September 9, 1946, "Hugh Bennett Day" in the scientist's native State. On that day, Bennett spoke to the farmers of Anson County's Brown Creek Soil Conservation District, the first Soil Conservation District in the nation.

Bennett is also a member of a number of agricultural and geographical societies, including the Association of American Geographers (of which he was president in 1943), the Soil Science Society of America, the American Society of Agronomy, Friends of the Land, the American Forestry Association, and the American Geophysical Union. In 1937 he was consultant to the Harvard University Graduate School of Business Administration. He has been married twice: in 1907 to Sarah Edna McCue, who died in 1909, leaving a daughter Sarah Edna (now Mrs. Eugene Akers); and in 1921 to Betty Virginia Brown. Their son is named Hugh Hammond, Jr. The tall, ruddy scientist finds his recreation in the outdoors, usually in gardening, hunting, or fishing.

References

Nation's Bsns 32:36 Ap '44
American Men of Science, 1944
Who's Who in America, 1946-47
Who's Who in the Nation's Capital, 1938-39

BERGE, WENDELL (bĕrj) Apr. 24, 1903-
United States Government official; lawyer
Address: b. c/o Department of Justice, Antitrust Division, Washington, D.C.; h. 9508 W. Stanhope Rd., Kensington, Md.

"Trust-busting, trust-crunching" Wendell Berge, as *Time* once called him, has inherited a controversial Governmental position. Made head of the Antitrust Division of the United States Department of Justice in 1943, Assistant Attorney General Berge not only handles national monopoly cases, but is faced with "the greatest antitrust issue of all at the moment"—international monopolies, or cartels.

Wendell Berge was born in Lincoln, Nebraska, on April 24, 1903, to Cora (Ott) Berge.

His father, George W. Berge, a lawyer, was in 1904 the unsuccessful Democratic candidate for Governor of Nebraska. He was sympathetic with the Populists, and, as his son was to do later, spoke out strongly against trusts. He wrote a book charging the railroads with using free passes to bribe state lawmakers, and, often accompanied by his son, toured the state making speeches on similar practices. After Wendell was graduated from the Lincoln High School in 1921, the youth entered the University of Nebraska. In the four years before he received his B.A., he was president of his freshman class, a member of the senior honorary society, a star debater, and the editor of the yearbook, on the staff of which he met his future wife. He was married to this coworker and fellow student, Laura Elizabeth Whelpley, in August of the year following his graduation, while he was studying for his law degree at the University of Michigan and serving as a member of the staff of the *Michigan Law Review*. He received the LL.B. the next year, 1927, and in 1928 the young couple left the West to establish themselves in New York City. (Berge, on a graduate fellowship, received his S.J.D. from Michigan in 1930.)

The Nebraska attorney's first legal position was with the well-known firm of Root, Clark, Buckner and Ballantine, not altogether an unfamiliar association for him, since Buckner had also been a member of the Nebraska university's debating fraternity. During Berge's two years with the New York firm he principally did research for the many corporate reorganizations which it handled; thus, as one writer pointed out, he had no opportunity for the courtroom work for which he had been trained. In 1930 he therefore accepted the offer made by John Lord O'Brian, chief of the Antitrust Division, of the post of special assistant to the Attorney General of the United States, in the Antitrust Division. The next year Berge was admitted to the District of Columbia bar.

He held a number of posts in the succeeding ten years. From 1935 to 1937, as chief of the division's Appellate Section, he was responsible for the briefs it filed with the Supreme Court. For a few months in 1937 he was chief of the Trial Section, after which he was made assistant to the then Assistant Attorney General, Robert H. Jackson [40], head of the Antitrust Division; in this capacity Berge supervised the operations of the division, and was responsible for gathering together a large staff of competent young lawyers. When Thurman Arnold [40] replaced Jackson, Berge in turn became his first assistant, as well as his alternate on Senator Joseph O'Mahoney's [45] Temporary National Economic Committee. In December 1940 he served as Acting Assistant Attorney General.

As the United States entry into World War II became imminent, it was evident that the Justice Department would be confronted with even more serious problems than before in its handling of subversive activities and the attendant problem of civil liberties. In January 1941 Berge was appointed Assistant Attorney General by President Roosevelt [42] and assigned

WENDELL BERGE

to head the Criminal Division, responsible for these cases. He has received praise for his work with this office, and at the same time it has been said that he lacked decisiveness. Berge remained with the division until August 1943, when he exchanged jobs with Tom Clark [45], then head of the Antitrust Division, who took with him many of the important wartime functions of the division.

In 1942, by agreement of the President and the War, Navy, and Justice departments, it had been decided to shelve certain antitrust cases when it was thought prosecution might endanger the war effort. The resulting disagreement over the extent to which this should be done led to the departure of Thurman Arnold in 1943. Clark filled this post for a number of months, until Berge took over in August as head of the Antitrust Division. "Despite all limitations," reported *Fortune* a year before V-J Day, the division "is far from impotent. In the year that ended June 30 [1944] . . . approximately eighty cases were filed and only a few less than that number settled." Later in the year another writer pointed out that Berge's office had twenty-seven cartel suits pending. These involved "the biggest corporations of the United States and other countries, and industries ranging from dyestuffs to aluminum to plastics to drugs to matches." And when the end of the war came, Attorney General Tom Clark announced that antitrust cases would be one of the principal concerns of the Justice Department, but that "witch hunting" was not its purpose.

To many businessmen, however, in the words of the *Saturday Evening Post*, "the Justice Department means witch hunts, patent wrecking, persecution of respectable men. Bitterness against Antitrust is matched only by bewilderment at the workings of the antitrust laws." To many other people, certain decisions won by the division have been welcomed: the de-

BERGE, WENDELL—*Continued*

cision making fire insurance companies subject to antitrust laws; "a judgment prohibiting motion picture exhibiting groups from using their combined buying power to force distributors to discriminate against the independents; and [a decision] restraining the Associated Press from enforcing bylaws that handicap nonmember newspapers competing with members of the association."

The Antitrust head is not opposed to capitalism, to "bigness" as such. He is against it, records a *Fortune* survey, "only if it is used to impair or prevent competition. But he thinks there is a point beyond which bigness in any industry ceases to promote efficiency, and he sees democratic advantages in keeping ownership dispersed." (As another measure to maintain a stable economy, he also believes in a policy of deficit spending, as advocated by Alvin Hansen '45.) "We try to concentrate on monopolies," says Berge himself, "that shelter inefficient or obsolescent industry or suppress new products or technologies needed to supply jobs and expand the economy. We believe profits are justified only as a reward for risk taking; we have no use for a corporation that entrenches itself behind a Siegfried line of illegal patent or monopoly weapons and still expects to draw down rewards appropriate to venture capitalism."

To the argument that the United States must inevitably adopt cartels in order to exist in a postwar cartelized world, he has replied that if America, with her tremendous productive resources and buying power were to remain outside the cartel system, the system itself could not survive. The effects of cartels on the nation's economy are several, Berge declares. They conflict with attempts of the Government at certain times to encourage imports by lowering tariffs; they interfere with the foreign policy, at one important period in the past having diverted valuable South American trade to Germany; and in World War II cartel agreements prevented some of America's allies from purchasing necessary war materials in the United States. If the Government refrains from regulating cartels, Berge warns, cartels will "come to exercise in effect the functions of Government itself. If, on the other hand, Government endeavors to control the cartels, governmental power must be built up to such proportions that it becomes incompatible with democratic institutions."

When World War II ended, Berge's antitrust bureau, unhampered by emergency wartime considerations, began an extensive investigation of industrial monopolies and cartels. It was found that economic power had become more highly concentrated in a few vested interests than ever before in history. In October 1945 Berge was one of the American representatives at British-American trade conferences in Washington. During these meetings the United States proposed the adoption of an anticartel agreement whereby all commercial nations would enact legislation preventing their citizens "from entering combines in restraint of trade." After that Berge became engaged in prosecuting, under the Sherman and Clayton Anti-Trust Acts, a number of companies in various industries. At the Senate Interstate Commerce Committee, Berge in April 1946 opposed the Bulwinkle bill, a measure amending the Interstate Commerce Act, and exempting railways and other transportation facilities "from antitrust laws in the fixing of freight rates by agreement among themselves." The Antitrust Division chief also directed in 1946 an investigation into the cause of high prices and scarcities of certain commodities. Later in the same year he urged the establishment of a national petroleum council to succeed the wartime Petroleum Administration for War, and to serve as an advisory and consultation committee to the Secretary of the Interior in petroleum industry matters.

Berge is a trustee of the University of Nebraska Foundation, Inc., and is a member of the Federal Bar Association, the American Bar Association, the American Judicature Society, the National Lawyers Guild, and Acacia. He is also a member of Phi Delta Phi and Delta Sigma Rho, and he is a Mason. In 1942 he was awarded a Distinguished Service Medal by the University of Nebraska. His political party is the Democratic, his church membership Unitarian. The attorney is a contributor to numerous legal journals and is the author of the book *Cartels: Challenge to a Free World*, published in 1944, and of *Economic Freedom for the West*, which appeared in 1946. In the second book Berge discusses the enforcement of antitrust laws as an aid to bringing "new and independent industry to the western States." It was called, in a New York *Times* review, a "lucid, challenging, and readable book on a problem of significance for all Americans."

Some writers have made certain comparisons between Wendell Berge and Thurman Arnold, his predecessor. "Judge Arnold," commented *Fortune*, "is dramatic and ebullient, Mr. Berge is methodical and quiet. Judge Arnold is as stagewise as an actor, given to double talk and double takes. Mr. Berge relies on direct, incisive speech. But in basic antitrust philosophy the two men are agreed."

The mild-mannered Berge is a stocky man, five feet nine inches tall and weighing one hundred and sixty pounds. He has brown eyes, thinning blond hair, and a cleft chin. Photographers often find him with a pipe, for straight-grained briars are an extravagance of his. With Mrs. Berge and their two sons, John Wendell and Douglas James, the attorney lives in the Rock Creek Hills section of Maryland. There, when work permits, the elder Berges are party and tennis enthusiasts and enjoy riding and hiking, while Berge himself occasionally goes mountain climbing. They also collect phonograph records of symphonies, operas, and dance music.

References

Fortune 30:136-41+ Ag '44 por
N Y Post Mag p5 Je 10 '44 pors
PM p2-3 D 26 '43 pors
America's Young Men, 1938-39
Who's Who in America, 1946-47
Who's Who in Law, 1937

BEVAN, MRS. ANEURIN *See* Lee, J.

BIFFLE, LESLIE L. Oct. 9, 1889- United States Government official

Address: b. The Capitol, Washington, D. C.; h. Westchester Apartments, 4000 Cathedral Ave., N. W., Washington, D. C.

"The Sage of Capitol Hill" is the title of an article Lewis Wood once wrote for the New York *Times Magazine* on Leslie L. Biffle, secretary of the United States Senate. "To the men of the upper chamber," said *Newsweek* of Biffle, "he is counselor, father-confessor, and savant . . .an encyclopedia of the national legislature. . . .Novices seek his guidance. Old hands heed his advice." Holder of an ordinarily obscure position, Biffle has gained public notice as an intimate of President Truman '45, who once said, "Les is worth ten votes on a roll call."

Leslie L. Biffle, of Scotch-Irish ancestry, was born October 9, 1889, in Boydsville, Arkansas, which the census of 1900 showed to have a population of one hundred. He was the first child of Billie B. and Ella (Turner) Biffle, who gave him the letter "L" for his middle "name." Billie Biffle, a storekeeper, was active in local Democratic politics, at various times holding the offices of sheriff and county clerk. Young Leslie attended the high school at nearby Piggott, a town about twice the size of Boydsville. In 1908, when United States Representative Bruce Macon was re-elected, he invited Sheriff Biffle's recently graduated son to come to Washington as his secretary. The youth accepted the offer, taking a course at the Keys Business Institute in Little Rock to prepare himself for his new duties.

In his *Times* article Wood described Biffle as having "retained an essentially small-town philosophy and point of view," although his working life since 1909 has been spent in the national capital. The year 1912 was Congressman Macon's last in the House, and after that young Biffle became secretary to Arkansas' Senator James P. Clarke. Clarke, a former Governor of Arkansas, died in office in October 1916, following which his secretary became superintendent of the Senate folding room, where documents are prepared for mailing. Biffle held this position for the next nine years except for the two (1917-19) he served with the World War I Army in France as auditor.

In 1925 Leslie Biffle became assistant secretary of the Democratic minority in the Senate. When the minority became the majority in the Roosevelt New Deal landslide of 1932, colorful majority leader Joseph T. Robinson of Arkansas chose Biffle as secretary for the majority, advising him to keep his eyes and ears open and his mouth shut. Biffle's new post had formerly been known as pair clerk, one of its principal duties being to arrange for pairing, by means of which members of opposite parties or opinions abstain from voting, thereby eliminating the effect of absences. When a vote is close, well-managed pairing may on occasion swing the decision.

Ever since his arrival in the capital city in 1909, Biffle has kept an indexed diary, jotting

Harris & Ewing

LESLIE L. BIFFLE

down items of interest on file cards under the names of Washington personages. The New York *Sun*'s Delos Lovelace has said that these notes, which Biffle has refused to show, tell "just why every Senator voted for whom and what." The "Arkansawyer" is credited with being on terms of personal friendship with Senators of both parties, and with having the ability to predict their actions and reactions. Carl Hatch '44 of New Mexico has been quoted as saying, "Biffle knows how I'm going to vote before I do myself."

According to Roger Butterfield in *Life*, Biffle is able to make his prophecies because he knows more than the obvious facts about national legislators. "He knows, for instance, just what little temperamental feuds are going on between members of the same party and how this will affect their votes. He is generally aware of the state of each Senator's digestion from day to day. He knows what financial or domestic upsets they are undergoing. Even the state of the weather enters into his calculations, for Senators with hay fever or sinus trouble often do unexpected things." During the days of the fight for New Deal legislation, *Newsweek* observed, "Les participated actively in the almost daily strategy conferences. . . . Les's comfortably furnished office on the gallery floor became a convenient gathering place where Senators could hold bull sessions before and after debates. . . .They came to him with their political troubles. Republicans as well as Democrats learned to trust him. Les never let them down." At the 1944 Democratic convention in Chicago, Biffle, as the sergeant at arms for the convention, is supposed to have worked with Senators Hatch and Minton '41 and Judge Schwellenbach '45 to win the vice-presidential nomination for Harry Truman.

After the death of Colonel Edwin A. Halsey, secretary of the Senate, Leslie Biffle was

BIFFLE, LESLIE L.—*Continued*

elected to succeed him in February 1945. The Republican minority omitted the usual formality of nominating an opposition candidate, and the Southerner was elected unanimously, an honor said to be unprecedented. This promotion placed Biffle in charge of more than a thousand employees, including a parliamentarian (also from Arkansas) to advise the presiding officer, assorted clerks, librarians, bookkeepers, pages, attendants, and the document, mailing, disbursement, and maintenance staffs. The Senate restaurants, the Capitol police, the little Congressional subway, and the pages' school—all are under his supervision. He receives and transmits all Presidential messages and vetoes, has custody of historic papers, and assigns desks to Senators after each election—there is keen competition for the historic ones, which Biffle allots strictly on a seniority basis. The Senate secretary's chief duty is to watch over the steps of legislation and resolutions through the chamber and to certify its action. Biffle is said to like his work so much that he has refused offers with salaries as high as five times his yearly eight thousand dollars. He has, however, been a member of the American Battle Monuments Commission since May 1941. In that capacity he made a three-week tour of Europe in September 1946 to report on American cemeteries overseas.

When Truman became President on the death of Franklin D. Roosevelt, one of the first things he did was send for Biffle, whom he had known since 1935. Before long the secretary of the Senate became known as one of the closest advisers of the new President, who reportedly spoke to him by direct wire many times daily, and who told newsmen, "They don't make them any better than Les Biffle." As a result, Biffle was besieged by favor-seekers and deluged with social invitations. His name appeared for the first time in the Washington *Social Register* in 1946, and he became the subject of articles in various publications.

An article on Truman and his Administration in *Fortune* (January 1946) described Biffle as "very important to the President. . . .He is one of Truman's few real intimates." He was, however, also a "profound handicap" to Truman, the article asserted, in that Congressional leaders were offended when the President repeatedly consulted the Senate's secretary rather than them. Another defect of this arrangement was that Biffle, while a shrewd adviser and "an extremely able legislative mechanic," did not think in terms of policy. Butterfield described Biffle "in action": "He is almost unnoticeable as he goes about his duties in the Capitol. . . . When necessary he can whisper without moving his mouth, like a ventriloquist. His job often requires him to step up to a Senator on the Senate floor and whisper something which another Senator, sitting three feet away, cannot hear or even read from his lips. . . .If a message is super-confidential Biffle will walk quickly past a Senator's desk, whisper without moving his lips, and keep going. He can do this in such an unobstrusive way that it looks as though he is just taking a stroll across the room."

The Senate secretary could be addressed as "Doctor." In June 1946 he was awarded an LL.D. by Dartmouth College, an honor extended then to former Governor Harold E. Stassen '40, Senator Warren R. Austin '44, Red Cross chairman Basil O'Connor '44, and industrialist Paul G. Hoffman '46. Biffle could also be called "Colonel," having been given that honorary rank as "military aide" on the staffs of Governors of Arkansas, New Mexico, and the Virgin Islands. Biffle is a member of the National Press Club, the Congressional and Army-Navy country clubs, and four other social clubs. His church affiliation is Methodist, and he is a member of the Masonic order.

Blue-eyed Leslie Biffle is five feet eight inches tall, a man of slight physique, and his curly brown hair is graying and receding. He lives in a five-room penthouse with his wife, who was Mary Glade Strickling of West Virginia. They met while she was attending Fairmount Seminary, in Washington, and were married in 1923. The Biffles have traveled a great deal, both on Congressional business and on their vacations. When at home, "Biff" raises tomatoes for his special "pick-me-up" in ten roof boxes, plays golf, and fishes. A sixty-nine-pound sailfish he caught at Miami hangs on the wall of the private dining room adjoining his office, where he gives daily luncheons for Senators and other personages. Biffle is known for his geniality, and Butterfield has remarked that he "conceals a somewhat romantic viewpoint behind his precise and modest manner."

References

Life 20:65-72 Je 10 '46 pors
N Y Sun p22 Mr 2 '45
N Y Times VI p18 Ag 26 '45 por
Newsweek 26:34 Jl 16 '45 por
Congressional Directory (2d ed., 1945)
Who's Who in America, 1946-47

BILLINGSLEY, (JOHN) SHERMAN
Mar. 10, 1900- Night club owner
Address: b. Stork Club, 3 E. 53d St., New York; h. 1130 Park Ave., New York

Many commentators on the New York scene have undertaken to explain how, in fourteen years, Sherman Billingsley has made the Stork Club the world's most famous night club. Russell Whelan in the *American Mercury* attributes Billingsley's prestige (Paramount Pictures paid a hundred thousand dollars for the use of the Stork Club name in a motion picture title) to a combination of "assured native shrewdness and the cooperation of helpful friends" like Steve Hannagan '44, ace publicity man, and widely read columnists who have featured the Stork in their columns. "It might be," suggests Lucius Beebe '40, "that the Stork is also a figment of the popular imagining and the factual realization of the vast and unabated hanker on the part of the American public for glamour, romance, and snobbishness in carload lots." Glamour and romance are furnished chiefly by the fact that the club is patronized by the famous from both the social and professional worlds. "If the celebrities should de-

sert Billingsley," says another Stork Club ap-
praiser, "so would almost everyone else, for
there is no entertainment. . . .The orchestras
are small and unknown. The show consists of
the common people looking at the celebrities
and the celebrities looking in the mirrors, and
they all sit pop-eyed in admiration." "It is the
genial host himself," says another. "He gives
his guests the best of whatever they may be
looking for, whether it be glamour, romance,
good food, good liquor, or good dancing."

John Sherman Billingsley, originally a
Westerner, was born March 10, 1900, in
North Enid, Oklahoma. His schooling ended
when he completed the fourth grade, and his
first earnings, of pennies, writes Jerome Beatty
in the *American* Magazine, came from the sale
of discarded whisky bottles to bootleggers.
When Sherman was twelve years old he moved
to Anadarko, where for several years he
worked with his elder brothers in their chain
of cigar and drugstores. These establishments
did a profitable business in Anadarko and other
small towns of the dry state of Oklahoma.
While still in his teens young Billingsley left
home to see America and eventually became
the proprietor of three neighborhood groceries
in Detroit.

At twenty-three Billingsley approached Manhattan by way of the Bronx. With five thousand dollars in cash he bought a drugstore
there and eventually owned a chain of twenty
in the Bronx and adjoining Westchester County. A monument to the Bronx period is Billingsley Terrace, a two-block long residential
street, where the young merchant built a number of apartment and private houses.

The first Stork Club opened its doors, shortly
before the 1929 stock market crash, on West
58th Street, the wrong side of Fifth Avenue.
"It was the first speakeasy," boasts Billingsley,
"that had a carpet on the floor and a canopy
out front." Prohibition agents ended the life of
this venture, but by 1932 Billingsley had crossed
Fifth Avenue, and established Stork Club
number two, at Park Avenue and 51st Street.
This was the beginning of his "six-cylinder"
clientele. Since the repeal of Prohibition, the
club's green canopy has marked its present site
at 53rd Street a few steps east of the Avenue.
The young man from Oklahoma then adopted
the "professional approach to society." He immediately began to attract the celebrated and
the rich; he told the prettiest debutantes and
those in a position to publicize the club that
they could expect "gentle treatment from his
totalizer. Simultaneously he went after the boys
in the Ivy League set by advertising in their
college publications and paying for the space
with due bills on the Stork. The boys and
girls came a-running, and soon, to Billingsley's
delight, their blue-blooded elders dropped around
for inspection, sniffed, liked what they sniffed,
and continued as regulars."

Billingsley's club seats 374 people at one time,
but since the Stork never closes its doors, the
average daily patronage is from two to three
thousand. The yearly intake is reported to be
in the neighborhood of a million and a half.
The club's foyer is neither large nor impressive,
but a red rope bars the way to the inner sanc-

SHERMAN BILLINGSLEY

tum. Although it is generally believed that only
"high hats" are welcome, it is not difficult for
unknowns to enter. They need only come under
Billingsley's own definition of "nice people,"
that is, sober, reasonably quiet, and well dressed.
Once past the rope, no restaurant patrons in
the world are said to receive more flattering
attention.

The rope, however, is not the only dividing
line in this famous club. There are five rooms
—Blessed Events, Loners', the bar room, the
main dining room, and the Cub room. The last-
named, said to be the world's most exclusive
room, is reserved for the famous, or important,
or beautiful. Among the privileged are the
James A. Farleys '44, George Jean Nathan '45,
columnists Leonard Lyons, Louis Sobol, Dorothy Kilgallen, and Walter Winchell '43. The
Darryl Zanucks '41, when in New York, make
the Cub Room their after-midnight haunt, as
do Orson Welles '41, Helen Hayes '42, Morton
Downey, and other luminaries from the Broadway and Hollywood worlds. Other habitués are
the Roosevelt sons and Jock Whitney '45. The
L-shaped main dining room has a dance floor,
fifteen by twenty feet, which is considered large
for a night club. Two bands, playing in shifts,
furnish uninterrupted music for the dancers.
The main dining room has a more elaborate
decor than any of the other rooms. Walls are
paneled with mirrors against dark blue velvet
and festooned with golden-silk draperies.

Billingsley runs the Stork Club with the aid
of two hundred and fifty employees, including a
world-famous chef and a night and day publicity staff. His weekly laundry bill is $600,
redecorating amounts to around $25,000 every
six months, florist bills come to $10,000 annually.
The figures are expected to soar when Billingsley, who own the two buildings that
house and adjoin his club, expands the club.
"It is a little like watching Farragut on the
bridge to observe Billingsley on the job," writes

BILLINGSLEY, SHERMAN—*Continued*

Russell Whelan, "his roving eyes noting a hundred details of service and conduct, the waiters and captains slithering up with a message or whispered questions, the orders quickly and quietly issued, the ship held steady on its course through the night." Samples of the messages which "hit the bridge" in the course of ten minutes are: A Hollywood star has just checked his hat—where shall he be seated; two chefs are threatening to behead each other; Leonard Lyons is ready for his nightly game of gin rummy; a man, calling from Kansas City, wants Billingsley to speak to his girl friend to prove that he is an old customer. *Life* Magazine has devoted a picture feature to the unobtrusive hand signals by which Billingsley transmits orders to an ever-present "shadow," who in turn orders a gift sent to a certain table, calls his employer to answer a nonexistent telephone call, or otherwise follows the semaphored command.

Although it is a time-honored custom for a commercial host on very special occasions to announce that the drinks are "on the house," Billingsley of the Stork has developed "gifting" to perfection. He does not limit his favors to special times or special people. If a guest comes under his favorite heading of "nice" and the benevolent boniface is in the mood, that person may be selected for favors. Unexpectedly a bottle of perfume or a Stork Club souvenir powder compact is placed with Billingsley's card before the lady guest. Before the guest has time to recover from this surprise the waiter may wheel champagne to the table and place Billingsley's card before the lady's escort. This flattery often gains another regular customer and much word-of-mouth advertising. To valuable guests—those whose beauty decorates the place or whose fame enhances it—Billingsley has been known to give anything from a gold cigarette case to an automobile.

Although there is a Billingsley character in the motion picture *The Stork Club* (1945), the role is not biographical. Further recognition of his eminence in the night club world appears in the *Encyclopædia Britannica*—its article on night clubs was written by Billingsley. He has also collaborated on articles which have been published in *Variety* and in the magazine sections of Sunday newspapers.

Billingsley was married in 1925 to Hazel Donnelly, who at one time was with Florenz Ziegfeld's *Follies*. There are three daughters in the family—Jacqueline, Barbara, and Shermane. In a short article on Jacqueline in *Good Housekeeping*, Nanette Kutner writes one characterization of Billingsley: "Around a steel core, his shrewd inner smartness, he seems disarmingly boyish, is sweetly likeable, remarkably young-looking." Because Billingsley never takes a vacation, his family remain with him during the summer in their Park Avenue apartment, except for excursions to Atlantic Beach, on Long Island. Despite the fact that he spends more than twelve hours a day at the club he manages to keep physically fit by abstinence from coffee, cigarettes, and liquor. He walks forty blocks from his home to the Stork Club

and between the dinner and after-theatre crowds has a shower, a rubdown, and a ten-minute nap, then changes to another of the one hundred suits in his wardrobe.

References

Am Mag 131:44-5+ Je '41
Am Mercury 59:357-65 S '44
Good H 119:29+ Jl '44
Time 44:73 Ag '44

BIRDSEYE, CLARENCE   Dec. 9, 1886-
Inventor; food-preservation expert

Address: b. and h. Eastern Point, Gloucester, Mass.

Clarence Birdseye, scientist and inventor, one of America's leading authorities on food, is responsible for two new methods of preserving food. The first method, called by *Fortune* magazine "one of the most exciting and revolutionary ideas in the history of food," is a process for quick-freezing meat, fish, vegetables, and fruit without altering the original taste. This method was perfected by the scientist-inventor in 1925 and now appears on the market under the trade mark Birds Eye Frosted Foods. The second idea, developed by Birdseye in 1945, is an improved method of dehydrating foods, which he calls "anhydrous."

The name Birdseye, which every housewife associates with packages of frozen food, originally became a family name when an ancestor of the inventor, a page to one of England's queens, served his royal mistress well by making a bird's eye shot. "One day," relates the twentieth-century Birdseye, "a hawk or some other big bird started to swoop down toward the Queen. And this page-boy ancestor of mine, according to the records, took out his trusty bow and arrow and shot that bird right in the eye. The Queen was so tickled she gave him the name right on the spot." With the name came the family motto, "Stay right on the target."

The son of Ada (Underwood) and lawyer Clarence Frank Birdseye, Clarence Birdseye was born December 9, 1886, in Brooklyn, New York. At the age of five the boy exhibited first signs of becoming a naturalist when he presented his mother with a mouse skin which he had dressed himself. By the time he reached "shotgun" age young Clarence considered himself an authority in taxidermy, and accordingly placed an advertisement in a sports magazine which announced that The American School of Taxidermy offered courses at a reasonable price. A few years later the young taxidermist left Brooklyn for Montclair, New Jersey, where he attended the high school and showed his first interest in food preparation by voluntary attendance at the school's cooking class.

After graduation from high school Clarence entered Amherst College (1908) but, owing to financial difficulties, his attendance was irregular, and in 1910 his formal schooling ended. (In 1941, however, Amherst gave him an honorary M.A. degree.) To help pay his expenses at college he had sold frogs (used for snake's food) to the Bronx Zoo, and supplied live rats, which he trapped in a butcher shop's bone room, to a Columbia University professor. Each year he had been forced to leave college early in the spring and return late in the fall because he worked for the United States Biological Survey as a field naturalist, work he continued to do during the spring, summer, and fall seasons from 1910 to 1912. Some of this time was spent in research on Rocky Mountain spotted fever in Montana and in trapping wolves in northern Michigan. On leaving college in 1910, for a time he was also an office boy in a New York insurance agency. For a number of weeks that winter he was a snow checker for the New York Street Cleaning Department, when he earned as much in one day as he had as an office boy.

In 1912 the young naturalist left for Labrador, where, under the auspices of the noted missionary, Sir Wilfred T. Grenfell, he engaged in fur trading. During his four years there he traveled thousands of miles in a small boat in the summer, by dog team in the winter. In an interview with Wambly Bald (New York *Post*) Birdseye told of being "snagged" for three days in an Arctic blizzard while traveling by sled. The snow and wind were so heavy, said Birdseye, that it was like being lost in a flour barrel. On another trip to Labrador, in 1916, he was accompanied by his wife, the former Eleanor Gannett of Washington, D.C., to whom he had been married the year before. *Pathfinder* relates that it was the presence of Mrs. Birdseye and their five-week-old baby which first aroused his interest in quick-frozen foods. Barrels of fresh cabbages had been taken along, and in order to preserve them Birdseye placed them in salt water and exposed them to freezing winds. Then he froze a winter's supply of rabbits, ducks, and caribou meat—"and an industry was born."

While the idea which was to revolutionize the perishable food industry was taking shape in its creator's mind, the United States entered World War I, and Birdseye became an assistant in the purchasing department of the Washington (D.C.) office of Stone and Webster (1917-18); during the following year he was purchasing agent of the United States Housing Corporation. Later on, relates Birdseye, he was, until 1922, assistant to the president of the United States Fisheries Association.

The next eight years were spent in experiments with the quick-freezing method. When Birdseye first began experimenting, Bald relates, he could afford only seven dollars for tools—an electric fan, buckets of salt brine, and cakes of ice. Later a friend lent him a corner of his ice plant to carry on his work. In 1924 Birdseye borrowed on his life insurance, found three partners, and formed the General Seafoods Company in Gloucester, Massachusetts. "My first quick-freezing trials," says Birdseye, "were with fish and rabbits, and I packed them in old candy boxes."

To quote *Fortune,* Clarence Birdseye "did not 'invent' quick-freezing," nor was his company the first of its kind. "The scientific principles underlying the method have been known for a long time, and whole fish were being frozen commercially in Europe before the First World War. Mr. Birdseye's contribution was

CLARENCE BIRDSEYE

a system of freezing perishable foods of all kinds in packages, by pressing them between refrigerated metal plates." The chief virtue of Birdseye's process was extremely rapid freezing, and one of the most important of the 168 patents which cover the Birds Eye process is "the procedure of freezing the product after it has been snugly packed in a square container. So whether it is a pound of lobster or a quart of strawberries it presents itself as a square hard brick, highly convenient to handle." Another advantage is the retention of food values, for vitamin values were not lost. In tests, reports a *Collier's* article, the vitamin content has been found to run even higher than in so-called fresh vegetables and fruits. No one knows how long they may be stored—a demonstration luncheon served meats and vegetables which had been packed ten years. The alterations in the taste of foods which have been frozen by ordinary means are usually the result of the rupture of food cells by slow forming ice crystals. In quick-freezing (under pressure at fifty degrees below zero) the ice crystals are about one-hundredth of the size of the slowly frozen crystals; the result is less rupture of the cellular structure of the food.

By 1925 Birdseye had perfected his process and was turning out fresh haddock in frozen packages in his newly formed company at Gloucester. His financial problem, however, was still with him, until Wetmore Hodges, son of Charles H. Hodges, vice-president of the American Radiator Company, became enthusiastic over the possibilities of the process. Hodges, reports *Fortune* magazine, first interested two members of J. P. Morgan and Company, and it was from this group that the first refinancing came of the "modest haddock-freezing General Foods Company." By 1928 Hodges "had so inflamed the imaginations of Postum Company, Incorporated, and Goldman Sachs Trading Corporation, that the latter solemnly

BIRDSEYE, CLARENCE—*Continued*

estimated that the process had a sales potentiality of one billion dollars a year." Negotiations for the purchase of Birdseye's process by these two concerns were completed in 1929. The financial arrangement, says *Fortune* (which gives a full account of the transaction), were extremely complex. Postum paid $10,750,000 for 51 per cent of the Birdseye General Food Company (and immediately changed its name from Postum to the General Foods Corporation). Goldman Sachs put up $12,750,000 for 49 per cent, and subsequently sold its interest to the former Postum company, which is now the sole proprietor. Under the new trade name of Birds Eye Frosted Foods, quick-frozen vegetables, fruits, seafoods, and meats were sold to the public for the first time in 1930 in Springfield, Massachusetts. Birdseye has acted as a consultant to General Foods Corporation ever since.

Having made a bird's eye shot in quick-frozen foods, the millionaire scientist turned to other fields. He invented the Birdseye reflector and infra-red heat lamps, now under the control of the Birdseye Electric Company, of which he was president from 1932 to 1936. His hobby of harpooning whales in waters off Gloucester inspired him to invent the "shoulder-fire harpoon gun," with which he "stayed on the target" with fifty whales during his six years of harpooning. When a hurricane wrecked his boat Birdseye returned to his cooking interests. He became president of Dehydration, Incorporated, and of Processes, Incorporated, which control his patents on Anhydrous, his second major contribution to perishable food preservation. "The new quick-drying method," says Clementine Paddleford (New York *Herald Tribune*), "extracts the water in approximately ninety minutes as compared to an average eighteen hours by other known methods. It removes virtually all the water content, semi-cooks the product and cuts in half the preparation time, as no soaking is needed. The finished product has the flavor, color, texture, aroma and nutritional qualities of vegetables and fruits, which are cooked fresh-picked from garden and orchard." Birdseye spent six years in developing this method. (Production of Anhydrous foods began in 1946.) Using the same principle of speed that had proved successful in quick-frozen foods he found that rapidly dehydrated foods retain their cell structure both physically and chemically. And like the frosted foods they have a distinct advantage in packaging. Servings for four are packed in cigarette-package-sized containers. The inventor, who holds three hundred United States and foreign patents, has announced that he originally organized Processes, Incorporated, for continuing research and development in the food preservation field.

Among the numerous articles and lectures he has contributed to the subject of food preservation are two chapters in the 1946 *Refrigerating Data Book*. In 1945-46 he acted as chairman of the Northeast Section of Institute of Food Technologists. Mr. and Mrs. Birdseye, who live in a high-school-size red brick house in Gloucester, have four children: Kellogg Gannett, Ruth, Eleanor, and Henry. Birdseye is of medium height—five feet seven inches tall—and his eyes and hair are gray. His diversions are "horse operas," Chinese checkers, and he likes to give large dinner parties. He has been described as good-humored and frank, and his speech as salty. "His success," wrote Bald, "has put no blisters on his ego."

References

N Y Post Mag p23 D 20 '45 por
Newsweek 26:72 N 19 '45
Pathfinder p 38 O 24 '45 por
American Men of Science (1938)
Who's Who in Commerce and Industry (1944)

BIRDWELL, RUSSELL (JUAREZ) (hwä'räs) Oct. 17, 1903- Public relations counsel; writer

Address: b. Russell Birdwell and Associates, 30 Rockefeller Plaza, New York; 200 S. Beverly Dr., Beverly Hills, Calif.

Nearly as well known as his clients is "idea man" Russell Birdwell, who has directed the publicity of such celebrities as ex-King Carol of Rumania, motion picture producers Howard Hughes and David O. Selznick; the stars Norma Shearer, Ronald Colman, Charles Boyer, Marlene Dietrich, and Dick Powell; the City of Yonkers; and business organizations such as The Tailored Woman, *Coronet,* Commander Air Lines, Celotex Corporation, Duotone Company (the largest manufacturers of phonograph accessories in the world), Playright Toys, Inc., and a score of others. The *New Yorker* devoted the longest of its famous "profiles" to him.

The name of the man who signs letters and contracts with a regally simple "Birdwell" is, in full, Russell Juarez Birdwell. Born in Coleman, Texas, on October 17, 1903, he is the son of Russell Juarez Birdwell, a colorful real estate dealer who disapproved of his son's violin lessons and wanted him to become a criminal lawyer. Russell's mother was the daughter of James Madison Mitcham, an equally colorful Texas landowner whose holdings were said to total nearly a million acres. When the boy was nine his father's health began to fail, and the Birdwells bundled their two sons and three daughters into a covered wagon and set out on travels through Texas and Mexico. Their trip ended with the elder Birdwell's death when Russell was twelve. (His only brother died at the age of seven.)

Little Russell, who had witnessed several scenes of violence during his childhood, "played hooky" from grammar school for three weeks to attend a murder trial. To get into the courtroom he pretended he was the sheriff's son, a device he used later to obtain admission to executions. At ten he was selling short articles at two dollars apiece to the *American Boy* on how to make money at home. At eleven he tried to sell his report of a lynching to the local daily paper. At twelve, according to the "profile" by Alva Johnston, he began to get inside information from jailers and prisoners whose friendship he had cultivated, and induced his condemned friends to add some reportable dramatic touch to the occasion. He was also editor of the school paper. When he was hired by the local newspaper for a regular job, however, it was for the delivery department. He became afternoon police reporter when he was thirteen.

Birdwell estimates that he worked for twenty-three newspapers and press associations in the course of twenty years: besides those in his native Texas, the list includes five dailies in New York, two in Mexico City, two in San Francisco, and six in Los Angeles. He did news reporting, wrote features, "sob stuff," columns, and fiction, was dramatic critic, ghost writer, and also "observed the first law of the craft by trying incessantly to escape to some other occupation." Thus:

At fourteen young Russell broke his routine of morning schooling, afternoon reporting, evening soda-dispensing, high school politics, dramatics, active social life and prize-winning oratory, by playing adult parts for some months with a touring stock company which had hired him by mail. After his graduation from high school he spent a year at the University of Texas, where he wrote and produced a musical play; his youngest sister, Dorothea (now deceased) traveled from New York to appear in it. (All three sisters—the other two are Cherie and Tomasita—became professional entertainers and toured in the United States and abroad.) At eighteen, Russell spent several months managing a jazz band in Mexico City, and for two or three months was a ghost writer for Mary Pickford. In October 1923, before his twentieth birthday, Birdwell was married to a young businesswoman, Mabel Condon. (They have a daughter, Joan. Their son Russell died at the age of twenty-two.) About three years after his marriage, Birdwell left his current paper for a fruitless literary collaboration with an imperfectly reformed forger and confidence man. Their unsuccessful novel was entitled *The Club of Failures*.

Birdwell tells in his autobiography that he has "lied and cheated, stolen and slugged, bulldozed and bribed to get a story"—and has had to risk his life, pay court to a towering housemaid, and has been knocked down by a police detective. In 1927 he "scooped" the world on Lindbergh's flight to Paris. One human interest story which he "planted" and reported proved salable in many other versions: he reworked and resold "The Eternal Honeymoon" as features for a number of newspapers, as a true story, a radio drama, a vaudeville sketch, and finally a movie scene. Used as a happy ending for an Unknown Soldier film, it brought him $5,000 besides $3,750 for three weeks' work on the script. While on the staff of the New York *Daily Mirror*, Birdwell wrote a "true story" nearly every day, adding twenty-five dollars for each to his income, but he always seemed to spend his earnings as fast as he received them.

In 1928 young Birdwell was struck with an idea for producing two-reel movie features at extremely low cost, and accordingly returned to Hollywood to put it into practice. Hailed as a genius by Charlie Chaplin [40], he directed Fox's *Masquerade* (1929), but re-

RUSSELL BIRDWELL

signed his $1,250-a-week job to go back to the Los Angeles *Examiner* when given an unacceptable assignment. Birdwell has also written and directed a radio program, *Hollywood on the Air*, for NBC. Back in Hollywood in 1933, with his depression-year salary of one hundred dollars cut to fifty, he directed RKO's *Flying Devils*, which turned out to be a box-office success—some time after the producer had fired Birdwell. In 1935, after more years of reporting and independent writing, the former "boy wonder" was hired by David O. Selznick to publicize Selznick-International Pictures, with which John Hay Whitney [46] was associated.

To advertise Selznick's first independent production, *Little Lord Fauntleroy*, Birdwell had the world's largest sign, more than two miles long, painted along a Culver City boulevard. For the next four years he got publicity for Selznick pictures by such means as latter-day Lady Godivas, previews before United States Senators, and Carole Lombard's defense of the income tax, which Birdwell says he did not instigate but merely publicized. He conducted the most outstandingly successful of all campaigns for *Gone With the Wind* (1939), making the search for a Scarlett O'Hara a topic of national discussion long after Vivien Leigh [46] had been signed for the role, and helping to roll up its record-breaking thirty-two-million-dollar gross (as of July 1943). Preparing to go into business for himself in 1939, Birdwell gained prestige by writing the rambling semi-autobiographical *I Ring Doorbells*. Screen rights were sold in 1944, and in late 1945 the screen version of *I Ring Doorbells* was released, the original story having been transformed into a "B" murder melodrama with a newspaper background. Birdwell's later writings include an unproduced play.

(Continued next page)

BIRDWELL, RUSSELL—*Continued*

Having established a modernistic, informal headquarters in Beverly Hills, Birdwell opened an office in New York, from which he directs industrial publicity. (Two rooms of the suite are modern, the third is furnished with centuries-old museum pieces.) His basic fees are twenty-five thousand dollars a year for individuals and fifty thousand for industrial concerns, exclusive of expenses. In 1943 he registered with the State Department as an agent for King Carol of Rumania, a relationship which brought Birdwell himself much publicity. Howard Hughes paid Birdwell fifteen hundred dollars a week for seven years to promote *The Outlaw*, which was completed in 1941 but not generally released until 1946. Sensational publicity made what Birdwell terms "a national issue" of its unknown leading lady, Jane Russell.

"Bird" has given his promotional services free to some promising young people and to causes, among them China Relief. An ardent and vocal interventionist in World War II, he was described by the New York *Daily News* as "the one-man campaigner for war." On his return shortly after Pearl Harbor from a three-week trip to England, where he had opened an office, Birdwell wrote a serious report, *Women in Battle Dress*, which was published without ballyhoo in 1942 and proved a literary and financial success. As a guest of the British Government on a corvette cruise in the North Atlantic, Birdwell supplied the entire flotilla with pictures of Jane Russell, and "cabled stirring accounts of the cruise to the Hearst papers, ringing in little references to . . . clients between German air attacks." Another signed Birdwell article, a full-page newspaper advertisement sponsored by one of his clients, the Military Order of the Purple Heart, in February 1946 urged that the experimental atomic bomb work be abandoned.

A prodigious worker himself, Birdwell has refused or canceled the accounts of individuals whom he considered social parasites or who had other characteristics which displeased him or which he thought might reflect on him. He is accompanied on his travels by two secretaries, and reportedly has living quarters in all his offices and offices in all his homes—a New York penthouse, a twenty-room house in Beverly Hills, and a one-acre "farm" in the San Fernando Valley. Whether dressed in "incredible" sports clothes in California or "chairman-of-the-board" suits in New York, Russell Birdwell usually has his pockets filled with office supplies.

The dapper, mustached public relations man, who is five feet ten inches tall and weighs 170 pounds, has been described as resembling a thin Robert Benchley or a delicate Wallace Beery. Because of his long hours of work Birdwell presents himself for medical examination twice each month. His health is excellent, he says, perhaps because one of his hobbies is sun-bathing. Another is collecting pepper mills.

References

New Yorker 20:26-30 Ag 19, '44; 26-30 Ag 26 '44; 24-8 S 2 '44; 20-4 S 9 '44 pors

Birdwell, R. I Ring Doorbells (1939) International Motion Picture Almanac 1943-44

BISSET, SIR JAMES G(ORDON) P(ARTRIDGE) (bĭs'sĕt) July 15, 1883-

Address: b. c/o Cunard White Star, Ltd., 25 Broadway, New York; h. 34 Cambray Ct., Cheltenham, Gloucestershire, England

Standing on the bridge when the world's largest luxury liner, the *Queen Elizabeth,* newly converted from war service, made her long-delayed maiden voyage as a civilian passenger ship, was Sir James G. P. Bisset, Commodore of the Cunard White Star fleet. Veteran of the days of sailing vessels, of service on nearly all the company's ships, and of two world wars, Sir James had been master of both the *Queen Elizabeth* and the *Queen Mary* during World War II.

James Gordon Partridge Bisset was born to a Scottish ironmonger and his English wife in Liverpool, England, on July 15, 1883, and began his career in the British merchant service at the age of fifteen. For four years beginning in October 1898 he was bound as an apprentice on the 1,000-ton bark or square-rigger *County of Pembroke* operated by William Thomas and Company of Liverpool. In her he made trips to Australia and the west coasts of North and South America, as well as one voyage with military supplies from Adelaide to Port Elizabeth during the Boer War. Passing the examination for second mate in 1903, he was then transferred to the same company's full-rigged ship *County of Cardigan,* with which during the next two years he made trips to Australia, New Zealand, Chile, and Peru. In 1905, having passed the examination for the next grade, first mate's rank, he left sail for steam.

Between 1905 and 1907 the young seaman served for short periods with Lamport and Holt, Leylands, Japp and Kirby, and the Holme Line, and in May of the latter year, having passed for master and extra master, he joined the Cunard Line as a fourth officer and was assigned to the *Caronia.* Between 1907 and 1946 Bisset served in various capacities, from fourth officer to captain and commodore, on all the ships of the Cunard Line, including the cargo vessels *Verbania, Brescia,* and *Phrygia* as well as the passenger (and cargo) carriers *Umbria, Saxonia, Carpathia, Carmania, Berengaria, Mauretania, Lancastria, Aquitania, Scythia, Franconia, Queen Mary,* and *Queen Elizabeth* among others. At the time of the *Titanic* disaster on April 15, 1912, when 1,502 lives were lost, he was second officer of the *Carpathia* which saved 706.

On June 1, 1910, Bisset had been commissioned a sublieutenant in the Royal Naval Reserve. In 1913 he was promoted to lieutenant and between May 1913 and May 1914 took his year's required naval training on

H.M.S. *Suffolk, Princess Royal,* and *Syren.*
During the first year of World War I he
served on the armed merchant cruiser *Caronia*
and then on the *Mauretania* when she was assigned to carry troops to the Dardanelles and
later when she was a hospital ship. For the
remainder of the war, transferred back to a
naval vessel, he was in command of the tor-
pedo-boat destroyer *Robuck,* patrolling the English Channel. In March 1919 he rejoined the
Cunard Line as a first officer.

In 1926 and 1927, as chief officer of the
Franconia, under the command of Captain Mel-
som, Bisset made two round-the-world cruises.
In June of 1927 he was transferred to the
Berengaria as staff captain, and later served in
that post on the *Aquitania.* Then, in May 1931,
while serving on the *Aurania* in the Canadian
trade, he was officially appointed a captain in
the company's service. (On July 15, 1933,
having reached his fiftieth birthday, he was
placed on the retired list of the Royal Naval
Reserve with the rank of captain. He had been
promoted to lieutenant commander in 1922,
commander in 1926.) In July 1936 Captain
Bisset of the *Ascania* took part in carrying
six thousand Canadian Vimy Ridge pilgrims
from Montreal to Le Havre, France.

A year and a half earlier, on December 14,
1934, the *Ascania* with Bisset as captain had
joined with the Belgian steamship *Jean Jabot*
in rescuing nine of the crew of twenty-four
of the British freighter *Usworth,* shipwrecked
and on the point of sinking during a hurricane
in mid-Atlantic. For this exploit Bisset had
received the Lloyds Medal, the Liverpool Ship-
wreck Society Medal, the New York Lifesav-
ing Benevolent Society Medal, and the Emil
Robin award, and was presented with a silver
tea and coffee service by the owners of the
Usworth and with a rose bowl by the Board
of Trade. For the Columbia Broadcasting System at Halifax and on the London radio program *In Town Tonight,* he broadcast the story
of the rescue, and with the ship's crew he appeared in Movietone News.

When World War II broke out in September 1939, Captain Bisset was in Boston with
the *Franconia.* On September 3, the day Great
Britain declared war on Germany, Bisset, returned to active duty, sailed for Liverpool, from
which he began transporting troops around the
Cape of Good Hope to the Middle East. Between that date and February 10, 1942, when
he left the *Franconia* at Trinidad, he had carried thirty thousand men. Then, from Trinidad he flew to Key West, Florida, there to relieve Captain John Townley of the *Queen Mary,*
which had been forced into the American harbor by submarine action after leaving Boston
on February 18. On this, her initial trip in the
ferrying of United States troops, she had on
board the first twelve thousand bound for Australia, routed via Rio de Janeiro and the Cape.

Except for one voyage on the *Queen Elizabeth* in September 1942, Bisset continued as
master of the *Queen Mary* until August 1945.
In December 1942 he left the Clyde with eleven
thousand troops for the El Alamein campaign.
In January and February 1943 he was engaged
in returning to Australia the remainder of her

SIR JAMES G. P. BISSET

troops in Egypt—and in this connection he
piloted the *Queen Mary* on her only run in convoy, when, as the commodore's ship, she was
escorted by the *Aquitania, Ile de France, Nieuw
Amsterdam, Queen of Bermuda,* and two cruisers from Massawa in the Red Sea. In May
1943 he commenced steady New York-Clyde
runs eastward with fifteen thousand troops each
voyage. From March 1940, when she went into
war service, to April 1945, the *Queen Mary*
had steamed approximately 600,000 miles carrying 600,000 troops, 500,000 of them Americans
and the remainder British. For three years the
man on her bridge had been Captain Bisset, who
had been made commodore in January 1945.

For her wartime task the huge 81,235-ton liner had been converted from a 2,000-passenger
floating hotel into a 15,000-passenger, blacked-
out, battleship-gray troopship housing GIs under what one reporter described as "sardine-
can conditions." Steel and canvas bunks had
been erected in tiers in every available space on
the ship, and a system of red, white, and blue
tickets and buttons, telling each man where
he could go, where sleep, where and when he
could eat, was instituted to deal with the very
serious traffic problem. At first he was a little
nervous about the possible behavior of American troops, Bisset told George Horne of the
New York *Times.* "I thought they'd be full
of victory spirit, and a little rambunctious. But
they were fine. I like them. They are all
right." The measure of this tribute, Horne
has said, can only be taken in relation to the
magnitude of Commodore Bisset's task.

In August 1945 the veteran shipmaster was
transferred to the *Queen Elizabeth* and thereafter had the honor of piloting her on her last
voyage as a troop transport in March 1946 and
on her maiden trip as a luxury liner, postponed for six years because of the war. Leaving Southampton on October 16, 1946, the
83,673-ton *Queen Elizabeth,* refurnished at a

BISSET, SIR JAMES G. P.—*Continued*

cost of five million dollars and carrying many United Nations delegates and other notables, steamed into New York harbor on October 21 amid "a Manhattan welcome befitting the world's largest luxury liner." Both the ship and her commodore appeared in newsreels and were the subject of press comment for days before and after.

During the war Captain Bisset carried Prime Minister Winston Churchill four times across the Atlantic in the *Queen Mary*. In the *Queen Elizabeth* in January 1946 he brought back to England the copy of the Magna Charta lent for the New York World's Fair of 1939-40. He succeeded Sir Robert Irving, R.N.R., as Commodore of the Cunard White Star fleet in January 1945; had been made a Commander of the Order of the British Empire by King George VI on November 3, 1942; and was knighted on July 19, 1945. From Cambridge University he received an honorary doctorate of laws on January 31, 1946, and from the Admiralty the Royal Naval Reserve Decoration in 1925.

Said to be an effective storyteller, Bisset has written for *St. Nicholas,* the *Christian Science Monitor Magazine,* the London *Saturday Review,* and other periodicals, and is the author of *Ship Ahoy,* "a book containing information valuable to prospective ocean travelers." Either alone or in collaboration he has also prepared guides on such subjects as lifeboat efficiency, fire at sea, and maritime insurance. Nearing the automatic retirement age in the Cunard line he hopes "they'll decide to waive it for a while"; if not, he thinks he may write a book; he thinks, too, that he may turn to gardening. "Genial" is an adjective often applied to him; and George Horne described him in the New York *Times* after an interview as "a stocky man with a bit of a roll in his gait and a rich mingling in his speech of the original Scottish burr with the salty sea jargon that knows no nationality."

References

N Y Herald Tribune Ag 29 '46 por
N Y Sun p12 O 21 '46 por
N Y Times p4 Ag 3 '42 por; p43 Ag 29 '46 por
Who's Who, 1946

BLALOCK, ALFRED Apr. 5, 1899- Surgeon
Address: b. c/o Johns Hopkins Hospital, Baltimore, Md.; h. 4204 Underwood Rd., Baltimore, Md.

TAUSSIG, HELEN B(ROOKE) (tou′sĭg) May 24, 1898- Physician
Address: b. c/o Johns Hopkins Hospital, Baltimore, Md.; h. 414 Lake Ave., Baltimore, Md.

Dr. Alfred Blalock, surgeon, and Dr. Helen B. Taussig, pediatrician and heart specialist, working together at Johns Hopkins Hospital, envisioned and perfected an operation to help "blue babies"—children suffering from anoxemia, a disease in which the blood is insufficiently oxygenated and which hitherto meant the child's invalidism or death.

The son of George Zadock and Martha (Davis) Blalock, Alfred Blalock was born April 5, 1899, in Culloden, Georgia, and reared in Jonesboro in the same State. After having received his B.A. in 1918 from the University of Georgia, Blalock served in the United States Army in World War I. In 1922 he was awarded his M.D. by Johns Hopkins School of Medicine in Baltimore. He continued as interne at the Johns Hopkins Hospital in 1922-23, and as assistant resident surgeon from 1923 to 1925.

In 1925 the young doctor became resident surgeon and instructor in surgery at Vanderbilt University Hospital, in Nashville, Tennessee. In the course of the next thirteen years he was appointed to three professorships at that medical school: as assistant in 1928, as associate in 1930, and as full professor in 1938. While at Vanderbilt, Blalock achieved national prominence in the field of vascular surgery. He and his associates pioneered in tracing the causes of shock, in either injury or surgery, to the loss of blood or body fluids, or both. Blalock was among the first to use large amounts of plasma and blood against shock, a technique which permitted new procedures in elective and emergency surgery in World War II. The surgeon also became known for his operations on "stone" hearts, which are characterized by thickened pericardia.

At Vanderbilt, too, Blalock completed a two-year experiment to determine whether any relation could be established between high blood pressure and hardening of the arteries. Since 1939 he had performed an operation of his own development on a number of dogs, in order to increase pressure in their lungs for experimental purposes. The operations themselves proved nothing, but Blalock noticed that the dogs whose circulation had been altered were doing well. While he found no relation between high blood pressure and hardening of the arteries, he had contributed an important technique with possible application to vascular surgery. In 1941, Blalock became professor of surgery and chief surgeon at Johns Hopkins Hospital, where he met Helen B. Taussig. She had developed a theory that "blue babies", whose condition she thought was caused by a lack of circulation to the lungs, could be cured by an operation similar to the one Blalock had performed on dogs at Vanderbilt Hospital. At Johns Hopkins, as one writer said, "Dogs bearing proof were about to make a junction with a brilliant theory."

Helen Brooke Taussig, the daughter of the late Harvard economist Professor Frank William Taussig and the former Edith Guild, who was among the first women to study at Radcliffe College, was born on May 24, 1898 in Cambridge, Massachusetts. Her family had a scientific and medical tradition on both sides: the chief interests of her mother (who died when the girl was eleven) had been zoology and other natural sciences; her paternal grandfather, a German immigrant who settled in Missouri and became a country doctor, specialized in the problems of children with defective eyesight. (The William Taussig School for

Handicapped Children in St. Louis is named for him.)

Reared in a university atmosphere, Helen Taussig received her early education at Cambridge School for Girls. Her summers, she says, were spent at Cotuit, on Cape Cod. From 1917 to 1919 she attended Radcliffe College, where she was a tennis champion. "In order to get a broader experience," in 1919 she transferred to the University of California, receiving her B.A. from that school in 1921. After graduation she took a half-course at Harvard Medical School as a special student because women were not admitted to the regular session until 1945. During the succeeding eight months Miss Taussig, her father, sister, and cousin traveled in Greece, Italy, Switzerland, Germany, and England.

Upon her return she resumed her studies at Harvard Medical School, then entered Boston University Medical School. The young medical student was started on her work in physiology of the heart by the late Dr. Alexander Swanson Begg '40, then dean of the Boston University Medical School, who told her, "It won't do you any harm to be interested in one of the larger organs of the body." Upon Dr. Beggs's advice in 1924 Miss Taussig continued her study at Johns Hopkins Medical School. As a second-year student there she published her first paper, entitled "On Rhythmic Contractions in Isolated Cardiac Muscle Strips," a report on work done at Boston University. In her fourth year at Johns Hopkins she completed a second paper on the heart. After receiving her M.D. from Johns Hopkins in 1927, Dr. Taussig worked in 1928 as an Archibald fellow at the heart station of the hospital. She interned in pediatrics at Johns Hopkins from 1928 to 1930, later receiving an appointment to the pediatrics staff. In 1930 the doctor became head of the Children's Heart Clinic of Harriet Lane Home (the pediatrics division) of Johns Hopkins Hospital. She has "always felt that there were three important purposes in such a clinic at a medical school: the first the care of the patients, the second the teaching of students, and third the advancement of knowledge and the study of disease."

Although best known for her work with Dr. Blalock in the treatment of "blue babies," Dr. Taussig states that she is "primarily interested in heart disease in children, the most important of which is acute rheumatic fever," which "remains a far more serious problem than that of 'blue babies' because it affects a far greater number of children and young adults." In July 1946 research into the causes and prevention of rheumatic fever became one of the main projects at the Harriet Lane Home of Johns Hopkins, under the joint research fund set up by one hundred and forty-six insurance companies. Dr. Taussig plans to continue her clinical work with child victims of the disease and also to study sociological factors which seem important in the spread of the fever. The results of fluoroscopic studies in the changes in the size and shape of the heart, Dr. Taussig is incorporating into a book ("Clinical Analysis of the Congenital Malformations of the Heart") to be published by the Commonwealth Fund.

ALFRED BLALOCK

Dr. Taussig considers her fluoroscopic studies as one of her two chief contributions to medical knowledge. "My other great contribution," she has said, "was an appreciation that many 'blue babies' died from lack of circulation to the lungs." Theories of others had lacked the precision of the last-named of Dr. Taussig's, but she had no way of proving her point until Dr. Alfred Blalock returned to Johns Hopkins Hospital in 1941. Of his coming Dr. Taussig writes, "It was extremely fortunate for me when Dr. Alfred Blalock was appointed professor of surgery as he was known as a vascular surgeon. It seemed clear to me that building an artificial ductus arteriosus for children dying of anoxemia would be even greater than the ligation of a ductus, an operation perfected by Dr. Robert Gross in Boston. Dr. Blalock accepted the challenge first to test the theory and then to perfect the operation. The results have been far more brilliant than we dared to hope."

In order to prove that cyanosis (blue coloring) in so-called "blue babies" was due to lack of oxygen in the blood stream, caused by narrowness or cloture of the ductus, and to test the success of his operation in correcting that defect, Blalock induced artificial cyanosis in dogs and performed an operation widening the artificially narrowed artery. The surgeon's experiments were successful, and on November 9, 1944, the operation was performed on a human patient for the first time. The procedure was described by *Newsweek* as follows: The child "was born with a defect of the large artery that supplied blood to the lungs. So little blood could be pumped through the narrow passage that the oxygen intake was painfully curtailed. To overcome this condition, Dr. Blalock cut one of the [systemic] arteries carrying blood to body parts outside the lungs. One end [of the artery] was pulled around and fastened to a slit made in the opposite (right or

BLALOCK, ALFRED, and TAUSSIG, HELEN B.—*Continued*

left) branch of the lung artery." While the one artery was being joined to the pulmonary artery, one of the child's lungs was collapsed. Since pressure in the systemic artery is about four times that in the pulmonary artery, blood was forced from the systemic to the pulmonary artery. "By this means blood was shunted from the general supply to one of the lungs, where it gathered enough oxygen to supply the rest of the blood in the body."

HELEN B. TAUSSIG

Although the first patient, a sixteen-month-old baby girl, died nine months later, it had been proved that the pulmonary artery could be by-passed. The second patient survived to become a healthy, normal child. As of February 15, 1946, the Blalock-Taussig operation had been performed eighty-five times, with remarkable success in 60 per cent of the cases and fair improvement in 11 per cent; 20 per cent of the patients died; in 9 per cent there had been no improvement. The first three operations, those on which Doctors Blalock and Taussing reported in the *Journal of the American Medical Association* of May 19, 1945, were performed over a period of nine weeks. The summary of the article reads in part: "Thus far the procedure has been carried out on only three children, each of whom had a severe degree of anoxemia. Clinical evidence of improvement has been striking and includes a pronounced decrease in the intensity of the cyanosis, a decrease in dyspnea [difficulty in breathing] and an increase in tolerance to exercise."

In 1946 the operations were being performed at the rate of four each week, on patients with lack of blood circulation to the lungs. The operation may be used with probable success on patients from the ages of three through twelve years, the time when the heart is usually strong enough to withstand the operation and

the additional load placed upon it by the altered circulation. Doctors have come from as far as Shanghai and Paris to witness the operations; one has already been performed successfully by another surgeon in California. After local doctors have made the preliminary examinations to determine whether the "blue babies" may be aided by the operation which Dr. Blalock performs, the patients are taken to the Johns Hopkins Hospital, where Dr. Taussig conducts preoperative diagnoses of patients. Each week about one hundred requests for help are received.

In addition to serving as professor and director of surgery of Johns Hopkins, Dr. Blalock is a member of the National Academy of Sciences, and surgeon in chief of the National Research Council. The surgeon is also a fellow of the American Medical Association and on the editorial board of its *Archives of Surgery,* and of the publications *Southern Surgeon, Surgery,* and *Gynecology and Obstetrics.* A member of at least eighteen local, regional, national, and international honorary, medical, and surgical societies, Blalock has published papers on collapse and paralysis of the muscular system, particularly the muscles of the face, neck, and throat; the control of circulation during operation; high blood pressure; and the "Principles of Surgical Care; Shock and Other Problems" (1940). He is coauthor with Dr. Taussig of the report on their work, "The Surgical Treatment of Malformations of the Heart Where There is Pulmonary Stenosis or Pulmonary Atresia."

After he had performed a successful Blalock-Taussig operation, one mother pleaded with Dr. Blalock for an indication of some service she could perform to repay him. Since she lived in Atlanta, not far from Jonesboro, where Blalock's mother resides, he said, "Yes, you can do me a favor. Go to Jonesboro and show your child to my mother." "Of medium height, with kindly eyes behind glasses, rather slow and deliberate of speech," Blalock has been described by *Collier's* as bearing "all the marks of a scholarly and reflective nature." He was married in October 1930 to Mary Chambers O'Bryan. They have three children, William (Bill) Rice, Mary Elizabeth (Betty), and Alfred Dandy. When his wife was asked how he spends his summers, she replied, "Why, he spends them the way he spends his winters—working." But the doctor likes to play tennis and golf, too, although the exercise he prefers, according to the Baltimore *Sun,* is chopping down trees.

Dr. Taussig has authored or coauthored articles on the Blalock-Taussig operation (with Dr. Blalock) and on rheumatic fever and congenital malformations of the heart. Her studies have appeared in the *American Journal of Physiology, Bulletin of Johns Hopkins Hospital, American Journal of Diseases of Children, Medical Clinics of North America, Journal of Pediatrics, American Journal of Nursing,* and *American Heart Journal.* She is assistant professor at Johns Hopkins University School of Medicine, a cardiac consultant to the State of Maryland and to the City of Baltimore, to St. Gabriel's and to Happy Hills convalescent homes. Her memberships in various societies include Phi Beta Kappa, Alpha Omega Alpha, Baltimore Medical and Chirurgical Society, Society of Pediatric Research, American Medical Association, and American Heart Association.

Since taking charge of the Johns Hopkins Children's Heart Clinic, Dr. Taussig has been so deeply absorbed with the "human detail" of her work that she seldom gets home until nine o'clock in the evening. The doctor has brown hair, blue eyes, a very feminine voice, a Boston accent, and a manner "at once high-strung and intensely earnest." Five feet ten inches tall, she "eats and swims heartily," according to a *Collier's* article. At her summer house on Cape Cod, built in 1935, Dr. Taussig records the work which she has done the preceding winter and follows her interests in poetry and nature. She has found the sensational reporting of the Blalock-Taussig operation by the press a major aversion. A Unitarian and unmarried, Dr. Taussig tells of two sisters and a brother and seven nieces and nephews to whom she is devoted. "My life has been enriched," she states, "by my long and close association with my father." It seemed fitting to a Baltimore *Sun* reporter that the two most prominent objects in Dr. Taussig's cluttered office at the clinic should be a plaster model of the human heart and a photograph of a portrait of her father.

References

Baltimore Sun Mag p5+ My 19 '45 pors
Collier's 117:20+ Ap 6 '46 pors
N Y Herald Tribune p21 F 15 '46 por
Time 46:71 D 31 '45
American Men of Science (1938)
America's Young Men, 1938-39
Who's Important in Medicine, 1945
Who's Who in America, 1946-47

BLANCHARD, DOC *See* Blanchard, F. A.

BLANCHARD, FELIX A(NTHONY)
1924- United States Army Cadet; football star
Address: United States Military Academy, West Point, N.Y.; h. Bishopville, S.C.

By playing in less than thirty football games, Felix A. ("Doc") Blanchard, a youth who had yet to begin his career as an artillery officer, became a fêted national figure and a target for autograph hunters in 1944-46. Voted in January 1946 the best amateur football player of 1945, the 205-pound West Pointer is judged by many as one of the greatest fullbacks of all time, a "human blockbuster" with unprecedented speed and remarkable ability in both offensive and defensive play.

Like most of his teammates, Felix Anthony Blanchard is a Southerner, born in his mother's home town of McColl, South Carolina, in 1924. He was brought up in the "turpentine town" of Bishopville (population 3,000), where his father, the late "Doc" Felix A. Blanchard, Sr., had his medical practice. The doctor's son was Anthony to his parents, but "Little Doc" to the townspeople. Young Blanchard's mother, Mary Gilchrist (Tatum) Blanchard, is described as exceptionally robust; his younger

sister Mary Elizabeth ("Butch") is a sturdy athlete whose basketball and tennis prowess makes her brother glow with pride; and his father had been an outstanding 240-pound fullback at Tulane University, playing under the name of Beaulieu so as not to alarm his conservative Louisiana-French parents.

From the beginning, Dr. Blanchard trained his son in football, and in baseball and tennis, too. He put a football into the baby's crib for luck, and started the boy's football lessons as soon as Anthony could toddle. "And Little Doc took to carrying a football with him wherever he went around Bishopville," Pete Martin has written in the *Saturday Evening Post.* Otherwise, his boyhood was "typically American. . . . At the age of four, he tried his father's pipe and set the barn on fire. In the summertime, he earned pocket money as a delivery boy for the corner grocery. . . .When he was old enough to drive, he shared a stripped-down jalopy with his young sister."

Less typically, Little Doc weighed 180 pounds by the time he was fourteen. "I wasn't anything special [in football] at Bishopville High School, because they made me play tackle," Blanchard says, "but I really had fun at St. Stanislaus Prep School in Bay St. Louis, Mississippi, where they let me carry the ball." On his fourteenth birthday the boy played for the Stanislaus Rokachaws throughout the New Orleans Toy Bowl Game, an honor which came to him twice. He was chosen for the All-Gulf Coast Region Class A team, and was considered the greatest football player in the school's history—although the All-American Marchy Schwartz was a predecessor. "During the next six months" (Stanislaus' Brother Peter is quoted), "a procession of big-time coaches came to woo him [with football scholarships], and the disappointment on various campuses was bitter when he finally chose North Carolina," where a cousin, Jim Tatum, was athletic director and freshman football coach.

At Chapel Hill, the burly six-footer ran the hundred-yard dash in ten seconds, and "cracked into the line like a locomotive." The freshman trainer recalls that "there were several men on the varsity who got so they wouldn't try to tackle him. Once he knocked out two would-be tacklers on the same play." Off the field, Martin recounts, Blanchard once ripped a hotel steam radiator from the floor with his hands when he was annoyed with the manager. But the athlete was turned down for the V-12 course by the University naval unit, because of defective eyesight, the result of a childhood accident, and overweight. At the end of his freshman year, in 1943, the eighteen-year-old enlisted in the wartime Army.

Basic training at Miami Beach was followed by study at the Army Air Forces ground school in Clovis, New Mexico, where Blanchard was assigned to Chemical Warfare. Meanwhile, his father secured for him a long-sought appointment to the Military Academy, and from Clovis the youth went to Pennsylvania to join the three-hundred-man pre-Academy unit at Lafayette College. But Dr. Blanchard did not live to see his son enter West Point in July 1944.

(Continued next page)

FELIX A. BLANCHARD

Cadet Blanchard was no longer "Little Doc," but simply "Doc," a nickname soon to be familiar all over the country.

The head football coach, Colonel Earl ("Red") Blaik '45, placed Blanchard on the second team, along with such brilliant plebe footballers as speedy Glenn ("Junior") Davis '46, tackle DeWitt Coulter, ends Barney Poole and Henry Foldberg, and center Herschel ("Ug") Fuson. Altogether, the West Point team was not only "the pride and dream of every heart in gray," but soon became something like a legend to the football public. Army mowed its opponents down with such ease in 1944 and 1945 that, Blaik reported, his first and second teams averaged only eighteen minutes of the hour's playing time in the first six games; the rest of the time Blaik used his third- and even fourth-stringers. Even so, Blanchard and Davis stood out in the sports columns like longtime stars. Blaik, who dislikes to single any player out for praise, once remarked, "I certainly never saw anybody like Blanchard before. . . .He has the weight of a fullback and the speed of a halfback." Blaik did not mention that Blanchard also had value to the team as a decoy—for the coach capitalized on the fact that games against Army were seen as a problem of "stopping Blanchard and Davis," by using him to distract attention from the ball carrier.

In one game, a 59-0 rout of Notre Dame in November 1944, an official who got in Blanchard's way was brushed aside—with a dislocated elbow—as the cadet went through him to make his tackle. The South Carolinian stood out, too, in Army's 23-7 defeat of Navy, its traditional rival, which was recognized as probably the next best team in the country. One leading sports writer held that "the real engine of destruction was Blanchard, 205 pounds of charging wild buffalo"; another wrote, "the

game failed to settle the argument whether Blanchard or Davis was most valuable to Army," but added that "they let him put on a performance that matched Nagurski, Nevers, or Standlee at their best." Blanchard was honored as one of the best players in the country— by the Associated Press, United Press, All-American Board, International News Service, *Sporting News*, and New York *Daily News*— these among other opinions; and his team was officially recognized as the best in the East by the award of the Lambert Trophy.

In 1945 Blanchard became a cadet corporal, and that April was chosen for the guard of honor at President Roosevelt's funeral. This is said to have meant more to the twenty-one-year-old than any football honors. But football honors continued to come to him. Playing fullback, he was considered to be even better than in 1944, "pretty close to being an all-time All-America fullback," exclaimed Arthur Daley. "He punts sixty yards a clip, he kicks off into the end zone, he's without a peer as a blocker, he's a deadly tackler, he's a sure-fingered pass-catcher, he splinters a line and then breaks loose in an open field with the speed and elusiveness of a halfback." Army repeated its one-sided 1944 campaign, winning every game of a crowded season against all types of defense. Blanchard and Davis, the "Touchdown Twins," were automatically selected for the All-American team, and linesmen Coulter, Albert Nemetz, and John Green were also chosen. The Cadets again won the Lambert Trophy, and Felix Blanchard received more than twenty national awards. Among them were selections as the only holdover from *Look* Magazine's 1944 team. He was voted the Maxwell, Heisman, and Touchdown Club awards as the year's best football player, with Glenn Davis the only other nominee who could be regarded as a serious rival. Earlier, he had been presented with a silver tea service by his Bishopville neighbors, and with the Sullivan Trophy for advancing the cause of good sportsmanship; and he and Junior Davis had appeared jointly on *Time*'s November 12 cover as Men of the Week, with the caption, "They make the Army's T boil."

Athletics are a required part of the rigorous Academy routine, and, in *Time*'s words, "Army's football heroes must do everything that every other cadet does, and do it just as right and just as quick. They have to take the standard three hours a week of physical training, in addition to their hour and a half of daily football practice." Blanchard's athletic schedule called for football in autumn, indoor track in winter, football practice in spring, and outdoor track after that. (The cadets spend their summers in the field, except for their single, second-year vacation.) When the 1944 football season ended, Doc Blanchard reported to the track coach with no particular specialty. A month of training, with the advice and help of the Point's leading shot-putter, his friend Ralph Davis, brought Blanchard's record with the sixteen-pound shot up from thirty to forty-one feet. In early March 1945 he won the Intercollegiate Amateur Athletic Association of America's indoor championship with a heave of 48 feet 3½ inches (Davis was runner-up), and in late May he established a new record for the Army-Navy Dual Meet of 51 feet 10¾ inches. The cadet also won the I.C.A.A.A.A. outdoor shot-put championship, was runner-up for the National AAU championship, and ran on Army's quarter-mile relay team. Blanchard was also a member of the team that won the third consecutive A.A.A.A. indoor track and field championship for the Army in May 1946.

In the split-up of the third class which accompanied West Point's reconversion from its accelerated wartime schedule to the normal four-year course, Blanchard and Davis were assigned to the class of 1947, rather than that of 1948. This meant that Blanchard would have a total of only three years as a varsity player. When their teammates heard the news, they immediately elected the fullback and the halfback as co-captains of the 1946 team, the first co-captains in Army football history. Blanchard missed several games of the 1946 season because of a knee injury sustained during the Army-Villanova game which opened the season. When he returned to the field, he alternated positions, sometimes playing fullback. Because of the injury, he scored ten touchdowns as compared to nineteen in 1945, and, the sports columns of the New York *Sun* reported, some scouts saw him as "just an extra good fullback instead of a cross between Buck Rogers and Superman." The heralded Army-Notre Dame game, which was scoreless, was the scene of the first successful attempt to curb the Davis-Blanchard power. Allison Danzig of the New York *Times* reported, "For the first time in three seasons of uninterrupted and overpowering success . . . Doc Blanchard and Glenn Davis . . . found themselves shackled and crushed like ordinary mortals through their full sixty minutes of devotion to duty."

To the surprise of most writers and fans, Navy made the same number of touchdowns (three) as the West Pointers in the traditional closing game of the season. Failure of Navy to make the extra points after the touchdowns resulted in the Army victory (21-18) bringing the total continuous triumphs for that team to twenty-seven in three years. For the third consecutive time, both "Mr. Inside" and "Mr. Outside" were named to the Associated Press All-American eleven. At the close of their football careers, the "Touchdown Twins" had scored 537 of the 1,176 points won by Army from the beginning of the 1944 season to the end of 1946.

"The hard life of a Point cadet did next to nothing to Doc's impish, hillbillyish charm," *Time* said. Various writers have mentioned his "Dixie drawl and Hollywood profile", "easy line of chatter," and fondness for Western stories and Betty Hutton movies. Although "mighty sincere about football," Blanchard is said to be calm and relaxed on the field, and "never gets tough until the going gets tough." Blanchard is scheduled to appear in a Columbia Pictures Sport Reel, a sports short featuring the Army team.

The impressively muscular six-footer has wavy black hair, brown eyes, a florid complexion which grows redder with emotion, and full lips which tighten into a straight line on such occasions. His best playing weight is 205 pounds, but it varies by as much as ten pounds in either direction. Blanchard is a member of Sigma Nu. He is a Catholic by faith, and adheres to West Point tradition by expressing no political preferences. When asked his favorite recreation, he says "Football."

References

Look 9:80 D 25 '45
N Y Herald Tribune p28 N 29 '45 por
N Y Sun p22 Ja 7 '46
Sat Eve Post 218:18 D 1 '45 ils pors
Time 46:57-62 N 12 '45 pors

BLANDING, SARAH GIBSON Nov. 22, 1898- College president
Address: b. c/o Vassar College, Poughkeepsie, N.Y.

For the first time in its eighty-five-year history, in October 1946 a woman was installed as president of Vassar College. Sarah Gibson Blanding, social scientist known for her administrative skill during her deanship of two colleges, was unanimously elected to the office by a committee representing Vassar's trustees and faculty. As might be expected of a social scientist, the new president places emphasis in education on "knowledge and understanding of the complex forces that operate in contemporary society." To this emphasis she adds a conviction that America's young women must be encouraged to enter public life, to participate in local and national politics, and to work for international understanding. Her career has revealed that she herself has consistently been "socially aware," an active, responsible citizen, not afraid to invade fields usually dominated by men.

The daughter of William DeSaussure and Sarah Gibson (Anderson) Blanding, Sarah Gibson Blanding was born on a small farm near Lexington, Kentucky, on November 22, 1898. Both her maternal and paternal ancestors fought the British in the American Revolution. Leaving his family home in Statesburg, South Carolina, her maternal grandfather, Major General Richard Heron Anderson, served through the Civil War as a member of General Lee's staff. Her other grandfather, Colonel William Blanding, also fought in the Confederate Army.

As a child Sarah liked to ride in the buggy of her country-doctor uncle as he made the rounds of his patients. She thought she might like to be a doctor herself, but her father, an internal revenue officer, died when she was fourteen, and she was forced to choose a quicker, less expensive education. Borrowing thirty-five hundred dollars, she enrolled at the New Haven (Connecticut) Normal School of Gymnastics (which has since become Arnold College). Two years later, in 1919, the twenty-one-year-old girl was graduated from the school, prepared to teach physical education. She sought a job that would enable her to pay back her debt, and to help her large family. But when two high schools offered her teach-

Delar

SARAH GIBSON BLANDING

ing positions, she refused them both in favor of a similar post at the University of Kentucky which paid eight hundred dollars annually, about half the salary the high schools would pay her. "I'm a horse-trader by nature," she later explained. "I told the university I'd take their job if they'd let me go to college in the mornings." The bargain was a good one for everyone concerned. Her work as teacher and student impressed university authorities so much that just before she received her B.A. degree in 1923 she was appointed acting dean of women, at twenty-four the youngest university dean in the country. The next year, reasoning that "a dean of women has to have the respect of her faculty," she left for New York to earn a Master of Arts degree at Columbia University. Her dissertation on Anglo-French rivalry in Siam won her that degree in 1926.

Two years later Miss Blanding went to England to study at the London School of Economics. During her year there (1928-29), she and her fellow students crossed the Channel to talk with the members of the League of Nations at Geneva, and to study the League in action. At the school she studied under Harold Laski, whom she remembers as the best teacher she ever had. At teas and week ends in the country Ramsay MacDonald, Rabindranath Tagore, Max Beerbohm, and the historian G. P. Gooch were among the people with whom she had "stimulating conversations."

In 1929 Miss Blanding returned to the United States to become dean of women and assistant professor of political science at the University of Kentucky. Promoted to associate professor in 1937, she held that rank as well as the position of dean of women until 1941. During these years the dean lived with her mother and two sisters near the campus on a 250-acre farm, where she raised tobacco of such high quality that it sold for twice the

price of an average grade crop. She wore her oldest farm clothes when she drove her crop to market—"I figured the poorer I looked, the better price I'd get." In these years she also worked as director of a girls' camp in Lexington. The dean served from 1933 to 1935 as chairman of the university section of the National Association of Deans of Women, and from 1934 to 1936 she was vice-president of the Kentucky chapter of the American Association of University Women.

Although Sarah Blanding was a social scientist, not a home economist, Cornell University offered her the post of director of the New York State College of Home Economics in 1941. At Cornell the thirty-place dinners she liked to cook and serve herself were evidence of her skill in the practical aspects of home economics. And her ability as an administrator was recognized within a year after her appointment, when Cornell's board of trustees elected her the first dean of the College of Home Economics. With America's entry into the world conflict, wrote the *Cornell Countryman*, "almost overnight the calls for the services of the college doubled, tripled, quadrupled. So pressing were the requests for help with food and nutrition, child care, conservation and preservation of materials, mass feeding, the upkeep and care of equipment, that a smaller calibered administrator of this new field must surely have become confused and swamped. The new Dean was steady of nerve and sure of aim, as she led the college work—resident, extension and research—into paths that would help to win the war on the home front."

During World War II Governor Thomas E. Dewey of New York appointed Dean Blanding to emergency posts in the State Government, naming her director of the Human Nutrition Division of the State Emergency Food Commission, and consultant to the Division of Volunteer Participation of the State Defense Council. She was also chairman of the education committee of the Women's Council in that State. In the national scene she served as the only woman member of the Joint Army and Navy Committee on Welfare and Recreation, and as a member of the Committee on College Women Students and the War of the American Council on Education. Her work in these posts, and at Cornell, earned for her a widening reputation as an able administrator.

In February 1946, when Vassar sought a president to succeed the retiring Dr. Henry Noble MacCracken [40], president since 1915, Dean Blanding was among the two hundred candidates, the majority of them men, whose names were submitted for consideration. Sarah Gibson Blanding was chosen unanimously as "the best possible person, man or woman . . . the outstanding candidate" by a committee of seven women and three men, equally representing Vassar faculty and trustees. The election of Miss Blanding was a break with tradition, since all of Vassar's five presidents, from the founding of the college in 1861, had been men. The New York *Herald Tribune* commented editorially that the choice was a happy one: "She is a fresh, vigorous and resourceful person with a mind of proved capacity, and, most, of all, balanced judgment." In full agreement that Miss Blanding was "an excellent selection by every educational standard" the New York *Times* noted that the election reversed "what seems to have been a recent trend toward naming men to administer women's colleges." Miss Blanding accepted the post as a challenging opportunity to devise "a better educational system for women." And Vassar broke another tradition: in order to help ease the overcrowding in men's schools as veterans applied for admission in unprecedented numbers, in April 1946 the college admitted men veterans, the first men to work for a Vassar degree. When the new president formally greeted the student body in October 1946 there were thirteen hundred and forty women and ninety non-resident men students at Vassar.

In a formal statement issued at the time of her election, Miss Blanding emphasized her belief that higher education must "inspire the young people of our country to assume the obligations of responsible citizens." Later she expanded on this theme to a *Christian Science Monitor* reporter: "Most of [our students] are still in adolescence—idealistic, responsive and impressionable. We have the opportunity to build on those idealisms, to develop spiritual values and qualities of leadership in these young people who respond so quickly. The world is facing as critical a period as we've ever gone through. The balance between good and evil is so precarious that the scales could be tipped in either direction. But the forces of good must win if we face our responsibilities." Stressing the need for women to participate in government, she added, "The place for them to prepare is back in their local communities. Sometimes I think women expect to achieve positions of prominence without going through the fatigue of learning what people do at the lowest level." Soon after her election to the presidential office, Miss Blanding was awarded honorary doctorates by Skidmore and Russell Sage colleges, and by the University of Kentucky. In June she was one of thirty appointed by President Truman to a National Commission on Higher Education, which was "to re-examine our system of higher education in terms of its objectives, methods and facilities, and in the light of the social role it has to play." And in July Governor Dewey named her to a thirty-member commission appointed to study the need for a State university in New York. At the end of October, Miss Blanding was elected a trustee of the Institute of International Education.

At her inauguration in October, Miss Blanding received the Civilian Service Award medal of the War Department "for exceptional service as consultant to the Secretary of War from March 1943 to June 1946, her tireless efforts and judicious foresight in developing welfare and recreational activities for the Women's Army Corps and her superior leadership demonstrated as a member of the joint Army and Navy committee on welfare and recreation." At the same time she was appointed to the War Department Civilian Advisory Council, which was formed to give advice on the arrangement of Army personnel, and to the Chief of Staff's National Civilian Advisory Committee for the Women's Army Corps.

Miss Blanding wears her graying hair drawn back severely into a knot. Those who meet her make note of her "twinkling, hazel eyes," her soft Southern voice, and deep laugh. Fern Marja reported in the New York *Post*: "Vassar's Blanding is tall, friendly, non-frightening, with casual, straight-from-the-shoulder speech, and startlingly beautiful eyes. She smokes, wears lipstick and is 'scared to death' of the press." Miss Blanding, who has a three-thousand volume library, describes her literary tastes as running to "the good, bad and indifferent." She prefers non-fiction, letters, mysteries, and poetry —Milton, Stephen Spender, and Auden. Fond of the theater, she especially enjoys Shakespearean productions. During her five years at Cornell, the former physical education teacher, who lived in a small, white house overlooking Cayuga Lake, was the first to brave its icy waters every spring, the last to stop swimming in the fall. A woman of "boundless energy," she likes canoeing and tennis as much as she likes swimming. She ends her working day by reading in bed, generally between midnight and two in the morning.

References

Christian Sci Mon p3 F 21 '46; p11 Mr 16 '46
Collier's 118:13+ N 23 '46 por
Cornell Countryman 43:3+ Mr '46
Ind Woman 25:128 Ap '46
N Y Herald Tribune p33 S 8 '46
N Y Post p45 Mr 22 '46
N Y Times p21 O 12 '46
N Y Times Mag p18+ Mr 31 '46 por
Time 47:65 Mr 4 '46 por
Who's Who in America, 1946-47

BLUNT, KATHARINE   May 28, 1876-
College president-emeritus
Address: 38 Glenwood Ave., New London, Conn.

Katharine Blunt, president-emeritus of Connecticut College, believes that a properly equipped college should imbue its students with "the finest, richest spirit possible" and at the same time advance their contribution, vocational or avocational, to the social fabric. Dr. Blunt's administration—approximately half the life thus far of Connecticut College— is known for its improvement of the college's physical equipment and the revision and expansion of the curriculum. Prior to becoming president, Miss Blunt, educated as a chemist, conducted research in nutrition and was professor of home economics.

The mother of Katharine Blunt was Fanny (Smyth) Blunt of New York; her father, Boston-born Stanhope English Blunt, an army officer and the author of technical articles and books in his field, was stationed at the Frankford Arsenal, Philadelphia, at the time of his daughter's birth, on May 28, 1876. After her preparatory education at "The Elms," Miss

KATHARINE BLUNT

Porter's school in Springfield, Massachusetts, Katharine Blunt attended Vassar College, where she received her B.A. in 1898, and was elected to membership in Phi Beta Kappa. Following a year of study at the Massachusetts Institute of Technology in 1902-3, she returned to Vassar as an assistant in chemistry. After two years she left Vassar to work for her doctorate in organic chemistry at the University of Chicago. Awarded her Ph.D. in 1907, Miss Blunt taught chemistry at Pratt Institute (Brooklyn, New York) in 1907-8 and at Vassar until 1913, when she was appointed to the University of Chicago home economics faculty. There, for the next sixteen years, Miss Blunt served as assistant professor (1913-18), associate professor (1918-25), and professor (1925-29).

Doctor Blunt became chairman of the university's home economics department in 1925, after having acted in that capacity informally during her associate professorship. In addition to teaching, Miss Blunt as chairman concerned herself with the development of home economics as a necessary part of undergraduate education and as a field for graduate work. Some years later, in 1936, when the educator was awarded an honorary LL.D. by Wesleyan University, the citation read, in part: "She developed in the graduate school at Chicago one of the best departments of home economics in our American universities." Professor Blunt believed that graduate work should offer opportunity for specialization and at the same time permit the student to "keep her perspective and . . . see the relation of her part to the whole [field]." The dietitian, the nutrition expert, the manager of home or institution, the home economics teacher, she declared (*Journal of Home Economics*, April 1923) could have the 'satisfaction that comes from "the highest intellectual labor, imaginative constructive thinking of the highest order . . . at the same

time . . . they may be making a direct contribution to wholesome living."

During World War I Miss Blunt was engaged in public service for the Federal Government as an expert in nutrition. Granted leave of absence from the University of Chicago, in the last four months of 1917 she wrote leaflets on food conservation for the office of home economics of the United States Department of Agriculture. Then, during the first half of 1918, in collaboration with Florence Powdermaker she prepared lessons for colleges which the United States Food Administration published under the title *Food and the War* (1918). At about this time Miss Blunt became an active member of the American Home Economics Association; she was to serve as president of its Illinois chapter in 1921-22, as national vice-president from 1921 to 1924, and then as president in 1924-26. In addition to her writings on the subject of the teaching and application of home economics, her articles on food chemistry and nutrition began to appear in 1919 in the *Journal of Home Economics* and other technical publications.

The book *Ultra-Violet Light and Vitamin D in Nutrition*, which Miss Blunt coauthored with Ruth Cowan, was published in 1930 by the University of Chicago Press. A summary of the literature in the subject through 1929, the book was described by the *Journal of Home Economics* as an "excellent analysis . . . useful to the student, the teacher, the nutrition worker, the dietitian, the medical man . . . and to the intelligent lay public concerned with matters of public health and welfare."

In September 1929 Professor Blunt was appointed president of Connecticut College, the third president of that institution, which, as the only one in the State offering a four-year college course for women, had admitted its first students in 1915. A privately endowed liberal college of the arts and sciences, that awards the bachelor of arts degree, Connecticut College, under the administration of Miss Blunt, gained maturity and "ceased to be or seem a 'new college.'" President Blunt's first objective was the building up of the college's faculty and second, its physical equipment and financial resources. She was given much credit for construction of eighteen buildings from 1929 through 1942, during which period she is said to have "displayed unusual ability to balance a constantly increasing budget." Appropriations for faculty study and research, the first named professorship, residential buildings, and salary increases and retirement funds were gained for the faculty. Benefits to students were: more scholarships; campus accomodations for all resident students; arrangements for summer apprenticeships in public affairs, economics, home economics, and business; a revised and expanded curriculum to encourage intellectual self-dependence, citizenship, and interest in public affairs. In 1943, attended by approximately 750 resident and day students, with a faculty of more than one hundred, the college had a physical plant, including its greatly enlarged library, consisting of twenty-one buildings. In September of that year sixty-seven-year-old Miss Blunt retired from the presidency of Connecticut College, but two years later, when the succeeding president, Dr. Dorothy Schaffter, resumed her nonacademic work, Miss Blunt was recalled to the post. At the close of the academic year, in June 1946, the educator again retired.

At her inauguration, in 1930, Doctor Blunt had emphasized that "man may not be a beholder of his world merely but its shaper." In their classroom work and reading, students were to be led to distinguish between facts and propaganda, to lessen prejudices on problems such as labor and taxation, and "to gain a sense that society is a constantly changing organism." Education was to advance women's participation in all fields open to them. The college should supplement courses in political science, for example, by providing for students' firsthand observance and participation in politics. The educator believes that "the days of confining college education to the campus are over," and that women, "with their belief in the force of education [and] their fresh political energy, can do much to serve the democracy which has helped them." The "real teacher," Dr. Blunt considers, is "a leader among the students, respected and admired by them . . . a research scholar, an educational authority, and a contributor to the community around the college." In the latter capacity, Dr. Blunt wrote (*Journal of the Association of American University Women,* October 1938) the teacher will be able to provide students with "the contacts with life which vitalize the theory and destroy 'ivory tower isolation.' "

In the summer of 1941, for the first time in the history of Connecticut College, three vacation enterprises were undertaken. One of these, the Latin American Institute, at which Miss Blunt presided, was organized at the request of Nelson Rockefeller '41, then coordinator of Inter-American Affairs. Miss Blunt stressed the importance to the student of international affairs of understanding Latin American trade relations, economics, and politics. Pointing to the battle of ideas in the Latin American countries, she asked that ties between the United States and its southern neighbors be strengthened against possible Axis footholds. The Secretarial School met for a six-week session that summer; at other times students at Connecticut may include elective courses in secretarial studies in their credited undergraduate program. In the summer of 1942 the college held an eight-week War Session for the training of secretaries, chemists, statisticians, accountants, and nursery school teachers. Many special lectures, concerts, conferences held at Connecticut College both in vacation and term time are attended by outside guests and speakers as well as by the faculty and students. The Institute of Women's Professional Relations has its research headquarters at the college. That organization was set up in 1929 to maintain a panorama of, and serve as clearing-house for, information on women's work and education for the college, business, and professional woman.

In 1943, Miss Blunt received Connecticut College's LL.D. The educator has also been awarded this honorary degree by Wesleyan University (1936) and Mount Holyoke College (1937), and in 1941 the University of Chicago, where she had studied, taught, and served as department chairman, cited her for distinguished achievement. Formerly a member of the Connecticut State Board of Education and chairman of the New London Red Cross War Fund (1944-45), since 1944 she has been a trustee of Russell Sage College (Troy, New York) and is a member of the New London Ocean Beach Park Board. Miss Blunt is a fellow of the American Association for the Advancement of Science, in which her father also held membership. The League of Women Voters, which for some years has held a two-day institute at Connecticut College, includes the administrator in its membership. She is also a member of the National Education Association, the American Association of University Women, the Biochemical Society, the American Chemical Society, and the honorary scientific society, Sigma Xi, as well as Phi Beta Kappa. Her clubs are the Cosmopolitan, in New York, and the College, in Chicago and Boston.

"A dynamic person . . . electric, in the sense of both magnetism and driving power," one interviewer said of the college president. *Chapters in the History of Connecticut College* (1943) paid tribute to Doctor Blunt as "a woman of judgment, of social instinct, of snap and vigor; sometimes imperious, sometimes flashing fire . . . a woman able to do a man's work with the encouragement a man needs, or without it; a cheerful hostess to perennial guests; in fine, a woman able to grapple with the impossible task of being President and Mrs. President, too."

References

Am Assn Univ Women J 32:2 O '38

National Cyclopædia of American Biography Current vol B p385

Nye, I. comp. Chapters in the History of Connecticut College (1943)

Who's Who in America, 1946-47

BOARDMAN, MABEL (THORP) 1861(?) —Mar. 17, 1946 Volunteer social worker, founder and "administrative genius" of the American Red Cross; director of Volunteer Special Services until 1940, active national secretary and member of central committee from 1940 to December 1944, honorary until death; served one term as a Commissioner of the District of Columbia. See *Current Biography* 1944 Yearbook.

Obituary

N Y Times p21 Mr 13 '46 por

BONTEMPS, ARNA (WENDELL) (bŏn-täm') Oct. 13, 1902- Author; librarian
Address: b. c/o Fisk University, Nashville, Tenn.; h. 923 18th Ave., N., Nashville, Tenn.

The Negro author and librarian Arna Bontemps is considered one of the foremost writers of his race. He is known for his poetry and

James L. Allen

ARNA BONTEMPS

his books for the juvenile and adult reader; and his adaptation for the stage of his first novel, *God Sends Sunday*, was presented on Broadway in 1946 as the musical comedy *St. Louis Woman*.

Arna Wendell Bontemps, whose first name was originally Arnaud, was born in Alexandria, Louisiana, on October 13, 1902, the son of Paul Bismarck Bontemps, a brick mason whose father and grandfather had been brick masons before him. The writer's mother was Marie Carolina (Pembroke) Bontemps, who taught school until the time of her marriage. When Arna was three years old the family left the South for the West Coast. They were to have gone to San Francisco but, coming first to Los Angeles, they remained there. When the boy was twelve years old his mother died.

In the meantime, Arna Bontemps had had an interrupted early schooling. Then, from San Fernando Academy, which he attended in the years 1917-20, he went to Pacific Union College, in Angwin (also in California), received his B.A. degree in 1923. Shortly afterward he went to New York to accept a teaching post. He had originally mapped out for himself a medical career, but this, after about a week's foretaste, was given up. The idea of a career in music, however, was harder to shake off, and even through the last of his college years he had not given up the idea entirely. On a somewhat different level, and for the sake of more immediate needs, he had been a newsboy, a gardener (in Hollywood), a post-office clerk (in Los Angeles), and a jubilee singer. His teaching position in New York City was at the Harlem Academy, from 1924 to 1931. In the course of these seven years, he says, were established some lasting friendships and associations, and 1931 saw his first novel published.

In 1926, too, he had been married to Alberta Johnson.

The three years following were spent in the South, in Huntsville, Alabama, where he taught at Oakwood Junior College. It was after this period that he "found" J. P. Morgan, a gay, adventurous, and sensitive Negro youth who became the prototype of his Slumber in *Sad-Faced Boy*. And it was in Huntsville that he and his wife and two of their children lived through almost unendurable summer heat. Their home was a cottage in which the hot-water tank had been placed above the ceiling and against the roof itself—to give "plenty of hot water without any fire," as the builder put it. Bontemps used to typewrite out of doors on a card table on the shady side of the house, and a towel and fly-swatter soon became far more essential than either shirt or socks. Several times in the course of a morning or an afternoon one of his children would "slip around the corner with ice water or lemonade."

In 1935 Bontemps returned to the North, to teach in the Shiloh Academy in Chicago for three years. A year later he was awarded a fellowship for study in the Graduate Library School of the University of Chicago. At about this same time he served for a while as editorial supervisor in the Illinois Writers' Project. During 1938 and 1939 he held a Julius Rosenwald Fund fellowship for creative writing and travel in the Caribbean. He received his M.A. degree from the University of Chicago Graduate Library School in December 1943, six months after having taken over his present post as the librarian at Fisk University in Nashville, Tennessee.

Bontemps's first published piece had appeared in *Crisis* in 1924, when he was "heading for New York." From this same magazine he received a poetry prize two years later. He also won an Alexander Pushkin poetry prize in 1926 and 1927 and another award offered by *Opportunity,* a journal of Negro life, in 1932—this last for a short story.

His first novel, *God Sends Sunday* (1931), was built around the short-lived luck of Little Augie, a tiny Negro jockey of the nineties. In it, critics felt, the author had "caught the light-heartedness and the soft melancholy of the Negro race" in "vividly intense pictures of common life in the Negro quarters." Five years later he wrote a historical novel called *Black Thunder,* a drama of what was known as the "Gabriel Insurrection," which took place (or was to have taken place, had it not been abandoned) in Henrico County, near Richmond. This book also received favorable reviews. For his third novel, *Drums at Dusk* (1939), he drew again upon a Negro revolt, this one in Haiti at the time of the French Revolution. Rose Feld, in the New York *Herald Tribune,* found that the book as a whole suffered "from a style . . . too lush and romantic and from writing . . . too often careless," but the Springfield *Republican* wrote that although the background and characters might have been developed more fully, the book was nevertheless "a welcome addition to the field of historical fiction."

The author's first book in the juvenile field was *Popo and Fifina* (1932), a story of two Negro children in Haiti, written in collaboration with Langston Hughes '[40]. Other collaborations were *The Fast Sooner Hound* (1942) and *Slappy Hooper* (1946), both with Jack Conroy. *Sad-Faced Boy* (1937), done at the suggestion of the Rosenwald Fund, and *You Can't Pet a Possum* (1934) are Bontemps's own, as are an anthology of poems for children called *Golden Slippers* (1941), and *We Have Tomorrow* (1945), a collection of career stories of Negroes, for older boys and girls. In progress is "A Little History of the Negro." The author's books for children are characterized by "beauty of style", "crisp humor," and skill in rendering Negro speech by "the use of appropriate rhythms."

St. Louis Woman, the musical comedy, was adapted by Bontemps from his novel *God Sends Sunday.* When this "all-Negro period piece of the eighties" made its appearance on Broadway in April 1946, critics were divided in their opinion. *Variety* mentioned a "gaudy undercurrent of the script," on which he had had the collaboration of the late Countee Cullen, Negro poet; the New York *Herald Tribune* found that "there are moments of exciting theatrical alchemy in the script, but they are random and infrequent"; and the New York *World-Telegram* thought "the whole 'shebang' quite beautiful and a great lot of fun." The show did well, running for 113 performances before closing in September 1946.

Two titles which lie outside the categories mentioned are *They Seek a City* (1945), a study of the Negro in American life written in collaboration with Jack Conroy, and *Father of the Blues* (1941), Bontemps's editing of the autobiography of W. C. Handy. He has also written two plays in addition to *St. Louis Woman: Creole* (with Schuyler Watts), and *Careless Love* (with Langston Hughes). Bontemps is a frequent contributor to periodicals—his writings have appeared in the magazines *Tomorrow, American Scholar, Negro Digest,* and *Contemporary Verse.*

There are five children in the Bontemps family: Joan Marie, Paul Bismark, Poppy Alberta, Camille Ruby, Constance Rebecca, and Arna Alexander. The author-librarian is of medium height, weighs 175 pounds, and has graying hair. He has been described as a man of "quiet aspect and sensitive features."

References

Horn Book 15:7+ Ja '39
Library Q 14:187+ Jl '44
Cullen, C. Caroling Dusk (1927)
Who's Who in America, 1946-47

BORGE, VICTOR (bôr'gä") Jan. 3, 1909-
Comedian and pianist
Address: b. c/o Music Corporation of America, Beverly Hills, Calif.; h. Chatsworth, Calif.

Victor Borge, the "quietly mad" comedian and musician billed as "The Unmelancholy Dane," has become a leading entertainer in America, where radio audiences have been amused by his "phonetic punctuation" and "inflated language." And of his hour-long night-club act, Paul Martin has said: "His drolleries, usually accompanied by a deadpan delivery, are the height of sophistication. . . .It is at the piano that Borge is his maddest best. . . .He plays a medley, concerto fashion, with the orchestra, and eats a ham sandwich during the rests. He composes by pasting together parts of scores from the masters Wagner, Strauss, Bach, and Mozart, with a result that sounds like something super out of Tin Pan Alley. . . .He's completely hilarious, and he winds up with a stirring and splendid finale of martial music."

Born in Copenhagen on January 3, 1909, Victor Borge was known in his native Denmark as Borge Rosenbaum. The youngest in a family of five boys, Borge was educated at the Borgerdydskolen, a public school in Copenhagen. His father, Bernhard, for thirty-three years a violinist in the Royal Symphony, planned to have Borge follow in his footsteps. This, however, did not appeal to the boy, who preferred the piano lessons his governess was giving him. In his liking for the piano he took after his mother, the former Frederika Lichtinger. After four years of music lessons, some time of which was spent in work with a pianist of the Royal Symphony, nine-year-old Borge entered the Copenhagen Conservatory on a scholarship. Another scholarship took him to the University of Berlin, following which he studied in Copenhagen with Victor Schüller, and in Vienna with the Scotch pianist Frederic Lamond and the Dutch pianist Egon Petri. Young Borge had made his concert debut in 1922, when he was thirteen, and until 1934 he continued to give concerts in the Scandinavian countries.

During these years the young pianist was gaining a reputation as a parlor comedian. In 1931 he was asked to substitute for the star of an amateur show for which he had written the music—Borge had been composing since the age of seventeen—and his spontaneous humor at the piano kept the audience laughing. With lucrative offers awaiting him in his new role, he abandoned his concertizing—although, *Newsweek* says, he still could not resist playing the organ at a few selected funerals. The tall, dark, twenty-three-year-old pianist made his professional comedy debut in 1932, and on Christmas Eve 1933 he was married to his American fiancée, Elsie Chilton of Long Island.

The next decade saw Borge rise to success as a Danish Noel Coward: he was actor, composer, pianist, writer, and director of stage, screen, and radio shows. For his appearance in six motion pictures, he was reportedly paid the highest salary given any Danish star. The column he wrote for Swedish newspapers had national circulation. One of the two leading comedians of Denmark, he was called on by the royal family for a number of command performances. Nevertheless, he continued to create his humor spontaneously, rather than plan it. "If I went on for a twenty-minute show," Borge recalls, "I would have only five minutes prepared. The rest would be impro-

Bruno of Hollywood

VICTOR BORGE

vised. . . .I used to have a man standing in the wings putting down every word I said. In the morning he would give me a script, word for word, with every laugh timed to find out which things people found funniest." Borge still prefers to begin slowly, saving the best jokes for the last, although he points out that the material is much less important than delivery in making people laugh.

From the beginning of Hitler's rise, Borge made the Nazis the butt of much of his humor. His reply to daily letters and telephone calls threatening reprisals was to hire a bodyguard and keep up the attack. One example was his comment on the signing of a non-aggression pact between Denmark and Germany: "Now the good German citizens can sleep peacefully in their beds, secure from the threat of Danish aggression." In April ·1940, when the Germans invaded Denmark, Borge had the good fortune to be in Stockholm with a touring revue, while his wife took advantage of her American citizenship to remain in Denmark with his hospitalized mother. After his mother's death, her son and daughter-in-law were able to get to the United States on August 28, 1940, having traveled in the hold of a much overcrowded ship. Everything they owned was left behind, except their Scotch terrier, so that the only customs duty they had to pay on arrival was three dollars on the dog.

While the Danish comedian could speak Swedish, French, and German, he knew no English. After trying unsuccessfully to learn from his wife and from a language school, he taught himself American English by going to inexpensive movies and sitting through many showings while he repeated the dialogue with the actors. This he did for months, sometimes picking up a gangsterism or comic dialect which he would later have to discard, but finally he was able to translate some of his Danish comedy routines into English and mem-

orize them phonetically. With his name changed to Victor Borge, the comedian obtained a twelve-minute spot in a Florida night-club show. His act "clicked," and his time was increased to more than an hour. Later, Borge was introduced in Hollywood to Rudy Vallée, who offered him an audition. It was a failure, but when Borge explained that he had never been able to be witty without an audience, Vallée gave him a chance to entertain the singer's studio audience before his radio show. After the performance—to which Vallée, a shrewd judge of talent, had invited Bing Crosby's radio sponsors—Borge was signed for a guest appearance on Crosby's *Kraft Music Hall* in December 1941. The guest appearance grew into a series, and Borge became a regular member of the *Music Hall* cast. "His comedy with Bing has been inconsistent," radio critic Alton Cook commented in January 1942, "but there has been enough fanciful drollery to mark him definitely the find of the season. . . .He still is none too fluent in the new tongue and likes to try his comedy routines on an audience before he brings them to a microphone." When Borge left the program in 1943 he had been on it fifty-six weeks. A national audience had become familiar with what *Time* called, "his droll, suave, teasing act, full of casually crazy asides ('The tenor comes in in single file')," which "culminates expertly at the piano." Two of his "specialties" are his "phonetic punctuation"—indicating commas, periods, and other marks by "appropriate" sounds—and his inflated language, in which "create" becomes "crenine", "wonderful" becomes "twoderful," and "the second lieutenant ate the tenderloin with his fork" comes out "the third lieueleven-ant nined the elevenderloin with his fivek."

Sufficiently well-established by that time to be booked for the "top-drawer" Wedgwood Room of New York's Waldorf-Astoria, Borge pleased its patrons enough for his appearances to become annual events. (In 1945 he played thirteen weeks there.) The pianist comedian was busy, too, with radio work, broadcasting on the Nelson Eddy show for two months, and for a time on MGM's daily broadcast program, *The Lion's Roar*; playing the piano on OWI broadcasts to Denmark; making personal appearances in a variety of theaters and night clubs; and conferring with his draft board (a chronic back ailment kept him out of the service).

When Borge, one of the highest paid of all night-club entertainers, went to Hollywood, Paramount Pictures cast him with Frank Sinatra in *Higher and Higher*—as an English crook. "How can I cultivate an accent that has taken centuries of head colds to produce?" wailed the Dane, but Paramount was firm. As Sir Victor Fitzroy Victor, Borge had a number of piano solos, but only one of them escaped the cutting room. He had had an even more disappointing experience with Metro over *Meet the People*, but the studio and he had been reported as reopening negotiations several times. Meanwhile, the Dane was well occupied, but found time for his hobby of flying, managing to get in flights at almost every stop when on the road. Beginning in July 1945, Borge had his own Tuesday night radio show over NBC, a three-month summer substitute for Fibber McGee and Molly, on which he was supported by orchestra and chorus and a girl vocalist, Pat Friday. *The Score* reported, "Victor Borge is making a big hit in this new series, both for his wit and his cleverness as a musician." In September 1946 he began broadcasting the *Victor Borge Show* over NBC. The Monday night show, scheduled to run for forty-three weeks, featured Benny Goodman's orchestra. As a guest artist, Borge has appeared on shows ranging from Hildegarde's *Raleigh Room* to *The National Barn Dance,* from *Stage Door Canteen* to *The Chesterfield Supper Club* and the Kate Smith hour. Borge also played many benefits and gave frequent performances for uniformed audiences. Perhaps his highest point of activity was reached on a Sunday in May 1944, when he gave five stage shows, entertained at two benefits and a testimonial dinner for Eddie Cantor, attended three rehearsals, and made his regular *Chamber Music Society of Lower Basin Street* broadcast. Later that year, Borge's activities included appearances at Roosevelt-Truman Presidential campaign rallies.

Victor Borge's American concert debut was made in October 1945. In the "august immensities" of Carnegie Hall he interspersed favorite comedy routines with his serious pianoplaying and conducting of a forty-piece orchestra. Here, as on the subsequent tour, Borge was reported to have "scored a solid success" with a large audience. All reviews praised his comedy, but there was a difference of opinion about his musicianship. Music critic Robert Bagar said that his playing and conducting were "neither comical nor satirical, but merely imperfect." A *Musical America* report from Baltimore a week later, however, called his music "smoothly performed"; and *Variety,* the journal of show business, headlined its review, "'Best Acts of All Play Carnegie Hall' Cued by Borge's Show." A concert piece of his own, "Blue Serenade," has been published for piano; and Columbia Records has put out an album, "A Victor Borge Program," which includes the pianist-comedian's interpretation of the classics as well as his "Blue Serenade," "Lesson in Composition," and "Phonetic Punctuation."

Described as looking like a handsome George Jessel, Victor Borge is tall (five feet eleven, 165 pounds), dark, and good-looking, with mobile features. "The first thing you notice about Borge," wrote Betty Moorsteen of *PM,* "is that he has no rough edges either in his appearance, dress, speech, or behavior. His dark brown hair . . . looks as if it might be kinky if it were not so well plastered down. . . .He uses his well-manicured hands in an expressive but controlled way during conversation. . . .Only his crowded room gave the impression that Borge is an exceedingly busy man despite his leisurely composure." In his free time, besides piloting an airplane, the comedian-pianist likes to drive a tractor or work with tools on the San Fernando Valley farm where he and his wife live. (In 1945 Mrs. Borge was voted one of the ten best-dressed women in the world by the French Congress of Fashions.) Borge has been listed as a "ten best" by the artist Frederic Varady, who classed him with nine other celebrities as having one of the most "exciting and symmetrical" male heads in the world. Other Borge distinctions include a Page One Award from the Newspaper Guild of New York, and an invitation to President Roosevelt's Birthday Ball for actors in January 1945.

References

    Collier's 111:38-40 My 15 '43 por
    N Y Times VIII p10 F 22 '42
    N Y World-Telegram p10 Jan 15 '42
    Newsweek 25:106-7 O 16 '44 por
    PM p13 Mr 15 '45 por
    This Week p17 O 28 '45 por
    Who's Who in America, 1946-47

BORZAGE, FRANK (bôr-zā'gē) Apr. 23, 1893- Motion picture director and producer
Address: b. c/o Republic Pictures Corp., Hollywood, Calif.; h. 400 N. Camden Dr., Beverly Hills, Calif.

"A name that is synonymous with fine understanding of human values," wrote *Motion Picture Producers and Distributors,* is that of Frank Borzage, Hollywood director and producer. The winner of two Motion Picture Academy Awards for direction, he was six times represented in the Ten Best Pictures of the Year awards of *Film Daily.* Borzage, formerly with Metro-Goldwyn-Mayer and Paramount, joined Republic Pictures early in 1945.

Frank Borzage was born in Salt Lake City, Utah, on April 23, 1893. He is the son of Lewis Borzage, "an expert stone mason, who gave the boy the inherent qualities of courage and integrity." His schooling was necessarily short; before he reached thirteen, young Frank had worked in the mines. After enrolling in a drama course with a correspondence school, which turned out to be worthless, he joined a touring company in 1906 as property-boy, errand-runner, and, as it is told, expediter of black coffee to the troupers. After three years of watching the actors at work, the sixteen-year-old Frank returned to the mining camps as a character actor in a small company's productions.

Early in 1913 Borzage arrived in California "strong and unafraid, burning with ambition," and soon began to play bit parts as a five-dollar-a-day extra. His first leading role in a "western," for which he was selected by Thomas Ince, one of the silent films' best-known producers, was followed by other cowboy pictures. Then, after "guiding" a series of westerns through production, Borzage emerged as a director with *Humoresque* (1920), believed by many to be one of the finest pictures of that year. Seven years later his *Seventh Heaven* (1927), which established the unknown Janet Gaynor and Charles Farrell as stars, won an "Oscar" (the Academy Award prize statuette) for 1927-28 and was judged one of the Ten Best Films in the annual contest conducted by *Film Daily. Street Angel* (1928), which Bor-

FRANK BORZAGE

zage also directed, was one of the Ten Best Films of 1928. His next award-winner was *Bad Girl* (1931), filmed at the Fox Studio, which won an "Oscar" for 1931-32, in addition to being judged one of the Ten Best. Between those two came *The River, Lucky Star, They Had To See Paris, Song o' My Heart, Devil With the Women,* and *Liliom.* Then, joining Fox Pictures, Borzage directed *Doctor's Wives* and *Young As You Feel*; after *Bad Girl* he directed *After Tomorrow* and *Young American.*

By the time he left Fox, Borzage was working on sound movies, the "talkies" having been launched in 1929. He went to Paramount Pictures to direct *Farewell to Arms* (1933), the Hemingway story he made into one of the Ten Best Films of 1933. Three other Paramount pictures were to follow: *Desire* (1936), *Disputed Passage* (1939), and *Till We Meet Again* (1945). During the same period, Borzage worked on *Secrets* (1933) for the Mary Pickford '45 Production Company, before going on to Columbia for *No Greater Glory* (1934) and *A Man's Castle* (1934). Warner Brothers acquired Borzage's directorial services for *Flirtation Walk* (1934), which was followed by *Stranded* (1935), the screen adaptation of A. J. Cronin's '42 *Green Light* (1936), and *Hearts Divided* (1936.)

For First International, Borzage directed *Living on Velvet* (1935) and *Shipmates Forever* (1935) before signing his contract with Metro-Goldwyn-Mayer. At that studio, where he spent the next seven years, he directed *Big City* (1937), *Mannequin* (1937), *Three Comrades* (1938), *The Shining Hour* (1938), *Strange Cargo* (1940), *The Mortal Storm,* another of the Ten Best (1940), *Flight Command* (1940), *The Vanishing Virginian* (1941), *Smilin' Through* (1941), and *Seven Sweethearts* (1942). *Smilin' Through,* based on the play by Jane Cowl and Jane Murfin, had been

made as a silent movie in 1922 and as a sound film in 1932. With added songs, the newly perfected Technicolor, and Borzage directing, the love story was again brought out in 1941.

Moving on from MGM to another United Artists release (his first had been *History Is Made at Night,* in 1937), Borzage made *Stage Door Canteen* (1943), his sixth pace-setter for the Ten Best Films award. The opinion of Howard Barnes of the New York *Herald Tribune* was: "Frank Borzage, who knows a thing or two about tear-jerking, has used his formula brilliantly in his direction of *Stage Door Canteen.*" Universal's *His Butler's Sister* (1943) utilized "the Cinderella formula" for a plot, moved with "consistently good pace" under Borzage's "sensitive direction," and earned *Variety's* praise as "topgrade." *The Spanish Main* (1945) for Radio Keith Orpheum, a romantic story of pirates, was Archer Winston's (the New York *Post*) nomination for "the most colorful waste of film of the month." It was generally agreed by the critics, however, that "this pretentious fable . . . [was] brightened by the Frank Borzage staging," as well as by his direction of "a multitude of realistic fight scenes." Following this was the "costly, fancy-dress opus," *The Magnificent Doll* (1946), based upon the life of Dolly Madison.

While Frank Borzage had been regarded primarily as a director, he had produced as well as directed *Little Man What Now?* (1934) for Universal, before producing and directing *Till We Meet Again.* This was called "just another melodrama" by some critics, a "delicately tender love story" by others; Alton Cook of the New York *World-Telegram* wrote that it was "a fragile, delicate wisp of a romance that called for wise and gentle hands on every small detail," which it found in Borzage's handling. John T. McManus of New York's *PM* raised a question of taste when he charged "misuse of the nun's habit [i.e. garb] to cash in on the Catholic cycle in films"; other reviewers felt that it had reached the stature of *The Song of Bernadette* and *Going My Way* through its "dominant religious aura." (*Till We Meet Again* was voted one of the Ten Worst Films of 1944 by *Lampoon,* Harvard University's undergraduate monthly.)

I've Always Loved You (1946) was Republic's first Technicolor venture as well as the first independent "package" production by Borzage. A businessman as well as a veteran director, Borzage became the first of three prominent directors to sign "semi-autonomous profit-participating" contracts with Herbert J. Yates, president of Republic. The five-year agreement calls for one picture a year, produced and directed by Borzage as a unit: he has complete authority in the selection of stories, the casting of parts, the purchase of material, and has also a financial interest in the outcome, which he may produce on a budget of from $1,500,000 to $2,000,000. Yates hailed the tendency to decentralize in the industry since men such as Borzage are thus enabled to "produce pictures on their own . . . free from assembly line methods." Borzage was also reported by a *World-Telegram* writer to have invested in the Mexican film industry, along with radio comedian Red Skelton and others.

Borzage has been called a "woman's director" by virtue of his success in projecting women's thoughts in motion pictures. His work with Janet Gaynor in *Seventh Heaven*, Helen Hayes '42 in *Farewell to Arms*, Sally Eilers in *Bad Girl*, Margaret Sullavan '44 in *Three Comrades*, Catherine McLeod, whom he "discovered," in *I've Always Loved You*, and Ginger Rogers '41 in *The Magnificent Doll*, has been cited in support of this particular quality. "Women are easy to understand. The biggest fool in history was the first man who said women were a mystery," Borzage told one interviewer (female). "A very wise man, who knew his women, once said: 'Treat a duchess like a charwoman and a charwoman like a duchess, if you want to be a successful lover,'" continued Borzage, "I think that applies to a director, too." Reducing rehearsal time to a minimum, since he believes that acting must be natural and that repetition is fatal to spontaneous artistry, Borzage generally gives his players preliminary instructions in conference. Whatever constructive criticism is needed comes during rehearsal, at which time Borzage softens his often biting remarks with a smile—he is said never to lose his temper.

Although he works for box-office appeal, the producer-director believes Hollywood has a moral obligation "to embody in the fundamentals of entertainment a point of view . . . designed to enlighten as well as entertain." He has urged that the Motion Picture Producers and Distributors Association eliminate glamorized gangster movies: "Our entire nation is working on a plan which will bring peace and prosperity and good will to all the world. . . . This is certainly an inopportune time for us to convey the impression that America is made up largely of gangsters, black-market operators, petty racketeers, and murderers." Borzage has suggested a system of voluntary censorship for the industry, and has pointed out that educational films such as *Wilson* bring "healthy profits."

After his divorce from the former Rena Rogers, Borzage was married on November 25, 1945, to Edna Marie Stillwell, radio "gag" writer, who is business manager for her former husband, Red Skelton. Borzage, whose curly brown hair is touched with gray, has hazel eyes, weighs 175 pounds, is five feet ten inches in height. Once one of Hollywood's "ranking" polo players, he has since given up both that sport and the piloting of his Waco F-2 plane; his favorite recreation is now golf. The bowl of Borzage's pipes are said never to be charred —he smokes as he works, a short stick in his hand, "burning neither too much energy, nor too much tobacco."

References

International Motion Picture Almanac, 1943-44
Who's Who in America, 1946-47

BOTHWELL, JEAN Author
Address: h. 161 W. 16th St., New York

Personal pleasure, and a desire to interpret the India she knew to the children of America, were the motives for writing *The Thirteenth Stone*, declared Jean Bothwell, when she received the New York *Herald Tribune's* Children's Spring Book Festival award (1946) for a book for children in the middle age-group. According to Miss Bothwell, "India is not the terrible place that publicity would sometimes have us believe." In her twelve years' residence in the country of the rajahs, the author came to know and love the land she portrays so authoritatively.

Underwood & Underwood

JEAN BOTHWELL

Jean Bothwell was born in Winside, Nebraska, the daughter of James Millward Bothwell, a Methodist minister, and Mary Emmeline (Batham) Bothwell. Her family is Anglo-Saxon on both sides, and the Bothwells trace their lineage back to the sixteenth century in Scotland. Educated in the Nebraska public schools, where she "found English themes fun and arithmetic a nightmare," young Jean grew up in a "leisurely environment of books and gardens." A few months' work as a secretary— to Edith Tobitt, librarian of the Omaha Public Library—preceded her college career. After taking her B.A. from Nebraska Wesleyan University in 1916, she taught history in a Columbus (Nebraska) high school for a year. Various business experiences followed, and in 1922 she went abroad, eventually going to India where she became a teacher in a girls' school. Her routine of teaching, and later of administrative work, was often varied by extracurricular activities which ranged from spanking the "wee inmates" of the school to "walking with kings" at the viceroy's garden party.

From the time of her grammar school days, Jean Bothwell had known that she wanted to

BOTHWELL, JEAN—*Continued*

write. She was a reporter for her college weekly, and was also a contributor to the annual. Before going abroad, she did a few pieces for publication, but she did not attain much of an output until after she was settled in India. While a teacher in an English-speaking girls' high school in Lucknow she was always ready to dash off a "drama" for the students' theatricals. There, too, she wrote a number of poems, articles, and short stories which found publication in newspapers and magazines in the United States, and in the *Pioneer,* an Indian paper. On furlough in 1929, she consulted a literary agent in New York City, who told her to write for children. Miss Bothwell, however, did not care to enter the juvenile field, and it was not until she returned to the United States permanently, in 1936, that she began to consider this advice.

Little Boat Boy (1945), her first book, grew out of her own experiences in a houseboat in Srinagar, a large city in the Himalayan province of Kashmir. Critics found this story of the Moslem boy, Hafiz, and his family a "satisfying book" whose "distinguished writing" should appeal to grownups as well as to children. M. B. Snow, in the *Library Journal,* compared Hafiz to the Chinese boy, Little Pear, in the popular book of that name. A second book, the prize-winning *The Thirteenth Stone,* in which "the fascinating background of India is richly portrayed with deep feeling for the country and its people," appeared in 1946. Concerned with the traditions and legends of several Rajputana states, this book has a more complex background than its predecessor, a fact which Ruth Hill, in the *Saturday Review of Literature,* found a bit confusing at times, though not retarding the story, which moves swiftly. According to the Chicago *Sun's Book Week,* "the color, the sounds, the very odors of India are to be found in these pages, so that the reader closes the book richer for experiencing life in a distant land." A sequel to *Little Boat Boy,* entitled *River Boy of Kashmir* (1946) continues the adventures of Hafiz, now at school. "Well-sustained story interest, combined with picturesque details of schoolboy life in India," commented May Lamberton Becker in the New York *Herald Tribune Weekly Book Review,* "brings that country close to an American schoolboy by the very differences between this River School and that in which he spends his days at eight years of age." A high spot in the story is the vivid description of a flood, actually experienced by the author. As with her previous books, much information on the life and ideals of the Indian people is skillfully woven into the narrative.

Miss Bothwell is a member of the National Book Women's Association, and of the Pen and Brush Club of New York City. In 1938 she was given Philadelphia's Review Club Poetry Award. In addition to receiving the 1946 award of the Children's Spring Book Festival, her *The Thirteenth Stone* was chosen as a May title by the Catholic Junior Book Club. The book is to be translated into the Dutch language in 1947. *Little Boat Boy* is on the

International Mind Alcove Booklist of the Carnegie Endowment for International Peace; it has also been transcribed into Braille for the blind children of the Chicago public schools.

Of medium height and weight, the author has green eyes and auburn hair. Horseback riding and cycling constitute her outdoor recreation, but she admits to being "mostly a spectator" in active sports. One of her hobbies is the making of handkerchiefs. She also collect postage stamps, and boxes of many sizes and shapes, a number of which she brought back from India. Although, or perhaps because, she has traveled so much—England and Scotland, Japan and China—she loves to keep house, and lives in an apartment in the old Chelsea district of New York City. A position with a literary agency keeps her busy during the day, but most of her free time is spent in writing. In 1946 she was finishing her fourth book, again about India.

References

N Y Herald Tribune p27 My 16 '46 por;
N Y Herald Tribune Books p7 My 19
'46 por
Pub W 149:2643 My 18 '46

BOULT, SIR ADRIAN (CEDRIC) (bōlt)
Apr. 8, 1889- Conductor
Address: b. c/o British Broadcasting Corp., London; h. Oxshott, Surrey, England

Sir Adrian Boult, conductor in chief of the British Broadcasting Corporation, has been called "the ambassador of musical good will between the two largest English-speaking nations," Britain and the United States. Under his baton the orchestra of the BBC performed over the radio as well as in the concert hall throughout World War II, even during the darkest days of England's bombing by the Luftwaffe. In December 1944 the conductor received the Gold Medal of the Royal Philharmonic Society. This Sir Adrian regarded not as a personal tribute but a tribute to all that his orchestra had done "during the war in its great effort of entertaining its radio public." In the United States he had become a familiar figure to concert-goers in the various cities where he had conducted before the war, and early 1946 saw his return to America as guest conductor of the Boston Symphony Orchestra.

Sir Adrian Cedric Boult (he was knighted in 1937), the only son of Katharine Florence (Barman) Boult and Cedric Randal Boult, a Liverpool businessman and justice of the peace, was born in Chester, England, on April 8, 1889. When he was two, the family moved to Cheshire. Until he was five the boy scarcely knew any English because both he and his older sister, Olive, his senior by several years, spoke the language of their German nurse. Sir Adrian says he always wanted to be an orchestra conductor. Before his eyes reached the level of the keyboard he could pick out notes with accuracy on the piano. His mother, herself a talented musician (although her frail health did not permit her to appear on the concert stage), encouraged the child's aptitude for music without pushing it. From her, and later from an

Austrian pianist, resident in Liverpool, the boy received his early instruction in piano.

At the age of twelve the boy was sent to Westminster School in London so that he might attend the various concerts in the city. The school, dating from olden times when it was conducted by monks, apparently did not consider music essential in the development of a child and therefore did not include the subject in its curriculum. However, the science master, H. E. Piggott, was devoted to music and it was he who became the boy's first music teacher outside the Boult home. The two spent much time in the study of harmony, counterpoint, and fugue. Adrian also had a season ticket to the concerts at Queen's Hall. There, score in hand, he eagerly followed the conductor, Sir Henry J. Wood, whose associate and successor he was destined to become. When he went home for weekends and holidays to Cheshire, a four hours' journey by train from London, his pockets were stuffed with the miniature scores he had begun to collect. By the time the boy was sixteen he was fairly familiar with the classical repertoire.

Eva Mary Grew, author of "Adrian Boult, the Story of his Life and Work" (a series of articles which appeared from August 1933 through June 1934 in the *British Musician*) believes the training the boy gave himself may have been more valuable than a conventional one—he appeared to be an observer rather than a participant. She also considers him fortunate in his development as a musician in turning later from "the exercise of simple observation to what may be called the practical amateurism" of Oxford University, which he entered in 1908 at nineteen. Believing that a conductor should have actual experience in singing, the youth joined choirs and choruses; in one of them, the Oxford Bach Choir, he sang bass solo parts. He also appeared as Don Fernando in a performance of *Fidelio* and as Samiel in the university's offering of Carl Maria von Weber's opera *Der Freischutz,* and in 1910 he was president of the Oxford Musical Club. When he left Oxford at the end of the four-year course, the future conductor had received his B.A. and M.A. degrees and had taken most of the examinations towards his doctorate in music. Procedure at Oxford, however, requires that a student must wait five years after he has been awarded his B.Mus. before he is eligible for his D.Mus. This ruling and the interruption of his studies by World War I prevented Boult from earning his advanced degree until 1921.

In 1912 Boult studied further at the Leipzig Conservatory for a year. While in the German city he had the good fortune to become accompanist for Marie Hedmondt, a teacher of many famous opera stars. At this time, too, the noted Hungarian conductor, Arthur Nikisch, was still conducting although he had given up his class at the conservatory. Remembering another young Englishman, Albert Coates, his pupil ten years earlier, he encouraged Boult to come to his rehearsals at the Leipzig Gewandhaus. Boult became a member of the choral society Nikisch directed there.

British Official Photo.

SIR ADRIAN BOULT

On his return to England in 1913, Boult joined the musical staff of London's Covent Garden Opera, where he remained for a year. Although he did not make his London debut as a conductor until the spring of 1918, he gave his first professional concert, with an orchestra he himself engaged, four years earlier in the town of West Kirby (not far from Chester), to which the Boults had moved in 1905. At the outbreak of World War I, the young conductor temporarily laid aside his music to work in the British War Office. There his knowledge of German made him particularly valuable. He was later personal assistant to the future Lord Woolton, then Frederick James Marquis, secretary to the Leather Control Board. In that capacity Boult also served with the Commission for Foreign Supplies (Commission Internationale de Ravitaillement) in London. When he was given permission in 1915 to conduct a concert of the Liverpool Philharmonic Society, he was the youngest leader the society had ever engaged. Toward the end of the war he gave four concerts in Queen's Hall. At that time he was engaged at the office all day; rehearsals were held on Sundays, and the concerts took place on Monday evenings.

In an appraisal of the work of Sir Adrian Boult, the British music critic C. B. Rees mentioned that it was the musician's interpretation of Vaughan Williams' *London* Symphony in 1918 that established him as a conductor. That same year Boult again won applause when, at a semi-private Sunday morning concert, he conducted the first performance of the work of another English composer, *The Planets*, by Gustav Holst. At the end of World War I a group of ex-servicemen musicians invited him to conduct their own orchestra, the British Symphony Orchestra, which had been in existence one year. By 1924, however, so many of the young musicians had been drafted

BOULT, SIR ADRIAN—*Continued*

into vacancies in the older orchestras, that the project had to be abandoned.

The record of Sir Adrian's direction of orchestras is long and varied. The Royal Philharmonic Society engaged him as one of three conductors for the 1919 season. He conducted at the Empire Theatre in London for Diaghilev's *Ballet Russe* with Massine, Karsavina, and Lopokova (now Lady Keynes) as the chief dancers. He taught a class for conductors for five years at the Royal College of Music, beginning in 1919. Instituted by Sir Hugh Allen, the director of the Royal College, it was the first class of its kind in England. When Sir Charles Standford, shortly before his death in 1924, retired as conductor of the senior orchestra at the college, Boult was given the post, which he held until 1930. From 1919 to 1929 he conducted the orchestras of the Patron's Fund, established by Sir Ernest Palmer at the Royal College of Music in 1903 so that British composers might hear their own compositions played for the first time. During a tour of the continent in 1923 Boult was guest conductor in Barcelona at the invitation of the Spanish cellist Pablo Casals. When the BBC appointed him its director of music in 1930 he resigned from the Birmingham City Orchestra, where he had held a similar post since 1924.

On the two occasions the British Broadcasting Company orchestra went abroad to give concerts, Boult was its conductor, leading it in Brussels in 1933 and in Paris, Vienna, Zurich, and Budapest in 1934. The following year he directed a program of English music at the Salzburg festival. At the coronation of King George VI, Boult, who was knighted the same year, led the orchestra which played before the ceremony. Also in 1937, when the National Broadcasting Company began its seasons of concerts, Sir Adrian was among the conductors invited to New York to lead its symphony orchestra.

Sir Adrian is the author of a *Handbook on the Technique of Conducting* and has contributed articles on the subject of music to various periodicals both in England and the United States. In "Orchestra on Parade" (*Musical America,* April 10, 1945) he gives an account of the activities of the BBC orchestra and himself during World War II. Early in the war Boult and his musicians were transferred from London to Bristol, which had its own broadcasting studio. With quiet humor he describes the orchestra's activities during the heavy night attacks to which the British Isles were subjected from the air by Nazi bombers. Once, at a late broadcast, the orchestra had to finish its program by the light of candles and oil lamps after the electric light had failed. "Although some of our valuable music was lost by enemy action . . . the members of the orchestra themselves stood the strain magnificently—never lowering the standard of their playing," said Sir Adrian. The orchestra suffered the loss of one player who was killed in a raid immediately following a broadcast. In July of the same year the orchestra was

transferred to Bedford, a small town in the Midlands surrounded by farming country. Sir Adrian and the BBC orchestra also toured service camps and factories in all parts of England as well as the naval centers at Southampton and Portsmouth. In addition to making provincial tours they visited London for the concert seasons in 1943 and 1944. In April 1942 Sir Adrian resigned from the post of director of music to the BBC in order to devote himself entirely to conducting the BBC Symphony Orchestra.

It was "with the greatest cordiality" that Sir Adrian was received on January 18, 1946, at his opening concert of the three full weeks he was the guest conductor of the Boston Symphony Orchestra. He gave the first Boston performance of *The Forgotten Rite* by John Ireland and Anthony Collins' *Threnody for A Soldier Killed in Action,* the latter based on musical sketches left by Michael Heming, a young Englishman who fell in battle at El Alamein. Elgar's *Enigma* Variations and the Brahms First Symphony completed the program. The music critic of the *Christian Science Monitor* responded warmly to the music of Elgar and Ireland and to Boult's interpretation, but felt that Collins had not had the "creative imagination to use the material [of Heming] to valid artistic purpose." Recalling Sir Adrian's "delightfully songful performance" of the Schubert C Major Symphony on his visit to the city eleven years earlier, the critic regarded his interpretation of Brahms as less successful, "except for the last half of the last movement when everything seemed to wake up." In May of the same year he conducted an English program at the Prague Spring Festival, which celebrated the fiftieth anniversary of the Czech Philharmonic Orchestra.

Among conductors Boult is known for his quiet bearing on the podium, his restraint, and his sparing use of the left hand, relying almost entirely upon the stick itself. In pianissimo it scarcely moves at all and has to be carefully watched by those who are some distance away. Believing that freshness at a concert is important, he does not tire his musicians with repetitious rehearsals. The principal viola player in the BBC orchestra, Bernard Shore, pays tribute to the conductor's "incessant striving after the most faithful approximation possible to the composer's mind" and to his dislike of showmanship. "He prefers to be an almost impersonal medium between the composer, orchestra, and audience rather than the central character." A musician of catholic tastes, Sir Adrian is reputed to be at his best in compositions of an "architectural character," less at ease in "the slighter music of phantasy and color." He is fond of the English custom of organizing a large number of choirs in adjacent villages and giving massed performances in some central town at a festival, in which he enjoys participating as conductor. In 1945, however, the pressure of work as conductor in chief of the BBC obliged him to give up this "hobby."

The heavy demands for space on transatlantic liners after the war made it impossible for the wife of Sir Adrian Boult to accompany him on his latest visit to the United States. Since their marriage in 1933 the former Ann Mary Grace Bowles has helped him to overcome the nervousness he still experiences before every concert. Lady Boult's best advice to her husband has been, "Go on to the platform as if you were going to enjoy yourself, as you are." She herself has sung in the London Bach Choir and is regarded by her husband as one of his most valuable critics.

At their home in England Sir Adrian likes to read his scores when he lies full length on the hearthrug. Over six feet, he walks with rapid stride and erect carriage. His eyes are hazel, and he wears a bristling mustache. Patience, economy of gesture, and "concentration to the nth" he considers the essentials of good conducting. His geniality and humor are traits appreciated by his orchestra. During a rehearsal that did not go off too well he once remarked, "I should lose my hair about this—if I had any hair to lose!"

References
Musical Am 65:5 Ap 10 '45 por
Shore, B. The Orchestra Speaks (1938)
Thompson, O. ed. International Cyclopedia of Music and Musicians (1943)
Who's Who, 1946
Who's Who in America, 1946-47

BOUTELL, CLARENCE B(URLEY) (boō-tĕl') Feb. 8, 1908- Columnist; writer
Address: b. c/o New York Post, 75 West St., New York; h. Glendale Rd., Harrison, N.Y.

The only literary gossip column syndicated in the United States is *Authors Are Like People,* by Clip (otherwise Clarence B.) Boutell, who originated the column for the New York *Post.* Clarence Burley Boutell was born February 8, 1908, in Washington, D.C. His mother is the former Avis Burley, and his father, Roger Sherman Gates Boutell, was a bookseller who had been law librarian at the Library of Congress. Boutell spent his childhood in Washington, in Saginaw, Michigan, and at St. Paul's School in Concord, New Hampshire. In 1926, at the age of eighteen, he was graduated from St. Paul's and in the same year entered Stanford University at Palo Alto, California. He never received his degree, for in 1927 he left Stanford to take a job in his father's business, the Tecolete Bookshop, in Santa Barbara. About two years later his career as a bookseller ended when he left the United States for a year of travel in Europe during 1929.

When Boutell returned to the United States in 1930, he remained in New York City. That year marked his first professional connection with the book-publishing field. For three years he was advertising manager for Alfred A. Knopf, Incorporated. When he resigned from this publishing firm in 1933, it was to take the position of promotion manager offered him by the *Saturday Review of Literature.* This Boutell left in 1937 to become advertising manager and publicity director of G. P. Putnam's Sons, Coward-McCann, Incorporated, and the

CLARENCE B. BOUTELL

John Day Company, posts he retained over a period of six years. In the meantime Boutell contributed articles to book-reviewing magazines and trade journals. One of the articles (in *Publishers' Weekly,* March 30, 1940) was an account of the methods by which Sir Nevile Henderson '40 was persuaded to write the memoirs of his experiences as British Ambassador to Germany from 1937 to 1939. (Boutell, then with Putnam's, directed the promotion for Henderson's book, *The Failure of a Mission.*)

Soon after the entrance of the United States into World War II, Boutell recognized the need for an organization to bring literary entertainment to men in service. Thus, in the spring of 1942, he started a project which developed into the Council of Books in Wartime, an organization composed of trade book publishers, booksellers, and librarians. During its early period Boutell acted as the council's first chairman. When the plans of the group had been formulated and its method determined by the summer of 1942, Boutell became a member of the board of directors as well as chairman of the program committee. The council met weekly for the duration of the war. Boutell's task as program committee chairman was to decide the type of entertainment the council was to provide, one of his responsibilities being the selection of books and chapters of books to be dramatized over the air as part of the campaign in the "war of ideas." The council distributed over ninety million books to "GI Joe" through the Armed Services Editions. In addition, it also published book lists on health and other subjects, for distribution on the home front.

Boutell's business connections with the book-publishing industry came to a close in July 1943 when he accepted the position of columnist on the New York *Post.* He and Sterling

BOUTELL, CLARENCE B.—*Continued*

North'[43], the book critic of the *Post*, started their weekly book page at that time. Boutell's literary gossip column, called *Authors Are Like People*, appeared under the by-line of Clip Boutell. The fare which the column offers includes brief interviews with authors, condensed evaluations of books, news about the publishing field, tidbits on literary teas, and quips. In 1946 Boutell's and North's *Post* material is being syndicated in twenty-one newspapers throughout the United States.

The columnist's writings have reflected his varied interests in books and publishing. Concerned as he is with all phases of his profession, Boutell once or twice has found himself involved in controversies such as that concerning the origin of the coined word "whodunit" for the mystery novel, and the ethics of revealing, in book reviews, the plots of detective and mystery stories, or of any other type of fiction. Pointing out in *Publishers' Weekly* for April 15, 1939, that such treatment not only spoils the suspense the plots have for the reader but also lessens the sale of the book, Boutell deplored the fact that this story-telling method of reviewing had grown widespread. In the *Saturday Review of Literature* (January 19, 1946), in an article called "Calamity at the Inkwell," Boutell described in detail the misfortunes or near misfortunes which befell some original manuscripts of the work of famous poets and authors, who, in most cases, recovered from their loss in commendable fashion. Boutell has also participated in discussions on the radio programs *The Author Meets the Critic* and *Books on Trial*.

Boutell and North collaborated on an anthology entitled *Speak of the Devil*, which appeared in the summer of 1945. The compilation consists of prose and verse selections on the Prince of Darkness, and became a Literary Guild dividend. In their choice of material, the editors were guided by two principal considerations: "readability in terms of the current taste and a sociological rather than a theological view of the devil." The appropriate keynote to the anthology was provided by a "jacket of horror," designed by Salvador Dali. Although *Speak of the Devil* was received favorably by most critics, to whom the novelty of the subject appealed, a reviewer in the *New Yorker* criticized the editors' attempts to please all tastes. The serio-comic mixture of philosophy, history, and personal views, with which the editors prefaced the various sections of the book, gave evidence of much research and was considered by Stewart Holbrook, writing in the New York *Herald Tribune,* often "more interesting . . . than some of the selections." Some reviewers chaffed North and Boutell because the anthology pointed out that the Evil One had been sympathetic with practically all creative artists, including writers.

A member and former president of the Booksellers League of New York, Boutell is also a director of Transportation Guides, Incorporated, publishers of the *Official Steamship and Airways Guide*. In his political allegiance he is a Democrat, and his church affiliation is Episcopalian. About five feet eight inches in height and weighing 155 pounds, the columnist has black eyes, a dark mustache, and graying hair. He lists his hobbies as pistol-shooting and cabinetmaking. Mrs. Boutell is the former Helen Paulsen, to whom he was married in May 1935. Their children—Patricia Carley, William Burley, and Christine Blodgett—are, according to their father, three budding literary geniuses. For them—and other young readers—Clip Boutell wrote *The Fat Baron* (it was published in October 1946), a tale concerning one Frederick Charles Henry Maximilian Francis Avoirdupois, whose slogan is "Avoirdupois or Die."

BOUTELL, CLIP *See* Boutell, C. B.

BOWES, EDWARD (bōz) June 14, 1874—June 13, 1946 Radio program director, corporation executive; real estate operator in San Francisco in 1906; major in the Intelligence Department in World War I; moved to New York to specialize in theatrical real estate, opened the Capitol Theatre there; was the first to encourage broadcasting; conducted an amateur hour from 1934 to 1946, voted the most popular on the air in 1935; radio audience estimated variously at from fifteen to thirty-seven million listeners. See *Current Biography* 1941 *Yearbook.*

Obituary

N Y Times p21 Je 14 '46 por

BRAGDON, CLAUDE (FAYETTE) Aug. 1, 1866—Sept. 17, 1946 Author, architect, and lecturer; practicing architect in Rochester, New York (1901-23); executed the sets for the plays of Walter Hampden after 1923; lectured on architecture at the Art Institute of Chicago and at Princeton University; well known for his books on theosophy; his autobiography *More Lives Than One* appeared in 1934.

Obituary

N Y Times p31 S 18 '46 por

BRANZELL, KARIN (brän'zĕl kär'ĭn) Sept. 24, 1891- Singer

Address: b. c/o Columbia Concerts, Inc., 113 W. 57th St.: h. 150 Greenway Ter., Forest Hills, N.Y.

"Singing as completely satisfying as that heard from Karin Branzell yesterday afternoon in Town Hall has become so rare nowadays that her recital must go on record as one of the red-letter events of the present musical season," wrote Noel Straus in the *Times* on the occasion of the Swedish contralto's first New York concert after her retirement from the Metropolitan in 1944. Recipient of the highest honors Sweden can bestow on a singer and a veteran of twenty years in leading roles on the Metropolitan stage, Mme. Branzell, who began her career under the patronage of the Crown Princess of her native land, will devote the coming seasons to *Lieder* recitals and the training of promising young artists at the Juilliard School of Music.

Karin Maria Branzell (she has since dropped the Maria) was born in Stockholm, Sweden, on September 24, 1891, to Anders and Jenny (Pearson) Branzell. Her father was principal of a school at Hjorthagen, a suburb of Stockholm, and volunteer organist in the parish church, in which capacity he also led the church choir. Outstanding among the choristers was his own teen-age daughter, then a high school student in Stockholm, who was frequently assigned the solo parts. One Sunday the services celebrating the completion of a new chapel were attended by the late Crown Princess Margaret of Sweden and from that day young Karin's career was assured: impressed by the girl's voice, and learning that she would like to become a singer, the princess arranged to sponsor her musical study. After several years as a pupil of Thekla Hofer in Stockholm, Karin Branzell made her debut with the Stockholm Royal Opera Company in 1912, singing the mezzo-soprano role of Amneris in *Aïda*. And in that and the following seasons she added to her repertory, among other roles, Nancy in Von Flotow's *Martha*, Carmen, Ortrud, even the soprano Brünnhilde in *Die Walküre*.

The singer remained with the Stockholm Royal Opera through 1918. Meanwhile, her first appearance outside her native land came at a Festival Concert in Copenhagen, to which she had been invited together with the noted Swedish baritone John Forsell. It was at this concert, relates *Opera News*, that the other artists made way as a distinguished figure came toward the nervous young guest: silently Jan Sibelius bent to kiss her hand in homage. A short while later in Gothenburg she earned new laurels when she sang the title role in Gluck's *Orfeo* eleven times in thirteen days to sold-out houses. Her success in Sweden attracted the attention of other opera companies and in 1919 Mme. Branzell was engaged for the Berlin State Opera. Because her performances had hertofore been sung in Swedish, this meant that she had to relearn her entire repertory in the new language, and the pronunciation of "ich" and "sch" gave her trouble, she admits, even though she had acquired a speaking knowledge of German while in school. Subsequent guest appearances in Stockholm, when she sang in the language of the opera presented, sometimes necessitated a third relearning of a role. During this period in Berlin Mme. Branzell also continued her vocal studies with Louis Bachner, with whom Marjorie Lawrence '40 and Sigrid Onegin likewise worked. (Later she was to study with Enrico Rosati in New York, and with the late noted teacher Anna Schoen-René.)

Several seasons after her German debut, Mme. Branzell received a telegram summoning her to an audition in Vienna with Giulio Gatti-Casazza and Artur Bodanzky of the Metropolitan Opera and their agent Norbert Salter, but she was not given a contract. "I sang rotten," she has explained to an *Opera News* interviewer. The next season, however, Bodanzky heard her as Ortrud and dispatched Salter to arrange a second audition. "My voice went

G. Nelidoff

KARIN BRANZELL

hoarse from fright," the singer relates. "I hurried to the doctor first, then I sang. I came away with a Metropolitan contract for five years." When she made her Metropolitan debut as Fricka in *Die Walküre* on February 6, 1924, New York critics hailed a "new, important, and admirable addition" to the company's ranks. "A woman of gigantic stature, she loomed over even Margaret Matzenauer on the stage," said the *Times* critic. "Not only that, her voice has the range, the power and the quality required by Wagner's orchestra and his treatment of ancient Nordic legend." "She seemed at her ease," wrote the *Sun and Globe* reviewer, "strong in her attacks, respectably capable in her use of a smooth voice. . . .She acts with regulation stir and Wagnerian gesture." And W. J. Henderson of the *Sun*: "She is a woman of fine presence . . . the fortunate possessor of a very beautiful mezzo-soprano voice which has the vein of contralto in its timbre. . . .The newcomer sang like an artist of fine instincts and intelligence. The passage 'Deiner ewigen Gattin heilige Ehre' was delivered with genuine grandeur of style."

In the three remaining months of the season Mme. Branzell demonstrated her versatility in the German, Italian, and French repertory, and the wide range of her voice, to New York audiences. Two days after her debut she sang her first Metropolitan Ortrud; in March her first Metropolitan Brangäne and again the soprano role of the *Walküre* Brünnhilde; in April, her first Metropolitan Amneris and Azucena in Verdi's *Aïda* and *Il Trovatore* and Dalila in Saint-Saëns' *Samson et Dalila.* The next season she added the Sexton's Widow at the second New York performance of Leos Janacek's *Jenufa,* the *Götterdämmerung* Waltraute and the *Rheingold* Erda, and at the Academy of Music in Brooklyn on January 27, 1925, having completed her own task of the

BRANZELL, KARIN—*Continued*

evening at the end of the second act of *Die Walküre,* she executed the unusual feat of stepping from the role of Fricka to that of Brünnhilde when Julia Claussen, the production's soprano, lost her voice. The following year the singer appeared as Laura in *La Gioconda* and as Venus in the performance of *Tannhäuser* at which Lauritz Melchior '⁴¹ made his debut, and subsequently as the *Siegfried* Erda, as Fides in Meyerbeer's *Le Prophète,* and as Maddalena in *Die Meistersinger.* On November 7, 1931, she created the part of the Queen at the American première of Jaromir Weinberger's *Schwanda.* The next season she sang her first Klytemnestra in Richard Strauss's '⁴ *Elektra,* and on January 29, 1934, her first Herodias in that composer's *Salome.*

The critics said she possessed "one of the most beautiful voices in opera" (New York *Evening World*), "a gorgeous and opulent voice" (Olin Downes '⁴³), "one of those round, thrillingly textured contralto voices" (Chicago *Tribune*). They praised her portrayal of Italian heroines and especially her "magnificent" Herodias, but they dwelt longest on the distinguished contralto's Wagnerian interpretations. Wrote Henderson in the New York *Sun*: "Mme. Branzell's Venus was . . . admirable vocally, impressive physically, and sung with rich golden tone." To which Irving Weil added in the *Journal*: "Karin Branzell is indeed the best Venus seen or heard on the stage since the stirring days of Olive Fremstad." The Philadelphia *Public Ledger* found her "a superb Brangäne in voice, drama, and stage presence . . . [interpreting] the role with that mixture of affection for Isolde and fierceness for those whom she believes to be her enemies which is so seldom adequately portrayed." In the opinion of Irving Kolodin her Maddalena in *Meistersinger* was "an impersonation better sung and acted than any other the role has had since the [First World] War." While Samuel Chotzinoff '⁴⁰ noted that here was an artist who had "not permitted experience to degenerate into routine. Her Waltraute was not only beautifully sung but it was a moving characterization of a very womanly goddess."

"Culture and intelligence," wrote Hanna Astrup Larsen, editor of the *American-Scandinavian Review* and a "confirmed Wagnerite," in 1935, "are the words that come first to mind in speaking of this admirable Swedish singer. Her voice is perfectly trained, every note full, round, and smooth. . . .Great versatility is demanded by the many contralto roles which in Wagner add so much to the effect of the whole. To each she brings her best, and her art lends distinction even to the minor parts. . . .[She] keeps her Fricka on the plane Wagner intended, always a goddess, though roused to angry defense of the established order against Wotan who yearns ever for the unknown. . . .Resisting the temptation to make Brangäne a second heroine, she dresses and acts the part of the faithful, affectionate maid, an effective foil to her young mistress, and by her careful adaptation of herself to the part she achieves distinction. . . .[In the distinguished

company of Kirsten Flagstad, Lauritz Melchior, and Friedrich Schorr '⁴²,] Karin Branzell holds a high place."

Success at the Metropolitan brought Mme. Branzell invitations from the world's leading opera centers: from London's Covent Garden (where Konchakovna in Borodin's *Prince Igor* was one of her roles) ; from the Teatro Colon in Buenos Aires (where during the summer of 1935 alone she participated in fifteen Wagnerian performances under Fritz Busch '⁴⁵ as well as in Bach's *Passion According to St. Matthew* and *B Minor Mass* likewise under Busch's direction) ; from the Vienna State Opera and from the Royal Opera in Stockholm. Until 1933 she also remained on the roster of the Berlin State Opera. In 1931 and 1932 she participated in the Bayreuth Festival; in 1937, in the Florence Festival; in the summer of 1939, in the Zurich Music Festival. Her Munich debut occurred in the fall of 1935 during a season—which she considers "one of the greatest successes" of her career—when she sang thirty-six times in a varied German, Italian and French repertory to enthusiastic acclaim. The next spring Munich also saw her first Adriano in Wagner's *Rienzi.* When not fulfilling operatic engagements Mme. Branzell toured in concert in the United States, South America, Europe and Russia, both as orchestral soloist and as *Lieder* singer, and she earned warm praise in presentations of Beethoven's Ninth Symphony, Mahler's *Kindertotenlieder,* and the *St. Matthew Passion* and *Mass in B Minor* of Bach. In 1932 she received from King Gustav V of Sweden the coveted Litteris et Artibus decoration and in 1936 (after a performance of *Carmen*) the even rarer title of "Singer of the Court"—the highest distinctions Sweden can confer upon a singer.

At the conclusion of the 1943-44 season, her twentieth, the contralto, one of the relatively few women to have continued in leading roles at the Metropolitan for that length of time, announced her retirement from the operatic stage, expressing the hope that she was thus making a place for some gifted young American artist. In the years that followed she toured the United States in a series of *Lieder* recitals. Occasionally she accepted a guest engagement in opera, one such being to sing in *Aïda* with the Stockholm Royal Opera in the summer of 1946.

It was her famous predecessor Louise Homer who predicted a brilliant recital career for Mme. Branzell, and her first appearance in Town Hall on February 4, 1945, after a long absence from New York's concert platform, impressed itself upon the critics as a "truly memorable" performance, a "red-letter" musical event. The next day Harriett Johnson wrote in the *Post,* "Karin Branzell's luscious contralto has the quality of irridescence. Like a prism, its vibrations send out an abundance of beauty. . . .A singer in her prime, richly mature." "It was not only in the technical perfection of her art that Miss Branzell excelled," reported Jerome D. Bohm in the *Herald Tribune.* "Her interpretations revealed flawless taste and musicianship, as well as apparently limitless imaginative resources that made her work a sheer delight."

In a more searching analysis, indicative of Mme. Branzell's artistry not only in this but in subsequent concerts, Noel Straus wrote in the *Times*: "The keen intelligence, deep understanding and ability to file down voluminous tones to the needs of a given song were nowhere more in evidence than in the superbly delivered 'Der Lindenbaum' and 'Der Tod und das Mädchen' among the Schubert *Lieder*. Not only was the atmosphere of each strikingly summoned forth, but every phrase was a marvel of sensitive coloring and expertly perfected tone, projected with the utmost sensitivity of feeling. On a high level, too, was the treatment of the four songs of the Mahler cycle, which reached its climax with a notably intense and tragic reading of the stormy 'Ich hab' ein glühend Messer,' in which the full glory of the voice, with its bright upper reaches and uniquely pure, rich lower tones, came into play with arresting effectiveness. And it was with a deftness beyond praise that Miss Branzell, with so ample a voice, was able to sing the lofty pianissimi in the final lyric of the set with such absolute command and assurance."

In early 1946 Mme. Branzell's appointment to the faculty of the reorganized Juilliard School of Music, to take effect October 1, 1946, was announced by its new president, the young American composer William Schuman. In September word was received in New York that she had been decorated by Denmark with the Medal of Liberation of King Christian X in appreciation of her contribution to the cause of Danish freedom during World War II. Since April 29, 1938, Mme. Branzell has been married to Fedya Reinshagen, a former operatic stage director who now acts as her personal representative. A tall five feet eleven, weighing a hundred and eighty pounds, with blond hair and green eyes, the Swedish singer was said by *Opera News* in 1942 to have remained as young in heart as her romping cocker spaniel Penny. She "confronts life with the wonder of a child," the magazine continued. "A sunset on her beloved coast of Maine, the skill of an amateur at the piano, the generosity of a friend, a swim, a flower, a compliment: they all elicit from her a wide-eyed delight. . . .Sorrow calls for a resignation that is in itself a thing of beauty. Joy is always unexpected and fresh to her touch. Routine does not exist at all. . . .It is Brangäne and Waltraute . . . which mirror her own personality and give to the public something of the impress of this generous woman whose affections run deep, but whose simple comradeship has made her one of the most beloved members of the Metropolitan family."

References

Opera N 4:16+ Mr 25 '40 por; 7:5 D 28 '42 por; 8:25+ Ja 31 '44 por
Ewen, D. ed. Living Musicians (1940) por
Macmillan Encyclopedia of Music and Musicians (1938)
Taylor, D. and Russell, K. eds. Music Lovers' Encyclopedia (1939)
Thompson, O. ed. International Cyclopedia of Music and Musicians (1943)
Who Is Who in Music, 1941

BRICE, FANNY Oct. 29, 1891- Actress; singer

Address: b. c/o Young and Rubicam, Inc., 6253 Hollywood Blvd., Hollywood, Calif.

America's radio listeners know Fanny Brice as the creator of the voice of an incorrigible little girl, the "Baby Snooks" who every Friday asks "Why-y-y, Daddy?" The older generation remembers Miss Brice as one of the greatest comediennes of the two decades after World War I: a star of Florenz Ziegfeld's *Follies,* the young singer of "demonaic vitality" with a gift for devastating mimicry. Today Fanny Brice continues to be among the most popular of American entertainers.

Fannie Borach changed her name to Brice when she went on the stage because she was tired of being called "More-Ache" and "Bore-Act" by waggish friends; and in recent years she has shortened the "ie" of her first name to "y." The daughter of Jewish parents—Alsatian Charles Borach and his Hungarian wife, Rose (Stern) Borach—Fannie was born October 29, 1891, on Forsyth Street of New York's lower East Side. Her father owned several saloons, which her mother helped to run and for which she prepared free lunches. "In those days," writes Niven Busch of Fannie in *Twenty-one Americans* (1930), "she used to steal beer from her father to give to neighboring women who were sick . . . her outward physical pity was supplemented by an altered but similar feeling directed toward herself. She wanted people to feel sorry for her." To the girls who worked with her, wrapping packages in a department store, she said that her father was blind and her family was starving—"I had them all crying and I loved it." She and her brother Lew would go to Coney Island, stop passers-by and tearfully ask directions for walking home to Brooklyn. Invariably the children were offered carfare, which they spent on "hot dogs" and merry-go-round rides.

Fannie was an occasional student at Brooklyn public schools—"I ran away from every school I ever went to, or if I didn't I was thrown out." It was people, not book learning, that interested her. "The steaming clothes strung across the tenement kitchens; bathing the newest baby; . . . the apartments without air, without light—there was never any ugliness or sordidness in all this for me." In the streets where she grew up (New York's lower East Side, St. Marks Place in Brooklyn, and 128th Street at the edge of Harlem) she learned the European accents she was later to use in comedy dialect songs. Fannie and the neighborhood newsboys sang for pennies in backyards and poolrooms. Urged by the "newsies," at thirteen she entered an amateur night contest at Keeney's Theatre in Brooklyn, at which she sang "When You Know You're Not Forgotten by the Girl You Can't Forget." For this she won the ten-dollar first prize and three dollars in coins the audience had tossed on the stage. By the time Fannie was fourteen she was averaging thirty dollars a week in amateur night winnings. Her first job, with a Cohan and Harris revue as a chorus girl,

FANNY BRICE

was short-lived; after watching her dance at rehearsal, George M. Cohan fired her. At fifteen she trouped through Pennsylvania in a show, *A Royal Slave,* in which she reposed on the boards in the role of an alligator.

Back in New York, Fanny Brice sang and danced in Hurtig and Seamon's *The Transatlantic Burlesque.* In 1910 the nineteen-year-old-performer was appearing in Max Spiegel's *College Girl* at the Columbia Burlesque House for twenty-five dollars a week, when young Irving Berlin gave her a song called "Sadie Salome" and suggested she sing it with a Yiddish accent. Into her interpretation of the song she put the spirit of "Loscha of the Coney Island popcorn counter and Marta of the cheeses at Brodsky's delicatessen, and the Sadies and the Rachels and the Birdies with the turnover heels at the Second Avenue dance halls." It was a hit with the audience. After Florenz Ziegfeld saw her performance he made her a headliner in the *Follies of 1910* at the Jardin de Paris in New York. ("I could never write the story of my life without half of it being Ziegfeld," Miss Brice has said.) Diamond Jim Brady gave a supper party for the stars of the *Follies* after the show's opening, and that night Miss Brice was ushered into a world "where ten-carat diamonds were used as buttons on underwear, and hundred-dollar bills were slipped under plates for no reason at all except that you were on the stage."

After 1910 Miss Brice appeared in most editions of the *Follies* produced by Ziegfeld—those of 1911, 1916, 1917, 1920, 1921, and 1923. She also played vaudeville, appearing in London in 1914, and she played in several farces, among them *The Honeymoon Express* (1913) and *Why Worry?* (1918). Ten years of success were behind her when Ziegfeld asked her one night in 1921, "Do you think you can

make them cry?" With that, he handed her "My Man," a lyric by Channing Pollock for the French song "Mon Homme." "She sang it without gestures," writes Busch, "her strong contralto giving an unforgettable reality to the crude words of the verse, the haunting repetitive tune." "My Man" was to become an almost legendary song hit and "the Brice trademark."

In the 1920's Miss Brice was being "discovered by the intellectuals." In his *Seven Lively Arts* (1924) Gilbert Seldes [41] announced that she and Al Jolson [40] were "geniuses." Burton Rascoe considered that Fanny Brice was the greatest comedienne he had ever been privileged to see. Famous for her skill at caricature and satire, her impersonation of "the vamp," her burlesques of classical ballet, modern dance, and "concert-room vocalism," and her rendition of songs such as "I Should Worry", "Second-Hand Rose," and probably most memorable of all, "My Man," she continued to star in the *Follies* until 1923. After *Music Box Revue* (1924), and a vaudeville tour in 1925-26, she decided to do something serious. Although her face, with its blue eyes and large mouth, could be handsome when she was not "mugging," her nose, she thought, was inevitably funny. Accordingly, she had it straightened by plastic surgery for her first attempt at a more serious play, *Fanny,* produced by Belasco in 1926. Of *Fanny* Busch has written, "Fairly successful in spite of its faults, it served principally to make people wonder what she could do if she ever got a good play."

In 1929 Fanny Brice played the Marchesa Vera Di Livio in *Fioretta*—"sword play and passion," reported the *New Yorker,* "in Earl Carroll's Venice of the eighteenth century." That year she was married to Billy Rose, in 1930 appeared in his revue *Sweet and Low,* and in 1931 headlined *Billy Rose's Crazy Quilt.* But Miss Brice made her biggest hit after the death of Ziegfeld, when she was starred with Willie Howard in the Shubert *Ziegfeld Follies* in 1934. "The skilled and subtle one, with an evil talent for sly dissection of all that is fake and preposterous," was *Literary Digest*'s description of her. "Miss Brice, with . . . a spirit which mounts plainly to genius, destroys such amiable cornerstones of the map as lady evangelists who run to flowing white garments, pop-eyed fan dancers . . . problem children."

Fanny Brice made her first film appearance in 1928, in *My Man,* for Warner Brothers. Subsequently she acted in *Be Yourself* (1930), lent a note of authenticity to *The Great Ziegfeld* (1936) by playing herself for Metro-Goldwyn-Mayer, performed in *Everybody Sing* (1938), and did a specialty in the picture *Ziegfeld Follies* (1946). Her radio career began in 1932—a "straight singing job" with George Olsen's orchestra in a short-lived radio series. Four years later, with Hanley Stafford as Daddy she introduced Baby Snooks to the air waves. Snooks was based on a character Miss Brice had spontaneously created at a party in 1921, and had used again for sketches in

Sweet and Low and in the *Follies* of 1934 and 1936. A second "Baby Snooks" radio series began in December 1937 (the *Good News* show), and since then Snooks has been on the air almost continuously. In 1946, Miss Brice at fifty-four celebrated Snooks's silver anniversary. While the character is the actress' creation, the chatter of the four-and-a-half-year-old *enfant terrible* is prepared by three writers —Miss Brice seldom ad libs. Paid $6,000 a week for her half-hour show, the comedienne considers it "stealing money" because she "could do Snooks blind." She says, "I don't have to work into it. It's part of me."

Fanny Brice's first marriage was annulled. By her second husband, Nicholas Arnstein, to whom she was married in 1918, Miss Brice has two children, William and Frances. This marriage ended in divorce in 1927. Two years later Miss Brice and Billy Rose were married; they were divorced nine years later. Fanny Brice is red-haired, five feet seven inches tall, and weighs 130 pounds. She has an active interest in the arts. Her collection of paintings by children was exhibited in the Associated American Artists galleries in 1944. Besides painting in oils herself, Miss Brice designs dresses—in her days on the stage she was known to say to a chorus girl, "Bring four and a half yards of silk to rehearsal tomorrow, and I'll make you a dress." Another of her talents is interior decorating. Among the homes she has decorated are those of the Eddie Cantors, the Ira Gershwins, Dinah Shore, and Katharine Hepburn. She also cooks with skill, specializing in Hungarian dishes. According to Busch, "her generosity is noted even in a profession in which generosity is a tradition."

References

Cosmopolitan 100:20 F '36 por
Good H 116:38 Mr '43 por
New Yorker 5:25-7 Ap 20 '29
Newsweek 27:60 Mr 11 '46 por
Seldes, G. Seven Lively Arts (1924)
Who's Who in America, 1946-47
Who's Who in the Theatre (1939)

BRINK, CAROL (RYRIE) (rī'rē) Dec. 28, 1895- Author
Address: h. 2243 Hoyt Ave., St. Paul, Minn.

A catholicity of interests distinguishes Carol Brink, whose career reconciles the duties of wife and mother with the activities of traveler, editor, historian, researcher, poet, and author of prose books for children and adults.

Carol Ryrie Brink's literary forebears include Lyman Abbott (a cousin of her maternal grandfather) and Jacob Abbott (her grandfather's uncle), who was the author of "The Rollo Books," the popular early juveniles. While she can also lay claim to descent from English nobility through her maternal grandmother (a member of the Woodhouse family), the author declares she values more highly the qualities she inherited from the peasant Scottish stock of her father, Alexander Ryrie. He

H. A. Fairchild
CAROL BRINK

had come from Scotland at the age of twenty, going West to settle in Idaho when it was not yet a State. There he had been married to Henrietta Watkins, the daugher of a pioneer doctor and had become the first mayor of Moscow, the Idaho town in which Carol Ryrie was born December 28, 1895.

Little Carol lost both her parents before she was eight, and went to live with her grandmother and an unmarried aunt in a comfortable old house with a large garden. Although she "had a good many troubles in those days—death, disaster, loneliness"—yet she had a happy childhood, "petted and spoiled" by her aunt, "a second mother" to her, and reveling in the reminiscences of her grandmother, whose qualities of "tolerance, impartiality, and a detached philosophical attitude toward life" endeared her to the child.

During her school days in Idaho and at the Portland (Oregon) Academy, Carol Ryrie became interested in writing, and some of her poetry was published in small magazines. This and other writing continued through her three years at the University of Idaho and her year at the University of California, from which she was graduated with a B.A. degree in 1918. On June 12 of that year she was married to Raymond Woodard Brink, a young mathematics instructor whom she had known for many years. They moved to St. Paul, Minnesota, where he taught at the university and where they still make their home.

When her husband went to Scotland to teach for a year at the University of Edinburgh, Mrs. Brink and their six-week-old son went along to her father's homeland. The nine months in Scotland were followed by travel on the Continent and several years' residence in France.

(Continued next page)

BRINK, CAROL—*Continued*

Her sojourn abroad provided Carol Brink with the material for her first book. She had begun to specialize in writing for children about 1925 and for several years her short stories had appeared in the *American Girl, Child Life,* and *Story Parade,* as well as in the children's story papers. *Anything Can Happen on the River* (1934) tells of the exciting adventures of a young French boy on the Seine and reflects many of the experiences of the Brink family in France. Anne T. Eaton, writing in the New York *Times,* thought that the book showed promise—she pointed out the individuality of the characters and the "lively and direct" style.

This book was followed by *Caddie Woodlawn,* in which Carol Brink "recreated her grandmother's pioneer childhood as a lively little girl on the Wisconsin border in Civil War days." "Writing the story," said the author, "has been like weaving a tapestry." A favorite with children, this book was awarded the John Newbery Medal in 1935 for the year's most distinguished contribution to juvenile literature. Later books were *Mademoiselle Misfortune* (1936), a return to the French locale; *Baby Island* (1937), a humorous account of two shipwrecked young girls who care for four infants; *All Over Town* (1939); *Lad With a Whistle* (1941), the story of a Scotch boy. All were well received with such comments as "lively", "amusing", "reads well," and praise for good character development and skillful writing technique. In 1944 the author resumed the pioneer theme with *Magical Melons,* a book of short stories featuring "Caddie Woodlawn." "The writing is fresh and the homely happenings ring true not only of a period and a way of life but of childhood any time and anywhere," was the opinion of the *New Yorker*'s critic.

Mrs. Brink's books for adults include *Buffalo Coat* (1944), a story of a small Idaho town in the 1890's. According to the New York *Times,* this novel "possesses what has always seemed . . . the first prerequisite of a good historical novel: the characters are timeless in their motivations, their emotions, their essential humanness, yet their destinies are molded and determined by the effect of a particular era and environment." "Harps in the Wind," scheduled for publication in 1946, is the tale of the singing Hutchinson family and required the historical research which Mrs. Brink enjoys as a hobby as well as a vocation.

At the same time that Mrs. Brink was occupied with her creative output, she was editor of *Best Short Stories for Children* in 1935, and editor of *Best Short Stories for Boys and Girls* from 1936 to 1939. She was also a member of the 1941 Yearbook Commission of the American Association of School Administrators and served as national chairman of juveniles for the National League of American Pen Women.

Mrs. Brink has found that books offer more opportunity than do short stories for the "leisurely character development" which she enjoys. She admits to liking books with "some solid foundation of truth or personal experience" as well as some imaginative writing. She has managed to crowd into her busy writing years the authorship of children's plays and of well over 150 stories for children which have been published by various magazines. She has also received numerous poetry awards, including a $100 prize for "The Men."

The gray-eyed, brown-haired author, who "finds life with her family and her friends a full and satisfactory experience," has a son, David Ryrie, and a daughter, Nora Caroline. She collects old juvenile books, and as hobbies enjoys painting, drawing, and various handicrafts. She also likes to hike, ride horseback, and travel.

References

Pub W 129:1954+ My 16 '36 por
American Women, 1939-40
Richards, C. N. and Breen, G. R. eds. Minnesota Writes (1945)
Who's Who in America, 1946-47
Who's Who in Minnesota, 1941

BROMLEY, DOROTHY DUNBAR, Dec. 25, 1896- Editor; writer

Address: b. c/o New York Herald Tribune, 230 W. 41st St., New York; h. 129 E. 10th St., New York

Dorothy Dunbar Bromley, author of books and articles on social, legal, and health topics, is the editor of a new kind of "woman's page" in a metropolitan newspaper, where discussions of local, national, or international significance occupy the space once given to club news.

The third of four children, Dorothy Dunbar Bromley was born Dorothy Ewing Dunbar, on a farm near Ottawa, Illinois, on Christmas Day of 1896. Her parents, Helen Elizabeth (Ewing) and Charles E. Dunbar had moved to the farm after her father had given up teaching. Later the family again moved successively to the northern Illinois towns of Grand Ridge and Plano, where the girl received part of her early education. She completed grade school in Toledo, Ohio, to which her father had taken his wife and children after he had abandoned farming to work in the insurance business. From Toledo the Dunbars went to Chicago, and there Dorothy attended the Hyde Park High School. In 1914 she won one of twenty-five scholarships awarded anonymously through the Chicago *American.* After her first year at Northwestern University, she earned her tuition by tutoring grade and high school pupils in English and mathematics; and by taking summer courses she completed the required four years' work for her B.A. degree in three. A Phi Beta Kappa student, she was graduated *cum laude* in 1917.

After teaching English for six months at the Antigo High School in Wisconsin, Miss Dunbar decided to change her vocation. Having minored in French at Northwestern, she enlisted, in the spring after the United States entered World War I, in the French-speaking women's telephone unit attached to the Signal Corps. She did not go overseas as she had anticipated, but she did enjoy the wartime duties she performed as long distance operator in Atlantic City for the American Telephone and Telegraph Company.

After the war, Dorothy Dunbar found employment in the statistical department of the Ford, Bacon and Davis Engineering Company at a salary of one hundred dollars a month. In the evening she took an accelerated course in shorthand and typing. Six months later, when she had completed her business studies, she left the job to live with her elder sister, a schoolteacher in Detroit. During the year Miss Dunbar lived in that city she was secretary to the editor of the Detroit *Free Press* and was given an opportunity to write book reviews. In August 1920 she was married to Donald C. Bromley, a graduate of the University of Michigan who was vacationing in Detroit from his YMCA job in East Orange, New Jersey. From New Jersey the young couple moved to New York City where Mrs. Bromley went to work with the publishers Henry Holt and Company, first as secretary, then as publicity assistant. She also read manuscripts and later did some editorial work for the firm, which was then small and offered numerous opportunities for advancement during the five years she was in its employ from 1921 to 1925. (In the meantime her husband and she had separated and were divorced.) She next devoted a year as advertising manager to the George H. Doran Company, the publishers, after which she resigned, in 1926, to write on her own time.

Mrs. Bromley received her first encouragement from the editor of *Harper's* Magazine, the late Thomas B. Wells. A supporter of the feminist movement, he suggested that she do research in the field of divorce for the purpose of determining under what circumstances women should receive financial support from their former husbands. In her investigations of divorce case histories, the writer received assistance from lawyer friends. In "Ethics of Alimony," the product of a month's study and the first of her writings to appear in *Harper's* (February 1927), Mrs. Bromley mentioned the suggestion, made by a member of the legal profession, that a signed ethical marriage contract would help to correct the injustices which some spouses inflicted on each other, and might eventually form the basis for sounder marriage and divorce laws. Mrs. Bromley has reported that before *Harper's* published her next article, "Market Value of a Paris Divorce," it submitted her study to an authority on international law, who found only a few minor errors in her presentation.

In the various articles Mrs. Bromley wrote for *Harper's* Magazine, particularly in "Feminist—New Style" and "Diogenes Looks At the Ladies," she enunciated what is still her philosophy on women in the modern world. Women should strive to become "complete people" working in harmony with men. In "Are Women a Success In Business" she declared, "These, then, are the virtues for which women must strive: a sense of fair play, a sense of values, and discretion. But greater than any of these, men say, is business acumen." Mrs. Bromley's commentary "What Risk Motherhood" (*Harper's* June 1929), one

DOROTHY DUNBAR BROMLEY

of a series she did on maternity deaths, was reprinted for use by doctors in maternity clinics. The editor of the *American Journal of Obstetrics and Gynecology*, Dr. George W. Kosmak, enabled Mrs. Bromley to obtain the information she required and also read her articles before they were published. Margaret Sanger, whom she esteems, also helped Mrs. Bromley, whose printed reports gave considerable impetus to the birth control movement. Mrs. Bromley also wrote for *Good Housekeeping*, the *Woman Citizen* and the New York Sunday *Times*. Because of her frequent contributions *Harper's* often printed her articles under a masculine pseudonym. During the years she free-lanced (1926-34) she averaged an income of five thousand dollars annually.

In 1932 Mrs. Bromley left the United States for a year to do further writing and research in Europe. She spent a month in England, three weeks in Denmark, and the rest of the time in France. In Denmark she observed the advance of the social services and the progress women had made in various professions. In France she interviewed a number of outstanding people, including Léon Blum. Later, in their Brittany home and in their Paris laboratory, she visited the co-recipients of the Nobel Chemistry Prize, Mme. Curie's daughter Irene, and her husband, Frédéric Joliet. Frédéric Joliet, who a short while earlier had helped to discover the neutron, predicted to his guest the eventual smashing of the atom. Mrs. Bromley also spoke with several French lawyers and feminist leaders in order to learn their reaction to the French woman's demand for suffrage.

On her return to the United States, Mrs Bromley became absorbed in the book her previous research on birth control had inspired her to write. *Birth Control, Its Use and Misuse* (1934) was the outgrowth of intensive study, visits to maternity clinics in New York City, and the letters she exchanged with similar

BROMLEY, DOROTHY DUNBAR—
Continued

institutions throughout the country. In a laudatory introduction to the book Dr. Robert Latou Dickenson, who worked closely with its author in the selection of the data, remarked: "Health and security hang on education and protection. When the teacher dare not teach and the doctor is threatened for instruction, the gap must be filled by the school of the book." He found Mrs. Bromley's book accurate, readable and opportune. A number of lay and medical critics commended *Birth Control* as a "valuable contribution to the welfare of humanity." (In 1946 its publishers sold the Spanish rights to the book.)

Mrs. Bromley's first book was partly responsible for her appointment as columnist on the women's page of the New York *World-Telegram* in 1935. Prior to this, the January 30, 1935, issue of the *Nation* had carried her article "The Newspapers and Child Labor," a reproof of certain papers for their indifference and, in many cases, opposition to the child labor amendment. During the three years Mrs. Bromley wrote for the *World-Telegram*, she collaborated with Florence Haxton Britten on another sociological book, published in 1938. In *Youth and Sex*, the authors, aided by replies to questionnaires and personal interviews, analyze the attitude of thirteen hundred college students toward the problems of sex. Said the authors: "We chose college students for the purpose of this study because they are easier to reach in large numbers, because they are more articulate, and because their academic training inclined them to be receptive to sociological inquiry which required their co-operation on an impersonal basis." The concensus of opinion, as expressed by Robert Bierstedt of the *Saturday Review of Literature*, was that the authors had accomplished a difficult job with unusual success.

After Mrs. Bromley resigned from the *World-Telegram* in 1938, she conducted a column in the New York *Post*, only to return to independent writing in 1940. Among the articles she wrote in that two-year period was "Education for Life or for College" (*Harper's* March 1941), wherein she declared: "It is time that we base our system of education on a democratic rather than on an aristocratic ideal." However, she missed her activities in the newspaper field, and when she was invited in 1942 to become editor of the Women's Activities Page of the Sunday edition of the New York *Herald Tribune,* she readily accepted. Her page soon gave evidence of the wide interests of the women of today. In her new position she has written on subjects requiring long investigation, such as the prisoner of war camps in the United States and the reforms required at the Walter Reed General Hospital in Washington, D.C. She has stressed the relief needs of the wartorn countries, equality for racial and religious minorities in the United States, and the need for reform in New York City's public schools. She has championed a minimum wage for store clerks and opposed

peacetime military training. In early 1946 she reminded her readers of the suffering of the people in the famine areas. In a plea for greater aid from Americans she wrote: "Every million tons [of wheat] that are not shipped abroad will mean that twenty million people will have to go without bread for six months. This will mean starvation and death since bread is the main article of diet in the European countries that are desperate for food. And along with Europe, there is India, in the direst need of all." Mrs. Bromley had an opportunity to see India's famine areas when she flew to that country as a press representative on a one-month trip with the American Famine Mission.

A member of the board of directors of the American Civil Liberties Union since 1938, Mrs. Bromley has won special recognition (in 1939 and again five years later) from the New York Newspaper Women's Club for her skill in presenting social problems. The second time she won a prize for the "best article of special interest to women" with her entry, "We Didn't Stop to Think," the story of two delinquent girls. In 1944 she was one of the speakers at a luncheon given to celebrate the fiftieth anniversary of the founding of New York's Town Hall. In June of the following year she participated in a *People's Platform* radio discussion on "Have We An Adequate Program for Disabled Veterans?" Shortly after the publication of *Strange Fruit*, Mrs. Bromley was the first to interview its author, Lillian Smith'", whom she considers a woman of great courage.

A trimly-built woman, Mrs. Bromley is of medium height and has blue eyes and light brown hair. She spends her leisure reading, when she is in the city. At other times she enjoys gardening on her New York farm in southern Dutchess County.

Reference

Women of Achievement (1940)

BROWNE, EDWARD E(VERTS) Feb. 16, 1868—Nov. 23, 1945 Lawyer; Wisconsin Republican Representative to United States Congress (1913-31); served in the Wisconsin State Senate (1906-12); drafted the first State Aid to Highways bill and a State Park law; leader of game conservation in Wisconsin.

Obituary

N Y Times p19 N 24 '45

BROWNE, GEORGE ELMER May 6, 1871—July 13, 1946 Artist; considered one of the foremost painters in the naturalistic school in the United States; won many awards, including the Altman five-hundred-dollar prize of the National Academy of Design, 1934, and the Gold Medal of Honor, awarded at the annual exhibition of the Allied Artists of America, 1928; conducted classes and exhibited in America and abroad; president of the Allied Artists of America, 1930-37, of Salmagundi Club, 1935-36.

Obituary

N Y Times p36 Jl 14 '46 por

BRUCE, WILLIAM CABELL Mar. 12, 1860—May 9, 1946 Senator and writer; won the Pulitzer Prize for biography in 1919 with *Benjamin Franklin, Self-Revealed*; Democratic United States Senator from Maryland 1923-29; fought against prohibition; often opposed the wishes of the majority of his party in the Senate; favored Federal antilynching legislation and opposed the Ku Klux Klan.

Obituary

N Y Times p19 My 10 '46 por

BUCKMASTER, HENRIETTA 1909- Author; journalist

Address: h. 63 W. 11th St., New York

Author Henrietta Buckmaster believes that historical events can be depicted in fiction form with the objectivity of the historical record and yet be presented in such a light as to give them meaning in terms of the present day. Her chief interest is the Civil War period in American history, which, together with the cause of the Negro, is the background and substance of her historical novels.

Henrietta Buckmaster, who chose another surname for her pseudonym, was born Henrietta Henkle in Cleveland, in 1909, the daughter of Rae D. Henkle and Pearl (Wintermute) Henkle. Her father was a newspaper publisher who died only a few years ago. His influence upon her early years was tremendous, she says: had he not been exceedingly patient in reading to her when she was very young and in showing her what a pleasant and exhilarating business writing could be, she might very well never have become a writer. When she was twelve, *Child Life* published one of her stories, and so far as she can remember she was trying to write something or other most of the time over the next five years.

She was educated privately—at the Friends Seminary and at the Brearley School, both in New York City. By the time she was about seventeen she had begun to do book reviews for the *Christian Science Monitor*, the New York *Sun*, the *Saturday Review of Literature*, and other magazines. She looks back on this achievement with considerably mixed feelings. For although it may have provided her with a sort of sustained stimulus, it developed what she now regards as an almost cruel self-indulgence. Once she became entrenched in her own novels her respect for an author's sensitivities made it difficult, if not impossible, to do any reviewing. She cannot, even now, with conscience, let herself "sit in judgment on other peoples' work." Only very rarely will she agree to review a book.

For some six or eight years after her reviewing stint Miss Buckmaster was occupied most of the time in editing for magazines— first for a number of McFadden publications and then for *Harper's Bazaar* and *Reader's Digest*. In the early thirties came her first novel, *Tomorrow Is Another Day* (1934), an introspective story of "youth's aspirations and ambitions, and its alternate moods of melancholy and discouragement." The critic of the

HENRIETTA BUCKMASTER

New York *Times* found it "thoughtful in conception . . . but lacking in incident," with "shadowy and unconvincing" characters. Her second book, *His End Was His Beginning* (1936), a novel of prewar and postwar Vienna, "has its moments of vivid and poignant drama," according to Lisle Bell in the New York *Herald Tribune Books*, "but it is written with a shrill intensity more exhausting than exhilarating." Following this she did some work with Ruth St. Denis on her autobiography (*An Unfinished Life*). But it was perhaps not until the publication of her third book, *Let My People Go* (1941), written around the Underground Railroad, that her direction became clearer, her style better defined. Louis Bromfield hailed the story as "exciting and illuminating . . .full of vitality as well as scholarly research."

From her early years Miss Buckmaster had been convinced of the rightness of the antislavery movement, and out of this had come a serious interest in the Negro and his place in the battle of minorities. When she had finished writing *Let My People Go* she was left with much material that had only an indirect application to that book itself. In going over these findings she began to piece together (with additional sources) a second book about virtually the same period: *Deep River* (1944), a picture of Georgia between 1859 and Secession. Orville Prescott, in the *Yale Review*, called the novel prolix and repetitious, but nevertheless a superior performance, written with beauty, with expert dialogue always in dialect. According to the New York *Times*, the book was "that rare thing, a historical novel in which events have moral values and are in themselves founded on ideas." This title won Miss Buckmaster the Ohioana medal for 1944; and because the book went into the Armed Services Editions it brought her mail from many GIs in all parts of the world. Their

BUCKMASTER, HENRIETTA—*Cont.*

letters, she says, were immensely meaningful, but what pleased her most was that many of these readers sensed the fact that from the point of view of social complexity the tale might well have been laid in 1940.

In November 1945 Henrietta Buckmaster went abroad as a representative of *Woman's Day*, to attend the International Women's Conference which met in Paris under the sponsorship of the Comité d'Initiative Internationale. This congress of eight hundred women representing forty-five countries was not a conclave of feminists, but of "citizens" of a tired and still chaotic world, about 90 per cent of whom had been in resistance movements over the long years of the war. Their purpose was to promote world peace, to combat fascism, and to improve the condition of women and children throughout the world. They gathered in Paris at what would seem to have been the most comfortless moment in modern times—the weather was bitter, fuel negligible, food scarce and unvaried, transportation nonexistent, and electricity completely unpredictable (almost never was it on after eight in the evening and French candles evidently give the impression of burning at both ends). Reports of the conference were run off on a broken-down mimeograph machine, and anything that had ever resembled paper was thrown into the mill. Yet, said Miss Buckmaster, the tone of the occasion, right through to the very end, was one of tremendous hope and vigor.

Miss Buckmaster, who in private life is Mrs. Peter J. Stephens, makes a hobby of the theater. She has two books in progress. The first of these is to be a portrayal of Southern women in the 1860's, and the second (the product of her 1944 Guggenheim fellowship) is a "biography of a period," as she puts it, a historical account of William Lloyd Garrison in terms of the age he lived in.

BUELL, RAYMOND LESLIE (bü'ĕl) July 13, 1896—Feb. 20, 1946 American writer, editor, commentator on international affairs; foreign affairs adviser to Time, Incorporated; lectured at leading colleges and universities from 1920; research director, Foreign Policy Association, 1927-33, president 1933-39; chairman Commission on Cuban Affairs, 1934; director of the Geneva Research Center 1935-36; chairman of the Public Affairs Committee 1936-38; member Wendell Willkie's campaign staff 1940; early anti-isolationist.

Obituary

N Y Times p21 F 21 '46 por

BULLIS, HARRY A(MOS) Oct. 7, 1890- Mill executive

Address: b. c/o General Mills, Inc., Minneapolis; h. 2116 West Lake of Isles Blvd., Minneapolis

Harry A. Bullis is president of the world's largest flour millers, General Mills, Incorporated, the creator of the cereals Wheaties, Kix, and Cheerios, of Softasilk cake flour, and Bis-

quick, and of the imaginary advertising personality, Betty Crocker. The company produces two hundred and forty varieties of bakers' flour, two hundred and fifty brands of family flour, and many kinds of commercial feeds sold through sixty-nine of its own farmservice stores. Of late years General Mills has begun a program of product diversification, producing soup concentrates and vitamins, as well as industrial products derived from soybeans and vegetable oils. During the war General Mills expanded its mechanical division, which had made the company's food-packaging machinery and special milling equipment, to be able to accept orders for naval ordnance; for the postwar market General Mills is readying a line of electrical appliances, including electric irons and pressure cookers. Bullis himself believes a chief executive should "inspire enthusiasm . . . and develop a high *esprit de corps*." His own story has been called with some humor and more truth "The Life of an Enthusiast."

Of English, Scottish, and Irish ancestry, Harry Amos Bullis was born October 7, 1890, in Hastings, Nebraska. His only brother, Roe, was a year older. While the boys were young, their parents, George Amos and Ella S. (Gould) Bullis, moved the home to Council Bluffs, Iowa. At eleven Harry was delivering the Council Bluffs newspaper *Nonpareil* on an early morning route. At sixteen he became office boy for the Citizens Gas and Electric Company in Council Bluffs, and in five years he was head bookkeeper. In those five years he studied mathematics by himself, and by taking examinations at the home of the high school principal, he secured his high school mathematics credits. Young Bullis was determined to study management engineering, which he decided could be studied best at the University of Wisconsin. He then left his job and enrolled at Simpson College Academy in Indianola, Iowa, in order to acquire the necessary high school diploma. His previously earned mathematics credits and extra courses at the academy made it possible for him to complete the four-year course in two years. He won the senior oratorical contest, was president of the graduating class, and "managed a boarding house on the side."

Immediately after his graduation young Bullis went to the University of Wisconsin, where he spent a summer as assistant university electrician. In the fall he enrolled in the College of Engineering. The next summer and the following two summers, he wholesaled sewing machines in Iowa and South Dakota. This experience, he later said, was the most vivid of his life, excepting only his army stint overseas in World War I. One of the three students at the top of the freshmen engineering class, as a sophomore he received permission to take a management engineering course of his own planning: he was permitted, in his four years, to finish all his mathematics and science courses in the College of Engineering, to take the required courses of the School of Commerce, and to complete a major in economics at the liberal arts college. In 1917, at twenty-six, he was graduated with a B.A. degree, and membership in Phi Beta Kappa, among other scholarship honors.

Since he had already had about seven years of business experience, upon his graduation Bullis received several offers of positions, one from the Chase National Bank in New York. One of Bullis' favorite stories describes his advent there. When he asked the newly elected vice-president, "What does a fellow have to do to advance in the bank, marry the president's daughter?" that official took him to the office of the president, who informed him that one of his daughters was married and the other engaged, but that there were other avenues of advancement. Learning that the vice-president had just come from another company, Bullis, who was to be his assistant, told him he preferred to start as a messenger and then spend a brief period in every department of the bank. "Don't you think one of us should know something about the operation of the bank?" Bullis asked—and answered, "I am going to go through the bank." He had gotten through one-third of it when he enlisted in the Army in World War I. He served overseas eighteen months as a sergeant, a lieutenant, and then a captain. On March 1, 1919, he was married in Paris to Irma Alexander, a financial secretary for the overseas YWCA, who had been his "girl" at college.

When he returned home, Bullis says, he had already decided that his success lay in fields other than banking. Learning that James F. Bell, vice-president of the Washburn Crosby milling company in Minneapolis, was looking for young men, he went out to see him. "After running the gantlet of executives for three days," Bullis has recalled, "I agreed to enter the service of the company if I could spend my first year at the mill and learn the business." At the end of a year at the Minneapolis mill Bullis became constructive accountant and head of the statistical department. With his staff he analyzed the operations of the company and devised a new accounting system and a new classification of accounts. Bullis was appointed auditor of the company in 1922 and comptroller in 1925.

Marketing considerations led Washburn Crosby to take the lead in merging more than a dozen well-established milling companies into a new corporation in 1928, to be known as General Mills. The parent company was to assume all responsibility for financing, taxes, insurance, accounting methods, and national advertising, while the associated companies were to have "local autonomy" in plant operations. Bullis was elected secretary and comptroller of the new organization, and three years later, in 1931, he became a vice-president, as well as comptroller, member of the executive committee and director of General Mills. In 1934 he became vice-president in charge of operations, in 1940 executive vice-president, and in December 1942 he was elected president. The president's chair, according to Time, was a "well-earned reward" for Bullis' foresight in "pushing the world's largest flour miller into munitions work long before any mill-sized war contracts were in sight."

Greystone-Stoller Corp.

HARRY A. BULLIS

The General Mills merger, according to an April 1945 Fortune article, "produced a blue-chip stock. Dividends have been earned and paid every year, and the regular dividend has not been reduced since 1929." Under Bullis' presidency General Mills intensified its diversification program, "mating a stable, low-margin business [flour]," as Fortune has said, "with a variety of risky enterprises [vitamins, produced by a company owned jointly by General Mills and Eastman Kodak, electrical appliances, chemicals, Navy fire control equipment, etc.] where the margins are wide. The result of the cross, the company very reasonably hopes, will be a hybrid vigor possessed by neither of the parents."

Bullis considers that personnel morale is one of the major concerns of a corporation president, although the president's first responsibility, he states, is to produce consistently "a satisfactory profit in relation to the investment" of the owners. He has also said, "I believe that the chief executive of a company should, insofar as it is possible, be a statesman in this world which is now so dominated by economics." Articles by Bullis setting forth arguments for the lowering of tariff barriers have appeared in Liberty magazine. In his August 1946 report to stockholders Bullis maintained it was essential that America achieve increased productivity per worker, through technological advances. This, he emphasized, did not mean the "speed-up" or "sweating" of labor. "As a matter of fact," he said, "it is management that must do most of the sweating." Approved by the board of directors in 1946, his program to rehabilitate and improve present properties and equipment and construct new facilities has been estimated to require a fixed investment of $22,000,000 over a five-year period.

(Continued next page)

BULLIS, HARRY A.—*Continued*

The milling executive has been a director and officer of the National Association of Manufacturers since 1933, and for three years he was chairman of its public relations committee. In 1932-33 he was national president of the National Association of Cost Accountants. He has also been at various times president of the Wisconsin Alumni Association, of the Wisconsin X Club, and of the Phi Beta Kappa Association of Minneapolis. He is a trustee of the National Planning Association and of the Committee for Economic Development. The other local and national boards and councils on which he serves include the Minneapolis Civic Council, the Foreign Policy Association of Minneapolis, and the Citizens Committee of Community Chests of America. Two honorary degrees have been conferred upon him: an LL.D. by the University of Wisconsin and a doctorate in business administration by Simpson College, both in 1943.

Bullis is two inches over six feet tall, and weighs two hundred pounds. Describing him as "nervous, voluble," a nonsmoker and a teetotaler, *Fortune* has reported that when he went to work for General Mills, "instantly he began making friends. He rarely forgot the birthdays or anniversaries of his associates or the names of their children. In another man this might have been taken for shrewd company politics. General Mills people insist Mr. Bullis does nice things only because he likes everybody." To his staff Harry Bullis has presented a code which includes among ten precepts: "Build men—big men. . . . Follow the three R's of creative business thinking: Research, Realism, and Resolute Reasoning." In a leader he looks for courage, competence, fair-mindedness, and cheerfulness. Bullis' personal motto is, "Drive straight ahead with a positive mental attitude."

References

Fortune 31:116-21+ Ap '45
National Cyclopædia of American Biography Current vol D p327
Who's Who in America, 1946-47
Who's Who in Commerce and Industry (1944)

BULLOSAN, CARLOS (bōō-lō'sàn) Nov. 24, 1914- Author

Address: h. 1562 Queens Rd., Hollywood, Calif.

The Filipino author and poet, Carlos Bulosan, has written a work of social protest in autobiographical form, *America Is in the Heart,* a nonfiction best seller in 1946. "It is a voice," wrote Albert Norton in *Book-of-the-Month Club News,* "of one of our own colonials reminding us that by no means all the exploitation and discrimination are found under alien flags."

Carlos Bulosan was born November 24, 1914, the son of Simeon and Autilia (Sampayan) Bulosan. In his native Philippine village of Binalonan in the province of Pangasinan, he helped his father to cultivate the land and his mother to sell salt fish. His attendance at the

Francisco Belandres

CARLOS BULOSAN

town school ended after three years when he began work at the age of eleven; at twelve he was employed in a bakery shop and at fourteen in an ice factory. (He had left home at thirteen.) The family hoped that an older son, Macario, might become a full-fledged schoolteacher, but the farm was lost and Macario went to work as a busboy in the United States.

In 1931 Carlos Bulosan followed Macario and another brother, Amado, to Seattle. On his first day there he was shanghaied by a hotel proprietor. Sold for five dollars to an Alaskan fish cannery, he was paid thirteen dollars for a season's work. He received nothing for months of apple picking in the Yakima Valley, which ended in white vigilantes' burning of the bunkhouse and Bulosan's flight in a boxcar to California. "It was the beginning of his long flight against fear," wrote Carlos P. Romulo in the New York *Times.* "It carried him into years of bitterness, degradation, hunger, open revolt, and even crime. The poolrooms and gambling houses, dance halls and brothels, were the only places he knew. They were the only places a Filipino could know."

To improve conditions for the Filipinos, Bulosan aligned himself with the labor movement and from 1935 to 1941 attempted to organize migrant workers into unions. Because of his union activities he was stripped, whipped, and driven out of various towns, harsh treatment which finally put him in the Los Angeles County Hospital for a two years' stay. Though he lost the ribs on one side of his body, and the use of one lung, he responded quickly in morale to the environment in the hospital.

For the first time Bulosan had the leisure and opportunity to read all he liked, and devoted himself to Hardy, Gorky, Tolstoy, Turgeniev, Malraux, and Jack London. Before becoming a tubercular patient Bulosan had written on a small newspaper in California, then had done some writing for a Filipino publication, the *New Tide*—he had started writing poetry in 1936, stories in 1938, and articles in 1939. After leaving the hospital and returning to the Philippines his first book of poems, *Letter From America* (1942), was published. *Chorus For America* (1942) and *The Voice of Bataan* (1943) followed.

Meanwhile, Bulosan's stories and articles on literature, culture, and politics, appeared in a wide variety of periodicals, among them the *New Yorker, Harper's Bazaar, Town and Country,* the *New Masses,* the *New Republic, Poetry, Books Abroad,* the *Saturday Review of Literature,* the *Saturday Evening Post, Voices,* and *Lyric.* In the spring of 1944 *The Laughter of My Father* (1944), a collection of family sketches reprinted from the *New Yorker, Town and Country,* and *Harper's Bazaar,* was received enthusiastically by reviewers, one of whom said, "His art seems so effortless as to be artless, but such casual tales are extremely tricky to spin." "I received letters from my countrymen telling me that I wrote about them and their times," Bulosan said. "These stories and eighteen others are now gathered in this volume. For the first time the Filipino people are depicted as human beings."

Bulosan's autobiography *America Is in the Heart* (1946) affirmed his loyalty to America, a loyalty which survived the years of cruelty and intolerance while he was a casual laborer and crop-follower in California, Oregon, Washington, and Idaho. It has been pointed out that this experience might well have permanently embittered a less sensitive and intelligent character. Of Bulosan's book, which ends with the attack on Pearl Harbor, William S. Lynch has written in the *Saturday Review of Literature*: "There is reason now to hope that what has happened in the past may only have been a prologue to a more decent period in the history of American social attitudes. If that is so, no small amount of the credit for a change will be due to the Carlos Bulosans who know the true unity of all people, who have worked to achieve it in labor circles, and who are using their special gifts to prove the talents of their own particular people." Bulosan in 1946 is planning a novel on American-Filipino marriage in California.

Carlos Bulosan has paid tribute to public libraries, recalling he once had nowhere to go except to the Los Angeles library, where he learned to read from books in the children's collection. It was a librarian, too, who gave him his first inspiration: In Baguio, in his native Philippine Islands, Bulosan had for a time been houseboy for Mary Strandon, a former librarian who had saved enough from her small salary in Spencer, Iowa, to go there to paint. "Fifteen years afterwards I went to Spencer, hoping to find her. But she had been dead for more than ten years. I wrote her name on a copy of my first book and donated it to the local library. I think she would have been happy to know that I would some day write a book about her country."

Reference
Bulosan, C. America Is in the Heart (1946)

BURGIN, WILLIAM O(LIN) (bûr′gĭn) 1877—Apr. 11, 1946   United States Democratic Representative from North Carolina; banker, businessman, lawyer; member North Carolina General Assembly, 1901, North Carolina Senate, 1903; mayor of Thomasville, 1910-12; elected to Congress in 1938.

Obituary
N Y Times p27 Ap 11 '46 por

BUSCH, FRITZ Mar. 13, 1890-   Conductor
Address: b. c/o Metropolitan Opera Association, Broadway and 39th St., New York; h. Alden Hotel, 225 Central Park West, New York

Fritz Busch, the conductor who made his Metropolitan Opera debut with *Lohengrin* on the opening night of the 1945-46 season, is no newcomer to the podium: a musician of high standing in the opera houses and concert halls of Europe and South America, he has led an estimated total of one hundred and twenty orchestras. In *Grove's Dictionary of Music and Musicians* he is designated "one of the most distinguished of living German opera and concert conductors." For his rejuvenation of the Dresden State Opera in pre-Nazi Germany and as musical director of the Glyndebourne operatic festivals in England he won world-wide notice, and his conducting of the Metropolitan's *Lohengrin* on November 26, 1945, established him at once in American critical opinion as an outstanding figure in the world of music.

Fritz Busch was born in Siegen, Westphalia, on March 13, 1890, the eldest son of Wilhelm Busch, a musician forced by economic circumstances to abandon his career in favor of carpentry and violin-making. The boy grew up in an atmosphere created by his father's wish to realize his own musical ambitions through his musically gifted children and pervaded by the music of a small orchestra led by the elder Busch which met regularly at its conductor's home. Together with his eight brothers (Adolf is the founder and violinist of the Busch Chamber Players and the Busch String Quartet; Hermann is a cellist and member of the Quartet) Fritz early received a comprehensive musical education and often joined his father in performances of chamber music. He could read music before he could read words, he says. His first musical instrument was a twelve-inch miniature violin made for him by his father, but when Adolf appropriated it Fritz turned to the piano, receiving his first lesson at the age of five. Two years later he was playing creditably at concerts. At the age of eight the boy announced his intention of becoming a conductor by placing a picture of Felix Weingartner in his room and carrying a conductor's baton in his sleeve so that he might be ready to practice at a moment's notice. By the time he was twelve years old, it is said, he had also

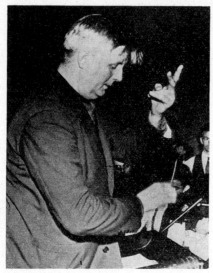

Ilse Bing

FRITZ BUSCH

become proficient on almost all the instruments of the orchestra.

Busch received his regular schooling at the *Gymnasiums* in Siegen, his birthplace, and in Siegburg in the Rhineland, to which the family moved in 1902. At the same time his systematic musical education was continued—even when the family's financial straits forced him and Adolf to seek work. In 1906 he was able to enter Cologne Conservatory. There he studied conducting with Fritz Steinbach, noted interpreter of Brahms and director of the conservatory; piano with Karl Boettcher and Lazzaro Uzielli; theory and composition with Otto Klauwell, composer and head of the piano department. In addition to being able to observe the great conductors of the day—Arthur Nikisch of the Berlin Philharmonic and the Leipzig Gewandhaus, Felix Mottl of Munich, Hans Richter, Felix Weingartner, and Steinbach—it was at the conservatory that Busch had his first real opportunity to conduct. Music, he says, occupied his entire day. "I was an ambitious musician, full of idealism, as I hope I still am, and I went to all the rehearsals and coached with piano. I lived in the music."

In the summer of 1909 Busch conducted two concerts at Bad Pyrmont, and in September of that year, at the age of nineteen, he received his first regular appointment, as conductor and chorus director of the Stadttheater in Riga. He remained in Riga until 1910 and then returned to Bad Pyrmont, where he conducted the summer concerts for the next three seasons, in 1911 also leading the Blüthner Orchestra of Berlin. During the winter seasons he made concert tours as a pianist and in the winter of 1911-12 led the choir of the Musikverein of Gotha. In 1912 the twenty-two-year-old conductor was engaged to succeed Eberhard Schwickerath as musical director in Aachen, and for the next six years he conducted the

town's orchestra, the peoples' concerts, and the Aachen Gesangverein. From August to October 1914 he had seen war service, but, wounded and invalided out of the army, he returned to his Aachen post in the latter month.

The young conductor's appointment as musical director of the Stuttgart Opera, to succeed Max von Schillings, was the result of a successful Max Reger festival which he conducted with the Berlin Philharmonic Symphony Orchestra in Jena in June 1918 and which constituted his first triumph. The following three years made his name known throughout German musical circles. And in 1922 his "extraordinary gifts as a conductor of opera" determined his engagement as general musical director of the Dresden State Opera. He thus succeeded Fritz Reiner '41 during the disastrous postwar inflationary period which had played havoc with the latter's management of the opera. But "it was in this position," wrote David Ewen, "that Busch acquired his worldwide reputation. . . .Under his guidance, the Dresden Opera became one of the great opera houses of the world."

The Busch seasons (1922-33) were noted not only for admirable performances of the standard repertoire, especially the works of Mozart and Wagner to which Busch seemed peculiarly responsive, but also for the introduction and sponsorship of modern operatic works. Kurt Weill's '41 *Der Protagonist,* Hindemith's '41 *Cardillac,* Richard Strauss's '44 *Intermezzo,* Busoni's *Doktor Faust* received their world premières at Dresden under Busch. (Hindemith's *Das Nusch-Nuschi* and *Mörder, Hoffnung der Frauen* had already been introduced by Busch at Stuttgart.) In 1928 the conductor offered the world première of Richard Strauss's *The Egyptian Helen* to inaugurate the festival celebrating the fiftieth anniversary of the opening of the opera house and the première of Strauss's *Tageszeiten,* a choral work, during the Schubert centenary program. Concerning the former, the *New International Year Book* noted: "As a matter of course, the performance was well-nigh flawless in all details." Busch's mounting of *La Forza del Destino, Don Carlos,* and *Macbeth,* Verdi operas which had till then been unknown in Germany, drew international attention and gave impetus to a Verdi renaissance in the country. Strauss's ballet *Joseph's Legend,* Puccini's *Turandot,* and others likewise received German premières at his hands. At least part of his success, he feels, was due to an adequate number of rehearsals, a point on which he has always been especially insistent. And with the Dresdner Staatskapelle, the principal Dresden orchestra, of which he was also conductor at this time, Busch likewise pioneered, giving first performances of works by Křenek, Bloch, Stravinsky '40, and others.

Although he had been awarded a life contract and although he is not a Jew, Busch terminated his connection with the Dresden Opera in 1933 because of his opposition to Nazism, just after Bruno Walter '42 was forced to relinquish his conductorial posts in Germany. Busch had first seen the Swastika at Bayreuth in 1924, reports *Opera News,* when he conducted at the reopening of the Bayreuth Festival after the ten-year suspension of its activities, and had thereupon refused Siegfried Wagner's invitation to return the following year. Until Hitler's '42 rise to power, however, he had retained his Dresden post. But in 1933 a successful revival of Verdi's *Masked Ball* in Berlin the previous year caused Hitler to order a production of *Rigoletto* at Dresden in March. On March 7, 1933, during a rehearsal of *Aïda*, Nazi storm troopers entered the opera house to demand the resignation of the ardently anti-Nazi conductor and that evening at the *Rigoletto* performance they occupied the front seats of the auditorium and chanted "Out with Busch." He learned later, the conductor says, that only a telegram from Hitler warning the SS men not to touch him—an action Busch has never understood—saved his life. Busch at once resigned and in a violent exchange of words with Göring '41 swore never to conduct for the Nazis again. In May he and his family were on their way to South America.

From August 8 to October 20, 1933, Busch conducted a season of German opera at the Teatro Colón in Buenos Aires. Shortly thereafter he became musical director of the Stats-radiofonie in Copenhagen and conductor of the Stockholm Konsertföreningen. Between 1934 and 1939 he directed and made famous the annual Glyndebourne summer operatic festival in England. And during these years of his exile from Germany he also conducted in Buenos Aires, Montevideo, Rio de Janeiro, and Chile, at the Royal Opera House in Stockholm and throughout non-Nazi Europe. In 1936 Arturo Toscanini '42 suggested Busch for the post he was vacating with the New York Philharmonic Symphony Orchestra and personally sent the younger conductor a cable to that effect, but Busch preferred to remain where he was. When the Nazis invaded Denmark, however, Busch, who happened to be in Stockholm at the time, once more left for South America.

In the fall of 1941 Busch came to the United States to conduct Mozart's *Cosi fan Tutte* and Verdi's *Macbeth* with the New Opera Company of New York, an organization inaugurated that season by Mrs. Lytle Hull and Mme. Merö-Irion for the dual purpose of providing operatic experience for young American singers while presenting distinctive and vital performances of opera. (His son Hans was stage director for these productions.) In January and February 1942 he was guest conductor of the New York Philharmonic-Symphony Orchestra. In both engagements he acquitted himself creditably, but, as in the 1927-28 season when he had been guest conductor with the Philharmonic's predecessor, Walter Damrosch's '44 New York Symphony Society, he received commendation but not acclaim from the New York critics and public. He did not have the magnetic stage personality of a Toscanini or a Stokowski '41, it was explained. Between the summer of 1942 and the autumn of 1945 Busch conducted opera and concerts in Argentina, particularly at the Teatro Colón in Buenos Aires, in Chile, Uruguay, and other South American countries, where he found the audiences avid for Wagner and Mahler and his demand for adequate rehearsal time satisfied.

Busch has attained his greatest fame as musical director of the Glyndebourne operatic festival, inaugurated in the late spring of 1934 by John Christie on his hereditary estate near Lewes in Sussex, England. It has been said that the New Opera Company was an attempt to transplant Glyndebourne to America, but in reality only the careful selection of the artists and the holding of adequate rehearsals reflected the latter. The English festival was the product of Christie's personal deep-rooted love of opera, which had led him to build the Glyndebourne theater adjoining his country house and to open his entire estate to music enthusiasts at regular intervals. Architecturally integrated with its surroundings, with an auditorium capable of seating approximately three hundred persons, a well-equipped though rather narrow stage, and an orchestra pit accommodating seventy players, the Glyndebourne opera house was designed for intimate performances of Mozartian opera.

With Busch as musical director and Carl Ebert, a colleague from Dresden, as stage director, Glyndebourne opened in May 1934 for its initial season of a fortnight with productions of *The Marriage of Figaro* and *Cosi fan Tutte*. During the following five seasons, each one longer than its predecessor, *The Abduction From the Seraglio, The Magic Flute, Don Giovanni,* and in 1938, after the stage had been deepened and the auditorium enlarged, Verdi's *Macbeth* and Donizetti's *Don Pasquale* were added to the repertoire. The performances which he had been able to give at Glyndebourne, outstanding for ensemble perfection rather than for individual display, were such as Busch had long been striving to achieve.

From the first both critics and audiences had been enthusiastic—the finest productions ever seen in England, the critics said. "Mozart's marvelous music was played with a clarity, a precision, and a verve that made it indescribably delightful." "The most striking feature . . . was the beautiful adjustment achieved between stage action and musical performance. . . .It was as if Fritz Busch, the musical director, had made a thorough study of the libretto, while Carl Ebert, the production manager, had memorized the musical score. . . . Music and action . . . became inextricably blended with each other, underscoring each other, giving new import and subtle meaning." Within a few years of its inception, Glyndebourne had become known as "the English Salzburg" and an appearance on its stage was recognized as a "hallmark of ability."

This success Busch attributes largely to the number of rehearsals. For example, reports *Opera News,* there were twenty orchestra rehearsals for *The Marriage of Figaro* alone. From the beginning, moreover, certain principles, evolved by Christie and endorsed by Busch, were strictly adhered to: the operas were to be sung in the original language; the star system was to be eliminated, no part of the production to be allowed to eclipse the unity of the whole; the best singers obtainable for each individual role were to be engaged irrespective of previous reputation, although an effort was to be made to uncover budding Eng-

BUSCH, FRITZ—*Continued*

lish talent; and rigorous rehearsal was to weld cast, chorus, and orchestra into a unified musical and dramatic ensemble.

These principles have always underlain Busch's conducting of opera. "The opera today," he wrote in *Etude* in April 1943 with a touch of understatement, "must stand or fall as a unified whole. That is to say, we have passed the day when sheer vocal magnificence alone was enough. We demand that the conductor shall conceive and organize a well-grounded, well-rounded performance; that the orchestral musicians shall play as ably as any symphonic body; that the sets and costumes shall be harmonious, convincing, and pleasing; that the stage director shall do more than indicate the moment when the performers rush to the footlights and throw out their arms; that the singers be actors in the sense of giving a sincere, true, and convincing characterization of the parts they play."

That the conception is an integral part of Busch's equipment as a conductor was again attested by the critical commentary on the *Lohengrin* performance of November 26, 1945. Wrote Robert Bagar in the New York *World-Telegram*: "The point and the thrust and the inner meanings of the music were made all too clear and life-like by the assiduous, penetrating, utterly assured conducting of Fritz Busch. There was no mistaking the fact that, although many elements entered into last evening's smoothly moving show, all emanated from a central intelligence, and that intelligence was right there in the pit, waving its hands over miracles. . . He has a supreme regard for the music in the first place. And he will not let one lyrical idea escape him, whether it is riding high on a leading singer's solo or hidden deep in the intricate maze of the orchestration. . . . Never once did he overshadow [the singers] by setting off explosions in the orchestra." Said the *Christian Science Monitor*'s roving reviewer: "The exceptional nature of this performance originated in the conducting of Fritz Busch. . . .At every point where musicianship was the key to dramatic realization, the interpretation was singularly impressive." Noel Straus of the New York *Times* reported: "One never lost the sensation that every measure of the opera would fall, as if by magic, into its right place in an exceptionally logical and revealing reading, as proved the case."

In subsequent 1945-46 performances—*Tannhäuser, Tristan und Isolde, Don Pasquale*—while some critics felt that Busch had lost a measure of the inspiration which infused this debut occasion, all continued to praise his musicianship. For the 1946-47 season it had been announced that he would add *The Marriage of Figaro* to his assignments and take over *Otello, Der Rosenkavalier,* and *Die Meistersinger* from George Szell [45], who left the Metropolitan to become permanent conductor of the Cleveland Orchestra. In performances of the first two of these, given in the first half of the season, he again drew critical acclaim. The *Otello,* wrote Francis D. Perkins of the New York *Herald Tribune,* "was the interpretation of a

conductor who knew this music drama thoroughly, and how to realize its music and emotional resources." "From the opening overture, played with flashing wit and spirit, *The Marriage of Figaro* was an accomplishment of high style and efficiency," said Irving Kolodin in the New York *Sun.* Of his *Tristan und Isolde* Noel Straus wrote: "Fritz Busch provided a sensuously textured, admirably adjusted account of the orchestral score, and his reading of the prelude could be as wholeheartedly commended for its transparency, sensitivity, and effectiveness as all that ensued in the orchestra pit."

Fritz Busch is described as having "bright blue eyes twinkling under a broad brow crowned with thick silvery hair." He is six feet tall, weighs one hundred and eighty pounds. On August 29, 1911, he was married to Margareta Boettcher, the niece of his former teacher. The couple have three children, Hans, a former soldier in the United States Army, later with UNRRA in Rome; Margareta Ruth, the wife of Martial Singher, French Metropolitan baritone; and Gisela, wife of the Danish Count Moltke of the Royal Horse Guards. Busch is an Argentine citizen, having been naturalized there in 1936. He is a member of the Royal Swedish Society of Arts and Sciences, was in 1934 a recipient of an honorary doctorate from the University of Edinburgh, and in 1945 was decorated as a Commendatore of the Chilean Government "in appreciation of his cultural work." With the Glyndebourne ensemble he has recorded the entire scores of *The Marriage of Figaro, Cosi fan Tutte,* and *Don Giovanni.* In 1946 he was preparing a volume of reminiscences for publication and again undertook to tour extensively throughout South America and Europe.

References

Etude 61:225+ Ap '43
Opera N 10:8+ N 26 '43
Ewen, D. Dictators of the Baton (1943); ed. Living Musicians (1940)
Grove's Dictionary of Music and Musicians, vol I; suppl vol (1940)
Thompson, O. ed. International Cyclopedia of Music and Musicians (1943)
Who's Who, 1946

BUTLER, SALLY Aug. 8, 1891- Lawyer; women's organization officer

Address: b. 832 Illinois Bldg., Indianapolis, Ind.; h. 171 W. 44th St., Indianapolis, Ind.

For some twenty years Sally Butler, an Indianapolis lawyer and United States Treasury Department official, has been active in furthering national legislation to provide social and economic equality for women. This she has done as an attorney and in her capacities as member and officer of a number of women's associations. Elected president of the National Federation of Business and Professional Women's Clubs in July 1946, Miss Butler stated that during her two years in her new office she will, among other things, devote her efforts to enlarging the membership of the organization—

in 1946 there were about 1,800 clubs and 102,000 women affiliated with the federation throughout the United States and in the territories of Hawaii and Alaska. In addition, she will aid the campaign for the passage of the equal rights amendment.

Born August 8, 1891, in Morgan County in the south central region of Indiana, Sally Butler is the youngest of thirteen children (she has six sisters and six brothers) of Tobias Daniel and Laura Ann (Asher) Butler. Tobias Butler was a progressive farmer and veterinarian. Sally Butler's maternal forebears were of Welsh and Dutch descent, her paternal ancestry Irish and English, the Butlers emigrating to the United States from North Ireland. Both branches of the family originally settled in Virginia and later moved to Indiana, where Sally Butler's paternal grandfather became a homesteader and acquired a large tract of farm land. This farm was her birthplace. After she was graduated from the Paragon (Indiana) High School situated in her home county, she matriculated at the Indiana State Teachers College in Terre Haute. There she specialized in history and English, receiving her B.A. degree in 1913. She then returned to Paragon to teach in its elementary school.

After a brief teaching career in Paragon, Miss Butler went to Indianapolis, the Hoosier State capital—she has lived there since—to pursue special training in Teachers College. At this period she became connected with one phase of the Indianapolis college's work, that of establishing free kindergartens in every section of the city where they were needed. The Indianapolis free kindergarten system, originally a private educational enterprise, was directed by Eliza A. Blaker, whom the young woman assisted. (Eliza A. Blaker and Tobias Butler are the two persons, she believes, who have influenced her life the most.) Altogether, Miss Butler spent about five years in the educational field. At the time of the United States entrance into World War I she became interested in civil service positions for women, partly in order to replace men who had been drafted into the nation's armed services. In June 1918 she herself entered the civil service, obtaining a position in the United States Postal Service, which she retained for twenty-five years.

About seven years after Miss Butler had become a Government employee she began the study of law in the University of Indiana. She had once wished to prepare herself for the medical profession; her father, however, had objected, maintaining that it was too difficult for a woman. Thus, she recalls, they compromised on a law career. While attending the university, she became a member of Iota Tau Tau, a legal society. As soon as she was graduated with her law degree in 1936 (she was admitted to the State of Indiana bar, the Federal bar, the American Bar Association, and the Indiana Women Lawyers Association in the same year), the attorney, described as being interested in equal rights for women "ever since she began to work" (*Christian Science Monitor*, July 13, 1946), specialized in lawsuits involving women's claims, such as

Delar

SALLY BUTLER

will, probate, and estate litigations. According to an earlier article in the same newspaper, she has taken a prominent part in her State in "defeating legislation designed to restrict the work of women." First her knowledge of working conditions and her association with various women's societies, including the Indiana branch of the National Federation of Business and Professional Women's Clubs, and later her private law cases provided her with the opportunities to influence legislation. Miss Butler, too, is the author of a number of articles dealing with legislation affecting women's interests.

During World War II the Indianapolis lawyer served as a Government official in another capacity: in 1942 she joined a branch of the United States Treasury Department in the Hoosier capital as vice-chairman of the women's division of the Indiana War Finance Committee. At this time she organized volunteer groups to promote the sale of bonds. Miss Butler was appointed executive director of the war bond program in Indiana schools in 1943 and established for herself a high record in war bond sales. In August of the same year she left the Postal Service. Then, at the end of the war in 1945 she was made deputy manager (afterward director) of the Community Service of the United States Savings Bond Division. In her latest work, which is concerned primarily with public relations, Miss Butler is required to administer an educational program for schools, colleges, and women's clubs in the State, and to lecture to these groups on the need for thrift, savings, and good budgeting, and on the individual's economic relationship with the Government.

In 1926 Miss Butler had first become associated with the National Federation of Business and Professional Women's Clubs in the Indiana State section of the organization. (The

BUTLER, SALLY—*Continued*

National Federation of Business and Professional Women's Clubs is one of the groups affiliated with the International Federation of Business and Professional Women's Clubs, the latter comprising organizations in twenty-six countries.) By 1940 she had held every office in the Indiana State Federation of Business and Professional Women's Clubs except that of treasurer, and during 1938-40 served two terms as its president. In 1938 Miss Butler also became North Central Region president, retaining the post for eight years. Meanwhile, she participated in the varied work of the national body as well, acting as its recording secretary at its convention in 1941, and holding the position of first vice-president from 1944 to 1946. The Indiana lawyer, too, has been a member of the executive committee of the nation-wide organization since 1941.

At the eighth biennial convention of the National Federation of Business and Professional Women's Clubs held in Cleveland early in July 1946, Miss Butler was elected to succeed former president Margaret A. Hickey [44]. In her speech of acceptance, Miss Butler "pledged that, under her leadership, the members will not rest until trained, equipped women, representing more than half our population, are elected in large numbers to both the Senate and the House and to leading posts in State, county, and local Government units." Declaring that the federation's goals were "jobs, justice, peace," the new president announced that among other aims of the organization for 1947 and 1948 were included appointment of United States women to all U.N. commissions; "extension of the merit system in Government, with promotion not dependent on employee's sex"; "adequate appropriations for the Women's Bureau of the United States Department of Labor"; "Federal aid in support of public education with state control of funds and policies guaranteed"; "universal jury service for women"; "enactment of the equal rights amendment" and of an equal pay for equal work bill; and "legislation restricting child labor." She closed with, "The road ahead is rugged, but it is plainly marked. We shall advance surely and steadily to make the world of tomorrow a man's and a woman's world."

When the twenty-second or equal rights amendment failed of adoption by Congress on July 19, 1946, Miss Butler promised that the fight for its passage would be carried into every State holding a Senatorial election in November and into the new Congress convening in January 1947. Speaking in support of the proposed amendment, she has remarked that American citizens living under the United States democratic Government should have equal rights under the law and equal responsibilities if individuals are able to assume them. In answer to the objection that the amendment would abolish special legislation for women (especially that for mothers), Miss Butler has asserted that the Government has passed, and will continue to pass even with the amendment, special legislation for individual groups as it has done, for example, in the case of the war veterans. Protesting against the paucity of wo-

men delegates sent to the U.N., she declared that women's talents and their capacities as "the natural peacemakers and harmonizers in the household" are needed in the world and in the making and keeping of the peace. (The national federation has appointed a staff specialist to the U.N. to report to its various member clubs on U.N. affairs.) A "firm and coherent backer" of working women, she believes that they "must not be pushed back into the kitchens" because the war is over, especially since many support their families. She maintains, too, that the shortage of domestic help could be corrected by granting higher wages to house workers and by making housework a profession, a "dignified business," through the establishment of homemaking training schools. At a meeting of the National Association of Manufacturers in December 1946 which paid tribute to the nation's career women, Miss Butler told her audience, as reported in the New York *Times*, "that women are essential to future business" and that they have a "high stake in the successful operation of the private enterprise system." She pointed out that they had "swayed the last election and put an end to the Office of Price Administration."

Miss Butler, by virtue of her position as president of the National Federation of Business and Professional Women's Clubs, is also a member of the board of directors of the international organization. Late in July 1946 she traveled to Brussels in the company of Dr. Lena Madesin Phillips [46] to represent the United States organization at a meeting of the international federation, at which twelve countries were represented. Among the projects discussed were the international exchange of business and professional women and the renewal of "activities before the United Nations for the removal of discrimination against women." Upon her return from her European trip in August, Miss Butler announced that she would recommend that each of the clubs in the national organization "adopt" at least one European child and contribute food and clothing to be sent to individuals abroad, in an effort to alleviate Europe's plight. (Her observations of European conditions and of the political and social consciousness of European women appear in the *Independent Woman*, September 1946.) Miss Butler also attended a conference of the International Assembly of Women held in South Kortright, New York, in the latter part of October. It was decided at the conference that the International Assembly of Women, a temporary organization, would set up a temporary volunteer information service group, with headquarters in London, to dispense "unbiased information and data" concerning world relations and understanding to women of all nations and to function until the UNESCO could perform the task. Miss Butler was selected a member of its newly formed advisory panel.

Aside from her professional and federation activities, Miss Butler is connected with the work of the General Federation of Women's Clubs, the Monday Club (Indianapolis), the Pilot International (a service club), and the

Delphian Society (a world-study group). Other organizations which claim her attention include Iota Tau Tau, of which she has served as dean, and Pi Omicron, a national sorority. She is a member of the Methodist Church and lists herself as a Republican. Miss Butler is a tall woman, slightly over five feet eight inches in height, and weighs 150 pounds; she has brown eyes and graying brown hair. Described as forthright and friendly, Miss Butler has said that she likes people. Golf and horseback riding are favorite sports of hers, and she has remarked that she is happy in her work partly because it involves much travel.

References

Christian Sci Mon p1 Jl 13 '46
N Y Times p18 Jl 13 '46

BUTTERWORTH, CHARLES (EDWARD) 1896—June 13, 1946 Film comedian; portrayed the man who could not make up his mind; featured in Broadway musicals; made film debut in *The Life of the Party* in 1930; acted in over thirty pictures, including *Forsaking All Others, The Magnificent Obsession, The Boys From Syracuse,* and *This Is the Army*; also appeared on the radio.

Obituary

N Y Times p42 Je 14 '46 por

CALDER, ALEXANDER (kôl'dĕr) July 22, 1898- Sculptor
Address: h. Painter Hill Road, R.F.D. Roxbury, Conn.

Alexander Calder, the "sculptural playboy" of modern art, developed a new art form, described as gay, fantastic, witty, and humorous, and more seriously (by art critic E. M. Benson) as an "original and substantial addition to the sculptural ledger of our time." From wrought metal and wire Calder makes constructions from one to fifteen feet high which gently tinkle when a breeze or the touch of a hand sets them in motion. The parts move into "unpredictable" patterns, and while one art critic remarked on how witty or entertaining are the results, another (James Johnson Sweeney) observed: "Through humor he satisfies the observer's appetite for feeling or emotion without recourse to direct representation. . . .At the same time the humor in his work is a protest against false seriousness in art, and the self-importance of the advanceguard painter, as well as of the academician."

While he is internationally known in art circles, Alexander Calder is considered by many critics peculiarly American, a product of his age and country. He was born July 22, 1898, in Lawnton, Pennsylvania, the son of Nanette (Lederer) and Alexander Stirling Calder. His father and his grandfather were well-known sculptors in the academic tradition, and his mother was a painter. Sandy, as he is known to his friends, grew up in the studios of his parents, with clay and paint always at hand.

But rather than take the obvious path to a career in art, he studied engineering. In 1915 he entered the Stevens Institute of Technology. (Art critics were later to remark of his work that only a sculptor with training in engineering could devise structures of such delicate mechanical balance.) For four years after his graduation from the Institute in 1919, Calder held a variety of engineering jobs. Then, in 1922 he left New York for San Francisco, shipping aboard a freighter as a fireman. On the west coast he worked in a Washington lumber camp for a time. While there he painted a few scenic views. He decided then to come East in the fall of 1923 to study art.

In New York, at the Art Students' League, he studied with Luks, Du Bois, Robinson, and particularly with John Sloan. Meanwhile, he did a half-page feature for the *Police Gazette,* compounded of "undistinguished" drawings and humorous captions. As a "newspaper artist" he was given a two-week pass to the Barnum and Bailey circus in 1925. After spending every night of the two weeks sketching in the menagerie tent, he published a small book entitled *Animal Sketching*. His interest in the circus was to be probably the most significant circumstance of his career. In 1926, after three years at the Art Students' League had resulted in an exhibition of his first oils at The Artists' Gallery in New York, he set out for Europe. He signed on a tramp steamer bound for England, and after three days in London, went on to Paris. There he illustrated books, designed wooden animals with movable parts for an Oshkosh (Wisconsin) toy company, and made several significant friendships among Paris artists. The sculptor, José de Creeft, persuaded him to exhibit some of his animated toys in the Paris Salon des Humoristes in the spring of 1927. From these toys developed the "phenomenal" Calder circus.

With ingenious figures created from twisted wire, a cork, a spool, or a piece of wood, Calder assembled a miniature circus. His semi-marionettes performed as acrobats, sword swallowers, lion tamers, trapeze artists, or bareback riders, and brought Calder's friends crowding into his narrow room. Leading French artists were regular vistors, too, with the result that from 1927 to 1930 Calder's circus was one of the most talked about events in Paris. At his circus parties Calder's wife, the former Louisa James, a grandniece of William and Henry James, played phonograph records to lend the proper background atmosphere, while Calder, in the role of the circus barker, expounded the acts and distributed peanuts. (Calder tells that he is in the habit of having ten-pound bags of peanuts in the shell for his guests.)

From the circus characters, which were fashioned partly of wire, came the idea of creating an entire figure in wire. Calder twisted his first caricature, a "statuette" of Josephine Baker, in 1926. In New York, at his first one-man show in 1928, Calder displayed a number of wire caricatures of well-known people. These pieces were not sculpture with the traditional appeal to the sense of touch; they were significant in a

Herbert Matter

ALEXANDER CALDER

new way. As the critic Sweeney has explained: "They were . . . three-dimensional forms drawn in space by wire lines, much as if the background paper of a drawing had been cut away leaving only the lines. The same incisive grasp of essentials, the same nervous sensibility to form, and the same rhythmic organization of elements, which are virtues of a drawing, were virtues of this new medium." When Calder returned to Europe in 1929 he exhibited his wood sculpture and wire caricatures in Paris and Berlin.

At about this time, Calder, who was known primarily as a wit and humorist in art, developed in a manner which caused men like the abstract painter Fernand Léger to declare him the most important living American artist. His meeting with Mondrian gave Calder what he calls "the necessary shock." After a visit to Mondrian's studio in 1930 he began to create stationary abstract sculpture using colored spheres and discs as well as wire. These pieces, labeled "stabiles" by the abstract artist Hans Arp, were followed in Calder's work by "mobiles." With mobiles Calder could make "two or more objects find actual relations in space." Constructing sculptures of spheres and curved wires, he added small electric motors, or hand cranks, which caused the spheres to move along the wires, forming new patterns with each new position of the parts of the construction. When two of Calder's mobiles were purchased for the Berkshire Museum in Massachusetts in 1934 the museum director wrote, "Whether or not they are the introduction of a new art form, I am sure they have real significance. I have watched with curiosity their effect upon the general public. People sit quietly before them apparently stilled and quieted by something, perhaps merely by the rhythm of the movement. But we have found it easy to make a Sunday afternoon

crowd understand 'abstract' motion where they would be blank before abstract painting." The mobiles were still further developed to the point where a puff of air, or a touch, would set them in motion, making the patterns and rhythms less predictable. Ingenious balance superseded the small motors and hand cranks. The bizarre possibilities of Calder's work are being utilized by Hans Richter, an independent producer of abstract motion pictures. Calder turned his collection of sculptures and mobiles over to Richter, who, by viewing them from unique camera angles and setting them in rhythmic movement to a musical score, has created a ballet.

The restrospective exhibit of Calder's work, given by the Museum of Modern Art in New York in September 1943, included drawings and paintings, mobiles, stabiles, jewelry made from various metals and containing no jewels, and "constellations," which were small pieces of wood linked by heavy wire, made to stand on a base or to hang from the ceiling. The Museum of Modern Art had been the second museum to purchase Calder constructions, acquiring several shortly after the Berkshire Museum bought two in 1934. Among many institutions which later bought his pieces were the Metropolitan Museum of Art in New York, the Museum of Lodz in Poland, the Honolulu Academy of Art, and the Washington (D.C.) Phillips Memorial Gallery. Calder was represented at the Paris Exposition of 1937 with a *Mercury Fountain*, a structure which was considered an outstanding creation at the Exposition. For the New York World's Fair in 1939 he designed a "water ballet" fountain display for the Consolidated Edison Building. Among the more sensational pieces he has exhibited are a ten-foot *Romulus and Remus* group, in which a wire wolf nurses a pair of wire children, and a wire goldfish bowl with wire fish swimming back and forth at the turning of a small hand crank. The sculptor has also illustrated books, *Fables of Aesop* (1931) and *Three Young Rats* (1944).

Calder's methods of work are as unconventional as the results he obtains would indicate. Speaking of his visit to Mondrian's studio, he once said, "I went home and tried to paint. But wire, or something to twist or tear or bend is an easier medium for me to think in." Instead of modeling or firing, he cuts and hammers. The *New Yorker* once quoted him on the subject of his materials: "I like broken wineglasses on stems, old car parts, old spring beds, smashed tin cans, bits of brass embedded in asphalt, and I love pieces of red glass that come out of tail lights." For his jewelry he rivets pieces of sheet metal in patterns, or twists wire into designs and then hammers the wire flat. The Museum of Modern Art has summed up the resulting "sculpture": "He combines nature with geometry, constructs balances operated by mechanics or the wind, and cuts fantastic and beautiful shapes out of air."

Frequently the newspaper and art magazine reviews of the exhibitions of Alexander Calder's work contain words to this effect—"I don't yet know if it is important as art, but it is certainly a lot of fun." *Art News* has several times termed him a man of first importance among non-objective artists. Edward Alden Jewell (New York *Times*) once referred to him as "that irrepressible and brilliantly imaginative playboy of the art world," while Henry McBride (New York *Sun*) thinks his work has "a strange and incalculable beauty." Another critic on the *Sun*, reviewing an exhibit of his paintings, warns away those who are "uninitiated in the vagaries of ultra-modern art."

Calder and his wife Louisa, to whom he was married in January 1931, have two daughters, Sandra and Mary. Much of the time they live on a farm in Roxbury, Connecticut, where, not far from the farmhouse, Calder maintains a barnlike workshop with enormous windows. Geoffrey T. Hellman, who "profiled" Calder for the *New Yorker* in 1941, spoke of his immense strength, and his enthusiasm for dining, drinking, and dancing. In his Paris days, Hellman said, he looked like "a gentle Stalin at a fancy-dress ball." According to Elizabeth Hawes, fashion writer, "He used to loom over the Left Bank in a lovely orange suit, and what with that and the large mustaches, one could hardly miss him." The artist—no longer mustached—has gray hair, and hazel eyes. He might still be said to "loom," with his five feet, ten and a half inches in height, and 210 pounds avoirdupois.

References

New Yorker 17:25-33 D 4 '41

Sweeney, J. J. Alexander Calder (1943)
Who's Who in American Art, 1940-41

CAPPER, ARTHUR   July 14, 1865-   United States Senator from Kansas; publisher

Address: b. Senate Office Bldg., Washington, D.C.; Capper Publications, 8th and Jackson Sts., Topeka, Kan., h. The Mayflower, Washington, D.C.

Arthur Capper, fifth-term Senator from Kansas, is known as the world's largest publisher of farm journals; his periodicals have more than four million average net paid circulation, as of 1946. Second only to President of the Senate Kenneth D. McKellar '46 in length of service in the upper chamber, the Republican has been a leader of the farm bloc, an isolationist, and opponent of the general New Deal program. It was he, incidentally, who appointed young Dwight Eisenhower to West Point.

The man whose name has been identified with his State for three decades was born in Garnett, Kansas, on July 14, 1865. His parents, Herbert and Isabella (McGrew) Capper, were Quakers. As a boy Arthur attended the local schools and learned the printing trade on the Garnett *Journal*. After graduation from high school in 1884, the nineteen-year-old youth went to Topeka and got a job as a typesetter on the *Daily Capital*. Later he became a reporter for the paper and, still later, city editor. In 1891 Capper went to work for the New York *Tribune*, and the next year he was back on the

ARTHUR CAPPER

Daily Capital payroll as its Washington correspondent. Later in 1892, the year of his marriage, the reporter became a publisher by purchasing the weekly North Topeka *Mail,* which he later merged with the *Kansas Breeze* to create the semimonthly *Kansas Farmer.*

Capper is president of Capper Publications in Topeka, a subsidiary of which produces two newspapers, the Republican *Daily Capital* and the independent Republican *State Journal*, with an approximate net paid daily circulation of 79,780 in 1946. Directly published by the company are *Capper's Weekly,* an agricultural and industrial journal with a circulation of 352,760; the semimonthlies *Kansas Farmer* (circulation 111,970) and *Missouri Ruralist* (118,280); and the monthly *Capper's Farmer* and *Household,* with a circulation of 1,241,680 and 1,853,410 respectively. Senator Capper also publishes the Kansas City *Daily Kansan,* which calls itself politically nonpartisan and has a circulation of 21,850, and, through the subsidiary, Capper-Harman-Slocum, three farm semimonthlies, in Michigan, Ohio, and Pennsylvania, with a combined circulation of 433,470. Capper's holdings also include radio stations WIBW and KCKN.

The publisher's entry into civic life came with his appointment to the presidency of the Board of Regents of Kansas State Agricultural College in 1910, a position he held for three years. He was the Republican candidate for Governor of the Sunflower State in 1912, but was defeated by twenty-nine votes. Two years later he was elected Governor, and in 1916 was re-elected. During his term of office, laws were passed to centralize the administration of education in Kansas, to create an industrial welfare and a highway commission, to provide compensation for persons injured in some industries, and to establish vocational education, a child hygiene department, and a budget system. His agricultural clubs for boys and girls, widely known as the Capper pig, calf, and poul-

CAPPER, ARTHUR—*Continued*

try clubs, had their genesis in 1916 when the Governor lent a young boy some money to buy a pig.

Governor Capper was elected to the United States Senate by a large majority in November 1918, and has been re-elected for four successive terms every sixth year. During his long service as a Republican stalwart in the upper chamber, Capper has generally been considered one of the most conscientious students of legislation on Capitol Hill. According to William Allen White, by 1942 the Kansan had the record of missing only ten of some two thousand roll calls and quorum calls, and one of his few boasts is that he has never dodged a vote. The legislator is a member of the Senate Committees on Agriculture and Forestry, Claims, the District of Columbia, Finance, Foreign Relations, and a special Small Business Committee. At various times he has supported Zionism, woman suffrage, sponsored a "truth in fabrics" bill, and year after year introduced two constitutional amendments: to provide for uniform national marriage and divorce laws, and another to exclude all aliens from the census counts in fixing the number of Representatives for each State.

The Senator's chief interests have been isolationism and agriculture. Capper first attracted attention as an isolationst in 1920 when he fought against United States entry into the League of Nations, unwilling to "relinquish . . . the constitutional right of Congress alone to declare war." Almost a decade later he proposed a resolution that would implement the Kellogg-Briand Pact for renouncing war, through a trade embargo on nations violating the treaty. Early assuming leadership of the farm bloc in the Senate, in 1922 Capper wrote *The Agricultural Bloc* for the "Farmer's Bookshelf" series, and sponsored a mass of farm legislation. He was joint author of the Capper-Volstead Act legalizing farm cooperatives; the Capper-Tincher Act, which was the first attempt to regulate trading in grain futures; the Capper-Jones Act for regulation of commodity exchanges; and the Capper-Ketcham Act, which broadened the provisions of agricultural extension work under the Smith-Lever Act to include boys' and girls' club work (organization and operation of the 4-H clubs). Capper continually demanded tariff protection for the farmer.

In the early years of the Franklin D. Roosevelt Administration, minority member Capper opposed priming the economic pump through relief programs and work projects. He voted for the Wagner [41] Labor Relations Act to guarantee the right of collective bargaining to labor, but against the forty-hour work week provisions of the Wages and Hours Act as being inequitable to small business. He voted for the Administration bill regulating holding companies and against the bill to "pack" the Supreme Court. It is characteristic, William Allen White wrote, that "when the gavel falls on a majority against him, his fight is done." As a basis for a national farm program, Capper favored the principle of the McNary-Haugen bill, twice passed and twice vetoed by President Coolidge, by which agricultural prices

would be artificially maintained by dumping surplus staples abroad (those farmers who lost by this would be compensated by an equalization fee collected from the beneficiaries). But when the new Secretary of Agriculture, Henry A. Wallace [40], instituted his controlled production and "ever-normal granary" systems, Capper accepted the new plan.

The Kansas Senator urged enactment of a permanent neutrality measure in 1936. He disapproved continuation of Secretary of State Hull's [40] reciprocal trade agreement policy, by which tariffs were lowered. One of the Senators who introduced resolutions for a constitutional amendment providing for a nation-wide referendum before war could be declared, he protested vigorously against scrap-iron shipments to Japan. The "war-stoppered isolationist," as Walter Davenport referred to him in a 1942 *Collier's* article, opposed revision of the Neutrality Act in 1939 and defended the arms embargo. "Why turn this country into an armed camp?" asked Capper, assailing Selective Service in 1940. He voted against Lend-Lease in March 1941, but in October of that year voted for the seven-billion-dollar allowance to implement it, explaining that as Lend-Lease had become the law of the land, it was entitled to a sufficient appropriation. However, in August 1941 he opposed extension of Selective Service, and in November voted a second time against the revision of the Neutrality Act to permit armed American merchant ships to enter combat areas and carry supplies to belligerent ports. He voted against every bill designed to strengthen the Navy and the Air Forces. In an article for *Scribner's Commentator* for February 1941, entitled "Time to Think American," Capper wrote: "There is no reason why we should not have peaceful relations with the world if we cease playing the role of international Meddlesome Mattie and confine our activities to our own proper sphere." According to Walter Davenport, Capper endorsed the Reverend Gerald L. K. Smith's [43] Committee of One Million at the time when it came out against President Roosevelt's foreign policy.

Although he exerted all his influence to keep the United States out of war, Senator Capper supported its prosecution, once the United States had been attacked. In October 1943 he stated that he favored the Fulbright [43] postwar collaboration resolution. In November he voted for the revised Connally [41] resolution providing that there be established "at the earliest practicable date a general international organization" —a commitment, however, so hedged about with references to constitutional process and national sovereignty that even the extreme isolationist Senator Nye [41] voted for it. Capper supported UNRRA in 1944 and the United Nations Charter in 1945, but voted against extension of the Reciprocal Trade Agreements Act to revive and stimulate international trade, against the Bretton Woods proposals for a world bank and world fund to provide foreign exchange and stabilize currencies, and against the British loan and trade agreements regarded by the Administration as an essential in the prevention of economic warfare.

On domestic issues during World War II, Senator Capper continued for the most part to oppose the Administration. He voted to prohibit the use of Federal funds to keep prices down by subsidy payments in 1943 and 1944; for overriding the veto of the pay-as-you-go income tax bill of 1944; against appropriations for the National Resources Planning Board, which had submitted a program to guarantee full production and employment in peacetime; for mass deferment of agricultural workers from the draft; for overriding the veto of the Smith '41. Connally Antistrike Act. He also opposed the confirmation of Henry Wallace as Secretary of Commerce and former NYA head Aubrey Williams '40 as head of the Rural Electrification Administration. On the other hand, Capper supported the Administration in favoring the increased appropriations for soil conservation, continuing the loan powers of the Farm Security Administration, and opposing the McKellar amendments to weaken the Tennessee Valley Authority. On the issue of civil liberties, he voted against a uniform Federal ballot for soldiers late in 1943, but for limiting debate during the poll-tax filibusters of 1942 and 1944, and he was against the amendment to eliminate the Fair Employment Practice Committee in 1944.

In the postwar period, Capper was one of the members of the Banking and Currency Committee who succeeded in weakening the full employment bill. He opposed the proposal to delay the return of the United States Employment Service to State control. He voted nay in a test on the Administration proposal to create housing for veterans by guaranteeing markets for prefabricated houses, and again voted with the real estate lobby on a bill that would have put price ceilings on existing houses and lots. Capper was among those voting against the draft-labor clause which the Senate struck from the labor bill in May 1946. The Kansan favored the Case '46 bill, which created fact-finding boards to settle labor disputes, a sixty-day cooling-off period, withdrawing Wagner Act rights from union members who engaged in "wildcat" strikes, and forbidding employee-controlled welfare funds. In late June he voted against the OPA extension bill passed by the Senate and, in the proposed compromise bills which followed, voted to eliminate livestock, poultry, and dairy products from price control. On the foreign relations front, in August 1946 he pledged his support of the Administration's foreign policy and expressed his confidence in Secretary of State Byrnes's judgment at the Paris Peace conference.

The "brisk, gay, and gingery" octogenarian, who has a reputation for keeping both ears to the ground, has expressed his life philosophy as, "Live and let live—and lift a little more than your share." He hopes that he still has "curiosity, tolerance, and good will," and adds, "I would hate to think I have become set in my ways, in my thinking, in my reactions." Senator Capper has been a widower for a number of years; his deceased wife was Florence Crawford, whose father had been Governor of Kansas during Capper's early childhood. The Senator-publisher's five-foot-eight-inch, 125-pound figure is a familiar sight on the golf courses of Washington and Topeka.

References

Congressional Directory (2d ed., 1945)
National Cyclopædia of American Biography Current vol C p58
Who's Who in America, 1946-47
Who's Who in Commerce and Industry (1944)
Who's Who in the Nation's Capital, 1938-39

CARMICHAEL, OLIVER C(ROMWELL) Oct. 3, 1891- Educator

Address: b. c/o Carnegie Foundation for the Advancement of Teaching, 522 Fifth Ave., New York

With the beginning of the year 1946 Oliver C. Carmichael, Southern educator and the chancellor of Vanderbilt University for the preceding eight years, assumed the presidency of the Carnegie Foundation for the Advancement of Teaching, of which he had been a trustee since 1937.

A descendant of Daniel Carmichael, who came to North Carolina from Scotland in 1773, Oliver Cromwell Carmichael is the son of the late Daniel Monroe Carmichael, a self-educated farmer, teacher, and Alabama state legislator, and Amanda Delight (Lessley) Carmichael. He was born on October 3, 1891, and together with his six brothers (three are now prominent educators, three are physicians) he spent his early years on farms near Good Water, his birthplace, and Thorsby, Alabama. The youth pursued his first two years of undergraduate studies at Alabama Presbyterian College from 1907 to 1909, then transferred to the University of Alabama, where he was awarded his B.A. and elected to Phi Beta Kappa in 1911. The year immediately following his graduation he taught French and German at the University of Alabama, and in 1912-13 he was acting professor of modern languages at the Florence (Alabama) Normal School in Birmingham. In 1913 Carmichael went as a Rhodes scholar to Oxford University, where World War I cut short his studies after one year.

Vacationing in Munich during the summer of 1914, Carmichael was caught in Germany at the opening of hostilities and managed to get out, relates the Nashville *Banner*, "only after a grueling thirty-six-hour train trip during which he had neither food nor sleep." Instead of returning to Oxford, he joined the Commission for Relief in Belgium directed by Herbert Hoover '43 and spent much of the next year on the Continent. In April 1915 he returned for one term to Oxford and then served in Bombay, Calcutta, and Hyderabad, India, with the British YMCA. After further service with the British Army, as assistant director of field force canteens, with the rank of captain, during the conquest of German East Africa, he returned to his university studies in England and completed the requirements for the B.S. degree in 1917, receiving in addition a diploma in anthropology. In August 1917 Carmichael resigned a proctor fellowship at Prince-

OLIVER C. CARMICHAEL

ton University to enter the officers' training school at Camp Oglethorpe, Georgia. Commissioned a first lieutenant in the Infantry in November 1917, he served first with the 321st Infantry and then, until March 1919, was a General Staff intelligence officer assigned to the Eighty-first Division as an interviewer of German prisoners in France. For his war service Belgium awarded him in 1915 the Queen's Medal, King Albert's Medal, and the medal of the Belgian national relief committee; and he received the British Army service medal in 1916 and the American service medal in 1918.

After the war Carmichael became chairman of the French department of the Central High School in Birmingham, Alabama; one year later, principal of the Henley High School in Birmingham; and in 1921-22 he was principal of the Woodlawn High School in the same city. In the autumn of 1922 he was appointed dean and assistant to the president of Alabama College, the state college for women at Montevallo, and in February 1926, after the death of President Thomas Waverly Palmer, Carmichael was elected to the presidency of the college. This position the educator held for nine years, while he improved and strengthened the college curriculum, managed to increase the annual appropriation from the state by almost 200 per cent, and added approximately a million dollars to the value of the college plant. During his presidency of Alabama College, Carmichael was also a member of the White House Conference on Child Health and Protection (1930) and of the President's Conference on Home Building and Home Ownership (1931). He was president of the Alabama Association of Colleges in 1927-28, of the Southern Association of Colleges for Women in 1929-30, and a member of the executive committee (1928-31) and of the research and legislative committees of the Alabama Education Association.

In 1935 Carmichael resigned from the Alabama College post to take up the duties of dean of the graduate school and senior college of Vanderbilt University, in Nashville, Tennessee. He assumed the additional responsibilities of vice-chancellor of that institution in 1936, and in June 1937 he was chosen chancellor to succeed James H. Kirkland. During his eight years' administration of Vanderbilt, greater flexibility was introduced into the curriculum, courses in aeronautical engineering were added, the Institute of Research and Training in the Social Sciences was established, and the Nashville School of Social Work was organized. Together with Peabody College for Teachers and Scarritt College, Vanderbilt University endowed and constructed a central university library, and with Peabody worked out a plan to avoid duplication of courses in those two institutions. A nine-million-dollar campaign for building and endowment funds for the liberal arts college was successfully promoted under Carmichael's leadership and a one-million-dollar campaign for the School of Law was organized. A women's dormitory was also erected. With the outbreak of World War II, Vanderbilt introduced an accelerated plan of study, cooperated with the Army's training program, and conducted research under Government contract. Before the end of Carmichael's tenure, arrangements had been completed for a permanent naval ROTC unit at the university and plans for a new engineering building and an ROTC armory were under discussion.

In administering both Alabama College and Vanderbilt University, Carmichael's goal was a broad cultural foundation as a preparation for a rounded life and as a necessary prerequisite to strictly professional training. "The contribution of the arts college to the development of youth," he has written, "is far more than merely getting them acquainted with useful knowledge. Its emphasis is on values and a sense of values rather than on facts and information. Essentially, its curriculum is a value-searching, value-creating program. In history, the classics, literature, foreign languages, and philosophy there is a search for values, the significance of events (history), an evaluation and understanding of the ideals and aspirations of ancient people (through the classics), the beauty of thought and expression (in literature), discrimination in the use of words (in foreign language study), and the evaluation of truth as sought by the philosophers (in philosophy). . . .Intellectual independence and initiative, social intelligence and understanding, accuracy of thought and expression, a sense of perspective and values— these are the qualities which have traditionally belonged to the liberally educated person . . . the qualities which the college years should develop."

In September 1945 Carmichael was named president of the Carnegie Foundation for the Advancement of Teaching, in New York, to succeed the late Walter A. Jessup. He took up his new duties in January 1946, acting also as special adviser to the Carnegie Corporation. At present, in keeping with the provisions of its charter—"to perform all things necessary to encourage, uphold, and dignify the profession of the teacher and the cause of higher education"—the Foundation sponsors or conducts research in education, publishes bulletins and reports on such research, and provides counseling services to institutions of higher education. The work of the Carnegie Corporation, which now has an endowment of a hundred and thirty-five million dollars, includes "granting aid to colleges and universities, support of educational and scientific research, scholarly publications, fine arts education, library service and training, and . . . related projects." For the post of president of the Foundation and adviser to the Corporation, said an editorial in the Nashville *Banner*, "Carmichael was chosen, beyond all question, for his grasp of education's needs, his experience in the broad field of world economics, and his administrative capacity, to all of which his record attests." One project initiated by Carmichael early in his tenure was a five-year experimental program—designed "to stimulate creative ability and to finance full or part-time research"—for the allocation of funds to individual faculty members of thirty-three participating Southern colleges and universities, to be administered by four designated university centers also interested in promoting personal, cultural, and scientific interchange among the teachers concerned. A second project was "to study existing nonprofit testing organizations . . . to determine the feasibility of merging their efforts to eliminate confusion and duplication." The Carnegie Foundation's first annual report under Carmichael's presidency (for 1945-46) contained his discussion of the "grave crisis in the teaching profession" brought about by the failure of monetary and cultural incentives for teachers to keep pace with curricular and administrative progress.

The educator is a linguist versed in Latin, Greek, German, French, Spanish, Italian, and Dutch, and he also knows some Urdu and Swahili. He has been the recipient of seven honorary degrees from Southern colleges and universities. He is a life member of the National Education Association; a trustee of the Carnegie Foundation for the Advancement of Teaching and of the Teachers Insurance and Annuity Association sponsored by the Foundation; a member of the Senate of Phi Beta Kappa (since 1940); a member of the Central Committee of the American Red Cross (since 1942); and a trustee of the Nutrition Foundation (since 1943). From 1919 to 1934 he was a member of the Alabama committee on the selection of Rhodes scholars; from 1936 to 1939, a member of the executive committee of the Southern Association of Colleges and Secondary Schools; in 1942-43, a member of the advisory council of the War Manpower Commission; in 1943-44, chairman of the American Council on Education. "As chairman of the Southern Association's committee to investigate irregularities in the Georgia university system," stated the Nashville *Banner,* "he was largely responsible for the dropping of the state school from the association's rolls," a circumstance which helped to pave the way for the defeat of the Eugene Talmadge [41] political machine by Ellis Arnall [45] in the Georgia gubernatorial

campaign of 1942. In July 1946 he was named to the reorganized board of trustees of the Committee for Economic Development, the C.E.D.

Carmichael is five feet eleven inches tall, weighs one hundred and ninety-five pounds, has blue eyes and auburn hair. He was married to Mae Crabtree on July 13, 1918, and their two sons are Oliver Cromwell and Fred Henry. Politically, the educator is a Democrat. He is fond of music, and a good golfer; and he is a member of Rotary, the Round Table, Coffee House, and Belle Meade Country clubs, of Kappa Delta Pi and Omicron Delta Kappa. He is the author of numerous articles on travel, education, and history, which have appeared in national periodicals.

References:

N Y Times p40 S 13 '45
Nashville Banner p1+ S 12 '45
America's Young Men, 1936-37
Leaders in Education (1941)
National Cyclopædia of American Biography Current vol F p312
Who's Who in America, 1946-47
Who's Who in American Education (1941-42)

CARR, ALEXANDER 1878(?)—Sept. 19, 1946 Stage and film comedian best known for his portrayal of Mawruss Perlmutter in the Montague Glass comedies, of which the first was *Potash and Perlmutter* (1913); his last motion picture role was in *Christmas in July* (1940).

Obituary
N Y Times p31 S 20 '46 por

CARTER, (WILLIAM) HODDING, JR. Feb. 3, 1907- Newspaper editor and publisher
Address: b. c/o Delta Democrat-Times, Greenville, Miss.; h. 504 Arnold Ave., Greenville, Miss.

"The South is so often damned for social backwardness, for reaction entrenched in smugness and lethargy, that it is a pleasure to introduce a young Southerner who represents a totally different school of thought—and action," the *Saturday Evening Post* informed its readers in its February 23, 1946 issue. The Southerner in question, Hodding Carter, editor and publisher of the *Delta Democrat-Times* in Greenville, Mississippi, won the 1945 Pulitzer prize for distinguished editorial writing. A novelist as well as a journalist, Hodding Carter has devoted himself to "flaying racism" wherever he finds it.

The son of William Hodding and Irma (Dutartre) Carter, William Hodding Carter, Jr., grew up in the Mississippi delta country. He was born February 3, 1907, in Hammond, Louisiana, and there received his early schooling. His summer vacations were spent at his grandmother's home on the Mississippi. In these years began his love of the river. He remembers how, as a fourteen-year-old boy,

HODDING CARTER, JR.

he would "dare" the Mississippi—with a row-boat near—until "the current and [his] heavy arms had pulled [him] across and a mile below." Left with him from this Louisiana boyhood were more disturbing memories also. "He was only six," *Time* magazine has related, "when he saw a yelping gang of white boys chasing a Negro kid. Several years later, he came upon the pendant body of a lynch victim. Those violent pictures never faded from his mind." At sixteen Carter went North to study. He was graduated from Bowdoin College in Maine in 1927 with a B.A. degree, and then entered Columbia University to study journalism for a year. When Columbia awarded him the B.Litt. degree in 1928, he also won a teaching fellowship to Tulane University in New Orleans for the 1928-29 academic year.

In 1929 Carter became a reporter for the New Orleans *Item-Tribune,* and in 1930, at twenty-three, the night bureau manager for the United Press in New Orleans. His next job took him to Jackson, Mississippi, where he was the fifty-dollar-a-week bureau manager of the Associated Press. In October 1931 Carter was married to Betty Brunhilde Werlein, and six months later he was dismissed from his job for "insubordination." Bent on publishing and editing a newspaper of their own, the newly-weds, whose funds totaled less than four hundred dollars, went to Carter's home town of Hammond, and there launched the *Daily Courier.* They struggled with a broken-down press and an antique kerosene-burning linotype machine, and traded advertising space for groceries. For three years, until he was killed in 1935, their *Daily Courier* attacked Huey Long, the most powerful man in Louisiana—according to *Time,* "theirs was the only district in the State that never sent a Long henchman to Congress." A year after Long's death, the Carters sold their paper for sixteen thousand dollars.

The Carters then moved to Greenville—a town in Mississippi with some twenty thousand inhabitants, of whom about half are Negroes—because Mississippi seemed to offer "the best fight in sight." Its Senator Theodore Bilbo '43, Carter felt, was making the "name of his state . . . synonymous with every evil prejudice that besets our democracy." In Greenville Carter established the *Delta Star* in 1936; two years later he bought out his competitor, and merged the two papers, becoming editor-publisher of the daily *Delta Demo-crat-Times.* In 1939 the Mississippi editor received a Nieman fellowship, a grant which Harvard University awards to seasoned newspapermen for a year's study in any fields the fellows may choose. At the close of his year's work at Harvard, Carter joined the staff of the newspaper *PM,* which had just been established in New York. He was *PM*'s press editor during its first months in the summer and fall of 1940.

"As a kind of personal protest against Munich," editor Carter had joined the National Guard in 1938. With his unit, an artillery outfit, he went into the Army in November 1940. For several weeks at Camp Blanding, Florida, he got out *Dixie,* the newspaper of the Thirty-first Division. An accident—according to *Time,* he walked into a palmetto in a training-camp exercise in Florida—cost him the sight of his right eye. In 1940-41 Carter served in Washington with the Army Bureau of Public Relations. Assigned to overseas duty, he went to Cairo in 1943 to launch and edit the Middle East editions of both *Stars and Stripes* and *Yank.* While in service Carter wrote three books—*Lower Mississippi* (1942), *Winds of Fear* (1944), and, in collaboration with Colonel R. Ernest Dupuy, *Civilian Defense of the United States,* which, when it appeared in 1942, was "highly recommended" for its material on "the part the volunteer can play."

At his discharge in mid-1945 Carter was a major in the Intelligence Division. Returning to his newspaper, which then had a daily circulation of 6,800, the thirty-eight-year-old editor took up the fight against bigotry in general and Senator Bilbo in particular. It was a lonely fight; according to *PM* only a small minority of Mississippians were publicly critical of such advocates of "white supremacy" as Senators Bilbo and James Eastland, and Representative John Rankin '44. "The chief reasons for the silence," *PM* added, "are the fear of being labeled 'Nigger lover,' or the feeling—even among many of those unsympathetic with such views—that the South should present a united front in racial matters." One example of Carter's editorial writing in his Mississippi paper was: "There was nothing in the Constitution or its Bill of Rights which reserved the blessings of America for 100 per cent Anglo-Saxon Protestants. . . .Here in America the sons and daughters of downtrodden illiterates have become lawyers and doctors and artists and musicians, businessmen, outstanding athletes, successful farmers, good citizens. . . .Apparently Senator Bilbo, like other disciples of the cult of the master race, finds this irritating. . . .It must take a great deal of courage to rampage against Italians and Catholics who in this State are in such a small minority, or against Jews whose numbers here are infinitely small, or against Negroes who don't vote or talk back." For his editorials on racial, religious, and economic intolerance, in May 1946 the Southern editor received a Pulitzer journalism award, the citation of which made special mention of his plea for fairness to returning Nisei soldiers. In the same year, Carter started the publication of a new daily, the Greenwood (Mississippi) *Morning Star*. The newspaper received national attention in August 1946 as a result of its story of the arrest of five white men for the fatal beating of a Mississippi Negro.

His understanding of conditions in the South was indicated in his book, *Lower Mississippi*, written in 1942 for the "Rivers of America" series. "He has dug below the surface ease and softness of the delta life to the savagery and pain which lie beneath them," commented Horace Reynolds in the New York *Times Book Review*. "His intimate, instinctive feeling and knowledge of the local scene and his careful research combine to make *Lower Mississippi* one of the best volumes yet published in the . . . series," wrote Orville Prescott.

Some of the complexities of the Southern interracial problem Carter dealt with in his novel *The Winds of Fear*, a story of interracial tension, rising terror, and violence in the fictional Southern town of Carvell City. "If you have not lived in Carvell City," he wrote, "it is too easy to denounce its masters, forgetting that they are also the slaves of the fear which impels them. If you have lived too long and too casually in Carvell City, it is too easy to accept the inevitability of its ways." The book, said Francis Hackett in the New York *Times,* was "immensely, brilliantly vivid [drama]...beautiful in its sincerity...a hard-hitting novel which is still essentially tender." It was pointed out by other critics that although too much the sociological document to be "great shakes as a novel" the book was one of the clearest presentations, yet to appear, of tension in the South: Carter was "balanced" and "detached," yet made "your blood run cold" with his story. Carter has frequently stressed that racism is not peculiar to the South, that it is fed by bigotry in other sections of the country. A character who sometimes speaks for the author in *The Winds of Fear* says: "They lynch up North, and a damn sight more people than we do. Only they call them race riots." However, Carter is aware that "within our country, it is principally through the South that the winds of fear are rushing today."

The Mississippi editor's analyses of intolerance in the South have appeared in national publications. In 1934 and 1935 he contributed a series of articles on Huey Long to the *New Republic*. His discussions of Southern problems and of Senator Bilbo have appeared in *PM* and in the New York *Times Magazine*. Others of his pieces have been published in the *Saturday Evening Post*, the *Nation,* and the *American Magazine*. Given a Guggenheim fellowship in literature in 1945 for use after his discharge from army service, Carter is in 1946 at work under the grant on an historical novel about the West Florida Republic in 1810. Another novel, "Flood Crest," in which a Mississippi flood is the protagonist, is also in preparation.

With his wife and three sons (William Hodding, 3d, Philip Dutartre, and Thomas Hennen), Carter spends his summers in Maine. Five feet ten inches tall, the Southerner weighs 190 pounds, has gray-green eyes, black hair, and a trim mustache. The Carters' friends," *Time* wrote, "know them as people who stick up for their ideals, but with no note of dreary, earnest dedication about them. The townspeople respect Carter's editorial policy, even if they don't always share it."

References

PM p10 Ag 5 '45
Sat Eve Post 218:4 F 23 '46 por
Time 47:50 My 20 '46 por

CARTIER (DE MARCHIENNE, EMILE DE), BARON (kär'tyā) 1872—May 10, 1946

Belgian Ambassador to London, dean of the diplomatic corps at the Court of St. James; after seven years as Belgian Minister at Peking, was appointed Minister at Washington in 1917 and became Belgium's first Ambassador to the United States in 1919; transferred to London in 1927; delegate to the Washington Disarmament Conference of 1921-22; largely responsible for successful negotiations of the Belgian War Debt Commission after World War I.

Obituary

N Y Times p27 My 11 '46 por

CARTOTTO, ERCOLE (kär-tô'tō ĕr'kō-lä)

Jan. 26, 1889—Oct. 3, 1946 Portrait painter; emigrated from Italy at sixteen, studied art in Boston, and opened a studio in New York; painted the portraits of figures in society and public life, and later specialized in portraits of women and children; his works hang in State Houses and leading museums; among his many medals are the Cross of Merit and Gold Medal of the art society of Bologna, Italy, and the Hallgarten Prize of the National Academy of Design.

Obituary

N Y Times p23 O 4 '46

CASE, FRANCIS (HIGBEE) Dec. 9, 1896-

United States Representative from South Dakota; businessman

Address: b. House Office Bldg., Washington, D.C.; h. 2345 Skyland Pl., S.E., Washington, D.C.; Custer, S.D.

In his ninth year in the House of Representatives, Francis Case's name became a household word in connection with the Case Labor Disputes Act which he introduced before the House in January 1946. The Republican Representative, one of two from South Dakota, has a rural constituency of 157,132, about half

FRANCIS CASE

the number represented by a Congressman from New York's Borough of Manhattan. His name had been on newspaper front pages in 1942, with an amendment to an appropriation bill requiring holders of military and naval contracts to file certificates of costs and agree to return to the Treasury by renegotiation all profits above 6 per cent.

Francis Higbee Case was born December 9, 1896, in Everly, Iowa. His parents were Mary Ellen (Grannis) and the Reverend Herbert Llywellen Case. The future Congressman's connection with South Dakota began in 1909, when his family moved to Sturgis. Young Frank was graduated from the Hot Springs High School in 1914 and from Dakota Wesleyan University with his B.A. in 1918. In that year he joined the wartime Marine Corps as a private; later he was to receive commissions in both the Marine Corps Reserve and the Army Reserve.

Resuming his studies at Northwestern University in 1919, the minister's son received his Master's degree in 1920. From 1920 to 1922 he continued his studies, while working as assistant editor of the *Epworth Herald,* published in Chicago by the young people's league of the Northern Methodist Church. He wrote *Handbook of Church Advertising,* published in 1921, and edited *Advertising the Church,* published in 1925. Case returned to South Dakota in 1922 as telegraph editor and editorial writer of the Rapid City *Daily Journal,* leaving in 1925 to become editor and publisher of the weekly Hot Springs *Star.*

According to *Business Week,* it was Francis Case, as a "thirty-one-year-old local booster," who invited President Calvin Coolidge in 1928 to spend his vacation in the Black Hills of South Dakota. Coolidge's famous statement, "I do not choose to run," was issued from the resort. In that year the publisher was joined as copublisher by his younger brother, Leland D. Case, later editor of the *Rotarian* magazine. Three years later Francis Case moved to Custer, where until 1945 he edited and published the Custer *Chronicle.* His first public office was that of a State regent of education, in 1931-33. During the next years he made enough friends to win a House seat from the incumbent Democratic Representative in the Democratic landslide of 1936. Case's district, the largely rural western half of South Dakota, is described by Scripps-Howard columnist Thomas L. Stokes as dominated politically, as well as industrially, by the wealthy Homestake Mining Company, which discouraged labor organization.

The newspaperman and rancher won his election to Congress by a vote of 34,812 to 32,549. A party-line Republican from a Republican State, Case won re-election with increased majorities every two years during his term of service in Congress. His one committee assignment is to the important Appropriations Committee, where the *United States News* says he has shown himself "a quiet, hard worker, with a bent for questioning Administration appropriation figures." An amendment of his to the War Department Appropriation bill in the spring of 1941 provided that none of the appropriated funds were to be used to pay the salaries of strike picketers. The renegotiation of war contracts, which he originated by an amendment to another appropriation bill, became standard practice and resulted in a saving of billions of dollars. Representative Case has succeeded in obtaining, for his thinly populated rural district, measures dealing with such matters as water conservation and the Japanese beetle; he supports the proposed St. Lawrence Seaway and opposes the Missouri Valley Authority.

Case's voting record is typical of Midwestern Republicans. His more important actions include offering in May 1941 a bill for the acquisition of French possessions in the Western Hemisphere; and voting, three weeks before Pearl Harbor, against amendments to the Neutrality Act which permitted American merchant ships to carry supplies to belligerent ports and to be armed for self-defense. One occasion on which Case's vote differed from the majority of his party found him, in March 1943, one of twelve Republicans voting against the debt increase-salary limit bill; on another, in February 1944 he was against a roll-call vote on the Worley Federal-ballots-for-servicemen bill and against sending the state-ballot bill back to committee (in March he cast his vote with the majority for the "compromise" soldier-vote bill). A year later he was one of sixty-five Republicans voting for limited national-service legislation for men aged eighteen to forty-five. In June 1945 he was against considering anti-poll tax legislation, although he followed his party program in voting for the bill itself. In general he was against price controls and subsidies, and in May 1945 he voted against the extension of the Reciprocal Trade Agreements Act. In July 1946, however, Case, with others, was to bolt his party to vote for the loan to Britain, an agreement supported by sixty-one Republicans and opposed by 122.

Among Case's proposals was one to investigate means of making the country self-sufficient in producing newsprint, another to set up wrecked warplanes as monuments, and yet another, in March 1944, to investigate the current situation of, and to "issue an emancipation proclamation" for, the American Indians (Case said that one out of eight citizens in his district was an Indian). In April 1943 Case blocked on a point of order the Farm Security Administration program for loans to tenant farmers to buy farms of their own, and in June 1944 he was voted down on requiring Senate confirmation of persons appointed to policy-making positions in any war agency.

In early 1945 the Representative from South Dakota was chairman of a committee of Congressmen from six Midwestern states who were seeking to have the Office of Defense Transportation pay state taxes on truck lines being operated by the Government under a War Labor Board ruling. That June the House voted down a suggestion of his to authorize the Secretary of Agriculture to allocate food from Army and Navy supplies to serve critical civilian needs; and in November Case pleaded the cause of the Black Hills, at the apex of South Dakota, Wyoming, and Nebraska, as the permanent seat of the United Nations. In January 1946, as part of an economy drive, Case introduced the proposal which prevented President Truman [45] from then building an addition to the White House which the President said was needed for Executive offices.

In March 1946 Case and Democratic Representative Brooks Hays of Arkansas introduced a resolution to appoint a House-Senate committee to investigate the number, character, and recruitment of the forces necessary to fulfill the country's international obligations—a matter then under the jurisdiction of several standing committees in each chamber. One answer to the problem was provided by Case himself; in April he introduced a bill for a United States Foreign Legion to carry out American commitments abroad. Patterned after the French Foreign Legion, it was to be a military force of five hundred thousand citizens of other countries, not more than one-fifth of them from the same country, to be paid somewhat less than American troops. "Properly presented to homeless and hungry people around the world," said Case, "a Foreign Legion of the United States would probably attract a larger number than the authorized strength and they would do a good job." By May 4 the number of persons applying to join "the Foreign Legion" in Europe was so great that American Army headquarters there were forced to issue an official statement denying that such a corps was planned. (Case's main Appropriations Committee work was on the subcommittee which handled the War Department budget.)

On May 13, 1946, Francis Case joined three other Republicans (Adams of New Hampshire, Bennet of New York, and Heselton of Massachusetts) in introducing legislation for a Presidential commission to investigate causes of labor disputes and recommend cures. This bill was brought in while rail and coal strikes were crippling activity and while another bill of his was a topic of lively discussion.

The proposed Act which he had introduced four months earlier "to provide additional facilities for the mediation of labor disputes, and for other purposes," known as the Case bill, was not written in its entirety by the man whose name it bears. "I am not brilliant enough," he has said. Commentators see in it also the hand of three conservative Rules Committee members: Democrats Howard W. Smith [41] of Virginia (the Smith of the Smith-Connally Act) and Eugene Cox [43] of Georgia, and Republican Charles A. Halleck of Indiana. "It is something new for him [Case] to take the lead in proposing legislation that labor considers restrictive," remarked the *United States News.* "In this connection, some have said it is significant that, in Mr. Case's thinly populated South Dakota district, there is virtually no labor vote." Case himself declared that the bill was not antilabor but was planned to overcome the alleged injustices of the Wagner National Labor Relations Act and "bring about mutuality of contract obligations and restrictions on the use of force and violence." Smith asserted, "there is nothing drastic in this bill," while liberal Republican Joseph Clark Baldwin termed it "entirely one-sided, against labor," and newspapers referred to it in their news columns as drastically restrictive labor legislation.

Instead of committing the bill to the Labor Committee, the normal procedure, the Rules Committee gave it immediate right of way on the floor of the House, as a substitute for Truman's proposed fact-finding bill. No hearings were held and no committee consideration given before the heated debate which preceded its passage by 258 votes to 155. This was in early February 1946. The House bill emerged in weakened form from the Senate Committee on Education and Labor, usually the graveyard of antiunion proposals, was rewritten on the floor of the Senate by Republican Senators Smith of New Jersey, Ball, and Taft, and in final form was passed by a 49-29 majority. Subsequently, on May 29, 1946, the House approved the amended version by 230 to 106, making the Case measure the first permanent restrictive labor measure in fifteen years. It then went to the President. (Four days earlier Case himself had voted also for the temporary strike-curb legislation requested by the President.)

The chief provisions of the Case bill, as presented to President Truman for signature, included: a new five-member Labor-Management Mediation Board. No strike, lockout, violence, or change in wages or working conditions except by mutual agreement would be permitted until sixty days after a collective bargaining conference had been asked. Employers violating this provision would be considered guilty of an unfair labor practice; workers violating it would lose their status as employees and their rights under the Wagner Act. Contracts between employers and unions would be enforceable through civil suits for damages in Federal District Courts, any judgments against a union being collectible only from union assets. Antitrust penalties were to

CASE, FRANCIS—*Continued*

be invoked against secondary boycotts, jurisdictional strikes by one union when another had an effective contract, and conspiracy with employers to fix prices or otherwise restrain trade. Union members would be subject to Federal Anti-Racketeering Act penalties if they obstructed interstate commerce by robbery or extortion through use or threats of force. Employer contributions to health and welfare funds were forbidden unless employers and employees were equally represented in their administration, and unless provisions were made for annual public audits. Foremen, timekeepers, and other "supervisory employees" could join unions, but with certain exceptions the union could not represent them as collective bargaining agents. The Norris-LaGuardia Anti-Injunction Act of 1932, passed under the Hoover Administration, was set aside, to give the district courts power to enjoin violations and threatened violations of the Case Act.

The Case proposals were condemned by union leaders, by Secretary of Labor Schwellenbach [45] and National Labor Relations Board chairman Paul Herzog [45]. The *Christian Science Monitor*, which desired correction of "union labor's unduly monopolistic power," remarked "there are alternatives to the Case bill considerably more promising of quiet on the labor front." Liberal columnist Marquis W. Childs, doubtful of its practicability, conceded that it "could never be described as a vicious bill." The New York *World-Telegram* called it "hasty, half-baked . . . an angry, punitive, and dangerous . . . measure." The New York *Times* thought its merits "mixed," some provisions being overdue and others unworkable. Proponents and opponents pointed out that most of the proposals had been repeatedly considered by Congress in the past. The American Farm Bureau Federation and the United States Chamber of Commerce were among those in favor of the bill; the Association of the Bar of the City of New York was among its opponents. "There is scarcely more than one worthwhile provision: that holding the unions responsible for their contracts," wrote the *Commercial and Financial Chronicle*. And finally the President in his veto message that June declared his support of most of the bill's objectives, but contended that the instrumentalities provided would not achieve their aims. Truman's veto was sustained by a vote of 135 to 255, five votes short of the two thirds required to override a veto.

Shortly after Case's renomination without opposition for a fifth term, he succeeded by a parliamentary maneuver in requiring Congressional approval for the estimated budgets of the thirty-three Government-owned corporations. The South Dakota Congressman was considered to face little trouble at the polls: he himself said that his Democratic opponent was running "just because he wants to run." After the November 1946 elections had resulted in a Republican landslide, Senator Ball told newsmen, "The Republican approach [to the labor relations question] will be that of the Case bill." When Schwellenbach called a conference on labor legislation for that Decem-

ber, Case attended as the delegate from South Dakota.

Francis Case is described as a slight, wiry, bespectacled man, rather bald, "iron-jawed" and "gimlet-eyed." Since August 1926 he has been married to Myrle Lucile Graves. The Cases have one daughter, Jane Marie; a son, Francis, Jr., died in April 1945, soon after birth. Representative Case, a former trustee of Dakota Wesleyan University, was awarded its honorary LL.D. in 1939. A Methodist and a Mason, he is a past commander of the Hot Springs American Legion, a member of the Pi Kappa Delta, Sigma Delta Chi, and Acacia fraternities, and an honorary member of Delta Sigma Rho. His home is in Custer, South Dakota—population 1,845—where he belongs to the Rotary Club. In Washington he is a member of the National Press Club.

References

   Bsns W p16 Je 15 '46 por
   N Y Sun p20 F 7 '46
   Congressional Directory (2d ed., 1945)
   Who's Who in America, 1946-47

CASE, FRANK 1870(?)—June 7, 1946 Hotel owner, host to literati; formed the Algonquin Round Table, an informal luncheon gathering that became a literary phenomenon in 1918 and continued into the thirties; assembled a cookbook in 1942 under the title *Feeding the Lions*; also wrote *Tales of a Wayward Inn* (1938) and *Do Not Disturb* (1940).

Obituary

   N Y Times p21 Je 8 '46 por

CASTANEDA, JORGE UBICO *See* Ubico Castañeda, J.

CASTILLO NAJERA, FRANCISCO (käs-tē'lyō nä'här-à frän-thēs'kō) Nov. 25, 1886-
Mexican Government official

Address: b. c/o United Nations, New York

Mexico's Dr. Francisco Castillo Nájera is a surgeon, an army officer, poet, and veteran diplomat. From 1945 to December 1946 he was his country's Secretary of Foreign Affairs, for ten years (1935-45) he was Mexico's envoy in Washington, and in 1946 he represented Mexico on the Security Council of the United Nations. His wide range of interests and vivid personality had led newsmen to describe him as "by all odds the most colorful of the Council figures."

Francisco Castillo Nájera was born November 25, 1886, in Durango, Mexico, and grew up there, the fourth of ten children. His father, Romualdo Castillo, was a prospector and mine manager. From his mother, who was Rose Nájera, he believes he inherited traces of Aztec blood, although in the main he is of Spanish lineage. He was graduated with a B.A. degree from the Instituto Juárez de Durango (the college of the State of Durango) in 1904. He might have attempted a career as a professional man of letters (*Albores,* a volume of his poems, written before he was twenty, was published in 1906), but an uncle, a doctor, interested him in a medical career, and Castillo Nájera thus entered the University of Mexico to study medicine. He received his M.D. from the Facultad Nacional de Medicina in Mexico City in 1912. By the next year the young Mexican surgeon was the author of a medico-legal work and an honorary professor of general pathology in the School of Medicine of Mexico. He furthered his medical studies in Paris, Berlin, and New York, specializing in abdominal surgery and urology. In Paris the doctor also took courses in the political and social sciences, and in Brussels courses in archeology.

Early in 1915 the twenty-eight-year-old surgeon was commissioned a major in the Mexican army. He survived "heavy shooting" in campaigns against insurgent peons led by Emiliano Zapata, and against the revolutionary *Villistas*. And he saw action in other minor battles of Mexico's civil disturbances. From 1915 to 1917 (after July 1916 a full colonel) he served successively as director of three military hospitals, and in various sections of Mexico as chief of sanitary services for the army. In 1918-19 he was director of the Juarez hospital in Mexico City. During the next three years (1919-21) he served as head of the Council of Legal Medicine of the Federal District, as a consultant in military hygiene, as a member of the international commission for the campaign against yellow fever (his only book in English, *The Campaign Against Yellow Fever in Mexico,* appeared in 1923—he worked with the commission from 1921 to 1925), and variously as director of Mexico's military medical school, head of the military medical bureau of the combined war and navy department, and professor of general pathology and of urology in national and military medical schools.

In 1922, by that time a brigadier general, Francisco Castillo Nájera commenced his diplomatic career. He was Mexican Minister to China from 1922 to 1924; then he went to Europe, where for two years he made various studies with a Mexican military commission. From 1927 to 1935 he was successively Minister to Belgium, Holland, Sweden, France, and Austria. A familiar figure in the halls of the League of Nations during the 1930's, Castillo Nájera headed several League commissions and once served as president of the Assembly. Also, while in Europe the doctor represented Mexico at conferences ranging from the International Congress of Medical Hydrology, Climatology and Geology to the meeting of the International Dairy Federation in Copenhagen. He headed the Mexican delegation to the 1931 disarmament conference, and was a delegate to the 1932 labor conference. Altogether, by 1945 he had represented Mexico at more than thirty international meetings of various kinds, and had attended numerous medical conferences in Mexico.

Castillo Nájera and Lázaro Cárdenas, the Leftist Mexican president, were close friends, Castillo Nájera supporting Cárdenas' program of social and agrarian reforms. In 1935 President Cárdenas appointed the diplomat-doctor to the strategic post of Ambassador to the United States. The Mexican diplomat's accomplishments as Ambassador were of far-reaching importance to the economy and security of his

FRANCISCO CASTILLO NAJERA

country. President Cárdenas' expropriation of American-owned oil wells in March 1938 seriously strained relations between the United States and its southern neighbor. No agreement could be reached on the amount of compensation to be paid the oil companies. The United States sent several sharp notes to the Mexican government and stopped buying Mexican silver. The matter was still hanging fire when Avila Camacho succeeded Cárdenas as Mexican president in 1940.

President Camacho retained Castillo Nájera in Washington, and the following year, in 1941, the Ambassador played what *Time* called "the biggest diplomatic game of his career." He negotiated with United States Secretary of State Cordell Hull [40] with these results: an agreement on payment to the oil companies was reached; the United States began again to purchase Mexican silver; the United States made available to the Banco de México $40,-000,000 to stabilize the peso; credits for road building in Mexico were made available by the American Export-Import Bank; Mexico agreed to pay in full the property claims, aside from oil, of United States citizens, amounting to $40,000,000. (It was not until October 1943, however, that a final settlement was reached on the oil claims—Castillo Nájera presented Harry Sinclair, president of Sinclair Oil, with a final check, and on the same day Standard Oil of New Jersey at last agreed on a settlement.) The 1941 agreement fanned dying embers of Mexican good will toward the United States, and was seen as a demonstration to the warring world of American hemisphere solidarity. Thereafter friendship between the two nations steadily strengthened, other disputes were settled (among them the Chamizal dispute, and the disagreement over the distribution of the waters of the Colorado, Rio Grande and Tijuana rivers), and trade agreements were negotiated.

(Continued next page)

CASTILLO NAJERA, FRANCISCO—
Continued

The doctor remained as Mexico's Ambassador until 1945, becoming dean of the diplomatic corps, and "the darling of Washington *bon vivants.*" Gourmets and intellectuals alike enjoyed the social affairs at the Mexican Embassy. The *Literary Digest* noted in 1937 that Castillo Nájera was unconventional enough to entertain "any one who interests him," that the versatile Ambassador directed the preparation of tasty tortillas, enchilada, tamales, or frijoles à la Castillo for his guests, and discoursed with them expertly on diplomacy, medicine, poetry, and art. Under his direction the Mexican Embassy was redecorated to become one of the most colorful in Washington, with modern Mexican murals on its walls, and a patio in which the coat of arms of each of Mexico's twenty-eight states appears in tiles.

While Ambassador to the United States, Castillo Nájera represented Mexico at important inter-American conferences, including the meetings at Lima (1938) and at Chapultepec (1945). He headed the Mexican section of the North American Joint Defense Council. During this time the international conferences at which he was Mexico's delegate, were usually of a diplomatic nature, but also included a meeting on migratory birds, and an assembly of the Pan-American Institute of Geography and History. He began to be less active in the medical and public health field about 1934—but he did not limit himself to diplomacy any more than he had to medicine. Literary criticism, and *corridos* (Mexican ballads) came from his pen.

Francisco Castillo Nájera was one of the Mexican delegates to the United Nations conference on international organization in the spring of 1945. The Mexican statesman fought in San Francisco for a "more democratic" U.N.—"We wanted the creation of a General Assembly with wider powers and a Security Council without permanent seats." After U.N. began to function, he expressed the fear that the right of veto of the big powers, proposed and accepted at San Francisco, would "hinder the application of the principles" of U.N. He was hopeful that the structure of U.N. might yet be changed: "If the present circumstances are prolonged, the life of the organization might become precarious."

In 1945, after ten years in Washington as Ambassador, Castillo Nájera became Foreign Minister of Mexico. And in March 1946 he was named the Mexican representative in the Security Council of the United Nations. Dr. Luis Padilla Nervo later became Mexico's permanent delegate on the council, but during Padilla Nervo's absence in Europe in connection with other duties, the Foreign Minister represented Mexico on the council. President of the council, in accordance with the alphabetical rotation rule, from June 17 to July 17, Castillo Nájera presided during the frequently bitter debates on Franco Spain and on the veto. In a farewell address as outgoing chairman, Castillo Nájera deplored the inaction on the Franco regime in Spain. (Mexico recognizes the Spanish Republican Government-in-exile.) Later

Dr. Castillo Nájera launched the small powers' fight against the big-powers veto at the October 24, 1946, meeting of the U.N. General Assembly. His argument was that because of the veto the big powers did not feel compelled to arrive at compromises, thus making unanimity impossible.

In his capacity as Mexican Foreign Secretary, Castillo Nájera disagreed with the United States that the government of Juan Perón in Argentina constituted a menace to world peace. "The Peron government," he said, in April 1946, after the publication of the American Blue Book setting forth Perón's pro-Axis activities, "was legally elected without external interference—that is the point. It is better to assume that Colonel Perón is going to be good than to assume that he is going to be bad. . . . Should the doctrines of the new Government overflow to neighboring countries . . . then a new situation will have been created which probably will require consultation and reorientation of our policy." When Miguel Alemán '46 took office in December 1946 as Mexico's new president, succeeding Avila Camacho, he assigned Jaime Torres Bodet to the post of Foreign Secretary formerly held by Castillo Nájera. Some observers believed it possible, however, that Castillo Nájera would be returned to the post of Mexican Ambassador to the United States.

The Mexican diplomat has received twenty-nine decorations from European and American countries, and honorary doctorates from George Washington University, Middlebury College, and the University of Southern California. His writings include poetry, and numerous articles in newspapers and special journals on medical, literary and historical subjects, archeology and education. Among his other books are included *Tratamiento Quirúrgico de las Epidemitis Agudas* (1920); *Tratamiento de la Espermatocistitis, por el cateterismo de los canales eyaculadores* (1920); *Piezas Americanas en el Museo Arqueológico de Madrid* (a translation of the work of Henry Davacheri, 1930); *Un Siglo de Poesía Belga, 1830-1930* (1931); *El Gavilan* (on the Mexican corrido, 1934); *Algunas Consideraciones sobre el español que se habla en México* (1936); *Una Voz de México en el Extranjero* (1936—a collection of his discourses); and *Treguas líricas* (1945—a compilation of his poems). He holds membership in thirty-nine North and South American and European scientific, literary, and cultural societies, and has been president at one time or another of many of them. These memberships include the Mexican National Academy of Medicine, the American College of Surgeons, and the New York Academy of Medicine.

The statesman's wife, the former Eugenia Davila, to whom he was married in 1917, headed the Latin American division of the Red Cross in Washington during World War II. The Castillo Nájeras have a daughter, married in Washington in 1942; and three sons, one an army officer, another a doctor, and the third a student of music. Their father is a tall heavyset man with a shock of iron-gray hair. Famous as host and conversationalist, a connoisseur of beer and an amateur chef, he is also known to be a master of chess and bridge. Explaining how Castillo Nájera has managed a multiple career, one interviewer reported that the Mexican sleeps only four to five hours a night, and has the power, as well, to concentrate on the matter at hand. As Castillo Nájera puts it, "When I am a doctor, I am a doctor; when I am a diplomat, I am a diplomat; when I play bridge, I play bridge." And he might add that when he smokes he smokes denicotinized cigarettes inserted in a foot-long holder—his smoking pose is as well known in Mexico as Franklin Roosevelt's was in the United States.

References

Lit Digest 123:6-7 F 27 '37 por
Pan Am Union Bul 69:277-79 Ap '35 por
Time 38:15 D 1 '41
Who's Who in America, 1946-47

CAYTON, HORACE R(OSCOE) Apr. 12, 1903- Sociologist; author
Address: b. Parkway Community House, 5120 South Parkway, Chicago

DRAKE, (JOHN GIBBS) ST. CLAIR Jan. 2, 1911- Anthropologist; author
Address: b. c/o Schomburg Collection of Negro Literature, New York Public Library, 104 W. 136th St., New York

Out of more than five years of collaborative research by two Negro social scientists has come a study of Negro life in Chicago, a study critics have pronounced "a landmark of research and scientific achievement" and "one of the best studies of urbanization that American scholarship has produced." This volume, *Black Metropolis,* is the work of St. Clair Drake, anthropologist, and Horace R. Cayton, sociologist, both of whom have had long experience in their respective fields.

The men who wrote the biography of Chicago's Black Belt both came originally to that city for university study. Neither is native to the region, Drake having been born in the South and Cayton in the Northwest. The elder of the two collaborators, Horace Roscoe Cayton, was born on April 12, 1903, in Seattle, Washington. His father, a mulatto, had migrated from the South in search of a free life and in Seattle had met and was married to Susie Sumner Revels, daughter of one of the only two Negroes ever elected to the United States Senate. The elder Cayton became prominent in his new home as a newspaper editor and publisher and as a political force in the State. With his sisters and brother, young Horace was brought up in a stimulating, cultured atmosphere. While the boy was attending Coleman Grammar School financial reverses forced the family to move from their comfortable home to a poor neighborhood, composed largely of recent immigrants. There the boy quickly made friends and at grammar school was elected president of the student body. When Cayton entered Franklin High School he encountered race prejudice for the

Arnl
HORACE R. CAYTON

first time, while at a freshman dance. This incident is related by Arna Bontemps in his book, *We Have Tomorrow* (1945). After the first bitter shock of experiencing discrimination, his old relationship with his white friends became strained. "When little things went wrong—as they do with high school kids— Horace found himself wondering, 'Has this anything to do with my being colored?'" Finally, in his junior year, confused and unhappy under the problem of prejudice, he sought an escape. He went to sea, signing up as messman on a coastal steamer bound for Alaska. During the succeeding four years his travels took him to the cities of Alaska, to California and Wyoming, Mexico, and Hawaii. These years were crowded with adventure and searching thought: he came to know people of all races while working on ships and in fields.

At the age of twenty Cayton returned home eager to prepare for what he saw as his lifework—helping young people who were beset by the same prejudices he had faced. For more than a year he studied at a YMCA preparatory school before entering the University of Washington. While studying sociology there he supported himself by working on the county detective force. In his senior year he met Robert E. Park, the eminent sociologist of the University of Chicago, who was impressed by the student and suggested he continue his work at the Illinois institution. After receiving his B.A. in 1932, Cayton therefore left for Chicago, where he became research assistant at the university. Two years later the young sociologist was appointed special assistant to the United States Secretary of the Interior. In 1935 Cayton became instructor in economics and labor at Fisk University in Nashville, Tennessee. After a year of teaching in the South he returned to Chicago to head a research project under the Works Progress Administration

CAYTON, HORACE R., and DRAKE, ST. CLAIR—*Continued*

which dealt with the Negro in that Midwestern city (1936-39). This research, co-directed by W. Lloyd Warner of the University of Chicago, marked the embryonic period of *Black Metropolis*. Awarded a Rosenwald Fellowship in 1939, Cayton traveled abroad for a while, but with the outbreak of war in September he returned to the United States.

The year 1939 saw the publication of Cayton's first book, written with George S. Mitchell, *Black Workers and the New Unions*. A study of the position of Negroes in industry, the volume proposed to "show how prejudice forms and is formed by economic relationships." Three industries were chosen as types to be analyzed: iron and steel, meat packing, and railroad car shops. The study also dealt with the participation of Negroes in unions and closed with the chapter, "Program for Negro Labor." Highly recommended by most critics, it was called a "must" book for all concerned with the Negro, the labor movement, and American democracy. The following year, 1940, the sociologist became director of Chicago's Parkway Community House, the largest institution of its kind, where he has since been applying his science to the many problems of a large Negro community.

The coauthor of *Black Metropolis*, John Gibbs St. Clair Drake, Jr., was born in the small town of Suffolk, Virginia, on January 2, 1911. His father had immigrated to the United States from Barbados, British West Indies, and while studying at Virginia Seminary in Lynchburg, was married to Bessie Lee Bowles, a student. The elder Drake became a Baptist minister, and when his son was two years old he took the pastorship of a church in Harrisonburg, Virginia. Then, two years later the family moved again when the minister decided to join the many Negroes who were migrating northward. The Drakes settled in Pittsburgh, where the minister's parishioners were principally steel and electrical workers. St. Clair, as the boy was called, entered grammar school, to remain through the seventh grade. During his childhood he lived in a mixed neighborhood, and while his knowledge of race prejudice was vague he recalls at least one fight he had when insulted about the color of his skin. From his father the boy learned how to handle tools and he developed an interest in woodworking. He also became a lover of books, and, encouraged by his mother, read many of the volumes in his father's large library. As the son of a preacher, he saw the church "from the inside" and this knowledge later proved valuable when Drake made the study of religious behavior his special subject. In his father's strict Baptist household no card playing or dancing was permitted, and motion pictures were also taboo. Drake says his father wanted him to consider himself a West Indian and brought him up to admire the British Empire, but subsequent experiences were to change the views of both father and son.

In 1923 the youth accompanied his father on a trip to the old home in the West Indies. Drake now credits his visits to the Virgin Is-

lands, Antigua, Guadaloupe, Granada, and St. Lucia with having first stimulated his interest in anthropology. Meanwhile, his father, appalled by the poverty of the people of the Indies and incensed by the attitude of the British ruling class, developed an antagonism toward the British Empire. He became associated with the movement led by the Jamaican Marcus Garvey, who, from his headquarters in the United States, fought for the freeing of Africa from imperialist domination and for an independent West Indian Federation. When the Drakes returned to the United States after a year of travel, the father resigned from the ministry to work as a traveling international organizer for the Garvey movement, and the son went with his mother to live in her home town in Staunton, Virginia. Here he attended high school until 1927 while he perforce learned "the facts of Southern life." Of his first contact with the Negro press, he remarks: "It was rather exciting, this learning that one is a Negro and what it means—also rather frustrating." He was no longer living in a rigid Baptist atmosphere, and like other high school boys he now enjoyed dancing and going to the movies with his friends. At this time, with the encouragement of his teachers, he began to write poetry, generally about nature, and in 1927 he edited the school yearbook. Upon graduation—he completed high school in three years —he entered Hampton Institute, in Virginia.

Majoring in biology and minoring in English, Drake also took many education courses to enable him to teach later if necessary. As a collegian he took part in debating, edited the school paper, and played intramural soccer and tennis. To meet expenses, he worked as a laboratory assistant and waiter. During this period he became familiar with the modern school of militant Negro poetry, especially the work of Langston Hughes [40], Claude McKay, and Countee Cullen. In 1931 he received his B.S., with honors, and the Calliope Medal for the highest scholastic average over the four years.

After graduation Drake made a chance contact which he says changed the whole course of his life—he joined the "peace caravans" sent out by the Society of Friends to win support for disarmament and world cooperation. Sent to Haverford College in Pennsylvania for a training period, he was one of three Negroes among two hundred white students. "For the first time since my Pittsburgh school days," Drake says, "I was meeting white people of my own age as equals." The speakers at the college included many Quakers and such eminent men as Norman Thomas [44] and W. E. B. Dubois [40]. Of this experience Drake has said: "A whole new world had opened before me— the world of the Left-liberals who dealt with Negroes as part of a larger socio-economic problem and who did not approach them as missionary wards but as collaborators in building a new world." Throughout the summer of 1931 Drake and a friend toured the South for this movement, speaking in schools, churches, and squares, distributing leaflets, and obtaining signatures for the petitions. It was a period of learning and adventure; the two met sharecroppers, saw the caste system in operation, and "just missed the lynching rope on several occasions." His observations quickly taught Drake that "Negroes were not interested in peace, but were primarily interested in justice."

Upon his return to Philadelphia Drake was offered a scholarship for one year of study at the Pendle Hill School, a Quaker "retreat" in Pennsylvania. He accepted, agreeing also to serve as speaker and consultant to the Race Relations Committee of the Society of Friends. That year he visited many Quaker schools, speaking on Negro poetry and "acting as Exhibit A for social studies classes that wanted a real, live, Negro to question about the Negro group." Drake almost became a Quaker himself, except for the fact, he explains, that he "found that even so liberal a group as the Society of Friends couldn't quite free itself of the incubus of American race prejudice." His desire to discover "just what made people tick" led to an interest in anthropology which developed together with the more practical desire to fight social injustice.

From 1932 to 1935 Drake was a high school teacher at Christiansburg Institute in Cambria, Virginia, a small boarding school where for three years he taught a variety of subjects, directed plays, coached the soccer team, and led prayers in the chapel. During this period he read a great deal—communist and socialist literature, religious and philosophical writings—and wrote articles and book reviews for Negro and Quaker magazines. In the summer he went North to work with the American Friends Service Committee summer camps. Then in 1935, on the invitation of a former professor, Drake became a research assistant in anthropology at Dillard University in New Orleans. In this position he spent much of his time in Adams County, Mississippi, where he did research on a study of class and caste divisions among Negroes and whites. He also worked secretly with the Southern Tenant Farmers Union and the Farmers Union, work which at times endangered his life. During the summer of 1936 he took courses in sociology and anthropology at Columbia University and later that year he taught those subjects at Dillard. But Drake wished to do more graduate work, and in 1937 therefore entered the University of Chicago on a Rosenwald Fellowship for further anthropological studies.

At the university Drake met Horace Cayton, who was beginning his WPA research, and after a year of study Drake, too, joined the WPA research staff as superintendent of a project studying the Negro church and volunteer associations. After three years of graduate work and research Drake, in 1940, became associate director of the Illinois State Commission on Conditions of the Urban Colored Population, a position which enabled him to collect further data for Black Metropolis, which was now taking form. In 1941 he returned to New Orleans to resume his teaching at Dillard and was soon involved in the struggle of the wartime community, where Negroes were denied decent jobs in the booming war industries. In the summer of 1942 he returned to Chicago, bitter against those who talked of destroying fascism abroad

Arni

ST. CLAIR DRAKE

but refused to fight it at home. He and Cayton were now working together on the manuscript of their book, and to bring it up to date Drake went to work in a Chicago war plant. For a few months he worked as a machinist's helper, learning firsthand much about Jim Crowism and anti-Semitism in the factories. Then Drake decided to join the merchant marine because, he says, "I did not intend to be shoved around in my country's uniform and I did not intend to submit to segregation in the Army." As a pharmacist's mate, first class, Drake served as a statistician in charge of X-ray statistical work. Drake then returned to the University of Chicago to complete his graduate work after his discharge from service in early 1946. (For a period, in 1945, he worked on a research project with Lawrence D. Reddick, curator of the Schomburg Collection of Negro Literature.) He was also appointed assistant professor in the social sciences at Roosevelt College in Chicago for 1946-47.

When Cayton and Drake decided to combine the anthropological and sociological techniques in a study of the urban Negro, they used the material gathered originally under the WPA project as well as a large amount of data which each author collected by himself. Cayton studied the upper and the upper middle-class strata of society while Drake's province was the lower class—and from their notebooks came several chapters of Black Metropolis. The completed book, which was published in October 1945, contains an introductory chapter by Richard Wright.[40] The Negro novelist wrote: "Black Metropolis is a scientific report upon the state of unrest, longing, hope among urban Negroes, and in writing it Drake and Cayton were working within the compass of the most normal ideas and moral imperatives of the West. A greater claim than that no American can make for the right to be heard."

(Continued next page)

CAYTON, HORACE R., and DRAKE, ST. CLAIR—*Continued*

Before examining the contemporary scene in the second largest Negro city in the world, the authors trace the historical development of Chicago from its first settler, a Negro, through the years of Negro migration from the slave States and the period between the two world wars to the present. Detailing the life of the Negro in "The Black Ghetto," they reveal the operation and effect of the color line, which is sharpest in employment and housing. The well-documented description of upper-, middle-, and lower-class life, covers many aspects of everyday existence. In the opinion of Wright, it is more than a picture of Negro frustration for it shows how "any human beings can become mangled, how any personalities can become distorted, when men are caught in the psychological trap of being emotionally committed to the living of a life of freedom which is denied them." Cayton and Drake point out the danger of racial outbursts in the postwar years and offer a program of prevention in their concluding chapter, "Of Things To Come." The authors also emphasize that the problem of the Negro is no isolated issue, but one which involves the entire nation and the world. Sounding the "One World" theme, they state: "The problems that arise in Bronzeville's Forty-seventh Street encircle the globe."

Black Metropolis was received with unanimous approval by the critics, who considered it an important contribution to American social history. Generally compared to such works as *Middletown* by Robert and Helen Lynd, and *American Dilemma* by Gunnar Myrdal [46], it was called "a landmark not only in race studies but in the broader field of social anthropology." In his review in the Chicago *Sun* Arna Bontemps found the book "a living portrait, a true likeness easily recognizable in a thousand details"; while in the *Nation*, Bucklin Moon called it "a rare combination of research and synthesis, a book to be deeply pondered." Writing in *PM*, Walter White [42] described it as "a lusty, raucous tale of a racial giant fighting to break his ghetto bonds." While this reviewer pointed out minor inadequacies, he emphasized the enormous value of the work. In an otherwise favorable review in *New Republic*, Thomas Sancton noted "proportionately too much repetitious material," and, similarly, Lewis Gannett [41] in his New York *Herald Tribune* column said the book "cries and groans for a popular condensation." Harry A. Overstreet, writing in the *Saturday Review of Literature*, called *Black Metropolis* "a book for all Americans to read, since the facts it presents—unfavorable though they are to most of us—are essential to a full, critical knowledge of ourselves." Of the same opinion, Louis Wirth in his New York *Times* review added: "Especially in the field of race relations . . . this volume makes a great contribution to the building of the future America and the free world." *Black Metropolis* shared with another book on race relations the Anisfield-Wolf Award of 1946, and on the basis of this work, Cayton and Drake received a citation by the Schomburg Collection for the same year. The

book was later chosen one of the five best on race relations, in a poll conducted by the *Negro Digest*.

Both authors have written articles for various publications and both are working on new books. Cayton, a columnist of the Pittsburg *Courier*, has contributed to the *Nation*, *New Republic*, the Chicago *Sun*, and the *American Journal of Sociology*. He is also planning to do a biography of his family. Articles and a few poems by Drake have appeared in *Crisis*, *Opportunity*, *Christian Century*, and the *Journal of Educational Sociology*. He has four projects in progress: an autobiographical book, "White Folks I Have Known"; a study of nationalist movements in Asia and Africa, for which he plans a research trip to the Orient; a study of the impression made upon the English by American Negro soldiers during World War II, financed by a Rosenwald Fellowship; a work on the economic factor in race relations to be written in collaboration with his wife, who holds a doctorate in sociology. (Drake has been married to the former Elizabeth Dewey Johns since June 1942.) Cayton, who is unmarried, is a muscular man, not quite six feet tall, weighing two hundred pounds. Of slight build, Drake is about five feet five, and weighs one hundred and fifty-eight pounds. Horace Cayton makes a hobby of collecting books, music, and paintings. Drake is an enthusiastic tennis player, and his special reading interest, he says, is Asiatic and African periodical literature dealing with the rise of nationalist movements.

References

Bontemps, A. We Have Tomorrow (1945)
Bontemps, A. and Conroy, J. They Seek a City (1945)

CHALMERS, PHILIP O(WEN) June 22, 1899–Feb. 15, 1946 American diplomat; acting chief of Division of Brazilian Affairs, Department of State, July 1944 to death; entered diplomatic service in November 1941; formerly represented American business firms abroad.

Obituary

N Y Times p13 F 16 '46

CHANDLER, RAYMOND July 23, 1888– Author

Address: b. c/o Paramount Pictures, Inc., 5451 Marathon St., Hollywood, Calif.

"A star of the first magnitude in the constellation of modern mystery writers," Raymond Chandler acquired additional fame when he completed his first original scenario, *The Blue Dahlia*. Filmed by Paramount with Alan Ladd and Veronica Lake in the stellar roles, the screen play was one of the sensations of the 1946 summer season. Chandler, who is an exponent of the tough school of crime fiction, was previously responsible for the "literate scripting" of James M. Cain's *Double Indemnity*, and *The Unseen*. He is one of the most sought after screen writers in Hollywood, with an income which runs to six figures. With the success of the author's *The Blue Dahlia* and with his four detective novels either currently showing on the screen or in process of being filmed, "Chandlerism," a cult once confined to the literati, is now, according to *Newsweek,* about to engulf the nation.

Raymond Thornton Chandler was born in Chicago, Illinois, on July 23, 1888, the son of Maurice Benjamin and Florence Dart (Thornton) Chandler, Quakers. At the age of nine, following his parents' divorce, he was taken to England by his Anglo-Irish mother. He studied at Dulwich College, London, from 1900 to 1905, and then was educated privately in France and Germany. A short period of teaching was followed by a spurt of journalism, but Chandler's career in this métier was a failure—he could never track down a story because he "always got lost." His subsequent efforts as reviewer and feature writer for such publications as the *Spectator* and the *Westminster Gazette* were more successful, but cut short by the outbreak of World War I. Enlisting in the Canadian Army, Chandler served in the Seventh Infantry Battalion. By the time the Armistice was signed he had won two medals and was training as a pilot in the Royal Flying Corps. Back in the United States in 1919, Chandler held various positions—accountant, tax expert, oil executive, and a six-week stretch on the Los Angeles *Daily Express.* About the time of the depression he became interested in the "pulps." His first story, "Blackmailers Don't Shoot," was bought by *Black Mask* magazine in 1933. Since then he has sold everything he has written.

In 1939 Chandler's first book, *The Big Sleep,* appeared, and established the author at once as a mystery writer of the first order. Critics were unanimous in recommending this "story of degeneracy in Southern California," although Will Cuppy in the New York *Herald Tribune Books* felt that "this unusual first novel" was "almost spoiled with a top-heavy cargo of lurid underworld incident." However, Cuppy found Chandler's next book, *Farewell, My Lovely* (1940), "the real thing in wickedness and the best hard-boiled mystery in ages. . . .Grade A." *The High Window* (1942) and *The Lady in the Lake* (1943) were followed by three collections of short stories— *Five Murderers* (1944), *Five Sinister Characters* (1945), and *Red Wind* (1946).

"Chandler writes in a hard-boiled idiom which is characteristically American," according to Charles J. Rolo, in *Town and Country,* who adds that the author's twin distinctions are that he is both a literary craftsman and an innovator. His work implies "a bitter critique of a certain segment of American society—the world in which big-time racketeers can still buy protection from crooked cops and politicians." As he delves into the more exotic forms of human depravity, the author piles lurid incident upon lurid incident with tireless invention. His writing has "tension and beauty and a crackling wit" with "logic and a quiet, controlled sort of passion that together propel the story with pace and drive." Concerning the detective story, the author himself feels

RAYMOND CHANDLER

that "the crime . . . is not half so important as its effect on the characters. . . .The reactions of the people to the crime are what makes the story." He also maintains that unless "relief is provided through character development, good dialogue, and humor," the mystery novel can be as dull as any other type of fiction.

Chandler's books have been published in England, France, Denmark, Spain, Portugal, and Latin America. They have been dramatized on the radio, and sold to the screen. *The High Window* was filmed as *Time to Kill* (Twentieth Century-Fox, 1942), *Farewell, My Lovely* became *Murder, My Sweet,* and the latest to be released, *The Big Sleep* (Warner, 1946), retained its original title. *The Lady in the Lake* will be a future production of Metro-Goldwyn-Mayer. In the fall of 1946 the author was at work on a screen adaptation of Elizabeth Sanxay Holding's *The Innocent Mrs. Duff.*

In 1924 the author was married to Pearl Eugenia Hurlburt. A devotee of the secluded life, Chandler has no convivial tastes—he does not drink, loathes bridge and golf. Described as resembling an Oxford don in appearance, he is six feet one inch in height, and weighs 180 pounds. His thick dark hair is touched with gray, and he uses heavy shell-rimmed reading glasses. Chandler likes travel, he says, and music, reading, walking, tea, pipe-smoking, and his private secretary—an eighteen-pound Persian cat. Although he feels that crime does not belong in the vicar's rose garden or the week-end parties of the upper classes, nevertheless it is the leisurely English detective story that the author reads for pleasure.

References

Newsweek 25:95 My 14 '45
Town and Country 100:160 O '45
Who's Who in America, 1946-47

CHAPMAN, FRANK M(ICHLER) June 12, 1864—Nov. 15, 1945 American ornithologist; curator of ornithology at the American Museum of Natural History from 1908 until his retirement in 1942, when he was appointed curator emeritus; originator of the habitat method of exhibition and of bird sanctuaries; known also as a conservationist, explorer, educator, and author.

Obituary

N Y Times p17 N 17 '45 por

CHARLES, PRINCE OF BELGIUM Oct. 10, 1903- Regent of Belgium

Address: Palace of Laeken, Brussels

When the Belgian elections in 1946 gave neither supporters nor opposers of exiled King Leopold III '⁴⁴ a majority, his younger brother Prince Charles, whom the Belgian Parliament had elected Regent of the Realm on September 20, 1944, remained in power. And in the opinion of Henri Rolin, Belgian Senator and professor of international law at the University of Brussels, unless Leopold abdicates or resumes the throne, Charles will continue as Regent even after Leopold's son Prince Baudouin comes of age or is freed from his father's control.

Medal by Verbanck

PRINCE CHARLES OF BELGIUM

His Royal Highness Charles Theodore Henri Antoine Meinrad, Count of Flanders, the second son of Albert I and Queen Elizabeth (a Bavarian duchess), was born in Brussels on October 10, 1903. Many stories are told of his happy childhood, about the normal play and training of the Prince, his elder brother Leopold, and his sister Marie José, who was to become the consort of Humbert of Italy '⁴³. After the fall of Antwerp to the Germans in World War I, Queen Elizabeth took the eleven-

year-old Charles and his brother and sister to England. There they were left in the care of Lord Curzon, a close friend of King Albert, while their mother returned to Belgium to continue her work in the Red Cross. After several months at "Hackwood," Lord Curzon's estate, the two princes were sent to English preparatory schools where, like other children, they were subject to the institutions' rules and regulations. With the coming of peace and their return to Belgium, their education was continued under King Albert's direction. Charles, who had inherited a talent for music from his mother, also studied the piano and violin. He underwent training in the Belgian Army and, for a period, in the British Navy.

Belgium's "bonnie Prince Charles" became known as "the-prince-in-overalls" because of his interest in machinery. This interest brought him to the United States in 1931 to work with Thomas Edison in the inventor's New Jersey laboratory, and later in the Baldwin Locomotive and Ford automobile plants. Traveling incognito, as Paul de Rethy or Charles Dawson, the prince mingled with Americans—attended dances, played golf, and did some fast automobile driving. His dancing partners thought Mr. Dawson rather shy, and his golf partners felt he could do better than his record of nine holes in forty-eight.

Belgians, *Newsweek* wrote, acclaimed Charles for the part he reportedly took in the underground war on the Nazis during World War II. But "no two Belgians are agreed" on the question of the return of his brother King Leopold. Rolin, in his analysis of the Belgian crisis in the January 1946 issue of *Foreign Affairs*, stated that few now condemn Leopold for his surrender of the Belgian army or for his decision to remain a prisoner of the Germans in preference to exile. He has been criticized, however, for not offering more resistance to German demands, and for his second marriage, in 1942, to Marie Baels, a commoner, whose father Leopold had removed from office in May 1940 for deserting his post as provincial governor. (Queen Astrid, to whom Leopold was married in 1926, had died in 1935.) On the other hand, Prince Charles worked with the resistance groups, and in at least one instance outwitted the Nazis. That was when Leopold was sent into Germany in June 1944. Charles pretended to be ill, and while the Nazis sought a doctor, he escaped. In September, on the return of Prime Minister Pierlot and most of the cabinet members of the Government-in-exile, the Belgian Parliament, with the exception of the Communists and Socialists, who did not vote, elected Prince Charles as Regent of the Realm. Although he had no administrative experience beyond routine duties as a member of the royal family, Charles was made Regent for the King, who was then a prisoner in Germany.

Prince Charles, since assuming the regency has gained in stature, though his political responsibilities are limited. ("In practice [in Belgium]," wrote Rolin, "it is not the King who acts with the counsel of his ministers, but rather the ministers who act with the counsel of the King.") But Charles is said to have successfully worked with Belgian political leaders "during a crisis of two complex factors—the regrouping of the nation's political forces" and the Leopold question.

One of the new Regent's first important acts was the choosing of a prime minister when, on February 7, 1945, Hubert Pierlot, premier during the four years of exile, resigned. Pierlot's party, the conservative Catholic party, in 1946 called the Christian Social party, had been the leading group in the Belgium parliament for sixty years. In 1945 the Leftist groups (Communists and Socialists) who had gained in power, and also the Liberal Party which traditionally represented the most conservative of business interests, demanded the resignation of the Pierlot government. Charles called upon Achille van Acker, a Socialist leader who had risen to prominence through his work with the resistance forces, to form a coalition government of the four major parties. But for a week the Catholic party resisted the admission of Communists to the Cabinet. They agreed finally only under the threat by a Communist union of continuation of the six-week-old strike in Belgium's vital coal industry. Before the end of February a four-party Cabinet was formed with Van Acker as premier.

On the involved dynastic question, Rolin wrote: "Although they belong to the Socialist Party, which is working for the establishment of a republic, both the Prime Minister M. Van Acker, and the Minister of Foreign Affairs (Paul Henri Spaak '45) declared in Parliament that they personally considered a monarchy preferable for a country like Belgium." But the King's reluctance and tardy execution of "certain token gestures" for the sake of "national unity" led Van Acker to change his mind about the return of Leopold. "Eventually," continued Rolin, "first the Socialist and Communist parties, later the Liberal party, which among them command a majority in Parliament, officially signified their opposition to the King's return. The Catholic party, on the other hand, affirmed its loyalty to the King, and cited the Constitution as authority for rejecting any discussion of his conduct." Rolin attributes the support of the Catholics to Leopold in part to the influence of the Catholic clergy, "preordained defender of venerable institutions." What makes the situation even more serious, it is pointed out, is that it divides the country ethnically—the Flemings are predominantly Catholic and the Walloons are predominantly Protestant. The Walloons, moreover, accuse Leopold of showing favoritism to the Flemings.

Although there have been reports that since 1940 Prince Charles and the King have not been on friendly terms, in June 1945 a royal plane was in readiness to leave Brussels to bring the King, then in Austria, back to Belgium. When the Van Acker government learned of the plan, they presented their resignation to Prince Charles, who refused to accept it. The King made an effort to form a new ministry. He failed to accomplish this, said Rolin, "since the majority of Parliament was sure to be hostile to anyone he designated. . . . Even this setback was not enough to convince the King of the necessity of abdicating. In a letter to Charles, dated July 18, he said that according to his information Parliament no longer reflected the opinion of the country and that, under these conditions, he would postpone any decision until it had been possible to hold a national consultation."

The "national consultation" or plebiscite on the question of his return, which Leopold had requested and which was advocated by the Christian Social party, was barred from the February 1946 elections by the Van Acker government on the ground that it was unconstitutional to decide by vote the fate of an hereditary monarch. The election, however, resulted in a plurality for the Christian Social group, and Charles called upon their leader to form a Right-wing coalition government. This was impossible since the other three major parties (Communists, Socialists, and Liberals) were united because of their opposition to Leopold's return. Charles next appointed Spaak to form a Cabinet. When the Spaak Cabinet, predominantly Socialist, failed to win a vote of confidence, the Regent again called upon Achille van Acker. After six weeks of political stalemate Van Acker returned to the office of premier (March 31, 1946) with a Cabinet which Randolph Churchill has described as "a somewhat uneasy coalition of Socialists, Liberals, and Communists." The Christian Socialists, despite their numerical superiority were not represented. On July 18 Van Acker resigned, having failed to obtain a vote of confidence from the Senate a week before. It was a month before Camille Huysmans, the Socialist mayor of Antwerp, who became Premier, could form a "stop-gap" Cabinet composed of Socialists, Liberals, of Communists. As the year closed, a stalemate in Belgian politics still existed, making it impossible for any one party to dominate the Cabinet.

Among foreign honors bestowed upon Prince Charles is President Truman's award of the Chief Command Degree of the Legion of Merit. The Prince is also a member of the Order of Saint Annunziata, holds the Grand Cross of Honor of Malta, and the Grand Cross of the French Legion of Honor. His military titles are major in the First Belgium Regiment of Guides, major in the Belgian Air Force, and honorary lieutenant of the British Navy. The bachelor Prince is a handsome man, six feet tall, well built, and blond. Two of his diversions are detective stories and his collection of jazz records.

References

N Y Sun p20 Ap 15 '46
Newsweek p60 S 25 '44

CHAVEZ, DENNIS (shä-vĕs) Apr. 8, 1888- United States Senator from New Mexico; lawyer

Address: b. Senate Office Bldg., Washington, D.C.; h. 1814 19th St., N.W., Washington, D.C.; Albuquerque, N.M.

Senator Dennis Chavez of New Mexico, a Democrat who seldom enters debate, has nevertheless been a leader in the struggle for a fair employment practice law during and after

DENNIS CHAVEZ

World War II. His state, New Mexico, has a population (1940) of 531,818, two-fifths of whom are Spanish-speaking, and his constituency includes many Mexican-Americans, who have a special problem of discrimination. Chavez himself is the only Spanish-descended United States Senator.

According to Delos Lovelace of the New York *Sun*, one of Dennis Chavez' relatives was the first *jefe político*, or governor, of the present New Mexico when it was part of Mexico after that country won its independence from Spain in 1821. At the time of the future Senator's birth, at Los Chavez, Valencia County, on April 8, 1888, it was a part of the United States Mexican Territory, and not until his twenty-fourth year was it admitted to the Union as the State of New Mexico. One of eight children in the impoverished Spanish household of David and Paz (Sanchez) Chavez in Albuquerque, the boy was baptized Dionisio, which was changed to Dennis at school. After he dropped out of the eighth grade at thirteen to go to work driving a grocery wagon, he served customers from many states, and came to prefer the American to the Spanish way of life. His job, which included "being a valet to a horse at six in the morning," paid two dollars and seventy-five cents a week. When the youth left that job in 1905 to join the Albuquerque Engineering Department, he was getting eleven dollars more. After his day's work, young Chavez would spend evenings in the public library reading about his hero, Thomas Jefferson.

"Before he could vote," writes Oliver Pilat of the New York *Post*, "Dennis was deep in politics. He became a Democrat because of Jefferson, and because he noticed that schools and teachers in Democratic districts were superior to those in Republican districts [in New Mexico]. Serving as Spanish interpreter for Senator A. A. Jones in the 1916 campaign gave

Dennis Chavez a major lift—a clerkship in the U.S. Senate." While clerking for the Senate in 1918-19, Chavez studied law at Georgetown University, in the capital, for which he had to pass a special entrance examination because he had never been to high school.

After receiving his LL.B. in 1920, the ambitious thirty-two-year-old lawyer returned to Albuquerque and followed the classic pattern of American political figures: he set up a law practice, campaigned and was elected to the New Mexico House of Representatives, and in 1930 to the United States Congress. Opposing the incumbent Albert Simms, a prominent banker, he became the sparsely populated state's only Representative.

Chavez was a minority member of the House in the last two years of the Hoover Administration, and won re-election on the Franklin D. Roosevelt ticket in 1932. In 1934 the forty-six-year-old Congressman fought hard but unsuccessfully for the Senate seat of Democrat Bronson F. Cutting in a bitterly contested and confusing campaign. The election of Cutting and Governor Tingley was challenged by the Republicans, and Chavez himself challenged the validity of Cutting's. After it had been certified by the State Canvassing Board, Chavez carried his fight to the Senate, filing in February 1935 a petition charging fraud. That May, while the case was still pending, Senator Cutting was killed in an airplane crash, and Governor Tingley appointed Chavez to take his place in the Senate, an appointment said to have been influenced by Democratic National Chairman Farley. As Chavez was being sworn in, five liberal Senators, including Norris and Wagner[1], expressed their disapproval by walking out of the Senate. The appointment, however, was confirmed at the polls in November 1936.

The Senator's chief legislative interests are shown in his committee assignments. As of 1945, in addition to the important Committee on Appropriations and the patronage-rich Post Offices and Post Roads, he was a member of the Committees on Education and Labor, Indian Affairs, Irrigation and Reclamation, and Territories and Insular Affairs. In general he followed the New Deal program, especially in housing, and he defended the President's much criticized 1937 plan for enlarging the Supreme Court to liberalize it. In the same year, Chavez led the Navajo insurgents in protesting the cut in grazing stock proposed by Indian Commission Collier for purposes of conservation, sought to oust Collier for alleged extravagance and coercion of his wards, and joined Wheeler of Montana in demanding an investigation of the Government plan to make the Indian tribes self-sustaining. In early 1938 Chavez was in the news because of the Chavez-McAdoo bill for a Federal radio station to compete with Nazi and Fascist broadcasts to Latin America. Later that year his name appeared in the news when several of his relatives, friends, and political protégés were among seventy-three persons indicted in a WPA political scandal. (Sixty-eight of the seventy-three were eventually freed.) According to *Time*, Senator Chavez had "gotten credit for most of the Federal funds obtained for New Mexico."

In 1939 Chavez urged that the United States recognize Spain's Franco. He urged the extension of trade relations with Latin America, and introduced a bill appropriating funds for construction of a Government radio station. The New Mexico Senator seldom attracted national attention because he rarely engaged in major battles; however, he was re-elected for six years on the Roosevelt third-term ticket in 1940, with 103,194 votes to his Republican opponent's 81,257.

Chavez voted against Lend-Lease in March 1941, but reversed himself to go on record for the second Lend-Lease Bill seven months later, in October 1941. That August he was paired against extending the service of draftees, National Guardsmen, and reservists; and in November 1941, he voted against the arming of merchant ships, though he was for permitting them to sail into combat zones and belligerent ports. In July 1942 he upheld the proposal for Senate confirmation of OPA appointments, and that October urged the Senate to "face the music" by voting on the prohibition amendment to a draft bill.

In November 1942, Chavez won Senate approval for a five-thousand-dollar investigation of social and economic conditions in Puerto Rico (the chamber had rejected a move to include political conditions). This was voted over the opposition of Secretary of the Interior Ickes [40]. Chairman Chavez selected Rafael Bosch as committee counsel, and in February 1943 he and his subcommittee (Senators Bone, Taft, Ellender, and Brewster) began investigating the island's food shortage and unemployment. Within two weeks Chavez reported that Puerto Rican distress was caused by overpopulation and wartime conditions rather than by the administration of Governor Rexford Guy Tugwell [40]. His suggestion that English, rather than Spanish, be the basic language of Puerto Rican schools was opposed by island newspapers and educators, who held that it would "destroy the cultural background" of the children. Nevertheless, Chavez' interest in island problems was said to have been much appreciated and to have won him the nickname, "Puerto Rico's Senator." In May 1943 he and Taft were instrumental in the Senate's passage of a bill to continue Federal works projects in Puerto Rico and the Virgin Islands after the expiration of the WPA; and two years later Chavez proposed native-born Major General Pedro del Valle of the Marines for the Governorship.

Meanwhile, in November 1942 Senator Chavez voted against closure, which would have ended the filibuster on the anti-poll tax bill. He voted with the farm bloc on various occasions, in the spring of 1943 for the mass deferment of farm laborers from the draft, and against recommitting the vetoed Bankhead [43] bill to increase farm prices. Other record votes in 1943 were for repealing the Presidential order limiting salaries to $25,000 after tax deductions; against American participation in a postwar international police force to preserve peace; for the Connally [41] bill outlawing strikes in Government-operated plants; for the modified Ruml [43] plan, which was described as providing more tax forgiveness for the upper brackets and less for the lower incomes than the House's Carlson-Ruml bill. In May he voted against funds for national planning; in June, to require approval of reciprocal trade agreements by a majority of both houses; for the Connally-Harness anti-strike bill and to override the veto; and for the McKellar [46] bill, generally considered "a barefaced patronage grab," to require Senate confirmation of most Federal employees paid more than $4,500 a year. He did support the Administration against prohibiting the use of subsidies to roll back food prices, against reducing Farm Security Administration appropriations, and for the Federal soldier-ballot bill, but was one of eight Democrats to join with the Republicans in requiring the President to appoint the War Ballot Commission from lists submitted by the two major parties. Early in the year Chavez was a co-sponsor of the Equal Rights Amendment: he said, "Wherever the common law, unmodified by statute, exists, there injustice to women exists."

In January 1944 Chavez voted to require labor unions, farm cooperatives, and other nonprofit, tax-exempt organizations to file financial reports with the Treasury. Other Chavez votes were for outlawing the Administration food subsidy program; for attaching a Federal war ballot amendment to the House-approved States-rights service vote bill; for overriding the tax bill veto; against closure in the anti-poll tax debate; against forcing the OPA to "assure cotton mills a reasonable profit"; and against the St. Lawrence Seaway Amendment. No vote is recorded for him on freezing the Social Security tax at 1 per cent, on the UNRRA appropriation, or on McKellar's "ripper amendment" to cripple TVA. In August 1944 Chavez spoke for retention of the two-thirds rule in ratifying treaties, and asked the Senate to assert and use its constitutional privilege of "advice" in treaty negotiations.

The voting record for 1945 includes Chavez' votes for confirming Henry Wallace [40] as Secretary of Commerce without removing the RFC lending agencies from his jurisdiction; for the O'Mahoney [45]-Kilgore [43] compromise "voluntary mobilization" manpower bill; against penalizing employers who violated manpower regulations. In March he was for confirming Aubrey Williams [40] as Rural Electrification Administrator; in April, against the automatic ending of Lend-Lease with the termination of hostilities, for the Mexican water treaty, and for barring the use of eighteen-year-olds in combat without a minimum of six months training. In June Chavez went on record for extending unimpaired the President's tariff-reducing power, including those on farm products, under the Reciprocal Trade Agreements Act. In July he voted for ratifying the United Nations Charter, and for participating in the financial agreements of Bretton Woods; in September, for Federal payments to raise unemployment benefits to a uniform maximum of twenty-five dollars a week for six weeks, and for the Wagner [41]-Murray [45]-Thomas [42] Full Employment Bill—but also for the unopposed Taft-Radcliffe amendment which reversed its original philosophy by

CHAVEZ, DENNIS—*Continued*

forbidding peacetime increases in the national debt. In November Chavez voted to delay the return of the United States Employment Service to the individual states.

The Senator from New Mexico introduced a bill in September 1943 to advance by one grade each year of their imprisonment all unpromoted prisoners of war below colonel who were serving in the Philippines, Guam, or Wake Island on December 8, 1941. (The bill was opposed by the War Department.) In January 1944 Chavez complained, "We've been trying for years to impress the War Department with the fact that the Pacific [theater of operations] is just as important as Europe." In August 1945 Chavez agreed with Senator Sheridan Downey that an expanded and intensive National Guard would be preferable to a standing army, but said a peacetime draft was better than keeping veterans on occupation duty. That July, incidentally, Chavez had become a co-sponsor of the Pepper '41 bill proposing that the country "devote the approximate cost of one day of war to a ten-year program of maternal and child health services."

It was his long fight for the Fair Employment Practice Committee which brought Chavez national attention. In 1944 he declared the Committee's five-hundred-thousand-dollar appropriation would be more effective in bettering relations with Latin America than the millions of dollars spent directly for that purpose. A member of the Democratic National Committee, he tried unsuccessfully to prevent the resolutions committee of the Party's July 1944 convention from "dodging the racial issue" in its platform. As head of the Education and Labor Subcommittee on FEPC, he opened its hearings by declaring his support of the measure, and pointed out that on twenty-three previous occasions Congress had outlawed racial and religious discrimination in legislating for public works projects. His bill for a permanent FEPC was approved by the full committee in May 1945, despite the nays of five Southern Democrats and a Republican. Meanwhile, Chavez and James M. Mead '44 of New York led the fight, against a three-day filibuster, to restore funds for the temporary FEPC, which were deleted in the House. The entire War Agencies Appropriation Bill, involving tens of thousands of employees in nearly twenty agencies, was held up, with both sides refusing to yield. Finally, after much pressure had been brought, a compromise gave the FEPC $250,000—half of the amount recommended by the Bureau of the Budget—with a "conditional" termination clause.

Chavez succeeded in calling his bill for a permanent FEPC off the calendar in January 1946, by a parliamentary maneuver. The bill would prevent an employer or labor union engaged in government work or interstate commerce from discriminating in employment of persons because of race, creed, color, national origin, or ancestry, and it provided for a five-man enforcement commission. Some of the finer points of the bill are said to have needed clarification or amendment, but the public never had a chance to find out. The next day, a group

of "white supremacy" Southern Senators opened a filibuster to prevent consideration of the measure; observers agree that the filibusterers were aided by the rulings of the Senate president, Kenneth McKellar of Tennessee, and its Arkansas-born parliamentarian, Charles L. Watkins. Chavez was floor manager for his bill, which had three other Democratic and three Republican sponsors, and which President Truman had listed as one of the twenty-one essentials of his legislative program. (In the course of the three-week filibuster, Chavez became ill and leadership was taken over by Senator Mead.) Finally Majority Leader Alben Barkley '41 offered a closure motion, which would have ended the filibuster by limiting debate to an hour a speaker. The 48-36 vote—eight short of the necessary two-thirds majority—cut across party lines, with twenty-two Democrats joining twenty-five Republicans and a Progressive for it. There was much ironic comment on the situation, as the Republican election platform had pledged a permanent FEPC, and the Democratic platform had included equal rights. Yet the fight was left to a few Senators—Chavez, Mead, Morse '42, Guffey '44, Ball '43, La Follette '44, Aiken of Vermont, Myers of Pennsylvania, and Smith of New Jersey. The final vote was delayed several hours, incidentally, to permit Senator Chavez to attend the wedding of his daughter Maria Gloria to Lieutenant Jorge Enrique Tristani, USNR, of Puerto Rico.

In the New Mexico contest in November 1946 Senator Chavez defeated Republican Patrick J. Hurley '44 for election to the Eightieth Congress. Some time before Dennis Chavez had become chairman of the Committee on Post Offices and Post Roads, succeeding Senator Kenneth McKellar '46. (Senator McKellar took over the late Carter Glass's '41 post as chairman of the Appropriations Committee.) Before the end of the Seventy-ninth Congress he opposed a rider to an appropriations bill, which would exempt certain agricultural workers from the Wagner Act; was one of a bipartisan group which introduced the Maternal and Child Welfare Act, which would provide Federal financial aid to States to improve maternity and child care; and was one of a group of Southern Senators who criticized the Administration for the curtailment of funds for flood control and river and harbor work.

"Swart, Spanish-blooded, poor-but-proud Dennis Chavez" and his petite wife, Imelda Espinosa, were married in 1911. They have two other children: Mrs. Stanley W. P. Miller, wife of an attorney, and Dennis Chavez, Jr., a lawyer, who served in World War II as a Marine lieutenant. Young Dennis made some news himself fighting the Japanese on Guam in 1944, and in May 1945 leading the first American patrol to enter a Japese city since the beginning of the war. His father's reading tastes run to history and biography. Chavez is said to dislike war movies and problem plays, preferring Bob Hope and Bing Crosby. The quiet, soft-spoken New Mexican continually smokes cigars, "maybe a dozen a day," reports Oliver Pilat, putting them down only to eat or legislate.

References

N Y Post Mag p5 S 30 '44 por
N Y Sun p18 F 18 '46
PM p13 Ja 29 '45 por
Congressional Directory, (2d ed., 1945)
Who's Who in America, 1946-47

CHEATHAM, KITTY 1864(?)—Jan. 5,
1946 American diseuse, lecturer, writer, composer; pioneer artist of children's concerts;
led community singing; specialized in children's songs and literature.

Obituary

N Y Times p40 Ja 6 '46 por

CHOU EN-LAI (jō' ĕn'lī') 1898- Chinese
Communist leader

Address: Yenan, China.

Since 1936 negotiations aimed at averting civil
war in China and uniting the country's political
factions have been taking place between National and Communist officials. General Chou
En-lai, recognized as China's No. 2 Communist
(General Mao Tse-tung [43] holds first rank
in the party), has taken a leading part in these
conversations, which were once again at an
impasse at the close of 1946. American
journalists who have met the Red leader generally agree with Edgar Snow's description of
him—"a pure intellectual in whom action is
perfectly coordinated with knowledge and conviction."

Chou En-lai was born in 1898 in Huaiyin, a
town in Kiangsu province, which in 1946 was
one of the centers of strife in China. The son
of a mandarin family that became bankrupt, he
was brought up in an atmosphere of scholarli-
ness—his grandfather was a high official in the
Manchu rule, his father was a teacher, and his
mother a well-read woman. Chou, who showed
literary genius as a child, attended a Nankai
middle school, where he first learned English,
then Waseda University in Japan. At Nankai
University in Tientsin, he was an outstanding
student, receiving scholarships for three of the
years he spent there.

The social ferment following the 1911 revolution against Manchu domination affected student circles and turned Chou En-lai to a life of
action. One of the founders of the Tientsin
"Awakening Society," an organization of radical youths, he was a leader in the student rebellion of May 4, 1919. He was arrested and imprisoned in Tientsin for a year together with
other agitators, among them Teng Ying-ch'ao, a
girl student who became his wife in 1925.
After his release Chou went to France and
studied in Paris for two years. At about the
same time that the Communist Party was formed
in China, he helped to found a Communist
group among the Chinese students in Paris.
He visited England for a few months and also
spent a year studying in Germany. Upon his
return to China in 1924 he immediately went to
Canton to join Sun Yat-sen, who had just
allied the Kuomintang with the Communists
and was preparing for the National Revolution.
The twenty-six-year-old Chou, whose abilities

as a revolutionary were already well recognized, became the director of political training
at the newly formed Whampoa Military Academy of which Chiang Kai-shek was appointed
president. Chou was also secretary and the
confidant of General Bleucher, the leading
Russian adviser at Whampoa.

The years 1925, 1926, and 1927 were the
period of the "Great Revolution" in China.
In the Northern Expedition, begun in July 1926
and led by Chiang Kai-shek as commander in
chief, the Northern war lords, who had subjugated the people for centuries, were overthrown. Although he had had little experience
with workers and no formal military instruction, Chou was ordered to organize the workers
of Shanghai and direct the seizure of the city
for the Nationalist Army. On March 21, 1927,
Shanghai's police stations, arsenal, and garrison
were captured and a "citizens' Government" was
proclaimed. But when Chiang, a bitter opponent of the increasing power of the Communists
and other Left-wing elements in the Kuomintang, arrived in the city, he took advantage of
the victory to stage his own coup d'état and
sentenced Chou and the other leaders of the
Shanghai insurrection to death. As it was, the
Communist leader managed to escape, fleeing
first to Wuhan, then to Nanchang. There he
took part in the organization of the uprising
(August 1, 1927) which marked the beginning
of China's Red Army. Next he went to Swa-
tow, a seaport in South China, which Communist workers had seized; under Chou's command, they held it for ten days.

Following the December 1927 failure of the
Canton Commune, which he helped to set up,
Chou had to work underground until 1931 when
he succeeded in entering the blockaded districts
of Kiangsi and Fukien where Chinese Communists had established soviets. He became
political commissar to Chu Teh [42], the commander in chief who led the Red Army in defeating Chiang Kai-shek in his four campaigns
against it. Later Chou was made vice-chairman
of the Revolutionary Military Council. Together with the other Communist leaders, he
planned military strategy, operated small ar-
senals and factories, organized smuggling of
supplies through the Kuomintang blockade, and
directed propaganda among the peasants. In
October 1933 Chiang began a fifth campaign
against the Communists which resulted a year
later in the retreat of the First Front Red
Army from the Southern soviets and in the
beginning of its epic long march to the North.
Chou was one of the generals at the head of
this army which tramped more than six thousand miles before it reached Shensi in October
1935.

In December 1936 at Sian, capital of Shensi,
Chou En-lai began the difficult task of trying
to form a democratic united front in China.
Since August 1935 the Communists had been
calling for an alliance among all factions
against the Japanese, who were continuing to
gain control of Northern China after their invasion of Manchuria in 1931. The forces of
"Young Marshal" Chang Hsueh-liang, ex-war
lord of Manchuria and commander of the Cen-

GEN. CHOU EN-LAI

tral Government's Northeastern armies, which had been sent to Shensi to eliminate the Reds, began to sympathize with the Communist anti-Japanese stand. When Chiang Kai-shek went to Sian to investigate reports that Chang Hsueh-liang was in collusion with the Reds, the Marshal's troops held Chiang captive and clamored for his death. Chang Hsueh-liang sent a plane which brought Chou En-lai and two other Communist delegates to Sian. In conversations with Chiang, who had once reportedly offered eighty thousand dollars for his assassination, Chou was able to convince the Generalissimo of the necessity to cease civil war and form an anti-Japanese united front. The Communist delegation also had to dissuade the Tungpei (Northeastern) army radicals from assassinating Chiang. In an interview with the Associated Press in 1945, W. H. Donald [46], Chiang Kai-shek's Australian adviser, asserted that "Chou En-lai was actually the one man who enabled the Generalissimo to depart unharmed from the 1936 Sian kidnapping."

In the months following the Sian meeting Chou flew back and forth between Yenan and Nanking, carrying out the negotiations for a united front. The Communists abandoned their land-confiscation policy as well as their soviet form of Government. The Provisional Soviet Republic of China which had been formed in 1931 became the Shensi-Kansu-Ninghsia Border Government. In September 1937, two months after Japan had attacked China, a united front manifesto was published. Under its terms the Red armies were reorganized as the Eighth Route Army, a part of the regular national forces, under the command of Chu Teh, the Communist General. However, formation of a coalition Government and the democratization of the country as well as certain other demands which the Communists made on the central Government remained unsettled questions. As the liaison officer between the Kuomintang and

the Chinese Communist Party, Chou was one of the Generalissimo's advisers on military decisions and in 1938 was made the vice-director of the political department of the National Military Council. When an academy patterned after the Communist school at Yenan was established in South Hunan to train Chiang's officers in mobile warfare, Chou became its principal.

But ties of unity were weak: the Central Government had not abrogated the edict which made the Communist Party illegal and the distrust that grew out of years of civil war could not be eradicated. In the summer of 1939 the Central Government's Ministry of Publicity no longer invited Chou En-lai to its press conferences with foreign correspondents; neither did the Government approve of journalists who sought information from Chou. In 1940 there were reports of armed clashes between National and Communist forces. When, on January 17, 1941, Chungking announced officially that fighting had broken out between the Communist New Fourth Army and Government troops, civil war seemed imminent. Relations between the two factions continued to grow worse as new outbreaks occurred in which each side blamed the other. Chou, in the words of Ta Kung Pao, Chungking's leading newspaper, remained "the only influential link between the Chinese Government and Yenan," but his meetings with Kuomintang representatives became less frequent. The parties could not come to an agreement on such important issues as the democratization of Chiang's Government, the legality of the Communist Party, the administration of Communist-occupied territory, and the size and control of Red troops.

To help break the deadlock which was hampering the war against Japan, President Roosevelt sent General Patrick Hurley [44] to China as his personal representative in September 1944. In meetings between Kuomintang and Communist negotiators arranged at Hurley's request, Chou, the head of the Yenan delegation to Chungking, again submitted the Communist proposals: "Immediate abolition of the one-party dictatorship, establishment of a democratic coalition Government and a united high command, recognition of the legal status of all anti-Japanese parties and groups, repeal of all laws suppressing popular freedom, abolition of the secret political police, release of political prisoners, cessation of the blockade of the border region, and recognition of the legal status of anti-Japanese troops and popularly elected Governments in the liberated areas." (Quoted from New Frontiers in Asia [1945], by Philip Jaffe.) Once more, however, negotiations ended in a stalemate.

In December 1945 General George C. Marshall [40] was sent to China to replace Hurley as truce-maker. When Chou En-lai, Marshall, and Chang Chih-Chung, the Government delegate, signed agreements in January and February of 1946, it seemed as if an accord had at last been reached. But soon new clashes were reported in Manchuria. Chou, who asked that the United States stop sending aid to China until a coalition government would be organized there, continued to meet with General Marshall and Government representatives; however, their efforts to negotiate a unity pact were unsuccessful. The two factions could not come to terms on certain issues relating to the "redisposition of troops" and the "more fundamental issue concerning the character of local governments" in the areas which would be evacuated by Communist troops. Although Chou had frequently expressed confidence in Marshall, he did not agree to Chiang's proposal that the American General should be the supreme arbiter. He believed that the entire question of local governments should be settled by the constitutional assembly. But, declared Yenan headquarters, Communist participation in the multi-party National Assembly to draft a democratic constitution, which Chiang had convoked for November 12, 1946, without consulting the Communists, depended on political and military developments. In August 1946 "the undeclared civil war [had] spread to parts of Kiangsu, Anhwei, Shantung, Shansi, Hopeh, Honan and Hupeh provinces." General Marshall and Dr. John Leighton Stuart, United States Ambassador to China, issued a statement declaring that it appeared "impossible for the [National and Communist parties] to reach a settlement of [certain fundamental issues] which would permit a general order to be issued for complete cessation of hostilities in all of China."

Despite this dark forecast, the two American diplomats continued their efforts to reconcile the Chinese factions. But Chou En-lai claimed that American mediation was no longer "fair or impartial" and laid the blame for the spread of civil war on United States assistance to Chiang. At the same time he denied charges that the Chinese Communists had connections with Moscow and were receiving help from the Soviet Union. As Nationalist forces, impeded by Communist guerrilla warfare, nevertheless made inroads on Communist-held areas, Yenan's negotiators remained adamant in their insistence that problems of Government reorganization could not be solved unless an armistice on all fronts were declared first. It was reported, however, that the Communist leaders were in disagreement on policy matters, that Chou was among those who favored compromise in negotiations which would lead to a coalition Government as opposed to a policy of uncompromising resistance to Chiang so as to establish a Communist China.

By November 12, the date for which the National Assembly had been scheduled, negotiations between Nationalists and Communists were still deadlocked despite mediation by third party leaders. On the military front Government forces had captured Kalgan and Antung, both important Communist strongholds. Chiang's cease fire order scheduled to become effective on November 11 was regarded as "a transparent ruse," said an Associated Press dispatch, and did not change their decision to boycott the National Assembly, which Chou En-lai called unilateral and nation-splitting. Of the other political groups, only the Young China and Social Democratic parties attended the Assembly, which convened on November 15, after a postponement of three days. Four days later Chou, leaving behind a liaison staff, left Nanking for Yenan, where preparations were being made for a possible attack by Government troops. When no answer seemed forthcoming to the Communist offer to resume negotiations on condition that the National Assembly be abolished and that all troops be returned to positions occupied before the January 1946 truce, Chou predicted the Communists would break "the back of the Kuomintang military offensive in six months."

Chou has also taken an important part in matters other than the issue of national unity. He worked for the introduction of modern medical practice among Chinese peasants and carried on negotiations which resulted in the reopening of Catholic missions in Communist-controlled areas. (Since 1941, however, there has been trouble between Catholics and Shensi Communists, charged Father Frederic McGuire, Shanghai head of the Frasciscan Mission, in August 1946.) A critic of the unfair distribution of UNRRA supplies in China (according to the New York *Times,* about five thousand tons out of total shipments to China of six hundred thousand tons were sent to Communist areas), Chou met with the director-general of Chinese relief in 1946 and reached an agreement designed to complete the Yellow River relocation project by the end of the year. (The river's dikes had been dynamited during the war.)

Chou's wife, Teng Ying-Ch'ao, is one of the foremost women Communists. She took an active part in the 1925-27 revolution, has held office in the Communist Party, and in 1946 was a delegate to the Political Consultative Council. (Chou was also a delegate to the P.C.C.) Mme. Chou En-lai was to participate in the 1946 Paris Conference of the World Women's Democratic Association and also in the International Assembly of Women meeting in New York City in October 1946, but was denied a Government passport. The Communist General is slender and of medium height. "He is boyish in appearance," wrote Edgar Snow, yet has "a kind of magnetism about him that [seems] to derive from a curious combination of shyness, personal charm, and the complete assurance of command."

References

N Y Herald Tribune p3 D 23 '45
China Handbook, 1937-43
Snow, E. Red Star Over China (1938)

CLAPPER, OLIVE EWING Feb. 4, 1896-
Writer; lecturer
Address: b. c/o Look Magazine, 511 5th Ave., New York; h. 2101 Connecticut Ave., Washington, D.C.

Olive Ewing Clapper, widow of Raymond Clapper [40], the nationally syndicated columnist and news analyst who died in an airplane crash in World War II, is a lecturer and the author of a nonfiction best-selling book. In *Washington Tapestry,* which is based on her husband's diaries and her own observations, she

Underwood & Underwood

OLIVE EWING CLAPPER

gives an "intimate record" of over two decades in Washington.

Born in Kansas City, Kansas, on February 4, 1896, Olive Ewing Clapper is the daughter of Edward E. and Janet (McKenzie) Ewing. Her father owned a retail grocery, and the family lived above the store, which was, according to Mrs. Clapper, "on the wrong side of the railroad tracks." She and her childhood sweetheart, Raymond Clapper, lived a block apart, in the packing-house district known as Armourdale, and they attended the same Presbyterian church, Sunday school, and high school. Although her parents had forbidden her to see young Clapper, on March 31, 1913, the couple "played hooky" from school, hid Olive's textbooks in the public library, added some years to their ages (since Raymond was not yet twenty-one and Olive was only seventeen), and were married. That September they hitchhiked into Lawrence to attend the University of Kansas, where they matriculated after making up the high school work they had failed to complete. To support themselves and pay their college expenses, for three years Olive Clapper gave piano lessons, and her husband was campus correspondent for the Kansas City Star. In 1916 Raymond Clapper was sent to Chicago by the United Press as an apprentice reporter, and Mrs. Clapper studied social work at the Chicago School of Civics and Philanthropy.

When the United Press assigned her husband to offices in Milwaukee and St. Paul, Mrs. Clapper found positions as a social worker in those cities. In the fall of 1917 the couple reached their geographical objective, which Mrs. Clapper called "the political reporter's heaven," Washington, D.C. She continued her career there as a case worker with United Charities, and in 1920 assumed charge of the home service of the American Red Cross's insular and foreign division. From 1923 until her hus-

band's death in early 1944 Mrs. Clapper was, in her own words, "a housewife and mother"; her daughter Janet Ewing (Mrs. Raleigh B. Hansl, Jr.) was born in 1923 and her son William (but always called Peter) Raymond in 1927.

In 1937 the Clappers made an extended tour of Europe, visiting England, France, Switzerland, Austria, Poland, Hungary, and Russia. Of their experiences in Germany Mrs. Clapper wrote: "We shuddered at the efficient iron thumb of the Gestapo and the factory chimneys belching smoke day and night to manufacture the instruments of war. . . .Anyone with half an eye could see that war was inevitable. We were scared to death." Although they had leaned to "Midwestern isolationism" earlier, the couple shifted to a state of "alarmed world consciousness" after Munich. Clapper defended this reversal of position with a syllogism: "I try to learn from events. Events are not consistent; therefore why should I be consistent?" Mrs. Clapper spent the war years as an active member of the American Women's Voluntary Services. As the wife of a nationally known newspaperman moving in political and social circles, she was able to observe many national and international personages.

The Navy Department announced on February 3, 1944, that Raymond Clapper had been killed in a plane collision while covering the invasion of the Marshall Islands for his Scripps-Howard syndicated column, Watching the World Go By. At the suggestion of friends, Mrs. Clapper spent the next six months shaping her late husband's newspaper columns into a book, Watching the World, which was published later that year. The book has as a preface Mrs. Clapper's biography of her husband, which has been compared with "the infinitely tender, moving story William Allen White [Raymond Clapper's idol] wrote about his daughter Mary when she died." In May 1944 Mrs. Clapper made her debut as a radio commentator in the Presidential election, broadcasting accounts of the Democratic and Republican parties' conventions for the Mutual network. (Her husband had also been a commentator for Mutual.) Mrs. Clapper, who says that she is without party affiliations although she was a consistent Roosevelt supporter, had a pair of politically significant andirons in her library fireplace. One was shaped like a donkey, the other like an elephant—designed for "the unbiased commentator."

Washington Tapestry, published early in 1946 (abridged in the July Book-Reader) is Mrs. Clapper's account of life in the nation's capital from 1917 to 1944, with emphasis upon the post-1932 period. Into the notes kept by her husband, Mrs. Clapper has woven her own reflections, stories, and humorous anecdotes about the important participants in the Washington pageant. She tells how the Clappers were attracted by Wilson's idealism, amused by Coolidge's shyness, repelled by Hoover's coldness, and impressed by Roosevelt's greatness, although not overfond of Roosevelt personally.

Mrs. Clapper called Washington Tapestry a history of her husband's years in the capital, which he would have written eventually, had he lived. "Yet it is a book that Raymond Clapper could never have written," said Gerald W. Johnson in the New York *Herald Tribune* of January 27, 1946. "His hand was stayed by innumerable considerations that do not weigh with her, he had understandings into which she did not enter, he was probably bound by promises that she did not share. She is, therefore, able to speak with a candor impossible to him." Clip Boutell of the New York *Post,* who felt that the book had attempted too much, wrote: "Good as it is (the author is a liberal and straight-thinking gal), it suffers from over-simplification." "It is best," said Lewis Gannett of the New York *Herald Tribune,* "when it is most feminine and gossipy." Turner Catledge of the New York *Times* pointed out that Mrs. Clapper resorted to no keyhole peeping, and displayed a striking lack of cynicism.

For the title of her platform appearances, Mrs. Clapper chose "Behind the Washington Scene." It was her husband who had helped her begin that phase of her career by recommending her to his lecture bureau: she had had experience in public speaking as a social worker. She is opposed to racial, religious, and class discrimination in the economic and social spheres, believing that the peoples of the world —white, black, yellow, and red—are locked together in one room from which there is no escape. She has expressed herself also on to-morrow's leaders: "The young men who forced air strips through the jungles, and were born into the age of jet propulsion and the atom bomb are the ones who are fitted to be our leaders. Send them to Washington; the time is short." In addition to lecturing, Mrs. Clapper, who is a member of *Look* magazine's editorial board, has written articles for national magazines. She is also one of the adult sponsors of Student Federalists, Incorporated, an organization of university and high school students "campaigning for a federal world government in our time."

While she says her favorite recreation is "sitting and reading", the gray-haired, blue-eyed writer also likes surf-bathing. An interviewer described her as a poised woman with a "tremendous calm strength"; Mrs. Clapper herself closed the interview with the remark, "Don't think I'm taking myself too seriously, please."

References

N Y World Telegram p11 Jl 11 '44
Clapper, R. Watching The World Go By (1940)

CLAPPER, MRS. RAYMOND *See* Clapper, O. E.

CLEMENT, M(ARTIN) W(ITHING-TON) Dec. 5, 1881- Railroad president
Address: b. c/o Pennsylvania Railroad Co., Broad St. Sta., Philadelphia; h. Rosemont, Pa.

M. W. Clement, who in 1935 became president of the Pennsylvania Railroad Company, —in April 1946 it celebrated its centennial— entered upon that post after thirty-four years of service with the organization. At the time that he assumed the presidency, Clement was one of the youngest men in the company's history to become its chief executive. Although the Pennsylvania Railroad controls little more than 6 per cent of the railway mileage in the United States, it carries more than 20 per cent of the country's passengers and over 11 per cent of the freight. Its more than 26,000 miles of track run through thirteen states of the thickly populated central-eastern regions of the United States. Among its subsidiaries are the Norfolk and Western and the Washington Terminal railway companies; it has a part interest in the New York, New Haven and Hartford Railroad, and owns the Long Island system. As president of the "largest privately owned transportation enterprise," Clement has been primarily responsible for various improvements in his company's lines and for outstanding transportation aid to the United States during World War II.

A descendant of early settlers in the United States who served their country in its wars since the American Revolution, Martin Withington Clement was born in Sunbury, Pennsylvania, on December 5, 1881. He is the son of Charles Maxwell and Alice Virginia (Withington) Clement. His father, who as a major general commanded the Pennsylvania National Guard and trained the famous 28th or "Iron Division" for World War I service overseas, was a lawyer. In addition to possessing an early American ancestry, Clement, too, is able to trace his lineage back to Runnymede, where the English barons forced King John to sign the Magna Charta in 1215. This gives him membership in the Baronial Order of Runnymede.

Young Clement spent his childhood in his native city, a Susquehanna Valley railroad community. There he was educated in the local schools, being graduated from the town high school when he was fifteen. He was salutatorian at his class's commencement. His secondary school education completed, he enrolled as an engineering student at Trinity College in Hartford, Connecticut. Soon he began to participate in the college's sports activities, playing end on its football team. While attending Trinity, Clement enlisted in the Pennsylvania National Guard's Company E, spending his summer vacations in military camps. (Some years later he became a staff officer in the guard, a post he retained until his increasing duties with the Pennsylvania Railroad obliged him to resign.) In 1901, at the age of nineteen, Clement received his B.S. degree in civil engineering from the New England college.

In the same year (1901), Clement obtained a job as rodman, the elementary engineering corps position, with the Pennsylvania Railroad Company. Since the days of Pennsylvania Railroad's first president, stated *Time* (March 16, 1936), "nearly every chief executive of the road has begun his career either as a rodman in the Pennsylvania engineering department or a mechanic in its shops. Mr. Clement followed the rodman tradition." In his first job Clement was engaged in the construction of tunnels under the Hudson River and in the building

M. W. CLEMENT

of New York City's Pennsylvania Station. He steadily advanced in the company, being successively promoted to the positions of transitman, supervisor (1910-14), division engineer (1914-17), and division superintendent (1917-18), among others. While working in Paoli, Pennsylvania, as assistant track supervisor he devised, in 1909, a new-type lantern handle for the trackmen which made the lantern easier to carry and conserved the use of the light. Clement's innovation is now standard on all of the nation's railways.

When the United States entered World War I, Clement proposed to relinquish his railroad position so as to join the ranks of the State militia then in the process of being mobilized; but he was persuaded that, by remaining at his transportation post, he would be performing a greater service to the United States in its war effort. During 1918-19 he was the railroad's superintendent of freight transportation, and during 1919-20, acting superintendent of passenger transportation (Eastern Lines) under the United States Railroad Administration. After Clement added to his roster of positions that of general superintendent of the Lake Division (1920-23), he was elected general manager of Pennsylvania's Central Region, with offices in Pittsburgh. Two years later he was stationed in Philadelphia as assistant vice-president in charge of operation. From 1926 to 1935, as vice-president in charge of operation, Clement had jurisdiction over the Pennsylvania's entire system. Meanwhile he was elected a member of the board of directors in 1929.

After two years in the vice-president's chair (he had been chosen vice-president of the company in 1933 but from July 1934 had also been acting president of the corporation), Clement was nominated in April 1935 to replace the resigning president, General W. W. Atterbury. Clement, who became president late in the

same month, was declared by Atterbury to be "unquestionably the ablest railroad executive in the country." Commented Atterbury: "Many of the improvements . . . in service and operations . . . effected in the last ten years have been due . . . to Mr. Clement's advanced thinking." (A May 1936 article in Fortune, discussing Clement's advancement, remarked that General Atterbury's attention as chief executive had been divided among "Republican politics, the electrification program, and consolidation maneuvers such as the formation of Pennroad Corp. Thus Clem has really been running the railroad since 1925.") One of the new president's first measures, according to Fortune, was to adopt a policy of resistance to all Republican political influence in the railroad's affairs. Although he is himself an "intense" Republican, his party affiliation is said always to have remained "a personal affair."

Unlike his predecessor, the "conservative-progressive" Clement was not concerned with "large financial strategies such as went into Pennroad Corporation." Although, according to Fortune, the larger railway systems' dearth of funds accounted mainly for the comparative absence of consolidation during the 1930's, Pennsylvania's "future consolidation policy," would be more cautious (Clement is known to be "skeptical of the advantages of owning roads" one does not "know intimately and operate directly"), but not less individualistic than Atterbury's. His major interest in the Pennsylvania Railroad has always been centered in problems involving train operations. "Operating a railroad," the chief executive is quoted as saying, "is simply the process of getting goods and people to their destination swiftly, smoothly, and on time."

Throughout the depression years during the 1930's, chiefly because of Clement's "skill and judgment" in management, and capacity for "selecting his associates," the Pennsylvania system was enabled to sustain its "sound financial condition" and to weather economic situations which had placed the majority of large railroads in receiverships. Even a decision in 1936 of the Interstate Commerce Commission demanding a reduction of passenger fares to a maximum of two cents a mile on coaches and three cents on Pullmans did not drastically affect the railroad's economy. (President Clement had termed the ICC order a "terrible disappointment" and had asserted that the reduction from Pennsylvania's standard 3.6 cents a mile would be a "terrific loss" to the company.) Pennsylvania Railroad continued to earn profits, though much reduced, and to pay its dividends; and it succeeded in carrying out the "largest improvement program in its history." Two hundred million dollars (seventy million were a PWA loan) were used for it. From 1930 to 1938, when the project was completed, Clement directed the electrification of the lines from New York to Philadelphia, Baltimore, Washington, and Harrisburg, an undertaking designed to provide greater capacity for overcrowded trackage.

In addition to promoting the electrification program, Clement directed the development of modernized passenger cars. He also helped reorganize freight handling so that shippers would be given faster service and the receivers prompt delivery: local freight trains were abolished and were replaced by motor trucks which carried shipments from all outlying districts and deposited them at central freight depots. Improvements in train schedules and in freight train classification and dispatching were introduced. Under the president's administration the GG-1 streamlined electric locomotive was designed and the 152-pound and 131-pound rails providing "higher beam strength" and "firmer, smoother riding track" were adopted for Pennsylvania lines. In the field of labor-management relationships, Clement recognized unionization for the 160,000 workers as being "axiomatic," and has maintained personal contact with many railroad labor leaders and employees' representatives. Although opposed to public ownership of the railways, Clement, in an address before the Pittsburgh Traffic Club (*Vital Speeches*, March 1, 1941) acknowledged that Government regulation was "a very necessary feature of the transportation industry."

At the outbreak of World War II in 1939, Clement acted promptly to acquire for his road new equipment and added electrification to an investment of seventeen million dollars. Thus the Pennsylvania Railroad was prepared to accommodate its heavy volume of wartime traffic (it transported 17,507,647) and supplies. In December 1943, in order to prevent a strike threatened by some of the railroad brotherhoods over wage issues, the United States Army was given "protective control" by the Government, of the United States railroads, to which emergency control the owners offered no objections. Clement, commissioned a colonel in the Army, was appointed technical adviser to Major General Charles P. Gross '46, chief of the Army transportation corps, who took charge of railway operations. This advisory position, his second Governmental post, ended in January 1944. In August of the same year, Clement criticized the railroad social insurance bill in Congress as being possibly destructive of the existing railroad pension plan. Before offering other proposals, the Administration, he believed, should correct defects in the standing law. Clement's 1944 salary, listed in an ICC report for December of the same year, made him the highest-paid railway president in the country. During the war the increased earnings of the Pennsylvania system made it possible for it to dissolve its $138,000,-000 debt. Aside from his wartime duties, Clement was active in a number of relief and entertainment organizations for servicemen.

Clement early in 1946 indicated his company's need for higher freight rates to cover the cost of Pennsylvania Railroad's postwar reconversion and rehabilitation program and to alleviate the decline in postwar revenue. (Later the ICC granted a 6 per cent emergency rate increase, the railroads demanding a further increase of 19 per cent.) He urged that the Congressional Bulwinkle bill, prohibiting the Department of Justice from bringing antitrust suits against transportation companies which combined to fix rates, should be adopted. Decreased postwar taxation on railroad income to allow more money for improvements was another of Clement's suggestions. (New direct-drive steam turbine locomotives and train-telephone systems were being installed in 1946 on many of the Pennsylvania's lines.) Railroad labor, he asserted, had remained "well-disciplined" and was settling any difficulties with management by collective bargaining, mediation, and fact finding between employer and employee. Prior to this, in 1945, Clement had suggested the establishment of disinterested fact-finding commissions to review, and make recommendations in, industrial disputes, while a fifty-day status quo would be maintained. Although the Pennsylvania Railroad and other railway systems have been, and continue to be, faced with competition of airlines, President Clement believes that the "airplane will stimulate travel in general," and that the railroads will share in it. The Pennsylvania previously handled bus line competition in its own region by obtaining a 50 per cent interest in the Pennsylvania-Greyhound bus lines.

The railroad president is affiliated with a number of the Pennsylvania's subsidiary organizations as director or president, often as both. Clement serves, too, as member of the executive committee and board of directors of the Association of American Railroads, and as a member of the Eastern Railroad Presidents' Conference and its committee on public relations. President Clement's other offices include those of director of the Insurance Company of North America, member of the board of managers of the Girard Trust Company (Philadelphia) and of the Philadelphia Saving Fund Society, and trustee of the Penn Mutual Life Insurance Company and of Trinity College. Numerous philanthropic and civic organizations, the Sons of the American Revolution, the societies of Colonial Wars and of the War of 1812, and the Philadelphia, Union, Rittenhouse (Philadelphia), and Merion Cricket (Haverford) Clubs also claim Clement's attention. He is the recipient of the honorary degrees of D.S., LL.D., and Doctor of Business Administration, and in October 1946, of the Vermilye Medal of the Franklin Institute for his contributions to the industrial management field as seen in "accomplishments in adapting railroad facilities under his administration to the taxation burden of the war years."

Martin Withington Clement has been married twice. His first wife was Irene Harrison Higbie (now deceased), to whom he was married in April 1910. Three children—Harrison Higbie, Alice Withington, and James Higbie—were born to them. His second marriage, in February 1931, was to Elizabeth S. Wallace. A leading Episcopal layman, he is a vestryman and rector's warden of the Church of the Redeemer in Bryn Mawr, Pennsylvania. Clement is a broad-shouldered, six-foot-tall man, with light blue eyes and thinning gray hair. His best-known characteristics, writers have said, are his geniality, forthrightness, and succinctness, and his belief in a "soldierly" self-discipline (periodically, for this reason, he gives up

CLEMENT, M. W.—*Continued*

smoking). For recreation he shows a preference for hunting, fishing (he enjoys sea food), some golfing, reading Western stories, and attending the motion pictures (his favorite actor was Will Rogers). He is also an avid gardener.

References

Bsns W p8 Ap 6 '46 por
Collier's 118:16+ D 28 '46
Fortune 13:76 My '36 por
N Y Sun p12 D 30 '43; p22 D 4 '45
Newsweek 5:30 My 4 '35 por
Time 27:46 Mr 16 '36 por

International Who's Who, 1945-46
Who's Who in America, 1946-47
Who's Who in Railroading, 1946

CLEMENT, RUFUS E(ARLY) June 26, 1900- University president

Address: b. c/o Atlanta University, Atlanta, Ga.; h. 691 Beckwith St., S.W., Atlanta, Ga.

Rufus E. Clement is the president of Atlanta University, one of the leading Negro institutions of higher education in the United States. Under its leadership seven schools of the Georgia city have set an example of a cooperative system which has attracted nation-wide attention. Emphasizing the role of educators in the maintenance of democracy and world peace, Clement has said that Atlanta University is "attempting to give leadership and direction in the field of race relations." Himself an author of numerous articles and a member of such organizations as the Southern Regional Council and the Southern Conference on Human Welfare, he has called upon his faculty "to make significant off-campus contributions" to the cause by writing, lecturing, and joining local and national organizations.

The mother of Rufus Early Clement is Mrs. Emma Clarissa Clement, who was chosen by the Golden Rule Foundation as the 1946 "Mother of the Year." Married to George Clinton Clement, whom she met while attending Livingstone College, in Salisbury, North Carolina, she reared a family of seven children, in whom she inculcated religious ideals and a love of learning. (All were to become distinguished in their fields of work.) The future university president was born June 26, 1900, in Salisbury, where his father was the minister of the African Methodist Episcopal Zion Church. As did his brothers and sisters, Rufus attended Livingstone College, where he was rated an excellent student and became a three-letter man in athletics for his prowess in football, baseball, and basketball. He received his B.A. with the class of 1919, of which he was valedictorian. During the three years which followed he studied for the ministry at the Garrett Biblical Institute, in Evanston, Illinois. Upon his graduation with the degree of B.D. in 1922, he was awarded the Kidder Prize. In the same year, he received the M.A. degree from Northwestern University, at which he had studied during his last year at Garrett.

Clement now returned to Livingstone College as an instructor in history. At the end of three years he was made a professor of that subject and dean of the institution. It was while Clement was dean that Livingstone became an accredited college. A former student remembers Clement as the best teacher he ever had—"without reservation." At the same time that Clement was teaching and carrying out his duties as dean, he was also the minister for two years (1929-31) of a small rural church at Landis, a town seventeen miles from Salisbury. His interest in athletics was still keen: he was football and baseball coach at Livingstone, a football official on the Colored Intercollegiate Athletic Association, and one of the founders of the Midwestern Athletic Association, of which he became commissioner. In 1930 Clement received his Ph.D. degree from Northwestern University, where he studied on a fellowship. In 1931 he left his position at Livingstone to direct the organization of the Louisville Municipal College for Negroes. Clement became the first dean of the new college, and he also served as professor of history. Under his deanship, in 1936 the college received its "A" rating.

The educator had been seven years at the Louisville college when, in 1937, he was unanimously elected by the board of directors of Atlanta University to succeed the deceased John Hope as its president. Hope had been president since 1929, the year in which Atlanta University had been reorganized as a graduate school and had become affiliated with six other Negro institutions of the city in a cooperative plan. By sharing equipment, exchanging professors, making use of the library of Atlanta University, and allowing students from one college to attend courses given at another, the schools of the Atlanta University Center have been able to make improvements and yet keep expenses low. The schools participating in the system are Atlanta University, the Atlanta University School of Social Work, Clark College, Gammon Theological Seminary, Morehouse College, Morris Brown College and Spelman College. Each has its own board of trustees and manages its own financial affairs; at least once each month Clement meets with the six other presidents to discuss common problems and educational policies for the University Center. Atlanta and its affiliated colleges also participate in the United Negro College Fund, for which a national drive to raise money for the thirty-three member colleges was begun in 1944 and conducted annually thereafter. As a member of the fund's board of directors Clement spends one month in the year organizing the campaign in the Los Angeles area.

Since Clement became Atlanta's president, two new professional schools have been opened at the university: in 1941, the School of Library Service and in 1944, the School of Education. The year 1941 also marked the beginning of a project in adult education for the Negro community in the city of Atlanta, which has been named the People's College. In his report for 1946 Clement stated that the university would make every effort to open a school of business administration in the fall of 1946. Such a school would help to fill a gap in Negro education, the field of business training having been neglected. Atlanta's decision was the result of a two-year survey sponsored in conjunction with the National Urban League (Clement is on the League's advisory committee), which had ascertained the high correlation between business success and business training among Negroes. Other activities which the university has undertaken have included an annual exhibition of the work of contemporary artists (begun in 1942) which has received favorable notices in the art journals and in *Time,* and the presentation of musical and theatrical programs. In 1940 the publication of *Phylon,* the university review of race and culture, was begun.

During the war, Atlanta was one of the few Negro colleges whose facilities were used by the armed forces in their training programs. Without contracts from the Army and Navy, many Negro colleges, which like other institutions throughout the country were losing their male students, struggled to survive. When, after six months the Government closed the Army Administration School at Atlanta University, Clement, through a series of conferences with Government officials, tried to persuade them to continue the program. In his report for 1944, Clement wrote: "History will record the fact that the great majority of the colleges and universities for Negroes in the United States were anxious to make their full contribution to the war effort during World War II but did not have the opportunity and the privilege of doing this, wholly because of the reluctance of policy-making officials to make use of their facilities." For the Negro student who could not see why he should fight side by side with men who discriminated against him, Clement sought to make clear the full meaning of the war. He also joined in efforts made to gain equal democratic rights for the American Negro. Since 1938 he has been a member of the board of directors of the Southern Conference on Human Welfare, of which the purpose is to secure equal rights and employment for all citizens irrespective of color; it had the first anti-poll tax bill introduced in Congress in 1938 and sponsored the creation of the National Committee to Abolish the Poll Tax.

From 1937 to 1942 Clement was a member of the executive committee of the Commission on Interracial Co-operation, an organization founded in the days of increased racial tension which followed World War I, and whose work Clement believes helped to prevent race riots in the South. Operating chiefly as an educational agency, the commission tried to stamp out race prejudice and solve interracial problems through conferences among white and Negro leaders and through the dissemination of literature on such subjects as lynching and the urban and other economic problems of the Negro. In a meeting at Atlanta University in February 1944 the commission transferred its property to the newly formed Southern Regional Council. With a broader program and a

Fabian Bachrach

RUFUS E. CLEMENT

wider membership (particularly of business men) than the commission had, the council has worked for similar objectives.

In an article on interracial committees Clement defended the dissolved Commission on Interracial Co-operation from the criticism of those who maintained that it had failed because it had concentrated too much on an educational program and not enough on a program of action. He has been a member of the executive board of the Southern Regional Council since 1942 when the Conference on Race Relations, out of which the permanent council gradually grew, first met. The council and the Southern Conference on Human Welfare work together with the NAACP on special issues such as the establishment of a permanent Fair Employment Practice Committee, the abolition of the poll tax, and the abolition of the white primary.

Clement has been active in many other organizations. In 1939 he became a member of the Committee on Colored Work of the National Council of the YMCA and since 1940 he has been on the advisory committee for the Southern Negro Youth Conference. From 1939 to 1943 he was on the board of directors of the National Public Housing Conference; in 1940 he became a member of the executive committee of the Citizens Conference on International Economic Union. He has been the president of the National Association of Deans and Registrars, the National Association of Teachers in Colored Schools (now the American Teachers Association), and the Association of Colleges and Secondary Schools for Negroes. He was on the advisory committee to the United States Office of Education in its survey of the higher education of Negroes (1938-42) and has been a member of the Commission on Citizenship of the Association of American Colleges since 1943; in 1945 he

CLEMENT, RUFUS E.—*Continued*

became the second vice-chairman of the American Council on Education. In his specialized fields of history and government Clement belongs to the American Historical Association, the American Academy of Political Science, and the Association for the Study of Negro Life and History. He has written numerous articles which have appeared in such publications as the *Southern Frontier, Journal of Negro Education,* and the *Negro Digest*; he has also contributed to the *Dictionary of American Biography.*

In December 1919 Clement was married to Pearl Anne Johnson; they have one daughter, Alice (Mrs. Robert P. Foster). Esteemed among his colleagues for "executive ability and tact," the university president relaxes from his work with a game of golf, tennis, or bridge. He is a member of Kappa Alpha Psi, Sigmi Pi Phi, and of the 27 Club and the Lincoln Golf Club in Atlanta.

References

Atlanta Univ Bul Jl '37
Who's Who in America, 1946-47

COFFEE, JOHN M(AIN) Jan. 23, 1897 United States Representative from Washington

Address: b. New House Office Bldg., Washington, D. C.; h. The Kennedy-Warren, Washington, D. C., 719 S. Grant Ave., Tacoma, Wash.

Leader of the liberal bloc in the House of Representatives, and in the opinion of liberal publications, one of the hardest-fighting legislators on Capitol Hill, Democrat John M. Coffee has been the representative of the sixth district of Washington from 1937 through 1946. (In the 1946 election he was defeated by a Republican.) Coffee has worked steadily for severing United States diplomatic relations with Spain and for the improvement of relations between the United States and Russia. Consistently supporting labor and the small businessman, he has attacked monopolistic abuses and warned against international cartels.

John Main Coffee, the son of William Buckingham and Anne Rae (Main) Coffee, grew up in the State of Washington. He was born in Tacoma on January 23, 1897, and attended the Stadium High School, from which he was graduated in 1914. After obtaining his B.A. (1918) and his LL.B. (1920) degrees from the University of Washington in Seattle, he went East to study at Yale University, where he received his J.D. degree in 1921. While at college he was captain of the debating team for a number of years. Admitted to the Washington bar in 1922, he opened a law practice in Tacoma and the following year took a position as secretary to Senator C. C. Dill of Washington, with whom he remained for one year.

Coffee was active in the affairs of his native city and State. From 1925 to 1934 he was counsel for the Tacoma Metropolitan Park District and during approximately the same period (1926-36), he was also counsel for the Washington State Civil Service League of Public

Employees. He was a member of the Tacoma Civil Service Commission in 1926. In 1931-32 he was chairman of the City-County Unemployment Relief Commission; from 1933 to 1935 he was secretary for his district of the Washington State Advisory and Recovery Board (NRA) and at the same time executive secretary of the Independent Progressive Clubs of Washington State, Incorporated. For six years (1928-34) he headed the legislative committee of the Federation of Improvement Clubs of Tacoma and is still a member of that organization.

Coffee was elected to the House of Representatives for the first time in 1936, the year that civil war broke out in Spain, and Hitler and Mussolini formed the Rome-Berlin axis. The Washington legislator, re-elected for four subsequent terms, generally supported Administration measures but was a severe critic of the mild stand taken by the State Department against the rising Fascist and Nazi dictators. One of a minority who opposed the Government's policy of nonintervention in Spain, he voted against the Neutrality Act of 1937 because it placed an arms embargo and other restrictions on both parties engaged in a civil conflict and failed to distinguish between aggressor and the invaded in international warfare. He urged a boycott against Italy, Germany, and Japan, advocating that the Neutrality Act be revised so as to provide for an embargo against aggressor nations. In 1939 Coffee stood with the House majority for the repeal of the arms embargo and for other modifications of the Neutrality Act which permitted more specific aid to the Allies although it did not prohibit the export of supplies to Axis countries. The Representative was also concerned about fascist elements within the United States: he vigorously opposed the continuance of the Dies Committee in 1939 because it had not made a thorough investigation of fascist organizations but had attacked "reputable citizens" and organizations like the American Civil Liberties Union as communistic.

The United States continued to drift further away from its policy of neutrality in 1940 and 1941, but Coffee was not always in favor of Administration measures. He did not vote for conscription in 1940, and a year later was against the House measure to extend the period of service for draftees. He also cast his vote against the Lend-Lease bill when it was passed in February 1941; nevertheless, he supported the first Lead-Lease appropriations measure. Although he favored the repeal of the ban on arming ships and the property seizure bill, he was against the removal of restrictions forbidding vessels to enter certain areas defined as combat zones.

In the years following Pearl Harbor the Washington Democrat voted against antilabor bills, backed legislation to prevent inflation, opposed the 1944 tax bill, which the President deemed inadequate for financing the war. A lecturer on racial and religious tolerance, he voted for the 1943 bill to eliminate the poll tax and raised his voice against discriminatory practices in the Army. He supported the Home Owners Loan Corporation, the Rural Electrification Administration, soil conservation, crop insurance, incentive payments to farmers, the Lucas-Worley soldier vote bill, nurse-draft legislation, and UNRRA.

An advocate of an effective full employment bill, of reciprocal trade agreements, and of the Bretton Woods proposal for a world bank, Coffee urged "eternal vigilance" against monopolies and cartels. In 1943 he introduced a resolution to investigate the handling of public power projects. Construction on the Grand Coulee and other public power projects in the West had been held up, he claimed, while critical materials were sent to build an American-financed private project at Shipshaw, Canada, which would enrich the aluminum trust at the expense of both the United States and Canadian peoples. Chairman of the Special Committee of the Decentralization of Industry, Coffee in 1944 introduced a resolution aimed against the concentration of industry in the northeastern part of the country. The Representative opposed the contract which the Government made with Standard Oil of California and the Texas and Gulf oil companies in 1944 for the construction of a pipe line through Saudi Arabia on the ground that it would lead to an international oil cartel. He also charged that petroleum executives in Federal agencies had prevented the United States from accepting information on Russia's method for manufacturing synthetic rubber and were using their influence to retain the oil industry's control over rubber. With his colleague Jerry Voorhis [41] of California, he investigated and brought to the attention of Congress the participation of United States and British bankers in the Nazi-controlled Bank of International Settlements, which continued to function during the war.

In 1942 Coffee was among those who favored the opening of a second front in the European war theater. At that time he also called for an investigation of the United States program of aid to Russia, for he believed it was being sabotaged by wartime profiteers and conservative Army officers. Following the end of the war in Europe, he was one of a group of Congressmen who campaigned for the maintenance of good relations between the United States and the Soviet Union. When, in 1946, suspicion and distrust seemed to be drawing the two countries further apart, Coffee denounced American foreign policy, which he said has become the "cat's-paw of Russia-baiters, most of whom are imperialists operating by and for the British Empire."

He was a critic of British policies in Greece and also objected to the American stand regarding the Balkan countries. One of six Pacific Coast Representatives who petitioned President Truman in November 1945 to seek accord between the Chinese Nationalist and Communist parties, he urged the recall of United States troops and supplies from China. He proposed legislation to establish a "West Point" for the training of diplomats and, in June 1946, opposed permanent military cooperation between the United States and Latin America as a step which would cause friction in the United Nations.

JOHN M. COFFEE

To the Washington liberal, the continuation of Franco's Government in Spain with its Falangist infiltration in other parts of the world was a threat to the ideal of future peace. In July 1943 he called for an investigation of the activities of the Spanish Falange in the Western Hemisphere. At each Congressional session since 1944, he introduced a resolution demanding the severing of diplomatic relations with Spain, and during the war he recommended American aid to the Spanish guerrilla armies for a revolt against Franco. Coffee charged that Germany was receiving American oil shipments via Spain and that Franco was aiding Hitler with other supplies as well as with propaganda and espionage in Latin American countries. In 1946, supporting Polish charges that German scientists were continuing atomic research in Spain, and demanding the publication of documents on Franco in State Department files, he again called for economic sanctions and a diplomatic break with Spain. He also urged the same measures against Argentina.

Coffee believes in the need "to build up . . . labor unions, liberal organizations, consumer groups, and cooperative enterprises, and to bring them into closer and more harmonious relations for united economic and political action." Maintaining that "the agencies which mold public opinion are completely under the sinister control of a selfish and unprincipled minority . . . corporate monopoly," he has sought to improve sources of information available to the public. In 1944 he proposed the establishment, by labor unions, of a research and publicity bureau in Washington, D.C., and later introduced a bill to authorize the broadcasting of Congressional proceedings. He was among those who attacked the House Committee on Un-American Activities for requesting the scripts of certain radio commentators and he

COFFEE, JOHN M.—*Continued*

continued to oppose the continuation of this committee.

Conservatives have accused the Congressman, who attacks monopoly and State Department policies toward Russia, of affiliation with "Communist-front" organizations. He was a sponsor of the 1946 "Win the Peace" conference, branded by some as Communist-inspired, and was also a sponsor of the Joint Anti-Fascist Refugee Committee, which came under questioning by the House Committee on Un-American Activities. When a twenty-five-hundred-dollar check which he had received in 1941 involved him in a probe by Senator Mead's War Investigating Committee, Coffee declared that Republican political motives were the basis for the charges against him. A Tacoma contractor claimed he had given the check to the Washington Representative as payment for services rendered in obtaining a war contract. Appearing voluntarily before the committee, Coffee asserted that it had been a campaign contribution with which he had reimbursed himself for his expenses in the 1938 campaign. At the end of the hearing he admitted that his acceptance of the check may have been foolish and involved "perhaps a question of ethics," but he denied that he had done anything criminal.

In the November 1946 elections, which gave the Republican Party a majority in Congress for the first time in fourteen years, Coffee was not returned to office. The Representative was a member of the House Committee on Appropriations and chairman of the District of Columbia Subcommittee on Appropriations as well as chairman of the Pacific Coast Democratic Steering Committee in the House. A speaker at rallies and on radio forums, he has contributed many articles to liberal publications and supplemented his salary from the Government by lecturing on political and economic subjects. A Mason, Elk, and Eagle, he lists membership in many organizations and clubs, including the Washington (State) Bar Association, the National Lawyers' Guild, the National Grange, the University Union Club and the Young Men's Business Club in Tacoma, the University of Washington and Yale alumni associations, Alpha Sigma Phi, and Sigma Upsilon. In his religious affiliation he is a Presbyterian. The Congressman, whose hair is thinning, is exactly six feet tall and balances the scale at one hundred ninety pounds. In his spare time he collects stamps, reads omnivorously, and enjoys swimming, boating, and hiking. He was married to Lillian Sly in November 1923; they have one son, John Main, Jr.

References

N Y Herald Tribune p3 Ag 4 '46
N Y Sun p14 F 29 '44
PM p5 Ap 7 '43
Who's Who in America, 1946-47

COLLET, JOHN C(ASKIE) (kŏl'lĕt)
May 28, 1898- United States District Judge
Address: b. c/o United States District Court of Missouri, Kansas City, Mo.; h. 200 W. 54th St., Kansas City, Mo.

In August 1946, for the second time within a year, President Truman [45] found it necessary to "borrow" Federal Judge John C. Collet from the Missouri bench to serve in Washington. Collet remained there for the four months from August through November as adviser to John R. Steelman [41], the director of the Office of War Mobilization and Reconversion. In September of 1945 he had been appointed to the key position of administrator of the Office of Economic Stabilization, where he joined fellow Missourian John W. Snyder [45], then director of the OWMR, in the task of maintaining a stabilized economy during the critical transition period. Collet sought to implement the President's economic policies, designed to hold the line against inflation.

Born in Keytesville, Missouri, on May 28, 1898, John Caskie Collet is the son of James Anderson and Mary Elizabeth (Miller) Collet. He was educated in the public schools of his home state, later entered Westminster College at Fulton, Missouri, where he studied during the years 1914-17. During World War I he served for a time (1917-18) in the United States Air Service. Admitted to the bar in 1920, Collet began his legal career the following year. The rising young lawyer became city attorney in 1925 and soon advanced to the post of prosecuting attorney for Chariton County, which he held until 1929. Collet then served as assistant counsel for the Missouri State Highway Department from 1930 to 1933, where he handled many matters which Truman, who was then a county judge, presented to the Department. The two men became friends. When Truman ran for the Senate, Collet collected a substantial amount of money which he contributed to Truman's campaign fund. In 1933 Collet became chairman of the Missouri Public Service Commission, an office he filled for two years. Meanwhile, Collet had become associated with the firm of Collet and Son and also worked in the Democratic Party. Appointed to the Missouri Supreme Court in 1935, he was elected to this position the following year for a ten-year term. But the jurist served in the office only for a short time: in 1937 he became judge of the United States District Court of Missouri, an appointment made by President Franklin D. Roosevelt [42].

In September 1945 Collet became "economic stabilizer," or Stabilization Administrator in the Office of War Mobilization and Reconversion, reportedly after considerable persuasion by the President. The New York *Times* disclosed that the Judge had been "borrowed" for the post by the Chief Executive after William H. Davis [41] had resigned as director of the Office of Economic Stabilization and the agency's functions had been taken over by the OWMR under Snyder. According to Delos Lovelace of the New York *Sun*, Collet "wouldn't pick up the Presidential proposition until he knew for certain that when stabilization was over he could go back to his lifetime seat on the bench." Assuming his new duties in October, the administrator arrived in the Capital, in the words of *Business Week*, "in time for fireworks over price and wage boosts, without the handicap or advantage of previous exposure to Washington pyrotechnics."

Coincidental with the President's radio address on October 30, 1945, on his wage-price policies, the Stabilization Administrator issued an explanatory supplement to the Truman proposals in the form of seventeen questions and answers. Writing in *PM* the following day, Alexander H. Uhl commented: "If anything, the Collet document was a whole lot more important than the President's speech, since it reduced some of the fine phrases down to actualities which were not so rosy from the workers' viewpoint." In November Collet announced a three-cent-per-pound rise in the price of green coffee to be absorbed by a subsidy paid by the RFC. The coffee subsidy, he stated, was designed to avoid a critical shortage of coffee during the coming winter but was interpreted by the press as United States compliance with the demands for higher prices by Latin American producers. That month an OPA-Agriculture Department study estimated a 10 per cent rise in eating costs with the termination of most Government food subsidies. It was pointed out that this estimate conflicted with Collet's claim that increases would be offset by decreases in other food items. Further developments on this issue came in late November when the administrator announced that food price subsidies would be gradually removed over a period. The end of these subsidies on June 30, 1946, however, is expected to cause a 10 to 40 per cent rise in the cost of basic foods, which, according to economists, can be prevented only by Congressional action re-establishing subsidies.

Further implementing reconversion Executive orders, Collet announced in early December that any pay increase raising wages to 33 per cent above those of January 1941 might be used as a basis for seeking higher prices. The 33 per cent figure, based on Labor Department statistics, "most accurately reflects the increase in the cost of living since January 1941," he stated. Operating under Collet, the newly created Wage Stabilization Board, successor to the War Labor Board, discarded the "little steel" formula which had been used by the WLB in considering wartime wage increases. The tripartite board, which does not handle labor disputes, is responsible for approving or disapproving wage rises which may affect price or rent ceilings or increased costs to the Government. In line with Administration policy, Collet declared his support of continuation of the OPA. He urged quick action to prevent hoarding by manufacturers and distributors in anticipation of the end of price control on June 30, 1946. A danger of inflation necessitates the continuation of the OPA, and failure to do so would cause a 40 per cent increase in the cost of living, the administrator's economists believe. A case in point was the price of citrus fruit: when the ceiling was suspended on November 19, the price doubled overnight. OPA chief Chester Bowles [43] requested the return of the ceiling but Secretary of Agriculture Clinton P. Anderson [45] and congressmen from fruit-growing states protested. After

JOHN C. COLLET

first refusing Bowles's request, Collet later authorized the restoration of price ceilings on citrus fruits in early January 1946.

The first weeks of 1946 found Collet in the midst of the turbulent industrial scene. He participated in White House conferences with other Government leaders in the case of the meat packing industry, involving two hundred thousand CIO packinghouse workers set to strike on January 16. In the steel industry dispute, affecting one million workers, Collet and Snyder granted a five-dollar-per-ton increase in the price of steel in an effort to avert a national strike. This decision on price increase overruled an OPA recommendation for an increase of two dollars and fifty cents per ton, which that agency believed to be consistent with Federal policy. (The company, United States Steel Corporation, had asked for a seven-dollar-per-ton increase.) The Collet-Snyder ruling was considered a significant modification of the Government price policy. According to Louis Stark [45] of the New York *Times*, the two officials "are understood to be of the opinion that the key to the present situation, given the steel price increase and possibly others that may follow, will lie in production."

Collet's policy as administrator was to let "prices and wages in a few selected industries rise a little higher." Wallace, Snyder, and Schwellenbach joined him in an attempt to convince President Truman that it might be wiser to "give ground" on price controls in order to speed up production and settle labor disputes. This plea drew heavy criticism and Collet let it be known, through a spokesman, that he resented any implications that he was wavering in his stand for price control. "There is," maintained the spokesman, "no disagreement between his office and the OPA."

On February 25, 1946, Collet resigned from his Office of Economic Stabilization post in

COLLET, JOHN C.—*Continued*

order to make way for Bowles's assumption of the administrator's job. Bowles, too, resigned a few months later during the battle over the OPA. Afterwards the work of the Economic Stabilizer was taken care of by the Office of War Mobilization and Reconversion, and the Office of Economic Stabilization was abolished. At the request of President Truman and Director Steelman of the OWMR, Collet returned to Washington on August 6, 1946, to begin (as Arthur Krock put it) "his second hitch as a trouble shooter." In November Collet went back to the Federal district court in Missouri, with the understanding that he would "hold himself available for future service." This occasion came within several weeks: on December 12 President Truman recalled Collet to formulate a plan for the liquidation of several wartime control agencies, among them the OPA and the Civilian Production Administration, which were still functioning under the War Powers Act. This new liquidation office was named the Office of Temporary Controls.

According to the *United States News*, Collet's friends say that he "brings to his task a judicial detachment." He is a tall, balding man, whose speech has been called forthright and forceful. Mrs. Collet is the former Hazel Elizabeth Bosworth, to whom he was married in November 1921. The Collets have two sons, William Anderson and John Caskie. A member of the American and Missouri Bar Associations, Collet is a Mason and a member of Kappa Alpha fraternity.

References

N Y Sun p30 O 10 '45
Who's Who in America, 1946-47

COMMAGER, HENRY STEELE (kŏm'-á-jēr) Oct. 25, 1902- Historian; university professor

Address: b. c/o Columbia University, New York; h. 30 Grace Church St., Rye, N.Y.

The author of *The Story of the Second World War,* published late in 1945, is Henry Steele Commager, professor of history at Columbia University, a member of the United States War Department's committee on the history of the war, a recognized historian of America, and an extensive commentator on current American and world problems.

The son of James Williams and Anna Elisabeth (Dan) Commager, Henry Steele Commager was born on October 25, 1902, in Pittsburgh, Pennsylvania. He received his early education in the cities of Toledo and Chicago. After his graduation from high school in the Illinois city, he enrolled at the University of Chicago, obtaining his Bachelor of Philosophy and Master's degrees in 1923 and 1924, respectively. A year of study at the University of Copenhagen in Denmark followed, after which he returned to the United States in 1925 to work on his doctorate. This he received from the University of Chicago three years later while he was an instructor at New York University.

Commager had joined the faculty of the New York university in 1926, shortly after his return from Copenhagen. From 1926 to 1929 he was an instructor of history; for the next two years he was an assistant, then an associate, professor; and from 1931 until his resignation in 1938 he was a full professor. When he left the university it was to accept his present post at Columbia University as professor of American history. For several summers before and after he also served as visiting professor in various universities, going to Duke in 1930, to Harvard in 1936, and to the University of Chicago in 1939. For six months of World War II, in 1942-43, Commager, on leave from Columbia, went to England to lecture on American history at Cambridge University. In October 1943 the educator, as one of ten experts chosen by the Office of War Information, returned to England to lecture on the various phases of wartime living in the United States. During the war, also, Commager served continuously as a consultant to the OWI, writing numerous articles, booklets, and broadcasts. He spent the spring and summer of 1945 in Paris serving in the Information and Education Division of the Army; at that time he held the assimilated rank of colonel. (He is also an active member of the War Department's Committee on the History of World War II).

In 1930 Commager, then an associate professor at New York University, had made his first book-length contribution to the literature of American history, in collaboration with Samuel Eliot Morison. Allan Nevins wrote in the *Saturday Review of Literature* that this work, *The Growth of the American Republic,* "may be pronounced the most entertaining, stimulating, and instructive single-volume history of the United States as yet written on the plane that meets a demand for all the principal facts as distinguished from the Beards'[41] commentary on the facts." The *Christian Science Monitor* said of the authors that their judgments, sometimes original, were always tolerant, and the London *Times Literary Supplement* considered it "a history of their country of which Americans may well be proud." Three years later, in collaboration with William Edward Dodd and Eugene Campbell Barker, Commager completed *Our Nation's Development,* one of the volumes in the "Our Nation" historical series. Also in that year (1934) Commager edited *Documents of American History,* a compilation of nearly five hundred representative writings, each supplied with a brief introduction and a partial bibliography. Said the New York *Times* approvingly: "The editor's final test of inclusion seems to have been the document's importance either as an influence upon the development of history or as a voice of its own time."

In 1936 the historian's *Theodore Parker* was published—a biographical study of the eminent New England preacher and abolitionist of pre-Civil War days. Once more approving, the critics commented: "a valuable and provocative study", "a major contribution to American historical scholarship", "a detailed and life-like portrait." *The Heritage of America,* edited with Allan Nevins and published in 1939, was Commager's next work, a selection of two hundred and fifty-two documents dating from Lief Ericson to Franklin D. Roosevelt '42. "Well arranged and edited," said the *New Yorker.* "The material, by no means conventional, traces, from an unusual angle, a profile of American history." Two years later, in 1941, Commager, with Barker, co-authored *Our Nation,* a senior high school history text considered interesting, readable, stimulating, and of high scholarship. In 1942, with Nevins as joint author, the professor wrote *America: the Story of a Free People,* a layman's history of the development of the United States from the earliest English settlement to Pearl Harbor. Francis Downing in *Commonweal* responded with the commentary: "An amazing piece of comprehension and compression. But what is even more amazing is the number of things they manage to include, and the variety of things touched upon. The authors insist that, despite Europeans, ours is a romantic and exciting history, possessed of beauty and grace. This they have made it." Later this work was published in England and then translated into French, German, and Italian under the United States Government auspices.

In 1943, with *Majority Rule and Minority Rights,* Commager left the path of straight history for discussion and special pleading. The *Nation*'s critic thought it "eloquent, forthright, and cogent" and termed it "an appeal for the unqualified acceptance of the majority principles as expressed through the democratic process. It is thoroughly Jeffersonian in spirit and meets squarely . . . all the arguments that may be raised against the position on the political and historical level." Other reviewers, however, while agreeing that Commager's sense of history was undoubtedly sound, thought his logic at fault. For his 1945 book, *The Story of the Second World War,* Commager was fortunate, through his work with the OWI and the War Department's committee on the history of the war, to have access to official documents relating to his subject. The volume, he explained in the foreword, was not, however, a systematic history because all the materials were not then available. "What this book does present is a series of stories, episodes, vignettes, descriptions, analyses, and historic statements by men and women who participated in or observed or analyzed the war, all bound together with a very general and, by any rigorous scholarly standards, uncritical running narrative." Nevertheless, commented Roiand Kilbon of the New York *Sun,* "down to the very end it is all there . . . [in] what is not only an interesting but also a valuable book."

Up to 1940 the educator had not been a prolific contributor to magazines, writing only infrequently for such periodicals as *Current History.* With the threat of war for the United States growing more menacing, however, he began a series of articles in *Scholastic* entitled *Today's Events in the Light of History.* In 1941 and 1942 he wrote a second series, entitled *Our American Heritage.* Meanwhile, he had become a frequent contributor to the New York *Times Magazine* as well as to

HENRY STEELE COMMAGER

Scholastic, and to various other magazines, among them the *American Mercury,* the *Nation,* and the *Atlantic Monthly.* He edited Tocqueville's *Democracy in America,* Franklin's *Autobiography,* Parkman's *Oregon Trail,* and Pike's *Prostrate State.* With Dr. Conant of Harvard, he was American coeditor of the Home University Library (Oxford University Press).

Commager is an associate editor of the *American Scholar,* the Phi Beta Kappa organ, and a contributing editor of *Scholastic.* He was elected to Phi Beta Kappa by Chicago University in 1923 and received the Herbert B. Adams Award of the American Historical Association in 1929. He is a Fellow of the American Scandinavian Society, and a member of the American Historical Association, the Massachusetts Historical Society, and the American Antiquarian Society. Commager, who classifies himself politically as an independent Democrat, edited one of the sections of *Franklin Delano Roosevelt: a Memorial* (1945). At present he is working on three books, "Joseph Story: a Biography", "The American Mind," and "Britain Through American Eyes." Since 1928 the historian has been married to the former Evan Carroll; their three children are Henry Steele, Elisabeth Carroll, and Nellie Thomas McColl. Commager is a man of medium stature and has brown hair and gray eyes.

Reference

Who's Who in America, 1946-47

CONDON, E(DWARD) U(HLER) Mar. 2, 1902- Physicist; United States Government official

Address: b. National Bureau of Standards, Washington, D.C.; h. 3535 Van Ness St., N.W., Washington, D.C.

After eight years as associate director of research for the Westinghouse Electric Cor-

(Continued next page)

E. U. CONDON

poration, E. U. Condon was appointed director of the National Bureau of Standards, of the United States Department of Commerce, in November 1945.

The birthplace of Edward Uhler Condon has become associated with the historic first detonation of the atomic bomb. The area chosen for that experimental explosion lies not far from the town of Alamogordo, New Mexico, where he was born March 2, 1902, to William Edward and Caroline Barr (Uhler) Condon. William Condon was a civil engineer, whose family accompanied him as he moved about in the West on various railroad construction jobs.

Young Condon was interested in science as a high school student in Oakland, California, but worked as a reporter for three years for Oakland and San Francisco newspapers before entering the University of California to study astronomy. His experience as a newspaperman probably contributed to his facility for translating his ideas into emphatic and readily quotable language. He was later to write numerous articles for popular scientific magazines, as well as research books and papers. According to his colleagues, even his research papers sometimes contain "a fillip of language unusual to such literature." In college he turned his main interest from astronomy to physics. He was awarded his B.A. degree with highest honors in 1924, and his Ph.D. degree in 1926, both from the University of California, at Berkeley.

The Rockefeller Foundation, in an effort to stimulate the development of trained research men in physics, chemistry, and mathematics, had established National Research Council Fellowships just after World War I. Awarded one of these fellowships, Condon studied in Göttingen and Munich in 1926-27. In the spring of 1927, on his return to America, he lectured in physics at Columbia University.

The next year he was appointed assistant professor of physics at Princeton University; this he left in 1929 to take a professorship at the University of Minnesota. When he returned to Princeton in 1930 he was to stay for seven years as an associate professor.

At Princeton Condon concentrated on applications of the new methods of quantum mechanics to problems of atomic and molecular structure and the interpretation of radioactivity. American industry was becoming increasingly interested in applied physics, and late in the thirties many physicists entered the field of industrial research. In 1937 Condon, too, left the classroom for the industrial laboratory. The Westinghouse Electric and Manufacturing Company in East Pittsburgh, Pennsylvania, appointed Condon associate director of its research laboratories, where research fellows dealt with pure science. Condon did not lose contact with the academic world, however; while at Westinghouse he served as advisory professor for the University of Pittsburgh. In an address at Purdue University in 1942, at the opening of the Charles Benedict Stuart Laboratory of Applied Physics, he said: "I feel sure that those who are entrusted with furthering scientific research at colleges see this problem of applied physics in all its broad implications. They recognize, as we do in industry, that all physics is applied physics—so-called pure physics being simply that part whose application is to satisfy the curiosity of the physicists."

At Westinghouse Condon directed the work of a group of young physicists doing research on the only large atom-smasher to be operated by an industrial research laboratory. With this equipment the group carried out studies on uranium fission before the Government's atomic bomb project was started.

From the fall of 1940 Condon was engaged full time on various phases of research for military purposes. Serving as a consultant to the National Defense Research Committee he helped to organize the Radiation Laboratory at the Massachusetts Institute of Technology, which conducted the research and development program on micro-wave radar. Later he organized and directed the research activities of Westinghouse in radar. Early in the war he assisted in organizing the rocket research program. Appointed to President Roosevelt's committee on uranium research in mid-1941, he helped in the studies which led to the launching in January 1942 of the major effort which culminated in the successful development of the atomic bomb. In the fall of 1943 Condon left the radar work at Westinghouse to devote his entire time to the work on the atomic bomb project at the University of California; his work involved separation of U-235 from U-238 with the use of large mass spectrographs.

In October 1945 Condon was nominated by President Truman as director of the National Bureau of Standards to succeed Dr. Lyman J. Briggs, who was retiring after twenty-eight years of service. The bureau, a division of the Department of Commerce, is the Government's principal agency for basic research in physics, chemistry, and engineering. Originally concerned mainly with the standards of length and weight, it now conducts basic research on fundamental science of great variety. Condon was also appointed by the President to the National Advisory Committee for Aeronautics, the Government research agency in the aviation field.

On November 5, 1945, two days after his appointment to the Bureau of Standards was confirmed by the Senate, Condon was named scientific adviser to the Senate Special Committee on Atomic Energy. This committee, which was headed by Senator Brien McMahon [45], reported unanimously to the Senate a bill providing for Federal operation of atomic energy plants by a civilian atomic energy commission. While not advocating the immediate disclosure of secret data on atomic weapons, Condon warned that "we cannot expect that the scientists of other nations will be long in discovering by their own studies what we now know and more, and therefore no sound policy can be permanently based on the idea of keeping secret our work in this field." He repeatedly emphasized the importance of developing international cooperation between scientists as it existed before World War II, and the need for an effective program of international control of the atomic bomb through the United Nations Atomic Energy Commission.

In March 1946 Condon brought into the open the conflict between American scientists and military men for the control of atomic energy in a speech before the Westinghouse Science Institute (reprinted in *Science,* April 5, 1946.) "Prominent scientists are denied the privilege of traveling abroad," he said. "Physicists are not allowed to discuss certain areas of their science with each other. . . .Information essential to understanding is being denied to students in our universities, so that, if this situation were to continue, the young students . . . will get from their professors only a watered-down Army-approved version of the laws of nature." Condon lashed out at army officers who were "without knowledge, and so without competence," and who yet were in a position to censor exchange of scientific knowledge. "War research is not true science," he wrote in the *Saturday Review of Literature* in June 1946. "Any attempt to perpetuate into peacetime the restrictive practices which were used during the war will have disastrous consequences : . . it spells death to our own activity."

Condon was one of several scientists who in May 1946 joined Professor Albert Einstein in forming the Emergency Committee of Atomic Scientists, which hoped to "help arouse the world to its danger." Two months later Condon served on the Presidential Evaluation Commission, which made an official report to the President of the results of the atomic bomb test at Bikini. He was elected to the National Academy of Sciences in 1944, is the 1946 president of the American Physical Society. He is the coauthor of two books: with P. M. Morse he wrote *Quantum Mechanics* (1929), and with G. H. Shortley, *The Theory of Atomic Spectra* (1935). He was also one of the seven-teen scientists who contributed to the book *One World or None* (1946).

Condon was married when he was only twenty years old, in November 1922, to Emilie Honzik. They have one daughter and two sons —Caroline Marie, Paul Edward, and Joseph Henry. The physicist has been described as "a chunky, square-built man with a closely cropped brush of black hair." *Time* magazine called him "approachable, colloquial, and jolly," adding that he "likes reading science books of all kinds, band music, complicated ice-cream sodas." Condon says his principal outside interest is symphonic and chamber music.

References

Time 35 :44-5 F 12 '40
U S News 20 :80-1 Mr 22 '46
Who's Who in America, 1946-47

COOK, FANNIE Oct. 4, 1893- Author
Address: b. c/o Doubleday and Company, Inc., 14 W. 49th St., New York; h. 400 Purdue Ave., St. Louis, Mo.

The first George Washington Carver award of $2,500 was won by Fannie Cook for her novel, *Mrs. Palmer's Honey.* Her story of a St. Louis Negro family was judged the most effective literary contribution "to the importance of the Negro's place in American life." This, Mrs. Cook's third novel, is characterized by the same social consciousenss which marks her other writings. She has studied the problem of race relations primarily in St. Louis, which she calls a "Northern city with a Southern exposure."

Fannie Cook was born on October 4, 1893, in St. Charles, Missouri, the daughter of Julius and Jennie (Michael) Frank. In St. Louis, where they lived later, she attended the Central and Soldan high schools, and was graduated from the latter. She was granted her B.A. from the University of Missouri in 1914. (She had spent the previous summer at the University of Wisconsin.) In 1916 she was given her M.A. degree by Washington University. A year before, on October 28, 1915, she had been married to a St. Louis physician, Dr. Jerome E. Cook. (They have two sons, Dr. Robert Jerome Cook and Howard Frank Cook, both of whom served in the armed forces, one as a doctor with the Seventh Army and the other as a B-17 pilot.)

In 1931 Mrs. Cook, her husband, and the two boys spent a memorable month in England. "I can still hear the voices of the people I met, see the designs on teapots in cottages. . . .I can smell dark carpeting in Bloomsbury, flowers at Oxford, shrubs at Salisbury, the lakes at Keswick. . . .Any mundane experience of my daily life is likely to light up with feeling and become memorable, so I can't pick out a 'first' unless it be the day I gained the courage to stop doing the many things I half wanted to do in order to do the one thing I most wanted to do—to write. I have taken an active part in the life of my own city and State but always as two persons: one partaking,

Todd Studios

FANNIE COOK

and one watching and reporting to the writer-self."

Apart from honorable mention in early years for a story sent to *St. Nicholas,* Mrs. Cook's first success as a writer came in 1935, when she won the first prize of $1,000 in a *Reader's Digest* contest for new writers. (To date the *Digest* has not published the article.) It was soon after this that she resigned an instructorship in the English department at Washington University to give her mornings to writing, two hours to doing water-color sketches (a portrait *Millicent* exhibited at the St. Louis Artists' Guild last spring was called "gay and delightful"), and the evenings to her husband and their two sons.

Mrs. Cook's first novel was *The Hill Grows Steeper* (1938), whose heroine makes a life of her own in St. Louis, starting as a factory worker and eventually becoming an executive of a woman's civic organization. Her second novel was *Boot-Heel Doctor,* published in 1941, for which Mrs. Cook had journeyed to southeastern Missouri, generally known because of its geographical contours as the "boot-heel," to do research for this story of hapless sharecroppers and tenant farmers. Rose Feld, in the New York *Times Book Review* called this a fine regional novel, "excellent not alone for its dramatic story but for its sympathetic treatment of humans caught in a grave national problem."

When *Mrs. Palmer's Honey* was published in February 1946 Mrs. Cook came to New York to receive the 1946 George Washington Carver award, established by the publishers Doubleday and Company in 1944. The story of Mrs. Palmer's Negro maid, Honey, whose horizons gradually broadened until she became the CIO's Honey, an expert in getting out the Negro vote, is a cheerful one. Lewis Gannett, in the New York *Herald Tribune,* voiced his relief at reading "a novel about Negro life

which neither treats Negroes as clowns nor ends in desperation and violence." One of the most enthusiastic critics was Barbara Klaw, also of the *Herald Tribune,* who thought it "a mature story of the growth of human dignity within an individual." Some critics, however, felt that labor propaganda tended to weaken the story: what started out, according to the *New Yorker,* as a "quietly perceptive study of a very lovable Negro girl" changes abruptly into "a sort of labor tract with characters." Orville Prescott, who had the same criticism, wrote in the *Yale Review* that "Mrs. Cook knows a great deal about the Negro problem and cares passionately about it."

It was an instance of injustice to a Negro houseboy in her own home, whom she vainly tried to save from a prison sentence and who eventually died of tuberculosis in jail, that impressed Mrs. Cook with the gravity of the problem of racial relations, as well as the fact that Negroes were barred from the University of Missouri. Her present contacts with her Negro readers include membership on the Mayor's Committee on Race Relations and work as adviser to the National Association for the Advancement of Colored People. After publication of *Mrs. Palmer's Honey* the St. Louis *Argus,* a Negro newspaper, gave the author a handsome trophy for her "Outstanding Contribution to Interracial Welfare."

Mrs. Cook herself has said of her writings: "The central characters of my novels have been big people spiritually who are lesser people in society. My short stories are usually humorous accounts of situations containing pathos, yet I am not a sentimentalist but a realist." Her stories have appeared in the *New Republic, Common Ground, Southwest Review, New Anvil, Coronet,* and *Mademoiselle.* She has also written numerous articles for *The Mirror of Public Opinion* in the St. Louis *Post-Dispatch.* One, "The Public Library Needs Help," was reprinted in pamphlet form and widely distributed. In recent years Mrs. Cook has given talks in the Noon-Day Series sponsored by the St. Louis Public Library. She is also a member of the People's Art Center in St. Louis.

Mrs. Cook likes to hike as well as to sketch and paint. An interviewer some years ago described her as a small, blond woman, with friendly blue eyes and a quick good-humored smile. Her interest in stories and how they are made, and her career as an imaginative artist date from the evening she saw Joseph Jefferson in *Rip Van Winkle.* "I remember how offended I was when the lights went on, and I had to recognize that there was a real world."

CORBETT, JAMES EDWARD *See* Corbett, J.

CORBETT, JIM 1875- Hunter; author
Address: Naini Tal, U. P., India; Kaladhungi, U. P., India

Man-Eaters of Kumaon, a best-selling book published in March 1946, is the account of seven high lights in the thirty-two years Jim Corbett devoted largely to ridding his native Kumaon Hills, in India, of man-eating tigers and leopards.

James Edward Corbett (he is "Jim" on his book's title page) was born in 1875 at Naini Tal, United Provinces, India, the beautiful hill station in the Himalayas where the United Province Government—and the Corbett family —spent the summer months. Jim was the second youngest of thirteen children; an older stepsister had survived the siege of Agra in the Mutiny of 1857. Their father, who served in the (British) Indian Army on the perennially explosive Afghanistan frontier, died when Jim was four, and the children were brought up by their mother on the Naini Tal estate and the "Irish cottage" at Kaladhungi, fifteen miles away but climatically very different, where they passed the winters.

The Corbett homestead was surrounded by jungle in which Jim studied wildlife, collected birds' eggs, and learned to hunt. When he was four, he and a younger brother were saved by their old collie from the attack of an infuriated Himalayan bear. The boy grew up without fear of the "jungle folk," however, and as a small boy, armed with an old wreck of a gun, wandered casually through the swampy, malarial, tiger-haunted country, sleeping by a small fire anywhere he happened to be. His hill training made him "as surefooted as a mountain goat," and an early desire to become a lumberman in Canada made him achieve "sufficient proficiency with an axe to split a matchstick." After attending school at Naini Tal, Jim wanted to become an engineer, but the Corbetts could not afford to send him to college.

At eighteen the tall youth was engaged by a railroad company to supervise several hundred villagers cutting wood to fuel its locomotives, a job which took a year and a half. For the next twenty years he remained with the company, most of the time at a rail junction in Bengal where his duty was to expedite the transshipment of material from broad-gauge to narrow-gauge cars. Funds for payment of the men under Corbett did not arrive for the first three months, but not a man left him. He later told an American visitor that the thousand Indian workmen he supervised never gave him a day's trouble.

When World War I broke out, thirty-nine-year-old Corbett gave up his railroad contract and went to Calcutta to offer his services. Rejected because of his age, he was later offered a captain's commission to recruit Indians for a labor corps, and led the five-hundred-man Seventieth Kumaon Labor Corps to France. Captain Corbett did not get to England, he said, because he would not leave his men even for a short time; nor did he trust the Hindu peasants with their Army pay in Europe, although he bought for them whatever souvenirs they wished. After the corps returned to India, he arranged to have them paid in full with freshly minted silver rupees. Next he was promoted to major and sent to the North West Frontier as commandant of the 114th Labor Battalion in the Third Afghan War

JIM CORBETT

From 1920 to 1936 Major Corbett spent half of each year in Africa, in Tanganyika, where he hunted big game and supervised the irrigation of his plantation on the slopes of Mt. Kilimanjaro. He still owns a share of the East African plantation, which produces such excellent coffee and maize that the Government buys its entire crop. In 1924, on the death of his mother, whom he had been supporting, Corbett gave up his other business interests (including partnership in a small engineering firm). Five years later he was given a sixteen-millimeter movie camera, and became so absorbed in photographing tigers and other jungle animals that he gave up hunting them for sport in 1930, after shooting the "Bachelor of Powalgarh," the most prized big-game trophy of the decade. He continued, however, to hunt man-eaters who were disrupting human communities.

Corbett had in 1907 brought down the first man-eating tiger in the Kumaon Division of India, after hunters deputized by the Government had failed to end its career of 436 known killings of human beings. This took him something over two weeks. "I have more than once been with him when villagers have come to complain of the ravages of a marauder," wrote Lord Hailey, who was Governor of the United Provinces in 1928-34. "Jim would weigh the indictment. . . .The killing of cattle and goats was not a capital offense; wilful homicide must be proved. But once proved, he would not stay his hand until the malefactor had been executed." When hunting man-eaters, Corbett would bring along two servants and might also engage a half-dozen hillmen to carry the equipment needed for a long expedition over rough terrain; but on the actual hunt he insisted almost invariably on being alone and he always went on foot. He also required all other hunters to leave the area and all rewards to be withdrawn. The last of Corbett's expeditions

CORBETT, JIM—*Continued*

against man-eaters was made in late 1938, when terror of the Thak man-eater had paralyzed all activities of a labor force of fifteen thousand men, in addition to the residents of all nearby villages and the hundreds of food suppliers.

"There have been occasions," says Jim Corbett in summary, "when life has hung by a thread, and others when disease resulting from exposure and strain has made the going difficult, but for all those occasions I am amply rewarded if my hunting has resulted in saving one human life." Nevertheless, he defends the tiger against charges of cruelty and blood-thirstiness: "A tiger is a large-hearted gentleman with boundless courage, and when he is exterminated—as exterminated he will be unless public opinion rallies to his support—India will be the poorer by having lost the finest of her fauna."

At the outbreak of World War II in 1939, the famous hunter was sixty-four. Again his proffered services were refused, and again he was later called upon, this time to become Deputy Military Vice-President of District Soldiers Boards. He was asked to organize a civil pioneer corps, but rather than take a desk job he went back to the hills of Kumaon to raise one of the ten battalions needed. Then he contracted tick typhus, spent three months in the hospital, and was discharged with the warning that he must never expect to do anything strenuous again. Under his sister's care, however, Corbett regained his strength, and in February 1944 was commissioned a lieutenant colonel to train British soldiers for jungle warfare in Burma. He spent a month studying the flora and fauna of that sweltering, disease-ridden land, and then returned to central and northern India for eighteen months of strenuous training. In September 1945 the seventy-year-old officer contracted malaria and retired again to Kaladhungi, where his sister was ill of the same disease. Together they regained their health. Since then Colonel Corbett has shown his jungle films and spoken before service audiences; and it is from Marjorie Clough, director of the American Red Cross at Agra, that his publisher, the Oxford University Press, finally got most of the biographical material on the shy author.

Man-Eaters of Kumaon, first published in India in 1944, was a Book-of-the-Month club dual selection in the United States in April 1946. All profits from the sale of the first Indian edition were devoted to St. Dunstan's, the training school for servicemen blinded in war, to whom the book is dedicated. It received almost unanimous praise from American reviewers, the one dissenting note being Edmund Wilson's "even the style, in spots, is like ruptured Kipling." Sterling North's New York *Post* comment was: "The format of the book was forbidding, and the photographs amateurish. But I wish to go on record as saying that in many years of book reviewing I have seldom been so carried away by a factual recital. . . .How Corbett could force himself to wade into chin-deep tangles of grass after wounded tigers . . . or track the big cats into jungles no native had dared traverse in five

years, not even the enthusiastic sponsors of this book can explain." The sponsors referred to are Governor Sir Maurice Hallett and former Viceroy Lord Linlithgow, who wrote the introduction and foreword. Christopher Morley characterized *Man-Eaters* as "a story of murder (by the tiger), of detective skill and courage (of the solitary hunter), but also of natural history, of the life of primitive people, of marvelous scenic beauty, and an unconscious revelation of rare human character. . . .The chapter on his half-breed spaniel Robin, who was an invalid with a bad heart . . . is one of the most charming tributes in all the peculiar literature of dogs."

By mid-May 1946, there were 536,000 copies of *Man-Eaters* in print, and Corbett had begun another book, "Man-Eating Leopards of Rudraprayag," which he was forced to interrupt to rid a village of a man-eater. Producer Monty Shaff had arranged to film Corbett's first book, and the septuagenarian author expressed his pleasure in this chance to justify the faith of his readers by showing them, he wrote, "men and women I have mentioned, and the streams, trees, and rocks I have drawn attention to." Two other book clubs (the Book Society and the Reader's Union in England) have selected *Man-Eaters of Kumaon,* and *Field and Stream* is to publish it in serial form. Arrangements have been made for its translation into six foreign languages.

Corbett's collection of tiger skins, never shown unless someone asks to see them, are stored at his home in Naini Tal. An erect, ruddy, mustached six-footer, the Colonel is described by Marjorie Clough as having "twinkling Irish blue eyes that laugh and are sad all at once. Though quite bald on top his hair is very white and abundant." Corbett's sister, Maggie, an amateur botanist and former piano teacher has, he says, devoted all her life to spoiling him. Asked why he never married, Corbett replied, "It has been my privilege—no, I have had the honor to make a home for the best mother and sisters in the world." Both Jim and Maggie Corbett have a paternalistic attitude toward the Hindu people of the hills, and Miss Corbett regularly administers medicine for "ailments ranging from malaria to hiccoughs" to "any villager who has the strength to crawl into the Corbett compound for medical attention." James Hilton found in *Man-Eaters of Kumaon* the self-portrait—"largely unconscious or it would not have been so clear"—of "a man in whom an intense kinship with nature has quieted many of the problems that beset the rest of us."

References

Book-of-the-Month Club N p7 Mr '46
    por
N Y World-Telegram p23 Ap 4 '46 por

CRAWFORD, JOAN Mar. 23, 1908- Actress

Address: b. c/o Warner Brothers Studios, Burbank, Calif.; h. 426 N. Briston Ave., West Los Angeles, Calif.

"A Hollywood headliner for twenty years," a star since 1929, Joan Crawford has appeared in about sixty motion pictures. Her story, she said, is a little embarrassing to tell—"the events of my life, set down in cold type, make me sound like such an unmitigated Cinderella."

Born Lucille LeSueur in San Antonio, Texas, on March 23, 1908, the actress did not meet her father until she was an established star. When the future Joan Crawford was a few weeks old, her mother, Anna (Johnson) LeSueur, re-married, and Lucille was brought up as the daughter of her stepfather, Henry Cassin, who owned a small vaudeville theater in Lawton, Oklahoma. At six she had an accident which kept her in bed for a year and threatened to cripple her permanently. Later the Cassins left Oklahoma for Kansas City, Missouri, where they leased a small hotel.

"Billie," as the little girl was called because of her tomboyish ways, was sent to the primary school at St. Agnes' Convent as a day student. When she had been there a few years the Cassins separated; her mother took over a laundry agency, her brother got a job, and nine-year-old Billie continued at the convent, paying her tuition there by waiting on tables and doing housework. After the sixth grade she went on to "a very fine private school" under a similar arrangement. "I was the only working pupil," Miss Crawford recalls, "and during my four years there I cleaned the fourteen-room house, cooked meals, made beds, and washed dishes for thirty boys and girls. When I attended a class I learned nothing because I was too exhausted to absorb anything I heard." Snubbed by the other girls, although popular with the boys, Billie did not try to go home because she felt that her new stepfather dis-liked her and was unkind to her.

Next came a period as a twelve-dollar-a-week salesgirl in Kansas City, in which the plump, lively teen-ager won the first of the many dancing contests which caused her to be nick-named "the Charleston Kid." For three un-happy months she attended Stephens College as a working student, but withdrew because she could not keep up with the studies, and returned to the department store. She had no money for dancing lessons, but being quick at picking up new steps she applied and was hired for the chorus of "a pathetic little revue." When she gave her name as Lucille LeSueur, the director chuckled, "Well, honey, you certainly picked a fancy one!" After the first week the troupe found itself stranded; but the sixteen-year-old chorine returned to Kansas City determined to try again as soon as she had saved enough money.

But she soon left home after a quarrel with her mother, and it was with only four dollars in her pocket that Miss LeSueur arrived in Chicago to find Katherine Emerine, the prima donna of the revue, who had offered to help her to get a job. Miss Emerine was out of town. Recalling the name of the producer, Erne Young, the future star found his office, begged him for a tryout, and got a job. (Eight years later she acted this scene almost exactly in Dancing Lady, and heard it called exag-gerated and overwritten.) The job was to do one song and one dance at an obscure cafe, for twenty-five dollars a week; two weeks later

JOAN CRAWFORD

Miss LeSueur was transferred to the chorus of the Oriole Terrace Club in Detroit. After about three months in that chorus line she attracted the attention of J. J. Shubert, when her billowing skirt swept a glass off his table. He invited her to join the chorus of his revue, Innocent Eyes, which opened in New York ten days later. This job lasted three months; then the chorus went into The Passing Show (1924). Through the stage manager, she also got a few weeks' engagement to dance after the show at the Club Richman. After eight months, Miss LeSueur was discovered by a Metro-Goldwyn-Mayer talent scout. She was unenthusiastic and refused to take a second screen test, as her ambition lay in the field of dancing, not acting; but on Christmas Day 1925 the studio wired her the offer of a five-year contract, beginning at seventy-five dollars a week, and on New Year's Day she left for Hollywood.

For the first few weeks Lucille LeSueur was kept busy posing for "cheesecake" publicity pictures, but after that she was ignored. Ap-pealing to the executive who had originally signed her, she recalls, she was cast as one of the chorus girls in the silent film Pretty Ladies (1925). (According to Elinor Hughes, however, the dancer's first role was in an un-important slapstick comedy, The Boob; her next was as Harry Langdon's leading lady in a full-length comedy, Tramp, Tramp, Tramp, and her third as an apache in Paris.) The studio, which considered the name Lucille Le-Sueur affected and hard to pronounce, spon-sored a contest to find a better one. To her dismay, Miss LeSueur was renamed Joan Craw-ford (she thought it sounded like "crawfish"), and the new name received its first screen credit in Sally, Irene, and Mary (1925). She had asked for the role of Irene, the dancer, which she calls her first real part. (The other title roles were taken by another stock girl, Sally O'Neil, and the star Constance Bennett.) After

CRAWFORD, JOAN—*Continued*

this Miss Crawford worked constantly; the studio took up her option and increased her salary, but her vehicles were confined at first to "quickies" and Westerns. Her reputation as the "Hot-Cha Girl" who danced each night away and had an entire room filled with prize cups held her back for a time, but the publicity it brought began to get her good parts in "A" pictures opposite some of the most important male stars, including Lon Chaney, John Gilbert, William Haines, and Ramon Novarro.

It was *Our Dancing Daughters,* released in 1928, which raised Joan Crawford to stardom. Her salary went up to five hundred dollars a week, and she bought a seven-room house in Brentwood. (Later remodeling has added twenty more rooms, and on the grounds are a swimming pool, a tennis court, and a theater.) The advent of sound in 1929, which ended many brilliant screen careers, did not disturb Miss Crawford's. In June 1929 she was married to Douglas Fairbanks, Jr. '41, whom she has described as having all the qualities she "most envied and admired." As gossip writers breathlessly informed the public, at first she was not welcomed by her father-in-law, Douglas Fairbanks '40, and his wife Mary Pickford '45. After her marriage the actress devoted much of her time to reading good books and to acquiring a knowledge of classical music and poetry. And Henry F. Pringle credits her with helping her husband to improve his acting.

Professionally, meanwhile, she was constantly busy, among her most memorable films being the silent *Our Modern Maidens* (1929) and the talking *Our Blushing Brides* (1930). From 1930 to 1936 Joan Crawford was voted one of the ten biggest money-making stars each year. But this was not enough—she wanted to be a dramatic actress. Finally Louis B. Mayer '42 gave her the chance by casting her in *Paid* (1931), an adaptation of *Within the Law,* in which she played the prison sequences in an ill-fitting dress, with uncombed hair and no make-up. This was well received. Later that year the hard-working actress added to her professional standing with *Possessed* (1931), her second picture with Clark Gable '45, and *Letty Lynton* (1932), opposite Nils Asther. For the first time, Adrian '41 decided to exaggerate her broad shoulders instead of playing them down in the costumes he designed for her as Letty. The star's fan mail increased by hundreds of letters, and from then on she was typed as a glamorous, sophisticated "clothes-horse." As such, she has introduced many Adrian innovations which have become fashionable. And the wide Crawford mouth set a fashion in make-up.

The failure of *Rain* in 1932, followed by the unsuccessful *Today We Live* (1933), damaged Miss Crawford's prestige; but that was restored by *Dancing Lady* (1933), in which she danced with Fred Astaire '45, "emoted" opposite Clark Gable. (A supporting member of the cast was Franchot Tone '40.) *Forsaking All Others* (1934), with Gable and Robert Montgomery, was the first of a series of drawing room comedies which came to be called "the

Crawford formula." After her marriage to Franchot Tone in October 1935 (she was divorced from Fairbanks in 1933), Miss Crawford became interested in activities like the Actors' Guild, in the Moscow Art Theater theories, and began to think seriously of going on the stage. This idea never got further than a recurrent rumor, although the Tones built a theater at the back of their Brentwood home where they rehearsed, and co-starred in radio performances of several well-known plays. They studied singing, too, and when they were divorced after four years the studio announced that Miss Crawford, a contralto, intended to seek a career on the operatic stage.

Despite her hard work and box-office drawing power, Miss Crawford was not "in the really big money" until 1941, when she signed a five-year contract with no lay-offs and no options. Moreover, she had little chance at the best parts: these went to the legendary Garbo or to Norma Shearer, "First Lady of the Screen," wife of the MGM production head. Miss Crawford did persuade the studio to give her one costume part, in *The Gorgeous Hussy* (1936), but after that came more routine roles in poor scripts. She asked for the part of Crystal, the home-wrecker, in *The Women* (1939), although it was only the fourth largest part, and this unsympathetic role restored her box-office appeal. Again she asked for a role, in *Strange Cargo* (1940), in which she appeared disheveled and without make-up; and, although this met with a mixed reception, it gave her a sense of achievement. Against studio objections, she played the selfish, notional mother of a teen-age daughter in *Susan and God* (1940), a great success, and then fought for the role of the brutal, horribly scarred blackmailer in *A Woman's Face* (1941). This brought much praise for her courage, as well as her acting ability. "In making that picture, I grew up professionally," says Miss Crawford. Next came one drawing room and one screwball comedy. (Replacing the late Carole Lombard in the latter, she turned her reported $112,500 salary over to Government relief.) But then Miss Crawford was cast in two more pictures with little to recommend them. Unable to win a chance at producing, which she wished to combine with her acting, the star left MGM, the lot where her contract still had three years to run.

A few months later Warner '45 Brothers offered her an even better salary, and she signed with it. For two years, however, the company did not offer a script to her liking; in January 1944 she asked to be taken off the payroll until she began to work. Meanwhile, the help shortage was such that Miss Crawford was doing the housework of her large establishment and caring for her adopted daughter and son; the cooking was reportedly done by her husband Phillip Terry, to whom she had been married in July 1942. (Her third marriage was terminated by divorce in April 1946.) Her war work included service as a Bundles for Britain volunteer and as War Dogs Fund recruiting chairman for the motion picture industry. Finally Miss Crawford found a satisfactory vehicle—James M. Cain's *Mildred*

Pierce (1945), which a commentator had once named as an example of a story Hollywood would not dare to touch. With the minimum blue-penciling necessary, it presented Miss Crawford as the mother of a girl old enough to take away that mother's husband.

The actress' style as Mildred Pierce, commented Alton Cook, "is intelligent restraint, leaving an impression of seething intensity held under rigid control. . . .Without doubt it has rejuvenated her badly undermined status among stars of the first rank." Most of the other reviewers agreed, *Look* declaring, "An all-time favorite . . . she returns with all the glamour and excitement that have made her a Hollywood headliner for twenty years. Her performance as the harried heroine of this turbulent emotional drama reveals a newly acquired acting finesse."

Variety added the comment that in this picture "Miss Crawford reaches the peak of her acting career." Praise also came from the *Christian Science Monitor*: "She made understandable every phase of Mildred's character"; and from Eileen Creelman of the New York *Sun* whose judgment was that "Miss Crawford, always playing down the scenes where she might have gone in for fireworks, is vividly effective. Her Mildred Pierce, far from an amiable or glamorous creature is a well-rounded person. Miss Crawford, in playing a 'Bette Davis' part has found the role she needed, one which requires tense, controlled acting." In March 1946 the actress, at home recuperating from the flu, received the Motion Picture Academy's award, the much-coveted "Oscar," for the outstanding feminine performance of 1945. Six months later the film star completed negotiating a new seven-year contract with Warner Brothers. By the terms of this contract, Miss Crawford is permitted to make one outside picture a year, which she will reportedly do under the aegis of the Skirball-Manning production unit at Universal.

To quote Sidney Skolsky, "Joan Crawford is a movie fan's idea of a movie star. . . .Even to the newcomers in the business, Joan Crawford is their idea of what a movie actress should be, and look like. . . .She came into the business when movie queens were just that, and she hasn't changed in this respect. She is surrounded by a retinue which includes a maid, secretary, hairdresser, wardrobe girl, make-up expert, chauffeur, and record changer," who plays popular and classical music for her between scenes. At the same time, she is consistently described as unaffected, kindly, and sentimental. She says of herself that she dislikes inactivity above all else. The Joan Crawford Fan Club is said to be the most active of all such organizations, and the Hollywood photographers have given her more than one testimonial dinner. Her large blue eyes, wide mouth, and thick reddish-brown hair are familiar to millions, as is her wide-shouldered, slim-waisted one-hundred-thirty-pound figure, which seems taller than its five feet four inches. The Crawford freckles, however, have to be hidden from the cameras. Despite her almost reverential attitude toward the stage, Joan Crawford loves the movies. "If I could get away with

it," she says, "I believe I'd stand in line with the fans and watch the stars go to a première. That's how much of a fan I am."

References
Collier's 114:13+ O 28 '44 por
Ladies' H J 59:13+ D '42 por
American Women, 1939-40
Hughes, E. Famous Stars of Filmdom (Women) (1931)
International Motion Picture Almanac, 1943-44
Who's Who in America, 1946-47
Women of Achievement (1940)

CULLEN, COUNTEE May 30, 1903—Jan. 10, 1946 American Negro poet and teacher; one of the most brilliant of contemporary lyric poets; won a national poetry contest while in high school with his "I Have a Rendezvous With Life"; awarded a Guggenheim Fellowship for study abroad (1928); assistant editor of the magazine *Opportunity*: *Journal of Negro Life* (1926-28); taught French in a New York junior high school (1934-45); among his principal works are *Ballad of the Brown Girl* (1928), *The Black Christ and Other Poems* (1929), a novel, *One Way to Heaven* (1931), *The Medea and Some Other Poems* (1935).

Obituary
N Y Times p23 Ja 10 '46

CUNNINGHAM, SIR ALAN (GORDON) May 1, 1887- British army officer; High Commissioner for Palestine and Trans-Jordan
Address: b. c/o Lloyds Bank, 6 Pall Mall, London

Britain's High Commissioner and commander in chief for Palestine and Trans-Jordan is a soldier who won fame in the East African campaign during World War II. Lieutenant General Sir Alan Cunningham drove the Italians out of Ethiopia in 1941, and afterwards held Army staff posts in England. His latest appointment, made in November 1945, continued a British policy of naming high military officers to the Palestine post.

Alan Gordon Cunningham was born May 1, 1887. His father, Professor D. J. Cunningham, a Fellow of the Royal Society, taught anatomy in Edinburgh and Dublin Universities; his mother was the former Elizabeth Cumming Browne. An elder brother Andrew [41] (now Britain's First Sea Lord) went into the Royal Navy, while Alan chose the Army as his career. After schooling at Cheltenham, young Cunningham entered the Royal Military Academy in Woolwich, and at nineteen was commissioned a second lieutenant in the Royal Artillery. Eight years later World War I struck Europe. For action in France and Belgium (1914-18) Cunningham was mentioned in dispatches five times, won the Military Cross in 1916 and the Distinguished Service Order in 1918. He became a brigade major in the Royal Artillery at thirty. After the

British Official Photo.

SIR ALAN CUNNINGHAM

Armistice, with the rank of general staff officer, second grade, he remained for five months in France. Serving next for two and a half years (1919-21) in the Straits Settlements, Cunningham was responsible for some of the initial plans for the base at Singapore. On his return to England, he took a course at the Naval Staff College, was graduated in 1925, and in 1928 was advanced to brevet lieutenant-colonel.

Between the two world wars, Cunningham taught, studied, and steadily rose in rank. From 1928 to 1931 he instructed at the Netheravon Small Arms School; in 1937 he was graduated from the Imperial Defence College —"It was a tribute to his abilities," states the British official biography, "that he was the only Army officer admitted to the course without having previously qualified at the Army Staff College, Camberley." The next year (1937-38) he was Royal Artillery commander with the First Division of the Aldershot Command. In September 1938, advanced to the rank of major general, he commanded the Fifth Anti-Aircraft Division of the Territorial Army. During the early months of World War II he commanded successively the Sixty-sixth, the Ninth, and the Fifty-first Divisions (the Fifty-first having been reorganized from the Ninth, after the original Fifty-first was decimated at St. Valery).

In the autumn of 1940 Cunningham was sent to Kenya as lieutenant general, commanding the East African Forces, which included South, East and West Africans, Somalis and Abyssinians. Finding only small forces and equipment at his disposal upon his arrival, the General expected not to be able to make any major offensive until the following summer after the rains—Ethiopia was known to be garrisoned by a modern army of two hundred thousand white and native Fascist troops. However, on

December 15, a raid which he essayed against El Wak, on the Kenya-Italian Somaliland Frontier, came off unexpectedly well. And meanwhile, General Sir William Platt, who commanded the northern arm of the British pincers which eventually crushed the Italian forces in Ethiopia, drove from the Sudan deep into Eritrea. Cunningham quickly changed his plans. He now thought it possible that a lightning attack by a comparatively small force might succeed, and gambling against the rains, struck in the full moon of February 11, 1941. The Cunningham forces swept across Ethiopia, following the route taken by Graziani's conquering Italians in 1936. They reached Addis Ababa, the capital, on April 6, 1941, and on May 5 Cunningham greeted Haile Selassie[41], Emperor of Ethiopia, the first victim of Axis aggression to regain his state. The campaign was termed "a well-organized miracle." Newspapers pointed out at the time that Mussolini's two biggest "headaches" were named Cunningham: while Sir Alan drove Italians from East Africa, his brother Sir Andrew, in command of the British Mediterranean Fleet, harassed Italian warships.

In August 1941 the General, who had been named Knight Commander of the Bath in recognition of his successful operations in East Africa, was transferred to the command of the newly formed Eighth Imperial Army. That month marked the opening of the second British drive through Libya. But Cunningham, who had intended to streak for Tripoli, had his timetable upset by the enemy's superior equipment—the German Mark III tanks had just made their appearance in the desert—and was stopped at Rezegh. On November 26 Cunningham was replaced by Major General Neil Methuen Ritchie; Winston Churchill reported to the House of Commons two weeks later, "General Cunningham . . . is . . . responsible for the planning and organization of the present offensive in Libya. . . .Reported by the medical authorities to be suffering from serious overstrain [he] has been granted sick leave." It was later disclosed that the General had been relieved because he had not believed he could carry out an order to sweep the enemy out of Cyrenaica, but had wanted instead to withdraw the British forces to regroup on the Sollum Line. After a few months of rest Cunningham went to the Staff College at Camberley to serve as its commandant during 1942. From October 1943 until the end of 1944 he commanded British troops in Northern Ireland, then returned to England to become general officer commanding of the Eastern Command, the post which he held until his appointment as High Commissioner and commander in chief for Palestine and Trans-Jordan in November 1945.

The fifty-eight-year-old Lieutenant General succeeded Field Marshal Viscount Gort[40], who resigned from the Palestine post because of ill health. As he took over his new post in Jerusalem on November 21, 1945, Cunningham said, "I have no preconceived ideas whatsoever, and I realize that the problems to be presented are human problems which I shall endeavor to treat humanly." In the months to follow Palestine problems became increasingly acute as the plight of the European Jews denied entrance to the Holy Land incited action by terrorist bands. In January 1946 extremists dynamited a Coast Guard station, which was to "operate against free immigration," wounding sixteen Britons; thousands of picked British troops searched for those responsible. The killing of seven British soldiers in Tel Aviv in April led the British to round up and question twelve hundred suspected terrorists, while Jewish authorities in Palestine deplored the violence and Cunningham termed it "cold-blooded premeditated murder." At the end of April Cunningham ordered almost all Jewish towns out-of-bounds to British troops following clashes with the soldiers in which Jews were injured. Arabs, too, were causing disturbances. Soon after the publication of the recommendations (later rejected by Britain) of the Anglo-American Committee of Inquiry on Palestine, Cunningham was forced to warn in the "strongest terms" against Arab strikes and violence.

Through June tension increased, outbreaks of violence were frequent, and strict curfews were enforced in some Palestine cities. On June 29 "military operations" were begun in which thousands of British troops struck suddenly, arresting nearly three thousand Jews, including Jewish Agency for Palestine leaders. "The object," stated Sir Alan, "is to restore those conditions of order without which no progress can be made toward a solution of the problem of Palestine." The British Government was "firmly resolved to root out terrorism and violence." Some days later General Cunningham commuted to life imprisonment death sentences imposed on two members of the *Irgun Zvai Leumi*, an underground extremist group, whereupon *Irgun* released three British officers it had held as hostages. Cunningham reported to the British Cabinet in London that he had placed nearly three thousand Jews in concentration camps, and proposed that the Jews be released except for about a dozen against whom charges would be brought. The Cabinet agreed to his plan. "It is to be hoped," Sir Alan said on July 11, 1946, "that there will be no further need for widespread military action, but it must be stated that . . . any further outbreaks of violence . . ., will be dealt with with the utmost vigor."

Eleven days later extremists bombed the King David Hotel, British military headquarters, killing ninety-three persons. Immediately twenty thousand British troops and police began a mass man hunt for members of Zionist terrorist groups. After the bombing all major questions of policy were referred to the Cabinet in London. Late in September the High Commissioner warned Jewish leaders against carrying out their announced program of non-cooperation in civil life and their plan to use the funds of municipal local councils to promote illegal immigration. The deportation of refugees from Palestine to Cyprus was upheld by the Palestine Supreme Court when the Jewish community of Haifa attempted to obtain a writ of habeas corpus for almost four thousand Jews who tried to enter the country in November. After other acts of violence against troops and police, the Zionists' press in Palestine attacked the terrorists. In December Sir Alan warned the acting head of the Jewish Agency that the British troops might be hard to control if terrorism continued.

Cunningham and his brother, the Admiral of the Fleet, are said to have always been "strong but friendly rivals." In Hampshire, where both men live, they are rivals in rose-growing, fishing, and the telling of tall tales. Sir Alan, who is unmarried, is a "bold rider to the hounds" and a confirmed smoker of cheroots, a habit he acquired in Malaya. He has the "swift appraising eye for country which belongs to the born tactician," and an "exact, retentive, pigeonhole memory for men and things."

References

N Y Herald Tribune p6 N 9 '45 por
N Y Times p5 N 9 '45 por
Time 37:24 Mr 10 '41 por
Who's Who, 1946

CURRY, JOHN STEUART Nov. 14, 1897—Aug. 29, 1946 American artist; his oils and water colors in major museums in the United States; he considered his best work the mural paintings he executed for the State House in Kansas. See *Current Biography* 1941 Yearbook.

Obituary

N Y Times p17 Ag 30 '46 por

DALUEGE, KURT (däl'ü"gĕ kŏŏrt) 1897—Oct. 23, 1946 Colonel General of German Nazi police; ordered the razing of the Czechoslovakian village of Lidice and the killing of over one thousand Czechs in retaliation for the assassination of Reinhard Heydrich, chief of the German State Secret Police; convicted in addition for the deportation of thousands of Czechs into Germany for forced labor; sentenced to death and hanged.

Obituary

N Y Times p13 O 24 '46

DALY, MAUREEN (PATRICIA) Mar. 15, 1921- Author; editor

Address: b. c/o Ladies' Home Journal, Independence Sq., Philadelphia; h. 905 Clinton St., Philadelphia

Maureen Daly, whose first page as editor of the *Ladies' Home Journal's* "Sub-Deb" department appeared in the October 1945 issue, was a nationally known short story writer at sixteen, a syndicated columnist at twenty, and a best-selling novelist at twenty-one. She has made her reputation by simply putting down in fiction form her own recent memories of teen-age hopes, experiences, and frustrations.

The third of four daughters, Maureen Patricia Daly was born to Joseph Desmond and Margaret Mellon (Kelly) Daly on March 15, 1921. Her birthplace is Castlecaufield, County Tyrone, in Ulster, but when she was two years old her family moved from Ireland to

MAUREEN DALY

the United States, where they made their home in the small town of Fond du Lac, Wisconsin. Maureen attended the public grade school and St. Mary's Springs Academy there. Her childhood was "pretty routine," she says, and her mother was very strict. When she began writing stories, Miss Daly has revealed, "it was not ambition but inhibition" that spurred her on: "I suffered from a permanent state of 'cat got your tongue,' wore my hair in a long braid twisted round my head, and was what is commonly known in Fond du Lac and surrounding counties as 'a complete drip.' The truth is, I just didn't date . . . and sort of drooped around at dances, no one dancing with me."

Maureen's story "Fifteen," a simple episode which happened and was written when she was that age, won fourth place in *Scholastic* magazine's national short story contest for high school students that year. She wrote "Sixteen" in March 1937, while waiting for a telephone call that never came: "It wasn't meant to be a short story at all, but rather I just wanted to get the experience down on paper to relieve the tense, hurt feelings inside of me." "Sixteen" was entered in the annual *Scholastic* competition that year and won first prize. Harry Hansen '42 chose it for reprinting in the *O. Henry Collection of Best Short Stories for 1938*, making Maureen the youngest author ever to be represented in that well-known annual. *Woman's Day* and *Redbook* magazines reprinted the story, as did a number of smaller magazines and newspapers; it was included in a half-dozen textbooks and anthologies, and adapted for radio broadcast. The young author continued to receive fan mail about it for three years, by which time she had been graduated from the academy as valedictorian (June 1938) and gone on to Rosary College, at River Forest, Illinois.

Her next story, rather pretentious, was rejected by *Redbook*. On the advice of Dorothy Canfield Fisher, Maureen then went back to writing about what she knew most. Her stories and articles were bought by national magazines, including *Vogue, Mademoiselle, Cosmopolitan,* and the *Woman's Home Companion.* In 1941 she submitted the first fifty pages of her novel *Seventeenth Summer* in the national intercollegiate competition for the first Dodd, Mead Intercollegiate Literary Fellowship. This fragment was the unanimous choice of the judges for the twelve-hundred-dollar advance against royalties, which made it possible for a beginning writer to complete a first novel. "When you get older," the twenty-one-year-old author said, "I believe you lose accuracy in remembering all the funny quirks and sadnesses and happiness you go through in adolescence. It is a wonderful and very important time. It is still so much a part of me I feel that I can write of it with truth and sympathy." Reviewers agreed with Miss Daly when the book appeared, using such terms as "limpid honesty and simplicity"; "sincerity, sound workmanship, and authoritative knowledge of her subject"; "poignant authenticity . . . utterly enchanting . . . true and sweet and fresh and sound." Published in April 1942, the novel had sold twelve thousand copies by July, and in November 1945 was in its twenty-third printing.

While she was finishing *Seventeenth Summer* Miss Daly was in her junior year at college. Majoring in English and Latin, she was the first junior ever to edit the literary quarterly, *Rosary College Eagle,* and also wrote a column for the campus newspaper. She was a member of *Mademoiselle*'s advisory college board, which meant, among other things, that she had to submit four satisfactory projects a year. In addition, the girl was working as a columnist and book reviewer for the Chicago *Tribune*—"but it isn't hard at all," she said, "and my grades are good and I have a wonderful time."

Her thrice-weekly column for teen-agers, *On the Solid Side,* started in 1941, was later syndicated to more than a dozen newspapers. Hundreds of letters a month came to the columnist, asking for advice. A collection of these articles, titled *Smarter and Smoother,* was published in 1944 and had gone into its ninth printing by July 1945. "Parents should be thankful to Maureen Daly," wrote reviewer Virginia Kirkus '41, "for she gives all the advice and counsel that teen-agers think is sermonizing from parents, but that they'll lap up in this form." The *Library Journal*'s critic thought that, "with slang and clichés, it often appears strained and self-conscious," but May Lamberton Becker '41 called *Smarter and Smoother* "the best book, all things considered, on our high school manners and ethics and their relation to those of later life, among many lately offered to the teens. One special advantage is the author's time of life; just old enough to look back on the teens, she has, as a novelist, already developed mature sympathy that lets her see them unclouded by the scorn the twenties often feel."

After her graduation from college Miss Daly continued her column and also was a police reporter for the *Tribune* in 1942-43. She declined an offer to go to Hollywood as a screen writer. Maureen Daly and her talented seven-years-younger sister, Sheila John Daly, shared a private office in Fond du Lac. When Maureen moved to Philadelphia to become associate editor of the *Ladies' Home Journal* in July 1945, her sister took over the column. (Kay Daly, two years Maureen's senior, is fashion editor of a Chicago daily newspaper.) Before this, in December 1944, Maureen had done "Meet a Sub-Deb" for the *Journal's How America Lives* series.

Some idea of Maureen Daly's working methods may be gathered from her statement, "It took me months longer than it should have to finish *Seventeenth Summer* because I was too soft with myself. I did a lot of rewriting and the parts I rewrote aren't as good as the parts I knocked off very fast. I'd make myself a stint—so much a day, about eight typewritten pages—and on a slip of paper I'd make a few notes of what points I wanted to make in those eight pages."

Miss Daly was married on December 28, 1946, to William McGivern of Chicago, a magazine writer. She is five feet six inches tall and weighs one hundred and twenty-five pounds. In politics she is a Democrat, in faith a Roman Catholic. She has listed her favorite recreations as swimming, skating, and dancing. "I still remember the first boy with whom I ever had a date," Miss Daly has told her sub-deb readers. "He was a tall blond fellow who worked for Western Union—and I've liked tall blond boys ever since. I've always liked to read a lot and can almost recite G. K. Chesterton and Thomas Wolfe backward. . . .The song which means most in my life is, of course, 'Stardust,' and I've learned to whistle part of the Sextette from *Lucia* because I like it and because it reminds me of someone. Most of the time I wear tailored clothes, suits and sweaters."

References

N Y Times Book R p2+ Jl 12 '42 por
Pub W 141:1582 Ap 25 '42 por
Scholastic 39:17 S 15 '41 por; 44:16
  Mr 20-25 '44 il

DANDY, WALTER E(DWARD) Apr. 6, 1886—Apr. 19, 1946 Brain surgeon, pathologist; considered one of the thousand Americans most important in the natural and exact sciences; introduced a number of diagnostic and surgical procedures; associate professor Johns Hopkins University, 1921-31, clinical professor of neurological surgery, 1931 until his death; author of several texts.

Obituary

N Y Times p13 Ap 20 '46 por

DANIELL, MRS. RAYMOND *See* Long, T.

DART, JUSTIN W(HITLOCK) Aug. 7, 1907- Business executive

Address: b. c/o Rexall Drug Company, 314 W. 6th St., Los Angeles, Calif.; h. Bel-Air, Los Angeles, Calif.

The president of the Rexall Drug Company, Justin W. Dart, would be an outstanding man among major corporation executives even if he were not one of the youngest of them. He was thirty-five years old in 1943, when he became head of the largest drug company in the world, with assets of seventy-odd million dollars. Formerly in charge of store operations for the Walgreen chain, Dart had revolutionized drugstore merchandising while living up to the advice he gives trainees, "Make money, but have fun doing it."

Justin Whitlock Dart was born on August 7, 1907, in Evanston, Illinois, the son of Guy Justin and Laura (Whitlock) Dart. An only child (two brothers died before he was six), Justin was reared in a comfortable suburban environment in Hinsdale. His father was in the clothing business. After graduation from the Hinsdale high school, young Dart went east to study at the Mercersburg Academy in Pennsylvania in 1924-25 before returning to enter Northwestern University. "During his prep-school track days," it has been said, "he carried a fifty-six-pound weight and a sixteen-pound hammer wherever he went and hurled them at the unlikeliest moments, endangering the public safety but enabling himself to set several local records."

At Northwestern, where the big, handsome Dart studied business administration, he played tackle on the football team and was selected for the All-Big-Ten-Conference teams in 1927 and 1928. (The coach was such a stern disciplinarian that Dart says he once received a tongue-lashing for smiling during a game.) A result of his "campus romance" with Ruth Walgreen, daughter of the Walgreen Company's founder-president, was that after Dart's graduation in 1929 he went to work as a $25-a-week stock clerk in the basement of a Walgreen drugstore. He and Miss Walgreen were married that October. (By this marriage there are two sons, Justin Whitlock, Jr., and Peter Walgreen.)

"For the first year," says Dart, "Mr. Walgreen practically carried me under his arm." In 1930 the young man was transferred to the supervision department; in 1932, at twenty-five, he was head of store operations for the entire 375 stores of the chain, and not long afterward he was elected to the board of directors. As his father-in-law's chief aide, Dart showed merchandising ability, accounts agree. (He could never expect to become a company officer, however, for Illinois law limits such positions in drug companies to registered pharmacists.) *Fortune* reported in a 1935 study of Walgreen that Justin and Ruth Dart owned some fifteen thousand shares of Walgreen stock; that one of the Walgreen-manufactured products, Dart's O'namel, was named for him; and that he was an able executive. Within a few years, Dart had set up new systems of keeping a finger on the chain's pulse, had made many changes in the purchasing and distribution systems, and "ruthlessly" eliminated stores which failed to show satisfactory returns.

More permanent in its effect was Dart's redesigning of stores to stimulate sales and to

Gladser Studio

JUSTIN W. DART

simplify merchandising of anything they could profitably handle. His first important step in this direction, considered revolutionary by the trade, was the soda booth and display unit, a low wall, flanked on one side by booths, which divided the soda fountain and luncheonette from the drug counters and the rest of the store, while its other side provided display shelves. Dart put a separate prescription counter at the back of the store, for privacy and to lead those who wanted drugs past the displays of other items. He paid particular attention to striking displays and to eye-catching packaging of the products of Walgreen's manufacturing subsidiaries. The climax was the "superstore," a huge establishment, highly departmentalized, which he hopes will be found everywhere some day. (The world's largest drugstore, as of 1946, is planned for the headquarters Dart is having built for United-Rexall in Los Angeles.)

Justin Dart was appointed general manager of the Walgreen Company in 1939. When Charles R. Walgreen died on Christmas Day of that year—eight months after his daughter had divorced Dart—he left a large share of the business to his former son-in-law. Dart remained as general manager and director during two years of disagreements with the other major stockholders, his ex-wife and her brother, before resigning in October 1941 to become president of the Liggett Drug Company.

The Liggett chain was a subsidiary of United Drug, Incorporated, which was then, in Robert Sellmer's words, a "large, formless, and [financially] unhappy conglomeration of chain stores, drug-manufacturing companies, candy factories, rubber manufacturers, stationery makers, and more than twelve thousand independent druggists [in the United States, Canada, England, and Ireland] holding franchises giving them the exclusive right to sell the Rexall line of

drugs and patent medicines." With twice the assets of Walgreen, United Drug made only two and one-half million dollars' profit in 1941 to Walgreen's three and one-third million. "Complete and almost mulish inefficiency was the order of the day" at United, according to Sellner. The chains owned by United, comprising about 585 stores, had completely separate organizations, and these were again duplicated in the Rexall setup. No dividend had been paid since 1937, although United, the largest drug company in the world, owned or had under contract one out of every five drugstores in the United States. A group of United stockholders, headed by Edward J. Noble '44, the Life Savers millionaire and Beta Theta Pi fraternity brother of Dart, had obtained control of the corporation and had offered Dart the Liggett presidency, with the understanding that it was to be a stepping-stone to presidency of the parent company.

Dart moved to Boston and took office in November, having won over the United stockholders who opposed him by confessing to several errors of judgment more serious than any which had been charged against him. In April 1942 the Midwesterner was elected a vice-president and director of United Drug, and a year later, at the age of thirty-five, he became president, one of the youngest men to hold so important a position.

The fact that United's manufacturing facilities were occupied with war production enabled the new president to concentrate his attention on long-range plans. He built up a team of subordinates of his age or younger, transferring or pensioning off the incumbents, raised salaries, and refinanced the company's outstanding obligations. And he changed the entire retail setup, placing all stores, including the Liggett, Owl, and Sontag chains, under a new retail division, thereby eliminating much wasteful duplication of effort. After a survey had shown that Rexall was the only one of United's many trademarks which the public recognized, Dart ordered all packaging redesigned to feature that name, although the seven manufacturing subsidiaries maintained their separate identities. Then he instituted the first national advertising campaign undertaken by any drugstore chain, including the sponsorship of the high-priced Jimmy Durante-Garry Moore radio show; and in 1944 he changed the corporation's name to the United-Rexall Drug Company.

Under Dart's leadership, United sales continued their rise from the all-time low of 1938. In 1943 the corporation paid its first preferred stock dividend in six years, and in 1944 paid more than double the 1943 amount, although no capital stock dividends were paid in 1944 or 1945 in order to build up the reserve. During the consolidation period, Dart was buying up bad leases, closing down unprofitable stores, thereby reducing the chains from 585 to 541 stores, and Rexall dealers from over twelve thousand to ten thousand. He spent $580,000 to move United-Rexall headquarters across the continent to Los Angeles in the fall of 1945. (He denies that this was a condition of his remaining as president at a reported seventy-five thousand dollars, rather than accepting Sewell

Avery's [44] offer to become president of Montgomery Ward at twice the salary.) First Dart sent agents to buy sixty-two houses and rent floors in hotels, persuaded his subordinates of the advantages of California, and obtained a converted B-17 to shuttle back and forth carrying key United executive and microfilm records. The firm's manufacturing activity was to continue in the East and Midwest, but Dart felt that southern California was a fertile field for new merchandising ideas and that United's business could be managed from there "just as efficiently and certainly more comfortably" than from Boston.

As part of his program for expanding United's retail outlets, Dart opened negotiations for the purchase of a number of small drugstore chains, including the nineteen-store E. T. Renfro chain in Texas. To avoid arousing the resentment of the independent Rexall dealers by this competition, he devised an "Opportunity Unlimited" plan to put them on the same basis as United-owned stores by extending them the same services in research, purchasing, advertising, and even financing of store improvements, and by urging them to reorganize their stores and services on the model of the chain stores. Having added women's hosiery to the twelve thousand items on his stores' shelves, Dart also purchased a Pennsylvania hosiery mill. Then, in late November 1946 he changed the organization's name to the Rexall Drug Company. President Dart concerned himself only with the establishment of broad policies, leaving their execution entirely to his associates. Dart's other business interests included membership on the boards of United Air Lines and of the American Broadcasting Company.

Just under six feet tall, heavily built Justin Dart has wavy black hair and blue eyes beneath light brown eyebrows. His politics are Republican. According to Robert Sellmer, the dynamic young executive is known to most of his women employees as "Superman," and when he goes through an office "papers blow off desks, doors slam, and minor executives jump. . . .Dart manages, in addition to getting through a day's routine in about four hours, to speak at dozens of conventions, prowl unceasingly through as many of his stores as possible, and occasionally play basketball with his Rexall trainees. . . . An abstemious man, he frowns on drinking by his employees, an attitude which has resulted in a tremendous increase in the consumption of gum and mints by all his associates."

The former football hero engages in half a dozen sports, including calf-roping, and he belongs to golf, polo, tennis, and ranch clubs. Since his first solo flight in 1935 Dart has earned a commercial pilot's license and has logged thousands of hours flying company planes around the country, often with his wife as copilot. Before their marriage on New Year's Eve 1939, Jane O'Brien Dart was the featured film player Jane Bryan, a protégée of Bette Davis. The Darts have two children, Guy Michael and Jane, and are now building a mountaintop home outside Los Angeles, to be called "Winds Aloft." Altogether the "super druggist" says of his life, "This guy Dart has an awful lot of fool luck."

References

Bsns W p8 Jl 13 '46 (por cover)
Life 21:90+ Ag 5 '46 pors
Time 48:82+ Jl 1 '46 por
Who's Who in America, 1946-47

DAVEY, MARTIN L(UTHER) July 25, 1884—Mar. 31, 1946 Political figure and businessman; president Davey Tree Expert Company, Davey Compressor Company, Davey Investment Company; United States Representative from Ohio, 1918-21 and 1923-29; Governor of Ohio, 1935-39; mayor of Kent, 1914-18; anti-New Deal Democrat.

Obituary

N Y Times p27 Ap 1 '46 por

DAVIS, GLENN Dec. 26, 1924- United States Army cadet; football star
Address: b. c/o United States Military Academy, West Point, N. Y.; h. Claremont, Calif.

"Mr. Outside" to sports writers—so named for the path he usually takes to a football touchdown—is Cadet Glenn ("Junior") Davis of the West Point class of 1947, in which Cadet Felix ("Doc") Blanchard [46] is "Mr. Inside." Co-captains in 1946, they were the most discussed stars of Army's unbeaten football team for two seasons before they were old enough to vote. Davis was awarded a prize as the outstanding football player of 1944, and in 1946 was called the greatest running ball-carrier of all time. The president of the Brooklyn Dodgers baseball club estimated that it would be worth seventy-five thousand dollars to a professional baseball team to hire Davis, a centerfielder with a "whiplike" throwing arm.

The day after Christmas is a triple birthday in the family of Ralph Davis, manager of the Claremont (California) branch of the Bank of America. On that day in 1924—his daughter's third birthday—identical twins were born to him and Irna Davis. The elder was named for his father, but it was Glenn Davis whom the family and friends called "Junior," because he was the younger twin. During their childhood in Claremont, a "citrus-belt town of well-manicured lawns and ivy-covered homes," the twins went to school together, played together, and got into identical mischief. Later they worked together during the summers and went out together on double dates.

At Bonita High School in La Verne, Ralph Davis caught the football passes thrown by his brother. Glenn, considered probably the greatest schoolboy athlete Southern California had ever produced, starred in football, baseball, basketball, and track, winning sixteen letters and the Knute Rockne track trophy. In one football game, when two passes of his were completed in succession, only to be called back on penalties, he picked up the ball and carried it fifty yards for a touchdown; and during his senior year he personally scored thirty-

GLENN DAVIS

six points. When approached by football talent scouts from colleges, Glenn would consider no offer that did not include his twin brother. Finally appointments to the United States Military Academy were procured for both.

On their arrival at West Point the twins were separated for the first time, assigned to different rooms and different companies, but spent as much time as possible together. On the football field Glenn established himself as a "gifted" runner at quarterback; at fullback against Notre Dame, however, he made three fumbles and permitted a Notre Dame tackle to steal the ball out of his arms on Army's seven-yard line. A reserve, he made three touchdowns in 1943. Scholastically, the first year proved too much for the eighteen-year-old Californian. Even getting up at four to study ninety extra minutes before reveille did not save him from being "found" (found deficient), and he had to leave West Point in December and study hard for several months to prepare himself for reappointment. (Thirty-nine years earlier the same thing had happened to another California cadet, George S. Patton [43].)

Davis' second try, at nineteen, was better. Continuing with his athletics—a required part of the academy routine, in addition to three weekly hours of physical training—he went in for football in autumn, basketball in winter, baseball in summer, football practice in spring, and earned varsity letters in all. In the Master of the Sword test of all-round physical efficiency, Glenn Davis scored 926½ points out of a possible thousand, setting an all-time record. (The average is about 540.) As a center fielder on the baseball nine, he was appraised at seventy-five thousand dollars by Branch Rickey [45], generally considered the best judge of baseball talent in the world. When fall came, Davis played intercollegiate football, while his twin was on the B squad.

According to Coach Blaik's [45] 1944-45 system of fielding entire alternate teams of first-stringers, Davis was assigned to the second team, on which were Blanchard and stalwarts like De Witt ("Tex") Coulter, Al Nemetz, and Herschel ("Ug") Fuson. Sportswriters and fans found it hard to believe that football occupied only an hour and a half of the cadets' sixteen-hour day, when they saw the Army team sweep through all opposition, running up a score of 59-0 against Notre Dame, 62-7 against Pennsylvania, and 23-7 against Navy. The names Blanchard and Davis became familiar even to persons who did not ordinarily follow football, and there was nation-wide discussion of their relative merits—this although Colonel Blaik held his first and second teams down to an average of eighteen minutes out of the hour of playing time in the first six games. In 1944 Glenn Davis scored more points than anyone else on the team, was voted the Maxwell Club award as the outstanding football player of the year, was runner-up for the Heisman Trophy, and was selected, with several other Army players, for the All-American "dream team." Commander Oscar Hagberg, the Naval Academy coach, said that Davis was the man who "ruined Navy." With an average carry of 11.1 yards, the Californian make a first down every time he got his hands on the ball.

Army ran its winning streak up to eighteen games in 1945, overcoming all types of defense. "Any coach who has the misfortune to face the West Pointers," said one such unfortunate, "is utterly helpless. If he jams up the middle alley to check Blanchard, Davis murders him with his sweeps. If he spreads his defenses to halt Davis, Blanchard pulverizes him on the inside. . . . And if by some stroke of genius he can distribute his strength evenly enough to bother them both, Army passes him dizzy." The "Touchdown Twins" appeared together on the *Time* cover of November 12, 1945, as Men of the Week, with the caption, "They make the Army's T boil." From *Time*'s article: "A jet-propelled gent named Glenn ('Junior') Davis . . . carries a special kind of speed that is all his own. After a brief show of [snake] hippiness, enough to get around the end, he simply leans forward and sprouts wings. Once outside, he makes would-be tacklers look ridiculous as they try to cope with his speed, his willowy change of pace, and starchy stiff-arm. He has gained a grand total of 1,777 yards in his fifteen games as an Army halfback for a breathtaking average of 12.2 yards a try. . . . Totally unlike most high-pressure halfbacks, he takes high delight in mowing down a rival tackler while running interference for somebody else (he cut down two Duke tacklers with one swoop to make way for a thirty-six-yard Blanchard touchdown run.)"

After the 1945 season had ended with the defeat of a previously unbeaten Navy team, the usually reserved Colonel Blaik said, "Glenn Davis can outrun any football player in America." Blanchard, who scored a total of nineteen touchdowns to Davis' eighteen, won 860 votes from sports commentators for the Heisman Trophy as best football player of the year, to 638 for Davis—and 187 for the third-place man. One writer explained, "Many sportswriters felt that flashy halfbacks such as Davis come along often enough, but a Blanchard only once in a generation." The two stars—again All-American—had amazed observers by coming out of each game uninjured, although both were prime targets for the opposition.

In the split-up of West Point's third-year class in early 1945, which accompanied the reconversion from an accelerated wartime schedule to a normal four-year course, Blanchard and Davis were assigned to the class of June 1947. When their teammates heard the news, they immediately elected the Southerner and the Westerner co-captains for 1946, the first co-captains in West Point football history. Glenn Davis was appointed, also, to the cadet post of regimental supply sergeant. (His brother, who was graduated in 1945, had established himself before departure as the champion college shot-putter, and had helped Doc Blanchard develop into one of the leaders.) "Even though Mr. Inside and Mr. Outside remain the most lethal twin engines of annihilation coupled on any eleven in the country," wrote Allison Danzig in September 1946, "take away Blanchard and Davis [this year] and West Point would be just another team" compared with the squads to be found at several other colleges. When injuries did take Blanchard away, Davis and quarterback Arnold Tucker joined forces to form "another irresistible combination," with Davis making four touchdowns in the twenty-two minutes and eight seconds the first team played against Cornell. (Blanchard and Davis shared another magazine cover, that of the September 16, 1946, *Life*.)

In October 1946 came the memorable 20-13 game against the heavily supported and cleverly deployed Michigan team of Coach Fritz Crisler. In this, wrote Stanley Woodward, "Statistics will show that Davis completed all of the seven passes he threw, made a touchdown on a fifty-eight-yard run, and gained 105 yards from scrimmage. They will not show what a great defensive game he played or what a horrendous beating he took. He played all but two or three minutes and gave the greatest one-man show this reporter has seen since 1935." The next Saturday saw Davis displaying "scintillating brilliance" in the Columbia game, Army's twenty-third consecutive victory, in which he played only twenty-three minutes. "It's impossible to conceive of anyone better than Junior," wrote Arthur Daley. Professional coach Steve Owen [46] remarked that only one thing could stop him—graduation; and Columbia coach Lou Little [45] declared flatly that Davis had been "the best running halfback I've ever seen in football." Little continued, "Davis has the uncanny knack of running at full speed and yet being able to make that sharp cut. . . . He never seems to tire or to be hurt. I never have seen anyone like him."

For the first time in his regular playing career, Cadet Davis was stopped in the scoreless Army-Notre Dame tie of November 1946. He came back the next week against Penn-

sylvania, scoring two touchdowns and passing for two more despite a blow on the head which caused him to lose his memory of the game afterward. At the end of his playing career that December, he had taken part in thirty-five college games, had not missed one of the twenty-nine games in Army's classic undefeated streak, and had contributed fifty-one touchdowns for 306 points. (Doc Blanchard's record stood at thirty-nine touchdowns and 231 points.)

Honors were again heaped upon the Army team and upon the left halfback individually. The sports reporters' Heisman trophy came to him by 792 votes to 435 for the runner-up (Blanchard was fourth with 267); he was named to various All-America selections, he and Blanchard being the only 1945 holdovers on the coaches' All-America; and he was considered "a cinch to win" the Sullivan Memorial Trophy for the outstanding amateur athlete of the year—except that his name was omitted from the list of nominees by oversight. (Another disappointment had been the loss of his chance to play one game in his native State: Army failed to receive the expected invitation to the postseason Rose Bowl game.) Davis was "drafted" by the Detroit club of the National Football League, which meant that if he decided to enter professional football, the other teams of the league had agreed to give Detroit first chance at his services. Despite the certainty of "glittering" offers from pro teams, as the year 1946 drew to a close both Blanchard and Davis maintained that any ball they might play in the future would be for an Army post team.

"Glenn is as bashful as a girl on her first date, even though he is All-American," Coach Blaik has said. The blue-eyed, brown-haired Californian is five feet nine inches tall, and his best playing weight is 170 pounds; he is regarded as little in comparison to other players, particularly the 205-pound six-footer Doc Blanchard, with whom he reportedly shares "true friendship and mutual admiration." Davis adheres to Army tradition in expressing no political preferences; his church is the United Brethren. After graduation he hopes to be able to join his brother, an Infantry officer. Good-looking and gentle-mannered, Davis is described as "the cool, brow-puckering type who insists on shouldering all the worries he can" on the playing field. Off it, said one writer, "West Point might make Glenn Davis an officer, but he's already a gentleman."

References

N Y Herald Tribune p29 N 8 '45
Time 56:57+ N 12 '45 pors

DAY, EDMUND EZRA Dec. 7, 1883-
University president

Address: b. c/o Cornell University, Ithaca, N. Y., h. 27 East Ave., Ithaca, N. Y.

Edmund Ezra Day has initiated a number of projects at Cornell University since he assumed the presidency of the institution in 1937. The first publicly supported labor school in the

EDMUND EZRA DAY

United States was opened there in November 1945. At that time, also, a Graduate School of Aeronautical Engineering was established in the Engineering College. Cornell was one of the first colleges in the country to offer a full course in contemporary Russian civilization. The president has also gone beyond the confines of his college campus to serve in Federal and State bodies, and on the boards of a number of organizations.

The son of Ezra Alonzo and Louise Moulton (Nelson) Day, Edmund Ezra Day was born December 7, 1883, in Manchester, New Hampshire. The boy went to public school in Worcester, Massachusetts. At Dartmouth, where he was awarded his B.S. in 1905 and his M.A. in 1906, Day was dubbed "Rufus" for having won a Rufus Choate Scholarship as a freshman with the exceptionally high scholastic average of 92 per cent. Day stayed on at Dartmouth as an instructor of economics from 1907 to 1910, except for two years at Harvard, where he received his Ph.D. in 1909. He also holds honorary LL.D. degrees from the universities of Vermont (1931); Syracuse, Pennsylvania, Dartmouth, and Harvard (1937); New York (1942); St. Lawrence, and Cincinnati (1943); William and Mary (1945); North Carolina, and Union College (1946).

In thirteen years, beginning in 1910, Day advanced from instructor to full professor and chairman of the department of economics at Harvard. During those years Day served as statistician in two Government agencies: for the Division of Planning and Statistics of the United States Shipping Board for seven months in 1918-19, directing the same division from June to August 1919, and for the Central Bureau of Planning and Statistics of the War Industries Board from September to December 1918. After leaving Harvard in 1923, for five years Day headed the department of economics at Michigan University. In 1925 he organized

and became first dean of its School of Business Administration. He was also appointed dean of the university, one of his chief duties being the preparation of the institution's budget. On leave in 1927-28, Day was associated with the Laura Spelman Rockefeller Memorial in New York, with which he remained through the year 1928-29.

Day served from 1929 as director for the social sciences in the Rockefeller Foundation, and from 1930 as director for both the social sciences and general education in the General Board of Education. Upon leaving these posts to assume the presidency of Cornell, Day expressed relief that he need no longer commute between his suburban Bronxville home and the city. According to *Time,* as one of the five "princes of the potent Rockefeller Foundation" dispensing $27,921,557 in Rockefeller money to United States colleges and research agencies, Day had not given any to Cornell.

In 1937, succeeding Dr. Livingston Farrand at Cornell University upon the latter's retirement, Day became fifth president of the then sixty-nine-year-old institution, the guide and guarder of its heritage (as expressed by the founding president) of avoiding "those who, in higher education, substitute dates for history, gerund-grinding for literature, and formulae for science." Discussing in his inaugural address the question of vocational training, which became an urgent problem in the depression years, Day affirmed, "It is the duty of a great university to serve the society in which it carries on. But it is equally the duty of the university to apply its resources so as to maintain that service durably. It is for the long pull that our universities exist." Thus, by making vocational education professional in character, specific and transient techniques would be learned on the actual job. "The largest vocational asset they [the students] can possibly acquire is the largest growth of intellectual power they can individually achieve."

On the first of November 1945 the State School of Industrial and Labor Relations was opened at Cornell as "New York's latest experiment in heading off strikes." Created by the 1944 legislature, it is the first of its kind in the United States to be supported by public funds. (Six months later it was given a one-thousand-dollar American Design Award by Lord and Taylor, New York department store, for its work in furthering human understanding.) In July 1946 the university acquired a modern aeronautical research laboratory as part of the Graduate School of Aeronautical Engineering, which was established the preceding November as an endowed division of Cornell's College of Engineering. Cornell was one of the first colleges in the country to offer a comprehensive course of study in current Russian civilization. Criticism which the course drew from some quarters was answered by Day's statement: "It is part of the respect we owe to our youth to deny it no knowledge that will enable it to bear, as it will bear resolutely and willingly, and in the enduring tradition of freedom, the weight of the world that is descending upon its shoulders." Inaugurated mainly through the efforts of Day, a formal gridiron pact was signed between

Brown University and the seven original members of the mythical Ivy League, so called by sports writers to indicate Columbia, Cornell, Dartmouth, Harvard, Pennsylvania, Princeton, and Yale.

Day is regarded as having answered in word and action the challenge to higher education by giving not merely information to students, but moral values, understanding, and a philosophy of pride in a job well done. In 1940 he changed a 7-3 football victory over Dartmouth into a 0-3 defeat when a motion picture of the game subsequently disclosed that Cornell's score had been made on an illegal fifth down. "I want no long count in Cornell's athletic history," he said. In 1941, wanting no "long count" in the nation's moral history, Day urged a speed-up of aid to Britain even if such policy involved the loss of American men and ships.

During the war years, Day was chairman of the Committee on Relationships of Higher Education to the Federal Government, constituted by the American Council on Education to work with officials of the armed services in the formulation of the Army-Navy college training programs. Important as education had been in war, Day declared in his first postwar commencement address, delivered at Cornell in June 1946, that "education broadly conceived is the most important base for a lasting peace." The future of mankind lies in "humane and intelligent control of scientific mechanisms in an atomic world," and Day believes, too, that it is the responsibility of the educators to find adjustments necessary for the reconciliation of the spiritual with the scientific levels of development. "The general confusion and bewilderment is not just a manifestation of postwar weariness or postvictory disillusionment, but a consequence of certain deficiencies in our national life in recent generations. Nothing short of a moral and spiritual awakening will save us. The bomb that dropped on Hiroshima less than a year ago called a turn in the affairs of mankind. Earlier ways of social organization and management will no longer suffice. We have no option but to rethink our habits, our interests, our attitudes, our ideals."

Day is a director of the National Bureau of Economic Research, and since 1939 has served as vice-president of the Association of American Colleges, counselor of the National Conference Board, and trustee of Tuskegee Institute. He serves as a member of the committee on school and college examinations of the Carnegie Foundation for the Advancement of Teaching, and as chairman of the board of directors for the Associated Colleges of Upper New York. Known as an authority in money and banking, Day was the United States representative on the preparatory committee of experts for the World Monetary and Economic Conference held in London in 1933, and from 1938 to 1942 he was a Class C director of the Federal Reserve Bank of New York. The educator is also active in New York State affairs. In August 1945 he was elected one of the eight vice-presidents of the State Citizens' Council, a group working to cultivate "in the State's average citizen belief in himself as one whose

opinion counts," with the ultimate goal of "an enlightened public opinion on community, State, nation, and world problems." Day also served on the Temporary State Commission Against Discrimination, which drafted the Ives report leading to anti-discrimination legislation, and he was appointed by Governor Dewey to study the need for a State university. Day is currently a member of the board of managers of the Memorial Hospital for the treatment of Cancer and Allied Diseases, in New York City.

The college president is the author of four books: *Index of Physical Production* (1920), *Statistical Analysis* (1925), *The Growth of Manufactures* (written with Woodlief Thomas in 1928), and *The Defense of Freedom*, a collection of four speeches (1941). Other of his association memberships are in the American Economic Association, the American Statistical Association, the Royal Economic Society (British), Phi Beta Kappa, Phi Kappa Phi, and Theta Delta Chi. His church is the Congregationalist. Day was married on June 5, 1912, to Emily Sophia Emerson, daughter of Charles Franklin Emerson, then dean of Dartmouth; their four children are Emerson, Caroline Louise (Mrs. Frederick C. Copeland), Martha Elizabeth, and David Allen. Bridge, tennis, and golf are listed as Day's recreations. The manner of the white-haired educator has been described as "usually quietly amused."

References

N Y Sun p22 N 16 '45 por
News Week 8:38 N 14 '36 por
Time 28:85 N 16 '36 por

National Cyclopædia of American Biography Current vol F p279
Who's Who in America, 1946-47

DE CARTIER (DE MARCHIENNE, EMILE), BARON *See* Cartier de Marchienne, E. de, Baron

DE CASSERES, BENJAMIN (dĕ kăs'ĕr-ĕs) 1873—Dec. 6, 1945 American journalist, author, poet; contributed book reviews and other articles to various periodicals since 1912; drama critic, motion picture company editor; columnist, editorial writer, and literary editor, Hearst papers, from 1933; his twelve books include a biography of his ancestor Spinoza.

Obituary

N Y Times p22 D 7 '45 por

DEUPREE, RICHARD R(EDWOOD) (doo-prē') May 7, 1885- Manufacturer; United States Government official

Address: b. c/o Procter & Gamble, Gwynne Bldg., Cincinnati, Ohio; h. Park Rd. nr. Shawnee Run Rd., Indian Hill, Cincinnati, Ohio.

Richard R. Deupree, president of the Cincinnati soap firm of Procter & Gamble, in February 1946 was named executive chairman of the Army-Navy Munitions Board, the agency responsible for plans for industrial mobilization in an emergency. In addition to his work in the

J. Anthony Bill

RICHARD R. DEUPREE

Government post, Deupree continues as head of Procter & Gamble, the company with which he has been associated since 1905.

A descendant of William Du Pre, a Frenchman who settled in Virginia in the early 1700's, Richard Redwood Deupree was born in Norwood, Virginia, on May 7, 1885, one of the six children of Richard Overton and Susan Elizabeth (Redwood) Deupree. He attended public schools in Covington, Kentucky, at sixteen becoming a clerk in the treasurer's office of the South Cincinnati and Covington Street Railway Company.

Seeking wider opportunities, young Deupree left the transportation company in 1905 for a clerical job with Procter & Gamble, the Cincinnati soap manufacturers. After four years, in 1909 he became a salesman for the bulk soap department, selling the company's products to laundries and textile mills. Promotions followed steadily. In another three years he was made manager of the western sales division of the company. Five years later, in 1917, he was general sales manager, and in 1924, when he was thirty-nine years old, he became a member of the board of directors. Thereafter, in rapid succession, from 1927 to 1930, he became general manager, vice-president, and then president. Selected for the last-named office by William Cooper Procter, who moved from the presidency to the chairmanship, Deupree was the first president of the firm who did not bear the name Procter.

In the depression of the 1930's, orders for soap fell off and production was reduced. In accordance with the company's guaranteed steady-work plan Procter & Gamble employees were not laid off. Instead, company employees cut grass, painted fences, repaired factory buildings, until production began to rise. In 1934 gross sales amounted to $116,593,142, and the figure soared to $352,336,632 in 1945. Statistics show that the company expends large sums on radio and publication advertising. Procter & Gamble was one of the first advertisers to use radio, sponsoring a program in 1923. By 1944 Deupree's company was alloting eleven million dollars for radio advertising, and in 1945 *Advertising Age* reported that Procter & Gamble had purchased more radio time and publication space than any other company in the country.

As president of Procter & Gamble, which manufactures Ivory Soap, Camay, Duz, Spic & Span, Oxydol, Drene Shampoo, Teel dentifrice, Crisco, and other soap and oil products, Deupree draws a salary of $188,600 a year. According to *Business Week*, "his stock interest in the company is small, which means that he depends squarely on his ability as an executive to maintain his position." A director of all Procter & Gamble companies, Deupree is chairman of the boards of two P & G subsidiaries, the Hewitt Soap Co., Inc., and Thomas Hedley & Co., Ltd., of Newcastle-on-Tyne, England. He is president of the Buckeye Cotton Oil Co., another P & G subsidiary. In addition to his positions in the Procter & Gamble organizations, Deupree is a director of the Baltimore & Ohio Railroad, the Coca-Cola Company, and the Cincinnati and Suburban Bell Telephone Company.

Deupree heads Procter & Gamble's labor relations program, which includes a profit-sharing plan, pension and insurance arrangements, and a steady-employment guarantee. In 1923, while Deupree was general sales manager, William Cooper Procter instituted a stabilized production plan which enabled the company to assure continuous work to its employees. Deupree at that time worked on sales plans, which had to be considerably altered to fit the new production schedules. When he became president of the company, Deupree continued the stabilized employment program and, in 1945, speaking before the American Management Association, he advocated the Procter & Gamble plan as a contribution toward a stable economy for the nation. He scored "producing to a buying hysteria," pointing out that "simply because those purchases are being made doesn't mean the goods are being consumed, and any manufacturer who supplies to that buying line is inevitably in trouble later on."

The P & G plan guarantees forty-eight weeks employment annually to every employee who has been with the company for more than two years. In periods when the retail dealer "is frightened into shrinking his inventory" the company arranges storage facilities for its products until buying is normal again. "I would say that the steady-employment plan is probably the greatest thing in our company, the greatest single factor—even greater than profit sharing—in producing good relationships," Deupree told the manufacturers. He also explained how, in the case of seasonal work, such as crushing cottonseed for oil, new methods of storing and handling cottonseed make it possible for the company to keep its mills in continuous operation. "The steady employment," he pointed out, "results in keeping trained men on the job, instead of having to train a new crew of men every crop season." To this type of management activity on behalf of labor he ascribed Procter & Gamble's record of sixty years without a major strike in any of its plants.

According to an official P & G statement, Deupree believes that "the first obligation of a business is to be successful. Success is based on good management and on cooperation of employees. . . .Employee plans and the resulting harmonious relations are factors in success, but they are results, not aims." He believes that it is up to industry to tackle the problem of "uncertainty in employment" if the nation is to forestall "untold trouble ahead." At the time he outlined to the American Management Association P & G's plans for avoiding alternating booms and shutdowns, he said, "I feel that this is the job of the manufacturer. I hope very much that neither the State nor the Federal Government attempts to guarantee steady jobs. I think such a program is doomed to failure before it starts, and will do nothing but make for trouble." Similarly, when the Senate Finance Subcommittee investigated profit-sharing systems in 1938, Deupree testified before it that he thought it would be impossible to dictate a fixed profit-sharing formula for all industry through legislation.

During World War II, P & G through a subsidiary, the Procter & Gamble Defense Corporation, designed, erected, and operated two shell-loading plants for the United States Government. In addition to his connection with this corporation, Deupree held several Government posts during the war. He was Chief of the Agricultural and Forest Products Division of the War Production Board, chairman of the Business Advisory Council of the Secretary of Commerce, and a member of a committee appointed by General Brehon B. Somervell to visit the European Theater of Operations in connection with military equipment problems. At various times he also served in Washington with the National Advisory Council, the Office of Production Management, and the War Labor Board.

In April 1946, Deupree took up his duties as executive chairman of the Army-Navy Munitions Board. He began the organization of a survey and study of the possibility of a dispersal of American industry, which would include moving key plants underground. Such a dispersal would be necessary to prevent their being wiped out by atomic attack in the event of war. The board also began work on a program of stock-piling critical war materials. It was commented in Washington that both activities were essential for national security, and that the dispersal study in particular involved problems of "staggering complexity," since American industry is "painfully" concentrated in a few areas. In August 1946 the board began the building up of a two-billion-dollar stock-pile of "the critical materials we would need first in an emergency," the purchases to be spread over five years. The drafting of a manual giving detailed instructions for fitting business and industry into a war program was under way in September. All plans were to be kept under revision to keep pace with scientific and industrial changes. "The better

prepared we are for industrial mobilization the less likely we are to be attacked," Deupree said. "A good mobilization plan will help prevent war." Beginning October 15, 1946, the chairman of the Army-Navy board was given full authority over purchasing for those services.

Active in civic affairs, the soap company executive several times served as chairman for Cincinnati community fund drives, in 1936, 1942, and 1945. In January 1946 he headed the Conference for Safeguarding Wartime Savings, as part of a nation-wide drive against postwar swindlers. He served on a committee of leading industrialists to spur the purchase of savings bonds between Armistice and Pearl Harbor days in 1946. Of his public service, *Business Week* has said: "Deupree is a favorite for such posts because he doesn't merely lend his name for letterheads. He gets in and pitches. The pressure of time contributed to public crusades is so great that his office hours are apt to be erratic." In his home city he is chairman of the executive committee of the Citizens Planning Association, president of the board of trustees of the Children's Hospital, a trustee of the Cincinnati Institute of Fine Arts, and a member of the Cincinnati Music Hall Association. He brings his experience in industry to the positions which he holds on the Visiting Committee of the Harvard Business School, on the advisory committee of the Soap and Glycerine Industry, and on the Business Advisory Council of the Department of Commerce. He is also a member of the board of trustees of the National Safety Council.

Richard Deupree was married to Martha Rule on October 18, 1913. Their four children are Richard Redwood, Jr., John Rule, James Young, and Elizabeth (Mrs. Richard E. Goldsmith). Mrs. Deupree died in August of 1943, and he was married a second time, in December 1944, to Emily Powell Allen. His recreations are horseback-riding, shooting, and golf—he holds memberships in a number of clubs, the Queen City, Commercial, Commonwealth, Camargo, and Cincinnati Country Club. *Business Week* describes the gray-haired, spectacled manufacturer as having a "general bearing . . . of Lincolnesque melancholy, his solemnity masking a combination of tolerance and humor." He likes simplicity and directness, "hates to read a letter of more than one page. If he wants an answer to something, he pops out of his office and goes directly to the person involved."

References

Bsns W p8 Ja 12 '46
N Y Sun p20 F 14 '46
National Cyclopædia of American Biography Current vol E p154
Who's Who in America, 1946-47

DIXON, THOMAS Jan. 11, 1864—Apr. 3, 1946 American author; member North Carolina legislature 1885-86; admitted to bar 1886; Baptist minister 1886-1909, preached in Raleigh, Boston, and New York; lecturer, 1889-1903; Federal court clerk, 1938-43; wrote twenty-two novels which sold more than five million copies;

DIXON, THOMAS—*Continued*

also nine stage and six screen plays; best known for *The Clansman* (1905), filmed as controversial *The Birth of a Nation* (1915).

Obituary

N Y Times p25 Ap 4 '46 por

DODD, MARTHA (ECCLES) Oct. 8, 1908- Author

Address: h. 115 Central Park West, New York

As the daughter of the American Ambassador to Germany, Martha Dodd was privileged to see history in the making from the vantage point of the American Embassy in Berlin during the fateful years from 1933 to 1937. She was able to gather a knowledge of persons of many nationalities—diplomats, industrialists,

MARTHA DODD

military men, and politicians; and when she returned home, an enemy of fascism, she recorded her memories in *Through Embassy Eyes* (1939) and in a novel, *Sowing the Wind* (1945).

Martha Eccles Dodd was born October 8, 1908, in Ashland, Virginia. She is the daughter of the late William Edward Dodd, historian, teacher, and diplomat, and of Martha (Johns) Dodd. Both sides of her family came of Southern stock, English colonists of the early seventeenth century, with strains of Welsh, Scottish, and German ancestry. Some of her forebears rose to prominence as landowners and clergymen. Almost immediately after birth the family moved to Chicago, and it was there that she was reared. She spent her summer holidays on a dairy farm, "Round Hill," in the Virginia foothills of the Blue Ridge. It was her father's belief that children should combine physical exercise with

productive work: the summer months were accordingly spent in gardening, preparing the produce for commercial markets, and picking fruit—such things as tennis and fancy diving were regarded as nonessentials.

At the time when Miss Dodd was growing up, her father was a ranking member of the history faculty at the University of Chicago; thus, she says, her strongest memories are of life as a professor's daughter in an academic environment. She early fell under the influence of the Russian writers; she was also, over a long period, engrossed in Nietzsche's *Anti-Christ*. And, in spite of her unsparing admiration for almost everything her father did, she was annoyed at his efforts to introduce his two children to the literary grandeur of the Bible. On this and on one other point, father and daughter did not see eye to eye: she could not share his high interest in, and concern for, the field of politics and economics. In fact, her indifference to it hung on through her college years.

Miss Dodd received her secondary school training at the progressive University of Chicago High School. She interrupted this to attend a finishing school in Washington, but disliked it intensely and soon returned to Chicago. At the University of Chicago, which she attended for three and a half years, the most valuable instruction she carried away with her was the influence of Robert Morss Lovett '43, who had been an acquaintance for some time and who continued to counsel her during the early 1930's before her father's appointment as Ambassador to Germany. In the midst of her college terms she made one long break—about a year—to go to Europe, and there took some courses at the Sorbonne.

When Miss Dodd left the University of Chicago she took a job as assistant literary editor of the Chicago *Tribune*, and found, in the course of reading Ella Winter's *Red Virtue*, a number of startling facts and interpretations that were entirely new to her. She wrote her review—which at best could be only a short one, since her small column was of necessity given over to several titles—and then discussed the book with her father. Even though her father's thinking about the book's subject did not encourage her in political sympathies (so far as Russia was concerned), this experience was evidently a starting point for some kind of social awareness. Her post on the *Tribune* left her some evening hours in which to try writing short stories, for she was intent upon carving out a literary career for herself. (It was during this same Chicago period that her first marriage took place; it was an unhappy one, and brief.)

In the early summer of the year 1933, William Dodd was appointed United States Ambassador to Germany, and with her older brother Miss Dodd accompanied her parents to Berlin. Up to this time Hitler had seemed, to her, a "clown who looked like Charlie Chaplin, who burned books, and against all the prophecies of mature and trained people had set up a dictatorship." To one whose political concepts of Nazism extended very little beyond this characterization, the prospects of life in the midst of Nazi Germany were primarily vague, and in that vagueness a little unwelcome. Yet the four years' residence in Germany during a historic period were to offer many advantages to the young girl from a literary point of view.

By the time Martha Dodd and her parents left Berlin in December 1937, her earlier lack of interest in politics had disappeared: she progressed from a mild admiration for the accomplishments of the Nazi regime (this on the basis of her first observations after her arrival in Germany) to a hatred for all fascism. In 1939 her first book, *Through Embassy Eyes,* appeared, a recital of her reactions to dictatorship and her inevitable exposure to the key personalities surrounding an American diplomat during four highly tense years. Rose Feld, writing in the New York *Herald Tribune,* recommended it "for its youth, its integrity, its indignation, its passion." Erika Mann in the *Nation* found that in the course of the book Miss Dodd "herself comes alive—unprejudiced and thoughtful, saucy and companionable, ready to help, eager to discipline herself through freedom."

In 1941, following her father's death, Miss Dodd and her brother, William E. Dodd, Jr., edited *Ambassador Dodd's Diary: 1933-1938.* For some months in 1944 she served as technical adviser in Hollywood on a film adaptation of her *Through Embassy Eyes,* which Twentieth Century-Fox had planned to produce. Late in 1945 came her third book, and first novel, *Sowing the Wind,* the story of the moral disintegration of a German airman. She had again drawn upon her four-year experience in Germany, but the materials did not, according to some of her critics, take on in fiction the form they might have. Lewis Gannett commented in the New York *Herald Tribune,* "Miss Dodd knows her Germany. But she seems more at home as a political commentator than as a novelist." The New York *Times* critic praised her book as "a contribution toward understanding the Third Reich" and felt that she had "succeeded well in what she set out to do." In 1946 the author was at work upon a second novel, dealing with the contemporary American scene.

Miss Dodd was married for the second time, in June 1938, to Alfred K. Stern; they have one son, Robert Dodd Stern. The author is five feet three inches tall, weighs 115 pounds, and has blond hair and blue eyes. Her favorite forms of relaxation are sea bathing, travel, and reading.

Reference

Dodd, M. E. Through Embassy Eyes (1939)

DOLIN, ANTON (dō′lĭn) July 27, 1904-
Dancer; choreographer

Address: b. c/o S. Hurok, 711 Fifth Ave., New York; h. 90 Madison St., New Bedford, Mass.

Dancer and choreographer Anton Dolin has been called "one of the most colorful and vital figures in modern ballet." As a member of internationally known ballet companies or as director of his own troupes, this British-born artist has toured Europe and America for the past twenty years.

Anton Dolin, christened Patrick Healey-Kay, was born on July 27, 1904, in Slinfold, Sussex, England. He is one of the three sons of George Henry and Helen Maude (Healey) Kay. His parents were born in England, his maternal grandmother was Irish, his paternal grandmother Hungarian, his great-great-grandmother Spanish—and he is said to exhibit characteristics of each nationality. The boy's father, who was known as a skilled cricketeer, was a master-owner of hounds. Pat, as he is still known to friends, was an athletic child, strenuously engaging in climbing, swimming, and bicycling.

When he was ten years of age his parents moved from Slinfold to Brighton. It was at about this time that the boy made up his mind to become a dancer. "As a child I longed to dance, and when I say that I could not hear music without my body wanting to respond, it is not exaggeration," Dolin tells in his book *Divertissement* (1931). Although his parents tried to discourage him from his ambition, he says, his constant entreaties and tantrums brought results. First they sent him to Miss Claire James' Academy of Dancing and later to the Misses Grace and Lily Cone, who came from London each week to give lessons in Brighton. After the boy danced and acted at the Brighton Hippodrome Theatre in a performance arranged by his teachers, the manager of the theater suggested that he be sent to London for training in dramatics. In the metropolis Pat studied under Italia Conti, and at the same time he attended the Pitman School for instruction in stenography and French. While at the Conti School he won the British Empire Shakespearean Society Prize for elocution, made his professional debut at the Prince's Theatre when he played the part of the Black Cat in *Bluebell in Fairyland* (December 1916), and appeared as John in *Peter Pan* (New Theatre, December 1917).

In 1917, a month after attending a performance of Princess Seraphina Astafieva's Swinburne Ballet, the thirteen-year-old boy registered for lessons with the Russian ballerina. A former pupil of the Imperial School and at one time principal dancer in the Diaghilev Ballet Russe, Astafieva was then conducting the only school of Russian ballet in London, which stressed the importance of the individual dancer in ballet. It was also she who helped to break down the legend that English dancers lacked the talent to advance beyond the corps de ballet. (Most of her pupils, including Markova[43], became well-known masters of pantomime.) After Pat had been her student for about four years, the famous Diaghilev visited the school one day in search of promising young dancers for extras in *The Sleeping Princess.* It was then that the seventeen-year-old youth was given his first dancing bit, a part in Diaghilev's chorus.

The Sleeping Princess had a three-month run, after which the young dancer returned to school for two more years of instruction. On

Maurice Seymour

ANTON DOLIN

August 26, 1923, under the name of the Anglo-Russian Ballet, Astafieva put on a large-scale production with her pupils as the principal dancers. For this first solo appearance Patrick Healey-Kay decided to choose a Russian name as he thought it would be an excellent joke. He found "Anton" in a Chekhov volume, but had difficulty in selecting an easily pronounced surname until someone at the school suggested "Dolin." The program for the performance thus announced that Anton Dolin would appear in two solo dances of his own composition: *Hymn to the Sun* and *Danse russe.* After this debut J. T. Grein wrote in the *Daily Sketch*: "Dolin is as light as a feather, as graceful as a fawn, as wing-footed as Mercury. I believe that Dolin ere long will be proclaimed the rival and successor of Nijinsky. . . .His great work is entirely free of pose." And Astafieva, feeling that her pupil was now ready to be accepted for Diaghilev's Ballet Russe, sent Anton Dolin to Paris, where she had arranged for an interview with the producer.

In November of that year (1923) Dolin was made a member of the Diaghilev company, which was then dancing in Monte Carlo. Before his next appearance before an audience, however, he devoted two months to intensive practice with Bronislava Nijinska, *maîtresse de ballet.* His debut was made on January 1, 1924, in the role of Daphnis in the classical ballet *Daphnis and Chloé.* (This was the first time that an Englishman had danced the principal role with the Russian troupe.) His next appearance, this time in a modern role, was as Beau Gosse in the production in Paris in June 1924 of Jean Cocteau's *Le Train bleu.* That ballet had been created especially for him after Cocteau, while one day watching the dancer do acrobatics, had conceived the idea of adapting these movements to the classical dance form.

In the next two years Dolin developed rapidly as a Diaghilev artist, but at the end of the 1925 season he and the impresario quarreled, causing Dolin, then the premier danseur, to leave the company. "Although I loved the Ballet and everyone in it," he has explained, "I was tired of being one of a band. The continual rehearsals and the restrictions imposed on me as a dancer annoyed and aggravated me." The following July Dolin appeared in *The Punch Bowl Revue* at His Majesty's Theatre, and after the show closed, at the beginning of 1926, he accepted an offer to dance in the musical revue *Palladium Pleasures.* Afterward, with Phyllis Bedells as his dancing partner at the Coliseum, he produced several "nursery rhyme" choreographies. Further ballet and revue engagements were followed in 1927 by an appearance in the revue *White Birds* (1927), a show considered one of the most widely publicized, most costly, and most talked-of failures in British theatrical history.

With Vera Nemchinova, one of his former colleagues in the Diaghilev company, Dolin next formed the Nemchinova-Dolin Ballet, dancing in *Swan Lake* and his own *The Nightingale and the Rose,* based on Oscar Wilde's fairy tale. During the following two years Dolin and Nemchinova toured Holland, Germany, France, and Spain, offering, among other compositions, Dolin's *Revolution,* founded on one of Chopin's etudes, *Espagnol,* and *Rhapsody in Blue.* The Gershwin ballet represents the struggle between classical music and jazz, with jazz the victor because "it is an expression of modern life." Describing it, Dolin has said, "Into this ballet I put everything I felt in my innermost soul, all my emotions, all my fears." The Nemchinova-Dolin company was disbanded early in 1929, Dolin rejoining the Ballet Russe. This second engagement lasted only a short while—Diaghilev's death in August 1929 causing the dissolution of the group. But Dolin had, with the Diaghilev company, created important roles—in Balanchine's [42] *Le Bal* and *Le Fils prodigue.* It was at about this time, too, that he danced with the budding ballerina Alicia Markova, eventually to be called "the greatest ballerina of our time."

Dolin's first New York appearance, on February 25, 1930, featured him, together with Argentinita and Gertrude Lawrence [40], in *The International Revue,* but the American critics were not enthusiastic and the revue closed after a few months. Dolin then returned to London, where he danced in two more revues, *Charlot's Masquerade* and *Stand Up and Sing.* His next engagement took him to Berlin as ballet master and dancer for Max Reinhardt's production of *The Tales of Hoffmann.* Upon returning to his native land, Anton Dolin joined the newly established Camargo Society Ballet, a British organization trying to revive ballet in England. It was with this group that Dolin danced the role of Satan in *Job* for the first time. After witnessing his interpretation of the Devil, the *Dancing Times* reviewer wrote that "Dolin, as Satan, was superb; he was the personification of the Fiend."

From 1931 to 1935 Dolin appeared in revues and was guest dancer with the Vic-Wells Ballet, of which Markova was the new première danseuse. After four years of this dual arrangement, Dolin and Markova in 1935 left the Vic-Wells company to form their own ballet troupe, sponsored by a patron of the theater, with Dolin as director and both the artists as the stars. From 1935 to 1937 the company toured the British Isles. Early in 1938, however, Markova left to become the principal ballerina of Massine's [40] newly organized Ballet Russe, while Dolin continued to dance in revues in England and later in Australia.

As principal dancers of New York's Ballet Theatre Dolin and Markova resumed dancing together in 1941, soon becoming, through the Ballet Theatre's annual national tours, much admired figures with American audiences. As choreographer with the troupe, Dolin recreated for modern audiences the nineteenth century classics *Giselle, Swan Lake, Les Sylphides,* and *The Sleeping Beauty,* and composed his own ballets, *Romantic Age, Quintet,* and *Pas de Quatre.* His art as a dancer was summarized by Robert Lawrence of the New York *Herald Tribune*: "He has that complete authority on stage that comes only with repeated seasons of first-class routine but from a highly acute and organized mind that dictates its will to the body. . . .Lyricism does not belong to Mr. Dolin as a performer, but marked sensitivity surely is there. His Albrecht of *Giselle,* his Prince Siegfried of *Swan Lake* do not depend so much on tenderness as on a lean and elegant pathos. Mr. Dolin's entire approach to the classical repertoire is that of the eighteenth century: line, structure, mood, rather than affecting detail. And it may be argued that he has right on his side. . . .None can approach him in comic roles [in Massine's *Don Domingo* or in *Bluebeard*]. . . .In the whole comic division of modern ballet Dolin, bolstered by his native sense of finesse, is supreme. Where his colleagues rely on careful planning for a humorous scene, he offers wit that is spontaneous and pointed." A New York *Times* critic expressed the opinion that Dolin was the only male principal of the company who was "capable of carrying classic roles" and that his contribution was "enormous and uncontradictable." He felt, however, that this gave Dolin an "ubiquity which neither his own art nor the repertory could stand."

In the winter of 1944-45 Dolin and his partner Markova were seen in Billy Rose's [40] production, *Seven Lively Arts,* in which, in addition to several ballet sequences, Dolin did some satirical and "shrewd emoting" in a scene with Beatrice Lillie [45]. During Ballet Theatre's engagement at the Metropolitan Opera House his appearance in the revue late in the evening made it possible for him also to dance with this group. In October 1945 manager S. Hurok [41] announced the formation of a new Markova-Dolin ballet troupe devoted to classical ballet, which he had booked for a first-season engagement of sixty appearances throughout the United States. The ensemble dancers, it was said, would be both selected and trained by Markova and Dolin. The group's initial tour, which began in November, had capacity audiences, reported *Dance News,* and its special booking arrangement brought it together for a joint appearance with Ballet Theatre in the larger cities of the United States.

In June 1946 Dolin ventured upon another acting experience and essayed the title role of the play, *The Dancer.* His performance was characterized by a reviewer as "absorbingly convincing"—despite a tendency "to enjoy being a bit of a ham in the Karloff manner." When the Original Ballet Russe returned to New York in October, Dolin was among the performers. Speaking of his dancing in the role of Albrecht in *Giselle,* John Briggs of the New York *Post* said, "Mr. Dolin, as usual, turned in an excellent performance."

Aside from his stage performances, Anton Dolin has appeared in several British motion pictures, which include *Invitation To Waltz, Chu Chin Chow, Forbidden Territory,* and *Dark Red Roses.* In 1945 Dolin and Markova were brought to the American screen in Republic Pictures' musical *A Song for Miss Julie.* The dancer has had two books published, *Divertissement* (1931), a book of reminiscences, and *Ballet Go Round* (1938), his autobiography. He has lectured at Oxford and Cambridge universities and over the radio in England, Australia, and the United States. In the summer of 1941, with Markova, he directed a ballet school and an international dance festival in the Berkshires.

Bachelor Anton Dolin is a well-built man whose muscular physique makes him appear larger than his five feet seven inches and one hundred and forty-four pounds. He has the characteristic black hair and dark eyes of a Spaniard, "a small Irish mouth." Tennis, motoring, and travel are his favorite recreations.

References

Christian Sci Mon p11 Mr 9 '40 por
Beaumont, C. W. Complete Book of Ballets (1941)
Dolin, A. Ballet Go Round (1938); Divertissement (1931)
Who's Who in America, 1946-47
Who's Who in the Theatre (1939)

DONAHEY, (ALVIN) VIC(TOR) July 7, 1873—Apr. 8, 1946 Politician and businessman; began as printer; Ohio State Auditor, 1912-20; Governor, 1923-29; United States Senator, 1935-41; president Donahey Clay Products Company and Motorists Insurance Company.

Obituary

N Y Times p27 Ap 9 '46 por

DONALD, W(ILLIAM) H(ENRY) June 1875—Nov. 9, 1946 Australian journalist and economist; adviser to Chinese Governments

Bulletin: W. H. Donald died on November 9, 1946.

From July 1946 issue:

W. H. Donald, known to the world for forty-four years as "Donald of China," and hated by the Japanese as "the evil spirit of China," has been political adviser and friend to China's leaders from Sun Yat-sen and

W. H. DONALD

Marshal Chang Hsueh-liang to Generalissimo Chiang Kai-shek'[40]. Released in February 1945 from a three-year imprisonment in the Los Baños Camp in the Philippines, the seventy-one-year-old "handyman to warlords . . . bottomless receptacle of more news information, chitchat, and . . . state secrets than any foreigner who ever lived in China" anticipates returning as unofficial aide to General Chiang.

"The friend of China," William Henry Donald, was born at Lithgow, New South Wales, in June 1875, the eldest in a family of seven sons and three daughters. From the early nineteenth century, when his dour, teetotaling grandfather left Scotland, the Donalds had lived in Australia. There the boy attended Cooerwull Academy. Whereas his father pursued a notable career as a politician, young Donald was trained to become a builder, the trade followed by his grandfather, constructor of many Government buildings.

The elder Donald had acquired part ownership of a local newspaper which William joined after an early accident had shattered his right arm. The printer's devil of the Lithgow *Mercury* became a reporter, and was graduated into positions on the Bathurst (New South Wales) *National Advocate*, the Melbourne *Argus*, and the Sydney *Daily Telegraph*. Arriving at the office of the *Telegraph* in 1902, it is said, Donald found a message from the editor of the English-language Hong Kong *China Mail* offering him a job and forwarding travel expenses. Only after his arrival in China did he discover that a friend had informed the Hong Kong editor that Donald was the strict teetotaler the *Mail*'s editor had sought for seven years.

Vivid dispatches written during the Russo-Japanese War of 1904-05 gained for Donald a reputation as crack correspondent. In 1904, the same year Donald was raised to the managing directorship of the *China Mail*, James Gordon

Bennett appointed him Shanghai correspondent and later Peking correspondent and press bureau chief for the New York *Herald*. Increased interest in the Nationalist cause of the Chinese people led Donald to join the revolution, as well as to help establish Hong Kong University, which he had long advocated. In 1911 he became editor of the *Far Eastern Review*, a monthly magazine dedicated to "breaking down the cake of custom" impeding China's modernization, and began working with Dr. Sun Yat-sen, later first president of China. Donald remained the leader's adviser through the revolution and his succeeding presidency (1911-12), writing several of Sun's early proclamations. Of their association it has been said, "The Nationalist leader had dreams, and Donald translated them into plans. He had ideas, and Donald translated them into words." A reporter once asked the visionary Sun Yat-sen whether he was a Socialist. The doctor turned to Donald. "Am I?" he asked. To this the realistic Donald promptly replied, "You are everything that is required as a Nationalist."

"Don," or "Gran," as his friends call him, found himself more and more the confidant of politicians rather than the "engineer of New China." Thus it happened that he had a seat at the negotiations over Japan's Twenty-one Demands upon China in 1915, which, if accepted, would have made China the vassal of the Japanese Empire. He helped considerably in having the demands modified and was ultimately the man to reveal Japan's dicta to the world. Donald's anti-Japanism is said to have originated in this affair. In 1915, too, Donald was instrumental in persuading the dictator Yuan Shih-kai to abdicate and go into exile. However, before he could abdicate, Yuan died just after the seventeen of the twenty-two Chinese provinces had revolted in favor of Nationalism and against the dictatorship.

"Almost single-handed," John Gunther reports in *Inside Asia*, "Donald brought China into World War I in 1917." At the time of the Wilson denunciation of the German submarine policy, an American minister to China, Paul S. Reinsch, heard the President's message and enlisted Donald's help in forming "The Flying Wedge," to win Chinese cooperation with President Wilson's wishes. Because Donald was "as influential a white man in Chinese affairs as there is in China or elsewhere," as Mrs. Theodore Roosevelt, Jr. once wrote, China endorsed Wilson's stand six days after it had been announced; and on August 14, 1917, China entered the war.

At the request of the Chinese Ministry of Finance, and in order to support himself in the Orient, Donald established the Bureau of Economic Information, to gather and disseminate little-known facts about China. When the Nationalist Government tried to turn the bureau into a propagandist organ in 1928, Donald answered the frantic calls of his friend the Old Marshal and warlord of Manchuria, Chang Tso-lin, by leaving China proper for Mukden, the Manchurian capital. There he served the Old Marshal, and acted as mentor to his son, Chang Hsueh-lin, the Young Marshal, who in

1936 figured prominently in the kidnapping of General Chiang Kai-shek. Donald set about rehabilitating young Chang, an opium addict, negotiated his rapprochement with Chiang-Kai-shek in 1929-30, took him to Europe, and, until Japan invaded Manchuria in September 1931, remained the Young Marshal's adviser in the modernization of his country.

Donald's credo of "unity and organization" allied his interests to those of Nationalist Chiang Kai-shek, leader of the modern republic, whom he joined in 1934 as personal adviser and unofficial envoy. In his work Donald "did what no one else had the courage to do. He stood up and told General Chiang what was the matter with his Government and his country." After escorting "Gissimo," as he calls the General, on his 1934 tour of the west of China, Donald in 1935 became ill for the first time in his life and spent six months in bed with a digestive malady.

His greatest mission was that of intermediary after the December 1936 kidnapping of General Chiang. The world thought that Chiang had been captured by Young Marshal Chang, who opposed Chiang's orders for war against the Chinese Communists. As mediator Donald persuaded General Chiang to satisfy Chang by uniting China to oppose Japan, according to Andrew C. Lang ("The Man Who Wouldn't Let Chiang Kai-shek Commit Suicide," *Fact*, January 1946). After the General's release on Christmas Day of 1936, Donald asserted that Chiang's own generals, rather than the Young Marshal, had probably engineered the abduction in an attempted coup d'état. When the generals later demanded that Chiang expel Donald, he refused. Because of Donald's constant declarations that "Japan cannot defeat China," the Japanese persistently hunted "the world's greatest Japanese-hater." They almost had him once, in July 1938, when seven Zeros attacked his plane over the Yangtze River, but it escaped in the mist.

In 1941, after thirty-nine years in China, Donald left for New Zealand, intending to write his memoirs. When war appeared inevitable, Donald, attempting to return to Chunking, was stranded in the Philippines. Captured when Manila fell, Donald was interned in Santo Tomás prison camp, then transferred to Los Baños internment camp south of Manila. He remained unrecognized even after Premier T. V. Soong '41 accidentally revealed that the famous W. H. Donald was a war prisoner, because the Japanese could not realize that this elderly, soft-spoken, bookish camp librarian was their "big, bluff, incorruptible" enemy. Prisoners in Los Baños, the Chinese Government in Chunking, and his relatives in Australia guarded the secret.

After a three-year incarceration, Donald was released in February 1945. He entered the 41st United States Field Hospital on Luzon to recuperate, and later in the same year he visited America. Following a brief trip to China to say goodbye to old friends until he should be able to return permanently, in 1946 he returned to Aiea Hospital, Honolulu, for treatment of a serious illness. When interviewed at the hospital, Donald expressed doubt that Chiang would relinquish leadership in the near future, declaring that the "Communists are creating a situation in which the General cannot lay down the reins of government without destroying his whole life's work at one stroke." Nevertheless Donald believes that an international commission should aid in solving Chinese administrative problems. The contest between Chiang and the Communists, Donald declared, "has not yet been settled." The decision of the United States "to make economic aid contingent upon certain dictated . . . changes," he warned, "is playing into the hands of Chinese Communists and might easily strengthen their position." Articles by Donald have appeared in *Asia, Collier's,* and *Living Age* magazines. A New York *Times* editorial said of him: "His honesty is unquestioned, and his testimony cannot be refuted." The Nanking Government awarded him the Order of the Brilliant Jade.

The man whose philosophy is "I expect nothing ever to happen according to logic or Hoyle—therefore I am never disappointed," has sung lullabies to the children of missionaries, plaited the pigtails of the very young Soong sisters and later played casino or rummy with Mme. Chiang for golf ball stakes. For her he reserves his highest compliment, "She thinks just like a man!" In the days before his imprisonment, Donald was, according to Ilona Ralf Sues, "tall, broad-shouldered, with a strong, ruddy face and curiously streaked gray hair, a willful chin, a determined mouth and extraordinary, world-conscious eyes that look right through people and things and cannot be fooled." He has no sense of smell. The Australian adviser is possessed of vitality, forthrightness, and a good humor which made him enjoy being the butt of General Chiang's collection of Scotch jokes. Called the "greatest enemy of 'face' in China," as well as the land's "best cicerone," "China's publicity-shy Richelieu," after almost forty years in the Orient, will not eat Chinese food, and does not speak a word of the language.

References

Asia　42:535+　S '42, 42:596+　O '42
Sat Eve Post　210:5+　Mr 19 '38 pors
Time　45:16 F 19 '45 por

International Who's Who, 1945-46
Who's Who in Australia　(1938)

DOWLING, EDDIE　Dec. 9, 1894-　Actor; playwright; director; producer
Address: b. 246 W. 44th St., New York; h. 38-24 213th St., Bayside, N.Y.

Eddie Dowling, a onetime song-and-dance man, a writer and producer of popular musical comedies, not only became a producer of and actor in serious dramas, but has achieved distinction in both capacities. The author and star of the musical *Sally, Irene and Mary* and *Honeymoon Lane* has in eight years won four New York Drama Critics' Circle awards and one Pulitzer Prize for his productions. In the 1945-46 season Dowling, as producer, director, and actor in *The Glass Menagerie*, achieved that

Talbot

EDDIE DOWLING

However, before he was to continue in vaudeville as a song-and-dance man, the young actor had a season in a New England stock company, where he received valuable training in the serious drama.

"The first real break in my life," Dowling has said, "came when I married Ray Dooley." In 1914 Ray Dooley's Ministrels was a headline act in vaudeville; Dowling was a song-and-dance man who had not yet arrived at star billing. Miss Dooley and her three brothers had been trained since childhood for the stage by their father, who had been a well-known clown in the British Isles. Although all the Dooleys were successful, it was generally conceded that Ray was the most talented. As a headliner in vaudeville and later in Broadway musicals, she commanded a weekly salary of four figures. This fact was to lead her husband, some years after their marriage, to begin writing motion picture scenarios—*The Life of Victor Herbert, The Rainbow Man*—and subsequently musical comedies.

Although for many years Dowling's name was closely associated with the forms of light entertainment, the actor had nursed an urge to turn to serious dramatic expression. One of his first recorded attempts was in a skit of his own that he used as the finale for his vaudeville turn. Entitled *The Stowaway*, this bit of pathos concerned a young immigrant who was about to be deported. The skit became the main feature of his vaudeville program, finally winning for him an engagement in the top variety house, New York's Palace Theatre. This change in fortune brought the Broadway showman, A. L. Erlanger, and his stage director, Edgar MacGregor, to see him, but the hoofer's comedy talents turned out to be the cause of postponing his debut as a serious actor. Erlanger and MacGregor, after seeing the actor in the song and dance part of his act, quickly decided that he was a young man worthy of encouragement. Sending word backstage to Dowling to call at their offices, they left the theatre before he had done *The Stowaway*.

That year, 1918, was nevertheless a milestone in Dowling's career. Erlanger engaged him for a part in the road company of the musical, *The Girl Behind the Gun*. The following year he made his Broadway debut in *The Velvet Lady*. Although Victor Herbert had written the score for this musical, the young comedian was permitted to sing two numbers of his own composition. His success—critics pronounced Dowling "the best since George M. Cohan"—carried him into Ziegfeld's *Follies of 1919*, which starred Will Rogers, Fannie Brice, and his own wife, Ray Dooley, who, with her brother Johnny, was one of the smash hits of the revue.

In 1922, after a period in Hollywood and appearances in a number of Broadway shows, including two more editions of the *Follies*, Dowling collaborated with Cyrus Woods on the musical comedy *Sally, Irene and Mary*. Serving as co-producer, co-director, and star as well, Dowling became what Broadway called "an overnight success." "A fresh little comedy of New York manners," said the New York *Times* critic of the play, "with screamingly funny lines and a flavor as sure as three-star Hen-

much desired goal, an artistic and financial success. Theater commentators have described him as "a wistful, reverent, and poetic leprechaun" and as "a force which has developed more leverage for the American theater than a lot of larger sounding organizations rolled into one."

The fourteenth of seventeen children, Eddie Dowling was born Joseph Nelson Goucher in Woonsocket, Rhode Island, on December 9, 1894. His parents were Charles Goucher, a French-Canadian, and Bridget Mary (Dowling) Goucher, who was Irish-born. The boy attended parochial school and earned pennies by singing Irish ballads outside the doors of barrooms. While still a child he ran away to Boston. Annoyed at the frequent mispronunciations of his surname and at the nickname "Canuck" for his French-Canadian blood, he decided to take his mother's patronymic, adding "Eddie" for no particular reason. In Boston, to quote Howard Dietz in *Cosmopolitan*, "he started his musical career by rendering in a ten-year-old soprano the ballads of another Rooseveltian day in a music store on Washington Street." At eleven he got a job as cabin boy on the Fall River Line. Later Eddie graduated to ocean liners, working again as cabin boy on the *Mauretania* and *Lusitania*. With the encouragement of Sir Harry Lauder's manager, the young American next joined the famous boys' choir of St. Paul's Cathedral in London. After that he made a world tour with a boys' choral group.

When Eddie's voice changed, ending his career as a choir boy, he worked for a time on a fishing schooner. He soon went back to entertaining, however, beginning as a "song plugger" who sang current numbers between acts in a theater and sold the sheet music to whomever he could interest. While he was working as a program boy, the youth was given his first stage role—in a vaudeville act which was playing Providence, in his home state.

nessey." Of the star, who today is noted for his style of understatement, critic Alan Dale observed, "If Dowling could be made to avoid shouting he could be fairly amusing." *Sally, Irene and Mary* ran a season on Broadway, two more on the road, and after earning for its producers a million dollars, was sold four times to Hollywood. *Honeymoon Lane* (1926), with Dowling in the threefold capacity of author, producer, and star, duplicated the success of *Sally, Irene and Mary,* but the next season's creation, *Sidewalks of New York,* failed to reach the hit class. This was the first production, incidentally, in which Ray Dooley shared stellar honors with her husband. The couple later appeared together in vaudeville, in 1931-32; then, after co-starring in *Thumbs Up* (1934), Ray Dooley retired from the stage —and Dowling made the final break with his song-and-dance past.

Although Broadway theater folk spoke "with wonder in their voices about the metamorphosis of Eddie Dowling, the song-and-dance man, into Eddie Dowling, the serious interpreter of poetic drama," the change was not so sudden as it seemed. Besides stock company training, and *The Stowaway* of his vaudeville days, the record shows that in 1925, between two musical shows, he had played a road engagement in the straight play *The Fall Guy,* and in 1933 he had produced *Big-hearted Herbert,* a comedy without music. Sidney B. Whipple (New York *World-Telegram*), for one, saw no revolutionary change in Dowling: "Eddie Dowling is doing today what he has always wanted to do . . . and what he has always been eminently fitted to do. He has found the niche into which his own character best fits and is most comfortable."

Dowling's production of Shakespeare's *King Richard II* (1937) included enough "firsts" to make Broadway prophets highly dubious of its success. Besides being the first serious production by Dowling, it was the first American presentation of the play since the days of Edwin Booth, the first major directorial job and the first professional appearance of Margaret Webster [40] in America; in addition, its star, Maurice Evans [40], had at that time been cast in only one Shakespearean role (Romeo) in the American theater. All doubt and uncertainty were gone, however, after the final curtain on its opening night. "Unanimous yells of enthusiasm" acclaimed the erstwhile song-and-dance man's first production of poetic drama as "one of the most startling triumphs in years."

For his second dramatic production Dowling chose Paul Vincent Carroll's play about the clash between "savage nationalism and worldly clericalism" in Ireland (William Lindsay Gresham, *Theatre Arts*), *Shadow and Substance,* which was well received when offered in Dublin by the Abbey Players in 1934. With a distinguished cast that included Sir Cedric Hardwicke, Julie Haydon, and Sara Allgood, the play won highly laudatory reviews on its New York opening (January 1938), captured the Critics' award and a place among Burns Mantle's [44] choices as the ten best plays of the season. Dowling's debut as a dramatic actor was made in his own production of Philip

Barry's *Here Come the Clowns* (1938). Richard Watts, Jr., pronounced Dowling's "the finest acting of the year," while a voice outside of the theater, the Reverend John Haynes Holmes [41], announced that the actor had risen to "real greatness in his tremendously yet utterly simple presentation" of the leading character. Despite the respect given the play by the critics, *Here Come the Clowns* operated at a loss from the beginning, and after eighty-eight performances was closed.

Another outstanding play among Dowling's serious productions was Paul Vincent Carroll's *The White Steed* (1939). The New York Drama Critics' Circle unanimously voted it the best play of the season and it also received a place among Mantle's "ten best." But an even greater honor came to the former musical comedy man when he won not only the Critics' award but the Pulitzer Prize (the first time that this double acknowledgment had been given a play) with his production of William Saroyan's [40] first full-length play, *The Time of Your Life* (1939). "Poetic vaudeville", "a prose poem in ragtime", "a goofy binge," and "cosmic vaudeville" are excerpts from critical reviews of this prize-winning play. Dowling, again in a triple role of co-producer, director, and actor, played Joe, the play's chief protagonist, an habitué of a barroom on the San Francisco waterfront. His acting of the dreaming, drinking, soul-helping Joe was hailed by critics as an histrionic masterpiece that ranked him as a second Edwin Booth.

One of the ambitions of producer Dowling has been to establish a repertory theater. With this end in view, in 1942 he took over the Belasco Theater, announcing that despite the fact that most producers were seeking escapist entertainment for war audiences, he thought that the serious times demanded uplifting drama. In keeping with his belief, Dowling revived for his first program G. K. Chesterton's short play *Magic,* which has the subject of faith for its theme. Saroyan's one-act play *Hello, Out There,* was its companion piece on the bill. Dowling's acting in, and his staging of, the playlets won praise, but again the producer-actor found himself on the wrong side of the ledger, financially. After forty-seven performances he closed the program and laid aside the idea of a repertory theater, an idea, however, which he still cherishes.

In October 1943 Dowling, reported to have lost a fortune in his effort to produce only the best in drama, returned to the stage as a member of the cast of *Manhattan Nocturne* (authored, produced, and directed by others). Ward Morehouse's [40] opinion that this was "a skimpy play," with Dowling's "quietly effective performance" as its only distinction, was echoed by the other reviewers. Although *Men to the Sea* (1944) by Herbert Kubly won no prizes, closed after a three-week run, and had only two admirers among the New York reviewers, those admirers championed the play's "intellectual effort" so strongly that it perhaps deserves a place among the showman's artistic successes. Unable to promote the money for its production, Dowling had turned *Men to the Sea* over to Dave Wolper, who thereupon engaged him as

DOWLING, EDDIE—*Continued*

assistant director of the play. "The drama," wrote Burton Rascoe (New York *World-Tele-gram*), "is quite an open acceptance of the fact that all wives of men in our armed forces overseas . . . have not been, and are not, true to their husbands. Their reasons are as varied as human nature," continued Rascoe. "All this is related with dignity, taste, poignancy, and sense." Credit for the skill of the cast, most of whom were new to Broadway, was given to Dowling by the critic.

The urge which has caused Dowling to persist in investing his time and money in prize-winning but not box-office-winning plays was finally rewarded when in 1945 he produced Tennessee Williams' '46 play *The Glass Menagerie*. This not only captured the critics' award but during its second season on Broadway still played to capacity audiences. (According to all estimates, it should make Dowling a rich man.) In an interview Dowling has related the story of his acquiring the play. He was in debt and had, therefore, signed a contract with Louis J. Singer to produce and direct "a strictly commercial play." In the midst of casting, Williams' agent sent Dowling the script of *The Glass Menagerie*, saying that the play had gone the rounds and was not a commercial possibility, but that it would give the producer an idea of the style of the playwright, an author worth watching. Dowling, enthusiastic about the script, turned to Mrs. Dowling for advice, pointing out that he did not think it would make money. "And we needed money," emphasizes Dowling now; "and I had a contract to do a play which would at least get us out of the hole financially." Her answer was, "Do the play your heart's in; you won't be happy otherwise; we'll get along somehow."

Laurette Taylor '45, co-starring with Dowling in the play, received high praise from the press for her "magnificent" portrayal of Amanda, the "decaying Delta belle, overfond of haranguing her two children, one a warehouse worker, played by Dowling, and the other a morbidly bashful maiden, played by Julie Haydon, upon their duty to rise above the drabness of their life in a St. Louis alley flat." Dowling, however, as co-producer, co-director, narrator, and actor, was given the major credit for the success of the production, considered the most distinguished the theater had offered in many seasons. Another honor to come to *The Glass Menagerie* company was its selection by President Truman '45 to present the play at the Washington benefit (January 27, 1946) for the National Foundation for Infantile Paralysis. Early in August 1946 the play's Broadway run ended. Two road companies, one containing members of the original cast, toured with the play in the fall of 1946.

With *Menagerie* a smash hit, Dowling and Singer took options on a number of other plays. The first of these to reach production was Dowling's adaptation from the Hungarian of Miklos Laszlo's *St. Lazare's Pharmacy* which opened in Chicago after Christmas of 1945. A divided press and the illness of its star, Miriam Hopkins, in the second week of January sent the box office receipts below the oper-

ating cost; and not long afterward the show closed. Late in the fall of 1946 producers Dowling and Singer dissolved their partnership, but Dowling retained his interest in *St. Lazare's Pharmacy* and *The Glass Menagerie*.

Among the actor-manager's other projects was Eugene O'Neill's *The Iceman Cometh,* which opened early in October 1946 under the aegis of the Theatre Guild. Although O'Neill had requested Dowling to play the lead as well as direct the play, which critic George Jean Nathan had predicted would be "one of the finest plays in the American dramatic record," Dowling committed himself only to serving as director. His direction was praised by critics as contributing to the play's triumph as "intelligent theater work." In the final months of 1946 Dowling was also under contract to direct *Mulligan's Snug* and Max Wylie's '40 *The Greatest of These*; he had purchased the rights to the latter.

Considered by many to be the American theater's most gifted director, Dowling says that he tries to achieve naturalness in his direction of players—his guide, Keats's "Beauty is truth, truth, beauty." His test for an actor is to ask him to say only the lines "I love you" and "I believe in God." "If he can say those lines naturally and with conviction," says Dowling, "the rest is easy." His greatest ambition has always been to produce the works of unknown, promising playwrights. Other plans of his are to be associated with repertory theater, with an American opera company producing the best (from a dramatic as well as musical standpoint) possible contemporary works in English, and with the fostering of American ballet.

Dowling has not been tempted by Hollywood offers since he has been concerned with serious plays. Between and during his theater engagements, however, he has made radio appearances. Among these were his role as master of ceremonies on *We, the People* (1941) and a thirteen-week engagement, also as "emcee," for *Wide Horizons* (1944). Some of his nonprofessional activities have been in the political field. A close friend of the late President Roosevelt '42 since World War I, Dowling stumped for him in his 1928 and 1930 gubernatorial campaigns. In his 1932, 1936, and 1940 Presidential campaigns Dowling headed the Democratic Committee for Stage and Screen Workers. Although *The Glass Menagerie* is Dowling's first "command" performance, he was guest entertainer at many of the Roosevelt Cabinet dinners. The actor has been given credit for first interesting Roosevelt in a work-relief program for theater workers, which resulted in the formation of the Federal Theater Project in 1935. Soon after the United States entered World War II, Dowling organized and became first president of the USO-Camp Shows.

Mr. and Mrs. Dowling live on a Bayside (Long Island) place, which they bought from John Golden '43. They have two children, John Graham and Maxine. John, who for two and a half years served as a war correspondent for the Chicago *Daily Sun,* was engaged in early 1946 in writing a play about his experiences.

Eddie Dowling is of medium height and slender; he has brown hair and "half-mystical gray-blue eyes, and an easy smile." A man of simple manner, he is called Eddie on first acquaintance by theater people. The success of *The Glass Menagerie* "couldn't have happened to a sweeter guy," say those who know him.

References

Cosmopolitan 119 :8+ S '45 pors
N Y Herald Tribune VI p2 N 1 '42
N Y Sun p24 S 23 '44
Theatre Arts 30 :632+ N '46
International Motion Picture Almanac, 1943-44
Who's Who in America, 1946-47
Who's Who in New York, 1938
Who's Who in the Theatre (1939)

DRAKE, (JOHN GIBBS) ST. CLAIR. *See* Cayton, H.R. and Drake, J.G.S.

DREISER, THEODORE (drī'sĕr) Aug. 27, 1871—Dec. 28, 1945 American writer and editor; considered one of the outstanding realistic novelists in the world; among his twenty-five books are *Sister Carrie* (1900), *Jennie Gerhardt* (1911), *The Financier* (1912), *The Titan* (1914), *The Genius* (1915), *Twelve Men* (1919), and *An American Tragedy* (1925); wrote on themes of social protest, involved in a number of controversies; editor of various magazines early in career.

Obituary

N Y Times p1+ D 29 '45 por

DU BOIS, GUY PENE (dü"bwä' gĭ pĕn) Jan. 4, 1884- Artist; writer
Address: h. 20 W. 10th St., New York; Stonington, Conn.

A frequent prize winner, Guy Pène du Bois lived up to past performance when he carried off top honors in the spring show of the Salmagundi Club of New York City in May 1946. The first prize of one thousand dollars was awarded to Du Bois for his painting, *After Dinner Speaker,* "a suave genre piece in charming color." Some critics chose to interpret the award as made, not so much for the single work—considered one of the artist's lesser canvases—but rather as an honor to a "long and distinguished career." A painter who presents "the passing show of life as he sees it—with humor, with detachment, and with that personal touch that gives distinction to him among American painters," Du Bois has had success both as an artist and as a writer. A social historian, according to W. B. McCormick in *Arts and Decoration,* his is a pictorial art based upon human experience, aided by his years of observing the human comedy through the eyes of a journalist.

Born in Brooklyn, New York, January 4, 1884, into an old French family which had become established in New Orleans in 1738, Guy Pène du Bois passed his early years in an environment thoroughly French in speech and tradition. His father, Henri Pène du Bois, a critic and writer, shaped his son's habit of thought and trained him in observation. His

Peter A. Juley & Son
GUY PENE DU BOIS

mother, Laure (Hague) du Bois, was the daughter of an English father and a French mother. The little boy was named Guy for the French novelist, Guy de Maupassant, an old friend of the family, who used to remember his namesake's birthday with books and notes. Young Guy went to the New York public schools, where he and his elder brother Raoul were called "the Frenchies" by their schoolmates. When he was fourteen, the family moved from upper Manhattan to Staten Island; there Guy attended the high school at Port Richmond. A year later, however, his father, who appreciated the lad's gift for drawing, sent him to art school. The youngest student at the New York School of Art, familiarly known as the "Chase School," he was put in the life class at once. During the next six years he studied with Carrol Beckwith, William M. Chase, Frank Vincent du Mond, Kenneth Hayes Miller, and Robert Henri. Fellow students in the Henri class included Gifford Beal, Edward Hopper, Rockwell Kent, and Walter Pach. In 1905 his father took him abroad, establishing him in a studio in the rue de la Grande Chaumière in Paris. There he studied with Colorossi, and also with Steinlen for a time; joined in the activities of the American contingent on the Left Bank; and everywhere, made sketches, by the hundred, of people.

In the spring of 1906 the elder Du Bois arrived in Paris, seriously ill with a heart condition. His death during the voyage home was a great shock to his son, who now had to shoulder some of the family responsibilities. He became a reporter on the New York *American,* his father's paper. Assigned at first to the "Tenderloin" district, he was given occasional opportunities to vary this sordid "beat" by covering auction sales of rare books and works of art, reviewing exhibitions of pictures, or making translations from the French. When the opera season opened, he was appointed music critic, a

DU BOIS, GUY PENE—*Continued*

post his father had held. "One of the most unenlightened music critics in New York," as he admits, he relieved the boredom of his evenings at the Metropolitan by sketching, or mentally recording impressions of the opera patrons, later to be utilized with telling effect. After seven years with the *American*, part of the time as art critic, Du Bois went to the New York *Herald Tribune* as assistant to Royal Cortissoz, from 1913 to 1914. On the publicity committee for the Armory Show, arranged by the Modern Art Association of American Painters and Sculptors to introduce to America the work of the School of Paris, he edited a special number of *Arts and Decoration* devoted entirely to the exhibition—"an enthusiastic blast in celebration of the new freedom in art." He continued as editor of the magazine intermittently until 1922. From 1916 to 1918 he was also art critic for the New York *Evening Post*. A prolific writer, he found time to contribute critical articles to various magazines, including *Vogue, Vanity Fair, International Studio*, and the *Craftsman*, as well as to prepare several monographs—on John Sloan and on William Glackens—for the "American Artists Series" of the Whitney Museum of American Art. In 1940 his autobiography, *Artists Say the Silliest Things*, appeared. It was well received by the critics, who placed the author among "those useful members of society, the artists who think." Royal Cortissoz called the book shrewd and provocative and professed to find, between the lines, traces of the mental stimulus that Du Bois had received from his father.

During the fifteen years that he devoted his major efforts to writing, Guy Pène du Bois continued to paint in his free time. At first he produced small sketches—"anecdotes in paint" —of racy incidents from his experience in the police courts, and later, witty and satiric representations of opera patrons in full dress. This early work, with its Daumier-like humor, attracted attention, and then began to sell. The artist had exhibited in Paris in the spring Salon des Beaux-Arts in 1906, and at the same time in the annual exhibition of the Pennsylvania Academy of the Fine Arts in Philadelphia. In 1910 he was represented in the Salon des Refusées in New York City. Participation in the famous Armory Show started him off on a long career in which his work appeared in all national annuals of importance, Paris and London exhibitions, the 1934 Biennial at Venice, and a number of one-man shows in New York City and throughout the United States.

For a time the artist had a studio in New York's Macdougal Alley, loaned to him by Gertrude Vanderbilt Whitney. There he painted the portrait of Jeanne Eagels, costumed for her part in *Rain*. Later, he bought a summer home in Westport, Connecticut, because it had "a very good studio in the back yard." But finding himself unable to work in so social an environment, he was obliged to commute to New York all summer to a studio in Lafayette Street. In 1924 Du Bois sold his Westport property and took his wife and young son and daughter and his three stepchildren, Virginia,

Donald, and Robert Duncan to France, with the idea of devoting himself exclusively to painting. Established in a small house in Garnes, in the Valley of the Chevreuse (which was later to be the subject of one of his prize-winning paintings), he remained abroad for the next six years, not returning to the United States until 1930.

Although he does an occasional landscape or flower piece, Du Bois is primarily a genre painter, interested in the human spectacle. "A cynical observer of life," according to Margaret Breuning of the New York *Post*, "he never becomes a propagandist, rather the detached amused looker-on who sees the pretense and absurdity, but also the colorful, animated pattern of urban life." His flair for character has been called the greatest contributory element to his success, although his satirical pieces are said to "lack the dramatic power of Daumier and Forain." Extremely personal in his point of view, Du Bois employs "luminous color and a subtle chromatic scale of values." An able draftsman, he has "marked plastic powers which give vitality to his figures." In the beginning of his career Du Bois was one of the group loosely designated as the New York Realists, but, he states, he has never since then belonged to or associated with any group of artists. Because his income was derived from other sources, he was free to use his painting as recreation and a means "to express things not easily said in print."

In 1938 the Kraushaar Gallery in New York put on a retrospective exhibition comprising a selection of Du Bois's work over a period of three decades, the earliest paintings dating from 1908. Edward Alden Jewell divides the artist's development into three phases—pre-Paris, Paris (1924-31), and post-Paris. The early period was marked by the dark tonality of Düsseldorf and also showed the influence of realists like Sloan and Henri. Notable canvases in this group were *Waiter* (1910), "a little epic of the arrogance of money"; the charming small *First Dinner Party* (1919); the hard-boiled *New York Girls* (1921); *Carousel* (1921), an imaginative piece; *Shovel Hats* (1923), a shrewd, satirical painting that hinted of his future style; and *The Subway* (1924), a "brilliant pattern of feet." In the Paris phase a "trend toward bigger and bolder design" appeared, and also an accentuation of the "wooden" quality of the figures. Outstanding works included the "splendidly composed" *Bal des Quatres Arts* (1929) with its bold color and strange forms, and *Grande Bleue, Nice*. In the 1930's Du Bois "stepped up his color scale, and added considerable play of light," *Art Digest* noted, while Edward Alden Jewell found in the canvases a "subtle loosening of design." *Yvonne in a Purple Coat* (1938), the strongly brushed *Portrait* (1938), and a "shimmery" *Beach Scene* (1938) were culminating examples of this later period. In subsequent exhibitions Du Bois's work, while retaining his "ingratiating satirical vein," took on "a more sensitive feeling, a more delicate linear habit." *Bouquet* (1939), *Solitaire* (1943), the "spirited, documentary" *Cocktails* (1945), *Parade* (1945), and *Landscape* (1945) are recent paintings. In November 1946

Du Bois's first one-man show in New York in three years was considered by Carlyle Burrows to be "more than usually notable" in quality and character. Seascapes in the exhibition included *Off Stonington* (1946), while among "incisive" figure paintings, in which Du Bois had caught "the languid mood . . . with particular elegance of style," were *Suspense* and *Vieux Marcheur*.

The "solidly modeled figures, depth of tone, and full-flavored characterization" of Du Bois's painting amply suited it to the mural. *Le Bal Masque*, decorations for the Jumble Shop restaurant in New York City's Greenwich Village, was a prelude to the more formal murals done for the United States Treasury Department's Section of Painting and Sculpture. The first of these were painted in July 1937 for the United States Post Office at Saratoga Springs, New York. The two panels—one a street scene in the town, the other a paddock scene at the racecourse—"involved an easy play of line and a clarity of contour" and "color with a fresh luminosity and charm which bring to his work both surface brilliance and depth of tone." The second mural, painted for the Post Office at Rye, New York, in 1938, depicted an incident in the life of John Jay, first Chief Justice of the United States.

Guy Pène du Bois is a member of the National Institute of Arts and Letters, and also an academician of the National Academy of Design, and a member of the board of editors of the *Magazine of Art* of the American Federation of Art. In addition to the Salmagundi Club prize, he has received the Purchase Prize of the Los Angeles Museum in 1928; the Norman Wait Harris Silver Medal and prize of $500 at the annual exhibition of the Art Institute of Chicago in 1930; the second Altman Prize, National Academy of Design in 1936; the second Clark prize of $1,500 and the Corcoran Silver Medal at the Corcoran Biennial Exhibition in 1937; the Altman Prize of $1,200 at the 120th annual exhibition of the National Academy of Design in December 1945; and the Limited Editions Club prize of $2,400 for his water colors illustrating *South Wind* in 1945.

The artist is represented in the Metropolitan Museum of Art, the Whitney Museum of American Art, the Museum of Modern Art, Galleries of Living Art, in New York City; the Newark Museum; the Brooklyn, New York, Institute of Arts and Sciences; Phillips Memorial Gallery, Washington; Milwaukee Art Institute; Los Angeles Museum; the Pittsburgh Athletic Club; the Cleveland Museum of Art; the Detroit Institute of Arts; the Pennsylvania Academy of the Fine Arts; and museums at San Diego, Andover, Baltimore, and Toledo.

On April 10, 1911, Guy Pène du Bois was married to Florence (Sherman) Duncan. Mrs. du Bois, for some years a fashion designer, gave up her career to minister to the needs of her gifted family. Yvonne, the daughter, now Mrs. Houghton Field Furlong, is a successful artist in her own right; William Pène du Bois, the son, writes and illustrates children's books. In the winter time the Du Boises live in New York's Greenwich Village; in the summer they migrate to Stonington, Connecticut, where the artist conducts a summer school of painting. In 1946 he was writing a book on realism, romanticism, and classicism for the American Artists Group, and "painting as usual."

References

Carnegie Mag 12:237-9 Ja '39
Life 8:58-9 Ap 29 '40
Cortissoz, R. Guy Pène du Bois (1931)
Du Bois, G. P. Artists Say the Silliest Things (1940)
Who's Who in America, 1946-47

DUCLOS, JACQUES (dü" klō' zhäk) Oct. 2, 1896- French Communist leader; Government official

Address: b. National Assembly, Paris

The Leftward swing of the political pendulum in Europe was sharply reflected in France in 1946 when for the first time in that country's history the Communist Party was the nation's strongest party. Prominent in the leadership of the French Communist Party was its secretary, Jacques Duclos, who in 1946 was serving as a Deputy in the first National Assembly elected under the constitution of the Fourth Republic. Long considered a significant figure on the international Communist scene as well, Duclos influenced the course of the American Communist movement in 1945 through his article, "On the Dissolution of the Communist Party of the United States." The political leader, who has been active in the Communist movement for more than two decades, played a vital role in underground work during World War II.

A native of southern France, Jacques Duclos was born in Louey in the Hautes-Pyrénées region on October 2, 1896. At the age of twelve the boy was apprenticed to a pastry cook and for a period worked in the pastry trade. Shortly after the outbreak of World War I, when Duclos was eighteen, he entered the service of his country. He was seriously wounded in the battle of Verdun and was taken prisoner at Chemin des Dames in 1917. Upon his release at the war's end young Duclos became a member of the Republican Association of Veterans. He was elected to the central committee of the veterans' organization in 1925. Earlier, when the Communist Party was formed in 1920, he had joined the party and within six years had risen to membership on its central committee. By 1931 Duclos was secretary of the French C.P. and four years later was named to sit on the executive committee of the Communist International.

From 1926 to 1932 Duclos was a member of the Assembly and in 1936, with the victory of the Popular Front, he was re-elected Deputy from the Seine (Montreuil). During this period, when he served as a vice-president of the Chamber, he was considered "one of the ablest technicians in economic and financial questions." Duclos was thus a Deputy during the turbulent period which preceded the downfall of France in 1940. Now in 1939, after

JACQUES DUCLOS

the outbreak of the war between France and Germany, anti-Communist feeling ran high because of the Communists' opposition to the conduct of the war. Communist Deputies, who had been elected by a million and a half French citizens, were arrested; about twelve escaped, Duclos among them. Then the Daladier '40 Government continued its "Red hunt" and on Labor Day of 1940 Duclos, in the company of several trade union leaders, was imprisoned in the Ile de Ré. He was, however, granted provisional liberty because of the wounds he had suffered in World War I. After the fall of France in June 1940 the party and its daily paper l'Humanité were suppressed. Immediately after the Pétain '40 capitulation to the Nazis Duclos, together with his colleague Maurice Thorez, called upon the people of France to fight the invader and traitors. According to Harry Pollitt, leading British radical, "It is to the eternal honor of the Communist Party of France that its voice was the first to call for resistance inside France."

Duclos joined the underground movement and played a significant part in the formation of the first groups of Francs-Tireurs. Communists worked with all organizations of the Resistance and cooperated with General de Gaulle's '40 National Committee of Liberation. They put at the General's disposal their organized bands of partisans, which harassed the Germans and the Vichy Government. While working for the liberation of France the party kept alive the Communist press through underground channels operating under the noses of the Gestapo. An article by Duclos printed in Cahiers du Communisme, theoretical organ of the C.P., was secretly distributed in France before the Allied invasion in June 1944. He declared: "Some day the people of France will know the tremendous toll of sacrifices made by all patriots, by thousands upon thou-

sands of Communists whom nothing could bend —neither torture nor promises nor bargaining." In the same article he analyzed the teachings and discipline of the party and "The Strength of Marxist-Leninist Theory"—which constitutes the party's guide to action.

The French Communist was one of the principal organizers of the Paris Insurrection in August 1944, in which Frenchmen and Allies freed the capital, while on all fronts the Nazis were being forced to retreat. With De Gaulle's Provisional Government established in Paris, growing Communist influence was observed. Writing in a mid-October edition of the New York Times, Harold Callender remarked of the situation: "The Communists are playing an important role in France today, partly because they took the leading part in the Resistance movement, but also partly because within the Government are some who sympathize with the Communist aims of socialization although taking exception to their methods." While two Communist ministers served in the Cabinet, the party was also well represented in the Consultative Assembly, formed by the union of the Resistance Council and former members of the Assembly. A delegate to the Assembly, Duclos was also a member of the Socialist-Communist Committee of Entente.

Participation in the Government, however, did not halt criticism from the radicals. The C.P. clashed with De Gaulle on the issue of disarming the Patriotic Militia. Duclos blamed the Government for disorders, attacking what he termed the slow and ineffective purge of Fifth Columnists and collaborators which led the people "naturally [to] take the law into their own hands." Meanwhile, the Consultative Assembly was devoting itself to re-establishing a republican government and planning the national election. On October 21, 1945, the results of the first French national election in nine years showed the C.P. to be the strongest single party, giving them the largest membership in the new Constituent Assembly—one hundred and fifty-three, headed by Duclos. Duclos was elected a vice-president of the Assembly, and as spokesman for the major party has wielded considerable power. On November 13 the Assembly elected the President of France: Most political leaders had previously declared themselves for De Gaulle, and the chamber waited in suspense for Duclos to announce the Communist choice. According to Newsweek: "In tones of mingled raillery, irony, and desperate sincerity, he jabbed all other parties present. An uproar broke out when he said placidly that the Communists had been ready to take full responsibility, under a Communist President." But Duclos concluded with the statement, "Your candidate is ours." Thus De Gaulle was unanimously elected.

To many this vote did not mean true solidarity. Volney D. Hurd of the Christian Science Monitor wrote from Paris after the election that it was "rather in the nature of lip service to General de Gaulle because there was no other candidate. . . . The Communists fought against General de Gaulle all through the election and have not changed their minds since then." In a later dispatch Hurd reported Duclos had promised his colleagues that for the sake of efficiency decisions made by commissions would not be questioned by the Assembly. This the Resistance paper *Combat* saw as an attack on the whole representative system.

The new President, moreover, was soon embroiled in a conflict with the Communists, who on the basis of their strength insisted on their democratic right to a key Cabinet post. De Gaulle refused to grant them the Foreign Affairs, War, or Interior ministries, and the infant government faced a crisis. The Communists withdrew their support of the President, and De Gaulle offered to resign. A compromise solution finally broke the deadlock: The Communists were given the Ministry of Armament and obtained also almost full control of the country's productive machinery by assignments to the ministries of National Economy, Industrial Production, and Labor. The reluctance of De Gaulle to give key posts to Communists had been viewed by their critics as a wise stand. Dorothy Thompson'[49] reported in November that their leader, Duclos, had served during the war as head of one branch of the Russian Intelligence in his own country. Emphasizing that the French Communist was strong enough to effect by his criticism the return of the American Communists to the Marxist class struggle, Miss Thompson wrote that it would be to the disadvantage of France, and the United States as well, to allow Duclos to become too strong.

One of the first acts of the Communists after the election was to present proposals for ten laws to the Assembly. This legislative program called for the establishment of a constitution and included measures to help civil servants, aged workers, young married peasants, and former war prisoners. Of the program, called a moderate one to encourage support of other parties, the Communists themselves observed "We will never say that what we are doing today is socialism." To anti-Communists, it is the party's initial attempt to make inroads among nonindustrial voters.

Duclos, representing his party, was an advocate of a constitution guaranteeing a figurehead president and a unicameral legislature. To mollify the Socialists, he was willing to compromise on a bicameral legislature if, as he said, one house be used "for study and not a political chamber." The French voters rejected the amended constitution in the June 1946 elections, thus causing the Communist vote to decline 5 per cent. With a view toward appeasing the militant Communists who did not desire to participate quietly in the Bidault Government, Duclos encouraged them in their attempt to prevent the seating of Rightist deputies (including ex-premier Reynaud) in July 1946. The results of the June elections, however, had indicated a reaction against the Communists; the vacillating peasant vote swung in favor of the Popular Republicans. In September of that year the weakened Communist power prompted Duclos to urge a coalition of the Socialists with the Communists against the resurgent De Gaullistes, but this proposal was rejected by the Socialists. Strong Communist support of the Socialist-Popular Republican coalition swung the October referendum on the constitution, and, despite De Gaulle's opposition, it was accepted.

Communist strength increased in the next month, so that the party received 28 per cent of the total vote in the November 11, 1946, election of deputies to the National Assembly. The party's plurality, determined by the French system of proportional representation (which conceded 26 per cent of the vote to the MRP and 17 per cent to the Socialists), brought 186 Communist deputies into the legislature, among whom was Duclos. Without the support of the entire body of 108 Socialist deputies, however, the Communists were not able to muster a working majority in the Assembly. Defeated in their efforts to secure the interim premiership for Maurice Thorez'[46], the Communist Party supported Léon Blum'[40], the Socialist leader, for the office, which also was the decision of the other parties. Duclos, however, speaking for his party in the Assembly in mid-December, implied that the Communists held their support subject to revision in the event that the policies of Blum's all-Socialist cabinet did not meet with their approval.

The April 1945 issue of *Cahiers du Communisme* carried the Duclos article "On the Dissolution of the Communist Party of the United States," which brought international reverberations. When a month later it was reprinted in the New York *Daily Worker* it was prefaced by a foreword by Earl Browder'[44] in which the American Communist leader stated that Duclos' words reflected "the general trend of opinion of European Marxists in relation to America." In his long treatise on the course of American communism in the war period, Duclos sharply criticized Browder's actions, declaring that nothing justified Browder's dissolution of the American C.P. He further scored Browder's "revisionist" attitude toward monopoly capital, or advocacy of cooperation between capital and labor, especially in the postwar period. Reaction within the Communist Political Association in America was immediate. After lengthy discussion the Communist program was redefined and William Z. Foster'[45] replaced Browder as the leader of the reconstituted Communist Party in America. The National Board of the C.P.A. in a resolution expressed its appreciation to Duclos for his "sound, fraternal, Marxist opinions."

Duclos, whom *Time* has called the "unofficial foster parent for national Communist parties outside of Russia," is seen as a possible leader of the Communist Internationale of the future. Duclos himself in a letter to the New York *Times* (September 15, 1946) asserted that he could not properly be considered "a center of international Communist leadership" and criticized the Paris *Tribune* for distorting his words in an interview. Supporters of Duclos argue that his policy of reparations, denazification of Germany, and security of French frontiers were not Mos-

DUCLOS, JACQUES—*Continued*

cow-inspired, but indigenously French and based on the peculiar political needs of France alone.

References

N Y Sun p22 O 30 '45
N Y Times Mag p7 Mr 24 '46

DUMONT, ALLEN B(ALCOM) Jan. 29, 1901- Radio engineer; manufacturer

Address: b. Allen B. DuMont Laboratories, Inc., 2 Main Ave., Passaic, N.J.; h. Montclair, N.J.

Allen B. DuMont, president of the Allen B. DuMont Laboratories, Incorporated, and pioneer in the field of television, is best known for the development of the cathode-ray tube, the basis of much of his subsequent research. His interest in the cathode-ray tube began in his student days, and his improvement of manufacturing methods made possible its use today not only in the perfection of television but also in the invention of radar.

Allen Balcom DuMont, a native of Brooklyn, New York, was born on January 29, 1901, to William Henry Beaman and Lillian Felton (Balcom) DuMont. He evinced an interest in electricity while still in elementary school, and an early illness which forced him into a more or less sedentary life encouraged this interest. At the age of fourteen he studied telegraphy, obtained a license as a first class commercial operator, and, during the years 1915-20, worked in the summertime on coastwise and transatlantic ships. When, in the latter years of that decade, wireless telephony, or radio, was making strides toward perfection and popularity, DuMont also built and operated amateur transmitting station W2AYR.

About the time that young DuMont was ready for college, he chanced upon a book published by the Rensselaer Polytechnic Institute (Troy, New York) to illustrate the work of its alumni. In the collection of pictures was one of the Brooklyn Bridge, which impressed the Brooklyn-bred youth, and, along with the other contributions of the graduates, influenced him to enter the institute in 1919. One year during his summer vacation from college, he went, as was his custom, to sea as a radio operator. The ship was bound for Copenhagen, but the ship's ports of call included more than those originally scheduled; DuMont did not return to school until Christmas, and thus, because of his enthusiasm for radio, was compelled to remain an additional year at the institute.

In those years at Rensselaer, DuMont first became interested in the wave forms appearing on the oscillograph in one of the laboratories and planned some day to put the cathode-ray tube, a scarce, costly, and complicated piece of mechanism, to use not only in the oscillograph but in many other devices as well. This was difficult because it called for the production of the cathode-ray tubes in great quantities and at a minimum of cost. Not having the resources needed then for inexpensive cathode-ray tube production, DuMont had to postpone his

manufacturing plans till a later date. In 1924 DuMont received his degree of Electrical Engineer from the institute.

The young man's first position after graduation was with the Westinghouse Lamp Company in Bloomfield, New Jersey, as engineer in the development laboratory, later as engineer supervising the manufacture of different types of radio receiving tubes. His inventiveness soon produced numerous improvements in tube and tube equipment—altogether he applied for ten patents on these new changes. One of the most important applications was for a "high speed automatic seasoning and testing machine which operated at the rate of 5,000 tubes per hour." In 1927 and again in 1928, for this invention, described as making production history, and for other accomplishments in the field, DuMont received the first award of five hundred dollars from the Westinghouse Lamp Company.

In 1928 the engineer joined the De Forest Radio Company of which Lee De Forest [41], inventor of the audion tube, was president. The Passaic (New Jersey) firm was in the process of being reorganized; it had not been in operation for almost a year, and its outdated machinery had to be discarded or remodeled. First as chief engineer, then as vice-president of the company, DuMont had "to supervise the design of a complete new line of receiving tubes, lay out and supervise the design of factory equipment necessary to produce 30,000 receiving tubes per day, and to get together and organize the necessary engineering and factory staff." His ability as manager and his aptitude for experimental work in electricity and radio helped him to achieve this goal within one year of the company's reorganization. Under his direction special new-type equipment was planned, assembled, and patented—the high speed sealing machine, improved automatic grid winding and welding machine, base branding machine, basing and wire cutting machine, high frequency tube bombarder, and numerous tube-characteristic tests sets and life racks.

While employed by the De Forest Company, DuMont had occasion to study and work with the De Forest television project which got its main impetus when De Forest took over the company belonging to Charles F. Jenkins, a pioneer in television and in the motion picture since 1890, who had managed thus far to transmit crude black and white images on a television screen. DuMont at this time put aside his other duties and concentrated entirely on television, becoming director of research and experiment in the field of "sight and sound" broadcasting. In 1930 the De Forest experimental transmitter, W2XCD, in Passaic, broadcast television programs, the first of the kind in the United States. DuMont realized that the equipment developed and employed in the De Forest studios was impractical. The images were transmitted by a direct pickup camera in outdoor work or by a flying spot scanner in the studio work. By means of whirling scanning disks the images to be televised were broken up at the transmitting end of the process and then "woven together" at the receiving end. This method only resulted in distortion and in lack of clarity of the televised images. Du-Mont was convinced by these early tests and imperfect effects that the only possible answer to perfected television was electronic scanning with the cathode-ray tube. His work along these lines, however, was halted by the depression: when he returned from a vacation he had been taking in Bermuda in 1931, he learned that the concern had failed and that he was without a job.

With only five hundred dollars, DuMont, who in all previous positions had experimented mainly with ordinary radio tubes, now returned to his earlier ideal of producing the cathode-ray tube and of applying it to many mechanisms. He studied all available literature on the subject. The cathode-ray tube itself, gradually developed by a number of technologists, was, because of its expense and its "life span" of about twenty-five hours, used only in a "few favored laboratories for the study of electrical phenomena." With his small capital and an equal sum contributed by a neighbor, in June of 1931 DuMont hired a few glass blowers and began his research into the simplification and manufacture of the cathode-ray tube in the basement of his home in Upper Montclair, New Jersey. Financial troubles dogged his efforts and for a time he maintained his business by borrowing money on his life insurance and from his relatives.

Yet the original purpose of DuMont's laboratory—to find a market for the cathode-ray tube in the television industry—was sidetracked. There was little demand then for such products and the company from its founding concentrated primarily on the making of cathode-ray tubes and equipment for oscillographs. DuMont's venture gradually improved and, as orders for cathode-ray tubes increased (he numbered his own college among his first customers), the laboratory expanded till it outgrew both the basement and the garage of DuMont's home. In 1934, DuMont, searching for a larger place for his firm, was offered aid by a friend, Mortimer W. Loewi, and the two men formed the business association known as the Allen B. DuMont Laboratories, Incorporated. Soon the laboratories became too large for the stores which housed them. More capital was needed and the solution was provided by DuMont's invention of the cathode-ray radio tuning indicator—the "magic eye." The rights to the invention were sold to RCA for twenty thousand dollars, and with this money the laboratories were moved into a large plant, formerly a pickle works, in Passaic. Until 1936 DuMont's company was the only one in the United States to carry on a large-scale manufacture of the cathode-ray tube. In 1946 the DuMont plants were four in number, two in Passaic and two in Clifton.

Once the DuMont laboratories were well established financially, DuMont and a few of his associates turned again to experiments in television. In the late 1930's Allen DuMont went to Europe to obtain valuable first-hand knowledge of the progress made in television by the British, French, and Germans. With the manufacture of commercial television receivers in 1938, the DuMont organization entered the first

Fabian Bachrach

ALLEN B. DUMONT

phase of its broadcasting career. A year later, when scheduled telecasting was inaugurated at the time of the New York World's Fair, only DuMont televisors could be obtained readily for installation in homes, hotels, and places of amusement. The next undertaking of DuMont and his associates was the designing of television transmitters. To facilitate their research, experimental television transmitters were set up in Passaic, and then in the DuMont studio now known as Station WABD, in New York City. WABD, originally W2XWV, served first as a testing ground for engineering problems. Ultimately, however, it was employed, through a series of telecast programs, as a means of gauging the artistic and commercial potentialities of telecasting.

When World War II began, the DuMont laboratories had to forego much of their regular business and to gear their plants to production for defense. With the entrance of the United States into the war, all their cathode-ray tubes and equipment were supplied to the Government. The experiments in television, nevertheless, were not neglected. In September 1944 the DuMont laboratories announced the opening of a new television studio in New York. Another step forward came when the John Wanamaker Studios of WABD were opened in New York in April of 1946. The program was telecast on the DuMont network from New York through Philadelphia to the experimental station in Washington. The performance, acclaimed the "year's outstanding contribution to the commercial development of television" obtained for WABD the top award of the American Television Society (June 1946). Asserting that even black-and-white television would not be available soon to the average citizen, DuMont in the spring of 1946 stated in newspaper advertisements that the color television phase was still a future accomplishment; denying that he was opposed

DUMONT, ALLEN B.—*Continued*

to it, he stated further that "the sincere scientist is not convinced by dramatically staged and carefully controlled laboratory demonstrations of any new art" and that "diligent research and exhaustive field experimentation in the years to come" would add "color television as a further refinement." The Allen B. DuMont Laboratories favor the simultaneous or electronic method of color television as superior to the sequential or mechanical method. In December of 1946 DuMont's company was one of several which opposed the Columbia Broadcasting System's petition to the FCC "for the establishment of commercial color television standards"—CBS wished to institute its own sequential-method color television broacasts at an early date. As stated by Allen B. DuMont, any standardization adopted too soon would deprive the public of "the ultimate in color television, as far as quality or cost of receivers is concerned."

In 1946 DuMont networks were being expanded to include stations in Pittsburgh, Cincinnati, and Cleveland; and regular programs of all types, including "on-the-spot newscasts," were being scheduled. DuMont engineers also had developed a method by which television shows could be transcribed. Plans to manufacture television sets to be on the market in large quantities by the end of the year 1946 and to produce image orthicon cameras in quantity proportionate to their demand were among the other main projects of the DuMont organization. DuMont television, too, was to be utilized in the motion picture industry, Paramount Pictures having financial interests in the corporation. In November 1946 the DuMont laboratories demonstrated a new type of television transmission whereby pictures and sound would be sent by light beam instead of by the radio waves now employed. This method, named photovision, is regarded as simplifying "the sending of color," as improving "the fidelity of telecast images," and as eliminating "the necessity of expensive coaxial cable hookups in network picture-sound broadcasts." One month later, in connection with the FCC color television hearings, the DuMont organization disclosed the development of a direct-view electronic color tube—the trichromoscope—embodying "new principles of color reception" and displayed a black-and-white high intensity cathode-ray "picture" tube "brilliant enough to be viewed" in a very bright light.

Although DuMont and his laboratories have had assigned to them many patents on inventions or improvements on inventions, the most far-reaching of all DuMont's contributions to science is considered to be the perfection of the cathode-ray tube as the "final link in practical radar." In April 1933 DuMont applied for a patent covering an indicating radio locater "employing numerous principles of radar." Requested by the War Department to "withold filing because of the military nature of the disclosures," DuMont complied. Previously he had illustrated in a publication and in his notebook how his cathode-ray tubes and associated

equipment might be utilized in determining altitude and the position of sounds, and in navigaton, in detecting and ranging objects on the sea. Realizing by 1939 that the fundamentals of radar were no longer unknown to many people, DuMont applied again for the patent and found, to his disappointment, that a French patent of 1937 covered many of his own discoveries and invalidated his claims.

DuMont's scientific interests are indicated by the many organizations to which he belongs. He is a fellow of the Institute of Radio Engineers, the American Institute of Electrical Engineers, the Radio Club of America, and the Television Society, and, in addition, a member of Sigma Xi, and a director of the Television Broadcasters Association, Inc. In August 1944 the honorary degree of Doctor of Engineering was conferred upon him by Rensselaer. In December of the same year he received an award from the Television Broadcasters Association for his technical contributions to television. DuMont is also the author of a number of articles on radio and television. Mrs. DuMont is the former Ethel Martha Steadman, to whom he was married in October 1926. Their two children are Allen Balcom and Yvonne.

References

N Y Herald Tribune IV p1 Ap 14 '46
Rensselaer Polytechnic Inst N O '43
Who's Who in Commerce and Industry (1944)

DUNBAR, RUDOLPH Apr. 5, 1907- Conductor; composer; journalist
Address: h. 19 Westbourne Ct., Orsett Ter., London

In the Hollywood Bowl on August 22, 1946, Americans had their first opportunity to hear Rudolph Dunbar, the young Negro conductor who has the distinction of being not only the first foreigner to conduct in both Paris and Berlin after the war, but also the first Negro ever to lead an important symphonic ensemble in either of those cities. Also a composer, and the author of the only published treatise on clarinet playing, Dunbar has, however, spent most of his time as a journalist, in particular covering the activities of Negro troops in Europe during World War II.

Although often mistaken for an American, Rudolph Dunbar was born in British Guiana, South America, on April 5, 1907, and holds British citizenship. At the age of nine his parents, Edward and Martha (Glasgow) Dunbar, apprenticed him to a British Guianan military band, with which he toured for the next several years and from whose English bandmaster he learned the rudiments of music. Three years later, in 1919, he entered the Institute of Musical Art of the Juilliard School of Music of New York, where he studied until 1928, being graduated at the age of twenty-one. The next six years the young musician spent in Paris, taking a postgraduate course in journalism at the University of Paris in addition to studying at the National Conservatory of Music, and in Leipzig and Vienna. His masters were Philippe Gaubert and Felix Weingartner in conducting, Paul Vidal in composition, Louis Cahuzac in clarinet. But he had not yet made his debut, and often he found it necessary to live on meals of bread and tea.

When he arrived in London in 1934, Dunbar has told Ted Poston of the New York *Post*. "I couldn't even pay my room rent or afford a penny bus fare." In time, however, his affairs took a turn for the better. In 1936 his journalistic training at the University of Paris enabled him to obtain a commission as a roving correspondent for the Associated Negro Press of America during the Italo-Ethiopian war. By 1942 he held an editorship in the A.N.P. and had served for a time as a music critic. He had also achieved some recognition as a composer, and in 1938 had come to the United States for the American première of his Negro ballet *Dance of the Twenty-first Century*, presented on the coast-to-coast network of the National Broadcasting Company. In 1939 his *Treatise on the Clarinet*, the first work of its kind, had been published in London. But he still wanted to be a conductor, and tried again at the height of the London blitz. "They laughed at me," he says. "I don't think it was a question of color. I was just unknown and they pointed out that no one would risk his life in a concert hall . . . to hear an unknown conduct an orchestra."

Then, because Singapore fell, Dunbar states, he got his opportunity. Talking about his disappointments at the Ministry of Information after the fateful February 15, 1942, reported the New York *Post*, he was reproved by Sir Donald Cameron, former Governor of Nigeria, with the exclamation, "Don't you realize we have just lost Singapore? Do you think anyone would underwrite a concert now?" Shocked, Dunbar could only reply, "Is that all England means to you? Singapore and lost investments? Well, forget my concert. I'll keep on fighting for a larger England than that." The next day he received from Sir Donald a letter to the noted British impresario Harold Holt, and on February 21 the newspapers reported that on April 26 Dunbar would lead the London Philharmonic Orchestra in a concert to raise funds for persons of African descent in the Allied fighting forces. The concert, stated the *Post*, was completely underwritten by Sir Donald. Given in Royal Albert Hall before an audience of more than seven thousand, it was an outstanding success, receiving favorable mention in the American as well as the British press. It was the first time since 1906, when Samuel Coleridge-Taylor, son of an African Negro father, had conducted the London Philharmonic in his own "African" Variations, that a Negro had led that orchestra.

After that Dunbar conducted the Liverpool Philharmonic Orchestra, the London Symphony Orchestra, the National Symphony Orchestra and National Philharmonic Orchestra, the Birmingham Symphony Orchestra, and the Bournemouth Symphony and Philharmonic orchestras. But with the Allied invasion of Europe imminent, he sought accreditation as a war correspondent for the A.N.P. Assigned to the all-Negro United States Army 333d Field Artillery Battalion, he covered its progress from the

Georges Saad, Paris

RUDOLPH DUNBAR

Normandy beaches to Brest, then rushed down to Paris, arriving one day before its liberation. In Paris he found that his newly acquired fame had preceded him, so that he was urged to conduct the city's first post-liberation concert. This he did on November 18, 1944, returning from the front to lead the Pasdeloup Symphony Orchestra at the Salle Gaveau and becoming, also, the first Negro ever to conduct in Paris. As a result he was asked by a delegation led by Claude Delvincourt to remain to organize a festival of American music—but he declined, preferring to return to the front.

One month later, he told the *Post* interviewer, he himself not only narrowly escaped death during the Battle of the Bulge, but unknowingly saved an entire battalion from extermination. Having left the Negro 969th Battalion to go in search of the 777th with only his jeep driver as companion, he had been lost for about nine hours in the vicinity of Marchin, Belgium (which the German radio had announced as fallen), when a group of excited civilians flagged him down, explaining that a German tank force was lying in ambush scarcely twenty-five yards around the bend in the road. Dunbar turned back to warn the 969th's intelligence officer, but it was not until months afterward that he realized the value of his warning. After this incident, until V-E Day, his assignment was to cover the American Negro troops advancing into Germany.

Later in 1945 the journalist-musician returned to the French capital to conduct the orchestra of the Paris Conservatoire in a gala performance, for the benefit of French colonial prisoners of war, at the Théâtre des Champs-Elysées, raising $60,000. He also led the orchestra of the Paris Opéra during the French-American festival, with Grace Moore as soloist. On September 2 (for German civilians) and the next day (for Allied military personnel), fol-

DUNBAR, RUDOLPH—*Continued*

lowing the invitation of the late Leo Borchard shortly before his accidental death, Dunbar conducted the Berlin Philharmonic Orchestra, winning "an ovation of astonishing warmth" from his audience, especially for his reading of fellow-Negro William Grant Still's [41] *Afro-American Symphony*, and the approbation of the orchestra's members. Again he had set precedents, being, as in Paris, the first Negro, and the first foreigner after the war, to conduct the leading symphonic organization.

In October, as musical director and conductor of a four-concert festival of American music (sponsored by the American Ambassador and the French Minister of Education but backed entirely by French funds), Dunbar aroused the enthusiasm of musical Parisians, who liked his "spirited and clean-cut" leadership even when they were startled by some phases of the works he presented. Said to have been an undertaking unique in French musical annals, the series gained further distinction from the utilization of four different important French orchestras, the Conservatoire, the Colonne, the Pasdeloup, and the National Symphony of Paris, which Dunbar had employed because he wanted as many French musicians as possible to become familiar with the American compositions. Immediately thereafter Dunbar went to Monte Carlo to conduct the Monte Carlo Symphony Orchestra, augmented to eighty players for the occasion.

As a boy in British Guiana, Dunbar recalls, he had resolved that some day he would lead an American orchestra. On August 22, 1946, he was given that opportunity when he conducted the Los Angeles Philharmonic Orchestra in the Hollywood Bowl. Almost everything went wrong at that concert, reported *Time*. Soprano Dorothy Maynor [40], soloist, withdrew at the last moment because of her mother's death, and both the substituted baritone and chorus were ill prepared. Nevertheless, the critics approved of Dunbar, praising his "crisp" and "authoritative" conducting.

Described as intense and staccato in manner, Dunbar has deep-set brown eyes, is five feet four inches tall, and weighs 140 pounds. A tennis and riding enthusiast, he does not, however, have the same fondness for golf. And while he likes the theater, he considers motion pictures a waste of time. "You could read a whole score in three hours wasted at the movies," he has said. In 1946 he was at work on a symphonic poem and a report on Negro troops in the invasion of Europe. That same year the British Guianan Government rewarded him with a grant of five thousand pounds for his "contributions to the Empire." But he does not expect to live on British, or even American, soil. "I think," he says, "I will make my home in Paris where, if you are good, they will applaud you whether you are pink, white or black, and if you are bad they will whistle at you."

References

N Y Post p31 Ag 19 '46 por
Newsweek 26:111 O 29 '45
Time 46:64 S 10 '45 por; 48:41-2 S 2 '46 por

DURANTE, JIMMY (dū-răn'tĭ) Feb. 10, 1893- Comedian

Address: Hotel Astor, New York

Ever since 1923 a good proportion of Broadway's night-club and musical-comedy chroniclers have considered Jimmy Durante the ranking American clown. Called "the Schnozzle" by reason of his great nose, he is "a high comedian who can convulse both children and sophisticates." Hollywood "rediscovered" Durante in 1944 after he had made a record-breaking reappearance in a New York night club and began to appear in a successful radio series over the Columbia network.

New York is Durante's town: he is the product of Manhattan's lower East Side where he grew up and of Manhattan's Broadway, of which he has been called the "personification." Born February 10, 1893, on the East Side's Catherine Street, James Durante was the youngest of four children (three boys and a girl). From his mother, Roséa (Millino) Durante, a devout Catholic from Salerno, Italy, he inherited his oversized nose. His French-Italian father Barthelmeo had a barber shop, in which Jimmy had lathered the faces of many Tammany politicians before he was twelve years old. Jimmy also delivered newspapers: "I'm passing the joints on Fourteenth Street between Third and Fourth Avenues. I peeps under the swinging doors and keeps thinking that the swellest job in the world is the guy what bangs away on the piano. I wants to be him." Father Durante bought Jimmy a piano, and provided a music "professor." Leaving school before he had finished the seventh grade, Jimmy became an errand boy, a dishwasher, finally a photoengraver. But he also spent much time at the piano, so that he was able to earn a couple of dollars a night playing at neighborhood parties and athletic club dances. At seventeen he got a job in one of "the wildest joints" in Coney Island, Diamond Tony's saloon—"Twenty-five bucks a week; hours from eight in the evening until unconscious." Then followed other jobs in saloons and dance halls on the Bowery, at Coney Island, and in Chinatown—once as an accompanist to a singing waiter named Eddie Cantor [41]. Young "Ragtime Jimmy" played by ear "in the classic razzmatazz style—heavy chording in the bass, and light finagling in the treble."

When he organized a five-piece jazz and novelty band for the Club Alamo in Harlem, he was about twenty-three. Durante did not yet sing or tell jokes, but devoted himself to the keyboard. One night a young singer named Jeanne Olson came in by mistake, her agent having booked her at a place around the corner. After hearing her sing, Durante hired her —and in 1921 they were married. At the Alamo, also, Durante met the sentimental singer Eddie Jackson, who was to become a member of the "greatest night-club act of all time"— Clayton, Jackson, and Durante. From Harlem, the pianist and his band advanced to Broadway's Club Nightingale. Frank Nolan, a headwaiter there, convinced Durante they could make "a million" with their own place, with the result that the Club Durant opened in a loft above a garage in January 1923. Then Lou Clayton, vaudeville actor and soft-shoe dancer, strolled into the club, "bought a piece" of the place, and worked out a comedy routine with Jackson and Durante. In this fashion the pianist discovered he was meant to be a comedian and a singer, and a new Broadway team was born, which for the next seven years, created "an uproar" in the night clubs of New York where celebrities gathered. Newsmen Walter Winchell, Robert Benchley, Gilbert Seldes, and Sime Silverman of *Variety* were among their early admirers.

For six months, until it was closed by prohibition officers, Club Durant flourished. The trio, at three thousand dollars a week, next went to the Parody Club, where they stayed two years. Durante's nose and Durante's hat became important props of wild, largely extemporaneous clowning, which was "notably clean." "The best entertainment in New York," Gilbert Seldes called it. "In whatever they do the rhythm of their movement gives it a special character. . . .Almost all their speech is shouting or half-whispered asides; they are always moving things or throwing things; they kid the piece, themselves, and the audience unceasingly." Durante himself, Seldes wrote in 1929, had "Harlequin's passion for words, which he picks out of the air and transforms to his own purposes," and "an instinct for gentle mockery and a natural sense of decency which gives him salvation from the hard gibes and meanness of most of Broadway's cracks." Durante wrote dozens of songs whose titles became catch phrases on Broadway, among them, "I'm Jimmy, That Well Dressed Man"; "I Know Darn Well I Can Do Without Broadway (Can Broadway Do Without Me?)"; "Did You Ever Have the Feelin' That You Wanted to Go, Still You Have the Feelin' That You Wanted to Stay?" The team played with "tumultuous success" in vaudeville (starting at the top—Loew's State and the Palace), made phonograph recordings, a motion picture (Paramount's *Roadhouse Nights*, 1930), appeared in Ziegfeld's *Show Girl* in 1929, and in December 1930 opened in Cole Porter's musical *The New Yorkers.*

After *The New Yorkers,* Durante accepted an offer from MGM to make films and the team broke up, Clayton becoming Durante's business manager. Durante's first motion picture, *Get-Rich-Quick Wallingford* (1932), was considered his best; it was written by "pioneer Durante fans" who knew the "nuances of his unique comedy style"—Ben Hecht and Charles MacArthur. But thereafter Jimmy received poor material; Hollywood played up "his more obvious buffoonery." "His performances," wrote Bosley Crowther, "were pitiable—just snips and tatters of the great Durante style." From 1932 to 1941 he made twenty-one films, most of them second-rate.

His stock on Broadway, however, continued high. In 1933 he appeared in *Strike Me Pink.* Two years later Billy Rose produced *Jumbo,* which was, according to Burton Rascoe, "a horrible flop financially, but a theatrical event in all other respects." Durante, its hero, had the

JIMMY DURANTE

role of the manager of a one-ring circus, sharing stellar honors with an elephant. The next year, 1936, Durante starred with Ethel Merman in *Red, Hot and Blue.* "In all of his mad career," wrote John Mason Brown, "the redoubtable Jimmy has never been as hilarious." In Great Britain that year, Durante broke attendance records in the theaters of Glasgow, Liverpool and London. *Stars in Your Eyes,* again with Durante and Merman on Broadway "at their incredible best," came three years later, in 1939. Otis Ferguson of the *New Republic* said its scenes were "constantly exploding into Jimmy Durante. . . .A good part of the fun of watching a man like Durante is in the way we're with him and love him, the way we spot him for a good and happy guy." Next was the 1940 *Keep Off the Grass,* about which a New York *Herald Tribune* drama critic wrote: "There is great gaiety . . . and it is almost entirely due to the presence in the cast of that incomparable funny man, the great Jimmy Durante . . . another of those comic spirits who make the world seem worth bothering about again."

Durante's "comeback" in 1943, after Hollywood had decided he was "through," was hailed by the reviewers who considered him one of the great clowns of the era. He "rode the crest," with night-club, radio, and motion picture successes, beginning in March 1943, just a few weeks after the death of his wife, to whom he had been "singularly devoted." Durante had found relief for his sorrow in a return, for the first time in twelve years, to "intimate, free-style" night-club entertaining; he was a sensational success at Manhattan's Copacabana. At about the same time he began a regular series of radio programs over the Columbia network, with Garry Moore as his partner and foil. The show was considered especially well constructed to take full advantage of Durante's comedy style—his exuberance and his gifts for split-

DURANTE, JIMMY—*Continued*

second timing in comic dialogue and for the whimsical "mangling" of the English language.

Then came a "rediscovery" of the comedian by Hollywood. In parts which gave him the opportunity to be himself Durante was eminently successful. In *Music for Millions* (1944), to the delight of the critics, Durante, playing José Iturbi's manager, several times "stole the show" as the picture "raucously slipped out of this world into Jimmy's own personal province." Of his part in *Two Girls and a Sailor* (1945), in which he played a veteran vaudevillian who makes a victorious comeback, Crowther wrote: "There. . .emerges. . .a sort of undertone of sadness which all great comedians usually have. . . .Jimmy has never wanted for affection, but he should be overwhelmed with it after this film." The fifty-three-year-old comedian drew similar plaudits for his performance as a Bowery pianist in the 1946 production *Two Sisters From Boston*. His new film success, it was said, was no "fluke" but the result of an intelligent handling of his talents by producer Joe Pasternack.

The Durante quips ("I've got a million of 'em," "Everybody wants to get into da act," "That's the conditions that prevail," "I'm mortified," "Surrounded by assassins") are "timelessly colorful" however often he repeats them, and are taken up by his audiences. "Umbriago," a Durante creation who came partly from the comedian's imagination and partly from Italian folklore about a "lusty, happy little man who is always the life of the party," has become a "popular substitute for swear words." In "an unadulterated accent picked right off the sidewalks of New York" Durante shouts malapropisms, adds, drops, and distorts syllables in long words with comic results. He has a prowling walk, a husky voice, "impudent" blue eyes, and incredible energy—"He performs until he is ready to drop." In a typical night-club routine he "insults waiters, lambastes bus boys, beats up the band, heaves lamps, flings around telephones, rips apart pianos," the last act of violence being one for which he is famous. But "there is no malice in him," wrote John K. Hutchens in the New York *Times*. "He is the man eternally baffled by this screwy world but never angry about it. He appears to fly into torrential rages. . .but his audience knows better."

"A sweet guy" (Broadway parlance for a modest, generous, top-ranking performer) is the phrase often heard as descriptive of Durante. His suite at Manhattan's Hotel Astor is "a kind of hotel within a hotel," always open, and always swarming with friends. Clayton and Jackson are still with him as manager and secretary. "The Schnozzle" is five feet seven inches tall, weighs 155 pounds, and has very little hair left. He eats little, sleeps about five hours a day. *Time* has called him "probably the hardest-working millionaire extant."

References

Collier's 113:24+ Ja 8 '44 por
Liberty 23:16-17+ Ja 19 '46 pors
N Y Times Mag p20+ Je 4 '44 por
Newsweek 27:92+ Je 17 '46 pors
PM p16 Ag 15 '46

Read Digest 44:43-4 Ap '44
Time 43:71-2+ Ja 24 '44 pors
Variety 162:33 Je 5 '46
International Motion Picture Almanac, 1943-44
Who's Who in the Theatre (1939)

DUTRA, EURICO GASPAR (dōō′trȧ ȧ-ōō-rē′kō gȧs-pȧr′) May 18, 1885- Brazilian Government official; army officer

Address: Catete Palace, Rio de Janeiro

In December 1945, at the first presidential election in Brazil since 1929, Major General Eurico Gaspar Dutra, former Minister of War in the Vargas [40] government, was elected chief executive of the largest country in South America. Only the Soviet Union, Canada, China with Manchuria, and the United States with Alaska have larger areas, and the United States of Brazil is larger than either China proper or the continental United States of America. Its population, not much less than that of Italy, represents a high degree of racial mixture and fusion. It is said that 60 per cent of the forty-five million inhabitants of this Portuguese-speaking country are illiterate.

Like the typical Brazilian army officer, Eurico Gaspar Dutra is the son of a small planter. He was born May 18, 1885, in Cuiabá, in the central Brazilian state of Mato Grosso. His early education was obtained in the municipal school of Cuiabá, a day school in that town, and the Cuiabá secondary school. Dutra "grew up in the saddle," riding over the plains of the cattle ranges. As a youth he was an avid reader of the lives of military heroes, and in 1902, when he was seventeen, he enlisted in the army as a private and was sent to military preparatory and tactical schools in Rio Pardo and Porte Alegre in 1904. Four years later the young man became an officer candidate, and in 1910, at the age of twenty-five, he was commissioned a second lieutenant and sent to Pernambuco where, *Newsweek* says, he acquired a northern accent which still persists.

By 1931 Dutra had attained the rank of full colonel. Seven years previously, in 1924, he had participated in an unsuccessful revolution. Six years later, however, he was a member of the military clique which put Governor Getulio Vargas into the presidency by a *golpe (coup d'état)* and in 1932 Colonel Dutra and General Pedro Aurelio de Góes Monteiro led President Vargas' forces to victory over the rebellious state of São Paolo. In that year Dutra was made a brigadier general and the director of military aviation. He became a general of division in 1935, and took over the command of the First Military Region.

President Vargas appointed Eurico Dutra Minister of War in his cabinet in 1936, with Góes Monteiro as chief of staff, and Dutra began work on a hundred-and-fifty-million-dollar defense program. Dutra mechanized the army and created its air corps. As Vargas' term approached an end (he had been elected in 1934, after four years as dictator) the army chiefs prodded him into demanding emergency powers. Karl Loewenstein of Amherst College (in his *Brazil Under Vargas* [1942], a Guggenheim grant study) states that Dutra and Góes Monteiro were in favor of eliminating the constitutional regime and setting up an authoritarian state. Without their approval Vargas could not have acted." On November 10, 1937, Vargas dissolved the Congress, proclaimed himself president, and promulgated the constitution of his *Estado Novo* (New State)—all by the use of military troops, but without the firing of a shot. "To the Brazilian people," comments Loewenstein, "the change of regime was at least acceptable if not actually welcome; this has been convincingly proved by later events." The key and perhaps the only significant article of Vargas' new constitution was Article 186: "in the entire country the state of national emergency is declared." In Brazil a state of national emergency automatically suspends the constitution. The presidential powers therefore included search and seizure without warrant, imprisonment or exile without intervention by the courts, censorship of all communications, and the issuance by decrees of all laws.

Vargas' cabinet remained substantially the same, with Dutra serving as Minister of War until 1945. He is described as "a competent and hard-working administrator," one of the few Brazilian officeholders without a bank account. Dutra and the chief of staff had control of all army appointments, commissions, and commands. They undertook to reorganize the army on the model of the German *Wehrmacht,* and were assisted by a large number of high-ranking German military attachés. After the outbreak of World War II, the army leaders closed down the influential pro-Allied newspaper *Carioca* for two days, and were prevented only by Vargas from closing another which took sides for Britain and thus indirectly against the army. In 1940, after a particularly large purchase of German armaments, General Dutra was decorated with the Grand Cross of the German Eagle for "valuable services" to the Nazis; he explained later that this referred merely to his purchases. The Japanese Embassy also presented the General with a set of bright Japanese furniture. Loewenstein says in his *Brazil Under Vargas* that the controlled press and radio were used to whip up resentment against Britain in several cases, and he gives instances of "open violation of the neutrality in favor of the Axis."

By mid-1941, however, Brazil began to lean toward the United Nations, with whom the sympathy of the people had been from the beginning; the Brazilians were said particularly to have a respect for President Franklin D. Roosevelt. When the Nazis began sinking Brazilian ships, Dutra talked war, and in August 1942, seven months after Pearl Harbor, Brazil joined the United Nations in making war against Germany and Italy. The United States Government proceeded to pour money and materials into Brazil to build up the army (Vargas' native state, in fact, was reported

EURICO GASPAR DUTRA

to be "one huge airfield") and many Brazilian officers were trained in the United States. Dutra himself was invited to Washington as an official guest in 1943, received the Legion of Merit decoration, and visited war plants and military training centers. Under his and Góes Monteiro's leadership, the peacetime army of one hundred thousand was brought up to nearly half a million—not too difficult in a country which has had universal conscription since 1912, and in which Army pay was from $2.50 to $25 (U.S.) a month. For the first time in its history, it was completely outfitted with modern weapons, by means of Lend-Lease from the United States. Army men were placed in charge of the Ministry of Transport, the National Planning Commission, and so many other key posts that a popular humorous definition of a Brazilian army officer was, "a man who, in wartime, takes a civilian job." A Brazilian Expeditionary Force was organized and sent overseas under General Mascarenha de Moraes. While inspecting troops on the front line in Italy, where they were part of General Mark Clark's [42] American Fifth Army, Dutra was given temporary command of a task force. The troops were brought home soon after V-E Day. In June 1945 Brazil declared war on Japan.

In October 1945 President Vargas was forced to resign by a group headed by General Góes Monteiro. However, he threw his support to Dutra as a candidate for the presidency, backed by the rightist Social Democratic party and by Catholic groups. Dutra's chief opponent was the more liberal Air Major General Eduardo Gomes. The largest number of voters in Brazilian history went to the polls on December 2, and long before the official tabulations everyone knew that Dutra had been elected for the six-year term. In January 1946 he was sworn in.

(Continued next page)

DUTRA, EURICO GASPAR—*Continued*

The constitution replacing Vargas' New State Charter of 1937 was passed by Dutra's Constituent Assembly in mid-September 1946, and in that month the Brazilian Congress convened for the first time in nine years. The constitution, which enables the State to outlaw any party "contrary to a democratic regime . . . and the guarantee of fundamental human rights," showed a trend toward a planned economy. Tacitly this strikes a blow at Brazil's fast-growing Communist Party, which mustered a vote of six hundred thousand in the presidential elections and boasts the largest membership of any C.P. in the Americas. The May 1946 arrival of Russia's Ambassador Serits in Brazil, after a twenty-six year lapse of diplomatic relations between the two countries, was greeted by a demonstration of 5,000 Communists. Dutra, alarmed by the role of the Communists in the food and anti-inflation riots of the summer of 1946, has enacted sternly repressive measures against the party, including seizure of its paper, the *Tribune Popular,* and police detention of the instigators of the riots. Luis Carlos Prestes, the Brazilian Communist leader, has indicated that they might form a coalition party with ex-president Vargas' Labor Party, since the suppression of independent labor unions and the outlawing of the right to strike has given the two parties similar grievances. In an effort to insure a supply of food to the large cities, President Dutra prohibited the export of food and eased customs duties on imports. The shortage was aggravated by Argentina's refusal to export wheat to Brazil in September 1946.

Eurico Gaspar Dutra is described as a stocky, gray-haired, impassive man with an "aggressive" face, thin lips, and a prominent nose. He is five feet eight inches tall. Although sworn in in full military uniform, he has assumed civilian clothes as president, and seems to have changed some of his attitudes with his clothes. In all his years as Minister of War, Dutra never gave a press interview, but as president he outlined his policies, answered questions with blunt directness, and showed flashes of humor. "He is so deliberate and slow-spoken," *Newsweek* reported, "that those who do not know him well sometimes get the impression that he is deaf—which is not the case. . . . He has no nicknames, and his only hobby is collecting guns and Japanese *objets d'art.* Speech-making is his pet aversion, probably because of his accent and poor speaking voice. . . . He used to be on the post by five in the morning, while his brother officers did not arrive until six. Today, he receives fellow generals standing." Dutra has a daughter, Emilia, and a son, Antonio João, who is in February 1946 a captain in the army. The General's wife, Carmela Leite, is a tall and energetic woman who is called *Santinha,* or "Little Saint," because of her devotion to the Catholic Church and her work with women's organizations.

References

N Y Herald Tribune II p3 Ja 27 '46 por
Newsweek 27:65 F 4 '46 por
Time 45:46 Mr 26 '45

EBERLE, IRMENGARDE   (ĕb'ēr-lē)
Nov. 11, 1898- Author
Address: 308 W. 20th St., New York

"A heightened awareness of our dependence on food for survival," brought about by wartime shortages, was the springboard for Irmengarde Eberle's latest book for children, *Basketful; The Story of Our Foods,* published in the spring of 1946. Miss Eberle, who had had the idea in mind for about two years, came to realize the "interdependence of the many peoples of the world, not only in present-day food production and distribution, but in the development and spread of food plants and animals throughout the ages." Her book is written with enthusiasm for the "rich and colorful" subject.

Irmengarde Eberle was born in San Antonio, Texas, on November 11, 1898, the daughter of Marcellus and Louise (Perlitz) Eberle. Both her parents died when she was still a baby. The little Irmengarde went to live with her aunt and grandmother in the suburbs of the city. Hers was a happy childhood, spent in the subtropical climate where outdoor play was possible all the year round. She and her two sisters walked a mile to school and back, and always "the road was full of adventure and interest." She learned to know the wild flowers, and all the small animals that later were to be described in her books. After finishing the San Antonio public schools, she took an art course at the Texas State Women's College, from which she was graduated in 1918. A position as designer with a New York manufacturer of drapery fabrics followed. But although Miss Eberle was successful enough to have her work displayed in an exhibition at the Metropolitan Museum, she eventually gave up her position to pursue a writing career.

As a child Irmengarde Eberle had begun to write little stories. When she was eight years old she won a prize of one dollar in a contest sponsored by a shoe company. Much later, when she was in her twenties, she had some verses published in the old *Smart Set.* After she gave up designing, she became an assistant editor of the Sunday magazine section of the Brooklyn *Eagle.* Subsequently Miss Eberle was editor of *Excella Magazine* (1924-26); editor, New York Theatre Programs (1927-28); and contributing editor, *New York Woman* (1937-38). All during this period she was a frequent contributor of "short shorts" to Franklin P. Adams' *Conning Tower* column in the New York *Herald Tribune.* There were also articles in the *Horn Book, Child Life, Seventeen,* and other magazines. While convalescing from an attack of influenza she wrote her first book, *Picture Stories for Children* (1926), a primer affair with small pictures by the author. A great success, it sold steadily for twenty years.

IRMENGARDE EBERLE

In 1937 appeared a little volume of nature stories, *Hop, Skip and Fly*, about the habits and behavior of frogs, lizards, bats, and other small denizens of earth and sky, "told simply and with a brisk natural humor." It "received literally hundreds of reviews" and definitely established Miss Eberle in the juvenile literature field. This was followed by *Sea-Horse Adventure* (1937). *A Good House for a Mouse*, which received an honor award in the New York *Herald Tribune*'s Children's Spring Book Festival in 1940, was written around an incident of Miss Eberle's childhood. Ellen Lewis Buell, in the New York *Times*, found this story, "told with beautiful simplicity . . . one of the most engaging books of the year." Outstanding among the ten or more books that followed are *Spice on the Wind* (1940); *Phoebe-Belle* (1941) the amusing story of one of Miss Eberle's childhood pets; *Through the Harbor, from Everywhere* (1938), a book which grew out of the author's love for the New York water front; and *Wide Fields: The Story of Henri Fabre* (1943). In 1945 *The Very Good Neighbors* was chosen as a Junior Literary Guild selection. In this story of a lovable Mexican family, "the author has drawn her characters vividly and affectionately," from memories of her days in San Antonio. Miss Eberle's latest 1946 titles were *Too Many Shoes and Stockings*, and *The Visiting Jimpsons*. Under the pseudonym Phyllis Ann Carter, she also wrote a factual book, *Spin, Weave and Wear; the Story of Cloth* (1941).

Miss Eberle, whose marriage terminated in divorce, has one son, Paul, whose "shining-eyed interest, as a small boy, in stories and facts, and whose enthusiasms and absorptions as a teen-age boy" have been very stimulating. She usually has her stories in mind for some time before putting them on paper, and she draws a map of the houses and the streets of

the region where the action takes place. Miss Eberle likes the variety of changing from fiction to facts, she says, but fiction is her favorite form. A capacity for enjoyment and integrity of approach to her subject are characteristic of Irmengarde Eberle. At present she is at work on the story of an American family, which will appear late in 1947.

The author, who lives in the old Chelsea district of New York City, is slender, with hazel eyes and chestnut hair. She has had a sojourn abroad, but most of her traveling has been up and down the Atlantic seaboard, between Texas and New England. Her recreation is painting, an activity for which she has little time. Of the books she likes, she says, perhaps Kenneth Grahame's *The Wind in the Willows* is the favorite. Miss Eberle is a member of the Woman Pays Club, and of the Authors' League of America.

References

Horn Bk 14:113 Mr-Ap '38
N Y Post p10 N 12 '41 por
Young Wings p8 Jl '45 por
Who's Who in America, 1946-47

EDE, J(AMES) CHUTER (ēd chōō'tēr)
1882-   British Government official

Address: b. Home Office, London; h. Tayles Hill, Ewell, Surrey, England.

Over-all superintendent of Great Britain's internal affairs and police system since August 4, 1945, is J. Chuter Ede, Home Secretary in the Labor Ministry of Clement R. Attlee '40. Member of Parliament for almost fifteen years, local government official, and former schoolteacher, Ede is, by virtue of his position, the new superior at Scotland Yard. He is also the man who must eventually determine, for example, what is to be done with the reviving British fascist organization led by Sir Oswald Mosley '40.

James Chuter Ede, the son of the late James and Agnes Mary Ede, was born in the English racing town of Epsom in the county of Surrey, in 1882. His father, a grocer, came of a family which had been engaged in honorable trade for over a hundred years—and in some smuggling before that, he admits with a smile; both his mother's and his father's ancestors had been active in municipal affairs. Young Ede was educated at Epsom National School and Dorking High School, winning a scholarship from the elementary to the secondary level and again to Christ's College, Cambridge. His stay at Cambridge was brief, however: lack of supplementary funds forced him to relinquish his scholarship before he had completed the requirements for the degree. (An honorary M.A. was conferred upon him by the University in 1943 for his subsequent services to education.)

From Cambridge the young man returned to Surrey, to teach in the elementary schools of Toolworth, Mortlake, and Ewell for a period of nine years. He soon became active in the Surrey County Teachers' Association, and in 1908, at the age of twenty-six, began his career in local public affairs as a member of the Epsom Urban Council. In 1914 he was elected

Daily Herald, London

J. CHUTER EDE

president of the Teachers' Association, and also became a member of the Surrey County Council. At the outbreak of World War I, however, he gave up teaching to enlist in the Fifth East Surrey Regiment as a private, and later, as a non-commissioned officer, he served with the Royal Engineers. Of this period of his war service he says, "At the time I was provost-sergeant their [the soldiers'] only feeling about me seemed to be regret that there were not enough cemeteries in France for the separate parts of me they wished to bury."

In 1918 the former schoolteacher, having become interested in politics through the sermons of a non-conformist minister, unsuccessfully contested, as a Laborite, the Parliamentary election from Epsom constituency. Five years later he tried again and was elected as the member from Mitcham Division, Surrey, in March 1923. In November of the same year, however, he lost his seat, remaining out of Parliament until the Labor victory of 1929, when he stood for election from South Shields. Together with the majority of Laborites, Ede lost his seat again in 1931; but since 1935 he has had a record of unbroken service as a member of the House of Commons from South Shields. In fact, reported the London *Daily Herald,* "for a long time he was known as the M.P. who never missed a division: his colleagues saying that, having won that fame, he had to maintain the record to avoid disappointing his constituents." In 1940 Ede was appointed Parliamentary Secretary to the Ministry of Education in the new coalition Government headed by Winston Churchill '42. It was in this post that, among other things, he helped guide through Parliament the new Education Act of 1944, which broadened Great Britain's free education system by raising the compulsory schooling age, providing more opportunities for education beyond the elementary

level, and placing school administration more completely under the local authorities.

Meanwhile, Ede was also devoting a large part of his time to local affairs. After World War I he had resumed his work with the Surrey County Teachers' Association, becoming assistant secretary—a position he still holds. Until 1927 he continued as a member of the Epsom Urban Council, with which he had become associated in 1908 and of which he was to be a member again between the years 1933 and 1937. After twelve years as a member of the Surrey County Council, he had in 1926 been elected an alderman; and from 1930 to 1933 he had served as its vice-chairman, from 1933 to 1937 as its chairman. Beginning in 1927 he had been a member of the London and Home Counties Joint Electricity Authority, its chairman from 1934 to 1940, and president of the British Electrical Development Association in 1937-38. In addition, for twenty-five years before 1945 he had been serving as a Justice of the Peace.

On August 4, 1945, in the new Labor Government of Prime Minister Clement R. Attlee, J. Chuter Ede became Secretary of State for Home Affairs. To many observers the appointment came somewhat as a surprise, as it had been expected that, in view of his background, Ede would receive the Education post. The London *Daily Herald,* however, pointed out that it regarded Ede's varied experience in local affairs as an "excellent groundwork for . . . his new task as Home Secretary." As chief of the Home Department, defined by *Whitaker's* as the "department of executive administration by which the internal affairs of the country are managed," Ede's "main functions are the maintenance of the King's peace, the enforcement of rules made for the internal well-being of the community, and the exercise of the prerogative of mercy." It is in the execution of the first and third that he will attract, and already (in early 1946) has attracted, the most public attention—the first instance being when he refused to commute the sentence of William Joyce, alias Lord Haw Haw; the second, when he was asked to curb the reviving activities of the British fascists under Sir Oswald Mosley.

In the latter situation, it has been noted, Ede could have requested special police powers to intern the fascists or special legislation prohibiting their assemblies and outlawing anti-Semitism. But he did not think that the correct approach to the problem. "The fascists," he explained to Overseas News Agency correspondent Claire Neikind, "are an incredibly small minority here, nothing like the number of Hitlerites before Hitler came to power. There is no evidence that they are growing. Drastic action against them, which they could represent as persecution, might martyrize some of them and give their doctrines a significance they certainly at the moment do not possess. We are a nation of doctrinaire liberals. Provided an individual makes his appeal to reason and not to direct force, I don't think we have a right to legislate against him." Although he recognizes the threat of anti-Semitism inherent in the Mosley activities, Ede believes that there is as yet no need for national legislation in the matter. "Whether it is better to make such an effort illegal and thereby drive its perpetrators underground, or to have the state combat them by argument and thus keep them overground, enabling authorities to know who distills the poison," he told the same interviewer, "this is the problem which will confront us if it becomes more acute."

Concerning the everyday police duties of his office, he has said: "More and more it is necessary for the police to have men of high intelligence. Real detective ability must be opposed to modern forms of crime, and above all there must be kindness, so that law-abiding citizens regard policemen as their natural friends." The aim of his reorganization of the police forces, he explains, is "to reform our criminal law so as to make it more human, less costly, and more remedial than it has ever been before; to make the administration of the law and the prison system more compatible with modern thought on the proper treatment of convicted persons."

The new Home Secretary is the author of two books, *Agricultural Labourers' Guide to Wages Award* (1918) and *Housing in Surrey* (1923). In 1937 he was made an honorary freeman of the Borough of Wimbledon and two years later of Epsom and Ewell. In 1943 he was given an honorary Master of Arts degree by the University of Cambridge, and in 1944 he was made a Privy Councilor. Since 1917 he has been married to Lilian Mary S. Williams. A teetotaler and nonsmoker who found his wartime recreation in reading and walking since gasoline for his motorboat and films for his camera were unobtainable, Ede is described as measured and deliberate in manner. The London *Daily Herald* wrote of him: "There is a hint of scholastic carelessness about the gray hair and mustache, a gentle academic irony in the way his bright brown eyes survey the world over his spectacles. Parliament expects and gets little shafts of humor in his speeches, and his fluent private conversation (with every part of every sentence in its right place) is similarly enlivened." Characteristic of him it is said was his first act upon arriving at his new office: from his desk he removed a copy of the *Report of the Ecclesiastical Commissioners* for 1925 and a volume of *Crockfords* for 1931; in their place he put the *Areopagitica* and the *Tenure of Kings and Magistrates* of Milton, whom he calls "the greatest advocate of freedom of thought" and regularly quotes.

References

N Y Post p33 Ja 24 '46
International Who's Who, 1945-46
Who's Who, 1946

EISENHOWER, MILTON S(TOVER) (ī'z'n-hou"ēr) Sept. 15, 1899- College president; United States Government official

Address: b. c/o Kansas State College, Manhattan, Kan.; h. The Residence, Kansas State College, Manhattan, Kan.

MILTON S. EISENHOWER

Milton S. Eisenhower, president of Kansas State College, was chosen permanent chairman of the United States Commission on Educational, Scientific, and Cultural Cooperation in September 1946. The commission, sponsored by the State Department and endorsed by Congress, was formed at the urging of the United Nations Educational, Scientific, and Cultural Organization, which desired a direct and permanent link between itself and each member nation. As chairman of the commission, Eisenhower, who had spent sixteen years in the service of the Federal Government, would bring his experience into activity on the international plane.

"The other Eisenhower", as Milton Stover Eisenhower has been called, was born at Abilene, Kansas, on September 15, 1899. His mother, Ida Stover, came of a family that had settled in Virginia about 1730, and his father, David Jacob Eisenhower, of one that had come to Pennsylvania in 1741. The parents of the six Eisenhower boys had met while they were fellow students at Lane University in Lecompton, Kansas, and were married in 1885. At the Eisenhower house on the outskirts of Abilene, the boys were each assigned household chores in weekly rotation, and in this way they learned to cook, garden, and care for animals. Although they were not a farmer's sons (their father was manager of the local gas company), the young Eisenhowers raised and sold their own produce—eggs, chickens, vegetables, and fruit—besides working on near-by farms during summer vacations.

Milton attended Abilene High School, where he was editor of the yearbook of the 1917 graduating class. His earliest ambition was to be a newspaper man, which was soon realized: while still a student at Kansas State College, he was city editor of the Abilene *Daily Reflector*—in 1918, and in 1920 and 1921. "Of inestimable help to me", Milton has said, was

EISENHOWER, MILTON S.—*Continued*

Charles Moreau Harger, the editor of that paper who gave him his start in journalism. Upon being graduated with the degree of Bachelor of Science in Industrial Journalism in 1924, Eisenhower remained at Kansas State for a short time as assistant professor of journalism. Later in that year he entered his first governmental position as vice-consul at Edinburgh, Scotland. During his two years there the young man continued his studies at the university in that city.

Dr. William Jardine, a former president of Eisenhower's college, had become Secretary of Agriculture by the time Eisenhower returned to the United States in 1926. From then until 1928 the young Kansan served on the staff of the Department of Agriculture as Jardine's assistant. He became director of information for the department in December 1928, a post which he held until 1941. One of his other duties during this period was to edit the *Yearbook of Agriculture,* which he did for the seven years between 1929 and 1936. At the request of Henry A. Wallace '40, then Secretary of Agriculture, in 1938 Eisenhower accepted the position of coordinating the land use programs of the Department of Agriculture.

Eisenhower's war service began in March of 1942, when President Franklin D. Roosevelt '42 appointed him to direct the War Relocation Authority. In this position Eisenhower's main responsibility was organizing and administering the evacuation of Japanese-American citizens from the strategic West Coast areas to relocation centers on lands owned by the Federal Government, where the evacuees could be provided with work. In conference with Secretary of War Henry L. Stimson '40, Eisenhower arranged wage scales for the evacuees and made provisions for their housing, maintenance, hospitalization, and medical care. At his suggestion a council for the relocation of Nisei students in inland colleges was formed.

After the evacuation of the Japanese-Americans was moving ahead efficiently, President Roosevelt, at Elmer Davis' request, named the Kansan associate director of the Office of War Information. OWI was an agency formed by the amalgamation of other Government information units in pursuance of a plan drafted by Eisenhower. The New York *Herald Tribune* reported that he had been chosen because he was "an expert in cutting snarled red tape" and had "a specialist's knowledge of which heads are useful and which should be lopped off." In the OWI, Eisenhower was to concern himself primarily with administrative and management details. It was incumbent upon him, for example, to eliminate the overlapping functions and responsibilities that the new agency had inherited from the parent agencies. His was the responsibility, too, of converting vague and generalized policy into action. In February 1943 the *American Political Science Review* assessed his year's work: "The product in large measure of the work of its associate director, M. S. Eisenhower, the OWI brings to

the public opinion problems facing the United States a degree of unified control and direction hitherto unattained."

Shortly after the Allied invasion of North Africa in December 1942, Eisenhower accompanied Elmer Davis to the war zone where his elder brother, Dwight D. Eisenhower '42, was in command of the AEF. Davis and Milton Eisenhower inspected the news and propaganda operations of the OWI and arranged for clear radio channels in Morocco to facilitate transmission of news to the United States. Eisenhower worked out arrangements for OWI and Army collaboration for distributing information in the Mediterranean theater; the OWI official was also charged with a special mission by the President to study refugee relief and relocation problems in Algeria and Morocco. On his return home, Eisenhower urged that food and clothing be sent to the people of North Africa immediately; failure to do so, he warned, would affect the military situation adversely.

On June 30, 1943, Eisenhower resigned from the OWI to accept the presidency of Kansas State College of Agriculture and Applied Science. Sometime later the college president enunciated his credo of education in a speech delivered at the Colorado Agricultural and Mechanical College: "Education in a democracy must at all times be concerned with human values and human growth. It must emphasize a unifying force which enables each student to synthesize fragmented knowledge into broad understanding and help him arrive at sound judgments on a multitude of issues both inside and outside his field of specialization. . . .A college or university that is aimlessly neutral, skeptical, or cynical with respect to human values and moral concepts is essentially nothing more than a glorified information booth." Eisenhower, who is a proponent of the technical—as opposed to the classical—college, is chairman of the executive committee of the Association of Land Grant Colleges and Universities. This committee looks after all matters which pertain to the member institutions and which come up before Congress and other Government agencies.

During the next few years the Kansas college president was called to Washington frequently to carry out various Government assignments. In June 1945 he assisted Secretary Clinton P. Anderson '45 to reorganize the Department of Agriculture. Upon Eisenhower's recommendation, after several weeks of study, the AAA and several minor agencies were consolidated into the Production and Marketing Administration, a new agency with broad powers to coordinate Government programs affecting production, pricing, and marketing of farm products. Secretary Anderson emphasized that Eisenhower would have a free hand in the reorganization of the department, because, he said, "He knows the department from top to bottom. Personally, I believe him to be the best-equipped man in the country to carry out the policies I have in mind for the producers of food and the consumer." Eisenhower from time to time spoke before various farm groups. In an address to the National Grange in November 1945, he advocated "a parity concept for all major economic groups similar to the parity index for agriculture," in the interests of economic equality. The agricultural expert pointed out that it is mutually advantageous for agriculture and industry to see that each gets a fair return.

In December 1945 and January 1946 Eisenhower served on President Truman's three-man, fact-finding board in the General Motors-United Automobile Workers wage dispute. Early in January the board recommended a pay increase of 17.4 per cent, which was a compromise between the 11.6 offered by the employers and the 30 per cent asked by the union. The union leaders were pleased because no commodity increase was recommended by the board, as the proposed wage increase, which the board considered noninflationary and "well within the national stabilization policy," did not require a price increase. President Truman then assigned the college official to the Government famine emergency committee, which was formed to make more food available for export to the starving people abroad. Delos Lovelace of the New York *Sun* later remarked: "Maybe what's needed in the battle against national food shortages is another Eisenhower. . . .He can tell you anything about agriculture from 'a' to 'e' because he knows his subject from the ground up."

Eisenhower in September 1946 was chosen permanent chairman of the United States Commission on Educational, Scientific, and Cultural Cooperation, which had its origin in the United Nations Educational, Scientific, and Cultural Organization. The national commission had a dual purpose: in the international sphere, to advise the State Department on cultural and educational policies; in the domestic, to act as a liaison between American organizations and UNESCO. Considered a powerful force for world peace, UNESCO will probably be instrumental in breaking down the traditionally nationalistic concept of education and replacing it by a wholly new one of international cooperation. The ideal inherent in UNESCO will be activated by the exchange of students and teachers, by allocating funds to the schools of the war devastated areas of Europe and Asia, and by serving as a clearing house for educational developments throughout the world. In mid-November Eisenhower left for Paris to attend the first session of UNESCO.

A member of the nongovernmental Committee for Economic Development since 1943, Eisenhower in 1946 was elected to its board of trustees, composed of twenty educators and publicists. The C.E.D. was organized by businessmen to stimulate American business to make its greatest possible contribution to sustained levels of employment and production in the postwar period. The educators and publicists, according to the New York *Times*, were chosen in order to direct "the work of C.E.D. along lines of national public welfare rather than the interests of business and industry alone."

Milton Eisenhower is also a member of the International Committee of the National Plan-

ning Association, a vice-president of the Society for the Advancement of Management, and a fellow of the Kansas Academy of Science. Honorary degrees have been given him by Wichita University (LL.D., 1944) and Colorado State University (D.Sc., 1945). His fraternities are Phi Kappa Phi, Sigma Alpha Epsilon, and Sigma Delta Chi, while his clubs include the Manhattan Country Club and the Rotary Club. Articles by him have been printed in *Collier's, Country Gentleman,* the *Scholar,* the *American Yearbook,* and the *Saturday Evening Post*; and he is a coauthor of *The United States Department of Agriculture: Its Structure and Functions* (1931). Writing and playing the piano are two of his pleasures. He also enjoys golf, but is more apt to wax enthusiastic over gardening—he is especially fond of growing flowers. While in Washington, he tilled several acres of the land around the suburban house where he lived with his wife, the former Helen Elsie Eakin, and their two children, Milton Stover, Jr., and Ruth Eakin. (The Eisenhowers, who had been fellow students at Kansas State, were married on October 12, 1927). In appearance Eisenhower resembles his brother, Dwight; the younger "Ike" (all the Eisenhower brothers have been nicknamed "Ike" at some time or other) is of medium height, weighs about 160 pounds, and has brown eyes and hair. He seldom attends the movies or the theater, prefers nonfiction for his reading.

Reference

Who's Who in America, 1946-47

EISENSTEIN, SERGEI (MIKHAILO-VICH) (ĭ'zyĭn-shtûĭn syĭr-gyā'ĭ myĭ-ĸĭ'lŭ vyĭch) 1898- Theatrical and motion picture director

Address: Moscow

Sergei Mikhailovich Eisenstein has been called "one of the few creative minds of filmdom." The Soviet director of such films as *Potemkin, Ten Days That Shook The World,* and *Alexander Nevsky* is known for his revolutionary treatment of the motion picture. A professor at the Moscow State Institute of Cinematography since 1929, he is the author of scholarly articles on the art and science of the cinema and of a book, *The Film Sense.* In the spring of 1946 his latest effort, *Ivan the Terrible,* made its foreign debut in Paris.

The son of a prosperous shipbuilder, Sergei Mikhailovich Eisenstein was born in 1898. Before he was nineteen, reports Evelyn Gerstein, he had acquired an interest in the Japanese theater and in the drawings of Leonardo da Vinci. While studying civil engineering and architecture he helped manage, at intervals, an experimental theater and a circus in Moscow. During the Russian Civil War he built trenches and dugouts for the Bolsheviki. Later he organized theatrical performances for the Red Army and also painted and designed the scenery. This in turn awakened his dormant interest in the Japanese theater, and he undertook the study of the language, adding it

SERGEI EISENSTEIN

to his list of foreign tongues which included French, German, and English.

After he was mustered out of the army twenty-two-year-old Eisenstein entered the Academy of the General Staff in Moscow where he specialized in "the Japanese section." While studying at the Academy he joined the first workers' theater, the Proletcult, as art director. A year later he went to work with the director of the newly organized Meyerhold Theater. Although Meyerhold, a former pupil of Stanislavsky, was considered an ultra-leftist, Eisenstein soon left him because he did not find him sufficiently "advanced." Returning to the Proletcult he successfully produced *It Is a Good Horse That Never Stumbles,* a comedy by the Russian classical writer Ostrovski. To bring the theater closer to life was the chief concern of the young Proletcult producer. As a step in this direction he took his next play, Tretiakov's *Gasmasks,* into a factory where it was produced with a cast composed entirely of workers. Still he was not satisfied. As a realist he felt that the theater had outlived its usefulness because it could not adequately present "chunks of life," and that the screen was a more suitable medium for his purpose. Having broken with the theater in 1924 he brought forth his first picture, *The Strike.* Subsequently this film won a prize at the 1925 Exposition des Décoratifs in Paris.

It was his next effort, *Potemkin,* which brought him to the attention of critics in the United States and England. Produced when he was twenty-six, it described the revolt of the sailors on the armored ship *Potemkin* during the abortive revolution of 1905. Like most of Eisenstein's work, *Potemkin* was definitely propaganda but, wrote Louis Fischer of the *Nation,* it was done so well that few were conscious of the fact. *October,* or *Ten Days That Shook the World* (1928), was inspired by the book of the American journalist John

Reed, who described the crucial period in 1917 culminating in the fall of the Provisional Government of Kerensky.

The young Eisenstein spoke contemptuously of the theater as a dying institution to be relegated to the past with the horse and buggy. Only the motion picture, he felt, could interpret the machine age of which it was a product. Ignoring the professional actor, he and his assistants scoured Russia for the exact type they needed for their films. For his next picture, *General Line,* they found the actors in night-lodging houses and "picked them up on the road." The picture had no love story and no heroine, for Eisenstein believed in making the masses his hero—he told Louis Fischer, "We want to develop the public, not the actor." Many critics in the United States felt that *General Line* did not have the intellectual breadth of his previous works, but they had praise for the beautiful scenes and his use of "astonishingly authentic types of the village witch, the priest, the rich peasant, the workers in the fields."

The Soviet director is known for the unique use he made of montage, a new method of cutting and mounting the film after the camera work has been completed, to produce a rapid succession of images to illustrate an idea. This consisted of "quick cross and back cutting and the selection of dominant characteristics best suited to illustrate the interplay of time and events." Louis Fischer reported him as saying: "Mounting—the interlacing of closeups, of side-views, top-views, bottom-views—is the most important part of our work. A picture is either made or unmade by it." According to Dudley Nichols, the Hollywood and Soviet directors have entirely different conceptions of the meaning and use of montage.

Both in his creative work and in his teaching Eisenstein reflects his many interests and his wide reading, which includes theosophy, psychology and Marxism. After an interview with Eisenstein in 1928 the critic Joseph Wood Krutch wrote that the director's views on art and the film were not representative of even the most radical of the Russian people. In the perfect world, as Eisenstein visualized it, there would not only be no theater but no movie since a perfect people do not need the instruction the cinema gives them. Nor do they have any unfulfilled desires which such entertainment must satisfy.

Long before he received an invitation to make pictures in Hollywood for Paramount-Famous-Lasky, an old corporate form of the present Paramount Pictures, Eisenstein had indicated his eagerness to work there for a time if he were allowed to do so without any interference. Having signed a contract for a weekly three thousand dollars in Paris, he arrived in New York in May 1930, and with his associate director and his camera man reported for work at the Hollywood studios of their American employers in September.

Almost from the start, Eisenstein met with difficulties. The day he began working for Paramount, the New York *Times* reported that a Congressional committee investigating communism in the United States had been warned of his activities as a film director. It took some time before Eisenstein and his employers could agree on a subject for him. After he had been assigned *Sutter's Gold* and Theodore Dreiser's *An American Tragedy,* Paramount, displeased with the scenarios he prepared, reassigned them to American directors. In the meantime a citizen whom Edmund Wilson characterized as "one of the Los Angeles professional patriots" began to attack the Russian publicly. He made Eisenstein "responsible for all the atrocities alleged to have been committed by the Soviets since the November Revolution."

It had previously been stipulated that the Soviet director's American visa was to expire with his Hollywood contract. At the end of a few months his employers released him without having assigned him a single picture, and gave him a return ticket to Russia by way of Japan. In his dilemma Eisenstein appealed to the California author Upton Sinclair, telling him that the artist Diego Rivera had whetted his interest in Mexico and that he wished to do a picture about that country. Sinclair got in touch with his "millionaire radical friends" and with their assistance made it possible for the Soviet director and his aides to go to Mexico in December. As outlined by Eisenstein his film project, *Que Viva Mexico,* was intended to be a living history of that country, from the pre-conquest days to modern times. He also tried to show that the feudal system introduced into Mexico by the Spanish conquerors was still alive.

Eisenstein and his associates had been working on the film for fourteen months from the scenario he wrote in collaboration with Alexandrov, his associate director, when his Government ordered him to return home because he had overstayed his leave. Since the United States granted him only a transit visa to New York en route to Russia, he was unable to return to Hollywood, as he had hoped, to edit his Mexican picture, of which the estimated length was more than two hundred thousand feet. Sinclair, not able to come to terms with Moscow, made an arrangement for its release by an independent producer as *Thunder Over Mexico.* Critics maintained that a great work had been mutilated, Sinclair that he had enabled the public to enjoy a rare cinema treat, and William Troy, the *Nation's* critic, wrote: "It has helped a few . . . to distinguish between the motion picture as a pile of celluloid and as a work of art."

After his return to Russia, the Soviet director resumed his teaching and his experiments with the motion picture. Among his unfinished works were a film on the Spanish Civil War of 1936 to 1938, and a *Modern Götterdämmerung* based on the life of the Swedish match king, Ivar Kreuger. He was at work on *Benzhin Mendow,* dealing with the controversial theme of collectivization in the country, when in March 1937, during the height of the "liquidation" of the Old Bolsheviks, the Central Administration of the Photo-Cinema Industry of the U.S.S.R. halted work on the picture. For a while Eisenstein was reportedly out of favor. He was, however, permitted to make pictures again and in December 1938, his new sound

film, *Alexander Nevsky,* with a brilliant score by the internationally known Soviet composer, Sergei Prokofiev [41], was released in Moscow. Shortly after the picture was finished the director received one of the highest honors in the Soviet Union, the Order of Lenin. Another decoration, the Stalin Prize, was awarded to him in 1941. In the United States the picture received a mixed critical reception. According to Franz Hoellering of the *Nation,* it proved that the famous director had been "subordinated to the orders of the monolithic state," while Joshua Kunitz of the *New Republic* wrote that Eisenstein had "achieved warmth and humanity and a simplicity verging on grandeur."

In November 1940, one year and three months after the signing of the Nazi-Soviet Pact, Wagner's opera *Die Walküre,* which Eisenstein had directed, had its première at the Bolshoi Opera House in Moscow. That presentation was evidence that he had broken with his early belief that the theater was obsolete. In March 1946 his newly completed film, *Ivan the Terrible,* had its first foreign showing in Paris, where, according to *Time* magazine, it was greeted with both boos and cheers. However, most of the critics received it with enthusiasm. Late in 1946, according to newspaper accounts, the second part of Eisenstein's film *Ivan the Terrible* was banned in Moscow (the first part had already been shown) because "the progressive army supporting Ivan the Terrible was depicted as a gang of degenerates and . . . Mr. Eisenstein portrayed Ivan the Terrible as a man with a strong will, but with a character weak and spineless—'something like Hamlet.'" Eisenstein reportedly received further official censure for an article published in Russia, which was called "erroneous, formalist, in essence advocating 'art for art's sake,'" and shortly afterward Eisenstein's presence in a hospital was announced. In October 1946 the New York *Times* reported the appearance of a new article by the producer, which stated, "We artists temporarily forget those sublime ideas to whose service our art is dedicated"; he said, further, that he had "permitted a distortion of historical facts which made the film [*Ivan the Terrible*] bad and ideologically defective."

Through the years Eisenstein's ideas have undergone considerable change, as he sets forth in his book, *The Film Sense,* which was published in the United States in 1942. The concensus of critical opinion, as expressed by Richard R. Plant of the *Saturday Review of Literature,* was that it was not easy reading. "But there also can be discerned a deep and profound knowledge of the arts, a really penetrating mind, and an approach to the problems of the movies that makes most of the writings of our Hollywood movie-makers look like high school exercises." Among the numerous articles the Soviet director has contributed to periodicals in Russia, England, and the United States are "The New Language of Cinematography," and "The Fourth Dimension in the Kino."

Eisenstein has been described as a man of exuberance, with expressive hands, blue eyes, and a mass of wavy dark hair. One interviewer wrote of him: "A serious student with a pen that prefers spirals to straight lines, he is

EISENSTEIN, SERGEI—*Continued*

essentially a comedian. His interests are catholic and his knowledge very broad; he is the most cultured man in the Soviet cinema."

References

Theatre Mag 52:16+ Jl '30 por
Eisenstein, S. M. Film Sense (1942)
International Who's Who, 1945-46

ELLENDER, ALLEN J(OSEPH) Sept. 24, 1891- United States Senator from Louisiana

Address: b. Senate Office Bldg., Washington ton, D.C.; h. 235 E. Park Ave., Houma, La.

In 1945 a bill was introduced in the Senate which embodied "the goal of a decent home and a suitable living environment for every American family." One of the sponsors of this measure was Allen J. Ellender, whose voting record has caused newspapermen to call

ALLEN J. ELLENDER

him "a relentless Southerner but sometime supporter of the New Deal." The Democratic Senator from Louisiana, a state with a population (1940 census) of 2,363,880 which includes 849,303 Negroes, has been a vehement opponent of anti-poll tax measures and of legislation for a permanent Fair Employment Practice Committee.

Allen Joseph Ellender was born in Montegut, Louisiana, on September 24, 1891, the son of a Dutch Pennsylvania immigrant, Wallace Richard Ellender, and a girl from the bayou country, Victoria (Javaux) Ellender. Allen attended St. Aloysius College in New Orleans, from which he was to receive an honorary M.A. degree, and took his LL.B. at Tulane University (also in New Orleans) in 1913. Admitted to the bar that year, he began the practice of law as the city attorney of Houma,

Louisiana, a position which he held until 1915. He then served for a year as district attorney of Terrebonne Parish. In Terrebonne he purchased several farms on which he raised potatoes so successfully that, according to *Newsweek*, the neighbors dubbed him King Potatus I. Under his direction the yield of land per acre was increased from eighty to three hundred and forty-seven bushels. When the United States entered the war in 1917, the lawyer-farmer became a soldier.

A delegate to the Constitutional Convention of Louisiana in 1921, in 1924 Ellender was elected to the State's House of Representatives. There he remained for twelve years, a figure in Louisiana public affairs which Huey P. Long, first as Governor (1928-30) and then as Senator in Congress (1930-35), dictated through the political machine. From 1928 to 1932 Ellender was the floor leader in the lower branch of his State's legislature; for the next four years he was its speaker. After the assassination of Long in 1935, Ellender, whom *Time* then described as one of those composing "the vote-getting political front of the Long machine which rarely lost a ballot battle in Louisiana," aspired to the governorship. Instead of gaining that office, however, he was elected in 1936 to fill the Senate seat left vacant by Long.

In his first year in the Senate Ellender was coauthor of the Agricultural Adjustment Act and supported the President's plan to enlarge the Supreme Court. He prevented the passage of the Administration's anti-lynch bill —for six days he held the floor of the Senate without interruption in a filibuster against the measure. In 1938 Ellender threatened another filibuster in the battle over the Fair Labor Standards Act unless special conditions for Southern employers were included. Allied with other Senators from the South, he forced a compromise favoring Southern manufacturers. The original provision, which would have set up an immediate minimum of twenty-five cents on hour to be increased to a minimum of forty cents within three years, was changed so that a thirty-cent minimum rate would become effective in two years, and a forty-cent rate in seven; in addition, the compromise provided for industry boards which would have the power to exempt employers from paying the minimum in any area where living costs were low and freight rates high. A member of the Senate Education and Labor Committee, the Senator from Louisiana supported legislation providing Federal funds for elementary schools, high schools, and vocational schools, and was also the author of a school-lunch bill.

In the tense years before the United States entry into World War II, Ellender was one of the five members of the Senate Naval Affairs Committee who voted to fortify Guam; he also voted for the repeal of the arms embargo and for conscription. When the White House-sponsored Lend-Lease bill created an issue in the early part of 1941, opponents of the measure who feared it might lead to the sending of another American Expeditionary Force tried to weaken it with restrictive amendments; Ellender proposed an amendment which provided that "nothing in the bill was to be construed as adding to the President's authority to send American troops outside the United States and its possessions." Under the pressure of Administration forces, which maintained that this amendment would reduce the bill to a mere gesture and raise the morale of aggressor nations, Ellender changed his amendment to read that "nothing in this act shall be construed to change existing law relating to the use of land and naval forces of the United States." Since "existing law" did not include anything to prevent the President from sending American troops to any part of the world, Ellender's substitute amendment was regarded as unnecessary.

Re-elected without opposition in 1942 (according to *PM*, only 6 per cent of Louisiana's potential voters went to the polls), the Senator was disturbed during the war because he felt that the United States was not receiving enough in return for its Lend-Lease aid. In 1943, excited by the reports brought back by five of his colleagues after a two-month world tour, he protested that the nation was being "penalized for [its] progressiveness"; as a result of aid to Great Britain and Russia, he maintained that the United States was only adding to the national debt. He called for an inquiry into Lend-Lease expenditures and demanded that the Allies make concessions to the United States in oil, tin, iron ore, and rubber. He also asked for immediate negotiations to grant the United States permanent possession of strategic bases in return for Lend-Lease aid. When the Lend-Lease program came before the Senate again in May 1944, Ellender nevertheless voted for its extension. He also voted for the extension of the Reciprocal Trade Agreements Act, for the UNRRA appropriation, and for the Green-Lucas soldier vote bill. In 1943 he supported the Farm Security Administration, the National Resources Planning Board, the National Youth Administration and the Smith[41]-Connally[41] antistrike bill.

The Louisiana Senator was a constant critic of Britain. He blamed the Tobruk disaster on "the continued inactivity of the British troops stationed in the British Isles, waiting for an attack that may never come." In 1944, when the British sent troops into Greece after the liberation of that country, Ellender again denounced Britain, charging that she was "taking the lead in causing disunity among the Allies" and that she was unnecessarily maintaining armies in reconquered countries which should have been used against Germany. The Southerner opposed the loan to Britain and worked with other Senators who sought to delay action on the measure.

In May 1945, when delegates were formulating the United Nations Charter at San Francisco, Ellender, who supported the Bretton Woods Agreement, gave them his full support. "The United States Senate," he asserted, "must, without delay, ratify and approve the charter of world organization that will be agreed upon at the San Francisco Conference... I make that statement unqualifiedly and without knowing what the charter will finally contain." Later

Senator Ellender did have certain reservations: when President Truman in an extemporaneous speech at Potsdam stated that the United States did not want "one piece of territory or one thing of a monetary nature out of this war," Ellender thought the President was "too liberal" and declared that the United States should have control not only over Pacific bases but also over some military bases in other parts of the world. Following a forty-two-day world tour which he made with several of his Congressional colleagues in 1946, Ellender, describing the situation in China as "hopeless," urged the withdrawal of American marines from the country as soon as repatriation of the Japanese was completed. He voiced approval of the conduct of the occupation in Japan and advocated that the United States follow a Monroe Doctrine policy in the Pacific, not for purposes of aggrandizement but in order to maintain peace. Maintaining that "graft" was preventing UNRRA shipments from reaching those in need, he asserted that he would not vote for any more appropriations for UNRRA or any similar organization.

A strong supporter of food subsidies and price control during the war, the "mid-road Louisiana Democrat" opposed the OPA's postwar effort to stabilize the price of raw cotton but otherwise favored continuation of the price-control agency. He was a sponsor of the fact-finding legislation recommended by President Truman at the end of 1945 to solve labor-industry problems, and in May 1946 after the national railway strike he voted for the Case[46] Labor Disputes Act, which provided for restrictions against labor. When the Senate confirmed the appointment of Judge William H. Hastie[44] as Governor of the Virgin Islands, Ellender, who had filibustered against the bill for a permanent FEPC, claimed that the selection of a Negro for the governorship was a mistake and would "retard the island." He attacked the Wagner[41]-Murray[45]-Dingell national health bill and again worked for the interests of Southern manufacturers by opposing an amendment to the Fair Labor Standards Act which would establish sixty-five cents as the minimum wage and gradually raise it to seventy-five cents. Ellender favored a minimum wage of sixty cents with no provision for further increase; the bill finally passed by the Senate provided for a sixty-five-cent rate which would remain at that level. At the same time the Senator approved the work of the Rural Electrification Administration among poor farmers and favored the confirmation of Aubrey Williams[40] as head of the REA. (Williams, a man who had tried to better conditions in the South, had been accused of Communist affiliations by the Committee on Un-American Activities.)

In conjunction with two other Senators of such opposite viewpoints as New Deal Democrat Robert F. Wagner and conservative Republican Robert A. Taft[40], Ellender, a member of the Senate Subcommittee on Postwar Housing and Urban Development, and always a supporter of housing legislation, sponsored a comprehensive housing bill which the *Christian Science Monitor* hailed as a measure

ELLENDER, ALLEN J.—*Continued*

that would "write a new chapter into the history of American housing." Through a program of slum clearance, urban redevelopment, low cost public housing, encouragement of private construction, and easy credit terms, the living standards of the general population would be improved. A central housing administration which would unify the many scattered Federal agencies already established would supervise the program. Such organizations as the National Association of Real Estate Boards, the National Association of Home Builders, and the Metropolitan League of Saving Associations opposed the Wagner-Ellender-Taft housing bill, which the Senate passed in April 1946 and sent to the House for consideration, where it was pigeonholed by the House Banking and Currency Committee. Housing officials claimed that Congress' failure to approve the bill was one of the factors retarding much-needed postwar housing.

Ellender was coauthor of a bill which would have provided compensation for the losses of loyal Japanese-Americans taken from their homes and businesses and placed in relocation centers during World War II. As chairman of the special 1946 Senate Campaign Investigation Committee, he was charged by Republicans with stalling the committee in its task of probing the primary campaigns of several Democratic Senators; Ellender denied the charges.

In 1946 Ellender was also chairman of the Senate Claims Committee and a member of the committees on Agriculture and Forestry, Banking, Post Offices and Post Roads, Territories and Insular Affairs; he was on the special committee for the Study and Survey Problems of Small Business Enterprises as well. In 1939 he had been the Democratic national committeeman from Louisiana. The Senator weighs 175 pounds and is five feet seven inches in height; he has been described as "usually somewhat combative in the presentation of his views." In 1917 he was married to Helen Calhoun Connelly; they have one son.

References

Congressional Directory (2d ed., 1945)
Who's Who in America, 1946-47

EMERY, DEWITT (MCKINLEY) Dec. 12, 1897- Businessman

Address: b. c/o National Small Business Men's Association, 39 S. La Salle St., Chicago; h. 2235 Central Park Ave., Evanston, Ill.

The president and founder of the National Small Business Men's Association, an organization established to give the "little man" of business an opportunity to voice his opinion in national affairs, is DeWitt Emery. Since the organization's inception in the latter part of 1937, Emery, an Akron stationery plant executive, has devoted his time, according to an association statement, "to preaching the gospel of small business," and to championing small

business "in its life and death struggle for existence, first in the maelstrom of the depression" and then in World War II.

DeWitt McKinley Emery was born to William Sylvester and Mina Elizabeth (Alexander) Emery in Grove City, Mercer County, Pennsylvania, on December 12, 1897. DeWitt's father, who enlisted in the Union Army at New Castle, Pennsylvania, when he was sixteen, served as a member of Company D, 109th Pennsylvania Volunteer Infantry, in some of the famous engagements of the Civil War. In 1899 the Emery family moved to Youngstown, Ohio, where young DeWitt received his education. He attended South High School from 1909 to 1913. After his graduation from secondary school, he was a student for the remainder of the year 1913 at Hall Business College. Emery's experience in business began at an early age: during the summer vacation before he entered high school he sold eleven automobiles for a garageman in his native city, and he continued to sell intermittently.

His first position after his schooling was completed was that of assistant trust officer of the Dollar Savings and Trust Company in Youngstown (1915). Emery remained at the bank until the United States declared war upon the Central Powers in April 1917, when he entered the United States Army and was stationed in the Eighth Division Training Company, First Officer's Training Camp, at Fort Benjamin Harrison, Indiana. Emery's sojourn in the Army was of only a few months' duration: he was disqualified for service because of his height—he is six feet six inches tall—and because he was underweight. In November of the same year Emery married Lillian Price, who died twelve years later. (Their two children are Marjorie Jane and Richard Lee.)

In 1918 Emery obtained the post of assistant district manager of the Ohio district of Boston's Stone and Webster Company. The office closed in 1920, ending Emery's association with the New England firm. About two years later Emery organized in Youngstown his own firm, the DeWitt M. Emery Company, business counselors. In October 1925 he joined the Monroe Letterhead Corporation of Huntsville, Alabama. There he worked as director of sales. When the Monroe company decided to function as two corporate organizations, each located in a different region of the United States, Emery in March 1929 moved one division of Monroe Letterhead Corporation to Akron, Ohio. From that year he has been president and controlling owner of the Akron firm. (His son Richard Lee, after service in World War II, became vice-president and treasurer.)

The stress of the depression had a telling effect upon the Monroe Letterhead Corporation. In 1937, when the organization had begun once more to thrive, its president is reported to have remarked that it was hit by social security, unemployment insurance, increased taxes, and higher wages. To learn how other small businesses were faring, Emery sent two hundred letters to business associates, friends, and executives of small firms. The first sentence of this form letter (according to the National Small Business Men's Association the letter "promises to become an historical document") read: "The sheriff is about to get my business. How are you doing?" In this correspondence, Emery proposed that the "little fellows" of business and industry form an organization designed "to protect their own interests and the interests of the great American middle class."

By January 1938 Emery had received replies from 80 per cent of those to whom he had written. They were inclined to agree that their business in general was bad and to favor his idea of associated action. As reported in *Business Week* (January 1, 1938), a ten-point program, demanding in part "an end of Government experimenting in business, taxes for revenue only, repeal of the undistributed profits and capital gains taxes, balancing the budget," and impartial law enforcement in all strikes, was drawn up early in the formation of the National Small Business Men's Association by Emery and his legal aides. Its membership policy was to accept those executives whose companies employed only up to one hundred workers.

DeWitt Emery was one among a number of businessmen invited by the United States Secretary of Commerce, Daniel C. Roper, to attend a conference of little business in Washington. The Akron executive called this February 1938 conference "a major blunder on the part of the New Deal, a great thing for the small business men because of all the publicity they received." (*Time* termed the conference a "circus"). Concerning the position of his association he remarked (in *Fortune*, April 1938): "We glory in being known as a pressure group." In September of the same year delegates of the National Small Business Men's Association met in Pittsburgh for their first national convention. Maintaining that at this meeting "there would be no fisticuffs, politics, or laughs like those at Washington," Emery declined to reveal the group's actual membership. As stated in *Time* (September 26, 1938), Emery declared: "If the membership is secret, no one knows how big a club you're swinging." Although this first convention's attendance was not large, Emery asserted that he was not discouraged: "After all, only thirty small business men attended the Boston Tea Party, and they played a pretty big role in history." Some time was spent in defining a "small business man," and a number of Congressional and labor officials delivered "anti-New Deal speeches." Included in the conference's resolutions were those supporting "the American system of free enterprise", "active and immediate cooperation of labor, business, agriculture, and Government," and "fundamental principles of antitrust laws."

Since the 1938 meeting, the membership of the National Small Business Men's Association has steadily increased. There were in 1946 more than thirty-five thousand members in the country. "DeWitt Emery," wrote the journalist Wythe Williams, "has made the National Small Business Men's Association a power to be seriously considered throughout the United States." The association maintains offices in Washington, D.C., and Los Angeles, and executive and national headquarters in Chicago and Akron, respectively. The president from the associa-

Fabian Bachrach

DEWITT EMERY

tion's founding through 1941, Emery resumed that office in June 1942. In 1941 Emery became a partner in DeWitt Emery and Associates, a public relations and management counsel firm.

Much of Emery's time has been employed in traveling from one region of the United States to another, addressing gatherings of all types of individuals on subjects pertaining to social and economic aspects of American life and obtaining from these people firsthand their opinions on vital matters. The greater number of his lectures and articles have been published as small pamphlets, among the titles of which are *The Awakening of Small Business*, *The Business Twins—Big and Little*, and *Our American Way of Life*. The year 1943 was the beginning of another phase of Emery's career: he undertook the writing of a syndicated column, *The American Way*, which appears in more than two thousand small-town newspapers, most of which are published weekly. Emery is also the author of a chapter of the book, *The Care and Feeding of an Executive* (1945) by Millard C. Faught and Laurence Hammond. The chapter attributed to him is entitled "How To Pound a Table."

When the United States entered World War II, Emery's addresses dealt with the obligations of Government, labor, and business during the war and in the postwar reconversion of industry. At that time he advocated the Government's giving the bonus to servicemen (*The Rotarian*, April 1942), condemned both profiteering and what he considered the Government's inefficient and discriminatory method of renegotiating war contracts to prevent excessive profits (*The Rotarian*, January 1943), and urged a Federal policy of *laissez faire*. Emery in July 1946 offered a new postwar proposal to aid business: he suggested, following the principle of the Bard tax plan, an amendment to the Internal Revenue Act allowing an owner

EMERY, DEWITT—*Continued*

or partner to pay corporate taxes on "income from capital directly ventured in the operation of business," and personal income rates on "income from nonbusiness or investment capital such as stock and bonds." Other of his proposals urge appointments to the Cabinet and the United States Supreme Court "on a basis of demonstrated ability and merit, political expediency to the contrary," a thorough and unbiased overhaul of the tax structure, decentralization of the accumulated powers of the central Government in accordance with the original terms of the Constitution, a foreign policy of national self-preservation and friendliness toward other countries, and practical, fundamental education emphasizing Americanism.

In the July 3, 1946, issue of the *Christian Science Monitor,* Dorothea Kahn sounded a critical note in discussing the policies of a number of the organizations of which the small business movement is composed. These groups, she found, did not champion the Senate Small-Business Committee for its warning "against growing concentration of power in the hands of big business," refused all offers of Government aid, and were pursuing a philosophy not basically different from that of large business organizations such as the National Association of Manufacturers. Emery's group, the writer stated, was one of those which opposed Government price regulation, demanded that organized labor be held more strictly accountable for its actions, and did not recognize "a sharp division of interest between big and little business." In an address (October 1946) to the National Association of Photo-Lithographers, Emery himself took issue with sections (reprinted from a standard economics textbook) of an economics manual used by the Army in an "educational program for service personnel." Objecting specifically to parts which urged adoption of a tax plan that would prevent the accumulation and inheritance of wealth and attacking the manual as being communistic, Emery asked for a "Congressional investigation" of "the whole War Department educational program and the personnel in charge"; and he criticized the State Department, which, he said, had tolerated radicals and Communists within its ranks.

The tall 240-pound Emery has gray eyes and graying red hair, a "large humorous mouth, and a deep resonant voice." He is described as energetic and genial. The business leader is a director of the Chicago Executive Club and a member of the Sunset Ridge Country Club. His recreations, he says, are golf and bridge, and he is a baseball and football fan. In July 1931 Emery was married for the second time. He and his wife, the former Florence Price, who is not related to Emery's deceased wife, have one son, James DeWitt. Emery's church is the Presbyterian, his fraternal organization the Masons.

References

Bsns W p28 Ja 1 '38 por
Who's Who in America, 1946-47

ERICKSON, JOHN EDWARD 1863—
May 25, 1946 Lawyer; Governor of Montana, 1924-33; United States Senator from Montana, 1933-34; the only person to win election as Governor of Montana for three successive terms.

Obituary

N Y Times p32 My 26 '46

ERSKINE, G(RAVES) B(LANCHARD)
June 28, 1897- United States Marine Corps officer; Government official

Address: b. Retraining and Reemployment Administration, Federal Trade Commission Bldg., Washington, D.C.; c/o Navy Dept., Washington, D.C.; h. 1003 Coast Blvd., La Jolla, Calif.

After serving as chief of staff to Marine General Holland M. Smith '45 in the Pacific and commanding a combat division at Iwo Jima, Major General G. B. Erskine, USMC, was named by President Truman to supervise the reintegration into civilian life of the thirteen million American veterans of World War II. "A nonpolitical figure with no ties to any Federal bureau," he is administrator of the Retraining and Reemployment Administration under the Secretary of Labor. His post is not connected in any way with Veterans Administration head Omar N. Bradley '42, whose duties often overlap his, but the two men are said to cooperate closely. In outlining his objectives General Erskine has said that jobs for veterans depended on "the tremendous fact that there must be jobs for all."

Graves Blanchard Erskine was born in Columbia, Louisiana, on June 28, 1897. At the outbreak of World War I he was working his way through Louisiana State University, planning to become a doctor. When the United States declared war, he was a sergeant trumpeter in the Louisiana National Guard but, wanting to see action without delay, he entered the Marines. The twenty-year-old Southerner was given a second lieutenant's commission in the Marine Corps Reserve in September 1917. When he was finally assigned to a combat unit he was enrolled as a probationary officer in the Regular Corps.

In France, as an officer of the Sixth Marine Regiment, Erskine led his men through some famous Marine battles, the Aisne-Marne, St. Mihiel, Belleau Wood, and Soissons; he was wounded at Marbache. After the war he returned wearing captain's bars, the Purple Heart, a French fourragère, and the Silver Star for gallantry in action. Between the two wars he studied and taught in service schools: he completed a postgraduate course in electrical engineering and one in general ordnance engineering. He was graduated from the Army Infantry School at Fort Benning, Georgia, and studied for two years at the second highest Army school, the Command and General Staff School at Fort Leavenworth, Kansas. At Quantico and Philadelphia he taught subjects ranging from machine-guns to tactics and strategy.

Erskine's assignments outside the continental United States were in Haiti in 1921 and Santo Domingo in 1922-24. He took part in the Second Nicararguan Campaign in 1928-30, and was awarded the Nicaraguan Medal of Merit for his services with the Guardia Nacional. From 1935 until June 1937 he was in China as executive officer of the Embassy Guard at Peiping, and during this period, in March 1936, he was promoted to lieutenant colonel. Colonel's rank was given to him in March 1941.

"When Pearl Harbor came," wrote Sutherland Denlinger in *Collier's*, "he was already an expert on amphibious landings and was applying knowledge gained at Guantánamo and at Quantico, as chief of staff of the amphibious corps, Atlantic Fleet." By mid-1942 Colonel Erskine had a total of eight years of foreign service. As deputy commander and chief of staff of the Fifth Amphibious Corps, he trained men to recapture the Aleutian Islands from the Japanese, and, according to an official release, "pioneered many of the doctrines for amphibious warfare . . . [later] employed so successfully in the Pacific." His work in this campaign, which won him the Legion of Merit, included personal participation in the Kiska operation of August 1943. This invasion, the last of the campaign, proved somewhat anticlimactic, for when the United States and Canadian forces stormed the beach, they found the enemy gone, presumably evacuated by submarine under cover of the heavy Alaskan fog.

In training the men who were to meet the same enemy in another extreme of climate, Erskine, as chief of the amphibious training staff of the Pacific Fleet amphibious corps and the Fleet Marine force in the San Diego area, "contributed greatly to the combat efficiency" of the troops which captured Tarawa Atoll and the other Gilbert Islands in November 1943. The 2,950 American casualties, a number which shocked the people at home, nevertheless compared favorably with upwards of 4,500 Japanese killed, wounded, or captured, especially as the latter had all the advantages of a strong system of fortifications. General Erskine took part in the successful Marshall Islands (Kwajalein Atoll) campaign of February 1944, under the amphibious command of Admiral R. Kelly Turner [44]. He did much of the planning for the famous Saipan and Tinian operations in the Marianas, serving as chief of staff of the forces which took those strategic islands halfway between Japan and the Philippines. According to Admiral Nimitz [42], over-all Pacific commander, the success of these invasions was due largely to Erskine's "tactical judgment and driving force." He was rewarded with a Gold Star in lieu of a second Legion of Merit, promotion to major general, and his first field command of the war.

Major General Erskine succeeded General Allen Hal Turnage in the command of the Third Marine Division, veterans of Bougainville and Guam. His first combat test came at Iwo Jima in the Volcano Islands, in the campaign which displaced Tarawa as the bitterest fight of the Marines in the one hundred and sixty-eight years of their existence.

From February 21 to March 15, 1945, the Third Marine Division fought grimly for the island under what Guam headquarters called "conditions that have had no parallel in this war." Erskine's "undaunted valor, tenacious perseverance, and resolute fortitude in the face of overwhelming odds," read the official citation accompanying his Distinguished Service Medal, "inspired his stout-hearted Marines to heroic efforts during critical phases of the bitter engagement."

After the Japanese surrender on August 14, 1945, Erskine directed all his men to take a compulsory course in the "GI Bill of Rights" (Servicemen's Readjustment Act of 1944). According to Denlinger, he supplemented this with a divisional program of voluntary education designed to fit his men for a world at peace, setting something of a record for educational programs of this kind, as it involved more than half of the men under his command.

The Marine General was flown nine thousand miles to Washington in October 1945, where his superior, the Secretary of the Navy, told him that the President had a new post for him. "It's only for a year or so," the Secretary said. The new assignment was to coordinate all Federal programs dealing with veterans except the Veterans Administration, as personal representative of the Secretary of Labor in charge of the Retraining and Reemployment Administration. A bill was soon introduced in Congress allowing Erskine to retain his Marine Corps standing while in this civilian post. Although the VA was specifically exempted from his control, Erskine's relations with the VA head, Army General Omar Bradley, were said to be a model of cooperation. The forty-eight-year-old Marine was to be the work-director called for in the Baruch [41]-Hancock report on the human aspects of demobilization. The RRA had been established sixteen months before Erskine's appointment, but the post had been vacant for about four months. General Erskine succeeded to what American Veterans Committee chairman Charles Bolté [45] summed up as "a Washington staff of fifteen executives, a two-year handicap in the race to humanize demobilization, practically no money, a tangled administrative structure with one agency overlapping the work of the next." Bolté continued, "And from the midst of this impossible situation he is supposed to initiate and administer plans for coordinating the human reconversion work of Government and the communities." The result, Bolté said, was that the veterans were being given the "run-around. . . . Unable to find the answers to their questions in their home towns, they are writing Washington for answers which Washington [likewise] cannot give them."

After taking office, Erskine paid particular attention to the Community Advisory Centers, which he defined as "community projects with joint Federal, state, and local cooperation... central points where veterans can go with dignity to learn what their rights are and how they can obtain them." Under Erskine's plan, every organization of any nature which offered

U.S. Marine Corps

MAJ. GEN. G. B. ERSKINE

help or advice to the returning veteran would join in the work of the advisory centers. Erskine advocated, too, that their facilities be extended to include nonveterans. Soon after entering upon his new duties, the administrator called together the heads of forty such centers and asked them to write a handbook for general distribution explaining how to organize and operate an advisory center. This assignment took two weeks to complete. Besides discussing whatever complaints the delegates had, Erskine sent an assistant around the country to confer with Governors, veterans' officials, and organization heads.

"The task of reintegrating the millions of people whose lives have been disrupted by war is considered to be primarily a community responsibility," said Erskine's RRA Order Number 3. In February 1946 he decentralized RRA operations, dissolving the committees of Federal officials under his jurisdiction within each State and ordering the officials instead to cooperate with State and local officials in setting up advisory centers. "A Federal agency," he said, "should refer an individual with a problem outside its own scope to an established advisory center if the problem is not sufficiently well-defined to make direct referral to another agency logical." By January 1946 fifteen hundred communities had such centers, although many needed expansion and improvement; four months later General Erskine reported that there were estimated to be about twenty-eight hundred of them. He pointed out, however, "since there are from six thousand to ten thousand communities in America which could support centers, it is obvious that many cities and towns are lax in meeting the need."

Another "top project" of the RRA was obtaining school credits for the in-service training

of veterans; and the forty-eight Governors were asked to assist this program. "Through such a program," Erskine commented, "a veteran whose prewar schooling was incomplete may qualify for a high school [or college] diploma or cut the time required to qualify, thus improving his job prospects.... This grant of accreditation is in no sense a 'gift' to a veteran, but a recognition of his qualifications... an asset which is 'frozen' until they take the steps necessary to apply it to their individual advantage." Recognizing the relationship of housing to education in a time of severe housing shortage, the RRA also sought to obtain priorities on surplus Government furniture, bedding, and housing facilities, for colleges and universities; and Erskine urged junior colleges and small colleges to expand their facilities during the crisis so that students could attend classes in their home towns instead of having to go to some overcrowded educational center. Erskine included under the heading of job opportunities the RRA program to obtain priorities on the sale of surplus war property for veterans, "at a cost of not more than 50 per cent of the normal charge for such properties." He attempted further to standardize, clarify, and supervise the on-the-job apprentice training program.

At a meeting of the Disabled American Veterans in September 1946, General Erskine voiced his concern over those veterans who have already exhausted their unemployment allowances "without making honest efforts to seek employment." According to the General, this was responsible for the paradox of labor shortages in certain areas and mass unemployment in others. General Erskine then estimated the unemployed of the nation at three million, including veterans who could not find suitable jobs and handicapped workers who were formerly employed in defense industries. On General Erskine's recommendation the Labor Department's Retraining and Re-Employment Administration urged industry to give handicapped veterans priorities on suitable jobs. Said General Erskine: "The disabled veterans who paid for our safety with their flesh and blood, and the handicapped workers who contributed materially to the sucess of our war efforts must not be the forgotten men and women of the postwar world." Several months later, the General asked that the manufacture and distribution of artificial limbs be put under his direction. He said that amputees' dissatisfaction with the limbs offered them had lowered morale in military hospitals.

Erskine, who has a California home, married the former Margaret Spratling, daughter of a Marine captain, and has three daughters. The General, who looks more like the usual conception of a Marine sergeant, is described by one writer as "without swagger, given to sometimes dryly humorous understatement... a tall, spare fellow with bright blue eyes in an affable, somewhat florid face.... He is pleasant and smooth and immaculate, the five rows of ribbons a splash of color against the perfectly tailored blouse, the eyes pleasant, alert, the big, well-kept hands relaxed on desk or table, the whole attitude one of easy, unhurried competence. . . .There is something of the quiet, confidently forceful schoolmaster in his manner."

References

> Collier's 117:34 Ap 27 '46 por
> Who's Who in America, 1946-47

ESTES, ELEANOR (ĕs'tēz) May 9, 1906- Author

Address: h. 344 W. 72d St., New York

A former children's librarian, and now a writer of children's books, Eleanor Estes has used the memories of her own childhood in New England to provide the background for her stories. Her "heart-warming" chronicles of "the Moffats" are presented "with genuine sympathy and truthfulness" and frequently classed with famous book families in the juvenile field.

Eleanor Estes was born Eleanor Ruth Rosenfeld in West Haven, Connecticut, on May 9, 1906. The child of parents who lived in the world of books, her early years hold memories of the works of Dickens, read aloud by her mother. The London of the nineteenth century was as vivid to the little girl and her family as if they had lived there. Young Eleanor went to the Union Grammar School, and then to the West Haven High School, from which she was graduated in 1923.

She then entered the New Haven Free Library training class, and after completing the six months' course, was appointed a junior assistant in the children's department. At first she was not conscious of any particular desire to work with children, but as time went on she became more and more interested in her young patrons. Storytelling and supervising reading clubs for boys and girls were the activities she enjoyed the most. In June 1928 she was appointed acting librarian in the children's room, and in October 1929 she became librarian, a post she held until 1931, when she received the Caroline M. Hewins scholarship, awarded in recognition of outstanding work in the juvenile field. After a year at the Pratt Institute Library School, she was offered a position at the New York Public Library, where she was children's librarian successively at the Chatham Square Branch, the West New Brighton Branch, and the George Bruce Branch.

While a student at Pratt, the young librarian met Rice Estes, also at the school; they were married on December 8, 1932. Eleanor Estes had always wanted to write, she says, and had made her first attempt at the age of eleven, when her class at school was instructed to prepare a "conversation piece." Eleanor wrote a little imaginative story called "Conversation Over the Back Fence." When the other children read their compositions, most of which were in the "Hello, Bill, how are you?" style, she became alarmed, because her own was so different. However, when the papers were returned she found that the teacher had written "Good" on her theme. Her desire to become a writer intensified. But it was not until after

ELEANOR ESTES

her marriage that Eleanor Estes began to put together material for a book.

Eleanor Estes and her husband have traveled much along the Atlantic seaboard, but mostly their vacations have been spent at Rockport, on Cape Ann, Massachusetts. There they met Louis Slobodkin, the sculptor. He was a sympathetic listener when Mrs. Estes discussed the book she was writing. When the manuscript had been placed, it seemed natural to ask Slobodkin to undertake the illustrations. Although he had done no work in this field, he was delighted to try, and Mrs. Estes and her publisher in turn were delighted with the results. *The Moffats* came out in 1941.

This story of an American family in a small town had nothing spectacular in it, as May Lamberton Becker wrote in the *Herald Tribune*, but it had "the difference that belongs to real life." The *Library Journal* found that "the style is deceptively simple; somehow the author has succeeded in conveying the large significance of small events in children's lives and has reported them as children experience them," while the *Christian Science Monitor* compared it to Margaret Sidney's *The Five Little Peppers and How They Grew*. According to Eleanor Estes the characters in the book are not counterparts of her family, as some critics have suggested, but a composite of all the children she has known. A keen observer, Mrs. Estes has garnered from memory all the little things that did happen and added to them possible happenings invented by a vivid imagination.

The adventures of the Moffat children were continued in *The Middle Moffat* (1942) and *Rufus M.* (1943). A. M. Jordan wrote in the *Horn Book* of the Moffat stories, "Eleanor Estes draws New England village life with genuine sympathy and truthfulness. Her Moffats, as Louis Slobodkin convincingly presents them, take their place among the book families

ESTES, ELEANOR—*Continued*

not soon forgotten." Also published in 1943 was *The Sun and the Wind and Mr. Todd,* a fantasy inspired by one of Aesop's fables. This book was a disappointment to some critics, who were far less enthusiastic about the adventures of Mr. Todd than they had been about the Moffats. Eleanor Estes' last book—*The Hundred Dresses* (1944)—is the story of a little Polish girl in New England. Called one of the most important books of the year, it is "beautiful in its softly colored spacious pictures, beautiful in its understanding of child character and belief in the essential goodness of a child's heart." *The Moffats* is being translated into several European languages, *The Hundred Dresses* into Turkish.

Eleanor Estes and her husband live in New York City. She employs her limited free time drawing, and painting in water color. She is also a lover of music. Her favorite books include such disparate choices as James Joyce's *Portrait of the Artist as a Young Man,* Andersen's fairy tales, and Plato. One of her pleasures is reading the fan mail that comes to her from all over the world, from children who look upon the Moffats as real people. She has many books in mind, she says; her current work is a novel of the contemporary scene. Of medium height, Eleanor Estes is youthful in appearance. She has gray eyes and dark hair.

ETHRIDGE, MARK (FOSTER) Apr. 22, 1896- Newspaper editor, publisher

Address: b. Louisville Courier-Journal, Louisville, Ky.; h. Prospect, Ky.

Editor-publisher Mark Ethridge of the only dailies in Louisville, Kentucky, the *Courier-Journal* and *Times,* "is universally regarded as one of the most forceful, intelligent, and progressive newspapermen in America," declared a Chicago *Sun* editorial in 1944. In recognition of his ability as a reporter, the Southern journalist in October 1945 was sent to Bulgaria and Rumania as Secretary Byrnes's [41] special representative, to observe the preparations made for the general elections in those countries. At the end of the following year, in December, Ethridge was appointed American representative on the United Nations commission assigned to investigate the reports of border friction between Greece and her three neighbors, Albania, Bulgaria, and Yugoslavia.

A native of the Deep South, Mark Foster Ethridge was born in Meridian, Mississippi, on April 22, 1896, one of the nine children of William Nathaniel and Mary (Howell) Ethridge. His father was a lawyer and, in company with the rest of the family, deeply interested in politics and government. Both parents were "voracious readers" and encouraged Mark along the literary path. Thus, he says, he grew up in a stimulating, intellectual atmosphere. While the boy was in high school his father gave him a horse and helped him to start a newspaper delivery route. Before he was graduated he was also reporting for a paper—writing sports stories for the Meridian *Dis-*

patch and a daily column, *Baseball Bubbles,* signed "Fanny," for which he was paid fifty cents apiece. During 1913, after graduation, he worked as a reporter for the Meridian *Star.* The next year he entered the University of Mississippi, but had only enough money for one year of study, after which he joined the staff of the Columbus (Georgia) *Enquirer-Sun.* While working in Georgia he was made aware of the progressive policies of the Macon *Telegraph* and managed to get a post on that paper. "I wanted to learn every darn thing about the newspaper business and I sought out the people I wanted to work for," he recalls. In this period in Macon, in addition to writing, Ethridge also attended Mercer University during 1916-17. (In later years the university awarded him an honorary degree.)

The First World War interrupted Ethridge's career and education, sending him into the Navy where he served first as a yeoman and later as an ensign. On release from service in 1919 he returned to the *Telegraph* as city editor. After four years in this position he became a writer for the Consolidated Press and the New York *Sun.* In 1925, however, he returned to the *Telegraph* as managing editor, there to remain for eight years. Then, in the year 1933, Ethridge went abroad on an Oberlaender Fellowship to study, as *PM* expresses it, "the ramifications of the Versailles Treaty, agriculture, and social security." Upon completion of his research on the Continent the journalist resigned from the *Telegraph* because the policies of the newspaper had been reversed. Leaving that paper, therefore, he went to work for the Associated Press for a brief period and then, "fascinated by the job Eugene Meyer [41] was doing with the Washington *Post,*" he transferred to Meyer's staff as associate editor, soon becoming assistant general manager (1933-34). In 1934 Ethridge turned South again to become general manager and publisher of the *Times-Dispatch* of Richmond, Virginia. Here he met Barry Bingham, son of Robert Worth Bingham, owner of the Louisville *Courier-Journal* and of the Louisville *Times,* who persuaded him to manage those newspapers. The elder Bingham, at this time United States Ambassador to the Court of St. James, announced the appointment of Ethridge as vice-president and general manager of the two papers in April 1936. On that occasion *Time* magazine reported the disappointment of *Times-Dispatch* reporters over Ethridge's departure from their paper. (His first official act had been to raise editorial salaries and he had encouraged colorful writing.)

In his study of the Louisville daily press for *PM* in 1945, Kenneth Stewart [43] described the *Courier-Journal*'s early fame under the editorship of Colonel Henry Watterson. "Once more," wrote Stewart, "the *Courier-Journal* has become a paper with a personality—and this time it is the personality of Mark Foster Ethridge" who, it was observed, "descended on Louisville like a tornado." One of the new editor's first acts was to make space for more news in his columns by dispensing with feature material designed primarily to promote circulation. In 1944 the two dailies gave up a possible $1,200,000 to keep "one of the highest ratios of news to advertising in the country." When Bingham entered the Navy in 1942 Ethridge assumed also the title of publisher. He has been commended for making both the *Courier-Journal* and the *Times* technically superior, more attractive in make-up, and better written, and for giving them editorial "punch." By increasing the picture and regional coverage, he has also increased circulation. Advocating full and honest news coverage in a speech in 1944, the publisher stated his creed: "We must as publishers come to what a few newspapers do now: we must root our policies in a philosophy rather than in economic or political alliances or prejudices."

The *Courier-Journal* is the policy-making paper of the two. "In some Northern and Negro eyes," Stewart wrote in *PM*, "the *Courier-Journal* has far to go before it can be regarded as a complete champion of racial justice, but it leads the way for its Southern contemporaries." On the other hand, as can be expected, Ethridge has been sharply attacked by die-hard Southerners for his work on behalf of the Negro's civil and economic rights. The editor believes that the poll tax and white primary, manifestations of the Southern "white supremacy" system, represent "a complete denial of the democratic process and a complete humiliation of all people who profess any faith in democracy." He favors economic opportunity for the Negro and maintains that the breakdown of all segregation can be attained only through education, not through legislation. (In December 1946 Ethridge became one of the members of the Wendell L. Willkie Awards for Journalism Corporation, which will provide three annual prizes to Negroes for achievements in journalism. The purpose of the corporation is to encourage cooperation among white and Negro writers and publishers.)

Other editorial policies of Ethridge's led to campaigns against the evils of farm tenancy, for lower freight rates and further social and economic improvements. As early as 1931, in the *Annals of the American Academy of Political and Social Science*, he stated his opinion on the Southern press's opposition to unionism. "Editors would rather not see the unions come," he said. "They would much prefer to see the manufacturers do what manifestly must be done to meet the standards of economic and social justice without having to be forced into it."

The *Courier-Journal* has been strongly Democratic in politics. Fully two years before the advent of the New Deal its publisher, speaking before several civic clubs in Georgia, delivered what has been called "a virtual blueprint of legislation of the first Roosevelt [42] Administration." "In this country," he declared, "people go hungry because there is too much wheat; ragged because there is too much cotton; homeless because too many homes have been built; penniless because too much money lies idle in the banking vaults of the nation; jobless because there are too many people willing to work. American capitalism has the greatest genius for obtaining production, but

MARK ETHRIDGE

it has made a monumental and disgraceful failure of obtaining distribution." "Communism," he observed on another occasion, "does not thrive where there is no need for change." A supporter of Henry A. Wallace [40], Ethridge joined the Businessmen for Wallace Committee during debate over the New Dealer's appointment to the Secretary of Commerce post early in 1945. But, Stewart points out, the *Courier-Journal* and its editor-publisher have "not followed the New Deal blindly; at times they have been openly critical and at times they have seemed to lead the New Deal."

In addition to the two Louisville newspapers, Ethridge is actively interested in WHAS, the largest radio station in the Louisville area, which Barry Bingham and his wife Mary also own. In 1938 the then general manager of the dailies was also president of the influential National Association of Broadcasters; in subsequent years he has continued his active affiliation with it. At the time of the controversy between the NAB and the FCC in 1941, President Roosevelt appointed Ethridge as investigator. The newspaperman resigned shortly thereafter, however, in disapproval of the FCC's order to split the Red and Blue networks, charging the Commission with using illegal powers; and he urged a Senate investigation. When on June 25, 1941, President Roosevelt by Executive order created a committee on fair employment practice in the Office of Production Management, to handle cases of discrimination in defense industries, he appointed Ethridge chairman of that pioneer body. The following September, as a result of the report turned in by Ethridge to the President, another Executive order was issued directing further that all Government departments and agencies hire without regard to creed, race, or religion. Late in 1944 the publisher was again in the foreground in his work in race relations: At the Atlanta meeting of the Committee of

ETHRIDGE, MARK—*Continued*

Editors and Writers of the South, called in anticipation of the revival of the anti-poll tax bill in Congress, he was one of the leaders of the committee, which soundly scored Southern devices for depriving the Negro of his vote.

In 1943 Ethridge served in an advisory capacity to the OWI. Recalled to Government service in October 1945 by the State Department and the President, he was made a special representative of the United States to survey the situation in Bulgaria and Rumania before the scheduled elections in those countries. He was selected, wrote Turner Catledge in the New York *Times,* "primarily . . . because he is a trained newspaperman and . . . for his particular ability to get at the factual roots of any given situation." In the political caldron of Sofia each of the various factions tried to impress Ethridge, but the journalist, who had termed this mission his toughest assignment, focused on his goal—"to arrive at the approximate truth." In November he brought back the report which caused the State Department to inform the Leftist-dominated Bulgarian Government that a new government elected under the projected conditions would not be recognized by the United States because such an election would not be considered free and democratic. Before returning to the United States from the Balkan capitals, Ethridge also visited Moscow for talks with Soviet Vice-Commissar Vishinsky '44.

Back in Louisville, Ethridge made his first unofficial report on New Year's Day in an address to the city's Board of Trade. Agreeing with Secretary Byrnes's decision against releasing the official report, Ethridge, however, emphasized that in so doing the Secretary was not suppressing "some great secret." The journalist reiterated his opinions concerning the Balkan countries, namely, that "neither country had a broadly representative government in the Yalta sense." Concerning Russian sentiment in the matter, he declared, "In spite of the fact that the Russian Government disagreed with my conclusions, I must say in all fairness that it made great concessions to the American viewpoint at Moscow. In fact, it went further in assurances to Rumania than I had thought it might." According to Ethridge, the Big Three promised Rumania a reorganization of the interim government and free elections, and the Russian Government would advise the Bulgarians to broaden their Cabinet to include representatives of missing democratic elements. Answering a common question, Ethridge further stated, "In spite of the fact that Russia has sometimes acted like an imperial power since the end of the war, I believe she does earnestly want an organization for international security."

At the request of Premier Tsaldaris '46 of Greece, a U.N. commission of investigation into Greek frontier problems was appointed in December 1946. Among its members, drawn from the eleven nations of the Security Council, was Ethridge. Three technical experts were assigned to assist him. The purpose of the investigation was to determine the veracity of Greek claims that Albanian, Yugoslavian, and Bulgarian guerrillas were assisting the underground warfare being waged by Greek rebels in the northern frontier provinces .

Ethridge is a member of two fraternities, Sigma Alpha Epsilon and Sigma Delta Chi, and his clubs are Rotary, Louisville Country, Pendennis, and River Valley. In 1944 he became a vice-chairman of the new national, nonpartisan organization, Americans United for World Organization. A small, rosy-cheeked man, Ethridge is liked for his hearty informality. His soft, Southern-flavored speech, quick movements, and understanding and sincerity are frequently described by interviewers. The publisher's wife is the author Willie (Snow) Ethridge, to whom he was married on October 12, 1921. They have four children: Mary Snow, Mark Foster, Georgia Cubbedge, and William Davidson. The Ethridge home is a century-old white brick house in the Kentucky hills, where the publisher enjoys walking. Known as a hard worker, alive to the responsibilities implicit in freedom of the press, Mark Foster Ethridge has been called "a newspaperman who wears no hat, and no man's collar." He once stated, "I think any liberal position I have taken has proceeded out of my own curiosity as to how and why things happen and if they are bad what can be done about them."

References

Newsweek 26:96 O 22 '45 por
PM Mag p13-14 Je 17 '45 por
Who's Who in America, 1946-47
Who's Who in Commerce and Industry (1944)

FAIRCHILD, BENJAMIN LEWIS Jan. 5, 1863—Oct. 25, 1946 United States Republican Representative from New York in 1895-97, 1917-19, and 1921-27; conducted a law practice in New York City when not serving in Congress; as realtor, he developed areas in Westchester County towns.

Obituary

N Y Times p17 O 26 '46

FAIRFAX, BEATRICE 1878(?)—Nov. 28, 1945 American author, newspaper columnist and reporter; originated idea of advice-to-the-lovelorn column in 1898; as Marie Manning, author of many short stories and several novels; her autobiography is *Ladies Now and Then* (1944). See *Current Biography* 1944 Yearbook.

Obituary

N Y Times p23 N 30 '45 por

FALK, MAURICE Dec. 15, 1866—Mar. 18, 1946 American industrialist and philanthropist; endowed the ten-million-dollar Maurice and Laura Falk Foundation (1929) for charitable, religious, and educational purposes; director of various corporations and Jewish charities.

Obituary

N Y Times p23 Mr 20 '46 por

FALLA, MANUEL DE (fä'lyä) Nov. 23, 1876—Nov. 14, 1946 Modern Spanish composer whose impressionistic music reflects the folksongs of his native Andalusia; became recognized as the foremost Spanish composer of the time with his *Nights in the Gardens of Spain* (1916); other of his best-known compositions are the ballet *The Three-Cornered Hat* (1919) and the operas *Life Is Short* (1905) and *Master Peter's Puppet Show* (1922), the latter presented with marionettes; died in Argentina, where he had gone in 1939.

Obituary

N Y Times p23 N 15 '46

FELLER, A(BRAHAM) H(OWARD)
Dec. 24, 1904- United Nations official
Address: b. c/o United Nations, New York; h. The Brooks, Roslyn Harbor, N.Y.

Since 1929 A. H. Feller has been representing the United States Government in various capacities in affairs of national and international importance. The attorney, who appeared before the Permanent Court of International Justice at the age of twenty-four, was given the position of general counsel to the United Nations with the rank of director at the age of forty-two.

Abraham Howard Feller is a native New Yorker. Born there on December 24, 1904, to Julius and Jennie (Klein) Feller, the boy attended school in that city, being graduated from Stuyvesant High School in 1922 and from Columbia University in 1925. He had earned membership in Phi Beta Kappa in college; and at Harvard Law School, where he was awarded an LL.B. in 1928, he served as editor of the *Harvard Law Review*. After receiving his degree, he studied international law at the University of Berlin in 1929-30. In 1929, also, he became an associate at the Institute of Foreign Public Law in Berlin, remaining there until 1931. Feller worked for the Weimar Republic in their relations with the United States and in 1931 was assistant counsel for Austria in the Customs Union case, which concerned an agreement between Germany and Austria to eliminate duties on imports and exports between the two countries. Strongly objected to by France and other countries, which saw in this proposal a step toward *Anchluss,* the plan was referred to the World Court where it was declared illegal because of a 1922 Austrian pledge not to make any economic commitments that might endanger her independence.

In 1931 Feller returned to Harvard to become an instructor in international law, and in 1932 he received the Thayer Teaching Fellowship, which he held for two years. Serving as special assistant to the United States Attorney General (first Homer Cummings and later Frank Murphy [40]) from 1934 to 1940, he took active part in the antitrust prosecutions involving the motion picture, building materials, milk, optical instruments, fertilizer, aluminum, oil, and newsprint industries; drafted several Federal statutes, and participated in the defense of the constitutionality of important New Deal measures (National Recovery Act, Agricultural Adjustment Act, National Labor Relations Act, and Social Security Act). During 1937 and 1938 he was again at Harvard, as a visiting lecturer. In 1939 Feller served as counsel to the Temporary National Economic Committee. Also known as the Monopoly Committee, with Senator O'Mahoney [45] as chairman, the group's function was to investigate American business for the purpose of uprooting evils in business practice, and to attempt to discover and correct the causes of business cycles.

Feller returned to teaching as an associate professor of law at Yale University and continued his activities with the Government during his four years at New Haven. In 1941 he was also named consultant to the Lend-Lease Administration and to the National Defense Mediation Board. The latter body, which was the forerunner of the War Labor Board and the Wage Stabilization Board, acted as a voluntary arbitrator in labor disputes, and in general attempted to adjust controversies. That same year (1941) the attorney was appointed a deputy director in the Office of Facts and Figures. Because of a growing need for a central office to disseminate information as well as to collect and coordinate it, the OFF was superseded by the Office of War Information in 1942. Of the importance of such an organization, Feller, who became a deputy director in that office, wrote: "The people of this country want all the things which a Government can provide them, but they want them all to contain at all times one common ingredient—the truth. . . .Our cause is good enough and our people firm enough to enable the truth to be told. And the telling of that truth is in itself a means of prosecuting the war." In charge of OWI matters dealing with production, man power, transportation, labor, and Lend-Lease, involving coordination with nine or more Government agencies, Feller was subsequently appointed OWI's general counsel in 1943.

After two years with OWI, Feller became general counsel to the United Nations Relief and Rehabilitation Association. In this post he served as an UNRRA delegate to the International Labor Conference at Philadelphia in 1944, the International Monetary Conference at Bretton Woods in 1944, and the United Nations Conference at San Francisco in 1945. He was chief drafting officer at UNRRA's meetings during 1944 and 1945. At the conference which drew up the United Nations Charter, Feller, representing UNRRA, made contributions to the drafting of social and economic clauses; he aided the head of the United States body in strengthening the wording of the human rights clauses of the charter. In 1945 Feller was an alternate on the United States delegation to the U.N. Preparatory Commission, which discussed the status of the League of Nations and selections for a permanent U.N. headquarters. Feller was present at the first meeting of the General Assembly in London as executive assistant to Edward R. Stettinius [40], United States delegate.

(Continued next page)

A. H. FELLER

In February 1946 Trygve Lie '46, Secretary-General of the United Nations, appointed Feller to the Secretariat as general counsel. The first American appointed by Lie to his staff, Feller has the title of general counsel and director of the legal department. It is this department which advises all groups of the U.N. on legal and constitutional matters, including the drafting of agreements and rules of procedure. Under Feller the body is undertaking the codification of international law. "Over several centuries international law has developed slowly through the writings of scholars, the practice of foreign offices of Governments, the judgments of international tribunals, and the conclusion of treaties between nations," the counsel pointed out, also asserting that international law is "in the same state common law was a few hundred years ago." Feller, as a member of the Secretariat, was concerned with the finding of a temporary home for the U.N. He also worked as counsel with the Security Council's subcommittee on Spain, which was investigating the Spanish Government-in-Exile charges that the Franco '42 Government is a menace to world peace. In September 1946 Feller was delegated by the U.N. to attend the International Labor Conference at Montreal. When the U.N. chose a New York City location for its permanent headquarters, Feller, as counsel for the body, requested the United States to establish that area as an international enclave to which law-enforcement could enter only with U.N. consent.

The author of two studies (*Diplomatic and Consular Laws and Regulations of Various Countries*, with Manley Ottmar Hudson as co-editor, published in 1934, and *The Mexican Claims Commission 1923-34*, published in 1935), Feller has also contributed numerous articles to magazines, among them the *Survey Graphic*, the *Nation*, and the *Public Opinion Quarterly*. Feller has a great deal of confidence in the

success of the United Nations. "Those big meetings were like Congress. You may object to something Congress does one day and approve what it does the next, but you always have Congress—that's fundamental." "Before the Security Council even knew its procedure," he declared in a newspaper interview, "they handled four major problems. And that is good, because the United Nations will grow not by structural arrangements, but through the work it will do."

Feller is a member of the executive committee of the American Society of International Law, the American Bar Association, and the Association of the Bar of the City of New York. Of the Jewish faith, Feller can recall "with irony" that Hitler's '42 Foreign Office tried to persuade him to represent Germany before the World Court. On August 14, 1932, he was married to Alice Klein—"I met her for the first time in Grand Central Station, the way all the movies arrange such meetings." The couple, who have traveled to many places in the course of Feller's career, have one daughter, Caroline Josephine. "Short, boyish-looking . . . with a high forehead," Feller likes to read and to play golf. Most of all, he says, "I like to see people, to listen to them, to talk to them. I like small groups where you can really concentrate on talking."

References

N Y Post p29 F 26 '46
New Yorker Mr 2 '46

Who's Who in American Jewry, 1938-39
Who's Who in Commerce and Industry (1944)

FERGUSON, (GEORGE) HOWARD
June 18, 1870—Feb. 21, 1946 Canadian businessman, barrister, and Government official; served in Ontario legislature 1905-31; Minister of Lands, Forests, and Mines 1914-19, Leader of Conservatives 1920, Prime Minister 1923-31, High Commissioner for Canada in London 1931-35; chancellor of the University of Western Ontario from May 1945.

Obituary

N Y Times F 22 '46 por

FLETCHER, SIR ANGUS (SOMER-VILLE) May 13, 1883- British Government official

Address: b. British Consulate, Buffalo, N.Y.; c/o United Nations Headquarters Commission, 51 Madison Ave., New York; h. Easthampton, N.Y.

Sir Angus Fletcher, the British consul in Buffalo, New York, is chairman of the United Nations Headquarters Commission set up in May 1946 to succeed Dr. Stoyan Gavrilovic's '46 original committee. Sir Angus was chosen to head the new nine-nation group which was assigned the selection of five alternate sites for a permanent world capital, after almost twenty years of service with the British Library of Information in New York.

Angus Somerville Fletcher was born May 13, 1883, on the island of Jura, which lies off the coast of County Argyll, Scotland. His father Patrick Fletcher was a geologist, who took his family to Africa. Angus Fletcher, who thus lived many years in South and Central Africa, received his education in law at the South African College in Cape Town. During World War I he saw action under General Botha, was wounded twice, and was commissioned a lieutenant in the artillery. He served with the First Rhodesian Regiment in 1914-15 and then with the Royal Field Artillery in 1915-19. Having gained a thorough knowledge of the administration and commercial development of the South African colonies, Fletcher was sent to the United States in 1918 on a British War Mission. He remained in America after his retirement from the British Army in 1919, to serve for the next three years as an economic expert on the American research organization, the National Industrial Conference Board.

Joining the staff of the British Library of Information in New York as an assistant director in 1922, two years after its creation by Britain's Under Secretary of Foreign Affairs, Fletcher helped in the expansion of this source of British official documents maintained by His Majesty's Government in the United States. He wrote of its functions: "The library is first an insurance against the misrepresentation of matters of fact (as distinct from matters of opinion) and second an instrument for the facilitation of the processes of trade and commerce. It does not seek to stimulate interest in British affairs, but, recognizing the practical value of authoritative information to international understanding and international trade, brings to the inquirer already interested an official answer to his question." In another magazine article Fletcher further described the official Government publications or "blue books" as having a high reputation for accuracy and, "when the opportunity is offered, [achieving] worthy literary style." By 1928 well-known in library and educational circles, Fletcher assumed the directorship of the institution in that year, and, in recognition of the value of his services, was decorated by his Government as a Commander of the Order of the British Empire in 1931. Ten years later he was created a Knight Commander of St. Michael and St. George.

Upon Sir Angus' retirement from the British Library of Information in August 1941, the New York *Times* printed an editorial expressing regret: "His readiness to provide authentic information about British affairs and his unfailing courtesy in dealing with requests for information have brought him a wide circle of friends. . . .Throughout the fourteen years of his directorship he has kept the library's activities strictly in line with the purpose for which it was established." Thus it has gained a reputation for being a center of British information, and not of British propaganda, which, as the *Times* observed, "is as it should be."

Sir Angus spent 1942-43 in Boston, Massachusetts, as the British consultant for the World-Wide Broadcasting Foundation. He left that position at the end of the year to assume the post of British consul at Buffalo, the terri-

Official United Nations Photo.
SIR ANGUS FLETCHER

tory of which covers the area of western New York, including Utica, Rochester, and Syracuse. He thus opened the consular office after it had been closed since 1932. Then, in May 1946, Sir Angus was granted a leave of absence to fulfill his duties as a United Nations committee member, becoming chairman of the nine-man Headquarters Commission seeking a site for a permanent world capital. His appointment to the group came at a time when he had been unable to find better than temporary housing accommodations for himself in New York City. This second United Nations "permanent home-hunting group" was confined by its terms of reference in its search for the area extending from Fairfield County, Connecticut, to Westchester County, New York, and later to five possible sites in Westchester County. Sir Angus mentioned one of his qualifications for his assignment: "I used to be a great walker"; his excursions on foot had taken him through all of Westchester and Connecticut.

Because of protests from persons living in those areas who would be evicted from their homes, the General Assembly voted to look outside Westchester and Connecticut. Offers of free sites from Philadelphia, San Francisco (Presidio), Boston, New York (Flushing Meadows), and Westchester, and Russia's objection to San Francisco threatened a new delay, until John D. Rockefeller, Jr., offered a new, New York City site. By a vote of 46 to 7 on December 14, 1946, the U.N. voted to build its home in a strip along the East River.

Fulfilling the New York *World-Telegram*'s hope that he would have "the wisdom to recognize in his report that citizens as well as nations have veto rights," Sir Angus has taken active steps to see that the communities affected by the sites taken under consideration are consulted. He is determined, he says, to give "all

FLETCHER, SIR ANGUS—*Continued*

due and friendly consideration to the problems of displacement of residents, payment of taxes, revenues, etc., which may be involved in the selection of any particular site," gauging the reaction of the local population to the United Nations should it be established there. Following World War I, Sir Angus (then Mr. Fletcher) had made an appeal for the Old World regarding war debts which is brought up to date with one minor change: "It is a pity that in the mischief-making frame of mind, now fashionable, people can find nothing but evil in everything and everyone. . . .[The United Nations organization] is craving for human sympathy, not backbiting. Europe needs more than money, more than food, the kindly word of encouragement, the cheery smile of the strong friend, the big brother, that Americans know so well to give. Do we look to you in vain?"

Sir Angus and Lady Fletcher (who is the daughter of Archibald Stewart, also of County Argyll) are the parents of three sons—Donald, Peter, and Angus, all of whom bear the middle name of Stewart. The Briton's clubs are the Savile, in London, and the Century and Lawyers, in New York. Of Sir Angus is told "one of those 'little incidents' that probably will always epitomize cross-border friendliness long after diplomatic exchanges of international assemblages are lost in weighty verbiage." It was precipitated by his wistful remark, made to the press, that he had lost all hope of finding any old-fashioned "sliding cord" or pulley-attachment suspenders. After an exhaustive search was undertaken by New York newspapermen, a pair of bright blue and white, farmer-style galluses of 1876 vintage was duly tracked down and mailed to the amazed and delighted Sir Angus as an "international gesture."

References

N Y Herald Tribune p11 My 8 '46
N Y Times p2 Jl 20 '46

International Who's Who, 1945-46
Who's Who, 1946

FLEXNER, SIMON Mar. 25, 1863—May 2, 1946 Physician; first director of the Rockefeller Institute for Medical Research, 1904-35; won world renown by his investigations in infantile paralysis, dysentery, and meningitis; former professor at Johns Hopkins, 1895-99; Eastman Professor at Oxford University; member of numerous scientific and educational institutions.

Obituary

N Y Times p21 My 3 '46 por

FORD, HENRY, 2d Sept. 4, 1917- Industrialist

Address: b. Ford Motor Company, Dearborn, Mich.; h. Provencal Rd., Grosse Pointe, Mich.

"To put the Ford Company back into first place in production and sales" was the objective of Henry Ford 2d, who in September 1945, after only two years of executive experience, assumed the direction of the billion-dollar, family-owned Ford industrial empire, estimated by *Time* in February 1946 to consist "of twenty-one major manufacturing and assembly plants, fifteen ships, four hundred thousand acres of timber and mining property, geared into one of the world's greatest production machines"—which he speedily began to streamline in the interests of more profitable operation. Already in early 1946 he had industry and labor applauding his call for a new era in labor relations marked by joint management-union responsibility, a concept said to be as historic today as Henry Ford's "" five-dollar daily wage a quarter of a century before.

Henry Ford 2d, eldest son of the late Edsel Bryant Ford (from 1918 until his death in 1943 president of the Ford Motor Company), and grandson of the founder of the Ford automotive empire, was born in Detroit on September 4, 1917. It is recorded that at the age of three he held the torch which lit the blast furnace at the new River Rouge plant, but little else about him was allowed to attract public attention during his first years. Fear of kidnappers kept the Ford children's pictures out of the newspapers and a husky bodyguard always close by. Thus the young heir's uneventful boyhood passed in the relative seclusion of the Italian-style home of Edsel and Eleanor (Clay) Ford at 7930 East Jefferson Avenue in Detroit with his brothers and sister, Benson, William, and Josephine.

Until he took over the direction of the Ford company, it seemed to observers that the boy had inherited little of old Henry Ford's ability: not only was he not academically inclined, but he likewise lacked the compensating mechanical aptitude which had made his grandfather's career possible. At the Detroit University School, where he received his early formal education, he showed himself to be reserved, good but not outstanding in football, only average in his studies. At Hotchkiss School in Lakeville, Connecticut, which he entered in 1933 at the age of sixteen, books still bored him and he was again better on the playing field than in the classroom. While his grades on the whole remained fair, a course in Cicero was too much for him—he had to take it over in summer school. But young Ford liked Hotchkiss, particularly the school's democratic atmosphere, and his common sense apparently impressed his schoolmates, for his photograph in the 1936 yearbook was given the prophetic caption, "You've got something there if you handle it right." (While at Hotchkiss his bodyguard had been inconspicuous as a swimming instructor, said *Time*.)

The summer of 1936 found the youth in England, France, and Germany with his parents and brother Benson. He visited Ford plants in both England and France in addition to vacationing but was not, recounts Gilbert Burck in *Life*, visibly impressed until the trip back across the Atlantic, when he met "a spirited, pretty girl named Anne McDonnell," one of the fourteen children of the James Francis McDonnells of New York and Long Island society and granddaughter of Thomas E. Murray, inventor and utilities magnate. When Henry 2d went to Yale University in the fall of 1936, Anne McDonnell was still uppermost in his mind. Throughout his four years of college she occupied his attention along with his extra-curricular activities to the point where books and academic matters meant little more to him than they had during his earlier schooldays. Taking precedence, it seemed, were Zeta Psi fraternity, the Book and Snake Club, management of the Yale crew, of which he was assistant manager during his first three years and manager as a senior in 1940, and Anne McDonnell. Having a position in the Ford company already marked out as his ultimate goal, he had begun his college career as an engineering student but had, after a year's trial, changed to sociology, mostly, he said, because he found in Professor Albert Keller an instructor who "did not use highfalutin' professorial language, but the people's own language." Although, according to Burck, he "thoroughly enjoyed" this latter work, Ford pointed out in 1945 that he had "not been able to reconcile academic and practical sociology." Had he, moreover, foreseen his destiny, he averred, he would have gone directly into the company after leaving Hotchkiss. As it was, he had not earned enough credits to obtain a degree when he left Yale in June 1940.

In July 1940 the young man made society headlines when he and Anne McDonnell were married just one day after he had, with his Methodist grandfather's full approval, embraced his bride's Catholic faith, for which he had been prepared by Mgr. Fulton J. Sheen '41 of the Catholic University of America. Then, following their Hawaiian honeymoon, young Henry Ford went to work in the Rouge plant to learn the automobile business from the bottom up. As a grease monkey, wrote Burck, "he insisted on doing the dirtiest tasks and resented being treated deferentially." Later he was assigned to the dynamometer rooms and experimental shops. There, despite limited mechanical aptitude, he felt at home and displayed, according to Laurence Sheldrick, then chief engineer at Ford and young Henry's adviser, "a terrific appetite for knowledge."

But in 1941 there was no particular reason for rushing his practical education, and so, when it looked as if he might be drafted, the young man enlisted in the Navy. Commissioned an ensign, he was assigned to Great Lakes Naval Training Station as an instructor in mathematics. He seems to have taught for a short while—for there is a picture of him in the classroom in *Life*—but then to have been reassigned as assistant to the director of the training office of the Ninth Naval District, in which capacity he helped establish and equip schools under the naval training program. Of this period of his life Burck writes: "He was definitely one of the boys. According to legend, he more than once broke the strict letter of the law when he decided that the spirit would be better served if someone were not held to inflexible accounting. He himself values most highly his experience with Navy discipline. 'I learned to do what I was told to do when I was told to do it,' he explains." By this time

HENRY FORD, 2d

a lieutenant, he wanted, however, to go to sea, and had just requested a transfer when his father Edsel Ford died on May 26, 1943. Apparently the family decided to keep the company (which was still entirely Ford-owned, with 58.5 per cent of the voting stock held by the elder Henry Ford) in Ford hands rather than to promote one of its other officials. Apparently, too, the late Secretary of the Navy Frank Knox was of the opinion that the youth could serve the United States better in the war-geared Ford plants than in the Navy, for it seems to have been at Knox's suggestion that the twenty-five-year-old Ford was placed on the inactive list on July 26 and on August 1 released from the Navy.

While the senior Henry Ford, then eighty years old, resumed the management of the Ford industrial empire, his grandson was set to work learning to replace him—this time from the top down. After his release from the Navy the young man reported to the Rouge plant in Dearborn. "Everyone was away," he recollects, "so I picked myself half a desk in somebody's office. I didn't even know what all the buildings were for." Under the guidance of Charles E. Sorenson, vice-president, director, and "production genius" of the company, and of Harry Bennett, Ford's bodyguard and righthand man, Ray Rausch and Mead Bricker, production chiefs, young Ford learned rapidly, "absorbed information as a Turkish towel absorbs water," it was said. Each day he appeared at 8:00 or 8:30 at the River Rouge, Highland Park, or Willow Run plants to study, ask questions, serve his apprenticeship. Meanwhile the elder Ford tendered advice and waited for his grandson to take the initiative. Then, on January 22, 1944, he announced young Henry's election to a vice-presidency, in charge of sales and promotion. (Company officials have since given the exact date of his election as December 15, 1943. He had been nom-

FORD, HENRY, 2d—*Continued*

inally on the board of directors since December 1938.) On April 10 it was announced that he had been promoted to executive vice-president, second in command to the founder himself. Other positions were given to him in quick succession. On May 11 he was elected to the board of directors of the Automotive Council for War Production, succeeding Charles E. Sorenson. On June 30 he became a vice-president of the Ford Motor Company of Canada, Ltd., of which he had been a director since April 1943. (This Canadian vice-presidency he resigned in April 1946 in order to be able to devote full time to his Detroit interests.)

After the spring of 1944 Henry Ford stayed in the background while the younger man set about making the Ford name once more first in the automobile industry, a position which the company's lack of salesmindedness during the years of Edsel Ford's incumbency had lost to Chevrolet and Chrysler. Up to this time Ford executives had had few titles and no properly defined jobs: anyone had been asked to handle anything; all reported to the president. Henry Ford 2d promptly installed a modern vertical type of administrative structure under which each person understands the responsibility and limitations of his power and knows exactly both his supervisors and the workers under him. He reorganized the sales department, completed a tour of Ford dealers throughout the country during which he assured the "astonished representatives" that the Ford company would henceforth recognize their functions, integrated sales, manufacturing and engineering; he expanded the engineering division, established a new research department and, at a specially convened meeting of Ford supervisors from shop superintendents up, gave his men more information about the company than they had ever been given in the past and explained his postwar plans. On July 2, 1945, just two days after the WPB-authorized date for the resumption of civilian automotive production, young Ford was the first manufacturer to exhibit a 1946 car. Before strikes in the factories of the automobile parts manufacturers cut off his supply and forced him to shut down in the early fall, he had produced approximately a thousand cars.

In September the elder Ford withdrew ("The critical period during which I again assumed office has passed," he said), leaving the presidency of the company to his grandson, who took the helm on September 21, at the age of twenty-eight. Six days later Ford 2d surprised Detroit observers by again reorganizing. Out went Harry Bennett, the elder Ford's aide-de-camp and strong-arm man, especially in labor relations; others were released, shifts in position were numerous, and for the first time men were brought in from outside the company. It had been expected that some changes would occur eventually, but not during the grandfather's lifetime. Detroit drew the conclusion that young Ford had really been given a free hand. The question asked everywhere, however, was—what would he do with strikes looming throughout the automobile industry over

the United Automobile Workers' demand for a 30 per cent wage increase? He was known to be friendly toward labor. Would he therefore give the union what it demanded, or would he team up with General Motors and the Chrysler Corporation in a fight to the finish with the UAW-CIO?

Before V-J Day, pointed out the New York *Post*'s labor commentator Victor Riesel following conversations with CIO leaders, UAW-Ford negotiations had proceeded smoothly, but they had been broken off as the industrial picture changed with the necessity for reconversion. From the middle of September to the middle of October, while Ford was forced to close down because of work stoppages in supplier plants, particularly in the Kelsey-Hayes Wheel Company, management and union did not meet. With the resumption of limited production in October the new president had invited the union leaders to a conference to become better acquainted with himself and his new right-hand man, industrial relations director John S. Bugas, thereby paving the way to a resumption of collective bargaining on November 20, just one day before the General Motors employees walked out. "In an atmosphere of tense, tight-fisted, but good-humored bargaining," as *Time* Magazine expressed it, negotiations continued for nine weeks. When they ended on January 26, 1946, the union had been granted an eighteen cents an hour, or 15 per cent, wage increase, in return for which it had agreed to guarantee the company against unauthorized strikes and worker inefficiency. (Three hours later Chrysler also signed with the union, leaving only General Motors to fight it out.) Not only had Ford not been struck, but the inclusion of company security guarantees in the new contract had opened a new phase in labor relations involving the co-responsibility of labor with management.

This concept of company security had first been raised by young Henry Ford in the early stages of the bargaining in November. When the management in 1941 had granted the union a closed shop and the check-off, Ford said in presenting thirty-one proposals for labor's consideration, it had expected an equal measure of freedom from production lag and stoppage in return. Instead, production costs had been forced to a new high because of frequent wild-cat strikes and the lowest productivity per capita in the company's history. While still executive vice-president he had expressed the opinion that "the job of the automobile industry after the war is not only to build a worthwhile product but also to provide its employees with a secure existence and to educate them to further progress" and that "no wage is too high if it is earned; fifty dollars a day would not be too high, provided it was earned, but one dollar a day is too high if it isn't earned." But first it became the responsibility of labor's leaders to give "the company the same degree of security as we have given the union itself."

While industry was still applauding this dictum, the young president of the Ford Motor Company, pursuing his thesis, delivered an address which observers at once compared with his grandfather's history-making introduction of the five-dollar daily wage. Speaking at the annual meeting of the Society of Automotive Engineers in Detroit on January 9, 1946, he called upon management and labor to cooperate in solving "the problem of human relations in industrial production" raised by the perfection of the mechanical factors in mass production without regard to the effects of concentration of labor and specialization on the workers and on employer-employee relations. From management, because it is "in charge" and "must manage," he asked the initiative in attacking the problem; from labor, because it has the "authority to affect industrial production on a vast scale," he asked the acceptance of the "social obligations that go with leadership"; from both, "industrial statesmanship." "If we can solve the problem of human relations in industry," he said, "I believe we can make as much progress toward lower costs during the next ten years as we made during the past quarter century through the development of the machinery of mass production." Commented one industrialist: "the best speech I've heard in ten years"; and George F. Addes, secretary-treasurer of the UAW: "one of the greatest industrial statesmen of the auto industry."

Labor relations, however, were only one item in the thorough overhauling of company administrative personnel, policies, and plans which young Ford carried out during his first two years of executive responsibility. Stating frankly that he thought the business of the Ford Motor Company was to produce automobiles and that his aim was eventual leadership of the low-priced car field, he began divesting the Ford empire of the many side lines instituted by his grandfather. All except five of the Ford fleet of lake and ocean-going vessels not already lost in war service were placed on the market; the Ford rubber plantation on the Amazon was sold; the soybean and antibiotin research projects were abandoned; and the experimental farms in Michigan and Georgia and part of the vast timber holdings were slated for disposal. No longer were Ford profits to be drained by expensive supplementary ventures which had little to do with the manufacture of automobiles and did not pay their way. At the same time, in June 1946, Ford announced that, as soon as Government regulations would permit, construction would begin on a new eight-building technical and "human," or personnel, research center, expected to cost fifty thousand dollars and to take eight years to complete. Earlier, in April, he had announced the formation of a new division to handle, exclusively, the new light model, projected since 1940, to be introduced to the public sometime after January 1947. By August 1946, also, despite several further shutdowns caused by strikes in supplier plants, Ford production was reaching 3,550 of a 1947 goal of 5,400 cars daily, a 20 per cent increase over February figures; the ultimate goal was 8,000. In advertising, he had discontinued the Ford *Sunday Evening Hour,* the radio symphonic program so long identified with the Ford Motor Company

under his grandfather, in favor of a program featuring popular music and comedy.

Henry Ford 2d, chosen "Young Man of the Year" by the United States Junior Chamber of Commerce in January 1946, generally formulates company policy, on which he is sometimes outvoted, with the aid of a seven-man advisory board. To keep production men alert he makes it a practice to drive to and from work in a new car each day, and once, it is told, when a car door he slammed sounded tinny, went down the production line slamming one after another, with the acid comment: "Don't you know that Chevrolet salesmen take prospects over to a Ford salesroom and slam a car door. When it sounds like this they just say 'see, tin,' then take them back and sell them a Chevrolet." Young Ford, says Burck in *Life,* "does have his grandfather's bluntness and impatience with diplomatic protocol, and it is possible to imagine his becoming as arbitrary as his grandfather when he gathers experience and confidence. It is easier, however, to imagine his combining his frankness with knowledge and experience in a way that will make him an unusually able practitioner of human relations. . . .He perhaps has a little of his grandfather's habit of devising oversimple solutions to complex problems and he gets very enthusiastic about new ideas very easily. But it is hard to imagine his going off half-cocked so long as he retains his present ability to value other people's knowledge more highly than his own."

Described as "solidly built, with a full mouth, a heavy nose, and a smooth left-side part in his hair," Henry Ford 2d, unlike his rather frail grandfather, stands six feet tall and weighs 190 pounds. Lefthanded, he plays a good game of tennis and golf, is fond of skiing and hunting, is an expert horseman, having won trophies in Bar Harbor and elsewhere, and can fly his own plane. He and Anne Ford, who, it has been estimated, brought him over a hundred in-laws, are the parents of two daughters, Charlotte and Anne.

References

Fortune 29:139-144+ Je '44 il pors
Life 19:108-110+ O 1 '45 il pors
N Y Herald Tribune p1+ S 22 '45 por
N Y Times p19 S 22 '45 por
Scholastic 48:11 F 11 '46 por
Time 57:75-78+ F 4 '46 por
Who's Who in America, 1946-47

FRANK, HANS May 23, 1900—Oct. 16, 1946 Nazi Governor General of Poland from 1939 throughout World War II; head of the legal department of the National Socialist Party; commissioner of justice from 1933-35; tried by the International Military Tribunal for war crimes, judged guilty of "willing [participation] in a program involving the murder of three million Jews"; condemned and hanged. See *Current Biography* 1941 Yearbook.

Obituary

N Y Times p1+ O 16 '46

FRAZER, JOSEPH W(ASHINGTON)
Mar. 4, 1892- Industrial executive

Address: b. Kaiser-Frazer Corporation, Willow Run, Mich.; Graham-Paige Motors Corporation, Willow Run, Mich.; h. Grosse Point, Mich.

The Frazer whose name and coat of arms appear on Graham-Paige cars and tractors, and who joined Henry J. Kaiser '42 to form the "fantastic" Kaiser-Frazer Corporation, is Joseph W. Frazer. A veteran of thirty-odd years in the automotive industry, he is not a produc-

JOSEPH W. FRAZER

tion man. His background, unlike that of most car manufacturers, lies in selling and finance— of the short-lived cycle-car as well as of leading vehicles. The Frazer motto, incidentally, is *"Je Suis Prêt"*—"I Am Ready."

Born in Nashville, Tennessee, on March 4, 1892, Joseph Washington Frazer is descended through his mother, Mary (Washington) Frazer, from George Washington's great-uncle. His ancestry also includes a share of what he calls "yowling reactionaries," who "thought Washington and Tom Jefferson were wild-eyed and dangerous Bolsheviks." Joseph's father was James S. Frazer, attorney for the Louisville-Nashville Railroad, who died when his son was six weeks old. The family was well-to-do, however, and sent the boy to the Hotchkiss School in Connecticut and the Sheffield Scientific School of Yale University. Entering the engineering course with the class of 1914, he left after a year to get into the automobile industry, where "everything moved."

The young Tennesseean obtained a job in the Packard Motor Car Company's Detroit factory in 1912. Beginning as a mechanic's helper, he was paid sixteen cents an hour for a week of six twelve-hour days—"they didn't get much out of me those last two hours of

the day." One result of this experience has been his liberal and advanced labor policy. After a time, Frazer was made an instructor in the Packard factory school, but he soon left to become a salesman in the Packard agency in New York. (In November of that year, 1914, twenty-two-year-old Joseph Frazer was married to Lucille Frost of Chicago, whom he had met while at Yale.) Next he returned to Nashville to become a partner in his brother's automobile agency, and in 1916 he acquired a dealership in Cleveland.

After World War I, in 1919 Joseph Frazer joined the Export Division of General Motors Corporation. Later he became assistant treasurer of the General Motors Acceptance Corporation, handling installment financing, and then went to the Chevrolet Motor Car Company as liaison officer with GMAC. "An energetic and successful salesman," he is said to have proved "from the first, a pioneer in the evolution of automobile sales paper and one of the leading architects of the general financial structure of the industry."

In 1923, at the request of certain New York banks, General Motors loaned Frazer to Pierce-Arrow (in Buffalo) to organize the Pierce-Arrow Finance Corporation, of which he was vice-president and general sales manager. When this was done, in June 1924, he became associated with Walter P. Chrysler in the old Maxwell-Chalmers Motors Company. They had a product which, Frazer recalls, was "about as poor a vehicle as was ever sold as an automobile." Before they could start production they had a supply of 1923 Maxwells to dispose of—and, as Frazer himself has asked, "Did you ever try to sell anybody a 1923 Maxwell?" In February 1927, when Maxwell was absorbed by the Chrysler Corporation, Frazer became general sales manager of Chrysler. Later he was elected vice-president of the Chrysler sales division, and of its Plymouth and DeSoto divisions. In 1930, incidentally, the Plymouth accounted for only 28 per cent of Chrysler's sales. In 1931 it was 41 per cent, in 1932— the year of its graduation into the company of the Ford and Chevrolet—it was 58 per cent, and in 1933 it reached 72 per cent. "Sales and production records have been broken with such monotonous regularity that it is needless to enumerate the breakage," wrote *Business Week*, which listed Frazer among some able lieutenants to the captains who engineered the corporation's rise.

After fifteen years with Chrysler, the forty-six-year-old Tennessean was elected president of Willys-Overland Motors, Inc., makers of low priced cars, and moved to Toledo to assume his duties in January 1939, taking along M. J. Golden and some other Chrysler executives. "No motor maker has made greater progress," commented *Sales Management* in June 1940. "In this year and a half Joe Frazer and his associates have transformed a foundering, largely demoralized outfit into a vigorous sales contender and a profitable business. . . . This has been done by retaining and revitalizing what was best of the old organization, by harnessing it to sounder policies, and then by expanding." When Frazer took over, Willys had little capital, many debts, unbalanced inventory—and less time to work out new models than usual, because the 1939 automobile shows were to be held early. By June all Willys' bank loans were paid off; in August the first models were shown to dealers and distributors; in September came private showings in larger cities; and by the time of the national shows in October, production was up to four thousand cars a month, and Willys showed its first profit in nearly two years. Then, in the first four months of the 1940 model year, Willys sold two and one-half times as many units as it had sold throughout the entire 1939 model year. Aware that "two-thirds of the cars on the road today are driven by people making less than $2,000 a year," Frazer emphasized the economy of Willys, "the lowest price standard size car in the world." When World War II broke out, he was busy getting an unusually low-weight and low-cost car established, but he laid these plans aside and converted all Willys-Overland facilities to war work within a few months after Pearl Harbor. According to the *American Machinist,* he was the first automobile manufacturer to do so.

Frazer's publicity agents did an effective job in making known Willys' connection with the rugged jeep. Not many people are aware that credit for the earliest pilot models must be shared with the Army Quartermaster Corps and the American Bantam Company, and credit for production, with Ford. Apart from this, however, the jeep may properly be credited to Willys' chief engineer, Vice-President Delmar ("Barney") Roos, working under Frazer's administration. From June 1941 the Willys president also served the Government as one of an unpaid but busy committee of eleven leading truck- and auto-makers assisting the Office of Production Management, later the War Production Board. (One of his fellow members was Paul G. Hoffman [46], president of Studebaker and later chairman of the Committee for Economic Development.) According to a report which Frazer submitted to the War Production Board in early 1942, questionnaires returned by some four thousand dealers revealed an untapped supply of machinery, skilled mechanics, and manufacturing space in the nation's small manufacturing shops.

The name of J. W. Frazer appeared in the news, too, in July 1942, when the House Military Affairs Committee investigated his complaint that the self-propelling anti-tank guns ordered by the Army were inferior to his company's; and in December 1942, when he declared to reporters that Henry J. Kaiser's plan for war bond payments on future cars was "the craziest thing I ever heard. We don't like a West Coast shipbuilder coming here to New York to tell us how to run our business," Frazer added. "Let him stick to his ships."

Frazer's 1942 salary of $123,183.80 was more than twice the sixty thousand dollars he earned in 1940. In less than five years under his administration, Willys' nine-million-dollar yearly business and eleven hundred employees had risen on the flood of war orders to one hundred seventy million dollars worth of business and sixteen thousand employees. (The company

was to reach its peak of two hundred and twelve million in 1944.) But Frazer's postwar plans disagreed with those of board chairman Ward M. Canaday, and in September 1943 he resigned, to be succeeded by Charles Sorenson of Ford.

In January 1944 Frazer was asked to help an Ohio war plant, the Warren City Tank and Boiler Company, which was having production trouble. He formed and became president of the Warren City Manufacturing Company, which took over the old company's assets, including a five-year lease on its nine-million-dollar, Navy-built plant. Capitalized at five hundred dollars—the legal minimum—Frazer's new company received a four-million-dollar loan from the Reconstruction Finance Corporation, guaranteed by the Navy. Frazer himself lent the company fifty thousand dollars, kept a controlling interest of 252 shares (par, one dollar) for himself and his family, and sold the rest to old business associates. Under his direction, Warren City's production quadrupled, rising to nearly two million dollars a month. After a few months, Frazer and some New York associates acquired 6 per cent of the Graham-Paige Motor Corporation (265,000 shares). Simultaneously, the Warren City company was sold to Graham-Paige, the owners receiving 150,000 shares of Graham common stock in exchange for 150,000 shares of Warren common stock. At current market value, this meant that $1,087.50 profit had been made in those few months on every share of Warren stock, or that an original investment of five hundred dollars was now worth one million. Frazer became the chairman of the board. "Some $540,000 belongs to Joe Frazer and family," *Time* reported, "and if he decides to sell out he pays not a sky-high income tax, but only a moderate capital gains tax of 25 per cent." (Frazer also took options to purchase several hundred thousand shares of Graham common at below-market prices.) He was elected chairman of the board of directors, serving without salary the first year.

"Getting back into the passenger automobile business will be a bigger job for Graham-Paige Motors Corporation than for companies which were building cars when the war started," *Barron's* financial weekly reported in May 1945. "It will be necessary to make a complete installation of facilities, and to obtain the necessary tools and dies for an entirely new model. It will take about six months longer for it to get back into peacetime production than the average. . . .Graham-Paige was able to carry to profit a substantial part of income in the past three years because of either loss carry-overs or unused excess-profits-tax credits, but no such unused credit is available for 1945 or subsequent years." (Graham's 1944 business had come to something over forty-three million dollars.) In the fall of 1944, Board Chairman Frazer announced that the company planned to enter the lower-priced car field. Graham would first produce farm implements, especially a flame-throwing weed killer and a Swiss-invented soil mixer called the Rototiller, which was planned to supersede the plow.

(Continued next page)

FRAZER, JOSEPH W.—*Continued*

After V-E Day, in the spring of 1945, Frazer looked for capital with which to expand Graham-Paige. Finally he met Henry Kaiser, who wanted to get into the automobile business, and within two days (according to a *Life* article by William Chapman White), plans for the Kaiser-Frazer Corporation were drawn up. The Kaiser interests and Graham-Paige were each to put in two and one-half million dollars, taking one-dollar-par shares at ten dollars each. Instead of merging, the new corporation would exist side by side with the old, using the same manufacturing, distributing, selling and servicing facilities as far as possible. Kaiser-Frazer would begin by making one product, the lightweight, low-priced Kaiser car; Graham-Paige would make the larger medium-priced Frazer car, and also produce agricultural machinery, including a Frazer tractor. Chairmanship of the board went to Kaiser, and the presidency to Frazer; as a preliminary, in July 1945 Frazer became president of Graham-Paige. His salary was reported at the time as $75,000, but White gave it, in late 1945, as $82,500 a year.

Kaiser-Frazer negotiated with the RFC for the use of its hundred-million-dollar, ninety-six-acre bomber plant at Willow Run—and Graham-Paige leased its old site to the RFC's Surplus Property Division for storage space. According to the Kaiser-Frazer prospectus, its operations would at first be limited to assembling the new car, with outside suppliers finishing parts and sections, including motors. No production was expected for at least six months, the offering was frankly labeled a risk, and yet a public offering of 1,700,000 shares, at ten times par value, was quickly oversubscribed by 650 per cent. "It's only with awe," wrote financial columnist Sylvia F. Porter, "that we can report the spectacle of thousands of presumably sane people scrambling to risk their savings in a new automobile company which hasn't even sold a single car." Another 1,800,000 shares, put on the market at $20.25 in January 1946, was oversubscribed within an hour. (Five thousand of them were bought by Frazer.) Yet the states of Michigan and Ohio had forbidden its sale, because the company had not earned any money since the first offering.

At the same time, nearly nine thousand orders for Kaiser and Frazer cars were placed within four days at prices yet to be approved by the OPA, by persons who had only seen the cars at a showing in New York, for which long lines of people waited in rain and snow outside the showrooms. The industrialists by this time had contracts with four thousand dealers, had signed an unprecedentedly generous contract with the various unions involved, and had "outlined, engineered, located, and designed" their own multimillion-dollar strip steel mill. "If we can't buy steel we'll have to make it," Frazer explained, and Kaiser added, "if there is no steel available, we'll try using glass plastics and aluminum."

The first Kaiser-Frazer production models appeared in dealers' showrooms in June 1946. The company expected to be able to produce six to nine thousand units by October and to increase monthly production to thirty thousand by March 1947. Like other automobile manufacturers, the Kaiser-Frazer Company was handicapped by shortages of basic raw materials. According to Frazer, a further handicap was "Governmental interference," which caused "industrial stagnation." The OPA established maximum retail prices for the Kaiser-Frazer automobiles in September 1946: $1,645 for the Frazer special four-door sedan and $1,795 for the de luxe Kaiser special. The construction of seven stamping presses for body parts at the Willow Run plant will increase production of these cars, since it will enable the company itself (rather than sub-contractors) to manufacture about 50 per cent of the fenders, doors, tops, and other parts.

A broad-shouldered man, largely bald, Frazer has "pixyish" blue eyes in a ruddy face, and a gray mustache. He is just under six feet tall, weighs two hundred and ten pounds, and is said to have "the build and energy of a plunging fullback, the freedom of speech of an impassioned coach at half-time," and "a lusty and ruddy charm that pulled men from jobs in the big motor companies to follow him to the empty spaces and mammoth hopes of Willow Run."

The Frazers, who have one daughter (widowed Mrs. Michael Strutt), live in a home in fashionable Grosse Point ("not lavish compared to other millionaire homes in that suburb"), and in 1945 Frazer became the only Detroit automobile magnate to own a Newport villa. His extra-industrial business interests have been few, except for a directorship of the Plaza Hotel in New York, writes William Chapman White, and he has had "the hobbies of a wealthy man: ranching in Arizona and a farm in Ohio where he raised walking horses." A hearty eater and drinker, convivial and congenial with all sorts of people, Frazer likes Rafael Sabatini adventure stories for his reading, and golf for recreation—"never broke a hundred in my life." The quotation, "Security is but an illusion, repose is not the destiny of man," is often on his lips.

References

Automotive Industries 80:5 Ja 28 '39 por
Life 19:72-9 D 31 '45 pors
Mag of Wall Street 71:485 F 6 '43 por
N Y Post Mag p33 Ja 30 '46
N Y Sun p32 D 8 '42; p18 N 19 '45
Borth, C. Masters of Mass Production (1945)
Who's Who in America, 1946-47
Who's Who in Commerce and Industry (1944)

FRICK, WILHELM Mar. 12, 1877—Oct. 16, 1946

Nazi Minister of the Interior from 1933 to 1943; Reich Protector of Bohemia and Moravia, 1943-45; tried by the International Military Tribunal, judged "largely responsible for bringing the German nation under the complete control of the Nazi party . . . for the legislation which suppressed trade unions, the church, and the Jews"; condemned and hanged. See *Current Biography* 1942 Yearbook.

Obituary

N Y Times p1+ O 16 '46

FRY, FRANKLIN CLARK, REV. Aug. 30, 1900- Clergyman

Address: b. c/o United Lutheran Church in America, 231 Madison Ave., New York; h. 57 Wellington Ave., New Rochelle, N. Y.

Dr. Franklin Clark Fry is president of the United Lutheran Church in America, an organization formed in 1918 with the merger of three Lutheran bodies, the General Synod, General Council, and United Synod of the South, and representing one and a quarter million church members. He is one of the youngest men to reach so high a place in church organization. Dr. Fry was one of three church leaders who went to Europe in 1945 to ascertain what steps Christian churches could take to fill the need for clothing, food, and medical supplies in war-torn countries.

The Fry family came to one of the first Lutheran settlements in America, to Trappe, Pennsylvania, early in the 1700's. Jacob Fry, grandfather of Franklin Clark, was ordained a Lutheran minister and in his sixty-seven years of service became known as a "distinguished son of the old Trappe Church." Jacob Fry was also professor of homiletics and pastoral theology at Mt. Airy Seminary, in Philadelphia. When Franklin Clark Fry was born in Bethlehem, Pennsylvania, on August 30, 1900, his father, Dr. Franklin Foster Fry, had been a Lutheran minister for twelve years; he later became the first executive secretary of the Board of American Missions of the United Lutheran Church in America. Franklin Clark's mother, the former Minnie Clark McKeown, was Mrs. Minnie Stormfeltz at the time of her marriage to Dr. Fry.

Young Franklin attended East High School, in Rochester, New York, where his father had become pastor of the Church of the Reformation. At seventeen he entered Hamilton College, in Clinton, New York, from which in 1921 he received the B.A. degree. A year of postgraduate work followed in Greece, at the American School for Classical Studies in Athens, where he was considered one of their most able students of Greek. Upon his return to the United States, Fry entered the Philadelphia Lutheran Seminary and three years later, on June 10, 1925, was ordained by the Lutheran Synod of New York and New England at Ithaca, New York. In addition to his D.D. degree from Muhlenberg College (Allentown, Pennsylvania), the clergyman holds several honorary degrees: an L.H.D. from Roanoke College (Salem, Virginia), Litt. D. from Wagner College (Staten Island, New York), and LL.D. from Wittenberg College (Springfield, Ohio), Thiel College (Greenville, Pennsylvania), and Gettysburg College (Gettysburg, Pennsylvania). In 1946 he was presented with an additional honorary D.D. by his alma mater, Hamilton College. Dr. Fry's other academic connections are his membership in Phi Beta Kappa, as well as his four-year service on the directorate of Wittenberg College between 1934 and 1938.

Dr. Fry's first pastorate was the Lutheran Church of the Redeemer, in Yonkers, New York. In the four years (1925-29) the young

REV. FRANKLIN CLARK FRY

pastor held that charge he became recognized as a brilliant speaker as well as a spiritual leader. After accepting the call to the congregation of Trinity Lutheran Church in Akron, Ohio, he remained there from 1929 to 1944. His career in church administration began soon after he came to Akron. From 1930 to 1938 he acted as secretary of the United Lutheran Church committee on evangelism; from 1934 to 1942 as a member of its board of American missions; and from 1942 to 1944 as a member of the executive board. In 1944 Dr. Fry also served as chairman of the examining committee of the Synod of Ohio.

The presidency of the United Lutheran Church in America, to which Fry was elected October 12, 1944, is a full-time, salaried position. The president is elected biennially. Thirty-two synods, as of 1945, represented a total adult membership of 1,250,000 in the United States and Canada. (Altogether, in the two countries there are over five million adherents of the church Martin Luther established.) Not included in the United Lutheran Church are the Scandinavian-descended American Lutheran Conference and the "ultra-conservative" Missouri Synod. When some five hundred U. L. C. A. delegates met at Minneapolis for the 1944 convention, they elected Dr. Fry president on the fourth ballot. Seventy-four-year-old Dr. Frederick H. Knubel, who had held the office since the unification of the churches in 1918, was chosen president emeritus for life. The comment of the Philadelphia *Inquirer* on the change in leadership was: "It was the consensus of the leaders that it was prompted by the increasing pressure of church activity . . . and the need for younger men to handle it." The induction ceremony of Dr. Fry as president took place on the following January 10, 1945.

As the representative of two commissions—the American Section of the Lutheran World

FRY, FRANKLIN CLARK—*Continued*

Convention and the Federal Council of the Churches of Christ in America—Dr. Fry made an inspection trip through Europe's war-devastated countries in 1945. With Bishop G. Bromley Oxnam [*], president of the Federal Council of Churches of Christ in America, and Bishop Henry Knox Sherrill, chairman of the General Commission of Army and Navy Chaplains, the Lutheran clergyman visited Denmark, France, Holland, Germany, and Switzerland. Upon their return the three clergymen joined those who were urging the Administration to send clothes, especially, to Germany since UNRRA did not operate in that country. On February 20, 1946, President Truman recognized the Council of Relief Agencies Licensed for Operation in Germany as the authorized agency for shipping contributions. Members of the council represented service and relief organs of American Christian churches of all faiths, as well as the A.F. of L. and the CIO.

The Lutheran leader opened the 1946 National Lutheran Council's campaign to raise ten million dollars for war relief and rehabilitation. (The council, formed during World War I, brings together the leaders of about two thirds of the American Lutherans for periodical consultation and action on matters of common concern.) The new program stressed the need for spiritual reconstruction in Europe. Defined in the New York *Times,* it included "efforts to restore and strengthen the ministry, alleviate the shortage of religious literature, replace ruined churches with temporary structures, provide offices and living quarters for missionary personnel, and equip clergy and lay officials of the church."

In midsummer of 1946 Dr. Fry was among the four clergymen representing the United States at a meeting of the Executive Committee of the Lutheran World Convention in Upsala, Sweden. The purpose of the meeting was to restore the convention "as the cooperative agency of Lutheran Churches in twenty-eight countries." Subsequently, he visited Poland, Hungary, and Finland, to return in August with a report that Europe would face its worst siege of hunger in the winter of 1946-47.

On October 5, 1946, Dr. Fry was re-elected to the presidency of the U.L.C. at its fifteenth biennial convention in Cleveland. In his opening address the clergyman spoke against an "artificial union of churches" without a solid basis of agreement on the meaning of the gospels and the sacraments. Referring specifically to the Communists and the conflict of ideologies today, Fry said that "a bright facade of union of churches" would deceive no one. On the contrary, he stated, Communists could only scoff at such an artificial front.

A frequent radio speaker, Dr. Fry appeared in May 1946 on a Town Hall program, "Are Church Creeds Essential to a Religious Life?" Broadcasting with a rabbi and a Roman Catholic priest, Dr. Fry maintained, "If anyone will look carefully at the church creeds before condemning them, he will see that they are simply a recital of the acts of God. In my judgment, there can't be a religion worthy of the name that is not based on God. . . . I firmly believe that the one thing America needs most religiously is a vertebrate religion. It needs a spine up the back that will hold the body together." Dr. Fry is a contributor to several books, which include *Great Sermons by Young Preachers, Sermons on George Washington, From Throne to Cross, Calling All Christians,* and *A Faith for These Times,* as well as to *Christendom,* an ecumenical review.

Dr. Fry holds a number of other posts in church organizations. He is president of World Relief, a member of the department of reconstruction and interchurch aid of the World Council of Churches, of the Church Committee for Relief in Asia, of the Church Committee for Overseas Relief and Reconstruction. In 1927 he was married to Hilda Adrianna Drewes. The family, in which there are three children (Franklin Drewes, Robert Charles, and Constance Hilda), lives in a suburban community of New York. The "Smiling Bishop", as he was called by his European associates, has been compared to Charles Laughton in the actor's more dignified and benign roles. He is a little over six feet in height, weighs 220 pounds, and has brown hair and brown eyes. A baseball fan, the minister is a strong supporter of the Yankees.

References

N Y Sun p30 N 28 '45
Who's Who in America, 1946-47

GAG, WANDA (gŏg) Mar. 11, 1893—June 27, 1946 Artist, author; wrote and illustrated *Millions of Cats* (1928), *The Funny Thing* (1929), *Snippy and Snappy* (1932), *The ABC Bunny* (1933), and *Gone Is Gone* (1936); illustrated her own translation of *Snow White and the Seven Dwarfs* (1938), from the original Grimm tale; represented as etcher and lithographer in many museums and other institutions in the United States and Europe; her autobiography, *Growing Pains,* was published in 1940.

Obituary

N Y Times p21 Je 28 '46 por

GALEN, CLEMENS AUGUST, CARDINAL, COUNT VON (gä'lĕn) 1878—Mar. 22, 1946 German Catholic prelate; leading anti-Nazi; Bishop of Münster from October 1933; elevated to College of Cardinals in February 1946; as a Monsignor, was president of the Berlin Workers Circle.

Obituary

N Y Times p13 Mr 25 '46 por

GALLAGHER, WILLIAM J. May 13, 1875—Aug. 13, 1946 United States Representative from Minnesota on the Democratic-Farmer-Labor Party ticket from 1945 until his death; before his election he was a pensioned Minneapolis street cleaner.

Obituary

N Y Times p25 Ag 14 '46 por

GALLICO, PAUL (WILLIAM) (găl'lĭ-kō)
July 26, 1897- Author; journalist

Address: b. c/o Harold Ober, 40 E. 49th St., New York; h. Sandy Ridge Farm, Stockton, N. J.

Paul Gallico, prolific writer of fiction and screen plays, whose unused middle name is William, was born in a New York City boarding house on July 26, 1897. His parents, Paolo and Hortense (Ehrlich) Gallico, were immigrants who loved their adopted country "naively but passionately." Paolo Gallico, a native of Trieste, had been to America at the age of fourteen, when he made his first appearance as a concert pianist in New York City. Returning a decade later as solo pianist with leading American symphony orchestras, he finally settled in New York as a teacher of the piano and composition. The Gallicos took little Paul on travels in what he recalls as "a luscious, rich, enchanting Europe, friendly and trusting, warm and gay, simple and colorful."

After attending New York City schools, Paul worked his way through Columbia College of Columbia University at a variety of jobs. A tall, sturdy youth, he helped load and unload ships at North River piers, worked in a library, was usher at the Metropolitan Opera House, a munitions plant worker, a gymnasium instructor, a tutor of German; and he wrote fiction for pulp magazines and newspapers. In his "spare time," he was a cheerleader, joined in several sports, rowed on the eight-man Columbia crew for four years, and captained it in his senior year. His studies were interrupted by service in the World War I Navy as a seaman gunner, but he finally received his B.S. in 1921. His first position was as review secretary for the National Board of Motion Picture Review.

That September the burly twenty-four-year-old athlete was married to redheaded newspaperwoman Alva Taylor. She was the daughter of Bert Leston Taylor, the Chicago *Tribune*'s best-known columnist. (By this marriage, which ended in divorce in 1934, there are two children, William Taylor and Robert Leston.) Bert Taylor's son-in-law was welcomed by the *Tribune*'s "cousin," the tabloid New York *Daily News*, which engaged him as motion picture reviewer in 1922. Not long afterwards Gallico was transferred to the sports department, and in 1924 he was promoted to sports editor and columnist, a position he held for twelve years. For a time, too, Gallico was assistant managing editor.

As a cub sportswriter, Gallico was sent to the camp where Jack Dempsey[45] was training for the Luis Firpo fight. Never having boxed before, Gallico asked the heavyweight champion to box a round with him. When it was over, the writer recalls, "I knew all that there was to know about being hit in the prize ring." During the next years, nevertheless, he made it his business to contest in nearly every sport he had not already tried—a total of some three dozen, including piloting airplanes—and also persuaded star players in various fields to let him play against them. Tennis with Vinnie Richards; golf with Bob Jones, Gene Sarazen,

PAUL GALLICO

and Tommy Armour; swimming against Johnny Weissmuller, Helene Madison, Eleanor Holm; trying to catch and hit the pitches of Dizzy Dean, Dazzy Vance, and Herb Pennock; skiing down an Olympic run at Garmisch-Partenkirchen; receiving the football passes of Benny Friedman; racing in Gar Wood's speedboat, Cliff Bergere's auto, and Lieutenant Al Williams' plane—all were included in Paul Gallico's self-education in "how it feels," and in the columns he wrote. Somewhere in his career, too, he promoted and staged an unsuccessful canoe marathon around Manhattan Island.

"Some sportswriters build up a following by the accuracy of their forecasts," says Gallico. "I built mine up by being wrong much more often than right. I didn't have to fake it. I just was. And then admitted it, worried over it, and marveled that I should not have seen what was apparently obvious to many thousands of readers." Gallico first suggested one of the most successful promotional activities of the *News*, the annual Golden Gloves amateur boxing tournament. Started in 1927, it was the first to prevent the matching of newcomers with more experienced lads. The sports editor shepherded the winning teams to Chicago each year for the big Inter-City championship bouts against the *Tribune*'s winners, an experience which helped to create in him a smoldering anger against Jim-Crowism.

By 1936 Paul Gallico was reportedly the highest-paid sports writer in New York, a field that included Damon Runyon, Grantland Rice, Westbrook Pegler, and Gallico's boyhood idol, W. O. McGeehan. Besides many articles, including some ghosted for Max Schmeling, he had had fourteen short stories printed in the *Saturday Evening Post* and one in the *American Magazine* since 1932. One of them, "Wedding Present," was bought by Paramount Pictures. (By this time, too, Gallico had been married to and divorced from Elaine St. Johns,

GALLICO, PAUL—*Continued*

daughter of the writer Adela Rogers St. Johns.) In 1936 Gallico left the *News* to become a free-lance fiction writer. His last assignment took him to the Reichs Sports Stadion in Berlin to cover the last Olympic games before Europe was plunged into World War II.

As a workplace, Gallico had chosen a small fishing village on the English Channel coast, where he spent three summers writing. In January 1937 he asked for and got a seventy-dollar-a-week job as a reporter attached to the *News* city desk, as he wished to round out his newspaper career by covering assignments like the Fisher Bodies strike in Detroit. After four months he went back to England, and continued to alternate summers of writing with winters of reporting for the International News Service. For Hearst's *Cosmopolitan* Magazine he wrote twenty-six chapters of reminiscences, *Farewell to Sport*. When Alfred A. Knopf put it between book covers in 1938, the New York *Times's* Robert Van Gelder called it "racy, thoroughly readable, and steadily interesting," while J. R. Tunis commented in the *Saturday Review of Literature*, "He is wrong sometimes, inaccurate sometimes (who of us isn't?) but dull, never." *Farewell to Sport* went into six printings, was published in Canada also, and in August 1945 Pocket Books gave it a test printing of a hundred thousand copies for distribution on the Eastern seaboard.

One of Gallico's stories was used in Columbia Pictures' *No Time to Marry* (1938), and eight of his humorous golf tales were collected as *Golf Is A Friendly Game* (1942), reaction to which seems to have varied with the reviewer's interest in golf. (This book was also published in Canada.) From January 1937 to March 1946 thirty-six of Gallico's stories and seventeen of his articles were printed in the *Saturday Evening Post, Collier's*, the *American Magazine, Good Housekeeping*, and the *Reader's Digest* (its October 1936 issue carried two Gallico reprints, from *Vogue* and the *American Legion Monthly*). His by-line appeared frequently in other magazines, too, including the *New Yorker, Esquire, Liberty, True*, and the *Cosmopolitan*. A whole series of his *Post* stories was built around the amusing plotting and mishaps of Swing and Audrey, two light-hearted Chicago debutantes. *Cosmopolitan*, on the other hand, ran his Hiram Holliday stories, which Knopf also published in book form. Gallico is said to have received as much as five thousand dollars for one story.

The Adventures of Hiram Holliday (1939) was pure escape fiction, in which a newspaper proofreader became involved in romance and international intrigue while on a European vacation. Lisle Bell in the *Herald Tribune Book Section* termed it "a rich chronicle of adventure, a swift panorama of events in half-a-dozen capitals of Europe in the months when the continent was edging toward the war . . . as crisp as an eyewitness report." The book was published in New York, in Toronto, and in London, where the *Times Literary Supplement* remarked, "the novel is an altogether unusual one, with a plot that flouts realism in the

grand romantic manner." Hiram Holliday was a foreign correspondent in *The Secret Front* (1940) which was similarly received as "frankly fantastic episodes which add up to a first class adventure yarn." Reprint editions of these books were also published in 1941 and 1942.

Quite different was *The Snow Goose* (1940), a technically difficult story of a hunchback, the girl he inarticulately loved, and the white goose which flew over his rescue craft at Dunkerque. As a short story, it was printed in the *Saturday Evening Post*, was chosen by Herschel Brickell for honorable mention as one of the *O. Henry Memorial Prize Stories of 1941*, and was adapted for broadcast on the *Treasury Star Parade* and reprinted in script form. It was issued in the English-speaking countries as a fifty-four-page-book, which William Lyon Phelps called "a little masterpiece both in its characters and in its style . . . a work of calm beauty all the more remarkable in these days of hell on earth." Robert Van Gelder's comment was "This is perhaps the most sentimental story that ever has achieved the dignity of a Borzoi imprint. It is a timely legend that makes use of every timeless appeal that could be crowded into it." *The Snow Goose* proved to be the most popular Gallico book, selling over three hundred thousand copies in the United States. "The Roman Kid" (1938), although not a mystery story in the strict sense of the term, was later reprinted in *Great American Detective Stories* (1945), giving reviewer Kurt Steel a chance to call it "the most brilliantly original story in the whole canon of American sportswriting."

"Simple, moving" plots for several screen plays have come from Gallico's typewriter. Besides an unproduced co-starring vehicle for Clark Gable and Mickey Rooney, he wrote *Joe Smith, American* (1942) for MGM, and *The Pride of the Yankees* (1942) for Samuel Goldwyn. The latter, a biography of the late Lou Gehrig printed in a fifty-cent edition that year, Gallico saw as a love story rather than a baseball story, treating the sport simply as his hero's profession. Paul and Pauline Gallico (Baroness Pauline Gariboldi, whom he married in February 1939) wrote the story of MGM's *The Clock* (1945) for Robert Walker and Judy Garland. Paul thought so little of this "thundering bit of cinematic sleeping potion" that he wrote in his monthly *Esquire* article, "There is no one at fault but the Missus and myself. We are ashamed of ourselves." The reviewers overruled him, using such phrases as "the simple and poignant love story", "sincere and touching", "charming", "tender and refreshingly simple"; and the picture made a fortune at the box office. At various times, the Gallicos have been reported as writing a musical for Vera Zorina.

In the summer of 1944 Paul Gallico was appointed European editor and war correspondent of *Cosmopolitan*. The author went to France to gather material for articles on the Maquis and the Allied troops fighting there; he was at the front at one time when, he recalls, "there was nothing between our side and the German Army except Ernest Hemingway." William

Randolph Hearst also sought Gallico for his Sunday newspaper magazine, the *American Weekly*, on which there reportedly was a "no limit" price policy for popular writers.

The ex-reporter is represented in several story collections; "What We Talked About" is his contribution to *While You Were Gone* (1946). He has also lectured on how to write, and on one of his pet topics, "Women and How to Improve Them." His frequently expressed opinion, that the United States is a matriarchy and its women are "a mess," seems to amuse rather than offend female audiences. (Of one 1943 lecture tour, Gallico said, "when a house full of thirteen thousand women laughs the way they did in St. Paul, the ham oozes out of me.") The lecturer added that he did not think his female characters were good—"Most of them are male wish projections."

Confessions of a Story Writer (1946) is the title of an anthology for which Gallico selected twenty-four of his own stories and novelettes to represent his best work at various phases of his development as a writer and in various styles of magazine fiction. The "confessions" of the title are explanatory comments telling how each story was conceived, developed, written, edited, and ultimately published. The work also includes a sixteen-page autobiography. At the end of 1946 plans were being completed for a radio series *Story—by Gallico*, featuring the writer as master of ceremonies; he will adapt his own stories for the series.

Paul Gallico is big and "bull-necked." Photographers never catch the six-foot-three-inch author without horn-rimmed glasses, and practically never without a pipe or cigarette; and interviewers who find him at home also find one or more dogs or cats. Gallico's favorite spectator sport is baseball; he likes to ski and still rides, flies, swims, plays golf—and admits that he has been sales-talked into buying several sets of golf clubs at different times, although he knows that one should last a lifetime. In addition to sets of golf clubs, he also collects symphonic records. "My wife and I are both very fond of deepsea fishing," the writer has also said, "and have an amazing amount of expensive equipment which we never get to use." They also share enthusiasm for fencing and dancing, particularly the rhumba, samba, and waltz. A member of the Authors' Guild, in 1946 he was elected to their thirty-man council. Gallico is also a member of the New York Athletic Club, the Dutch Treat Club, and the Quiet Birdmen. In 1941 the Gallicos bought an old 144-acre New Jersey farm, complete with ghost.

References

Esquire 19:22 My '43 por
N Y Post Mag p3 N 16 '46 por
Scholastic 42:17 Mr 8-13 '43 por
Time 30:45-6 D 13 '37 por
Gallico, P. Confessions of a Story Writer (1946); Farewell to Sport (1938)
Who's Who in America, 1946-47

GARNSEY, ELMER ELLSWORTH (gärn'sĭ) Jan. 24, 1862—Oct. 26, 1946 American artist; decorated many private homes and public buildings, including the Library of Congress; awarded a bronze medal as one of the designers of the Chicago Exposition of 1893; received a silver medal and honorable mention for his decoration of the United States Pavilion at the Paris Exposition of 1900.

Obituary

N Y Times p26 O 29 '46 por

GASCH, MARIE MANNING. *See* Fairfax, B.

GASPERI, ALCIDE DE (gäs-pĕ'rē äl-chē'dĕ) Apr. 3, 1881- Italian Premier

Address: b. Palazzo Viminale, Rome; h. 21 Via Bonifacio VIII, Rome

Prime Minister of Italy and leader of one of his country's strongest political parties is Alcide de Gasperi, whose name has been connected with Italian politics since his youth. The eldest of four sons of a minor Government official, he was born on April 3, 1881, in the Italian-speaking portion of the southern Tyrol called Trentino by Italians. The province, then under Austrian rule, was, during Gasperi's youth, the center of pro-Italian agitation on the part of the local political party Italia Irredenta (Unredeemed Italy); and at the age of seventeen De Gasperi joined the movement. A few months later, and again in 1904, as a result of his participation, he spent a short period in jail, as did other young Irredentists, but this did not deter him from continuing the struggle for Italian minority rights. After graduation from the University of Vienna, by which he was awarded a degree in modern philology in 1905 (he now speaks fluent French, German, and English), he became editor of the Trento Irredentist newspaper *Il Nuovo Trentino*, a post he filled for approximately the next five years.

In 1911 De Gasperi was elected by the Irredentist population of Trento to the Austrian parliament. There he fought openly for Italian minority rights until, after May 1915 when Italy repudiated the Triple Alliance and declared war on Austria-Hungary, he protested Austria's counterdeclaration of war against Italy; according to an official information bulletin, he was imprisoned by Austria for two years, but from a summary of his career in *World Report* it appears that technically he remained a member of the Austrian parliament until 1918. And also between 1914 and 1918 he helped organize an underground Italian National Committee in Vienna.

The Versailles Treaty of 1919 awarded Trentino to Italy. As an Italian, De Gasperi then joined the Popular, or Catholic, Party, organized that year by Luigi Sturzo. Two years later, in 1921, he presided over its congress and was elected to the Italian Chamber of Deputies under its banner. He remained a member of parliament—in opposition—until 1924, while conditions described as resembling

ALCIDE DE GASPERI

anarchy prevailed: as the communists and extreme socialists expropriated estates and introduced their economic reforms unopposed by the Government (in 1921 and 1922); and, after October 30, 1922, while Mussolini seized control of the Government and assumed dictatorial powers. When in 1924 Mussolini, in his first moves to crush all political opposition, exiled Sturzo, De Gasperi became acting secretary of his party. Finally, after an unsuccessful concerted parliamentary revolt of a hundred deputies and an appeal to King Victor Emmanuel '43 had failed, he was forced to leave the political scene, and retired to the Tyrol to do research and to write.

In 1926 an attempt on Mussolini's life was followed by more repressive measures on the part of the Fascists. De Gasperi, among those hunted, fled the police only to be betrayed by those whom he supposed to be friends. Arrested and sentenced to prison, he managed to obtain his release through the intervention of an influential friend. Still he was not safe, and fled first to Milan and then to Rome. Attempting later to return to Trento, he was again arrested and this time served a prison term of sixteen months, being released in 1931. It has been said by official sources that De Gasperi was twice offered the vice-presidency of the Council of Ministers by Mussolini but unconditionally refused. After his release from confinement, De Gasperi took a position in the Vatican library and for a decade devoted most of his time to the study of European economic and social conditions and wrote essays and books "emphasizing the Vatican's role in advancing social legislation."

From his refuge in the Vatican, De Gasperi in 1939 began organizing the resistance group, with branches throughout Italy, which later became the nucleus of his Christian Democratic Party. For a short while after Mussolini's downfall in July 1943, recorded *World Report,*

the group was able to operate in the open; then the German occupation of Italy again forced it underground. De Gasperi and the other leaders hid near St. Johns Lateran Cathedral in Rome and met there daily. By an Allied submarine they dispatched a delegate to the congress of anti-Fascist parties held at Bari and joined the six-party Committee of National Liberation. Thus, when liberation finally came to Rome in June 1944 they were ready to participate in the six-party coalition interim Government then formed. De Gasperi became minister without portfolio in the first Bonomi Cabinet, Foreign Minister in the second Bonomi '44 and Parri '45 Cabinets, and in December 1945 Prime Minister.

The Italian statesman came into power as a result of a Cabinet crisis brought about by the withdrawal of the three Rightist parties in the coalition from the Parri Cabinet over Liberal Party demands that an independent be added to the ministry and that defascistization procedures be liberalized and freed of abuses. Ferruccio Parri resigned as Premier on November 24, 1945, but it was more than a week later when all six parties agreed on De Gasperi, the Liberals finally consenting to enter the new coalition Government because of "great esteem for De Gasperi," and another week before De Gasperi was able to present his completed list of ministers to Crown Prince Humbert '43, Lieutenant General of the Realm. The New York *Times* commented editorially on December 11, "De Gasperi inherits domestic problems before which most men would quail."

Politically and economically, observers pointed out, there was deep-seated unrest. Although in comparison with other countries Italy had suffered little destruction of industry, lack of coal and other strategic supplies permitted operation of only about 25 per cent of capacity. Rioting for bread or jobs in all the large urban centers was frequent, and in the predominantly Leftist north armed bands roamed the country. The lira was unstable and inflation threatened to become ruinous. Politically, there was a deep split between the three parties of the Left (the Socialists, Actionists, and Communists) and those of the Right, among which De Gasperi's Christian Democrats stood closest to the center. Complicating the situation were the nationalist feelings aroused by the proposed peace treaty and the question of monarchy versus republic soon to be decided.

This was the situation which preceded the general elections for a Constituent Assembly (to draw up a constitution and govern in the interim) and the plebiscite on the monarchy both set for decision on June 2, 1946. On May 9 King Victor Emmanuel abdicated in favor of Crown Prince Humbert, but the move, interpreted as a bid for popular support for the monarchy, failed of its objective, and after some delay over the counting of the votes and Humbert's refusal to leave the throne until the count had been completed, the Republic of Italy came into being on June 21. Pending formal proclamation, De Gasperi had been made provisional chief of state, and on July 2, the Christian Democrats having polled the largest number of votes in the general elections, he was asked to form the Government by the country's new president Enrico de Nicola. Because the Christian Democrats had not won a clear victory, the second De Gasperi ministry, like its predecessor, was a coalition and was formed only after a prolonged Cabinet crisis resulting from Communist demands. De Gasperi retained the Foreign Ministry portfolio with the stipulation that it would go to deputy premier Pietro Nenni after the peace treaty had been signed.

The change in Government, however, brought no appreciable tranquillity to Italian internal affairs. Strikes and riots continued unabated or increased in violence; with four Communist ministers in the Cabinet, the Communist Party disavowed Governmental responsibility and felt, reported one New York *Times* correspondent, "completely at liberty to undermine the Government's position by agitating against its fundamental policies." Several times during the summer De Gasperi received votes of confidence from his Cabinet or the Constituent Assembly, but on September 2 the resignation of Minister of the Treasury Epicarmo Corbino, an independent and the target of the strongest Communist attacks because of his financial policy, precipitated a crisis while the Premier was attending the Paris peace conference. This was settled two weeks later by the replacement of Corbino and a vote of confidence by the Constituent Assembly. However, local elections held throughout Italy in October and November showed a definite increase in strength for the parties of the Left and a corresponding decline for the Christian Democrats, while some observers, not too confident of his future, interpreted De Gasperi's elevation from secretary-general to president of his party to indicate a party attempt to shelve him. At the end of the year the Italian Premier was about to leave for a visit to the United States to attempt to hasten approval of the hundred-million-dollar Export-Import Bank Loan pending since early 1946 and to seek additional shipments of food to Italy after the expiration of UNRRA.

At the Paris peace conference as leader of the Italian delegation, De Gasperi was able to effect only a few minor changes in the Italian treaty as written; he was not able to prevail on questions of territorial apportionment or to change the attitude which resulted in a preamble which Italians charge completely ignores their two years of Allied co-belligerency. However, together with Austrian Foreign Minister Gruber, he worked out a compromise on the Tyrol question which left the Italo-Austrian boundary as approved by the Foreign Minister's Council but gave to the German-speaking populace of the southern Tyrol virtual self-rule and to both the border provinces freedom of economic interchange. This agreement, presented as an amendment to the Italian treaty, still must be approved by the Foreign Ministers writing that document, but it was at once hailed by observers as the first real peace treaty of World War II.

De Gasperi has been described as conscientious and tireless. His face is lined and bears the scars inflicted by an enraged bird high in the Dolomites, an experience which nevertheless did not dampen his enthusiasm for mountain climbing. In December 1945 he fought the Cabinet crisis although he was ill with influenza and fainted at one meeting. He lives simply, with his wife Francesca and his four daughters; he himself is said to turn out the lights in the Government offices after work each day. A devout Catholic, he attends Mass daily, in small churches and early in the morning to avoid attracting attention.

References

Scholastic 49:13 S 30 '46 por
World Report 1:33-4 Ag 1 '46 por
International Who's Who, 1945-46

GAUMONT, LEON ERNEST (gō″môɴ′) May 10, 1864—Aug. 11, 1946 French-born pioneer and inventor in the motion picture industry; produced the first synchronized talking films, which were shown at the Academy of Sciences of Paris in 1910; introduced colored motion pictures by a three-color method in 1912; founder of the Gaumont Company in London which became the Gaumont-British Distributing Company; honorary president of French film societies and a member of the Legion of Honor.

Obituary

N Y Times p21 Ag 12 '46

GAVRILOVIC, STOYAN (gä-vrĭ′lō-vĭch stō-yän′) Aug. 22, 1896- Yugoslav Government official
Address: b. c/o United Nations, New York

A delegate to "virtually every important international assembly from the League of Nations on," doctor of international law, and the author of books and essays on international relations, Stoyan Gavrilovic is Yugoslav delegate to the United Nations General Assembly, as well as Yugoslav Under-Secretary for Foreign Affairs. He was chairman of the U.N. inspection committee which toured parts of the eastern United States to find a site for permanent U.N. headquarters.

Stoyan Gavrilovic was born in Belgrade, of an old Serbian family, on August 22, 1896. His father, the noted Dr. Bogdan Gavrilovic, mathematician and physicist, is president of the Academy of Sciences in Belgrade and of the University of Belgrade. His mother, the former Ruzica Markovic, came of a family active in government affairs: her father had been a cabinet minister during the reign of King Milan in Serbia; her brother was Yugoslav Finance Minister in 1927-28. Young Gavrilovic attended high school in Belgrade and took his law degree at the University of Belgrade in 1923. From 1916 to 1919 he was in London, on military duty in the War Office.

Gavrilovic first attracted attention as a newspaperman, while working on the Belgrade *Politika*. He wrote a political exposé, but "exposed too powerful a personage," and lost his job. This taught him that "even the greatest

STOYAN GAVRILOVIC

of exposés is of no use unless it is properly timed. Timing—ah, that is everything!" In December 1923 he entered the diplomatic service as an attaché in the Belgrade foreign office. The next year he began a long service with the League of Nations, acting at various times as Yugoslav delegate in the Council and in the Assembly at Geneva, and as a member of the League's International Opium Commission. But since stability is hardly one of the attributes of the Balkan "cloak-and-dagger" school of politics, Gavrilovic's career was far from smooth. In 1929 General Peter Givkovic abolished the constitution and established a military dictatorship in Yugoslavia. Because the General did not like his views, Gavrilovic "departed" from the service. "I call it departure to be diplomatic," he has said. The next two years he spent at the University of Geneva earning a doctorate in international law. His treatise, *The Organization of Conciliation Commissions*, was written in French and published in Paris in 1931. That same year he rejoined the Yugoslav government service, becoming in 1935 the head of the League of Nations Division in the Ministry of Foreign Affairs in Belgrade, and in 1938 Assistant Political Director. From 1935 to 1940 he attended all the meetings of the Political Council of the Little Entente and the Balkan Entente, and was prominent in the formulation of the policy of Balkan unity. He early foresaw a need for Yugoslav and Allied understanding with Russia, and in December 1939, as Yugoslavia's delegate to the Council of the League of Nations, refused to vote for the break with Moscow.

Germany invaded Yugoslavia April 6, 1941, and in a few weeks the Nazis were in complete control. Two days before the April 6th bombing of Belgrade, Gavrilovic's wife, the former Vera Prendic, and their eleven-year-old son Ivan escaped from the city in a small boat and made their way to Palestine. Gavrilovic soon afterwards was taken by British plane and warship to Cairo. Almost immediately he left Cairo for Cape Town, where, as the first Yugoslav representative in that part of the world, he opened diplomatic relations for Yugoslavia with the Union of South Africa and with Northern and Southern Rhodesia. He was consul general in the Union of South Africa when his wife and son joined him in June 1941. Eight months later he sent Mrs. Gavrilovic and Ivan to the United States aboard a freighter. The ship was torpedoed, with the loss of forty-two lives. Gavrilovic's wife and son, after two days on a life raft in a rough sea, were rescued by an American Coast Guard cutter. Gavrilovic was reunited with his family a year later when he came to New York to be Chief of the Yugoslav Information Service.

Gavrilovic was dismissed from the information post in September 1943, by the Puric Government, which he considered "very much the same as that of Givkovic." From October 1943 to January 1944 he lectured at the University of Pittsburgh. Until the middle of 1944 he wrote and spoke in the United States on international problems, and worked for the cause of the National Liberation Army in Yugoslavia. Early in 1944, at a meeting of the Foreign Policy Association in New York, he contended that in the Yugoslav political struggle there were "on the one side the old, disunited and disuniting political groups which are personified by the prewar dictatorial and oligarchical regimes. On the other, there are the new and strongly united forces of Marshal Tito '43 which have rallied the democratic, liberal, and progressive elements in all the parts of the country." Then, in August 1944 he became Under-Secretary of State for Foreign Affairs in Premier Subasitch's reorganized Yugoslav Government-in-exile in London and was sent as Minister Plenipotentiary on a secret mission to Marshal Tito's headquarters in Yugoslavia. His discussions with Tito were part of the negotiations which eventually resulted in the Tito-Subasitch agreement, an accord between Tito's Provisional Government and King Peter's Government-in-exile.

In the United Yugoslav Government formed under Marshal Tito in March 1945, Gavrilovic retained the post of Under-Secretary of State for Foreign Affairs. The veteran League of Nations diplomat dedicated himself to working toward "a great and true international organization of the world." He was among the jurists of thirty-eight countries who assembled in Washington in April 1945 to draft a statute for the new International Court of Justice. In the same month he proceeded to San Francisco, a deputy delegate from Yugoslavia to the United Nations Conference. There he served on the coordination committee which drafted the Charter of the United Nations. When the United Nations preparatory commission met in London in November and December 1945, Gavrilovic attended as head of the Yugoslav delegation. During the London negotiations he was prominent among the supporters of the proposal to place the United Nations headquarters in the United States, believing that "new and modern trends can only be safeguarded in a new world away from the old scenes of power politics and colonial exploitations." He was next appointed Yugoslav delegate to the United Nations General Assembly which met in January and February 1946.

Gavrilovic was chairman of the U.N. committee which in November 1945 received twenty-three United States delegations, all of whom had come to London to urge that their localities be chosen for the United Nations permanent headquarters. Then, in January 1946, the diplomat went in search of a "capital of the world." Gavrilovic came to America as the chairman of an international inspection committee of seven instructed to recommend sites for a U.N. home twenty-five to eighty miles from New York City or within sixty miles of Boston. During his search Gavrilovic thought of the world capital as it would be fifty years in the future; he envisioned a world mecca, "studded with magnificent buildings." Of immediate concern was the fact that within five years permanent facilities would have to be available for the General Assembly (which it was estimated would bring approximately five thousand people to the capital probably once each year), for the numerous permanent councils, agencies and committees of U.N., and for the secretariat (at the time already totaling twenty-two hundred persons). Each of fifty-one nations would want an "embassy" building. An airport, a railroad station, utilities, hotels and shops, and radio and televison stations would be necessary. Thousands of visitors would have to be accommodated. "Our idea," said Dr. Gavrilovic, "is that this development must maintain its identity and must not be engulfed by a growing city. Accordingly we have to provide a buffer in the way of belts of landscaping against encroachment from outside communities."

After conferences with mayors, governors, prominent citizens, and real estate salesmen, the committee decided to recommend a site cutting across the North Stamford-Greenwich area of Connecticut and Westchester County in New York. For interim headquarters the group considered New York City the best choice. The committee flew to London in February to report to the General Assembly. But Gavrilovic's troubles as a home-seeker were only just beginning. Residents of the chosen area, distressed because their quiet suburban estates might soon be part of a international capital, registered opposition in a referendum vote of 5,505 to 2,019, and informed the United Nations, with some heat, that it was not welcome. Gavrilovic's comment was: "There were officials everywhere we went wanting us. . . .If we had heard the protests we would have taken them into account." Partly because of the attitude of the residents, the site was not approved by the Assembly. Instead, a headquarters commission was directed to find another site in Westchester and Fairfield counties. Gavrilovic, who had "stood firmly" for the New York area as the best location for the U.N. throughout considerable Assembly opposition, immediately flew back to the United States as temporary

chairman of this second commission. On May 7 Sir Angus Fletcher '46 of Great Britain was elected chairman, while Gavrilovic became vice-chairman. In mid-August the commission announced it had selected five Westchester County areas to recommend. When protests of residents made further consideration of those regions unfeasible, the search widened to Philadelphia, Boston, New York, San Francisco, the cities which had offered sites. Then, on December 11, John D. Rockefeller, Jr., offered a strip of land along the East River in New York City. On December 14, 1946, the General Assembly accepted the gift.

Besides his diplomatic and political activities, Gavrilovic for many years was associated with the Red Cross, the Young Men's Christian Association, various institutes in Yugoslavia, the International Law Association, and British and American clubs in Europe. He has often been a member of the executive boards of these organizations. He has been awarded numerous Yugoslav and foreign orders, and a Red Cross Order. In 1944 he was elected a member of the Academy of Political and Social Science in Pittsburgh, and of the American Political Science Association. His published works include his doctoral dissertation and a translation of *Oppenheim's International Law*, with interpretations and additions, published in part in Belgrade in 1938.

"It is wonderful to be a politician," Gavrilovic once said to John Hohenberg of the New York *Post*. "You win so many battles and you kill nobody." The Yugoslav politician is tall and thin (five feet, ten inches in height, 150 pounds in weight). He has brown hair, but very little of it, "overhanging eyebrows, a sharp nose, and an ascetic face." He smiles frequently "even when he is ripping into political opponents," because, as he explains, "You can say the most terrible things when you smile." He lost his home in the bombing of Belgrade, but is not interested in being a propertied man. To one newspaperwoman he declared: "I have no possessions myself. No securities, no real estate, no furniture, no bank account. All I have is my wonderful wife and son and friends—friends all over the world."

References

N Y Post p7 Ja 26 '46 por

Who's Who in Central and East-Europe, 1935-36

GILLETTE, GUY M(ARK) Feb. 3, 1879-
President of the American League for a Free Palestine; former United States Senator from Iowa

Address: b. c/o American League for a Free Palestine, 2315 Massachusetts Ave., Washington, D.C.; h. Cherokee, Iowa

After four years in the House, eight years in the Senate, and five months as Surplus Property Administrator, in 1945 Guy M. Gillette accepted the presidency of the American League for a Free Palestine: "Not because my love or sympathy for the Jews is in any degree greater than that of the average American. . . .I consider the so-called Jewish problem, not as a

GUY M. GILLETTE

Jewish or a Hebrew question, but as an urgent problem of the United Nations and of the decent portion of mankind." While in the legislature as the Democratic Senator from Iowa, Gillette had become known as an Administration critic.

Guy Mark Gillette grew up on a farm in Cherokee, which is the name of a town and county in northwestern Iowa. There he was born February 3, 1879, to Mark Daniel and Mary (Hull) Gillette, and there attended high school until 1896. After serving as a sergeant in the United States Volunteer Infantry during the Spanish-American War Gillette earned an LL.B. degree at Drake University in Des Moines, and in 1900 was admitted to the Iowa bar. He began practice in the town of Cherokee, served as city attorney in 1906-7, and as Cherokee County prosecuting attorney from 1907 to 1909. Elected on the Democratic ticket to the State Senate in 1912 by a first count of 52,851 votes, one vote more than his opponent received (a recount gave Gillette a larger lead), he represented his county for four years.

The thirty-eight-year-old lawyer became a captain in the infantry when the United States entered World War I. Returning from France in 1918, he was surprised to learn that in his absence he had been nominated—and defeated—for the office of state auditor. In any case, politics and law no longer appealed to the Iowan—he returned to farming for fourteen years of "happy days." "I had the satisfaction of producing something I could see, smell, taste, and touch, not to mention never having to worry about who was going to knife me next," he has recalled. "Milked a dozen cows myself night and morning. . . .That's darned good farming. I wasn't one of those gentlemen farmers."

Re-entering politics in 1932, when Roosevelt first ran for President, the dairyman and "dirt farmer" gained election from the ninth Iowa

district to the United States House of Representatives, and was re-elected in 1934 with a majority of twenty-six thousand votes. In November 1936 the fifty-seven-year-old lawmaker crossed the Capitol Building to the upper chamber, having been elected to fill the vacancy caused by the death of Senator Louis Murphy. President Roosevelt purportedly sought to "purge" Gillette (who had opposed the Supreme Court reorganization plan) in the 1938 primaries. But supported, according to *Time,* by the A.F. of L., Catholics, and the State political machine, Gillette defeated his primary opponent (who had been endorsed by Iowa-born Harry Hopkins and by out-of-state CIO leaders) by a two-to-one margin, and in the elections was returned to the Senate by usually Republican Iowa for a six-year term.

"His chief legislative efforts have been in behalf of farmers, and he has fought particularly to expose semimonopoly and profiteering by middlemen in the food industry," wrote a New York *Post* interviewer of the Senator in January 1944. The Iowan's efforts for the farmers frequently came in conflict with the Administration's; he was a leader in the fight against the Government price-holding food subsidy program, and voted with the farm-bloc advocates of broad deferment from military service for farm laborers. In 1944 he sponsored a bill for taxes on the resale of farm land to head off a threatened land boom and introduced one of the several bills to create a Missouri Valley Authority. In October of that year he put before the President a program for postwar development of agriculture and industry in the Middle West; he said he found Roosevelt "very sympathetic" toward that project.

Chairman of the agricultural subcommittee seeking new uses for surplus agricultural commodities, in 1942 Gillette sponsored legislation designed to further production of synthetic rubber from grain alcohol. His committee began a wartime investigation of the synthetic rubber program which lasted for almost three years. Gillette held that selfish and powerful petroleum interests had won a monopoly on contracts for the production of butadiene (from which synthetic rubber was made) to the detriment of the national good. Petroleum, he maintained, was essential for other purposes, while butadiene could also be produced, probably faster and more cheaply, from alcohol derived from agricultural products. This was the report of his committee after one hundred hours of public hearings. Although some contracts were allocated to alcohol plants, Gillette continued to criticize the War Production Board, for failing, he felt, to take full advantage of the possibilities of using grain for rubber production.

Gillette voted against the Lend-Lease bill (March 1941), against draft extension legislation, and in opposition to the modification of the Neutrality Act in November 1941. In February 1943, the "implacable pre-Pearl Harbor isolationist" introduced a resolution to put the Senate on record as approving the basic principles of the Atlantic Charter, and to advise President Roosevelt to negotiate by treaties with others of the United Nations for a "postwar peace charter." "The Administration does not want to have its hand forced," commented Raymond Clapper, "by anything like the Gillette resolution" (which raised the issue of the non-legality of the Atlantic Charter and U.N. agreement, neither ever formerly ratified by the Senate). The resolution still pending, in May his good friend and fellow-Iowan Vice-President Wallace '⁴⁰ shook his hand in congratulations on the Senate floor after Gillette proposed an amendment to the Constitution which would make Senate majority approval, instead of a two-thirds vote, sufficient for treaty ratification.

The Gillette resolution on the Atlantic Charter, along with others on international collaboration, was turned over to the Connally '⁴¹ subcommittee (on which Gillette was one of eight members) of the Senate Foreign Relations Committee. In November of 1943 the subcommittee's "Connally resolution" (approving American participation in world government) passed the Senate 85 to 5, the chief opposition coming not from isolationists but from those who felt it was too "hedged about with references to constitutional processes and national sovereignty" to mean anything. The one member of the Foreign Relations Committee and one of the seven Democrats in the Senate who voted against the authorization of funds for UNRRA in February 1944, Gillette was again termed a die-hard isolationist. Emphasizing his sympathy with the objectives of the legislation, he ascribed his solitary stand to the fact that the relief provisions were contained not in a treaty, but in an agreement, of a sort which he felt did not permit Congress to retain sufficient control over the use of the funds. Two months later Gillette was chosen by Connally for an eight-Senator bipartisan liaison committee to confer with Secretary of State Hull '⁴⁰ on international organization and peace problems.

Other legislation which the Senator introduced included a 1943 bill designed to expose and curb the use of racial prejudice in political contests, and to provide for the creation of an office of minority relations. Chairman of the committee that investigated the 1940 national campaign, Gillette accused both parties of overspending in their campaigns, and in 1944 he introduced legislation which would limit more stringently than did the Hatch '⁴⁴ Act the expenditures for a Presidential contest. In 1944 he also proposed and fought for a constitutional amendment guaranteeing equal rights for women. His anti-Administration stand included his support of the Smith '⁴¹-Connally antistrike bill; he also voted in 1944 to abolish the FEPC.

The creation of the War Refugee Board in 1943 was the result of the legislative efforts of the Iowan. In the last months of 1943 Gillette also introduced two resolutions, the first directing the State Department to seek British and neutral cooperation in sending aid to the children of Nazi-occupied countries (passed early in 1944, the resolution was in effect an "expression of sentiment"), and a second proposing to the President that he set up a commission of experts to "formulate and effectuate a plan of immediate action" to save surviving European Jews. At many rallies in behalf of European Jews, the Senator was a principal speaker, contending that the problem of bringing them out of Europe was not one for Jews alone, but for Christians everywhere. In an April 1944 address Gillette attacked British policy in Palestine as "political," and proposed that the United States use its influence to have the immigration-restricting White Paper nullified. In the Senate he proposed that the United States provide temporary care for war refugees at Ellis Island and in other "free ports." Mrs. Gillette, meanwhile, became chairman of the Washington Emergency Committee to Save the Jewish People of Europe. Gillette declared in December 1944: "It is my belief that the attitude of Great Britain as well as that of the United Nations, must be re-examined in the light of the urgent need for asylum for such refugees as can still be saved."

His Senate term drawing to a close, Gillette withdrew as a delegate to the 1944 Democratic National Convention, announcing, "I could not conscientiously vote for the renomination of President Roosevelt." (In 1940 he had similarly opposed a third term for Roosevelt.) While easily winning in the 1944 Iowa primaries, Gillette was defeated in the election by Iowa's Republican Governor Hickenlooper, whereupon President Roosevelt nominated Gillette one of the three members of the Surplus Property Disposal Board. Becoming chairman of the board, Gillette was expected to dispose of one hundred billion dollars worth of surplus war property. *PM* called him the "little fellow's best friend" on the SPB, and the New York *Post* ran a story indicating that his policy was to use surplus goods to provide the "greatest good for the greatest number": for example, sheets discarded by the Army would be sold to badly equipped hospitals in the South at low rates rather than to big New York department stores for "white sales." Gillette resigned five months later following a disagreement with the two other members of the board, who, he felt, were favoring large businesses in the disposal of machine tools. His minority stand had been that, regardless of warehouse and other possibly avoidable expense, the Government should attempt to make the tools available to all who needed them.

Offered a Federal judgeship by President Truman, a fifty-thousand-dollar corporation post in private industry, and a War Department job in Germany with the rank of major general, the sixty-six-year-old former legislator refused them all to accept, in August 1945, a ten-thousand-dollar-a-year (he refused twenty-five thousand) presidency of the one-year-old American League for a Free Palestine; he was also to be political adviser to the Hebrew Committee for National Liberation. The nonsectarian American League for a Free Palestine advocated the establishment of a democratic Government in Palestine, with the Arabs as well as the Jews fully represented. It contended that there is a distinction between being of the "Jewish religion" and being of the "Hebrew nation," whose national territory is Palestine, and held that all the Jews of

GILLETTE, GUY M.—*Continued*

Europe wishing to become Palestinian citizens should be given the opportunity to do so at once. In the closing months of 1945 Gillette and six other Americans, including three Congressmen, visited Prime Minister Attlee '40 to urge him to open Palestine immediately to Jewish refugees. At a league-sponsored conference in February, Gillette charged Great Britain with persistently violating "the letter and spirit" of her mandate power in Palestine, and urged that a blueprint be evolved to aid Palestine to become a free and independent state. In July 1946 Gillette journeyed to Palestine "to circumvent the news blackout imposed by the British" and to observe conditions for himself. On his return in August, he said he had found "every evidence" that Jews and Arabs could work together in a free country "if the British would get out."

In the fall of 1946 the league sponsored the production of the play *A Flag Is Born,* by Ben Hecht, one of the cochairmen of the league. Receipts from the play, which starred Paul Muni, were to finance the transportation of Jews from Europe to Palestine. In October, on behalf of the league's one hundred and thirty thousand members, its executive committee asked President Truman to give Prime Minister Attlee "a specific deadline of October 15, 1946, to begin action." Should action not be taken by that time, the league urged that the American Government "actually inaugurate the movement of Hebrews to Palestine."

Slightly over six feet tall, and weighing 190 pounds, the handsome, silver-thatched former Senator, whom his colleagues find "warmly human," is a renowned amateur softball pitcher. A teetotaler and a nonsmoker, his chief "vices" are playing poker and eating candy. He relaxes best at the piano, which he plays by ear. One of the most faithful of the "bus boys" at the Washington Stage Door Canteen during World War II, Gillette has written, staged, and acted in minstrel shows for the American Legion. He belongs also to the Veterans of Foreign Wars and the Spanish War Veterans; a Presbyterian in religion, he is also a Mason and member of the Knights of Pythias. His wife, the former Rose Freeman, was teaching school in his home county when they met. Married in June 1907, they have a son Mark Freeman. There are few activities the three members of the family do not share. However, although mother and son like Washington, Gillette himself wants to get back to farming.

References

Esquire 19:122 Je '43
N Y Post p7 Ja 22 '44 por; p5 Ag 18 '45 por
N Y Sun p29 Ap 20 '43; p6 Jl 15 '44
Time 31:16 Je 13 '38
International Who's Who, 1945-46
Who's Who in America, 1946-47
Who's Who in the Nation's Capital, 1938-39

GIRAL (Y PEREIRA), JOSE (hē-räl′ ē pĕ-rä′ē-rá hō-sä′) Oct. 22, 1879- Premier of the Spanish Republican Government-in-Exile

José Giral, refugee from Franco Spain, and once professor of chemistry at the University of Madrid, became Premier of the unrecognized Spanish Republican Government-in-exile in August 1945. A Liberal Republican or "moderate Leftist," Giral has been working from headquarters in Paris to win the recognition of the major powers for his Government. In May of 1946 he presented charges against the Franco regime before the United Nations Security Council committee which was investigating the Spanish Government as a possible menace to world peace.

José Giral y Pereira was born in Santiago de Cuba, on October 22, 1879, when Cuba was a Spanish colony. As a boy he was sent by his father, Antonio Giral, to Spain to live with his uncles. Lack of funds ruled out the ten-year engineering course José wished to take. But, supporting himself by tutoring and aided by scholarships, he managed to attend the University of Madrid and was graduated at twenty-one with doctorates in chemistry and pharmacy. Even as a student, according to Jane Morgan, a New York *Post* writer who interviewed Giral in Mexico, he was engaged in political conspiracies against the monarchy. And after his graduation, while taking a series of examinations which would win him his teaching certificates, he learned that Government officials were searching for him. "By staying up two nights and days he foiled his pursuers, and went to jail four days later—a full-fledged professor," wrote Miss Morgan.

In 1905 Giral was appointed a professor of organic chemistry at the University of Salamanca, where he remained until 1920, carrying on research in organic and biochemistry, writing scientific treatises, and spending evenings in his laboratory with friends quietly plotting against the regime in power. Before the Republican Government was established in 1931, he was a "jailbird" seven times, according to Miss Morgan, and escaped an eighth imprisonment by undergoing a pretended appendectomy. In 1920 Professor Giral became the head of the chemistry department of the Instituto Español de Oceanografía. He held that post through the dictatorship of Primo de Rivera (1923-29) and the subsequent ministry of Berenguer (1929-31), who proclaimed the Constitution but continued the policies of the oppressive monarchy. Also, from 1927 until 1939, Giral was a professor of biochemistry on the faculty of pharmacy at the University of Madrid. Meanwhile, intellectuals throughout Spain were conspiring against the Government of King Alfonso, and Giral is said to have had an important part in organizing the successful 1931 revolt, which led without bloodshed to the abdication of King Alfonso and the establishment, on April 14, 1931, of the Republic of Spain.

Professor Giral was elected a deputy to the Cortes, the new Republic's single house of parliament, in 1931. Under the prime ministry of Azaña, founder of the Liberal-Republican party, Giral served as Minister of the Navy

(1931-33). But the "honeymoon of the Republic" came to an end in 1933, when reactionary elements united in an "Anti-Marxist Coalition" and won control of the Government. This group held power until the elections of February 1936. The results of the 1936 voting showed a decisive parliamentary victory for the Popular Front, which, moderately Left (Communists had won only 4 per cent of the electoral vote), was led by Giral's good friend Azaña. In May 1936 Azaña took over the presidency, Casares Quiroga became Prime Minister, and Giral, in the Casares cabinet, was again Minister of the Navy.

That July, Francisco Franco, with Moorish troops transported by Italian airplanes from North Africa to Seville, led the revolt against the Republican Government. At this critical juncture José Giral replaced Casares as Prime Minister. According to Gerald Brenan (*The Spanish Labyrinth*, 1943) the Government— composed of Liberal Republicans and led by Giral in order "to impress foreign opinion"— soon lost all authority in Spain. "The workers, through their party and trade-union organizations," Brenan contends, "became the real rulers of the country and the organizers of the war." At the end of August, Prime Minister Giral resigned. Alvarez del Vayo, foreign minister of the Republic during the Civil War, recalls in his book *Freedom's Battle* (published by Alfred A. Knopf in 1940): "Señor Giral, on meeting me one day in the War Ministry, told me that he wanted to broaden the basis of the Government. . . .There is no doubt that it was only the two most prominent Socialist leaders, Largo Caballero and Indalecio Prieto, with whom Señor Giral wished to share his grave responsibilities. But in the meantime the military situation had deteriorated to such an extent that a complete change in the administration of the war seemed inevitable, and Señor Giral decided to resign. Very generously he took it upon himself to persuade the President of the Republic to dispense with his services, although Señor Azaña was reluctant to part with a man to whom he was bound by close political and personal ties and who had taken over the Government at such a critical time."

Largo Caballero, Socialist, succeeded him as Prime Minister, but Giral remained in the cabinet as Minister without portfolio. Then, in May 1937 a cabinet crisis was precipitated by the resignation of two Communist cabinet members. Largo Caballero was succeeded by Juan Negrín [45] as Prime Minister, and in the reshuffled cabinet, José Giral became Foreign Minister, replacing Alvarez del Vayo. Giral, as Foreign Minister, worked in Paris and in Geneva before the League of Nations to inform the world of the extent of Italian aid to Franco in the Spanish Civil War. He also strove to tap every possible source of arms for his people. In April 1938 a second reorganization of the Negrín cabinet returned Alvarez del Vayo to the post of Foreign Minister, and José Giral once again became minister without portfolio. In the latter capacity he served on the Supreme War Council, in which the various shades of political opinion in the Government were represented. A Socialist, a Communist, a member of

JOSE GIRAL

the CNT (National Confederation of Workers), and Giral, who represented the Left Republicans (or Liberal Republicans), were Council members.

In February 1939, when the fall of the elected Government to the Franco forces was only a matter of time, Giral was asked to accompany President Azaña to Paris. Negrín and other Republicans were forced to follow in March. Meanwhile, President Cardenas of Mexico made it easy for the Spanish political refugees to obtain visas and other necessary papers for entrance into Mexico. (Mexico and the U.S.S.R. were the only countries which did not recognize Franco.) Thousands of Spanish Republicans, among them Giral, accepted Mexico's hospitality. Thus, toward the end of 1939 Giral was living in Mexico City with his wife and four children, in a furnished flat while he made a scanty living as professor of chemistry at the Instituto Politécnico de México, in Tacuba. He was also active in the Committee to Aid Spanish Republicans, which organized a medical center, opened an elementary school, aided the needy, the war widows and old people, and granted scholarships to needy refugee students, using funds of the Spanish Republican government.

Spanish Republican exiles in Mexico met in a Cortes in the summer of 1945 and elected Martínez Barrio president. In August Barrio asked José Giral, the "moderate Leftist," to form a new Government. While the 185 Cortes members gave majority approval to Giral, criticism of the President's choice came from Spanish Communists, and from backers of the Socialist leader, Juan Negrín, last Premier of the Spanish Republican Government. When Negrín refused a post in the Giral cabinet, his supporters pointed out: "Dr. Negrín's political significance would have been neutralized had his name appeared side by side with those of the persons now in the Cabinet—very honorable

GIRAL, JOSE—*Continued*

men but some of them representing a policy utterly different from and even contrary to what we believe indispensable at this moment." What many of the exiles objected to was the "mildness" and "respectability," of the Giral group. Giral was thought to lack sufficient force for the task of re-establishing republicanism in Spain. On the other hand, Giral's supporters expected that a moderate cabinet might win recognition from Washington and London; but this hope was not fulfilled. In the spring of 1946 Giral decided to broaden his Government to include representatives of the Communists, and some Rightist groups as well. The Communist Santiago Carillo, and the Catholic Right-wing leader, José Sanchez Guerra, who had been active in the resistance movement in Franco Spain, joined the cabinet in Paris, to which the exiles had moved their Government early in 1946. Recognition for the Government-in-exile came first from Poland and later from Hungary and Bulgaria. In August Juan Negrín pledged his support to Giral, asserting that although he disagreed with some of its policies, the Giral Cabinet was truly representative of Spain.

The sixty-six-year-old Spanish Republican Premier flew to New York in May 1946 with 350 pages of anti-Franco evidence for the U.N. subcommittee investigating charges that Spain was a menace to world peace. Giral held that Franco could be overthrown without civil war or military intervention if other countries would break off commercial and diplomatic relations with Spain. Republicans inside Spain were strong enough and numerous enough to overthrow Franco by civil war, he added, but they were anxious to avoid bloodshed. In June, after the Security Council had failed to agree on action against Franco, Giral warned that internal strife might turn his country into "the focus of a third World War." On December 12 a resolution denouncing the Franco regime in Spain and recommending that the members of the U.N. recall immediately their chiefs of mission in Madrid was adopted by the U.N. General Assembly. Giral considered this "a step forward" although he had hoped for a complete diplomatic break with the Franco Government.

· Just before the Giral Government left for Paris in January 1946, its Premier defined his policies to New York *Times* writer Thomas J. Hamilton: He pledged that the Republican Government would hunt down fugitive Nazis in Spain, and would repudiate the Spanish fascist "Hispanidad" program. A restored Republic would reform the Spanish Army and would revive the agrarian laws so that great estates might be run on a cooperative basis by their tenants. As to the Republic's relations with the Catholic Church, Giral said his Government would maintain freedom for all religions at the same time that he emphasized that the Church would be kept out of politics. Giral also pledged social security legislation, plans to bring education to the working classes, and a program of public works directed toward developing Spain's water power resources and improving her standard of living.

Giral is a member of several French, American, Mexican and Spanish scientific societies. His writings include: *Análisis orgánico funcional* (Madrid, 1913), *Ración alimenticia higiénica y social* (Madrid, 1914), *Tratado de química orgánica* (Madrid, 1926), *Fermentos* (Mexico, 1941), and a translation of twelve volumes of Muspratt's chemical encyclopedia (1920). In September 1910 he was married to María Luisa Gonzáles de la Calle. Their four children are Francisco, Antonio, who serves as his father's secretary, María Luisa, and Concepción. Giral is of smaller than average height, gray-haired, "gentle, both in appearance and voice."

References

N Y Post p41 S 28 '45 por

Who's Who in Latin America; Part I, Mexico (1946)

GLASGOW, ELLEN (ANDERSON GHOLSON) Apr. 22, 1874—Nov. 21, 1945 American novelist; winner of Pulitzer Prize in 1942 for last novel, *In This Our Life*; has been called an "ironic idealist", "ironic tragedian," and a "realist"; first novel, *The Descendant*, was published anonymously when she was twenty-three; her more than a dozen other books include *The Voice of the People* (1900), *Barren Ground* (1925), *Vein of Iron* (1931).

Obituary

N Y Times p35 N 22 '45 por

GLASS, CARTER Jan. 4, 1858—May 28, 1946 Democratic United States Senator from Virginia from 1902 until his death, except for one year as Secretary of the Treasury under President Wilson; sponsor of the Federal Reserve Act; disagreed with President Roosevelt because he thought the President was favoring unsound fiscal measures; appeared last on the Senate floor in 1942; termed "one of the great men of this age." See *Current Biography* 1941 Yearbook.

Obituary

N Y Times p1+ My 29 '46 por

GLENNON, JOHN, CARDINAL June 14, 1862—Mar. 10, 1946 Irish-born American Roman Catholic prelate; Archbishop of St. Louis from October 1903 until death, elevated to College of Cardinals in February 1946; considered one of the country's greatest orators and one of the Church's greatest architectural builders.

Obituary

N Y Times p1+ Mr 10 '46

GLINTENKAMP, H(ENDRIK) Sept. 10, 1887—Mar. 19, 1946 Painter, sculptor, etcher, engraver; teacher from 1908; cartoonist on the Hudson *Dispatch,* 1912; and on *The Masses,* 1918; represented in Metropolitan Museum of Art, Museum of Modern Art, Cleveland Museum, Baltimore Museum, New York and Newark public libraries; wrote *A Wanderer in Woodcuts* (1932).

Obituary

N Y Times p24 Mr 20 '46

GODOY ALCAYAGA, LUCILA *See* Mistral, G.

GOLDSBOROUGH, PHILLIPS LEE Aug. 6, 1865—Oct. 22, 1946 Republican Governor of Maryland from 1912 to 1916; United States Senator from 1929 to 1935; director of the Federal Deposit Insurance Corporation from 1935 until his death; supported the Smoot-Hawley tariff law, the prohibition law; opposed President Roosevelt's exchange stabilization fund.

Obituary

N Y Times p27 O 23 '46 por

GOLDSTEIN, ISRAEL, RABBI (gōld'-stĕn) June 18, 1896- Zionist leader

Address b. 270 W. 89th St., New York; h. 300 Central Park West, New York

Dr. Israel Goldstein is the rabbi of the Congregation B'nai Jeshurun, the oldest synagogue of the conservative branch of Judaism in America. Cochairman of the United Jewish Appeal (a fund-raising body for the Palestine movement), member of the governing council of the World Zionist Organization, and former president of the Zionist Organization of America, he has been an ardent Zionist all his life.

Even in the days of his early childhood Israel Goldstein knew a great deal about the cause of the Jewish national state. His Russian-born parents, David L. and Fannie (Silver) Goldstein, were Zionists. Born in Philadelphia on June 18, 1896, Israel attended both the public and Hebrew schools in that city. Violin lessons were added to this full program from his sixth to his ninth year, for his father, a merchant who had been educated for the rabbinate, wished his son to be a child prodigy. In 1911 he was graduated from Gratz College, a school for the training of Jewish teachers, and three years later he obtained his B.A. degree from the University of Pennsylvania, from which he was graduated with honors. The eighteen-year-old Goldstein, who had decided to become a rabbi, then entered the Jewish Theological Seminary in New York City. He also attended Columbia University, receiving his M.A. degree in 1917, the year before he was graduated from the seminary, where he was valedictorian of his class. A member of the B'nai Jeshurun Congregation in New York, which needed a rabbi at that time, was present at the seminary's commencement exercises; much impressed with Goldstein's valedictory, he recommended the young man for the post.

In the summer of 1918, soon after he was married to Bertha Markowitz, whom he had met through friends at the seminary, Goldstein assumed his duties as rabbi of B'nai

RABBI ISRAEL GOLDSTEIN

Jeshurun. His activities were not limited to ministering to his congregation, however. From 1922 to 1925 he served as the first president of the Young People's League of the United Synagogue of America, which was organized for the purpose of keeping traditional Judaism alive in Jewish youth. From 1925 to 1933 he was chairman of the committee on social justice of the Synagogue Council of America. In 1925 he was head of a committee to raise a special fund for a Jewish division in the New York Public Library. As a member of the administrative committee of the Palestine Foundation Fund, in 1926 he raised money for the Jewish Agency for Palestine. (He is chairman of the board of directors of the Palestine Foundation Fund in 1946.) The rabbi also continued his studies at the Jewish Theological Seminary, receiving his degree as Doctor of Hebrew Literature in 1927.

The first time Dr. Goldstein visited Palestine was in 1928. He went there again in 1932 with his wife and children, a son named Avram Shalom, and a daughter, Vivian Rose. When Mrs. Goldstein and the children revisited that country four years later, they worked in an agricultural cooperative for a year. The rabbi, a city-dweller, also learned much about farming as president of the Jewish National Fund of America, an organization which buys land in Palestine for Jewish agricultural settlement. After Goldstein became president in 1933, the number of branches in the fund doubled and contributions also increased. American contributions, which amounted to one hundred forty-four thousand dollars in 1933, were one million nine hundred thousand in 1942. At a banquet celebrating his tenth anniversary as head of the organization, it was agreed to purchase a tract in Palestine and name it for Goldstein, who was then elected honorary chairman of the organization.

(Continued next page)

GOLDSTEIN, ISRAEL, RABBI—*Cont.*

The rabbi was also active in other Zionist agencies: In 1936 he became the national co-chairman of the United Palestine Appeal and of the United Jewish Appeal, both fund-raising organizations. Since 1937 he has been a member of the council of the Jewish Agency for Palestine, the body which the League of Nations designated as the supreme national authority for the building of a Jewish home in Palestine. He is also a member of the American commission of the agency. A delegate to the World Zionist Congress in 1935, in 1937 and 1939 he served on its actions committee. As chairman of the board of the Palestine Pavilion at the New York World's Fair, he directed an exhibition at which millions saw the progress made by the Jews in building cities and reclaiming wastelands in Palestine.

When Hitler began his extermination of the Jews, the importance of Palestine as a Jewish national home was overshadowed by its immediate significance as a refuge. With admission to non-fascist nations still much restricted, Palestine became almost the sole hope of increasing numbers of persecuted Jews. Impeded by dangers and by the British White Paper policy, Zionists and non-Zionists made organized efforts to rescue as many Jews as possible from death in Nazi concentration camps. A member of the Council for German Jewry since 1936, and also a member of the American Zionist Emergency Council since 1940, Goldstein was cochairman of the interim committee of the American Jewish Conference. This was organized in 1943 to plan the immediate rescue of European Jewry, solve their postwar problems, and secure Jewish rights to Palestine. The rabbi was a sharp critic of the 1943 Bermuda Conference on refugee problems, which he felt had resulted in failure. The conferees, according to Freda Kirchwey of the *Nation,* had listed the difficulties involved in saving the Nazi victims of occupied Europe but had done little toward their solution.

In February 1944, two months before the British White Paper took effect, Dr. Goldstein, then president of the Zionist Organization of America and of the Synagogue Council of America, made a trip to England to consult with Chaim Weizmann [42], president of the World Zionist Congress, and other leaders. Goldstein's interviews with British officials indicated that there would be no immediate change in the White Paper policy and that solution of the Palestine question would have to be postponed until the end of World War II. The rabbi urged that this stand should not be accepted passively, but despite protests, the doors of Palestine were closed to all Jews except those allowed to enter on quotas not filled by April 1, 1944, and on special quotas fixed by the British Government from time to time.

In the summer of 1945, Dr. Goldstein toured the liberated countries of Europe and attended London consultations of the American Jewish Conference, the Board of Deputies of British Jews, and the World Jewish Congress. His tour convinced him that the problem of the Jews in a postwar Europe, where pogroms still occurred in Poland and difficulties hindered the return of Jewish property, was a special one and could not be solved as part of the general European problem. He estimated that of one million four hundred thousand surviving Jews, one hundred thousand wanted to leave for Palestine immediately and one million wished to settle there eventually. When Britain, claiming that the United States should share the burden of the Palestine problem, did not take steps to permit at least one hundred thousand to emigrate, Jews began to get into Palestine by other means. Goldstein refused to recognize their entry as illegal, alleging that those who tried to keep the Jew from Palestine were acting illegally.

He viewed the appointment of an Anglo-American Commission to investigate the feasibility of allowing additional Jews into Palestine, as "patently a delaying tactic." Following the committee's unanimous report advising the immediate entry of one hundred thousand Jews, a report which provoked threats from the Arab League, Ernest Bevin [40], British Foreign Minister, asserted that another division of British troops would be needed to carry out such a proposal. The United States promised financial and transportation aid to implement the committee's recommendation but said nothing about the military assistance which Britain also sought. In the summer of 1946 Dr. Goldstein attended an executive meeting in Paris of the Jewish Agency for Palestine. Commenting upon the living conditions of European Jewry, he urged that Great Britain cease her reported aggressions against Palestinian Jews, to avoid, he said, "an embittered struggle against the British Government." In September the detention of four Jewish Agency for Palestine officials, among the many Jews arrested by the British, was seen as the main obstacle to Zionist attendance at a British-sponsored conference of Arabs and Jews. Dr. Goldstein has criticized the United States Government for not influencing the British to open Palestine to displaced Jews, and declared (New York *Times,* October 29) that the Nazi war criminals' slate of crimes will not be abrogated "unless and until their chief victims, the Jews, will be able to live a life of dignity in their national home in Palestine." Subsequent to the November elections in the United States, the rabbi commented that in 1947-49 "the American system of checks and balances can be vindicated . . . with devotion to our national interest as the paramount criterion of the leaders of both political parties." His comment on Henry Wallace's letter to President Truman on United States foreign policy (made public in September) was that it should help America to understand why Russia distrusts and fears our intentions. . . . Either the United States or Russia must break this vicious circle of distrust."

Dr. Goldstein, who defines religion as "international-mindedness" and concern with "world salvation," was in October 1943 one of one hundred and forty-four leaders of the Protestant, Catholic, and Hebrew faiths to sign a joint declaration of basic principles of peace: These called for "practical recognition of the moral law, the dignity of the individual and the rights of small peoples and minorities; establishment of an international society with power to make and enforce its laws; economic collaboration between states, and a just order within each state to insure adequate living standards for all." The religious leader has participated in interfaith groups since 1928, when he became a member of the National Conference of Christian and Jews; in 1946 he is a trustee and cochairman of its commission on religious organizations. Vice-chairman of the Interfaith Committee for Russian War Relief, he was also chairman of the Jewish Section of the Interfaith Committee to Aid the Democracies, which cooperated with the British War Relief Society. As the first president of the Albert Einstein Foundation, for a brief period in 1946, Dr. Goldstein announced that a Jewish-sponsored, nonsectarian university, supported by funds from Jewish organizations and individuals, would open in October 1947 on a site which has been procured in Waltham, Massachusetts. The university, as yet unnamed, whose single prototype is the Hebrew University of Jerusalem, is to be open to students and faculty members without regard to race or religion.

The rabbi has written several essays on Biblical subjects, has contributed to the *Universal Jewish Encyclopaedia,* and is the author of two books: *A Century of Judaism in New York* (1930), and *Toward a Solution* (1940). In 1945 he received the honorary degree of Doctor of Divinity from the Jewish Theological Seminary where he had lectured on homiletics in 1938. He became the first person to establish a lectureship during his lifetime at the seminary in 1946. The British War Relief Society has named an English children's nursing home in his honor. Since 1929 he has been the president of the Jewish Conciliation Board of America. He has also belonged to the national council of the Joint Distribution Committee, the board of directors of the National Jewish Welfare Board, and the Jewish Advisory Committee for the Boy and Girl Scouts. Interested in Government affairs, Dr. Goldstein was a member of the Citizens Committee on Unemployment Relief in 1933 and also served on the Department of Labor Committee on Immigration and Naturalization. In 1946 he is the public representative for the meat, poultry, and dairy industry in the Wages and Hours Division of the United States Department of Labor. He lists himself as a member of the Liberal Party.

A tall, heavy man with brown eyes, Dr. Goldstein is described as having a "dignified demeanor" which is "lightened by a sense of humor." He likes to stretch out on the grass in Central Park, which he considers his "front yard," and enjoys the theater and movies; however, he conscientiously tries to use what little spare time he has for reading history, biography, and the newspapers.

References

N Y Post p29 My 29 '44
Who's Who in America, 1946-47
Who's Who in American Jewry, 1938-39

GOODSPEED, EDGAR J(OHNSON)
Oct. 23, 1871- Biblical scholar; author
Address: h. 551 Perugia Way, Bel-Air, Los Angeles, Calif.

For more than forty years the educator and biblical scholar Edgar J. Goodspeed has been engaged in the study and collation of pre- and early-Christian Greek, Latin, and Semitic manuscripts. The results of this scholarship are best evident to the general public in Goodspeed's American Translation versions of the New Testament and of the Old Testament Apocrypha, which have been well received and have been reprinted in a number of new editions. For his translations, Goodspeed made use of newly discovered sources and background material, and for the purpose of language clarification attempted to approximate as nearly as possible the English idiom of twentieth century America. In providing more accurate interpretations of biblical episodes and theology and a simplified phraseology, he has rendered a service to readers and students of the Bible.

Edgar Johnson Goodspeed was born on October 23, 1871, the younger of two sons of Thomas Wakefield and Mary Ellen (Ten Broeke) Goodspeed. His birthplace was Quincy, Illinois. The Goodspeed family is of Oxfordshire origin, the family's first emigrant to American shores having been Roger Goodspeed, who settled in Barnstable on Cape Cod, Massachusetts, in 1639. Edgar's grandfather founded the village of Goodspeedville in New York State. Thomas Goodspeed, an eminent Baptist clergyman, helped to establish the present University of Chicago, subsequently becoming historian of the institution and a biographer; Mary Goodspeed was herself the daughter of a minister of the same denomination. Young Edgar during the ages of nine to twelve was tutored by his cousin, George S. Goodspeed. For two years after this, Edgar attended the college preparatory department of the Old University of Chicago. He was graduated with the final preparatory class in 1886, at the time that the Old University was obliged to close.

The fourteen-year-old student matriculated in the same year at Denison University (Granville, Ohio.) There he specialized in the classics—Latin and Greek—played baseball on his class's team, and became president of the Calliopean Literary Society in his senior year. Denison awarded no prizes to its students, but Goodspeed "showed best" in Greek, Latin, modern languages, and physiology. He was graduated with the B.A. degree in 1890. (It was during 1886-90 that Thomas Goodspeed was working to re-establish the University of Chicago. He interested John D. Rockefeller in donating funds to this project, and, with the secretary of the American Baptist Education Society, raised the remainder of the required money. Later Thomas Goodspeed became one of the university's incorporators, 1890-91, and served as registrar for a time and as a member of the board of trustees.) Then, for one year the clergyman's son studied Semitics at Yale Uni-

DeHaven Studio

EDGAR J. GOODSPEED

versity under Professor William R. Harper, later the University of Chicago's president, who had long urged the youth to become his student.

Goodspeed returned to Chicago to teach the classical languages at Morgan Park Academy (1891-92), and at South Side Academy during the school years 1894-98. Meanwhile he had entered, in 1892, the University of Chicago, where he remained six years as a postgraduate in linguistics and religion. A junior fellow in Semitics (1892-93) and an honorary fellow in the New Testament (1895-96), Goodspeed was the author of two theses: the first, for his Bachelor of Divinity diploma (1897) was entitled *An Unpublished Syriac Manuscript of the Gospels,* and the second, for his Ph. D. degree, *The Newberry Gospels.* In 1898 he received a two-year position as assistant in biblical and patristic Greek. While at the university, Goodspeed, whose career henceforth was primarily to involve biblical and philological research, joined the Alpha Delta Phi fraternity.

During the summer of 1895 Goodspeed's graduate studies at Chicago had brought him under the tutelage of Professor Caspar René Gregory, an American connected with the University of Leipzig. Gregory influenced him to pursue manuscript study and Greek paleology, and Goodspeed obtained for himself "a collection of undeciphered Greek papyri from Asiut, Egypt." These he edited and published (he was the "first American to take up the decipherment of Greek papyri"), his further investigations into the field leading, for a time in 1898-99, to work at Berlin's University and National Museum. His interests also brought him the friendship of the Oxford fellows Bernard Pyne Grenfell and Arthur Surridge Hunt, who later were to be acclaimed outstanding papyrologists. Their camp was stationed in Tebtunis, Egypt, where, in 1899-1900, financed by the University

of California, they were excavating manuscripts from an archaeological site. There they discovered crocodile mummies wrapped in papyri, and it was there, too, that Goodspeed visited the papyrologists. In the summer of 1900 at Oxford University, the American paleographer edited with Grenfell and Hunt part of their find, which, under their three names, appeared seven years later as the second volume of *Tebtunis Papyri.*

These Greek papyrus documents, uncovered mainly in Egypt late in the 1800's and after, were letters, deeds, contracts, and the like— seldom was any manuscript found bearing directly on the New Testament story—dating from the New Testament era and written by people in Egypt. Because the Greek of extant New Testament manuscripts and of these contemporary daily accounts was identical, Goodspeed and other scholars were able to conclude that New Testament Greek idiom, hitherto somewhat of a linguistic enigma, was the vernacular—informal, colloquial—Greek of the period. (Goodspeed develops this thesis further in "The Original Language of the Gospels," an *Atlantic Monthly* article for October 1934.) By means of studies in comparative philology and with the information, revealed by the papyri, about life in early Christian epochs, Goodspeed and a number of co-workers were able to examine and to translate, with a new understanding, the actual sources of the Christian Scripture.

When he returned to the University of Chicago, Goodspeed resumed teaching. Associate (1900-2), then instructor (1902-5) in biblical and patristic Greek, he was advanced to an assistant (1905-10), and later to an associate (1910-15), professorship. In 1915 the educator was made a full professor, and five years after became secretary to the university's president, retaining the latter post until 1924. During this period Goodspeed numbered among his publications *Greek Papyri from the Cairo Museum* (1902), *Homeric Vocabularies,* in conjunction with W. B. Owen (1906, second edition in 1909), *Index Patristicus* (Leipzig, 1907), and *Chicago Literary Papyri,* the following year. In 1908, to the *Patrologia Orientalis,* whose redactors were the Roman Catholic scholars Nau and Graffin, Goodspeed contributed *The Conflict of Severus.* He had edited it from Ethiopic manuscripts preserved in the British Museum. Among other Goodspeed works to appear were the *Index Apologeticus* (Leipzig) and the *Catalogue of University of Chicago Manuscripts,* with M. Sprengling, both in 1912, *Die aeltesten Apologeten* (Goettingen, 1914), *The Story of the New Testament* (it was published in 1916 and was translated afterward into Chinese and Japanese), and *Harmony of the Synoptic Gospels,* with E. D. Burton (1917).

With the groundwork already supplied by his inquiries into New Testament sources and contemporary records, Goodspeed completed, and published in September 1923, his transcription of the New Testament into the American Translation version. He dispensed with the anachronisms of the widely accepted King James or Authorized text of 1611 (the English Revised Version of 1881 and the American Standard Bible of 1901, though textually more accurate than the King James, had not been enthusiastically greeted because they lacked beauty of language) and omitted chapter and verse divisions. Insisting that the Scripture's message and meaning should outweigh considerations of literary form, Goodspeed employed (as he stated in the preface) "the simple, straightforward English of everyday expression" similar in essence to the Scripture's original idiom and not to the King James Elizabethan English, now to a great extent archaic. Goodspeed's work met with a mixed reception. Although a Boston *Transcript* reviewer thought he went beyond any modern translator in destroying the Testament's "rich language of reverence," most critics commended his thorough scholarship and the version's dignified tone. In praising the American Translation style, a *New Republic* review declared that Goodspeed's text "deserves to take its place as a standard of English prose as we speak it today."

Three parallel quotations taken from the King James and Goodspeed versions, respectively, illustrate some of the differences. Luke, Chap. 2:14: "Glory to God in the highest, and on earth peace, good will toward men"; "Glory to God in heaven and on earth! Peace to the men he favors!" John, Chap. 1:1: "In the beginning was the Word, and the Word was with God, and the Word was God"; "In the beginning the Word existed. The Word was with God, and the Word was divine." I Corinthians, Chap. 13:1: "Though I speak with the tongues of men and of angels, and have not charity, I am become as sounding brass, or a tinkling cymbal"; "If I can speak the languages of men and even of angels, but have no love, I am a noisy gong or a clashing cymbal."

Since its first publication, Goodspeed's New Testament has been reprinted fully or in part in the American Translation series, including the Bible (1931), the Short Bible (1933, now one of the Modern Library books), the Junior Bible (1936), the Complete Bible (1939), containing Goodspeed's translation of the Old Testament Apocrypha published alone a year previous, and the Goodspeed Parallel New Testament, with the Authorized Version (1943). By 1946 Goodspeed's translation had sold a total of 830,000 copies in its various forms. During World War II Army and Navy editions were distributed to servicemen. The Bible, for which J. M. Powis Smith, a University of Chicago biblicist and Goodspeed's collaborator, had directed Hebraic scholars in their Old Testament research, was the sole translation made from Greek and Hebrew original manuscripts. This version also marked the first occasion when biblical experts in both languages worked in conjunction on such a project. Although William Tyndale for his sixteenth century Bible—and most later English Protestant Bibles had reproduced his work to a certain extent—had employed Hebraic and Greek sources, Goodspeed, Smith, and their associates had the "advantage of eight thousand original manuscripts" (*The Literary Digest,* October 24,

1931, gives the figures) discovered since 1611. Goodspeed and Smith added the former's Apocrypha to their Complete Bible on the basis of historical precedent (discussed in the preface to the Apocrypha).

When the Revised Standard Version of the New Testament (for this new version the research, directed by Luther Weigle [46], was undertaken by the American Standard Bible Revision Committee of the International Council of Religious Education at the request of Protestant denominations in the United States and Canada) made its appearance in February 1946, it was lauded for its "direct, familiar, and yet beautiful diction." Goodspeed, a member of the committee since 1930, was one of the revisers, it was said, whose "influence" was felt throughout the work.

In the year that his New Testament first appeared, Goodspeed was appointed chairman of Chicago's New Testament department, a post he retained until his retirement as professor emeritus in 1937 at the age of sixty-five. From 1933 to 1937, his official university title was that of distinguished service professor. A year after his departure from the University of Chicago, Goodspeed became a lecturer in history at the University of California at Los Angeles where he remained for four years (1938-42), teaching also during the summers of 1945 and 1946. Other such posts of his were those of Richard lecturer at the University of Virginia (1939) and of lecturer in biblical literature at Scripps College during the year 1941-42.

Goodspeed's articles, dealing with historical and philological as well as biblical subjects, are to be found in periodicals such as the *American Journal of Theology,* the *American Journal of Semitic Languages, Biblical World, Classical Philology,* and the *Atlantic Monthly.* Among his other books—there are more than forty-five in all—are *Strange New Gospels* (1931), *A Greek Papyrus Reader,* aided by E. C. Colwell (1935), *The Story of the Bible* (1936)—it comprises his *Story of the New Testament* (1916), *Story of the Old Testament* (1934)— *Christianity Goes To Press* and *Four Pillars of Democracy* (1940), and *History of Early Christian Literature* (1942). These writings with his two volumes of essays, *Things Seen and Heard* (1925) and *Buying Happiness* (1932), called entertaining, whimsical, witty, and ironic, and his mystery novel, *The Curse in the Colophon,* which drew almost unanimous praise from the reviewers, attest to Goodspeed's versatility and variety of interests. In November 1946 appeared another of his works, *How to Read the Bible,* called by John Haynes Holmes in the New York *Herald Tribune* the "perfect 'reader's guide' to the Bible." Later in the year a complete bibliography of all the writings of the author who has gained the reputation for being "America's foremost biblical scholar" was to be published.

The professor emeritus is actively associated with, and has served as president of, the Society of Biblical Literature and Exegesis, and the Society of Midland Authors (Chicago), and is a member of the board of directors in

GOODSPEED, EDGAR J.—*Continued*

the Chicago and Los Angeles P.E.N. His clubs are the University (Chicago) and the University and Lincoln in Los Angeles. A regular member of Phi Beta Kappa, Goodspeed has also received the honorary degrees of D.D. and Litt.D. (Denison), and of L.H.D. and LL.D. from the universities of Redlands and California at Los Angeles, respectively. He is a deacon of the Baptist Church, and a Republican in his political affiliation. In December 1901 he was married to Elfleda Bond, daughter of Joseph Bond, after whom a University of Chicago chapel is named. Goodspeed collects early printings of the English Bible ("I have most of the editions from 1537 on," he stated), the Greek Testament, and Greek papyri. During one of his trips abroad he discovered, in 1927, in a Paris antique shop the "most richly miniatured Greek manuscript of the New Testament known," which Mrs. Edith Rockefeller McCormick bought at his urging. Edited by Goodspeed and others, it appeared in 1933 as the three-volume Rockefeller McCormick New Testament. The gray-eyed and white-haired scholar, who is five feet ten inches tall and weighs 153 pounds, lists his outdoor recreations as automobile touring and motor boating.

References

International Who's Who, 1945-46
Who's Who in America, 1946-47

GORING, HERMANN WILHELM (gû'-rĭng) Jan. 12, 1893—Oct. 16, 1946 Most powerful Nazi, Hitler's chosen heir; commander in chief of the Luftwaffe from 1933; field marshal, 1938; tried by the International Military Tribunal, judged "a leading war aggressor . . . director of the slave labor program. . . .He developed the Gestapo, and created the first concentration camps"; condemned to be hanged; committed suicide. See *Current Biography* 1941 Yearbook.

Obituary

N Y Times p1+ O 16 '46

GORT, (JOHN STANDISH SURTEES PRENDERGAST VEREKER, 6TH) VISCOUNT July 10, 1886—Mar. 31, 1946 British Army officer; entered the Grenadier Guard in 1905, rose to field marshal; chief of Imperial General Staff, 1937-39; commander in chief of British Expeditionary Force in France, 1939-40, led famous rear-guard action at Dunkerque; Governor and commander in chief of Gibraltar, 1941-42, of Malta, 1942-44; High Commissioner and commander in chief for Palestine and High Commissioner for Trans-Jordan, October 1944-November 1945; "most decorated officer in thirty years." See *Current Biography* 1940 Yearbook.

Obituary

N Y Times Ap 1 '46 por

GOUIN, FELIX (gwăn fã"lĕks') Oct. 4, 1884- French political leader and Government official

Address: War Ministry, Paris

Until the June 1946 elections, the provisional President of France was Felix Gouin, a veteran Right-wing Socialist and one of the few members of the French parliament who dared to oppose Hitler, Laval, and Pétain after the fall of France. Elected in January 1946, when he was sixty-one, Gouin had served fifteen years in the Assembly, and had been president of the Free French Provincial Consultative Assemblies in London, Algiers, and Paris. His full title was President of the Council of Ministers.

Born October 4, 1884, in Peypin, a town in the Mediterranean-bounded department of Bouches-du-Rhône, Félix Gouin is of the Provençal middle class. Both of his parents were school teachers. After receiving his Bachelor of Letters degree from the Lycée of Marseille, which he had entered as a scholarship student, young Gouin began the study of law at the near-by city of Aix and was admittted to the bar in 1907. He was not twenty when he joined the Socialist Party in 1904, and ever since he has been one of the most faithful workers of the party's Right wing. The first seventeen years of his career (except for his service throughout World War I as a private), were those of a successful lawyer with political ambitions. During this time he was elected Councillor General of Bouches-du-Rhône (1911) and mayor of Istres (1923). In 1924 he was elected to the Chamber of Deputies by the voters of Aix, and was re-elected with ever increasing majorities in 1928, 1932, and 1936. From 1924 to 1936 he was a member of the Chamber's Commission on Civil and Criminal Law; from 1936 to 1940 a member of its Finance Commission, which, at the outbreak of war, appointed him to a subcommittee for the control of armaments, in charge of inspecting war industries. His expertness as parliamentarian, says Jan Hasbrouck of the Paris *Post,* secured him the leadership of the Socialist parliamentary group in the Léon Blum[40] regime.

After the fall of France to the Germans in June 1940, Gouin showed himself to be "a courageous militant." He was one of the eighty parliament members who refused to vote full power to Marshal Pétain. After Pétain came into power, Gouin, with a few trustworthy friends, attempted to reorganize the Socialist Party in the unoccupied zone. He was also responsible, reports *Free France,* for organizing the liaison between the reborn Socialist organizations and the southern resistance movements. In 1941, when Blum went on trial before the Nazis at the High Court of Riom, Gouin was one of the defendant's three lawyers. In 1942 he was chosen representative of his party in the De Gaulle Government-in-exile in London, following which the fifty-eight-year-old patriot braved the dangers of illegal departure from his home. He escaped from France into Spain by shaving his full black mustache, posing as an Englishman with the aid of a 1939 British ration card which gave his name as "Gouib." His wife, to explain his absence, complained to all who would listen that Gouin had eloped with another woman. Once inside Spain, however, he was less fortunate—he was detained for three months in Miranda, a Spanish concentration camp. Finally, he reached England in August 1942. During his year's stay there the Socialist headed the State Reforms Commission which drew up the draft text of the Consultative Assembly's constitution. He was also made president of a French Parliamentary group, composed of ten deputies and one senator.

When De Gaulle moved his Government to Algiers in September 1943, Gouin accompanied him. There he made the material arrangements for the Provisional Consultative Assembly, and on the following November 10 was chosen its head, a post to which he was re-elected in May 1944. He was similarly elected on November 8, 1944, after a new Assembly had been formed in Paris. The members of these Assemblies had not been elected by the people of France, but by the parties separately. However, the assemblymen elected by the people in October 1945 (the first national election held in France in nine years) gave Gouin 512 votes for the presidency out of 543. Gouin's popularity with his colleagues, in the opinion of the *Christian Science Monitor,* is due to his defense of parliamentarism against authoritarian trends in De Gaulle's Fighting France Movement.

In February, before the 1945 national election, Gouin called for consolidation of France's nineteen political parties into two or three strong groups. This consolidation, he said, would give the administration a stable majority and enable the country to maintain "continuity" in internal and foreign affairs. As a first step, Gouin urged completion of the then current negotiations to merge the Socialist and Communist parties into one great Left-wing party. Although the Socialists "overwhelmingly rejected fusion with the Communists" in August, two months before the national election, France emerged with three major parties, of almost equal strength—the Communists, with 152 seats in the Assembly, the Socialists with 142, and the new left-of-center Catholic party (Mouvement Républicain Populaire), the MRP, with 141 seats. All three parties were of the Resistance; and all three, commented the New York *Times,* "are of the Left, though in varying degrees. At present all agree on certain fundamental principles, including wider socialization. . . .The primary task of the Assembly is to replace the Constitution of 1875 with a new one to be submitted to the people in a national referendum," which was to take place seven months after the October 21 elections. At this time a new Assembly was to be elected, and in turn it would elect a new president of the Republic.

The Socialists, Gouin's party, and the Communists joined the MRP in electing General de Gaulle to the presidency in November 1945. But France's liberator soon found himself in conflict with the Leftist Assembly. A "moderate bloc" of Socialists and MRP's sustained

French Press & Inf. Service

FELIX GOUIN

him in his first clash with the Communists, the strongest single party. De Gaulle took the view that French Communists were not truly representatives of a national party, and refused to give them one of the key ministries. Gouin was proposed for the presidency by the Communists, but refused the nomination, and the Socialist caucus decided against forming a two-party government. The Communists were voted down 400 to 163. New Year's Day of 1946 brought a final break, on the old issue of legislative power versus executive power. The Constituent Assembly, which was writing a constitution for the Fourth Republic, wished to give future parliaments "almost absolute" power, while De Gaulle insisted that France needed a strong executive. Another cause of dissension was the Socialist-Communist demand for a 20 per cent cut in the Army budget, which De Gaulle felt would reduce France to the level of a Balkan state.

On January 22, 1946, De Gaulle resigned. After other candidates were found unacceptable, the MRP went on record as holding that only the Socialists represented "a middle around which extremes could gather"; the Communists nominated Félix Gouin, and he was elected, 497 to 55. "It is a bad situation, but I'll try to do my best," said the new President of France.

Editorial comment from the French press darkly predicted that Gouin would be facing the same situation as that which confronted De Gaulle, but with "none of the latter's strong leadership with which to hold hopelessly ill-mated horses together." *Figaro* described the new Government as "a transitional ministry" which would serve the chief purpose of speeding up the constitutional action and thereby new elections. Editorial comment from the American press was no more sanguine. "The net result of the change," said the New York

GOUIN, FELIX—*Continued*

World-Telegram, "is a weaker executive and worse instability." Regarding Gouin as a Communist puppet, that editorial declared: "If the Communists succeed in making France weak in the military and economic fields, and a Russian stooge politically, she will lose her international influence and succumb to chaos at home." In the opinion of the New York *Herald Tribune* Gouin had been chosen because, being colorless, he offended fewer members of the Assembly than other candidates, and not because he was expected to be a strong executive. "The Assembly has, in fact, taken the Government into its own hands." The *Christian Science Monitor* regarded Gouin's election as "an expression of embarrassment rather than of strength" on the part of the Assembly—a compromise candidate, as none of the parties accepted the real leader of one of the others as head of the Government. Randolph Churchill declared in his syndicated column that if nothing else, De Gaulle's dramatic gesture in resigning "will force every Frenchman to make up his mind once and for all where he stands on the fundamental issue of whether France is to be governed by Frenchmen or Russians." In his opinion, the decision of the Socialists to cooperate with the Communists had been "an abandonment of their principles for the sake of party advantages." The New York *Times,* on the other hand, said that while Gouin was not a "spectacular character," he was "courageous and level-headed," and might be "able to hold the Government together where the less adaptable De Gaulle could not."

Wearied by three days of bickering over his Cabinet selections, Gouin sent an open letter to leaders of the three major parties in which he said that France faced a grave financial peril and had to take drastic action to meet it. In conclusion he warned that unless his plan for retrenchment were accepted he would abandon efforts to form a government. The plan included deflationary budget cuts, wage and price freezing, limits on nationalization, crushing of black markets, speed-up of food and other commodity distribution. For the French public it meant that there would be less meat, less wine, fewer potatoes, and no increase in the limited amount of bread.

Gouin's program, John O'Reilly of the *Herald Tribune* pointed out, was, with slight modifications, the same program presented by the Radical Socialist Pierre Mendès-France. It was he who had turned down the finance portfolio when his proposals did not meet with full three-party approval and who had resigned from his post of Finance Minister in the De Gaulle Cabinet when the former President refused to consider his program. The agreement of the three major parties to his plan for retrenchment marked Gouin's first victory. On January 26 he announced that he had formed a new Cabinet. André Philip replaced René Pleven as Finance Minister, but eleven of the ministers chosen by Gouin had held posts in De Gaulle's Cabinet. (Six, including Gouin, who retained the Defense Ministry, had never

before held a Cabinet post.) The major parties were represented by seven Socialists, eight Communists, six MRPs and one independent. Gouin, as president, was considered to be of no party.

More drastic cuts than even Gouin had proposed were announced in the first weeks of the new regime. The French Army budget was cut in half and an equal slashing of civil expenditures also was announced. "To show how near France has been to bankruptcy," writes Volney Hurd (*Christian Science Monitor*), "it is pointed out that with the deficit prior to the announced cuts running to one billion francs a day and the Bank of France having a reserve of only 116 billion francs, that in four months France would have faced a financial breakdown." Gouin's chances for re-election were seen as depending upon the success of his deflation plan. He had won praise for his courage in making plain the facts about France's financial crisis to the people, and his program to offset it was considered strong.

Public opinion changed, however, when Gouin advocated an Anglo-French pact and entered into negotiations with England's Foreign Secretary Ernest Bevin [40]. As a concession to the British, Gouin was willing to forego a settlement of the Ruhr problem, involving detachment of the Rhineland from Germany proper, but unanimous opposition of his Cabinet, led by Georges Bidault [45], overruled him in April 1946. Opposition also came from the Communists who suspected that the French, German, and British Socialists were planning a Western bloc. This was the beginning of a breach between the Communists and the Socialists.

His Cabinet's veto meant a loss of prestige to Gouin. Although he had offered a compromise draft, in May 1946, the referendum on the constitution was rejected by an increasingly anti-Leftist electorate of nineteen million. An American loan of nearly one and a half billion dollars, obtained for the French nation by ex-Premier Blum, salvaged the Socialist position somewhat, but even so, their support declined by 11 per cent. Gouin had already tendered the resignation of his Government in a constitutional step to prepare the way for the formation of a new Government of which Georges Bidault was chosen provisional president. Gouin became his Vice-Premier.

The consistent foreign policy of the De Gaulle, Gouin, and Bidault Governments was given a sharp rebuff in July 1946 by Russia's refusal to detach the Ruhr from the Rhineland and place it under French administration. But this withdrawal of support had been hinted at by the attitude of the French Communists during the electoral campaign, when they attacked the Gouin Government's program of stabilizing wages, the American loan, and the revised constitution. The French Socialists, refusing to join the Communists because of their association with Moscow, took control from Blum's "Old Guard" in September 1946 and formed a new board of directors from a group of "insurgent and nonparliamentary" leaders.

Gouin declined to be a candidate. Two months later the veteran Socialist was elected for a five-year term as deputy to the new National Assembly, the first legislature to meet under the terms of the constitution ratified in September. The deadlock between Rightists and Leftists in December led to Gouin's name being mentioned as a possible choice for a coalition Premier; Gouin had previously endorsed Maurice Thorez [46], the Communist candidate, who was defeated for lack of Socialist support. A Socialist Premier was eventually chosen, but he was, however, Léon Blum rather than Gouin. In the Cabinet formed by the new Premier, Gouin was named Minister in charge of the Four Year Economic Plan, responsible for stabilizing France's economy and for implementing the nationalization of industry.

"France's Calvin Coolidge", "the man without any enemies," are the phrases applied to "Smiling Félix" Gouin. He is described as likable, forthright, voluble but unflowery, and "utterly unspectacular, with little of the dash and vehemence one associates with Frenchmen of the South." He is, however, considered typical of the solid French middle class. Five feet five inches tall (the average height of the French soldiers) Gouin is stout, "penguin-shaped," clean-shaven, and dressed unassumingly in dark suits. His black eyes are rimmed in heavy horn-rimmed spectacles; his gray hair was once black, too. The Socialist leader is said to be a crack marksman who does not waste a shot in his hunting. His love of good food, especially Provençal dishes, extends to considerable skill at cooking. Other Gouin interests are collecting paintings—he has a hundred of them, some quite valuable—and playing bridge with his wife, who is one of France's most noted furniture designers. Described as a systematic, hard-working politician who seldom loses his sleep or misses his meals, nor indulges in unbridled partisanship, Gouin has no eccentricities, except for often getting up at five in the morning to do some work in the quiet hours.

References

Christian Sci Mon p9 N 11 '45
Free France 6:497 D 15 '44
Life 20:43-4 Mr 25 '46 por
N Y Herald Tribune II p3 Ja 27 '46
N Y Post p2 Ja 24 '46
N Y Sun p22 N 16 '45
Time 47:28 F 4 '46

Dictionnaire National des Contemporains (1936)

GOULD, ARTHUR R(OBINSON) (gōōld)

Mar. 16, 1857—July 24, 1946 United States Republican Senator from Maine, 1926-30; pioneer industrialist of Aroostook County; operated a lumber mill; built a hydro-electric plant and railroads serving the lumber industry.

Obituary

N Y Times p21 Jl 25 '46

GRAHAM, SHIRLEY

Nov. 11, 1907- Author

Address: h. 3111 Broadway, New York

Shirley Graham, author and composer, is best known for her biographies of famous Negroes, written for young people. The story of George Washington Carver [46], which she and George Lipscomb coauthored, was said to "accomplish the seemingly impossible . . . a book which is

Calhoun

SHIRLEY GRAHAM

written in a popular, almost lyrical vein, which is yet a searching character study." Miss Graham is also the author of a biography of Paul Robeson [41].

Shirley Graham's great-grandfather was freed from slavery by his owner before the Civil War. An industrious blacksmith, he earned enough money to buy a farm near Evansville, Indiana, where his farmhouse was subsequently used as a station on the underground railway by means of which runaway slaves escaped to Canada. Born there on November 11, 1907, Shirley Graham was thus a fourth generation Hoosier, with a storied family tradition. Her late father, the Reverend David A. Graham, was a Methodist minister. He and his wife, the former Etta Bell, reared their daughter and four sons in parsonages all over the country. The girl's first memories were of New Orleans. She remembers her father as a remarkable storyteller: he did not read fairy tales to her, but novels like *Ben Hur* and *Quo Vadis*, interpolating colorful explanations which "brought the Bible world to life." Her father eventually went to preach in the West, to which large numbers of Negroes had newly migrated. She was graduated from the Lewis and Clark High School in Spokane, Washington. The class poet, she also won first prize in writing for an essay on Booker T. Washington. Soon after graduation Miss Graham was married. Her husband

GRAHAM, SHIRLEY—*Continued*

died three years later, leaving her with two baby sons.

In 1929 her father was made head of a mission school in Liberia, Africa. She accompanied him across the Atlantic but remained in Paris, where for a year she studied music composition at the Sorbonne. She has told how she was fascinated by the French-Africans of Paris, "colored people who couldn't speak a word of English." Following them about she learned their "strange rhythms and haunting melodies," which were neither African nor European, but a combination of both. On her return to the United States in 1930 she became a music teacher at Morgan College, a Negro school in Baltimore. She taught for two years, then entered Oberlin College in Ohio to work for her Bachelor's degree, earning expenses by sorting clothes and doing clerical work in a laundry.

While at Oberlin she wrote and composed a musical play, *Tom-Tom*, for a school production. At the suggestion of Ernst Lert, director for the Cleveland Summer Opera Company, she built *Tom-Tom* into an opera, a sixteen-scene dramatization of the Negro's coming out of Africa to America, which opened in the African jungle, and closed with a scene in New York's Harlem. All its music she developed from centuries-old African themes and rhythms, some of them brought from Liberia by her brother. The long chant of the old-style Negro preacher replaced the traditional opera recitative, and tom-toms were important in the score. Produced by the Cleveland Company in July 1932, with Jules Bledsoe in the lead, it brought her critical attention as a folk-poet and an offer from a prominent musician who wished to finance her studies in Vienna. She decided, however, to remain in America with her young sons. Oberlin awarded her a Bachelor's degree in 1934, and a Master's in 1935; the title of her thesis was "Survivals of Africanisms in Modern Music." During 1935-36 she taught music and arts at the Tennessee State College in Nashville.

In the summer of 1936 Miss Graham became interested in the Negro unit of the Chicago Federal Theater, which at the time was almost inactive. Accepting the position of supervisor, she remained with the unit three years, directing and designing productions, organizing acting classes, and writing musical scores for plays, thereby helping to build the unit to a position of national theatrical importance. She directed and designed, and wrote the music for its 1937 production of *Little Black Sambo* for children. "Critics put it on the 'must' list for children, commented on the skill and understanding of its direction and the vivid jungle quality of sets and music," Hallie Flanagan wrote in *Arena*, the story of the Federal Theater. In 1938 the same unit produced *Swing Mikado*, which the Chicago *Tribune* called the hit of the season, and which was subsequently brought to Broadway. Awarded a Julius Rosenwald Fellowship for creative writing, Miss Graham spent most of the next two years (1938-40)

at the Yale School of Drama, where her three-act *Dust to Earth* was produced in January 1941. Other shorter plays by Miss Graham were put on by various university groups and by the Gilpin Players in Cleveland. Her radio play *Track Thirteen* was heard over the Mutual network. From 1941 to 1943 she was a USO director at Fort Huachaca in Arizona, where she planned and directed theatricals and art exhibits, and started a camp magazine.

Miss Graham collaborated with George Lipscomb to write *Dr. George Washington Carver: Scientist* (1944) for teen-age readers. Its readability for adults as well as children, its lyricism and dignity impressed reviewers. "There is inspiration in the poignant picture the authors paint of Carver," wrote the *Christian Science Monitor* reviewer, while the comment of the *Saturday Review of Literature* was, "Their book has the simplicity and dignity that is necessary to interpret Dr. Carver accurately to the public." Miss Graham's second biography for young people, *Paul Robeson, Citizen of the World*, was published in 1946. "Shirley Graham has somehow known how to combine in her story the strong forward march of Paul Robeson's career," Carl Van Doren wrote in his introduction to the book, "with a sympathetic account of his own daily difficulties and uncertainties. . . .His story is a hero story, because it had to be." Scheduled for early 1947 publication is her next book, "There Was Once a Slave," an historical novel for adults built around the life of Frederick Douglass, the escaped slave who became an abolitionist leader. The manuscript of Miss Graham's book won her in December of 1946 the Julian Messner Award of $6,500—of this sum $3,500 was contributed by the Lionel Judah Tachna Foundation—for "the best book combating intolerance in America." The judges were Clifton Fadiman, Lewis Gannett, and Carl Van Doren. Miss Graham's next book will be a biography of Anne Newport Royall, the pioneer American woman journalist, who early in the nineteenth century was a newspaper publisher in the nation's capital.

A petite woman (she weighs 128 pounds, is five feet two inches tall), the author becomes shining-eyed and as enthusiastic as a schoolgirl when she discusses her work. She is likely to turn the conversation with some pride to her son, David Graham McCanns, who was discharged in 1946 as a lieutenant after three years of military service. (Her older son is deceased.) Articles by Miss Graham have appeared in *Common Sense* and *Etude*, and in other publications. In 1946 she was completing her doctorate in English and education at New York University. She likes to think of herself as a teacher in the broadest sense: she hopes to inspire the young people of minority groups to optimism and achievement with her stories of the great men of the Negro race, of whom she says, "These are Americans young people ought to know about."

Reference

Christian Sci Mon p4 Ap 8 '46 por

GRANGER, LESTER B(LACKWELL)
Sept. 16, 1896- Social agency executive

Address: b. c/o National Urban League, 1133 Broadway, New York; h. 270 Convent Ave., New York

Lester B. Granger, race relations expert active since 1919 in social work and related educational service, is the executive secretary of the National Urban League for Social Work among Negroes. The Urban League primarily works to develop economic opportunities for Negroes in large industrial centers. Granger himself perhaps best summed up the ultimate objectives of the League when, at a meeting of the American Civil Liberties Union, he proposed four freedoms for the members of his race—"the right to work, the right to vote, the right to physical safety, and the right to dignity and self-respect."

Lester Blackwell Granger was born September 16, 1896, in Newport News, Virginia, which was also the birthplace of his schoolteacher mother, the former Mary L. Turpin. His father, William Randolph Granger, a native of the Barbadoes, West Indies, had sailed from the Indies as a cabin boy, and had jumped ship in an American port. In the United States William Granger earned an M.D. degree by working his way through Bucknell University and the University of Vermont. Lester is the only one of the doctor's six sons who did not study medicine or dentistry. Instead, after taking a B.A. degree at Dartmouth College in 1918, he applied for admission to Harvard Law School. World War I interrupted his plans, however, and he enlisted in the Army, sailing to France with the Ninety-second Division.

By the time Lester Granger received his army discharge he had changed his mind about studying law. In April 1919 he took a job in the Newark Urban League's industrial relations department, which in effect serves as an employment agency for Negroes in its area. Realizing that his background was inadequate for the work, he resigned after seven months, "to the politely concealed relief of my superior," he says. After this young Granger taught for a time in 1920 in North Carolina schools—at the Slater Normal School in Winston Salem and at St. Augustine College in Raleigh. During 1921 he took graduate studies at New York University.

In 1922 the twenty-six-year-old Negro became an extension worker for the New Jersey State Manual Training School at Bordentown. He remained with the school until 1934, counseling, handling publicity, coaching the athletes, and working with parents' groups. The school's chief bookkeeper, Harriet Lane, became his wife on August 11, 1923. During his twelve years at Bordentown, Granger became increasingly interested in professional social work: he took courses at the New York School for Social Work and, in 1930, after obtaining a year's leave from Bordentown, he organized the Urban League in Los Angeles. Finally, in 1934 he left the New Jersey State School and joined the staff of the Urban League in New York.

In the national offices in New York Granger first was business manager of the League's magazine *Opportunity*, and then headed the Worker's Education Bureau for four years. Given a two-year leave of absence in 1938 he served as secretary on Negro Welfare for the New York City Welfare Council. (Granger was elected to a one-year term as vice-president of the council in June 1946.) Upon his return to the National Urban League in 1940 he took the post of assistant executive secretary, becoming executive secretary in 1941. He later became a member of the board of directors of the Union for Democratic Action. During his years in New York he was active in social service organizations. A member of the National Board of the American Association of Social Workers from 1940 to 1942, he was first vice-president of that association in 1942. He served, as well, on the executive committee of the National Conference of Social Work and on the advisory committee on social service of the United States Children's Bureau.

With the coming of World War II, Granger felt that the League had "attained an importance unsurpassed in its whole history." The League urged that jobs be made available to Negroes in war industry, fought discrimination in the armed forces, and, at the same time, combated the cynicism or indifference of the many Negroes who suffered disillusioning experiences. Early in 1943, at the end of the nation's first year at war, Granger prepared the annual report of the League. "The influence of the League's leadership," he wrote, "has been placed against cynicism and defeatism within the ranks of Negroes, as well as against that blind racial prejudice that puts barriers in the way of Negroes as they come to their country's defense." The League had been acting as "a trouble shooter in solving knotty racial problems," he explained. "We have fought against attempts in war industry to extend the physical segregation of Negro workers from whites. We have insisted upon housing for Negro workers in all war industry centers on the highest possible rather than on the lowest plane of interracial relationships. We have pointed out the mistakes and weaknesses in organizing Negro civilians for various defense programs."

As a man considered "one of the best informed Negro spokesmen on the subject of the Negro's problems" by newspapers like the *Christian Science Monitor*, Granger was several times interviewed on race problems during the war years. He presented graphic pictures of critical housing conditions, animosity between races in war industries, and the difficulties of Negroes who migrated to industrial areas to work in war plants. He warned of greater difficulties to come if these problems were not faced with honesty and practicality during the war. Soon after his 1943 report was made public, Granger was called on for comment by the newspaper *PM* when Secretary of the Navy Knox declared that the Navy's "experimental" Negro program had been approved by Negro leaders. Granger said, "The League sees no reason why the use of Negro sailors,

Blackstone Studios, Inc.

LESTER B. GRANGER

marines, and members of the Coast Guard should be an 'experiment' in a democracy. Neither does the League approve the over-timid and frequently contradictory policies which the Navy Department has instituted."

In the spring of 1945 the Navy Department adopted a new policy which disavowed all theories of racial superiority and urged the fullest use of Negro manpower. Secretary of the Navy James Forrestal selected Granger as a special adviser on the new nondiscriminatory policy. From June until September 1945 Granger toured naval bases, traveling fifty thousand miles in three trips which took him to the Great Lakes, the Pacific Coast, and to many Pacific islands. He spoke with high ranking Naval officers, and with Negro and white enlisted personnel, and returned to report that the Navy's policy was "absolutely sound," but that it needed "vigorous policing." He found that Naval officers were increasingly eliminating segregation and discrimination in accordance with official policy. After the end of the war, in April 1946 he became a member of the Navy's civilian advisory committee to study methods for making naval service a better career for young men.

On December 31, 1945, Granger was awarded the Navy's highest civilian decoration, the Distinguished Civilian Service Award, in recognition of his counsel on Navy policy toward Negro personnel. The citation from Secretary of the Navy Forrestal reads, in part: "By inspection of continental and overseas naval activities during which his tactful and forthright advice won the respect of men and officers alike, Mr. Granger personally evaluated the position of the Negro in the Navy, suggesting general policies as well as solutions for specific cases. Courageous and fair in criticism, honest and temperate in praise, Mr. Granger has performed a delicate and important

task in a manner deserving of the Navy's highest civilian award." This honor was not the first recognition of his work. In 1944 the Congress of Industrial Organizations presented him with an award for outstanding work in race relations, and in 1943, for the same reason, he was cited by the New Jersey Organization of Teachers of Colored Children. A nationwide poll conducted by officials of the Schomburg Collection of Negro Literature of the New York Public Library during Negro History Week in February 1946 named Granger one of the twelve Negroes and six white men who had contributed most toward bettering race relations.

Granger has written articles for such magazines as *Survey Graphic, The Annals of the American Academy of Political and Social Science, Survey Midmonthly,* and *Opportunity.* Among the pamphlets he has written, or collaborated on, are *Occupational Opportunities For Negroes,* one of the "Color Line Series" of the Urban League, and *Toward Job Adjustment,* written for the New York Welfare Council. The League's publications, to which Granger frequently contributes, are considered by social workers and students as important source materials for the study of Negro life. Granger also serves as a member of the editorial board of the *Social Work Year Book,* and on the editorial advisory board of *Survey Graphic.*

An inch under six feet tall, Granger weighs over two hundred pounds. He wears two pairs of glasses when he reads, which gives him "a most scholarly look." Dartmouth College, his alma mater, awarded him an honorary Doctorate of Humane Letters in June 1946. As a student there, Granger had become a member of Alpha Phi Alpha. He is an Episcopalian in religion, a Democrat in politics.

References

N Y Post p21 My 8 '45
PM p23 Ja 18 '46
Who's Who in America, 1946-47

GRAYSON, DAVID *See* Baker, R. S.

GRIFFIN, BERNARD (WILLIAM), CARDINAL Feb. 21, 1899- Roman Catholic prelate

Address: Archbishop's House, Westminster Cathedral, London

Spiritual father to the nearly two and a half million Catholics in England and Wales is Bernard Cardinal Griffin, Archbishop of Westminster. The youngest prince of the Roman Catholic Church when he was elevated to the purple in 1945, just one year after he had been appointed to the See of Westminster, he is regarded as an outstanding British liberal, a man of strong convictions who does not hesitate to state his views.

Characterized as a typical son of the English Midlands, Bernard William Griffin was born February 21, 1899, in the industrial city of Birmingham, to William and Helen (Swadkins) Griffin. His father, a devout Catholic, was a bicycle manufacturer and a city councilor. Of the five children, three daughters and two sons, two others also became servants of the Church, one a nun, and the Cardinal's twin a Benedictine monk. Revealing a noticeable "ease of scholarship," young Bernard attended first Cotton College, the Midlands Catholic preparatory institution in Staffordshire, and later Oscott in Birmingham. Although his intention was to become a priest, during World War I he interrupted his studies to join the Naval wing of the Royal Flying Corps, which in 1918 was merged with the Army branch to form the Royal Air Force. Having entered the service without a commission, he found the experience deepened his insight into the ways of the ordinary man; also from the war years dates his keen interest in aviation.

After his discharge from the RAF at the end of the war, Griffin returned to Oscott, where, wrote Douglas Newton, British author, "his fervor and his brilliance carried him forward so forcefully that he was sent to Rome to complete his studies." From 1921 to 1926 Griffin was a student at the Venerable English College in Rome, the second oldest national college in the Eternal City, from 1926 to 1927 at Beda College, also in Rome, obtaining doctorates in divinity and canon law. He had been ordained in 1924, and in England he was soon to gain recognition as a leading canon lawyer.

In Birmingham in 1927 the young priest became private secretary to Archbishop John McIntyre, from 1929 to 1937 continuing in that capacity under his successor, Archbishop Thomas L. Williams. At the same time, beginning in 1929, he served as Chancellor of the Archdiocese of Birmingham and assumed the added duties of director of studies of the Catholic Evidence Guild and Catholic representative on the Religious Advisory Committee of the British Broadcasting Corporation. In 1938, to fill the need for an assistant to Archbishop Williams, Griffin was consecrated Bishop of the titular See of Abya and appointed Auxiliary Bishop of Birmingham by Pope Pius XI. One year earlier the active young churchman had been made administrator of Father Hudson's Homes, the largest Catholic orphanage in England, situated in Coleshill in the environs of Birmingham. There, during the eight years of his incumbency, he completely reorganized the government of the institution, added new nurseries, erected a new church, and won the affection of the children, to whose individual cases he brought a deep concern.

Then, on December 22, 1943, word was received in England that Pope Pius XII had chosen Bishop Griffin to succeed the late Cardinal Hinsley as the sixth Archbishop of Westminster since the restoration of the Catholic hierarchy in 1850. The appointment, which made him Roman Catholic primate of England and Wales as well as ordinary of the Diocese of Westminster, was as welcome as it was unexpected, according to the commentators. Although Griffin's reputation was primarily local, they said, he is regarded as one of the most liberal and progressive of English Catholics. In particular they pointed to his administration of Father Hudson's Homes, to the fact that he was perhaps the only Catholic bishop to par-

Vandyk, London
BERNARD CARDINAL GRIFFIN

ticipate as an active air-raid warden in the civilian defense effort, and to his appearances before immense crowds in Birmingham's Bull Ring, an open-air arena for controversial speakers comparable to London's Hyde Park or New York's Columbus Circle.

At the enthronement ceremonies in Westminster Cathedral on January 18, 1944, Archbishop Griffin delivered an "outspoken, unconventional" sermon—denouncing "easy divorce" and birth control as destructive of "the sanctity of the marriage bond and the sacredness of the family" and attacking the proposed education bill as "gravely affecting" the prerogatives of parents in the education of their children and as discriminating against Catholics. For family allowances as outlined in the Beveridge report he expressed his approval, "providing always," he added in a qualification, "that the freedom of the individual and the family is secured."

While Auxiliary Bishop of Birmingham, he had had an important part in the drafting of the pastoral letter issued by the Archbishops of Westminster, Liverpool, Cardiff, and Birmingham in 1942 condemning, among the malpractices of the social system, the failure of industry in many instances to pay a wage sufficient for comfort and saving and the consequent denial of security to larges masses of workers. As Archbishop of Westminster, in 1946 he summarized his views on labor-industry strife with a strong defense of the right of working men to organize, agitate, and strike for a living wage and better working conditions; but he issued an equally strong warning that labor, too, may be guilty of injustice. "In the old Christian guilds," he said, "master and man sat together and it was not considered essential . . . to foment conflict between employer and employed. . . .There is a just price for work as well as for goods. Men engaged in essential services can throttle their fellow

GRIFFIN,   BERNARD,   CARDINAL
—*Continued*

citizens. . . .Remember, while the worker is right to fight injustices which would seek to victimize him, he in turn must observe justice not only to his employer but to the whole community."

On the international front, Griffin has aroused the ire of Russian and Polish newspapers, especially of *Izvestia*, for his rejection of the Yalta agreements on Poland, his championship of the Polish forces in Britain, and his plain speaking concerning Soviet policies and the growing rift between West and East. "We are disturbed in our own consciences," he said on one occasion, "when we receive reliable reports from many countries which fought with us in the war which show that these countries are still in fetters and under the domination of a foreign power." On another: "It is false to describe as democratic a system where liberty is refused to the individual and where elections are held with no choice of candidates allowed to the electors. It is difficult for us to imagine freedom existing in countries where secret police and the dread of concentration camps are the most potent sanction of a nation's law." As guest speaker at the Charter Centenary Dinner of Fordham University during his visit to the United States in 1946, he voiced a similar opinion.

Exactly two years after his elevation to the throne of Westminster, Archbishop Griffin received one of the Church's highest honors when he was named by Pope Pius XII as one of thirty-two prelates from nineteen countries to become Cardinals at the history-making consistory of February 18, 1946. For the first time since the Great Schism of the fourteenth century the traditional Italian majority in the Sacred College was broken, and for the first time in history a representative was allotted to each of the continents of the world. Only forty-six years old at the time, the English prelate also had the distinction of becoming the world's youngest Cardinal.   In May 1946, when he flew to the United States to receive an honorary doctorate of laws from Fordham University and to address the guests at Fordham's Charter Centenary Dinner, he became the first English Cardinal to visit the United States and the first to celebrate a pontifical Mass in New York's St. Patrick's Cathedral.

The Cardinal Archbishop of Westminster is described by Robert Wilberforce in the *British Magazine* as "a short ruddy-faced man with rust-colored hair and friendly eyes that impress you with their sincerity." Wilberforce, former secretary of the British Legation to the Vatican, attributes the ecclesiastic's influence in affairs beyond the immediate spheres of the Church to "his tremendous energy, the restlessness of his mind, his eagerness to receive new ideas" and his willingness to listen to the point of view of the ordinary man in the street. A familiar, gregarious figure in the bomb-scarred parish of Westminster, Griffin obtains results in everyday tasks, continues Wilberforce, because he has the rare faculty of imbuing all engaged in the work with the belief that they are doing something highly stimulating.

References

British Mag p71+ My '46
N Y Sun p26 My 9 '46
N Y Times p1+ D 23 '43
Catholic Who's Who, 1941
International Who's Who, 1945-46
Who's Who, 1946

GROSS, CHARLES P(HILIP) Mar. 14, 1889- New York City official; retired United States Army officer

Address: b. c/o Board of Transportation, 250 Hudson St., New York; h. 22 E. 36th St., New York

Chairman of New York City's hard-pressed Board of Transportation is Major General Charles P. Gross (retired), who came to his task from the monumental problems of the Chief of the United States Army's Transportation Corps in World War II. His position is of greater national and even international importance than its title would indicate, for the New York transit system is the heart of the United States' greatest seaport, communications center, and manufacturing area, as well as the country's leading financial and amusement center. Any interruption of transit service might have widespread repercussions.

After thirty-five years of Army life, Gross returned to New York City, where he was born, March 14, 1889, to Frederick Charles and Elizabeth (Stoetzer) Gross. His elder brother Felix became an Army officer in the Coast Artillery Corps. Charles was graduated from Cornell University with the degree of M. E. in 1910, and then entered the United States Military Academy. Graduating from West Point with the high standing of third on the scholastic list, he was commissioned a second lieutenant in the Corps of Engineers on June 12, 1914. Eighteen days later he was married to Eleanore Marion Hubach of Bay Ridge, Brooklyn.

For twenty-seven years Gross served in various Army engineer posts. After the United States entered World War I, he was promoted to captain and later to major (temporary), and in April 1918 he sailed for France in command of a new outfit, the 318th Engineers. On arrival he was promoted, and in September led his Engineers in the occupation of the Gerardmer sector, where he was awarded the Purple Heart (which was then a merit decoration). After a week's rest, Gross's men entered the Meuse-Argonne offensive, fighting until the end of the war. The Colonel remained in the Army of Occupation in Germany until June 1919. In October 1919, while in charge of fortification work on the coast defenses of Long Island Sound, he reverted to his permanent rank of captain, but was promoted to major the following July. The next years saw Gross in command of the Thirteenth Engineers (1920-22), teaching at West Point (1922-26), receiving the Army's highest training at the Command and General Staff School (August 1926-

June 1927) and the Army War College (August 1931-June 1932). He served as District Engineer at Los Angeles (1927-29), commanded the Twenty-ninth Engineer Battalion in Virginia, and supervised field work on the Nicaragua Canal Survey (October 1929-August 1931). In August-November 1939, Lieutenant Colonel Gross was called from his work as director and teacher of tactics at the Engineer School in Virginia to do further survey on Nicaraguan canals and highways, and his work there won him the Presidential Medal of Merit. In March 1941 Gross left Rock Island, Illinois, where he was District Engineer, to become General Staff chief of transportation, serving in the Supply Division (G-4). The fifty-two-year-old New Yorker was promoted to full colonel six months before Pearl Harbor.

When a Special War Supply Mission, led by W. Averell Harriman '41, was sent to Russia in September 1941 to study the needs and transportation problems of the then sorely beset Red Army, Gross, now a temporary brigadier general and permanent colonel, went along. In February 1942, the Services of Supply was organized under General Brehon Somervell '42, and Gross became Chief of Transportation in that section. Finally, in August 1942 he was named chief of the newly organized Army Transportation Corps at Washington with the rank of major general (temporary).

The experiences of World War I showed the importance of a highly coordinated transportation service because bottlenecks had then caused costly delays in the movement of troops and equipment. Under Gross's guidance, in World War II there were no similar stoppages in traffic despite a far greater volume of movement and supplies than in World War I. Between Pearl Harbor Day and August 31, 1945, the ports of embarkation of the Transportation Corps dispatched 6,902,000 troops and 126,-700,000 measurement tons of supplies and equipment overseas. Greatest of these ports of embarkation was New York City, commanded by General Homer N. Groninger '45. Although about half of the equipment and three-fifths of the men passed through New York, its safety record was the finest of any port in the country. A plaque and a pennant for having the least number of accidents among major Transportation Corps ports during the three-month period July to September 1945, was presented by General Gross and accepted by Major General Clarence H. Kells, who had exchanged posts with Groninger.

The return of troops and supplies was, of course, accelerated by the end of the war in the Pacific. There were complaints about inadequate train facilities, delays at overseas ports, and the withdrawal of sleeping-car facilities for civilian travelers, but the immense job of Army transport was considered to have been accomplished with a minimum of delay and hardship. On November 30, 1945, with the Transportation Corps "over the hump," General Gross ended his thirty-five-year Army career to accept appointment by Mayor Fiorello LaGuardia '40 as chairman of his native city's Board of Transportation. The three-man Board was responsible for some 241 route miles of rapid transit (subway and elevated) lines, 192

U.S. Army Signal Corps
CHARLES P. GROSS

miles of trolley lines, and 110 miles of bus routes; the subway and elevated lines alone had carried a 1944 total of nearly two billion revenue passengers. "If you think war is hell," said the Mayor, "then you have something waiting for you in this job."

Only in comparison with the transport problems of the greatest and most far-flung army in history could General Gross's new task be considered easy. The one fact about the New York subways on which all groups agreed was that they were substandard, overcrowded, and run at a loss of fifty-seven million dollars a year. The actual deficit reached forty-one million dollars in 1945. What to do about the problem was a hotly disputed question, involving basic political philosophies. One faction, which included many of the property owners, 23 per cent of whose taxes were earmarked for the subways, maintained that the city transit system should be considered as a business corporation and should charge a fare large enough to meet its expenses. In support of this idea, they pointed out that the five-cent fare had been set in 1904, when incomes and operating costs were half those of 1945; that New York was the only city among the twenty-five largest (except Newark) to maintain the five-cent fare, the others charging seven, eight, or ten cents; and that "185,000,000 out-of-town residents and commuters take 330,000,000 rides at less than cost fare," with New York taxpayers making up the difference. Others countered with the argument that raising the fare would decrease the use of subways for short hauls—the very fares that did show a profit—and would further decrease revenue by causing others to use the already fully-loaded surface transport system. Still others felt that a five-cent fare was not a business proposition but a public service, provided by the city on the same basis as schools and parks, and that raising it would remove

GROSS, CHARLES P.—*Continued*

the burden from the backs of the large real estate holders to those of the lower-income groups who used the subways constantly.

Gross was not, however, directly responsible for the financing of the system. He prepared a seven-point plan for improvement of subway service: For the next three years, Gross estimated, $260,000,000 would be needed to reduce crowding through the provision of additional equipment, provide better lighting in cars and stations, improve ventilation, reduce noise in existing equipment, install escalator service for all stations that were a considerable distance from the street, improve sanitary arrangements, and keep the subways clean and attractive. He stated that a ten-cent fare would be necessary to accomplish this if the subways were to be self-sustaining. Rises in the pay of transit workers have caused him to urge speedy passage of the necessary fare increase.

Hardly was Gross out of his two-starred uniform and in his new office when he was faced with a threatened strike of fifteen hundred workers in the city-owned power plants which supplied part of the electric power for the subways. The president of the local Transport Workers Union (CIO), Councilman Michael Quill [41], demanded a referendum on Gross's proposed sale of the plants to private operators, and after a short but tense period, Mayor William O'Dwyer [41] agreed to submit the question to the city's voters for settlement. The threat of a strike, this time of all thirty-two thousand transit workers, arose again in early 1946, when the TWU made sixteen demands, including a two-dollar-a-day wage increase and recognition of the exclusive bargaining rights which it had enjoyed under the previous private ownership of the subways. As summed up in a New York *Post* editorial, the workers' situation was this: During the war "24,000 workers had had to do the work of the prewar 32,000. And during the five years since 1941, while living costs have risen by 28 per cent here, the wage of the transit worker (which ranges from seventy cents to $1.15 an hour) was raised exactly five cents an hour. Or a maximum of 7 per cent. So that today our town's transit workers are actually earning 21 per cent less than they did five years ago." The right to strike against the city was also involved, as was the question of a municipal contract to bargain exclusively with one union, a right which had been extended in several other American cities. General Gross apparently took the view that the city should not accept one union as the exclusive bargaining agent for its transit workers, for he wrote to all the transport unions, including some minor "splinter" groups, asking them to submit their demands for a hearing. The TWU responded by offering to prove its right to speak for all the workers in a secret-ballot election, and the question went to the Mayor for settlement. A committee appointed by O'Dwyer approved an increase in October, but made no mention of collective bargaining rights. A new strike was threatened when the Citizens Budget Commission filed suit against the Board of Transportation to prevent payment of retroactive pay,

and when the Transit Workers Union demanded collective bargaining elections. When O'Dwyer obtained the retroactive pay for the transit workers, the union yielded on the bargaining issue and voted not to strike at that time. William H. Davis, dissenting from his colleagues of the Board of Transportation, expressed his belief that a collective bargaining election would be legal and suggested that a court be asked to determine this question.

The rugged-looking, straight-haired transit chairman and his wife make their home in midtown Manhattan. Their five grown children are Lucy Helen, Dorothea Katherine, John Edward, Nancy Ellen, and Sheldon Harley. One son was in the World War II Navy, and all the daughters are married to Army officers.

References

N Y Sun p10 O 27 '45
Who's Who in America, 1946-47

GROSVENOR, GILBERT (HOVEY) (grōv′nĕr) Oct. 28, 1875- Editor; geographer; educator

Address: b. c/o National Geographic Society, 1146 16th St., N.W., Washington, D.C.; h. "Wild Acres," Grosvenor Lane, Bethesda, Md.

Under the leadership of Gilbert Grosvenor, the National Geographic Society has grown from a small technical group to one of the largest scientific and educational organizations in the world. Its researches, explorations, and publications are financed by the million and a half members who in 1946 pay four dollars a year dues and receive the monthly *National Geographic Magazine,* the travel magazine known for its lavish use of illustrations. Grosvenor introduced this policy when he became editor in 1903, about thirty years before the development of the modern picture magazine.

Although Gilbert Hovey Grosvenor was born in Constantinople, which is now Istanbul, his Massachusetts ancestry dates back to 1624. His grandmother, Harriet Sanborn Grosvenor, wrote popular juvenile books; his father was Edwin Augustus Grosvenor, the historian. Through his mother, who was Lilian Hovey Waters, Grosvenor is descended from two victims of the Salem witchcraft trials of 1692, Rebecca Nurse and George Jacobs. Gilbert, a second cousin of President William Howard Taft, was one of identical twins born October 28, 1875, while their father was teaching at American-endowed Robert College on the Bosporus Strait, where Europe is only eight hundred yards from Asia. At three the twins were taken to the United States by their mother to escape the Russo-Turkish War, and lived in their grandparents' home at Millbury, Massachusetts, for four years. Later, from 1884 to 1890, they were back in Turkey, attending the elementary department of Robert College, where their classmates were boys of many nationalities.

When his sons were fifteen, Professor Grosvenor returned to his native State to teach at Amherst College. Gilbert and Edwin entered Amherst, where in their first three years Gilbert received three prizes for writing, a two-hundred-dollar prize in mathematics, and divided the first and second Latin prizes with Edwin (Grosvenor now says that he cannot translate even the Latin motto on his family coat of arms). Gilbert also won a hundred-dollar prize for oratory in his senior year. At Amherst the twins, who enjoyed confusing people by their identical dress, were elected to the scholastic honor fraternity Phi Beta Kappa, and to Psi Upsilon, constituted the varsity doubles tennis team, and were graduated *magna cum laude* in 1897.

In February 1899 Alexander Graham Bell asked his friend Professor Grosvenor if either of the Grosvenor twins would care to become assistant secretary of the National Geographic Society and assistant editor of its *National Geographic Magazine,* then an irregularly published brochure of abstruse technical articles. The offer was accepted by Gilbert, who was then teaching three languages, algebra, chemistry, and public speaking at the Englewood Academy for Boys in New Jersey. (Edwin, who went on with their original plan of entering law, died in 1930.) The twenty-three-year-old teacher moved to Washington and took up his new duties that April; nineteen months later, on his parents' wedding anniversary, he was married in London to Elsie May Bell, elder of Alexander Graham Bell's two daughters, who had been educated in France and Italy. The following year (1901) Grosvenor received his M.A. from Amherst.

When Gilbert Grosvenor joined the National Geographic Society, he was its only salaried officer. One of his duties was to address all the envelopes in which the magazine was sent to its nine hundred subscribers; after doing this once by hand, he spent twenty dollars for an addressing machine. For five years President Bell paid the young editor's salary out of his own pocket, making a gift of sixty-nine hundred dollars to the society for the purpose. Bell's and Grosvenor's idea was to continue the magazine as a prerogative of membership, rather than as a separate commercial venture, but to broaden its appeal to the layman. (The membership plan is largely responsible for the society's classification as a nonprofit educational institution and its consequent exemption from taxes.) The society was able to move from its rented half-room in September 1903, when the Bell and related Hubbard families presented it with a building of its own; but the National Geographic organization was not able at the time to pay for proper lighting and maintenance of the new building.

Under Grosvenor, who became managing editor in 1900 and editor-in-chief in 1903, the magazine began to employ the new and expensive process of photoengraving on an unprecedented scale. In 1910 came the first of the many *Geographic* series of four-color illustrations, of which Grosvenor claims to have published more than any other magazine editor; and the *Geographic* pioneered, also, in aerial, undersea, and wildlife photography. From the first, Grosvenor's policy has been to print only kindly, noncontroversial material, stressing the picturesque and adventurous, avoiding the

Underwood & Underwood

GILBERT GROSVENOR

trivial and impermanent, and planning the content of each number with a view to timeliness and human interest.

By 1905 membership had risen from less than a thousand to ten times that number, and the society was self-supporting; seven years later, membership had reached one hundred and seven thousand; in 1946, it is a million and a half. Advertising revenue exceeded a million dollars in 1923, and since then has been proportionately high, going above two million in 1929 and topping a million during five of the eight depression years. Grosvenor, who avoids tobacco and stimulants himself, refuses to accept advertising for wine, liquor, cigarettes, patent medicines, real estate, or stocks and bonds, giving as his reason for this exclusion the wide use of the *Geographic* in schools. Moreover, he confines the advertising matter entirely to certain pages before and after the editorial content.

Because the *National Geographic* is published by a nonprofit educational institution, all its profits go toward the gathering and diffusion of geographic knowledge, which Grosvenor interprets in the broadest sense—he states, for instance, that the *Geographic* has published more articles about aviation than any other periodical of general circulation. Besides the financing of exploration and research, the methods used include the printing of books that are sold at low prices, most of them compilations of material used in the magazine; the preparation and distribution to members of from four to six large ten-color maps each year, which cartographers consider among the best made for laymen; and, for the benefit of specialists, technical monographs on the research treated more popularly in the magazine articles. Since 1914 a free daily news bulletin service on places in the news has gone to hundreds of writers and editors, and since 1917

GROSVENOR, GILBERT—*Continued*

illustrated lessons for each school day have been sent to thirty thousand teachers. To house its staff of eight hundred, in the early thirties the society built a modern air-conditioned headquarters three blocks from the White House; it also established a reserve fund which in 1946 approximates fifteen million dollars.

From its inception, the National Geographic Society has enjoyed the prestige and news value of influential names, among them seven Presidents of the United States. Many of the personages served as officers or trustees, and many contributed articles and photographs. In addition, staff members made trips totaling as much as a quarter million miles in a year, and the society has financed, in whole or in part, more than a hundred expeditions. Its flag, designed by Mrs. Grosvenor, has been carried to both poles and to the highest altitude and lowest ocean depth reached by man.

From its establishment in 1920—the year Grosvenor became president—the National Geographic Society library has been open to the public. As many as two thousand requests for information have been answered by its staff in one year. In World War II, the nearly four hundred thousand photographs of other parts of the world and other data in the society's files proved valuable to the Government for purposes ranging from planning strategy to unmasking camouflage; thirty-five thousand photographic prints were made in the society's laboratories and presented to the Government, and ten thousand copies of a book on the South Pacific area were printed for the Navy. Several million copies of Geographic maps were requisitioned for the services and more reproduced by the British War Office.

As of 1946, the *National Geographic Magazine* has run 288 pieces of text by Grosvenor, printed 218 photographs taken by him, and published 101 map supplements edited by him. A dozen books have his name on the title page, and his name is also borne by a Peruvian glacier, a blind Peruvian fish, a Greenland seashell, an Alaskan island and lake, an Antarctic trail and mountain range, a Chinese mountain and plant—all named for Grosvenor by their respective discoverers. Other honors which have come to him include seven doctorates (he is known as Dr. Grosvenor); medals from, and honorary memberships in, various geographical societies; trusteeships of several colleges; and election to the managing boards of five associations. France made him an officer of the Legion of Honor, and Norway, a commander of the Cross of St. Olaf. In the business world Grosvenor is a director of the American Security and Trust Company and of the Chesapeake and Potomac Telephone Company, and has served also on other corporation boards. He has a wide range of club and association memberships, and belongs to the Presbyterian Church and to the Republican Party. Grosvenor and his wife enjoyed a stay in Hollywood in 1939, during which they had the titles of technical advisers on *The Story of Alexander Graham Bell*.

The editor's enthusiasm for birds had its beginning in his thirty-ninth year, when he acquired the hundred-acre Maryland farm from which he commutes to Washington; he is still proud that a count in 1915 showed fifty-nine pairs nesting within the acre around his house. At his Nova Scotia and Miami homes, Grosvenor enjoys sailing the fifty-four-foot yawl given to him years ago by his father-in-law. (He is a founder of the Cruising Club of America, which runs the Bermuda yacht races.) Other recreations of his include traveling by air, golfing at the Chevy Chase and Burning Tree clubs, and playing bridge at the Cosmos Club, of which he was president in 1922. Grosvenor gives his wife credit for reading hundreds of manuscripts and examining thousands of page proofs and photographs. Their son Melville Bell is assistant editor of the magazine (another son is deceased); and four of the five daughters are married. On Sundays the elder Grosvenors are likely to be surrounded by children and by grandchildren, of whom they have eleven. The slender, spectacled geographer (five feet ten inches, 170 pounds), has blue-gray eyes, a florid complexion, and his hair and mustache are gray. Geoffrey Hellman, who "profiled" him for the *New Yorker* in 1943, reported that all subordinates call him "Chief" and look upon him with great respect. Hellman described the editor as having a "sprightly" air and a "mixture of business sagacity, intellectual curiosity, regard for tradition, and tolerance of temperate innovation."

References

> Nat Geog Mag 69:136+ Ja '36 pors
> New Yorker 19:26+ S 25 '43 por; 19:27+ O 2 '43 por; 19:27+ O 9 '43 por
> Encyclopædia Britannica (1946)
> National Cyclopædia of American Biography Current vol A p309
> Who's Who, 1946
> Who's Who in America, 1946-47
> Who's Who in Commerce and Industry (1944)

GROVES, ERNEST R(UTHERFORD)

May 6, 1877—Aug. 28, 1946 Sociologist and educator; taught the first college class in marriage in the world in 1925; founded the annual University of North Carolina conferences on conservation of marriage and the family in 1934; among his books are *The Marriage Crisis* (1928), *Parents and Children* (1929), and *The American Family* (1934). See *Current Biography* 1943 Yearbook.

Obituary

> N Y Times p18 Ag 30 '46 por

GRUENING, ERNEST (HENRY) (grēn'-ĭng) Feb. 6, 1887- Governor of Alaska

Address: b. Federal Building, Juneau, Alaska; h. Governor's House, Juneau, Alaska

With twenty-three years of newspaper and magazine work behind him, Ernest Gruening in 1939 became the Governor of Alaska, the

Territory which may become the forty-ninth star in the United States flag. Looking forward to the time when Alaska will be "an integrated part of North American civilization," Gruening calls for hardy pioneers to settle in Alaska and "relive the American epic." In 1946 the Territory of Alaska, approximately one-fifth the size of the United States, has a population estimated at eighty-five thousand, a number which includes Eskimos, Indians, Aleuts, Japanese, and white people (the last-named comprised about 54 per cent of all in 1940). The region, once known as "Seward's icebox," has a climate similar to that of Scandinavia and is considered capable of supporting twelve million people.

Although he now uses his early medical training only incidentally on gubernatorial visits to isolated villages, Ernest Henry Gruening in his youth seemed to be following in the footsteps of his German-born father, who was a well-known eye and ear surgeon in the United States. The son of Emil and Phebe (Fridenberg) Gruening, Ernest was born on February 6, 1887, in New York City, where he attended several local schools. In 1903, after being graduated from Hotchkiss, a private school in Lakeville, Connecticut, the sixteen-year-old boy entered Harvard, there earning his B.A. degree in 1907 and then studying at the medical school. He received his M.D. degree in 1912, but by that time he had already worked a year as a reporter for the Boston *American* and decided that journalism was the field for him. He continued to report and write special articles for the *American* until 1913, after which he became, successively, assistant editor of the Boston *Herald* (1913-14), managing editor of the Boston *Traveler* (1914-16), and managing editor and editor of the Boston *Journal* (1916-17).

Upon the entry of the United States into World War I Gruening went first to Washington to assist in organizing the bureau of imports under the War Trade Board; then to Louisville, Kentucky, where, after having enlisted in the Field Artillery, he was stationed at Camp Zachary Taylor. When the Armistice was signed he was a candidate for a commission. The thirty-one-year-old newspaper man now joined the staff of the New York *Tribune* (today the *Herald Tribune*), as managing editor, a position he left in a year to become president of the Prensa Printing Corporation and general manager of *La Prensa,* the only Spanish-language daily newspaper in the United States. Next, from 1920 to 1923 he was managing editor of the *Nation.*

A crusader against "dollar diplomacy," Gruening called for the evacuation of American marines from Nicaragua and wrote articles which, according to Richard L. Neuberger (*Collier's* December 23, 1944), helped bring about a Senatorial investigation of American military occupation in Haiti and Santo Domingo. His visit to these countries in the fall of 1921 with Senator Medill McCormick, who headed the investigation, confirmed his opposition to United States intervention in Latin American affairs; and in the pages of the *Nation* as well as such magazines as *Forum, Century,* and *Current*

History, Gruening urged that the United States pursue a policy of "good will and equal dealing" with its southern neighbors. His position in general, however, said Neuberger, was "a strictly middle-of-the-road one." While he attacked interference by American industry and finance in Latin American countries, he also warned against the influence of extreme radicals. In the 1924 Presidential campaign Gruening was the national director of publicity for Robert La Follette, Progressive Party candidate.

By this time the newspaperman was already at work on his book *Mexico and Its Heritage.* Seeking the causes of Mexico's revolutions, its "backwardness," its Government's friction with the United States, he read extensively in Mexican history and literature and traveled through twenty-four of that country's twenty-eight states at various intervals over a period of six years. (In 1922 he had gone to Mexico to represent *Collier's* and several metropolitan newspapers.) When Gruening's book appeared in 1928 it was generally acclaimed as "the most vigorous, useful, and comprehensive picture yet made of the complex present conditions below the Rio Grande."

Gruening was "a critic of the sins of the commercial press." "Twice," wrote one of his colleagues, "he . . . resigned the managing editorship of important daily newspapers because his high sense of honor made it impossible for him to work on in those shops." In the tendency toward newspaper consolidation he saw a threat to the freedom of the press and a consequent threat to American democracy. When he founded the Portland (Maine) *Evening News* in 1927, he became the editor of the only newspaper in Portland which, according to a *New Republic* writer, was not controlled by the Guy P. Gannett press and was not the instrument of the "power trust." Gruening's campaign against the high electricity rates and other abuses of the Insull-owned utility companies in Maine did not help to sell advertising space in the *Evening News.* Its editor continued in this position until 1932, when he became a contributing editor. In *The Public Pays* (1931), "an easily digestible book" summarizing the findings of the Federal Trade Commission in its three-year investigation of public utilities, Gruening further exposed power monopolies.

In 1933 President Roosevelt, whose election Gruening had actively supported, sent him to Montevideo to act as general adviser to the United States delegation to the seventh Pan American conference—an event which marked the adoption of the "Good Neighbor" policy as the official policy of the United States. For the newspaperman it meant the realization of an objective toward which he had long been working as well as the beginning of a new trend in his career. In 1934, after about three months as editor of the New York *Evening Post* (he had been editor of the *Nation* in 1933-34), Gruening left the newspaper field to direct the Division of Territories and Island Possessions in the United States Department of the Interior. This post gave him jurisdiction

ERNEST GRUENING

over Alaska, Hawaii, Puerto Rico, the Virgin Islands, the Philippines, and the Pacific islands of Jarvis, Baker, Howland, Canton and Enderbury. From 1935 to 1937 the Government official was also the reconstruction administrator for Puerto Rico and, in 1935-36, the island's Federal emergency relief administrator.

It was in the spring of 1936 that Gruening first visited Alaska. By that time, he has written, "I had reached the age of forty-nine and had seen many interesting and beautiful places in Europe and the Americas. But no region ever gave me quite the profound thrill that did Alaska." Three years later he was appointed Governor of this peninsula which the United States had purchased from Russia in 1867. Except for the mining and fishing industries, financed largely by absentee capitalists, its resources were still but little developed. It was said that a man could live there the year round without seeing a tax collector, and in this land of rugged individualists, wrote *Newsweek*, Gruening was "a confirmed New Dealer." But the ability which he demonstrated as an executive, reported a *PM* correspondent, won him the favor of most Alaskans. When he proposed to supplement Federal support with the imposition of personal and corporation net income taxes, however, the Alaskan legislature opposed him with a bill which would have taken from him his territorial (non-Federal) powers.

World War II made Alaska a strategic military outpost as well as an important source of peat and such essential products as airplane spruce, nickel, chromite, antimony, and tin. In 1941, stated *Newsweek*, the peninsula became the scene of "the greatest surge of activity since the (1898 Klondike) Gold Rush." Following the 1942 Japanese invasion of the Aleutians, an Alaskan War Council (this was similar to the United States Office of Civilian

Defense) with Gruening as chairman was created. Gruening, who had in 1940 formed the first Alaskan national guard, in 1942 also organized and became commander in chief of the Alaskan Territorial Guard. Indians and Eskimos also demonstrated their loyalty to the United States by purchasing war bonds from the Governor. In 1942 the highway connecting the United States with Alaska, which had first been discussed by a Government commission in 1930, was finally built— Gruening called it the new Northwest Passage. (He had been a member of the Alaska International Highway Commission since 1938.)

In the several hundred thousand soldiers, sailors, and Coast Guard men who served in Alaska during the war, the Governor saw "the Alaskan frontiersmen and settlers of the future." He envisioned a land in which farming communities, small retail businesses, a tourist trade, mining, and a lumber industry would flourish. At the end of the war, however, Alaska was a land of high prices, high interest rates, and housing shortage; the Governor warned the thousands of veterans eager to settle in the territory not to come unless they had twenty-five hundred dollars, a job or an idea for an enterprise, and a place to live in. Gruening felt that a plan sponsored by the Federal Government was necessary to help solve the problems of new settlers.

An important goal toward which Gruening and other Government officials worked was Alaskan statehood. In October 1946 the inhabitants of the Territory voted two-to-one for admission as a State, but before this could be accomplished Congress would have to register its approval and Alaskans take another vote. A forty-ninth state would add to United States Government expenditures, but statehood would give Alaska the greater Federal benefits accorded to all States and hasten its development. Before World War II, stated William H. Stringer of the *Christian Science Monitor* in trying to show how Alaska "has stagnated," the region had never received an appropriation for new roads. When Governor Gruening in September 1945 sought the establishment of a Veterans Administration branch for the more than seven thousand Alaskans who had served in the armed forces of the United States during World War II, a VA staff, reportedly consisting of three, was sent to Alaska. The Governor's request for roads received support from President Truman [45] and from Secretary of Interior J. A. Krug [44], who announced that his department had undertaken a long-range program for improving the transportation system in Alaska. Confronted with a high tuberculosis death rate and a lack of adequate facilities for the care of tuberculars, Gruening in 1946 also sought a Congressional appropriation of $2,775,000 for the building of a sanatorium. A serious problem with which he had to cope in the fall of 1946 was the virtual "blockade" of Alaska, the result of the Pacific Coast maritime labor conflict. Almost entirely cut off from outside sources of food and other vital supplies during the loss of 127 days of shipping, Alaska, according to Edwin G. Arnold, director of the Interior Department's Division of Territories, suffered "the most serious setback in the territory's history."

In 1946 Gruening was among those who urged that General Draja Mikhailovitch [42], the Yugoslav military leader, be tried by an international tribunal. The Governor is a member of the Council on Foreign Relations, the American Academy of Political and Social Science, and the Foreign Policy Association, of which he was a director from 1932 to 1936. He participated in the latter organization's Cuba Commission in 1934. The editor of *These United States,* a symposium, he has also been a contributor to the *Dictionary of American Biography,* the *Encyclopedia of Social Science,* the encyclopedias *Britannica* and *Americana,* the *American Year Book,* and many magazines. In 1934 he was a lecturer on inter-American relations at the New School for Social Research in New York. That year he also lectured in Mexico. He holds membership in several clubs : St. Botolph in Boston, Harvard in New York, and Cosmos in Washington, D.C. The Governor's wife is the former Dorothy Elizabeth Smith, to whom he was married in 1914. They have two children, Huntington Sanders and Peter Brown; a son, Ernest, is deceased. A former colleague on the *Nation* has described Gruening as a man of understanding, knowledge, good will, and tact.

References

Am Mag 142:133 O '46
Collier's 114:11+ D 23 '44 por
Scholastic 25:23 N 24 '34 por
Columbia Encyclopedia (1935)
National Cyclopædia of American Biography Current vol F p394
Who's Who in America, 1946-47

GUERARD, ALBERT J(OSEPH) Nov. 2, 1914- (gā-rärd') Author; educator
Address: h. Warren House, Cambridge, Mass.

The diversity of approaches open to the writer of psychological novels is in the way of being almost as bewildering as the personality variations of the people he chooses to write about. Albert J. Guérard, author, faculty instructor in English at Harvard University, and recipient, in 1946, of a Rockefeller postservice fellowship, reserves, admittedly, a primary interest in individual psychology; but he would like to think, he adds, that his novels "also reflect or face the main spiritual difficulties of our times: solitude, an absence of moral order, dislocation. We are all 'displaced persons,' and our various dislocations must be described and defined before we can remedy them."

Albert Joseph Guérard was born in Houston, Texas, on November 2, 1914, the son of Albert Léon and Wilhelmina Emmeline (McCartney) Guérard. His father is professor of general literature at Stanford University, a writer, and an authority on French literature and history. Young Albert went from the elementary schools of Houston to the Ecole Pascal and the Lycée Montaigne in Paris;

ALBERT J. GUERARD

and following his return to the States entered high school in Palo Alto, California. Again he broke into his American education for a year's stay (1929-30) in Paris, where he studied at the American High School. At twenty he received a B.A. degree from Stanford University, where during his undergraduate years he had been a college correspondent of the United Press. In the course of the next two years he received a Master's degree from Harvard (1935) and was assigned to a teaching post at Amherst before setting out for London to study at King's College (1936-37). He returned to Stanford, received his Ph.D. in 1938. From 1938 to 1941 he served on the Harvard faculty as instructor in English; and was thereafter advanced to faculty instructor in the same field. He was granted leave to join the Army in 1943.

The suddenness of Guérard's break from a college environment left him in a position to regard the early part of his military training as "fantastic and wonderful." He was placed in the Army Specialized Training Program, and between "spells of guard duty and K.P." he was detailed to "write, edit, stencil, and mimeograph a little company newspaper." As he advanced from private to staff sergeant he moved from the Psychological Warfare Division (Intelligence Section) to the Office of War Information, Cultural Relations (in Paris), and his knowledge of France and the French was called into play. He had maintained rather intimate connections with the French underground—so much so, indeed, that in August 1944 he was in the first car to enter Paris with the left wing of General Leclerc's division. He was discharged from the Army early in 1946, and subsequently returned to the Harvard faculty.

At one time Guérard was urged to go into newspaper work or to make a stab at the cotton export business, but by the time he was

GUERARD, ALBERT J.—*Continued*

fourteen he had won a second prize in the National Scholastic Awards—and the notion that writing might be more than a diversion began to enlarge itself (he had written a story when he was eight, but there was nothing especially indicative in this early flash). While he was still an undergraduate at Stanford his "Davos in Winter" won him first place in the *Hound and Horn* college story contest in 1933. And on the momentum of that he turned out a variety of short tales for publication in little magazines, all the while strongly under the influence of the Hemingway school. Beyond 1934, however, he wrote nothing more in this form but concentrated on the writing of articles that found their way into *Harper's, Yale Review*, and other American periodicals as well as several French journals.

In 1937 came his first novel, *The Past Must Alter*, which had a mixed reception. Critics, on the whole, were inclined to agree that this "story of the delicate relationships of a boy to his father and mother was moving and right in tone. . . .Not a great novel, but a competent one." There followed a critical work, *Robert Bridges*, a study of traditionalism in poetry. "A brilliantly written book," according to the New York *Times*, it is "highly provocative, and the first of its kind." *The Hunted*, Guérard's second novel, is a psychological piece, set in a New England college town and involving a waitress and her unhappy marriage to a neurotic college English instructor. An "original and brilliantly written study of evil," this book displays "a genuine gift of style" and is based on "a thoughtful analysis of the meaning of character in action." (This and his first novel appeared in French translations and the second has been done also into Portuguese.)

Maquisard (1945) was written in France while Guérard was still in the Army, and although he affirms the fictitiousness of its "characters, events, and military situations," even an undiscerning reader is aware of the snatches of semi-autobiography. It is a tale of France at the time of the Battle of the Bulge, when news from the Western Front threw the whole structure of the Maquis into a state of reversal, confusion, and weariness. And the book's subtitle—*A Christmas Tale*—serves as something of a reminder for those to whom Christmas 1944 came easily and pleasantly. Another book to come out of his Army days—but presumably quite unrelated to the military—is an anthology of American short stories, which he edited and which was published in Paris in 1946.

The blue-eyed, brown-haired author is five feet ten inches in height and weighs 150 pounds. He has no hobbies, he says, but likes to play tennis and is fond of travel. In July 1941 he was married to Mary Maclin Bocock.

Reference

Who's Who in American Education (1941-42)

GULLION, ALLEN W(YANT) (gŭl'yŭn) Dec. 14, 1880—June 19, 1946 Major General in World War II; an American delegate to the international conference at Geneva in 1929, the sole United States delegate to the Congress of Juridical Experts at Luxembourg in 1938; Judge Advocate General of the Army from 1937 to 1941; organized and became first chief of the Provost Marshal General's department in 1941; chief of the displaced persons branch of Allied Headquarters in World War II. See *Current Biography* 1943 Yearbook.

Obituary

N Y Times p23 Je 21 '46 por

HAMILTON, ALICE Feb. 27, 1869- Physician; authority on industrial diseases *Address*: b. c/o Little, Brown & Co., Boston, Mass.; h. Hadlyme, Conn.

A pioneer in the field of occupational diseases, Dr. Alice Hamilton has been an authority on the hazardous industries since 1910. Her books *Industrial Poisons in the United States* and *Industrial Toxicology* are considered classics among the studies which eventually led to the passage of workmen's compensation laws.

"I always have to give New York City as my birthplace, most inappropriately, for I left it at the age of six weeks and I really belong to Indiana," says Alice Hamilton in her autobiography, *Exploring the Dangerous Trades*. The second of five children of Montgomery and Gertrude (Pond) Hamilton, she was born on February 27, 1869, at the home of her maternal grandmother. Her maternal ancestors were Dutch, with English and Irish "admixture." Her paternal forbears were Scotch-Irish and English, her grandfather Allen Hamilton having come as a young man from Northern Ireland to settle in Fort Wayne when it was still a military post in the frontier state of Indiana; there he was to become one of the leading citizens. The child Alice grew up in a sheltered but mentally stimulating environment. She, her three sisters (her only brother was not born until she was seventeen), and the Hamilton cousins, who lived in the neighboring house, lived in a little world of their own. However, this exclusiveness was modified by the intellectual curiosity of her parents, to whose home came some of the leading socially conscious citizens of the day.

Although the girl's early education (in languages, literature, history and some mathematics) under the tutelage of her parents, assisted by a governess and a teacher, was "very uneven," it provided her with the background for the career she chose in later life. Her father encouraged her in research, training her sisters and her, she says, "in habits of scientific approach. We were not allowed to make a statement which could be challenged unless we were prepared to defend it." At the age of seventeen, in accordance with family tradition, she went for two years to the finishing school conducted by Miss Porter in Farmington, Connecticut.

Outside of marriage there were few careers open to girls in the latter part of the nineteenth century. Alice Hamilton chose medicine, and after she returned to Fort Wayne took her preparatory studies at one of the "little third-rate medical schools" which were common before medical teaching was reformed. Later she enrolled at the coeducational Medical School of the University of Michigan, from which she received her M.D. in 1893. After an internship at the Hospital for Women and Children in Minneapolis and at the New England Hospital for Women and Children near Boston, Dr. Hamilton decided to devote her career to bacteriology and pathology. In the fall of 1895 she went to Germany for another year's training. While women were barred from higher education, the American girl was allowed to attend the universities of Leipzig and Munich on condition that she make herself inconspicuous. On her return to the United States she continued her study and research at the Johns Hopkins Medical School. Then, in the summer of 1897 she received her first appointment as professor of pathology at the Woman's Medical School of Northwestern University.

Shortly after she took up her new post at the university the young doctor received permission from Jane Addams to live at Hull House, the mecca of many of Chicago's visitors in the nineties. The years she spent there were both useful and rich in human contacts, with a roster which included the names of H. G. Wells, Prince Peter Kropotkin, Emma Goldman, Eugene Victor Debs, and Sidney and Beatrice Webb. Since every Hull House resident was required to do some social work in her spare time, the young Northwestern University professor devoted Saturday mornings to bathing the neighborhood's babies in the basement of the settlement. From these beginnings she succeeded in starting Chicago's first baby health center.

During her first five years in Chicago Alice Hamilton, besides teaching, carried on research in the laboratory of the University of Chicago. Later, after the Women's Medical School closed in 1902, she joined the newly founded Memorial Institute for Infectious Diseases, as assistant to the eminent pathologist Dr. Ludwig Hektoen. Before taking up her new duties she was able for a brief period to take further study at the Pasteur Institute in Paris. When she returned to Chicago in the autumn of 1902, Dr. Hamilton found it in the midst of a serious epidemic of typhoid fever. As a result of her investigations the Health Department of the city was completely reorganized. She also won considerable praise for the paper she wrote for the Chicago Medical Society on the part flies played in the spread of the contagion.

Through her activities at Hull House Dr. Hamilton learned that many of the neighborhood's immigrant workers had been made incurable invalids by the poisonous fumes they inhaled on their jobs in the steel mills, factories, and foundries. Subsequently Dr. Hamilton found that these conditions prevailed throughout the country. "The chief method of protection was to encourage a large labor turnover (so that no one worker would be exposed too long) which was not then regarded

Bradford Bachrach

ALICE HAMILTON

as poor industrial practice." Dr. Hamilton's interest in the hazardous trades was stimulated by her reading of Sir Thomas Oliver's *Dangerous Trades,* and at the John Crerar Library she read all the material she could find on the subject.

In 1910 Governor Deneen of Illinois established the Occupational Disease Commission, the first of its kind in the United States. Dr. Hamilton was invited to join the commission and later became its managing director. A direct result of the commission's year of investigations was the passage in the State of Illinois of a workmen's compensation law. While these investigations were still in progress Dr. Hamilton was sent to Europe to attend the International Congress on Occupational Accidents and Diseases in Brussels. A paper she read on conditions in her own country brought her to the attention of the United States Commissioner of Labor in the Department of Commerce. (The Department of Labor was not organized until 1912.) On her return to Illinois he asked her to undertake a similar survey for the Federal Government. Although Dr. Hamilton's new assignment took her to Washington and other parts of the country, Hull House remained her home until 1919. After that she continued to spend several months of each year there until the death of Jane Addams in 1935.

Dr. Hamilton remained in her non-salaried Federal post from 1911 until the time of the Harding Administration in 1921. However, the Government agreed to purchase her report when it was ready to be published "at a price to be decided on." In an age when an interest in the physical welfare of workers was considered "socialism" even by doctors, she managed to conduct her investigations without antagonizing either employers or employees. Before visiting a plant the newly appointed

HAMILTON, ALICE—*Continued*

Federal agent would thoroughly familiarize herself with the industry. As a result of the pioneer work most of the states today have made legal provision for workmen's compensation.

An ardent pacifist, Alice Hamilton favored the American plan of "continuous mediation" in World War I. In April 1915 she and Jane Addams went as delegates to the peace meeting of the International Congress of Women at The Hague, later visiting leaders and government officials of the warring as well as neutral countries. When the United States entered the war, the Federal Government retained her services despite her avowed pacifism, and the doctor now added to her earlier investigations a study of the munitions industries and observed the effects upon workers of a number of new poisons.

The increasing interest in industrial hygiene during and after the war was responsible for Dr. Hamilton's appointment as assistant professor of industrial medicine in the Medical School of Harvard University in 1919. She has said with amusement that because she was "the only candidate available" she became the first woman on the faculty in this "stronghold of masculinity." As she taught for only six months of each year she was able to continue her surveys for the Federal Government. In the years after she ceased to be a Federal agent she made two outstanding investigations for Washington in 1937-38 and 1940 at the request of the Secretary of Labor, Frances Perkins '40. The first was a detailed study of the new and then dangerous rayon industry and the second an analysis of silicosis and the other diseases common to miners. Again in Washington in 1946, Dr. Hamilton testified before the Senate Education and Labor Committee in defense of the Wagner '41-Murray '45-Dingell national health bill. "That health insurance is necessary, if adequate medical care is to be provided for all our people, is no longer controversial," she said. "I have seen the great blessings the old-age pension has brought to our country. . . .I long to see us make the same approach in the alleviation of the burden of sickness."

During her long association with Harvard, from 1919 to 1935, Dr. Hamilton watched with deep concern the developments in the postwar world both in Europe and the United States. The only woman member of the League of Nations Health Committee, on which she served from 1924 to 1930, she visited the Soviet Union in 1924 at the invitation of its Department of Health and noted the achievements it had made in the field of industrial hygiene. She was in postwar Germany on three occasions. In 1919 she made a study of the famine conditions in that country for the Quakers; in the spring of 1933, on an exchange fellowship of the Carl Schurz Foundation, and again in the fall of 1938 during the period of the Munich crisis, as a United States Department of Labor delegate to the International Congress of Occupational Accidents and Diseases held in Frankfort on the Main, she was able to observe the effects of the Nazi Government in Germany.

In the many articles Alice Hamilton has contributed to publications in the United States and in her books she has shown that her social consciousness knows no boundaries. She has contributed to the *Survey Graphic*, the *American Journal of Public Health*, *New Republic*, *Living Age*, and other magazines. Among the numerous articles she has written are: "Hitler Speaks—His Book Reveals the Man" (*Atlantic*, October 1933), "The Plight of the German Intellectuals" (*Harper's*, 1934), "Healthy, Wealthy—if Wise—Industry" (*American Scholar*, winter 1938), "Death in the Factories" (*Nation*, July 17, 1943), and "Why I am Against the Equal Rights Amendment" (*Ladies Home Journal*, July 1945). Her books *Industrial Poisons in the United States* (1925) and *Industrial Toxicology* (1934), regarded as valuable contributions in the field of public health, received a favorable reception from her colleagues. More accessible to the lay reader is her autobiography *Exploring the Dangerous Trades* (1943), which was regarded by a reviewer as "more exciting than any fiction."

Since 1935 Dr. Hamilton has been professor emeritus of the Medical School of Harvard University. Honorary degrees have been conferred upon her by Smith and Mount Holyoke colleges and the universities of Michigan, and Rochester, and by Tulane. She is a member of the American Association for the Advancement of Science as well as the American Public Health and Medical Associations. The president of the National Consumers League, she also belongs to the National Women's Trade Union League, the League of Women Voters, and the American Association of University Women.

After she retired from teaching, Dr. Hamilton moved to Hadlyme (Connecticut), a "loose collection of groups of houses," too small to appear on the map. There the doctor is able to pursue her hobbies of painting and gardening. Alice Hamilton has been described as hazel-eyed with classical features set in a frame of soft white hair. To one writer she appeared as "wine, silver, and homespun."

References

American Men of Science (1944)
American Women, 1939-40
Hamilton, A.   Exploring the Dangerous Trades   (1943)
Sergeant, E. S.   Fire Under the Andes (1927)
Who's Who in America, 1946-47
Yost, E.   American Women of Science (1943)

HAMILTON, CLAYTON (MEEKER)
Nov. 14, 1881—Sept. 17, 1946 Critic, playwright; dramatic critic on magazines from 1907 to 1920; since 1912 served on sixteen annual juries which chose the year's Pulitzer Prize play; wrote *The Stranger at the Inn; The Big Idea* with A. E. Thomas; and *Friend Indeed* with B. H. Voigt.

Obituary

N Y Times p31 S 18 '46 por

HANSENNE, MARCEL (FERNAND)
(än″sĕn′ màr″sĕl′ fĕr″nän′) Jan. 24, 1917-
Track athlete; sportswriter

Address: b. c/o Elans, 15 Rue Montmartre,
Paris; h. 122 Boulevard Murat, Paris

France's middle-distance track champion,
Marcel Hansenne, came to New York in February 1946 to compete for the first time in indoor racing. Rated by experts the best runner
France has developed in a score of years, he
was cited three times from 1943 to 1945 for
giving the "best performance in track and field"
in France. The "feather-footed" Frenchman
lost several races in New York, but the American track probably never had a more popular
foreign visitor, his lively sense of humor and
modesty winning for him the good will of track
fans and sports writers. An amateur athlete,
his profession is writing on sports for two
Paris newspapers.

Marcel Fernand Hansenne was born in the
French capital on January 24, 1917. When he
was eleven years old he entered his first sports
competition, a swimming meet in Lille. He attended the Ecole Industrielle et Commerciale
de Tourcoing, in the north of France, where,
as he tells it, he busied himself with "wool
studies and foreign languages—English, three
years, and German, two years." When he was
nineteen years old he entered the French army,
and while in service the tall, agile young Parisian played a good deal of basketball. Then he
made a discovery: "My basketball teammates
used to get all fagged out toward the end of
a match. They longed for the final whistle to
blow. Me, I felt fresh as a field flower. So I
said to myself, 'Marcel, if you are strong
enough to play a second basketball game right
now, you should have the endurance to run
distance races.'" Whereupon, in 1937 he entered his first race. Fifteen minutes before that
race was to begin he asked that someone be
substituted for him, because he was too nervous
to compete. His request was refused—and he
won the race. Two years later, in 1939, he
became France's middle-distance (400 to 800
meters) champion, setting an 800-meter record
of 1:50.2. He also won the 1500-meter championship in Paris, clocking 3:49.4.

An air force ground crew corporal, Hansenne
was stationed in southern France when France
fell to Germany in June 1940. In September
he was released from the Army, and during
the early part of the Nazi occupation he lived
in Paris. With him were his wife, Alberte
Braye, to whom he had been married in August
of 1941, and their baby daughter Michèle. The
family moved to Lille in May 1944, and soon
afterward Hansenne joined the Maquis, the
French underground fighters. When the Americans marched into France, Hansenne was with
the Maquis in Auvergne. To sportswriter
Arthur Daley (New York *Times*), he later
reminisced: "I just wish I could have run a
race the day of the invasion of Normandy. I
was so happy, I could have run a four-minute
mile with ease." The voluble young French
athlete became a sportswriter after the liberation. He began in September 1944 on the Paris
morning paper *Aurore*, and in 1945 changed to

MARCEL HANSENNE

l'Etoile, an afternoon paper. He also writes
for the sports paper *Elans,* specializing in boxing and basketball.

The French champion ran the mile for the
first time in the summer of 1945 in Sweden.
His time, 4:08.2, was the fastest ever set for the
mile by a Frenchman, and it might have been
better were it not for the peculiar circumstances
of the race. With Gunder Hägg, Arne Andersson, and Lennart Strand in the race, Hansenne entered "for the experience." He later
explained that Hägg objected to having him
in the race, but finally agreed to let him run
on condition that he promise to stay behind the
leaders and not get in anybody's way. The race,
it was expected, would be a "private, cutthroat"
rivalry between Hägg and Andersson. On the
last lap, however, the Frenchman noticed that
Hägg was beginning to "wobble" and decided
to forget the agreement. With a soft "Adieu,
monsieur," he spurted past the Swedish champion. To everyone's surprise Strand came in
first, Andersson second, Hansenne third, and
Hägg trailed in fourth. A footnote to the
story comes from Arthur Daley: "Afterward,
Gunder the Wunder remarked that if it hadn't
been for the agreement which handcuffed the
Parisian, Marcel would have beaten Andersson
for second place. 'But you must consider,' says
the Frenchman 'that maybe Gunder was just
being nasty to Arne.' Quite a sense of humor
this lad has."

In the winter of 1945, as New York track
writers bemoaned the "dearth of fleet milers"
for the coming indoor meets, Daniel Ferris of
the Amateur Athletic Union conceived the idea
of bringing Hansenne to New York to lend
excitement to the races. By arrangement with
the International Amateur Athletic Federation,
Hansenne was permitted to come in February
1946. Since the I.A.A.F limits the amount of
time an athlete may spend abroad (in order to
prevent athletes from living off track ex-

HANSENNE, MARCEL—*Continued*

penses), Hansenne was allowed only two weeks' time for training on indoor boards in New York. The Frenchman had never even seen an indoor track, and his only experience running the mile had been in the Swedish meet the summer before. Experts said Hansenne had "Olympic class on cinders," but doubted that he could "get the hang of board-track racing in two weeks." The pessimists proved right. Wearing his first pair of indoor track shoes, Hansenne ran the Wanamaker Mile in Madison Square Garden in February 1946 and trailed in a poor third. (Leslie MacMitchell [46] won the race, and Tom Quinn was second.) Offering no excuses, Hansenne insisted that he enjoyed running on a board track, and that the heated, smoke-filled air of the Garden, the undoing of many outdoor runners, had not affected his breathing. However, sports writers noted that his feet had been badly blistered because he was unaccustomed to the pinpoint spikes of the shoes used in indoor racing. A week later Hansenne ran the Hunter mile in Boston, with the same results: MacMitchell first, Quinn second, and Hansenne third. Track writers reminded their readers that with one or two exceptions, notably the famous Paavo Nurmi of Finland, champion European runners were disappointing failures on indoor planks.

On March 2, 1946, MacMitchell, as had been predicted, won the Zamperini Mile in the American Athletic Union meets at Madison Square Garden. "The surprise, and a welcome one that the crowd liked," reported the New York *Times,* "was that second place went to Marcel Hansenne, Frenchman. Staying up with the pace all the way, he finally showed his stretch sprint wallop that gave him a 4:08.2 clocking last year outdoors. He ran down Tommy Quinn, and beat him for second by a yard." The following week, in the Columbian mile at Madison Square Garden, Hansenne gave his best American performance. He crossed the finish line behind MacMitchell, again passing Tommy Quinn for second place, and clocked 4:15.8. Though he couldn't catch MacMitchell on the track, Hansenne, after passing the finish line, "kept on sprinting and draped his arms around Leslie's brawny shoulders." In his dressing room later, Hansenne grinned at reporters. "I feel better out there tonight. More life in the feet." The next day he boarded a plane for his transatlantic trip home.

Marcel Hansenne's "cheerful manner, ingratiating ways, and sense of humor," made him a favorite with all reporters. They quoted him at length, discovered he was a "boogie-woogie fiend," and that he sang "Hotchayson, Topeka, and Santa Fe" by the hour. As for Hansenne, he announced "I lahv America!" Though he liked Yankee food, he avoided overeating, an indulgence catastrophic for many visiting European athletes, and went to bed at eight o'clock. Hansenne is tall and reedy (five feet eleven inches in height, 150 pounds in weight), with "a hawklike profile, a chiseled chin." His eyes are brown—"Very nice eyes, says my wife." He writes that his *première passion* is his family, and lists his other *passions* in the order of their importance: sports; books by Baudelaire, Gide, De Montherlant, and Poe; music, and his work. Track and field competitions (he represents the Club Athletique Français) and basketball are his favorite sports, but "for look at" he prefers prizefighting and soccer.

References

N Y Herald Tribune p20 Ja 21 '46; p24 F 1 '46
N Y Times p26 Ja 22 '46

HANSSON, PER ALBIN (hàn'sôn pâr ăl'bĭn) Oct. 28, 1885—Oct. 5, 1946 Prime Minister of Sweden from 1932 until his death; a self-educated Social Democrat, he was elected to the Riksdag in 1918 and served as Minister of Defense from 1920 to 1923 and from 1924 to 1926; in 1929-32 he was a member of the Public Debt Administration. See *Current Biography* 1942 Yearbook.

Obituary

N Y Times p59 O 6 '46 por

HARGROVE, MARION (LAWTON, JR.) Oct. 13, 1919- Writer; lecturer
Address: h. New City, Rockland County, N. Y.

Marion Hargrove, ex-soldier, author, and lecturer, achieved fame as the bungling rookie of *See Here, Private Hargrove,* which he wrote during his first year in the Army. Former feature editor of *Yank,* the Army weekly of World War II, he was also a contributing editor of *Salute,* a magazine similar to *Yank* in make-up, which first appeared on newsstands in March 1946. After his discharge from the armed forces, Hargrove, who claimed that he had "almost no interest in politics as such," gained attention for his lectures on "the need for democratic and humanitarian reform in the Army."

The son of Marion Lawton and Emma (Jernigan) Hargrove, the junior Marion Lawton was born October 13, 1919, in Mount Olive, North Carolina, his family having come to that section from Virginia "a couple of hundred years ago." While attending Central High School in Charlotte, also in North Carolina, he was a feature writer on, and then editor of, the school paper; he was also the student director of the dramatic society, for which he played Tom Sawyer. During his junior year, a job with the Charlotte *News* as high school reporter gave him some professional experience. A member of the class of 1938, young Hargrove, whose nickname was "Colonel", failed to graduate because he lacked a half-point credit. In June 1946, however, the high school ruled that his service in the Army would be accepted in lieu of the credit, thereby making him eligible to receive a diploma.

After four months as a student at Belmont Abbey, in North Carolina, Hargrove went to Washington, where he worked for a while as a soda dispenser. Upon returning to Charlotte in March 1939, he held various jobs: he was an usher in a movie theater, a printer's devil, and a publicity man. He then went back to the Charlotte *News* as a proofreader and worked his way up to become the city editor's assistant and feature editor. In *See Here, Private Hargrove* he later wrote that he was "the feature editor, the obituary editor, the woman's page editor, the hospital editor, the rewrite man, the assistant to the city editor, the commissar for paste and copy paper and Coca-Colas, the custodian of oral memoranda . . . the guest artist for ailing columnists, the tourist guide for visiting school children . . . the butt of the office jokes."

A letter which began "The President of the United States—to Marion Hargrove: Greetings!" rescued Hargrove from the mountain of work: on July 18, 1941, he was inducted into the United States Army at Fort Bragg, North Carolina. On July 19 he was classified as a semiskilled cook. In the training camp Hargrove saluted the noncommissioned officers, tripped over himself during calisthenics, spoiled drill exercises,—and received some additional practice in K.P. duty. He capitalized on his experiences as a rookie by writing about them for the Charlotte *News* in a column called *In the Army Now*. When playwright Maxwell Anderson visited Fort Bragg in March 1942—he was in search of local color for his play *The Eve of St. Mark*— Hargrove made friends with him and showed him numerous clippings from his column. Anderson returned to New York with soldier dialogue for his play (Hargrove is reported to be the prototype for the character of Francis Marion, the Southern soldier) and with Hargrove's columns. These Anderson showed to William Sloane, then the editor of Henry Holt and Company. The result was the publication in July 1942 of *See Here, Private Hargrove*.

In general, the critics thought Hargrove's account "a delightful book about the trials and tribulations of a rookie" and recommended it as "an antidote" for parents and brothers in the service. "It approaches Army life with just the right touch of hard-boiled banter to take the sting out of it," said *Time*. Regarding the author's talents as a writer, opinions differed. While John Chamberlain saw "a latent novelist in the character of Marion Hargrove," the *New Republic* thought the author had "no more talent or imagination than a phonograph record, but like a phonograph he [could] pick up stuff fine."

With the public, *See Here, Private Hargrove* immediately became a best seller. In consideration of its value as a morale builder for soldiers and civilians alike, Holt released the book to Pocket Books, which sold more than two million copies of it as a twenty-five-cent reprint. Hargrove reportedly made two hundred thousand dollars. (Alice P. Hackett, in her *Fifty Years of Best Sellers,* placed the book as sixth among eleven record best sellers in a list of one hundred and fifty all-time American best sellers.) Hargrove's escapades gained even wider popularity when MGM made a motion picture adaptation of his book, first shown in March 1944. The soldier received twelve thousand dollars for the film rights; upon the tremendous success of the motion picture, it was reported that MGM would make an adjustment later, which Hargrove said did

MARION HARGROVE

not materialize. Hargrove was wise enough to retain the sequel rights, for which he received fifty thousand dollars after eighteen months of negotiating. The contract provided for an additional amount if the picture grossed three and a half million at the box office.

In May 1942 Hargrove was transferred to New York to work as a staff writer on *Yank*. Before leaving Fort Bragg he had been promoted to the rank of corporal and, to his relief, placed in the public relations office of the Fort Bragg Field Artillery Replacement Center. In March 1943, Hargrove, now a sergeant, was sent to China as staff correspondent for *Yank* and afterwards became managing editor of the CBI edition of the magazine in India. In May 1944 he returned to New York as *Yank*'s feature editor; fifteen months later he again received an assignment as staff correspondent, this time going to the Philippines. His work took him to every continent except Europe—he was the first person to go around the world for *Yank*. The writer also contributed articles to other magazines and wrote the foreword to George Baker's *The Sad Sack*. In 1944 Hargrove, together with John Hersey and Lieutenant John Mason Brown, was a member of the advisory council of the "GI Joe Literary Award" of five thousand dollars for the best book manuscript written by a service man or woman wounded in action. Articles which Hargrove had written for *Yank* were included in *The Best from Yank*, a book published in 1945. A letter he wrote to explain why he could not accept the invitation to write a foreword for Barrie Stavis' Army satire, *Chain of Command*, actually became the book's foreword.

After being discharged from the Army in October 1945, Hargrove, who had "planned to lead a calm civilian life in the country writing novels and plays" went on a lecture tour. To some audiences he spoke about his Army ex-

HARGROVE, MARION—*Continued*

periences—a "light" subject—but he preferred to speak on what to him was a more stimulating and important subject: the need for democratizing the Army. He pointed out some abuses of the court-martial system, the disproportionate differences between the living conditions provided for officers and those for enlisted men, the practice of compensating only officers for lost leave. After a speech on the subject before corporation presidents and directors in Pelham, New York, Hargrove was accused of being a Communist and a rabble-rouser. The ex-soldier replied that such name-calling was "not only dirty fighting" but "a lazy man's way of disposing of a problem without having to think about it." Calling for a bill of rights for the enlisted man, he also presented his criticism before a military board which heard complaints against the Army caste system.

Hargrove was one of the "critical outsiders" whom the National Association of Manufacturers invited to its Golden Anniversary Congress of American Industry in December 1945. The veteran, in phrases pointed with sarcasm, did not mince words: "I can't remember offhand a single contribution the organization itself has made or a single constructive thing it's done in the time I've been reading or hearing about it." He was also concerned with the problem of housing for veterans: as spokesman for "Operation Housing," the American Legion committee working on this issue, Hargrove criticized Robert Moses '40 of New York for "creating a displaced persons problem" with a plan for the construction of a highway which would cause the eviction of five hundred families. Once active in the literature unit of the Independent Citizens Committee of Arts, Sciences and Professions, Hargrove also lent his support to a pledge of "unequivocal support" of American workers in their fight to secure better wages.

Hargrove was the commander of the American Legion Duncan-Paris Post, which in September 1946 became the subject of sharp controversy. At that time it was announced that the Legion's New York State executive committee refused the post (which had been organized in March) its "application for permanent charter." In the words of the Legion's New York adjutant, the action was taken against the post—which had not received a bill of particulars or a hearing—because "the American Legion doesn't want within its membership any veterans who advocate Communism and are identified with it either in a professional or political capacity." Hargrove asserted that there was no "Communist or any strong influence in the post," that perhaps half a dozen among the 273 members were Communists. The issue was an illegal basis of expulsion, he declared—"the Legion Constitution states that expulsion on religious, racial, or political grounds is not allowed." He appealed to the Legion's national executive committee, which subsequently rescinded its approval of the revocation of the charter, but did not reinstate the post. Composed largely of writers and artists, including many former staff

members of *Yank, Stars and Stripes,* and other Army publications, the Duncan-Paris post, according to Hargrove, was the first Legion affiliate to take action on Congressional housing bills. Hargrove withdrew from the American Legion in November 1946.

In December 1942 Private Hargrove was married to Alison Pfeiffer of Brattleboro, Vermont, whom he had met at a party held for the staffs of *Yank* and *Mademoiselle*. Miss Pfeiffer had gotten the job as a guest editor on *Mademoiselle* while a senior at Smith College. The Hargroves' children are Christopher and Stephen. Mrs. Hargrove, who enjoys dancing and golfing, bemoans the fact that she has done neither since the evening she met her husband. He dislikes parties and exercise—sleeping is his favorite pastime. Although he described himself to a newspaperwoman as the reticent type, the interviewer did not get this impression. "He has a quick wit and a fine sense of humor," she wrote, "and is rarely at a loss for a subject." While his lectures against the Army caste system were halted by doctor's orders, in June 1946 he was reported to be at work on a serious novel.

References

N Y Post p27 Mr 30 '44

Who's Who in America, 1946-47

HARMON, ERNEST N(ASON) Feb. 26, 1894- United States Army officer

Address: b. c/o War Department, Washington, D.C.; h. Vienna, Va.

As commander of the American Constabulary in Germany, which by mid-1947 is expected to be the only United States Army force in the American zone of occupation, Major General Ernest N. Harmon is building a distinctive corps. Highly mobile, with a specially trained personnel, the Constabulary is distinguished by a shoulder patch designed by the General himself—a blue "C" crossed by a red bolt of lightning—blue and gold striped helmets, a Sam Browne belt. The Constabulary's development and the change from full military occupation to "police-force" occupation in the American zone, are being observed by other occupation forces with a view toward possible duplication. The General—"Old Gravel Voice" to the men of the "Famous First" and "Hell on Wheels" Second Armored divisions—reportedly has to his credit the greatest number of major victories of any Allied tank commander of World War II.

Ernest Nason Harmon, the son of Ernest Josiah and Junietta (Spaulding) Harmon, was born in Lowell, Massachusetts, on February 26, 1894. Until the death of his parents in 1904, the family, in which there were another son and daughter, lived in Lowell. Under the care of John Durant and his wife, Ernest then left his birthplace for West Newbury, Vermont; from there he was sent to Bradford Academy in the same State. Then, after one year at Norwich University (Northfield, Vermont), young Harmon was appointed to the United States Military Academy at West Point.

A few days after the United States entered World War I in 1917, Harmon was commissioned a second lieutenant and assigned to the Second Cavalry stationed at Fort Ethan Allen, Vermont. A month later (May 1917) he was promoted to the rank of first lieutenant, and when his regiment was transferred to Camp Devens, Massachusetts, in August, he had received the temporary rank of captain. Following his December 1917 graduation from the School of Musketry at Fort Sill, Oklahoma, Captain Harmon began a tour of duty at Fort Ethan Allen which ended when he sailed for France in March 1918. From the Baccarat sector in Vosges, where he served in April and May, he was transferred to Camp de Valdahon. He participated in the St. Mihiel offensive (September) and the Meuse-Argonne offensive (September to November). Returning to the United States from France and Belgium in June 1919, the New Englander was assigned to duty with the Second Cavalry at Fort Riley, Kansas. While at that post, he attended the Cavalry School, enrolling a month after his promotion to the permanent rank of captain in August 1920; he was graduated in June 1921. In August he reported for duty as instructor at the United States Military Academy, where he remained for four years.

Following two years with the Sixth Cavalry at Fort Oglethorpe, Georgia, Captain Harmon went back to teaching as professor of military science and tactics at Norwich University, his old school. In 1931, after four years at Norwich, he began three years of study at advanced Army schools. He completed a two-year course at the Command and General Staff School at Fort Leavenworth in June 1933, a year's course at the Army War College in Washington the following June, and two months later the Field Officers' Course of the Chemical Warfare School in Maryland. Major Harmon—he had been promoted in November 1932—was next assigned to command a squadron of the Eighth Cavalry in Texas. He served on the War Department General Staff in Washington from August 1935 to June 1939, then spent a year with the First Cavalry at Fort Knox, Kentucky, where the nation's gold bullion had been deposited in 1937.

Colonel Harmon is said to have been one of the pioneers, along with General George S. Patton '43 and General Alvin C. Gillem, who tried in the thirties to convince the Army that it should concentrate on tanks. When the first United States Armored Force was activated in July 1940, Harmon, promoted to lieutenant colonel, became assistant chief of staff for supply of the First Armored Corps at Fort Knox. He subsequently served (November 1941 to June 1942) as chief of staff of headquarters for the Armored Force, and was later cited, with the addition of an oak leaf cluster to his Legion of Merit, for being "of incalculable value in the initial organization and subsequent expansion of the Armored Force." Eight months after Pearl Harbor, with the emergency rank of major general, Harmon became commanding general of the Second Armored Division.

In November 1942 Harmon led troops in the invasion of French Africa, conducting a rapid attack on the harbor and town of Safi, French Morocco, with "complete success." He was awarded a Silver Star for personally directing, under enemy fire, the unloading of ships in the harbor of Safi. "After the town and harbor were captured he continued the attack with dash and drive," read the citation accompanying his Distinguished Service Medal. The citation noted further a ninety-mile march through hostile country, the forcing of a river crossing, and the General's advance alone across a defended bridge to inform the enemy that an armistice existed, in all of which Harmon demonstrated the "highest character of combat leadership."

From May 1943 to July 1944 General Harmon commanded the First Armored Division in North Africa and afterward in Italy. The First Armored opened the way into Bizerte, taking forty-two thousand prisoners. In May, when stubborn enemy defense of a defile in Tunisia was delaying his advance, Harmon went forward by truck, exposing himself to intense fire, and "so encouraged his men that the defile was promptly forced." This "extraordinary heroism" won him the Distinguished Service Cross. A story that became legendary was General Harmon's reply to five captured German generals who demurred at riding in a truck with their troops: "You are free to walk, gentlemen. I am too busy at the moment to consider military delicacies." In Italy the First Armored saw action at Cassino, broke out of the Anzio beachhead to fight a "savage engagement" in the area of Cisterna and Campo Leon, and fought what Homer Bigart, New York *Herald Tribune* correspondent, called "one of the greatest tank battles of the war" at Lanusvio, below Rome. The first to cross the Tiber, General Harmon's division rolled into Rome in June 1944. It had "distinguished itself repeatedly" in Africa and Italy.

In August, after a month in the United States as commanding general of the Thirteenth Corps at Camp Bowie, Texas, Harmon was assigned to SHAEF in the European theater. Preferring action to rank, he had asked for a combat assignment in a personal letter to General Omar N. Bradley '43. Offered the "Hell on Wheels" Division, the Second Armored, (known to the Germans as "Roosevelt's Butchers") Harmon returned to the field in October. The closing phase of the war was "an armored force field day." Harmon's Second was among the three veteran divisions spearheading the offensive into Germany: the Second Armored broke the Siegfried Line above Aachen, and in December and January fought in the "Belgian Bulge" in blizzards and bitter winter cold, wiping out Marshal Gerd von Rundstedt's '41 Second Panzer Division in a furious battle. That January a *Newsweek* correspondent reported that Harmon was the man the Germans dreaded most among the Allied armored field commanders—"at fifty probably the most profane, wisest, and sprightliest tank leader in the army. He has never lost an armored battle and has won more major victories than any other Allied tank commander. . . .He has a fighting philosophy based on the premise that tanks are expendable but human lives are not. He said that he has kept careful records of

U.S. Army Signal Corps
MAJ. GEN. ERNEST N. HARMON

casualties which show that tank break-throughs are costly in armor but relatively cheap in lives."

At the end of January 1945 General Harmon was assigned to the Fifteenth Army Group, and in February assumed command of its Twenty-second Corps. The first American military governor on German soil in World War II, in April 1945 Harmon took over the northern half of the Rhine province, where he introduced a system for the screening of Nazis. But faced with a choice between letting the six million Germans in the area starve and freeze in a coming food and coal crisis, and permitting a few Nazis to retain their positions, Harmon chose the latter course. "You can't run railroads with drug clerks, or run factories with bootblacks. So in some cases we had to keep the Nazis who had the know-how." That summer a United Press correspondent reported that Harmon had done "a notable job" in the Rhineland, which had been crowded with tens of thousands of liberated slave laborers. "Harmon settled bitter fights between Poles and Russians, set them up in camps, and is shipping them home at the rate of thousands each week. . . . All major Nazi war criminals in the area have been rounded up, tried . . . and probably will be executed."

The new Constabulary, which was eventually to be the only security force in Germany, was placed under General Harmon's command in January 1946. He set out to build a mechanized force of efficiency and dignity, its motto to be "Mobility! Vigilance! Justice!" Seventy per cent of his organization, which was built around mechanized cavalry units of the Third Army, would be new men from the United States all "keen to serve in the new force." The General developed an intensive training scheme; his men were to use light tanks, ar-

mored cars and jeeps, motorcycles, horses, and small liaison-type aircraft. A Constabulary "West Point" was established in the Bavarian Alps in buildings designed originally for the education of future leaders of the Third Reich. The four week courses covered subjects from constabulary tactics and law to geopolitics. The General established his mobile staff headquarters aboard what was dubbed "Harmon's Lightning Bolt"—formerly Hermann Göring's special train—which he used while inspecting scattered units of the Constabulary. Until it took over complete responsibility, the Constabulary was to collaborate with other occupation forces in security patrols, border patrolling and "search and seizure" operations. Thus, in February 1946 the Constabulary raided Displaced Persons camps to stop attempts by Poles and Yugoslavs to form underground armies hostile to the Governments in Warsaw and Belgrade, and in May conducted "Operation Grab-Bag," the seizure of almost four hundred Danube River craft to break up a suspected smuggling ring and underground railroad for escaping SS (Elite Guard) men. But Harmon viewed with alarm the large turnover of men that had made it necessary for him to train two constabularies in four months, and that had lowered his high standards for personnel.

General Harmon was married to Leona Tuxbury on August 15, 1917; their children are Barbara Ruth, Halsey Winans, Ernest Nason, Jr., Robert Spaulding, and Jeanne Leona. His favorite spectator sports are football and polo, and fishing and hunting are likely to fill any leisure time he may have. The "dynamic, restive" Harmon has close-cropped gray hair, a trim brown mustache, piercing hazel eyes. He talks, according to *Newsweek*'s Roland C. Gask, with a cigarette in his mouth, one eye closed, and the other fixed on his listener. "Every other sentence," Gask reported, "he threw in a purple epithet." In battle the New England General was apt to be "firing off expletives like a semi-automatic gun . . . yet all the time he was skillfully directing daring tactics." Nicknamed "Old Gravel Voice" because of a rasping voice, Harmon often "bums" cigarettes or candy from GIs for the sake of having some conversation with the men.

References

Christian Sci Mon p9 Jl 6 '46
N Y Sun p22 Ap 24 '46; p19 Ap 26 '46; p24 S 4 '46
Newsweek 25:24+ Ja 15 '45 por
PM p3 Je 7 '45
Who's Who in America, 1946-47

HARRIMAN, W(ILLIAM) AVERELL Nov. 15, 1891- United States Secretary of Commerce

Address: b. c/o Department of Commerce, Washington, D.C.; c/o Brown Brothers, Harriman and Co., 59 Wall St., New York; h. Harriman, N.Y.

NOTE: This biography of W. Averell Harriman supersedes the one which appeared in *Current Biography* in 1941, when he was Lend-Lease coordinator.

To W. Averell Harriman's career of banker, railroad director, diplomat, and nonelective Government official, President Truman added in September 1946 the post of Secretary of Commerce, vacated shortly before by Henry A. Wallace '⁴⁰. Under the Roosevelt Administration, Harriman had served as Lend-Lease coordinator between the United States and Britain, and as Ambassador to Russia; under President Truman, he had been Ambassador to Great Britain for a short period. Harriman, who had been born and bred a Republican, became a Democrat during Al Smith's '⁴⁴ campaign for the Presidency. He was also a close friend of President Roosevelt and was associated with the New Deal after its inception in 1932.

The son of financier Edward Henry Harriman (who "feared neither God nor Morgan") and his philanthropic wife, Mary W. (Averell) Harriman, William Averell Harriman was born on November 15, 1891. At seventeen, just when he was entering Yale from Groton, his father died, leaving him and his brother E. Roland Harriman various railroad holdings and a fortune reputed to be between seventy and one hundred million dollars. During summer vacations from college, the young millionaire worked as a clerk and a section hand in the Union Pacific Railroad yards at Omaha, Nebraska. Upon graduation from college in 1913, he once again went to work for the railroad, and in less than two years had risen to be vice-president in charge of purchases and supplies for Union Pacific.

Shortly before the United States entered World War I, Harriman bought a small shipyard at Chester, Pennsylvania, where he built the first partially prefabricated ships in the country. Out of this grew the Merchant Shipping Corporation, of which Harriman was chairman of the board. In 1920 the twenty-nine-year-old railroad and shipping magnate established W. A. Harriman and Company, a private bank. For the next decade Harriman was chairman of the board of this concern, but when it was merged with the Brown Brothers firm in 1931 to form Brown Brothers, Harriman and Company, he accepted a partnership in the new corporation. (He had already disposed of his shipping interests in 1927 in order to devote more time to finance.)

Harriman became chairman of the board of the Union Pacific Railway in 1932. During the depression of the thirties, while other railroads were retrenching, he poured millions into streamlined aluminum trains, low-priced diner meals, and trained-nurse stewardesses. As a result, at the lowest point of the depression, in 1934, Union Pacific's receipts from passenger traffic rose 66 per cent. Two years later board chairman Harriman called in public relations man Steve Hannagan '⁴⁴ to look into the possibilities of establishing a winter resort on some thirty-three hundred acres of Idaho valley land owned by the railroad. The result was the famous playground Sun Valley.

Through a chance meeting on the croquet field at the Long Island estate of Herbert Bayard Swope '⁴⁴, which initiated Harriman's friendship with Harry Hopkins '⁴¹, the rail-

Harris & Ewing

W. AVERELL HARRIMAN

road magnate was brought to the attention of President Roosevelt '⁴². "Harriman," said *Time,* "reacted to the New Deal like a weathercock in a gale." Roosevelt, while not yet completely convinced of Harriman's talent for organization, appointed him Administrator of Division II of the NRA in January 1934. In dealing with business problems, Harriman showed himself to be a middle-of-the-road arbitrator, with a capacity for ironing out the trouble spots between the Administration and industry. In March 1934 he was appointed special assistant administrator for the NRA, and two months later, when General Hugh Johnson '⁴⁰ resigned, he became administrative officer, a post which he held until the following year. At Secretary of Commerce Roper's invitation, Harriman joined the Business Advisory Council for the Department of Commerce in 1933, and was eventually chosen chairman of the council for the years 1937 to 1940. In this capacity, as *PM* put it, he spent a good deal of time trying "to get Government and business to swap concessions." Harriman's diplomacy was double-edged: in business conventions, he would block anti-Administration moves, and at the White House, he would complain about tax and labor legislation.

Harriman brought his experience as a transportation and procurement man into the service of the national defense while the United States was still neutral in World War II. When he was chosen chief of the raw materials branch of the Office of Production Management in 1941, he introduced a speed-up system of armaments production. With proof of Harriman's executive ability, President Roosevelt appointed him "defense expediter" in London shortly before the passage of the Lend-Lease Act in March 1941. As liaison officer between the American and British Governments, Harriman was entrusted with keeping the President in-

HARRIMAN, W. AVERELL—*Continued*
formed of British needs and the British apprised of American production.

Although Roosevelt gave Harriman the rank of Minister, he told newspapermen that the job "did not conform to any job reporters had ever heard of." Harriman was supposed to devote his attention to three problems: transportation, financing, and purchasing. Gradually the orbit of his activities widened and he was soon shuttling to the Near East (May 1941) to make surveys for the installation of American supply bases and to Russia (August 1941) on a joint Anglo-American mission with Lord Beaverbrook '40 in order to discuss Lend-Lease aid to the Soviet Union. The joint mission agreed on the immediate necessity of sending material aid to Moscow, and Harriman promised that hundreds of planes and tanks would be sent to Russia. "The flow," he said, "will be constantly increased and eventually will be limited only by problems of transport." Returning in October to report to President Roosevelt, he told reporters that "Hitler will never destroy Russia." In the following three years, he frequently reiterated this statement, calling for "quick and increasing" aid to Russia.

During 1942 Harriman often accompanied Prime Minister Churchill '42 on missions. One of these was another trip to Moscow in August 1942, when Churchill and Premier Stalin discussed the question of the second front. Meanwhile, "work-minded" Harriman continued his activities as Lend-Lease expediter, and to them added the duties of representative in London of the Combined Shipping Adjustment Board (February 1942) and of member of the London Combined Production and Resources Board (July 1942). At Casablanca in January 1943, he joined President Roosevelt and Harry Hopkins. (Harriman was present at the conferences in Quebec, Casablanca, Moscow, Teheran, San Francisco, and Potsdam.)

President Roosevelt on October 1, 1943, named Harriman Ambassador to Russia. By then the American financier, who had already met Stalin '42 twice, renewed the acquaintance toward the end of that month when he and Secretary of State Cordell Hull '40 conferred with Stalin and Molotov '40. Throughout the three years of his ambassadorship, Harriman consulted with Stalin an average of once a month—a courtesy supposedly not accorded any other diplomat. The new Ambassador completely reorganized the American Embassy in Moscow, both as an office and residence, and installed Kathleen, his daughter by his first wife, as hostess.

Harriman worked closely with Russian Foreign Minister Molotov and the English Ambassador, Sir Archibald Clark Kerr '42. At his first press conference in the new post, Harriman said: "One matter I think deserves the greatest possible consideration at this time is the assistance the United States can give to the Soviet Union in the rehabilitation of devastated areas and the repairing of other dislocations caused by the war." Toward the end of his embassy, however, it became increasingly evident that the United States and Russia were not agreeing about postwar policy. The American Ambassador often acted in concord with the Russians, as when he told the Polish Committee of National Liberation that the United States would not oppose Russian wishes in regard to the Polish question. In February 1945 he was appointed to the committee conferring in Moscow with the various Polish factions. He attended the conference at Potsdam in July and soon after Christmas of 1945 transmitted the terms of the peace treaty to the Rumanians, which facilitated the broadening of the Bucharest Cabinet as a condition of recognition.

After Harriman had tried several times to resign, according to the *Christian Science Monitor,* President Truman acceded to his wish in February 1946 by accepting his resignation. Harriman returned home via Chungking (where he conferred with Chiang Kai-shek '40 and General George C. Marshall '40), Korea, and Tokyo. The ex-Ambassador reported to the President, the Secretary of State, and the House Rules Committee before holding a press conference. To the reporters he said, "Russia does not want war with the United States and is trying to cut off avenues of invasion by surrounding herself with friendly small nations." Through the press, Harriman warned the country that the "chief hope of the world is collective security through the United Nations organization." He added: "It is a fact that the Russian ideology is completely different from ours, but if we both adopt the attitude of live and let live, as to internal affairs, and if we both respect the right of all people to choose their own way of life, this barrier needn't be insurmountable. Most of the people of the world know that this is the attitude of the United States and are counting on us to stand firm against any nation that won't abide by this principle." Harriman also voiced his disapproval of Russia's failure to carry out certain agreements. (It was assumed at this time that he was referring to Russia's failure to withdraw her troops from Iran by March 2, 1946.) About a month after Harriman's return to the United States he and his daughter received a gift of two thoroughbred horses from Stalin.

The last week of March 1946, when John Winant '41, Ambassador to England, was sent to the United Nations Economic and Social Council, President Truman appointed the fifty-four-year-old Harriman to be Winant's successor at the court of Saint James, thus making him the only man in United States history to have held the rank of Ambassador both to Moscow and London. In this way, commented *Time,* the former polo player's "diplomatic rating was raised to a ten-goal top." Harriman knew London from long familiarity ("I have been there on and off ever since I was a boy"), and was described by the British press as a "very close friend of Britain."

Scarcely seven months later, at the end of September 1946, the Ambassador was called home to enter President Truman's Cabinet as Secretary of Commerce. The previous incumbent, Henry Wallace, had been forced to resign after broadcasting a proposal for a changed foreign policy toward Russia, in which he spoke against "getting tough" with the Soviet power.

Harriman's appointment was variously regarded as "a consolidation of Truman's decision to intensify a diplomatic challenge of Russia" (*PM*), and as an Administration attempt "to cultivate more cordial relations with American business" (New York *World-Telegram*); Arthur Krock wrote in the New York *Times* that "his [Harriman's] record, the present value of his past political sponsorship, and his educated realism as to Soviet Russia have produced the general expectation that the Secretary will effectively meet his new responsibilities." The new Secretary is expected to revitalize the forty-five-member Business Advisory Board of which he was once chairman. He will have the task of reorganizing the Commerce Department to be what it was originally intended to be, said Krock further—"a liaison between American business and the Government of the United States," without a policy "designed to proclaim the faults of capitalism."

Immediately after his appointment, Secretary Harriman announced that he was in complete accord with Secretary of State Byrnes's [41] foreign policy. (It is believed that Harriman's reports at the San Francisco conference helped to shape Secretary of State Stettinius' [40] policy of firmness toward Russia, a policy Byrnes inherited.) In reference to Russia, he declared, "A country which attempts to gain security through unilateral action, through aggressive independent action, is only opening the gates of disaster." Referring to his work in various missions, the Secretary of Commerce said, "I had an opportunity to learn first-hand the grave economic problems that face the people of Europe and Asia. . . .In playing our part in world reconstruction, development of a stable and expanding economy at home is of primary importance."

On October 11, 1946, Harriman held his first conference with members of the Department of Commerce. He assured the war veterans in the department that "experience overseas is just as important in developing men as sticking to the job at home is. Therefore, the experience of service men will be recognized in department promotions." To the women employees, Harriman declared: "There will be absolutely fair treatment in the department as to race and religion and as between men and women." In his capacity as Secretary of Commerce, Harriman will also serve on the Presidential Research Board, which will determine "the allocation of research resources between the universities, research foundations, industry, and the Federal Government."

Toward the end of November, Harriman served as the United States representative at the Paris peace conference, participating in the negotiations on the Rumanian treaty. He returned to the United States in December, and at the opening session of the NAM's Congress of American Industry brought out that this country's internal affairs are of vital importance to the rest of the world; he urged businessmen to prevent enactment of legislation that would unduly restrict labor. Turning his attention to international topics once again, the Secretary exhorted the International Red Cross to take leadership in "international human sympathy," for, he told its board of incorporators, "this country has determined to take political responsibility in international affairs." At the end of 1946, Harriman was among the six men who met at the White House to advise President Truman on his revised labor policy. Among subjects discussed were amendment of the Wagner Act, mediation, and improvement of labor-management relations.

Harriman considers himself a public servant, hired by the American people to promote the commercial interests of the whole nation, without favoritism to either "big" or "little" businesses. He intends to continue ex-Secretary Wallace's plans for the reorganization of the Commerce Department. (Congress had substantially curtailed the annual appropriation of the Department under Mr. Wallace's administration, and he had therefore not been able to complete his plans.) A reorganization of the Bureau of Foreign and Domestic Commerce is projected. It will be organized into five divisions: domestic trade, international trade, small business, field operations, and business economics, with new secretaries appointed to the first three branches.

As his father did, Harriman has devoted a good deal of his time to his railroad interests. From 1931 to 1942 he was chairman of the executive committee of the Illinois Central Railroad Company; he was a director in 1946, was also chairman of the board of the Los Angeles and Salt Lake Railroad Company, the Oregon Short Line Railroad Company, and the Oregon and Washington Railroad and Navigation Company. On becoming Secretary of Commerce, Harriman resigned these various offices, retaining only a limited partnership in Brown, Harriman and Company. Harriman is the father of two daughters, Mary and Kathleen, by his first wife, the former Kitty Lanier Lawrance. After their divorce, in 1930 he was married to Mrs. Marie Norton Whitney. The Harrimans are collectors of modern art, and have acquired paintings by Van Gogh, Renoir, Cézanne, Picasso, and Derain. The Secretary of Commerce used to be an outstanding polo player, with an eight-goal rating. He is described by *Time* as a "glossy," young-looking man, with "an ingratiating if aristocratic charm."

References

N Y Herald Tribune p1 S 23 '46
N Y Times p1 S 23 '46
Newsweek 22:24+ N 15 '43; 27:20 Ap 1 '46
Time 42:17 S 27 '43 por; 48:25 S 30 '46 por
U S News 20:20+ Mr 29 '46 por; 21:62-64 O 4 '46 por
Who's Who in America, 1946-47

HARRIS, WILLIAM, JR. July 22, 1884—Sept. 2, 1946 Theatrical producer; excepting for 1926 and 1927, brought out at least one play a year from 1919 through 1930; among his successful productions were *Robert E. Lee,*

HARRIS, WILLIAM, JR.—*Continued*
In Love With Love, Outward Bound, The Outsider, and *The Greeks Had a Word For It.*

Obituary
N Y Times p19 S 3 '46 por

HART, WILLIAM S. Dec. 6, 1872—June 23, 1946 Stage and screen actor; leading man with Mme. Modjeska in several Shakespearean dramas; played role of Messala in *Ben Hur,* 1899-1901; turned to motion pictures in 1914, and became Wild West idol during the era of the silent screen; starred with his pinto pony Paint in the films *The Toll Gate, Wagon Tracks, Sand, Tumbleweeds* and many others; his autobiography is *My Life East and West* (1929).

Obituary
N Y Times p21 Je 25 '46 por

HASLUCK, PAUL Apr. 1, 1905- Australian Government official
Address: b. c/o United Nations, New York

The Australian representative to the United Nations Security Council is a former newspaperman and history teacher who entered his country's diplomatic corps in 1941. When Colo-

PAUL HASLUCK

nel W. R. Hodgson '46 found it necessary to leave New York suddenly in April 1946, Paul Hasluck, familiar with Hodgson's problems as his adviser, succeeded him.

Hasluck is a native of Western Australia, a state of almost a million square miles in which live only about four hundred and eighty thousand persons, almost half of them in Perth, the capital city. Great tracts of its territory are still unexplored and some twenty-seven thousand of the state's inhabitants are ab-

origines. Born in Fremantle, the port city for Perth, on April 1, 1905, the son of E. M. C. Hasluck, Paul Hasluck attended the Perth Modern School, and then the University of Western Australia. In his school and university days he was active in athletics, a particularly good swimmer. In 1922, at seventeen, he became a member of the literary staff of the *West Australian,* Perth's morning daily, writing about "everything from chaff markets to foreign news." He got his Master of Arts degree at the university while working on the paper. Later, as the paper's drama critic, he earned "a considerable reputation" in his state and in 1937 he organized the West Australian Drama Festival, which annually offers prizes for the writing and production of plays.

Hasluck was also interested in Australian history and the aborigines of present-day Australia. During 1939 he lectured in Australian history at the University of Western Australia. His first book on the aborigines, *Our Southern Half-Castes* (1938), was followed in 1942 with *Black Australians,* a survey of native policy in Western Australia from 1829 to 1897. Hasluck is also the author of *Into the Desert,* a sixty-four page book of verse published in 1939. In 1944 he was given the assignment of writing that volume of the Australian official history of World War II which will deal with the political and social developments of the war years.

The thirty-six-year-old newspaperman joined the rapidly growing Department of External Affairs in Canberra in 1941, the year when World War II spread to the Pacific. Hasluck was sent abroad in 1942 as a member of the Australian delegation to the Institute of Pacific Relations Conference in Canada. Within the same year he became officer in charge of the postwar section of the department's publications and research branch. Two years later, in 1944, he was appointed the director of a branch of the Department of External Affairs, the Post-hostilities Division. At the Australia-New Zealand conference in Canberra in January 1944, he served as secretary; the following October he attended a similiar conference in Wellington, New Zealand, as adviser to his country's delegation. He was again an adviser for the Australian group at the British Commonwealth meetings in London in April 1945, and in the same capacity he served from April until June with the Australian delegation at the United Nations conference in San Francisco. His posts soon became more responsible. From August until October he was Australian delegate on the executive committee of the United Nations. In November and December he was alternate delegate on the Preparatory Commission, in January 1946 he was named alternate delegate to the United Nations General Assembly, and then, in March 1946, Hasluck was appointed counselor in charge of Australia's permanent mission to the United Nations. While in this capacity he served as the Australian representative on the Committee of Experts of the U.N. Security Council, meeting in New York.

Hasluck took the place of the Australian Security Council representative, Lieutenant Colonel W. R. Hodgson, when the latter was suddenly called to Paris, where his wife was seriously ill. Half an hour after Hasluck first took his seat at the Council table on April 28, he was in the international limelight; since the inquiry had been an Australian proposal, he was named chairman of the Council's first investigating body, the five-nation subcommittee to investigate Spain. The forty-one-year-old Australian promised that the investigation, condemned by Russia as a device of delay and inaction in the case of a proved fascist menace, would be "practical and forceful." Whereas Russia had insisted Spain was a threat to peace, and Great Britain and America that it was not, the committee held, after a month's inquiry, that Spain was "a potential threat." It recommended that if the Franco regime were not withdrawn by September the Security Council should propose that the U.N. General Assembly vote a recommendation for the collective breaking of diplomatic relations with Spain. "By inventing the tenuous notion of a threat-of-a-threat," *Time* commented, "the subcommittee had achieved at least a promise-of-a-promise of world order."

Australian policy was an attempt to "democratize" the U.N. by narrowing Big Five control and broadening the power of the fifty-two-nation General Assembly. In Council meetings Hasluck maintained the Australian reputation, gained by Herbert V. Evatt [42] and Hodgson, for forthrightness in discussion. His was the first "open and frank" discussion in Council of the Soviet refusal to attend meetings at which the Iranian question was discussed. "It looks as though we may be on the way to establishing dangerous procedures for the work of this organ," he said. Speaking for his Government he demanded to know what the Soviet Union expected to achieve by "ignoring" the Council. When the rules committee proposed that a Council subcommittee consider in private new applications for U.N. membership, Hasluck dissented, on the ground that the United Nations was not "a club" with an executive committee —the Council—to receive "the applications in private and decide whether or not the candidate is a cad or an acceptable person."

On June 7, Evatt, Australian Minister of External Affairs, temporarily replaced Hasluck on the Council. During July Hasluck served on the United Nations Atomic Energy Commission as chairman of the commission's legal committee, charged with making a long-range study of the veto and treaty questions which were key points of difference between the American and Russian plans for the control of atomic energy. He was also on the membership committee, which was composed of one delegate from each of the nations on the Security Council. Unlike others on the committee, Hasluck took no stand for his nation on the advisability of admitting any of the nine applicants (Albania, Afghanistan, Eire, Iceland, the Mongolian People's Republic, Portugal, Sweden, Thailand, and Trans-Jordan) ; Australia believed, he said, that the committee's only task was to gather information to enable the Council to reach a decision. When the U.N. Council met in late August, Hasluck was again in the Australian seat, Evatt having left for the Paris Peace Conference.

Hasluck joined Russian representative Gromyko [43] in the opposition which defeated the American proposal that all eight applicants for U.N. membership (Thailand had withdrawn) be accepted. Objecting to this "easy way out" in which the United States was indicating she would not veto Albania and Outer Mongolia as she had intended, if Russia, in turn, withheld the veto on Eire, Portugal, and Trans-Jordan, Hasluck insisted the applicants be examined on their merits. But the Australian abstained from voting on any of the eight (only Iceland, Sweden, and Afghanistan won admission), protesting that the applications should have first gone to the General Assembly for the necessary two-thirds vote of that body. In accordance with his belief that the "primary and final responsibility" for admitting new members lay with the Assembly, the Australian proposed to the General Assembly's Political and Security Committee that a joint committee of the Assembly and Security Council be set up to work toward that end.

In November Hasluck condemned excessive use of the veto as having "stultified the work of the Security Council . . . undermined confidence in it and lessened the council's ability to deal effectively with the matters brought before it." In an October *New Republic* article, he had expanded this idea, criticizing the United Nations charter for vesting certain powers in the unanimity of the Big Five, rather than recognizing the equality of all nations. After weeks of discussion, the political committee of the General Assembly passed a resolution calling upon the Security Council to formulate new procedures to reduce the use of the veto. In the United Nations Atomic Energy Commission Hasluck endorsed the Baruch [41] plan for international control, which was passed late in December 1946.

With Hasluck in New York are his wife, the former Alix Darker, to whom he was married in 1932, and his two sons, Rollo and Nicholas. Five feet ten inches tall and weighing 173 pounds, Hasluck has a ruddy complexion, a small brown mustache, and brown eyes. American newsmen described him as "boyish looking," but also remarked on his "poise, coolness, affability, and quick mind." An official Australian statement ascribes his swift rise in the Department of External Affairs to "great industry and energy, combined with thoroughness, powers of concentration, and knowledge of history and current affairs that make him invaluable." A devotee of the theater, the Australian lists his other recreations as printing and riding. In rurally situated Canberra, the capital of Australia, he is said to have been a "familiar figure on his tall black horse roving the avenues of blossoms and the outlying hills in his few leisure hours." He was honorary secretary of the West Australian Historical Society from 1930 until 1936, and makes a hobby of collecting the stories of the old colonists of Australia.

References

N Y Herald Tribune p16 Ap 30 '46
N Y Times p7 Ap 30 '46

HAUPTMANN, GERHART (houpt'män) Nov. 16, 1862—June 8, 1946 German writer; novelist and poet best known for his plays; *The Weavers* (1892), considered his greatest work; awarded the Nobel Prize for Literature in 1912.

Obituary

N Y Times p27 Je 12 '46 por

HAUSHOFER, KARL (ERNST NIKO-LAUS) (hous'hō-fĕr kärl) Aug. 27, 1869—Mar. 10, 1946 German Army officer and geographer; served in World War I; lectured at the University of Munich from 1919, where one of his students in geopolitics was Rudolf Hess; Hitler appointed Haushofer to the presidency of the German Academy in Munich and subsidized his research organization; among his many books are *Wehr-geopolitik* (1932) and *Weltpolitik von Heute* (1934); a suicide. See *Current Biography* 1942 Yearbook.

Obituary

N Y Times p3 Mr 14 '46

HAWLEY, PAUL R(AMSEY) Jan. 31, 1891- United States Army officer and Government official

Address: b. c/o Veterans Administration, Washington, D.C.

Major General Paul R. Hawley has been an army officer almost as long as he has been a physician. He has seen service in the two World Wars; in the course of World War II he became Chief Surgeon in the European Theater of Operations, winning, in recognition of that service, the Distinguished Service Medal and the Legion of Merit. In August 1945 he was appointed Chief Medical Director of the Veterans Administration and adviser to its Administrator, General Omar N. Bradley '43.

The "country doctor" whose grandfather and father were practitioners in the town of West College Corner, Indiana, was born there on January 31, 1891, the son of William Harry and Sabina Cora (Ramsey) Hawley. After he received his B.A. degree from Indiana University in 1912, young Hawley prepared himself for the medical profession by further studies at the College of Medicine of the University of Cincinnati. At twenty-three the young man, now an M.D., returned home to practice with his father as a family doctor, and at twenty-four he was married. Having been attracted to military medicine, he accepted a commission as a first lieutenant in the Army Medical Reserve four months later, in August 1916. By October he was on active duty as a student in the Army Medical School at Fort Thomas, Kentucky.

Six days before the United States declared war against Germany in April 1917, Hawley was appointed a first lieutenant in the Regular Army Medical Corps, and later that year he became a medical officer in the Eighty-fourth Division. In March 1918 the Hoosier doctor was transferred to Camp Taylor, Kentucky, for three months' duty with the 309th Sanitary Train, and the same day was promoted to the rank of captain and immediately thereafter to major. After duty in Ohio, Major Hawley sailed for France with the 334th Infantry. He served with the Second Depot Division and with the Service of Supply, then returned to the United States in June 1919. The Major was next ordered to Fort Benjamin, in his native state, and in September of that year to Camp Grant (Illinois) as surgeon for the Fourteenth Infantry and sanitary inspector for the Sixth Division. Having enrolled in the Army Medical School in the national capital, he was graduated in December 1921. After a brief tour at Fort Sheridan (Illinois) Hawley was transferred to Camp Custer, Michigan, as a sanitary officer. From 1921 to 1924 he was a medical inspector in the Sixth Corps area. During that period the thirty-one-year-old Major enrolled in a course in preventive medicine at Johns Hopkins University and there was awarded the Doctor's Degree in Public Health in 1923.

In 1924 Major Hawley left the United States for overseas duty as assistant to the surgeon of the Philippine Department at Manila. After serving there for three and a half years he was reassigned as chief of the Medical Service at Fort Riley in Kansas. Then, having been appointed Chief Surgeon of the United States Army troops in Nicaragua he moved in 1929 to his new headquarters in Granada, Nicaragua. The Major noted with satisfaction the advances made in the field of preventive medicine in the Nicaragua Canal area and described his impressions in "The Investment of the United States in Tropical Hygiene," which appeared in the April 1930 issue of the *Pan American Magazine*. The rapid progress, he said, was not so much due to humanitarian impulses as to the fact that human life has a certain economic value, as illustrated by the medical service maintained by great commercial and industrial enterprises in the tropics.

Hawley's Nicaraguan assignment ended in 1931, when he appointed executive officer of the Army Medical Center (Washington, D.C.), where he was instructor. In August 1934 he entered the Command and General Staff School at Fort Leavenworth, Kansas, and was graduated in June 1936 after completing the two-year course. Promoted to the rank of lieutenant colonel, he became director of the Department of Administration at the Medical Field Service School at Carlisle Barracks, Pennsylvania, and was later appointed commanding officer of the First Medical Regiment there. In September 1938 he was ordered to the Army War College in Washington, which gives the service's highest training. Colonel Hawley was graduated the following June and two months later returned to Carlisle Barracks as director of the Army Extension Course at the Medical Field Service School. From January to May 1941 he served as commanding officer of the medical department replacement training center at Camp Lee, Virginia. Returning that same year as a colonel (temporary) to Carlisle Barracks, Hawley acted as assistant commandant of the Medical Field Service School until September, when he was ordered to Europe as one of the military group of special observers, a few months before the United States entered World War II.

In January 1942, following Pearl Harbor, Colonel Hawley received a new assignment as Chief Surgeon of the United States Army Air Forces in the British Isles and the European Theater of Operations. Reports in American newspapers told of the work of the new Chief Surgeon: One of his first moves had been to establish cooperation with the health authorities of the United Kingdom, and to see that the American medical units worked with the British civilian and military units in all matters pertaining to the health of the American servicemen. The problem of food, water, housing, sanitation, and the prevention and treatment of communicable diseases were all included in the program mapped out by Hawley and the British.

The American doctor (given the single star of a brigadier general in September 1942 and another to mark him as major general in February 1944) was responsible for the installation of a general medical laboratory and the supervision of medical, technical and nursing staffs. In a chapter he wrote for the book *Doctors At War* (1945) he praised the assistance he received from the British authorities and the preparations that were made against D-Day for the care of the wounded. Mobile medical units which traveled in motor trucks gave the wounded the care they required before they could be removed to the base hospitals a few miles behind the front. Hawley and his staff compiled the *Manual of Therapy* to insure constant and unaltered medical treatment even when medical officers were shifted.

Hawley's appointment as Medical Director of the Veterans Administration brought him from France to Washington to assist the Administration's chief, Omar N. Bradley. Hawley was frank in his discussion of the difficulties he faced on his new post. Criticisms of the inadequate care the sick and disabled veterans were receiving had made the Veterans Administration a national storm center. "I have fallen heir to a long neglected house, and that house has to be remodeled," the new medical chief told reporters. Out of a needed thirty-four hundred doctors, the VA had only twenty-three hundred to care for its eighty-five thousand patients in September 1945. Of these doctors seventeen hundred had been in the wartime service and only 35 per cent intended to remain permanently with the VA. To cope with the immediate problem of overcrowding in the veterans' hospitals, the General planned to use the facilities of civilian hospitals and those of the Army and Navy.

Hawley planned a long-range program covering a period of ten years for his department, and waited only for the necessary Congressional appropriation. He hoped to have a permanent medical corps patterned after the United States Public Health Service. An alteration of this plan, subsequent to the enactment of Public Law 293, followed Civil Service grading, but provided higher base pay. By offering better security and a higher remuneration, he also hoped to attract specialists and capable doctors

Drawing by C. Engel
MAJ. GEN. PAUL R. HAWLEY

to the VA and thus be enabled to weed out the incompetent from his medical personnel. One of his first acts was to appoint eleven physicians as consultants in the veterans' hospitals. In answer to the complaints of amputees he also planned a three-year program of prosthetic research, for which an appropriation of a million dollars would be needed annually. At one time, when it appeared that Congress might not approve the necessary appropriation for the work of the Veterans Administration, the Washington bureau of the New York *Sun* reported that it seemed certain that General Hawley would resign if funds were not forthcoming. On March 5, 1946, the House of Representatives voted a VA appropriation of $114,000,000.

A "bright spot in the VA picture," wrote Albert Deutsch (*PM*, November 14, 1946), Hawley "has shown extraordinary ability as a farsighted planner and administrator. . . .He has infused the whole hospital program with a spirit of modern scientific medicine. . . .The Hawley revolution is far from completion . . . but Hawley and his aides know where . . . the flaws in the system . . . are, and they are gradually being eliminated." Early in his first year as VA Medical Director, when Public Law 293 had released key VA medical personnel from the jurisdiction of civil service and placed them under the VA Department of Medicine and Surgery, Hawley procured the cooperation of private medicine. He was said to have "sold" his program to the American Medical Association, when he promised (*Newsweek*, August 12, 1946) that the profession would "be given free rein" if it would "pitch in and help." (Addressing graduates of the Syracuse University College of Medicine, Hawley had declared that "the United States will have socialized medicine soon unless the medical profession forgets its indifference and attacks the problem from the

HAWLEY, PAUL R.—*Continued*

angle of insuring that the highest standards of medicine are available to every citizen.")

The quality of medical care was raised by placing responsibility in the hands of the leading specialists in the country. Physician-residency programs were put into operation in thirty-two VA hospitals through the participation in the program of "Grade A" medical schools deans' committees, which recommended resident physicians and senior consultants who became responsible for the supervision, consultation, and teaching done in the hospitals. More significant than the increase in hospital space, Dr. H. A. Rusk '46 commented in the New York *Times,* was "the increase in available beds, made by drastic reduction in duration of treatment time . . . in many hospitals, particularly those affiliated with schools of medicine." In most hospitals, Dr. Rusk observed, the additional staff increased the patient-day cost, but this was more than compensated for by the reduction in the total time necessary for the treatment of the patient. In August, at the end of Hawley's first year as VA Medical Director, there were set up the first outpatient clinics to care for disabled veterans not requiring hospitalization, and arrangements had been completed in sixteen States to provide outpatient care by local physicians for service-connected cases. An expenditure of over five hundred million dollars was planned for the construction of new hospitals, which would be located near medical schools and centers, to insure the procurement of "first-class medical care . . . the principal objective of the [VA] Department of Medicine and Surgery."

In recognition of his earlier services in England and later in the European Theater of Operations, General Hawley was awarded the United States decoration of the Legion of Merit in July 1943, of which the citation read in part: "General Hawley displayed marked professional ability, keen judgment, and devotion to duty, and rendered service of outstanding value to the Government." The General also holds the Distinguished Service Medal and the Bronze Star. The British made him an honorary Companion of the Bath and conferred the Order of St. John of Jerusalem upon him. Other foreign decorations he has received are: Officer of the Legion of Honor and Croix de Guerre with Palm (French); Commander of the Order of the Crown (Belgian); Presidential Medal of Nicaragua. His honorary degrees include LL.D.'s from Indiana University, the University of Cincinnati, and the University of Birmingham, England; and he is a Fellow of the American Medical Association, and of British societies: of the Royal College of Physicians, Royal Society of Medicine, and Royal College of Surgeons in Edinburgh. Hawley is a member of Delta Omega, Phi Delta Theta, and Phi Rho Sigma. He is a Mason and belongs to the Army and Navy clubs in Washington and Manila.

Paul Hawley has been married to the former Frances Katharine Gilliland since December 1915, and is the father of two children—Barbara (Mrs. Thomas Grant Tousey, Jr.), and

William Harry. The military surgeon, who has been described as solidly built and freckled, is five feet nine inches tall and has hazel eyes and graying sandy-colored hair. For recreation he enjoys golf and polo, and his favorite reading is Pepys's Diary.

Reference

Who's Who in America, 1946-47

HAYNES, GEORGE EDMUND May 11, 1880- Sociologist

Address: b. c/o Federal Council of the Churches of Christ in America, 297 4th Ave., New York; h. 411 Convent Ave., New York

As the first executive secretary of the Department of Race Relations of the Federal Council of the Churches of Christ in America, George Edmund Haynes has maintained his reputation for "always being first." The co-founder and first executive director of the National Urban League, Haynes was also the first Negro to graduate from the New York School of Social Work as well as the first to receive a Ph.D. from Columbia University. In addition, he has the distinction of being the founder and first secretary of the Association of Negro Colleges and Secondary Schools, serving as Director of Negro Economics for the United States Department of Labor, and writing many articles and books which have "inspired a new Negro philosophy."

Born May 11, 1880, in Pine Bluff, Arkansas, Haynes received his secondary school education in near-by Hot Springs. He attended the Alabama State Normal School and then Fisk University in Nashville, Tennessee, from which he was graduated with a B.A. degree in 1903. Upon receiving an M.A. degree from Yale University in 1904, he studied for two summers, in 1906 and 1907, at the University of Chicago. His interest in sociology then prompted his desire to specialize in that subject, and in 1910 he was graduated from the New York School of Social Work. In 1912, the Columbia University Press published Haynes's doctoral thesis, *The Negro at Work in New York,* and conferred the title of Doctor of Philosophy upon him. "Not only was Dr. Haynes the first Negro to receive a doctorate at Columbia," one writer declared, "but his thesis, which is a study of the manner and causes of migration, makes man more aware of his fellow men. This is the greater distinction." Haynes's *The Negro Newcomer in Detroit, Michigan,* appeared in 1917.

Before completing his education, Haynes set out upon his career by serving as student secretary to the Colored Men's Department of the International Committee of the YMCA from 1905 to 1906. While he was attending school he had also made studies of Negro life in New York City, stressing the questions of employment and social welfare. His interest in urban migration led to the formation, in 1910, of the National League on Urban Conditions Among Negroes (now called the National Urban League), which he cofounded with Mrs. William H. Baldwin, mother of the present president of the league, William Henry Baldwin '45. In addition, Haynes served as the first executive director of this league until 1918. In 1910 he was appointed to the chair of economics and sociology at Fisk University, which he also held until 1921. Founding the Association of Negro Colleges and Secondary Schools in 1910, Haynes was its first secretary until 1916.

Immediately following World War I, the United States Secretary of Labor wished to stimulate Negro workers to full-time production during the postwar period, and to improve their relations with white workers and employers. To this end the Department of Labor formed the Negro Workers Advisory Committees, which were composed of representatives of Negro wage earners with cooperating white employers and, wherever possible, of white wage earners. In 1918 Haynes was granted leave from his professorial duties to serve as the Director of Negro Economics for the United States Government. As special assistant to the Secretary of Labor, he investigated Negro affairs, observed all that occurred in the advisory committees, and developed the work of these committees, bringing together the welfare agencies and organizations among Negroes that were working for race adjustment. While working in this capacity until 1920, Haynes also assisted the Children's Bureau of the Department of Labor, fighting child labor.

During the following year, Haynes served as an official member of the President's Unemployment Conference and, from 1920 to 1922, he was made adviser for a special survey for the Inter-Church World Movement of North America. At this time Haynes completed his book, *The Trend of the Races,* which was published in 1922. In the introduction to this book, James H. Dillard wrote: "Its author is a man of education and high intelligence, whose peculiar opportunities of seeing all conditions of life among his people, and of knowing their thoughts, entitle him to be a spokesman and interpreter—he presents 'things as they are' as he honestly sees them."

The sociologist believes there is a real challenge to the churches of America to "champion the cause of justice to the minorities if their Christian professions mean anything to the outside world." Becoming executive secretary of the Department of Race Relations in the Federal Council of Churches of Christ in America in 1922, Haynes has since led in the promotion of a nation-wide program to enlist the churches on the side of interracial justice in the fields of industry, civic rights, and education. In a magazine article, written in 1938, he declared that "the churches were made for the people and not the people for the churches." The church should then act, he insists, for the elimination of racial tensions by serving as a means of educating all. Haynes has been acknowledged as a leader of a new development in Negro philosophy. In *The Trend of the Races* he asserted that the only solution to the question of race in America is the application of good will as set forth in the gospel of Christ. Haynes's theories, one writer points out, have their largest audience among white people, particularly among the members of the interracial bodies of the South.

Haynes's work with the churches in the Federal Council has led his department to: 1)

GEORGE EDMUND HAYNES

hold interracial clinics with national, state, and local leaders; 2) recruit, inform, and inspire church and community leaders for programs to improve race relations; 3) sponsor the National Conference of Church Leaders for exchange of thoughts, views, and plans; 4) contribute articles on racial problems to the press and magazines; 5) promote Race Relations Sunday, the second Sunday of each February, marking Brotherhood Month, now set apart by sixteen national church bodies for fellowship and cooperative community activities; 6) strive for equitable civil rights for all races; 7) serve as a clearinghouse of advice and information on interracial questions.

The Negro sociologist is a member of the American Sociological Society, the American Association for the Advancement of Science, the National Geographic Society, the National Conference of Social Work, the Church Conference of Social Work, the Association of Church Social Workers, and he is a trustee of Dillard University and the Atlanta University School of Social Work. He was formerly vice-moderator and first vice-president of the Home Missions Board of the Congregational Christian Churches. In 1930 he conducted a field survey for YMCA work among natives of South Africa, and he has studied missions in the Belgian Congo and in Angola. He directed the development of the William E. Harmon Awards for Distinguished Achievement, which recognize Negroes who do significant work in the arts, industry, education, science and religion; and honor both Negroes and white people who have contributed to improved race relations.

As an authority on race relations, Haynes contributed the article on American Negro economic life for the 1929 and 1939 editions of *Encyclopædia Britannica* and for the 1938 and 1939 *Britannica Book of the Year.* He is the author of the section entitled "The Negroes"

HAYNES, GEORGE EDMUND—Cont.

in the 1935 and 1939 volumes of *Social Work Yearbook,* and was the coauthor of studies *Cotton-Growing Communities* (Study No. 1, Alabama, 1934; Study No. 2, Arkansas, 1935). His articles have appeared in most of the leading magazines, among them *Christian Century, New Republic,* and *Survey.* In 1946 were issued *Clinical Approach to Race Relations* and *Enlistment for Interracial Brotherhood,* manuals on methods in dealing with racial tensions.

George Edmund Haynes and Elizabeth Ross were married in December 1910, and have one son, who is named after his father. Described as a "genial friend with a ready smile but a firm will," Haynes is of medium build, wears glasses, and his hair is conspicuous for its absence of gray. Fishing and archeology are his chief after-hours recreations.

References

Who's Who in America, 1946-47
Who's Who in Colored America, 1941-44

HENKLE, HENRIETTA *See* Buckmaster, H.

HENRY, MELLINGER EDWARD 1874(?)—Feb. 1, 1946 American educator; collected, edited, and published volumes of American folksongs; author of articles on folklore; taught in a Jersey City high school (1911-1937).

Obituary

N Y Times p24 F 1 '46 por

HERRIOT, EDOUARD (e″ryō′ ä″dwàr′) July 5, 1872- French statesman and political leader

Address: 1 Cours d'Herbouville, Lyons, France.

Edouard Herriot, onetime Premier of France and Mayor of Lyons since 1905, has been a figure on the international political scene for more than twenty years. Leader of the "not very radical" Radical Socialist Party and president of the Chamber of Deputies during the Nazi occupation of France, he was imprisoned in 1942 for his refusal to yield to or recognize the German-dictated Vichy Government. Herriot's first oration since his 1945 liberation was made in the Constituent Assembly of January 1946, where he was helping to shape France's new Constitution and her future.

A native of Troyes, in the province of Champagne, France, Edouard Herriot was born on July 5, 1872. His father was a captain in a Zouave regiment of the French Army, and his grandfather was also an Army officer; his uncle was a country priest. A precocious boy, he won a scholarship at the age of fifteen to the College of Sainte-Barbe. This was followed by another scholarship to the well-known Lycée Louis Le Grand in Paris where he was to prepare for entrance to the military school at St. Cyr, for his parents assumed that their son would follow the family tradition by entering the Army. However, young Herriot, interested more in academic studies, entered l'Ecole Normale Su-

perièure (Paris), from which he was graduated in 1894 with highest scholastic honors. (This school is considered the most important institution of higher learning in France and was known for its courses in politics and liberal arts.) After graduation Herriot became a professor of rhetoric and taught in the Lycées at Nantes and Lyon from 1896 to 1905. Meanwhile, in 1904, he received the degree of Docteur des Lettres with his thesis in music, *Madame Récamier et ses amis.* But politics had attracted the thirty-three-year-old teacher, and that same year he began his political career as a member of the municipal council of the city of Lyons.

In 1904 he was elected Mayor of Lyons, the office to which he has since been re-elected and has therefore held uninterruptedly except for the period he was a prisoner of the Nazis during World War II. Herriot's next post, to which he was elected in 1912 and which he held concurrently with his mayoralty, was as Senator from the department of Rhone. While there was a French tradition that a man must be well over forty before he could expect to be an able legislator, Herriot's career in the upper chamber of the National Assembly was distinguished, and from December 1906 to March 1917 he was Minister of Public Works in the Briand Cabinet. Immediately after the close of World War I he left the Senate, having been elected in 1919 to represent Lyons in the Chamber of Deputies.

As leader of the Radical Socialist Party Herriot brought about the first major electoral victory of the liberals in postwar France. By overthrowing the Poincaré Cabinet, a regime marked by widespread discontentment in France because of the French march into the Ruhr, Herriot's Leftist coalition appointed him Premier, an office he held from June 1924 until April 1925. The fifty-two-year-old Premier's program was: the reduction of military service, trade unionism for state employees, and the evacuation of the Ruhr. In his first message to the National Assembly Herriot announced the party's plan to sever diplomatic relations with the Vatican: no papal nuncio would be welcome in Paris, and the French would not be permitted to send an ambassador to the Vatican. In addition to his anti-clerical policy, Herriot announced his intention of substituting "the laws of the Republic" for the Concordat which was still in force in Alsace-Lorraine. Herriot and British Prime Minister Ramsay MacDonald, both crusaders for international peace, set about to reach an agreement which would improve strained Franco-British relations and at the same time conciliate Germany. Within two months the Ruhr was evacuated and the Dawes plan in operation.

Herriot and MacDonald then drafted a formula whereby "arbitration, security, and disarmament" would be recognized as a basis for all future relations with foreign countries. In September of 1924 the French and British statesmen introduced the Geneva Protocol to the League of Nations, a document which offered a pacific setttlement of international disputes by clearly defining an aggressor nation as one which does not submit her dispute to the

Council, and by providing guarantees to defeat the aims of potential aggressors. The League unanimously adopted the resolution on October 2, 1924, but it was never ratified by Great Britain. (When the protocol was brought before the House of Commons, it was under the leadership of Prime Minister Baldwin and Foreign Secretary Chamberlain, who did not approve of world-wide commitments and apparently distrusted compulsory arbitration as a means for preserving peace.) This rejection, declared James T. Shotwell [44], "dealt the blow from which the Protocol and the League never recovered." It has been thought that, had the Protocol been accepted, Europe would have been spared the Nazi scourge and World War II.

France was going through a period of inflation in the mid-twenties. By April 1925 the note issue had exceeded its legal limit, and the people were reluctant to make additional loans to the government. Herriot's Left group demanded a capital levy on the rich, a heavier direct taxation, and a reduction of expenditures by lowering the interest rate on government bonds. The Right element agitated for more indirect taxation, heavier taxes on the middle classes, and a reduction of expenditures by the lowering of government salaries. The National Assembly did not pass either group's resolutions, thereby causing an increase in paper currency. The financial situation grew so critical that Herriot was forced out of office. Poincaré was restored as Premier for the purpose of saving the franc, and Herriot served in his Cabinet as Minister of Public Education (1926-28). However, the fifteen months after his resignation in 1925 were marked by such a rapid succession of six different ministries, while the country was still in a bad state of inflation, that Herriot became Premier for a few days in 1926.

Again, in the spring of 1932, the Left coalition won a decisive victory at the election polls, and Herriot, as their leader, was again Premier of France and Minister of Foreign Affairs. Championing the principle of international unity, he negotiated the Lausanne settlement, which ended reparations, and he sought the good will of England, Germany, the United States, and Soviet Russia. (It was Herriot who signed the Franco-Russian non-aggression treaty.) He felt that France ought to pay at least some of its war debt to the United States, and in a memorable speech before the Chamber of Deputies he declared: "Today we have heard a great deal about morality, and it has even been said that in the name of morality we are justified in refusing to pay the American war debt. For me, morality is a simple thing. . . . In deep respect for our word, written or spoken, no matter what the circumstances or the terms, lies the true France." However, the National Assembly did not agree with Herriot, and in December of 1932 he was again forced to resign.

President Roosevelt [42] invited the French statesman to visit the United States in April 1933, when they conferred on the French debt, disarmament, and monetary problems of international scope. Upon returning to France, Her-

EDOUARD HERRIOT

riot resumed his plea for the payment of the war debt and said that he "found President Roosevelt not only a great democrat, but a man well disposed to France." Between February 1934 and January 1936, Edouard Herriot held the post of Minister of State in the Cabinets of Doumergue and Flandin [41]. When the election of 1936 brought the Popular Front (of which the Radical Socialist Party was a main constituent) into power, Herriot again received a post of importance. He became president of the Chamber of Deputies and presided until 1942, when collaborationist Pierre Laval [40], under pressure of the Nazi occupation forces, dissolved the legislative body.

France fell in June 1940, having been betrayed by Marshal Pétain [40], who became Chief of State, and Pierre Laval, his Chief of Government. Although the Government, set up in Vichy, did not disband the National Assembly immediately, the Assembly's powers became much weakened. Herriot, as president of the Chamber of Deputies, waged a constant battle against the collaborationist policies and refused to recognize the Vichy Government. In September 1941 Vichy reported that Herriot was heading a "subversive rump parliament" which was to be a permanent organization in opposition to the Nazi-powered regime of Pétain. When the Chief of State dissolved the French parliament (August 31, 1942) and tried to draw France into war against the United Nations, Herriot and Jules Jeanneney, president of the suppressed Senate, sent a joint letter of protest to Pétain. The historic document asserted: "If without authorization of parliament you try to draw France into war against our Allies. . .do not make the foolish mistake of believing that you can win the adhesion of France's spirit or its heart. . . .You have substituted unlimited dictatorship for guarantees that all civilized nations grant to accused persons. . . . Everywhere you have abolished the

HERRIOT, EDOUARD—*Continued*

principle of elective representation. . . . You have wiped out general councils that reflected the wisdom of our provinces and you have substituted men of your own choice. . . .It is impossible for liberty to die in the country of its birth, from which it spread all over the world." (Simultaneously, Herriot resigned from the Legion of Honor because he had learned that the award was being given to collaborationists, specifically to several French officers who had been killed while fighting with the Nazi Army in Russia.)

Fearful that Herriot might try to leave France after his public denunciation of the Pétain-Laval regime, Vichy demanded that the politician pledge himself, in writing, not to leave the country. "You insult me," Herriot retorted. "You can tell your masters that I am not obliged to take any engagements." He added that his only purpose was to serve France, and that the manner in which he chose to do this did not concern the Vichy government. Within twenty-four hours, on October 2, 1942, he and his wife were arrested. They were interned in various parts of France, until August 1944, when Herriot was brought back to Paris. Laval offered Herriot "the opportunity to form a government which would save Vichy," but despite threats and orders to work for Vichy, Herriot emphatically refused to consider any such proposition. Edouard Herriot was finally removed to Germany. Before leaving he wrote a note in which he said: "I did not give in to Nazi demands or Laval's blackmailing methods." When the letter was given to his friends, they suggested that he might be given milder punishment if he were to cooperate in a small way, but the former president of the Chamber of Deputies replied that it was his duty to share the fate of the other freedom-loving patriots of France. While in Germany, in a sanitarium near Berlin, the Nazi news agency, DNB, falsely reported his death on three different occasions. On April 22, 1945 Herriot and his wife were liberated by the Red Army, and in a few days a Russian plane brought him to Moscow.

Within another month Herriot was back in France, in the city of Lyons, where the citizens greeted him with an elaborate ceremony and re-elected him their Mayor. At the trial of the French traitors he appeared as one of the chief witnesses, accusing Pétain of turning the French Republic into "a full-fledged and illegal dictatorship." Furthermore, he charged, Pétain's plan was to block the movement of France's Republican Government to North Africa until the Armistice with Hitler '[42] had been signed—a plan aided by Laval.

Elected an honorary president and political strategist in chief of the Radical Socialist Party in the late summer of 1945, Herriot then announced that he would be a candidate for the Chamber of Deputies on his party's ticket. The veteran Mayor's Radical Socialists managed to win only nineteen seats in this election, Communists winning the majority of seats. According to William Simms of the New York *World-Telegram*, the Radical Socialists "have been all but wiped out."

This opinion was invalidated by the slight resurgence that the Radical Socialists showed in the June 1946 elections. In the spring of that year, Herriot had formed a coalition of his party and several other minor groups under the name of the Rassemblement Republicain, and thus was able to muster thirty-thousand votes more than in the October elections. The Rassemblement Republicain, or Republican Group, characterized themselves as "anti-Leftist" and "anticlerical." This party of the Center refused, under Herriot's leadership, to participate in the Cabinet formed by provisional President Bidault.

At the Radical Congress, held in Lyons in May 1946, Herriot had proposed a program at variance with the plans of both the Communists and the Catholics (the MRP). It called for the defense of individual liberty and private property, the safeguarding of secular schools (the MRP had advocated clerical control of the national school system), the prevention of state domination by big business, and the limited nationalization of trusts and monopolies. Most probably, the increase in voting support of the Radical Socialists shown in the June election was caused by the Herriot stand on the education problem, which became a paramount issue in the election.

Throughout the first nine months of 1946, Herriot held out against the proposed constitution. He appealed for the retention of the Bill of Rights, arguing that its validity had been proven ever since the French Revolution, and that, with amendments protecting the rights of women and workers, it was still practicable. He also fought long and unsuccessfully to have a specific guarantee of the freedom of the press written into the constitution, since French law requires Government licensing of newspapers and thus makes them subject to the whims of the party in power.

In the elections held under the new constitution in November 1946, Herriot was elected a Deputy to the National Assembly for Lyons. Since the Communist and Socialist parties together did not control a majority in the Assembly, they extended an invitation to Herriot's Radical Socialists and the other parties of the Rassemblement Republicain to join the Leftist united front. Acceptance would mean that these moderately Left parties would swing the balance of power in the new Government.

Edouard Herriot is reputed to be one of the most cultured men of France. An orator, he is also an historian and a writer. His book, *La Vie de Beethoven* (*Life and Times of Beethoven*), published in France in 1929 and in the United States in 1935, has been called one of the best biographies of the composer. As a traveler he has recorded his impressions in *La Russie nouvelle* (1922), *Orient* (1934), *Lyon* (1937), and *Impressions d'Amérique*. In the fields of philosophy, history, and literature, he is the author of: *Créer* (1919), *Lyon pendant la guerre* and *Dans la forêt Normande* (1925), *La Porte Océane* and *Nos grandes ecoles normales* (1932). Several of Herriot's political books have been translated into English and published in the United States: *United States of Europe* in 1930, *Eastward from Paris* in

1934, *Wellsprings of Liberty* in 1939, and *Message to the Free Countries* in 1942. In recognition of his scholarly historical work, Herriot was elected to the French Academy on December 6, 1946.

One writer has described Herriot as "fat and friendly," with deep and penetrating eyes in a square head. He likes good food and good wine, and is a constant pipe-smoker. His wife is the former Mlle. Rébatel.

References

Collier's 90:26-8 Ag 20 '32 pors
Time 43:27 Mr 27 '45 por
Dictionnaire National des Contemporains (1936)
Gunther, J. Inside Europe (1940)
International Who's Who, 1945-46
Simone, A. J'accuse! (1940)
Who's Who, 1946

HERTZLER, ARTHUR E(MANUEL) July 26, 1870—Sept. 12, 1946 Surgeon, author; conducted research on diseases of the peritoneum since 1894, and made important discoveries in the field of local anesthesia and the diseases of the thyroid gland; his reminiscences, *The Horse and Buggy Doctor,* appeared in 1938.

Obituary

N Y Times p7 S 13 '46 por

HIBBS, BEN July 23, 1901- Editor; journalist

Address: b. c/o The Saturday Evening Post, Independence Sq., Philadelphia; h. 713 Braeburn Lane, Penn Valley, Narbeth, Pa.

"One of the blessings of America has been that a boy might dream his aspirations and then live his dreams," says Ben Hibbs, who became the editor of the *Saturday Evening Post* in 1942. This national weekly, which is "trademarked" by a profile of Benjamin Franklin, in 1946 has a circulation of more than three million seven hundred thousand.

A descendant of Pennsylvania-Quaker colonists, grandson of a Kansas settler, and son of a retail lumber merchant, Ben Hibbs was born July 23, 1901, the first of the three children of Russell and Elizabeth (Smith) Hibbs. The family soon moved from Fontana, Kansas, the town of Ben's birth, to Pretty Prairie, population four hundred, in the same state, where the boy attended Kingman High School and edited the school newspaper. By this time young Ben had decided upon the career of editor. Told by the elder Hibbs that a man should do what he wants in the world, he determined to fulfill his ambition, knowing that his father had spent a large part of his life dreaming of a career as architect and regretting his failure to become one.

After his graduation from high school, Ben spent a year working in his father's lumber yard to earn his tuition for a higher education. Too young to fight in World War I, Hibbs arrived at the University of Kansas at Lawrence in 1919, when jobs for students were plentiful. At various times he worked in a brick plant near Lawrence, served as janitor of the Methodist Church, cashier of a cafeteria, and keeper of supplies in the psychology laboratory. During vacations he harvested wheat and worked in lumber yards. At the same time, Hibbs maintained an extraordinary scholastic and extra-curricular record, earning membership in Phi Beta Kappa; Sigma Delta Chi, journalistic fraternity; and Sachem, senior men's honor group. (In April 1942 he received a "distinguished service award" from the university, in lieu of an honorary degree, which the university does not confer.) During his junior year he was sub-instructor in English, and as a senior he was in charge of the newsroom of the *Daily Kansan.* Hibbs held in succession the various editorial jobs on the *Kansan,* achieving the post of editor in chief. All this, he says, "was easy!" attributing his early and late successes to getting "the breaks." One of these he feels was membership in and residence at the Sigma Phi Epsilon House in Lawrence at the time when his older fraternity brothers were returning from the war. From them, he has said, he learned both tolerance and assertiveness.

The graduate, who regarded William Allen White '40, editor of the Emporia (Kansas) *Gazette* as his idol, sought work on Midwestern newspapers. He joined the Fort Morgan (Colorado) *Evening Times* in 1923, and after part of a year returned to Kansas as news editor of the Pratt *Daily Tribune.* In 1924 he became professor of journalism and English at Hays (Kansas) State College, spending two years at what he has called "pale experience." Returning to active Kansas journalism in 1926-27 Hibbs was editor and manager of the Goodland *News Republic* and later in 1927 managing editor of the Arkansas City *Daily Traveler.* E. H. Taylor of the *Country Gentleman* magazine saw the editorials of "the most quoted young squirt in Kansas," as the Kansas City *Star* called him, when his opinions were reprinted in that paper's *Kansas Notes,* and was instrumental in bringing Hibbs into the Curtis Publishing Company in Philadelphia, publishers of the *Country Gentleman,* the *Saturday Evening Post* and the *Ladies' Home Journal.* Characterized as having a sense of humor, and "the clever optimism and buoyancy of youth," Hibbs's pieces, whether praising Kansas legislators, requesting new garbage disposal plants for Arkansas City, new waterworks for Wichita, or extolling Kansas sunsets and jack rabbits, were said to be "clever, erudite, and entertaining." When Hibbs left Kansas in 1929, his admirer William Allen White wrote: "Philadelphia is taking from us the white-headed boy of Kansas journalism. He is blessed with great talents, whose developments his confreres have watched with envy and admiration. He is cursed by the little gnarled demon of industry, which perches on his shoulder eighteen hours a day, digs its sharp teeth into his neck, driving him on to tremendous feats of work and enabling him to produce a greater volume of first-rate stuff than any other man in the state."

At twenty-seven Kansas' Ben Hibbs became associate editor of the *Country Gentleman,* and at thirty-three its fiction editor as well. During

BEN HIBBS

what the *Post* prints," to the statement that the preface forms " a keenly analytic appreciation of the contents of the volume."

During Hibbs's management of the *Post* two incidents brought extended newspaper notice. The first was the strong censure of the *Post* by advertisers and readers for its publication in 1942 of Milton Mayer's article, "The Case Against the Jew," bought and published by Hibbs's predecessor. Three years later in December, when associate editor Edgar Snow [41] was barred from China by the Nationalist Government, Hibbs forwarded Snow's protest to American officials. The Chungking Government lifted its ban and allowed Snow to enter China at any time. Hibbs's political convictions were reflected first in the *Country Gentleman*, and later in the *Post*. The editor is a Republican, favored social security and some New Deal legislation, but "doesn't much fancy Americans living according to a bureaucratic Government-planned economy." His later articles have been praised as more urbane than his early efforts, and as remindful of the *New Yorker*, comments to which he objects. He still employs "the amiable retort" which early critics admired.

Occasionally Hibbs discusses a matter of national policy in a signed editorial. In January 1945 he wrote approvingly of peacetime military training for national defense. The postwar period he termed "a time for patience" in September of that year, opposing those who would have abandoned all rationing, price controls, and other wartime measures immediately. "Journey to a Shattered World" is Hibbs's report on a visit to Germany and the Dachau and Buchenwald concentration camps (the *Saturday Evening Post*, June 9, 1945). The author proposed what he believed to be right and necessary precepts for Allied activity within the Reich: elimination of war criminals, no shrinking from the grim task of occupation, and non-participation in the rebuilding of German industry, while avoiding the starvation of its people. "Starvation isn't a pretty sight," he said. "I have seen it....We must not forget that human misery is almost the most fertile seedbed for fanaticism.... Justice and world security, not vengeance, must be our guideposts in delaying with this defeated land." The November 1942 Sigma Phi Epsilon *Journal* reported that "Hibbs thinks Walter Lippmann the soundest of the newspaper columnists, but that Westbrook Pegler is readable, and quite occasionally, too, is right." The *Journal* also said, "The editor does not listen to the radio often, but believes Lowell Thomas to be the best of the newscasters and John W. Vandercook one of the most authentic of the commentators."

Hibbs lives in a Philadelphia suburb with his wife, the former Edith Kathleen Doty, a Kansas schoolteacher to whom he was married in 1930, and their son Stephen, born in 1935. The lean, bespectacled editor looks younger than his years, with his brown hair, blue eyes which give the impression of "restrained boyishness," and a hesitant smile. Six feet one and one half inches tall and weighing 170 pounds, he appears both lanky and athletic, although lack of time does not now permit his preferred recreations

these years he toured the country and wrote editorials and feature articles. In September 1940 he was made editor in chief of the magazine whose style he modernized and whose circulation he raised to the all-time high of 2,275,000. Upon assuming leadership of the *Country Gentleman*, Hibbs wrote of himself: "It need be said only that he is Kansas-born; that he grew up out on the wide prairies where wheat is king and the autumn sunset flares crimson.... It might be added that he loves America and all it stands for; that he still has an abiding faith in the ultimate triumph of human liberties over the brutality and blood and ruin which darken half the world." In April 1940 Hibbs was elected a director of the Curtis Publishing Company.

When Wesley Winans Stout [41], also a Kansan, resigned in March 1942 from the editorship of the *Saturday Evening Post*, Hibbs was selected as his successor. Hibbs had previously contributed articles to the magazine, including two on the itinerant trucker of the Corn Belt and the fate of the Dust Bowl. When *Time* announced "mild Ben Hibbs" as the new editor, Hibbs, to whom the adjective "modest" is often applied, was surprised by the comment, remarking, "The least I had expected was 'horse-faced, ulcerous Ben Hibbs.'" As *Variety* predicted, anti-isolationist Hibbs, with his dislike of obsolete design, revised and brightened the format of the *Post* to include more color layouts and shorter stories, radically changed the isolationist policy of the publication, and modified its anti-New Deal attacks—in its editorials and articles it continued to take a firm stand on nearly all major issues. Hibbs's standard for *Post* fiction, quoted in his preface to *Post Stories 1942-1945*, has been, "a story does not have to be dull or incomprehensible to be good—current critical opinion notwithstanding." It must, however, entertain. Critical response to Hibbs's foreword has varied from "Ben Hibbs need not be self-conscious about of tennis and hunting. The editor enjoys long, lonely walks in the country and his brief visits home to Kansas, but dislikes bridge, extreme sophistication, and making talks, although considered a good speaker. His colleagues describe his anger as cold and silent, giving the impression that "in an intellectual world his emotionality has been trained down to a courtly [and homely] quietude." Although he generally prefers subtler humor, of the "regulars" in the *Saturday Evening Post* family Hibbs is especially partial to Alexander Botts, supersalesman for the Earthworm Tractor Company, and the cartooned doings of Hazel, the maid.

References

Sigma Phi Epsilon J N '42 pors
Who's Who in America, 1946-47

HILL, GEORGE WASHINGTON Oct. 22, 1884-Sept. 13, 1946 Manufacturer

Bulletin: George Washington Hill died on September 13, 1946.

From June 1946 issue:

As president of the American Tobacco Company, George Washington Hill has made a reputation as one of the world's most successful salesmen. He is identified with the company's advertising, particularly with its Lucky Strike cigarette promotion, and is given credit for much of the tremendous increase in cigarette consumption in the decades since he became head in 1925. His company and its subsidiary, the American Cigarette and Cigar Company, manufacture several hundred kinds of cigars, cigarettes, smoking and chewing tobaccos. Besides Lucky Strikes, their best-known brands are Herbert Tareyton and Pall Mall cigarettes, and Half and Half and Bull Durham pipe tobaccos.

Born in Philadelphia on October 22, 1884, George Washington Hill is the son of Cassie Rowland (Milnes) Hill and the "classic magnate" Percival Smith Hill. When George was eight, his father became sales manager of the Blackwell Durham Tobacco Company, which the American Tobacco Company absorbed; and when George left Williams College in his sophomore year to go to work for American Tobacco, Percival Hill was vice-president of its cigarette business.

Beginning in 1904, young Hill spent three years in the factories and tobacco leaf markets of North Carolina. "His fellow boarders at the old Mangum House in Durham found him serious-minded almost to the point of being unsociable," *Fortune* recounted. "They recall that in their penny ante games (the only study George allowed himself time for besides tobacco) he kept strict track of his winnings and losses in a little vest-pocket notebook." In 1907 American acquired a small company which produced expensive Turkish cigarettes under the brand name of Pall Mall, and vice-president Hill put his son in charge of Pall Mall sales. Under George Hill's management Pall Mall rose to first place among higher-priced Turkish brands.

GEORGE WASHINGTON HILL

As the outcome of an antitrust suit, the Supreme Court ordered the American Tobacco Company monopoly dissolved in 1911. This divorcement, which carved the trust into fourteen companies, gave American its first competitors of comparable size: Lorillard (Old Golds), Liggett and Myers (Chesterfields), and Reynolds (Camels). The two last-named constitute, with American, the "Big Three" of the cigarette industry. Percival Hill was appointed president of the shorn but still large corporation, and his son was named vice-president and sales manager. In 1917 they brought out the Lucky Strike cigarette, retaining the name of a smoking tobacco the company had owned for eleven years. Inspired by the success of Camels, the first blended cigarettes, Percival Hill was, his son says, "anxious to put out the brand of Lucky Strike cigarettes and I was not willing to put it out because . . . I didn't have a reason for it." After spending hours in their Brooklyn factory, he found a "reason," meaning an advertisable attribute, in the use of heat to dry the tobacco. "It's toasted" became the Lucky slogan.

"In an account of the rise of the Lucky Strike cigarette," said *Fortune*, "you must watch Mr. Hill very carefully. The two stories can be told as one because Mr. Hill has little life outside the Lucky Strike, and the Lucky Strike is almost wholly the creation of Mr. Hill." Its advertising introduced a note of sharpness and sensationalism, but leading brands thrived under Hill's methods, and by 1923 cigarette sales had risen to seventy-seven billion from the ten billion of 1911. After G. W. Hill succeeded his father as president in 1925, he supplied the company's advertising agency "not only with almost unlimited funds and a fertile advertising mind of his own, but a boyish

HILL, GEORGE WASHINGTON—*Cont.*
readiness to back to the limit every idea on which he was sold."

The American Tobacco Company's net profit for 1926, after the forty-two-year-old George Hill had taken over the reins, was $22,500,000, and Lucky Strikes amounted to 20.14 per cent of the country's total cigarette production (Camels came to about 45 per cent). Concentrating on Luckies, Hill leased some of the company's lesser cigarette brands to Whelan's Union Tobacco Company. In January 1927 Lucky Strike opened an advertising campaign which doubled the potential cigarette market by appealing to millions of women as well as to men. Testimonials from prominent persons of both sexes were obtained; the first of the women endorsers were foreign opera stars, and later recommendations came from "good wholesome American actresses" like Alice Brady. Sophisticates had smoked cigarettes before then, but, *Fortune* has asserted, "public cigarette smoking by women in America can be correctly dated from that year."

Next year came the "Reach for a Lucky Instead of a Sweet" campaign, which immediately alienated the whole candy industry and caused Senator Smoot, from beet sugar-producing Utah, to denounce the entire tobacco industry. The Federal Trade Commission called Hill to Washington and got his promise to stop buying testimonials and not to advertise Lucky Strikes as a reducing agent. Hill therefore eliminated the word "sweet," letting future advertisements read, "Avoid over-indulgence if you would maintain that modern, ever-youthful figure. Reach for a Lucky instead." And Hill's was one of the few concerns to report improved business during the depression that followed the 1929 Wall Street crash. In 1930 Luckies represented 38.1 per cent of the country's total production and pushed Camels out of their long-held first place.

The company's 1930 earnings amounted to forty-three million dollars. President Hill received a $168,000 salary, plus "special cash credits," a bonus, and a stock allotment which brought the total remuneration for the year just under two and a half million dollars. The stock subscription plan was fought up to the Supreme Court by some stockholders but was upheld as within the company's authority. However, in 1933 Hill sent a letter to the stockholders stating that, because he believed in the principle of rewards to stimulate key men, he was renouncing his allotment of 13,440 shares; and in 1936 it was reported that he and the entire board of directors, all of them company officers, owned less than 1 per cent of the voting stock.

Hill has retreated from his position on a few other occasions. In the summer of 1931 he abandoned the five-cent Cremo cigar after making a twelve-million-dollar appropriation to promote it, and left the low-priced cigar field entirely. In 1932, however, he broke precedent by transferring American's fine-cigar production from Havana to New Jersey, thereby saving a great deal on import duties and taxes,

and freeing himself from temperamental and comparatively high-paid Cuban cigarmakers.

The year 1932, one of demoralization in the cigarette business, saw Hill's memorable "Nature in the Raw Is Seldom Mild" advertising series. More recent campaigns have emphasized the "teaser" and the "triphammered commercial." When the need of dyes in World War II transformed the Lucky Strike package from green to white, "Lucky Strike green has gone to war," repeated three times, was dinned into the ears of puzzled radio listeners. "The best tunes of all go to Carnegie Hall," similarly repeated, was the oblique way of announcing that the radio program *All-Time Hit Parade* was to originate from Carnegie Hall. "LS/MFT," clicked in Morse code over the air, repeated in dramatic crescendo by announcers and printed in advertisements and on the packages was intended for: "Lucky Strike means fine tobacco, so round, so firm, so fully packed, so free and easy on the draw." Hill, who is credited with authorship of the slogans, is reported to think that it is good business to use advertising themes which attract satirical observations.

Hill has had to spend some time in the law courts and has had skirmishes with the Government. In 1937 he dropped his fight to prevent the Securities Exchange Commission from publishing his company's sales data. In 1940 he held the antitrust action against him and other leading tobacco manufacturers was an attempt "to repudiate established economic principles and to promote economic theories wholly foreign to American principles of fair competition and individual enterprise." While it was pending, he fought a number of stockholders' suits, brought in objection to his salary ($458,415 in 1940, which was exceeded only by those of Louis B. Mayer [43] and Bethlehem Steel president Eugene G. Grace [41]) and in 1941 he clashed with OPA chief Leon Henderson [40] over cigarette prices. In June 1946 the Supreme Court unanimously upheld the Sherman Act conviction and fines of the "Big Three" tobacco companies and top officers, including Hill, for having set up a price monopoly on leaf tobacco.

For years the tobacco executive successfully avoided personal publicity: in 1930 *Business Week* predicted that he would never be quoted in print nor photographed for publication. In the decade and a half which followed, however, a few facts and rumors circulated. Hill became particularly well known to readers of *Variety,* the show business bible, because of his lavish radio sponsorship. In February 1946 the estimated program cost of the Lucky Strike-sponsored Jack Benny show, the highest-priced of all programs then on the air, was $22,500 a week, and American Tobacco was also paying an estimated $11,500 a week for *Your Hit Parade.* This was exclusive of air time, which added a few million dollars a year to the advertising budget. The company also had programs on other radio systems, in 1946 paying particular attention to that in Venezuela. (Hill himself had Kay Kyser leased to Colgate on a three-year personal contract.) Lucky Strike pays two tobacco auctioneers

$25,000 a year each just to chant one and a half minutes of the opening and closing commercials."

This "rugged individualist in matters programmatic," discoverer of organist Ethel Smith for the radio, first national sponsor of Frank Sinatra, and first to have Lawrence Tibbett sing popular songs, feels 90 per cent of a program's value to the sponsor lies in its commercials and 10 per cent in entertainment. From his pioneer days in sponsorship, he has insisted on loud, lively, heavily syncopated music, a demand which some of the musicians are said to have found irksome. *Your Hit Parade* has involved the sponsoring company in complaints brought by music publishers and writers who felt that some song of theirs had been slighted in the selections of the nation's most popular music. Hill's direct control over the production is said to be complete; in March 1944 he refused to allow the network to give it a free "plug," reportedly because he wished to control "all wordage relative to the show." A new *Hit Parade* idea, beginning in February 1946, was to leave the new male vocalist a mystery, giving him no billing whatever.

George Washington Hill is described as a dynamic, commanding man of stocky build, known for wearing a hat indoors and for other eccentricities. Commentators have compared the manufacturer to the character of Evan Llewelyn Evans in *The Hucksters* (1946), the novel by Frederic Wakeman '46, formerly an advertising account executive for Lucky Strikes. *Fortune* has called Hill "a salesman without a flaw. He believes everything he says and everything he writes, and he writes a good many of his own advertisements. . . .When he sells Lucky Strikes to dinner guests who have the bad grace to want a rival brand, it is pure conviction that burns away any desire he may have to be obliging. . . .His only close friends are people who have reason to share his zeal. . . .His wife was once his secretary and she still sometimes takes dictation at home of a Saturday afternoon." She is the former Mary Barnes, to whom he was married in July 1935. (Hill's son George, by an earlier marriage, is a vice-president and director of his father's firm; there is also a younger son, Percival.) The senior Hill is fond of salmon-fishing, dancing, and detective stories, is said to be "a knowing amateur of shrubs and trees." Despite his concentration on Luckies, he lists himself in *Who's Who in America* as "officer or director of various other companies."

References

Bsns W p39-40 F 22 '30
Fortune 14:97+ D '36 por
N Y Sun p12 Mr 2 '40
N Y Times p7 II Ap 22 '45
New Outlook p55-6 Ja '35
Who's Who in Commerce and Industry (1944)
Who's Who in America, 1946-47

HILL, PATTY SMITH 1868—May 25, 1946 American authority on progressive education; professor emeritus of education at Columbia University; introduced medical care and mental tests in the kindergartens; author of the verse, "Happy Birthday," and many magazine and newspaper articles on child education; organizer and first chairman of the National Association of Nursery Education.

Obituary

N Y Times p32 My 26 '46 por

HILLMAN, SIDNEY Mar. 23, 1887—July 10, 1946 Labor leader; pioneer advocate of constructive cooperation between workers and employers; president of the Amalgamated Clothing Workers of America since 1915; member of the National Defense Advisory Commission, 1940; associate director of the Office of Production Management, 1941; chairman of the CIO Political Action Committee, from 1943 to his death; New York State chairman of the American Labor Party; called by President Truman "one of the most effective and devoted exponents" of the cause of democracy. See *Current Biography* 1940 Yearbook.

Obituary

N Y Times p1+ Je 11 '46 por

HINES, DUNCAN Mar. 26, 1880- Author; publisher

Address: P.O. Box 548, Bowling Green, Ky.

Duncan Hines, who will travel five hundred miles for a good meal, has been America's where-to-eat expert since 1936, when at fifty-six he turned a hobby into a profitable publishing enterprise. Before Pearl Harbor, thousands of American vacationists traveled with a gastronomic Baedeker—Duncan Hines's *Adventures in Good Eating,* a directory of two thousand selected eating places. During World War II, when non-essential travel was taboo, servicemen on furlough in strange towns let Hines's book be their guide. When the war was over, according to *Publishers' Weekly,* bookstores received requests for the latest edition of the Hines book on the day gas rationing was lifted. More than half a million copies of his books have been sold. Duncan Hines is thus one of the nation's best-selling authors— and an author who is his own publisher.

In Bowling Green, Kentucky, Duncan Hines was born March 26, 1880, the son of Edward L. Hines, a Confederate army captain, schoolteacher and lawyer. When young Duncan was four years old, his mother, Cornelia (Duncan) Hines, died. He remembers well the Negro cook who prepared the meals for the Hines children, five growing boys and a girl. "We ate all the time," said Hines years later, as he recalled the home-baked bread, wild turkey, venison, fried chicken, sausage, and jam and molasses for biscuit topping. During the summer the children would visit their grandmother's farm, where marvelously prepared stuffed fowl—turkey, chicken, guinea, or geese—and hickory-smoked hams were tribute to their grandmother's skill at the cookstove.

Duncan attended school in his native town, and when he was sixteen entered the Bowling Green Business College. But he left after two years without a diploma: "As a boy the only

DUNCAN HINES

thing I was really interested in was eating." And next to eating, he liked to travel, so he took a job with the Wells Fargo Express Company in 1898 and thereafter, until 1905, he worked in the West, usually for mining companies. He never stayed in one town for more than three months. In 1905, when he was twenty-five years old, Hines came to Chicago with a young wife, and there became associated with an advertising and printing firm. The couple always spent their weekends and vacations traveling. By 1938 they had covered a million miles of America's highways together, partly on business trips (Hines sold "creative printing" ideas to industrial firms), and partly for relaxation. But Hines found a barrier to his complete enjoyment of traveling—"the library paste served as gravy in short-order places was a personal insult."

While on their motoring trips, Hines and his wife began to explore the country for good eating-places. They made a game of their explorations, kept lists, took notes, and exchanged comments with other motorists. Hines's business acquaintances began to come to him, before leaving on trips, for advice about where to eat, for instance, in Indianapolis, or Fort Worth. Word spread that Hines knew the best inns and restaurants in the country. Suddenly he realized that he was spending half his time answering telephone queries. By Christmas of 1935 he had worked out a little scheme which he hoped would quiet his phone and leave him some time for his printing business. In lieu of greeting cards he mailed to about a thousand acquaintances a printed list of his entire roll of seven hundred "superior eating places." He was hardly prepared for what happened next—he was deluged with requests for extra copies of his list. The next year, "in self-defense," Hines published his listings in a paper-covered book. To defray expenses, he charged a dollar and a half per copy. For

two years he lost money on his hobby, but by March 1938, word-of-mouth advertising had increased sales to the point where Hines was making a profit. He realized that his "sideline" had become a valuable property. In 1938 he added to his enterprise *Lodging for a Night,* a directory of accommodations "for discriminating guests." Giving up his work with the printing firm that year, Hines became a full-time author and publisher, with his offices in Chicago.

When Mrs. Hines died in 1939 Duncan Hines moved his new business from Chicago to his boyhood home at Bowling Green. There he added the third book to his list—*Adventures in Good Cooking and The Art of Carving in the Home,* which grew out of repeated requests for the recipes of the eating-places those who "traveled by the book" had visited. Included was a supplement on the carving lore he had learned from his Kentucky grandfather. In 1940 he built a colonial house at Bowling Green, which included office facilities as well as living quarters. His sales were mounting steadily. By 1946 his three books had gone through twenty-nine printings, and had sold over half a million copies. Besides publishing at Bowling Green he also prepared hickory-smoked hams, and shipped them to buyers all over the country. From four hundred to six hundred letters came to his office every day, with requests for advice, recommendations of new restaurants, criticisms of some of his selections, and an occasional heartfelt thank-you from a dyspeptic traveling salesman.

Hines's guides cover Alaska, Mexico, Hawaii, and Canada, as well as the United States. "Written from the traveler's point of view, without the slightest effort at literary style," his listings nevertheless make sprightly reading at times. He includes comments such as "Imagine you will have to elbow your way through the honeymooners to register," or an exuberant "Service is plain but, oh, such pie!" Hines prints no advertising, and accepts no fees for listings, though he is said to have received "fabulous offers" for advertising space in his books. He determines who is to be listed by touring the country to investigate new lodging and eating-places, and to make sure the places he has already recommended have not relaxed their standards. (The books are constantly revised.) When he eats in a new restaurant, Hines uses an assumed name, orders all the entrees on the menu, and samples a little of everything. After he has paid for the meal (he consistently refuses gratuitous meals, even in the places he has been recommending for years), Hines announces that he would like to inspect the kitchen and dishwashing department. It irks him to see food wasted; and the way the food is prepared, with attention to cleanliness and conservation, is as important to him as its taste.

Even though he spends only three to four days a month at home in Bowling Green, and travels the rest of the time, Hines would never be able adequately to cover old listings and investigate new ones. He relies for assistance on about four hundred volunteer "detectives." They include singer Lawrence Tibbett, cartoonist Gluyas Williams, radio commentator Mary Margaret McBride, and professors, bank presidents, brokers, and corporation executives —all of whom sleuth for Hines without pay. "A young Western millionaire is one of Hines's most enthusiastic mashed-potato spies," reported Milton MacKaye in a *Saturday Evening Post* article about Hines. However, the travelers who buy his book are Hines's most important source of information. The hundreds of his readers who recommend new places for his investigation and who keep him informed as to whether places listed continue to qualify, he calls the "Duncan Hines Family."

"A famous chef told me," wrote Frank J. Taylor in *Scribner's Commentator* of June 1941, "that Duncan Hines has done more in four years to lift the level of the American cuisine than all the cooks had done in the previous forty." Because of Hines, many restaurants, which he had refused to list because the kitchens did not meet his standards of cleanliness, have "modernized and cleaned up." They are now in the book. Numerous out-of-the-way inns where Hines discovered good cooking are able to stay open only because motorists "traveling by the book" turn off the main highways to seek them out.

Hines, who believes in moderation, maintains that Americans overeat. As for American cooking, he says there is more good food in New England than in other sections of America. Averse to long menus which include nothing outstanding, he campaigns for regional dishes, thinks it tragic that many inns have abandoned regional specialties in order to serve, with finger bowls, and pretty candles, "just as good and up-to-date a dinner as you can get in New York." Food must have "loving care," he says. "We Americans have got to get away from the 'bolt it and beat it' idea of eating. We've got to give the cooks more time to prepare the food properly." And he does not believe in bargain dining: "Usually the difference between a low-priced meal and one that costs more is the amount you pay the doctor or the undertaker"; but, he says, some of the best chicken he ever tasted came out of the basket of a Negro peddler who cried, "Fried chicken— twenty cents a hunk!" For the diner who is in doubt, he recommends ordering ham and eggs, since no cook can disguise a bad egg, and very few cooks can spoil a slice of good ham.

The dinner-detective was married again, in March 1946, to Clara Wright Nahm. Mrs. Hines, a trim, blond Kentuckian, takes turns with her husband at the wheel of the car, and enjoys sampling entrees with him. Hines is solidly built, but not overly stout—he stands five feet, eight and a half inches tall, and weighs 178' pounds. With his silver-rimmed spectacles and his gray hair, he looks more like a genial business executive than a gourmet. "He may look like a lawyer, he may have the attitudes of a businessman," wrote Milton MacKaye, "but there runs through his conversation a tender and touching attachment to such items as unsweetened corn bread, white, first-run maple syrup, and properly cured hams, which

at once stamps him as a sentimentalist and poet."

References

Am Mag 131:80-1 Ap '41 por
Bet Homes & Gard 23:30-1+ Mr '45 pors
Read Digest 38:59-62 Je '41
Sat Eve Post 211:16-17+ D 3 '38
Scrib Com 10:13-18 Je '41
Who's Who in America, 1946-47

HODGSON, W(ILLIAM) R(OY) May 22, 1892- Australian Government official
Address: b. Australian Legation, Paris

Lieutenant Colonel W. R. Hodgson, the Australian Minister to France, was his country's delegate to the first meetings of the Security Council of the United Nations in New York, where he won a reputation as a forthright diplomat and a "stormy petrel" within a week after the session opened in March 1946. When he returned to his legation in Paris at the end of April, the New York *Times* commented, "Three points made him second only to Andrei A. Gromyko '[43] of Russia as a center of public interest: his peppery, aggressive manner during a Council session, his broad accent in speech, and the determination to investigate and prod. He became known as 'the needle of the Council.'"

The son of Robert Hodgson, headmaster of an Australian public school, William Roy Hodgson was born May 22, 1892, in Kingston, Victoria. As a boy Hodgson became an expert rifle shot, the champion of his club. This interest, with the encouragement of his father, prompted him in 1911 to enroll in the Royal Military College at Duntroon, the Australian "West Point" founded by Lord Kitchener. He took competitive examinations to gain admission, and came out eighteenth among the forty candidates selected. Although of small physique, at school he was a star athlete, winning tennis and welterweight boxing matches and playing cricket, rugby, and Australian league football. (After 1918, war injuries kept him from participating in most sports, but he became an enthusiastic lawn-bowler, representing his Australian club in championship tournaments.) In 1914, at the outbreak of World War I, Hodgson was graduated and received a commission in the army.

A twenty-three-year-old lieutenant in the Australian Imperial Forces, Hodgson was with the original Anzacs (men of the Australian and New Zealand Army Corps) who made the first Gallipoli landing in the Dardanelles, in April 1915. He was a forward artillery observer, among the first to scale the cliffs and direct the fire of Royal Navy battleships. A Turkish sniper shattered his hip, but he lived to have "the pleasure of reading" his own obituary notice. For his part in the Gallipoli action, he received the Croix de Guerre with palm. In 1917 he was invalided home to Australia, and for several years underwent major operations, which left him with a short-

W. R. HODGSON

ened left leg—"My legacy in the cause of peace," he once called it.

Hodgson served on the permanent Australian military staff from 1917 to 1934. After 1921, attached to the General Staff at Army Headquarters, Melbourne, he worked in training operations and intelligence sections. He specialized in foreign affairs, particularly the problems of the Pacific and the Far East. In 1934 Colonel Hodgson resigned from the army to become assistant secretary of the Australian Department of External Affairs, and a year later moved up to the post of secretary.

Secretary Hodgson did the spadework for the expansion of the Australian diplomatic service, serving under Minister for External Affairs Dr. Herbert Vere Evatt '42. At the Imperial Conference in London in 1937 Hodgson was adviser on foreign affairs to the Australian delegation, after which, according to an official statement, he returned to Australia and "built a solid foundation" for Australian world activities. In 1942, when Java fell to Japan, the country "down under" was in mortal peril for the first time in her history, and her people realized how much they were dependent for security on the cooperation of other nations. Thus, Australia's Department of External Affairs grew rapidly during the war. A need for trained diplomats was foreseen, and in 1943 Colonel Hodgson began to work out the details of a unique scheme of "diplomatic cadetships."

Young people were to be chosen by written and oral competitive examinations, then specially trained at a university for service as counselors, secretaries and aides in the diplomatic corps. They were expected eventually to take over diplomatic posts on the highest levels. "When we first called for applicants we received 1,500," reported Colonel Hodgson. "The chance was offered to both men and women,

and preference given to those in the services. The written examination enabled us to select eighty people, and after that a board, of which I was a member, traveled many thousands of miles between far northern military establishments interviewing young soldiers. We were interested in character, appearance, personality, quality of mind, sporting and recreational inclinations, and just about everything else, and by the time it was over we had a dozen of the finest young people it would be possible to find anywhere."

In September 1944 the Colonel left Australia to attend aviation conferences in New Zealand and Montreal and, subsequently, the first international conference on civil aviation in Chicago. He next crossed the Atlantic to represent Australia at Dominion and Foreign Office talks in London, then returned to North America in January 1945 as temporary Australian High Commissioner to Canada. Two months later, in March 1945, when the French Foreign Office opened diplomatic relations with Australia, he was named Australian Minister to France.

Before going to France Colonel Hodgson first went to San Francisco as adviser to the Australian delegation to the United Nations Conference. He then returned to Australia for a gallstone operation, which culminated in an attack of pneumonia. As soon as he was well he left, not for Paris, but for London, as leader of the Australian delegation to the U.N. preparatory committee meeting, and as Australian delegate to the first meeting of the U.N. Assembly. He was also delegate to the United Nations Educational, Scientific, and Cultural Organization (UNESCO), and to the intergovernmental committee on refugees. Between London meetings he visited Paris to attend to affairs at his legation. After the U.N. Assembly voted Australia one of the six temporary seats on the Security Council, Hodgson left for New York as Australia's representative to the first meeting of the U.N. Security Council in the United States.

The Colonel took an active part in the discussions concerning the selection of a temporary site for Security Council meetings. "New York is one of the most stimulating and exciting cities of the world," he said, "but it has always seemed to me that the U.N. needs a place for deliberation conducive to objective calm, rather than a seething political and commercial center." The Colonel took the same tack throughout the first meetings of the Council—he wanted "objective calm." He warned of the dangers of rushing into decisions, advocated that the young world organization "make haste slowly" and sharply criticized the Council's handling of its first problem, Iran's dispute with Russia.

The Australian delegate proposed that the Council, in dealing with the Russian-Iranian dispute, first request written reports from both Moscow and Teheran, and, when all facts were available, then discuss the situation. However, the British and American Council members considered that the principle of whether small nations had a right to be heard was the real issue, while the substance of the particular question was only incidental. A resolution calling for an immediate hearing for the Iranian Ambassador was adopted. The Iranian was asked to prove a dispute existed without discussing the substance of the dispute, but he found it impossible not to move over the nebulous line between procedure and substance. Gromyko refused to appear at the session when the Iranian spoke. "That's the thing I was trying to avoid—a walkout," Hodgson told reporters. "You can't call witnesses to the bar without getting testimony from both sides." Finally the Council asked both Russia and Iran for additional information, as Hodgson had originally suggested.

After a closed executive meeting, the Council adopted the "Byrnes resolution," postponing further action on the dispute until May 6, 1946. The vote was 9 to 0, with Australia abstaining, and the Soviet delegate absent. While other delegates were unanimous in praise of the way the problem had been handled, Hodgson delivered a scathing attack on the action. He was especially critical of the closed session the Council had held, which he felt had weakened the prestige of the Council in the eyes of the world. He directed barbs against Russia for leaving the sessions and "thus prejudicing the work, efficiency and authority of the Council," and against the Council itself for following "a disorderly procedure of expediency in a hasty handling of the case." Newspaper observers were impressed with his independent stand, and on the whole favorable to his point of view. "It was only the Australian delegate," wrote Sumner Welles in the New York *Herald Tribune*, "who courageously insisted upon the realities underlying the mirage."

In the Council's second test—the consideration of Poland's charges that Spain under General Franco was a menace to world peace—the doughty independent from "down under" again demanded facts, "orderly, methodical examination" of information, and judicial dignity. "We have here at this table two schools of thought," he said at the Council meeting. "One school says let us without investigation impose certain sanctions. The other says we won't do anything because it is a matter of domestic jurisdiction. The Australian delegation accepts neither proposition. We want an investigation." Hodgson proposed that a five-member committee determine whether the Spanish situation was a matter of international concern, and that the Council act in accordance with the report of the committee. "Finally . . . a proposal that makes some sense," was the comment in the New York *Post*, while the *New Yorker's* Howard Brubaker remarked, "Australia's delegate . . . is rapidly acquiring a reputation as an ecentric character. The Colonel seems to think that the U.N. should learn the facts before it makes its decisions, instead of afterwards." Hodgson's proposal was accepted 10 to 0 (Russia did not vote). But the Australian vote was not placed by the Colonel; he left New York suddenly to join his wife, who had become critically ill in Paris. Paul Hasluck [46] took Hodgson's place at the conference table. (Not long after the Colonel took up his duties as

Minister to France, Mrs. Hodgson died, on August 8, 1946.)

When Hodgson left the Council, it was remarked that he would be greatly missed. His legacy to the Security Council was more than an "Austrylyan" accent (variously described as Cockney, and Australian-Bronx), commented John Hohenberg in the New York *Post*. "Hodgson wasn't one for other nations to run interference for him," Hohenberg added, "nor did he go in for private hotel room skull practice sessions. He played the game solely as his country saw it, and he played it wide open for all to watch."

As a member of the Australian delegation to the Conference of Paris in 1946, he served on the Finnish Political and Territorial Commission, which drafted the treaty and the constitution for Finland, and on the secretariat committee, which dealt with such matters as fixing the agenda for the conference. He was opposed by the Soviet delegates on various proposals; and during a debate on Trieste in the Italian Political and Territorial Commission, he denounced as "arbitrary, irresponsible, dictatorial," the use of the veto in the United Nations Security Council.

Lieutenant Colonel William Hodgson is an Officer of the Order of the British Empire (O.B.E.). He has an LL.B. degree, is an Associate of the Federal Institute of Accountants, and an Associate of the Australasian Institute of Cost Accountants. Hodgson is five feet, six inches tall, and weighs 147 pounds, has blue eyes, an impressive forehead, and a "fighting jaw." His associates call him a "tiger for work," and add that he "certainly gives the impression of a man whose job is his life." The hard-hitting diplomat's favorite pastime is collecting china and old silverware, a hobby he acquired from his wife, the former Muriel Bruce of Mentone, Victoria, to whom he was married in 1919. (Colonel Hodgson has two children, a son Rodney, and a daughter Cynthia.) In sports the Colonel likes action: "Ice hockey as played by the Montreal Canadiens is my idea of the best game played any place in America. Your football is, in my opinion, a sissy game."

References

N Y Sun p26 Ap 10 '46
N Y Times p3 Mr 30 '46
N Y World-Telegram p4 Mr 30 '46
PM Mag p2 Ap 14 '46
Who's Who, 1946

HOFFMAN, PAUL G(RAY) Apr. 26, 1891- Industrialist

Address: b. c/o the Studebaker Corporation, South Bend, Ind.; c/o Committee for Economic Development, 285 Madison Ave., New York; h. 3123 Miami Rd., South Bend, Ind.

President of the Studebaker Corporation and chairman of the important Committee for Economic Development, Paul Gray Hoffman was born in Chicago on April 26, 1891. He is the son of George Delos and Eleanor (Lott) Hoffman. "As a boy," says *Time*, "he learned about cars from a decrepit secondhand Pope-Toledo

PAUL G. HOFFMAN

that he heckled his inventor father into buying." After graduation from the LaGrange (Illinois)High School, Paul entered the University of Chicago, where he studied in 1908-09. But he soon decided that there were already enough lawyers, and left college to enter the derided automobile business, then in its infancy.

The eighteen-year-old boy began work as a porter for the Chicago distributor of Halladay cars. According to the January 15, 1938, *Sales Management,* young Hoffman became foreman of the repair shop. Then he turned to Studebakers, selling them "on the hoof"—which means that he would start out in a car, show it to prospect after prospect until he had sold it, and then return to headquarters for another car to sell.

The enterprising young salesman (then twenty years old) moved from Illinois to the West Coast in 1911. "He picked Los Angeles as a site for operations even before its citizens recognized its manifest destiny as the world's greatest automobile market," *Time* comments. "He also learned to love competition by practicing it; auto selling in those days was a murderous free-for-all. Angelenos still remember that even so noble-minded a salesman as Hoffman bought up wrecks of competing makes, regaled his customers with lurid tales about the fate of their hapless owners." It is remembered, too, that Hoffman's way of celebrating a sale was to make another one, so he sold more cars than anyone else. In 1915 the Chicagoan became sales manager of the Los Angeles Retail Branch. (That December he was married to Dorothy Brown of Pasadena.) Two years later Hoffman was promoted to branch manager of the district. According to his Committee for Economic Development associate William Benton [45], he was also running, two small businesses of his own.

In 1917 the twenty-six-year-old executive enlisted in the World War I Army as a private. By 1919, when he was discharged, Hoffman was a first lieutenant of field artillery. Soon afterward he purchased the Los Angeles branch; and in six years, says Benton, he "made the Paul G. Hoffman Company of Los Angeles famous throughout the automobile business." He is still chairman of the board of the Paul G. Hoffman Company and of the Hoffman Specialty Company.

By 1925, he was doing a reported seven million dollars' worth of business a year as a Studebaker distributor (wholesaler), and is said to have made a million dollars. He had also been active in forming the present Automotive Safety Foundation. According to *Newsweek,* "in 1924, when no one could sell Studebakers, Hoffman could." The president of the Studebaker Corporation, Albert R. Erskine, sent for Hoffman to find out why—and discovered that the thirty-three-year-old "boy wonder" had added accessories to the cars after they left the factory. The upshot was that Erskine persuaded Hoffman to leave Los Angeles in 1925 and to return to South Bend as his vice-president in charge of sales, and member of the board of directors.

On March 18, 1933, the corporation went into receivership; the receivers were Hoffman, Ashton G. Bean, head of the White Motor Company, and Harold S. Vance, vice-president in charge of production. At one o'clock the next morning, as *Newsweek* tells the story, Hoffman telephoned the referee in the case to ask for a hundred thousand dollars for expenses. He got it—and spent it in advertising "Studebaker Carries On!" Sales manager Hoffman also dubbed Studebaker the "Friendliest Factory," inviting dealers to come to him with any complaints they might have about the car. He and his coreceiver divorced Pierce-Arrow from Studebaker in 1933, reportedly selling that property for a million dollars. When the Studebaker Corporation emerged from receivership in March 1935, Paul Hoffman was president, and he has remained its president ever since. Few other automobile company presidents came up through the sales department. They are usually production men.

H. S. Vance is chairman of the board of directors, and Hoffman gives him, as well as their loyal employees, the credit for making Studebaker the first automobile company ever to emerge from receivership under the same management. For the first nine months of that year, 1935, Studebaker sales totaled 30,194, which put the company fourth among independent (non-General Motors) producers of passenger cars—behind the giants, Ford [44] and Chrysler, and the smaller Hudson, but ahead of the seven other American manufacturers of any consequence. Hoffman is said to consider himself a successful small businessman, not a big businessman, although he directs a seventy-million-dollar corporation.

President Hoffman inherited four decades of untroubled labor relations. In a *Public Opinion Quarterly* article, reprinted in the October 1940 *Printers' Ink Monthly,* Glenn Griswold tells how Hoffman and Vance have preserved this amity through years in which the automotive industry has been torn by bitter and costly labor strife. Exact figures on costs and profits are available to the employees, with the result, Griswold writes, that the men are not only keenly desirous of keeping up the quality of Studebaker cars, but often think of ways of increasing sales. This was strikingly demonstrated in the spring of 1938, when Hoffman climaxed three years of study, planning, deficits—and finally of convincing the bankers—by entering the low-price field with the Studebaker Champion. On their own initiative, the union leaders dipped into their funds to hire an advertising man and put half-page Studebaker advertisements in the local paper. Unintentionally, they created a public relations problem for the startled corporation—it had to reassure indignant merchants that the ads were not an appeal to all good unionists to boycott non-users of Studebakers.

Competing with Chevrolet, Ford, and Plymouth, the Champion put its manufacturer back on the profitable side of the ledger. World War II kept the company there, with Studebaker selling military trucks to the French Government. Net profits for 1939 were figured to be nearly at the three-million-dollar mark. Following Pearl Harbor, in January of 1942 Studebaker began to investigate the possibilities for dealers who wished to go into war production, and undertook to assist and advise dealers in turning to war work during the straitened sales period. Such production was not exclusive with Studebaker dealers, but Studebaker was described in the October 22, 1942, *Iron Age* as "well on the way to becoming the focal point of the first real bits and pieces manufacturing program in the nation's war effort."

As for the Studebaker Corporation itself, Hoffman says that in early 1941 it contracted to construct and operate for the Government three entirely new plants for the manufacture of aircraft engines under license from the Wright[45] Aeronautical Corporation, having found its car manufacture facilities unsuited for the purpose. Not long after Pearl Harbor, the Corporation obtained Government contracts totaling more than three hundred million dollars. By the end of the war, Studebaker had turned out 63,789 Wright Cyclone engines for Flying Fortress bombers at one of the lowest unit costs, and 197,678 heavy-duty military trucks, which "took punishment by weather and terrain from the Persian Gulf to the Arctic Ocean" and "played a vital part in the crushing of Nazi armies on the Eastern front." For use in the Asiatic theater, Studebaker made the Weasel, which was developed for use in Europe, where it first saw action in combat, and which the manufacturer describes as an amphibious personnel and cargo carrier that went where no other vehicle made by man could venture. "Some manufacturers turned out munitions of war in greater volume than Studebaker," said an advertisement under Hoffman's signature in the fall of 1945. "But it is doubtful whether any other manufacturer carried out such difficult assignments with complete success as did ninety-three-year-old Stude-

baker. . . .These assets—management, brains, engineering genius, craftsmanship—made it possible for Studebaker to deliver *on schedule* every engine, every truck, and every Weasel ordered. My own responsibility at Studebaker," Hoffman continued, "has been administration rather than production. The credit for these accomplishments does not go to me as president but to Studebaker's matchless production and engineering organization. Therefore, I feel free to publish this tribute to men who deserve it." In 1944 Studebaker improved its postwar competitive position and asserted its claim to leadership by eliminating the distributor from its system, leaving a higher profit margin for the dealer. By the end of the war, Studebaker was recognized as the leading independent in the car field. Its president had already become "a sort of industrial statesman." Active not only in business but in the safety movement, Hoffman was chairman of the Automotive Safety Foundation and vice-president and safety chairman of the Automobile Manufacturers' Association. He received honorary doctorates from four institutions. He was asked to join the Department of Commerce's Business Advisory Council, and became vice-chairman. Early in 1942 he organized an outstandingly successful ten-million-dollar drive for United China Relief, and he is still honorary chairman.

At the suggestion and with the active co-operation of the Secretary of Commerce, Jesse Jones[40] (this included free office space), Hoffman joined several other businessmen in June 1942 to form the Committee for Economic Development. He is board chairman of this privately-financed nonprofit organization. Its 18-man original board included William Benton[45], Will Clayton[44], Eric Johnston[43], Chester Davis[40], Charles F. Kettering[40] of General Motors, and Harry Scherman[43] of the Book-of-the-Month Club. Their purpose was to stimulate American business to the bold planning necessary to create a higher level of peacetime employment than the nation had ever known. Commented *Business Week*: "These men are on the board as realists, not stuffed shirts; as working directors, not window dressing. Predominantly on the liberal side of political and economic thinking in business, they see ahead a tremendous task of preparing the nation's business to withstand the shock of peace."

The CED Research Division was headed by a full-time, $20,000-a-year director, Theodore Yntema of the University of Chicago, a "moderately conservative economist of top professional standing"; it included Hoffman, Beardsley Ruml[43], Thomas W. Lamont[40], and a paid advisory group of university economists. The CED determined that fifty-three to fifty-six million civilian jobs would be needed to provide abundant peacetime employment. This meant that seven to ten million more jobs than existed in 1940 would have to be created, and the Field Division set out to do so. Hoffman has expressed the CED ideas in some articles and in innumerable speeches, delivered in as many as six cities a week. To quote an *Atlantic Monthly* article of his (July 1945 issue):

HOFFMAN, PAUL G.—*Continued*

"These new jobs can be created only through an increase in our national output of goods and services to a level of 30 per cent to 45 per cent above that of 1940. . . .Stated in terms of 1943 prices, it means we must achieve a gross output of from $155,000,000,000 to $170,000,000,000. . . .That means bold expansion, not cautious temporizing. . . .I think it the quintessence of horse sense to accept and strive for a goal high enough to meet our social and fiscal needs. Anything short of that will, I fear, prove tragic." Hoffman further pointed out that most business expansion would have to come in the field of distribution, trades, and services. He and the other CED leaders decided that the program would have to be carried out community by community, and in the late fall of 1942 they asked the businessmen and leaders of three cities to become the pioneer local CED's.

Within three years, there were nearly three thousand local CED's, with more than 75,000 volunteer members. "Since no employer can fill out a check sheet intelligently until he has actually sat down and done some postwar planning, the [CED] surveys are frequently the first real spur to postwar thinking among many employers," Hoffman reported. "Once a committee has its 'job budget' down in black and white—and particularly when the budget shows a job deficit looming after victory—then the local planning program begins to take on real individuality." For practical advice from top businessmen, local groups could then turn to the CED's Industrial Advisory Board, organized by David C. Prince of General Electric.

To help produce the "healthy economic climate" favorable to high productive employment, in the fall of 1945 the CED presented to President Truman '45 plans for a "compensatory" budget, balanced over the business cycle instead of over the year. They warned against premature removal of wartime restrictions as tending to start "an inflationary price boom beyond the power of added production to check." Other proposals advocated by Hoffman and the CED include decreasing corporate and eliminating most excise taxes, as "a restoration of rewards for risk-taking on the part of business and industry," and Hoffman holds that "both business and government must make every effort to see that competition is put back into the competitive system to the fullest extent possible." The CED asks also for lowered tariffs and an end to cartels, and for liberalized unemployment compensation. In January 1946 the chairman again recommended the immediate formation in the executive branch of Government and in Congress of a working group to develop "a coordinated and progressive program of measures, designed to meet the responsibilities of the federal government for a more stable and prosperous society."

In July 1946, CED outlined a postwar program to mobilize businessmen, economists, and educators to plan for a high level of production in an attempt to eliminate the "boom-bust" business cycle. The group also planned to continue its research program. At a convention of bankers two months later Hoffman asserted,

"We know that as of today our system is producing the highest standard of living the world has ever known. I predict it can be doubled within the next twenty-five years under our free capitalistic system provided the world remains at peace." Writing on "The Great Challenge to Capitalism" in an article in the New York *Times Magazine,* the manufacturer stated that "the function of Government is to create conditions under which free labor and free business can work effectively in the public interest." He advocated Government planning with the cooperation of business, labor, and the individual. "For distinguished achievement in industrial management as a service to the community," Hoffman received the Gantt Memorial gold medal, awarded by the American Management Association and the American Society of Mechanical Engineers. He also received a 1946 award from the National Association of Public Relations, and Dartmouth College conferred an honorary LL.D. upon him.

In June 1946 Hoffman was named by President Truman to a twelve-man committee of industrialists and bankers to survey foreign trade conditions and to make recommendations on the financing of international reconstruction. (He is also serving on a similar committee for the Twentieth Century Fund). The executive has also been appointed to the hundred-man commission which will advise the United Nations Educational, Scientific, and Cultural Organization. Under the sponsorship of the International Chamber of Commerce, Hoffman headed a committee of businessmen from several countries who studied world employment conditions.

Hoffman is the author of *Marketing Used Cars* (1930), *Seven Roads to Safety* (1939), and a number of articles on safety, postwar planning, and other topics. Several of his talks have been printed in *Vital Speeches.* He is a Republican, a Mason, a member of Delta Tau Delta, and was president of the fraternity in 1940-42. The Studebaker president belongs to the Chicago Club, The Tavern, and the local country club, and also to three clubs in Los Angeles. He has property in California, and the California influence is also to be found in his house, which is "probably the only dwelling in Indiana built around a roofed-over Mexican patio with palms, with rooms opening off surrounding balconies." The manufacturer is a director of the Federal Reserve Bank of Chicago, a member of the visiting committee of the Harvard Department of Government, a trustee of the Tax Foundation, of Kenyon College (Ohio), and the University of Chicago, and a and Encyclopædia Britannica Films, Inc. (Hoffdirector of the latter's *Encyclopædia Britannica* man's directorships also include United Air Lines, the New York Life Insurance Corporation, and the Chicago Corporation.)

As might be gathered from the extent of his activities, Paul Hoffman is, in William Benton's words, " a dynamo of energy and resourcefulness." In *Time*'s words, he is "a mildmannered, mildly good-looking, nonsmoking, teetotaling man of medium size, whose most distinctive feature is a pair of startlingly blue eyes." His personal statistics include a height of five feet nine and one-half inches, a weight of one hundred and seventy pounds, and graying hair. The Hoffmans have seven children; the five sons—Hallock Brown, Peter Brown, Donald Gray, Robert Cheseboro, and Lathrop Gray—served in the World War II forces. The daughters are Barbara and Kiriki. According to a *Cosmopolitan* article by Bogart Rogers, Hoffman's home life (in a "mildly exclusive" part of South Bend and in summer at unpretentious Lakeside) has in the past been "a bedlam of seven Hoffman children, other people's children, and dogs. . . .As proof of his powers of concentration, friends say that Mr. Hoffman can, and has played intricate bridge hands—like grand slams redoubled—with a junior Hoffman on his knee and a minor dogfight going on under the table." He is fond of, and good at, golf, bridge, and poker.

References

Cosmopolitan 119:8+ O '45 por
Newsweek 6:31 N 2 '35 por
Sales Management 52:40 Ja 15 '38 pors
Scholastic 44:7 Ap 10-15 '44 por
Time 26:72 N 4 '35 por; 42:75 S 6 '43 (por cover)
Who's Who in America, 1946-47
Who's Who in Commerce and Industry (1944)

HOLADAY, WILLIAM PERRY 1882—Jan. 29, 1946 American lawyer and legislator; Republican United States Representative from Illinois (1923-1933); previously member Illinois House of Representatives.

Obituary

N Y Times p25 Ja 30 '46

HONJO, SHIGERU, BARON May 1876—Nov. 20, 1945 Retired general of the Japanese Army; considered leader of the Manchurian conquest; saw action in the Russo-Japanese war; regimental commander with the Siberian Expeditionary Forces (1919); committed harakiri after his arrest had been ordered by the Allied powers.

Obituary

N Y Herald Tribune p2 N 21 '45

HOPKINS, HARRY L(LOYD) Aug. 17, 1890—Jan. 29, 1946 United States Government official, social worker; considered the most trusted adviser and most intimate friend of President F. D. Roosevelt; Federal Administrator of Emergency Relief (1933), Works Progress Administrator (1935-38); Secretary of Commerce (1938-40); Lend-Lease Administrator (1941); special assistant to President, member War Production Board, Pacific War Council, special envoy on various delicate diplomatic missions, 1942 until resignation in July 1945; impartial chairman, Cloak and Suit Industry, September 1945 to death. See *Current Biography* 1941 Yearbook.

Obituary

N Y Times p19+ Ja 30 '46 por

HORMEL, JAY C(ATHERWOOD) (hôr' měl) Sept. 11, 1892- Meat packer
Address: b. c/o George A. Hormel and Company, Austin, Minn.; h. Austin, Minn.

At the head of George A. Hormel and Company, the largest independent meat-processing establishment in the United States, is Jay C. Hormel. Known as the "Spam man," for the most successful of his luncheon meat products, he is an executive whose interests extend beyond Spam (actually only one of the more than three hundred items on the Hormel list) to business administration, advertising, and

Pach Bros.

JAY C. HORMEL

labor relations, in which he has likewise been an innovator. President since 1929, in July 1946 he succeeded his late father as chairman of the board of directors.

The only son of the founder of the Hormel meat-processing interests, George Albert Hormel, and the former Lillian Belle Gleason, Jay Catherwood Hormel was born in Austin, Minnesota, on September 11, 1892. This was less than a year after his father, a buyer of wool and hides and a meat retailer in his early years, had established George A. Hormel and Company, pork packers, in a remodeled creamery on the Cedar River at Austin. Young Jay, who received his early education in the Austin public schools, first became associated with the company on March 29, 1907, at the age of fourteen, when his employment card records that he was receiving ten cents an hour in the lard room. The job lasted only two days, however, for on April 1 it is recorded that he left to return to school. A second entry on the card is "February 24, 1909: fifteen cents an hour," but it was not until 1910 that he began to work in the plant during his summer vacations, excepting only the summer of 1911, the year he graduated from Shattuck Military

HORMEL, JAY C.—*Continued*

Academy at Faribault, Minnesota. In the autumn of 1911, aged nineteen, he went east to attend Princeton University, but at the end of his junior year, in June 1914, he abandoned his college career for the family business. On November 17, 1914, he was made a company director. Two years later, almost to the day, he was elevated to the first vice-presidency.

Then, on September 5, 1917, young Hormel was inducted into the Army, becoming the fourth drafted man and the first from Minnesota to report to Camp Dodge, Iowa, and the first enlisted man in the 351st Infantry, 88th Division. Assigned to Company G, in nine days he was made a corporal; eleven days after that, regimental sergeant major; and in another fourteen days, second lieutenant. In November, because of his background, he was assigned to Ice Plant Company 301, with which early in 1918 he went overseas, to be stationed first at the quartermaster's depot in Gievres, and later in Tours, France. Having always been "a little overwhelmed" by his very energetic and strong-willed father, points out Frances Levison in an article in *Life*, it was here that he "demonstrated for the first time his [real] administrative talents." And when continued shipping losses were depleting the cargo space available for overseas shipments, it was Hormel who together with his commanding officer evolved a plan to save 40 per cent of shipping space by the simple expedient of boning the beef before it was frozen. A cable dispatched to Washington brought acceptance of the solution, and the newly promoted First Lieutenant was sent home "to compose uniform orders for American packers on how to bone, freeze, and pack beef."

Discharged from the Army on December 10, 1918, the young man returned to Austin, said Miss Levison, "with a lot more confidence and a little more prestige." Then, in July 1921, his prestige was greatly enhanced when he found an entry in the company's books which led to the discovery that the assistant comptroller, had, over a period of years, embezzled a total of $1,187,000. Up to this time Jay Hormel had been working most of the time in the plant. Going through some operating figures in the accounting department one day, he came across a seeming discrepancy which he could not understand, and, already suspicious, asked the aid of a banker friend. Late that night he approached his father with the announcement, "I think we're broke." The money which had been stolen was borrowed money; besides its investment in building and equipment, the assets of George A. Hormel and Company had been reduced to a net value of $14,000 less than nothing. It was a hard blow for both the firm and the town, which had grown up on its prosperity, but the elder Hormel, with his son beside him, faced a creditor's committee of bankers in Chicago and convinced them of the basic soundness of the business and its value to the community. He offered to pledge his personal property as surety. Credit was extended and the business saved.

But with the credit went a supervisory committee which greatly restricted the management's freedom of action. Hence, at the first opportunity, George A. Hormel floated a bond issue, which confirmed the Hormel reputation for integrity by being disposed of on the first day of sale. At the same time the elder Hormel made administrative changes, detailing a large share of the responsibility to his son Jay, who at this time was also engaged in helping to set up the duplicate set of books, "designed to give quicker knowledge of profit or loss and better control of operations," which subsequently became the basis of the Hormel accounting system. One year later, in 1923, vice-president Jay Hormel took on the additional position of company treasurer.

In the decade that followed, he initiated a gradual modernization of the packing house's organization and methods. In 1926, the year the last of the bonds were retired, he startled his father by announcing that he had signed contracts for a half-million-dollar advertising campaign. Casting about for an idea to attract nation-wide consumer attention to the Hormel name, he set the workers to experimenting with processes for canning frankfurters and sauerkraut. But during the summer, spent in Hamburg, Germany, he encountered Paul Jörn, who had successfully canned ham in Germany and whose United States patents for the process, confiscated in World War I, were lying unclaimed in the custody of the Chemical Foundation. Abandoning the earlier plan, therefore, he brought Jörn to Austin and early in the year 1927 launched Hormel canned whole ham, followed soon afterward by canned half and quarter hams to meet varied consumer needs.

This was only the first of several products with which Hormel was to pioneer. Later in 1927 the young executive placed on the market canned spiced ham, "an outright Hormel invention consisting of a loaf of chopped ham, salt, sugar, nitrate, and pepper"; and following that, still in bulk form, a canned luncheon meat made largely from the shoulder of the hog. With the latter item he performed a double service, increasing the over-all value of the hog by making more desirable the shoulder cut and extending the market by overcoming the "very considerable difficulty" of preserving the pork meat in the can. With both he initiated a whole new line of packing house staples, the canned luncheon meat loaves, for in this innovation he was imitated by the entire packing industry, whereas only a part of the industry had followed his canned ham pioneering. Despite the competition, however, surveys show that the Hormel products retained the leadership, only the canned soup line of 1931, designed to succeed the poorly selling luxury item canned whole chicken of 1928, being forced into third place by Campbell and Heinz.

Meawhile, on November 19, 1928, the younger Hormel, who had already been acting as president since 1927, assumed the full duties of that office, while his father retired to California, whence, as chairman of the board of directors, he continued to supervise the business until his death in June 1946. By 1929, also, the large expansion program of the previous several years had been virtually completed, and the new president began an administrative reorganization of the firm. Four divisions were created, vertical in administrative structure, each designed to function as an autonomous business, buying from or selling to the others or unaffiliated concerns. They are: abattoir, the hog slaughtering unit; beef, the beef, veal and lamb slaughtering unit; packing, the processing unit for most of the meat; and "Flavor-Sealed," the canning unit, which although it has the lowest volume of sales, is best known to the public.

Two years later, in order to mitigate the hardships of seasonal employment, the enterprising Hormel proposed a straight-time plan of remuneration under which, to quote the explanation in *Fortune,* "the company [would] contract with the men of any department for a year's work based on the ten-year average of output of product of the department and the number of man-hours required to produce it. The men would then receive their pay in fifty-two weekly checks of equal size, whether there was heavy work for them, light work, or none." Instituted in the smoke-house division because that had the greatest seasonal variation, the plan soon won favor with other departments and became the basis for payment throughout the company. Only one complaint has been leveled against it—that at times it constitutes too much of a speed-up arrangement.

Although the "Flavor-Sealed" products, including the Dinty Moore line of stews and spaghetti and meatballs, begun in 1936 and responsible for Hormel's conversion to the small package idea, increased sales, their sponsor had not yet achieved either the goal of his earlier advertising campaign or his aim of marketing an unique nonperishable canned pork product when he introduced Spam in 1937. Actually perfected in 1935, "the special high-grade compound of ham and pork shoulders" had been held up by a search for the perfect name, which Hormel specified had to be short, different, nondescriptive, copyrightable, and pronounceable in any language. Contests brought no solution until at Hormel's New Year's Eve party "a fellow felt sufficiently inspired" to suggest "Spam." Immediately the advertising campaign, utilizing one of the first singing commercials, the services of George Burns and Gracie Allen, and such inventions as "Spamwich", "Spambled Eggs," and "Spam good idea," got under way. The result, reported *Life,* was a change in the gustatory habits of the United States, with 70 per cent of urban Americans using canned meats in 1940 in comparison with only 18 per cent in 1937, while "more than twice as much Spam was sold as the analogous products of its closest competitors" and this time no close rival appeared for nearly two years.

However, it took World War II and GI jokes, jingles, and *Yank* cartoons to make Spam internationally "notorious." "Undeservedly," insists Hormel, for the pink luncheon meat which appeared all too frequently on GI menus and was called by them "Spam" was not, he declares, his product, but a similar and "inferior" preparation made by other companies from a recipe furnished by the United States Army Quartermaster Corps. What Spam the soldiers did get was "fine food [with] nothing in it but shoulder of pork and chopped ham and the knowledge of cooking it —none of the mysterious ingredients soldiers claim to have found in it." But actually, he adds, Spam was sold primarily for Lend-Lease. For the Russians it became "the second front" or "Roosevelt sausage," and its frequent appearance on English tables, sometimes as "Escallope of Spam," caused that country to be renamed "Spamland." Nevertheless, Spam, like the Ford "Tin Lizzie," which in its day was the butt of American humor, found every knock a boost, and throve.

"An original thinker who had put his novel economic ideas into practice," in the words of Frances Levison in *Life,* Jay Hormel pays higher wages than the average for the packing industry and has gained the loyalty of his workers through such beneficial arrangements —in addition to straight-time—as incentive payments, a joint earnings plan, and a fifty-two-week written notice of intended dismissal. And though some clashes have occurred— notably the strike of 1933 against compulsory insurance deductions—it is to these policies that observers attribute the company's immunity from the 1946 industry-wide work stoppage. Others of his ideas have crystallized in the Hormel Chili Beaners, a costly song and dance show which he sent barnstorming throughout the West to advertise chile con carne, and in the Hormel Research Institute, situated on his estate, affiliated with the University of Minnesota. But some, like a plan for a tax on savings instead of profits, have fared less well.

So numerous have his ideas been that his competitors, it is said, have been led to wonder whether he "operates a butcher business in order to exercise his social convictions or practices social beneficence in order to stay in the butcher business." A businessman first, he has answered, "I'm well situated. I don't want to get removed....The community must eventually hold me responsible. I couldn't live out in that cottage [the Hormel estate] unless people figured that they were getting some good out of me."

Hormel is active in civic organizations, many of which deal with the problems of labor and management, and also lists among his extramural interests those of travel and music. He likes to conduct the family trio of piano, clarinet and drums, consisting of his three sons, George A. 2d, Thomas Dubois, and James Catherwood, while their mother, the former Germaine Dubois, whom he met in France, looks on. Though of mild disposition, with an easy good humor, he has, comments the *New Yorker,* become increasingly "tired of being identified as the man responsible for Spam. He feels sure that he has heard all the Spam gags worth hearing, and on occasion he has the

HORMEL, JAY C.—*Continued*

drawn, trapped air of a man who knows he is certain to hear a good many thousands more."

References

Fortune 16:127-32+ O '37
Life 20:63-6+ Mr 11 '46
Who's Who in America, 1946-47
Who's Who in Commerce and Industry (1944)

HORTON, EDWARD EVERETT Mar. 18, 1887- Actor

Address: b. 1103 El Centro, Hollywood, Calif.; h. 5521 Amestoy Ave., Encino, Calif.

Edward Everett Horton, the "fluttery" comedian who is master of the grimace and the "double-take," by 1946 had appeared in a hundred films, including two-reelers. A character actor in constant demand by the major Hollywood studios, Horton was one of the few to

EDWARD EVERETT HORTON

survive the transition from silent films to "talkies." He learned his craft in stock company theaters before the advent of the motion picture, and has returned often to the "straw-hat" or summertime circuit and the road company, usually in revivals of *Springtime For Henry,* in which he has played over nine hundred times.

When Edward Everett Horton was born on March 18, 1887, in Brooklyn, his father, for whom he was named (and who, in turn, was named for Edward Everett Hale) was foreman of the composing room of the New York *Times.* His mother is Isabella (Diack) Horton. One of young Edward's first memories was visits to Manhattan to see the first linotype machine. From the "stupendous beer parties" which his father used to give for proofreaders, printers, and reporters, the boy became "saturated with

thoughts of newspaper work." At the same time, however, he was spending all his spare money for theater tickets.

Young Horton was graduated from Boys' High School in Brooklyn, and later attended Columbia University. At Columbia he studied history and German, but had no particular vocational ambition; although the family urged it, he preferred not to be a teacher. He was still at Columbia when he took a part in a Kenneth and Roy Webb show in Newport, Rhode Island. According to Kyle Crichton, writing in *Collier's,* he "got nothing out of it but a lot of cuts which eventually resulted in his being busted out of college." The twenty-year-old ex-college student immediately took a job as a member of the chorus of the Dempsey Opera Company, which was then presenting Gilbert and Sullivan comic operas on Staten Island.

A year later, in 1908, Horton joined Louis Mann in New York City as a bit player and stage manager, making his first appearance on the New York stage with a walk-on part in *The Man Who Stood Still.* Three years with Mann—during which his salary rose from twenty-five to seventy-five dollars a week—gave Horton a good grounding in acting, voice placement, and stage presence. Leaving Mann, he joined the Chestnut Street Stock Company in Philadelphia, said to be the best of its day, to play juvenile leads at twenty-five dollars weekly. When that company's theater was closed for infractions of fire regulations Horton went first to Beulah Jay's Little Theater, which was also in Philadelphia, and from there to a stock company in Portland, Maine, with which he played eighty-eight consecutive weeks. Then the Wilkes Stock Company in Los Angeles hired him at two hundred and fifty dollars weekly. After six years with Wilkes, Horton formed his own company.

"A visit to L.A. without seeing Horton," according to Crichton, "was accounted a social error in Southern California." For years the actor played to a loyal following, earning for himself as much as one thousand dollars a week. Among his successful roles was that of the lead in Booth Tarkington's *Clarence,* which ran for forty-four weeks in 1923. Another notable presentation was his production of *Springtime for Henry* in 1932. He was deep in debt at the time, following the presentation of several experimental productions. Then twelve weeks of success as the philandering bachelor, Henry Dewlip, brought him "out of the red."

At regular intervals, meanwhile, Horton was appearing in silent films. These included *Ruggles of Red Gap, The Front Page Story, To The Ladies, The Beggar on Horseback,* and *Marry Me,* all financial failures, according to Crichton. "The polite comedians in the silent days were handsome fellows," Horton has said in explaining these early failures. "The other comics had their distinct peculiarities. Harold Lloyd had the glasses. Lloyd Hamilton was the goofy type. Buster Keaton had the dead pan. I wasn't handsome or funny-looking—at least not funny enough. They couldn't make me out. . . .The early films were two-reelers and you had to come right out and hit the ball." With the introduction of sound, Horton's stock with producers rose considerably. His first sound film was *Miss Information,* with Lois Wilson. He made a number of two-reel talking pictures, and appeared in *The Terror,* the second full-length "talkie." Other Vitaphone Productions in which he played were *The Hottentot, The Victor, The Sap, Wide Open,* and *Sonny Boy.* Then, for a year, producers "forgot about him." He filled in the time, as usual, with his stock company. Lewis Milestone brought him back by casting him in *The Front Page* (released in 1931).

After 1930 Horton was continuously in pictures for the major producers, making well over fifty films in fifteen years. He was the mad hatter of *Alice in Wonderland,* the American crook in *Lost Horizon,* and Fred Astaire's [45] best friend in half a dozen Astaire-Ginger Rogers [41] musicals. By 1936 he was earning as much as most stars. According to Crichton, the audience blamed the star for a poor picture, and if it was very bad, Horton would usually "stand out triumphantly," since he was "a technical actor of vast proficiency."

In the summer of 1939 Horton decided to revive Benn Levy's *Springtime for Henry.* He left Hollywood for the straw-hat circuit in the East. The revival was so successful that Horton took the farce from coast to coast and to Canada and Cuba, playing Henry for ninety-six weeks. In the role, said *Time* in 1940, Horton had "plenty of opportunity for the jittery mugging that averages him eighty to one hundred thousand dollars a year in Hollywood."

The seven films Horton made in 1941 included *Ziegfeld Girl* (MGM) in which he played Ziegfeld's agent, and the successful fantasy-comedy *Here Comes Mr. Jordan* (Columbia), in which Horton was Celestial Messenger Number 7013, assigned to bringing souls to heaven. The next year saw him in *I Married An Angel* (MGM) supporting Nelson Eddy [43] and Jeannette MacDonald. He also appeared in *The Magnificent Dope* with Henry Fonda, and in the musical *Springtime in the Rockies* (both Twentieth Century-Fox).

Horton's films in 1943 included *Her Primitive Man,* in which he played a "double-talk role that couldn't possibly exist, but is a wonder to behold." In *Summer Storm,* a 1944 United Artists release, he was a landowning Russian aristocrat. Others of his films were *Cinderella Jones, Brazil, San Diego—I Love You,* and *Arsenic and Old Lace,* all made in 1944; and *Steppin' In Society* and *The Town Went Wild,* released in 1945. "In pictures," Horton told Ward Morehouse [40] in 1945, "I have my own little kingdom. I do the scavenger parts no one else wants, and I get well paid for it."

In 1945 Horton revived *Clarence* for a three-week engagement at the Montclair Theater in New Jersey. And in the summer of 1946 he again played in *Springtime for Henry;* he was the "busiest player on the summer theater for 1946." *Life* reported in August, "Clowning and mugging without shame, Horton's Henry still seems as enjoyable to summer audiences as

a tall Tom Collins." The play had become a "straw-hat classic," and Horton was "king of all the Henrys" who ever played the role. Between tours as Henry and his film engagements, Horton was often heard on the air.

The comedian, who is unmarried, is said to be a "demon collector"—particularly interested in rare flowers and antiques. He buys fine old furniture for "Belleigh Acres," the San Fernando Valley estate which he bought in 1925. His house has "overflowed a hilltop in all directions"—the addition of rooms has almost kept pace with the appearance of the actor's successful films.

References

Collier's 98 :22+ Jl 18 '36 pors
N Y Sun p22 O 5 '45
N Y World-Telegram p13 Jl 7 '42 por
Time 36 :62 Jl 22 '40 por
International Motion Picture Almanac, 1943-44
Who's Who in the Theatre (1939)

HOUSTON, ROBERT GRIFFITH 1867—Jan. 29, 1946 American businessman, lawyer, newspaper editor and publisher; former Government official; held various state offices, 1900-1904 and 1921-25; United States Republican Representative from Delaware (1925-31).

Obituary

N Y Times p25 Ja 29 '46

HOVDE, BRYN(JOLF) J(ACOB) (hŭv'dă brĭn) May 17, 1896- Education; social service administrator

Address: b. c/o New School for Social Research, 66 W. 12th St., New York

When seventy-year-old Alvin Johnson [42] announced his intention to retire from his post at the New School for Social Research, in New York, he and the board of trustees searched for a new president. They found him in Bryn J. Hovde, then chief of the Division of Cultural Cooperation in the State Department's Office of Public Affairs. Before he was elected to the presidency, which he assumed in mid-December 1945, the school authorities consulted with various organizations and individuals in Pittsburgh, Hovde's home before he accepted the Washington assignment. The president of the local Chamber of Commerce, the CIO, the American Civil Liberties Union, the A. F. of L., Negro groups, department stores, steel companies—all endorsed Hovde. And a banker observed, "Hovde is grand, but he's radical as hell!"

Hovde, who was given the name of Brynjolf Jakob, is an only son and the oldest of four children; he was born on May 17, 1896, in Jersey City, New Jersey. His mother, Marie (Jacobson) Hovde, was a music teacher; and his father, Christian J. M. Hovde, was a clergyman in the Norwegian Lutheran Synod. Later the family moved to Decorah, Iowa. To supplement her husband's small income, Mrs. Hovde taught the piano for twenty-five cents a lesson, and her son at an early age earned a little money working in neighbors' gardens.

Parry

BRYN J. HOVDE

Young Hovde attended public and parochial schools in Iowa and Wisconsin. Later he studied at Decorah's denominational Luther College, "one of the oldest, best-equipped and largest Norwegian-American colleges." From his mother the boy inherited a love for music and during his student days he played the alto horn in the college concert band. In 1914 Hovde and his fellow musicians made a six months' national and international tour. Of their performance at New York City's Carnegie Hall the music critics wrote that they compared favorably with Sousa's band. Norway was observing its Centennial Exposition when the band toured that country between May and July. Afterward they gave concerts in Sweden, Denmark, Germany, England and France, departing from Europe only a short time before the Continent was swept by World War I.

Hovde remained at Luther College for a year after he had received his degree in 1916 to teach. In World War I he served as a second lieutenant in the Coast Artillery Corps. All his service was in the States. In 1919 he returned to serve as instructor and acting dean of men for a four-year period. He had already been awarded his Ph.D. in modern European and American history in 1924 by the University of Iowa when he was appointed assistant professor of history and political science at Allegheny College in Meadville, Pennsylvania. With the young professor went his wife, the former Theresse Arneson (who until their marriage in 1921 had been a trained nurse) and their son Christian Arneson. Two other children were born to them: Ellen Margrethe in 1925, Carl Frederick in 1926.

Three years after he came to Allegheny College the peripatetic educator was appointed associate professor of history at the University of Pittsburgh, a post he held for nearly a

decade, until 1937. In addition to teaching undergraduates and graduates in modern American and European history, he did research in the development of the Scandinavian countries. Two fellowships, one from the Guggenheim Foundation, another from the American-Scandinavian Foundation, enabled Hovde to spend about two years (1930-31 and 1932) in research and travel in Norway, Sweden, and Denmark. Out of these years of study was to come two thick volumes, *The Scandinavian Countries, 1720-1865; the Rise of the Middle Class*, published in 1943. In its spring issue the *American Scandinavian Review* described the volumes as "truly scholarly work", "a first-rate study contributed by a foreigner to the history of the Scandinavian nations." It also praised the author for his avoidance of "obtrusive doctrinarism." Previously, in 1921, Hovde's *Diplomatic Relations of the United States With Sweden and Norway From 1783 to 1905* had been published. Among his shorter writings is an article Hovde contributed on Norwegian-Americans to *One America* (1945), a symposium edited by F. J. Brown and J. S. Roucek. He was editor of the *Evergreen House Report on Urban Planning* in 1944.

During the depression Hovde's concern for the distress of large numbers of his fellow citizens in Pittsburgh impelled him to start a relief campaign. This obliged him to accept the directorship of the Public Relations Office, which he organized for the Allegheny County Emergency Relief Board, for a year (1934-35). As Director of Public Welfare in Pittsburgh from 1936 to 1938, he was responsible for the administrative supervision of city physicians as well as hospitals with three thousand mental patients and fourteen thousand general hospital patients and "indigents." Under his jurisdiction came also nurses, accountants, farmers, and coal miners, as well as an electric generating plant and a thousand-acre farm.

These civic activities of the college professor made him acutely aware of the housing needs of Pittsburgh. In his capacity as administrator of the Pittsburgh Housing Authority from 1938 to 1944 he directed the planning, construction, and management of 5,463 family dwelling units, into which was poured an investment of thirty million dollars. In the April 1944 issue of the *Survey Graphic*, Hovde reminded his readers that, according to the United States census of 1940, there were ten million substandard houses in the country. Inasmuch as these were the homes of the lowest income groups, whom private enterprise could not supply with decent low-cost homes, he believed the solution of the problem should be the concern of the Government. "If we can lay aside our narrow-mindedness, there is so much public interest in private housing, so much private interest in public housing, that agreement should be easily possible on the common objective of decent housing for all our people," he wrote. He also contributed articles on the subject to the *American City* and the *Public Administration Review*. During his association with the Pittsburgh Housing Authority, Hovde also held the post of special consultant and director of the Management Division of the United States Housing Authority in Washington (1939-40). In 1941 he also devoted several months to the problem of housing the defense workers in Pittsburgh. Contracts for the fourteen projects involving the construction of five thousand public housing units were drawn up under his supervision. He became president of the National Public Housing Conference in 1943 and has been urging Congress to act in the housing shortage by passing the Wagner '41-Taft '40-Ellender '46 bill. In 1938, Hovde's interest in public affairs had led him, a Democrat, to manage the Allegheny County campaign on behalf of the unsuccessful labor candidate, Tom Kennedy, who ran for Governor of Pennsylvania.

To his Washington appointment as chief of the Division of Cultural Cooperation in October 1944, Hovde brought his particularly keen interest in the exchange of cultures between the United States and other lands. Cultural exchange, he explained, was not limited to the fine arts. Every effort was made to assist Americans and other nationalities to acquire an understanding of each other's social, economic, and political life. The visit of a South American worker to a North American factory in order to improve his craftsmanship and the trips of foreign technicians and engineers to the United States to explore American methods of production all came under the heading of "cultural intercourse." In April 1945 Hovde accompanied the American delegation to the United Nations conference in San Francisco as its technical expert. He was also technical secretary to the delegation when it later went to London in November. There he was responsible for the minutes of proceedings, for supplying the delegation with the basic documents it needed to participate in the discussions, and for keeping it informed of all United States Government policies on the various problems presented at the conference. One of the subjects the conferees considered was the exchange of students among the members of the United Nations. At a press gathering which Alvin Johnson had arranged to introduce the New School's president-elect, Hovde pointed out that before World War II there were ten thousand foreign students in the United States. So that "missionaries and friends of peace" might be developed throughout the world he suggested that the number of exchange students under UNESCO's auspices be increased. In a newspaper article written in the summer of 1946, Hovde urged the speedy establishment of the United Nations Educational, Scientific, and Cultural Organization, which would coordinate such exchanges and organize international cooperation in cultural and educational activities. In the fall of the same year he proposed the establishment in the United States of a foundation for international education, under private auspices, which would train American teachers in educational methods of promoting international understanding.

The New School for Social Research, which Hovde now heads, was founded in 1919 by "four intellectual mavericks," historians Charles A. Beard '41 and James Harvey Robinson, philosopher John Dewey '44, and economist Thor-

stein Veblen. Its purpose is to assist "the intelligent adult toward educating himself to a better understanding of a rapidly changing world." In his inaugural speech on December 27, 1945, Hovde pointed out that neither freedom nor liberal education could exist without the other and that "a liberal education would enable us to distinguish clearly and in time the meaning of such movements as fascism and nazism and predispose us to deal with them before they can do us harm." Hovde admitted that he was "rather appalled" at the thought of succeeding Alvin Johnson, whom he calls "one of the foremost educators in the United States today." The greatest problem his predecessor transmitted to him was that of finding additional space for a healthy, growing institution which was "bursting at the seams."

The New School president, a tall, strongly built man with graying hair, impresses interviewers with his soft-spoken manner. Although he has for years been too busy to play the alto horn, he has not lost his fondness for music; and his two other hobbies seem to lie close to his work—they are books and people.

References

PM Mag F 20 '46 p47 por
Time 46:68 D 17 '45
Biographic Register of the State Department, Sep 1, 1944

HOVING, WALTER (hō'-vǐng) Dec. 2, 1897- Corporation executive

Address: b. 10 Rockefeller Plaza, New York; h. 435 E. 52d St., New York

Walter Hoving is president of the Hoving Corporation, which is forming a new national retail empire expected to reach an annual business volume of one hundred and fifty to two hundred million dollars. Formerly president of Lord and Taylor, the New York department store, Hoving is the author of *Your Career in Business.*

The son of the Finnish physician Johannes Walter Wilhelm Hoving, Walter Hoving was born on December 2, 1897, in Stockholm, Sweden. Dr. Hoving, of Swedish descent, was, according to his son, "a man of definite convictions" whose home was in Helsingfors but whose four children were born in Stockholm. "Father," Hoving has said, "didn't want us children born under the Russian flag"—Finland at that time was under the rule of the Czars. Helga (Adamsen) Hoving, Walter's mother, was a prima donna of the Swedish Royal Opera before her marriage, and, Hoving relates, "she took great pains to instill in her children a love for, and understanding of, the best in literature, music, and art." Brought to the United States by his parents in 1903, Hoving attended the Barnard School and the De Witt Clinton High School in New York. At Brown University he was a member of the Naval Reserve in 1918-19, receiving his Ph.B. degree in psychology in 1920. His college societies were the Cammarian Club and Delta Kappa Epsilon.

After leaving college, Hoving relates, he drifted about in the accounting, insurance, publishing, and importing fields, remaining in one

WALTER HOVING

position in the latter field for two years. In 1924 Hoving joined R. H. Macy and Company's "rigorous training squad for aspiring merchandisers," at a salary of twenty-five dollars a week. It was while at this New York department store, one of the largest of its kind in the world, that he discovered what work he wanted to do in life. He submitted an unsolicited research report which streamlined his department, nearly doubled its merchandise turnover, earned a raise, and, says Hoving, taught him "early in the game that a valuable idea is as welcome to any boss as finding a hundred-dollar bill." At the age of thirty Hoving was a vice-president and merchandising director of the store. Although he had taken courses in college on the appreciation of art and painting, Hoving felt that he knew little about those subjects, so important in the merchandising field. Accordingly, he went to the Metropolitan Museum of Art two nights a week for four years taking courses on painting, color and textile design, furniture, old silver, and rugs, until he considered his background adequate.

Leaving Macy's in 1932, Hoving spent the next four years in Chicago at Montgomery Ward and Company as vice-president in charge of sales. According to an article in *Business Week,* "one of his major achievements—and one of the sound reasons for Ward's gains in recent years—was the establishment of a bureau of design to overhaul the [then] fifty thousand-odd items in Ward's catalogue." A member of their board of directors in 1934, Hoving left the mail order house in 1936 after having modernized its catalogue, redesigned its packages, and broken its traditions by hiring women junior executives because he felt their good taste was invaluable to the business.

In April 1936 Hoving joined Lord and Taylor as chairman of its board of directors, becoming president of the store on January

5, 1937. As an executive of the "big, plush" affiliate of the Associated Dry Goods Corporation, Hoving became a member of the parent organization, serving on its executive committee from 1942 until his resignation from Lord and Taylor nine years after he became part of the organization. "The importance of design in moving merchandise has been something of a fetish with Hoving," wrote *Business Week.* This conviction of Hoving's resulted in his establishment in 1937 of four annual one-thousand-dollar awards for outstanding work in merchandise design. "We must have original creations and not just copies of higher priced things . . . [to] build a great tradition of clothes designing in this country," asserted Hoving. "Originality," he said, "wore no price tags."

Hoving's resignation from the presidency of Lord and Taylor, an office with a salary of one hundred and thirty-five thousand dollars a year, became effective on January 5, 1946. Five months later the Hoving Corporation was formed with the backing of a firm of Wall Street investment bankers. Stock shares were offered to the public, and the corporation announced plans for national merging of properties including department, chain, and specialty shops. The amalgamation was to emphasize individual store differences rather than attempt to follow the chain store tactics of standardization, since it is Hoving's belief that people prefer one store to another "because of its personality." The concern will offer its subsidiaries research facilities, giving small stores and those far from large merchandising areas access to new trends and developments in advertising, styling, and labor relations. The new corporation began operations by acquiring rights from the Atlas Corporation to buy, according to *Business Week,* "Manhattan's swank Bonwit Teller specialty store . . . as mother hen for a brood of chicks in other cities."

Your Career in Business, Hoving's book, was published in 1940. The writing of it, tells Hoving, took a year and a half of hard work, preceded by the same length of time thinking about it and threatening to do it. Taking as its theme "Find out what you've got—and use it!", the book is based on Hoving's philosophy that success comes through "making a hell of an effort." Hoving writes: "The modern world is built to the scale of the average man. It's his oyster. But it's up to him to open it." This calls for the affirmative quality of aggressiveness for the man who aspires to responsibility; it is the extrovert who makes the best executive. Hoving assures the man who knows his aptitudes and who applies them to his greatest advantage: "There is a place for you!" An article in *Newsweek* described the book as a "clear, common-sense volume that should be required reading for all college seniors." "Essentially practical, it holds a genuine inspiration for a business career," wrote a New York *Times* reviewer. Harry McNeill in *Commonweal* criticized what he considered to be Hoving's undue optimism, which dates from the days when small enterprises predominated. That reviewer suggested that, were Hoving's ideas effected, the huge department store "might . . .

disintegrate into a hundred small independent bazaars each presided over by a midget Mr. Hoving."

Hoving accepted the Brown University Alumni Association presidency for the year 1939-40, because he felt "that the only important thing the alumni can do is to put their experience at the disposal of the undergraduates." Perfecting a plan to facilitate exchange of information between students exploring various fields and men experienced in those fields, Hoving also financed a three-hundred-and-sixty-five-dollar "Keep the Wolf From the Door" essay scholarship. This award relieved the winning graduate of pressure to "take any kind of . . . job" by giving him what was then a subsistence wage of $1 a day while he looked about for work in keeping with his aptitudes. Brown University made Hoving one of its life trustees on October 25, 1943. In the previous June Hoving affirmed his belief that research foundations and universities are the institutions wherein to forge the "instruments for peace": "We must plan now carefully and methodically for the 'shape of things to come.'"

In 1930 Hoving became a director of the National Retail Dry Goods Association and a vice-president of the Mail Order Association of America in 1933. A director of the American Arbitration Association and of the New York Commerce and Industry Association, he also headed the Better Business Bureau from 1937 to 1939. He was president from 1939 to 1943 of the Fifth Avenue Association, of which, in 1946, he was serving as chairman of the board of directors. His objectives were to improve traffic conditions, eliminate "tin-can" solicitations by pseudo-charitable organizations, and prevent "going-out-of-business retailing." As chairman of the 1943 New York City Anti-Sales Tax Committee, Hoving became involved in a heated "battle of the budget" which was marked by strong words between the department store executive and Mayor Fiorello H. LaGuardia [40]. After he had secured the legislative defeat of the proposed raise in the tax, Hoving organized and became chairman of the Committee to Balance the (1943-44) Budget Through Sensible Economies, which suggested ways to cut the resulting deficit. Hoving has also maintained business connections with firms in various fields: he is a director of the General Reinsurance, North Star Reinsurance, and Home Life Insurance companies.

The executive headed the organizing committee to form the United Service Organizations, was its first president and in 1946 the chairman of its board. From 1941 to 1943 he served as chairman of the board of directors of the USO camp shows. He was a director of the National War Fund in 1943. Chairman of the 1939 Citizens Appeal drive, and recipient of the Salvation Army Distinguished Auxiliary Service gold medal in June 1942, Hoving was both president of the Salvation Army Association of New York and vice-chairman of its New York Advisory Board from 1939 to 1946. During the Salvation Army's million-dollar fund-raising campaign in the winter of 1946, Hoving accepted the chairmanship of the commerce and industry committee of the drive. In 1939 Hoving was chairman of the organized hospitality unit of the National Advisory Committee for New York's World's Fair and a director of the New York Safety Council in 1943.

Hoving was married to Mary Osgood Field on November 4, 1924. There are two children: a son and daughter, Thomas Pearsall and Petrea Field. After a divorce, Hoving was married a second time, to Pauline (van der Voort) Dresser Rogers on April 30, 1937. The executive is an Episcopalian and a thirty-second degree Mason. He has blue eyes and dark hair "whose natural tendency to curl is sternly repressed." Over six feet tall, Hoving, according to a New York *Sun* interviewer, could easily model for a statue of a Viking. Twice mentioned in Walter Camp's All-American football selections, he was a member of the Brown University swimming team, and captain of his football and swimming varsities in high school. He has kept trim physically by shooting, golfing, and swimming at his various clubs.

References

Christian Sci Mon Mag p7 Jl 22 '40 por
N Y Sun p23 Ap 23 '40 por
National Cyclopædia of American Biography Current vol E p31
Who's Who in America, 1946-47
Who's Who in Commerce and Industry (1944)

HUNTER, GLENN 1896—Dec. 30, 1945 American actor; made debut in 1916; scored success in title roles of *Merton of the Movies* (1922-24) and *Young Woodley* (1925-27); last stage appearance in *Journey's End* in 1939; starred in many motion pictures.

Obituary

N Y Times p17 D 31 '45 por

HURLEY, CHARLES F(RANCES) Nov. 24, 1893—Mar. 24, 1946 Politician and real estate dealer; receiver-general (treasurer) of Massachusetts, 1931-37; Governor, 1937-39; member of Cambridge School Committee, 1919-31.

Obituary

N Y Times p25 Mr 25 '46

INGLIS, JOHN J. Aug. 26, 1867—Sept. 2, 1946 Dublin-born landscape artist; exhibited at the London Academy, Royal Hibernian Academy, and Scottish Academy; his visit to Canada early in the 1900's lengthened into wanderings during which he worked as lumberjack, prospector, and canal mule driver, before he settled in Rochester, New York, and resumed painting; he received prizes in Dublin and Rochester.

Obituary

N Y Times p23 S 4 '46

IRENE Dec. 8, 1907- Fashion designer
Address: b. c/o Metro-Goldwyn-Mayer Studios, Culver City, Calif.; h. 1124 Manning Ave., West Los Angeles, Calif.

"Fashion impresario" at Metro-Goldwyn-Mayer Studios, Irene must approve all gowns used in the film company's motion pictures. The designer, whose creations have won praise for their naturalness and originality, is considered the originator of the dressmaker suit and has

IRENE

also become known for her designing of figure-revealing gowns with draped or gathered lines.

At an age when most girls are conscious of feminine clothes, Irene was wearing outdoor togs almost exclusively. She spent the first sixteen years of her life on her father's Montana ranch near the town of Baker, where she was born December 8, 1907, to Emil and Maude (Watters) Lentz. After attending Baker High School, Irene, who wanted to become a pianist, registered for music courses at the University of Southern California. There she enjoyed planning her campus wardrobe and helping her friends with theirs, although she did not yet think of abandoning a musical career for one of clothes designing. That came when she happened to attend a class in designing: to please a friend who wished to study at the Wolfe School of Design but was too shy to go alone, Irene went with the class's first meeting. She came away with the decision to become a fashion designer.

After completing the course at the Wolfe School, Irene opened a dress shop on the campus of the University of Southern California. The shop, with its piano around which the college girls practiced amateur musicals, soon became a gathering place for the coeds. The day that Dolores Del Rio chanced upon it was a fortunate one for Irene: the actress told

her friends about the dresses at Irene's, and it was soon frequented by Hollywood's screen stars. Another result was the designer's meeting with Richard Jones, a movie director, to whom she was married. Recognizing her talents, he installed her in a fashionable shop in Hollywood. Not long afterward her husband died, and Irene, not caring to continue it alone, closed the shop. For a year and a half she traveled in Europe, studying designing and learning as well all the operations of dressmaking.

Upon her return from Europe, Irene was asked to head "the ultra-swank, custom-made salon" at Bullock's Wilshire store, where her seasonal openings became important events in the fashion world. At these openings, Irene, who had sold dresses in her campus shop at a maximum price of $29.50, was always embarrassed by the fabulously high prices which were now being charged for her creations. "She could never look a woman squarely in the eyes and say of a simple white piqué dress 'It's only two hundred and sixty-five dollars.'" To avoid this, she employed an assistant for opening days to answer questions about prices.

In the course of her seven years at Bullock's Irene planned wardrobes for many screen players, and designed the gowns in a number of their films. In 1938 her talents were employed by MGM in *Merrily We Live*, by United Artists in *Topper Takes a Trip*, and by Columbia in *You Can't Take It with You*. The following year Irene was responsible for the gowns in RKO's *Bachelor Mother* and *In Name Only*, and United Artists' *Intermezzo* and *Eternally Yours*; in 1940 she designed for RKO's *Lucky Partners*, Universal's *Hired Wife* and *Seven Sinners*, and United Artists' *The House Across the Bay*. The film credits for the wardrobe in such 1941 productions as *Twin Beds, Skylark, Bed Time Story, The Lady Is Willing, To Be or Not to Be* and United Artists' *That Uncertain Feeling* read "Gowns . . . by Irene."

In July 1942 Irene left Bullock's to succeed the renowned Adrian [41] as executive designer at MGM's Culver City studios. In this position she heads a staff of designers, each of whom she assigns to a different picture while she supervises them and designs "a bit here and there where it pleases her." To her mirror-lined office come such famous figures as Hedy Lamarr, Greer Garson, Judy Garland, Lana Turner, and Irene Dunne. She likes to help develop a new star's style in clothes: young actresses who often prefer low heels and sweaters outside the studios are transformed into the "glamorous type."

The fashion designer considers herself lucky to be able to design clothes for beautiful women. However, she maintains that "an actress doesn't really have to have a good figure to look entrancing on the screen. It's all in the way she carries herself and walks. If there is rhythmic music in her movements, it needn't matter that her shoulders are too broad or narrow, her waistline not slim enough; her hips too heavy, her ankles slightly thick." Irene advises the screen players to type themselves by always wearing the particular style that best suits them. "If you look best in ruffles, wear them on everything," she recommends. For herself she prefers suits. She also believes that hats are a necessary part of an outfit—"but not the silly type."

No matter how much a star may wish to buy a gown which she has worn in a film, she is unable to do so because of the studio's policy of keeping all the costumes used in pictures. After being re-used by bit players and then by extras, the dresses are hung in a storeroom. This is a policy of which Irene approves, for future designers may be asked to work on period pictures of the 1940's, and will find it much easier to reproduce a dress from the actual model itself than from a picture of it. While Irene's work is devoted almost exclusively to actresses, she is called in for consultation on costumes for men in period pictures. When she first came to MGM she wanted to avoid such films but has since come to like them. From the clothes angle, *The White Cliffs of Dover* was a particularly interesting picture to the Hollywood designer. Despite skillful make-up to give her a middle-aged appearance, Irene Dunne, in the short modern dresses of the 1940 scenes, looked younger than in the hobbleskirts of the 1914 scenes. Away from her work, Irene does not like to "talk shop": she will not criticize the gowns worn by women she may know unless she cannot possibly avoid it.

In 1936 the "statuesque, attractive" designer was married to screen writer Eliot Gibbons. They had met the year before at a party given by Dolores Del Rio, who was then married to Eliot's brother Cedric Gibbons, the supervising art director at MGM. A captain in the Air Transport Command during World War II, Eliot Gibbons still likes to pilot a plane in his free time and has persuaded his wife to take up flying. On their frequent hunting trips, she and her husband join such of their "Hollywood Who's Who" friends as the Gary Coopers and Clark Gable. Irene, who learned to shoot when she lived in Montana, also excels in bowling and skiing.

References

N Y Post p21 N 13 '43
N Y Sun p29 N 19 '43
International Motion Picture Almanac, 1943-44

IRWIN, MARGARET   Author

Address: b. c/o Harcourt, Brace & Co., 383 Madison Ave., New York

"The straight historian," says Margaret Irwin, the English writer of historical novels, "has only got to say a thing happened, and can give alternative possibilities for the reason; he can write 'he might have done this' or 'we may wonder why he didn't do that.' To which the historical novelist replies, like Dr. Johnson, 'Sir, you *may* wonder!'" For the novelist, she holds, must deny himself the luxury of speculation: he is "writing a story which happens to be true; and has got to re-create the scene and people from their point of view." Miss Irwin, whose latest historical novel is *Young*

Navana, Ltd., London

MARGARET IRWIN

Bess, has been described by Rose Feld in the New York *Herald Tribune* as possessing "the rare gift of charging her image of the past with the beat of the immediate present."

Margaret Irwin was born in England, the daughter of the late Andrew Clarke Irwin. She was brought up by her uncle, classics master at one of the English public schools. It was he who first stimulated her interest in history. She subsequently went to Oxford and there received her degree in English language and literature. After graduation, she turned to writing historical plays for children, which brought her considerable attention in England.

In the early 1920's she began writing a ghost story, but put it away for months or more at a time, bringing it out only when some new twist of plot had occurred to her. It was finally finished and published, in England in 1924, as *Still She Wished for Company*. Most of the first edition as well as the printing blocks were lost in a fire. However, it was reprinted nine years later and has been popular ever since. (It has never been issued in the United States.) *Still She Wished for Company* has remained Miss Irwin's favorite of her own writings.

Miss Irwin's first historical novel, *None So Pretty*, won her the publisher's (Chatto and Windus') historical novel prize in 1930. News of the award reached her on her wedding trip: she was married, evidently near the end of 1929, to John Robert Monsell, the artist. *The Royal Flush* was published in 1932, and *The Proud Servant* three years later. In 1937 came *The Stranger Prince*, the story of Rupert of the Rhine. (Rupert's sister—who appears also in *The Royal Flush* and again in a third and later book—is one of Miss Irwin's favorite characters, because "she painted and sold pictures to pay the butcher's bills.")

(Continued next page)

IRWIN, MARGARET—*Continued*

The Bride, published in 1939, is, according to the author, the "most maligned" of her books. It has been called unhistorical for the reason that its love story of Montrose and the Princess Louise was based on the written evidence of Louise's own sister, the Electress Sophia, in her private *Memoirs*. That evidence, the author explains, had been discussed by one historian, some time before she wrote it, as an "idle tale." She believes that historians, while on oath to tell the truth, do not always tell the same truth, simply because their estimates of their authorities differ. "I deny," she adds, "that it is 'unhistorical' to rely on informal writings such as letters, diaries, private memoirs of the time; if one dismisses these, there is little left to bank on but 'Acts of Parliament.'"

Her love story of Mary Queen of Scots—*The Gay Galliard*—was issued in 1942, and from it she has selected her "cherished" villain, Bothwell (if, she adds, he *is* a villain), "for although he abducted Mary Queen of Scots by force, he married her by persuasion." From this book she has also singled out one scoundrel for whom she has very little affection—"Good Lord James," bastard brother to Mary Queen of Scots. Cunningham Reid once told the author: "The best shot ever fired in Scotland was the shot that killed the Good Lord James." Critics were unanimous in their praise of this novel. Iris Barry wrote in the New York *Herald Tribune* that "there steals through it the unmistakable savor of a past which was once so terribly alive; seldom does one experience as keenly as here the momentary sensation of seeing and feeling into a long-ago yesterday."

Young Bess, a Literary Guild choice for April 1945, was written almost of necessity: the more she found out about the fabulous Queen Elizabeth, the more convinced she was that much of what cannot be actually explained about this figure is at least illuminated by a close study of her extraordinary childhood. Miss Irwin praises Tom Seymour, the gay soldier, sailor, and lover, for one thing if for nothing else—he was "the only man known to have smacked Queen Elizabeth." The work of ending the tale of *Young Bess* (which is being carried through to a later stage in her next book, along with another work on Sir Walter Raleigh) was something of a puzzle, and when the end came, it came suddenly. She wired her husband, "Have finished Bess," but the news was delivered as "Have finished the bass." *Young Bess* was, on the whole, well received by the critics, who agreed that Miss Irwin had "sketched a colorful background and created a warm and lively cast of characters." The author was criticized, however, for modernizing the dialogue. Concerning this, she says, "I constantly insert actual sentences used by the characters into my invented dialogue; and I could not do this if they did not slide in quite naturally as part of the general talk. Elizabeth's letters and sayings . . . have often an amazingly 'modern' ring."

Miss Irwin tells that she has had more accidental triumphs than planned ones. She was once waiting for the luncheon gong in the library of an Irish country house, and pulled out a battered old book without any title. For no good reason she "opened straight on an eye-witness account, in 1641, of Alasdair Macdonald walking down a street in Belfast with his wrist in a sling, having 'somewhat tired it, with killing fifty Scots and forty-five English in a day'"—and this at the very time she was writing of Alasdair and his campaign with Montrose.

IVES, BURL June 14, 1909- Ballad singer; actor

Address: b. c/o Twentieth Century-Fox Studios, Hollywood, Calif.

"I'm not an academic folklorist; I'm just a guy who sings," says Burl Ives, whom Carl Sandburg [40] calls "the mightiest ballad singer of any century." Ives has been singing the songs of the American people most of his life; and of late, in night clubs, theaters, and on the radio and records, the public has been hearing these tunes which the guitar-strumming minstrel has gathered through the many years of his wanderings up and down the land.

Like many of the songs he sings, the troubadour is a product of the Midwest, where he was born in Hunt Township in Jasper County, Illinois, on June 14, 1909. He was named Burl Icle Ivanhoe Ives, and while he does not know why he was given his unusual first name, he has remarked: "Webster says it's a knot in a stick of wood. That suits me all right." With an American ancestry dating back to the seventeenth century, Ives is a descendant of farmers and an "occasional preacher"—of English stock on his father's side and Kentucky Irish on his mother's. At the time of his birth his parents, Frank and Cordella Ives, were tenant farmers whose arduous existence never interfered with their singing. With their six children they were known to the neighbors as "those singing Iveses." From his grandmother, Kate White, who smoked a stone pipe, chewed tobacco, and looked, in his opinion, as though she stepped from an Elizabethan print, Burl Ives learned many of his songs. "I don't remember when I started singing," he says, "there wasn't any beginning. Ballad singing has been going on ever since people sang at all. It comes up like an underground stream and then goes back again. But it always exists." At an early age the boy was sent to a small school four miles from his home, where he had a new audience for his songs. Even earlier, at four, he had made his first public appearance at an old soldiers' picnic, singing the ballad "Barbara Allen," for which he was given a quarter.

The migratory life of tenant farmers meant hard work, hunger, and cold for the Ives family. With their possessions piled on a horse-drawn wagon, for many years they moved from farm to farm in southern Illinois, always returning to Hunt Township. But Frank Ives was ambitious: he studied engineering between seasons and before very long was helping to build bridges. The family moved to Newton, where the father established a business and their fortunes improved. Thus, by the time he was a high school sophomore, Burl found the going easier. During his first two years in the Hunt high school he had waited at table to pay for his meals, but now he could earn twenty-five dollars by singing and playing the banjo at the Robinson (Illinois) Rotary Club. (In Newton the young man was known as "Misery," from a role he had acted as a child, and it is a name which the people there still call him.) As a boy Burl had wanted to become a preacher, an ambition that fired him after attending an evangelistic meeting. But his first high school dance made him change his mind. "There they were," he recalls of his fellow students, "a-dancin' and a-singin' and a-laughin'. I said to myself, 'Boy, this ain't religion! It's music!' And I decided not to be a preacher." However, although Ives thereupon put aside the idea of entering the church, he did not turn immediately to music. He was quite sure, following his success as a fullback on the Newton high school eleven, that he wanted to become a professional football coach. After his graduation from high school in 1927 he entered the Eastern Illinois State Teachers College at Charleston, where he played football, sang in the college quartet, but "never did take to studies."

After two years of college, in June 1929 he started on his first cross-country trek, taking along his banjo, on which he had painted in collegiate fashion, "Burl Ives, the Vagabond Lover." These trips were to take him through Canada and Mexico and forty-six of the United States. In his own words, "I was curious to see what America looked like, so I found out the hard way. I bummed from one end of the country to the other." By his music the minstrel wanderer earned his meals, and sometimes a night's lodging during that summer. In the winter he returned to college. But his vagrant spirit prevailed, and shortly before he was graduated in 1931 he was on the road again. During the next two years he traveled thousands of miles, in the Northwest, the South, New England, always listening to and remembering the songs the people sang. The days he did not earn enough with his music he waited on tables or washed dishes in order to eat. Then for two years he lived in Terre Haute, Indiana, where he made radio appearances and played professional football. Momentarily prosperous, he bought a motorcycle on which he "roared lustily up and down the prairie." About this time he met Mrs. Clara Bloomfield, who aroused in him an interest in the great music and literature of the past. Of this friendship he once said, "I believe she has been the most important single influence in my life to date."

When Ives again resumed his roving, he visited steel mills and logging camps, and for a period was a singer with the Reverend J. Frank Norris' traveling company of evangelists. Finally he made a temporary home in New York at Columbia University's International House, where he worked as a bus boy and on Sundays sang at the Church of St. Mary the Virgin or Riverside Church. Oc-

BURL IVES

casionally, however, the wanderlust would seize him again and he would set out on another hitchhiking interlude. During his stays in New York he sang in bars, cafes, and Greenwich Village night clubs—until he got an urge to go on the stage. In 1938 he played his first professional roles at the Rockridge theater in Carmel, New York, taking character parts in Ah, Wilderness, Pocahontas Preferred, and Flight. This experience led to Broadway in 1938, when he was given the part of a tailor's apprentice in The Boys From Syracuse, George Abbott's '40 musical comedy based on Shakespeare's Comedy of Errors. Later that year he played another straight role in a musical, appearing as a retired general in the road company of the Rodgers '40 and Hart '40 musical I Married an Angel. Early in 1940 he played on Broadway in Heavenly Express, Albert Bein's fantasy in which ballads were sung, ironically enough not by Ives, but by actor John Garfield.

Thus far in New York Ives had been recognized only as a character actor. Not until two years after his arrival was he given a chance to sing. At this time Sigmund Spaeth '42, who had been impressed by his balladry, helped arrange for a radio appearance for him. On an eventful June day in 1940 he sang on an NBC broadcast, but nobody heard him: while he sang into a "dead" microphone special news flashes announced the fall of France. Subsequently, however, he was heard on several NBC programs. In the fall he was signed by CBS to sing his ballads on the program Back Where I Come From. When this series ended he remained with the network for his own show, The Wayfarin' Stranger. His first appearance on a stage as a singer was as a member of the GI chorus of Irving Berlin's '42 This Is The Army—after he was drafted into the Army in April 1942. While stationed with the show in New York he also did a radio

IVES, BURL—*Continued*

program, *G.I. Jive,* which was shortwaved from the studios of OWI to all Army bases overseas. After a nationwide tour with the Army show, Private Ives requested a transfer to the Air Corps. But in October 1943 he instead received a medical discharge and his war service was thereafter confined to entertaining servicemen and making recordings for OWI. He also recorded Russian folk songs as part of a cultural exchange program with the U.S.S.R., and in 1945 he introduced Frank Loesser's [45] tribute to the Infantry, "Rodger Young."

In the summer of 1944 Ives began a long night club engagement at Cafe Society Uptown, where his enthusiastic audiences were largely composed of cosmopolitan sophisticates. At the end of the year he opened in the Theatre Guild's *Sing Out, Sweet Land.* This unconventional show featured him and Alfred Drake [44] in an historical pageant of American music. While the critics generally welcomed it for its musical content, some found it handicapped by a poor script. But the same reviewers were unanimous in their praise of the balladeer: According to *Variety* "it was Ives who set the tone, created the atmosphere and proved the affinity between a minstrel and the people"; and Lewis Nichols declared, "The theater probably can offer nothing finer than Burl Ives singing 'Big Rock Candy Mountain' or the 'Blue Tail Fly'." (This last song is said to have been the favorite of Abraham Lincoln and is one of the folk singer's most popular numbers.) During rehearsals Ives had objected to singing "Frankie and Johnnie," which later proved to be the hit of the show. As a result of his performance in *Sing Out, Sweet Land,* the singer was chosen by his colleagues as "the outstanding supporting actor" of the 1944-45 season, which gave him the Donaldson Award.

In 1945 Ives appeared in his first film, cast as a singing cowboy in the Twentieth Century-Fox production of Will James's *Smoky,* which starred Fred MacMurray. Ives also appeared in a folk song feature with Josh White [44], Winston O'Keefe, and others. Twentieth Century-Fox "loaned" him to Walt Disney [40] for a film to be based upon *Midnight and Jeremiah,* written by Sterling North [43]. Before leaving for the film colony the singer gave a party for his friends aboard his houseboat which was pictorially reported in *Life* (July 2, 1945). His home at the time, the *Water Gypsy* is a reclaimed barge anchored off Whitestone Landing in Long Island Sound and is the realization of a childhood dream of the land-locked Midwesterner. Back in New York after his film work, Ives made his concert debut at Town Hall on December 1; a reviewer from *Musical America* praised Ives for employing "all [the] emotional fervor . . . usually associated with the finest interpretations of Brahms and Shubert *Lieder.*" His midnight concert the next year, December 15, 1946, was similarly successful. Record albums of Ives's music have been issued by Columbia, Asch, and Decca, and are preserved in the Library of Congress. It was the last company which released *The Lone-*

some Train, Earl Robinson's stirring Lincoln cantata, with Ives singing a principal part. The folk singer has sung at the White House, has appeared as guest performer on many radio programs, and for a period in 1945 was a weekly star on the *Radio Reader's Digest.* His own weekly show, a recorded song series originating in Hollywood, received its radio première over the Mutual Broadcasting System on October 18, 1946.

After Ives had become popular in New York he took a course in music dictation at New York University in order to be able to put on paper any unfamiliar folk songs he hears. He has written songs himself, including "Where Is the Old Man?," inspired by the plight of an old neighbor who was arrested for making corn liquor. The balladeer can spend hours "reeling out the mayhem and murder, the cradle ditties and love murmurs of six centuries," all of which he refuses to embellish. According to MacKinlay Kantor, "he is completely catholic in his taste and in his repertoire because of a natural desire to embrace and interpret simple people in every clime and century." A sponsor of the People's Songs Organization, Ives believes that American women have preserved their country's musical heritage by handing down the old songs through their children. One kind of folk music he does not sing is the Negro spiritual, because, he says, he has never heard a white person "give to a spiritual what it deserves." The minstrel considers hillbilly music synthetic—"It's written in New York by guys who never saw a hill."

The friendly, informal balladeer is a six-foot, two hundred-seventy-pound man with blue eyes and reddish brown hair. The bachelor became a benedict on December 6, 1945, when he was married to Helen Ehrlich, his former radio script writer. Ives enjoys eating and likes to prepare his own meals—he boasts of his fried chicken. On the subject of exercise, in the words of Mary Braggiotti of the New York *Post,* "when he feels the need of it he lies flat on the floor and relaxes." Occasionally the singer returns to his home town where his family still lives. Of his three sisters, two are teachers and one is married, while one of his brothers is a farmer and the other a mailman. Comments Burl Ives: "I'm the only one who didn't turn out to be much."

References

Collier's 113:77+ Ap 15 '44 por
Look 9:78 Ap 17 '45 por
N Y Herald Tribune V11 p2 N 26 '44
N Y Post Mag p29 O 5 '44 pors
N Y Times II p1 F 25 '45
N Y World-Telegram p25 D 16 '46
Sat Eve Post 217:12-13+ Ap 14 '45 pors

JACKSON, WILLIAM K(ENNETH)
Nov. 18, 1886- Businessman; lawyer; chamber of commerce executive

Address: b. c/o Chamber of Commerce of the United States, 1615 H St., N.W., Washington, D.C.; c/o United Fruit Company, 1 Federal St., Boston

William K. Jackson, "social-minded conservative," in May 1946 succeeded "progressive and aggressive" Eric A. Johnston '43 as president of the Chamber of Commerce of the United States of America. Founded in May 1912, this national body, as of 1946, is composed of 1,883 local chambers of commerce and 517 trade associations throughout the country, and lists its 1946 resources at more than five million dollars. More than one million businessmen and businesswomen comprise the membership of the twenty-three hundred organizations. Jackson also holds the offices of vice-president and general counsel of the United Fruit Company, with which he has been associated for about twenty-five years.

William Kenneth Jackson, the third of six children of William Kendrick and Medora Elizabeth (Montgomery) Jackson, was born November 18, 1886, in Denver, Tennessee. The boy's father was in the commission business, buying and selling grain, peanuts, and other produce in Denver, the town nearest which was a railway flag station. Six years after William's birth the family moved to Florida, where the elder Jackson raised fruit and mined phosphate, and William attended the Inverness public school in Citrus County. A high school graduate at thirteen—"the school wasn't like modern institutions," Jackson has insisted—he entered the University of Florida, where in 1904 he received his B.A. degree. At the university, Jackson was manager of the football team, and major of the land-grant institution's cadet battalion. Supplied with a free uniform and working in the president's office, the young man was able to meet his college expenses with his father's three-hundred-dollar contribution.

In 1905 Jackson got a job in the Florida legislature, in both houses of which his father served several terms. Appointed recording clerk for the lower house, he substituted occasionally for the reading clerk and studied stenography in his spare time. When the legislature adjourned, to help pay his way through the University of Virginia Law School he took a forty-five-dollar-a-month job in a Jacksonville law office. Then, during his first year at the university, he worked in the law library, tutored, and put his stenography to use, but had to do another stint at the law office to maintain his budget. After fifteen months he returned to the university, and in 1908 was awarded its LL.B. degree and elected to Phi Beta Kappa. He passed the Florida bar examination that year, formed a partnership, and started his practice in Jacksonville.

This was interrupted when, in 1909, upon the recommendation of his former law school, he went to Panama as an attorney on the staff of General George Goethals, chief engineer for the Panama Canal. In his first year in the tropics, Jackson was assistant attorney for the Isthmian Canal Commission and for the Panama Railroad Company, as well as assistant prosecuting attorney for the Canal Zone. In 1910, at the age of twenty-four, he became prosecuting attorney and, after four years, United States District Attorney of the Canal Zone District in 1914-15. Since Jackson had learned Spanish during his six years in Panama, he served as an inspector for the United States in the elections there. The attorney left

Chase-Statler Photo

WILLIAM K. JACKSON

Panama in 1915 and resumed his Florida law practice. Soon afterwards he went into the World War I Army and became a captain in the Chemical Warfare Service, fighting, he says, "in the bloodless battle of Washington."

After the war, in 1919, Jackson was commissioned by a client to inspect a mahogany concession in Honduras, to which a New Orleans group claimed prior rights. When settlement was made out of court, Jackson and the opposing attorney, Walter Spencer, "developed a vast mutual respect." Spencer, a counsel for the United Fruit Company, later called on Jackson for United in Colombia, whose laws are similar to those of Panama. Upon his return to the United States in 1922 with "a familiarity with Central American law codes, [and] an easy skill in dealing with Latin Americans," Jackson joined United Fruit's tropical division as a general attorney. He had moved to an office on State Street in Boston by 1926, and had taken his place on the board of directors as secretary of United Fruit. A few years later the executive became general counsel and vice-president of United Fruit, the positions he still holds in 1946.

Jackson had been president of the Boston Chamber of Commerce for a year when in May 1946 the directors of the Chamber of Commerce of the United States in its annual election chose its four-term vice-president for the office of president. When Jackson replaced retiring president Eric A. Johnston who, commented Time, "had probably made the most eloquent and effective exposition of the new social consciousness of many businessmen," there was "speculation on whether the chamber wasn't . . . turning back to its old hidebound ways." Business Week thought that "since he is a Democrat in politics and a middle-of-the-roader in economics, he can be counted on as a peacemaker between John-

JACKSON, WILLIAM K.—*Continued*

ston's young Turks and the chamber's conservatives. . . .Competing elements in the chamber expect him to negotiate acceptable compromises."

Upon his election Jackson classified himself as "a social-minded conservative": "Leaders of big business," he said, "are merely trustees today. They can't have a proprietary interest in their business like the rugged individualists we used to know. They . . . must be objective. . . .Business leaders must face and work for the solution of vital social problems." The new executive projected a three-point program: to "initiate a vigorous campaign" to revise the Wagner Labor Relations Act (former president Eric Johnston had "led and won a backstage fight which killed a proposal calling for repeal of the . . . act after the states had passed legislation to fill the gap"); to eliminate Federal control on building (productive capacity . . . must be released by 'price adjustments,'"); and, by October 31, to liquidate the Office of Price Administration.

On May 23, reported the New York *Times,* Jackson called for legislation which would outlaw "coercion and violence in the conduct of strikes and suggested that new consideration be given to compulsory arbitration, Government seizure and operation, with appropriate penalties for conspiracy or concerted activities designed to interrupt service or production, and application of antitrust laws to 'labor conspiracies which are in restraint of trade.'"

Then, on June 3, Jackson urged President Truman to approve the Case [46] Federal Mediation (Labor Disputes) Bill. The same day he announced his support of the three-and-three-quarter-billion-dollar loan to Great Britain to "check rather than aid some of the world tendencies toward socialism." A week later he urged that management "keep the public fully informed on industrial issues," be "realistic" with "whatever group" is "running things in Washington," and learn to "educate Washington bureaucrats and not antagonize them." Five weeks after his White House visit, he asked Congress in a statement to override the presidential veto of the Case bill. The executive office of the Chamber of Commerce announced June 30 that the national board of directors would "spearhead a large-scale advertising campaign to promote 'American opportunity.'" The directors would assist all national advertisers to "do some selling of the American economic system." In a radio speech on July 11, the Chamber of Commerce head said about price control: "Consumers should get out of their minds the thought that without OPA they were at the mercy of merchants, manufacturers, and farmers."

Later, again in reference to the labor situation, Jackson warned that labor would start "a vicious surge of inflation" if it attempted "another round of strike-enforced wage increases" (in order to make the Government "roll back" prices and liberalize wage stabilization standards). When the OPA decided to restore price ceilings on meat and promised "an all-out assault on the meat black market"

by an augmented OPA enforcement staff, Jackson predicted that the Government "could not prevent lawlessness in the meat industry" and that "the consumer will not be the gainer by price ceilings if meat returns to the black market" (New York *Post,* August 22, 1946). His group also asked for a cessation of Government food subsidies.

The United States Chamber of Commerce is one of the nonprofit trade organizations, according to Peter Edson of the New York *World-Telegram,* which is "worried" by the passage of the Congressional Reorganization Act. Hitherto not required to pay income taxes, the United States Chamber of Commerce, if it registers as a lobby and discloses the sources of its income, Edson stated, might find itself besieged by Federal income tax collectors. Jackson's organization has also asked for a "balanced Federal budget to be attained at lower than the current level of expenditures and taxation." A Federal curb on its own expenditures, Jackson asserted earlier at a meeting of the National Institute for Commercial and Trade Organization Executives, could "wield the country's most powerful weapon against inflation." (Late in November the Chamber of Commerce stated that it favored a 1947 Federal budget of less than twenty-five billion dollars.) Among other measures which would produce prosperity in the United States, Jackson believes, are "revision of the tax structure to encourage capital investment and to give a program of taxation for revenue instead of taxation for social reform," and "international cooperation to stabilize currencies, revive credits, and restore world trade" (New York *Sun,* September 26, 1946).

About two months after, he maintained, according to a New York *Herald Tribune* article (November 14, 1946) that the "United States must throw the full weight of its economic power into the scales of world affairs" since "an invasion of American dollars, machinery, industrial efficiency, and technical talent now will obviate the necessity for military measures later." The Chamber of Commerce head earlier had advocated closer military cooperation between the United States and Canada because of the division of the world into two separate spheres of influence, although at the same time he expressed the belief that the United Nations "still held the key to permanent peace." Among his other public statements in 1946, Jackson approved of the naming of W. Averell Harriman [46] as Secretary of Commerce, asked for "cooperation among Government, management and labor to make the free enterprise system, now virtually restored, work for full production," and predicted that if there were no strikes the year 1947 would see a record amount of goods being produced for consumer use, with supplies in many commodities balancing demand, all of which "points to an easing of pressure for higher prices."

William Jackson is a member of the American Bar Association, the American Society of International Law, and the Foreign Law Association. He was married in September 1916 to Katherine Mitchell, a sister of the well-known American airman General William (Billy) Mitchell. The business executive is a "spare, square-jawed . . . man with shoots of silver in his dark hair." Friendliness and modesty are two characteristics often attributed to him, as are "incisive reasoning" and "legal imagination." He spends his free time on his Dublin (New Hampshire) farm, sometimes accompanied by the five children, Danforth, Katherine Mitchell Bass, Richard Montgomery, Joan Jackson Mason, and Alexander, and his five grandchildren. Stonewall Farm has dairy cattle; and the greenhouse there, his Boston rose garden, and the hobby he developed in Panama of collecting rare orchid plants have given the businessman the nickname, within his family, of "Green Hands."

References

Bsns W p8 My 4 '46 por
N Y Sun p6 My 18 '46
Nation's Bus 34:56 Je '46 por
Time 47:85 My 13 '46 por
Who's Who in America, 1946-47

JAMES, ALEXANDER R. Dec. 22, 1890—Feb. 26, 1946 American painter of figures, portraits, and landscapes; some of his works are in the Metropolitan Museum of Art and other institutions; son of William James.

Obituary

N Y Times p25 F 27 '46

JAMES, W. FRANK May 23, 1873—Nov. 17, 1945 Former United States Republican Representative from Michigan (1915-35); served as chairman of the House Military Affairs Committee; Mayor of Hancock, Michigan (1908-9); state Senator (1911-14).

Obituary

N Y Times p44 N 18 '45

JEANS, SIR JAMES (HOPWOOD) Sept. 11, 1877—Sept. 17, 1946 English physicist, astronomer, and author; worked on kinetic theory of gases and on radiations; among his scientific works are *Radiation and the Quantum-Theory* (1914), *Introduction to the Kinetic Theory of Gases* (1940); widely known for his books for the layman, among them *The Universe Around Us* (1929), *The Mysterious Universe* (1930), *Through Space and Time* (1934). See *Current Biography* 1941 Yearbook.

Obituary

N Y Times p7 S 17 '46

JEWETT, FRANK B(ALDWIN) Sept. 5, 1879- Electrical engineer
Address: b. c/o National Academy of Sciences, 2101 Constitution Ave., N.W., Washington, D.C.

The president of the National Academy of Sciences, Frank B. Jewett, has been called by the *Journal of Applied Physics* "a pioneering prophet of the application of the research

methods of science." In the forty years that he spent as an executive engineer with the American Telephone and Telegraph Company before 1944, he effected advances in the fields of transcontinental and transoceanic telegraphy, aircraft communications, radio, and television.

Frank Baldwin Jewett was born on September 5, 1879, in Pasadena, California. His mother was the former Phebe Mead; his father, Stanley P. Jewett, was descended from a Yorkshireman who had settled in Massachusetts in 1632. Stanley P. Jewett was one of the civil engineers who built the Atchison, Topeka, and Santa Fe Railroad. After his elementary education in the public schools of his native State, young Jewett decided to follow his father's profession. He received his B.A. in 1898 from Throop Polytechnic Institute (now the California Institute of Technology) and his Ph.D. from the University of Chicago four years later. He has since been awarded honorary D.Sc. degrees from Dartmouth and New York (1925), Columbia and Wisconsin (1927), Rutgers (1928), Chicago (1929), Harvard (1936), Pennsylvania (1940), and Boston (1944) universities; honorary LL.D. degrees from Miami (1932), Rockford (1939), Norwich (1944), and Yale (1946) universities; and an honorary D.Eng. degree from the Case School of Applied Sciences (1928).

While working for his doctorate at the University of Chicago, Jewett was research assistant to Professor A. A. Michelson there in 1901-2. Afterward he went to the Massachusetts Institute of Technology as an instructor in physics and electrical engineering. His career in teaching lasted until 1904 when the American Telephone and Telegraph Company offered him a position as transmission and protection engineer at sixteen hundred dollars a year (then a high salary for a beginner). In 1912 he was sent to the Western Electric Company, part of the American Telephone and Telegraph parent company, as assistant chief engineer, becoming chief engineer four years later, and a vice-president of the firm in 1922. In this period, he constructed many of the company's long distance telephone lines, the most notable of which is the transcontinental from New York to San Francisco. He also introduced and developed the loading coil for telephone lines, did development work on the vacuum tube for use in telephone repeaters, and directed work which resulted in the first successful transatlantic telephone call in 1915.

Much of the work Jewett did at Western Electric was designed for military use in World War I. In 1917 he was a major in the Signal Officers' Reserve Corps of the United States Army, advancing to the rank of lieutenant colonel in the Signal Corps on December 1, 1917, in which grade he served during 1918. He worked on the telephone system for the AEF in France and later developed their aircraft communications. While his radio wireless telephone experiments at Montauk Point, Long Island (1914-15), set the standard for later apparatus and systems, the first actual tests of radiophones for airplanes were at Langley Field, Virginia (June-July 1917), when Jewett supervised the establishing of contact

FRANK B. JEWETT

between planes, and between planes and the ground. At Western Electric Jewett put the manufacture of the vacuum tube (essential to military signaling) on a quantity basis for war production for the Government. He was one of four advisory members on the special submarine board of the United States Navy, as well as a member of the State Department's special committee on cables. In 1919 he was awarded the Distinguished Service Medal "for exceptionally meritorious and conspicuous service with the development of the radio telephone and the development of other technical apparatus for the Army."

After the end of the war, Jewett continued in the American Telephone and Telegraph Company as the vice-president in charge of the company activities in research and development, for nineteen years beginning in 1925. In the same year he assumed the presidency of the Bell Telephone Laboratories, the official research organ of the Bell Telephone System, part of the American Telephone and Telegraph Company (Jewett had been chief organizer of the laboratories originally). His engineering advances there include pioneering work in the dial system, radio broadcasting, television, sound motion pictures, the electric phonograph, and the high-speed submarine telephone cable. On October 1, 1940, the former president became chairman of the laboratories' board of directors, remaining in that capacity until he reached the retirement age in 1944. (Upon Jewett's retirement, the American Telephone and Telegraph Company established five annual fellowships in his name to be used for post-doctorate work in the physical sciences.)

Leaving private industry, Jewett was able to devote more time to the National Academy of Sciences, of which he had been elected president in 1939. The association, described by *Newsweek* as "the nation's most exclusive scientific body" (restricted to 450 scientists), was

incorporated by Congress in 1863 to assure to the Federal Government a continuous flow of scientific information. According to its charter, the academy is an official adviser without any delegated powers; Jewett, however, points out that "the strongest authority you can give to anybody is the authority of distinction without power." In 1916 the National Research Council was created as a permanent subsidiary agency of the National Academy of Sciences. Jewett was chairman of the council's division on engineering and industrial research from 1923 until 1927, was a member of the physics division's committee on radio, and is now, in 1946, a member of the National Research Council's committee on scientific aids to learning.

Jewett, who had been a member of President Roosevelt's [42] Science Advisory Board from 1933 until 1935, was appointed to the Office for Emergency Management when it was created by executive order in 1940. In June of the same year the National Defense Research Committee of the Office of Scientific Research and Development was created with Jewett as one of eight members—there were five civilians, one representative each of the Army and Navy, and the United States Commissioner of Patents. Jewett was in charge of the group's research in transportation, communications, and submarine warfare, directing its submarine warfare laboratories. During the years that followed, Jewett was a member of the coordination and equipment division of the Signal Corps, and consultant to the Chief of Ordnance of the United States Army. In 1944 he was one of twelve civilian, Army, and Navy members of a committee to create a high command in science, equivalent in rank to the Army and Navy high commands. At the request of the armed services the following year, Jewett set up the Research Board of National Security, composed of twenty civilian and twenty military scientists, to continue the development of weapons. (This group served the interim period between the expiration of the Office of Scientific Research and Development, and the creation of a new group by Congress.)

In discussing the atom bomb Jewett has said that he knows of no defense against it, nor does he anticipate an early application of atomic fission to commercial use. He favors civilian rather than military control of scientific research and, while he is not opposed to direct or indirect Government aid "when it is clear that the public interest demands it," he was against the proposed Federal Research Foundation. The prime essential of "first-class fundamental scientific research, the only kind that is worth while," is "complete freedom for experimentation and operation unhampered by the limitations of a politically controlled agency." He favors the free flow of scientific information both nationally and internationally, keeping "secrets" at a minimum; he had scored the 1942 war secrets bill for providing more secrecy than was "really justified."

Called "one of the ten men the world could least afford to lose in 1930," Jewett has received a number of citations: he was awarded the Fourth Order of the Rising Sun (1923) and the Third Order of the Sacred Treasure

(1930) from Japan; the Edison Medal (1928); the Faraday Medal (1935), awarded by the British Institute of Electrical Engineers, of which Jewett is a member; the Franklin Medal (1936); the Washington Award (1938); the John Fritz Gold Medal (1939), the highest American engineering honor, which both Edison and Marconi had received; and the Medal for Merit (1946). Jewett is the author of many brochures, articles, and public addresses on physical and electrical subjects, including vapor density of sodium vapor, the magnetic change of resistance in bismuth, and the effect of pressure on insulation resistance.

The president of the National Academy of Sciences was vice-chairman of the Engineering Foundation from 1919 until 1925. He is a fellow of the Academy of Arts and Sciences, the American Physical Society, the American Institute of Electrical Engineers (he was president in 1922-23), the Acoustical Society of America, the Institute of Radio Engineers, and the Telephone Society (he was president in 1914). The engineer is also a member of the Society for the Promotion of Engineering Education and of the New York Electrical Society. The president and a trustee of the New York Museum of Science and Industry, he is also a member of the American Philosophical Society and serves on the Council of Eye Banks for Sight Restoration, which aids those with corneal defects by the grafting of healthy corneas.

His work with colleges brought Jewett to the chairmanship of the Milton Fund at Harvard, beginning in 1924; and to the trusteeships of Princeton University, the Carnegie Institute of Washington, the Carnegie Institue of Technology (Pennsylvania), the Woods Hole Oceanographic Institute, and the Tabor Academy. He is a life member of the Massachusetts Institute of Technology Corporation, and was president of the M.I.T. alumni association in 1939-40. In the suburban township where he lives, Jewett was president before becoming vice-president of the Millburn, New Jersey, board of education, and serves as a director of the First National Bank of Millburn. His fraternities are Delta Upsilon, Sigma Xi, and Tau Beta Pi; his clubs are the University, Railroad-Machinery, Engineers, and Century (New York), Cosmos (Washington, D.C.), and Short Hills (New Jersey); and he is an American Legionnaire. Jewett was married on December 28, 1905, to Fannie C. Frisbie of Rockville, Illinois. Their children are Harrison Leach and Frank Baldwin, Junior. The gray-haired engineer and scientist looks happiest when smoking his cigar.

References

American Men of Science (1944)
National Cyclopædia of American Biography Current vol C p272
Who's Who in America, 1946-47
Who's Who in Commerce and Industry (1944)
Who's Who in Engineering, 1941

JODL, ALFRED (yō'd'l) 1892(?)—Oct. 16, 1946 Chief of German General Staff, initialed all Nazi war orders; tried by the International Military Tribunal, judged "in the strict military sense the actual planner of the war . . . active in planning the attack on Czechoslovakia . . . in preparing the [Norwegian] attack . . . in planning against Greece and Yugoslavia"; condemned and hanged.

Obituary

N Y Times p1+ O 16 '46

JOHNSON, CHARLES SPURGEON July 24, 1893- College president; sociologist

Address: b. c/o Fisk University, Nashville, Tenn.; h. 1611 Meharry Blvd., Nashville, Tenn.

Director of the Julius Rosenwald Fund's interracial relations program is Charles Spurgeon Johnson, a sociologist whose work has been that of interpreting Negroes to white people and white people to Negroes, Southerners and Northerners, country people and city dwellers, to each other. Three important appointments came to him in 1946: he was sent to Japan by the State Department as a member of a group to organize the Japanese educational system; was appointed a delegate to the United Nations Educational, Scientific, and Cultural Organization; and elected president of Fisk University.

Charles Spurgeon Johnson, born in Bristol, Virginia, on July 24, 1893, was named after a Baptist preacher of that day, Charles Spurgeon. He was the oldest of five children of the Reverend Charles Henry Johnson, an emancipated slave whose former master had drilled him in Latin, Greek, Hebrew, and in English and American literature. The minister, who "carried his gospel straight into the quarters of sin and riot," once set his "five feet four inches of moral courage" in the path of a lynch mob in an unsuccessful attempt to stop it. The boy's mother, Winifred (Branch) Johnson, wove spirituals and work songs into hymns, some of which are still sung in Bristol today.

Young Johnson, who had read many of the classical and theological works in his father's library, in 1909 was sent to the Wayland Academy, a Baptist mission school for Negroes (the school was then a part of Virginia Union University in Richmond). His academic career there was enlivened by many quiet pranks which, according to Edwin R. Embree in *Thirteen Against the Odds*, the studious Johnson perpetrated by "bending" rules without "breaking" them. After his graduation as valedictorian in 1913, Johnson went on to the university itself. From the time when he was fourteen he had worked in the summer months as stevedore, ditchdigger, and as messboy and night watchman on a New York-Providence steamboat. During the college semesters he worked as dormitory helper, waiter, and library monitor; and he also found time for playing tennis, managing the football and baseball teams, singing in quartets, debating, editing the college journal, and serving as president of the student council. A sociology major, with some field work at the Richmond Welfare Associa-

Fabian Bachrach

CHARLES SPURGEON JOHNSON

tion to his credit, Johnson completed the four-year course with honors in three years, receiving his B.A. from Virginia Union University in 1916. (His father had received his Bachelor of Divinity degree at the same institution in 1883.) Johnson earned his Ph.B. in 1917 on a fellowship at the University of Chicago, where he was greatly influenced by Robert E. Park, who was called "the father of American sociology."

Johnson enlisted in World War I early in 1918, served in the AEF infantry in France (he fought in the Meuse-Argonne offensive), and received his discharge as a regimental sergeant major after a year. While on his way home, Johnson saw the riots in Brest, Norfolk, and Washington. He arrived in Chicago a week before "the worst of them all," the Chicago race riot of 1919 in which 578 persons were wounded or killed. The catastrophe, Johnson has said, was in part a result of the "mass migration, like unto the flight of children of Israel out of Egypt," which had moved half a million Negroes north from the Southern states. Johnson, who was among those shot at in the riot, was appointed an aide to the Governor's committee which investigated the riot, and became coauthor of the committee's report of the disturbance, *The Negro in Chicago* (1922). The book has since been described as "one of the landmarks in social research."

Although he had created and had directed the research and investigations department of the Chicago Urban League from 1917 until 1919, Johnson dates his career in sociology from 1919, when he joined the Chicago Commission on Race Relations as associate executive secretary. He left that position two years later, in 1921, to direct the research and investigations of the National Urban League in New York. This social service agency helps Negroes in urban centers to find employment.

In 1923 Johnson founded *Opportunity,* the National Urban League's "Journal of Negro life," and was its editor until leaving the league in 1928. The magazine became a channel for Negro expression in literature, art, and music.

In 1928 Johnson became director of the department of social sciences and a professor of sociology at Fisk University in Nashville, Tennessee. About eighteen years later, on October 29, 1946, Johnson succeeded Dr. Thomas E. Jones as president of the university (the term of office to begin on July 1, 1947). Dr. Charles Spurgeon Johnson thus becomes the first Negro to hold that administrative post since the institution's founding eighty years earlier by the American Missionary Society and the Western Freeman's Bureau. Biracial in faculty and student body, Fisk University has been a leader in the study and betterment of interracial relations.

The college president, who was codirector of the racial relations program of the Julius Rosenwald Fund in 1942, became director of the program in 1943. Activities of the organization have been directed toward stimulating and supporting other agencies concerned with Negroes and Negro-white relations in America. The fund, of which Johnson is also a trustee, makes financial grants to such groups, prepares studies and reports, distributes books and pamphlets, arranges conferences and consultations, and awards approximately seventy annual fellowships to exceptionally promising Negroes, white Southerners, and race-relations workers. Evolved from a plan to construct schools for Negro children, the fund now supports an education program for teachers in all rural schools in the South. Its ultimate aim is the elimination of racial friction everywhere in the United States.

Johnson believes that "the pathological aspects of race relations will not be solved simply by fellowship or good will, or by concentration on the issue of race alone, but will have to be worked out as a part of the general social and economic framework"—a high level of employment is one of the indispensable conditions for permanent improvement. Many of his ideas may be traced back to the investigations of Negro migration which he did for the Carnegie Foundation in 1918; he has been able to explore the ideas further at the Swarthmore College institute of race relations which he first directed in 1933, and at New York University where he lectured in 1938. In 1943 Johnson also became director of the racial relations program sponsored by the American Missionary Association of the Congregational Christian Churches, which had established the first schools for Negroes in the South following their emancipation.

One of the earliest Government missions upon which Johnson has been sent was the three-man League of Nations commission sent in 1930 to investigate charges of slavery in Liberia, then Africa's only republic. His report exposed the exploitation of natives through domestic and debt slavery, "pawning" of relatives for collateral, and labor conscription. After World War II Johnson became a member of the education mission sent to Japan by the State Department at the request of General Douglas MacArthur '41. One of twenty-six educators who participated, Johnson helped to recommend changes desirable for the structure of that country's school system. President Truman '45 later appointed him a delegate to the United Nations Educational, Scientific, and Cultural Organization scheduled to meet in Paris in November 1946.

Johnson was secretary of the Negro housing committee at President Hoover's '43 Conference on Home Building and Home Ownership in 1931, later worked on President Roosevelt's '42 Farm Tenancy Committee in 1936-37, and aided the Department of Agriculture to formulate plans for "the extension of the democratic process to rural areas." Johnson also served on the Department of Labor's Fair Labor Standards Committee as a representative of the public, and on its National Commission on Children in Wartime, which reviewed all aspects of children's needs during the war and in the transition to peace.

In education, Johnson is a member of the National Education Association, a trustee of Bethune-Cookman, LeMoyne, and Tillotson Colleges, and a board of directors member of the Colonial Students Advisory Commission. He is associated with the Social Science Research Council, the editorial board of the *American Sociological Review,* the *Encyclopedia of the Negro,* and the Schomburg Collection of Negro Literature at the New York Public Library. His work with the Negro has also taken him into the National Tuberculosis Association as a member of the committee on that disease among the Negroes, and into the Committee on Minority Groups in Economic Reconstruction. In the South, he is director of the Southern rural division of Negro youth for the American Youth Commission of the Council on Education, a member of the Southern Sociological Society (until 1945 he was first vice-president, in 1945-46 he served as president), and a member of the executive committee of that society's commission to study lynching. He was on the organizing committee and then became a co-head of the new Southern Council on Regional Development, and is leader and spokesman for the Congress of Southern Negroes. A member of the Tennessee Valley Authority's sociology committee in 1934, Johnson was in 1946 a member of the advisory board of the National Youth Administration of Tennessee, and a trustee of the Delta Cooperative Farm.

Johnson has been the author, coauthor, and editor of books and magazine articles on racial sociology. *Shadow of the Plantation* (1934), which analyzed "one of the cancers on our body politic," was a best seller among social texts. In *Growing Up in the Black Belt* (1941), prepared for the American Youth Commission, Johnson writes of the "pervasive strain of resignation and futility" found in many Negro youths interviewed. "Moving and often shocking," wrote a reviewer in *Newsweek* on February 17, 1941, the book illustrates that "the American Youth Commission researchers have the knack of dressing up their sociological data in readable English." *Patterns of Negro Segregation* (1943) is a study of the institu-

tions, the ideology supporting segregation, and the behavioral response such practices evoke in the depressed tenth of the nation's population. "Whatever fury the author, himself a Negro, may have experienced in the preparation of this volume, he has effectively sublimated in the writing," wrote Henry Lee Moon in the *New Republic* of March 8, 1943. *To Stem This Tide* (1944) was compiled at Fisk University with aid from the Julius Rosenwald Fund to help remove the "sins of caste" from American life. The sociologist's analysis of the country's areas of racial tension drew praise for what a *Christian Century* reviewer called Johnson's "rare skill and Christian statesmanship." With two new books in progress, Johnson is also revising his text *The Negro in American Civilization* (1930).

Among the awards that Johnson has received are the 1930 William E. Harmon gold medal for distinguished achievement among Negroes in science, the Wolf-Anisfield prize of 1938 for his book *The Negro College Graduate* (1936), and a citation for public service by the Alumni Association of the University of Chicago. He was awarded the honorary degrees of Litt. D. by Virginia Union University in 1928 and of Doctor of Humane Letters by Howard University in 1941. Alpha Phi Alpha is his fraternity, and the political independent is a member of the Congregational Church. Johnson was married on November 6, 1920, to Marie Antoinette Burgette, then a teacher at a Chicago girls' school, who had a reputation for being one of the most progressive citizens in her native Milwaukee. They have three sons, Charles Spurgeon, Robert Burgette, and Jeh Vincent, and a daughter, Patricia Marie. The brown-eyed, black-haired sociologist is no pedant: according to Embree, he also enjoys the lighter moments of life.

References
Embree, Edwin R. Thirteen Against the Odds (1944)
Leaders in Education (1941)
Who's Who in America, 1946-47
Who's Who in Colored America, 1941-44

JOHNSON, ED(WIN CARL) Jan. 1, 1884- United States Senator from Colorado
Address: b. Senate Office Bldg., Washington, D.C.; h. Craig, Colo.

The year 1946 marks the tenth year that Kansas-born Ed Johnson has served his adopted State, Colorado, as Democratic member of the United States Senate. A former railroad man and cattle rancher, Senator Johnson was a State official, in a number of capacities, for thirteen years before he was elected to his Congressional post in 1936. Although an outstanding, avowedly anti-New Deal Democrat, he has, nevertheless, supported many of the Administration's measures.

Edwin Carl Johnson was born on January 1, 1884, on a farm in Scandia, Kansas, to Nels and Annabelle (Lunn) Johnson. His parents were Swedish immigrants; and, according to their son, "the proudest day of their lives" was that on which both became naturalized citizens of

ED JOHNSON

the United States. Young Johnson was reared
on a cattle ranch in western Nebraska, where
he remained until he was seventeen. Then,
during the years from 1901 to 1909, Ed Johnson worked as a railroad section hand, next as
a telegrapher, and lastly as a train dispatcher.
Meanwhile, in between his railroad trips to,
and assignments in, a number of Midwestern
States, he found time to attend the Lincoln
(Nebraska) High School from which he was
graduated in 1903.

Because of ill health, Johnson in 1909 was
obliged to leave his railroad post. So that he
might recover, he went to Colorado with his
wife, the former Fern Claire Armitage of
Kearney, Nebraska, to whom he had been married in February 1907. In the northwestern
region of that State Johnson became a homesteader and built a sod-and-log house on his
acres. After Johnson regained his health, there
followed a varied career for the industrious
homesteader during which he tended his cattle
ranch (1910-20), directed, as manager, a farmers' cooperative milling elevator and produce
business at Craig, Colorado (1920-30), and
for a time taught school. Johnson was attracted to politics, too: in 1922 the Kansas-
born Coloradan was chosen a Democratic member of the State legislature, to which, until
1930, he was subsequently re-elected. For the
1930-32 term of office, Johnson was Colorado's
Lieutenant Governor; and the State elections of
1932 and 1934 resulted in two terms of governorship for him.

In 1936 Johnson was elected to the United
States Senate. An isolationist in foreign affairs and a "consistent" New Dealer in the
majority of the Democratic Administration's
domestic measures, he first parted company
with the New Deal, according to Arthur
Krock '⁴² (New York Times, March 23, 1944),
when the Roosevelt Administration sought, by
means of a Congressional bill, to enlarge the

Supreme Court in 1937. A few years later
when the question of the validity of a third
term was brought up, Johnson began attacking
the chief executive's silence on the issue and
opposed his renomination. Asserting that
Rooseveltian foreign policy was warmongering
in nature, the Coloradan maintained that only
Senator Burton Wheeler '⁴⁰ could defeat Wendell Willkie '⁴⁰, the Republican Presidential candidate, and advocated establishment of an isolationist third party. Four years later, the increasingly critical opponent of the New Deal
labeled Roosevelt's 1940-44 Presidential office
the "term of appeasement" in home and foreign
relations (New York Times, March 22, 1944),
and criticizing what he termed one-man party
control, declared that a fourth term, "if it ever
materializes," would be called the "term of
defeat and frustration." Earlier, in November
1943 Senator Johnson had urged his party to
draft General George C. Marshall '⁴⁰ as the
Democrats' next Presidential candidate.

Senator Johnson, some months before the Japanese attack on Pearl Harbor, had advocated
extensive national defenses and a modern mechanized army and was interested in bettering
the conditions for soldiers. A Military Affairs
Committee member and head of a subcommittee
studying Army-recommended pay increases,
Johnson with the aid of his colleagues formulated (October 1941) a bill doubling the
previous salary for all entering servicemen,
and providing for a more rapid advancement to
the rank of corporal and sergeant. To aid the
families of men taken in the general draft of
fathers (begun October 1, 1943), Johnson introduced a bill, subsequently adopted, which allowed for a substantial increase in allotment
for each child. In March 1944 Senators Johnson and Reynolds became the authors of a
soldier bonus bill bestowing maximum bonus
payments of $3,500 on men and women serving
in continental United States, $4,500 on those
serving abroad. Their proposal was superseded by the GI bill. During 1943 and 1944
Johnson also introduced a number of measures
providing for the appointment of women physicians into the Army and Navy, for "real instead of relative" ranks for members of the
Army Nurse Corps (he objected to the proposed nurse draft), and for Army commissions for women dietitians and therapists. Before this he was a sponsor of free postage for
men and women in the services.

World War II posed other domestic issues
for the Senator from Colorado. When an unsettled strike among certain railway brotherhoods prompted the Government to give control of the railroads to the Army late in December 1943, Ed Johnson, called an expert
in railroad labor problems, protested that the
"seizure" was unnecessary and premature since
he believed the recalcitrant brotherhoods would
have come to an agreement shortly. In the
same year, six months earlier, he had voted in
favor of an amendment increasing soil conservation payments to farmers, thus supporting
Henry A. Wallace's '⁴⁰ wartime crop program,
and had helped to defeat an amendment designed
to terminate the FSA, had opposed the antilabor Smith-Connally antistrike bill, and had

upheld the NYA. The projected national service system, under Congressional consideration in January 1944, he objected to on the grounds that it was "labor conscription," and in the same month the Senator voted for the continuation of price control and upheld an amendment abolishing a requirement that labor unions and cooperatives file income reports for taxation purposes. Bills to end the poll tax and to grant unemployment benefits to former war workers during the reconversion period also gained his support. Johnson's other activities included his taking issue with the Administration on "livestock ceilings, mineral controls, and a highway-construction policy that departed from the former State-Federal equal division of cost," and his favoring, for the soldier vote, the "use of the Federal ballot . . . only on application and when State ballots were not available." The Surplus Property Act, which Johnson drew up (based on the suggestions of Bernard Baruch), was passed in the fall of 1944.

Originally opposed to United States entry into the world conflict, Johnson, after the United States had entered the war, rejected in a radio address (May 1943) the proposed postwar international police force (it might be used to preserve "international injustices," he thought) and remarked that the war was imperialistic. "We are in this war to preserve the British Empire and the Soviet Union and to liberate the so-called Republic of China." He questioned, too, President Roosevelt's right to make postwar commitments. When the Morgenthau plan to deindustrialize Germany was published Johnson denounced it as being "poorly conceived" and as rousing the Nazis to a greater display of fighting force. Insisting that "something more" than unconditional surrender and the Morgenthau plan was needed, Senator Johnson in October 1944 advanced a seven-point program dealing with the treatment of a defeated Germany. Among the points were included the restriction of Germany's borders to those of 1932 (except for East Prussia), transfer of all German-speaking populations to Germany, trial of Nazi war criminals (he limited the number to fifty thousand), and disarmament of Germany and prohibition of rearmament. Violation by Germany of any of the clauses should result in immediate occupation by all three Allies. The same month witnessed his recommendation for postwar military intelligence measures to keep the United States public informed of possible war preparations elsewhere.

As chairman of the veterans affairs subcommittee of the Senate Finance Committee, Johnson, in the spring of 1945 and following the end of the European phase of the war, launched his campaign to reduce the number of men in the armed forces. He called for a speedy replacement of all servicemen entitled to discharge in the Army. In January of 1945 the now ranking member of the Senate Military Affairs Committee was named chairman of a special subcommittee to "explore" the demobilization situation when United States soldiers began to register protests against being retained in the service after the end of the war.

Reducing Army appropriations, he suggested, would force demobilization. Johnson proposed, too, that the Army attract volunteers (instead of relying upon conscripts) by improving the status of enlisted men and by abolishing its caste system. He favored "additional corrective and liberalizing legislation" for disabled veterans; and he introduced legislation for an increase in veterans' pensions to meet the rising cost of living, and for terminal leave pay for enlisted personnel. In 1946 he supported the Thomas bill creating a unified military and naval command and bureaus for "industrial mobilization" and scientific research under a Department of National Security. The Senator has opposed universal military training as being "Fascist conceived, calculated to destroy democracy and the free enterprise system." Denying in the Senate late in December 1946 that he was a pacifist and indicating that he would support "whatever national defense is necessary for our full and complete protection," Johnson added, as reported in the New York Times, December 24, 1946: "Our first line of military defense should be an intelligence corps; next we should have an industry which is easily convertible to war production; then a first-class scientific research department, and, last, well-trained technicians in aeronautics, nautics, electronics, logistics, and the operation of military weapons. . . .One chemist or one physicist is more valuable to our defenses than are 10,000 foot soldiers."

During 1945 and 1946 Senator Johnson's international policy record included his vote against the Reciprocal Trade Agreement Act of 1945 designed to decrease tariffs by agreement an additional 50 per cent; his indictment of British actions to debar further Jewish entry into Palestine; and his attempt to block the $3,750,000,000 loan to Great Britain. The Senator who visualizes no hope for humanity except through an "organized world effort to stop war backed by force" upholds the U.N. and in 1946 favored a contribution of United States troops to the U.N. international force. Appointed a member of the Senate Special Committee on Control of Atomic Energy (early in August 1946 Johnson was made a member of the permanent joint Congressional committee on atomic energy), the Senator introduced (but did not support, he said) in the Senate the May-Johnson atomic control bill, providing for an administrator and a part-time committee of nine. Its opponents stated that it would permit military instead of civilian or part civilian control of the atom. He did support, however, a modified version of the McMahon[45] atomic control bill, to which he had introduced an amendment. Late in June that year the Colorado Senator, who has stressed that it is the opportunity of the United States, by employing the atomic bomb, "to compel mankind to adopt a policy of lasting peace or be burnt to a crisp," placed himself on record as favoring international atomic development and control as given to the U.N. in the Baruch plan.

Aside from his membership on Senate military, finance, and atomic control committees, Senator Johnson has served on the Interstate Commerce, Mines and Mining, and Public Lands

JOHNSON, ED—*Continued*

and Surveys committees. He is also serving on a special committee investigating petroleum resources. In 1945 he proposed compromise manpower legislation involving a job "freeze" for all individuals as against the labor draft (April), supported the FEPC (June), voted against an amendment to the full employment bill which would have abolished the TVA and the Rural Electrification Administration among other bureaus (September), and favored an extension of time for the United States Employment Service to remain "an efficient national service for reconversion" before it was returned to the States (November). Among his other measures has been his furthering of anti-Petrillo legislation; previously he had introduced bills to "outlaw the advertising of alcoholic beverages on the air" and to license United States radio commentators. In August 1946 Johnson resigned as acting chairman of a Senate committee on campaign expenditures as a protest against the committee's inaction in investigating Senator Theodore Bilbo's '43 renomination. In December he urged a Treasury Department inquiry into Robert R. Nathan's '41 report to the CIO that "business could support a 25 per cent rise in payrolls" in order to ascertain whether the report's allegations were true or false. If true, the Senator suggested action by the Government in the form of a "special further corporate taxation measure against profits" might be taken. The Coloradan also proposed that General George C. Marshall '40, Secretary of State James F. Byrnes '41, or General Dwight Eisenhower '42 be drafted as the Democratic Party's 1948 Presidential candidate if Truman declined to run.

Earlier, in August 1946, Senator Johnson had announced that he would retire from politics at the end of his second term in the Senate in January 1949 (he was re-elected in 1942). Stated Johnson: "I'm going to retire before I get to the age when perhaps I would not have the discretion to get out of politics. I am not suffering from 'Potomac fever.' It's 'Rocky Mountain fever.'" At the same time he recommended adoption of a Constitutional amendment restricting Senators to two terms in Congress. Senators, he declared "too often succumb to 'Potomac fever' after twelve years in the capital and show all the symptoms of 'Presidentialitis'. . . .When a Senator begins to think he may be Presidential timber, he becomes just dead wood to the people back home."

The Colorado Congressman is a Freemason, and a member of the Elks, Odd Fellows, Redmen, and Modern Woodmen of America. In 1946-47 Johnson was serving as president, without pay, of the Western Baseball League. His church is the Lutheran. Senator and Mrs. Johnson have two daughters, Janet Grace (Mrs. Robert Howsam) and an adopted one, Gladys Marie (Mrs. Henry J. Arrance). A large man, six feet two inches in height and weighing 220 pounds, Johnson has blue eyes and brown hair. He has been described as an even-tempered, good-natured individual who "hits out hard," however, when he is roused. According to Arthur Krock, Johnson has the reputation among his Congressional associates of being a man "whose word is good and whose convictions are deeply rooted." He has been characterized, too, as a man of "great faith," with a firm conviction in the efficacy of prayer.

References

Lit Digest 121:5 My 2 '36 por
N Y Sun p4 N 13 '43; p22 Ag 9 '44
Congressional Directory (2d ed., 1945)
International Who's Who, 1945-46
Who's Who in America, 1946-47
Who's Who in the Nation's Capital, 1938-39

JOHNSON, HERSCHEL V. May 3, 1894- American Government official

Address: b. c/o United Nations, New York; h. Charlotte, N.C.

When appointed deputy to the American delegate of the United Nations in April 1946, Herschel V. Johnson, "skilled career diplomat," was Minister to Sweden. It was Johnson's twenty-sixth year in the foreign service, and Stockholm was the sixth capital in which he had been a United States diplomatic official. In June, upon the resignation of the American delegate Edward R. Stettinius '40, Johnson became temporarily—until January 1947—his country's representative at the Security Council table of the United Nations. His official rank is that of Ambassador.

Of Scottish-English lineage, Herschel V. Johnson was born in Atlanta, Georgia, on May 3, 1894. He and three sisters are the children of William White Johnson, who was in the insurance business, and of the former Arabelle Kenan Horne. Johnson, who still retains Southern inflections in his speech, grew up and attended public schools in North Carolina. At eighteen he entered the University of North Carolina, where he majored in history and also concentrated on languages and literature. He was graduated in 1916 with a B.A. degree, then taught French at the Chamberlayne School for Boys in Richmond, Virginia, until 1917, when he enlisted in the Regular Army. From 1917 to 1919 he served overseas, a lieutenant and then a captain in the Infantry, fighting with the Sixth Division in the Vosges Mountain battles and in the Meuse-Argonne offensive of World War I.

The twenty-five-year-old veteran entered Harvard Law School in 1919, but left the next year. "He can't think of any particular book—or person, either—that directed him into a diplomatic career," William O. Player, Jr., of the New York *Post* wrote, "but by the time he'd reached college, Johnson had made up his mind what he wanted to do." After he had passed an examination, in November 1920 came the wished-for appointment to the United States Diplomatic Service (now called the United States Foreign Service). His first assignment abroad took him to Switzerland as third secretary to the American legation in Berne during 1921. In 1922-23 he was second secretary at the legation in Sofia, Bulgaria.

Johnson came home to the United States in 1924 to serve three years with the State Department's Division of Near Eastern Affairs. Then, for seven years, beginning in 1927-28 when he was second secretary at the legation in Tegucigalpa, Honduras, Johnson's province was Latin America. As first secretary of the Embassy he next served under Ambassador Dwight W. Morrow in Mexico City. This was during a period when Ambassador Morrow was effecting cordial relations between the United States and its southern neighbor for the first time in decades. (Morrow had taken the post in 1927 when bitter resentment smoldered in Mexico on the question of American oil concessions.) After working from 1929 to mid-1930 with Morrow, whose "quick sympathy and deep understanding" were winning the esteem of the Mexican people and initiating a new era of good will between the neighboring nations, Johnson returned to Washington where for four years he was chief of the State Department's Division of Mexican Affairs.

Seven years in England followed. Johnson went to London as first secretary of the American Embassy in February 1934, and two and a half years later, in July 1937, became counselor, or "second man" there. International meetings in London, which Johnson attended for his Government, were the meeting of the Governing Body for Assistance to Refugees Coming from Germany in 1934; the Conferences on Whaling in 1937, 1938 and 1939; and the Sugar Council meetings, 1937-41. As counselor and later as minister-counselor, he was for various short periods, totaling over two years, chargé d'affaires—or, in effect, acting Ambassador. This was the case from the time when, late in 1940, Ambassador Joseph Kennedy[40] resigned from his London post, until John Winant[41] was named the new Ambassador in February 1941. In the same month of Winant's appointment, Johnson was given ministerial rank. He was thus American minister counselor in Great Britain when, in October 1941, President Roosevelt nominated him for the post of Envoy Extraordinary and Minister Plenipotentiary to Sweden. The forty-seven-year-old career diplomat left bomb-shattered London for neutral Sweden, arriving in Stockholm three days before Pearl Harbor.

Sweden, America's best "listening post" in Europe during the years of World War II, was an important diplomatic assignment—"a hot spot during the war with the enemy all around," Johnson told a PM interviewer. "The legation grew from forty to about three hundred people, all of whom had to be flown in." One of the Minister's duties was that of discouraging, as far as possible, Swedish trade with Germany. In April 1944, after Secretary of State Cordell Hull's[40] warning to neutrals against trade with the Nazis, Johnson delivered a note to the Swedish Foreign Office demanding that Sweden halt the exportation to Germany of ball bearings and related machinery. Sweden refused to accede to the demand. Throughout 1944, however, the Swedish Government and public sentiment in Sweden be-

HERSCHEL V. JOHNSON

came increasingly hostile toward Germany; by the fall of the year it was announced that the export of ball bearings had ceased. Johnson figured in the dramatic news of the days in May 1945 when the collapse of the Reich was hourly imminent. He and Sir Victor Mallet, the British envoy in Stockholm, received from the Swedish Count Folke Bernadotte[45] the German offer of unconditional surrender to all the United Nations except the Soviet Union, an offer which the Count delivered from Heinrich Himmler in Denmark. Himmler was, of course, unsuccessful in his attempt to split the Allies, and the unconditional German surrender followed.

Johnson had been in Sweden four and a half years when, in April 1946, President Truman called him home to serve as deputy to the United States representative on the Security Council of the United Nations. On his departure the Stockholm newspaper Svenska Dagbladet commented editorially: "During a very important and critical period Mr. Johnson has handled the frequently delicate negotiations between his country and Sweden with an understanding of Sweden's position which his keen intelligence quickly gave him. Many Swedes hoped that his tenure would be extended. With genuine regret they now see him leave."

"When President Truman and Secretary Byrnes started looking for a deputy to Edward R. Stettinius, Jr.," wrote Player, "they decided that—unlike Stettinius—he ought to be an outstanding foreign service officer, a seasoned diplomat and a highly skilled technician. . . . It was almost entirely on the strength of his record and reputation along those lines that [Herschel Johnson] got the job." Asked about his new duties, Johnson explained, "In the absence of the chief, I'll take over all his functions. When he's here I'll help him all I can." On June 3, a little more than a month after Johnson arrived in the United States, Stettinius

JOHNSON, HERSCHEL V.—*Continued*

resigned as U.N. representative. The man chosen by President Truman to succeed Stettinius, Senator Warren R. Austin '44, because of a constitutional technicality would be unable to take his place on the council before January 1947. Johnson was named to serve in the interim, while Austin, with ambassadorial rank, was given the position of adviser to Johnson. The problem of what action to take in regard to the Franco Government in Spain was before the Security Council when Johnson joined it on June 6, 1946. His "persistent effort" resulted in the formulation of a plan—later vetoed by Russia—whereby the question would be submitted to the General Assembly in September.

"The most perfect machinery cannot work without the faith and determination of the people to make it work," Johnson declared to the American Legion national executive committee on June 6. "Given such determination, courageous leaders can be found to express this faith and determination and with it they would at least have a fighting chance to make the imperfect machinery work. . . .We must all help America measure up to its responsibilities for peace and security." To this he added: "We will invite aggression and encourage war if we do not determine now to make whatever sacrifice may be necessary to hold ourselves in readiness to take our full share of military responsibility for world security."

Johnson has called for restraint in the use of the veto in the Security Council of the U.N., but at the same time has pointed out that it was not only Russia but all of the major powers who established and agreed to that power. As United States representative on the Security Council, he proposed a plan whereby the eight applications for membership in the United Nations would be forwarded to the General Assembly for ratification, claiming that membership in that organization should be universal. The proposal was rejected, and on the ensuing one-by-one vote, he favored the admission of Iceland, Sweden, Afghanistan, Trans-Jordan, Eire, and Portugal (the admission of the three last-named was later vetoed by Russia), and opposed the acceptance of the application of Albania and Outer Mongolia (the applications did not receive the necessary two-thirds vote and therefore will not be sent to the General Assembly for approval). In September he favored placing Ukraine's complaint against Greece (that British troops were occupying that country and interfering in its affairs, and that Greece was a menace to international peace) on the agenda, but also voted affirmatively on the Australian plan to drop the discussion on the basis that the complaint was unfounded. Three months after a similar proposal had been vetoed by the U.S.S.R., in late 1946 he proposed that a group be sent to investigate Balkan strife; a board of inquiry was set up.

It was while Johnson was acting delegate to the Security Council that the United States Senate registered its acceptance of the jurisdiction of the World Court. Following the alphabetical rotation system of selecting presidents of the General Assembly, Johnson, as acting chairman of the United States delegation, served as the presiding officer over that body in December 1946. No longer chief United States delegate after January 1947, the diplomat will, nevertheless, appear before the Security Council representing Warren Austin '44.

A thickset man—he is five feet ten inches, and about 175 pounds in weight—Johnson has a ruddy complexion, gray eyes, and sandy hair. The bachelor diplomat "whether in Bern, Sofia, Mexico City, London, or Stockholm . . . seeks a home worthy of the name—a flat or house that he can decorate according to his tastes." He describes himself as a "student by temperament," remarking that he gets "more intense pleasure out of reading than anything else"; his favorite reading is history, historical analysis, and an occasional modern or classic novel. A legal resident of Charlotte, North Carolina, Johnson thinks Southern cooking "is the best in the world if it's done right."

References

Christian Sci Mon p2 Ja 8 '46 por
N Y Herald Tribune p1+ Je 5 '46 por
N Y Post p49 My 22 '46
PM Mag p2-3 My 14 '46 por
Biographic Register of the Department of State, Sep 1, 1944
Who's Who in America, 1946-47

JOHNSON, JACK Mar. 31, 1878—June 10, 1946 American Negro heavyweight pugilist;

won championship by defeating Tommy Burns in 1908; defeated James J. Jeffries in 1910 and lost his title to Jess Willard at Havana in 1915; one of the craftiest boxers in the ring.

Obituary

N Y Times p1+ Je 11 '46

JOHNSTON, ALVANLEY May 12, 1875- Labor leader

Address: b. Brotherhood of Locomotive Engineers Bldg., Cleveland; h. 3197 Warrington Rd., Shaker Heights, Cleveland

Alvanley Johnston became Grand Chief Engineer of the Brotherhood of Locomotive Engineers in 1925. This "aristocrat of rail unions" had over 80,000 members in 1946, when a rail strike led by Johnston and A. F. Whitney '46 of the Brotherhood of Railroad Trainmen put the Grand Chief Engineer's name on newspaper front pages.

Alvanley Johnston was born May 12, 1875, in Ontario, Canada, in a county bordering on New York State. His parents, both citizens of the United States, were David and Annie (Jarrell) Johnston. He attended the elementary school in his native town of Seeleys Bay from 1882 to 1888, and then went to the United States. Two years later, when he was fifteen years old, he returned to Ontario to attend, during 1890-91, the Brockville Business College. Then, in 1892, at the age of seventeen, he became a railroad employee; he was successively a call-boy, engine wiper, a clerk in the master mechanic's office, fireman, and finally in 1897, a twenty-two-year-old locomotive engineer on the Great Northern Railroad.

In 1909, after twelve years as an engineer, Johnston became General Chairman of the Brotherhood of Locomotive Engineers of the Great Northern road. He occupied this office for nine years. In 1918 he became Assistant Grand Chief Engineer of the Brotherhood in the national offices in Cleveland, a post he held until 1925, at which time he was elected Grand Chief Engineer. In this capacity Johnston was in charge of the "protective" or labor activities of the organization.

The Brotherhood organized the Locomotive Engineers Cooperative National Bank at Cleveland in 1920. In subsequent years certain officials of the Brotherhood were instrumental in organizing a number of other banks and investment companies. These latter, according to an official statement, were not organized by the authority of the union, Johnston himself contending that the Brotherhood should confine itself to labor activities.

In 1927, when the "outside" institutions were encountering financial difficulties, the Brotherhood voted to eliminate the offices of president and first and second vice-presidents, and re-elected Johnston as Grand Chief Engineer, thus making him chief executive officer of the Brotherhood. In 1930 Johnston became a member of a three-man committee whose duty it was to continue the liquidation of the financial holdings of the Brotherhood. Three years later (1933), after the Cleveland bank had failed, Johnston, together with nine bank officials, was indicted under an Ohio statute for misapplication of funds and making false entries. Although Johnston was found guilty in the lower court, on appeal the Court of Appeals exonerated him when it found that "there was no instance of direct knowledge on the part of Johnston of the claimed irregularities, that the incidents referred to concerning misapplication did not indicate a possibility of guilt, and that the verdict was manifestly against the weight of evidence."

Despite the Brotherhood's large losses in the failure of the bank and the "outside" institutions, it regained its "financial health" under Johnston's administration. Its membership rose from the 1933 low of some 60,000 to approximately 80,000 in 1946. Its Insurance Association, a separate corporation which furnishes life, accident, and health insurance to its members, was reorganized and placed upon an adequate reserve basis. Following the trend of the times, and in view of the movement for Federal railroad retirement and pension legislation (which culminated in 1935 in the passage of the Government's Railroad Retirement Act), the Brotherhood's Pension Association was discontinued. (Recent amendments to the Act, supported by Johnston, have brought additional benefits to railway employees.)

As to the Brotherhood's financial condition, Johnston explained to Morris Markey (who sought information about the union's finances for an article in the January 5, 1946 *Liberty*) that the Brotherhood's constitution made it impossible to make public a record of

ALVANLEY JOHNSTON

expenditures; but he added: "Suffice it to say that at present we have about $1,000,000 in what is known as the operating fund of the labor organization itself. The assets, reserves, and general expense funds of our insurance association total approximately $17,500,000. We own two of the principal office buildings in . . . Cleveland. . . .Also, we own a modern apartment hotel."

In 1943, after the machinery provided in the Railway Labor Act had failed to settle differences between railroad employees and the managements, President Roosevelt offered to act as arbitrator. Johnston, as directed by the Brotherhood's wage committee, accepted the President's offer for the Brotherhood of Locomotive Engineers, as did President A. F. Whitney for the Brotherhood of Railroad Trainmen. The Engineers' and Trainmen's controversies were promptly decided by President Roosevelt, and no strike was called by these Brotherhoods. However, the three other operating unions (the Brotherhood of Locomotive Firemen and Enginemen, the Order of Railway Conductors, and the Switchmen's Union) refused arbitration and called a strike. The Government took over the railroads, and Johnston and Whitney were appointed labor consultants for the Government-operated roads. After an interval of Government operation the latter three unions yielded and called off the threatened strike.

During World War II the Brotherhoods withheld requests for general wage or rule changes. After the conclusion of hostilities, however, wage-increase movements were begun, the Brotherhoods who represented the "operating" men presenting both wage and rule demands. Negotiations on these requests reached a deadlock in January 1946, and three of the five operating unions (The Firemen, the Conductors, and the Switchmen) agreed to postpone discussion of the work-rule changes.

JOHNSTON, ALVANLEY—*Continued*

Johnston and Whitney, acting upon the direction of their respective committees, declined to abandon the request for rule changes and insisted that both wage and rule changes be brought to a conclusion.

After Johnston's and Whitney's committees had negotiated with the railroads on these issues for more than a year without gaining a concession, the "obstinacy of the carriers" led the committees to take a strike vote. The procedures of the Railway Labor Act were invoked, and the dispute between the employees (of the two Brotherhoods) and the carriers were heard and reported publicly before President Truman's Emergency Board for about a month, beginning March 12, 1946. The board reported to the President on April 18, recommending an increase in wages and the granting of certain rules demands made by the two Brotherhoods. When the railroads refused to place interpretations upon the recommendations which were deemed "reasonable and proper" by the Brotherhoods, the unions called a strike, effective on May 18.

The two-day strike, which stopped all rail traffic, brought heavily headlined articles and pro and con editorials in the press; and in a radio address to the nation President Truman described Johnston and Whitney as being responsible for the crisis. To this charge the unions replied that the action taken was authorized and directed by the union committees, that the two leaders were thus only carrying out of the duties of their offices, and that the settlement of the strike without the granting of their demands was forced by the President in repudiation of the recommendations of his Emergency Board. Johnston's office made the statement, "In the interest of averting further tie-up of transportation, the Brotherhoods had lost, for the time being, their case for rule changes. . . .Johnston is content in the conviction that the cause of the Brotherhood of Locomotive Engineers was just and that he had fulfilled his duty and exercised his best efforts on behalf of the men he represented." Drawing a parallel between the emancipation brought by the Civil War and the union's efforts for its membership, Johnston saw the 1946 movement for wage and rule changes as a continuation of that effort.

The labor leader's fondness for quoting Washington and Lincoln is a product of his "deep delving" into American history. On the occasion of the 150th anniversary of Washington's Farewell Address, Johnston gave something of his personal philosophy in a message (published in the *Locomotive Engineers Journal*), in which he pointed out that "Washington's counsel is immortal. . . .He believed in constitutional government and understood the needs of the common man. . . .One of the great truisms that he repeatedly emphasized is —our nation cannot survive as a true democracy if all power and authority is concentrated in the central Government." In a later article Johnston expressed the view that capital and labor should be able to reconcile their differences without legislative injunction and warned that such action would cause organized labor to revolt and "probably wreck 'the best system on earth.'"

Johnston's home is in suburban Shaker Heights, where he lives with his daughter, Anna Maud (Mrs. Harry C. Saddington), his son-in-law, grandson, and his other daughter, Marian Jean. Mrs. Johnston, the former Maude Ethel Forsythe, to whom the labor leader was married in July 1917, died in 1934. Johnston is described as a ruggedly built man with graying hair, "solid and conservative in appearance, forceful in speech and action at a conference table." His one outdoor hobby is fishing in his favorite Canadian waters with a few friends.

References

New Repub 78:123-5 Mr 14 '34
Time 47:21-2 Je 3 '46
U S News 20:52-4 My 31 '46 por
Who's Who in America, 1946-47

JOLIOT-CURIE, FREDERIC (zhô"lyō′ kü"rē′ frä"dä"rēk′) Mar. 19, 1900- French chemical physicist

Address: b. c/o Collège de France, Paris

The most prominent in political affairs, and the most active, of contemporary French scientists is Frédéric Joliot-Curie, who with his wife Irène Curie '40 won the 1935 Nobel Prize for the discovery of artificial radioactivity. During World War II he was a leader in the French Resistance movement. In 1946 he is director of the French National Center of Scientific Research, French High Commissioner for Atomic Energy, and alternate French delegate to the United Nations Atomic Energy Commission.

The son of middle-class parents who came to Paris from Alsace-Lorraine, Frédéric Joliot was born in that city on March 19, 1900. Morally and intellectually, he says, he is especially indebted to his mother; for his deep love of nature, in particular to his father. Only ten when he made up his mind to become a scientist, after preliminary schooling he entered the Paris Ecole de Physique et de Chimie, from which he was graduated in 1923 with an engineer's diploma. The next two years he spent in heavy industry and military service. Then, in 1925, at the recommendation of Paul Langevin, famous French physicist and professor at the Collège de France, Joliot was engaged as an assistant to Marie Curie, director of the Radium Institute of the University of Paris. At first he worked as a preparator, meanwhile continuing his studies with more exclusive concentration on atomic physics and chemistry. Investigating the properties of alpha rays from radioactive elements, he obtained a second bachelor's degree and in 1927 his *Licence ès Sciences*.

One year earlier the young scientist had been married to Irène Curie, the elder daughter of Pierre and Marie Curie, who was his fellow assistant in her mother's laboratory. Until 1930, when he completed his dissertation—setting forth the results of his electrochemical explorations of the properties of radioactive and in-active elements in extremely diluted solutions—and received his *Docteur ès Sciences* degree, Joliot continued his researches independently for the most part. After 1930, following the path of Irène's parents, he and Irène worked as a team, symbolized by their now hyphenated name Joliot-Curie. During the next five years their experiments helped lay the groundwork for James Chadwick's [45] discovery of the neutron in 1932 and resulted in their own production of artificial radioactivity in 1934, scientific events of the first importance recognized by the award in 1935 of the Nobel Prize in physics to Chadwick, the Nobel Prize in chemistry to the French couple.

Together the Joliot-Curies began atomic bombardment experiments, in particular firing alpha particles at the light metal beryllium. In 1930 experiments of a similar nature had been carried out by the German scientists Bothe and Becker of the University of Giessen and had unexpectedly produced beryllium radiation of a penetrating power approximately equal to that of the powerful gamma rays of radium. Mystified by this radiation, the Joliot-Curies repeated the German experiments, placing an absorption screen of lead between the beryllium and the ionization chamber. Then, substituting paraffin for the lead they observed with amazement the expulsion of protons at speeds exceeding eighteen miles per second, a phenomenon compelling the conclusion that the activating agents, if rays, had the unbelievable energy of fifty million electron volts. At this point Chadwick took up the investigation, and it was his experiments which established that the supposed rays released from the beryllium by the alpha particles were not rays at all but streams of neutrons, particles of weight equal to the proton, deriving their penetrative power from the electrical neutrality which prevents their influence by any magnetic field at which they may be aimed. Subsequent work by the Joliot-Curies produced further confirmation of this.

After the discovery of the neutron in 1932, the Joliot-Curies turned their attention to the other recently discovered particle, the positron, or positive electron, probing its method of production. This time, when they bombarded the element boron with alpha particles obtained from polonium, they observed that positrons seemed to be accompanying the resultant neutrons. But upon further investigation, explains an article in the British scientific magazine *Nature*, they realized "that while the neutrons were emitted simultaneously with the bombardment by the alpha particles, the emission of positrons was an entirely separate process occurring after the source of alpha particles had been removed." The boron had been transformed into radioactive nitrogen which, after the removal of the polonium, emitted a positron and thereby disintegrated to form a stable, or nonradioactive, nucleus of carbon. Chemical tests confirmed the production of artificial radioactivity, and the official announcement was made on January 15, 1934. The Joliot-Curies were also able to induce artificial radioactivity in magnesium and aluminum, but more important, they opened up a fruitful new avenue

French Press & Inf. Service
FREDERIC JOLIOT-CURIE

for scientific research, pursued in particular by Enrico Fermi [45] of Italy, whose experiments led indirectly to the final splitting of the atom.

Recognition for their achievements came early to the Joliot-Curies. In 1933 and 1934 they were co-recipients of the Henri Wilde and Marquet prizes of the Académie des Sciences. In 1935 they received the forty-one-thousand-dollar Nobel award in chemistry. Again, in 1940 both were honored by the award, made only once in five years, of Columbia University's Barnard Gold Medal for Meritorious Service to Science. At the Centre National de la Recherche Scientifique, which he had joined in 1930, Frédéric Joliot-Curie was designated chief of research. At the same time he was made secretary of the Société Française de Physique and a member of the International Commission on Radium. In 1937 he was made a professor at the Collège de France, was appointed to the Commission du Poids Atomique for the International Union of Chemistry, and was elected vice-president of the Haut Comité des Recherches Scientifiques. Meanwhile, he and Irène Curie continued their researches in atomic physics, in February 1940 being among the first experimenters to attain the long-sought chain reaction in nuclear fission.

Five months earlier, after France had declared war on Germany on September 3, 1939, Joliot-Curie had been given the rank of captain in the French artillery and the task of coordinating the work of the atomic research laboratories of the University of Paris, the Collège de France, and the Centre National de la Recherche Scientifique, then asked by the Government to concentrate on research for war. One of his first acts was to send a representative to Norway to negotiate for the sale to France of Norway's stock of heavy water, the world's largest, and important in atomic research. Just prior to the April invasion Norway complied with a loan of the precious ma-

JOLIOT-CURIE, FREDERIC—*Continued*

terial which was then entrusted to the Collège de France, where French scientists immediately set to work. When France fell several months later, it was Joliot-Curie's quick action in sending his two principal assistants with it to England which once again saved it for the Allies. Later, during a twelve-hour session with the Gestapo, he also was able to dissuade the Nazis from seizing France's only cyclotron and her valuable store of radium.

After the liberation of Paris it was revealed that throughout the occupation the scientist had been in the forefront of underground activities as a leader of the Front National, the Resistance movement in university circles of Paris. Under pretense of theoretical investigation of the atom, he had directed the manufacture of explosives and radio equipment for the use of the Maquis, often with the Nazis working in rooms close by or on the next floor of the laboratory buildings. Some aid came from an unexpected quarter with the unintentional appointment by the Vichy Government of a French patriot as director of the Municipal Laboratory of Paris, where were stored the arms and explosives confiscated by the Vichyites; and on Joliot-Curie's staff was an engraver of the Bank of France whose perfect forgeries eventually made the Germans realize the futility of continuing to inspect identification papers. In addition, after some of its organizers had been killed by the Germans, Joliot-Curie assumed the risk of keeping in hiding in his laboratory the remaining members of the staff of the clandestine fortnightly *L'Université Libre*. Not until four months before the Paris insurrection did the Germans become suspicious: then Joliot-Curie went into hiding while his wife fled with their children to Switzerland.

Just two days after the liberation of Paris in the fourth week of August 1944, Joliot-Curie's part in the Allied war effort was recognized by his appointment as director of the Centre National de la Recherche Scientifique. Soon afterward he was appointed Front National representative to the Provisional Consultative Assembly, a post he held until February 1945, when he resigned because he considered its duties incompatible with his functions as director of scientific research. In January 1946 General Charles de Gaulle named him French High Commissioner for Atomic Energy, heading the newly created Commission on Atomic Energy. Later he was appointed assistant French delegate and scientific adviser to the United Nations Atomic Energy Commission, attended its sessions in New York in June and September 1946. In May he had been made a Commander of the Legion of Honor by France and had been elected a foreign member of the Royal Society by Great Britain. In August he was elected to the presidency of the newly formed World Federation of Associations of Scientific Workers, dedicated to the "initiation of action to insure that science plays its proper part in helping to solve the urgent problems of our time."

Frédéric Joliot-Curie has been said to express the "human side of science" because of his profound interest in people. "In the laboratory," he told James Aronson of the New York *Post*, "I give a great deal of thought to the persons with whom I associate. For a scientist it is necessary not only to know people, but to work with popular organizations. When he formulates ideas, they often stem from his associations. I do not care for an intellectual vacuum." A member of the Communist Party, he joined in 1940, because, he said, "I was impressed by the generosity, courage, and hope for the future that these people in my country had. They seemed willing to do the most to give France social reform." His statements concerning atomic energy reflect the same attitude. "French science," he said, "does not want to have anything to do with atomic research other than for peace. All our efforts are being utilized in the development of this tremendous energy for the advancement of humanity." Furthermore, he maintained, international cooperation and free circulation of scientific knowledge are prerequisites for the accomplishment of this objective, so much so that scientists should boycott atomic research if they continue to be curtailed.

Described as a slight, dark-haired man with a sensitive and kindly face and a patient, easy manner, the Frenchman has one great desire: to live in a world freed of social problems wherein he may devote his entire thoughts and efforts to science. He takes vacations only seldom, but he then is apt to spend them living the life of his fishermen friends on the north coast of Brittany. Daily relaxation he finds in reading and smoking. In the family the question presents itself: will the son and daughter of Frédéric and Irène Joliot-Curie continue the Curie tradition? In 1946 they were studying science—"they heard so much talk about our work around the house."

References

N Y Post p33 Je 25 '46 por
MacCallum, T. W. and Taylor, S. eds. The Nobel Prize Winners and the Nobel Foundation, 1901-1937 (1938)

JONES, ROBERT EDMOND   Dec. 12, 1887- Theatrical designer; artist

Address: b. c/o The Players, 16 Gramercy Pk., New York

Theatrical historians have pointed out that so accustomed have audiences become to the "new stagecraft" which superseded the old realism epitomized by David Belasco that they have all but forgotten that it was Robert Edmond Jones, "the most influential artist-designer in the modern American theater," who effected its introduction in 1915 with his first assignment, *The Man Who Married a Dumb Wife*. In the practice of Jones and the younger men whom he has inspired it has meant a wholly new integration of the background with the spirit of the play in order more fully to project the playwright's thought, an emphasis upon essentials by the elimination of all obscuring detail, and thereby, as Jones himself has noted, the achievement of a fluid and imaginative dramaturgy comparable to that of the Shakespearean stage. In the case of Jones himself, it has likewise meant on the one hand the painter's feeling for color and texture which distinguished his investiture of *Lute Song*; on the other, the "superior realization of the mystery of space, the drama of shadows, and the poetry of the undecorated" which John Mason Brown found in his settings for Eugene O'Neill's *The Ice Man Cometh*.

Those who know him well say that beneath his cosmopolitan exterior Robert Edmond Jones is a true native of the New England in which he spent his first nineteen years, which as it left its imprint on his sensitive nature was, in his own words, at once "violent, passionate, sensual, sadistic, lifted, heated, frozen, transcendental, Poesque." He was born on December 12, 1887, in the village of Milton, New Hampshire, the son of Fred Plummer and Emma Jane (Cowell) Jones. But he had no inclination or aptitude for the rugged farm life of the community: he was a dreamer, retreating into a world of his own imagining, finding refuge among the family's few books, and always drawing. Had it not been for his mother he might have had a hard time. But as a prospective concert pianist who had renounced her career to become the wife of a poor farmer and the mother of six children, she responded with sympathy to his artistic temperament and sought to channel his gift with lessons on the violin. When, a high school youth, he was playing at village concerts, it was said that he was not like other boys; already at ten his drawing had been singled out as possessed of remarkable talent.

It was not, however, until he entered Harvard University that Jones had his first contact with the stage, and then he found his way into the midst of things theatrical, in the words of Kenneth MacGowan, "through the most rearward of all back doors." As a violinist in the college orchestra, he was in the pit at a rehearsal of MacGowan's student production of Percy Mac-Kaye's *The Scarecrow*. "The next thing we knew, he was making up the faces of the actors." He attended Harvard from 1906 to 1910, taking odd jobs on the side to earn expenses, was graduated *cum laude*, and stayed on for another two years as an instructor in the Fine Arts Department. It was for him a period of discovery, of reveling in the extravagant theatricality of Valeska Suratt, Gertrude Hoffman's Russian ballet company, and the other attractions which drew him to Keith's vaudeville house in Boston whenever he could spare the time. He came to know Gordon Craig's visionary theories, and his friends saw a flood of sketches for costumes and settings in which he gave himself up to "smashing" color schemes and a need for magnificence and nobility for the eye.

Yet most of this activity and enthusiasm was sporadic. In the opinion of Hiram Kelly Motherwell it was pretty clear that neither at Harvard nor when employed as a costume designer by Comstock and Gest in New York was he finding full scope for his talents. And then, early in 1913, he left for Europe and, after being rebuffed by Gordon Craig's school of theatrical art in Florence, went to Germany.

Through the influence of one of Max Reinhardt's associates he was given the freedom of Reinhardt's Deutsches Theater, and there in Berlin he found himself. "He found life keyed high, craftsmanship professionally dignified, and artistic creation bold and free," wrote Motherwell. "He felt a constant pressure of bold tendencies to be adopted, criticized, or fought. He came home a trained and mature artist of the theater. . . .In short, he woke up."

The outbreak of World War I drove the young designer back just in time to place some sketches in the exhibition of the "new stagecraft" which MacGowan and Sam Hume had brought to New York from Cambridge. Seen by Emilie Hapgood, president of the Stage Society, which was preparing a production of Anatole France's medieval comedy *The Man Who Married a Dumb Wife*, these won for Jones an invitation to design the settings for the France play. Harley Granville-Barker, on tour from London, saw the one-act piece in rehearsal, bought it as a curtain raiser for Shaw's *Androcles and the Lion,* and thereby made possible the event which theatrical historians regard as marking the beginning of a new period in the history of the American theater. On January 27, 1915, at Wallack's Theatre, Jones's setting showed for the first time what could be done when the designer's imagination was freed from the demands of an exacting realism, a demonstration which was eventually to lead to the recognition of the contribution of the designer as equal to that of the director or the producer. The façade of a house, balconied, with one large window through which the interior was just visible, rectilinear and slightly conventionalized in design, bare of excess detail, posteresque in its simplicity, it was done in black and gold against a light gray. Down to the painting of the scenery and the pinning and basting of the costumes on the actors themselves, it was all the handiwork of its creator. "The beauty of it literally took everyone's breath away. . . .It was so utterly right that criticism had no place."

Arthur Hopkins saw the production and the young man of twenty-eight began the most fruitful of his associations. His first production for Hopkins, *The Devil's Garden,* opened in December 1915 and is still remembered for one severely plain set in which the three judges sat in comfortable familiarity on one side of the stage while the accused occupied a lone, straight-backed chair on the other. His second, *The Happy Ending,* included one in which he "vividly suggested the palpable darkness of a forest" by means of "many hanging clumps of dark canvas in heavy folds." Then, because Nijinsky [40] saw *The Happy Ending,* Jones in the fall of 1916 became the first American to design for the Russian ballet, producing one of his most memorable settings when he represented a medieval Gothic town not as it was but as it appeared to the distorted imagination of his hero, Till Eulenspiegel. Between 1915 and 1920, when at the Bourgeois Galleries he became the first scenic designer to give a one-man show of his drawings, Jones was responsible for the

ROBERT EDMOND JONES

arresting *décor* of seventeen plays, most of them for Hopkins, two ballets, and five masques.

Ruth Woodbury Sedgwick said in 1935 that seldom had Jones equaled and only once surpassed the settings he made in 1918, 1919, and 1920 for Hopkins's productions of *Redemption*, *The Jest*, and *Richard III*, when the participation of John Barrymore completed one of the greatest teams in American theatrical history. Because Jones made them, she wrote, "the guttering of a candle in a dark room has for this generation become symbolic of Tolstoi's Russia; a column stabbing the sky, an arched window harboring doom, mean the Renaissance; an abstraction of the Traitor's Gate with a gibbet waiting before it holds all of the significance of Bosworth Field." But, whereas *Redemption* and *The Jest* were both recognized as employing Jones's by now familiar unliteralness, *Richard III*, dominated by its brooding Tower of London, was singled out by Kenneth MacGowan as "absolutely revolutionary" in method because of its "creation of settings from mere scraps of background dropped in the midst of a permanent setting, and emphasized, individualized, and sublimated by light." What has become a commonplace of the theater in 1946 was startlingly new in 1920.

Then, in 1921, five years after the psychological *Till Eulenspiegel*, came the controversial *Macbeth*, with its abstract suggestion of an emotional idea rather than a physical reality, which Hopkins and Jones hoped would establish a new esthetic for the theater. Wrote Kenneth MacGowan in *Theatre Arts Magazine* for April 1921: "Jones has seen as the dominant element of *Macbeth* the abnormal influence of the powers symbolized by Shakespeare in the witches. He has tried to visualize the superhuman nature of those mystic forces in gigantic masks appearing high in the air above the blasted heath. . . .For the first scene of the witches there are only the three silver masks hanging above and three similarly masked figures in red

standing motionless in a pool of light below. For most of the scenes in Inverness, he uses one or two sets of arches, curiously and disturbingly aslant. . . .When Macbeth is reaching the highest point of his success the two groups seem to lunge upward and away toward triumph . . . when he hears of the coming of Birnam Wood, only one set of arches remains and it seems almost toppling to the ground. . . .Never has Jones shown more power and beauty in such work." But confronted with something it could not understand, as well as a pictorial conception with which the acting was at variance, the public emphatically repudiated it. Commercially, *Macbeth* was Jones's most complete failure; artistically, many consider it his greatest triumph.

The year 1921 also marked Jones's first professional association with Eugene O'Neill when Hopkins produced *The Hairy Ape*. Thereafter, he was designer for O'Neill's *Anna Christie* (1922), *Desire Under the Elms* (1924), *The Fountain* (1924), *The Great God Brown* (1925), *Mourning Becomes Electra* (1931), and the last on Broadway before *The Ice Man Cometh*, *Ah, Wilderness!* (1933). Similarly, in 1925 he created the *décor* for Philip Barry's *In a Garden* and then went on to set the stage for Barry's *Paris Bound* (1927), *Holiday* (1928), *Joyous Season* (1934), *Philadelphia Story* (1939), and *Without Love* (1942). Among other plays which bore his name as designer after 1921 were the John Barrymore *Hamlet* (1922), *Machinal* (1928), *Green Pastures* (1929), *The Green Bay Tree* (1932), the Walter Huston *Othello* (1936), *The Sea Gull* (1938), the Paul Robeson *Othello* (1943). Musical events saw his name connected with John Alden Carpenter's ballets *The Birthday of the Infanta* (1919) and the jazz *Skyscrapers* (1926), with Leopold Stokowski's production of Alban Berg's opera *Wozzek* (1931) and Stravinsky's opera-oratorio *Oedipus Rex* (1931).

In 1917 the designer had attempted direction for the first time when in association with Emilie Hapgood he had produced three one-act plays of Ridgely Torrence with an all-Negro company. From 1923 through 1925, together with Kenneth MacGowan and Eugene O'Neill, he was an associate director of the newly organized Experimental Theatre which took over the famous Provincetown Playhouse and later the Greenwich Village Theatre. Each year between 1932 and 1935 he produced, directed, and set the summer festivals at Central City, Colorado. Also, between 1933 and 1936 he was in Hollywood, pioneering for John Hay Whitney in the new three-color Technicolor process, using color as an emotional medium in *La Cucaracha* (1934), *Becky Sharp* (1935), and *Dancing Pirate* (1936).

On June 21, 1933, Jones had been married to Margaret Huston Carrington, singer, voice teacher of John Barrymore, Lillian Gish, and others, and sister of Walter Huston. After her death in August 1942, he passed through a period of comparative quiescence: he "just didn't feel like working," he has said. But when he returned to Broadway in the spring of 1946 it was to hear "magnificent", "stunning", "superb", "a production of extraordinary loveliness" from every side. Together with Michael Myerberg he had worked a year on the ancient Chinese play which was produced as *Lute Song* and had outdone himself in the "mad hues" of the costumes, a "kaleidoscopic mélange" which he presented against pastel drops. In the representative words of John Chapman: "Dominating everything is Robert Edmond Jones. His scenes range from complete simplicity to overpowering color and richness. His beggar's costumes are rags indeed, his princely raiments exotic beyond any dream but his own. And by the use of drop curtains which are themselves part of the story, he has given *Lute Song* complete fluidity in spite of a great number of scene changes." His settings for *Lute Song* resulted in what Jones called his fourth "discovery," but the extravagant publicity did not please him half so much as the simple comment that his investiture of his next play, O'Neill's *The Ice Man Cometh,* was "supremely right." Following *The Ice Man Cometh,* the Theater Guild has announced, it will produce O'Neill's *A Moon for the Misbegotten* and *A Touch of the Poet,* on which Jones worked concurrently with the first-named from January to September 1946.

Jones was awarded the Howland memorial prize by Yale University in 1925 and the Fine Arts Medal by the American Institute of Architecture in 1936. In his much praised book *The Dramatic Imagination* (1941), which one critic called "a flint to strike fire from the dullest stone," he has elaborated his beliefs concerning the theater. He conceives of drama as "man's creative spirit, in action, before our eyes"; as "a dream—an excitement, a high, rare mood, a conception of greatness" more real than reality because truth in the theater is not mere accuracy to fact but art, a heightening of reality. And he conceives of stagecraft as the "evocation"—his favorite word— of a mood or an atmosphere; as a part of the communication of the essence of the author's thought; as the omission of the details and prose of nature in favor of the spirit and the splendor.

What distinguishes Jones's work, Gilbert Seldes has said, is a "combination of vigor with taste." "A romantic rather than a realist, a mystic rather than a literalist," in the words of John Mason Brown, at the Bergman Studios which execute most of his settings Jones is esteemed as a craftsman as well as an artist, as one who can be relied upon to provide a hundred diagrams in various scales if necessary and to provide them on time. Because he prefers to do work which has meaning for him as an individual, Jones often designs only two or three plays a year instead of the seven or eight of many other designers, and, he says, each scene takes on reality in his mind's eye long before he begins to sketch. But the sketch is still only a small part of his job. Just as in the days of his first successes, Jones still prefers to do most of the work himself, exploring lower Manhattan for atmosphere, hunting, for instance, in all sorts of out-of-the-way places for exactly the right prop, the right

material for a costume, then fitting the costumes with his own hands. Those who have known him long say that Jones has not changed much over the years, only mellowed a little. Friendly and accessible as his friends find him, the tall, youthful-looking man, whose hair is scarcely touched with gray, still gives the same general impression of reticence and aura of mystery which surrounded him in his younger days.

References

Creative Art 10:289+ Ap '32 il por
N Y Herald Tribune V p3 D 29 '46
New Yorker 7:25+ My 9 '31 il
PM p20 Mr 3 '46 por
Stage 12:36+ Jl '35 il por
Theatre Arts Mag 1:51+ Feb '17 il; 4:103+ Ap '30 il
Theatre Arts Mo 9:720+ N '25 il
Columbia Encyclopedia (1935)
International Motion Picture Almanac, 1943-44
International Who's Who, 1945-46
Sergeant, E. S. Fire Under the Andes (1927) por
Who's Who, 1946
Who's Who in America, 1946-47
Who's Who in American Art, 1940-41
Who's Who in the Theatre (1939)

JUDD, CHARLES HUBBARD Feb. 20, 1873—July 18, 1946 Psychologist, author, educator; professor and head of the department of education at the University of Chicago from 1909 to 1938; author of many textbooks, including *Genetic Psychology for Teachers* (1903), *Psychology of Secondary Education* (1927), *Problems of Education in the United States* (1933), *Education and Social Progress* (1934).

Obituary

N Y Times p19 Jl 19 '46

KAGEY, RUDOLF 1905—May 13, 1946 Educator and author; wrote ten mystery stories under the name of Kurt Steel; became instructor in philosophy at New York University in 1928; assistant professor and acting director of the evening division at his death; wrote stories about Hank Hyer, private detective; his books include *Judas, Inc., Murder Goes to College,* and *Ambush House.*

Obituary

N Y Times My 14 '46 por

KALININ, MIKHAIL IVANOVICH (kŭ-lyē'nyĭn myĭ-ĸŭ-ēl' ĭ-vȧ'nŭ-vyĭch) Nov. 20, 1875—June 3, 1946 Russian statesman; president of Union of Soviet Socialist Republics from 1923 until his retirement on March 19, 1946, because of illness; "salesman" of the first Five Year Plan. See *Current Biography* 1942 Yearbook.

Obituary

N Y Times p23 Je 4 '46 por

KALTENBRUNNER, ERNST 1901—Oct. 16, 1946 Chief of the Gestapo or Nazi Security Police from 1943 through World War II; a general in the Elite Guard; tried for war crimes by the International Military Tribunal, which found his office "played a leading part in the extermination of the Jews"; condemned and hanged. See *Current Biography* 1943 Yearbook.

Obituary

N Y Times p1+ O 16 '46

KEANE, DORIS Dec. 12, 1881—Nov. 25, 1945 American actress; made debut in 1903; scored one of the greatest modern theatrical triumphs as star of Edward Sheldon's *Romance* (1913), in United States and England; last stage appearance in 1929.

Obituary

N Y Times p21 N 26 '45 por

KEENAN, JOSEPH B(ERRY) Jan. 11, 1888- United States Government official

Address: b. 520 Woodward Bldg., Washington, D.C.; h. 10 Hesketh St., Chevy Chase, Md.

Following the surrender of Japan in August 1945, Joseph B. Keenan, a lawyer with a national reputation as a "gangbuster," was appointed chief prosecutor for the International Military Tribunal in the Far East before which wartime Premier Hideki Tojo '41 and twenty-seven other Japanese militarists were to be brought to trial. In these trials, Keenan saw the means of establishing a valuable precedent under international law for punishing perpetrators of "crimes against peace", "conventional war crimes," and "crimes against humanity."

The son of Bernard A. and Sarah (Berry) Keenan, Joseph Berry Keenan was born in Pawtucket, Rhode Island, on January 11, 1888. He received his B.A. and M.A. degrees from Brown University in 1910; in 1913 he won his LL.B. degree from Harvard Law School, where he had attended classes with Robert A. Taft '40 and Owen Brewster. Soon after graduation he was admitted to the Ohio bar and began to practice law in Cleveland. In 1916 the twenty-eight-year-old lawyer served on the Mexican border with Troop A, 107th Ohio Cavalry, known as the Cleveland "Black Horse" cavalry troop. When the United States entered World War I, Keenan was a member of the same troop, which became the 137th Field Artillery of the AEF. In France, where he was commissioned a first lieutenant and transferred to the Judge Advocate General's Office, he earned citations for distinguished service from both General Pershing and the French Government.

Upon his return to Cleveland in 1919, Keenan entered the firm of Day, Day, and Wilkin, but before he had worked there long, Governor James M. Cox appointed him to assist the attorney general of Ohio in the investigation of crime conditions in Cleveland. His success in prosecuting the gangsters of the Lake Erie metropolis was still remembered fourteen years later. In 1933, three years after he had established the prosperous firm of Keenan and Butler, he was called to Washington as a special assistant to Attorney General Homer S. Cummings in the drive against the nation's kidnappers and racketeers. Within about four months after his arrival in the capital, Keenan had convicted "Machine Gun" Kelly and others of the "mob" for the kidnapping of a wealthy oilman, and became a regular assistant attorney general in charge of the Justice Department's criminal division. In 1936 he was promoted to the post of assistant to the Attorney General.

Keenan's activities in Washington were not confined to his role as a prosecutor. "A knack for winning friends," wrote *Newsweek* in 1938, "made him the Justice Department's key lobbyist." He helped gain the passage of laws which gave the Federal Bureau of Investigation more power in pursuing criminals. President Roosevelt, whom Keenan had supported in 1932, also recognized his talents (he called him "Joe, the Key") and made him a "contact man" between the White House and the Capitol. In the fight over the Administration's bill to enlarge the Supreme Court, Keenan worked hard to win votes in support of the Administration. While the measure was not passed, he aided in "resurrecting parts of it." Legislation was secured to provide for the retirement of Supreme Court justices on full pay at seventy, for the shifting of Federal judges from one district or circuit to another when congested dockets made it necessary, and for the direct appeal from a District Court to the Supreme Court in cases involving the constitutionality of a Federal law. Keenan also won votes for the omnibus judgeship bill which created fifteen District Court and five Appellate Court judgeships. It was his task to help in the selection of the new appointees.

The "efficient political fixer," as two *Saturday Evening Post* writers called Keenan, was also of assistance to the President when he made his famous "purge" of the Democratic Party. *Time* maintained that Keenan's efforts for the Administration "were known to be based more on loyalty than conviction" and therefore did not affect his good standing with "anti-Administrationists." In February 1939 Keenan resigned from his position in the Department of Justice to return to a private practice in Washington. He refused an offer for a twelve-thousand-five-hundred-dollar judgeship on the grounds that the salary was not high enough to enable him to provide a college education for his four children, William Quigley, Joseph Berry, Betty Jean, and John David. (Keenan had been married to Charlotte Quigley in July 1920.)

In the fall of 1945, however, when President Truman appointed him chief prosecutor at the trials of the Japanese war criminals, Keenan again left his law practice. He and his staff of thirty-eight arrived in Tokyo on December 6, 1945. They wished to open the trials as soon after that date as possible, but met with a number of delays. These, Keenan told reporters, were caused by a lack of sufficient documentary evidence such as was available in the Nuremburg trials, and of an adequate translation staff, together with the difficulties involved in probing into the lives of men who had not occupied prominent positions but had worked "under cover." Not until the end of April 1946, when the staffs of all the nations participating in the tribunal (Australia, India, China, the Philippines, New Zealand, France, the United Kingdom, the Netherlands, Russia, Canada, and the United States) had arrived, was he able to start the proceedings; in a fifty-five-count indictment he charged twenty-eight former Japanese officials with plotting aggressive war from 1928, when a plan was made for the seizure of Manchuria.

But the beginning of the trials was further delayed when the defense counsel, ignoring the Briand-Kellogg pact, which renounced war except in self-defense and had been signed by Japan, challenged the jurisdiction of the court on the grounds that waging warfare could not be considered a crime because there were no international laws against war. In the hearings which were held on the question, Keenan countered that lack of precedent was not sufficient reason to free the accused. Finally, on June 4, 1946, with an opening statement lasting three hours and fifteen minutes, which the New York *Times* described as the "bluntest condemnation" of former Japanese rulers and the entire Japanese imperial system since the beginning of the American occupation, Keenan began the trial proceedings. A continuance of ten days, however, was granted to give the defense more time to prepare its case.

Keenan himself left Tokyo for more than a month to examine further evidence in the United States. While he was in Washington, D.C., a decision was reached "on high political levels" not to bring the Japanese Emperor to trial. Up to that time the question of whether to indict the Emperor had remained unsettled. New evidence showed that Japan's wartime Premier Tojo had blocked the efforts of Japan's special United States "peace" envoy to prevent war by arranging a direct exchange of views between Hirohito '42 and Roosevelt in November 1941, about two weeks before Pearl Harbor; therefore, although some of the other prosecutors disagreed, Keenan felt that Hirohito was more "a figurehead and a fraud perpetrated on the Japanese people" than a war criminal. In November 1946 the tribunal heard evidence, obtained in an examination of Tojo, showing that Hirohito had opposed an attack on the United States without a previous declaration of war; according to the prosecution, Tojo had also confessed "responsibility" for the July 1941 Imperial Conference, which reached the decision that Japan was prepared to wage war on the United States and Britain.

Some of Keenan's colleagues were critical of the chief prosecutor's departure for the United States at a time when the trials at Tokyo were not progressing smoothly—the proceedings were slowed down by exhaustive interrogations by the attorneys and disagreements over procedure which the presiding justice attempted to curb. One member of the prosecuting staff—who, according to Keenan, had resigned because he failed to receive a promotion—criticized the leadership of the tri-

JOSEPH B. KEENAN

bunal and declared "the Allied prosecution of Japanese accused warmakers [had] fallen victim to maladministration, neglect and inefficiency." A spokesman for General Douglas MacArthur, Supreme Commander for the Allied Powers in the Japanese Empire, however, declared that Keenan, who returned to Tokyo at the end of July 1946, was handling "a most difficult international situation in a successful way" and still held the General's confidence.

The chief prosecutor, who is a member of the Ohio State, Cuyahoga County, and Cleveland bar associations, did not always support the Democratic Party. Once he sought election as a delegate to the Republican National Convention, but was defeated. In his religious affiliation he is Catholic. The "beefy, square-jawed" attorney weighs 170 pounds and is five feet seven inches in height. Upon his arrival in Tokyo, reported the New York *Herald Tribune,* he went to a hospital to try to lose ten pounds so as to put himself in "fighting trim" for the trial.

References

N Y Herald Tribune p3 Je 23 '46 por
N Y Sun p30 Nov 30 '45
Who's Who in America, 1946-47
Who's Who in Law, 1937
Who's Who in the Nation's Capital, 1938-39

KEITEL, WILHELM (kī'tĕl) Sept. 22, 1882—Oct. 16, 1946 Chief of the high command of the Nazi armed forces; tried for war crimes by the International Military Tribunal; the verdict stated that he "put pressure on Austria . . . initialed Hitler's directive for the attack on Czechoslovakia . . . signed the orders for the attacks on Belgium and the Netherlands"; condemned and hanged. See *Current Biography* 1940 Yearbook.

Obituary

N Y Times p1+ O 16 '46

KEMMERER, E(DWIN) W(ALTER)
June 29, 1875—Dec. 16, 1945 American economist and educator; Walker professor of International Finance at Princeton University from 1928 to 1943, Professor Emeritus since 1943; financial adviser to fourteen countries, including Mexico, Colombia, Poland, Guatemala, China, and Turkey; author of several books, among them *High Prices and Inflation* (1920); *The ABC of Inflation* (1942). See *Current Biography* 1941 Yearbook.

Obituary

N Y Times p21 D 17 '45 por

KENDRICK, BAYNARD (HARDWICK)
Apr. 8, 1894- Author
Address: b. c/o Willis Kingsley Wing, 522 5th Ave., New York

A popular author who gave up writing for a whole year to assist in carrying out the program of the Blinded Veterans Association during its first crucial months is Baynard Kendrick, former honorary chairman of BVA's board of directors. The only sighted adviser of the group, Kendrick, who had been active in the Army's rehabilitation program for blinded soldiers, served as liaison with businessmen and industrialists. After the association had become well organized, he resigned, but was elected an honorary member of the group for life.

Baynard Hardwick Kendrick was born in Philadelphia on April 8, 1894, the son of John Ryland Kendrick and Julia (Lawton) Kendrick. Much younger than his four brothers and sisters, he always accompanied his parents when his father, who traveled for the St. Louis Exposition, made business trips. By the time the Exposition opened, young Baynard had seen most of the southeastern part of the United States. His favorite amusement on trains and in hotels was reading, and before he was eleven years old he had devoured about five hundred books. Later, he went to the Tome School in Port Deposit, Maryland, and then to the Episcopal Academy in Philadelphia, from which he was graduated in 1912.

Soon after leaving school, Kendrick went to work at the Packard automobile plant in Detroit. He roomed with a young friend, just across the border, in Windsor, Ontario. It was there that he heard the declaration of World War I in August 1914. One hour later he enlisted in the Canadian Army, the first American to volunteer. He saw service in France with the First Canadian Battalion in 1915, was wounded, and later transferred to the Medical Corps, going to Salonika with the Fourth Canadian General Hospital. Invalided a second time, he returned to England via Egypt in 1916. Subsequently he was stationed in London with the Royal Canadian Army Service Corps. Awarded the 1914-15 Star, Kendrick also received the Canadian War Medal and the British War Medal. After four and a half years in the Canadian Expeditionary Forces, he was demobilized in Ontario and returned to New York on New Year's Day 1919.

Back in the United States, Kendrick had a variety of business experiences. He was secretary of the Selden Cypress Door Company in Palatka, Florida, from 1921 to 1927; president of the Trades Publishing Company, Philadelphia, in 1928; general manager of Peter Clark, Inc., New York City, 1929; general manager, Bing and Bing's Hotels, New York City, 1930-31. While in Florida he found time to read law, but although he passed his bar examinations, he never practiced. He also studied accounting, became a certified public accountant and a member of various accounting firms. Always commanding a large salary, he amassed a considerable fortune; but most of it was lost in the crash of 1929.

The depression crystallized Kendrick's desire to work for himself, to have a profession that could be carried on wherever he happened to be. In 1932, he left the business world to become a full-time free-lance writer. He had had some contact with publishing, in both editorial and executive capacities. Moreover, he had long been a devotee of the detective story, and had thought of writing one himself. It seemed natural, then, that he should choose this field. He began with the pulps, writing a number of short stories and more than forty novelettes for such magazines as *Black Mask, True Detective,* and others. In 1934, his first novel, *Blood on Lake Louisa,* appeared. Of this book, which won the third prize in *Liberty* Magazine's first serial contest, Isaac Anderson wrote in the New York *Times,* "It would be interesting to know what novels won the first and second prizes over so thrilling a yarn as this one." Continuing in the Florida locale, his next story, *The Iron Spiders* (1936), introduced Stan Rice, the lanky sheriff who had figured in so many of Kendrick's short stories. Rice is the protagonist in two other books, *The Eleven of Diamonds* (1937) and *Death Behind the Go-Through* (1938).

In *The Last Express* (1937) Kendrick created a new sleuth, blind Captain Duncan Maclain, a character inspired by an incident which had occurred twenty years earlier in London, when the author was serving in the Canadian Army. He had volunteered to play the piano for the blinded soldiers at St. Dunstans Home during their recreation period. One of the inmates, a young sergeant, had traced Kendrick's entire war record by fingering the emblems on his uniform. In response to Kendrick's surprise, the boy had replied, "I don't see anything remarkable about that. . . .The blue tabs—they feel different from the others—show you were in the first battalion. You're wearing medics' insignia on your shoulders, and a Middle East patch. The only Canadian hospital out there is at Salonika. One of my brothers was there and came back through Egypt. And you're wearing a Service Corps cap badge, which shows your present unit." This example of sensory perception made a lasting impression on Kendrick and, years later, gave him the idea for his now famous blind detective. In order that his character should do nothing fictionally that any blind man could not do with proper effort and training, Kendrick read more than thirty books about the blind. He also paid many visits to the school in Morristown, New Jersey, where the Seeing Eye dogs are trained.

Long intervals between books confirm the author's statement that he works slowly and carefully because he wants each detail to be correct. When several books appear in one year, they have been simmering for some time. Kendrick prepares no story outline beforehand; he lets his characters make the plot—and the logical person is the murderer. Incidents occur as the story progresses and eventually everything falls into place. The author revises as he works. But in the Maclain books, Kendrick feels that there should be a definite reason for a blind man to be the detective. Thus, in *The Last Express*, Maclain is the friend of the murdered man's sister's fiancé; in *The Whistling Hangman* (1937) he is playing chess with the hotel manager when the tragedy occurs; *The Odor of Violets* (1941) concerns the safety of the city in the blackout, so Maclain, an intelligence officer in the last war who now lives in perpetual darkness, is the proper person; in *Blind Man's Bluff* (1943) the victim is a blind man, therefore Maclain is called upon to reconstruct his possible reactions; *Death Knell* (1945) concerns friends, as does *Out of Control* (1945). The plot of this last book has been hailed by critics as most nearly approaching the legendary "perfect crime."

Of the many dollar-a-year men employed by the Government in World War II, perhaps none has been assigned to his job for a more unusual reason than has Baynard Kendrick. His stories about Captain Maclain and his Seeing Eye dogs attracted the attention of the Library of Congress and the American Foundation for the Blind because the author was "able to get across to the public, while entertaining it, ideas which workers for the blind have striven for years to instill." When the education of soldiers blinded in the war became one of the Army's problems, the Library of Congress suggested to the Red Cross that Kendrick give a talk at Old Farms Convalescent Hospital at Avon, Connecticut, where special courses are offered to blinded veterans. This and other talks led to a full-time job as civilian consultant and instructor at Avon and at Valley Forge General Hospital at Phoenixville, Pennsylvania. Kendrick taught the more than seven hundred veterans in his classes English, accounting, and creative writing.

Lights Out (1945), a dramatic and poignant portrayal of the rehabilitation of a blinded soldier, Larry Nevin, is Kendrick's first serious novel. "Describing to the layman the difficult and fascinating routines with which the blind are made to see," this book is the result of the author's experiences at Avon and Valley Forge. "Mr. Kendrick," writes Enid Griffis in the New York *Times*, "probes the mind and heart of Larry Nevin, and reports what he finds there with skill, accuracy, and deep feeling." The novel also contains social implications, for Larry "begins to think for the first time in his life, and in thinking, discovers new and important values." "*Lights Out*," continues Miss Griffis, "will do harrowing things to the emotions, but it should be placed on the list of

BAYNARD KENDRICK

required reading for all those who still have eyes with which to see, and a brain with which to think."

In addition to his novels, Kendrick has contributed articles, short stories, and novelettes to a number of periodicals, among them the *American* Magazine, *Coronet*, *Esquire*, *Good Housekeeping*, *Liberty* Magazine, and *Red Book*. His novels have been made into Talking Books, transcribed into Braille, and translated into many foreign languages. Two of his books were made into motion pictures by Metro-Goldwyn-Mayer—*The Last Express* and *The Odor of Violets* (filmed as *Eyes in the Night*). MGM also bought the right to feature Duncan Maclain in one of their own plays, *The Hidden Eye*.

In November 1940, Baynard Kendrick was married to Martha Pomeroy, his second wife. His first marriage, in 1919, to Edythe Stevens, the mother of his three children—Baynard, Jr., Edith, and Julia—ended in divorce. Kendrick is a Mason, a member of the Authors League Council, and in 1945 was first president of Mystery Writers of America, Inc. A large man, Kendrick stands six feet three and weighs one hundred and ninety-five pounds. His wavy brown hair is still thick. An ardent hunter and fisherman, as one might infer from his Florida novels, Kendrick has also such recreations as chess, and bridge, in which he is an expert of professional standing. He is a member of the Marshall Chess Club of New York.

Reference

Who's Who in America, 1946-47

KEYNES, (JOHN MAYNARD KEYNES, 1ST) BARON (kānz) June 5, 1883—Apr. 21, 1946 British economist of international influence; financial adviser to the British Treasury; opponent of Versailles Treaty policy; proponent of full employment theory; represented

KEYNES, BARON—*Continued*

his Government at international conferences; vice-president of World Bank and Fund; orator, historian, farmer, bibliophile; books include *The Economic Consequences of the Peace* (1919), *A Treatise on Money* (1930), *The General Theory of Employment, Interest, and Money* (1936). See *Current Biography* 1941 Yearbook.

Obituary

N Y Times p1+ Ap 22 '46 por

KEYSERLING, HERMANN (ALEXANDER), COUNT (kĭ'sĕr-lĭng hĕr'män) July 20, 1880—Apr. 26, 1946 Philosopher, author, and lecturer; born in Estonia, left when dispossessed in the 1918 Soviet revolution; traveled extensively but considered Germany his home; published *Travel Diary of a Philosopher* (1925), *The Book of Marriage* (1926), *Europe* (1928), and *America Set Free* (1929); the exponent of an intuitional "popular mysticism."

Obituary

N Y Times p22 Ap 29 '46 por

KINDLER, HANS (kĭnd'lēr häns) Jan. 8, 1893- Conductor

Address: b. c/o National Symphony Orchestra, Woodward Bldg., Washington, D.C.

In the National Symphony Orchestra, Washington, D.C., has a musical ensemble which, it is said, ranks with the best American organizations and which throughout its fifteen years of existence has been a zealous sponsor of modern composers. Its guiding genius and founder is Dutch-American Hans Kindler, formerly a cello virtuoso.

A native of Holland, Hans Kindler was born the son of Carel and Jeannette (Hanken) Kindler in Rotterdam on January 8, 1893. On his mother's side he is descended from a Polish-Russian noble family, one member of which, the Countess Evelina Hanska, was the idol and inspiration of the French novelist Honoré de Balzac; and through this relationship he is a second cousin of the late Hendrik Willem van Loon. Both parents were musical, his father an oboist and English horn player, and his mother a pianist. Young Hans received his musical education at the Rotterdam Conservatory of Music, and in 1908, at the age of fifteen, was graduated with first prize in both piano and cello. Later he was to study the cello with Mossel, Pablo Casals, and Jean Gerardy, for like many another famous conductor, Hans Kindler began his career as an instrumentalist. To round out his education he also studied literature, art, the classical languages, and Italian.

At the age of ten he had made his first public appearance in Rotterdam; his enthusiastic, boyish approach to the study of the cello during those early days he recalled in an article written for *Etude* in 1925: "To me there was [at this time] a great fascination, a kind of artisan's excitement, in the struggle with and the conquering of the technical difficulties of the cello. When I was a boy of fourteen to fifteen, I loved to make that which was difficult already, more difficult still . . . to come to the next lesson with a new technical difficulty 'subjugated' gave me a real thrill. It was not till later that I came to the realization that . . . to phrase a melody beautifully or to play a simple scale smoothly is just as difficult if not more so than to be able to play the 'Witch's Dance.' "

At the age of seventeen Kindler made his official debut as soloist with the Berlin Philharmonic. Then, until 1914 he appeared with orchestras and in recitals in Germany, Austria, Poland, Holland, and England, playing under the batons of Mengelberg, Sir Landon Ronald, Kunwald, Pierné, and others, and in joint concerts with such artists as Busoni, Schoenberg, and Julia Culp. At the same time, from his nineteenth year he not only occupied the position of first cellist in the Berlin-Charlottenburg Opera orchestra but was principal teacher of his instrument at Berlin's Klindworth-Scharwenka Conservatory. At the age of eighteen, records David Ewen, his reputation had brought him an invitation to play before the Queen of Holland.

In 1914 the youthful virtuoso took time from his many pursuits to cross the Atlantic to visit his mother who was then in New York. Before he could return to Europe, war had begun, preventing him from going back. With newly acquired first American citizenship papers and a musicians' union card in his possession, therefore, he secured the position of first cellist of the Philadelphia Orchestra, conducted by Leopold Stokowski. Soon he was also solo cellist with the orchestra and had begun a second concert career. Five years later, in 1919, yielding to demand, he relinquished his Philadelphia connection so as to devote himself exclusively to solo work. For two seasons he toured only the United States, but in 1921 he returned to the concert platforms of England and subsequently toured also Holland, France, Belgium, Czechoslovakia, Austria, and Italy. He appeared with orchestras led by conductors Stock, Furtwängler, Monteux, Rodzinski, Reiner, and Bodanzky; with artists Caruso, Rachmaninoff, Ravel, Gabrilowitsch, Thibault, and Cortot—in trio performances; and he introduced the cello works of composers Bloch, Schoenberg, Ravel, Malipiero, Pizzetti, Casella, and Ornstein—some of which were dedicated to him or written especially for him. In London the *Daily Telegraph* characterized him as the "Kreisler of the violoncello." And James Gibbons Huneker wrote, "I do not expect in my life to hear duplicates of an Elman or a Kreisler, a Casals or a Hans Kindler."

Kindler's first opportunity to conduct came in 1927, when he was invited to lead the Philadelphia Orchestra during one of its special Sunday night concert series. Shortly thereafter he was chosen by Mrs. Elizabeth Sprague Coolidge '41, the well-known music patron, to conduct a series of concerts of contemporary music which she was sponsoring in Milan, Rome, Vienna, Prague, Paris, Amsterdam, Brussels, London, and elsewhere. As a result, his reputation as a conductor of the modern idiom established, Kindler next found himself selected to conduct the première of Igor Stravinsky's ballet *Apollon Musagète* at the Library of Congress in Washington, D.C., on April 27, 1928. This was the period which Kindler later characterized as his "hybrid career," when he often combined a solo performance on the cello with the leadership of the remainder of the program.

It was also the period during which he made up his mind to abandon the career of a cellist entirely for that of the conductor. Two considerations influenced his decision, it was noted in an article in the *Knickerbocker Weekly*. The first was his fear of the effect on his art of the constant repetition of familiar works which is the lot of the recitalist. "To think," he expressed it, "that really great artists like Paderewski and others, at sixty-five, would have to practice, for purely material reasons, the same pieces which they played, probably better, when they were eighteen years old, seems to me disgraceful, and, to tell the truth, anti-artistic. For the ideal artist, every performance should be but a stepping stone to the next one." Secondly, for some time, he said, it had bothered him that the capital of a nation as great as the United States should have no musical organization of its own, and an orchestra for Washington became his dream. Thus, though at the height of his career as a virtuoso, during the next two years he gave his final programs as a cellist, ending in 1929-30 with his most extensive tour, a hundred and ten concerts which took him around the world from California to the Indian Archipelago.

The next year, 1931, in spite of the fact that the United States was in the grip of the depression and that a number of similar ventures in Washington during the preceding decade had failed, Hans Kindler set about building the National Symphony Orchestra. In defiance of pessimistic forecasts he managed to obtain the necessary backing from nearly one hundred persons. Then, with a carefully selected personnel, he launched a first season of twenty-four concerts—and, "much to the amazement of his friends, and to his own quiet satisfaction," wrote David Ewen, was able to return 31 per cent of the original investment at its close. Equal or greater success attended the orchestra's subsequent seasons. The number of patrons steadily increased until it approached ten thousand—to make the National, as Kindler wished it to be, a real people's orchestra. The schedule of concerts in Washington was greatly expanded and the organization departed on tours which took it north into Canada and south to Florida, giving in the nine years between 1932 and 1941 two hundred and sixty-three concerts in ninety-four different cities. The orchestra's recording schedule likewise grew. In 1935 it inaugurated free summer concerts on the Potomac, in 1940 it organized students' concerts and, more recently, early autumn "Pops" concerts and operatic performances.

At the same time, like Stock, Stokowski, and Koussevitzky, Kindler made a practice of

Harris & Ewing. Courtesy of Musical America
HANS KINDLER

introducing to his audiences the works of contemporary musicians. (He believes they fail of their just recognition primarily because the apathy of newspapers, in denying preperformance notes and in slighting critical reviews, makes it doubly hard for the interested conductor to attract public attention.) In 1943, for instance, it was estimated that the repertoire of the National Symphony included approximately seven hundred scores, a good proportion of them seldom-performed modern compositions. These, a critic said, were played with the same dignity and appreciation as were the classics. What Kindler would like is some method of improving the chances of survival in the repertoire of this contemporary music, and in 1944 he suggested as a solution a forum on modern works held every four or five years.

For the critic of the Boston *Transcript* the National Symphony Orchestra was, after one performance, "in sonority, technical facility, flexibility and the various essential virtues . . . approaching the standards of the best symphony orchestras in the world." After its benefit performance for the Hendrik Willem van Loon Scholarship Fund at the Metropolitan Opera House in December 1944, Olin Downes wrote in the New York *Times*: "It would be a pleasure to hear the Washington symphony orchestra again in a concert hall . . . for no orchestra can do itself justice on the stage of the Opera House, where the most brilliant fortissimo sounds like chamber music, and the resonance is prevailing faint and dry. This orchestra has had thirty of its regular members inducted into the armed forces, but it gave highly creditable performances, and these with special conscientiousness and care for detail on the conductor's part." As a guest leader of other orchestras, Kindler has achieved equal recognition, Mexico City reporting, for instance, that "he possesses a keen sense of style

KINDLER, HANS—*Continued*

and a special gift for getting from an orchestra a mellow, velvety tone."

Kindler conducts without a score, and complains of his phenomenal memory which annoyingly recalls to his mind errors made by a player as many as ten years earlier. Of his performance David Ewen has written: "He may not rise to those empyrean heights to which some other conductors soar, but at the same time it can also be said that he never descends to . . . cheapness, superficiality, or sensationalism. He is a self-respecting and respected musician who does justice to the . . . music he performs, and serves his art with humility. . . . .Beyond everything else the National is his orchestra . . . responding to his every demand with amazing resilience." Among the honors which have come to Kindler are an honorary doctorate of music from George Washington University (1932), the Elizabeth Sprague Coolidge Medal for "eminent services in the field of chamber music" (1939), the Mahler Medal (1944), and the Officer's Degree of the Order of Orange Nassau, the highest award bestowed on citizens of other lands by the Dutch Government (1944). He also possesses a sapphire ring given him by the Italian poet Gabriele d'Annunzio after a private cello recital. At the New York World's Fair of 1939 his name was inscribed on the special panel honoring outstanding foreign-born contributors to American culture.

Naturalized in 1921, Kindler has written: "I applied for my final papers out of gratitude and loyalty to a country which had been so generous to a strange boy." He was married in 1920 to Alice Riddle, and has three children, Jan, Helen Yvonne, and Don. Tall, blue-eyed, and now gray-haired, he reports that the exertion of conducting regularly causes him to lose twenty pounds during the season. When not otherwise occupied, he finds his recreation in wandering through the countryside with a gun—though he rarely shoots—and in reading. In the corridor outside his office hang caricatures of instrumentalists, of which he is the artist. And invariably on visits to "Nieuw Veere" in Connecticut the cello would reappear to join in duets with that "determined amateur" but "excruciatingly bad" violinist, Hendrik van Loon—when the professional and the amateur were not insulting each other, "in the nicest possible spirit, of course."

References

Knickerbocker W 3:20-25 Mr 29 '43 il pors
N Y Post p7 O 27 '45 por
America's Young Men, 1938-39
Ewen, D. Dictators of the Baton (1943) por; ed. Living Musicians (1940) por
Grove's Dictionary of Music and Musicians Suppl vol (1940)
Parkhurst, W. and De Bekker, L. J. eds. The Encyclopedia of Music and Musicians (1937)
Pierre Key's Musical Who's Who (1931)
Thompson, O. ed. International Cyclopedia of Music and Musicians (1943)
Who Is Who in Music, 1941
Who's Who in America, 1946-47

KONOYE, FUMIMARO, PRINCE (kō-nō-yĕ foo-mē-mä-rō) Oct. 1891—Dec. 16, 1945 Japanese Premier in 1933, 1937-39, and 1940-41; attended Paris Peace Conference in 1919; elected vice-president of the House of Peers; joined Rome-Berlin-Tokyo Axis; committed suicide rather than surrender as a suspected war criminal. See *Current Biography* 1940 Yearbook.

Obituary

N Y Times p1+ D 16 '45 por

KORDA, SIR ALEXANDER Sept. 16, 1893- British motion picture producer; industrialist

Address: b. c/o London Film Productions, Inc., London; 350 5th Ave., New York

Sir Alexander Korda, British motion picture producer and director, whose cinema work during the past few years has of his own choice been limited, re-established himself early in 1946 as an independent producer when he formed his new company, London Film Productions. The British motion picture magnate, who first attained recognition as the man primarily responsible for the prestige of the British film industry since 1933, thus presented a challenge to the domination of English films by J. Arthur Rank [45].

The son of Henry and Ernestine Korda, Alexander Korda was born in Turkeve, Hungary, on September 16, 1893. His well-to-do father was employed as land agent on the estate of a bishop. Young Alexander, who at fourteen began to work as a schoolteacher, was educated further in Budapest, first in the Reformist College, then at the Royal University, receiving his degree from the latter institution.

Although Korda chose to become a journalist, this profession, at which he had worked even in his teens, gradually lost its main attraction for him. Instead, he decided in 1915 to cast his lot with the motion picture industry (as yet, the silent films) in Hungary. In his new work he found his experience as a journalist very valuable to him, for he began by translating subtitles. Soon after, however, he began to write and direct pictures of his own, his first vehicle for the screen being an "inferior epic based on the Freudian theory of dreams." Having attained a measure of fame in Hungary by the end of World War I, Korda went next to Vienna where he made the successful film, *The Prince and the Pauper*. From there he went to Berlin to work for UFA, and then to other European capitals. While he was trying to establish himself internationally in the motion picture field, in 1919 Korda was married to Maria Farkas, an actress. One son, Peter, was born to them, and the marriage subsequently terminated in divorce.

After more than ten years' connection with European cinema companies, Korda arrived in Hollywood in the mid-twenties, at about the time that sound tracks were being added to the films. He was first associated with First National Pictures, whose name and assets the Warner brothers had acquired in 1925, then with the Fox Film Corporation, among other companies. *The Private Life of Helen of Troy* was the most notable of his early films. One critic wrote of it, "Judged by any standard, it was a superb production. Judged by Hollywood standards, it was three years ahead of its time." However, it found little favor with the public. During his sojourn in Hollywood Korda had gained scant recognition; by 1930 he had left for Europe where he had little success until he took a job in Paramount's Joinville studios in France to produce *Marius*.

Korda arrived in England in 1931 to make the picture *Reserved for Ladies* for Paramount-British Films. He remained there to organize, a year later, with his brother Vincent, the author Lajos Biro, and a film salesman, the enterprise known as London Film Productions, Limited, of which Korda became chairman and managing director. London Films planned to make pictures for release by Paramount and the Gaumont-British companies. Meanwhile, Korda was occupied with directing *Wedding Rehearsal, The Girl from Maxims, Counsel's Opinion,* and *Men of Tomorrow.* With the knowledge that there was "no quota barrier on British films" in the United States and with the assurance that he would receive financial aid from the British, Korda decided to produce English films, hitherto inferior to American films, that would be equal or superior to those produced in the United States. In 1933 came the first fulfillment of Korda's plans, when his studios released *The Private Life of Henry VIII.* With Charles Laughton, Robert Donat, Binnie Barnes, Wendy Barrie, and Merle Oberon as the main players (their film careers were launched in this picture) the "considered, intelligent" film, produced at a minimum of cost, became an immediate success in England and in the United States, and Korda was "credited with the amazing task of lifting British film production into the front ranks on a solidly, proudly competitive basis with Hollywood."

Encouraged by their success, Korda and his company sought new triumphs in the field. For this purpose, they imported well-known American motion picture scenarists and performers, and at the same time sponsored the film careers of British players and writers. *Catherine the Great* (1934), with Elizabeth Bergner, was Korda's next production, followed in the same year by *The Private Life of Don Juan* (with Douglas Fairbanks, Sr.), and in 1935 by *The Scarlet Pimpernel* with Leslie Howard, *Sanders of the River* with Paul Robeson, and lastly the film *Congo Raid.* With the profits obtained from these films, together with the capital (almost a million pounds) provided by the Prudential Assurance Company, Limited, a "model motion-picture production plant" on an estate in Denham, Buckinghamshire, was completed for Korda's organization by January 1936. Vincent Korda became art director, and another brother, Zoltan, was also made a director.

In 1935 Korda became a stockholder in a Hollywood company, the United Artists Corporation, along with three of its founders, Mary Pickford, Douglas Fairbanks, Jr., and Charlie Chaplin. Before this, United Artists had distributed British films, Korda's among them, in the United States and Europe. Korda's shareholding facilitated this distribution; his action was then viewed in some quarters as a British move to gain some control of the American film industry. Following this negotiation, Korda's productions for United Artists included, in 1936, *The Ghost Goes West,* a much-discussed comedy directed by René Clair; *Things to Come,* a screenplay written by H. G. Wells depicting the history of the world for the next one hundred years; *Rembrandt*; and *The Man Who Could Work Miracles.* Among later films were: *Fire Over England, Knight Without Armour, Paradise for Two,* and *The Return of the Scarlet Pimpernel*; in 1938, *The Divorce of Lady X* and *South Riding*; and in the following year, *Over the Moon,* and *Four Feathers.*

Because he found it "frightfully hard to meet the American pace from abroad" in the midst of war difficulties and because many of his players had assignments in the United States, in 1940 Korda established another motion picture company, Alexander Korda Films, in Hollywood. Pictures made there and released by United Artists were the Technicolor fantasy, *The Thief of Bagdad,* and a film dealing with the history of aviation; *That Hamilton Woman* which Korda directed as well as produced, and *Lydia* (1941); *The Jungle Book,* adapted from a Kipling fable, and *To Be or Not To Be* (1942). The Alexander Korda Films organization was only a temporary arrangement and was discontinued late in 1942.

During this same period, while Korda was traveling between the two countries to fulfill picture commitments, he also produced movies with a decidedly propagandist trend. The producer, who was already a naturalized British citizen at the outbreak of the war, maintained close contact with the Ministry of Information and the service film units so that he might aid the war effort of his adopted country. Always a "fervent liberal," Korda had more opportunity than ever to apply his ideas "assailing war and tyranny" to motion picture art. Among his war dramas, screened under trying wartime disruptions and shortages, was the first British propaganda film to be shown in the United States, *The Lion Has Wings* (released in 1940). (Previously, Korda's production of Wells's prophetic *Things to Come* presented a "reductio ad absurdum of fascism"; *To Be or Not To Be* was a comedy-satire on the Nazis in Poland.)

In March 1943 Korda became affiliated with Metro-Goldwyn-Mayer as head of the organization's production division which was amalgamated with his own London Film Produc-

SIR ALEXANDER KORDA

tions, Limited. (Korda's interests in this company and in United Artists were reported at the time to be under investigation by the antitrust division of the Department of Justice. Later he sold his United Artists holdings.) Begun as an "artistically independent" unit, the association between Korda and MGM lasted two years. Before he withdrew in October 1945, however, Korda had produced *The Perfect Strangers* in 1944 (its American release in 1946 was under the title *Vacation from Marriage*). He also prepared to film about fourteen scripts, but the screen work on these was held up by the delayed reconditioning of his new studios, the Denham Studios having been sold to Rank.

In the early months of 1946, Korda again allied himself with British films when his independent British motion-picture producing and distributing company was organized. The corporation, known as London Film Productions, has a controlling interest in British Lion Film Corporation, Limited (a distributing agency which makes the producer a seller as well), and is also comprised of Regina Films (French producing company) and Tricolore Films, Incorporated (American distribution outlet for French and possibly other foreign pictures). Korda became the possessor of the second largest studio space in England with the combination of his recently acquired Worton Hall and Sound City studios. When much of the rivalry between the American and British motion picture industries resumed with the end of World War II, the monopoly by American pictures of the greater part of the playing time of movies shown in Great Britain gained widespread attention. In the spring of 1946 Korda predicted that British producers would soon supply 50 per cent of English theaters' screen time. In addition, he emphasized the need for British pictures that would "excite and interest the public." In an article

appearing in the New York *Times* (December 1, 1946) the producer alleged, among other things, that American domination of the world market in matters of distribution was cluttering the market with often worthless pictures, thus preventing better films from reaching the general public.

As some of his associates in his new enterprise Korda secured Julien Duvivier, Herbert Wilcox, Orson Welles, and Carol Reed. A number of well-known actresses and actors, both American and English, have signed contracts or have negotiated to make films in partnership with Korda, who initiated, too, an interchange between American and British technical specialists. In 1946 Korda held screen rights to Thomas Mann's *The Magic Mountain,* Daphne du Maurier's *The King's General,* the successful French picture *Les Enfants du Paradis,* and, in addition, rights to Jules Verne's *Around the World in Eighty Days,* to be adapted for a musical. He had undertaken to buy back from MGM-British certain stories prepared during the years of his association with them. *Bonnie Prince Charlie, The True Story of Carmen, Man About the House, The City of Bells,* and *Hungarian Rhapsody* (the film biography of Franz Liszt), and Oscar Wilde's *Salome* and *An Ideal Husband* are among the future productions scheduled for Korda's studios. In September the British magnate, with other British independent producers, signed a contract with Twentieth Century-Fox under which the American company was to distribute their films in Australia, New Zealand, and Tasmania; in 1946 Korda, too, was understood to be contemplating a distribution-company project with Samuel Goldwyn "⁴. In 1947 Korda films will be in two categories: low budget (about 150,000 pounds) and high budget (about 350,000 pounds) pictures. According to one of Korda's representatives, it is hoped that the low budget series "will be dropped altogether after the initial year of operation."

Called the most scholarly of producers, Korda was characterized by C. A. Lejeune in a *Fortnightly* (March 1935) article as possessing "the kind of fecund and adventurous spirit" found "among the artists of the Renaissance." This spirit prompted Korda to attempt overcoming many "realistic restrictions" inherent in sound films by producing "spectacle" pictures in which fantasy, imagination, and varied Technicolor effects predominate. Korda is known, too, for his story flair, and "like all good journalists . . . he senses the right moment to publish, and the apt method of presentation to a special audience." A true romantic, Korda has often permitted historical inaccuracies, as those in *That Hamilton Woman,* in order to emphasize "universal" yet personal elements in the story. He also "collects" writers since he believes that "young, fresh writers are the life-blood of the screen." At times he has criticized producers for underestimating the intelligence of the movie public and has called for a more serious attitude toward picture-making.

Korda, described as a distinguished-looking man, is six feet tall and has graying hair and gray-blue eyes. The spectacled producer is noted for his knowledge of literature and painting, familiarity with music, and sense of humor. He is interested in the formation of "drama and instructional film" groups in English universities, and later in 1946 became a member of the committee of the newly-formed British Film Academy, a "nonfactional and nonpolitical" group whose purpose is to enhance the prestige of the British motion picture industry. He holds membership in the American Motion Picture Association. In 1939, Korda was married, for the second time, to Merle Oberon "⁴¹; six years later the film celebrities were divorced. In June 1942 the producer-director was knighted for his contributions to the British film industry. Early in 1946 Sir Alexander acquired a Holbein portrait of Henry VIII, declaring that, for him, it was "an ancestral, family portrait."

References

Lit Digest 122:19-21 Jl 18 '36
N Y Times II p3 Ap 14 '46
Stage D '35 por
Time 26:44+ S 9 '35 por; 27:43-46 Ap 6 '36
International Motion Picture Almanac, 1943-44
International Who's Who, 1945-46
Who's Who, 1946

KRAVCHENKO, VICTOR A(NDRE-YEVICH) (kråf-chăn'kô ŭn-dryå'yĕ-vyĭch) Oct. 11, 1905- Russian writer; industrial engineer
Address: b. c/o Charles Scribner's Sons, 597 5th Ave., New York

Victor A. Kravchenko, the Russian industrial engineer who made front page news in the spring of 1944 by leaving his position in Washington as an official of the Soviet Purchasing Commission and severing his connection with the Communist Party, two years later completed the writing of his memoirs in the volume he named *I Chose Freedom*. The book continued to be listed among best-selling titles through the spring and summer of 1946.

His personal declaration of war against the Soviet regime had its roots, writes Victor Andreyevich Kravchenko, in the passion for freedom he imbibed in his early youth when revolution and civil wars swept through his home in the Ukraine. On the night of his birth, on October 11, 1905, his father, Andrei Fyodorovich Kravchenko, narrowly escaped capture by the Czar's police. (Andrei Kravchenko was the leader of the general strike of the railway men in Yekaterinoslav, which ushered in the Revolution of 1905.) The boy knew poverty and hunger during the first nine years of his life, when his father was the fascinating stranger who lived with the family in intervals of freedom. When Victor was five, Tatiana Alexeyevna Kalyadina, his mother, sent him to live with Grandfather Fyodor Panteleyevich, an ex-czarist soldier, in the provincial town of Alexandrovsk. There he entered the public school, and in 1916 returned to his native city to continue his studies in the Gymnasium, or higher school. That winter, when the collapse of czarism was imminent, Victor's home often served as a stopping-off place for fugitives from Siberia.

The turbulence of civil war lasted for several years in the Ukraine until the Bolsheviks had consolidated their regime there. Early in 1919 Victor's family was among the hundred from Yekaterinoslav who were settled on a near-by fertile estate on the Dnieper, which was turned into an agricultural cooperative or "commune" for city workers. In the autumn of 1920, at the close of the commune's second harvest, he enrolled with his brother at Erastovka Agricultural School at Komissarovka. Fired by the eloquent idealism of a Communist Party lecturer, he decided to become a miner shortly afterward, and in the summer of 1922 was sent to a mine in the Alchevsk district; but instead of a pick he was put to wielding a pen and an abacus in one of the administrative offices, because of the lack of literate men. Kravchenko dates his conversion to communism from the arrival at the mines of Comrade Lazarev, who gave a series of lectures on the problems of socialism: that year he joined the Comsomols (the Communist Union of Youth, a branch of the Communist Party). An ardent member, he was soon an "activist," writing, speaking, serving on committees. He was transferred to work in the pits, but after a serious accident returned to the city and obtained a position in the Petrovsky-Lenin metallurgical factory, where from the mechanical laboratory he was promoted to the pipe-rolling mill and in less than a year became a foreman. Late in 1927 he answered the call to the Red Army, but a fall from a horse cut short his military career.

Kravchenko was formally admitted into the Communist Party in the middle of 1929. "I was no longer an individual with a free choice of friends, interests, views," he writes. "I was dedicated forever to an idea and a cause. . . .There were many defects, extensive suffering. But there was also the lift of terrific excitement, and inflamed hopes. . . .I belonged to the minority that was stirred by the ideas behind the great effort." Selected along with thousands of young men for training as an engineer to carry on the task of industrializing the vast country, Kravchenko matriculated at the Technological Institute in Kharkov early in 1931. Not long afterward transferred to the metallurgical institute in his native city, now renamed Dnepropetrovsk, he received an assignment to go as part of a commission to expedite the work at the Nikopol metallurgical construction plant. Then the central committee of the party chose him as a member of a committee to oversee the harvesting and secure the bulk of grain for the Government, in one of the communities of the Ukraine. This was the collectivization followed by the famine of 1932-33. Kravchenko says his mission was a success chiefly because he treated the peasants humanely. "Inwardly, in the secret recesses of

KRAVCHENKO, VICTOR A.—*Continued*

my being, I must have begun to break with the party at this time," he reveals in his book.

At twenty-nine Kravchenko was launched in his engineering career as one of the chiefs in the new industrial enterprise at Nikopol. From 1935 on, he continued to advance in the ranks of the bureaucracy as party "trouble-shooter" in other enterprises which, he says, had been initiated in haste or had been corruptly administered. Although he found the atmosphere more and more onerous, he was successful to a large degree. After being shunted about to various plants and having narrowly escaped the purges of the GPU a number of times, he was finally made an executive in the central Government, elevated to the directorship of a department in the Sovnarkom, with an office in the Kremlin. During his brief elevation in the Soviet hierarchy, the idea of going to the United States began to take shape in his mind. Soon after being investigated for some months, he was commissioned to go to the United States to expedite Lend-Lease. He arrived in Washington in August 1943 as a member of the Soviet Purchasing Commission, regarding himself as a "fugitive from injustice."

Placing himself "under the protection of American opinion," in April 1944 Kravchenko gave up his job and Russian citizenship and issued a statement to the New York *Times* assailing Soviet domestic and foreign policies. The Soviet Embassy formally repudiated Kravchenko as only one of the U.S.S.R.'s three thousand employees in the United States, a mere "inspector of pipes," and deserter from the Russian Army, who refused to return to his country for military service.

Kravchenko stated he worked on the manuscript of his book, *I Chose Freedom, the Personal and Political Life of a Soviet Official,* "under harrowing conditions of persecution and threats." Written in his native tongue and translated by an unnamed writer, the autobiography was published in April 1946. In denouncing the U.S.S.R. as a police state which has usurped the political and civil freedoms of her citizens, Kravchenko has elaborately reconstructed his emotional past, written detailed conversations, and named innumerable people, places, and circumstances, except when he felt obliged to alter some of this material to protect people in Russia.

Reviewers of Kravchenko's arraignment of the U.S.S.R. were essentially in agreement with Elizabeth Simon of the New York *Times Book Review,* who wrote: "The most important question in evaluating such a book as this, that of its accuracy, is impossible to answer finally." "Mr. Kravchenko," she continued, "has not only presented a remarkable account of his own experiences but—implicitly and explicitly—challenged liberal American apologists for Soviet Russia to sustain, in equally concrete terms, their defense and justification of its regime." Taking a more objective view of the book's impact, Henry Seidel Canby observed: "Neither the American Communists, who hold up the Russian way of life for our imitation, nor the Russia-baiters who wish to involve us in a war with the Soviets, will get much comfort from

this account." Lewis Gannett wrote: "Some readers ready to accept most details of his appalling picture of a police state may yet wonder how, if matters were as bad as he pictures them, and as he is fiercely independent, his own rise was possible. . . .Mr. Kravchenko is as obviously sincere as he is without perspective." The historian Frederick L. Schuman, appraising the volume in the *New Republic,* also condemned it for what he considered a lack of balanced perspective and pointed out, too, the fact that although Kravchenko broke "inwardly" with the party in 1932 he continued to profit from his membership for twelve years thereafter. In all, criticisms ranged from Dorothy Thompson's estimate of the book as "dynamite under illusions" and "the most remarkable and most revelatory report to have come out of the Soviet Union from any source whatsoever" to the view of the New York *Herald Tribune* critic, Walter Kerr, that the book was "a diatribe written by a passionate and disillusioned man who is incapable of reflection and evaluation."

There are no available photographs of Victor Kravchenko, but his publishers reveal that he is a fairly tall, brown-haired man of average weight. They give his marital status as "divorced."

Reference

Kravchenko, V. A. I Chose Freedom (1946)

KROLL, JACK June 10, 1885- Trade union leader

Address: b. c/o Political Action Committee of the Congress of Industrial Organizations, 205 E. 42d St., New York; h. Oak and Burnet Sts., Vernon Manor, Cincinnati

Appointed director of the Political Action Committee of the Congress of Industrial Organizations in July 1946, veteran trade-unionist Jack Kroll succeeded the late Sidney Hillman [40], whose philosophy he has summarized: "An individual worker has an investment in his industry—we are an essential part of the industry and our stake is equal to the employer's. We contribute everything we have to the industry, our lives depend on it, we have a right to a voice in it." A "Hillman man," Kroll intends to translate the philosophy into political ideas by "helping to create in the American people a broader understanding of political responsibilities and of the importance in their daily lives of fuller and more effective participation in the formulation of the policies of our Government."

John Jacob Kroll was born June 10, 1885, in London and brought to the United States as a child by his parents, Mark and Julia Kate (Blumberg) Kroll. Following the example of his father and six brothers, who were working in Rochester (New York) tailor shops, Jack Kroll entered the trade as a cutter in 1900, after having attended high school. By 1903 he had become a union member. Because of the part he took in an ill-fated strike in 1904-05, young Kroll was forced to leave Rochester. He went to Chicago, where it was necessary for him to find work under an assumed name, which he used for eighteen months. "I couldn't get a job—they had my record already. That's how I learned about the blacklist. It's not funny when they catch up with you one thousand miles away to stop you from earning a dollar. . . .I didn't have to read any books to know where I stood."

In 1910, a member of Cutters' Local 61 of the United Garment Workers of America, in Chicago Kroll became acquainted with Sidney Hillman and with him led the Hart, Schaffner and Marx strike of forty thousand predominantly foreign-born garment workers. The strike, the immediate cause of which was the company's failure to settle a grievance involving sixteen women employees, lasted from October 1910 to January 1911, and resulted in the Impartial Arbitration Plan, forerunner of similar boards of negotiation which were later set up throughout American industry. Kroll remained with the insurgent Hillman faction which, dissatisfied with the excessively "conservative tactics and autocratic officers" of the UGW, seceded from that organization in 1914 to form the independent Amalgamated Clothing Workers' Union of America. Starting as a small, "somewhat militant group of exploited urban workers," Amalgamated, under the presidency of Sidney Hillman, grew to a union of one hundred and seventy-seven thousand members by 1920.

After having helped to complete the organization of the men's clothing market in Chicago, during which time he saw "the inside of most of the jails around Chicago . . . [without having been] convicted of anything," Kroll became a national organizer for Amalgamated in 1919. He was "summoned to Cincinnati to salvage the pieces of a losing . . . strike," and remained for seven years as an "organizer, trouble shooter, and administrator" for the union. Concerning his work as union-builder, Kroll has said, "I know I'm no star. I don't proclaim that I am. But I like to work with people. That's what I've done all my life." Others have since affirmed Kroll's "knack of befriending and winning the confidence of industrialists and conservatives." Amalgamated's policy was so successful that one manufacturer, "Golden Rule" Nash, invited the union to organize his Cincinnati clothing plant in the mid-twenties, when production quality had fallen off during the rapid decrease of business.

Kroll was elected a manager of Amalgamated's Cincinnati joint board, and several years later, in 1928, became a vice-president and a member of its executive board. The independent Amalgamated, after nearly two years as an outcast, returned to the A.F. of L. in 1933 (the United Garment Workers from which it had withdrawn in 1914 was an A.F. of L. affiliate). In 1935 the Amalgamated Clothing Workers' president, Sidney Hillman, helped to found the original Committee for Industrial Organizations. When, in the following year, Amalgamated was suspended from the A.F. of L., it became a CIO union. Three years later Kroll was elected a vice-president of the Ohio CIO Industrial Union Council, and in 1939 he became its president.

Underwood & Underwood

JACK KROLL

Kroll came to New York in 1940 to head the joint board of the Laundry Workers' Union, an Amalgamated affiliate with twenty-five thousand members. When the Political Action Committee of the CIO was formed in 1943, Hillman, the national chairman, called on Kroll to be regional director for the Ohio-Kentucky-West Virginia area in the 1944 Presidential campaign. (While Kroll voted Socialist in his early years and carried a Roosevelt banner after 1932, he holds no card in any political party.) In 1944 Kroll was appointed vice-chairman of the PAC, and in the same year won the CIO national award for outstanding work in combatting racial discrimination. In the early part of 1946 the "tenacious, hard-working" Kroll was made assistant director of the CIO drive to organize the South, under Van A. Bittner, the "bitter-tongued old mine-union hand from West Virginia." Kroll resigned from this post upon his appointment to the chairmanship of the CIO-PAC.

On July 18, 1946, seven days after Sidney Hillman's death, Jack Kroll was designated by the CIO executive committee in Washington as director of the executive board of the Political Action Committee. A newly adopted five-man executive board is composed of the secretary-treasurer of each of four CIO unions with Kroll as the administrative head, replacing the original one-man control arrangement which prevailed under Hillman. "In recognition of its responsibilities in the field of political action, the CIO has decided to . . . enlarge the apparatus for conducting political action work," CIO president Philip Murray [41] said as he announced the further extension of the CIO-PAC from seven to eleven members, including the secretary-treasurer of the CIO and Murray himself. The executive board of five, with the eleven-man group, constitutes the steering committee of CIO-PAC.

(Continued next page)

KROLL, JACK—*Continued*

Not one of "labor's beetle-browed glamour boys," wrote James A. Wechsler in the New York *Post,* Kroll accepted the PAC assignment "with the same mellowness of spirit he would have shown if he were told to organize the shop down the street." His quiet demeanor is deceptive, for, a shrewd adversary, "when Kroll hits he hits hard," and he has already served notice that he will fight any Congress which passes antilabor legislation. "We are faced with a situation in which a reactionary coalition is seeking to dominate our political life for selfish and sinister ends. The CIO is deeply aware that the work of Sidney Hillman must be carried forward and completed because the nation's interest so desperately requires it." In policy a "middle-of-the-roader," Kroll asserted, "It will be our job to see that the public knows who's who in Congress and is able to distinguish the villains from the heroes. . . . We will .tell our people the issues. When they go to the ballot box they will use their own judgment. We feel the issues will be so clear and their effect on their futures so obvious that they will know how to vote." The raising of funds to finance the PAC functions, through voluntary contributions from the six million members of CIO unions, is to "get immediate emphasis, and for two reasons: Money is needed and when a man contributes, his heart is a little closer to PAC."

PAC claimed credit for defeating sixteen Congressional incumbents who sought renomination in the August 1946 primaries, and at least part credit for forty-four "improvements" in the quality of Congressional candidates at that time. It was irrelevant, Kroll declared, whether the Eightieth Congress is Republican or Democratic—but it must "serve the interests of the people." The organization listed as significant issues a candidate's position on inflation, housing, discrimination, foreign policy, and industrial and social security. Stating that the course of the Seventy-ninth Congress must be reversed and that "labor and the common people have the power to reverse it," Kroll pledged that PAC would work for the return to Congress of "a militant group of fighting progressives" and the retirement of members "who have spearheaded the reactionary onslaught." In September Kroll was one of three cosigners of a joint open letter to President Truman, asking that the President call an "emergency" session of Congress, to act on desired legislation. Kroll described the November election of many candidates considered unfavorable to labor as "not an affirmative . . . rather, a negative vote." "We have just begun to fight," the labor leader declared. "We shall emphasize day-to-day activity in wards and precincts. . . We are to stay as a vital and growing influence carrying forward the Roosevelt tradition and . . . program." Kroll had written earlier, in the New York *Times Magazine* (October 27, 1946) that labor is in politics to solve "all community problems subject to legislative control. . . .What the CIO asks for politically must be tested first on how good it is for the people as a whole."

An active participant in the Conference of Progressives, the organization which brought forth the resolution to "mobilize the most effective liberal-progressive coalition ever," Kroll, in December, was elected a vice-chairman of the Progressive Citizens of America. The PCA, formed from the dissolution and subsequent merger of two Conference sponsors, the National Citizens Political Action Committee and the Independent Citizens Committee of the Arts, Sciences, and Professions, proposes "to expand the existing progressive groups into a nationwide framework of community political organizations." The program does not "rule out the possibility of a new political party."

Kroll, who continues as a vice-president of Amalgamated and president of the Ohio State CIO Industrial Union Council, has made his home in Cincinnati for twenty-five years. Sent there originally because he was foot-loose, unattached, and therefore free to travel, Kroll arrived in Cincinnati on August 3, 1919, went to a union picnic, met a girl striker named Sarah Sylvia Rabin, and was married to her the following January 19, thus supporting one writer's statement that "all the landmarks in Kroll's life bear a union label." The Krolls have one son, Mark Harold.

Kroll's associates, the newspaper *PM* wrote, find he has a "talent for leading a group to a decision and making most of those present feel that they have played an important part. . . . One of the big surprises of the coming political wars is likely to be Jack Kroll." To one interviewer, the stocky, gray-haired, brown-eyed labor leader looks like "a solid citizen who probably just left a weighty board of directors' meeting." Kroll is a continuous pipe-smoker and a moderate whisky drinker—"but please, no beer." A friend of his remarked, "It's hard to say exciting things about him—he's all serious in business, a guy with moderate tastes, a small middle-class flat in Cincinnati, a quiet home life." Kroll, who has recovered from a once rabid case of baseball enthusiasm, gives his favorite recreation as fishing.

References

N Y Herald Tribune p15 Jl 26 '46
N Y Post p40 Jl 19 '46
N Y Post Mag p38 Jl 24 '46 por
N Y World-Telegram p9 Jl 20 '46
PM p5 Ja 19 '46 por
Who's Who in Labor (1946)

KROLL, JOHN JACOB *See* Kroll, J.

KUHN, IRENE (kün) Jan. 15, 1900- Radio executive; journalist

Address: b. c/o National Broadcasting Company, 30 Rockefeller Plaza, New York; h. 45 Christopher St., New York

In the closing chapter of her autobiography, *Assigned to Adventure,* Irene Kuhn remarks, "If I've heard it once, I've heard it a million times. 'It must be wonderful to be in the newspaper business because you meet so many interesting people.' Yet strict honesty impels me to confess that while reporters gag on the 'interesting people' cliché and pretend a cynicism they don't feel about the unusual character of their work, they do meet interesting people—the most interesting ones everywhere." Meeting interesting people has been Mrs. Kuhn's lifelong hobby and the source of her livelihood as well. Her years have been crowded with reporting from widely separated spots, from Syracuse, in New York, to Shanghai in China. She has been a fashion editor, a foreign correspondent, as well as a scenario and publicity writer. Since 1944 she has been assistant director of information for the National Broadcasting Company.

Most stories of successful Americans follow the familiar pattern of the small-town boy or girl whose first goal is the big city. This tradition was broken by Irene Kuhn, who was born Irene Corbally on January 15, 1900, in New York City, which was not to be the scene of her apprenticeship or early success. Her parents were Patrick J. and Josephine (Connor) Corbally. Young Irene grew up in a large brownstone house which her family shared with her aunts and uncles in New York City's Greenwich Village, "when that lovely section was a village in fact as well as in name." She received her early education in Catholic schools and convents in her native city. At sixteen, before she had finished high school, she decided that secretarial work would provide her with a short-cut to writing because she would be meeting people and would "learn about life." With the hard-won consent of her grandfather who, according to the honored Irish custom, was the "head man of the clan," she enrolled at the Packard business school in New York City. After seven months of studying stenography she "emerged into the great world of business" and secured her first job at a weekly salary of nine dollars.

A series of jobs followed, but none seemed to bring the aspiring writer any closer to her self-appointed role in life. It was while she was secretary to Dr. William J. Gies, then professor of biological chemistry in Columbia University's College of Physicians and Surgeons, that she changed her approach toward her objective. Having convinced her of the necessity of a formal education, he obtained for her a fellowship at Marymount College in Tarrytown-on-the-Hudson, a school directed by French nuns for girls of wealthy families. In the fall of 1918 the teen-aged girl resumed her interrupted studies. At the end of the first term she returned to New York to take college subjects in the Extension Division of Columbia University because she wished to be "among people who for the most part were paying for their own education, people who wanted an education because of an inner urge and not just because it was traditional procedure."

Through the help of a newspaper acquaintance who recommended that the girl acquire her "cub" experience on a newspaper in an upstate town before she ventured into the offices of the metropolitan dailies of New York City, twenty-year-old Irene Corbally secured her first reporting job at eighteen dollars a week

IRENE KUHN

with the Syracuse (New York) *Herald* in 1920. Had her family suspected the nature of her first assignment they would probably have regretted the reluctant assent they gave to her leaving home. So "green that she didn't know copy paper from cleansing tissue," she was sent out on her first day to inquire of the various male citizens of the community, "Do you wear a nightshirt or pajamas, suspenders or a belt? And why?" a few months later, while covering the State Fair in Syracuse, the young reporter ventured her first airplane flight as a passenger.

Shortly afterward the young reporter returned to New York City to work for the *Daily News* which made its first appearance on newsstands on June 26, 1919, as the "offspring" of the Chicago *Tribune*. Philipp Payne, who was then its city editor, taught the girl that the reactions of the "gum-chewers" were virtually the same as those of the upper classes "except that the former are more honest." "On such hard and realistic beginnings did I cut my second set of journalistic teeth." The financial difficulties of the new tabloid brought an end to her job. She thus went to Paris in 1921 to write advertising copy for a New York manufacturer of perfumes and patent medicine. Before long, however, she resigned from this job but did not return to the United States. The Paris edition of the Chicago *Tribune,* the paper owned by Colonel Robert McCormick [42], gave her a good reason for remaining in France. Its fashion editor and reporter, Rosemary Carr, was leaving to marry the poet Stephen Vincent Benét and she readily persuaded the editor, John Clayton, to let Irene Corbally take her place. The New York girl who had once conducted a column, *I'll Tell the World,* in a New York neighborhood paper, the *Greenwich Village Home News,* in 1921 found herself telling Americans in Paris about such diverse subjects

KUHN, IRENE—*Continued*

as the marriage of the heir of a "Tin Plate King" to the daughter of a Russian Grand Duchess, about an evening of music and Dada art at the Galerie Montaigne. The latter assignment she handled with "satire and humor" under the heading "Evening of Dada-ism." As for the first-named assignment, the sumptuous wedding she reported made her determine that, when she married, "it would be with a minimum of fuss."

Not long after this, Irene Corbally was able to keep her vow. In Shanghai, where she had gone on the Japanese freighter *Inaba Maru* in search of adventure, she met a newspaperman, Bert L. Kuhn of Chicago. They were married in June 1922 at the Église de St. Joseph in the French Concession in Shanghai. During the wedding ceremony the bride, who was dressed in a four-dollar dress and a hat that didn't belong to her, was unconsciously composing her own story for the next day's edition of the paper for which she and the groom reported—the *Evening Star* of the China Press.

Not long afterward, the Kuhns obtained a year's leave of absence from the China Press and sailed for Hawaii. In Honolulu, where both did newspaper work, Mrs. Kuhn as a foreign correspondent for the International News Service, their daughter Rene Leilani was born in March 1923. When the child was six months old, her father's restlessness took them back to Shanghai. En route the Kuhns stopped in Yokohama, and in Kobe, on September 1, 1923 they felt the earthquake which did so much damage to Tokyo and its environs.

Back in China, in 1925 Mrs. Kuhn helped to organize the Women's Volunteer Motor Canteen Service during student riots in Shanghai. These followed the shooting down of Chinese students protesting the conviction of Chinese strikers who had left their work in Japanese-owned cotton mills. Radio had come to China in 1924, and Mrs. Kuhn was its "first voice, radio-casting from Station KRC in a sheet-draped vacant room in the China Press offices in Shanghai." In an article she wrote for the China Press she predicted that "the introduction of a small instrument which can bridge the gap with the human voice may change the entire fortune of China." Among the people she interviewed were Chiang Kai-shek [40], Madame Chiang [40], (then Mei-ling Soong) and Margaret Sanger [44], who came to China on a mission in 1922. At one time Bert Kuhn entertained some Lama priests, emissaries of the High Lama, and Mrs. Kuhn, her little girl, and the child's nurse had to remove themselves from the home because of the religious ruling that no Lama was permitted to come into a house if a female were present. On another occasion Mrs. Kuhn visited the palace of the former boy emperor Hsuan Tung in the Forbidden City in Peking (now Peiping). In 1926 Bert Kuhn died in China while his wife and child were on a visit to relatives in the United States.

After the death of her husband Mrs. Kuhn returned with her daughter to New York City. There she joined the *Mirror* as a staff writer, but a year later she went back to the *Daily News,* where she remained for two years. In the fall of 1929 she took a leave of absence, and she and six-year-old Rene went back to Honolulu. They spent a year there while the mother reported for the Honolulu *Star-Bulletin.* Mrs. Kuhn had returned once again to the *News* when she received a summons to write scenarios for the new "talking pictures" in Hollywood. There she worked on various occasions between 1931 and 1933 (and again in 1939) for MGM, Twentieth Century-Fox, and Paramount studios. Her experience, she remarked, ran true to form: she made a "grand entrance" then "suffered immediate and complete obliteration except on the payroll."

While vacationing in New York in 1933, Irene Kuhn accepted an invitation from Roy W. Howard [40], head of the Scripps-Howard chain of newspapers, to become a feature writer on the New York *World-Telegram.* Mrs. Kuhn remained with that paper until 1936. Out of her varied experiences came her autobiography, *Assigned to Adventure* (1938), the first of its kind written by a newspaperwoman. Robert Strunsky of the *Saturday Review of Literature* summed up the critics' friendly reception of this book when he described it as "warmly and colorfully" written and added that it "properly belongs among the best of personal newspaper histories of the past few years." Mrs. Kuhn was twice elected the only woman vice-president to the Overseas Press Club and contributed a lively essay on the suffragette movement "They Wanted the Vote" to *The Inside Story* (1940), a collaborative work of the club's members. Of this book the *Saturday Review of Literature* remarked that "the spontaneity and journalistic bonhomie that marked the founding of the Overseas Press Club is also reflected in these newspaper yarns," while Joseph Barnes of *Books* wrote that "it possibly reflects more truly than many intelligent books the real nature of American public interest in the foreign world."

Miss Kuhn, who was associate director of publicity for the Republican National Committee during the campaign in 1940 and again in 1944, joined the National Broadcasting Company in 1940 as a special writer and assistant to the vice-president in charge of the press. During the four years (1940-44) she was director of program promotion she visited Mexico (1942) to secure special material for the Good Neighbor series of broadcasts she introduced. She also broadcast for NBC from Rio de Janeiro and in New York conducted her own radio column, *Irene Kuhn's Feature Page.* Since 1944 she has been assistant director of information for the National Broadcasting Company.

In September 1945, twenty years after her first broadcast in Shanghai, Irene Kuhn was the first person to broadcast from the liberated city. Among her other "firsts" was that of being the first woman to broadcast from a United States Navy vessel, the *Rocky Mount,* flagship of Admiral Thomas C. Kinkaid [44] of the Seventh Fleet anchored in the Whangpoo River in China. She was the first woman to broadcast from Manila in October 1945 and the only civilian to write for *Stars and Stripes* (China edition, September 1945). Mrs. Kuhn has done considerable flying since the day she hazarded her first airplane flight in Syracuse in 1920. As an accredited war correspondent for NBC in the China-Burma-India theater of war in 1945, she flew a total of 24,277 miles in planes of the Air Transport Command. In addition to her membership in the Overseas Press Club, Mrs. Kuhn holds membership in the Women's National Press Club (Washington, D.C.), the New York Newspaperwomen's Club and in Town Hall, as well as the National Association of Public Relations Counsel, Inc., to whose board of directors she was elected for a five-year term.

Five feet five inches tall with dark brown eyes and hair, Irene Kuhn still regards life as "high adventure" and her daughter, Rene Kuhn, a prizewinning author in her own right, as her "assignment from life." Believing firmly that "to live close to reality is really to live" she has said, "I would not give up one heartache or trade any part of the agony . . . for a chance to live my life in security and peace."

References

American Women, 1939-40
Kuhn, I. Assigned to Adventure (1938)
Ross, I. Ladies of the Press (1936)
Women of Achievement (1940)

KUNZ, STANLEY H(ENRY) (koonts) Sept. 26, 1864—Apr. 23, 1946 United States Democratic Representative from Illinois, 1920-34; served in the Illinois House of Representatives from 1888 to 1890 and in the Illinois Senate from 1902 to 1906.

Obituary

N Y Times p21 Ap 25 '46

KURTZ, EFREM (koorts ĕf'rĕm) Nov. 7, 1900- Conductor
Address: b. c/o Kansas City Philharmonic Orchestra, Kansas City, Mo.

One of the younger men who have been gradually demonstrating their competence in the orchestral field is Efrem Kurtz, permanent conductor of the Kansas City Philharmonic Orchestra. After an impressive debut in Berlin in 1920 as a last-minute substitute, he became known as a conductor of symphony, and as musical director of the Ballet Russe de Monte Carlo, in Europe, South America, Australia, and the United States.

One of four children, all musical, Efrem Kurtz was born in St. Petersburg, Russia, on November 7, 1900. He is the son of Aron and Sima Kurtz. His father, a storekeeper, loved music but did not play an instrument. His mother, however, played the piano, and his grandfather had conducted a military band for Czar Nicholas I. Through his grandmother he is distantly related to Mendelssohn. Young Kurtz received most of his musical education at the conservatory in St. Petersburg, where he studied with Tcherepnine, Glazunov. and Vitol.

In 1918 he was graduated from the Peter the Great High School there, and from 1918 to 1920 he was a student at the University of Riga. When the Kurtz family was later forced to flee Russia because of the Revolution, the young musician resumed his studies at the Stern Conservatory in Berlin, with special classes in conducting under Carl Schröder, and was graduated in 1922. His first big opportunity had come in 1920 when at the last moment he was asked to substitute for Arthur Nikisch as conductor of a recital by Isadora Duncan. A highly successful debut brought the novice an immediate guest contract for three performances with the Berlin Philharmonic.

During the next several years Kurtz followed a heavy schedule which took him to forty-eight German cities and later to Italy and Poland. Then, in 1924 he was appointed chief conductor of the Stuttgart Philharmonic and musical director of the radio station servicing all southern Germany. In these posts Kurtz remained for nine years, until the rise of the Nazis to power. His activities, however, were not confined to Stuttgart. In 1927, for instance, Anna Pavlova, the dancer, heard his conducting and engaged him to conduct her ballet company at Covent Garden. The ten-day season was followed by a South American tour with the Pavlova Ballet, during which period Kurtz also conducted symphony concerts in Buenos Aires and Rio de Janeiro. The South American engagement led to an invitation to wield the baton in Australia, and the Australians were so enthusiastic that they extended to him three separate offers to remain. Kurtz, however, preferred to return to Europe. While permanent conductor at Stuttgart he also filled engagements in Holland, Belgium, and other European countries, and in 1931 and 1932 he conducted a series of Handel concerts at the Salzburg Festival.

In 1933 Kurtz, a Jew, left Germany for France. There, in Paris, Colonel Wassily de Basil asked him whether he would aid in an emergency by conducting the Ballet Russe de Monte Carlo without rehearsal, and on the strength of his performance appointed Kurtz musical director of the Ballet Russe. This position the young conductor was also to occupy for nine years, touring extensively throughout Europe, South America, and the United States, and at intervals appearing as guest conductor in Melbourne and Sydney, Australia, with the New York Philharmonic-Symphony Orchestra at Lewisohn Stadium for several seasons, and with the Los Angeles Philharmonic, the NBC Symphony, the Cleveland Orchestra, the Detroit Symphony, the Philadelphia Orchestra, and others. His ballet work encompassed both the classical repertoire and new choreographies, some composed to the music of the great symphonies. Although, unlike some balletomanes, he believes that the latter should be included in the repertoire, of ballets utilizing symphonic scores the Ballet Russe's former musical director was on one occasion reported to have remarked, "Oh, I never see them. I keep my eyes closed. But it is not so cruel to use the music that way, because it is experimental. [Although] it is true that when I am conducting

EFREM KURTZ

something like Brahms's Fourth I do not want to see a Mickey Mouse come out and cavort."

Kurtz has, however, written seriously of ballet. "The ballet as an art form," he said in 1941, "offers to the conductor problems which are inherent in the combination of two heterogeneous elements: bodily movement and tone. The ballet requires absolute synchronization of music and physical movement, and in this synthesis lie the problems peculiar to the ballet. . . .I am a conductor and a musician first, but ever since the days when I was associated with Anna Pavlova I have been impressed by the manifold possibilities involved in the relationship of music and the dance. If the conductor is sensitive to the problems involved, he might very well come to the point where he doubts his ability to preserve the highest standards of musicianship while, at the same time, maintaining interpretation, synchronizing the accompaniment to the movements of the dancers, and fully expanding the choreographer's ideas. . . .When one conducts classical ballet, he must follow the dancer in finest detail. He must be thoroughly conversant with the steps of the dancers; more, he must have developed an intuitive feeling for equilibrium. . . .All the problems involved in classical ballet are pertinent to the modern with an additional important element. As contrasted to the classical ballet which is merely the projection of a mood, the modern is conceived for the execution of a story. . . .Composer and choreographer have produced the modern ballet in closest collaboration. Tempo becomes a matter of a work's content, of a dance's very essence. The dancer becomes the instrument of the choreographer who, in turn, is as much the servant of the composer's ideas as the composer is willing to integrate his composition with the potentialities of pantomiming. . . .Music originally written as ballet music is without doubt better than music arranged for ballet. The possibilities for

young composers in the field of ballet music are tremendous."

Kurtz has been called "the finest of ballet conductors," but although he enjoyed his work with the Ballet Russe, he readily admitted his preference for symphonic conducting. In the autumn of 1943, therefore, he accepted an invitation to become conductor of the Kansas City Philharmonic Orchestra, to succeed Karl Krueger who had left for Detroit. The next season Kurtz was re-engaged for another two years. His first thought on taking over in Kansas City, he has said, was how to bring his music to the masses, how to make them come to understand and like it; and despite opposition he began to offer "pops" concerts featuring good music at very low prices, annual free concerts, "name" soloists, and special concerts for school children in an endeavor to attract audiences. "The most important thing is to get them in," he said, "and then sell myself and the orchestra." The response proved that he was right, for by the end of his second season the orchestra was out of the red for the first time in many years and seemed well on its way to becoming self-sufficient.

He moves Kansas City audiences, it is said, because "he knows how to inject his dramatic flare into programming, at the same time maintaining the highest musical standards." Both in Kansas City and during his guest appearances it is his habit to include modern compositions and the works of the Russian masters on his programs, and he has won commendation for his conducting of these works as well as of the standard repertoire. (Igor Stravinsky [40] Kurtz has known for many years; he has seen "many of the composer's works come into being and has been their consistent advocate.") He is likewise eager to foster new instrumental and vocal talent, in this regard being a sponsor of Carol Brice, contralto, and William Kapell, pianist, both of whom have been especially well received by the critics; and for 1947 he planned engagements for eight young American soloists during the Kansas City winter "Pops" season. In 1944 Kurtz's Kansas City Philharmonic was selected as the first orchestra to be presented on NBC's new radio program *Orchestras of the Nation*, with reappearances scheduled for the following seasons.

In addition to his regular tasks Kurtz has led a specially assembled orchestra for several Warner Brothers' shorts of the Ballet Russe and has conducted the London Philharmonic Orchestra in the scores for two motion pictures starring Elisabeth Bergner. A "tall, gaunt Russian," Kurtz was married in 1933 to Katherine Jaffé, whom he describes as an authority on cooking, ceramics, and painting. Kurtz himself makes a hobby of art, specializing in water colors and caricature. So well known has his interest in art work by children become that, it is pointed out, mothers now send him the paintings of their talented offspring for criticism. In addition, he collects letters from famous contemporaries, possessing many from Einstein [41], Hindemith [41], Prokofiev [41], and others; and he has built up an unusual collection of stamped letters which have some interesting historical significance. Of one of his constant companions, his French poodle Dandy, the conductor says, "You can talk to him and he understands, but he doesn't answer. That is so good sometimes."

References

Newsweek 19:65 Ap 20 '42
Ewen, D. ed. Living Musicians (1940)
Who's Who in America, 1946-47

LAING, HUGH (lăng) Dancer

Address: b. c/o Ballet Theater, Inc., 25 W. 45th St., New York; h. 52 W. 52d St., New York

A dancer who has been called outstanding in the modern wing of ballet is Hugh Laing, known for his "darkly intense delineations" in the Antony Tudor [45] ballets. The repertoire of this dancer, who has become well known to American audiences through his appearances with the Ballet Theater since 1940, is not restricted to the work of that English choreographer. Laing has also been termed "wonderfully poetic" by critics, who commend his sensitive interpretation and keen sense of the dramatic.

Hugh Laing was born Hugh Skinner, the son of Donald Morris and Beatrice (Aleeyne) Skinner, on Barbados Island in the British West Indies. He received his early education there, but in 1931 he went to London, where he attended the Grosvenor School of Modern Art. While he says he had once planned to become a doctor, he had always been interested in ballet and in the theater. Consequently, he decided to study the dance after he had met Mme. Marie Rambert, founder of the Mercury Ballet, in 1932. This "love of line, color, form and drama," wrote Margaret Lloyd of the *Christian Science Monitor,* "stayed with him and pervades his work. . . . It is evident in his distinguished line and bearing, his sensitivity of dramatic values, his flair for theater dance."

During the year 1932-33 Laing studied in London with Mme. Rambert and Margaret Craske, and in Paris with Olga Preobajenska. By 1933 he was dancing with the Mercury Ballet, which also gave small Sunday night performances as the Ballet Club. While with this company, Laing met Antony Tudor, and in 1935 he appeared in the first performance of the choreographer's *Descent of Hebe.* In 1936, he danced in *L'Après-midi d'un faune,* bringing to it, said the *New Statesman* critic, "an ideal presence and a very exciting intensity." That same year, Laing appeared for the first time in Tudor's *Jardin aux lilas* in which he still may be seen. Of Laing's appearance in its American production with the Ballet Theater in 1940, Grace Robert writes in the *Borzoi Book of Ballets,* "American audiences . . . were at once aware that Ballet Theater had acquired a dancing actor of distinction and remarkable power of projection." Laing and the other dancers in this, the only modern ballet which has been in the Ballet Theater's repertoire since that company's inception, have performed it on a stage with an eighteen-foot proscenium and, without any change in chore-

HUGH LAING

ography, on stages with huge prosceniums such as that of the Hollywood Bowl.

Before leaving Rambert's Mercury Ballet in 1937, Laing danced in the London debut of Tudor's *Dark Elegies.* Meanwhile, a new theater had been built in the Toynbee Hall section of East London, and in 1937 Laing and Tudor embarked on plans for the formation of a new ballet company there. By 1938 the London Ballet opened the theater and inaugurated its first season by introducing *Gala Performance,* which good-naturedly mocked classic dancers—the London Ballet had been organized to present modern, theatrical ballet. Introduced that same season was the "bitterly ironic, jesting" Tudor ballet, *Judgment of Paris,* for which Laing had contributed the scenario and in which he appeared.

It was in 1939 that Hugh Laing first went to the United States, there joining the Ballet Theater when it was formed by Richard Pleasant in 1940. As the name implies, the aim of the Ballet Theater is to present modern ballet against a background of fine theatrical production. On that score it has come under some criticism: Irving Kolodin, writing for the New York *Sun,* observed, "The Ballet Theater has gone just about as far as it should go in its theater trend and should now show a little interest in the ballet again." In 1941 the troupe appeared at the Metropolitan Opera House under the management of S. Hurok [41], with whom they were to remain until the fall of 1946. In October 1941 Laing accompanied the Ballet Theater to Mexico City where he appeared in the first performance of *Bluebeard,* a Michel Fokine [42] ballet, which was performed later in the same season in New York.

Three ballets in which Laing has earned distinction were introduced in 1942. In April Laing danced the role of the Young Man from the House Opposite in Tudor's *Pillar of Fire,* a performance which was called "remarkable."

LAING, HUGH—*Continued*

"There are many times," Grace Robert writes, "when Laing is called upon to make a dramatic point without the aid of dancing steps or stylized movements—at one point simply by walking across the stage." Two days later, the company presented the *Romeo and Juliet* ballet in its entirety (a partial performance had been given shortly before). Creating "one of his very best roles," Laing gave Romeo "a new youthfulness and harebrained impetuousity, and built the role from its rather tentative beginnings into a full and finished character." Having already produced *Aleko* in Mexico City, Ballet Theater introduced this ballet about gypsies to New York audiences in October 1942. Hugh Laing, as the Young Gypsy, "danced with keen dramatic sense as well as stunning execution." The New York *Herald Tribune* wrote, "Hugh Laing was, as usual, superb."

Dim Lustre, a Tudor ballet, is among Laing's favorites. His performance in it caused John Martin to comment in the New York *Times*: "Hugh Laing, always excellent, has outdone himself this year [1943]. Here, indeed, is one of the most distinctive talents in the ballet field. From the strictly orthodox point of view he is perhaps limited, but within his own theater world, in which modern ballet tends more and more to live, his range is wide and his quality incontestably high. It is a long way from the evil young man of *Pillar of Fire* to the suave, witty gentleman of *Dim Lustre,* but it would be difficult to improve on either of them." In that same year, Laing appeared in Agnes de Mille's [43] *Tally-Ho,* and two years later in Fokine's *Carnaval.* In 1945, the leading role in Tudor's provocative *Undertow* was danced by Laing "with all the dark tension of his remarkable theatrical power."

In 1945 Laing appeared in his first classic dance before American audiences as he temporarily replaced Anton Dolin [46] in *Giselle.* His interpretation was called "excellent in line and expression," bringing "new dramatic colors to the role, giving not only to Albrecht but also to the work as a whole, qualities of pathos which it had not had before, and that sense of the supernatural which belongs so closely to the romantic nineteenth century Gothic ballet." In October of that year Laing had the ballet lead of *The Day Before Spring,* a musical comedy for which Tudor did the choreography. This was the only season in which Laing did not appear with the Ballet Theater. Returning to that company, he went to London in the summer of 1946—the Ballet Theater was the first American troupe to go abroad after the war. In the fall of the same year, when the Ballet Theater broke away from Hurok's management because of policy disagreements (losing some of its dancers), Laing remained with the organization and appeared in their performances of *Les patineurs* and *Facsimile.* The New York *Herald Tribune* compared Laing's dancing in *Facsimile* with that of Jerome Robbins, the choreographer, who had appeared in the debut of that ballet: Laing's interpretation "is less mercilessly sardonic . . . and makes for a somewhat more even balance with the performance of John Kriza in the other male role."

Hugh Laing is a slight, dark man, with intense blue eyes. Fond of sports, he goes swimming as often as he can, and regrets that the strenuous physical demands of dancing make his participation in riding and tennis undesirable. The bachelor spends a good deal of time reading "anything but best sellers," visiting art museums throughout the country, going to the theater or the movies. By birth a British subject, the dancer plans to become an American citizen, having found that the United States is "well suited" to him.

LAIRD, DONALD A(NDERSON) May 14, 1897- Psychologist; author
Address: h. Homewood, Lebanon, Ind.

Dr. Donald A. Laird, author of more than a dozen books and about seven hundred articles as of 1946, is an indefatigable popularizer of psychological discoveries. His style of writing is "folksy": he leans over backward to avoid the technical; but he has an academic background of some distinction, and subscribes to every English-language journal in the fields of psychology, psychiatry, and psychoanalysis. He has written special sections for medical books and one of his articles is in the Time Capsule, which was deposited at the World's Fair in New York to give future archeologists a picture of twentieth-century American life.

Of "diluted" Scottish descent, Donald Anderson Laird was born on his grandfather's farm in Steuben County, Indiana, on May 14, 1897. His father, Allan Max Laird, who later became a minister of the Disciples of Christ, was then a student. When the boy, an only child, was about three, his parents were divorced; Laird does not remember seeing his father until eleven years later. He was brought up by his grandmother and his mother, Grace (Anderson) Laird, who taught in the one-room schoolhouse where her son learned the "three R's." While in the eighth grade, the boy wrote local news items for a Fort Wayne daily. Later he had a summertime job as a printer's devil for fifty cents a week; and still later he worked in a general store in a small Iowa town.

As a freshman at the University of Dubuque, Laird began teaching as a part-time assistant in the physics laboratory. He was absorbed by chemistry at this time and, as he recalled in *The Technique of Building Personal Leadership,* was "working overtime in the laboratory, starting one experiment before another was finished" and getting "hopelessly tangled up in them." A faculty member advised the eager chemist to carry a memorandum pad and jot down the stray ideas that occurred to him, instead of attempting to follow them all up at once; and this simple device—he still carries a similar pad—was the beginning of Laird's application of management to himself. One day a philosophy and psychology professor asked Laird to help him set up some new apparatus, and the would-be natural scientist became so interested that he turned to psychology. (A member of Theta Chi, Laird has since been made an honorary member of three other Greek-letter societies.)

Young Laird did field work at a large mental hospital at Independence, Iowa. There he met Hilda Drexel, a psychiatric nurse to whom he was married in November 1916, when he was nineteen. Mrs. Laird worked with him in many experiments. Laird served in the World War I Navy as psychological examiner at the Great Lakes training station. Having received his B.A. in 1919, he became an assistant at the Iowa State University's Child Welfare Research Station (1920-21). He says he worked part of his way through graduate school as janitor of an old ladies' home. While in graduate school, incidentally, the left-handed student lost his left middle finger in a laboratory accident.

Donald Laird began his "authoring" in 1920. Convinced that one of his course papers was so important that it deserved to be published, he sent it to one magazine after another. At the end of two years, it was finally accepted by the *Yale Review*, which paid him thirty-five dollars. It was less than the total cost of postage and retyping, but Laird was pleased with the moral victory he had won. He considered it a triumph for his "three-foot rule," a yardstick he kept to remind himself, by allusion to a story he had heard, not to give up when discouraged. The psychologist was an instructor at Iowa in 1921-22, and in 1923, while teaching at the University of Wyoming, he received his Ph.D. from Iowa. For his dissertation, Laird had done research in the field of optics, on binocular summation. In 1923-24 he was national research fellow in biological sciences at Yale, and during the former year two of his books were published. Written for the layman in popular style, they were *Applied Psychology for Nurses* and *Psychology of Selecting Men*.

Next Laird joined the faculty of Colgate University at Hamilton, New York, where he taught psychology for fifteen years. He had a horror of getting into a rut: he has said, "I never taught the same course twice in the same way. . . .When I found I was considered a specialist in one field, I intentionally broke off for another and am irritated when people remind me of the works of an earlier year. . . . I am one of those folks who have to work at being progressive." When he moved away from a place, he always sold any property he had there for whatever he could get for it, preferring a financial loss to "being tradition-bound to the past." He would not visit his old home town for the same reason. During the summers he continued his own education. At his birthday, and again at Christmas, he would take inventory of himself to see if he had any "sidetracks." As he approached his thirty-seventh birthday, Laird was unable to find any time-wasting habits except shaving, so he eliminated that—although, as he recalls, "I was then employed by a university which basked in the financial support of a shaving-cream family." The crop of reddish-brown whiskers, as he calls them, apparently did not retard his advance, for in 1936 he became head of the psychology department at Colgate.

DONALD A. LAIRD

In 1925 Professor Laird had become director of the Colgate psychological research laboratory. That year his laboratory developed the Colgate mental hygiene tests for intro-extroversion and in 1927, the first measurement of city noises and their effect on personality. (In 1940 he was to become a technical adviser to the National Noise Abatement Council.) Awarded a D. Sc. by Dubuque in 1927, Laird turned his attention to the psychology of digestion and the study of sleep, inventing the somnokinetograph in 1932, and directed the sleep and fatigue laboratory demonstration at the Century of Progress Exposition in Chicago in 1933. Meanwhile, during summer vacations Laird secured cadavers from the Syracuse University medical school and began dissecting them to increase his knowledge of the brain, nervous system, sense organs, and glands, and devised a new method for coloring specimens. Laird's work in the psychological laboratory was the subject of many articles, a number under his signature. The director applied findings to himself whenever they were relevant.

At the same time, the psychologist was an industrial relations consultant to a number of corporations, mainly on problems of reducing fatigue and of relations with employees. His clients included the Order of Sleeping Car Conductors, the Dictaphone Corporation, the Hotel New Yorker, the Hood Rubber Company, and the N. W. Ayer and Son advertising agency. Concurrently he lectured and wrote hundreds of articles and a stream of books. *Increasing Personal Efficiency* came out in 1925, *Psychology and Profits* in 1929; *Why We Don't Like People* (1931) was followed by *What Makes People Buy* (1935), *More Zest for Life* (1935), *How to Use Psychology in Business* (1936), *We Can Rest and Sleep Better* (1936), and *How to Improve Your Brain Power* (1939). For several years the professor "wrote, managed, edited, and dug

LAIRD, DONALD A.—*Continued*

in pockets to pay the bills" of the *Industrial Psychology Monthly*, which he finally discontinued. He was for a time with the *Health Digest;* was chairman of the Health Guild of America's mental health committee; and in 1937-39 was a member of the executive council of the Acoustical Society of America. When Laird took his semiannual inventory in Christmas 1938, he decided that his goals had become hazy, so he "cleared them up" by resigning his "soft job" at Colgate in January 1939. A week later he was appointed director of the new Ayer Foundation for Consumer Analysis in Philadelphia, which the advertising agency hoped would reduce selling costs by discovering the surest ways to appeal to the consumer. Laird had already done some work in this field. After Mrs. Laird's death in 1938 he was married in April of 1940 to Eleanor Childs Leonard, a distant cousin of his from Massachusetts, who was then county librarian of Arlington, Virginia. She became his literary assistant, research librarian, proofreader, and collaborator.

Later in 1940 Laird's association with the foundation ended; he remained an industrial consultant until 1945. Before then, however, he had resigned from most of the numerous organizations to which he belonged and moved from his Philadelphia penthouse to the country to get away from the distractions of the city. The task he set himself called for concentrating on books and articles to help people understand themselves and each other, as he felt that lack of such understanding is and has been the main problem of society. He also went on brief lecture tours. In 1941 Laird wrote and appeared in a movie short, *Let Yourself Go*, and collaborated with C. G. Muller on the book *Energy and Sleep*. In 1942 he and Mrs. Laird coauthored *The Psychology of Supervising the Working Woman*. During the war came the first of a planned annual series of five self-help books, the ones published so far being *The Technique of Handling People* (1943), *The Technique of Building Personal Leadership* (1944), and *The Technique of Personal Analysis* (1945). Early in World War II Laird's only child, David, had joined the RCAF, becoming one of its youngest flying officers; he was killed in July 1944 while on reconnaissance over the Gothic Line in Italy.

A brown-eyed, 180-pound six-footer with a fringe of white hair, Dr. Laird keeps himself "gaunt." His sharp nose and his white beard, which parts itself in the middle, combine to lend his smile a somewhat Mephistophelean quality. Over the mantel in Laird's study is the motto *Ancore Imparo* (I Am Still Learning), and in his living-room *Aequo Animo* admonishes him to keep calm. The psychologist rises early and prepares his own big breakfast (he lives up to his finding that a heavy breakfast and a very light lunch make for greatest efficiency), plays with the fox terrier, and then turns out twelve hundred words of first-draft writing. After this he works for two hours in his ten-acre woodlot, which he is gradually transforming into a private park; rewriting,

reading and planning come in the afternoon and evening.

In order to increase his own personal efficiency, Laird avoids the "detour" of rolling up his sleeves by having them all cut off above the elbow and avoids writing long letters by using postal cards or half-size letterheads for his prompt answers to letters. "Every person should belong to a social group and attend at least one meeting a week," Laird wrote in 1945, but he himself accepts not more than one invitation a month, and says, "If someone leaves a party before I do, I know I am on the detour of staying too long." To save the time he spent on his hobbies, he sold his camera and guns, and gave up detective stories. However, he still seeks and finds errors in dictionaries and encyclopedias. His radio listening he confines to news broadcasts at meals, using a device which automatically turns on the radio at these times. He avoids the "boresome details" by having his wife edit, correct, and read proof on his writing. Laird says of himself that he lacks natural tact, and must be careful not to offend others, that he avoids arguments, is hard to embarrass or insult, has to prevent himself from "running on forever," and constantly overcomes a tendency to move slowly and deliberately. "I can't figure out," he has written, "whether my inclination is due to laziness, dignity, or introversion."

References

American Men of Science (1944)
Who's Who in America, 1946-47

LAMONT, CORLISS (là-mŏnt') Mar. 28, 1902- Author; educator
Address: h. 450 Riverside Dr., New York

The author of *The Peoples of the Soviet Union* (1946), Corliss Lamont has for more than a decade lectured and written about the U.S.S.R. A professed socialist, since 1933 he has been writing, as an "independent radical," on political and economic affairs, always with a special interest in the Soviet Union's experiment in state socialism. From its inception in 1943 until June of 1946, he served as chairman of the National Council of American-Soviet Friendship. Lamont has also written in the field of philosophy, and is a lecturer in philosophy at Columbia University.

Corliss Lamont is a descendant of men who fought in the American Revolution and a son of one of America's most influential financiers. He was born March 28, 1902, in Englewood, New Jersey, the son of the former Florence Haskell Corliss and Thomas William Lamont [40], chairman of the executive committee of J. P. Morgan and Company. Young Lamont grew up in Englewood, a mile from the summit of the Palisades on the Hudson River. He has called the area "beautiful and exciting," and to this day finds refreshment in tramping the Palisades. In 1920, after attending Phillips Exeter Academy, he entered Harvard University, of which he later wrote, "It is obvious from the very atmosphere of the university that its practices and traditions favor, in comparison with other educational institutions, the critical and dissenting mind." In 1924, graduated as a member of Phi Beta Kappa with a B.A. degree *magna cum laude,* Lamont went to England for a year's graduate work at New College of Oxford University. He was married in 1928 to Margaret Hayes Irish, and the same year became an instructor in philosophy at Columbia University, where he taught for the next four years.

While at Columbia Lamont wrote his first book, in the form of a doctoral thesis, and his Ph.D. was conferred in 1932. The thesis, an analysis of "certain definitions and descriptions of immortality together with some of the supporting arguments," was published as *Issues of Immortality.* The book was on the whole well received by reviewers, one of whom wrote, "It is the most devastating survey of the idea of immortality that I have ever read." Thirty-year-old Lamont, already being referred to as "the socialistic son of banker Thomas Lamont," and his wife, a writer and research worker who was associated with *Living Age,* in the summer of 1932 made a six-week tour of Russia. Together they wrote the book *Russia Day by Day* (1933), which was a travel diary. Reviewers found it "smooth and pleasant reading," a book friendly to the Russian experiment, written with an "accuracy" which "would seem to be fairly guaranteed by Mr. Lamont's wide academic reputation."

Next came Lamont's major work in philosophy, *The Illusion of Immortality* (1935), in which with "logic and scholarship" he maintained that belief in immortality is a harmful illusion, and presented "an affirmative philosophy of life based on the this-earthly enjoyment of human existence." The wide comment which greeted the book included a favorable review by John Dewey in the *New Republic*; and another by George Lawton in the *Journal of Philosophy*: "The ethical idealism . . . [pervading the work] . . . [is] another refutation of the claim that atheism demeans man and stultifies human endeavor." Another critic felt that "in spite of his philosophy" he had written "a remarkable book." Lamont, "in order to make the job complete," in 1936 edited an anthology of poetry, *Man Answers Death,* "centering around this same philosophy of humanism. It is, I believe," he has written, "the only anthology of poetry which fully presents the more realistic side of what the poets of the race have had to say about death." His next book, *You Might Like Socialism: A Way of Life for Modern Man* (1939), was the result of his "turning to the question of *how* the two billion inhabitants of this planet can attain the humanist goals of peace, freedom, and happiness." The year before (1938), he had again visited the Soviet Union, and had witnessed "the tremendous economic and cultural progress" achieved since his first visit. "I do not believe, however," the author has said, "in any mechanical imitation of Soviet Russia, since socialism must necessarily differ from country to country."

But he did not confine his independent radicalism to his desk top and typewriter. In 1934 the writer was arrested in Jersey City and charged with being a "disorderly person" for

Mayfair Photographers

CORLISS LAMONT

picketing on behalf of the American Civil Liberties Union in a test of Mayor Hague's law against free speech, a law which the Supreme Court later declared unconstitutional. Maintaining, as he phrased it, "a general though critical sympathy for the Soviet Union," Lamont was early active with such organizations as The American Council on Soviet Relations and the Friends of the Soviet Union. This activity was "dissected" and labeled "Communist" by Eugene Lyons in his book *The Red Decade,* subtitled *The Stalinist Penetration of America.* In October 1941 Lamont filed a libel suit against the Bobbs-Merrill Company, Lyons' publisher, complaining that he had been depicted as "a contemptible tool for Communist politicians," and a leader of "an espionage organization." The suit was settled out of court in 1942 "to Mr. Lamont's satisfaction."

Lamont resumed teaching in 1940 at the New School for Social Research, where for two years he lectured in philosophy. Then, in 1943 he went to Cornell University to participate in what Cornell's president called "one of the most significant projects staged in an educational institution that I have seen in a lifetime" —the university's program for an intensive study of contemporary Russian civilization. To both army and civilian students Lamont taught the orientation course, "Social Institutions and Life." The next year, 1944, he was a lecturer in the Social Studies Workshop on Soviet Russia at the Harvard Graduate School of Education. In 1946, as lecturer in philosophy, he again joined the Columbia University staff.

Lamont's book on the U.S.S.R. as an "ethnic democracy," *The Peoples of the Soviet Union,* which appeared in 1946, is regarded as "a useful and highly informative handbook." The author drew praise for making the Russian political structures "intelligible in terms of their human units," brightening his work

LAMONT, CORLISS—*Continued*

with folklore and native proverbs. In the preface to that book Lamont writes, "I believe that study of how the diverse peoples of the Soviet Union work and live together can cast considerable light on the problem of minorities in the United States and other countries." In 1946 the author was at work on another book of philosophy, tentatively entitled "The Philosophy of Humanism"; he gives the same name to the course he will be teaching at Columbia in 1946-47.

The writer's other works include numerous brochures on Soviet Russia and articles in periodicals. He is on the advisory council of *Soviet Russia Today*. A director of the American Civil Liberties Union, and of the Trade Union Service, the author is also a member of the American Philosophy Association, the New York Teachers Union, the Columbia Faculty Club, and the Harvard Club of New York. From 1939 to 1941 he was on the advisory board of the American Humanist Association.

Lamont was chairman of the Congress of American-Soviet Friendship in 1942, and of the National Council of American-Soviet Friendship from 1943 to mid-1946. Though he remains a member of the board of directors of the last-named organization, he retired from the chairmanship in June 1946 to devote his time more fully to teaching and writing. Before this time, however, Lamont and Richard Morford, executive director of the council, refused to submit council financial records to the House Committee on Un-American Activities on the grounds that the Committee's attempted investigation was "beyond its scope, improper and unconstitutional." Because of this, in June 1946, Lamont was cited for contempt by the House of Representatives, and his case went before the District of Columbia Federal Attorney for prosecution. This was still pending at the end of 1946.

Brown-haired and brown-eyed, Lamont weighs 145 pounds and stands five feet eight and one-half inches tall. "My chief personal problem," Lamont once wrote of himself, "is to find time for all the things I want to do both in the field of creative writing and of pure enjoyment in the exciting worlds of literature and art, drama and music, travel and sport, social intercourse, and family relations. I try to keep abreast of all these worlds, though the presence of four children in the house [Margaret Hayes, Florence Parmelee, Hayes Corliss, and Anne Sterling] sometimes threatens to disrupt the process."

References

Kunitz, S. J. and Haycraft, H. eds.
Twentieth Century Authors (1942)
Who's Who in America, 1946-47

LANG, COSMO GORDON, 1ST BARON LANG OF LAMBETH *See* Lang of Lambeth, C.G.L., 1st Baron

LANG OF LAMBETH, COSMO GORDON LANG, 1ST BARON Oct. 31, 1864—Dec. 5, 1945 Former Archbishop of Canter-

bury and Primate of All England from 1928 until retirement in 1942; Archbishop of York (1908-28); appointed Privy Councilor in 1910; became a temporal peer in the House of Lords in 1942; said to have played a large part in bringing about abdication of Edward VIII, now Duke of Windsor'". See *Current Biography* 1941 Yearbook.

Obituary

N Y Times p27 D 6 '45 por

LANGE, OSCAR (RICHARD) (län'gĕ ôs'kär) July 27, 1904- United Nations official
Address: c/o United Nations, New York

Poland's delegate to the United Nations is a member of the faculty of the University of Chicago, Oscar Lange, professor of economics on leave of absence. Lange was also the first Ambassador to represent the postwar Polish Government in the United States. The Polish-born economist, a naturalized citizen of the United States, gave up his American citizenship to accept the diplomatic post, which he held from December 1945 to the end of 1946. A member of the Polish Socialist Party, Lange has been called a "Russian puppet" by anti-Soviet Poles. He wrote and spoke in the United States in the cause of Russian-Polish friendship for several years before he became Ambassador.

The only son of a textile manufacturer, Oscar Richard Lange was born in Tomaszow, Poland, on July 27, 1904. Stricken with tuberculosis of the hip when he was seven, the boy spent two years in bed. The Ambassador's wife thinks that his "scholarly ways" date from this illness, which crippled his right leg. Oscar's mother insisted that he study music, and "to relieve the tedium" of practicing on the piano he studied mathematics and Chinese as well. (One of the few delegates to the United Nations who knows a little Chinese, he also speaks Polish, Russian, English, German, French, and Spanish, and carries on a voluminous correspondence in Latin with several Jesuit priests.) Lange attended the University of Posen in 1922-23. For ten years thereafter, except for a trip to England in 1929 to study at the London School of Economics, his life centered around the University of Cracow. There he earned an LL.M. in 1926, worked as research assistant during 1927, received his LL.D. in 1928, and in 1931 became a lecturer in economics and statistics. There, too, he met and married his wife Irene, who was soon to receive her Ph.D. in literature. His family was "scandalized" when he joined the Socialist Students Organization at Cracow. Later he worked with the Polish Socialist Party, serving as a member of its educational committee. Active in the labor movement, for a time he did some work for the Ministry of Labor in Warsaw.

Two years after his marriage in 1932, the thirty-year-old economics instructor made his first trip to the United States, as a fellow of the Rockefeller Foundation. He studied at Harvard and at the University of Minnesota, and in 1936 he was a lecturer in economics at the University of Michigan. After a brief sojourn in his native Poland (1936-37), he once again visited the United States, in the fall of 1937, this time intending to become a naturalized American citizen. During his second visit he was at first lecturer in economics at the University of California, and then at Stanford University. In 1938 the University of Chicago appointed the thirty-four-year-old economist an assistant professor, promoted him the following year to associate professor. In 1943, the same year he received his final citizenship papers, he was named a full professor of economics, the position he still holds and from which he is on leave.

"He was drawn into Polish politics by development," Lange's wife once explained to Betty Moorsteen in an interview for the newspaper *PM*. "He just spoke a few times, and wrote a few things which he felt had to be said." In May 1943, Professor Lange was to be one of the principal speakers at a rally in New York sponsored by the National Council for American Soviet Friendship. A member and one of the organizers of the Chicago branch of the Council, Lange was in New York (1942-43) as a visiting professor at Columbia University. He suddenly withdrew from the rally, because advertisements in the Communist newspaper the *Daily Worker* had led him to believe his speech might be misinterpreted. Questioned by reporters on his withdrawal, he emphasized his full support for the objectives of the meeting, at which Senator Claude D. Pepper [41] and Leland Stowe [40] were among those who would answer to "anti-Soviet propaganda." He added that he had intended, in his speech, to urge the formation of a new Polish Government-in-exile, to replace the London group. The Poles in London were headed by General Sikorski, whom Lange considered an honest but ineffective leader, "sabotaged by the reactionary emigrés upon whom he had to rely." Lange was thus on record as one of the few early, articulate critics of the Polish Government-in-exile in London. In November 1943 he proposed that the liberals in the London Government break away to form a coalition government with the Union of Polish Patriots. This was the plan ultimately approved by the Big Three at the Crimea conference in February 1945, when it was agreed that the Soviet-recognized Lublin government, established with the aid of the Union of Polish Patriots, should join with the liberal elements in the London group to form a new Polish Government with a "broader base."

In September 1943, in a long "letter to the editor" which the New York *Herald Tribune* featured prominently on its editorial page, Lange outlined a program for postwar Poland, presenting ideas he frequently reiterated in the two years before he became Polish Ambassador to Washington. Prefacing his statement with an attack on "the follies of the anti-Soviet emigrés," as he described the actions of the Polish Government-in-exile (at that time headed by Stanislaw Mikolajczyk [44] in London), he set forth five requirements for Poland's future. First, he said, Poland needed a close understanding with the Soviet Union, and Soviet military support "in a similar way as say, Can-

OSCAR LANGE

ada, or Mexico needs the military support of the United States." Secondly, he thought smaller nations, such as Poland, could not be assured of freedom and security unless the Soviet Union, Great Britain, and the United States reached close understanding and established a "nuclear alliance." Thirdly, postwar Poland must have "a democratic form of government and agrarian reform which will eliminate the feudal elements in the country by giving the land to the peasants." His fourth point was that "Polish sovereignty over East Prussia is necessary for the peace of Europe. . . . A democratic Poland will have to expropriate the Junkers, to ship them out of the country and to settle their estates with peasants. This will break once and for all the social basis of Prussian militarism." He wanted Poland to acquire, as well, other German territories which had "a prevailingly Polish population."

The final proposal in Lange's program was a suggested solution to the Polish boundary dispute with the Soviet Union. He would have Poland give back to the Soviets those areas with Ukrainian and White Ruthenian populations, but he would expect Poland to retain ancient Polish cities, such as Lwów, although situated in "ethnographically Ukrainian or White Ruthenian territory." Fundamental to his hopes for an amicable agreement between the two nations was his view of Poland as an essential part of the Soviet Union's plans for military security. "The strategic frontiers of the Soviet Union will coincide with the western frontiers of Poland (and Czechoslovakia). This should enable the Soviet Union to be very generous with Poland in matters of territory, a policy which the Soviet Union will find to turn out to its own good advantage." (The following year, after an interview with Stalin, Lange indicated that the Russian leader held a point of view similar to his own on these points.)

(Continued next page)

LANGE, OSCAR—*Continued*

The stand Lange had taken apparently was known in the Kremlin. In February 1944 Frederick Kuh of *PM* reported from London that "Moscow is said semi-officially to have intimated a desire for the inclusion in a reshuffled Polish cabinet of three or four Poles whose good faith toward Russia is thought to be assured. These include Professor Oscar Lange of the University of Chicago." Lange had received his American citizenship papers the year before, in 1943, but apparently neither Moscow, nor the correspondent, considered him any the less a Pole. Then, in April 1944 front page stories appeared about the unprecedented invitation to Moscow which the Soviet Government had extended to two Americans, Father Stanislaus Orlemanski "[4], a Roman Catholic priest who had been working in America for Polish-Soviet amity, and Oscar Lange, University of Chicago professor. At the request of Premier Stalin, the United States Department of State furnished passports for the two Americans, but stated publicly that the priest and the professor were acting as private citizens, without official status of any sort. The known feeling between the Catholic Church and the Communist State, and the fact that Father Orlemanski was visiting Russia without the permission of his Bishop, centered attention on the meeting of the priest with Premier Stalin. Lange's six weeks in Russia and his two-hour-and-twenty-minute visit with Stalin, though less publicized, is now seen as having had more significant results.

Lange spent four days on the Russian-Polish frontier, visiting units of the Polish army organized on Soviet soil under the Union of Polish Patriots. He talked with Polish soldiers, visited schools established in Russia for Polish children, and conferred with Polish leaders in Russia. Five American and English correspondents accompanied the professor on his trips to the Polish army units. Correspondent Edmund Stevens, in his book *Russia is No Riddle*, has described these visits. The newspaper stories of the correspondents accompanying Lange agreed that the Polish army retained its national character, and that it was "not a communist organization." The United Press report added: "All the Poles [in the army units in Russia] supported the idea of Poland's expansion westward at the expense of Germany, and asserted that the German population of East Prussia, Silesia and Pomerania should be deported." (These last ideas Lange himself had advanced in his letter to the *Herald Tribune* some months before.)

Aware of the pro-Soviet sympathies of Orlemanski and Lange, London Poles were uneasy about the "mission to Moscow," suspecting that both men might be "destined for important roles under Russian auspices" in the near future. Following his conference with Stalin on May 21, 1944, Lange proceeded to London, where, it was rumored, he would present Stalin's terms to the Polish Government-in-exile. Lange was convinced that, as he had always supposed, Stalin was interested in a strong and independent Poland, that Stalin had "not the slightest intention" of dictating the political, economic or social forms of the Polish state, but wanted only the resignation of certain anti-Soviet men in the Polish Cabinet-in-exile, the inclusion of Poles from the Moscow Union of Polish Patriots in the Polish cabinet, and territorial adjustments. Apparently Lange managed to impress the London Poles to some extent with his own belief in Stalin's sincerity; Frederick Kuh reported from London in June 1944 that "leading Poles are saying Professor Oscar Lange . . . made a valuable contribution toward easing the whole position."

The Polish Government in London "ceased to exist" in July 1945: Great Britain, the United States, and the Soviet Union recognized the Provisional Government of National Unity in Warsaw, a coalition government which included the Lublin group. In August rumor had it that Professor Oscar Lange of the University of Chicago might be named the first postwar Polish Ambassador to Washington. There was some criticism on the score that Lange was an American citizen. John C. Metcalfe (New York *Herald Tribune*) reported from Washington that the State Department would probably accept him but would be "far from enthusiastic" if Lange were chosen. State Department officials, according to Metcalfe, expressed "misgivings" about a man "who is a citizen of one country today, another tomorrow and returns to his native land the third." However, the ambassadorship was offered him in the fall of 1945, and Lange flew to Warsaw for instructions, explaining to friends that he had decided to relinquish his American citizenship and to accept the diplomatic post, because of a desire to "better relations between the land of his birth and the land of his adoption." In Warsaw he regained Polish citizenship, and familiarized himself with national conditions. Then, in December 1945, he returned to the United States as Polish Ambassador.

In presenting his credentials to President Truman, the new Polish envoy reviewed conditions in his nation (New York *Times*, December 22, 1945). He told about social and economic changes under way in Poland, with the Government taking over the operation of large and medium-sized industry, planning further industrialization but at the same time breaking up large estates to spread private ownership of farms among the people. Asked about anti-Semitic violence in liberated Poland, he said the Government was "dealing sternly with the problem," and ascribed the outbreaks to underground, anti-government fascist organizations.

Poland was among the six nations elected by the General Assembly of the United Nations to serve on the Security Council with the "Big Five," and, as Ambassador to the United States, Lange was Poland's delegate when the Security Council met at Hunter College, New York, in March 1946. The only supporter of the Russian position during the discussion of Iran's grievances, his Government was called by many observers "Soviet-dominated." Ambassador Lange denied such charges. Anything that "creates understanding between the big powers," he said, "and keeps us friendly with our closest neighbor, Russia, and with the Western powers too, we favor." He later added, "Our very life and existence depend on it [peace between the Western powers and the Soviet Union]. Any conflict will be fought on our soil. Even a diplomatic conflict involves us." Joseph G. Harrison of the *Christian Science Monitor* explained Lange's attempt to act the conciliator between Russia and the Anglo-Americans as follows: "His actions so far have shown that he is under stringent instructions from Warsaw not to find himself in opposition to the Soviet Union in Council deliberations. At the same time, however, as a former United States citizen, Dr. Lange is personally drawn to the latter country and to the viewpoint it expresses."

In April, Lange precipitated a heated controversy by asking the Security Council to recommend that all members of the United Nations break off diplomatic relations with Spain, on the ground that the Franco regime was a threat to world peace. Finally, in November the Franco issue was dropped from the Council agenda, thus freeing it for discussion by the General Assembly. For the original Polish resolution calling for an outright diplomatic break was substituted a modification which denounced the Franco Government and urged that chiefs of diplomatic missions be withdrawn from Madrid. This resolution was approved December 12, and Lange heralded it as a victory for the United Nations.

In June Lange gave full support to the Soviet plan for the outlawing of atomic weapons. Taking his seat after a month of conferences in Warsaw, by the rule of rotation Lange was president of the Security Council from mid-August to mid-September. In December the Polish Foreign Ministry nominated a new Ambassador to the United States so that Lange could devote his full time to the United Nations. He was meanwhile serving as chairman of the U.N. General Assembly Economic and Finance Committee.

Politics has not distracted Lange from his academic work. In 1946 he is working on a treatise on theoretical economics. Besides numerous articles on economics in scholarly journals, he has written the studies, *On the Economic Theory of Socialism* (1938), *The Rate of Interest and the Optimum Propensity to Consume* (1938), *Economic Mobilization* (coauthor; 1940), *The Foundations of Welfare Economics* (1942), *The Theory of the Multiplier* (1944), *The Working Principles of the Soviet Economy* (1944), *Price Flexibility and Employment* (1944). His special interests in his field are socialist economic theory, and economic fluctuation.

Ambassador Lange and Mrs. Lange, who retains her American citizenship, have a son, Christopher. Edmund Stevens described Lange as "a mild-mannered little man—an extremely shrewd observer... a man of the world, a typical Mid-European liberal intellectual." "He is one of the most relaxed delegates at Council meetings," Betty Moorsteen reported, "chirping greetings to reporters on the way in, walking faster than would seem comfortable on his crippled right leg which gives him a painful-looking gait, carrying always a brown leather briefcase in his small, almost child-sized hands." The Polish delegate has blue eyes and thinning fair hair. "Small and round," he is five feet three inches tall, weighs 176 pounds. He is said to be "always accessible to reporters" and "not a stickler for formality." Once he wandered into the U.N. press lounge, "put down his walking stick and proceeded to give an impromptu interview to eighty reporters." According to Frank Gervasi, writing in *Collier's,* Lange is a "voracious reader of everything that comes his way, from esoteric treatises on economics down to 'whodunits.' Otherwise his principal avocation is eating."

References

> Collier's 118:27 O 19 '46
> PM p8 Ap 7 '46
> International Who's Who, 1945-46

LANVIN, JEANNE (län"văn' zhän) 1867(?)—July 6, 1946 French dressmaker; founder of La Maison de Couture, the small Paris fashion group which, with a few other designers, set the mode for the world.

Obituary

> N Y Times p36 Jl 7 '46

LARGO CABALLERO, FRANCISCO (lär'gō kä'bä-lyä-rō frän-thēs'kō) 1869—Mar. 23, 1946 Spanish Socialist leader, "the Lenin of Spain"; sentenced to life imprisonment in 1917, but released to assume seat in legislature; minister of Labor during April, October, and December of 1931, June-September 1933; imprisoned for complicity in revolt October 1934, acquitted and released November 1935; was first Socialist Prime Minister of Spanish Republic and Minister of War, September 1936-May 1937; fought in Loyalist ranks against Franco troops; fled to France, imprisoned by Germans in World War II.

Obituary

> N Y Times p13 Mr 24 '46 por

LA ROCQUE, FRANÇOIS DE (là rôk frän"swà' dĕ) 1886—Apr. 28, 1946 French colonel; founded the Croix de Feu and the French Social Party; on the staff of Marshal Foch in World War I; headed the intelligence service of the French Army in the Riff War; interned in Germany for twenty-six months in World War II; held "collaboration" essential for European peace; supported Marshal Henri-Philippe Pétain.

Obituary

> N Y Times Ap 30 '46 por

LASSER, J(ACOB) K(AY) Oct. 7, 1896-Certified public accountant; tax authority
Address: b. 1440 Broadway, New York; h. 307 West End Rd., South Orange, N.J.

To ease the headaches which beset them each spring as they approach the income tax return deadline, Americans since 1936 have had a

J. K. LASSER

paper-bound best seller entitled *Your Income Tax.* "The most widely used tax guide" in the country, selling over eleven million copies in ten editions, it has since 1939 been the work of J. K. Lasser, tax authority and senior partner of a well-known New York accounting firm.

Jacob Kay Lasser, the son of Morris and Rebecca (Traub) Lasser, was born in Newark, New Jersey, on October 7, 1896. Educated in the New Jersey public schools, he was graduated from Newark's Central High School in 1915, after taking the usual general high school course. That same year he went to work as a part-time reporter for the Newark *Star* and also began studying in the evening session of New York University. After approximately a year with the paper, he obtained his first accounting job with the Breeze Manufacturing Company of Newark. But the next year, 1917, he transferred from NYU to Pennsylvania State College—and the day session—in order to take advantage of Penn State's nationally known courses in industrial engineering. Three years later he was awarded its B.S. in engineering, and in 1922 he received the I.E. (industrial engineering) degree from the same institution. During World War I, for a period in 1917-18 he had served in the United States Navy; and between 1920 and 1923 he also took further graduate work in the evening session of New York University.

In 1923 Lasser passed the New Jersey C.P.A. examinations and became entitled to practice as a certified public accountant. His own accounting firm, J. K. Lasser and Company, he established in 1926 in New York City. (In 1934 he was also licensed as a C.P.A. in New York; in 1939, in California.) In partnership with Lasser are David Boyd Chase and Harry Silverson, attorneys, Harold Kenneth Marks and Lawrence W. Bell, C.P.A.'s, and A. F. Adams. (As does Lasser, the first three devote consid-

erable time to writing, teaching, and lecturing.) Approximately seventy experts, including many accountants and some attorneys, complete the staff. When an attorney enters the company, Lasser reports, he turns from general law to concentrate on the particular problems of the firm: his background has been excellent preparation for the new work. Specializing in Federal taxation and in matters of concern to book and magazine publishers, some two hundred and fifty of which are numbered among its clientele, J. K. Lasser and Company is said to be one of the nation's best known accounting organizations.

Lasser, wrote Edward N. Polisher in the *Phi Epsilon Pi Quarterly,* soon drew to the forefront of his profession, acquiring a reputation as a pioneer. He was one of the first to recognize the growing importance of Federal, especially Federal income, taxation. He took the lead in awakening his colleagues in accountancy and law to their responsibilities in the new field and in making available to the layman and businessman alike a practical tax guide which they could understand. Taking over from Hugh Satterlee and I. H. Sher, whose experimental *Your Income Tax; How to Keep It Down* was published in 1936, Lasser in 1939 brought out the first edition of his manual *Your Income Tax,* which, revised each year, has come to be regarded as an "indispensable stand-by . . . without which one might say no home is complete." Modifying the more theoretical approach of his predecessors, which included an explanation of the principles of tax laws as well as, in the words of the New York *Times,* "many examples of various income-tax calculations which should prove helpful to the person who prepares his own return," Lasser concentrated upon the practical problems of the taxpayer.

"Written in simple you-style," said *Time,* "*Your Income Tax* treats the befuddled lower-bracket taxee very much as a psychiatrist would handle an alarmed patient. The hundred and twenty pages of text lay every bugaboo from Who-Must-File-a-Return to What-to-do-if-They-Get-After-You. You can hardly go wrong unintentionally." And the Atlanta *Journal* commented, "What this book is is a tax consultation service between two covers. . . . Mr. Lasser is a genius at streamlining the essential facts of our tax obligations to our Government and the rules whereby we shall know where we stand. . . . This book . . . explains in a level-headed fashion the minor intricacies which without help can become major annoyances. Nor is it necessary to read the entire book or to wade through page after page that bears no relation to your individual tax problems. A convenient index locates the answers to your questions, and a reasonable facsimile of the official treasury form is arranged to guide you at every step of your task."

Lasser's annual *Your Corporation Tax,* first issued in 1941, and in 1946 revised as *Business Tax Guide,* performs a similar service for the businessman and is also highly regarded. Meanwhile, with the aid of several of his colleagues and in cooperation with New York University, Lasser had begun to work out plans for the Institute of Federal Taxation, directed toward familiarizing tax men with the latest developments in this increasingly important sphere. Assembled, under Lasser's chairmanship, to lecture before the first session at New York University in December 1942 were the nation's foremost authorities in all phases of Federal taxation. Annual enrollment quickly rose to capacity (over three hundred people from all over the country) and today, wrote Polisher in 1945, "the Institute of Federal Taxation [still under the chairmanship of J. K. Lasser] ranks as the most notable achievement of its kind in postgraduate education in Federal taxation." Since early 1943, as editor of the *Journal of Accountancy*'s monthly feature "The Tax Clinic," which he originated, the accountant has also been providing his colleagues with a popular medium for discussion of current tax problems.

In addition to the writings already mentioned, Lasser has contributed both simplified and technical articles to such popular magazines and trade journals as the *American Mercury, House Beautiful, Publishers' Weekly, Advertising and Selling, Dun's Review, Sales Management*, and *Aero Digest*, the popular articles bearing such titles as "How Tax Cheaters are Caught", "In Fairness to the Small Taxpayer", "Maybe Those Excess Profits Taxes are not so High as They Seem." Regular columns edited or written by Lasser have also appeared in *American Business*, the *Wall Street Journal* (1942-43), and the New York *Herald Tribune* (1942-43). In 1934, together with J. A. Gerardi, he published *Federal Securities Act Procedure*; in 1943, *Handbook of Accounting Methods*; in 1945, *How to Speed Up Settlement of Your Terminated War Contract* and *Business Executive's Guide*. The second of these, "a cooperative undertaking with accounting authorities in some seventy different industries bringing their specialized knowledge to the project . . . was prepared to meet the practical needs of public and private accountants, system designers, executives and others interested in accounting procedures," and has been acclaimed as a "landmark among accounting publications." The last, "the result of notes made during twenty odd years of advising people on their duties and rights growing out of business problems that confront them," was intended to "provide a practical guide and check list to which businessmen can turn when confronted by a business problem."

The accountant has also taught at the University of Miami Conference on Federal Taxation and at New York University, and in 1942-43 was Blue Network commentator on taxes. In addition, he is active in the programs of the American Institute of Accountants, the New York State Society of Certified Public Accountants, of which he is a director, the New Jersey Society of Certified Public Accountants, and the National Association of Cost Accountants, and is a director of Tax Institute, Incorporated. Blond, blue-eyed, and of medium height, he lists his favorite recreation as golf and his clubs as the Engineers (New York)

and Mountainridge (West Caldwell, New Jersey); he is a member of the fraternity Phi Epsilon Pi.

Lasser and the former Terese Reuben, to whom he was married on January 1, 1924, are the parents of two children, Donald Judd and Barbara Ann. Known as "J.K." to his intimates, Lasser is, said Polisher, "a human dynamo . . . friendly, generous, willing at all times to lend a hand, and refreshingly unassuming. . . .The roster of his friends and acquaintances in the field of Federal taxation would make a veritable Who's Who of tax men in the country."

References

Phi Epsilon Pi Q Je '45 por
Who's Who in America, 1946-47

LAUSCHE, FRANK J(OHN) (lou'shē)
Nov. 14, 1895- Governor of Ohio
Address: b. State House, Columbus, Ohio

While casting their votes for the Republican candidates for President and Senator in the 1944 elections, the people of Ohio chose as their governor a Democrat, Frank J. Lausche, who was to hold that office for one term. Running on the Democratic ticket, although organizing his own campaign (without the aid of the party machine), it was the second time Lausche won election in a year of Republican victories. In 1943 he had been re-elected as mayor of Cleveland, in the midst of a landslide of Republican victories throughout the country.

The son of immigrants from Slovenia, now part of Yugoslavia, who came to the United States in 1885, Frank John Lausche was born in Cleveland on November 14, 1895. His father, Louis Lausche, worked in the steel mills to support a family of ten children. At the age of thirteen (his father and older brother having died), Frank became the mainstay of his widowed mother, Frances (Milavec) Lausche. To help care for the family he got a job lighting street lamps, for which he was paid two dollars a week. In course of time he was able to find work as a court interpreter; it was at this job that he first became interested in the law. In those days, however, law was not Lausche's primary interest. After starring as third baseman on the city's baseball lots, he made his mark as a professional baseball player in Lawrence, Massachusetts, and Duluth, Minnesota. With his earnings he helped to send two brothers and a sister through college, and he attended the Central Institute in Cleveland in 1915-16. A batting slump put an end to his ball-playing career with Duluth just before the entry of the United States into World War I. In 1918 Frank joined the Army, from which he emerged at the end of the war as a second lieutenant. Upon returning to civilian life, he received an offer to play with Atlanta in the Southern League, but doubts as to what the future might hold for a baseball player made him decide to become a lawyer instead.

(Continued next page)

FRANK J. LAUSCHE

After receiving his LL.B. in 1920 from the John Marshall School of Law, of which he is now a trustee (he received his LL.M. in 1936), he went to work for the law firm of Locher, Green, and Woods. Cyrus W. Locher, the late United States Senator, helped him to become one of Cleveland's best trial lawyers and encouraged him to enter politics. Lausche then joined the Democratic Party, and in 1922 he ran for the State legislature, but was not elected. Two years later he was a candidate for the State senate; once more he was defeated.

Not until 1932, when he was appointed to fill a vacancy on Cleveland's municipal bench, did he enter public office. The following year he was elected to the same post from among ten candidates, and in 1937 he was elected to the Cuyahoga County Court of Common Pleas. As judge, Lausche won much acclaim but also made some enemies. He accepted the labor cases other judges were apparently afraid to handle because of the antagonism which decisions in such cases were likely to arouse among the electorate. In the Crosby Restaurant Case, Lausche handed down a decision which alienated him from certain A.F. of L. unions. The employees of the Crosby Restaurant were not union members and made no attempt to unionize; however, the Hotel and Restaurant Alliance of the A.F. of L. wanted to organize the restaurant and picketed it. Declaring that "there was no legitimate trade dispute and that picketing by 'strangers' was unlawful," Lausche handed down an injunction against the union. (This ruling, at first upheld by the United States Supreme Court, has since been reversed.)

Lausche's work as a judge was not limited to making decisions on the bench. In the fall of 1940 he took the initiative in closing three large gambling houses in the metropolitan section of Cleveland. When county officials were uncooperative and the gambling operators were mysteriously warned, he organized a special police squad, which caught the gamblers redhanded. Such action won him much public attention, and he was asked to run for mayor. Resigning from his $12,000-a-year position in the Court of Common Pleas, a position which he might have kept for life, he accepted and was elected in 1941 by a 61 per cent majority.

In his campaign speeches Lausche promised such improvements as better sanitation and transportation, lower taxes, and city beautification. But with the attack on Pearl Harbor one month after he took office, the mayor found that he had more vital tasks to perform. He faced numerous problems in organizing Cleveland to help fight a war. More than half the city's population of nine hundred thousand were foreign-born or first or second generation Americans, and their loyalties were divided; also, they were of many different nationalities. The majority of the people were employed in industry at low wages, and strikes were frequent. In addition to these problems were those caused by discrimination against Negroes, with the consequent danger of riots.

Avowing a principle of being "on the level with everybody" and working "always for the good of the whole, never for any special group," Lausche was able to steer clear of trouble. Before the proposal came from Washington, he organized the Mayor's War Production Committee, consisting of the representatives of management, of labor, and of the mayor himself. Its purpose was not to settle strikes but to persuade the strikers to return to work while the disputes were being resolved by the proper authorities. By convincing the workers that their contribution to winning the war was just as important as the soldiers', the committee usually succeeded in getting the strikers back to work after twenty-four hours. Racial problems were solved by another special committee which the mayor set up. Still another special committee was organized to deal with transportation problems. And a fourth committee, the Mayor's Health Committee, which took measures to improve the war worker's health, was established; the plan was so effective that it was advocated as a model for other cities in the United States. By increasing the number of playgrounds from forty-eight to sixty-four and by adding more men and women to the police force, Lausche tried to combat juvenile delinquency. His successful efforts in fighting the black market won him praise from the Office of Price Administration.

In 1943, with a campaign promise to the effect that he would make every effort to be "a wholesome influence," Lausche was re-elected to serve until 1944, by a 71 per cent majority. (In this election, the total number of votes cast was at an all-time low.) Such a political victory was achieved under conditions which most politicians considered unfavorable. Lausche's relations with the Democratic County chairman were distinctly cool. He therefore organized his own campaign, and at the same time announced that none of those campaigning for him could expect any reward. Just before election day he risked his chances of winning by vetoing a pay increase for city building employees. The measure would have made their pay equal to that of workers in the private building industry, a provision Lausche maintained was not necessary since city building employees' work was not seasonal. This stand increased the antagonism which his decision in the Crosby Restaurant Case had already aroused among A.F. of L. unions. On the other hand, he was backed by the CIO as well as by other diverse groups. His support of a Negro candidate for judge, because he felt that an able Negro should be on the bench, rallied the Negroes of Cleveland to his side. (The candidate, incidentally, was not elected.) Lausche also received support from big business, from the Bar Association, and from some Republicans.

The record which the Cleveland mayor established as a vote getter attracted the attention of national Democratic leaders, who, it has been said, saw his value to the party as Governor of Ohio. Nevertheless, when he contested for that office, Lausche again waged his campaign independent of party help: it was run by friends at a cost of about $25,000, the largest contribution, $1,000, coming from Marshall Field [41]. At a time when the campaign committee was running out of money for stamps, a news story brought in small contributions from the public. (For the days Lausche campaigned he returned his salary as mayor to the city treasury.) Lausche's popularity was so great that Thomas Dewey, Republican candidate for president, hesitated to speak in Ohio; the reason given was that it would have been necessary for him to endorse the Republican candidate for Governor, and that, Dewey felt, would have cost him votes in Ohio. (Many of those who voted for Dewey cast their votes for Lausche.) Lausche's election as Governor in 1944 represented a victory over tradition. It was the first time a Catholic and a son of immigrants had been elected to the Governor's office in Ohio. When Lausche took office January 8, 1945, he outlined his four principles of administration for Raymond Moley, who devoted a *Perspective* in *Newsweek* to the new Governor of Ohio: "First, law and order. Second, economy. Third, equality of treatment among conflicting economic groups. Fourth, the development of unity between city and rural interests."

Lausche ordered no general dismissal of Republicans from office after he was inaugurated as Governor, retaining a Republican in the important position of director of finance. He opposed a bill to raise the Governor's salary, which is less than the $15,000 he received as mayor. The Governor was almost as hard on other State employees—he vetoed a bill which would have made pay increases for them retroactive because "it smacked of pork." As Governor, Lausche also continued his efforts toward winning the war. In June 1945 he directed the Ohio Selective Service to induct strikers at the Goodyear Plant in Akron into the armed forces. Protests came from C. V. Wheeler, local president of the CIO United Rubber Workers at Akron. The Governor further antagonized labor on Lincoln's Birthday in 1946 when he did not receive a "bill of grievance" asking for unemployment benefits for strikers. (He had told

their leader in advance, however, that he would not be in his office that day.) With the CIO strikers were war veterans who asked for a soldiers' bonus and for low-cost housing for veterans; a thousand strong, the workers and the ex-servicemen marched two blocks to the State House. The result was that the Governor was branded as unfriendly to labor and veterans.

In the November 1946 elections Lausche's personal popularity could not deflect the wave of Republican votes that swept Ohio. The Democratic Governor lost to Thomas J. Herbert by a narrow plurality of thirty-eight thousand votes. Shortly before the election it seemed as if the incumbent Governor would be re-elected, but a shift of sentiment, supposedly attributable to dissatisfaction with postwar conditions in the State, caused Lausche's defeat. His successor was to take office in January 1947.

Although his office has brought him chiefly into municipal and State affairs, Lausche has taken a stand on both national and international issues. An interventionist long before Pearl Harbor, he believes in the necessity for a world organization "able to deal decisively with those nations which harbor ambitions for world domination." As an honorary member of the Committee of Catholics for Human Rights, he has come out in favor of "retributive justice for war criminals." In the national issue of free enterprise versus government control, it is reported that he stands for free enterprise with a limited amount of government control.

Lausche, who was awarded the honorary degree of Doctor of Laws by Kenyon College (Gambier, Ohio) in 1945, is a member of the Cleveland Bar Association as well as of the Cuyahoga Bar Association; he is also a member of Delta Theta Phi and of the City Club in Cleveland. In 1928 he was married to Jane O. Sheal, an interior decorator and designer, who is described as "pretty, always smartly dressed, and quietly clever"; they have no children. Before coming to live in the Governor's Mansion, they had a small home next to a Chinese laundry in an unfashionable section of Cleveland, where they lived quietly. Tall, rather handsome, and bushy haired, the Governor retains a figure befitting a former baseball player. His early love for baseball has been replaced with an interest in golf, but he still plays the violin in the small orchestra of which the other members are five of his brothers and sisters. Lausche is described by admirers as a "man of great strength, character, and firmness"; and by critics as one who "takes himself pretty seriously and hasn't much sense of humor." When he is faced with a particularly knotty problem he turns to poetry for "new strength": he shuts the door of his office, silences the telephone, and reads Shakespeare, Burns, and Keats.

References

Am Mag 137:38-9+ Mr '44 por
N Y Sun p24 F 20 '46
Nation 159:95-6 Jl 22 '44
Newsweek 25:88 Ja 8 '45
Sat Eve Post 218:17+ Jl 7 '45
Who's Who in America, 1946-47

LAWRENCE, SIR GEOFFREY Dec. 2, 1880- British jurist

Address: b. Royal Courts of Justice, Strand, London; h. Hill Farm, Oaksey, Malmesbury, England

The presiding judge of the International Military Tribunal at the Nuremberg trial of the Nazi war criminals was Lord Justice Sir Geoffrey Lawrence, for many years prominent in the British judiciary. Lord Justice of Appeal and former Attorney General to the Duke of Windsor '44, he has taken part in numerous famous cases in the course of his legal career.

SIR GEOFFREY LAWRENCE

He was appointed senior British member of the international tribunal in September 1945 and later chosen chairman of what became the greatest trial of modern times.

The youngest of the three sons of the first Baron Trevethin, Sir Alfred Tristram, and Jessie Elizabeth (Lawrence) Lawrence, Geoffrey Lawrence was born on December 2, 1880. His father had risen high in the legal profession, becoming Lord Chief Justice of England, and the son was early destined for the law. After receiving his education at Haileybury and at New College, Oxford, he was in due course called to the bar at the Inner Temple, where in 1906 he began to practice under Sir John Simon. Later Lawrence became junior counsel to Lord Finlay, in whose chambers he worked on important constitutional cases. The barrister subsequently acquired a knowledge of income tax cases, turf litigation, ecclesiastical issues, international arbitration, and Privy Council appeals. When his country entered World War I he was commissioned a second lieutenant in the Hertfordshire Royal Field Artillery, with which he served in France, Palestine, and Gallipoli. Twice mentioned in dispatches while commanding a brigade, he was wounded and won the Distinguished Service Order. With the close of the war, he resumed

his civilian profession, meanwhile continuing his military service as commander of the Eighty-sixth Royal Artillery Brigade of the peacetime Territorial Army. In 1926 he retired from this service with the rank of colonel and the Territorial Army efficiency decoration.

Lawrence built up a large junior practice after the Armistice, largely of cases from the Dominions and the Colonies, which were heard before the Judicial Committee of the Privy Council. (One of his other clients was the Jockey Club, for which he was counsel from 1922 to 1932.) In 1924 he became justice of the peace for the county of Wiltshire. That same year he was also named Recorder of Oxford (1924-32) and a year later a King's Counsel. His professional status was considerably elevated with his appointment in 1928 as Attorney General to the Prince of Wales (now the Duke of Windsor). In this position, for the next four years he was adviser to the Prince's Council, which manages the affairs of the Duchy of Cornwall. At the same time Lawrence served as Examiner in Ecclesiastical Causes from 1927 to 1932. In the last year in this post he became a judge of the High Court of Justice of the King's Bench Division, and was sworn in in the presence of three generations of his family. Shortly thereafter the new judge was knighted and elected Master of the Bench of the Inner Temple. Sir Geoffrey served as chairman of the Quarter Sessions Appeal Committee in 1936.

A moderate and cautious judge, Sir Geoffrey was known for handling cases with scientific objectivity before rendering a decision. In 1933, for instance, at Manchester, the judge, fully robed and accompanied by his Marshal and two King's Counsels, mounted the top deck of a bus to discover whether a passenger had any means of preventing his being swept off when the vehicle rounded a bend. His judicial decisions created precedent; one of them was that a man whose marriage had been annulled could nevertheless not be taxed as a bachelor during the years in which he was actually married. Another decision, issued in Manchester in 1932, held that it was illegal to pay in England any money won in the popular Irish Sweepstakes because it was a foreign lottery.

In the Second World War the jurist once more took up active war work, serving as a private in the Parliamentary Home Guard. During the London blitz of 1940 he was wounded twice while on duty at the House of Commons. His war service also included the chairmanship of the advisory council of the Women's Transport Service, a volunteer organization which performed canteen and ambulance duties for the British Home Guard, the American Ambulance in Great Britain, and the Polish Army. In 1944 Sir Geoffrey was named Lord Justice of Appeal. At that time he was also appointed by the Crown to membership in the Privy Council in recognition of his public service. In September of the following year came his appointment as British member of the International Military Tribunal.

The London agreement of August 8, 1945, signed by the United States, Great Britain, the Soviet Union, and France, had established the four-power military tribunal and the legal basis for the trial of war criminals. By early October the judges were in Berlin, prepared to accept indictments. The tribunal consisted of four judges: Lawrence, Francis Biddle [41] for the United States, Major General I. T. Nikitchenko for the Soviet Union, and Henri Donnedieu de Vabre for France, in addition to an alternate for each member. (Sir William Norman Birkett was made Sir Geoffrey's alternate.) The long-awaited trial began on November 20, with indictments against twenty-four Nazi war leaders. Heading the list were Göring [41], Hess [41], von Ribbentrop [41], and Keitel [40]. Declared the chairman, Lord Justice Lawrence: "the trial is unique in the jurisprudence of the world." The London agreement had defined war crimes as crimes against humanity. In opening the British case on December 4, Sir Hartley Shawcross [45], the chief British prosecutor, charged the Nazi defendants with "planning and waging a war of aggression." As German violations he listed twenty-six specific international treaties, agreements, and assurances dating from the Hague Convention of 1899 to the German assurances to Yugoslavia in 1939.

When, in September 1946, Justice Lawrence summarized the charges against the defendants and announced that a verdict would be handed down at the end of the month, he had passed through ten months of a trial notable for Göring's brilliant self-defense and adroitness, and for Hess's occasional flurries of madness. In March, Justice Jackson, the American prosecutor, had appealed to the Chief Justice to curb Göring's "discursive oratory"; he said that these eulogies of Hitler and Nazism had a renascent propaganda value, as reports of the trial were being broadcast and published in Germany. Justice Lawrence disregarded this plea. Later, however, growing impatient with Göring, Lawrence ordered defense counsel to frame his questions more narrowly. On the last day of the trial Justice Lawrence declared that the tribunal would take into consideration the fact of Hess's insanity. At 10 A.M. September 30, Justice Lawrence began to read the summary of the tribunal's findings against the defendants, and then turned it over to the judges and alternates representing France, the United States, and Russia. All except three of the defendants were sentenced to death or imprisonment. In the honors list of December 1946, Sir Geoffrey was made a baron, not however, in recognition of his work at the Nuremburg trial (which will be mentioned on a special honors list in 1947), but in recognition of his many years of service to British law.

The British jurist is described as a strong, stocky, genial man, "thoroughly representative of all those values which are associated, especially by foreigners, with the Victorian English gentleman." According to a writer in the London *Observer*, Sir Geoffrey, "bristling with common sense," is suspicious of extravagance in word or action and dislikes the fanciful and fantastic. He was married to Marjorie Robinson on December 22, 1921. They have one son, John Geoffrey Tristram, and three daughters, Mary Elizabeth, Enid Rosamond, and Anne Jennifer. Sir Geoffrey's club is Brooks's. He spends much of his leisure at his country house, busy with his horses and his famous herd of Guernseys. A good judge of animals, he is reputed to have an astonishing memory for their pedigrees and in his spare time will "go off to some committee of the Guernsey Society and discuss for hours whether certain progeny, although from a nonpedigree stock, should be admitted into the stud book." Another hobby of Sir Geoffrey's is the collection of antique china and art treasures. During the years of his court service he would "often slip out at lunchtime and be found at Christie's —bidding for a rare cup or a sporting print."

References

Burke's Peerage (1936)
International Who's Who, 1945-46
Who's Who, 1946

LAXNESS, HALLDOR (KILJAN) (läks'-nĕs häl'dôr kyïl'yän) Apr. 23, 1902- Author
Address: P.O. Box 664, Reykjavik, Iceland

Halldór Laxness, author of *Independent People*, the epic novel of peasant life compared by some critics to Hamsun's and Hardy's finest tales, is Iceland's foremost contemporary novelist and poet. He has traveled widely and covered many subjects in his books; his works have been translated into all the major European languages and have been well received in England, France, Holland, Czechoslovakia, and the Scandinavian countries. But despite American publication of *Salka Valka* in 1936, Laxness had been little known in the United States prior to the appearance of *Independent People* in 1946. With the favorable reception of this novel, Laxness became an important figure in world literature.

A native of Reykjavik, Iceland, Halldór Kiljan Laxness was born in 1902, on April 23, Shakespeare's birthday, and was christened Halldór Gudjonsson. He spent his boyhood on his father's prosperous sheep farm, "Laxness." ("Laxness," which literally means "salmon peninsula," later became the writer's pen name.) There the boy heard his father recite the great Icelandic sagas and there he read the forty volumes, mostly of epic poetry, of which the family library was composed. Aspiring to a career in music, the boy received violin lessons from his father and studied the piano in Reykjavik, where he attended school. At this time Halldór composed verse much like the Icelandic poetry he had read, and later, while at the Icelandic Latin School, wrote romantic tales which he kept secret. When Laxness was seventeen, his first story, "The Child of Nature," was published.

After his graduation Laxness began the trips which have made him probably the most traveled living Icelander. In Denmark he wrote short stories for a Copenhagen newspaper. The next year he returned home to become a teacher in a country school. Then he plunged himself into introspection, philosophy, and religion, following the thought of Gunnarsson's, Undset's, and Strindberg's novels. According to Stefán Einarsson, the Icelandic critic, Laxness "represented the young urban population of Reykjavik,

Jóns Kaldal, Reykjavik

HALLDOR LAXNESS

cut loose from the secure moorings of the thousand-year-old farm culture, searching vigorously for a new mode of living among the possibilities of the postwar world." From 1920 to 1921 Laxness roamed through Austria and Germany, becoming deeply affected by German internal strife. In France he participated in the surrealist movement and, according to the New York *Times* reviewer, because of his "own inner turbulence," retired to Clairvaux monastery, where he wrote *Undir Helgahnúk* ("Beneath the Sacred Mountain"), published in 1924. Following a year and a half at Clairvaux, he studied with the Jesuits in Paris, and with the Carthusians in Sussex, England. From his impressions of these and other visits to Catholic centers, Laxness wrote several books concerned with religion.

Following a brief visit to Iceland, Laxness in 1925 traveled to Taormina, Sicily, where he wrote his first long novel, *Verfarinn Mikli frá Kasmir* ("The Great Weaver of Cashmere"), disclosing, according to Robert Gorham Davis in the New York *Times*, "stormy intellectual and spiritual development." In this Laxness is seen as expressing his own disillusionment. Subsequently he returned home to meet national criticism for his use of expressionistic form and foreign words in that book—tantamount, at a time when his country was arguing over the advisability of admitting foreign influences into its life and classic tongue, to approval of foreign infiltrations. Meanwhile, Laxness wandered through Iceland's small fishing villages and over its mountains. Much of his experience of these years among the country's poor appears in Laxness' later works, among them *Independent People*.

In the late 1920's Laxness came to America and lived for several years in Canada and the United States. While in Canada he wrote a short story about the difficult life of Icelandic immigrants in Manitoba, a story which led to a demand for the author's deportation. He visited California next, where he met author Upton Sinclair. Laxness has since written: "I arrived there as a rather conservative European, but getting acquainted with America, I turned socialist, finding it the only thinkable reaction of an intelligent being to the state of affairs in that country." A "communistic" thesis became apparent in his writings, beginning with the satiric essays in *The Book of the Common People* (1929). Laxness also wrote a "revolutionary" volume of poems in 1930. In his verse, Laxness is said to have helped to establish the new poetic school by continuing an earlier modern author's *Letters to Laura*.

Laxness returned to Iceland in 1930 for the thousandth anniversary of the Althing, the island's Parliament. After further travel in Germany, Republican Spain, Scandinavia, and Eastern Europe, including the Soviet Union, Laxness' next book, a small work on Russia called *I Austurvegi*, appeared in 1933, and in the same year a volume of short stories was published. Two stories, of folklore quality, "The Defeat of the Italian Air Fleet in Reykjavik" and "Lily" have been published in English in the *American Scandinavian Review*. Early in the Hitler regime Laxness' books were banned in Germany. Given the chance to retract his anti-Nazi statements, the author replied with a speech delivered in Iceland on May Day, 1937, the defiance of which resulted in the permanent blacklisting of his works by the Nazis.

Salka Valka, the first Laxness novel to appear in America, was issued in Iceland in the early 1930's, brought out in an English translation of the Danish edition, and published in the United States in 1936. The book, whose title is the name of its "vigorous" heroine, received mixed reviews, but most critics declared it "sharply satirical", "elemental", "unrelenting." Frank Swinnerton asserted that "while translation always heightens crudity in an original, enough power remains . . . to make it seem authentic and alive."

In the author's opinion, his chef d'œuvre, the biggest and by far the most important of his books, is the tetralogy about the Poet, the four volumes of which are titled "The Light of the World", "The Château in Summerland", "The Poet's House," and "The Beauty of the Sky."

Unlike Hamsun, to whose work Laxness' has been compared, the Icelandic author is interested in political and economic problems, a fact reflected in *Independent People*. The first part of this book was published in Iceland in 1934, the second, completing the work, in 1935, and an American edition in 1946. Ernestine Evans in the New York *Herald Tribune Weekly Book Review* said that Laxness "dissects the warm body of the universal political crisis . . . tells a love story tragically beautiful and almost hidden in the chronicle of peasant life, and . . . sets a vision of independence as man's goal to be brooded over, questioned, and perhaps to be discerned, after all, in interdependence." The *PM* review of the novel, the August 1946 selection of the Book-of-the-Month Club, states that from *Independent People* "you have the feeling of power in reserve, of the author having so much more to tell if only there were sufficient time, which is the mark of a major novelist." "A hard but truly great novel, which goes far to explain an entire nation," according to Roger Butterfield writing in the *Saturday Review of Literature*, "the book is drenched in the cold beauty of the northern landscape. . . .Through it all runs the pattern of Icelandic folklore. . . .Finally, *Independent People* is richly symbolic of the entire life span of the Icelandic nation."

Publication of *Independent People* and other of Laxness' writings revived the Icelandic controversies over both revision of the language and what is said to be Laxness' presentation of an "exaggerated idea of the hardships of farm life" in Iceland. One of the author's former schoolmates is quoted by the *Book-of-the-Month Club News* as emphasizing the cleanliness of Icelanders: "Halldór is such a fastidious man himself that it is strange that he can describe so much dirt. The last time I asked him about that he just smiled and said, 'I must be getting old—it isn't as much fun shocking the bourgeoisie any more!'"

In Laxness' later works, Robert Gorham Davis found, the author "has shown himself capable of the same ironic, perceptive, sympathetic and yet detached attitude toward communism as toward so many of the movements in which he has participated in his varied career." His *Islands Klukkan* ("The Bell of Iceland"), the beginning of a new trilogy, appeared in 1943. A second volume, "The Fair Maiden," was published in late 1945. In 1946 Laxness finished the third volume, "Fire in Copenhagen."

An industrious and prolific author, during the six years of World War II Laxness translated Voltaire's *Candide* from the French, five novels from the Danish, edited for publication several of the longer Icelandic sagas, and in 1940 translated Hemingway's *A Farewell to Arms* into the Icelandic. Since 1931, except for several prewar winter vacations on the French Riviera, in Spain and Italy, and once in South America (1936), Laxness has made his home in Iceland. Even in the prosperous war years, Iceland's most popular authors could not make their living by writing, because of the small, though highly literate population. Laxness and others of his contemporaries therefore received an annual stipend from the Government. In his case, this supplemented extensive foreign royalties. But there have been some years in which Laxness has not accepted this stipend because he considered its reduction a reflection upon his honor as an author. This was true in 1946.

The author, who is married to a young hospital technician, his second wife, spends the winters in a Reykjavik apartment, and summers writing at the modern house he built on his father's farm. Called "world-conscious", "resourceful," and "highly civilized," Laxness opposes, on principle, ownership of any extensive personal belongings, including books. He is not quite six feet in height, has thinning fair hair, and is admired as "impressive" rather than as handsome.

References

Book-of-the-Month Club N p4 Jl '46 por
Books Abroad 16:254-9 Summer '42
N Y Times Book R p1+ Jl 28 '46
Sat R Lit 29:12 Jl 27 '46
International Who's Who, 1945-46
Lindroth, H. Iceland; A Land of Contrasts (1937)

LAZZERI, TONY Dec. 6, 1903—Aug. 6, 1946 New York Yankees' famous second baseman, 1925-37; record hitter and one of the most popular of contemporary baseball players.

Obituary

N Y Times p21 Ag 8 '46 por

LEA, CLARENCE F(REDERICK) July 11, 1874- United States Representative from California

Address: b. House Office Bldg., Washington, D. C.; h. 719 North St., Santa Rosa, Calif.

Clarence F. Lea has represented California in Congress for thirty years, a record unmatched by any other member from the Pacific coast. In all except two of his terms, Lea, a Democrat, has won both his party's and the Republican Party's nominations. He is author of the Lea-Bailey [45] civil aviation bill of 1943 and of the controversial "anti-Petrillo [46]" bill of 1946.

CLARENCE F. LEA

Clarence Frederick Lea, a descendant of Missouri pioneers, was born near Highland Springs in Lake County, California, on July 11, 1874. His parents were James Madison and Elizabeth (Trower) Lea, who had gone West in the 1850's. The boy attended public school in his native county and Lakeport Academy. After studying at Leland Stanford Junior University from 1895 until 1897, he went to law school at Denver University, where he received his LL.B.

LEA, CLARENCE F.—*Continued*

degree the following year. In 1898 he also was admitted to the bar and began his law practice at Santa Rosa. His political career began there in Sonoma County when he became district attorney in 1906. He was re-elected in 1910 and in 1914, but resigned in his third term, in December 1916, to enter the United States House of Representatives as a Democrat from California's first district.

Arriving in Washington before the passage of the Eighteenth Amendment, Lea opposed the prohibition measure when it was brought before the House. The following year he supported agricultural appropriations, and in 1919 the Californian introduced a resolution calling for a national redwood park. After supporting a minority report in a spruce production investigation, Lea filed his own minority report on an aircraft production investigation. By 1924 he had become a member of the House Committee on Interstate and Foreign Commerce, and the next year he blamed the lack of funds for halting that committee's aircraft investigation. Lea later favored a proposal to encourage travel in the United States by the creation of a Federal agency for that purpose. He spoke against some of the railroad restrictions which he considered needless, and urged Government regulation of interstate shipment of natural gas. In 1921 the Senator was first made a member of and later (1937) became chairman of the House Committee on Interstate and Foreign Commerce.

During the depression years of the thirties, Lea supported the public works projects, the National Youth Administration, and the food stamp plan to utilize farm surpluses. While he voted to continue the Home Owners Loan Corporation, to give more funds for hydroelectric power and for rural electrification (he had pressed for action on the Boulder Dam bill in 1927), he opposed grants requested by the Administration for soil conservation, crop insurance, incentive payments on certain crops, and similar subsidies. In 1946 he was to protest against a budgetary cut in flood control appropriations.

In 1939 Lea supported appropriations for the Guam naval base, and for military planes. He favored the peacetime draft, the property-seizure bill giving emergency powers to the President, repeal of the arms embargo, liberalization of the neutrality act, and Lend-Lease. To implement Lend-Lease activities, in 1941 he supported the use of armed ships and the lifting of belligerent zone restrictions on deliveries. After the United States had entered World War II, Lea voted to extend the draft to "limited service" men and to women nurses. He supported the Fulbright [43] resolution to continue international cooperation after the war, the United Nations Relief and Rehabilitation Administration, the loan to Britain, and the Reciprocal Trade Agreements Act of 1943. The 1945 Reciprocal Trade Agreements Act did not receive his support as it would have increased the power of the President: the Chief Executive would be enabled to reduce tariffs, fixed by Congress, from 50 to 25 per cent.

Lea has supported legislation to bring labor unions under the Hobbs Anti-Racketeering Act and to keep them out of politics. While some of the drastic labor amendments he favored in 1940 were defeated, the Smith [41]-Connally [41] War Disputes Act was passed with Lea also voting to override President Roosevelt's veto of the measure. When Lea several years later proposed repealing that antistrike bill, it was in order to suggest other labor restrictions in its stead. Lea supported the Case [46] antistrike Labor Disputes Act, of February 1946, added a rider to the War Labor Board appropriations bill excluding agricultural processing workers from the board's jurisdiction, and voted to freeze the social security tax at 1 per cent. On the other hand, he voted to use Federal funds for aiding stranded war workers, supported the Ramspeck bill to increase the pay of Federal employees, and opposed returning the United States Employment Service to heterogeneous State control.

Although he opposed the Wolcott amendment to limit the scope of the 1942 Price Control Act, Lea later became known as a strong opponent of the Office of Price Administration. Lea was author of a move to strip the OPA of all save rent control; while the measure was defeated, it resulted in the June 1946 bill establishing the Price Decontrol Board. The previous year Lea had favored giving authority for all Government orders and for preserved food to the Secretary of Agriculture. Lea voted for the cost-plus-"reasonable profit" formula in OPA ceilings and against a bill to curtail speculation in home pricing. In 1944 Lea supported an income tax bill which Roosevelt said helped the "greedy" rather than the "needy," after having rejected the Carlson-Ruml [43] pay-as-you-go plan in favor of the Robertson-Forand compromise tax proposal. Lea also opposed setting a limit on salaries of $25,000 after taxes.

An expert on aviation, Lea proposed the Lea-Bailey civil aviation bill in 1943 to make the Civil Aeronautics Board independent of the Department of Commerce, to make aviation subject to Federal regulation, to provide airport zones for abating the hazard of tall obstacles, and to exclude surface transportation companies from engaging in aviation except where incidental to surface transport operations. This was a reversal of previous attempts to synthesize surface and air commerce under the same transportation control, which air transport companies felt would constitute a "transport monopoly." Again in 1945 Lea proposed legislation for national regulation of air commerce and in the same year made a trip to Paris to investigate the possible need for an assistant Secretary of State for air, who would handle international problems. In rail transportation, Lea favored payment by the Government of full transportation rates; he believed that the railroads, by allowing 50 per cent discounts, in return for lands granted by the Government in the nineteenth century, had "already paid their debt."

As chairman of the House Committee on Interstate and Foreign Commerce, Lea also conducts the national transportation survey, authorized by Congress to study the problems arising after World War II. Lea believes that "without economical transportation, our whole economy can bog down no matter how much energy, wisdom, and capital . . . [are] put into the other phases of reconversion." In 1944 Lea had succeeded Eugene Cox '43 of Georgia as chairman of a House committee to investigate what *Newsweek* called the Federal Communication Commission's "death grip over radio." Lea's committee commended the way in which the FCC had functioned, but urged revision of the Federal Communications Act "to meet the developing needs of the radio industry." The report recommended that Congress, rather than the FCC, decide whether newspapers should be banned from operating radio stations. Lea is also chairman of the House oil committee and of the subcommittee to implement the Holding Company Act of 1935.

Lea twice voted to extend the Dies '40 Committee to Investigate Un-American Activities, but was against making the House committee a permanent one when the issue came up in 1945. He voted for the Smith Committee, to investigate the executive branch of the Government, which was led by a strong critic of the Administration. While Lea missed a Congressional attempt to outlaw the poll tax, he voted for the original soldier vote bill for 1944 to provide a Federal ballot for servicemen in the Presidential election (the Federal ballot would have enfranchised many of those disfranchised by the poll tax).

One of the most controversial bills sponsored by Lea was his "anti-Petrillo" bill signed by President Truman in April 1946. The law provides severe penalties (imprisonment and/or fine) for union officials who "coerce, compel, or restrain" a broadcast licensee to hire more employees than he needs; to pay more than once for the same service; to pay stand-by fees; and to refuse noncommercial, educational, or overseas programs. Unions are also barred from demanding royalties on transcriptions, from restricting the number of records made or used, and from charging fees for the use of transcribed shows. Lea pointed out that the bill does not prevent collective bargaining by the unions; contracts embodying the extras, fees, royalties, and specific prohibitions are valid.

Although James Caesar Petrillo is nowhere mentioned by name, Lea admitted his bill was designed to curb activities of the American Federation of Musicians president. *Broadcast* wrote that the bill marked "an end to A.F.M. pillaging of radio," while Representative Vito Marcantonio of New York called it "the most extreme antilabor measure brought out in this country." Petrillo violated the law in June 1946 and charges were subsequently pressed by United States Attorney J. Albert Woll. These were dismissed that December by Judge Walter J. La Buy, of the United States District Court in Chicago, who held the Lea Act to be unconstitutional, a violation of the First, Fifth, and Thirteenth Amendments on five separate counts. Woll announced that he would appeal directly to the Supreme Court, the country's highest tribunal.

Lea has long advocated a Constitutional amendment of the electoral college system, because he regards it as both burdensome and dangerous. The unit vote, whereby the total electoral votes of a State are given to the candidate receiving a majority, operates to disfranchise the minority. (The discrepancy between the popular vote and the electoral votes actually given a candidate has ranged from 3 to 40 per cent since the beginning of the century.) The Lea resolutions of 1933 and of 1936 would retain the present allocation of electoral votes (the number of votes equal the total number of Senators and Representatives for the State) but would abolish the electoral college itself, and give to each candidate his share of the electoral votes in the exact proportion to the popular vote he receives. In 1944 Lea proposed another amendment to lengthen the term of office for Representatives to four years, since he felt that biyearly elections "emphasized the political phase of membership and minimized the importance of service."

Both the Democratic and Republican parties nominated Democrat Lea in fourteen of his sixteen Congressional primaries (he had failed to receive Republican backing for his first and ninth terms). Thus, Lea writes, "Throughout my Congressional career, I have maintained an independence in voting." He was chairman of the House Democratic caucus in 1933 (the year of his ninth term) at which committee memberships for the incoming Administration were assigned. He was president of the District Attorney's Association of California in 1916-17.

Married to the former Daisy A. Wright on July 18, 1907, Lea and his wife had a son Frederick, who died at the age of six. Lea is a Baptist Church member. Brown-eyed, he has gray hair, stands five feet nine inches tall. The Congressman plans to retire in 1949 after thirty-two years of service; he looks forward to other useful years home in Sonoma County, "still blessed with good health."

References

N Y Sun p17 F 23 '43
Sunset 58:49 F '27 por

Congressional Directory (2d ed., 1945)
Who's Who in America, 1946-47
Who's Who in the Nation's Capital, 1938-39

LEA, LUKE Apr. 12, 1879—Nov. 18, 1945 Former United States Democratic Senator from Tennessee (1911-15); organized and became a lieutenant colonel in the 114th Field Artillery in 1917; led an unsuccessful expedition into Holland to kidnap the Kaiser (1918); publisher of the Nashville *Tennesseean, Commercial Appeal,* and the Knoxville *Journal.* Imprisoned (1934) for defrauding bank, paroled (1934), and pardoned (1937).

Obituary

N Y Times p21 N 19 '45 por

LEAO VELLOSO, P(EDRO) (lä'oun vä-lō'sō pä'thrōō) Jan. 13, 1887- Brazilian Government official; delegate to the United Nations Security Council

Address: b. c/o United Nations, New York

The "watchful Brazilian" of the United Nations Security Council sessions, Pedro Leão Velloso has been in his Government's foreign service since 1907. "Velloso is a diplomatic hang-over from the Vargas regime," wrote Frank Gervasi in *Collier's* in July 1946, "but is responsible to an obviously democratically oriented Brazilian Government." Under Vargas

Official United Nations Photo.

P. LEAO VELLOSO

the "shrewd" and "seasoned" envoy was Minister to China, Ambassador to Japan and to Italy, and Secretary General of the Ministry of Foreign Affairs before he became Foreign Minister in 1944.

Since the establishment of the federal republic of Brazil, São Paulo, a "cow, cotton and coffee" state, has been politically and economically one of the two most powerful of the twenty Brazilian states. In São Paulo's town of Pindamonhanguba, Pedro Leão Velloso was born on January 13, 1887, two years before the Empire of Brazil was changed by a bloodless revolution into the Republic of the United States of Brazil. The boy's mother was the former Virginia De Oliveira Castro; his father, also named Pedro Leão Velloso, owned and edited a newspaper. Young Pedro attended Kopke College, which is comparable to an American high school. Graduated in December 1903, he entered the university in Rio de Janeiro. His Bachelor of Laws degree was awarded him by the faculty of juridicial and social sciences in December 1907, shortly before his twenty-first birthday. To embark on a career as a diplomat he gave up work as a newspaper reporter, although he still writes

articles for Brazilian newspapers. His first assignment in the Ministry of Foreign Affairs came in 1907, as assistant to the Brazilian-Peruvian Court of Arbitration.

Appointed second secretary in the Foreign Office in January 1910, in the next eight years he saw foreign service in Brazilian legations at Rome, Paris, and Berne. In Paris in 1918 he was appointed secretary of the Brazilian Delegation to the Peace Conference at Versailles. After that he was chargé d'affaires in Copenhagen (1919), and counselor in Rome (1921) and in Paris (1923). Returning to Brazil in 1926, the thirty-nine-year-old career diplomat was named chief of cabinet of the Ministry of Foreign Affairs, under Foreign Minister Mangabeira. Three years later he again went abroad, this time to the Far East; he was Minister Plenipotentiary to China until 1935, and Ambassador to Japan from 1935 to 1939. "He apparently learned more about the Japanese character than some of our own diplomats," Gervasi has written. "At the San Francisco Conference Velloso predicted they'd fold up at the first hard blow 'like the submissive, servile people they are. And once you've beaten them, watch out. They'll do their utmost to ingratiate themselves.'" The Ambassador was transferred to Italy in 1939, where he remained until 1941, when he was recalled on the insistence of the Italian Government after he had criticized its policy. On his return to Rio de Janeiro two years later, he was appointed Secretary General of the Ministry of Foreign Affairs (or Undersecretary of State for Foreign Affairs) under Foreign Minister Oswaldo Aranha, who pursued a policy of collaboration and friendship with the United States.

With Aranha's resignation in August 1944, Leão Velloso became Acting Foreign Minister in the Government of Getulio Vargas, strongman president of Brazil since 1930. Officially it was stated, "The Government of the republic judges it opportune to reaffirm the directives of his [Aranha's] foreign policy of continental solidarity and strict cooperation with the Allied Nations." The next year, representing his country at the Inter-American Conference on Problems of War and Peace in Mexico City, Leão Velloso unbagged "an unseemly cat," according to *Time,* with his "bald" assertion "that a prime purpose of the conference was to line up 'a solid bloc of votes' for the forthcoming world security conference in San Francisco." He later declared: "At the Mexico City Conference, where momentous decisions were taken to strengthen the union between our countries, what we had in view was to equip them better to fulfill the mission that will be incumbent upon them in the organization of peace and in the re-establishment of the disrupted balance of the world. It is with this in mind, and desiring to give our frank and loyal cooperation, that we shall soon attend the San Francisco Conference."

At the head of the Brazilian delegation to the 1945 San Francisco conference, Leão Velloso was a member of the important coordination committee. In common with other Latin-American delegates, he was particularly concerned with the problem of "regionalism"; though a believer in world organization, he was loathe to see his nation give up the security provided by Pan-American unity. The formula finally adopted by the conference permitted regional systems to settle their own disputes, the world organization to take over only when regional efforts failed. The Brazilian was one of the drafters of the memorandum committing the American republics to the admission to the U.N. of Argentina despite its fascist Government. To this Gervasi pointed as an example of why "both fellow diplomats and correspondents rate him [Velloso] a conservative rather than a liberal." Gervasi added, however: "Velloso has privately expressed his regret that Argentina was allowed to come into the United Nations." Brazil was also one of the leading opponents of the veto provision of the charter. When that fight was lost Leão Velloso said, "We are not disappointed because we did not expect too much. The important thing is to have a charter and to keep unity among the Big Three (let's be polite and call them the Big Five)."

Brazil, meanwhile, had a change of Government. "A rebirth of democratic fervor" came to the nation as Vargas gave up office in the fall of 1945. Eurico Dutra[46], the president elected to succeed Vargas, retained Leão Velloso as Foreign Minister, according to the New York *Herald Tribune* "because of his international prestige and thirty-eight years' experience in foreign affairs." Thus, when the United Nation's Security Council met in New York in March 1946, the veteran statesman was present as his Government's representative; Brazil had been elected to a nonpermanent Council seat by the Assembly. The "most passive, self-contained and deliberate" delegate, Leão Velloso was notably silent during the first sessions. His longest single speech, made in April in support of the Byrnes resolution requesting information from Russia and Iran, contained less than twenty-five words. The least voluble of the Council members opposed the Polish proposal that relations with Franco Spain be broken on the grounds that Brazil could not accept interfering in the internal affairs of other countries, but withdrew his objections under instructions from his Government. Leão Velloso also served on the U.N. Atomic Energy Commission.

After the killing of five American fliers in Yugoslavia, the Brazilian delegate denounced the Soviet Union as being guilty of the "same aggressive methods as the onetime Nazi-Fascist states." And two months later, when Albania, a nonmember of the United Nations, sought a voice on the Security Council to second the Ukrainian attack on Greece (her argument was to include a listing of Albanian-Greek border incidents and an objection to British troops in Greece), Leão Velloso announced that Brazil planned to follow her attitude at the London Council of "not considering the presence of British troops in Greece as a menace to peace, since these troops are there at the request of the Greek Government." He took the same stand in September 1946, when the Russian delegate claimed that the British and American

troops scattered all over the world were a menace to peace. Leão Velloso replied that most American troops had been withdrawn from Brazil, but that the few radio technicians still remaining were there upon "the express desire of the Brazilian Government." If there were any trouble with them, the Brazilian delegate continued, Brazil would submit the case to the Pan American Union first, and then to the Security Council if no solution were reached.

The Brazilian diplomat considered the disarmament proposal the most important issue placed before the United Nations Assembly; he also endorsed the American proviso that guaranties of the principle be established: "No country is going to disarm today without due guaranties that all others will do the same. And the only method of obtaining such guaranties, without suspicions, is through establishment of an inspection system which enables all to join in the same spirit of cooperation."

"As a diplomat," Gervasi has noted, "Velloso plays his cards close to his bulgy belt. His colleagues and newspapermen who've known him for years agree about his shrewdness." The Brazilian was a conspicuous figure at the Council table, "easily identified by a magnificent baldness.", In the spotlights the stocky, five-foot-three Latin American wore green smoked glasses, and his head glistened "in mahogany splendor." With his French wife, Germaine Leão Velloso, the diplomat plans to retire some day to private life, to their home in Rio de Janeiro and their summer villa in Petropolis.

References

Collier's 118:60 Jl 20 '46
Who's Who in Latin America (1940)

LEE, JENNIE Nov. 3, 1904- Laborite Member of Parliament
Address: 23 Cliveden Pl., London, S.W., England

"Britain's first man-and-wife Parliamentary team," was the comment when both Jennie Lee and Aneurin Bevan[43] were returned as Labor members of the House of Commons in July 1945. But Jennie Lee, it is pointed out, is more than merely the distaff side of this team. She is, it is said, a personage in her own right—having been the youngest member of the House of Commons in the 1929-31 Labor Government and having since then, as she phrases it, "hoboed all over the world," lecturing, writing, and working steadily to advance the socialist doctrines.

A collier's daughter who considers miners her people and their life her life, Jennie Lee was born on November 3, 1904, in Lochgelly, Fifeshire, Scotland. Her father, himself an active trade unionist and member of the Independent Labor Party, was a son of the famous Scottish trade unionist Michael Lee, pioneer of the Fife Miners' Association and member of the Scottish Miners' Executive. It was her father, she says, whose "critical socialist attitude" influenced her entire outlook on life. Her mother's family, on the other hand, were hotel owners

LEE, JENNIE—*Continued*

in Cowdenbeath two miles away, and it was in the Arcade Hotel, located on the floors above an entertainment and meeting hall to which she was a frequent and unregulated visitor, that Jennie spent her third to her eighth years. "The Arcade," she wrote in her autobiography, "was my real nursery school. Its actors and actresses, rats and ventriloquist's doll, its toy shop and Chinaman with a real pigtail, form in my memory a frieze of as grotesque and brightly colored pictures as any child's artist could devise." In 1912, however, her parents discontinued the operation of the hotel, and her father resumed his occupation of coal mining.

Jennie Lee received her first schooling at the Cowdenbeath Elementary School, at which a first place in the final examinations, resulting in a scholarship, enabled her to attend the Cowdenbeath Secondary School instead of going to work; for by this time she had made up her mind that she wanted more schooling. Then, with the aid of grants from the Fife Education Association and the Carnegie Trust and of numerous prizes won whenever she applied herself to her studies instead of to the socialist activities and argumentation which she found much more interesting, she put herself through the University of Edinburgh, graduating in 1926 with an M.A., a diploma in education, and a teacher's certificate.

That was the year of the General Strike in Great Britain, and young Jennie Lee's last term at the university was divided between studies and work at strike headquarters in Edinburgh, while her summer was spent in Ireland raising funds for a miners' soup kitchen. She does not know quite what she had expected from a university education, she says in her autobiography, *This Great Journey*, but it was not the memorizing and cramming for examinations, the routine collecting of degrees, and the complete absence of any relation to life which she had experienced at Edinburgh and which had become the "least important part of student life" for her. Emotionally and intellectually, she points out, (although she admits she was biased in their favor) her stimulation during these years came during the long summer vacations spent among the leaders of the vigorous Fife socialist movement, men whose "eager, questioning, purposeful kind of knowledge" formed an "exhilarating contrast to the dead, disconnected parroting that earned us our university degrees."

After the failure of the General Strike of 1926, Miss Lee went back to Edinburgh to complete her studies for the LL.B., which she received in 1927. Then, for approximately two and a half years, while unemployment and poverty in the Scottish coal districts were at their worst since hard times had begun about 1921, she taught school near Lochgelly and bore the burden of family support because her father had been blacklisted by the mineowners for his part in the General Strike. But "I had no bent for this kind of teaching," she writes. "I was too impatient; too much at war with my whole environment. I did not believe in what I was doing. I did not believe that

there was any good reason why either the children or myself should come to terms with life as we found it in that bleak mining village. Most of the misery I saw around me in school, in the streets, and in private homes, had its roots in the poverty of the place. I did not see how, within the four walls of a classroom, I could ever hope to change any of that." Thus, when in 1928 she was offered a chance to become the Independent Labor Party's Parliamentary candidate from North Lanark in the 1929 general election (in which Labor came to power for the second time), she put aside her misgivings of youth and inadequacy to accept. Several months before the scheduled general election, however, the death of the sitting member from North Lanark precipitated a by-election, and in March 1929 she was returned by the district with a majority of 6,578 votes.

Jennie Lee was only twenty-four when, a few weeks after she took her seat in the House of Commons, she "broke into the budget debate like a hurricane"—in the words of a contemporary. She knew clearly, however, why she was in London. "I had been sent there," she says, "because I vehemently resented the poverty and slums and unemployment that was sapping away the very life of the industrial population of Scotland. And had persuaded the majority of the electorate of North Lanark that these were not acts of God about which nothing could be done but man-made evils that men could also remedy." She became identified with the Left wing of the Labor Party and rapidly proved herself a forceful and vivid exponent of the advanced Labor viewpoint. Weekends she would spend in North Lanark among her constituents, and many hours on weekdays she spent in answering their letters. In August 1929 she went to Vienna to study the Austrian socialist youth movement. In 1930, together with Labor M.P.'s Aneurin Bevan, John Strachey, and George Strauss, she visited industrial and mining centers in Russia, with characteristic independence managing to leave the "conducted tour" to accompany a group of Russian workers bound for a holiday in the Caucasus.

But by its second year in office the depression-aggravated economic crisis was fast overtaking the ineffectual MacDonald Government. "These are bad days for Labor," Miss Lee told an I.L.P. meeting in November 1930, "and they will become worse unless the government gets right back to its own policy and its own philosophy instead of imagining that it can save the country by reaching compromises with the Liberal or Tory parties. There is no use in putting up a paper parasol as a shelter from a world-wide blizzard." Together with a few others she tried to rouse her Parliamentary colleagues to a sense of their individual responsibility, she says, but "they would see nothing, do nothing, listen to nothing that had not first been given the seal of MacDonald's approval." In August 1931, "with economy and the upholding of British credit," in the language of the *New International Year Book*, "as the most pressing of national issues, the question arose as to how the required sacrifices were to be distributed among the population. Labor demanded that the cost be borne by the rich, through higher taxes, and lower returns on fixed investments. The industrialists and financiers stood firm for a reduction of wages to enable British industry to compete more successfully in foreign markets, and a tariff to protect the domestic market." On August 24 the Labor Cabinet resigned, and Ramsey MacDonald, sacrificing the leadership of his party, formed a coalition ministry. Two months later, on October 28, a general election swept a National (coalition) Government into power with a majority of 554 to 61, again under MacDonald, and the young M.P. lost her seat. In the Labor Party split which followed the election rout, she went over to the Independent Labor Party.

Although she stood for Parliament again in 1935 and at a by-election in 1943, Jennie Lee did not return to Commons until the third Labor victory in 1945. Instead, she became a lecturer and free-lance journalist. Beginning in December 1931, she made frequent lecture tours of the United States, Europe, and the Soviet Union, and, as before, ignored convention to reach the workers. On her first American tour, for instance, disregarding her agent's schedule, she went to the South, where she addressed cotton workers making their first tentative attempts to form a union without color distinctions and a group of Kentucky miners. As a journalist she covered the Popular Front elections in France in 1936, revisited Russia, contributed to the American *New Republic* as well as to British periodicals and newspapers. For a time during World War II Miss Lee was lobby correspondent in the House of Commons for the London *Mirror,* and, after the fall of France in 1940, at Lord Beaverbrook's suggestion, she was assigned to the Ministry of Aircraft Production, where it became her responsibility to keep production lines moving even with German planes overhead. She had also been during these years an active member of the I.L.P.

In 1939 Jennie Lee's autobiography *Tomorrow is a New Day* appeared (enlarged and published in the United States as *This Great Journey* in 1942), and in 1941 she published *Our Ally, Russia.* In 1942, however, the Labor rebel resigned from the I.L.P. because she could not accept its antiwar attitude. Two years later she rejoined the party she had left in 1932, and in the Labor landslide of July 1945 she was elected to Parliament from Cannock with a majority of approximately twenty thousand votes. In November 1946 she was one of fifty-nine Laborites who signed an amendment to a speech by King George when he opened Parliament. The addition, considered a rebellion against Secretary Bevin's foreign policy, asked for a change in international relations to the extent that Great Britain would encourage and collaborate with all nations working toward socialism, "thus providing a democratic and constructive socialist alternative to an otherwise inevitable conflict between American capitalism and Soviet communism, in which all hope of world government would be destroyed."

"Politics, for me, means the fight against poverty." the Laborite has written in her auto-

JENNIE LEE

biography. "For Libertarian principles, 'democracy', 'civil liberties,' lose all vitality whenever an attempt is made to call a truce in the fight against poverty. . . .I had taken it for granted in all my growing years that my special job in life was to fight coalowners and all they stand for. I loved that particular fight. It raised no divisions inside myself. It was unanswerably, triumphantly worthwhile. It was a fight for bread. . . .It was a fight for status too . . . [for those who were the] underdogs, mere workbeasts laboring for the greater glory and profit of a caste-ridden plutocracy." American critical comment on the book was favorable, although its, at times, strong language and partisan nature were recognized. "Written with ease and humor, with insight, sympathy, anger, and understanding," said the *Atlantic Monthly*, "it has all the strength and weakness of the common people." "Her book is like Jennie—," said Varian Fry in the *New Republic*, "passionate, stubborn, violent and intensely sincere." "Hers is the memory of a class rather than an individual," Rose Feld pointed out in the New York *Herald Tribune*, "and it is that memory, clarified by knowledge and experience, which colors and directs her thinking." The book will explain, wrote R. E. Roberts in the *Saturday Review of Literature*, "the peculiar genius of the socialist movement in Britain; it will explain why neither communism nor Nazism can ever gain a strong foothold in that country." Orville Prescott of the New York *Times* was less sure, however. "No fears of the super state, no qualms about bureaucracy, no knowledge of the sorry lot of the average man in nations where the means of production are already completely under State control, have ever bothered Miss Lee," he wrote.

Black-haired, hazel-eyed Jennie Lee was married in 1934 to Aneurin Bevan, Labor M.P. from Ebbw Vale and Minister of Health in the Attlee Cabinet. She likes to go walking, to attend the ballet, but outside of politics her

LEE, JENNIE—*Continued*

husband is, she says, her main interest. Their home in London, one reporter felt, is "the kind of a house into which people pop without formal invitation."

References

N Y Post p11 Oct 7 '41
N Y Times p15 Aug 14 '42 por
Lee, J. This Great Journey (1942)
Who's Who, 1946

LEIGH, VIVIEN (lē) Nov. 5, 1913- Actress

Address: h. Durham Cottage, Durham Pl., Chelsea, S. W., London

With a brief British stage and screen career behind her, Vivien Leigh went from comparative obscurity to world fame in the role of Scarlett O'Hara in *Gone With the Wind*, the film seen by more people than any other in screen history. After several less successful

VIVIEN LEIGH

films, Miss Leigh achieved new importance as an actress in the 1945 London stage production of *The Skin of Our Teeth*, directed by her husband Laurence Olivier '46, and with the 1946 release of *Caesar and Cleopatra*, the British film adaptation of George Bernard Shaw's play.

Vivien Leigh, who was born in Darjeeling, in the cool mountain region of India, on November 5, 1913, was given the name Vivian Mary Hartley. Her parents, Ernest Richard Hartley, an English stockbroker of French descent, and his wife Gertrude, whose family had come from Ireland, spent six months of the year in India, and the remaining months in England. When five years old, Vivian enrolled as a boarding pupil at the Sacred Heart Convent in Roehampton, half an hour's ride

from London. There, at the age of eight, she first appeared on a stage, as a fairy in a school production of *A Midsummer Night's Dream*— "I loved it, because even then I wanted to be an actress. I can't remember when I didn't." Vivian completed her education in Europe: at a finishing school in Paris, in San Remo, Italy, where she studied languages, and at a girl's seminary in Bavaria. The young schoolgirl was always enthusiastic about dancing and elocution; while in Paris she studied dramatics with Mlle. Antoine of the Comédie Française; and when she was eighteen her parents sent her to the Royal Academy of Dramatic Art.

In November 1932, after a year at the dramatic school, nineteen-year-old Vivian Hartley was married to Herbert Leigh Holman, a London barrister, and two years later the couple had a daughter, Suzanne. Later that year the young mother set out to realize her ambition, taking her husband's middle name for her stage name, and making a slight change in her given name. She first appeared as one of the schoolgirls in the British motion picture *Things Are Looking Up,* and next played small roles in the films *The Village Squire, Gentleman's Agreement,* and *Look Up and Laugh.* Her first role in the theater came in February 1935, in a suburban presentation of *The Green Sash,* which, though it did not get to London's West End, was to lead to a "big break." A West End producer, Sydney Carroll, who had heard about her performance, decided Miss Leigh might be suitable for the role of a cocotte in his new production *The Mask of Virtue,* which was to open in May 1935. In that play she achieved what *Who's Who in the Theatre* calls "sensational success," although "the more discerning critics," Sewell Stokes pointed out, "were in agreement that it was her youthful beauty, rather than any exceptional ability as an actress, that caused her to shine so brightly in the public's favor." A few days after the opening, Alexander Korda signed Miss Leigh— "London's latest dramatic discovery"—to a five-year film contract for two hundred and fifty thousand dollars.

During the next three years Miss Leigh continued to be seen, between film engagements, in stage roles, "no one of which," W. A. Darlington of the New York *Times* has recalled, "was good enough to stamp her as a star performer, nor bad enough to let anybody suggest she had nothing to offer but her looks." She played the Queen in a Gielgud-directed *Richard II* with the Oxford University student drama group; then Jenny Mere in *The Happy Hypocrite*; Anne Boleyn in *Henry VIII* in an outdoor theater production the summer of 1936; and early in 1937 Pamela in *Because We Must* and Jessica Morton in *Bats in the Belfry.* She was Ophelia to Laurence Olivier's Hamlet in the Old Vic production given in Denmark in June 1937 at the invitation of the Danish Government. With the Old Vic company that year she also played Titania in *A Midsummer Night's Dream.* The following year she had the title role in *Serena Blandish,* her last London stage appearance before she won international fame in *Gone With the Wind.*

Her film work in those years did not attract much attention. As a lady in waiting to Flora Robson's Queen Elizabeth in Korda's *Fire Over England,* she was wooed by Laurence Olivier in the role of a stalwart in the Queen's cause. *Dark Journey* followed, then *Storm in a Teacup,* and in 1938 *A Yank At Oxford* with Robert Taylor, a film which served principally to prove that Taylor was a "he-man"—Miss Leigh was referred to as one member of "an extraordinarily fine cast of British players." In 1938 she also appeared with Charles Laughton in *St. Martin's Lane* (released in America in 1940 as *The Sidewalks of London*) playing a "mean, selfish, grasping, petty-minded and completely unscrupulous" heroine. Miss Leigh next went to Hollywood, largely because Laurence Olivier was there. The two, who had been strongly attracted to each other while making *Fire Over England,* were awaiting divorces from their spouses so that they might marry.

Meanwhile, despite ballyhoo and feverish hunts by talent scouts, David O. Selznick '41 was still without an actress to play one of the most publicized roles in the history of the cinema, Scarlett O'Hara in *Gone With the Wind.* Production of the film, however, had already begun. One night, Selznick's agent-brother Myron asked Olivier, who was under contract to him, if he would like to see a huge bonfire of old movie sets which was to be filmed as the burning of Atlanta. As Bennett Cerf tells the story, Olivier brought along Miss Leigh. David Selznick saw her watching the fire, gave her a screen test the next day, and shortly afterward (it was January 1939) announced that he had found a Scarlett.

One of the longest, most expensive, and most publicized films ever produced, the Technicolor Civil War drama was, said the reviewers, a major event in the history of the industry, "first and last, a great entertainment." Miss Leigh brought to life "with thorough conviction, the mercurial and unpredictable . . . Scarlett." For this performance, called "flawless" in reviews, she won the Academy Award as the outstanding actress of 1939. Cinema-goers made her their newest idol, and anxious to take advantage of her popularity, MGM rushed the actress through *Waterloo Bridge* (1940), in which she was a ballet dancer involved in a tragic story with a British officer played by Robert Taylor. "Miss Leigh," declared a *Newsweek* writer, "manages the highly emotional Myrna beautifully and will doubtless tighten the hold she has on the movie public."

In May 1940 Miss Leigh went to New York to star with Olivier in *Romeo and Juliet.* Not yet a great Juliet—the extremely emotional scenes were considered disappointing—Miss Leigh made the character "so lovely and winning a young girl and so pathetic a victim of tragedy" that she was "one of the brighter spots" of an otherwise unhappy production. Commented one critic: "It is one of the sad things about the theater that by the time she has learned . . . to play Juliet with proper emotional skill she will probably have ceased to look the part ideally."

When their respective divorces became final in August 1940, Vivien Leigh and Olivier, who had been placed by newsmen in "the select company of great . . . lovers" along with Romeo and Juliet and the Duke and Duchess of Windsor, were married. Shortly after the marriage the couple played Lord Nelson and his Emma in the film *That Hamilton Woman* (1941), in which, except for an aside from *Time* ("For anyone who left *Gone With the Wind* believing that Vivien Leigh was an accomplished actress, *That Hamilton Woman* will come as a nasty shock"), Miss Leigh received enthusiastic notices. In December 1940 Miss Leigh and her husband sailed for blitzed England, where she worked with the British equivalent of the American USO, while Olivier served in the air arm of the Royal Navy. In March 1942 Vivien Leigh returned to the West End stage as Jennifer Dubedat in a revival of Shaw's *The Doctor's Dilemma.* Darlington reported to the New York *Times* from London that "she showed a great improvement over anything she had done before"; but Stokes later commented, "it was undoubtedly the public's eagerness to see their film idol in the flesh that kept . . . [the play] running for a year in London."

Miss Leigh worked in the latter half of 1944 with Claude Rains in Gabriel Pascal's high-budget motion-picture production of Bernard Shaw's *Caesar and Cleopatra.* Her role was that of the "siren of the Nile" at sixteen. Early in September 1946 the film was released in the United States, where *Variety* reported it "doing record biz." While critics were divided in their opinions of Pascal's direction and of Shaw's adaptation of his own witty lines for the screen, their judgments of Miss Leigh were: "Slim, elastic", "fascinating, artful", "a constant delight"; "she has cultivated shadings of expression that help to give depth and variety to her portrayal."

The Shaw film completed, she next appeared in the London production, directed by her husband, of *The Skin of Our Teeth,* and was pronounced "pretty as a peach, and as clever as a cat," while "little if anything seemed lacking in her interpretation." After this, according to Stokes, "the majority of the critics were undivided in their belief that when Miss Leigh stepped on to the stage, she knew very well what she was about." An illness, however, forced a closing of the play in July 1945, and also necessitated the indefinite postponement of *Lottie Dundass,* a Korda film in which Miss Leigh was to star. Doctors ordered her to take a long rest. In early 1946 she was convalescing at the country home in Buckinghamshire; by May, though not yet well enough to act, she was able to accompany her husband when he brought the Old Vic company to New York for a six-week engagement. In June they flew to England, immediately after engine trouble had forced their first plane down in Connecticut. Back in London, Miss Leigh resumed her starring role in *The Skin of Our Teeth.*

Of petite build—she weighs not much more than one hundred pounds and is five feet three and a half inches tall—Miss Leigh is so well-proportioned that she appears larger. Wasp-waisted and "tilt-browed," she has reddish-brown hair, gray-green eyes. "As positive as

LEIGH, VIVIEN—*Continued*

a bolt-action pistol," she works at "an almost frantic tempo," is likely to insist: "Let's be on with it. Let's leave off the fuzz-buzz, and do."

References

> Life 8:74 My 20 '40 pors
> N Y Herald Tribune VI p2 Je 2 '40
> N Y Sun p24 My 6 '40 por
> N Y Times Mag p9 Je 9 '40 pors
> Theatre Arts 29:711 D '45 por
> Time 35:59 Ja 15 '40 por
> International Motion Picture Almanac, 1943-44
> Who's Who, 1946
> Who's Who in America, 1946-47
> Who's Who in the Theatre (1939)

LEWIS, ETHELREDA (ĕth'ĕl-rē'dá) 189?—July (?), 1946 South African novelist; her first novel, *The Harp* (1925), was followed by *Flying Emerald* (1926); became widely known as the editor of the best-selling book of adventures in the African wilds, *Trader Horn* (1927), the autobiography of Alfred Aloysius Smith.

Obituary

> N Y Times p19 Ag 2 '46 por

LI LIEH-CHUN (lē lē-ă'-chōōn) 1881—Feb. 20, 1946 Chinese Army officer and revolutionary; early follower of Sun Yat-sen, leader in the establishment of the Chinese Republic; fled to Japan after failure of the 1913 revolt against Yuan Shi-kai, returned to become a leader and hold high Government posts.

Obituary

> N Y Times p13 F 23 '46

LIE, TRYGVE (HALVDAN) (lē trĭg'vŭ hälv'dän) July 16, 1896- United Nations official

Address: b. c/o United Nations, New York; h. 123 Greenway North, Forest Hills, N.Y.

The Secretary-General of the United Nations, Trygve Lie, elected thereto on February 1, 1946, came to his new post with a "recognized talent for negotiating." Legal adviser to Norway's Trade Unions Federation thirteen years, he entered the Cabinet with the Nygaardsvold Ministry of 1935 and after 1941 had been Norway's Minister of Foreign Affairs. In the latter post, observers point out, he was equal to the delicate task of maintaining friendly relations with both Great Britain and Russia.

Trygve Halvdan Lie was born in Oslo, the capital of Norway, on July 16, 1896. His father, Martin Lie, a carpenter, died while Trygve was only a small boy, but his mother saw to it that her son received a good education. Young Lie helped out by working as an office boy at the national headquarters of the Norwegian Labor Party in Oslo, a job which he held through both his Gymnasium and college years. He had early acquired an interest in politics, and while still in high school, at the age of sixteen, he was elected president of the Aker (a suburb of Oslo) branch of the Labor Party. In 1914 he entered the University of Oslo as a law student, retaining both the Aker presidency and his job as office boy. And in 1919, the same year that he graduated from the Oslo University Law School, Trygve Lie was appointed secretary in charge of administration of the Norwegian Labor Party. He was then twenty-three years old.

In 1922 the lawyer, who the previous year had been elected president of the regional branch of his party in the province of Akershus, of which Oslo is the capital, was appointed legal adviser to the Trade Unions Federation. Thus it fell to his lot to deal with the disputes and controversies which arose between labor and management as the workers gained in power, and to fight many test cases for the federation in court. He occupied the position until 1935 and is given much of the credit for the peaceful settlement of disputes usually effected. During his last five years in the post, from 1930 to 1935, it has been noted, the Norwegian economy was almost entirely free from strikes (a condition which lasted until the actual outbreak of World War II). And since in 1926 he had also been made a member of the national council of the Labor Party, which during these years grew to be Norway's largest political party, Lie, it is further pointed out, was in the forefront of the entire, rapidly developing, labor movement.

The growth of the Norwegian Labor Party between 1919 and 1935 was in large part an expression of the Norwegians' discontent with existing economic conditions. Economic troubles and unemployment beset the country almost continuously after the abrupt cessation of her war-born prosperity in 1918. The first Labor ministry, however, established January 26, 1928, had fallen after two weeks in office when it attempted to implement its radically socialistic program. Thereafter a coalition government had succeeded in stemming the flow of capital from the country and in restoring prosperity for a brief period. But mounting unemployment after 1931 finally brought the Labor Party to power a second time on March 20, 1935, when the Agrarian Party joined with it to overthrow the Liberal Government, headed by Prime Minister Johan Ludwig Mowinckel, on the immediate issue of increased taxes. Johan Nygaardsvold became the Prime Minister of the new Government, in which Lie received the portfolio of the Ministry of Justice. Economic improvement followed the ascendancy of Labor, and at the triennial elections to the Storting (the Norwegian parliament) on October 19, 1936, the Labor Party, although failing to secure a clear majority and therefore still dependent upon the cooperation of the Agrarians, received popular endorsement.

The socialist lawyer served as Minister of Justice until June 1939, when a Cabinet reorganization made him Minister of Commerce. At the outbreak of World War II in September of that year, however, the Storting, having learned the lesson of the blockade in World War I, established a Department of

Shipping and Supply with Cabinet status, to which post Premier Nygaardsvold appointed Trygve Lie on October 1. Lie began at once to build up Norway's stores of supplies, and at the beginning of the German attack on April 9, 1940, it was calculated that food supplies were sufficient for three years to come. "The fact," said an official Norwegian source after the liberation, "that the Norwegian population has fared comparatively well as far as food is concerned during five years of occupation— in spite of German plunder and requisitioning— is to a large extent due to Mr. Lie's foresight."

On April 9, at an emergency meeting, the Nygaardsvold Cabinet tendered its resignation to King Haakon '⁴⁰ and the Storting but was refused. Instead, before adjourning for the duration of the occupation, the Storting designated the Nygaardsvold Cabinet the lawful governing body of the kingdom and directed it to continue the fight from outside the country if necessary. During the two months of fighting before the final capitulation, the King and Government remained in Norway, and, although forced to flee before the advancing Nazis, were able to organize Norwegian resistance, bolster morale, and carry on necessary administration. While the Government was thus being hounded from place to place, Lie was busy organizing supplies for both military and civilian use in the unoccupied areas of the country. By adroit management he was able to salvage large quantities of supplies from occupied southern Norway—enough, it is said, to have carried on the campaign in the north through the summer and succeeding winter had adequate military support been available. To Lie must likewise go the credit for saving Norway's huge merchant fleet for the Allied cause: working in a small village in the Romsdal valley, the Minister of Shipping and Supply, with characteristically swift decision, drew up the provisional regulation placing that part of the shipping not yet in German hands (about 85 per cent, approximating one thousand ships totaling more than four million tons) under Government administration—recording it originally on a piece of paper torn from a scrapbook. (One of the last of the ministers to leave Oslo, he had moved on, just out of the reach of the advancing Germans.)

Finally, on June 7, 1940, the Government was forced to leave Norwegian soil for England: on June 10 King and Cabinet established themselves in London, where for the duration of the war they bent all their efforts toward aiding the Allies. In addition, in accordance with a further direction of the Storting at its last session on April 9, the Government reorganized to provide a broader national basis, distributing thirteen portfolios among the representatives of all of Norway's political parties except Quisling's Nasjonal Samling (National Union). In this reorganization Lie retained his post as Minister of Shipping and Supply. In November, when Minister of Foreign Affairs Halvdan Koht was granted a three-month leave of absence, Lie also became acting Foreign Minister, and on February 21, 1941, after Koht's resignation because of ill health, Lie was appointed Minister of Foreign Affairs.

Norwegian Official Photo.

TRYGVE LIE

As Norway's Foreign Minister, Lie has been outspoken for international cooperation at the same time that he has avoided having his country drawn into either an eastern or a western bloc. Observers point out that he has accomplished the difficult feat of maintaining equally friendly relations with both Great Britain and Russia, of remaining not only geographically but politically "as nearly as possible equi-distant between the two centers of attraction," despite the fact that the Norwegian Government-in-Exile's leftist policies were viewed with some suspicion by the conservative Churchill '⁴² Government in England and that Russia's war with Finland tried the feelings of Finland's sympathetic neighbor. Diplomatic relations at times took Lie away from his London headquarters. In the spring of 1943 he came to Washington to confer with American officials. Early in 1945 he was in Moscow to discuss the practical problems contingent upon the joint Russo-Norwegian liberation of parts of northern Norway. In April 1945 the Foreign Minister was chosen to head the Norwegian delegation to the United Nations Conference at San Francisco. At the conference itself he was chosen chairman of Commission III which was charged with drafting the charter of the Security Council of the United Nations, "the organ . . . which would have the power to act against aggressors."

At the eighth plenary session on May 2 the chairman of the Norwegian delegation, speaking realistically, yet with typical Norwegian idealism, expressed his nation's hopes for the postwar world for which the Conference was breaking ground. "We Norwegians," Lie said in English, "have come here to assist and not to offer negative criticism. We know that the Dumbarton Oaks Proposals are not perfect, and we welcome a number of the amendments that have been suggested. But even if the

LIE, TRYGVE—*Continued*

Charter as molded at this Conference will not correspond to all our desires and ideas, we hope that the building of a new security order will be started under such conditions that in the future it may be further developed in a process of continuous creation. . . .In any new world order the great powers will have to shoulder the main burden of providing military and material means for maintaining peace, and we are prepared to grant them an international status corresponding to their responsibility and power. But at the same time, we have a strong feeling that also moral standards should be taken into account. . . .It seems [to us] essential that this Conference should include among the principles of its organization the aspirations expressed in the United Nations declarations: to defend life, liberty, independence, and religious freedom, to preserve human rights. . . .I would like to stress that economic, social, and intellectual cooperation form a whole. Without such cooperation, our efforts might prove futile in the years to come. . . .The nations of the occupied countries have proved in their struggle that there are certain invisible privileges of mankind without which life is not worth living. It is not sufficient for countries to be peace loving. Our brothers and sons are fighting and dying because they and we love justice and human decency even more than peace. Daily bread turns to stone unless eaten in freedom and with human dignity."

On May 7, before the end of the Conference, Lie and C. J. Hambro [40], president of the Storting, returned to London, where Lie's first task was the expediting of shipments of food and clothing to his liberated countrymen. On May 31 he accompanied the Government back to Oslo, and on June 12, together with the other members of the Government-in-exile, submitted his resignation to King Haakon. Two weeks later he was reappointed to his post in the interim coalition ministry of Einar Gerhardsen, and after the sweeping Labor victory in the national elections in October 1945 his reappointment as Prime Minister Gerhardsen's Minister of Foreign Affairs was confirmed.

In London in January 1946, at the first convocation of the U.N., Lie again headed the Norwegian delegation and again emphasized his country's advocacy of internationl cooperation, the elimination of power politics and spheres of influence, and its recognition of the large powers' right to leadership because of the responsibility they must of necessity assume. Almost at once he found himself in the limelight, when, at the opening session on January 10, Andrei Gromyko, acting chief Russian delegate, seconded by Polish, Ukrainian, and Danish representatives, unexpectedly and spectacularly nominated him for the presidency of the General Assembly in opposition to the Anglo-American nominee, Belgian Foreign Minister Paul-Henri Spaak [45]. Some observers believe the action was an attempt on the part of the Soviet Union to test future reactions to its proposals, but the vote—28 for Spaak, 23 for Lie—left no doubt as to the Norwegian's popularity with the delegates.

About a fortnight later Lie was nominated by unanimous vote of the Security Council as compromise candidate for the post of Secretary-General of the United Nations, to which he was elected by a vote of 46 to 3 in a secret ballot of the Assembly on February 1. This broke a prolonged deadlock. Originally the American policy had been to back a European for Secretary-General inasmuch as the permanent site of the U.N. was to be in North America, and at that time Lie had been a possible American choice. Consideration of the personal qualifications of the candidates, however, had led Byrnes and Stettinius to favor the British candidate, Canadian ambassador to Washington Lester B. Pearson. Meanwhile the Russians put forward the names of both Stanoje Simitch, Yugoslav ambassador to Washington, and Polish Foreign Minister Wincenty Rzymowski, but remained adamant against a Western Hemisphere nominee. The deadlock was finally broken with the suggestion by Stettinius in an unofficial conference of Trygve Lie of Norway, and his unanimous acceptance by the Security Council then meant virtual confirmation of his election. (It has since been noted that earlier in San Francisco the United States delegation had suggested Lie as a possible nominee for either Assembly president or Secretary-General.)

The United Nations charter stipulates that the Secretary-General is to be the chief administrative officer of the organization, that he is to act in that capacity at all meetings of the General Assembly, the Security Council, the Economic and Social Council, and the Trusteeship Council, and to perform such other functions as these groups may designate; and that in accordance with Article 99 he "may bring to the attention of the Security Council any matter which in his opinion may threaten the maintenance of international peace and security." In accepting the U.N. post at the official induction ceremony on February 2, the former Norwegian Foreign Minister said: "I am the servant of you all. You can count upon my impartial approach to all your problems. I am determined to merit your further confidence through my work for the cause of the United Nations. Certain of your support, I look to the future with confidence. It will be my duty always to act as a true international officer. . . .We may find difficulties and obstacles ahead of us. But the harder the task, the higher the prize. It is the future of the whole civilized world which is at stake."

As Secretary-General (the term of office is five years, with re-election permittted), Lie's first task was to recruit a staff of eight assistant secretaries-general and an international secretariat, a task rendered difficult by the need for securing the highest standards of efficiency, competence, and integrity while at the same time observing an equitable geographical distribution of personnel, and further complicated by the reluctance of national governments to part with some of their ablest men. This he began at once. But his silence at meeting after meeting during the first three weeks of the Security Council's session in New York caused some commentators to wonder exactly when he would begin to exercise the powers conferred upon him by Article 99 of the U.N. charter. Then, after Lie on April 16 had submittted to the Council a memorandum suggesting that it might not have the authority to continue the Soviet-Iranian dispute on its agenda since both nations had asked its withdrawal, others, as well as United Nations representatives, questioned his right to intervene. And although on April 19 the Council's Committee of Experts ruled that, once a matter has been submitted to the Council, it is for the Council itself to decide when to drop it from the agenda regardless of any other considerations, it was not until June 1 that the same committee finally established that "the Secretary-General, or his deputy acting on his behalf, may make either oral or written statements to the Security Council concerning any question under consideration by it." The uncertainty as to his powers thus ended, Lie thereafter seized the opportunity to present his views on the admission of new members (which favored the United States recommendation for blanket approval), to reserve his right to re-open the Greek border question any time he deemed this necessary, to turn his attention to the Council's continued failure to take positive action in any of the major cases brought before it—which he thought constituted the chief factor in the U.N.'s ineffectiveness in 1946.

Lie, who will receive a salary of twenty thousand dollars annually and another twenty thousand for expenses in his important new full-time post, has been described as a burly, handsome man, jovial and friendly in manner. He stands six feet one inch tall, weighs two hundred and twenty pounds, and likes to eat and drink well, but in moderation, say friends, who also point out that he was known as a connoisseur of wines in pre-war Oslo. He speaks fluent English and some German; and he is the author of two books, both published in 1931, *The Anti-Labor Laws and the Battle Against Them* and *The New Labor Arbitration Law* (with Viggo Hansteen).

In 1921 Lie was married to Hjördis Jörgensen, a social worker and fellow Party office-holder, whose ability and enthusiasm in the cause of the labor movement Lie considers to have been invaluable to his own political advancement. The Lies, whose open hospitality has been called proverbial, are the parents of three daughters. The eldest, Sissel, widow of a Norwegian airman, was secretary to the Norwegian delegation at San Francisco; the second, Guri, took over that function for the Norwegian delegation in London; while the youngest, Mette, attracted attention because until 1944, when she was spirited from Norway by the underground, she had remained in Norway with a relative, in constant danger of German "retaliatory measures" whenever her father spoke on the radio. An enthusiastic sportsman—he says he was "practically born on skis"—Trygve Lie was once a good wrestler, still plays a good game of tennis, likes to hunt and ski, and before 1940 was prominent in the Norwegian Sports Association. His life of continuous hard work, it is said,

has given him the ability to concentrate exclusively on the problem in hand and then to relax completely during his rare periods of leisure. In 1946, when Princeton University during its bicentennial celebration conferred upon him the honorary degree of Doctor of Laws, the citation read: "A statesman distinguished in the service of his own country who has now been entrusted with a major role in the great undertaking of world cooperation."

References

Christian Sci Mon p5 Ja 30 '46 por
Liberty 23:13+ My 11 '46 por
N Y Herald Tribune p12 Ja 30 '46
N Y Post p31 Mr 26 '46 pors
N Y Times p10 Ja 30 '46
N Y Times Mag p11+ Mr 24 '46 por
New Repub 114:403-4 Mr 25 '46 por
PM p6 Mr 24 '46 por
Sat Eve Post 218:24+ Je 15 '46 por
International Who's Who, 1945-46
Who's Who, 1946
Who's Who in America, 1946-47
Who's Who of the Allied Governments, 1943

LIEBMAN, JOSHUA LOTH, RABBI
Apr. 7, 1907- Jewish religious leader; author
Address: b. Temple Israel, Boston; h. Somerset Hotel, Boston, Mass.

Enthusiastically hailed by experts and the general public alike, Joshua Loth Liebman's *Peace of Mind* has been declared one of the most useful books of our time by leaders in religion and psychology and has achieved, and long held, a place at the top of the national nonfiction best-seller list. Written by the young radio preacher and rabbi of Temple Israel in Boston, it is an attempt to solve the ordinary individual's inner conflicts by means of a union of the techniques of the hitherto antagonistic spheres of psychology and religion.

Born to Simon and Sabina (Loth) Liebman on April 7, 1907, in Hamilton, Ohio, Joshua Loth Liebman is a descendant of noted rabbis on both sides of his family—great-grandson of a distinguished German rabbi, great-nephew of Moritz Loth, first president of the Union of American Hebrew Congregations, and grandson of Rabbi Lippman Liebman, one of the early American Reformed rabbis and founder of the first synagogue in Youngstown, Ohio. He attended elementary school in Hamilton through the third grade, when the family moved to Cincinnati and he became a pupil at the Avondale Public School in that city. In 1922, at the age of fifteen, he was graduated from Walnut Hills High School in Cincinnati, and from 1922 to 1926 he attended the University of Cincinnati. At the first-named he had received the Harvard Prize for the highest academic record in his class; at the latter he made his mark both in scholarly and extracurricular activities, winning election to Phi Beta Kappa at the end of his junior year and becoming captain of the debating team and an active member of the university's dramatic society, the Mummers.

(Continued next page)

RABBI JOSHUA LOTH LIEBMAN

At the same time, beginning when he was thirteen, during the years that he was attending high school and college the youth was pursuing the eight-year rabbinical course of Hebrew Union College in Cincinnati, the oldest Jewish theological school in the United States and a chief center of American Reform Judaism. Joshua Liebman says that it was his paternal grandfather, Rabbi Lippman Liebman, whose influence on his life has been especially strong, who had first directed his thoughts to a rabbinical career when he expressed the hope that his nine-year-old grandson would follow in his footsteps. Twelve years later, in 1930 Liebman received the title of rabbi from Hebrew Union, having during his last two years also taught philosophy on a Taft Fellowship at the University of Cincinnati.

By the time he departed in 1930 for the Hebrew University of Jerusalem as a Leo W. Simon Traveling Fellow of Hebrew Union College, Liebman had become imbued with the philosophy set forth in the college's catalogue, that "Judaism is both in spirit and fact a continuously progressive religious discipline and that it must be kept constantly liberal and spiritually alert . . . that if it is to live and expand in America it must be open to every positive influence of modernism, must square itself with every advance in scientific thought, and must engender that type of religious devotion which will evoke the uncompromising loyalty of every Jew."

Returning from Jerusalem in 1931, Liebman was chosen rabbi of Temple Israel in Lafayette, Indiana. This position he occupied until 1934, going thence to the KAM Temple in Chicago, the Windy City's oldest synagogue, where he remained until he was called to Temple Israel in Boston in 1939. In addition to ministering to his congregations for these eight years he continued his formal studies, during the remainder

of his fellowship, until 1934, serving as instructor in Bible and rabbinics as well as research worker in Jewish philosophy at Hebrew Union College, which awarded him the doctorate in Hebrew letters (D.H.L.) in 1939. His dissertation, *The Religious Philosophy of Aaron den Elijah*, some six hundred pages in length, dealt with the major concepts of medieval Jewish philosophy in relation to the influence of Plato and Aristotle. He had taken his doctorate under Professor Zevi Diesendruck, formerly of the universities of Vienna and Jerusalem, whom he characterizes as "one of the greatest Jewish philosophic minds of our age," and in 1943 he completed his translation of one of the professor's important philosophical works, retitling it *Teleology and Attributes of God*. (In 1946 it was in process of publication.)

In 1944 the rabbi of Boston's Temple Israel became visiting professor of Jewish philosophy in the Graduate School of Boston University and visiting professor of Jewish philosophy and literature at Andover-Newton Theological Seminary, a position which his publishers believe denotes the first time that a rabbi has ever been a regular faculty member of a Christian theological school. In 1945 he served as Samuel Harris Lecturer on Literature and Life at the Bangor (Maine) Theological Seminary, becoming the first rabbi ever to hold this lectureship. Since about 1939 Liebman's sermons have been reaching millions of listeners from coast to coast over the Columbia, National, and American networks, and from Boston stations WBZ and WBZA alone each Sunday an estimated one to two million in the six New England States. Also during the last few years, he has acted as university guest preacher at Harvard, Cornell, Vassar, Dartmouth, Wellesley, Smith, and other leading institutions.

Peace of Mind was published on March 22, 1946. Within three weeks it was in twelfth place on the New York *Times* nonfiction bestseller list. Four weeks later it had climbed to sixth place, and by the third week in July it had outsold all other titles to reach second place, directly after Betty MacDonald's '46 *The Egg and I*. At the end of October it stood at the head of the nonfiction list, with 205,000 copies in print. It had been selected for condensation in the May issue of *Reader's Digest*; was the May choice of the Religious Book Club, distributed by it on the anniversary of the Nazi burning of the books on May 10, 1933; and, although not originally chosen by the Book-of-the-Month Club, became one of their book dividends.

Intended to aid the unhappy, fearful, and perplexed to find that "one ingredient lacking which each possession becomes a hideous torment and [the acknowledged "goods" of life] as a whole an intolerable burden," *Peace of Mind* imparts to the layman the discoveries of a spiritual counselor who is also a modern psychologist, in particular a student in the new field of depth psychology. The book was originally presented in the form of six lectures, collectively entitled "Dynamic Psychology and

Living Religion," given by Rabbi Liebman under the auspices of the Charles W. Eliot Foundation of the Jewish Institute of Religion in October, November, and December 1944. It aims, by leading men to a new and proper evaluation of their capacities and limitations, to restore their belief in their own worthiness as a necessary prerequisite to that adult serenity of mind, "the shockproof balance [against the pummelings of fate and fortune] achieved *inside* the soul," which is both the sign of a healthy human being and the goal of the considered life.

With one or two exceptions, critics of *Peace of Mind* were enthusiastic. "In these times," wrote Franz Alexander in the Chicago *Sun's Book Week*, "in which the most diabolic attempt has been made to make use of psychodynamic knowledge for psychological warfare and for the education of youth to evil, destruction, and the cynic adulation of the law of the jungle, in times in which we are using our mastery of nature's forces primarily for destruction, this book fills a need of unparalleled urgency." "Dr. Liebman shatters the long-standing myth that religion and psychology are necessary antagonists," pointed out Gordon W. Allport, chairman of the Department of Psychology of Harvard University. "With eloquence he proves that they converge upon a single goal—the enhancement of man's peace of mind." "Almost uniformly excellent," was the opinion of John Haynes Holmes of the Community Church of New York; "more human than most books on psychology, more practical than most books on religion," was the judgment of Chairman Edgar S. Brightman of the Department of Philosophy of Boston University; "beyond all else, a useful book," wrote Rabbi Milton Steinberg of the Park Avenue Synagogue of New York.

Rabbi Liebman, who during World War II also served on the Committee on Army and Navy Religious Activities of the National Jewish Welfare Board, is a member of the Massachusetts Committee for Racial and Religious Understanding, chairman of the Massachusetts Governor's Committee of Clergymen, and Grand Chaplain of the Grand Lodge of Masons of Massachusetts. Since July 1928 he has been married to Fan Loth Liebman, his first cousin. Of a stocky build, he has brown eyes and hair. Although his favorite hobby as well as mental relaxation is reading, he has not lost his early love for the theater. His physical relaxation he finds in a game of golf.

Reference

Liebman, J. L. Peace of Mind (1946)

LIGGETT, LOUIS KROH Apr. 4, 1875—June 5, 1946 Founder of the Liggett chain of drug stores; founder and chairman of the board of directors of the United-Rexall Drug Company; Republican national committeeman for Massachusetts from 1928 to 1932.

Obituary

N Y Times p19 Je 7 '46 por

LINCOLN, LEROY A(LTON) Aug. 18, 1880- Life insurance executive

Address: b. c/o Metropolitan Life Insurance Co., 1 Madison Ave., New York; h. 49 E. 68th St., New York

Leroy A. Lincoln is the president of the Metropolitan Life Insurance Company, the largest life insurance company in the world—in an article in the April 1946 issue of *Fortune*, on the total assets basis of seven and a half billion, it is considered the largest privately managed corporation in the world. According to statistics of December 1945, its policyholders, who are insured for a total of $31,261,969,817,

Pach Bros.

LEROY A. LINCOLN

number 31,208,000 or one-fifth of the population of the United States and Canada.

Leroy Alton Lincoln was born in Little Valley, Cattaraugus County, New York, on August 18, 1880, to Charles Zebina and Lusette (Bonsteel) Lincoln. A prominent lawyer, his father was the legal adviser to three of New York's governors: Levi P. Morton, Frank Black, and Theodore Roosevelt. He was also the author of several books on law, among them a history of the constitution of the State of New York, which is regarded as an authority. Until 1895, when the family moved to Albany, Leroy was a pupil at schools in Little Valley. After graduation from Albany High School, he attended Yale College and received his B.A. degree in 1902. Following in his father's footsteps, he decided to make law his profession and accordingly entered Albany Law School, where he remained for one year; a Buffalo law office was the classroom for the rest of his legal training. Admitted to the bar in 1904, he began a general practice in Buffalo and soon became a prominent figure in the legal circles of that city.

(*Continued next page*)

LINCOLN, LEROY A.—*Continued*

In 1915 Lincoln was a delegate to the New York State Constitutional Convention. It was at this time that he first became connected with insurance. Jesse S. Phillips, also a delegate to the convention, who had just been appointed State Superintendent of Insurance, asked the Buffalo attorney to become the counsel for the State Insurance Department. In this position Lincoln played a major part in settling many significant cases, a number of which arose during World War I. When the Pittsburgh Life and Trust Company failed in 1917, Lincoln was instrumental in developing a plan whereby all policyholders of the bankrupt company willing to accept reinsurance by the Metropolitan Life Insurance Company had their matured endowments and death claims paid in full. He was also largely responsible for bringing about an agreement between the fire insurance companies and the State Insurance Department on the matter of a standard policy and for obtaining legislation to enforce this agreement.

Upon receiving an offer for a position with the New York insurance law firm of Rumsey and Morgan in 1917, Lincoln resigned from the State post. Soon afterward he was also asked to join the Metropolitan Life Insurance Company as general attorney. This invitation he accepted but, feeling that his commitment did not permit him to leave the law firm, he filled both positions for two years. He then resigned from Rumsey and Morgan to give his full-time attention to Metropolitan. In 1926 he became general counsel for the Metropolitan; three years later, when Frederick H. Ecker was elected president of the company and Robert Lynn Cox was elected vice-president, Lincoln was appointed first vice-president and general counsel. That same year, 1929, he was elected to the board of directors. Cox died in January 1930, and Lincoln was now elected vice-president and general counsel. Six years later he was elected to succeed Ecker, who became chairman of the board.

While Ecker, persuaded by the board to remain beyond his retirement age, has been absorbed in Metropolitan's large-scale housing projects, Lincoln has carried the main load of administrative detail for his company. This covers three main categories of activities: the writing of insurance, the investment of funds, and welfare work. Directly connected with the writing of insurance are such functions as selling, actuarial calculations, and the servicing of policies. A large part of the policyholders' payments is put into investments and all money remaining at the end of the year after benefits and expenses have been paid is returned to them in the form of dividends. The problem of investments is solved in part by profitable investments in large-scale housing projects. To reduce mortality, Metropolitan conducts various services for its policyholders, a program which also helps public welfare: the company distributes pamphlets on health and safety measures, runs health advertisements in magazines, and maintains a nursing service for insured industrial workers.

As president, Lincoln heads a staff of 42,500 field-men and office employees. Like his predecessors, he has made an effort to become better acquainted with the field personnel. By visiting every section of the United States and Canada and holding group meetings, he has met the thousands of managers, assistant managers, agents, and clerks working for Metropolitan. (The employees in New York are members of the Industrial Insurance Employees Union, a branch of the CIO United Office and Professional Workers Association.)

When social security legislation was passed under the New Deal Administration Lincoln did not agree with a view expressed in *Nation's Business* which foresaw the possible elimination of life insurance as a private enterprise. In an interview with *Scholastic,* the president of Metropolitan stated that his company viewed "with friendly eyes some nationwide provision for old age retirement." He interpreted the old age pension system of the Social Security Act as an attempt "to copy in a limited way for a large group what had been done in a smaller way by those who had 'taken thought for tomorrow.'" Asked to criticize the Act, he replied that the chief problem raised by the legislation was how to use the large reserves which the Government would accumulate. The main difference between the social security plan and private insurance, Lincoln maintained, is that "the Government program is compulsory. . . .Uncle Sam will always have customers." A private life insurance company, he said, operating on sound business principles cannot depend on payments made by future policy holders to provide pensions for current policyholders upon their retirement, whereas, in the Federal program, "compulsion takes the place of reserves."

In February 1939 the Temporary National Economic Committee, which had been set up by the joint resolution of Congress in 1938 to make a complete study of monopoly and its effects on the national economic structure, began an investigation of the operations of insurance companies. Lincoln was among those who attended the TNEC hearings at which evidence gathered by the Securities and Exchange Commission was presented. Among the charges made by the SEC were: that self-perpetuating interlocking directorates had misused their position to further their own interests; that industrial insurance sold to low-income groups was the most expensive kind of insurance; that the big companies attempted to eliminate rate competition; that in investing their funds, insurance companies discriminated against small business. In August Lincoln submitted a statement on behalf of the life insurance companies to answer the criticism. Charging that the TNEC hearings had been based on insufficient evidence, Lincoln defended the companies on every point; he emphasized their security, pointing out that despite the serious depression suffered by the nation in the thirties, the safety record of the life insurance companies during those ten years was unparalleled. "Policyholders want safety," he stated, "and experience demonstrates that the institution of life insurance has not failed them, either in good times or bad."

At the annual meeting of the Institute of Life Insurance in December 1946, Lincoln remarked that American business was entering a new phase, that of the third industrial revolution. Interdependence of industry and the public has increased, with the public subjecting mass production to a more personalized scrutiny than heretofore. "They study its social and economic significance, services, effectiveness and general usefulness," said Lincoln, "whereas few knew what went on in any business in prewar days." This new attitude, he brought out, will serve "to entrench democracy against the attacks of less personalized philosophies. It will mean better citizens, and fewer crises, fewer dislocations, fewer personal and business disasters."

The head of a business in which improving health and reducing mortality are primary aims, Lincoln is also connected with health programs other than those maintained by Metropolitan. He helped to organize the Citizens Planning Committee of the National Health Council for the purpose of unifying fund-raising programs of voluntary health organizations. Lincoln is also a member of numerous business associations. In December 1945 he was elected chairman of the Institute of Life Insurance. He was president of the New York State Chamber of Commerce for two consecutive terms which expired in May 1946. In addition, Lincoln belongs to the American Bar Association, the New York State Bar Association, the Association of the Bar of the City of New York, the Commerce and Industry Association of New York, and others. In politics, he is a member of the Republican Party. His religion is Presbyterian.

For relaxation Lincoln enjoys a game of golf: his clubs are the Links Club in New York City, the Garden City (Long Island) Golf Club, and the Huntington Valley Country Club in Philadelphia. In 1930 he was married to Miss Hilda F. Deyoe of New York. (He had been widowed twice.) The executive is the father of two sons: Charles Waters, who is associated with a firm of insurance brokers, and Thomas Ridgely, an attorney.

References

National Cyclopædia of American Biography Current vol E p37
Who's Who in America, 1946-47

LITTLEDALE, CLARA SAVAGE Jan. 31, 1891- Editor; writer

Address: b. c/o Parents' Magazine, 52 Vanderbilt Ave., New York; h. 5 Sniffin Ct., New York

Herself the mother of two children, Clara Savage Littledale, the editor of *Parents' Magazine,* has advised thousands of mothers and fathers in the vital occupation "of bringing up the nation's children." It has been her goal not only to give parents practical suggestions on how to meet the everyday problems of child care, but to make them aware of the intangible fundamentals of happy living.

Halsman

CLARA SAVAGE LITTLEDALE

Clara Savage Littledale, born in Belfast, Maine, on January 31, 1891, was a year old when her parents, John Arthur and Emma (Morrison) Savage, moved to Medfield, Massachussetts. There she spent her childhood and began to attend high school. Upon her father's retirement from the Unitarian ministry, the family moved to Plainfield, New Jersey, where a married daughter lived. It was her brother-in-law, a newspaperman, who first turned Clara's thoughts toward journalism. A student at Plainfield High School, she worked on the school magazine; and at Smith College she was a member of the Press Board and sold short feature articles to such papers as the New York *Times.*

Upon receiving her B.A. degree in 1913, the twenty-two-year-old Miss Savage applied for a teaching position (as did most women college graduates in those days), but her aspirations were not in the field of education. She went to see the woman's news editor of the New York *Evening Post*—the result was a job for both Clara Savage and a friend, in the city room of the *Post,* which had never before employed women reporters. The men on the staff eyed them skeptically at first, but came to accept them as able coworkers. Miss Savage was later made the editor of the woman's page.

Assigned to woman suffrage conventions and parades, the young journalist became acquainted with the leaders of the National American Woman Suffrage Association, who in 1914 offered her a job as press chairman. After "carrying the banner" for the suffragists for a year, Miss Savage came to the conclusion that she really did not care for publicity work. Through the old College Bureau of Occupations she found a position as associate editor of *Good Housekeeping.* General editorial work, however, was too tame for Miss Savage, and she persuaded her superiors to send her to Washington

LITTLEDALE, CLARA SAVAGE—*Cont.*

each month to report on the political scene from the woman's angle.

In June 1918, about five months before the end of World War I, the magazine sent Miss Savage overseas to write special articles. Arriving in Paris when "Big Bertha" was bombarding the city, she spent her first night in a hotel where she amused the French guests by coming down to the basement with her pillow at the sound of the alarm, calm and ready for sleep. Her interview with Cardinal Mercier of Belgium, her stories on Chateau-Thierry and other war scenes, in the opinion of William Bigelow, the editor of *Good Housekeeping*, "made some of the best articles [he had] ever printed." When the magazine summoned her home at the end of the war, Miss Savage cabled her resignation, for the chance to remain in Europe and observe the postwar turmoil as a free-lance writer was too good to give up. At one time she lived in the Soviet House in Bolshevist Hungary and interviewed political prisoners.

In 1920, not long after her return to the United States, Miss Savage was married to Harold Aylmer Littledale, a newspaperman whom she had met while working for the New York *Evening Post*. She continued her freelancing—her articles and stories, among them "Adam at Home", "So This Is Marriage," and "Sublimation" were published by *Good Housekeeping*, the *New Republic, McCall's* and other popular magazines. In a whimsical style they imparted sound advice to broken-hearted maidens and worried wives. When, in 1926, she was offered a full-time position as editor of *Children, the Magazine for Parents*, which George Hecht, the publisher, was then launching, Mrs. Littledale refused. She was not interested in a career, she said, wishing to devote herself to her household, which by that time included a four-year-old daughter, Rosemary. Hecht, seeking an editor who was a mother and an experienced magazine writer, persuaded to her reconsider and accept the editorship.

In the years that followed, Mrs. Littledale found much satisfaction editing the magazine which counseled thousand of perplexed parents. (The original name was changed to *Parents' Magazine* early in the periodical's history.) In its pages, in lively, interesting style appeared accurate accounts of the advanced findings on child development; information, formerly presented in technical reports, was made understandable to the layman. In addition, the contents covered many phases of the field, from prenatal and infant care to book selection, movie guidance, and relations between the child and the community. While a number of university professors immediately lent their cooperation (Teachers College at Columbia University, the State University of Iowa, the University of Minnesota, and Yale University became stockholders in the company formed to publish the magazine), there were other experts who were skeptical at first. In the magazine's tenth year, however, the circulation was four hundred thousand, and

by 1946 it had almost a million subscribers. Because its articles became the basis for group discussions, the magazine established a Group Service Bureau to aid mothers' clubs, parent-teacher associations and similar organizations in planning programs for discussion and further reading.

In selecting material for publication, Mrs. Littledale's aim was "to give parents a realization of what underlies successful living—understanding between husbands and wives as well as between parents and children," the recognition of values transcending daily routines, the need for self-knowledge on the part of parents, an awareness of "national problems and developments which affect the security of homes and the future of youth." Her own articles and those of other contributors called attention to such important questions as legislation against child labor, better vocational guidance and training, improved health measures, hot school lunches, nursery schools, play schools, a bill providing Federal aid for education. During the war she urged parents to contribute to agencies working for the relief of European children. She also advised them on how to explain the war to their children and tried to make them aware of the need to take measures providing for "the health and well-rounded development" of the many children aimlessly drifting into jobs.

Mrs. Littledale's work has brought her into many activities related to the field of child development. She became a member of such organizations as the Child Study Association of America, the American Association for Adult Education, the National Commission for Mental Hygiene, and the National Council of Parent Education. She attended conferences and meetings, gave speeches and radio talks, and had discussions with the many people engaged in child welfare and parent education who came to her office. While counseling parents that "using the rod" might "spoil the child," and urging them to be "constantly flexible, imaginative, quick in understanding, and ready to meet new situations in new ways," she applied the theories which her magazine expounded with her own children. (The Littledales' son, Harold, had been born in 1927.)

Politically an independent, Mrs. Littledale is a member of the New York League of Women Voters and the American Association of University Women. One of her associates has described her outstanding trait—an ability "to do a difficult job easily. . . .She has the proper light touch in handling a complex situation." The editor, who is five feet one inch tall and weighs 110 pounds, wears her gray hair swept back from her face. The Littledales' son was stationed on Okinawa in 1946; their daughter is married to a physicist who worked on the atomic bomb project at Los Alamos. Mrs. Littledale lives in a tiny seventy-year-old house in the midst of New York's towering buildings. She likes to spend some of her leisure time in her house-top garden.

Reference

Who's Who in America, 1946-47

LITTLEJOHN, ROBERT MCG(OWAN)
Oct. 23, 1890- United States Government official

Address: b. c/o War Assets Administration, Railroad Retirement Bldg., Washington, D.C.; h. 1851 Columbia Road, N.W., Washington, D.C.

After handling huge and complex supply and procurement operations as Chief Quartermaster in the European Theater of Operations, Major General Robert McG. Littlejohn was retired from the Army so that he might direct one of the most "colossal" disposal tasks of all time. Appointed head of the War Assets Administration in July 1946, the former professional soldier who had spent twenty years with the Army's Services of Supply, began to dispose of America's tens of billions of dollars' worth of surplus war material—from "white elephants with wings" (obsolete aircraft) to pup tents, pipe lines, and industrial plants.

Robert McGowan Littlejohn was born in Jonesville, South Carolina, on October 23, 1890. His parents were Catherine (whose maiden name became her son's middle name) and Samuel Littlejohn. During 1906-7 he was a student at South Carolina's Clemson Agricultural College, then, in 1908, entered the United States Military Academy at West Point. Commissioned a second lieutenant at his graduation in June 1912, he joined the Eighth Cavalry in the Philippine Islands. Three years later he returned to the United States, having been assigned to Fort Bliss, Texas. In July 1916 Lieutenant Littlejohn was transferred to the Seventeenth Cavalry at Fort Bliss for patrol duty on the Mexican border. Three months after the United States declared war in 1917, the twenty-six-year-old cavalry officer, by that time a captain, was made an instructor at West Point. He taught from July 1917 until May of the next year, when he joined a machine gun battalion at Camp Wadsworth, New York. In June he was given the temporary rank of major in the 332d Machine Gun Battalion, and in September, two months after his marriage to Smith College graduate Mary Lambert, he sailed for Europe. During the final weeks of World War I Major Littlejohn served with the machine gun unit in France, but entered Germany in November 1918 with the Thirty-ninth Infantry. Remaining overseas for seven months after the armistice, part of the time he commanded a machine gun battalion in Germany, and for the last two months served in the Quartermaster Corps in France.

For a year after his return to the United States in 1919, Littlejohn was stationed in Raleigh, North Carolina, where he was assistant inspector of an R.O.T.C. district. But from August 1920 to the end of World War II he was concerned exclusively with army supply —the "procurement, storage, and issue" of food, clothing and supplies (but not weapons, vehicles, or signal equipment) to army troops. After serving briefly with the Quartermaster Corps in South Carolina and in Georgia, the Major (it was now a permanent rank) completed the six months' course at the Quarter-master Corps Subsistence School in Chicago. At his graduation in June 1921 he became a director of the school. From July 1922 to August 1925 he was its assistant commandant. For the next four years, Major Littlejohn was at the Command and General Staff School, in Fort Leavenworth, Kansas, first as a student (1925-26) and then as an instructor (1926-29). He attended the Army War College in Washington, D.C., in 1929-30, and then remained in Washington to serve five years (1930-35) in the Operations and Training Branch of the War Department General Staff.

With the rank of lieutenant colonel, he was post quartermaster at West Point for two and a half years (1935-38), next went to Manila as assistant to the quartermaster (1938-39); then was quartermaster and superintendent of the Army Transport Service for the Philippine Department. In June 1940, when France had fallen to the Nazis, he was assigned to the Office of the Quartermaster General in Washington, D.C., as chief of the clothing and equipage division. Although "official plans concerned less than a million men," according to *Time*, "Robert Littlejohn privately planned and organized for twice that number." In May 1942, a brigadier general (he was given that temporary rank a month after Pearl Harbor), Littlejohn went to Britain, where he became Chief Quartermaster for the European Theater of Operations.

The Services of Supply in the European theater was then being organized; six months later, in November 1942, came the Allied invasion of North Africa. In that half year, General Littlejohn, who by October was Acting Chief of Staff in the Services of Supply as well as Chief Quartermaster, created an organization which solved "seemingly insurmountable problems of supply," to make possible the successful landing of the African task force. Littlejohn's "marked aggressiveness" and "superior quality of leadership" were cited when he was awarded the Distinguished Service Medal for the accomplishment. The General procured 40 per cent of his supplies from the British on reverse Lend-Lease; his anti-waste campaign cut shipping space 12 per cent without reducing rations. "But to K.P.'s there is a single, better reason for the [D.S.M.] award," reported *Time*. "Waste-hating Quartermaster Littlejohn abolished the peeling of potatoes."

"The most complex and huge supply operations of all times" became Littlejohn's responsibility in mid-1944, with the Allied landings in Normandy. General Littlejohn believed that the German General Staff was depending on supply problems to defeat the Allies when they reached the Nazi West Wall, since supplies came to front-line soldiers from bases two hundred to three thousand miles away. These supplies included guns and tanks; food, of which 95 per cent was transported from the United States; five-gallon cans of gasoline (thirteen million of these to power the armored forces of General Patton before pipe lines and heavy carriers were available); and heavy winter clothing as the fighting stretched into a cold, wet winter.

MAJ. GEN. ROBERT MCG. LITTLEJOHN

That year at Thanksgiving relatives at home were cheered to know that General Littlejohn had guaranteed every soldier a roast turkey dinner; a man on the front lines would get his dinner later. To be sure of no shortage, the Quartermaster Corps had alloted 20 per cent overissue. Littlejohn was also the major general who sent a captain to investigate the complaint of a private: when the private wrote *Stars and Stripes* that he couldn't get ammunition out of his cartridge belt, the captain was dispatched to take him a new belt and bring back the defective one. "This office . . . has three teams in the field whose duty it is to investigate, report upon and recommend corrective action in cases of this nature," the General wrote to *Stars and Stripes*. "I appreciate your forwarding questions . . . for all my resources are available twenty-four hours a day to give aid to GI Joe." By V-E Day General Littlejohn was "providing subsistence, clothing and equipment for over seven million persons." The citation accompanying the Oak Leaf Cluster to be added to his Distinguished Service Medal read: "He not only maintained anticipated requirements but he exceeded them and established a new record for Quartermaster service."

Upon his return from Europe in February 1946 General Littlejohn was assigned to Detachment of Patients in the Walter Reed General Hospital. Five months later, in July, he was retired in the grade of major general so that he might accept an appointment by President Truman as head of the War Assets Administration. The WAA had taken over from the Surplus Property Board the largest-scale, most complicated selling job in the world. The WAA, then being investigated by five Congressional committees, was hampered by tight Congressional priority legislation, its own vast size,

and the many opportunities for corruption, as brokers vied for scarce commodities. Veterans were complaining that they were being cheated of their priorities, while others accused the former soldiers of "fronting" for groups without priorities. Also, brokers and middlemen were charged with making unnecessarily high profits. In the face of these conditions, "Washington politicos," reported *Time*, "were most impressed by Littlejohn's courage in taking on the thankless job." The new administrator set July 1947 as "target date" for all disposable properties to be out of Government hands. He reorganized entire departments; changed rules; increased the WAA enforcement staff to clean up admitted "widespread irregularities, favoritism and criminal misconduct"; decentralized sales responsibility among three hundred subregional offices. By various means disposal operations were speeded up; commercially nonflyable aircraft, for example, were sold on a mass basis for scrap and salvage.

By September 1946 Littlejohn had established five advisory boards to guide top WAA officials on contracts, controversies, and sales. To forestall a repetition of veterans' charges of favoritism, he planned to form a veterans' committee, composed of representatives from the various veterans' organizations, to advise on the disposal of surplus property. Both Littlejohn and the WAA were criticized by the House Committee on Surplus Property sales during August and September of 1946. Under a legal precedent established in wartime, international organizations received purchase priorities on goods, which aroused adverse comment in the House, especially when it was revealed that UNRRA was sending ice machines to Yugoslavia soon after the Yugoslavs shot down five American fliers. In the future, all sales were to be submitted to WAA for review. As a consequence, Littlejohn wanted to amend WAA regulations which grant "international organizations the right to acquire surplus property on the same basis as national organizations." Representative Slaughter, chairman of the House committee, suggested that the WAA establish a more efficient method of inventory, omit delays in offering property for sale, eliminate turnovers in personnel, and create a constant policy.

The last two months of 1946 witnessed Littlejohn's appearance before the Slaughter Committee to explain the delay in the sale of the Big Inch and Little Inch pipelines, used during the war for the transportation of oil from Texas to the East. After stating that the bids so far received were inadequate and that a report submitted by his predecessor, W. Stuart Symington [45], had not completely covered the potentialities of the pipelines, the WAA administrator was instructed to permit the immediate sale to the highest bidder. Despite its criticisms of the handling of the sales, the Slaughter Committee's report said that the WAA's business was being conducted in a far more efficient manner than was the case when the committee began its deliberations. General Littlejohn expected an even greater increase in efficiency to bring the agency's work to a close by 1948.

The Southern-born General belongs to the Army and Navy City and Country clubs. He has contributed articles on subsistence to technical publications. "It will be my policy to hide nothing," Littlejohn has said about his duties as chief of the WAA. "Every successful businessman does make mistakes, admits them, profits by them, does not repeat them." As an undergraduate at West Point the six-foot 210-pound Army man won the heavyweight wrestling title and played tackle on the football team. He likes to quote his wrestling coach, who maintained, "There ain't no hold that can't be broke." On his office memo paper the "gruff and crusty" administrator has had inscribed in capital letters the slogan of the Quartermaster service in Europe—"It will be done."

References

PM p16 Je 19 '45

Who's Who in America, 1946-47

LOGAN, HARLAN (DE BAUN) Apr. 30, 1904- Publisher; publishing consultant

Address: b. 1060 5th Ave., New York; h. Mayapple Rd., Stamford, Conn.

Described in a *Special Libraries* (December 1944) article as "a man of vision whose creative ideas converted the early *Look* of garish pictures into a family magazine of unquestioned respectability and national importance," Harlan Logan, general manager and editor of *Look* magazine from 1939 to November 1946 (it has a circulation of nearly two million), has been regarded by colleagues as a rare phenomenon— a college athletic hero and Rhodes Scholar who has made a success in the business world. He was formerly a university professor, magazine analyst, publicity writer for a Swedish physical culture institution, and even deputy sheriff of Chinatown for three months. Late in November 1946 Logan resigned from the staff of *Look* magazine and established two new enterprises of his own—a publishing company and a firm of publishing consultants to magazines and newspapers.

Harlan de Baun Logan was born on April 30, 1904, in Starkville, Mississippi. His father, William Newton Logan, a professor of geology at Mississippi State College, was descended from one of the English families that settled Virginia in the seventeenth century. His Kansas-born mother, Janette (de Baun) Logan, was of Flemish descent. The Logans lived on the campus, midway between the library and the athletic field, both of which attracted their son. When he was not in the library, young Harlan could be found on the field, where he was the mascot of the college football and baseball teams. At the age of seven he entered fourteen events in an elementary school track meet and won thirteen, coming out second in shot put. In 1916, when Harlan was twelve years old, his father accepted a position as head of the geology department of the University of Indiana, and the family forthwith moved to Bloomington, Indiana.

HARLAN LOGAN

There the youth attended high school and later the University of Indiana. At both he was a star athlete, named basketball as his favorite sport, and English composition and chemistry as his favorite subjects. At the university he majored in science and received his B.A. in 1925 after three years of study, also winning a Phi Beta Kappa key. Described as "a tall, skinny kid with long arms, deft hands, a fair amount of speed, and an accurate shooting eye," during his final year he had been chosen all-Conference forward in the "toughest college basketball league of the country," the Western (Big Ten) Conference, and he had also won his varsity letters in track, baseball, and tennis. At twenty-one, Logan also received the Big Ten medal for scholarship and athletics. After the completion of his undergraduate studies he remained for another year at the university, studying for his M.A. and coaching the tennis and freshman basketball teams (for which he was paid the sum of $360). In 1926 Logan went to Columbia University to begin work on his Ph.D., but two years later, having been selected as a Rhodes Scholar from Indiana, he left for Oxford without completing his study. By 1930, however, he was back in the United States, apparently cured of all further desire for an academic career. Although he had played on the Oxford tennis team and had made friends among the English students, he reported himself disappointed with Oxford life and said that, having found himself "aging at an alarming rate," he had decided to return home to "lead a more active life with less wear and tear."

Now twenty-six years old, Logan took stock of his assets and decided that he was equipped with a sound academic background, a considerable amount of fame as an athlete, but with no business experience. He turned therefore to the field he knew best, becoming an instructor of

LOGAN, HARLAN—*Continued*

English at New York University. It was a routine English assignment which first gave him the idea of analyzing magazines for their publishers. He had asked his students to make an analytical survey of some sixty American magazines. Receiving studies and analyses of articles, story techniques, and mechanical requirements, he wondered if periodicals could not use efficiency experts as industry did, and thereupon set out to conduct a magazine analysis service in his spare time. His venture proved successful, for by 1935 he had analyzed approximately one hundred and ten periodicals, including *Life*, *Liberty*, and *Vanity Fair*, and had been retained as an editorial consultant by some of them. He had not left New York University, however: in 1935 he was made director of its division of unified studies; in 1936, associate professor of English with a position in the adult writing center he had helped to establish.

In the spring of 1936 Logan was offered five hundred dollars to analyze the declining *Scribner's Magazine*. When he reported that the publication might survive if it were modernized, he was given the opportunity to direct the modernization. He then resigned from his university post—which he had never liked, he says—to become editor of *Scribner's*. Within five months (June–October 1936), it is pointed out, *Scribner's* was "transformed from an old-fashioned literary magazine into a streamlined venture in modern journalism." It employed photographs, color, and attractive layouts, increased its fiction content and focused its attention on the contemporary American scene. Nevertheless, while its circulation rose from 46,000 to 115,000 in two years, the magazine was forced to suspend publication in the spring of 1939. Logan still believes that, had the new *Scribner's* had another year to impress itself upon advertisers, it would have succeeded.

While the editor-publisher was trying to keep *Scribner's* alive, he was invited to conduct the experiments in policy and make-up that were thought necessary to rejuvenate *Look* magazine, and in the summer of 1939 he joined the staff of that periodical. *Look*, a sensational semi-monthly picture magazine, was being published at a loss by the Cowles brothers, owners of Des Moines and Minneapolis newspapers. Under Logan's guidance "the lusty liberalism, along with blood and bodies," which had constituted most of its fare, disappeared from its pages, and *Look*, wrote Kenneth Stewart [43] in *PM*, "became more conservative in subject matter, treatment and social consciousness." It also began to make money, showing a profit for the first time in 1943.

By that time Logan had risen from assistant to Gardner (Mike) Cowles, president of Look, Incorporated, to general manager (1940) and editor (1942); in 1944 he also became vice-president of Cowles Magazines, Inc., the newly expanded company. Speaking of his editorial policy with regard to the magazine he told an interviewer: "Here at *Look* we are hanging our hats on the visual presentation peg. Other magazines have become what they are because of a gradual and accidental accretion of things. My contention, however, is that a publishing house should have a central idea, like General Motors or any other big organization that is selling an established product, a core to build around. We plan everything we do. Nothing just happens." The planning, it might be added, was done mostly in conference, with Logan demonstrating on proof sheets pinned on the walls of the conference room.

The change of name from Look, Inc., to Cowles Magazines, Inc., was made in 1944 to indicate the expanding operations of the organization. By that year the company had produced, besides *Look*, six movie shorts, which have been shown in about one hundred newsreel theaters. The subjects of the shorts were based on features that had appeared in the magazine, among them one on the dangers of inflation. The editors of *Look* have prepared several books, profusely illustrated with photographs, for publication by other firms. Among the titles were *Air Power*, *How To Be Attractive*, *Woodrow Wilson*, and Shirley Temple's [45] *My Young Life*. Their *One Nation*, described by Logan as a "survey of racial and religious stresses in wartime America," was well received by the critics, who found it "unsentimental, hard hitting, and practical," "much more than just a picture book." Another such work published by the company was *Look at America* (1946), compiled by the *Look* editors. While Harlan Logan was the operational head of the organization, much of this extra task was directed by himself, but when he applied pressure, as he frequently did, it was not resented, said his colleagues, "because it always has meaning—it's productive rather than nervous, personal or whimsical."

In late 1946, when he and Cowles disagreed about Logan's conception of *Look* as a family magazine—Logan believed it should be a "combination of entertainment and instruction," Cowles, that it should be more "news-minded"—Logan resigned as editor and general manager and Cowles took over his posts. Logan then began organizing his own company, Visual Enterprises, Incorporated, which was to assume the function of publishing the type of "picture" books which had been issued by the *Look* book department. At the same time he formed the firm of Harlan Logan Associates, publishing consultants to magazines and newspapers.

Logan, who is over six feet tall, is no longer the gangling youth of his basketball days. He is pleased with the fact that his tennis is still good enough for him to hold his own at the River Club in New York, where he likes to play with Alice Marble [40], former women's national champion. Logan is also a member of Sigma Delta Psi, Sigma Delta Chi, and Phi Kappa Psi. The blue-eyed, brown-haired Logan says he likes people, but is loath to face large audiences. This is said to account for his innumerable small conferences with his staff and his preference for the seminar rather than the lecture hall when he taught at New York University. His religious affiliation is Methodist. He was married on June 14, 1930, to Barbara Rollins, daughter of a Massachusetts circuit court judge. Their four children are Deborah, Lois, Penelope, and Mary Haven. Although Logan's formula for success is "planning and teamwork," he is forced to admit, he says, that in his home life "five women are too much for any man's planning."

References

Newsweek 7:29 Je 27 '45
America's Young Men, 1938-39
Who's Who in America, 1946-47
Who's Who in Commerce and Industry (1944)

LOMBARDO, GUY (ALBERT) June 19, 1902- Band leader
Address: b. c/o David Alber Associates, Inc., 654 Madison Ave., New York; h. 710 S. Grove St., Freeport, N. Y.

Although Guy Lombardo's style has remained much the same during the years of changing jazz rhythms, and swing fans consider his music "strictly corny," he has retained his place as one of the top band leaders in the United States. Twelve times his Royal Canadians, who, according to the November 1945 issue of *Time*, gross almost a million dollars a year, won the annual New York *World-Telegram* radio editors' poll for "the sweetest music this side of heaven."

The Royal Canadians have their roots in Canada—it was in London, Ontario, the town of his birth, that Lombardo first organized the band. The son of Guy and Lena (Paladino) Lombardo, Guy Albert Lombardo was born on June 19, 1902. His father, a tailor who had left his native Italy for Canada at the age of fourteen, had studied voice and wanted his children to have a musical education. Almost as soon as he could hold the instrument, Guy began taking lessons on the violin. In the afternoons, when classes at St. Peter's, a Catholic school which Guy attended from 1909 to 1920, were over, he and his brothers would play together on their instruments. The two eldest, Guy and Carmen, performed duets for their mother's club, and soon Freddie Kreitzer, the son of one of the other club members, joined them at the piano. Thus, at the age of twelve Guy had a three-piece band. When the boys were a little older they filled minor engagements at parties and dances.

In 1921 the nineteen-year-old band leader, encouraged by the success he had had thus far and by the popularity of Paul Whiteman, added about six other musicians to his band, including his brothers Carmen and Lebert. In the summer of 1923 they played at Lake Erie resorts, and the following year they crossed the border to try their luck. Lombardo was convinced that radio could make his band famous; in the United States, where broadcasting was a growing enterprise, he felt that he might have the opportunity to go on the air. After the Canadians had succeeded in getting an engagement at the Clairmont Cafe in Cleveland, Lombardo persuaded a local radio station to let him broadcast without pay. It was at the Clairmont Cafe that "the Lombardo style was born." Jerome Beatty in an August 1946 article in *American Magazine* gave an account of how the young musicians, who had not had enough experience with difficult songs, al-most lost their first job in the United States. After avoiding complicated numbers like "Sentimental Over You" and "Street of Dreams" for several evenings, it occurred to Lombardo that if the tunes were played at a slower tempo, the band would be able to play all the notes. He then arranged to have the lights dimmed while the melodies were played; and the dancers commented on the romantic effect.

In 1927 Lombardo was engaged by the Granada Hotel in Chicago. In that city, which was then "the jazz mecca of the bootleg era," he made his first network broadcast for CBS. At about this time the band, which had been known as the "Canadians," became the "Royal Canadians," because Lombardo's theater manager felt that a more colorful name was needed for advertisements. Since 1926, when the musicians had been drawing record crowds to Cleveland's Music Box Restaurant, the Music Corporation of America, a new booking agency whose executives thought they "could enter portals still closed to them and force those places to take lesser bands as part of the price of getting Lombardo," had been trying to persuade the young band leader to become its client. But Lombardo felt that he was doing well without an agent, and not until 1929, when M.C.A. offered to procure a New York engagement for him, did he employ the services of the agency, which became a powerful element in show business.

A week before the stock market crash in the fall of 1929 the Royal Canadians came to New York to play at the Roosevelt Hotel where they replaced "Ben Bernie and his Lads." The Roosevelt Grill, which was later enlarged to accommodate five hundred and decorated by Lombardo's only unmusical brother Jo, became the band's annual winter stand; in 1945 they opened their seventeenth season there at forty-five hundred dollars a week. Engagements followed at other New York dance spots such as the Waldorf-Astoria's Starlight Roof, and in the ballrooms and motion picture theaters of many other cities. These, in addition to phonograph recordings, sponsored radio programs, and films, made the Royal Canadians one of the five biggest money-making bands of all time, according to a 1946 article in the New York *World-Telegram*. Lombardo's income was reported as more than two hundred thousand dollars a year. His broadcasts—which began with his first radio contract in 1928—included programs for the Wrigley Company, the General Baking Company, Lady Esther Cosmetics, Colgate-Palmolive-Peet, Bond Bread, and Chelsea Cigars. In 1946 he was featured on the Mutual Network's *Spotlight Bands* program on Monday nights. Among the films in which Lombardo and his band appeared were *Many Happy Returns* (1934), *Stage Door Canteen* (1943), and *No Leave, No Love*, which was not yet released in August 1946.

Besides winning the *World-Telegram* radio editors' poll for twelve years, the Royal Canadians were rated first in polls conducted by *Radio Daily* and *Motion Picture Daily* in 1944 and by *Billboard* in 1946. In 1944 Lombardo received a special citation from *Orchestra*

GUY LOMBARDO

World for introducing ten of the twenty most popular songs for the year. Since Cleveland days, when he introduced "Give Me a Little Kiss, Willya Hon?" which became a nation-wide hit, Lombardo has played a new tune each week on his broadcasts. It is estimated that about two hundred and fifty of the melodies he has introduced became best-selling records. In some instances, however, his judgment has erred. When Latin-American rhythms first became popular, he refused to play them until his arranger persuaded him to try the "Peanut Vendor," which immediately became a hit. "Mairzy Doats," a nonsense song about mares and lambs, was another number whose popular appeal Lombardo did not recognize.

The band leader attributes much of his success to the fact that many of his musicians have been with him for a long time—seven were members of his original group. Columnists speak of the band as a family affair: Lombardo's brother Carmen sings, plays the saxophone, reeds, and flute, and has written the music for "Boo-Hoo" "Coquette", "Sweethearts on Parade," as well as other tunes; Lebert, two years younger than Carmen, is a "Royal" trumpeter; Victor, who is the youngest of the brothers and did not join them until 1930, played the clarinet and saxophone until he left to form his own band in 1946; Rosemarie, the boys' sister, is one of the vocalists.

Although it has had little effect on his success, comment on Lombardo's music has not always been favorable. Robert Goffin, who is the author of a book on jazz and lectured at the New School for Social Research, told his students that they should "hear Lombardo to have a notion of what not to do in jazz." Some have called the player of sweet music "King of Corn." His answer to these critics is that he "plays for people in love, not acrobats." While most band leaders emphasize

rhythm, Lombardo, whose primary aims are balance and a sweet tone, stresses melody. It is this lack of rhythmic emphasis which makes the music seem slow even though the band does not play at a very slow tempo. Dewey Bergman, the arranger who has been described as "the man behind the scenes," follows Lombardo's rule for lyric phrasing: the tunes are rendered so that the instruments will sound much like the vocalists. For many years the Royal Canadians were a "brass and reed choir"; after he stopped playing his violin with the band, Lombardo used no strings and his only bass was a single tuba. But when he felt that a more sonorous foundation was necessary, he added a bass viol. A unique instrument in the band is the fozophone, a hybrid trombone-mellophone, which was invented by Dick Fosdick, one of the Royal Canadians. This collection of instruments led to Lombardo being named "King of Corn" in a poll conducted in December 1946 by *Down Beat,* the professional musicians' magazine.

Lombardo, who became an American citizen in 1937, has engaged in a number of other enterprises. He has an interest in the London Music Company, an affiliate of Broadcast Music Incorporated, which was set up during the feud between ASCAP and BMI. In July 1946 he and his brothers launched the Long Island Airlines, which flies commuters from the east tip of Long Island to Manhattan in about fifty minutes. Lombardo himself cannot pilot a plane, but he is an expert in running a speedboat and has competed in races since 1939. He came in second in the Fite Memorial Trophy Race at Ocean City, New Jersey, in 1941, and in 1946 won races at Davenport, Iowa. He won the National Sweepstakes championship at Red Bank, New Jersey, in August 1946, and the much coveted International Gold Cup in a ninety-mile race at Detroit a few weeks later. He is a member of the Columbia Yacht Club and hopes to win more prizes with a new jet-propelled model which is still in the experimental stage. In September 1926 the band leader was married to Lilliebell Glenn, whom he met while playing in Cleveland. Dark and well-built, Lombardo was selected in 1941 as one of the ten best-dressed men in the nation by the Custom Tailors Guild of America. But the musician, whom an interviewer described as "quiet, suave, unhurried. . . like his music," prefers "to be out on his boat in a pair of old trousers and a pair of old shoes."

References

Am Mag p32-33+ Ag '46
N Y World-Telegram p13 Mr 11 '46
Eichenberg, R. Radio Stars of Today (1937)
Who's Who in America, 1946-47

LONG, ANDREW THEODORE Apr. 6, 1866—May 21, 1946 Rear-Admiral of the United States Navy from 1918 to 1930; veteran of all types of service, decorated by numerous countries.

Obituary

N Y Times p21 My 23 '46

LONG, TANIA Apr. 29, 1913 Journalist
Address: b. c/o The New York Times, 229
West 43d St., New York; h. 92 King's High-
way, Westport, Conn.

Tania Long, in 1946 correspondent in Germany for the New York *Times,* has earned the
praise of her fellow journalists as "both a
leading war correspondent and a woman of
ideas." The New York Newspaper Women's
Club, at their February 1941 Front Page Ball,
awarded her a prize for her stories on the
bombing of London, which were judged the best
news stories written by a woman in 1940. At
the end of World War II, Miss Long turned
her attention to conditions in conquered Germany. Her articles in the New York *Times
Magazine,* and her news stories, attracted considerable comment for the picture she presented
of the dangerous effect of fraternization by
American troops in Germany on the American
occupation policy.

Tania (an abbreviation of Tatiana) Long
was born on April 29, 1913, in Berlin, Germany. Daughter of Russian-born Tatiana
Mouraviev and British Robert Crozier Long,
she early gained a broad linguistic background
which was of value in her later work. By observing and assisting her father, who served
as New York *Times* financial columnist and as
Berlin correspondent of the *Economist* of London, Miss Long received her first journalistic
training. After several years of living in Scandinavian capitals and attending the Lorenz
Lyceum in Berlin from 1920 to 1924, young
Tania studied at the Ecole des Jeunes Filles at
St. German-en-Laye, near Paris, until 1927.
From then until 1930 she was a student at the
Malvern Girls' College in England. In her
post-graduate work at the Sorbonne in Paris
(1930-31), and at the Paris Ecole des Sciences
Politiques, Miss Long specialized in history and
economics.

Although most of her life thus far has been
spent in Europe, she began her career as a
journalist in America in October 1936. For
two years she worked on New Jersey's *Newark
Ledger,* reporting everything "from fires to police blotter." These early general assignments
were useful in her later role as correspondent, she points out: "It was a full year before I
was assigned to war news in London, and most
newspapers cannot afford to keep a foreign
correspondent who specializes in only one form
of story. It's smarter to learn technique and
newspaper judgment under your own city editor before embarking for further points."

Returning to Berlin in October 1938, Miss
Long obtained a position with the New York
Herald Tribune bureau in that city, largely because of her "previous long residence in the
German capital . . . a consequent wide circle
of friends and contacts . . . combined with her
linguistic abilities and thorough knowledge of
many other European countries." Her first
duties consisted of reading approximately forty
daily German newspapers, selecting significant
articles from them, and rewriting these for
the *Tribune.* Her skill in writing both quickly
and well soon led to her becoming assistant
chief correspondent, under Ralph Barnes, Wal-

N.Y.Times

TANIA LONG

ter Kerr, and Joseph Barnes, each of whom
headed the bureau at different times during the
year before the war.

When World War II began in September
1939, the journalist left Berlin for Copenhagen,
where she helped to relay stories from Germany. Then she went to Paris; and before
the end of September she was assigned to the
Tribune bureau in London, where in 1941 her
coverage of the bombing of the city won her
the Newspaper Women's Club award. Among
Miss Long's best stories, the judges held, were
accounts of the sinking of a British liner transporting refugee children, of the conditions of
London's poor during the war, and of the bombing of the Hotel Savoy while she was living
there. Of the bombing of her hotel she wrote
in a dispatch to the *Tribune*: "I was sitting in
my third-floor room ready to get into bed when
I heard the bombs coming. The second or
third of the sticks landed in the street right
outside my window. Only a split second later
the next bomb hit the cornice of the hotel and
went off, and almost immmediately after that
the other one hit the rear of the building. When
one hears bombs coming that close there is no
time to do anything. One hasn't time to be
afraid, that comes later."

At the time of the obliteration bombing of
Coventry, the correspondent worked for thirty-
six hours at a stretch. As told in *Mademoiselle*
(March 1942), she completed her regular office stint in London at one in the morning, then
traveled at snail's pace by car through blackout and bombing. She reached Coventry several
hours later, and since, in any case, she could
find no hotel accommodations or food, she kept
on working through the day. From Coventry,
she went on to Birmingham, which was also being blitzed—"Almost two-and-a-half days, sleep-
less and practically foodless (except for a
few forlorn snacks) was her record this time."

LONG, TANIA—Continued

Before meeting Miss Long, Raymond Daniell[*], New York *Times* correspondent in London whom she was later to marry, had considered newspaper work in London a man's job; but, he wrote later, she "provided us with as much competition as any man in London." And in his book *Civilians Must Fight* (1941), he noted: "One of the two American newspaperwomen in London, she looked after us all with a sort of motherly care. Her calm and her courage during the frightful early days of the blitzkrieg helped us all to keep our nerves steady."

Miss Long joined the staff of the New York *Times* in February 1942. She continued reporting on wartime London, and in 1944 became London representative of the Sunday supplement department of the *Times*. With the termination of the war, she returned to Germany as a *Times* correspondent, assisting Daniell, by that time her husband, in the coverage of the Nuremberg trials. In her articles on postwar Germany, the correspondent told of the growing black market and "wholesale" fraternization by United States occupation forces. "The average GI and officer," she warned, "has forgotten why he came here at all . . . and unless something is done . . . there is a serious threat that our occupation policy toward Germany will be weakened and once more the Germans will have succeeded in taking the Americans into camp." She attacked, too, the seeming lack of a definite policy toward Germany by the United States Government and the diffusion of "pity Germany" propaganda by the hypocritically friendly residents of Berlin, a city about which she had never cared, although, she has pointed out, she had lived and worked there for years and life had been pleasant until the Nazi encroachments. In December 1946 Miss Long was awarded a campaign ribbon for service in the European theatre by Secretary of War Patterson.

Among her articles for the New York *Times Magazine,* those on postwar Germany include: "Spawn of the Nazi Code," a discussion of the problem of the demoralized German youth; "They Long For a New Fuehrer," in which Miss Long declared that German women were bitter, hostile, fearful of the future, yet still steeped in Nazi poison; "Goering's Home Town Under American Rule"; and "Little Man, What Next?" the story of Siegfried, fourteen-year-old man of affluence in Germany's booming black market. Others of her *Times* Magazine articles are: "Over the Nazi Lines With a Gun Spotter," which she and her husband co-authored in December 1944; "Women of Three Armies," about American, Russian, and English army women in Berlin; "It's Still The Same Glowing Paris"; and "Education of a Queen To Be," on Princess Elizabeth of Great Britain.

Tania Long's marriage to Raymond Daniell (in 1946, chief correspondent for the New York *Times* in Germany) took place on November 22, 1941. Later he wrote of their meeting in London in 1939: "I saw an attractive girl with the most strikingly alert eyes and the most infectious smile I have ever seen." Of slender build (125 pounds, five feet four and a half inches tall), Miss Long has brown hair and hazel eyes. Her son Robert M. Gray is the child of a previous marriage. Reading, gardening, and swimming are her chief recreations.

References

    Ind Woman 20:8 Ja '41 por
    Mademoiselle Mr '42
    N Y Post p3 F 15 '41
    N Y Times p13 F 15 '41

LUCE, ROBERT Dec. 2, 1862—Apr. 7, 1946 Public official and businessman; United States Representative from Massachusetts, 1919-35, and in 1937-41; began as a reporter; cofounder, president of Luce Press Clipping Bureau; member Massachusetts legislature, 1899, and in 1901-08; admitted to bar in 1908; lieutenant governor, 1912; author of eight books.

Obituary

    N Y Times p27 Ap 8 '46

LYNCH, J(OHN) JOSEPH, REV. Dec. 6, 1894- Seismologist; educator
Address: b. c/o Fordham University, New York

The Jesuit order numbers among its members the leading scientists in the Roman Catholic Church, and about one hundred Jesuits are among the four or five hundred seismologists active in the world today. Of these men who are engaged in the study of the movements of the earth's crust, America's best known is Father J. Joseph Lynch, director of the Fordham University Observatory, considered the largest and best-equipped in the world, where the "heartbeat of the earth" is recorded and analyzed. Father Lynch's instruments record the intensity, distance, and direction of about one hundred and fifty major earthquakes a year. Probably thirty thousand quakes of measurable intensity occur yearly; most of them are in ocean beds, or sparsely inhabited parts of the earth. "Earthquakes are like snakes," says Father Lynch, who is also a teacher at the university, and the author of a popular book on quakes. "They avoid human beings more than is generally realized." Once or twice a month newsmen waken the priest at odd hours, whereupon he rushes to his subterranean vault to determine the "address" and seriousness of whatever quake has been reported on the news wires.

John Joseph Lynch was born in London on December 6, 1894. His parents, Patrick and Marianne (Hayden) Lynch were both Irish, and both had relatives in the Roman Catholic Church: four of the boy's aunts became Sisters of Mercy (later one of his sisters became a nun in the same order), and an uncle was a secular priest in Point Pleasant, New Jersey. While John was on a summer vacation with his mother's relatives in Ireland when he was nine years old, his left hand was caught in the main driving cogs of a threshing machine on their Kilkenny farm. When a doctor wished to amputate his smashed fingers, his father insisted that, even at the risk of infection, the hand be given a chance to mend. "The bone fragments knit into fine shape. Had [the fingers] been amputated I couldn't have been ordained," the priest has said. (The "canonical fingers" are needed in the celebration of Mass.) As it was, he became a Jesuit scientist, instead of a secular priest, largely because of his injury.

At ten the boy entered St. Ignatius College in London, where he studied for eight years. He became captain of the football team in his last year (1911-12). He wished to join the Westminister Diocese as a secular priest, but was told his maimed fingers (which might cause him to drop the chalice) would bar him. For a year the eighteen-year-old youth clerked in the office of an East End leather factory, meanwhile making plans to go on a mission as a priest to the western United States. Advised to spend a year at an American college to become accustomed to American ways, in 1913-14 he attended St. Joseph's College in Philadelphia. While there the tall student was anchor man on the relay team. Before the year was out, it was suggested to him that he join the learned Jesuit order. This he did in July 1914, when he was not yet twenty. For the next three years he studied classics at St. Andrews-on-Hudson in Poughkeepsie, and followed that with three years of philosophy and physics at Woodstock College in Maryland. After Woodstock had awarded him his B.A. and M.A. degrees in 1920, he was appointed instructor in physics at Fordham University and director of its seismograph observatory. The observatory then consisted of a Weichert, a primitive inverted pendulum device which scratched records of distant quakes on smoked paper, but which was insensitive to local disturbances. He had been at Fordham three years when his superiors sent him abroad for the advanced study required of those in the Society of Jesus.

The Jesuit scholastic (his rank after his novitiate) was in Europe from 1923 to 1927. For those four years he studied theology at St. Ignatius College in Valkenburg, Holland. There he also studied with Father Theodor Wulf, noted for pioneer work which led to the discovery of cosmic rays. Under Professor Herbert Hall Turner, the greatest seismologist of the day, for five summers Lynch worked at the Oxford University seismic observatory. He also devoted one year to studying ascetic theology in Wales. While abroad, he was ordained a priest of the Roman Catholic Church in Dublin on July 31, 1926. Father Lynch returned to Fordham University in 1928 to become a professor of physics, and director again of the observatory. He received his Ph.D. in 1939, following three years of graduate work at New York University.

The new Fordham Observatory was blasted out of bedrock on the Fordham campus in the Bronx in 1935. Almost hermetically sealed in layers of brick, sand and concrete, and topped by a stone Gothic-style building, the vault houses nine seismographs, representing every known design. "Probably the greatest thrill I have had at the observatory was the installation of our Benioff seismograph," Father Lynch has written. "This is our Giant of Palomar [California's two-hundred inch telescope]. It magni-

REV. J. JOSEPH LYNCH

fies about one hundred thousand times and as soon as we had installed it we began to record vibrations we had not known to exist. It opened up for us a new field of exploration within the earth." The seismographs each have a pendulum which sends a light beam to a roll of photographic paper fastened around a rotating drum, which in turn is anchored deep in the bedrock. The vault, with only one dim red bulb near the door, acts as a darkroom. As the earth "pulses," the drum vibrates, and the beam from the pendulum traces a "cardiograph." Each morning Father Lynch and his assistants spend an hour interpreting the 1,650 feet of "squiggly lines" on the newly developed rolls of photographic paper. The priest-scientist of necessity is an expert on New York's "pulse" rate—the vibrations of its milk trains, highway traffic, explosions and blastings—because he must be able to distinguish local disturbances from earthquakes. Quake data from seismograph stations around the world are collated at Oxford, where the "quake's final biography" is prepared.

"It is quite a thrill to stand in the dim vault and watch a tiny light spot move back and forth, and realize that the light spot is being activated by an earthquake in far-off Japan or Turkey," says Father Lynch. Less satisfying are the spiders and bothersome people he classifies as "sighs of a seismologist." The "cranks" write letters; one actually threatened "dire consequences" if the priest did not remove the observatory building and stop producing earthquakes. The spiders provide more serious difficulties. Once having entered the sealed vault in some unknown manner, they dance on the delicate instruments causing earthquake "forgeries" which might seriously interfere with the records of the beginning of a real quake. Father Lynch has never found out why they like seismographs or what they feed on, but he has

LYNCH, J. JOSEPH, REV.—*Continued*

spent many hours dismantling instruments and creeping through the vault on spider hunts.

The composition of the earth's interior and the basic causes for quakes are still unknown. "We give you as our candidate for the earth's core—a solid solution," Father Lynch has written, "a metal occluding many thousands of times its volume of a gas." His experiments with gas forced into a metal, which led to his theory, were described in the paper *The Effect of Occluded Hydrogen on the Rigidity of Palladium* (1940). He is also the author of *General Physics* (1933) and *Our Trembling Earth* (1940), "an informative story of earthquakes and the men who study the earth's restless interior," and is a frequent contributor to scientific journals. In September 1946 Father Lynch headed a mission to the Dominican Republic to study the effects of recent earthquakes and tidal waves there.

The "handsome" and "robust" priest is over six feet tall, has thinning light hair, and wears yellow-rimmed spectacles. A naturalized American since 1935, echoes of London and Oxford speech remain in his pronunciation. Father Lynch has a weakness for puns—his physics classes at Fordham are apt to hear of "the sweet music of ohm, sweet ohm." He also likes to quote excerpts from old English ballads and Victorian poetry. Explaining how he finds particular satisfaction in the study of earth tremors, he has written: "By encouraging men to learn the laws of nature, as written in the faults and folds of the earth, one can lead men to a knowledge of the Author of those laws."

References

Good H 120:38+ F '45 por
Life 20:59-60+ Ap 15 '46 por
American Men of Science (1944)
Lynch, J. J. Our Trembling Earth (1940)
Who's Who in America, 1946-47

MACALARNEY, ROBERT E(MMET) Dec. 30, 1873—Nov. 15, 1945 American author, educator, and newspaper editor; associate, then full professor of journalism at Columbia University (1912-20, 1943-45); city editor in succession of several New York newspapers (1906-16); editor of the *Ladies' Home Journal* (1923-28); director of public relations for the National Committee on Food for Small Democracies (1940-42).

Obituary

N Y Times p19 N 16 '45 por

MCCAREY, (THOMAS) LEO Oct. 3, 1898- Director; producer; scenario writer

Address: b. c/o RKO Radio Studios, Inc., 780 N. Gower St., Hollywood, Calif.; h. 1018 Ocean Front, Santa Monica, Calif.

Going My Way and *The Awful Truth*, two of Leo McCarey's many film successes, have won for the director-writer three of the coveted "Oscars" from the Acadamy of Motion Picture Arts and Sciences. In 1937 he earned one award for the "comic touch" in his direction of *The Awful Truth*, and in 1944 one each for writing and directing *Going My Way*, the biggest box-office surprise of the past several years.

Thomas Leo McCarey was born in Los Angeles, California, on October 3, 1898, the son of Irish Thomas J. ("Uncle Tom") McCarey and the former Leona Mistrot of Pyrenean-French blood. His father, a prominent West Coast sports promoter, was determined that his boy should become a lawyer and, after his son's graduation from Los Angeles High School, sent him through the University of Southern California Law School. Young McCarey, then one of the best amateur middleweights on the Coast, was more interested in a career of prize fighting. His first money came, however, not as a result of his legal pleadings or of his boxing, but from damages received when he fell down the elevator shaft of the University Law School and suffered a broken leg. McCarey invested the five thousand dollars in a copper mine, entered the San Francisco offices of Rufus Thayer, attorney for the Jacklin copper interests, and later, after the mine failed, put in a year as mucker in Montana mines for a weekly ten dollars. The mining company offered him a chance to represent the firm in the Southern California courts, but in his first trial McCarey was ruled down in the brief time of fifteen minutes. He then opened a new Los Angeles law office, which he closed after his third case, the last of his legal career.

Song-writing next attracted McCarey, but that proved unsuccessful. Then, becoming keenly interested in the growing motion picture industry, he persuaded his friend, director (then actor) David Butler, to introduce him to Tod Browning, director of melodrama at Universal Studios. In September 1918 McCarey became Browning's third assistant (the equivalent of script girl) for the picture *Virgin of Stamboul*, continuing to work with Lon Chaney and on other films. Under Browning, McCarey learned the writing-directing skills he was to use at the Hal Roach Studios from 1923 to 1928. He directed about three hundred shorts for Roach, including the Charley Chase and other comic series. McCarey's idea of teaming the studio's fat and lean comedians resulted in the many Laurel and Hardy films. He also originated a new technique, utilized in their later comedies: until then the main plot was a romance, with Laurel and Hardy providing only comic relief; now McCarey made the laugh-getters the principals. As a reward for his successful ideas, Roach Studios made him vice-president in 1926. He remained in that position until 1928.

In 1930 McCarey signed with Fox Studios, for which he directed *Roadhouse, Shepper Newfounder, The Kid From Spain, Indiscreet* (for United Artists release), *Wild Company*, and *Part Time Wife* for Fox. His sole 1933 production was the Marx Brothers' *Duck Soup* for Paramount, the studio with which he remained until 1937. There he produced or directed *Six of a Kind, Belle of the Nineties*

(1934), *Ruggles of Red Gap* (1935), *Milky Way,* and *Make Way for Tomorrow* (1937). For his direction of *The Awful Truth* (1937) for Columbia, McCarey received his first Academy award. In the same year, he collaborated on the story for *The Cowboy and the Lady.*

Serious injury in an automobile accident interrupted McCarey's direction of *Love Affair* in 1940 for RKO—he had helped to write it—and necessitated his wheel chair supervision of *My Favorite Wife.* The director had come to be known as "one of the all-around boys": he had proved himself to be a capable director of love stories when he supervised and collaborated in *Love Affair;* his light touch had been apparent in *Ruggles of Red Gap* and in *The Awful Truth. Make Way for Tomorrow,* thought by many to be his finest early film, had shown his ability to direct tragedy. Now, according to *Time,* he tried "to mix a box-office Mickey Finn out of these disparate ingredients: topical tragedy, pulmotored patriotism, slick paper romance, and anything-for-a-laugh comedy." While his *Once Upon a Honeymoon* (1942) generally received poor reviews, there was constant praise for "McCarey's sleight of hand" in the direction of Cary Grant '41 and Ginger Rogers '41. It was a personal triumph for McCarey, but otherwise a failure.

The desire to make a picture about a music-loving priest, to star his friend Bing Crosby, resulted in *Going My Way,* a Paramount release, "a comically tender story of a young priest's efforts to modernize a run-down parish and its old-fashioned pastor." Produced for less than one million dollars, the film by 1946 had earned more than that amount for McCarey alone. Critics hailed him for his writing of the original story and his direction with "all the skill and artistry which distinguished that memorable offering of his *Ruggles of Red Gap.*"

Going My Way garnered seven Academy awards in 1944: two to McCarey personally, as director and original story writer; and five others, including one as best picture of the year. The picture headed the New York Film Critics' list for 1944, won a special Greek Academy of Arts and Sciences award, was placed first among the *Playbill* list of 1944's best motion pictures and, among other recognitions, brought to McCarey a special GI "Oscar" for directing the film which most "maintained in the minds of the American home front the principles for which American soldiers . . . [were] fighting."

A sequel, *The Bells of St. Mary's* (1946), was directed and produced by McCarey for RKO release, in return for that studio's allowing him to direct *Going My Way* for Paramount. The production was a box-office success. "Warmly sentimental," *Variety* wrote, *The Bells of St. Mary's* "has a simple story that hits home." The film was the first venture of an independent company, Rainbow Productions, formed with McCarey as president, and

LEO MCCAREY

with Bing Crosby, David Butler, Buddy De Sylva '43, and Hal Roach, Jr., as officers. Rainbow Productions plans to produce two or three pictures a year.

The producer has no set formula for his pictures: "I only know I like my characters to walk in clouds. I like a little bit of the fairy tale. . . .As long as I'm there behind the camera lens," says McCarey, "I'll let somebody else photograph the ugliness of the world." Songwriting remains a great love. McCarey has composed a prodigious number of ditties, only a few of which have been published. His most popular tune, "Why Do You Sit on Your Patio," netted him two dollars and fifty cents. Leo McCarey was married to Stella V. Martin on July 29, 1920, and they have a daughter Mary Virginia, in 1946 a student at the University of Southern California. "The bargain-basement edition of Cary Grant," as McCarey has been called, is five feet ten inches tall, has dark brown hair and eyes, and would "probably win . . . hands down, in any beauty contest among Hollywood directors." Referred to as that "easy-going, good-natured, soft-spoken Irishman," he has penchants for dungarees and tweeds; for Bull Durham and for "rolling his own"; for swimming, tennis, and golf; and for hearty breakfasts of "seven eggs, hot cakes, bacon, and coffee."

References

Esquire 19:57+ My '43
Liberty 22:20+ My 26 '46 pors
Motion Pict Mag 68:58+ Ja '45 por
N Y Times VIII p3 Mr 29 '42; p44 Je 17 '46
Sat Eve Post 219:14+ N 30 '46
International Motion Picture Almanac, 1943-44
Who's Who in America, 1946-47

MACDONALD, BETTY Mar. 26, 1908-
Author

Address: b. c/o J. B. Lippincott Co., East
Washington Sq., Philadelphia; h. Vashon
Heights, Vashon Island, Wash.

The author of the best-selling book *The Egg
and I* (1945), Betty MacDonald, has delighted
readers with her account of her life as a young
bride on a forty-acre chicken ranch, complete
with an unromantic log house, an abandoned
well, explosive stove, and chicken houses in
need of repair. From the point of view of one
looking forward to life on a similarly equipped
ranch, it is a warning against any back-to-the-
farm longings.

BETTY MACDONALD

A native of Boulder, Colorado, Betty Mac-
Donald was born Anne Elizabeth Campbell
Bard on March 26, 1908, to Darsie Campbell
and Elsie Tholimar (Sanderson) Bard. (She
did not actually become Betty MacDonald
until her second marriage, in 1942.) The
daughter of a mining engineer, Betty spent her
earliest childhood in some of the more rugged
mining towns of North America—in Mexico,
Idaho, and Montana. When she was nine her
father's work took the family to Seattle, Washington, and in this city Betty lived until shortly
after her marriage. Her parents were determined that their children should grow up to be
healthy, useful, and cultured individuals. Betty
and her sister Mary were therefore given instruction in singing, ballet, piano, French, dramatics, body-building exercises, cooking, shooting—and roof-painting. "If they had only
known what the future held, at least for me,
they could have saved themselves a lot of
money and effort because, for my life on the
chicken ranch, a few hours a day shut in the
icebox contemplating a pan of eggs would
have been incalculably more useful training,"
the author has lamented. Her formal educa-

tion was received at the Roosevelt High School
in Seattle, where she was labeled for posterity
in her class yearbook: "An honor roll student
and true friend." After this accolade from
her classmates she entered the University of
Washington to major in art. But at the age
of seventeen Betty Bard fell in love with "tall,
very handsome" Robert Eugene Heskett, and the
next year, 1927, they were married.

The newlyweds set up housekeeping in
Seattle, where Heskett was a promising
insurance salesman. He confessed, however,
to a long-cherished childhood desire to own a
chicken farm, and the bride thought of her
mother's advice—that a wife's first duty to her
husband is to make him happy in his work
and that she must accept any inconveniences
his job might entail. But, wonders Mrs. Mac-
Donald in her book, "Why does everyone
want to go into the chicken business? . . .Is
it because most of men's lives are shadowed
by the fear of being fired—of not having
enough money to buy food and shelter for their
loved ones—and the chicken business seems
haloed with permanency? . . .There is one
thing about the chicken business: if a hen is
lazy or uncooperative or disagreeable you can
chop off her head and relieve the situation once
and for all."

This particular pair of chicken farmers
found an isolated ranch in the Olympic Mountain area of Washington. By pooling their
wedding gifts of money, their savings, and a
small legacy, they managed to scrape together
fifteen hundred collars—enough to purchase
the forty-acre ranch with its log house, entirely without modern conveniences, a barn,
two small chicken houses, and a woodshed. The
cost was four hundred and fifty dollars; the
remainder of the capital was to be used for
buying and raising chickens. As Mrs. Mac-
Donald describes the ranch in her book, "it
was the little old deserted farm that people
point at from car windows, saying, 'Look at
that picturesque old place!' and then quickly
drive by toward something not quite so picturesque but warmer and nearer to civilization."

The young bride was quite unprepared for
the near-primitive life she was to lead. She
found herself beginning her day at four in
the morning—housekeeping without electricity
or running water, cooking in a menacing mon-
ster which she called "Stove," carpentering,
helping her husband to clear the fields and
plant, and taking care of a young baby. But
perhaps her most distressing task was attending to their main sources of income, whose
primary object in life, as chicks at least, seemed
to be to destroy themselves. She fed them
several times a day, nursed them through their
illnesses, fussed over the temperature of their
living quarters, and performed autopsies. The
vital statistics she kept about them in her
"Death and Food Record Book" listed the
causes of the numerous deaths as Chickenpox,
Eggzema, and Suicide, opinions which her husband Bob Heskett firmly changed to "Not determined." All in all, she could never really
like these chickens. She felt that they were
unappreciative specimens of fowl, who would
permit themselves to be fed and nursed and

yet show no affection in return. Perhaps this was, she reasons, because "I couldn't get close to the hen either physically or spiritually, and by the end of the second spring I hated everything about the chicken but the egg."

A few years after its beginning, however, her chicken ranching experience was over: in 1931 Betty was separated from Robert Eugene Heskett and later they were divorced. She now turned to a business career, beginning as a secretary in March 1931. In July of the same year she became the only woman labor adjuster in the National Recovery Administration, and two and one half years later she began work for the procurement division of the United States Treasury Department. Having contracted tuberculosis she was forced to spend the months between September 1938 and June 1939 in Firland Sanatorium, but in October of the latter year she returned to the business world as supervisor of publicity for the National Youth Administration, a position which she then held until June 1942. Before returning to the status of housewife early in 1943—her second marriage, to Scotsman Donald Chauncey MacDonald, had taken place on April 24, 1942—she had worked for the United States Office of Emergency Management as an assistant purchasing agent and for the West Construction Company as chief clerk. (This, as well as, the other positions was in Seattle.)

The Egg and I, her reminiscences of those early trials, appeared first in serial form in the *Atlantic Monthly*, then were published in book form late in 1945. She inscribed the book to her older sister Mary—"who has always believed that I can do anything that she puts her mind to." Mary's faith in her sister has been justified in this case by the immediate success of the book. Ten days after the book was reviewed the publisher prepared for five printings, totaling sixty-six thousand copies, with a British publication planned later. By August 15, 1946, the number of copies reached the million mark. The story will be filmed by Universal-International Pictures, with Claudette Colbert and Fred MacMurray playing the leads, and with Mrs. MacDonald's daughter, Anne, also appearing.

In Barbara Klaw's opinion (*Weekly Book Review*), Mrs. MacDonald's story "is extremely funny and the picture she paints in crisp good humor of loneliness, endless work, and the overrated rigor of simple life is appealing." The Springfield *Republican* reviewer similarly pronounced the book "entertaining and instructive." Virginia Kirkus '41 compared it to Louise Randall Pierson's '43 *Roughly Speaking*, which she had found "as exhausting as entertaining." "Men readers with soft hearts will grow indignant at her husband —an unbearably efficient fellow—for working his wife so hard," wrote Clifton Fadiman '41, "while female readers, always tougher, will probably feel a certain impatience with the author for sacrificial passivity." Fadiman adds, however, that all readers will enjoy the book because of its "infectious humor and vigor." Regarding Mrs. MacDonald's style of writing,

the *Booklist* critic commented that "the wry humor is a woman's, but the language is masculine, outdoing realistic farm novels in calling a spade a spade, and there were plenty of spades." Frances Alter Boyle of the *Library Journal* wondered, "Could this be the Margaret Halsey '44 of the chicken world?" And the *Commonweal* critic summed up the book by calling it "a good antidote for back-to-the-land romancing."

The author, who is described as a "comely woman," has auburn hair and green eyes, is five feet seven inches tall and weighs one hundred and thirty-five pounds. With her husband and two daughters by her first marriage, Anne Elizabeth and Joan Sydney, she lives in a log house on Puget Sound fronted by a clam beach and salmon fishing grounds; there is a stand of timber for a backdrop. Mrs. MacDonald lists the other members of the household as "a dog that sleeps on the beds and a cat that always jumps in the laps of people who dislike cats." Having inherited a talent for drawing from her mother, she likes to make crayon portraits of children. Her other recreations she gives as gardening, eating, talking, and drinking coffee. Her immediate writing plans include a book of stories for children, and a description of life in a tuberculosis sanatorium. Both daughters, Betty MacDonald says, "have not quite made up their minds whether writing is another glaring fault of their mother's, which they must eventually correct, or whether it is a harmless form of senile diversion."

Reference

MacDonald, B. The Egg and I (1945)

MACDONALD, WILLIAM J(OSIAH)
1874—Mar. 30, 1946 Lawyer; practiced in Illinois, 1916-39; United States Representative from northern Michigan, 1913-15.

Obituary

N Y Times p46 Mr 31 '46

MCGOVERN, FRANCIS EDWARD Jan. 21, 1866—May 17, 1946 Republican Governor of Wisconsin from 1911 to 1915; engaged in a program of constructive legislation which became known as "the Wisconsin Idea"; changed his political allegiance and was Democratic candidate in 1940.

Obituary

N Y Times p19 My 18 '46

MACHADO (HERNANDEZ), ALFREDO (mä-chä'thō ĕr-nän'däth äl-frä'thō) 1889—Aug. 3, 1946 Venezuelan diplomat; Finance Minister of Venezuela, 1941; the republic's representative at the San Francisco United Nations conference, 1945; Ambassador to the United States at the time of his death.

Obituary

N Y Times p21 Ag 5 '46 por

MACK, WALTER S(TAUNTON), JR.
Oct. 19, 1895- Business executive
Address: b. c/o Pepsi-Cola Co., 47-51 33d St., Long Island City, N.Y.; h. 907 5th Ave., New York

Walter S. Mack, Jr., who believes that industry must take an active part in the community life of the country, has brought the Pepsi-Cola Company, of which he is president, into several fields of civic activity. These interests include a *Paintings of the Year* contest, which yearly offers the largest prize purse ever awarded in any American competition in art; three centers for the armed forces

WALTER S. MACK, JR.

during the war; four Junior Clubs for New York's teen-agers; the Voice Record Program through which soldiers could send home spoken messages free of charge; 117 college scholarships, distributed annualy throughout the United States.

The son of Walter Staunton and Alice (Ranger) Mack, Walter Staunton Mack was born on October 19, 1895, in New York City. He attended the city's public schools and was graduated from the De Witt Clinton High School. At the age of eighteen he matriculated at Harvard University, where in 1917 he received a B.A. degree. With the United States entrance into World War I, he enlisted in the Navy and was appointed to Officers' Training School. Graduating third in a class of three hundred, Ensign Mack was assigned to destroyers and transports operating in the Atlantic. Upon his return to civilian life he became a salesman for the textile house of Bedford Mills, Inc. By 1926 the young salesman had risen to the presidency of the company.

In 1931 Mack entered the investment banking house of William B. Nichols and Company as vice-president. About the same time he became vice-president of Equity Corporation

and president of the Phoenix Securities Corporation. As head of the last-named company, Mack, who has always been a pioneer in business methods, reversed the order of things —instead of investing in prosperous concerns, he sought out "anemic" corporations. In payment for "financial blood transfusions" and a daily diet of "hard-headed management," the ailing companies gave Phoenix options on shares. The wisdom of this innovation was shown in the corporation's February 1939 semi-annual report, which listed investments with a book value of $6,481,682, and "noted the information that their market value was $5,976,867 greater."

In 1939 Mack announced that three years before Phoenix had become interested in Loft, Inc., a ten-million-dollar candy and restaurant chain in New York City. Phoenix had loaned Loft $600,000 and put up securities for some $400,000 more in bank loans. "For such help in a crisis," reported *Time,* "Phoenix got options on 300,000 shares of Loft at $1.50, on 200,000 shares at $2. But since Loft had lost money every year since 1934, this did not look like too promising an investment." However, with the aid of the Phoenix loan, the candy concern brought suit against its onetime president, Charles Godfrey Guth, on the grounds that Guth had bought 237,500 shares (91 per cent) of the Pepsi-Cola Company with Loft money. When the courts decided against Guth the Pepsi-Cola Company became the property of Loft, and Walter S. Mack, Jr., president of Phoenix, the security company holding the major share of Loft stock, became president of the Pepsi-Cola Company. The net profits of the soft drink company in 1938 had been almost three million dollars. One year later the company's earnings under Mack's presidency had increased by 76 per cent, and its stock had gone from $70 to $190 a share. Of the thirty-five "cola" drinks on the market in 1946, Pepsi-Cola ranked second in sales.

In his second year with Pepsi-Cola, Mack began the first project of his educational program. This, with little actual publicity from the company itself, has proved to be most effective advertising. In celebration of the company's thirty-fifth anniversary in 1940, the president announced the Walter Mack Job Awards for American Youth. These provided jobs, with salaries of thirteen hundred dollars a year each, in the Pepsi-Cola company for about twelve college graduates who were selected in a competition conducted among seniors in 254 colleges. Mack, in making the announcement, expressed the hope that other companies would be encouraged "to emulate our example." The awards were repeated in 1941, but with America's entrance into the war, were suspended.

Pepsi-Cola's second social service project was the establishment of three centers (in New York City, Washington, D.C., and San Francisco) which provided recreation facilities and other conveniences for seven million or more service men and women. Another honor extended to members of the armed forces was the gala Navy ball for twenty-five hundred officers and their guests at the Ritz-Carlton

Hotel in New York during Navy Week in 1945. The Voice Record Program, also sponsored by Pepsi-Cola, enabled members of the armed forces to "speak" a letter home. More than one million records, reports Pepsi-Cola, were sent out during the war. In announcing the opening of the company's three Junior Clubs in New York City, Mack said, "I'm sure we all have sufficient faith in our young people . . . to feel that if they are given a place they can call their own, with games, dancing, refreshments, and activities they enjoy, so-called 'youth problems' can be effectively met."

Five thousand canvases were submitted by three thousand artists in the *Portrait of America* painting contest which Mack established in 1944. In a *Magazine of Art* article Mack stated that his company did not participate in any way in either preliminary or final selections of the contest. (This was done by Artists for Victory, a wartime organization.) "Our part of the program," he explained, "was simply to award the prizes, pay the expenses, agree to reproduce the pictures, and to distribute at least five hundred thousand free calendars to the public, as well as pay for the resulting exhibitions at the Metropolitan Museum of Art and eight other leading museums around the country." The contest, considered an artistic success, awarded $11,000 in twelve prizes and selected 138 other paintings for exhibition. The plan which had worked so beneficially in 1944 the following year made "a sort of record in its general mistakenness." Artists for Victory had originally represented artists of all schools, but with the end of the war it was controlled primarily by architects and old-time mural decorators who, said *Newsweek,* "have little if any influence on painting." Leading art critics considered the choice of paintings poor, and the exhibition space, method of hanging, and lighting were criticized. The disappointing quality of the pictures on view, said Emily Genauer (New York *World-Telegram*) was not Pepsi-Cola's fault. The company, she pointed out, had spent money lavishly to bring living American art to the people of America. "It was the artists—or the predominant voices in their organization—who made the competition a political football." In 1946 the title of the contest was changed to *Paintings of the Year,* thus eliminating any restrictive connotation the first name might have had; cash prizes and fellowships amounting to $27,750 were awarded to twenty-seven artists.

In June 1945 the company began its largest educational program by awarding "the first of an annual batch of 117 college scholarships. The scholarships will pay tuition, fees, traveling expenses, and twenty-five dollars a month for four years to two students from each state and the District of Columbia, plus nineteen additional Negro students from the South. Winners are chosen through tests given to the candidates elected by their own high-school classmates. A board of eleven, headed by Professor Floyd W. Reeves of the University of Chicago, has full control of the program." This newest expression of Mack's belief that industry owes more to the community than jobs, represents, in the total value in scholarships each year, almost a quarter of a million dollars.

Walter Mack also has his personal list of civic and welfare interests. In 1942 and 1943 ne took over the chairmanship of the New York Police Athletic League's benefit, held in Madison Square Garden. (Funds are raised by the League for playgrounds and other provisions for recreation for the teen-aged in a movement to combat juvenile delinquency.) During the war he acted as vice-chairman on the Industrial Salvage Committee for Greater New York, was honorary and active chairman of various committees of the Red Cross and USO, of the Beverage Division of the National Safety Council, Inc., of the War Production Fund to Conserve Manpower, of the 1943 War Fund Drive, and a member of the Fire Protection Committee of the New York City War Council. During Mayor La Guardia's [40] administration Mack served on the mayor's Local Defense Council and Business Advisory Committee and was an incorporator of New York's City Center of Music and Drama. He is a trustee and treasurer of Temple Emanu-El (New York), a trustee of Mt. Sinai Hospital and was a member of the advisory committee of the New York's World Fair. He is also a director of the Mexican, Cuban, and Queens County Chambers of Commerce and of the China-American Council for Commerce and Industry.

The Pepsi-Cola president has been active in both national and local politics. In 1932 he was an unsuccessful candidate for state senator on the Republican ticket; he has acted as treasurer of the Republican County Committee of New York and in the same capacity has served two different campaign committees on the La Guardia ticket. As a delegate to the convention which nominated Wendell Willkie [40] for President in 1940, he played an important part. On the third ballot, Mack rose and demanded an individual roll call of the ninety-two New York delegates—"a maneuver which immediately swung ten extra votes from New York State to Willkie and turned the tide of the whole convention."

In May 1922 Mack was married to Marion Reckford, granddaughter of the philanthropist Adolph Lewisohn. By this marriage he has two children, Anthony Reckford and Florence Ann. Upon the termination of the marriage by a divorce in 1944, Mack was married to Ruth Juergensen, an American of Norwegian descent, in February 1945. They have one daughter, Alice Ruth. The executive is an inch over six feet tall, weighs 180 pounds, and has blue eyes and black hair. His recreational pursuits are golf, riding, and swimming.

References

American's Young Men, 1938-39
Who's Who in America, 1946-47
Who's Who in American Jewry, 1938-39
Who's Who in Commerce and Industry (1944)

MCKELLAR, K(ENNETH) D(OUGLAS)
Jan. 29, 1869- United States Senator from
Tennessee; lawyer
Address: b. The Capitol, Washington, D.C.;
h. Mayflower Hotel, Washington, D.C.; 1138
Peabody St., Memphis, Tenn.

When Vice-President of the United States
Harry S. Truman '⁴⁵ succeeded to the Presidency
in April 1945, seventy-six-year-old Senator
K. D. McKellar took over the duties of Senate
president pro tem. To "K.D.," as he is known
to the Tennessee constituents who have made
him the dean of the upper chamber, this meant
that to his power and prestige were added:
recognizing speakers, appointing the members
of special and conference committees, interpreting the rules, and generally presiding over
the Senate deliberations. Unlike a Vice-President, McKellar retained all the rights of a
Senator; and in May 1946 he received the
chairmanship of the powerful Appropriations
Committee, of which he had been acting chairman. President Truman had also given Mc-
Kellar the unprecedented privilege of sitting
in on Cabinet meetings.

The son of Caroline (Howard) and James
Daniel White McKellar, Kenneth Douglas Mc-
Kellar comes of "an educated and moderately
well-to-do rural Alabama clan." According to
Don Taylor and Lynne Brannen (in *Liberty*),
his father was a country attorney and farmer
who had served in the Confederate Army.
Kenneth was born in Richmond, Dallas County,
Alabama, on January 29, 1869, less than four
years after the Civil War, and grew up in the
impoverished postbellum South. He worked his
way through the University of Alabama in
three years by clerking in a store, teaching
school, and farming. In 1891 McKellar was
graduated at the head of his class, *magna cum
laude*, with both a B.A. and M.A. Taylor
and Brannen write that the owner of a large
store where the youth worked during the summer offered to give him a half-interest, worth
the then impressive sum of three thousand dollars a year, but McKellar went back to the
university to study law. He emerged with his
LL.B. in 1892, six hundred dollars in debt to
his brothers. (One of those brothers is now
postmaster of Memphis; another served the
Government as Senator McKellar's secretary
and clerk on the Post Offices and Post Roads
Committee until his death.)

The twenty-three-year-old lawyer settled in
the growing city of Memphis, Tennessee, where
he went into practice with Colonel William H.
Carroll. In nineteen years of law practice, his
friends say he accumulated $300,000. He was
active in Democratic politics, and for several
years served as chairman of the Tenth Congressional District Democratic Committee. In
1904 he was elected a Presidential elector, and
cast his ceremonial ballot against Theodore
Roosevelt. Four years later McKellar was a
delegate to the Democratic National Convention
which again and unanimously nominated William Jennings Bryan. In 1911 the lawyer won
election to fill the unexpired term of General
George W. Gordon, Shelby County Representative in the Sixty-second Congress. One of

McKellar's first speeches was in support of the
radical idea that the Federal Government should
help the states to construct highways. (McKellar had had personal experience with this lack
when going East: his new Packard had to be
shipped by rail, as there were no roads from
Memphis.) Later the Tennessean helped to
win a very large appropriation recommendation
from President Wilson for the purpose.

McKellar was a faithful supporter of Woodrow Wilson's Jeffersonian liberalism. As a
Representative, he worked for the Sixteenth and
Seventeenth Amendments, providing for the income tax and for direct election of Senators
(formerly elected by the State legislatures).
He helped pass the Federal Reserve Act, as well
as the Act establishing the Department of Labor
with a Secretary of Cabinet rank, and other
Administration measures. With the help of
political boss Ed Crump, he was re-elected in
1913 and 1915. Then, in the first popular election of Senators, Representative McKellar ran
successfully against Governor Ben W. Hooper.

Entering the Senate at the beginning of 1917,
McKellar began several decades of uninterrupted service which made him eventually the
most powerful figure in the chamber. Rising by
seniority, by 1945 he was chairman of the
politically important Committee on Post Offices
and Post Roads, acting chairman of Appropriations (because of the long illness of Chairman
Carter Glass '⁴¹), second-ranking majority member of Civil Service, in line for the chairmanship of the all-powerful Rules Committee, and
an important figure on the Byrd '⁴¹ Joint Committee on Reduction of Nonessential Federal
Expenditures. His other assignments included
the Senate and Joint Library Committees and
the Washington-Lincoln Memorial Commission;
and he had recently applied, without success,
for a seat on the Foreign Affairs Committee.
Upon Glass's death, Acting Chairman McKellar became chairman of the Appropriations
Committee, and his Post Offices and Post Roads
chairmanship went instead to Senator Dennis
Chavez '⁴⁶.

According to Crump, "Senator McKellar
probably has more personal friends in his
State than any other Senator has. He answers telephone calls promptly; he responds
to every telegram within the hour and in most
cases earlier. He answers his mail every day
and follows up his answers. He is courteous
and polite to every man and woman who visits
Washington from Tennessee. Therefore, no
one can beat him." Others add that McKellar
does innumerable political favors for his constituents, that he is expert at obtaining appropriations for dams, bridges, post offices, and
other public works, and that he gets the very
most out of the patronage (appointment and
bestowal power) accruing to him. It is frequently said, in fact, that the Senator is a
"patronage-grabber": *Time* calls him the premier spoilsman of the Senate. "Patronage has
been the worst asset I ever had," McKellar re-
torts. "My colleagues must be a very weak
lot of Senators if they have not any more
patronage than I have." According to a *Saturday Evening Post* article by Hugh Morrow,
McKellar has also "religiously practiced the

quaint custom of logrolling with such skill that he has led the entire Senate in an about-face when he changed his mind about a piece of legislation in which he was interested personally."

Appointed to the Military Affairs Committee in his first Senatorial term, McKellar was a co-author of much of the country's World War I legislation. Before passage of the Eighteenth Amendment, he had proposed prohibition amendments to the army reorganization and espionage bills; he introduced bills to prevent profiteering, and interested himself in postal, food, and agricultural questions. The Tennesseean was an ardent supporter of the League of Nations, opposed all proposals to cancel war debts, and strongly favored veterans' benefits and the retention of a navy equal to that of Great Britain. Contrariwise, in 1921 he urged reduction of the Regular Army. One of his minor bills would have required all aliens to learn the English language within five years of landing in the United States. Among the liberal measures backed by McKellar was woman suffrage; he claims to have personally persuaded the Tennessee Legislature to ratify the Twentieth Amendment. He opposed intervention in Nicaragua, although in favor of the Nicaraguan canal treaty of 1916.

McKellar was a member of the minority during the terms of Presidents Harding, Coolidge, and Hoover [42], from 1920 through 1932. He repeatedly charged that Secretary of the Treasury Andrew Mellon was ineligible for that office because of his business connections; he introduced bills to control campaign contributions and expenditures; he took an energetic part in investigations, attacked the war debt settlements, filibustered against the Muscle Shoals bill and the ship subsidy bill, but sought to encourage the use of American vessels by tariff reductions. He was for ratification of the Four Power Treaty of 1922 with Great Britain, France, and Japan, he supported the McNary-Haugen farm relief bill and other farm measures, and was active for cutting postal rates. In 1928 he opposed the flexible provisions of the tariff, and assailed the limitation of armaments; in 1931 he attacked the Hoover moratorium, advocated repeal of the Hawley-Smoot tariff, and suggested a plan for reciprocal reductions. He also attacked the Reconstruction Finance Corporation as a pork-barrel project.

Sixty-two-year-old "K. D." advocated the nomination of Governor Franklin D. Roosevelt for President as early as 1931; and when the Democrats finally returned to national power in January 1933, his seniority made him a leader of the Senate. Although the new President did not please McKellar by proposing to put postmasters under civil service and was prepared to repeal his cherished prohibition, McKellar was a thoroughgoing Administration man until about 1940, and continued to campaign for Roosevelt in each election. He defended the Roosevelt economic program, favored recognizing the Soviet Union, and introduced the McKellar-Black [41] bill bringing air mail carriers and their subsidiaries under the jurisdiction of the Interstate Commerce

K. D. MCKELLAR

Commission and the Department of Commerce. He was in favor of the wages and hours legislation and the other important New Deal acts, including the much-criticized 1937 plan for enlarging the Supreme Court to liberalize it. On the other hand, he continued his effort to remove postal employees from civil service, claiming that "a public servant will do a better job when he knows that any incompetency may result in his party's defeat at the polls and the loss of his own job."

McKellar is perhaps best known for his connection with the Tennessee Valley Authority, the huge and hugely successful Government corporation which controls floods, develops navigation, and manufactures fertilizer and cheap electric power for the people of the Valley, which includes parts of seven States. While a Representative he had sponsored the construction of Wilson Dam at Muscle Shoals, Alabama, the first of the big power dam developments on the Tennessee River, and he has said, "I've spent the best years of my life working my fingers off for TVA." President Roosevelt's request that Senator George Norris introduce the bill authorizing TVA was said to have been one of McKellar's greatest disappointments. Throughout the long struggle for the experiment, he won most of its appropriations, going farther than the board chairman had asked. But since 1941 he has become known as an enemy of TVA. Every year has seen "McKellar's spring offensive"—his recurrent "ripper bill" to abolish TVA's revolving fund, forcing the corporation to turn its profits into the Treasury and come to Congress for all needed moneys. This measure, and its perennial companion bill to require Senate confirmation of all except a few Government employees earning more than $4,500 a year, passed the Senate in 1944 and lost in the House, to an almost universal sigh of relief from both

MCKELLAR, K. D.—*Continued*

parties, all civic groups, and the unanimous Valley residents.

Observers generally date McKellar's "feud" with TVA chairman David Lilienthal [44] from October 1941, when a dam site was chosen over his protests; but Morrow suggests that it began earlier, when the Tennesseean was pushing legislation for four of the present dams, and Lilienthal favored waiting for public demand before increasing facilities. When Lilienthal (who had headed the State Department committee which worked out the Government policy on international control of atomic energy) was mentioned in October 1946 for appointment to the new Atomic Energy Commission, McKellar said, "I will do everything I can to see that he is rejected."

The Southerner was to disagree with the liberal Democratic Administration on another issue in the latter part of "FDR's" Administration. The New Deal program of equal rights and opportunities for "the forgotten man" struck home when it was applied to Negroes, victims of lynchings, and citizens disfranchised by the poll-tax and/or intimidation. Kenneth McKellar helped defeat such measures with his vote, his fiery invective, his expertness at parliamentary maneuver, his personal influence, and his willingness to filibuster.

As president of the Senate, McKellar ruled for the anti-FEPC filibusterers on technicalities from which Majority Leader Barkley filed an appeal. Other points of disagreement with his party's program were: his vote for immediate removal of price controls from all farm products and for restoring 1941 price markups, one of the items most severely criticized by President Truman in his veto; his support of the Case [46] labor disputes bill of January 1946; and his leaving the presiding officer's chair in February to lead the fight to halve the Civilian Production Administration's funds. McKellar was one of the lower Mississippi Valley Congressmen who persuaded the President to reconsider his curtailment of flood control and river-and-harbor work for economy and because of the shortage of materials—they challenged his right to stop a project for which the money had already been appropriated. McKellar was also one of the committee chairmen who opposed the La Follette-Monroney Congressional Reorganization bill, objecting particularly to the nonpatronage system of appointing Congressional clerks and other nontechnical personnel.

On one occasion in 1943, when opponents of an anti-poll tax bill were staying away from the Senate to prevent a quorum, majority leader Alben Barkley [41] had a sergeant-at-arms bring McKellar to the chamber. This caused a breach between the two old friends which was not healed until Barkley's short-lived but dramatic "revolt" against the Administration in February 1944. McKellar led the successful 1942 fight to abolish the NYA and CCC—a dispute which resolved into a tug of war between the Byrd Economy Committee and the Truman War Investigating Committee, for the defense. The next year McKellar helped block

nomination of NYA head Aubrey Williams [40] as Rural Electrification Administrator. McKellar also introduced a bill requiring all agency surpluses to be returned to the Treasury immediately, not impounded nor reallocated by the Bureau of the Budget—a proposal attacked as discouraging all economy, and tending to increase spending to the limit appropriated.

In foreign affairs "K. D." was an interventionist and an internationalist. In September 1941 he advocated outright repeal of the Neutrality Act. A consistent supporter of the League of Nations, he urged the Senate not to repeat its earlier mistake by staying out of the United Nations organization. At the same time he insisted that the United States must maintain the largest navy in the world, and in October 1943 said, "our allies as well as our defeated enemies should put in our hands such naval and air bases and make such agreements for adjoining land, sea, and air routes as will make our aid in keeping world peace effective." Specifically, he meant all Pacific islands formerly mandated to the Japanese, and all islands west of the Galapagos. "Thus far," as one commentator puts it, "he has achieved only angry editorials in Argentina, anguished and hasty action by Ecuador to prevent disposal of any of her islands, and a ribbing from London." To this, the Senator calmly answered, "This is no time to be quarreling with our allies."

Youthful for a man of his age, the president of the Senate continues to raise his "foghorn" voice in spirited debate. He "works as hard as any other Senator," despite an occasional physical weakness, and his temper and command of invective are famous. In his usual formal morning attire—frock coat, pin-striped trousers, white-edged waistcoat, and black bow tie—and with his more or less flowing hair, McKellar looks strikingly like a cartoonist's idea of a typical Southern Senator. He has never married—"a hundred and one women turned me down," he says. A Presbyterian, he neither drinks nor smokes, boasts that he has never had time for a hobby, but enjoys reading history, Shakespeare, and the Bible. At the end of his seventy-hour work week, says Morrow, McKellar likes a Saturday afternoon "double-feature dose of horse opera and the weekly chapter of cliff-hanger"; his favorite stars are reportedly Roy Rogers, Gary Cooper [41], and the long-retired "It Girl," Clara Bow. McKellar has been awarded three honorary degrees, by the University of Alabama, Tusculum College, and Lincoln Memorial University. He is a member of Delta Kappa Epsilon, is a thirty-second-degree Mason (Shriner) and an Odd Fellow, and has written a 625-page book, *Tennessee Senators*.

References

Liberty 22:17+ Je 23 '45 por
Life 20:98 Mr 11 '46 por
N Y Herald Tribune p1+ Ap 22 '45 por
PM p8 O 9 '45 por; p5 Jl 28 '46
Sat Eve Post 217:23+ Je 2 '45 por
Congressional Directory (2d ed., 1945)

National Cyclopædia of American Biography, Current vol C p427
Who's Who in America, 1946-47
Who's Who in the Nation's Capital, 1938-39

MACLENNAN, (JOHN) HUGH Mar. 20, 1907- Canadian novelist

Address: b. c/o Duell, Sloan & Pearce, 270 Madison Ave., New York; h. 1178 Mountain St., Montreal, Canada

Hugh MacLennan was awarded the Governor General's Literary Award in 1945 by the Canadian Authors' Association for his novel, *Two Solitudes*. Dealing with the essentially Canadian problem of the disunity between French and British thinking in Canada, this novel was praised by American critics as a real contribution to an understanding of the author's country. J. Donald Adams wrote in the New York *Times* that he believed Canada had found in MacLennan "a novelist of great potentialities."

John Hugh MacLennan was born at Cape Breton, Nova Scotia, on March 20, 1907, the son of the late Samuel J. and Katherine (Mac-Quarrie) MacLennan. They moved with seven-year-old Hugh at the outbreak of World War I to Halifax, where, when he was ten, two ships, one loaded with TNT, collided in Halifax Harbor with a consequent terrific explosion that destroyed a tenth of the city and killed nearly three thousand people. MacLennan attended Halifax Academy, and Dalhousie University granted him a B.A. degree in 1929. Following his graduation he was named a Rhodes Scholar representing Canada at large and studied at Oriel College, Oxford University, where he read "Classical Mods. and Greats," his particular interest then, as now, being history. He received a B.A. degree in 1932, and an M.A. in 1935. During his time at Oxford, MacLennan traveled all over Europe. "By the time I was ready to come home," he writes, "I knew Germany and Italy more intimately than any part of Canada west of the Maritime Provinces. Since then I have traveled over most of the United States and gone east as far as Moscow."

In 1935 MacLennan returned to America, where he had been granted a fellowship in the Princeton Graduate School. In this most academic year of 1935 he garnered another M.A. and his Ph.D. degree from Princeton for a thesis, *Oxyrhynchus* ("God forbid that you should have to read it!"). A study of a town in Roman Egypt, based entirely on more than five thousand papyri found on the site, "it was an attempt to examine the decline of the Roman social and economic system in the provinces through the large end of the telescope, and as such succeeded to some extent. . . .It often gives me shivers," he has said, "to remember the evidence and to compare it with what one sees today." Since leaving Princeton the author has taught classics and history at Lower Canada College, Montreal.

HUGH MACLENNAN

For his first novel, *Barometer Rising*, published in 1941, MacLennan drew on his own memories of the Halifax explosion. This story of the effect of the catastrophe on the life of a deserter in World War I was called by the New York *Herald Tribune* "a first novel of unusual quality, essentially a novel of inner drama." The New York *Times* praised the author: "Mr. MacLennan is a young man but, except perhaps in one instance, the book is distinguished by maturity of thought, not invariably found in writers of his years."

Two Solitudes, a study of the conflict between French-Canadian and British ideas and ideals, and with a title derived from Rainer Maria Rilke, was published in 1945. Written on a Guggenheim fellowship, it was a selection of the Canadian Book-of-the-Month Club, was received with critical acclaim, and has sold nearly seventy-five thousand copies. It has been translated into French for the Montreal market, and is to be translated into Swedish, Dutch, and Spanish. *Two Solitudes* was appraised by Leo Kennedy in the Chicago *Sun Book Week* as "a clean-cut novel of great warmth and skill, peopled with flesh-and-blood characters whose personal lives and problems are skeined with the racial and religious life and problems of their homeland, in a way perhaps unparalleled anywhere else in the world."

The whole position of a writer in Canada is a peculiar one, MacLennan himself has written, "owing to what may be a time lag in social development between this country and the United States, and what may also be (and I hope it is) a difference much deeper than most Americans suspect. Anyway, this makes the task of a Canadian who writes in large part for an American audience somewhat difficult. Americans not only don't know our frame of social reference, they are apt to dismiss Canadian social values as old-fashioned. Only time

MACLENNAN, HUGH—*Continued*

will tell whether Canada is a real social entity, or merely a reflection of what the United States used to be forty years ago." In 1946 the author was working on a third novel, which he says depends more directly on character than did the other two, and he hopes "will cut deeper." Its scene is laid both in Canada and the United States.

Hugh MacLennan is a Presbyterian, but he lists no political affiliation. "Party and political labels mean nothing," he says, "unless one is a die-hard conservative, a fascist, or a Communist, and I am none of these." He was married to Dorothy Duncan on June 22, 1936. (Mrs. MacLennan, who is American-born, has published four books since 1939 including *Blue-nose; a Portrait of Nova Scotia* and *Here's to Canada!*) The MacLennans live in Montreal and have a summer place at North Hatley in the Province of Quebec. As a youth the novelist played a good deal of Rugby football, basketball, and hockey. He is an expert tennis player; he was champion of the Maritime Provinces from 1929 to 1931, and played tennis for Oxford against Cambridge in 1931 and 1932. Chess, walking, and boating are his other recreations.

References

Book-of-the-Month Club N p14 F '45
   por
Pub W 140:1843 N 10 '41 por

MACMITCHELL (THOMAS) LESLIE
Sept. 26, 1920- Track athlete

Address: h. 1521 Unionport Rd., New York

Leslie MacMitchell, in 1940 a nineteen-year-old New York University track star, was then being talked about as the greatest potential mile runner the world had ever seen. Quentin Reynolds predicted: "One day he'll be hailed as the greatest runner of all time; the only man ever to accomplish that Miracle Mile, running the distance in four minutes flat. . . .No one will do it until our boy Leslie MacMitchell reaches his peak. . . .Give MacMitchell another two years." But two years later MacMitchell, having won most of the big mile races in the 1942 indoor season, was building up a creditable record for himself as a lieutenant in the United States Navy. Leslie MacMitchell came back to the track in 1946, a civilian again, hoping to make good the predictions of his coaches, track experts, and sports writers, who were expecting him to set new records for the mile.

Thomas Leslie MacMitchell is a city-bred athlete. He was born in midtown Manhattan on September 26, 1920, only child of Thomas Lesley MacMitchell, Scotchman, and the former Mary Thom. Stricken with diphtheria when he was seven years old, Leslie spent four months in bed, then had to learn to walk all over again. Stanley Frank writes in *Collier's* that when the boy was finally able to walk in the streets, "the neighbors' children wouldn't play with him." Said he . . . couldn't run fast enough to be a good guy in cops and robbers. Now the same brats pay to see their old chum run." (The fact that he had to learn to walk twice puts MacMitchell in a class with almost every great miler in the recent history of the sport. Glenn Cunningham, Bonthron, San Romani, Mangan, and Venzke all suffered crippling accidents when they were young.) When Leslie was nine years old his father died, and, to support her son, Mary MacMitchell became housekeeper for a doctor.

When he was fourteen years old, in the summer of 1935 Leslie won several 100-yard races at Camp Pequot, in New York. After he returned to Manhattan's George Washington High School in the fall, a friend urged him to try for the track team. As Stanley Frank told it: "Presently Tommy Greenwald [the high school coach] was experiencing that tremendous bang which visits a coach upon seeing a natural athlete for the first time." While at high school the young runner won the national interscholastic 1000-yard and cross-country championships, but he was defeated six times in the mile. Coach Greenwald had urged him to race cross-country to improve his stamina, but he did not take the coach's advice until 1937 when he returned from a summer at camp twenty pounds over his best running weight. He took to the hills to remove the excess poundage, and discovered he could run three to five miles with ease. After that he was never defeated in a cross-country race, setting the national record for the event. In 1937 he won the mile at the Stuyvesant meet, and thereafter he was invincible among schoolboys. New York University's coach Emil Von Elling later said, "Cross-country made MacMitchell what he is today." Von Elling pointed out that the punishing stints over hilly country had made MacMitchell "strong enough to bear down for a long stretch without losing the sharp edge of his speed."

When MacMitchell entered New York University in 1938, record-holder Glenn Cunningham had already named him the mile king of the future. In his first big-time race, the Wanamaker Mile in Madison Square Garden in February 1940, MacMitchell made a poor showing, while Chuck Fenske won in 4:07.4, equaling Glenn Cunningham's record. The next year, on the same Garden track, in the famous Baxter mile, MacMitchell raced past Chuck Fenske to clock 4:07.4 himself. What excited track experts was the fact that winner MacMitchell was only twenty years old. Cunningham never hit 4:07.4 until he was twenty-eight; milers usually do not give top performances until they are about twenty-five. The N.Y.U. youth, it was predicted, might be the man to run the legendary four-minute mile. In March 1942, six hundred sports authorities voted MacMitchell the highest award in amateur athletics, the James E. Sullivan Memorial trophy. Twenty-one-year-old Les MacMitchell was the youngest athlete and the first college undergraduate ever to win the trophy, which in former years had been given to such famed athletes as Bobby Jones, Cunningham, and Don Budge.

In 1942, his last indoor season before he joined the Navy, MacMitchell won nineteen mile competitions in a row, including the Metropolitan A.A.U. mile (4:13.3), the Wanamaker mile (4:11.3), the Hunter mile (4:11.8), the Baxter mile (4:09.8), the ICAAAA mile (4:13.7), and the Columbian mile (4:08.0). MacMitchell lost one major race, however, his twentieth of the season, in the National A.A.U. championships, when Gilbert Dodds shot ahead of him to win in 4:08.7. Never a pace-setter, MacMitchell had let Dodds take the lead, and had discovered in the final quarter that he could not overtake him. In two subsequent races MacMitchell left Dodds several yards behind him.

MacMitchell's "miler's heart" caused Navy doctors twice to reject him for military service. Like all great milers, he has an unusually slow heartbeat, which makes it possible for him to expend tremendous energy and then to recuperate quickly. The average heart beats seventy-two times a minute, whereas MacMitchell's count is 38 to 43. (Other famous distance runners have had similarly low pulse counts, e.g., Glenn Cunningham's 49, Gunder Hägg's 46, and Paavo Nurmi's 45.) Finally convinced that his unusual heart was sound, the Navy accepted MacMitchell when he was graduated from N.Y.U. in June 1942. He attended Northwestern V-7 school, and entered service in July 1942. For three years a deck officer on the Navy cruisers *Houston* and *Philadelphia,* MacMitchell earned ribbons for the American, the European-African, and the Asiatic-Pacific theaters, and the Philippine Liberation, a citation from Admiral Halsey, and five battle stars. With the dream of running that four-minute mile, Lieutenant MacMitchell kept in condition in strange ways. He ran on the steel forecastle decks of ships, on the wingwall surfaces of drydocks in the South Pacific, on coral islands and Hawaiian beaches, and on Italian breakwaters. His spiked racing shoes were with his gear when he participated in the North African invasion, the Sicilian and Salerno invasions, and in South Pacific campaigns.

When he was discharged from the Navy in September 1945, he trained for his comeback by running forty miles a week in Van Cortlandt Park. In the 1946 indoor season he won seven mile races in a row, with a better clocking each time he ran. His slowest was the Wanamaker mile when, with no one willing to be pacemaker, MacMitchell took the lead, to amble to the tape in 4:19. MacMitchell explained, "I'd rather not blast out a fast mile yet." He did not need to. With little competition he won all the big mile events of the season, setting his best time 4:12.3, in the Baxter mile on February 16. A week later he won the National A.A.U. mile championship, the one title he had failed to take in 1942. At the end of his first indoor track season after three years in military service, Leslie MacMitchell was still the "unquestioned mile king of the country." In February 1946, Arthur Daley wrote in his New York *Times* column: "The era of the fast miles is back to stay, and the modest, self-effacing MacMitchell is just the lad to fashion them. Welcome home, Leslie."

Without fast competition MacMitchell seldom sets a good clocking. He runs a race to win, with his eye "on the tape, not the watch."

LESLIE MACMITCHELL

"It takes the incentive of competition to make Leslie really exert himself," coach Von Elling has commented. Letting his rivals determine the pace, MacMitchell depends on his finishing kick and stamina to carry him across the finish line a winner. George Trevor, track writer for the New York *Sun,* has written: "What he must cultivate is the ability to sustain a stiffer pace over the first three quarters of a mile race. That's the key to a four-minute-flat clocking." The twenty-five-year-old MacMitchell in 1946 is confident that he will cut the mile time to a new low. To Jesse Abramson of the New York *Herald Tribune* he has remarked: "In 1942 I thought a 4:04 mile would satisfy me, but the Swedes have changed things, haven't they?" (Gunder Hägg, now no longer an amateur, ran the mile in a 1945 outdoor meet in Sweden in 4:01.4 The fastest indoor mile to date was set by Gilbert Dodds in Chicago, 1944, at 4:06.4). At the end of June 1946 he was defeated by Lennart Strand, the Swedish runner, in a fifteen-hundred meter race. Strand's time was 3:54.5, the equivalent of a 4:12 mile. MacMitchell was thirty yards behind Strand at the finish.

"MacMitchell looks smooth only when he is driving on his toes," Von Elling has said. "At cruising speeds, so to speak, Leslie gives the impression of crudeness. His heavy shoulders make him appear to be lumbering. He hasn't the light feather duster stride of a Hägg, a Hansenne [46], or a Lovelock." "Loping Leslie," or "the Bronx Express," as he has been dubbed by sportswriters, stands five feet eleven inches tall, weighs about 158 pounds, and takes a running stride of six feet six inches. The good-looking, black-haired runner maintained an above-90 scholastic record at New York University, majoring in physical and health education. He plans to teach, after taking a Master's degree; in the spring of 1946 he is an assistant to the registrar at New York Uni-

MACMITCHELL, LESLIE—*Continued*

versity. He was married in his first year in the Navy to Mary Lee, an N.Y.U. alumna. Both are active members of the Presbyterian Church—MacMitchell was a deacon at the Fourth Presbyterian Church, in Manhattan, before he entered the service. When he is not running, MacMitchell swims and boats and likes to watch baseball and football. He also enjoys taking motion pictures.

References

Collier's 105:32+ Ap 27 '40 por; 107-19+ Je 7 '41 por
N Y Herald Tribune p28 Ap 19 '45 por
N Y Times p17 D 23 '46

MCNEIL, HECTOR Mar. 10, 1910- British Government official

Address: b. The Foreign Office, London; h. 4, The Croft, Primrose Gardens, London

Hector McNeil, a thirty-six-year-old Scotsman from Glasgow, became Minister of State of Great Britain at the beginning of October 1946. He succeeded Philip Noel-Baker ''', for whom he had substituted as leader of the British delegation to the United Nations Economic and Social Council meeting at New York in June. During the August session of the Paris Peace Conference, McNeil was prominent as an observer on the staff of Sir Harold Alexander, who was then deputizing for Attlee as chief of the British mission. The reorganization of the British Cabinet brought McNeil out of his position as understudy to the two senior Ministers and placed him in a rank second only to Bevin's in the administration of Britain's relations with foreign countries.

The second child of a family of seven, Hector McNeil was born on March 10, 1910, in the village of Garelochhead in Dumbartonshire, Scotland, to Donald McNeil, a shipwright, and his wife, Margaret. Early showing evidence of a talent for politics, even as a schoolboy McNeil astonished his teachers at the Woodside School in Glasgow by entering into lengthy and knowledgeable political arguments with them. At Glasgow University, McNeil in the beginning vacillated between studying for a political career and studying for the Presbyterian ministry. (It is a Scottish tradition that the clever boy of a family enter the church.) The death of his father in 1929 finally determined his choice, for the widowed Mrs. McNeil received a pension of only $125 a year from her husband's firm. "That," *Time* quotes her son as saying, "was when I turned to socialism."

The young Scotsman attained a certain undergraduate glory as a debater, and in 1931-32 toured Newfoundland, Canada, and the United States as a member of the British universities' debating team. After being graduated from college, he worked on a free-lance basis for the Allied (now Kemsley) Press of Glasgow, until he joined the staff of the Scottish *Daily Express* as a "leg-man" in 1934. At first, McNeil covered only general news, but he tended more and more to specialize in labor, industrial, and political articles. Once the news editor of his paper plucked him out of a union meeting to report a murder in Fifeshire, where a man had "clouted his uncle with an ax and taken to the hills." McNeil, it is said, is still "modestly proud of the story he telephoned his newspaper." In 1938 McNeil was transferred to the *Express* London office as an editorial writer, but returned to Glasgow soon afterward to take over the night news editorship of his paper, a post which he held until he entered Parliament.

Meanwhile, McNeil's political career had been developing concurrently with his career in journalism. While still a student, the twenty-two-year old debater had been requested by the Glasgow Labor Party to run for the traditionally Conservative ward of Whiteinch in the 1932 municipal elections. Much against his expectations the young socialist won the election and held his district for three years. After losing Whiteinch, he was returned to the Corporation of the City of Glasgow for Springburn ward. In 1936 McNeil was made a bailie, or magistrate, for the city of Glasgow, but, on going to London for his paper two years later, had to resign from his seat on the city council.

McNeil was unsuccessful in his first two attempts to enter Parliament. During the 1935 general election, at the age of twenty-five, he contested Walter Elliot for the Kelvingrove division of Glasgow, but was defeated when a re-count of disputed ballots showed 149 votes more for Elliot. Several months later, in January 1936, the Glasgow Laborite opposed Malcolm MacDonald, Randolph Churchill, and Dr. Russell Thomas in the by-election for Ross and Cromarty in the North of Scotland. McNeil ran ahead of Churchill and Thomas, but did not defeat MacDonald. Not until 1941 did McNeil reach Westminster—in the by-election of that year he was returned unopposed for the burgh of Greenock. Four years later, in a four-cornered contest between McNeil, Lord Malcolm Douglas-Hamilton, a Liberal, and a Communist, the Scottish Labor member for Greenock was re-elected to Parliament by a majority of eight thousand votes in the general election.

In 1943 McNeil became Parliamentary Private Secretary to Philip Noel-Baker, who was then Parliamentary Secretary to the Minister of War Transport. The Scotsman quickly established a reputation for keen debating, frequently speaking on subjects pertaining to his own country. He did not hesitate to criticize the foreign policy of the Churchill coalition Government, even though it was politically inexpedient and might have harmed his career. When he was promoted to Under Secretary of State for Foreign Affairs after the 1945 election, McNeil had an opportunity to present his own party's foreign policy. Speaking before the Fabian Society in London soon after the election, he said: "The principle of it is that we shall seek to use our prestige, our economic power, and our diplomatic interests to insure not only that freedom of speech, of publication, of assembly, and of election is guaranteed in the countries with which we are in treaty but that these same powers will be used by us to uplift the conditions of the common men and women in every country with which we maintain friendly relations. Our policy is not to press down but to uplift." For some time it was McNeil's duty to interpret and defend the Labor Government's foreign policy in the House of Commons while the senior ministers, Foreign Secretary Bevin and Secretary of State Noel-Baker, were attending U.N. meetings. In various sessions of Parliament between December 1945 and October 1946 the Under Secretary of State discussed Greek, Egyptian, Rumanian, Czechoslovakian, Polish, Bulgarian, and Italian affairs. Of Spain, he said at one time: "Franco represents a thoroughly unpalatable and repugnant regime." On another occasion, McNeil referred to Leon Degrelle, the Belgian fascist leader, as an "obnoxious quisling."

Foreign Minister Bevin sent McNeil to Greece on a "visit of general inquiry" in November 1945. At a time of upheaval, McNeil's presence in Greece was resented, particularly when he could give no definite promise of increased financial aid to the devastated country; the prospect of a British loan, McNeil stated, would depend upon Greece's ability to put "its own house in order first." Concerning the presence of British troops in Greece (which had been criticized in Parliamentary debates), the Under Secretary of State declared that they would be withdrawn as soon as "conditions permit." It is believed that Britain's policy towards Greece was based upon the report brought back to England by McNeil.

Appointed a British alternate delegate to the United Nations organization in January 1945, McNeil in March 1946 was named to represent Britain on the Committee on Refugees and Displaced Persons established by the Economic and Social Council of the U.N., and was unanimously elected its chairman at the opening meeting. Throughout the seven-week life of the committee, dissension prevailed between the Soviet Union and the Western powers over the major issues of financing a new refugee agency to succeed UNRRA and of the forcible repatriation of displaced persons. In the report presented by Chairman McNeil to the Economic and Social Council at New York in June, only one definite recommendation was made: that an international refugee organization be created to assist and resettle exiles. During this visit, McNeil substituted for Philip Noel-Baker as leader of the British delegation, since it was necessary for Noel-Baker to administer the Foreign Office while Ernest Bevin was absent in Paris. Against the opposition of the Soviet Union and the Soviet-influenced countries, McNeil and the American representative, John Winant [41], worked out a financial arrangement for the proposed International Refugee Organization at the closing session of the Economic and Social Council at New York in October. By the terms of this agreement, the United States and Great Britain were to pay three-quarters of the costs of operating the IRO, with the remainder to be provided by the other members of the U.N.

At the Paris Peace Conference in August as a British observer, McNeil was drawn into an argument with Soviet Foreign Minister Molotov [40] about the procedure of voting on treaty recommendations. It was eventually de-

British Official Photo

HECTOR MCNEIL

termined, after a nine-hour, all-night debate, to settle substantive matters by a two-thirds majority (advocated by the Russians) and to settle matters of procedure by a simple majority (recommended by the British and Americans). Later in the session McNeil spiritedly defended the independence of Trieste. "We'll honor our bargain," he declared, "but if the statute is so changed as to impair the conception of a free territory, we will have to reconsider our whole agreement." McNeil emphasized that the solution of the Trieste problem must involve a consideration of "ethnic, economic, and political factors" and warned that change of only one of the three factors would render the compromise unacceptable.

In a shake-up of the Attlee [40] Cabinet at the beginning of October 1946, Hector McNeil was made Minister of State, succeeding Noel-Baker, who became Air Minister. Long groomed for the post under the tutelage of Bevin and Noel-Baker, McNeil would now rank next to the Foreign Secretary in administering Britain's relations with other countries. In his new capacity, the Scotsman joined his former superiors as a member of the British delegation to the United Nations General Assembly meeting in New York at the end of October.

McNeil's vocabulary still shows traces of journalistic vividness. A cut in a Governmental expenditure, for example, provoked him to shout, "A miserable bit of cheese-paring." McNeil's letters to his constituency are often transcribed in shorthand by his wife, the former Sheila Craig, an erstwhile fellow student at Glasgow University, to whom he was married in 1939. Mrs. McNeil has also done the research for many of her husband's speeches. During their engagement, she helped him with the campaign for Ross and Cromarty, where they returned for their honeymoon. The McNeils have one son, Craig Russell.

(Continued next page)

MCNEIL, HECTOR—*Continued*

A tall, sandy-haired, smooth-shaven man who utters dryly humorous remarks with "a rolling Glaswegian burr," McNeil moves about the House of Commons "on the double." McNeil's recreations—aside from boxing, golf, and swimming—are inclined to be sedentary, for he most enjoys intelligent argument and chess.

References

Time 48:30 Ag 19 '46

International Who's Who, 1945-46

Who's Who, 1946

MCREYNOLDS, JAMES CLARK Feb. 3, 1862—Aug. 24, 1946 Associate Justice of the United States Supreme Court from 1914 to 1941; earned a reputation as a "trust buster" while Attorney General in 1913-14; after the death of Associate Justice Pierce Butler in 1939 Justice McReynolds became known as "the lone dissenter" in the Supreme Court, opposing the New Deal and fighting for the "written Constitution."

Obituary

N Y Times p1+ Ag 26 '46 por

MADDY, JOSEPH E(DGAR) Oct. 14, 1891- Musician; educator

Address: b. 303 S. State St., Ann Arbor, Mich.; h. 3122 Geddes Ave., Ann Arbor, Mich.

"To make America genuinely musical, one man without money has done more in the last ten years than all our musical foundations put together." Thus wrote Francis Rufus Bellamy of Dr. Joseph E. Maddy in the *North American Review* for December 1934. Today the founder of the National Music Camp at Interlochen, Michigan, is described as the idol of the three million young people who comprise the hundred thousand school bands and orchestras throughout the United States. Maddy, who is convinced that music must become a part of every American's life, has long been regarded as an important influence in making music a regular part of the school curriculum and in fostering the growth of the American school orchestras. His latest crusade began in 1942 when James C. Petrillo[40] banned student broadcasts from Interlochen. Commentators see the Lea bill, "To Prevent Control of Radio Broadcasting by Coercive Practices," written into law on April 16, 1946, as inspired by Maddy and aimed at Petrillo.

Joseph Edgar (or Joe, as his mother insists and he prefers) Maddy was born on a farm on the outskirts of the town of Wellington, Kansas, on October 14, 1891. His father, William Henry Maddy, had come to Kansas in the early seventies "with a shot-gun under one arm and a violin under the other." There the elder Maddy became a school teacher and was married to Mary Elizabeth Harrington, also a school teacher as well as a pianist and singer. The parents wished their talented children, Joe and Harry, to have a non-professional musical education and hence started the boys on violin duets although little Joe was only five years old.

Soon he was playing as a member of the family quartet. For his formal schooling the youth attended the Sumner County High School in Wellington, but he did not complete the course. Instead, he spent a year at Bethany College in Lindsborg, Kansas (1906-07), and another (1907-08), together with his brother, at the Wichita College of Music and Art. It was while rehearsing with the Wichita College string quartet that the brothers attracted the attention of the manager of the Minneapolis Symphony Orchestra. Projected plans for further study either in New York or Europe were abandoned and the youths joined the orchestra, with which Joe performed as viola and clarinet player from 1910 to 1914. Whereas Harry Maddy has been content to remain a member of the Minneapolis Symphony throughout his career, Joe Maddy even then looked toward other horizons and continued his musical studies, from 1909 to 1911 attending the Minneapolis School of Music and thereafter receiving private instruction from Richard Czerwonky (for five years) and from other teachers.

In 1915 Maddy accepted his first teaching post as director of the Wichita Falls (Texas) College of Music. But he was dissatisfied. "It was too formal, too sedate, too foreign, if you must know," he told an interviewer. "I was sure America had something to offer, so I went down to Chicago to look around." This was in 1917. He found work giving advanced music lessons to several well-known Chicago musicians. In one case he exchanged lessons in orchestration for more study with the violin. But he also needed a steady job; hence, when the Bismarck Garden needed a clarinetist, Maddy became a member of its jazz orchestra. It was this work which had the strongest influence on his subsequent career, he believes: it showed him that there were other approaches to music besides the classic. The young musician remained in Chicago for approximately a year, and was for a while also instructor in wind instruments at the Metropolitan School of Music there.

Then, near the end of 1918 Maddy was appointed supervisor of instrumental music (as distinct from supervisor of music) for the Rochester (New York) public schools, becoming the first to hold such a position in the American public school system. Before he resigned from the Rochester post in 1920, he had introduced into the Rochester schools the first system of class instruction in heterogeneous musical instruments and had secured from George Eastman the fifteen-thousand-dollar student instrument fund which later formed the basis of the endowment for the Eastman School of Music in Rochester. From Rochester Maddy went to Richmond, Indiana. During the next two decades he was to be successively: supervisor of music and director of municipal music in Richmond (1920-24); head of the public school music department of Earlham College in Richmond (1922-24); supervisor of music in the Ann Arbor (Michigan) public schools (1924-27); head of the public school music department of the University School of Music in Ann Arbor (1924-30); professor of public school music in the University of Michigan (1930-38). In 1946 he is professor of radio music instruction at the University of Michigan, a post which he has held since 1938. He has been a guest instructor in the summer sessions of the Chautauqua Summer Schools (1920-21), of the University of Southern California (1922-24), and of Teachers College of Columbia University (1926-28). Since 1928 he has devoted his summers to the National Music Camp at Interlochen, Michigan, of which he is founder, president, and music director.

Although Maddy's unique career of service to music really began in the Richmond school system, it looked for a time as though he might not have a chance to experiment in its liberal atmosphere. Maddy still lacked a high school diploma when he went to Richmond in 1920, while a new State law required certification of all teachers based on high school graduation. But, he discovered, although teachers needed the certificates, superintendents did not. He therefore resigned—as a teacher—and waited. Immediately there were protests, and before long Maddy was appointed an assistant superintendent of Richmond schools. Then, while the legislators rushed to close the loophole, Maddy crammed the equivalent of a four-year high school course in the 1920 summer session at Chautauqua, returned to pass the high school examinations in Richmond, and was awarded the necessary document.

That hurdle leaped, Maddy turned his attention to the possibilities of a student orchestra. At a convention of music supervisors in Missouri in 1921, he had heard with amazement a forty-piece orchestra made up of high school students from Parsons, Kansas—a town of about ten thousand inhabitants—and had learned that this group practiced every day for an hour with full school credit. Why not, he asked himself, as did his colleagues, and went back to Richmond to demand academic credit for orchestral performance. By 1922 he had developed a complete symphony orchestra of seventy pieces, the first full orchestra in any American high school. Then, to show what his players could do, Maddy took them to the next Music Supervisors National Conference at Nashville, Tennessee—on funds raised by the students' sales of their own recordings. "Once more the supervisors of the nation went home with a new determination—to develop complete symphony orchestras in their high schools."

The next big step came in 1926 when the musician-educator "accepted an assignment to attempt to assemble an all-American high school orchestra, designed to demonstrate the value of school orchestras [and the possibility of developing them in the high schools of the United States] at the Music Educators National Conference in Detroit." The task was dismaying, he says, but challenging. It meant finding among high school students the correct number of good players of even the most neglected orchestral instruments; finding boys and girls willing and able to pay their own expenses and to miss a week of school for the sake of practicing music; choosing them on the basis of mail applications, since no funds for auditions were available; making it possible for all of them to play when they arrived in Detroit.

"The only solution," says Maddy, "was to have an orchestra within an orchestra—a very large orchestra for massive effects, with a smaller selective orchestra for delicate effects, permitting all the players to play in the large orchestra and only the best ones in the smaller. So the first National High School Orchestra numbered two hundred and thirty-odd players, from thirty states. . . .The effect was stupendous."

The next year, 1927, the second National High School Orchestra assembled in Dallas, Texas, for the school superintendents' convention, which, in response to the enthusiasm engendered by Maddy's first undertaking, had been organized around the theme of music. The second demonstration was as successful as the first, and the superintendents passed a resolution urging that music be given equal status with the three R's in American schools. "Thereafter the road was comparatively easy, for music was no longer considered a fad or frill." And from the youthful musicians then congregated came the stimulus for the National Music Camp. Into the concluding festivities of the week, relates Maddy, there came without warning "an intangible and suddenly solemn note. . . .The thrill of this intensive week of music was being snatched away—and forever! . . . .There was no response to my appeal that each return to his own school with the glorious achievement of the National Orchestra as an ideal. . . .Then the . . . voice of a young boy: 'Why can't we all get together somewhere for a long time this summer and play all the music we want to play?' What would you have done?" he continues. "Here they were demanding a summer camp for the National High School Orchestra—and demanding it of me! Well, I did it. I promised them I would move heaven and earth to establish a summer camp where they could play to their hearts' content. . . . Those youngsters went home happy. I had to keep my promise."

Maddy has told the story of the growth of the National Music Camp at Interlochen in the *Saturday Evening Post* of August 31, 1940, as well as in literature on the camp. From a hastily built encampment financed with borrowed money on land Maddy and his colleague T. P. Giddings did not own, it developed into a "modern city built in the woods" representing an investment of about $400,000 and accommodating approximately a thousand music enthusiasts—despite recurrent indebtedness, depression, and war. It came in time to be his life work and kept him struggling when any sane man, he notes, would have sought relief in the bankruptcy courts. For, wrote Karl Detzer in the *American Magazine,* "Maddy believes, with evangelical fervor, that music must become a part of every American's life." Its greatest value, Maddy believes, is as a socializing force, teaching teamwork and unselfishness, and as a medium for personal enrichment through self-expression.

Interlochen, "established for the purpose of testing and developing talent in music and related fields," has as its goal the provision of "an ideal environment wherein the arts become

Kaiden-Keystone

JOSEPH E. MADDY

the principal theme in a life situation created to stimulate artistic endeavor and growth of personality." A "work" camp, which in 1945 produced in their entirety Mozart's *Cosi fan Tutte* and an original ballet, *Storybook*, it is designed only for the musically gifted, since they can best profit from its opportunities. The boys and girls live in separate camps, meeting only for group participation in music. There is a junior exploratory division, a more advanced high school division, and a college division affiliated with the University of Michigan. Radio, dramatics, script-writing, art, dance, crafts, photography, physical education, and recreational leadership enhance the program, which is served by one hundred and sixty buildings on a five-hundred-acre tract, an outdoor theater (Interlochen Bowl), workshops, a radio studio, an art gallery, a $40,000 music library, and numerous other facilities. The staff is drawn from leaders in every field and a number of well-known musicians have exchanged their services "for room and board," among them Frederick Stock, Carl Busch, Percy Grainger, Ossip Gabrilowitsch, Howard Hanson, Walter Damrosch.

Orchestral broadcasts from Interlochen first went on the air, with a short commercial contract, in 1930. Permission had been obtained from the International Executive Board of the American Federation of Musicians. Thereafter, for eleven years, the commercial program was replaced by "public service sustaining programs" for which the radio stations received no income. Then, in July of 1942, James C. Petrillo, president of the American Federation of Musicians (A.F. of L.), threatened a strike of all union radio musicians, whose means of livelihood he declared was being impaired, and thereby effectively banned the childrens' concerts from the air. When, in the following autumn, Petrillo imposed a ban on all programs

by nonunion music students, an investigation was begun by the Interstate Commerce Commission. "But when all the shooting was over," wrote *Newsweek*, "there was still no school band or orchestra on the networks." After Maddy had been off the air for two and a half years, Petrillo in February 1945 placed the camp on the "unfair" list, an action which meant that no union member could teach there and retain his union membership; and in January 1946 Maddy was expelled from the union (of which he had been a member for thirty-seven years) because he continued to act as the camp's director. His own campaign, Maddy pointed out, was not to suppress the union, with whose members he said he was in sympathy, but to establish the principle of freedom of the air in the spirit of the other freedoms guaranteed by the Bill of Rights.

Beginning in May 1944 with a measure sponsored by Senator Arthur H. Vandenburg of Michigan, three bills to curb the musicians' union chief were introduced in Congress. By early April 1946 the Lea bill, subtitled "To Prevent Control of Radio Broadcasting by Coercive Practices," had been passed by both Houses and sent to the President for his signature, or veto. Meanwhile, strenuous objection to the measure had arisen among such unions as the American Federation of Radio Artists, the Radio Directors Guild, the American Guild of Musical Artists, Actors Equity, the Screen Actors Guild, and the International Brotherhood of Electrical Workers. Maintaining that the measure's provisions outlawing the employment of "stand-by" musicians and payments beyond first broadcasting rights would seriously interfere with their means of livelihood, they planned to bring strong pressure to bear on President Truman to veto the Lea bill. Criticism of another sort—to the effect that the bill was too narrow in scope—was voiced in editorials in the New York newspapers, specifically in the *Times* on February 8, 1945, and April 11, 1946: "Congress will never do anything to curb Mr. Petrillo until it sees him as a symptom of a larger situation . . . of which his personal dictatorship is merely a part."
time was 3:54.5, the equivalent of a 4:12 mile.

On April 16, 1946, the Lea bill was signed by President Truman without comment. Contrary to Maddy's expectations, however, this did not alter the situation: radio stations continued to observe Petrillo's demands and, pleading full schedules, refused to grant time on the air to Interlochen. Then, in June Petrillo violated the law in order to force a test case to have the Lea act declared unconstitutional, and in December of the year Federal District Judge Walter J. La Buy ruled against United States District Attorney J. Albert Woll, upholding Petrillo in his contention that the act violated the First, Fifth, and Thirteenth Amendments to the Constitution. Woll then planned an appeal to the United States Supreme Court. Maddy meanwhile was considering plans to make Interlochen a year-round college of fine arts, since the camp's facilities could be made habitable in winter. The Interlochen plan, he said, is to gather together persons of like interests so that they may work in their chosen fields free from "the conflicting interests and distractions which characterize many schools," and this "principle of grouping students by interests," he thinks, is one which "may revolutionize our whole educational system when thoroughly understood and appreciated."

Maddy, who received an honorary doctorate of music from the Cincinnati Conservatory of Music in 1930, the year he joined the faculty of the University of Michigan, continued to organize and conduct a National High School Orchestra for the annual meetings of superintendents until that year. He also organized and conducted all-state high school orchestras and bands in more than thirty states, as well as three all-Southern high school, two all-Southern, and two North Central high school orchestras. In 1931 he originated radio instruction in musical performance, broadcasting from the University of Michigan studios, and from 1936 to 1939 conducted nation-wide radio music classes over the NBC network. From 1926 to 1934 he was also organizer and supervisor of the nation-wide school orchestra and band contests. His publications include *Universal Teacher* (1922), *Instrumental Technique* (1926), and *Instrumental Class Teaching* (1928), all with T. P. Giddings, *Radio Music Course*, and other texts, and he has invented an aluminum violin, the quality of which is said to compare favorably with good wooden instruments. He was married to Fay Pettit in 1938, has three children by a previous marriage; he is a Methodist and a Republican. Maddy is gray-haired, brown-eyed, and weighs 165 pounds to his height of five feet eight and a half inches. He is, says Marcia Davenport, essentially a "quiet, rather inarticulate man who has the brainstorms of a true genius."

References

Am Mag 114:46-7 D '32 il por
Cosmopolitan 109:23 S '40 il por
No Am Rev 238:565-7 D '34
Sat Eve Post 213:16 Ag 31 '40 il
Who Is Who in Music, 1941 por
Who's Who in America, 1946-47

MAGNER, THOMAS F(RANCIS) Mar. 8, 1860—Dec. 22, 1945 Former United States Democratic Representative from New York (1889-95); New York State Assembly (1887-88); assistant corporation counsel in Brooklyn (1914-17); partner in the law firm of Magner and Connolly since 1925.

Obituary

N Y Times p18 D 23 '45

MAKIN, NORMAN J(OHN) O(SWALD) (mā'kĭn) Mar. 31, 1889- Australian Ambassador to the United States

Address: b. Australian Embassy, Washington, D.C., h. Carlton Parade, Torrensville, South Australia

The first person to attain the rank of Australian Ambassador to the United States is the Honorable Norman J. O. Makin, former mem-

NORMAN J. O. MAKIN

ber of the Commonwealth Parliament, who assumed his new post in September of 1946. Previously, Australia was represented in Washington by a Legation. Makin, also chief of his country's delegates to the United Nations, served as president of the United Nations Security Council for one month, beginning January 15, 1946. He came to the U.N. conference with experience gained from twenty-five years in the Australian Federal Parliament, two of them as Speaker of the House of Representatives. As Minister for Navy and Munitions, he was an important figure in the Dominion's World War II organization.

Norman John Oswald Makin was born at Petersham, New South Wales, on March 31, 1889, to John Hulme and Elizabeth Makin. He was in his second year when his native colony had its first Labor party Government, and in his twelfth year when New South Wales became a state by joining five other British colonies (Victoria, South Australia, Queensland, Tasmania, and Western Australia) to form the Commonwealth of Australia. The new constitution provided for a government much like that of the United States in regard to types of representation, elections, terminology, judicial review, etc., with the Crown-appointed governor-general in place of an American President; but it was, nevertheless, a cabinet or parliamentary type of government.

Norman Makin's parents, who had emigrated from Lancashire, England, were of the working class. At the age of thirteen the boy was forced to leave the Superior Public School, at Broken Hill, to go to work. His first job was delivering parcels. His next, in a bookstore, gave him an introduction to great books, and he read much of Ruskin, Emerson, and Carlyle. The boy came into contact with Labor politics, also, when he was called as a witness at the trial of a Labor publicist in connection with "industrial upheavals." (Indus-

MAKIN, NORMAN J. O.—*Continued*

trial upheavals were nothing new to the mining town of Broken Hill, which was strongly unionized even for a country which has been called "the working man's paradise.") Active in the Shop Assistants' Union, Makin was its delegate to the local Barrier District Assembly of the Labor Party.

At seventeen, Makin gave up bookselling to become a patternmaker in engineering, a better-paying trade. After moving to Melbourne four years later, he was a regular visitor at the evening sittings of the Federal Parliament. When he returned to that city from South Australia in 1919, it was as a member of the House of Representatives for Hindmarsh—although the Labor Party, which had been divided over the conscription issue in 1916, was badly beaten in that "khaki election" of 1919. Makin has been returned to Parliament by a comfortable majority at each successive election since then, and has one of the longest records of membership in that body.

The member for Hindmarsh served as a member of the Joint Committee on Public Accounts from 1922 to 1926, and as temporary Chairman of Committees from 1923 to 1929. That year he became Speaker of Australia's House of Representatives in the Scullin Government, a post he held until 1932. Before that, for one year (1931) he had been secretary of the Federal Parliamentary Labor Party. In 1935 Makin was selected by the Empire Parliamentary Association to attend King George V's Silver Jubilee celebration in London, from which he went home by way of Russia, Poland, Germany, Belgium, and France. During 1936 he was president of the Labor Party, which he represented at the coronation of George VI in 1937, a visit he topped off by a stay in South Africa. After the outbreak of World War II, in 1940, the Australian labor leader was a member of the Advisory War Council. Within another year, in October of 1941, Laborite John Curtin [41] became Prime Minister. Norman Makin was then given the portfolio of the Ministry of Navy and Munitions, in the first Labor Government since 1932.

"As Minister for the Navy in the most critical period of World War II for Australia," says an official news release, "Mr. Makin played a big part in helping to direct the expansion of Australia's naval forces from a total strength of sixteen ships at the outbreak of the war in 1939 to its present [1946] total of 350 ships in commission. Matching this expansion in naval tonnage has been the growth in personnel from the prewar total of approximately five thousand to well over thirty thousand." As for munitions, the program reached "saturation point" by early 1945, and in a Cabinet reshuffling Makin was given the additional portfolio of aircraft production. As of early 1946, the Australian aircraft industry had delivered more than three thousand planes to the Royal Australian Air Force. In the absence of Dr. Herbert V. Evatt [42] on various overseas missions, Makin was also acting Minister for External Affairs, duties which began almost as soon as his elevation to the Government.

The name of N. J. O. Makin came into the international news in January 1946, when the Australian delegation head was elected to preside over the United Nations Security Council meeting in London, because his country's name headed the alphabetical list. (The United Nations Security Council each month appoints a new chairman, the rotation being determined by the names of the nations.) The other countries and their representatives were the United States (Edward Stettinius [40]), Britain (Ernest Bevin [40]), France (Georges Bidault [45]), the Soviet Union (Andrei Y. Vishinsky [44]), China (Dr. Wellington Koo [41]), and five "non-permanent" members—Mexico, Brazil, Egypt, Poland, and the Netherlands. Besides organizing itself, the first major tasks before the Security Council were to recommend a nominee for the Secretary-Generalship, and to draw up plans for the military force which each nation would be asked to provide. Speaking before the Political and Security Committee of the United Nations General Assembly, Makin questioned the wisdom of limiting the Atomic Energy Commission to members of the Security Council and Canada, and pointed out that if UNO members were to agree to provide "armed forces, assistance, and facilities" to the Security Council, it might become necessary to consider the question of atomic weapons.

Meanwhile, Makin was presiding over the stormy Council sessions at which Iran made charges against the Red Army in Azerbaijan, and the U.S.S.R. similarly accused the British of helping reactionaries in Greece and Indonesia. By February 12, the New York *Times* correspondent James B. Reston reported: "The Security Council has mastered the technique of starting arguments and debating them, but under the rules as they now stand—or the lack of rules—it has much trouble ending them. . . . The President of the Council is put in the position of having to improvise as he goes along. . . . It is almost impossible to apply in all cases the standards of international law, even if the new Court of International Justice were operating. . . . All this leads to a lot of irritable debate. But the general opinion here is that it is merely one of the consequences of the fact that this is the first session of a Council of independent states who are dealing with delicate political questions at a time when the map of the world is being redrawn."

In April 1946 the Australian Government, "recognizing the need for strengthening its representation diplomatically," selected Makin to become Australia's Minister in Washington. The post is regarded as the "most senior appointment in the representation of Australia abroad." At the time, the elevation of the status of the Washington Minister to the rank of Ambassador was being considered; and, a few months later, before he was to undertake his new duties, Makin was made Ambassador. (The United States appointed Robert Butler as its first Ambassador to Australia.) Soon after his arrival in Washington early in September, Ambassador Makin, as his first official act, presented Under Secretary of State William L. Clayton with a check for twenty million dollars. This was to be partial payment of his country's Lend-Lease settlement. The balance, seven million dollars, is to be paid "in the form of real estate needed by United States Embassy and consular offices and in scholarships for United States students studying in Australia." Expressing hope that "American investments in industry would be made in his country and that greatly increased trade between the two nations would ensue," Makin also stated that he favored emigration of United States veterans to Australia. To a question on postwar Pacific naval bases, he replied that he thought the problem "would be settled by conference between the two nations most concerned" and that the settlement "should contain reciprocal rights provisions." Earlier in 1946, at a commemoration of the fourth anniversary in May of the Battle of Coral Sea, which proved a "turning point in the Pacific war and undoubtedly saved Australia," Makin had paid tribute to Australia's American allies to whom his countrymen "give credit for victory." Bilateral air transport agreements were concluded in December between the United States and Australia, and New Zealand.

The Australian Ambassador to the United States resumed his duties as Australia's chief representative to the U.N. in October 1946. In his addresses to the General Assembly in the same year, Ambassador Makin charged that the Soviet Union was attempting to "thwart the will of the clear majority" of the Security Council with its use of the veto, and maintained that the elimination of the veto would not permit "groups of nations to further their own policy" as Russian Foreign Minister Molotov had charged. "In our opinion," Makin asserted, "the United Nations would function not less efficiently, but more efficiently, as an instrument for peaceful international cooperation if the veto were restricted to matters of enforcement action only." The Australian delegation in November submitted a formal resolution asking that the "use of the veto be restricted to cases involving threats to the peace, breaches of the peace and acts of aggression." In addition, Norman J. O. Makin stated that his country favored the United States Baruch atomic control plan and insisted that "no system of veto could be permitted in any international atomic agency," in which organization, every nation "must be bound by all its obligations." He supported the establishment of the U.N. Trusteeship Council which will determine the policies of nations toward their mandated territories, and upheld the principle of disarmament on which program he believed much detailed planning was needed. The chief of the Australian delegation had opposed the selection of New York City as the permanent site for the U.N. headquarters, his group favoring San Francisco.

"A graying, professorial man," slightly built, Norman Makin has a rather stern manner and a rhetorical style of speaking. He has been married to the former Ruby Florence Jennings since 1912, and has two sons. Makin is a prominent Methodist lay preacher and a strict teetotaler, drinking fruit juice while his guests at official dinners are offered wine and liquor. The Ambassador is the author of a treatise entitled *A Progressive Democracy*.

References

N Y Herald Tribune II p3 F 10 '46
N Y Sun p18 Ja 31 '46
Who's Who, 1946

MANKIN, HELEN DOUGLAS (măn'-kĭn) Sept. 11, 1896- United States Representative from Georgia; lawyer
Address: b. House Office Bldg., Washington, D.C.; First National Bank Bldg., Atlanta, Ga.

Congresswoman Helen Douglas Mankin, Democrat, was chosen at a special Georgia election in February 1946. A lawyer, she is one of the few women elected to Congress from Southern States who are not widows of Congressmen. Mrs. Mankin is the tenth Representative of her sex in the Seventy-ninth Congress. She was greeted with much enthusiasm by the liberal Democratic wing and viewed with disfavor by Representative Rankin '44, on the basis of her ten-year record as a member of the Georgia Assembly.

Representative Mankin was born Helen Douglas in Atlanta, Georgia, on September 11, 1896. As far as is known, she is not related to her fellow-Congressman Helen Gahagan Douglas of California and Emily Taft Douglas of Illinois, who "showed discernment by acquiring their Douglas through marriage." Her parents, Hamilton Douglas, Sr., a Virginian, and Corinne (Williams) Douglas, an Iowan, were schoolteachers who studied law together at the University of Michigan. "There were five good reasons why my mother did not practice," says Mrs. Mankin. "I was one of them." But Mrs. Douglas did organize the first department of commercial studies in the Atlanta high school for girls, while her husband became president of the Board of Education and founder and dean of the Atlanta Law School. Their home was a center of intellectual life, and their visitors included Jane Addams, William Howard Taft, and Charles W. Eliot, president of Harvard University. Mrs. Mankin's great-grandmother had been a member of the original faculty of Rockford College, in Illinois, and the girl followed her grandmother's and mother's example by attending Rockford. From the day when she was first baseman on a baseball team (she was the only girl member), Helen Douglas said, "I was going to college, become a lawyer, and go to the State legislature."

After she had been graduated from Rockford College in 1917 with a B.A. degree, twenty-year-old Helen Douglas joined the American Women's Hospital Unit, attached to the French Army. For thirteen months she drove an ambulance in France. Returning home she earned an LL.B. at the Atlanta Law School, the school her father had founded, and of which her brother is now dean. After her admission to the Georgia bar in 1921, she and a sister drove on dirt roads across the United States and back, a story told in her article "Thirteen Thousand Manless Miles." With their mother they traveled for a year in the Western Hemisphere,

HELEN DOUGLAS MANKIN

after which they toured Europe by automobile. During both these trips Helen Douglas did some writing for newspapers. In 1927, vacationing from her law practice in Georgia, Miss Douglas took a trip to Havana. She happened to stop at the same boarding house as Guy Mankin, a mechanical engineer in Cuba on an engineering job. Six months later, Helen Douglas and Guy Mankin were married. Subsequently the couple returned to Atlanta and several years later opened joint offices which they still maintain. They have lived successively in Cuba, the West Indies, Brazil, and Argentina, but their permanent home is a farm west of Atlanta.

Bringing up their son, Guy, Jr., did not prevent her from maintaining her law practice. One reason for the high percentage of support she received from the few Negroes who voted was her reputation for fair treatment of her Negro clients. The tall, brown-haired attorney began her political career when, in the year 1935, she lead an unsuccessful fight for passage of a child labor law, then "thought she might do more if she were on the inside." Mrs. Mankin took one hundred and fifty dollars she had saved toward painting the house, posted it, and declared herself a candidate for the Georgia General Assembly from Fulton County. "Nobody thought I had a chance," she recalls, "but I got an eight-hundred-vote plurality." And she was re-elected four times to the legislature, which meets for sixty days every second year.

As one of the 205 Georgia Representatives (all Democrats), Mrs. Mankin "worked diligently and intelligently for progressive legislation," to quote the *Christian Science Monitor*. Her particular interests were education and child welfare. She worked for improved salaries for teachers, a non-political basis for the university system, segregation of youthful prisoners, and modern health legislation. She also acted for better state policing, expanded civil service provisions, permanent registration laws, a state department of labor, and a truly secret ballot. When in 1942 Ellis Arnall [45] succeeded Eugene Talmadge [41] as governor of Georgia, he had Helen Douglas Mankin as an ardent supporter. In February 1945 Governor Arnall warned that unless the legislature repealed the poll tax, he would suspend it by executive decree. Mrs. Mankin supported him in his fight; she was on the winning side when the Georgia House voted 141 to 51 to abolish the poll tax. In the first Georgia election to follow the repeal of the voting restriction Mrs. Mankin was voted into the United States Congress from the Fifth Georgia District.

In February 1946, Georgia's Fifth Congressional District was left without a Representative, since Robert Ramspeck had resigned from Congress to take a position with the Air Transport Association. Of the eighteen candidates who ran for the post in the special election, Helen Douglas Mankin was the only woman. The campaign was a "rough" one, but Mrs. Mankin was determined to win. Governor Arnall backed her, and, although she did not solicit it, the Congress of Industrial Organizations (CIO) gave her its support after she had begun to campaign. The campaign was particularly bitter over the question of the equalization of railroad freight rates, but Mrs. Mankin says she fought it "on a very high plane." As election returns began to pile up the contest narrowed to a duel between Mrs. Mankin and Ramspeck's former secretary Thomas L. Camp, executive secretary of the Georgia Railroad Association. The final tally was 11,099 votes for Mrs. Mankin, a plurality of 770 over Camp, who had received 10,329 votes. Altogether, in a particularly heavy turnout, about 32,000 cast their votes. In this first election since Georgia abolished the poll tax, the Negroes' votes went almost exclusively to Mrs. Mankin, including those of the city of Atlanta and of Decatur. Mrs. Mankin herself pointed to what she considered the decisive factors in the election. "In the legislature," she said, "I have been a stanch supporter of Governor Arnall's liberal program. My main opponent, Mr. Camp, comes from a part of the county that is overwhelmingly pro-Talmadge. Here in Atlanta we regard Mr. Talmadge as the Bilbo [43] of Georgia. I think the deciding factor was that the voters were simply disavowing old dogmas and embracing new ones."

Interviewed after her election, Mrs. Mankin said that freight-rate equality for the South and Federal aid to education would concern her most while she was in Congress. Of the bill for a Fair Employment Practice Committee, a part of the Administration program which was hotly opposed by Southern Democrats, she remarked that she needed to give the matter study, but that newspaper accounts of the legislation had led her to believe it was "ill-advised." Asked if she would support President Truman's Administration, she answered, "I am a Democrat." The *New Republic*, under the heading "Good News Down South," was unequivocally enthusiastic about the new Congresswoman. "She carried on an imaginative campaign which brought the vital issues home to the people. Thus with the support of women's and church groups, organized labor, progressive individuals and organizations, and helped by a heavy turnout at the polls, she demonstrated that liberal sentiments can find political expression in the South." The *Christian Science Monitor* reported that Mrs. Mankin had opposed the socialization of medicine, whereas she offered her support to price controls, a Federal housing program, and international cooperation to maintain peace. She also voted for the United States loan to Great Britain. On labor issues, she went on record against the Case '46 antilabor bill; she voted for the Hobbs bill, which was directed against the CIO's Teamsters' Union. During her "freshman" term in the House, she served on the Civil Service, Revision of the Laws, Claims, and Elections No. 2 committees.

In the 1946 primaries Mrs. Mankin won the popular vote from her nearest opponent Judge James C. Davis (53,000 to 43,000) but was defeated under the Georgia unit vote system which gave her six units to Judge Davis' eight. In parallel suits in a Federal District court brought by herself contesting the Congressional race and by individuals protesting the defeat of James V. Carmichael in the gubernatorial race, the decision was handed down that the Georgia unit vote was constitutional. Later, her nomination was certified by the Executive Committee of the State Democratic Party, but then rescinded by the State convention. Mrs. Mankin, nevertheless, conducted a campaign, and received 16,000 write-in votes; Davis received 22,000 regular votes. Failing election to the Eightieth Congress, she made plans to contest the nomination and election procedures.

Newspaperwomen in the capital were favorably impressed by the newcomer from the South. After Mrs. Mankin's first press conference, Doris Fleeson (New York *Post*) remarked that she spoke in a manner "more than slightly reminiscent of such stalwarts as Frances Perkins and Eleanor Roosevelt." And Josephine Ripley (*Christian Science Monitor*) said, "It is obvious that an individual as vibrant and vocal as Mrs. Mankin will play no wallflower role in the House." Mrs. Mankin is a tall woman (five feet, nine inches), usually weighs 148 pounds. While campaigning she lost twenty pounds, because she worked as her own campaign manager, slept four to five hours a night, and lived on eggs and milk. (Her son, who had assisted her in all her previous campaigns, was in the North Atlantic as a third engineer on a Maritime Service tanker.) A "magnolia smile," "really lovely" blue-gray eyes, brown hair touched with gray, a "strong, mobile" face, and a "throaty contralto" characterize the Representative, whose feminine Southern manner contrasts with her brisk, "almost masculine" carriage. Mrs. Mankin is a teetotaler, does not smoke, and claims to be a "good cook and a good housekeeper." She adds, "My husband likes to fish. He says it is painful for him to sit out in a boat and look up and find me swinging a grass cutter. He says I lack the ability to relax. Maybe he is right." A baseball enthusiast since childhood, she holds one of the few gold passes good for all Southern Baseball League games.

References

Christian Sci Mon p8 F 21 '46
N Y Herald Tribune II p4 F 17 '46
N Y Post p33 Mr 4 '46
N Y Sun Mr 5 '46
Who's Who in America, 1946-47

MARBURG, THEODORE July 10, 1862—Mar. 3, 1946 American writer on international politics and leader of universal peace movement; Minister to Belgium 1912-14; officer of several social science organizations and international peace societies; author of eleven books.

Obituary

N Y Times p23 Mr 5 '46

MARION, GEORGE July 16, 1860—Nov. 30, 1945 American actor and theatrical director; played character parts on stage, and from 1914 in motion pictures; directed a number of Ziegfeld productions in the nineties; among the plays he staged for other producers were *The Merry Widow, Madame X, The Yankee Consul, The College Widow,* and *The Prince of Pilsen*; as an actor, was starred in 1917; perhaps most memorable screen appearance was in his stage role in *Anna Christie.*

Obituary

N Y Times p46 D 2 '45 por

MARTIN, CHARLES H(ENRY) Oct. 1, 1863—Sept. 22, 1946 Governor of Oregon, 1935-39; United States Democratic Representative from Oregon, 1931-35; major general in the Regular Army; he commanded the Blackhawk Division and the Fifth Corps in the Argonne during World War I, served as assistant chief of staff under General John J. Pershing, 1922-24.

Obituary

N Y Times p30 S 24 '46 por

MASSEY, RAYMOND (măs'ĭ) Aug. 30, 1896- Actor; producer
Address: h. 132 E. 80th St., New York

Off to an auspicious start in December 1945, Theatre, Inc., the new producing company, presented veteran actor Raymond Massey in Shaw's *Pygmalion* opposite Gertrude Lawrence '40 for its first offering. Massey, known as "the man who took the face of Lincoln off the penny and put it into the hearts of millions of Americans" because of his outstanding portrayal of the Emancipator in *Abe Lincoln in Illinois,* in the Shaw comedy played one of the relatively few light roles in his long career on the English and American stage and screen.

Considered an Englishman by Americans and an American by the British, Raymond Hart Massey, now an American citizen, was born in

RAYMOND MASSEY

Toronto, Canada, on August 30, 1896, of American and Canadian stock. Through his mother, Anna (Vincent) Massey, of Erie, Pennsylvania, he traces his ancestry to forebears who fought in the American Revolution and for the North and South in the Civil War. His paternal ancestor Geoffrey Massey was one of a group of English Nonconformists who came to Massachusetts and settled in Salem in 1629. Later Masseys emigrated to Canada in 1810, where they founded the Massey family fortune in the Massey-Harris Agricultural Implement Company, of which the actor's father, the late Chester D. Massey, afterward became head. (Massey's older brother is the Rt. Hon. Vincent Massey, who was the first Canadian minister to Washington and is now High Commissioner for Canada to the United Kingdom.)

Young Massey received his early education at Appleby School, a private school in Oakville, Ontario, where he joined the other boys in amateur shows in the loft of an old barn "just for the fun of it." When World War I broke out he enrolled in the Canadian Officers' Training Corps at the University of Toronto, and in 1915 was commissioned a lieutenant in the Canadian Field Artillery. Sent to France, he was wounded at Ypres in 1916, but six months later had recovered sufficiently to serve with the British Military Mission to the United States as an instructor in gunnery practice at Yale and Princeton universities. His final service of the war was with the Expeditionary Force in Siberia in 1918 and 1919, where he attracted his commanding officer's attention by organizing a minstrel show in the officers' mess. This was promptly followed by an order to devote his talents to entertaining the troops. Although he admits that he always had had stage ambitions, he says "the bug really bit then."

Mustered out of the army in 1919, Massey went to Balliol College, Oxford. There he rowed for his college and tried out for the dramatic society. Although that society thought his accent "too American," he did get a small part, he told Lewis B. Funke of the New York *Times* in 1944. "I put the blanket over Nelson when he died and mouthed some stuff when Napoleon abdicated. I was pretty lousy." Some time later he was back in Canada selling farm implements, but he was not happy at his work, preferring the amateur theatricals at Hart House, the little theater built for the University of Toronto by his family. Hence, though "we were very Methodist and my uncle was a bishop," Massey determined to broach the matter of an acting career to his father. Somewhat unexpectedly, writes Funke, "it was agreed that he might serve God and the theater, provided he didn't rehearse on the Sabbath." The young man was soon on his way to London, directed thither by veteran actor John Drew, and at the twenty-ninth stage door he found his opportunity: he made his professional debut in July 1922 at the Everyman Theatre in Hampstead as Jack in Eugene O'Neill's *In the Zone.* Then followed the roles of James Bebb in *At Mrs. Beam's* (1923), Jones in *The Rose and the Ring* (1923), Stanley Pitt in *The Audacious Mr. Squire* (1924), and both Captain La Hire and Canon D'Estivet in the world première of George Bernard Shaw's *St. Joan* with Sybil Thorndike (1924). (It was his appearance in *St. Joan* which fully reconciled the elder Massey, who was in the audience, to his son's stage career.)

By March 1925 Massey had also become a producer, staging *Tunnel Trench,* in which he also played Lieutenant Gaythorne, at the Prince's Theatre for the Repertory Players. He deserved, said Ivor Brown of the *Saturday Review,* "the highest praise for his contrivance of movement and his control of tone." In January 1926, together with Allan Wade and George Carr, Massey entered upon the management of the Everyman Theatre. "The Everyman," noted *The Nation* shortly afterward, "is assuming the important function of an experimental station, where interesting plays are tried in short runs on a select and mainly local audience, and then passed on to the West End if they are found to have a popular appeal." During the next year Massey's roles at the Everyman included Robert Mayo in Eugene O'Neill's *Beyond the Horizon,* Rufe Pryor in Hatcher Hughes's *Hell-Bent for Heaven,* Edmund Crowe in Noel Coward's "*The Rat Trap,* Mr. Man in *Brer Rabbit,* Tommy Luttrell in *The White Chateau.* Much, both of the acting and the staging, of the new venture elicited high praise from the critics. And Massey received such plaudits as: "Mr. Massey's fine acting leaves no doubt that Rufe is never a deliberate hypocrite, but deceives himself with the rest"; and "Out of the dreaming duffer for whom spades can never be trumps, Mr. Massey makes an exquisite study of futility."

In the five years which preceded his New York debut in the fall of 1931, Massey produced, in West End theaters, thirteen plays and took twelve roles, four of them in his own productions. He made a "notable hit" as the

Khan Aghaba in H. M. Harwood's *The Transit of Venus* (April 1927); played among other parts the Reverend Macmillan in *An American Tragedy*, which he produced for the Venturers (June 1927); Reuben Manassa in Harwood's *The Golden Calf* (September 1927); Austin Lowe in S. N. Behrman's '⁴³ *The Second Man* (January 1928); Joe Cobb in *Spread Eagle* (June 1928); Lewis Dodd in a revival of *The Constant Nymph* (September 1928); Randolph Calthorpe in *The Black Ace* (May 1929); Raymond Dabney in Harwood's *The Man in Possession* (January 1930); the title role in *Topaze* (October 1930); Randall in *Late Night Final* (June 1931). He produced in addition *The Crooked Billet* and *The Squall* in 1927; *Blackmail* in 1928; William Somerset Maugham's *The Sacred Flame*, Beverley Nichols' *The Stag*, and Sean O'Casey's *The Silver Tassie* in 1929; *Dishonoured Lady* in 1930; *Lean Harvest* in 1931.

His performance as actor and producer caused the *Nation* to comment in 1927 that he was rapidly increasing his reputation as both; and led Ivor Brown of the *Saturday Review* to write in 1928 that "Mr. Massey's work has matured rapidly in the last two years" and in 1929 to speak of the "steady brilliance which one has come to expect from . . . Mr. Massey's productions." In 1927 the *Nation's* reviewer noted that "the best acting comes from Mr. Massey, almost unrecognizable in his clever make-up as a Jewish financier [in *The Golden Calf*]." Of *The Silver Tassie*, which Massey produced after its rejection by the Abbey Theatre, it was said: "This is not a realistic play; but in writing it Mr. O'Casey has employed two distinct methods, one purely symbolic and the other, though superficially realistic, symbolic in terms of realism. . . .Mr. Massey's production is superb. He is in perfect sympathy with his author, having and communicating to the actors a perfect accord with the spirit and sense of the play." On his production of *Late Night Final* Gilbert Wakefield of the *Saturday Review* congratulated Massey "both on his brilliant handling of a difficult play and on his fine performance in a far from easy part."

The actor made his New York debut on November 5, 1931, in the title role of Norman Bel Geddes' '⁴⁰ expressionistic *Hamlet*. Prevailing critical opinion thought it a far from happy choice. "It is an old theatrical saying," wrote Otis Chatfield-Taylor in *Outlook,* "that no actor has ever failed as Hamlet. Well . . . Raymond Massey is certainly put to a test of the adage and only just succeeds in maintaining its verity. . . .The whole show can be summed up as hardly *Hamlet* as we have previously known it, but a pretty good thriller with trick lighting." In Brooks Atkinson's '⁴² opinion Geddes and Shakespeare disagreed "most violently" about the play's theme. Hence, Massey's "boyish affable Hamlet has nothing of Hamlet's melancholia. It has none of the nobility of a prince, and none of the sickly wonder of a thinker. . . .It is not Mr. Massey's fault altogether. By staging and cutting this production . . . [Geddes] has done everything possible to rob the chief part of its grandeur and the play of its meaning." Richard Lockridge of the New York *Sun* found Massey's Hamlet "in this instance . . . entirely unequal to Mr. Geddes' Hamlet, although it is the interesting and flexible performance of a skilled modern actor." But while Stark Young of the *New Republic* considered Massey's portrayal of Hamlet scarcely worth discussing, Gilbert Gabriel of the New York *American* recorded a vote for the other side with the opinion that this was a plausible and human characterization in a refreshingly alive production.

In 1934, after a period on the boards in London, Massey returned to the New York stage as David Linden in his own production of Keith Winter's *The Shining Hour,* which he had bought after reading the first two acts. Although Stark Young thought him "even worse miscast" than in *Hamlet*, critical opinion both in New York and later in London was on the whole highly favorable. "*The Shining Hour*," wrote Cy Caldwell in *New Outlook,* "is the one play of this past month which lifted me completely out of myself. . . .Here were more than actors. . .; here were the characters themselves." For Hiram Motherwell, editor of *Stage*, it was a production "informed, in every detail, with an alert theatric intelligence which is rarely equalled in New York." Two years later Guthrie McClintic's '⁴³ *Ethan Frome* received mixed notices. Said Ruth Woodbury Sedgwick of *Stage*: "Mr. Massey makes the tortured bewilderment of Ethan, caught in the web of his poverty, his love, the inexorable tentacles of his wife's possessive spirit, as actual as the shadows across his gaunt face." But *Time* reported: "A reorientation of Zenobia required a general softening up of the other characters. Actor Massey . . . who knows how to wear a sheepskin coat as if he realized its usefulness, thus loses some of his customary forceful directness." The London production of Robert E. Sherwood's '⁴⁰ *Idiot's Delight* in early 1938, on the other hand, was regarded, in the words of Derek Verschoyle of the *Spectator,* as a "personal triumph for Mr. Massey, who has directed it in addition to playing the leading part."

In October 1939 Massey opened in New York in the role with which he is invariably identified, Abe Lincoln in Sherwood's *Abe Lincoln in Illinois,* a part written especially for him. The play itself, although it was awarded the Pulitzer Prize, was generally regarded as an indifferent effort of the playwright, but opinions of Massey's performance were, with few exceptions, expressed in glowing superlatives. "His performance," wrote Rosamond Gilder '⁴⁵ of *Theatre Arts Monthly,* "is truly exalted, informed with an inner passion that molds the very contours of his face. The round boyishness it exhibits in the early scenes is tempered and worn down until in the last act it takes on the gaunt and harrowed nobility of the familiar life mask. His body, at first thin and loose-jointed . . . draws together, becomes more solid. His shoulders round under a weight too great to be borne. His eyes, at times wild, almost frantic, reflect in the end an acquaintance with grief, a knowledge born of suffering which is both his own and that of all the world." Even

MASSEY, RAYMOND—*Continued*

Stark Young applauded: "By all odds this is the top of Mr. Massey's performances on the American stage." His portrayal of Lincoln brought Massey the New York Drama League medal for "the most distinguished performance of the season."

Following *Abe Lincoln,* the actor appeared in three plays with Katharine Cornell [45]: as Ridgeon in George Bernard Shaw's [44] *Doctor's Dilemma* in 1941; as Morell in Shaw's *Candida* for the joint benefit of the Army Emergency Relief Fund and the Navy Relief Society in 1942; and as Rodney Boswell in Dodie Smith's *Lovers and Friends* in 1944. All three were hits, although some critics maintained that Massey was again miscast in the Shaw plays and that the *Lovers* role was "thankless" at best. On December 26, 1945, the newly organized repertory company Theatre, Inc., presented its initial offering, Shaw's *Pygmalion,* with Massey in the role of Henry Higgins and Gertrude Lawrence [40] as Eliza, for a limited engagement of eight weeks. Excellent reviews and a demand for tickets caused the management to announce an extension of the run.

Increasingly in recent years the actor has also devoted much time to screen and radio work. He has appeared in such films as *The Scarlet Pimpernel* (1935), *The Hurricane* (1937), *The Prisoner of Zenda* (1937), *Reap the Wild Wind* (1941), *Arsenic and Old Lace* (1941), *The Invaders* (1941), *Desperate Journey* (1942), *Action in the North Atlantic* (1942), and others; and he has been especially commended for his work in *Things to Come* (1936), *Fire Over England* (1937), *Abe Lincoln in Illinois* (1939), and *Santa Fé Trail* (1940). His motion picture commitments took him to England in the fall of 1946, to play the role of Abraham Farlan, "the first man killed in the Boston massacre, a man who never got over his anti-British prejudice," in the fantasy film of the hereafter, *Stairway to Heaven.* The *Christian Science Monitor* called Massey's performance "appealing."

In addition to reading Lincoln's Gettysburg Address and other Americana items at various civic and patriotic gatherings and over the radio, he has played the part of Lincoln on the air; has been guest artist on the *Kate Smith Hour,* the *Philip Morris Playhouse,* NBC's *Eternal Light,* Mutual's *Arch Oboler Drama,* and other programs; in the summer of 1944 was narrator of CBS's *The Doctor Fights;* at present is narrator and master of ceremonies on NBC's *Harvest of Stars.* For his participation in programs furthering democracy, Massey was awarded a gold medal by the Women's National Radio Committee in 1941. In November 1942 the actor rejoined the Canadian Army as a major but eight months later was placed on the inactive list because of ill health. On March 21, 1944, he took the oath of American citizenship. And during the 1945 mayoralty campaign in New York City Massey took time out to campaign for the "No Deal" candidate Newbold Morris.

The actor says he is interested in the one-dimensional quality of broadcasting, which he describes as "pure emotional work" and "photography" as opposed to the stage's "portraiture." Between the stage and the screen he finds only one point of contact and that is that "they are both show business." To the question whether he feels the part he is playing, Massey has answered "no": his job, he says, is to make people feel that he does, and that takes a sense of proportion and control which is aided by the ability to remain, so to speak, "on the outside looking in." He is not afraid of type casting. The man who is Lincoln to so many persons is six feet three inches tall, weighs one hundred and eighty pounds, and has black hair. He was married to Dorothy Ludington Whitney on July 15, 1939. (Previously he had been married to Peggy Fremantle and to English actress Adrianne Allen, and he is the father of two sons and one daughter.) He is a member of the Garrick, Bath, Bucks, and Green Room, London clubs; and of the Century, Lambs, and Coffee House, in New York. If he has any hobbies, he says, they are golfing and reading play scripts. Despite the somberness that is usually his lot on the stage and screen, he is, writes Lucius Beebe [40], "a hilarious laugher, a mad wag, and a wonderful raconteur." A writer in *Stage* has described him as a mercurial man who nevertheless has been known to fall asleep "so charmingly at parties that hostesses apologize to him." Opening nights are likely to find him in a jittery state, and there is a famous example of his absent-mindedness: he once signed some checks with a gracious "Yours sincerely, Raymond Massey."

References

    Christian Sci Mon p4 F 23 '45
    N Y Times II p1 F 6 '44
    Stage 11:18-21 Ap '34
    Who's Who, 1946
    Who's Who in America, 1946-47
    Who's Who in the Theatre (1939)

MATSUI, KEISHIRO, BARON (mä-tsōō-ē kä-shē-rō) Mar. 1868—June 4, 1946

Japanese diplomat; Ambassador to France from 1915 to 1922; Foreign Minister, 1924; Ambassador to Great Britain, 1925 to 1928.

Obituary

    N Y Times p23 Je 5 '46

MATSUOKA, YOSUKE (mät-sōō-ō-kà yō-sōō-kĕ) Mar. 1880—June 27, 1946

Japanese statesman; head of the Japanese delegation to the League of Nations, 1932-33; walked out of the League after the council condemned Japan for its Manchurian policy; president of the South Manchurian Railway, 1935-39; Foreign Minister of Japan, 1940-41; signed the Tripartite Pact with Germany and Italy; on trial with war criminals on charges of conspiracy to rule the world. See *Current Biography* 1941 Yearbook.

Obituary

    N Y Times p21 Je 27 '46 por

MAXTON, JAMES June 22, 1885—July 23, 1946 Labor Party member of the House of Commons, from 1922 until his death; a Left-wing pacifist, he led the three-man representation of the Independent Labor Party.

Obituary

N Y Times p27 Jl 24 '46 por

MEAD, GEORGE H(OUK) Nov. 5, 1877- United States Government official; corporation executive

Address: b. c/o Price Decontrol Board, 20th St. & Constitution Ave., N.W., Washington, D. C.; c/o The Mead Corporation, 131 N. Ludlow St., Dayton, Ohio; h. Oakwood, Dayton, Ohio

As a member of the Price Decontrol Board, created by Congressional legislation in June 1946, George H. Mead is one of the three men destined to decide which, if any, of the national price ceilings will be maintained. Organizer and chairman of the Mead Corporation, a leading pulp- and paper-manufacturing firm, Mead was described by *Business Week* as "a private businessman with a public conscience." He is regarded as industry's representative on the board.

George Houk Mead was born in Dayton, Ohio, on November 5, 1877, the son of Harry Eldridge and Marianna Phillips (Houk) Mead. His father was founder of the original Mead Paper Company of Dayton, and young Mead was employed there in 1897-98 after he received his LL.B. degree from Hobart College in 1897. Continuing his formal education, Mead was awarded his B.Sc. by the Massachusetts Institute of Technology in 1900. In the few years following, Mead worked in various cities and dealt with different aspects of the pulp industry: he was with the Cellulose Products Company from 1900 until 1902 in Boston; with the Mead Paper Company in Chillicothe, Ohio, the following year; and with the General Artificial Silk Company in Philadelphia, from 1903 until 1905.

On November 1, 1905, Mead organized the Mead Pulp and Paper Company of Dayton (now the Mead Corporation of Chillicothe). He was vice-president and general manager of the new company until 1912, when he became president. He served in that capacity until the firm's incorporation in April 1942, at which time he was elected chairman of the board of directors. Under Mead's leadership, the corporation (a descendant of the first Mead Paper Company established in 1846) became one of the nation's leading papermakers, doing a business of nearly forty-one million dollars gross in 1945.

Mead was sworn in as a member of the Price Decontrol Board, the "high court" of the Office of Price Administration, on July 30, 1946. Taking office with him were chairman Roy L. Thompson '46, a land bank president, who is considered a representative of agricultural interests, and former Government career man Daniel W. Bell '46, regarded as the public's representative. The three men who, according to *Time*, "bravely picked up the [price control] coals hot-handled them by Congress," were not previously involved in the price control situation; they were "not the prisoners of past pol-

GEORGE H. MEAD

icy," wrote the New York *Times* editorially. Appointed by President Truman as "men in whose judgment and fairness the Congress and the country will have complete confidence," they aim to liquidate controls and return the country to a free price economy as soon as is feasible. This end is in accord with Mead's personal political philosophy of free enterprise: the pulp and paper manufacturer believes an uncontrolled economy can function efficiently when the extreme differences between Government and business are reconciled. Mead's reputedly "nominal" affiliation with the Republican Party makes him that political group's representative on the bipartisan but, in Republican Senator Albert W. Hawkes's opinion, "New Dealish" board.

The board, created by the OPA Extension Act of June 1946, had, as its first "unenviable task," that of deciding within twenty-one days of its inception whether grain, livestock, soybean, cottonseed, and certain dairy products should remain exempt from price regulation. The fulfillment of four conditions before ceilings could be restored was prescribed by law: the price of a given commodity must have risen "unreasonably" since June 30, 1946; the item must be of "short supply"; its recontrol must be "practicable and enforceable"; and its regulation must be in the "public interest." Mead, Bell, and Thompson received Government research agency reports and heard the testimony of individual, agricultural, and consumer groups and individuals before formulating their decision. Their report, delivered five hours before the midnight August 20 deadline, drew praise for its promptness, but criticism for its contents. That only livestock and seed-oil products were to go back under price ceilings at a date fixed by the OPA was considered by some critics as removing too much control, and by others as unsound for allowing any commodities to remain under regulation. The War

MEAD, GEORGE H.—*Continued*

Stabilization Board had previously warned the board that it "could not hold the line on wages unless the prices of essential foods were recontrolled and rolled back to levels as close to those of June 30 as the new OPA law would allow." Attempts at this were abandoned in October 1946 when the decontrol program was speeded up; the Price Decontrol Board was cut to the legal minimum in anticipation of its impending liquidation.

Appointed to President Roosevelt's Committee of Business Men in November 1944, Mead had remained a member of the advisory board of the Office of War Mobilization and Reconversion. As an industry representative on the National Defense Mediation Board, later called the National War Labor Board, Mead's "too prolabor" stand brought him what James A. Wechsler of the New York *Post* called a reputation for being "a heretic in industrial circles." Said *Business Week*: "His business friends sometimes think that . . . [he has become] over-receptive to Government and labor viewpoints." While Mead stated that he does not consider labor's position as radical as industry believes it to be, he has not "gone down the line" with labor—he hailed the Case "anti-strike bill as "the first sound piece of labor legislation" in many years. Mead was a member of the business advisory committee of the United States Department of Agriculture for 1933-39 (chairman, 1936-37) and was chairman of the Industrial Advisory Board under the National Recovery Act in 1934. A member of the Committee on Industrial Analysis in 1937, Mead was president of the American Paper and Pulp Association in 1942-43. He is also president of the G. H. Mead, the Mead Sales, and the Mead Investment companies.

Mead was married on November 22, 1914, to Elsie Louise Talbott. They have five children: Elsie Louise, Harry Talbott, Nelson Talbott, Katharine, and Marianna. (Another son, George Houk, died in combat in World War II.) Mead's clubs are the Metropolitan, in Washington, D.C.; the Racquet and Tennis, Meadow Brook Hunt and Polo, River, and Cloud, in New York; the Miami Valley Hunt and Polo, Dayton Country, and the Engineers, in Dayton; and the Mount Royal in Montreal. Mead, who neither smokes nor drinks, plays a vigorous game of golf. "Quiet, personally unassuming, a shunner of publicity," the gray-haired official wears double-breasted suits sometimes enlivened by a bow tie.

References

Bsns W p8+ Ag 17 '46 por
Time 48:22 Ag 5 '46 por
Who's Who in America, 1946-47
Who's Who in Commerce and Industry
    (1944)

MEANS, MRS. ALAN HAY   July 11, 1897-   Youth leader

Address: b. c/o Girl Scouts of America, 155 E. 44th St., New York; h. 1283 E. South Temple St., Salt Lake City, Utah

Trout Ware, Inc.

MRS. ALAN HAY MEANS

The national president of the Girl Scouts of America, an organization numbering nearly 840,000 girls and women in its membership, is Mrs. Alan Hay Means of Salt Lake City, who has been active in the Scouts since 1928. Mrs. Means sees Scouting as a medium for developing both self-reliance and tolerance in future generations of American women; hence, her postwar plans for the organization call for increased emphasis upon camping and group activities and for a more intensive drive for the enrollment of leaders and sponsors so that every girl who wants to be a Scout may have the opportunity.

Born Helen Hotchkin on July 11, 1897, in Chicago, to Benjamin Lincoln and Lillian (Windes) Hotchkin, the girl grew up in that city and its environs. After graduation from Northwestern Academy in Evanston, she left the Middle West to attend Smith College, where she took the first case work ever offered by the college. Her interest in social service work led her to major in that subject and in political economy. After obtaining a B.A. degree from Smith in 1919, young Helen Hotchkin found her first job as a social case worker with the home relief division of the Red Cross in Springfield, Massachusetts. Later she returned to Chicago to become personnel director for Sears, Roebuck and Company. While working with the mail-order house Miss Hotchkin discovered that her real bent was for recreational leadership rather than for social case work, and during lunch periods she succeeded in organizing and directing tennis matches among employees.

Marriage then interrupted her career for some time. Alan Hay Means, a mining engineer, and dark-eyed, slim Miss Hotchkin were married on August 28, 1920. Their honeymoon was spent in Mexico, in the jungles of Guatemala, and in following the trail of

Pizarro into the interior of Peru. The bride perforce learned how to make yeast and bread in cooking for the seven engineers in her husband's metallurgical exploring party in Guatemala, while this and subsequent expeditions with her husband through South and Central Americas, Canada, and Alaska prepared Mrs. Means for future leadership in Girl Scout camping activities.

Mrs. Means's association with the Girl Scouts began in 1928 when a friend asked her to take over the leadership of a Girl Scout troop as a favor. "I never had so much fun in my life," recalls Mrs. Means. This enthusiasm, retained throughout her many volunteer jobs as a troop leader during the years between 1928 and 1935, induced the organization to offer the young matron the office of deputy commissioner of the Salt Lake City Girl Scout Council, a position she held until 1939 when she was made an honorary member of the council. During 1936, 1937, and 1938 she also acted as regional camp chairman. In 1937 she was made a member of the National Board, which membership she held until she was elected second vice-president in 1939. Two years later the former volunteer troop leader was made national president, an office to which she was re-elected for another two-year term in October 1943, at the Girl Scout biennial convention.

The Girl Scouts of America, although following the "Scout-way" devised by Sir Robert Baden-Powell for the Boy Scouts and Girl Guides of England, is an American organization. It was founded in Savannah, Georgia, in 1912, by Mrs. Juliette Low, who had for many years known Sir Robert and his sister Lady Agnes Baden-Powell in England. Its program embraces homemaking, health, citizenship, and out-of-door activities. The Girl Scout oath pledges: "On my honor, I will try to do my duty to God and my country, to help other people at all times, to obey the Scout laws." Through the Juliette Low World Friendship Fund the goal of the founder of the United States organization—a world-wide sisterhood—is being carried out. There are Girl Scout groups in Brazil, Cuba, and Mexico. In August 1945 a group of twenty-three women from North, South, and Central Americas joined forces to "evaluate how they could best adapt the flexible Girl Scout program to meet the diverse needs of growing girls in the Latin American countries, where, with the exception of Brazil, Mexico, and Cuba, Scouting is [as yet] virtually unknown."

Mrs. Means, as wartime president of her organization, has received her share of the credit given to the Girl Scouts for their war record. Scouts did volunteer work for the Red Cross, the War Finance Committee of the Treasury Department, and the American Women's Voluntary Services. They operated Victory gardens, sold war bonds and stamps, collected scrap, sewed and knitted for the soldiers and for relief groups, assisted in canning centers, did errands for air wardens, distributed recruiting materials for the women's services,

did clerical work for hospitals and home front agencies, and performed other duties. In Greater New York alone, reported the New York *Times* in April 1945, they aided 224 agencies for a total of 611,160 hours in 1944. On the farm front they were organized as "farm aides"—a program in which physically fit Scouts over fifteen stationed in Girl Scout camps were transported each day to different farms in the neighborhood in order to relieve the critical labor shortage. "They were, of course," explains Mrs. Means, "under proper supervision all the time and were allowed to perform only the lighter tasks."

During the years from 1930 to 1932 the Salt Lake City matron, in addition to her Scouting work, served as president of the Salt Lake City Junior League. Her hobbies range from the finest needlework to skeet and trap shooting, in which her average is twenty, and to golf, in which she plays with a handicap of four. Her skill as a golfer won her the Utah State Women's Golf championship of 1931-32. Mrs. Means is five feet six inches tall, weighs one hundred and forty-two pounds; she has dark brown hair, deep-set merry dark eyes, and is described as "pleasingly slender."

References

N Y Herald Tribune p16 Mr 29 '43 por
Who's Who in America, 1946-47

MEANS, HELEN HOTCHKIN   *See* Means, Mrs. A. H.

MECHAU, FRANK, JR. Jan. 26, 1904— Mar. 9, 1946 American painter and teacher; received Guggenheim Fellowship in 1933, 1934, and 1938; won medals in 1936 and 1938; director of art classes at Columbia University 1939-43, associate professor of architecture and director of drawing, painting, and sculpture from 1943; *Life* war artist-correspondent 1943; represented in Museum of Modern Art, Metropolitan Museum, and other museums.

Obituary

N Y Times p45 Mr 10 '46

MECHEM, MERRITT CRAMER Oct. 10, 1870—May 24, 1946 Lawyer; Governor of New Mexico from 1920 to 1922; recommended the passage of a land ownership act excluding Japanese and a drastic "blue sky law."

Obituary

N Y Times p32 My 26 '46 por

MERCK, GEORGE W(ILHELM) Mar. 29, 1894- Chemical manufacturer
Address: b. c/o Merck & Co., Inc., 125 Lincoln Ave., Rahway, N.J.; h. Prospect Ave., West Orange, N.J.

George W. Merck is the president of Merck and Company, Incorporated, producers of fine chemicals for medical, pharmaceutical, laboratory, and industrial uses. The firm is also a manufacturer of pure vitamins and of sul-

Fabian Bachrach

GEORGE W. MERCK

fonamides. Merck, a special consultant to the Secretary of War, formerly directed American research in biological warfare.

George Wilhelm Merck was born in New York City on March 29, 1894, the son of Friedrike (Schenck) and George Merck of Darmstadt, Germany, who came to the United States in 1891. With his sisters, Elsbeth (now deceased), Lynn, Olga, and Magda, the boy George was reared at Llewellyn Park in West Orange, New Jersey. He entered Newark Academy in 1905, and after three years went on to preparatory school at the Morristown Academy, also in New Jersey. After his graduation in 1911, he attended Harvard University, distinguishing himself as editor of the Harvard *Lampoon.* Awarded his B.A. degree in 1915, he began his career the same year in the packing and shipping department of the family chemical business.

The Mercks had an early start in chemistry: the first member of the family to open a pharmacy shop did so in 1668 "At the Sign of the Angel" in Darmstadt. In 1816 the family began manufacturing alkaloids, in 1827 became the first commercial producers of morphine, and of cocaine in 1862. The first American house of Merck and Company was founded at Rahway, New Jersey, in 1891 by George W. Merck's father, who was president of the firm until his health failed in 1925. In that year, young Merck, after having worked in most of the departments and branches and served as manager of the plant during World War I, succeeded his father as president and director. Two years later the firm merged with the Powers-Weightman-Rosengarten Company of Philadelphia, which had been in business since 1818, and on December 28, 1934, articles of incorporation were signed to form the present Merck and Company, Incorporated, of Rahway. In 1941 the stock of the company, which was not listed on any exchange, was divided among one thou-

sand holders, the Merck and Rosengarten families controlling 75 per cent of the voting shares. After redistribution later that year the founding families retained what *Business Week* (April 19, 1941) estimated to be 58 per cent of the voting stock.

Under George W. Merck's presidency and directorship, the Merck company grossed over fifty-five million dollars in sales for 1945, eight million dollars of which was earned profit before taxes (*Barron's,* August 12, 1946). Merck's domain is a fifty-five-acre main plant and offices at Rahway, and he supervises the work of over twenty-eight hundred employees of plants and warehouses in New York, Philadelphia, and St. Louis. Since January 1930 there have been Canadian branches in Montreal and Toronto.

Merck is a manufacturer of chemicals, as distinct from makers of pharmaceutical products, many of whom are his largest customers. The firm supplies over twelve hundred fine chemicals (e.g. of high grade) to physicians, dentists, pharmacists, industry, laboratories, and to the general public, exclusive of special orders. The company conducts research laboratories for the synthesis of complex organic compounds, for the isolation and purification of natural products. Credited with the synthesis of ephedrine after the Chinese natural supply had been cut off, the laboratories have also synthesized vitamin B_1 (1936); vitamin E (1938), which the laboratories were first to identify; vitamin B_6 or pyridoxine (1939); and collaborated with others in synthesizing pantothenic acid (1940), another vitamin B complex which the Merck laboratories first identified. (Merck and Company was the exclusive producer of pantothenic acid and vitamin B_6 in 1941, also putting out vitamins C, E, and K.) The laboratories also introduced the sulfonamide derivatives, sulfanilamide, sulfapyridine, and sulfathiazole, used to control infectious disease. The company produces these, antibiotics (penicillin is one), narcotics, arsenicals, quinines, bismuths, iodines, mercurials, and insecticides (such as DDT), in addition to other organic and inorganic compounds.

The Merck Institute for Therapeutic Research, of which Merck is board of trustees president, was founded on April 26, 1933, to conduct investigations into the nature and cause of diseases in men and animals, as well as into their means of prevention and cure. One of the institute's chief duties, in association with the Merck laboratories, is to determine the therapeutic value and safety of new drugs. In original investigation, the institute is credited with the development of vinethene, an inhalation anesthetic, and of mecholyl, a vasodilator used in nervous disorders. Among Merck and Company's widely circulated publications are *The Merck Index,* an encyclopedia of chemicals and drugs; *The Merck Manual of Therapeutics and Materia Medica,* a reference book for the physician; and a service quarterly in pharmacy and medicine.

Early in World War II the United States suspected the enemy of forming task forces to drop microorganisms upon Allied territory, using disease as a large-scale weapon. Biological warfare, which Merck defines as "the use of bacteria, fungi, viruses, Rickettsias (e.g. typhus fever, Rocky Mountain spotted fever), and toxic agents derived from living organisms . . . to produce death or disease in men, animals, or plants," had its modern roots in World War I. In 1915 German saboteurs injected horses and cattle leaving the United States for Allied countries with disease-producing bacteria. The Japanese were accused of dropping plague germs upon China, having worked on offensive experiments since 1936. In February 1942 President Roosevelt '42 established a civilian agency to take full charge of biological warfare activities—it was given the noncommittal name of War Research Service to maintain secrecy—of which Merck was appointed director.

Attached to the Federal Security Agency, WRS physiologists and bacteriologists worked on both defensive and offensive measures, opening laboratories and plants in November 1942. The WRS worked with thirty-eight hundred Army and Navy men, and, at the height of activities, Merck reported that thirty-nine hundred persons were working "under high pressure and [under] the strictest secrecy." In December 1943 it was reported that the Germans were planning germ warfare. This led to both an acceleration of work and to a partial transfer of responsibility to the War Department's Chemical Warfare Service, which transfer was completed by June 1944. Merck was named chairman of the United States Biological Warfare Committee for 1944-45, and was also retained as the Secretary of War's special consultant.

In January 1946 Merck warned that the possibility of germ warfare "cannot be discounted by those who are concerned with the national security." The United States, he said, must continue research in this field during the peacetime years since any other nation might easily prepare for biological warfare under the guise of legitimate medical or bacteriological research. Germ clouds deemed more deadly than the atomic bomb are possible; Merck tells of one chemical in particular that acts upon plants, which then grow "normally" but fail to yield any harvest, their roots having withered. (Merck's speech, "Peacetime Implication of Biological Warfare," delivered at the Westinghouse Centennial Forum in May 1946, is to be published in book form, along with the other forum addresses.) On May 20, 1946, the special consultant was decorated by War Secretary Patterson with the Medal for Merit, the country's highest civil award, for services in the direction and development of biological warfare. In 1939 Merck became a member of the chemical advisory committee of the Army and Navy Munitions Board, which post he continues to hold in 1946.

In addition to his presidency of Merck and Company, Merck is a director of the Colgate-Palmolive-Peet, the New York and Long Branch Railroad, and the United New Jersey Railroad companies. A member of the governing body of the National Industrial Conference Board and of the board of trustees for the Navy Industrial Association, Merck is also a member of the National Association of Manufacturers, having previously served as a director for that organization. He was vice-president of the Manufacturing Chemists' Association, of whose executive board he had later become chairman. Formerly an executive committee member and vice-president of the American Drug Manufacturers Association, he has also held membership in the American Pharmaceutical Association. The corporation executive has worked in local business affairs as director of the Regional Plan Association of New York City, as vice-president and director of the New Jersey State Chamber of Commerce, as a member of the Oranges and Maplewood (New Jersey) Chambers of Commerce, as a member of the Zoning Board of Adjustment for West Orange, and as a member of the Banking Advisory Board of the State of New Jersey from 1935 until 1937.

The Philadelphia College of Pharmacy awarded Merck an honorary Doctor of Pharmacy degree in 1938. A fellow of the American Geographic Society and a member of the American Chemical Society, he has worked to further chemical education on the Princeton University advisory committee for the chemical engineering department, on the Harvard University committee to visit the chemistry department, and on that university's committee to visit the biology department and Bussey Institution. From 1942 until 1945 Merck was a member of the committee on drugs and medical supplies for the National Research Council; his other activities in medicine have been as a member of the national executive council of the American Cancer Society, and as a director of the American Foundation for Tropical Medicine. He is on the board of governers for the Orange (New Jersey) Memorial Hospital, in addition to having served on the board of managers of the New Jersey State Prison.

Merck is a member and former director of the National Conference of Christians and Jews—he is a Unitarian. A Republican in politics, he is treasurer and an executive board member of the New Jersey Republican Committee. Before the prohibition repeal, in the thirties Merck was the New York chairman and a national director of the Association Against the Prohibition Amendment. His clubs are the University, Harvard, Chemists', Down Town, and Railroad-Machinery (New York), the Metropolitan (Washington, D.C.), and country clubs in New Jersey, Pennsylvania, Vermont, and Florida.

By his first marriage to Josephine Carey Wall, of New Jersey, on September 22, 1917, Merck has two sons, George and Albert. After a divorce Merck was married to the former Serena Stevens, of Virginia, on November 24, 1926. Their children are Serena S., John Henry Carrington, and Judith Frederica. The blond, six-foot-five, 250-pound executive enjoys outdoor activities—his favorite sports are surf swimming and tennis.

(Continued next page)

MERCK, GEORGE W.—*Continued*

References

America's Young Men, 1938-39
National Cyclopædia of American Biography Current vol F p174
Who's Who in America, 1946-47
Who's Who in Commerce and Industry (1944)
Who's Who in New York, 1938

MERIVALE, PHILIP Nov. 2, 1886—Mar. 13, 1946 British actor of stage and screen; made debut in 1905; played with Sir Herbert Tree, Mrs. Patrick Campbell, and George Arliss; best known in America for portrayal of title role in *Death Takes a Holiday* (1929), also for *The Swan, The Road to Rome, Mary of Scotland, Valley Forge*; made film debut in 1932.

Obituary

N Y Times p25 Mr 14 '46 por

MERRITT, MATTHEW J. Apr. 2, 1895—Sept. 29, 1946 United States Democratic Representative at large from New York, 1934-44; a member of subcommittees of the House Military Affairs Committee which inspected United States military bases in Central and South America in 1943 and in Europe in 1944.

Obituary

N Y Times p25 S 30 '46

METZMAN, G(USTAV) June 23, 1886-Railroad president

Address: b. c/o New York Central Railway System, 230 Park Ave., New York

After forty-one years of practical training within the railroad industry, Gustav Metzman was made president of the New York Central Railway System in September 1944. In succeeding Frederick E. Williamson in that office, Metzman left unbroken the tradition which, since 1899, has seen only men from the ranks preside over the nation's second largest railroad.

Gustav Metzman was born in Baltimore, Maryland, on June 23, 1886, the son of Louis and Sophia (Shultz) Metzman. While studying engineering in the evenings at Baltimore Polytechnic Institute, in 1903 he began his career as a copy clerk with the Baltimore and Ohio Railroad, but was soon made a traveling car agent, at which work he met the men whose jobs were "tough and practical." Metzman, who heretofore had spent all his free time in technical study, says, "I thought I could learn all there was to know by myself. I made the mistake, very common among young men, of thinking that all the answers could be found in books." Working with the Baltimore and Ohio until 1916, he discovered that practical understanding of the business picture is something one must learn firsthand, that "the men at the throttle can tell you plenty," and that "the answers to today's problems can best be found with the men facing them." By 1916 Metzman was on the staff of the Eastern Railroad Presidents

Conference, and from 1918 through 1919 he served on the World War I Railroad Administration.

Released from Government service on March 16, 1920, thirty-three-year-old Metzman joined the New York Central Railroad as transportation assistant to the vice-president. Two years later he was chosen transportation assistant to the president, advancing on January 1, 1929 to the position of manager of freight transportation in New York. He was at that time a member of the general committee, transportation division, of the Association of American Railroads.

Metzman was assistant vice-president with headquarters at Chicago from February 1, 1940, to March 1942, when he was granted leave of absence to serve in Washington, D.C. as chief of the rail division, Transportation Corps, United States Army. On his return in August 1942, in the first of a series of promotions which took him to New York Central terminal points throughout the country, Metzman was sent to Cincinnati, Ohio, as assistant vice-president and general manager, and vice-president and general manager, successively. Transferred to Chicago, Metzman was made vice-president, with jurisdiction over the New York Central lines west of Buffalo, the Big Four, Michigan Central, Indiana Harbor Belt, and the Chicago River and Indiana Railroads, the position he held when elected president in 1944.

Metzman's most serious problem on assuming the presidency was the maintenance in peacetime of the bulk of the New York Central's wartime freight and passenger traffic. Williamson, his predecessor, had led the company through a depression by maintaining a policy of retiring more and more debt, rather than using profits to purchase large quantities of new equipment. In one of his first presidential statements on September 2, 1944, Metzman declared, "The healthy plan of debt reduction . . . will be continued as long as the company is allowed to keep some of its earnings in the till," adding that he did not believe the lines to be in need of a recapitalization plan. He announced the start of an intensive study of the financial structure of the system, and the purchase of new Diesel engines for hauling fast freight, and for use on passenger trains in 1945. Metzman was "noncommittal on the future matter of rates, Pullman service, and the relation of air transport to the rail companies." Viewing with encouragement the addition of new industrial plants along the New York Central lines, he felt that many would remain as peacetime industries, boosting freight traffic and ending the temporary slump in railroad transportation which would come with the end of the war.

On March 15, 1946, Metzman broke his silence on rate policy. As principal speaker for the railroad interests he addressed the combined arbitration boards set up in Chicago by President Truman to determine whether or not to grant pay demands of the fifteen nonoperating and three operating unions. Of the demands affecting one million four hundred thousand employees of one hundred thirty railroads, Metzman said, "It is manifest that the railroads will not approach, much less attain, in 1946, a reasonable or fair return on the investment in the industry." Asking the maintenance of a policy of static wages unless freight and passenger rates are increased, he declared, "The primary consideration . . . is no longer whether an increase will produce for the carriers an excessive return on investment. . . .Rather the primary question is the capacity and readiness of traffic to bear the increase and the possible diversion of certain classes of traffic to competitive facilities." A wage structure beyond the capacity of the carriers would mean suspension of the program of modernization of facilities, a reduction in service, and a corresponding reduction in employment, Metzman asserted.

The executive asked for a 25 per cent increase in freight rates for the railroads after May 15, 1945. Metzman told the Interstate Commerce Commission that the pay rises which had been granted, together with increased costs and declining traffic had created a situation "which can with entire accuracy be characterized as critical." To support his statement Metzman cited figures showing that the New York Central's earnings had declined each year since 1942, despite increasing gross revenues.

Metzman in October 1945 stated that the employment of public funds in creating and maintaining transportation facilities constitutes the country's primary transportation problem, one which can best be met by cooperation among shipper, transport agency, and public. The solution is currently threatened by the antitrust prosecution of the railroads directed at rate-making practices, he held, urging passage of the bill advanced by Representative A. L. Bulwinkle, Democrat from North Carolina, which would remove railroads from under the jurisdiction of the antitrust laws. Criticizing Metzman's stand that "it would be entirely possible for the competition of tax-subsidized transportation so to undermine America's railroads that the Government would have to take them over," along with other forms of transport, former Assistant Attorney-General Thurman Arnold '⁴⁰ stated that railroad exemption from antitrust laws would lead to similar exemptions for other industries and would open this country's doors to the "cartel system."

When in 1945 the Pullman Company was declared to be a monopoly in restraint of trade, Metzman testified before a United States District Court in Philadelphia, supporting the bid by railroad lines including the New York Central System to purchase the company. "From a business point of view," he said, "it does not seem to me the railroads can properly be denied the opportunity of themselves owning and controlling the sleeping-car business to be rendered on their lines. If . . . an outside organization is armed with the ownership of the only present available sleeping cars, the railroads are robbed of the opportunity of protecting their important financial interests and public service obligations, and are not even in position themselves to choose the one they think will render the most satisfactory service." Although the carriers were granted the right to purchase, the sale was opposed by Holmes

G. METZMAN

Baldridge, special assistant to the United States Attorney, who felt that carrier ownership would mean another monopoly substituted for the one condemned by the court.

While guiding the New York Central System, the railroad president is a director of J. P. Morgan and Company, elected on January 3, 1945; of the Cleveland, Cincinnati, Chicago and Saint Louis Railway, under lease to New York Central, and of numerous other companies comprising the New York Central System; of the Association of American Railroads; of the Railway Equipment and Publication Company, New York. He is chairman of the Eastern Railroad Presidents Conference and has been chairman of the railroad contact committee, Atlantic States Shippers Advisory Board. His clubs are New York Railroad, Masons, Siwanoy Country, and Union League; the Union Club of Cleveland, and the Chicago Club. According to the Interstate Commerce Commission, the president of the New York Central received ninety thousand dollars in 1944, the second highest income of railroad presidents in the United States.

In line with his policy that "the chap who goes ahead keeps so busy at his job and reading about it that he seldom had time to form habits which undermine vigor" (quoted by Donald A. Laird in *Technique of Personal Analysis*), the six-foot-two, 190-pound "commandingly erect" railway president makes his work his chief hobby. He still enjoys riding along the Central line in a private car, "a business car," as he calls it. Golf, bridge, theater, and opera are among his recreations. "When younger," says Metzman, whose brown hair is not even tinged with gray, "I liked to play amateur baseball." He smokes moderately, usually a pipe. Politically Metzman is an independent; in religion, a Protestant. In 1933 he was married to Marie S. Smale Hutchinson.

METZMAN, G.—*Continued*

His two stepchildren are Nancy (Mrs. Arthur J.) Pegler, and Charles L. Hutchinson. "I've never met an executive," he has remarked, "any bigger than the sum total of the personnel under him."

References

Newsweek 29:64+ Ag 28 '44 por
Who's Who in New York, 1936
Who's Who in Railroading, 1946

MIELZINER, JO (měl-zē'nẽr) Mar. 19, 1901- Scenic designer
Address: b. 1430 Broadway, New York; h. 1 W. 72d St., New York

The scenic designer Jo Mielziner is known for his versatility, particularly for his talent for giving his settings a rich feeling of occupancy, and his effective use of lighting. When he closed his New York studio in May 1942 to enter the United States Army Air Forces as a camouflage officer, he left a record of eighteen years of creative work. During that period hardly a season passed without a Broadway theater housing at least one of his settings for a drama or musical; and New York critics hailed his return in the 1944-45 season with his scenery for *The Glass Menagerie*. With his contribution to Elmer Rice's [43] *Dream Girl* he finished his one hundred and fiftieth setting.

Born in Paris on March 19, 1901, Jo Mielziner spoke French until he was ten. Sometime before his birth his parents, Ella MacKenna (Friend) Mielziner and Leo Mielziner, a portrait painter, had gone with their older son, Kenneth, then two, to live in France. Mrs. Mielziner was the first woman member of the Foreign Press Association; and the designer's paternal grandfather, Rabbi Moses Mielziner, was the author of a book on marriage and divorce upon which the present divorce laws of the State of Ohio are based. Since he had a successful artist as father and early teacher there seemed to be no doubt about the career the boy would choose for himself. After the family's return to New York Jo studied for a year at the National Academy of Design and the Art Student's League, where his father was an instructor. A Cresson traveling fellowship from the Pennsylvania Academy of Fine Arts in Philadelphia, at which he had been a student for four years, enabled the youth to return to Europe in 1920.

Two years of study and travel convinced young Mielziner that, while art would continue to be his world, it would be the art of the theater. After a tour of the Continent he remained in Vienna to work under Professor Oscar Strand, the Ringtheatre designer who was famous for his creation of the rotating stage. The boy drew further inspiration from a visit to Gordon Craig in the Italian city of Rappalo. In the studio of the famous designer, Robert Edmond Jones [46], Mielziner on his return to the United States set himself to master the mechanics of scenic painting and to acquire a craftsman's knowledge of the stage. Later he

joined the Theatre Guild, where he continued his apprenticeship under Lee Simonson and acted in minor roles in 1923 in *Saint Joan* and *The Failures*. To this day Mielziner believes that every designer should have some experience in acting, however brief.

After his successful debut with his settings for the Theatre Guild's offering of *The Guardsman* in 1924, he completed an auspiciously busy season with the scenery for *The Awful Mrs. Eaton, Nerves, Mrs. Partridge Presents—, Buccaneer,* and Ibsen's *The Wild Duck*. In a review of Mielziner's creations, reprinted in the *Literary Digest*, John Mason Brown wrote: "His work has the balance and beauty and sanity of fine prose, but it never flies to the heights or falls to the depths of poetry." Early in his career Mielziner established a reputation for ingenuity, with the result that an uninformed person would never have suspected that the settings for *The Guardsman* and *The Wild Duck* were the creation of the same mind. He also won praise for his ability to establish the particular mood of a play without "any noisy tricks of interpretation." Mielziner's work, in fact, expressed the new trend in the theater both in the United States and abroad. According to Lee Simonson, until World War I, theatrical designing, with few exceptions, had "reflected the faded traditions of perspective painting of the eighteenth century in expanses of literally painted detail, drab in color, without atmosphere or illusion, particularly in out-of-door scenes that usually presented symmetric rows of wood wings and overhead borders." Modernism in the theater was an outgrowth of the experiments of the modern easel painter and of a new and growing interest in plays, both American and European, of a less conventional nature than had been previously offered to the public.

At thirty-three Mielziner was considered a leader among the second generation of American stage designers, and his sets for *The Barretts of Wimpole Street* (1931) "among the best American contributions to theatrical art." Constantly experimenting, he did not always see eye to eye with the playwrights. Consequently, when much against his will he was obliged to follow "the concrete road of realism" in his settings for *Street Scene* (1928) he was "astounded to receive the most enthusiastic press of his career to date." He also designed the settings for the musicals *Of Thee I Sing* (1931), *The Gay Divorce,* and for the operatic version of Eugene O'Neill's *Emperor Jones* (1932). Each time he strove to capture the mood of the drama, comedy, or musical for which he was designing, Mielziner revealed a different facet of his art. According to *Theatre Arts Monthly,* in doing his scenery for the Katharine Cornell production of *Romeo and Juliet* (1934) he "abandoned the traditional Elizabethan or Renaissance manner in his designs . . . in favor of the earlier Italian primitive school of decoration because the latter offers a suitable lightness of key and purity of color and frees the designer from the restrictions of so-called true perspective by which later schools were bound." That same year he did settings for *By Your Leave, Merrily We Roll*

Along, Spring Song, Accent on Youth, and *Dodsworth.*

His erstwhile mentor, Lee Simonson, has commended Mielziner for his able use of lighting by which he helped create an environment to heighten the play's dramatic action "and sustain its emotional effect." He also spoke of "his poetic power which transfigured the scene under an East River bridge in *Winterset,* the decorative opulence of *Romeo and Juliet,* and his gay and witty investiture of musical comedies and reviews."

By 1936 the modern trend in the theater had entered another stage of its development. Of this Mielziner declared in an interview he gave that year, "The stage is becoming as streamline-minded as architecture, or interior decoration, or sculpture. We are rediscovering the limitless power of suggestion and illusion. After all, there's no use spending, in this breathless world, a lot of time, energy and agony fussing with details and superfluities that will, in the end, only serve to confuse and obstruct." More important than authenticity he claimed was the need to capture the mood of a play. Thus, in Shaw's *Saint Joan* (1936) he tried to convey "the insensate coldness and merciless bestiality" of the Dark Ages. He also sought to express the lyrical quality of the dramatized version of Edith Wharton's novel of New England, *Ethan Frome* (1936), by arranging to have the constellations over the bleak snow covered land change in accordance with the hours of the night. It was one of the plays which gave him his greatest satisfaction.

Streamlined stage designing, Mielziner pointed out, called for greater subtlety of thinking and planning. "If you shave a set down to the barest essentials, these essentials must be doubly significant." As a practical application of this theory he referred to his work in Maxwell Anderson's drama *Winterset* which he had done the year before. "I wanted to make the bridge the focal point of the set, and I tried to do this by building everything, as imperceptibly and subtly as possible, up to it and then suggesting the bridge itself as a backdrop. . . . In this way I hoped to make the audience *feel* the bridge, be aware of its continual presence, be drawn beneath its shadow, acknowledge it as a symbol of the real meaning of the play." Similarly in a later play by Anderson, *High Tor* (1937), he used the device of the steam shovel to obtain this effect. Scenery, he believes, should exist only to enhance a play and should not demand more than thirty seconds of the audience's conscious attention.

In March 1942, a few months after Pearl Harbor, Mielziner became chairman of the Camouflage Society of Professional Stage Designers (Unit 1) which he helped to organize. In May of that year he closed his studio in New York to take his place as captain in the United States Army Air Forces. Later he rose to the rank of major and was attached to the staff of Lieutenant General Barton Kyle Yount for whom he wrote a technical manual on camouflage for the use of the Air Forces. Describing this experience two years later, he said that camouflage was merely taking the rules of stage designing and operating them in reverse,

that is, the attention of the enemy was to be diverted by the use of decoys.

After thirty months of duty in the United States the scenic designer was released from service; whereupon he returned to Broadway to do the settings for Tennessee Williams' *The Glass Menagerie,* which was later given the New York Critics' Circle award. The critics also praised Mielziner for his "non-realistic" settings which they found in harmony with the symbolism the author used in the play. In April 1945 he was retained to do the lighting of the main conference room of the United Nations in San Francisco. Aware that a later production, *Carousel,* would probably go on the road after its Broadway appearance, he designed all the furniture not to exceed five feet nine inches, the average width of freight-car doors. According to *Variety,* he turned another production, the *Firebrand* of Kurt Weill and Ira Gershwin, into a "visual pleasure." He also created the settings for Robert Sherwood's *Rugged Path.* In addition to the sets he designed for *Dream Girl* at the end of 1945, Mielziner in 1946 did those for Robert Ardrey's *Jeb,* Anita Loos's play for Helen Hayes, *Happy Birthday,* Lillian Hellman's *Another Part of the Forest,* and the musical *Annie Get Your Gun.* He was also commissioned to do the scenic designs for 1947 productions, *The Big Two, Finian's Rainbow, The Fourth Little Show,* and the musical version of *Street Scene.*

To express his dissatisfaction with the functional inadequacy of most modern theaters, Mielziner contributed an article to the June 1946 issue of *Theatre Arts.* "Adequate storage and handling facilities for productions other than the one currently playing are . . . imperatives," he wrote. The rest of the article suggested that the theater of the future be used in the morning for performances for children and in the afternoon for lectures and concerts. Its patrons would enter "an enormous lobby, which has already earned its keep as a display showcase for luxury goods during the eight preceding hours of daylight. From the lobby they enter an attractive restaurant and bar." Mielziner concluded his argument in favor of a multiple-function theater by saying: "For a nation with our proud record of architectural and engineering achievements, we have the worst theaters of any country in the world."

Among Mielziner's other recent activities have been the planning, with director Margo Jones and Tennessee Williams, of a theater project in Texas—the Dallas Civic Repertory—to the board of trustees of which he was elected in January 1946. In February of that year, he, together with artists Lee Simonson, Robert Edmond Jones, Cleon Throckmorton, and Adolphe Appia, held an exhibition of stage designs at the Hudson Park Branch of the New York Public Library. In May *Variety* chose him as the best scenic designer of the 1945-46 season; a similar award came to him two months later from *Billboard* magazine. That summer he delivered a series of lectures at the Fordham University Theater seminar and was preparing a book on stage design.

(Continued next page)

MIELZINER, JO—*Continued*

Mielziner was married to the actress Jean MacIntyre in 1938. They have three adopted children, Michael, Neil, and Jennifer Ann. The designer has been described as a tall boyish-looking man with puckish features and gray-blue "nondescript" eyes. When he can take time off from his work he likes to turn to one of his few hobbies, book collecting.

References

> Lit Digest 86:25-6 Jl 18 '25; 117:13 Ap 28 '34
> N Y Herald Tribune p13 Mr 12 '42
> N Y Times p12 Mr 28 '42
> N Y World-Telegram p5 N 6 '44
> PM p2 D 10 '44 por
> Variety p45 O 18 '44; p46 Ja 20 '46
> Who's Who in America, 1946-47
> Who's Who in the Theatre (1939)

MIKHAILOVITCH, DRAJA (mē-hī′lō-vĭch drä′zhä) 1893(?)—July 17, 1946 Yugoslavian general, leader of the Chetniks, who offered the first Yugoslav resistance to German invasion; War Minister of the Yugoslavian Government-in-exile and commander in chief of the Free Yugoslavian Army, 1942; executed for treason and collaboration with the Germans. See *Current Biography* 1942 Yearbook.

Obituary

> N Y Times p1+ Jl 18 '46

MILLAND, RAY (mĭ-länd′) Jan. 3, 1907- Actor

Address: b. c/o Paramount Pictures, Hollywood, Calif.

Ray Milland has set a record for length of service among top-ranking male players with Paramount Pictures. The star, who has appeared in more than fifty pictures in the course of fourteen years in Hollywood, won the Motion Picture Academy Award for the best lead performance in 1945, this for his portrayal of the dipsomaniac Don Birnam in *The Lost Weekend*.

Ray Milland was born Reginald Truscott-Jones, on January 3, 1907, in Neath, Glamorganshire, Wales, and spoke only Welsh until he was five. After his mother's second marriage, to a "semi-itinerant" structural engineer and steel mill supervisor, the boy was known by his stepfather's surname of Mullane. (Not until he went on the stage was he known as Milland and then he used the first name of Jack; "Ray" was a later development, and his friends still call him Jack.) The future star spent much of his boyhood on his uncle's horse breeding farm in Wales, and worked also on a Channel potato boat, in steel mills, and as cabin boy on an uncle's Mediterranean steamship. He went to "public" schools, but only sporadically, as the family moved frequently; however (Jerry Asher reports in *Photoplay*), at the age of ten the boy had already read "everything of Chekov, Tolstoy, and Blasco Ibañez." For a time he attended King's College, in Cardiff, but left at the age of eighteen without finishing his course and went to London.

There he was "auditioned" for the Household Cavalry, one of the exclusive regiments guarding the Royal Family, and after "nine months of grueling training in horsemanship" was admitted to their ranks. The guardsman learned to shoot, to box, and to fence, and joined in their gay social life, but disliked sitting like an equestrian statue. After three years, Milland relates, "my father couldn't afford to support me. To be employed in the Household Cavalry required an independent income." An injury he received may also have helped him to reach this conclusion. Some writers have stated that Milland inherited seventeen thousand dollars from an aunt, resigned from the cavalry and toured the Continent; but a *Liberty* interviewer reported that he had not received such a legacy. Nevertheless, in London with ten pounds in his pocket, he spent it on an evening's entertainment of Estelle Brody, the English film star. Through her he got work as an extra, and this led to walk-ons and bits in several provincial companies, reaching his highest point with a touring company of *The Woman in Room 13*. Jobless in London once more, Milland was hired by a movie studio as an expert marksman, a typical task, being to shoot a small mirror out of Lys DePutti's hand from offscene. The illness of Cyril McLaglen gave Milland a chance at the lead in *The Flying Scotsman*. Then a Hollywood talent scout discovered him, and off he went to the film capital.

Ray Milland's first American picture was MGM's *Polly of the Circus*, with Clark Gable and Marion Davies. No long term contract followed, however, and he returned to England. It was there that another scout "discovered" him in a London stage revue, and before long Milland traveled back to California to play opposite Constance Bennett in *Bought* (1931). Shortly after his second arrival in the United States a friend advised him to get rid of his very broad British accent, suggesting that he learn "plain American" by cultivating the friendship of an American girl. Milland took the hint and in a few months, he says, he was "the only Englishman in captivity" who could speak with a Georgia accent—the girl came from Atlanta.

Milland met his future wife, Muriel ("Mal") Weber, a Hollywood showgirl, at a bridge party. They were married in 1932 after a brief courtship. But times were hard for the young Welshman, promising roles had not materialized, and pictures scheduled for production did not reach the camera. At the end of a year he decided to return to England, while his wife remained in Hollywood. He next appeared in several British pictures (one of them was *Orders is Orders*) and between times added to his income by riding in steeplechases twice a week. On his last race he came a cropper over the three-and-a-quarter-mile at the Sandown park course of thirty-two jumps. When his horse refused the jump seven riders crashed, while the newsreels recorded one of the most spectacular falls in steeplechase history.

By 1934 Milland was back in Hollywood, for the third time. He was living on credit in a furnished room, about to go to work in a garage, when he obtained a role in *Bolero* (1934). This resulted in a long-term contract with Paramount, which renewed it in 1943, when the actor signed a new, straight seven-year contract with no options. (According to *Variety*, by 1944 his annual salary was $169,000.)

In the meantime Milland had become re-united with his wife, and had paid off debts to friends who had helped him through his "on the cuff" days. In 1934-35 he had good parts in Paramount's *We're Not Dressing*, in *Menace*, and *The Gilded Lily*, starring Claudette Colbert '45. *Next Time We Love* followed in 1936 and *Three Smart Girls* in 1937. But it was not till he played opposite Loretta Young in *The Doctor Takes a Wife* (1940), that his talent for comedy was given free play and he won praise from the critics. Claudette Colbert insisted that he should be her leading man in *Arise, My Love* (1940), and for the first time Milland was recognized as a true star, with great box-office appeal, not just a good leading man. Next came *I Wanted Wings*, with Veronica Lake, and *Skylark* with Miss Colbert. He was co-starred with Ginger Rogers '41 in the light comedy, *The Major and the Minor* (1942), concerning which Bosley Crowther said, "Credit Mr. Milland with making a warm and nimble fellow of the major." Of his acting in *Are Husbands Necessary?* (1942), in which he starred opposite Betty Field, Howard Barnes wrote that Milland "handled a difficult assignment with more than a little skill." Other Milland 1942 pictures were *The Lady Has Plans* and *Reap the Wild Wind*, both with Paulette Goddard. The former was a weak comedy thriller, the latter a lavish De Mille '42 prestige picture.

In 1943 Milland again costarred with Paulette Goddard in *The Crystal Ball*, which Joseph Pihodna called in the New York *Herald Tribune*, "an attempt at a farce that doesn't come off." He was starred in *Ministry of Fear* (1943), played in the all-star *Star-Spangled Rhythm* (1934), and the all-British, all-star *Forever and a Day* (1943). The actor received good notices for his performance in the ghost drama *The Uninvited* (1943). One critic called Milland and his co-star, "a very realistic and courageous pair," while Alton Cook of the New York *World-Telegram* said, "Ray Milland came along with two beautiful performances in *The Uninvited* and *Lady in the Dark*." Of the latter, a lavish musical in which Milland won Ginger Rogers, the actor was said to "bring a pleasantly exuberant mirth with him every time he stepped into the picture." His acting opposite newcomer Barbara Britton in the war drama, *Till We Meet Again*, led a critic to remark, "Ray Milland, who never gives a bad performance, gives a better one here." In 1945 the hard-working actor made a number of pictures, two opposite Teresa Wright '43, and another period extravanganza, *Kitty*, with Paulette Goddard. In this, commented *Variety's* Brog, "Ray Milland has the more difficult task of keeping the unpleasant foppish character of Sir Hugh Marcy consistent," while making

A. L. Whitey Shafer
RAY MILLAND

Kitty's love for him credible, and "does well by it."

But Milland's great triumph was *The Lost Weekend*, adapted from the Charles Jackson '44 novel—a clinical study of an alcoholic, a frustrated writer, who is trying to escape from reality. While the critics disliked the semi-happy ending of the film, they were unanimous in calling the film an artistic triumph, honest and straightforward, breaking many long-established movie taboos. They called Milland's performance "splendid": "he catches the ugly nature of a 'drunk,' plumbs the depths of degradation and shame, revealing the inner torment of a weak yet respectable man." Howard Barnes wrote in the New York *Herald Tribune*, "The book was sensational as well as fascinating. The picture is a far more universal and lasting reflection of human experience. . . Ray Milland gives the finest performance of a not uncelebrated alcoholic." In January 1946 the New York Film Critics formally presented their awards to Milland and to producer Charles Brackett and director Billy Wilder for their parts in the picture. Another kind of tribute came from the House of Seagram, whisky distillers, which took full-page newspaper advertisements complimenting Milland, urging everyone to see the picture, and emphasizing that it expressed "our own long held and published belief that some men should not drink." In March 1946, Milland received the coveted "Oscar" awarded by the Motion Picture Academy to the best actor of the year. At the International Film Festival held at Cannes, France, *The Lost Weekend* was voted the best American film of 1945, and Ray Milland received individual tributes. The actor was also honored by the Foreign Language Press Film Critics of New York.

On his own time, Milland headed a troupe which, in the spring of 1944, made the tour of

MILLAND, RAY—*Continued*

the South Pacific for the Hollywood Committee and USO-Camp Shows. The entertainers opened their Solomon Islands circuit with three weeks on Guadalcanal, then went on to Tulagi and the Russell Islands. Leaving the USO girl performers at the Russells, Milland and the Foxhole Foursome played advanced areas from Munda through the Treasury Islands, sometimes doing as many as four shows a day. The actor is also well known to radio audiences, having acted in broadcast adaptations of screenplays over the Columbia Broadcasting System. He speaks Spanish fluently and has frequently served as Spanish-speaking commentator in Government-sponsored broadcasts to Latin America.

After appearing in *The Lost Weekend*, Milland was costarred in *The Well-Groomed Bride* with Olivia de Havilland and in *Kitty* with Paulette Goddard. Paramount releases in which he will be starred are: *The Big Clock*, *Whenever I Remember*, *Imperfect Lady*, *The Trouble With Women*, *California* (the star's fiftieth picture), *Golden Earrings*, and *Variety Girl*. He has made guest radio appearances with Jack Benny, Louella Parsons, Fred Allen, Edgar Bergen, in *Theatre Guild on the Air* and *Information Please*. Heading a group of eight American film stars, Milland appeared in a command performance before the King of England in November 1946. He will return to Great Britain in May 1947 to star in the British production *For Her To See*.

Ray Milland is six feet one and a half inches tall, weighs somewhere in the neighborhood of one hundred eighty pounds, and has dark brown hair and blue eyes. In March 1946 his name appeared on the list of America's ten best-dressed men. Milland lives in a Tudor-style house in Beverly Hills with Mrs. Milland, their son Daniel David, and a Llewellyn setter. Milland is said to be impulsive, impatient with small talk and "stuffed shirts," fond of parties and informal entertaining, but disinclined to commit himself to engagements in advance. He rides, hunts, sails, fishes, and enjoys puttering about the garden; and he can become so absorbed in a book as completely to ignore his hosts or guests. The Milland record library contains more than two thousand records, and its owner has a wide range of musical tastes. He has described himself, perhaps not entirely seriously, as a rabid Welshman; and there are still traces of Welsh accent in his speech.

The star says he learned to act by going to the movies to watch Fredric March[43] on the screen. "I admired the frank theatricalism of March, and still do. His overacting is admirable," Milland says. From Walter Huston and Edward G. Robinson he learned economy of expression. "Learning to act at all is hard. In one picture I spent two full working days trying to walk naturally through a door." Milland likes to go to the movies, but he still "shudders" to see himself on the screen, and claims that his fans are all under fourteen or over forty.

References

Liberty 23:12-13+ Mr 9 '46 pors

N Y Post p43 F 11 '44
N Y Times VIII p3 S 20 '42
Photoplay 20:50-1+ My '42

International Motion Picture Almanac, 1943-44

MILLAR, MARGARET Feb. 5, 1915-
Canadian author

Address: b. c/o Random House, 20 E. 57th St., New York; h. 2124 Bath St., Santa Barbara, Calif.

Margaret Millar is not only a mystery writer, but a novelist whose gamut runs from farce to horror. She began writing in 1940 and by 1946 had turned out seven notable mystery novels. The author has been called an outstanding exemplar of good prose—a fact which makes her mystery stories, especially *Wall of Eyes* and *The Iron Gates*, not merely time-killers and spine-chillers, but genuine novels in their own right, worthy of a permanent place on any *aficionado's* bookshelves.

Born February 5, 1915, in Kitchener, Ontario, and still a Canadian citizen, Margaret Millar (she does not insist on the "ar" pronunciation) is the daughter of Henry W. Sturm, a coalyard operator and twice mayor of the town, and of Lavinia (Ferrier) Sturm, whose father was a high school principal. When she was four she began playing the piano without instruction, and by the time she was a student in the Kitchener Collegiate Institute she was playing on local radio programs and being encouraged to prepare for a professional career as a musician. Two things deflected her: a classics teacher, Margaret Dale, turned her ambition to archaeology, and taught her enough Greek in one year for her to win a scholarship to University College, University of Toronto; and the stirrings of the literary urge became evident. Her first stories appeared in the Institute's literary annual, one of whose editors was a fellow student, Kenneth Millar.

In college, though she maintained an excellent scholastic record, she decided against archaeology as a career, and left in 1936, after three years, without a degree. She and Kenneth Millar were married on June 2, 1938, the day after he had been graduated from the University of Western Ontario. The following year their daughter, Linda Jane, was born.

In the fall of 1940 Mrs. Millar had to endure several weeks' illness in bed. She put the enforced leisure to use: in fifteen days, writing in longhand, she completed *The Invisible Worm* (1941). Will Cuppy, in the New York *Herald Tribune*, found this "weird, impressive and most amusing tale of multiple murder . . . a mystery find of considerable voltage." Its appearance coincided with the Millars' move to Ann Arbor, Michigan, where Kenneth Millar was a graduate fellow in English. (He has published two novels, *The Dark Tunnel* and *Trouble Follows Me*, in 1946 had another ready for publication, and was finishing a fourth.)

The Weak-Eyed Bat and *The Devil Loves Me*, Mrs Millar's next efforts, were both published in 1942 and were well received. "Now

Cotton Studio

MARGARET MILLAR

is the time," said Will Cuppy reviewing *The Weak-Eyed Bat*, "for all good fans to realize that Margaret Millar is a humdinger right up in the top rank of bafflers, including the British." *Wall of Eyes*, a serious mystery novel dealing with psychiatric problems, followed next, in 1943. This book was hailed by the *New Republic* as one of the mystery classics of the decade.

After *Fire Will Freeze* (1944), a return to farce, came *The Iron Gates* (1945), in the same genre as *Wall of Eyes*. Though to one reviewer it seemed that the author had "stayed too long in the clinic with her victims," another found the book a masterpiece of horror, with some of the brooding terror of Mabel Seeley, some of the psychological insight of "Francis Iles." It has been filmed by Warner Brothers, who hired Mrs. Millar to write the script. She had a good time in Hollywood, she says, and was offered contracts by two other studios, but turned them down—"I hate to write with someone breathing Basic English into my ear."

Meanwhile Millar, who is a United States citizen because he was born in California during the temporary sojourn of his Canadian parents, had been commissioned in the Navy, and was sent to Princeton and then to Harvard for training. Mrs. Millar and Linda Jane followed him to both colleges, and later to San Diego. When he was ordered to duty in the Pacific, Mrs. Millar bought a house in Santa Barbara, California, to which he returned after his discharge.

Mrs. Millar's new novel, "Experiment in Springtime" (not a mystery, but "a tragicomic study of an unsuccessful marriage") will appear early in 1947. Another, tentatively called "Priscilla"—"a comedy about a twelve-year-old

girl with a terrific imagination and demonic energy"—was in progress. Her first editor and most acute critic, her husband, writes: "Margaret doesn't know whether she has abandoned murder for good; the chances are she hasn't. But she writes out of mood, as she plays the piano, and her mood at present is too gay to permit her mind to dwell on murder. . . .She takes her writing seriously, sometimes spending a morning on a sentence, and she is an ardent student of good prose."

The Millars expect to stay in California. The only thing Mrs. Millar misses is figure skating, but she can still swim and sail, her two other sports enthusiasms. Of medium height and build, the author has green eyes and brown hair. Her favorite authors are Evelyn Waugh, Katherine Mansfield, Rosamond Lehmann, and William Faulkner (with Raymond Chandler, Agatha Christie, and John Dickson Carr among mystery writers); her all-time favorite book, *Tender Is the Night,* by F. Scott Fitzgerald. The author claims her life is remarkable only for its omissions: "I have never broken a limb, been divorced or arrested, never had anything stolen, and the only thing I ever lost was a phonograph needle."

MISTRAL, GABRIELA (mēs-träl' gäb"rē-ä'lä) Apr. 7, 1889- Poet; educator
Address: b. c/o Ciudado del Ministerio de Relaciones Exteriores, Santiago, Chile

Latin America's leading contemporary poet, Gabriela Mistral, long internationally recognized, received the world's highest honor in literature when she was awarded the Nobel Prize for 1945. A native of Chile, the prize winner is also widely known for her work in education, having begun her career as a teacher and devoted her talents, both pedagogic and poetic, to children. Much of her poetry is religious in tone, personal and lyrically passionate. Following the Hispanic-American custom of appointing leading writers to foreign posts, in the course of the past decade Chile has appointed Gabriela Mistral to consulates in several capitals.

Gabriela Mistral was born Lucila Godoy Alcayaga on April 7, 1889, in Vicuña, a small town in the valley of Elqui in northern Chile. Of humble parentage, she is the daughter of Jerónimo Godoy Villanueva and Petronila Alcayaga, both Chileans of Spanish and Basque blood, with probably "more than a touch of Indian." Her father was a village school teacher, well known in the neighborhood as a "pallador," or minstrel who composed verse for festivals and joined in singing competitions with other village troubadours. Lucila grew up in the country among simple farm folk, and was educated by her father and an older sister, also a teacher. She attended the town's *Liceo* or high school, and later the Pedagogical College in Santiago, Chile's capital. At the age of fifteen she became a primary school teacher and for several years taught poor children in rural areas. She then turned from primary to secondary education, becoming Professor of

GABRIELA MISTRAL

Hygiene in the Traiguen secondary school in 1911. Shortly thereafter she was given the post of inspector general and Professor of History in the Antofagasta school, where she remained for a year. In 1912 she was appointed inspector and Professor of Castilian in the Liceo de los Andes, a post she held for six years.

During this period, before 1920, the young teacher first gained recognition as a poet when she entered and won a poetry contest conducted by a writers' society in Santiago. Under the name Gabriela Mistral—a composite pseudonym taken from two eminent European poets whom she admired, Gabriele D'Annunzio, the Italian, and Frédéric Mistral, the Frenchman (also a Nobel prize winner)—she submitted three *Soñetos de la Muerte* ("Sonnets on Death"), for which she won the highest prize, a laurel crown and a gold medal (1914). These poems were subsequently published in Chile, and later appeared in translation in other countries. Gabriela Mistral, as she was henceforth known, had written her first poetry in 1907, stirred by a tragic love affair which found expression in sorrowful lyrics. A year later she utilized the material of her own experience in the composition *La Voz de Elqui* ("The Voice of Elqui"). She also dealt poetically with what has been the great interest of her life—children. Her poems about and for children, such as *Canciones de Cuna* (lullabies) and *Rondas de Niños* (Children's songs), were published in newspapers and magazines. After winning the 1914 poetry award she rapidly took her place among South America's foremost poets. Some of her poems and prose pieces were included in a five-volume set of school readers and also in a volume of the translated work of the great Hindu poet Rabindranath Tagore.

Her fame as a poet spread, and brought her the public adulation bestowed on leading poets in Latin America, where huge crowds will turn out to hear a favorite read a new composition. But Gabriela Mistral continued her educational work. In 1918-22 she was director and Professor of Spanish in three schools successively. On the invitation of the Mexican Government, she was commissioned by Chile to assist in the reorganization and development of Mexican libraries and rural schools, in which she was associated with the Minister of Education, Dr. José Vasconcelos. She delivered a series of lectures on Hispanic-American literature and other subjects, dedicated a school named for her, had several of her children's songs set to music by a noted composer for use in children's education, and published a selection of reading for use in girls' secondary schools. The problems of the Indian masses also impressed her deeply.

Miss Mistral's two busy years in Mexico were followed by European travel. On her return to Chile she was welcomed with official honors and has since served her country in consular and other posts. The poet was named Chile's delegate to the League of Nations Institute of Intellectual Cooperation, with headquarters in Paris, of which she later became secretary. In 1927 she was the Chilean Teachers' Association delegate to the Congress of Educators at Locarno, and the following year she represented both her own country and Ecuador at the Conference of the International University Federation at Madrid. In 1931 she returned to teaching for a brief period when she came to the United States as professor of Spanish history and civilization at Barnard and Middlebury colleges. The next year she was visiting professor of Spanish studies at the University of Puerto Rico. Her consular service began in 1933 with her appointment to Madrid, where she remained for two years. Since then she has been stationed in many important cities, including Lisbon, Genoa, and Nice. In December 1945 the poet was serving in Petropolis, Brazil's summer capital. The writer Olive Holmes has said that on occasion, during the last twenty years, the poet has "preferred to absent herself" from her country when unsympathetic to the political administration. However, Miss Mistral's position has generally been undisturbed by political changes within Chile. In the words of her compatriot Clarence Finlayson, "so great is her reputation that each successive government feels honored to have Gabriela as its representative abroad."

The first volume of Gabriela Mistral's poetry had been published, not in Chile, but in New York where Dr. Federico de Onís, professor of Spanish literature at Columbia University, had stimulated interest in the work of the Chilean poet. According to the professor, his students "wanted to know where they could get her poems, and all I could give them was a handful of clippings. I told them that if they wanted a volume, enough of them would have to subscribe to copies to pay for the printing." Thus the first edition of *Desolación* ("Desolation") was published under the auspices of the Spanish Institute in New York in 1922, and a year later was reprinted in the poet's native land. Her next volume, *Ternura* ("Tenderness"), published during her first sojourn in

Spain, consisted of poems for children. The poet's verse has been collected in *Desolacion* and in *Tala* (Buenos Aires, 1938). Her poems have been translated into French, German, Swedish, Italian, and English. Among her works are a series of sonnets, *Preguntas* ("Questionings"), *Nubes blancas* ("White Clouds"), and *The Prayer of the Schoolmistress*, both first published in Barcelona in 1930; she has also written a life of St. Francis of Assisi. In the United States her poetry has appeared in various magazines, including *Commonweal* and *Poetry*, and in 1938 was reprinted in two anthologies, *Some Spanish-American Poets* and *Anthology of Latin-American Poetry*. Other selections of her work are *Lectures for Women* and *Destruction*, and "Gabriela Mistral's Anthology" is being translated. The poet has also served on the editorial staff of a Bogotá newspaper, *Time*.

Considered the founder of the modern poetry movement in Chile, Miss Mistral enjoys "universal favor" among her countrymen. Her style is direct and personal, her imagery rich and earthy, and her words simple and vigorous, "a valuable contribution to the enrichment of the Spanish language." Her chief literary influences have been the Bible, Tagore, the Mexican Amado Nervo, and the Nicaraguan Rubén Darío. Finlayson (writing in *Commonweal*) finds in her work "a unique delicacy, gentle resignation, and an inclination that is spontaneously ethical." "Gripping dramatic power" and "apostolic intensity" have also been noted in her work and she has won the appellation, "the best-loved of living Spanish mystic poets." While most critics stress the strong religious quality of her poetry, Mildred Adams points out that although an ardent Catholic, Miss Mistral is "an avowed anti-clerical." According to another critic, her poetry reveals "a universal maternal instinct for children, the poor and the unfortunate." This feeling and her political consciousness impelled her to give the proceeds from the sale of her book *Tala* (1938) to the Basque orphans of the Spanish Civil War. The gesture incurred the displeasure of dictator Franco's'⁴² supporters, a displeasure which, however, failed to dampen the poet's sympathy for the child victims. She has glorified the mission of the teacher in her work, revealing at the same time her profound understanding of children and idealistic approach to teaching. While she has treated many themes, creating beautiful love and nature lyrics, she has generally written "out of sorrow." Wrote one Chilean critic: "Her best claim to enduring fame lies in her making articulate and moving the tragedy of the childless woman." Her writings include many prose poems, short inspirational stories of a Biblical quality.

The poetry of Gabriela Mistral reflects many moods and a wide range of sensitivity. In minor key are these lines from the early *Sonnets of Death* (translated by Alice Stone Blackwell):

> From that cold ledge where they have laid you by,
> I shall take down and lay you in the ground,
> Where humble and alone myself shall lie,
> Where we shall share dream-pillowings profound.
>
> Beside you stretching I shall show you all
> A mother's yearning for her child asleep,
> So earth shall cradle your pale body's pall,
> And sweetness smother half the sobs you weep.

Pitched to a lighter key is the opening stanzas of the inspirational lyric, *"Hymn to the Tree"*:

> O Brother tree, fast fixed in earth
> By brown hooks 'neath the soil that lie,
> Yet raising thy clean brow aloft
> With fervent yearning for the sky!...

The prose poem "To the Children" is typical both of her use of this form and of her feeling for children. It begins:

> Many years hence, when I am a little heap of silent dust, play with me, with the earth of my heart and of my bones!

A frequent contributor to periodicals in Spanish America, Europe, and the United States, Miss Mistral has written articles on sociological and cultural subjects. *Living Age* (August 28, 1926) carried her study "Mexico's Educational Effort," the *Bulletin* of the Pan American Union (October 1938) published her tender "Farewell to the Children of Brazil," and in April 1931 the *Pan American* Magazine published her "Message to American Youth." Long an enthusiastic worker for harmony and understanding between the Americas, the poet-teacher in this last article declared: "We of North and South America have accepted with our heritage of geographic unity a certain common destiny which should find a threefold fulfillment on our continent in an adequate standard of living, perfect democracy, and ample liberty." Writing in *Free World* in February 1943, she "sharply, yet eloquently" analyzed the differences which hinder inter-American unity in her article "The Gulf and The Bridge." Primary among these isolating factors she found race prejudice—"that great paganistic and collective evil, racial superstition, the idolatry of the skin, exists both within and between the Americas." Egocentric cultural attitudes, Miss Mistral says, also contribute largely to disunity, for the average North American, confusing culture with civilization, "does not believe the average man in Latin America has a cultural rank equal to his own." She concludes: "I write as a prophet when I say that the century of the common man will be built in the Americas only on common ground in education, regardless of race, creed, or language."

The Chilean poet has been widely honored for her literary and poetic work. Her first visit to the United States, in 1924, was marked by an impressive official reception and an interview with President Coolidge at the White House. She holds an honorary diploma from

MISTRAL, GABRIELA—*Continued*

the University of Chile, and membership in the Committee of Arts and Letters of the League of Nations. Her most recent honor, the 1945 Nobel Prize, placed her in the ranks of Kipling, Tagore, Yeats, Mann, and Galsworthy. (Five years earlier she had been proposed for the Nobel award by the Peruvian newspaper, *La Cronica.*) When she accepted the award in Stockholm in December, she said, "The New World has been honored through me. . . .The victory is not mine, but America's." On her Swedish visit the poet found that country's social democracy "a century ahead of everything else" and was reported by *Time* Magazine to have been the "lioness of social Stockholm."

After her European visit, in March 1946 Miss Mistral was received by President Truman and feted in Washington and in other cities. The United States, the poet had remarked on her arrival, possesses the "strongest pulse of life and creation" in the world today. She has, too, praised the qualities of American men and expressed the "highest kind of admiration" for American women. Formerly a member of the United Nations Subcommission on the Status of Women, Gabriela Mistral, after attending meetings once, resigned from it in May 1946. One of the reasons she gave for her action was her disagreement with the aim of the subcommission. She did not believe, she said in an interview, that the way for women to obtain equality with men was through special protective legislation. "It [special protective legislation] does not equalize. It lowers women. Common legislation raises womanhood's standards, gives it equality." Miss Mistral explained that she was neither a fighter nor an "official feminist." Later in the year Gabriela Mistral was named as one of the Latin American women sponsoring the Inter-American Congress of Women to be held in May of 1947. Earlier, in January 1946, press reports revealed that her countrymen planned to make her birthplace a cultural center. Many South American schools and libraries have been named in her honor. As for her poetry, Miss Mistral has revealed that "for years she has had material for two or three new books of verse."

Gabriela Mistral is a tall, handsome woman with strong features, straight hair, a dark complexion, and a "captivating smile." She dresses simply. One interviewer has remarked, "Only her clear eyes contrast with the pointedly Araucanian [Indian] characteristics, and betray a remote Spanish ancestry," while another says, "She is of the Basque type that predominates in Chile." She has impressed reporters with her sincerity and simplicity. The poet revealed the key to her philosophy and lifework when she said, "I am a Christian, a total democrat. I believe that Christianity, in its profoundest social sense, can save the peoples of the world." To this she added, "I have written as one who speaks in solitariness."

References

Bul Pan Am Union 58:647-61 Jl 24 por
Chilean Gaz p10+ D '45 por

Commonweal 35:160-3 D 5 '41
Free World 5:191 F '43
Liv Age 323:495-6 N 29 '24
Columbia Encyclopedia (1935)
Who's Who in America, 1946-47

MITCHELL, WILLIAM D(E WITT)
Sept. 9, 1874- Lawyer

Address: b. 20 Exchange Pl., New York; h. Syosset, N.Y.

As its first official act the Joint Congressional Committee Investigating the Pearl Harbor Attack on September 26, 1945, selected William D. Mitchell as committee counsel. A former United States Solicitor General and Attorney General, with a large private practice in New York City, the septuagenarian lawyer, many of whose colleagues include him among the half-dozen best practitioners at the national bar, was chosen by unanimous vote. He presided at the hearings until shortly after the Christmas recess of the committee.

William De Witt Mitchell was born on September 9, 1874, in Winona, Minnesota, the son of William and Frances (Merritt) Mitchell. His paternal grandparents had emigrated from Scotland to Ontario, Canada, but his father, a native of Ontario, received his education in the United States and eventually settled as a lawyer in Winona in 1857. For twenty years the elder Mitchell was a distinguished justice of the Minnesota Supreme Court, and today many of the opinions he rendered are used in the case books of the country's principal law schools. Young Mitchell left Winona at the age of fourteen to attend the Lawrenceville (preparatory) School in New Jersey and then, not yet attracted to law as a profession, enrolled in the Sheffield Scientific School of Yale University to study electrical engineering. Vacations he spent with his father, absorbing the legal discussions and arguments of the attorneys, judges, and justices who were his father's companions. And after two years at Yale he transferred to the University of Minnesota and a pre-law course. He received his B.A. from Minnesota in 1895 and, after a post-graduate night law course, his LL.B. in 1896. In that year he was admitted to the Minnesota bar and began his career as a law clerk with the firm of Stringer and Seymour in St. Paul, to which city the family had moved while he was in school.

At the outbreak of the Spanish-American War in 1898, Mitchell interrupted his career to serve as a second lieutenant in the Fifteenth Minnesota volunteer infantry. Subsequently, he became acting judge advocate for the Second United States Army Corps (1898), engineer officer of the third brigade, First Division, Second Army Corps (1899), and captain and adjutant of the Fourth Regiment of the Minnesota National Guard (1899-1901). Upon being mustered out of the Army after the end of the Spanish-American War in February 1899, the young man returned to the firm of Stringer and Seymour, with whom he now remained for approximately a year. But in the 1898 elections the elder Mitchell had failed to receive the Republican endorsement as state supreme court justice (which in previous elections had been his along with the Democratic and Populist endorsements) and was thus defeated by the Republican candidate of the strongly Republican state. At the expiration of his term in December 1899, therefore, father and son set up their own law partnership in St. Paul. Then, after his father's death in August 1900, the younger Mitchell entered the firm of Palmer, Beek, and Mitchell as junior partner. He was then twenty-six years old.

Within a short time, however, both Palmer and Beek left the firm and Mitchell found himself (wrote Theodore G. Joslin, Boston political observer, in *World's Work* in 1930) with a large law practice which he had not himself built up. Believing a connection with an older firm to be desirable, Mitchell then became junior partner of How, Taylor, and Mitchell. When Pierce Butler returned to general practice in 1905, after representing the Chicago, St. Paul, Minneapolis and Omaha Railway as attorney for six years, the firm was reorganized as Butler, Mitchell, and Doherty. The practice of Mitchell and his partners, consisting entirely of private cases, grew so that it became one of the largest west of Chicago. During these years (and until 1925) Mitchell held no public office. While "there were occasions when he aspired to the office of corporation counsel and to a seat on the state bench," reported Joslin, "such opportunities came after the time had passed when he felt that they would be of advantage to him." When the United States entered World War I, Mitchell again interrupted his legal practice, to help organize and serve as colonel in the Sixth (later the 206th) Minnesota Infantry assigned to home guard duty, and in 1918 he entered the Field Artillery Officers' Training School at Camp Taylor, Kentucky, where he remained until the Armistice.

Rejoining his law firm in 1919, Mitchell reentered upon a varied and remunerative practice. And in 1922, when President Warren G. Harding appointed Pierce Butler to the United States Supreme Court, Mitchell became senior partner of the reorganized firm of Mitchell, Doherty, Rumble, Bunn, and Butler of St. Paul. Three years later President Calvin Coolidge appointed him, a Democrat, to the position of Solicitor General of the United States, one of the most highly prized Federal legal posts. The appointment had come about in a curious manner, notes Joslin. Shortly after the war, when Mitchell was apprehensive lest his continued occupation in private practice result in stagnation, an influential friend in Washington asked him if he wished to have his name considered for a vacancy as circuit judge. Mitchell, says Joslin, truthfully and without ulterior motives replied that only the position of Solicitor General would interest him. When the vacancy occurred some time later, therefore, Mitchell's friend presented the lawyer's name to Coolidge and the President passed over the Republican aspirants in his choice of Mitchell.

"Under the direction of the Attorney General," states the United States *Government Manual*, "the Solicitor General has special

WILLIAM D. MITCHELL

charge of the business of, and appears for and represents, the Government in the Supreme Court. When requested by the Attorney General, the Solicitor General may conduct and argue any case in which the United States is interested, in any court of the United States, or may attend to the interests of the Government in any State court or elsewhere, conferring with and directing the activities of the Federal law officers throughout the country when the occasion so requires. No appeal is taken by the United States to any appellate court without the authorization of the Solicitor General." "When he came to Washington in 1925 as Solicitor General," wrote Joslin, "it was with the understanding that he would contest for the Government only when he believed the Government was in the right. During the . . . years that he held the office . . . he or his subordinates . . . went before the Supreme Court of the United States on thirty-four occasions and expressed the solemn opinion that the lower courts had erred in rendering decisions in favor of the Government. Equally important and equally significant, the Supreme Court accepted the recommendations made in thirty-three of the cases. It was not that he made the Government an easy adversary. He contested tooth and nail when he was convinced the Government was in the right, but when he believed it in the wrong he said so unhesitatingly."

Mitchell at first intended to hold the solicitor generalship for only two years, but his interest in the work kept him in office for another year and in 1928 Attorney General Sargent's refusal to accept his resignation extended his period in office to the end of the Coolidge Administration. At this point Mitchell again intended to return to private practice; however, "his quiet but masterful pleadings" before the Supreme Court had earned the respect of that body and it was the Supreme Court Justices' recommen-

MITCHELL, WILLIAM D.—*Continued*

dations which prompted President Hoover '[43] to appoint Mitchell, rather than former assistant Attorney General William J. Donovan '[41], to his Cabinet as Attorney General. In this post, which he held until the defeat of the Hoover Administration in the 1932 campaign, Mitchell was head of the Department of Justice, chief law officer of the Federal Government, and a member of the President's Cabinet. It was his responsibility to represent the United States and when requested to advise the President and heads of executive departments in legal matters generally, to supervise Federal district attorneys and United States marshals and to oversee criminal investigations involving Federal laws. "In cases of exceptional gravity or importance," notes the *Government Manual*, "the Attorney General himself represents the Government in the United States Supreme Court." Among the cases which Mitchell himself pleaded as Attorney General was the so-called "Pocket Veto Case" (279 U.S. 655).

At the close of the Hoover Administration, Mitchell returned to private practice in New York, on April 1, 1933, joining the firm of Taylor, Blanc, Capron, and Marsh, which was then reorganized as Mitchell, Taylor, Capron, and Marsh. For twelve years the lawyer again took no part in public life. Then, on September 26, 1945, the Joint Congressional Committee on the Investigation of the Pearl Harbor Attack, as its first official act, selected Mitchell as committee counsel by unanimous vote, because he was one of the few who could fill the committee's designedly exacting qualifications for: "(1) an experienced lawyer familiar with Government procedure and investigating technique and (2) a man of vigorous health and sound integrity with no handicapping Administration affiliations." (It is said that Mitchell offered to serve without payment, but that a fee was to be worked out at a future date.) As reported in the New York *Times,* the technique of inquiry agreed upon gave Mitchell sole access to all departments, records, and personnel, including access to the Joint Chiefs of Staff and to President Roosevelt's '[42] papers at Hyde Park; individual committee members might not, on their own, probe where they would. And to expedite the hearings, Mitchell was authorized to conduct the first questioning of each witness without interruption, after which each member of the committee would individually continue the questioning, also without interruption.

On December 14, 1945, however, Mitchell announced his resignation from the committee, though he agreed to remain until the Christmas recess or till the new counsel could familiarize himself with the testimony already taken. He gave as his reasons the fact that the committee, although scheduled to present its complete findings to Congress on January 3, 1946, had heard only eight witnesses in a month's time, leaving approximately sixty still to be heard, and that he as counsel had not been permitted to present evidence which he thought pertinent. "It has become increasingly apparent," he said, "that some members of the committee [meaning, according to observers, the Republicans whom Mitchell accuses of unnecessarily prolonging the daily questioning] have a different view than that entertained by counsel, either as to the scope of the inquiry or as to what is pertinent evidence."

Determination and fearlessness are, in the opinion of Joslin, two of Mitchell's outstanding characteristics. "Mitchell is not the type," he says, "to move juries or to captivate the imaginations of men. Rather he is the intellectual type, appealing almost entirely to reason and at his best before appellate tribunals, where his work is calm, his expositions temperate, and his arguments possessing the power which moderation and balance give." *Newsweek* reports that "lawyers call him a lawyer's lawyer—an able consultant and adviser on legal problems." Mitchell served on the first Charter Commission for St. Paul in 1900, as regional counsel to the U.S.R.R. Administration in 1919, and on the Citizens Charter Committee of St. Paul in 1922. He is a member of the American Bar Association and the Bar Association of the City of New York (of which he was president from 1941 to 1943); of the Central Committee of the American Red Cross, of the Spanish War Veterans, and of the American Legion.

On June 27, 1901, he was married to Gertrude Bancroft, and their two sons are William and Bancroft. Mitchell's clubs are the Somerset, the White Bear Yacht (St. Paul), the Metropolitan, the Burning Tree (Washington), the University, and the Century (New York). Politically he is a Democrat, but he does not hesitate to vote outside of his party for a better candidate; and in religion he is a Presbyterian. "A slender, graying man with a springy step," he was for many years an enthusiastic golfer, winning amateur championships, a tennis player and a marksman; he used to play the mandolin, guitar and clarinet, and has taken up movie photography as a hobby.

References

Law Notes 33:6-8 Ap '29
World's Work 59:68-71 F '30

International Who's Who, 1945-46
National Cyclopædia of American Biography Current vol C p10
Who's Who in America, 1946-47
Who's Who in Law, 1937

MOMSEN, C(HARLES) B(OWERS) (mŭm'sĕn)   June 21, 1896-   United States Navy officer

Address: h. 2436 39th Pl., N.W., Washington, D.C.

During World War II the escape device called the "Momsen lung" saved the lives of many men who would otherwise have been suffocated or drowned while trapped in disabled submarines. Rear Admiral C. B. Momsen of the United States Navy, the man chiefly responsible for the successful development of the "lung," and after whom it is named, was made Administrator of the United States Naval Shipping Control Authority for the Japanese Merchant

Marine in November 1945. About a year later, in October 1946, he was appointed commandant of the Naval operating base at Guam.

Charles Bowers Momsen was born in Flushing, New York, on June 21, 1896. After attending high school in Washington, D.C., and St. Paul, Minnesota, he received his appointment to the United States Naval Academy from the Fourth District of Minnesota and began his training May 29, 1916. While a midshipman at the Naval Academy, "Swede" Momsen played football and baseball. He served, in the summer of 1918, aboard the battleship *Kansas* which operated on escort duty during World War I. In June 1919 he was graduated and commissioned an ensign with the class of 1920. Until September 1919, Momsen remained on duty at the Naval Academy, leaving the next month to join the battleship *Oklahoma*.

After June 1921 Momsen was assigned to the *Maryland* during and after the time she was fitted out at Newport News (Virginia) Shipbuilding and Drydock Company. He left the ship in September 1921 for instruction at the New London, Connecticut, Submarine Base. In January 1922 Momsen joined the submarine O-13 based on Coco Solo, Canal Zone, serving there beyond June 7, 1922, when he was promoted to lieutenant (junior grade), until June 1923. During the next four years he consecutively commanded the submarines O-15, R-24, and S-1, earning the rank of lieutenant on June 7, 1925.

From July 1927 to June 1929 Momsen served in the design division of the Bureau of Construction and Repair (later combined with the Bureau of Engineering and designated the Bureau of Ships). Duty followed with the officer in charge, Submarine Safety Tests, and with the commander, Submarine Safety Test Unit; the latter aboard the salvaged submarine S-4, which sank in December 1927 with a loss of forty men off Provincetown, and had been reconditioned as a floating laboratory. At this time Momsen, who had been captain of the S-4's sister ship, was engaged with others in the invention of a submarine escape device to allow occupants of a too-long submerged ship to breathe and escape. Lieutenant Momsen participated in the diving tests held off Key West, using the "lung" he had helped devise. Before the trial the experimenter entered a steel, barrel-like escape hatch, high enough for a standing man. He then let water enter through a valve until the air inside the hatch became compressed to equal the pressure of the water outside, and the water stopped coming in. Then the "lung," bearing an attached breathing tube and filled with oxygen and soda of lime to absorb the noxious carbon dioxide, was placed around the chest. The diver next opened a door into the sea from the escape hatch, and came to the surface, guided by a line with a buoy which had been released from within the hatch. On the surface of the water the oxygen-filled bag served as a life preserver until the man was picked up by a rescue ship. Later tests showed that, wearing the "lung", men could blow out the water in the S-4's ballast tanks and bring her to the surface. The New York *Times* reported that, as a result of the experiment, "men

U.S. Navy

REAR ADM. C. B. MOMSEN

will not be trapped like rats when a damaged submarine sinks to the ocean floor."

For his meritorious service to the Government in the perfection of the "lung," Momsen received the Distinguished Service Medal, the citation of which reports: "During the early stages of its design and development Lieutenant Momsen, one of the inventors, courageously, repeatedly, and voluntarily risked his life in conducting experiments of a nature such that there was little or no information available as to their probable results. In the later tests of the device when escapes were made from the U.S.S. S-4 submerged to depths as much as 206 feet, Momsen was not only the first person to venture the escape but was also the leading and guiding spirit in all subsequent ones. It is through the initiative, courage and perseverance of Lieutenant Momsen that the development of the 'lung' . . . has reached a successful conclusion and the device been adopted as part of the regular equipment of all our submarines."

Transferred to the submarine base at Pearl Harbor, Momsen served in Hawaii until March 1934, when, as a lieutenant commander, he joined the *Ogala*, a minelayer, on which he was engineer until January 1935. In February of that year he reported for duty as executive officer of the submarine *Canapus*, operating with Squadron 5. A year later he was transferred to the *Augusta* as engineer officer. He served as her first lieutenant and damage control officer from March until June of 1937.

Momsen became officer in charge of the experimental diving units at the Washington, D.C., Navy Yard in August 1937. During this assignment he proved that helium is superior to nitrogen as a diluter for oxygen in diving. In a long series of tests he worked out a new set of decompression tables for various depths and for dives of varying length, in order to prevent the post-diving "bends." Divers were now able

MOMSEN, C. B.—*Continued*

to descend five hundred feet with safety and full consciousness.

For the successful salvage and rescue of crew members of the submarine *Squalus,* which sank off Muscle Shoals, Momsen received a letter of commendation from the Secretary of the Navy which stated that he had, in May, 1939, as diving officer on the staff of the commander of the Squalus salvage unit, "demonstrated a high and outstanding measure of ability, exceptional coolness, judgment, specialized knowledge and a responsibility . . . which resulted in the successful rescue of the thirty-three survivors from a depth of 240 feet of water and the salvage of the stricken submarine." An attached report stated, "This was a period of the greatest diving effort in the world's history. That, in six hundred and forty dives, under the most severe conditions, there was not a single loss of life or a serious personal injury, speaks for the eternal vigilance, professional skill, technical knowledge and rare judgment and initiative of Commander Momsen." He had been promoted to commander in July 1939, in which rank he continued his work until September of that year.

When assigned duty in the Fourteenth Naval District, Pearl Harbor, in October 1941, Momsen was commanding the *Sirius,* on which he had served since September 1939. He remained at Pearl Harbor until after the Japanese attack of December 7, 1941, and in July of the next year was assigned additional duty as assistant chief of staff to the commander, Hawaiian Sea Frontier and as War Plans Officer. Detached from that assignment on February 5, 1943, Momsen served as commander of Submarine Squadron 2 until one month after his promotion to rear-admiral on October 6, 1943, and as commander of Submarine Squadron 4 until June 1944. For his contribution to submarine warfare he was awarded the Navy Cross with a citation praising his command of ships which had sunk five enemy vessels and damaged eight.

In June 1944 Momsen reported for duty in the Office of the Chief of Naval Operations, Navy Department, Washington, D.C. From December 9, 1944 until July 30, 1945, he was at sea commanding the *South Dakota.* Under his direction the ship operated in the Pacific area and participated in pre-invasion operations against Japan, attacking enemy installations in the Tokyo area. Momsen returned to the headquarters of the Fleet commander in chief, in Washington, and in November 1945 was designated administrator of the United States Shipping Control Authority for the Japanese Merchant Marine. As administrator he has supervised the evacuation of the first of an eventual three million three hundred thousand Japanese from China, Manchuria, Formosa, and Pacific islands. Nearly two hundred surplus Army and Navy ships, most of them manned by Japanese crews guarded by United States service personnel, are participating in the operation.

In addition to the Navy Cross and the Distinguished Service Medal, Admiral Momsen has earned the Legion of Merit, the Victory Medal, Escort Clasp (U.S.S. *Kansas*), American Defense Service Medal, Fleet Clasp (U.S.S.

Sirius), the Asiatic-Pacific Area Campaign Medal, the American Area Campaign Medal, and the World War II Victory Medal. The Admiral and his wife, the former Anne Lyles Offutt, have a son, Lieutenant Commander Charles Bowen Momsen, Jr., a 1942 graduate of the Naval Academy.

MONTEUX, PIERRE (môn″tû′ pyâr)
Apr. 4, 1875- Conductor
Address: b. c/o San Francisco Symphony Orchestra, San Francisco, Calif.; h. Fairmont Hotel, San Francisco, Calif.; Domain of the Great Pine, Hancock, Me.

Responding to demand, Pierre Monteux, conductor of the San Francisco Symphony Orchestra, during the season 1946-47 will lead his men on an eight-week tour of the United States. The circumstance, it is believed, will go far to satisfy those critics who have for years been complaining that the unspectacular Monteux has never received in America the full measure of popular acclaim which is his due as one of the world's outstanding musicians. Conductor at one time or another of sixty-some orchestras in Europe and the United States, the septuagenarian Frenchman began his career as an instrumentalist, introduced controversial modern scores with the Diaghilev Ballet Russe, founded several orchestras of his own, and finally rebuilt the San Francisco Symphony Orchestra. Applauded by the critics whenever he conducts the classical scores of Beethoven and Brahms, Monteux has likewise earned high praise as an "apostle of new music."

"Frisco's Frenchman," as Pierre Monteux has been affectionately called by the press in recent years, was born in Paris on April 4, 1875, the son of Gustave and Clemence (Brisac) Monteux. Hearing a Mozart violin sonata as a child, he first decided to become a violinist. At a relatively early age he entered the Paris Conservatoire, where he studied violin with Maurin and Berthelier, solfeggio and harmony with Lavignac, counterpoint and fugue with Lenepveu. At his graduation in 1896 he was awarded first prize for his violin playing, but two years earlier he had begun his instrumental career by playing the viola in public concert with a string quartet. Between 1896 and 1911 he was first a violinist with the orchestras of the Opéra Comique and the Société des Concerts Colonne in Paris, then, in succession, concertmaster, assistant conductor and conductor of the Colonne orchestra. This experience equipped the young musician to organize his own Concerts Berlioz in Paris in 1911, which attracted the attention of Serge Diaghilev, impresario of the Ballet Russe.

Thus, a few months after launching the Concerts Berlioz, Monteux was engaged as a principal conductor of the Ballet Russe, which Diaghilev and Michel Fokine had founded in 1909 in protest against the stereotyping of Russian ballet. "It was no sinecure—that conductorial post with the Diaghilev Ballet," writes David Ewen in *Dictators of the Baton.* "The music of Stravinsky [40], which then burst on the world of music like a bolt of lightning, demanded an exacting technique. With its enormous rhythmic and harmonic complexity it called for all the resources of a conductor's science." The familiar repertoire was interspersed with new works, and Monteux's first assignment was to prepare Stravinsky's second ballet, *Petrouchka*, for its première on June 13, 1911. On June 8, 1912, Monteux conducted the première of Ravel's *Daphnis et Chloé*. Then, on May 29, 1913, came the sensational première of Stravinsky's revolutionary *Sacre du printemps*. The first bars of the prelude, says Stravinsky in his *Chroniques de ma vie,* "evoked laughter and mockery." Protests and counter-protests produced an uproar above which the music could scarcely be heard. Saint-Saëns and the Paris critic André Capu were loud in their denunciations of the work, while Maurice Ravel and Claude Debussy were equally vehement in their championship of the score. Incidents such as a lady slapping the face of a man who was hissing were frequent. Meanwhile, in the wings Stravinsky was holding Nijinsky [40], the choreographer of the work, by the collar to prevent his reaching the stage, and from the conductor's pit Monteux was throwing desperate glances at Diaghilev who signaled to him to continue playing. But whatever the public thought of the music, Stravinsky approved Monteux's conducting of his ballets.

The Frenchman remained with the Diaghilev troupe through four tours, approximately from 1911 through 1914, and conducted also the première of Debussy's *Jeux* in 1913 and of Stravinsky's *Rossignol* in 1914. His fame was increasing, however, and beginning in 1913 he accepted a series of guest invitations with the Paris Opéra Comique, at Covent Garden and Drury Lane in London, in Berlin, Budapest, and Vienna. In February 1914, to remedy the neglect of modern French and foreign scores by his contemporaries, he organized the Société des Concerts Populaires, often known as the Concerts Monteux, at the Casino de Paris. It was with this group that he gave the first full concert performance of Stravinsky's *Petrouchka* on March 1, 1914, and on April 5 and 26, 1914, barely a year after the première, two concert performances of *Le Sacre du printemps* which were well received.

In World War I, from August 5, 1914, to September 10, 1916, the conductor served as a private in the 35th Territorial Infantry of the French Army, participating in the battles of Verdun, Rheims, Soissons, and the Argonne. In January 1916 the Ballet Russe, without Monteux, arrived in New York for its first short American season of ballet under the sponsorship of Otto H. Kahn, a director and chief patron of the Metropolitan Opera Company. In the autumn the troupe, engaged for a forty weeks' transcontinental tour sponsored by Kahn, returned, and this time—Kahn's intercession with the French authorities at Nijinsky's request having succeeded—it was again under the baton of Pierre Monteux. Monteux's release from the armed forces was granted, it is said, because the tour was considered propaganda for the Allied cause. Almost at once, however, Monteux became the center of controversy and criticism when he refused to conduct the ballet *Till Eulenspiegel* which used the

PIERRE MONTEUX

music of Richard Strauss's tone poem, saying that he would under no circumstances play the music of an enemy national. To Americans, not yet at war, the attitude seemed extremely questionable, but peace was restored when Kahn ordered that a second conductor be engaged to direct the offending work. Monteux's success with the Ballet Russe in the United States brought him first an invitation to appear as guest conductor with the Civic Orchestra in New York in the summer of 1917 and later that year a contract to conduct the French repertoire at the Metropolitan. (Ernest Ansermat, the Swiss conductor, succeeded him with the Ballet Russe but was, according to Romola Nijinsky, not nearly so well liked as Monteux.)

In 1918, after public opposition to his alleged enemy sympathies had driven Karl Muck from his post as conductor of the Boston Symphony Orchestra, and while the orchestra was awaiting its new conductor Henri Rabaud, Monteux was asked to take over the Boston podium. So deep was the impression he made on the Bostonians that at the termination of Rabaud's trial contract in 1919 they chose him as their new permanent conductor. Terminating his relation with the Metropolitan, therefore, Monteux began a reorganization of the Boston Symphony, which had recently lost twenty of its best members, including the concertmaster, during an unsuccessful strike for unionization. Despite many difficulties, points out David Ewen, Monteux's concerts during his five years' incumbency, which included first American performances of many of the works of Stravinsky, Debussy, Ravel, Roger-Ducasse and other moderns, "were admirable both for the vitality of his programs and the musicianship with which they were presented." Before he left Boston in 1924 the French conductor had succeeded in restoring to the orchestra some of its former brilliance and he bequeathed

MONTEUX, PIERRE—*Continued*

to Serge Koussevitzky at least the foundation on which the latter was to build the present world-famous ensemble.

Returning to Europe, Monteux began a ten years' association with Willem Mengelberg and the Concertgebouw Orkest of Amsterdam, conducting also the Amsterdam Wagner Society and traveling widely as a guest conductor on the Continent. In 1928 he returned to the United States to appear with the Philadelphia Orchestra during a leave of absence of Leopold Stokowski, but the experience was an unhappy one. Although the critics praised, the public remained indifferent, and Monteux left America with the acid remark that he was through with a country that wanted only "slim, well-tailored conductors." Musical historians explained afterward that he had encountered a "Stokowski-dazzled audience" which remained unmoved when not given the "sensationalism" of the Philadelphia leader. Two years after this Monteux became the conductor of the Orchestra Symphonique de Paris, which had been founded by Ernest Ansermet in June 1928. Until 1938 Monteux continued as its regular conductor, dividing his time after 1935 between it and his new post in San Francisco. Just before the outbreak of World War II in 1939, he led the Paris Symphony Orchestra for the last time, as a guest conductor.

Known to San Francisco both by reputation and from guest appearances in the West Coast city, the Frenchman was invited to undertake the rebuilding of the San Francisco Symphony Orchestra in 1935. This organization, founded in 1911 under the sponsorship of the Musical Association of San Francisco and led until 1929 by Alfred Hertz, had since the depression been drifting both economically and artistically under a series of guest conductors. The fact that the orchestra had been able to give only four concerts during the 1934-35 season, and these only because the municipality had agreed to guarantee payment of the bills, provoked a reorganization of the Musical Association, and a vigorous public campaign resulted in a vote for partial subsidization of the orchestra by the city. Now a conductor of established reputation and organizational talent was needed, and Monteux, with world-wide recognition and the Boston experience behind him, was chosen. After the first trial year, he was given a new three-year contract. Today the revitalized orchestra forms the backbone of San Francisco's musical life, giving twelve pairs of concerts each season either at the opera house or in the Civic Auditorium, as well as special concerts for university students. Each year since 1943 a series of festival concerts has been devoted to a single classical composer. At least one contemporary work is included on each program and conductor Monteux has made a habit of sponsoring promising young talent, such as Carol Brice, Leon Fleischer, and William Kapell. He is also active with his orchestra in the recording studios. Moreover, "as a result of his benevolent protectorate," said the New York *Times* in 1944, his men still like music enough to form chamber music ensembles and quartets when off duty, while Monteux spends his time away from San Francisco in guest conducting with other orchestras. (On November 13, 1937, he inaugurated the new NBC Symphony Orchestra established for Arturo Toscanini.) During the summer he holds conducting classes at his summer home in Maine, continuing a practice he began in Paris.

"For a period of more than three decades," wrote David Ewen in 1943, Monteux "has been among the elect of the baton." "A musician of soundness and breadth of perception if ever there was one," said Olin Downes, at another time comparing Monteux's musicianship to Toscanini's. "The salient characteristics of his work," noted Henry Simon in *PM*, "include an unquestioned authority over the men, a clarity of design, a steady and inevitable feeling for the tempo of the music and an ability to underscore its drama without distortion." One New York concert drew from Virgil Thomson of the *Herald Tribune* the comment: "It has remained for Pierre Monteux to achieve what many of us thought hopeless. He has made the Philharmonic play with real beauty of tone, many kinds of it, and with perfect balance and blending—to sound, in short, like an orchestra, a real, first-class orchestra requiring no apology." Another caused Olin Downes to grow lyrical: "Mr. Monteux's interpretations of the works of Brahms [Third Symphony] and Beethoven [Third Leonore Overture] were the most musically and stirring performances of those scores that the present writer has heard from any conductor in a considerable number of years in this city. . . .Lo, we heard again the veritable voices of Beethoven and Brahms—the passion of Beethoven, the power and the glory of his spirit—just as one distinguished, with the first two chords of the symphony, and the lightning flash of the theme that leaps from the strings, the inalienable manner of the rugged individualist, the modern classic, the congenial romantic of the greatest German symphonies since the Nine. The spaciousness was back in the Brahms symphony, and the deep breath of it, and the bear's hug of it, too; and the mountain vistas." Of his conducting of Hindemith's *Mathis der Maler* Jerome D. Bohm said: "Mr. Monteux's interpretation was highly convincing, realizing the exalted mysticism implicit in the music with unerring perception, the final climax reaching incandescent heights of intensity."

To San Franciscans, says *Time* Magazine, the portly figure with the dyed black hair, blue serge suits and pearl stickpins, has "long since become a civic feature." And so enthusiastically does he return the city's regard that on one occasion the New York *Times* found it necessary to remark that he was not employed by the San Francisco Chamber of Commerce. With "sprightly" Mme. Monteux (the former Doris Hodgkins, to whom he was married on September 26, 1928, in Brussels, Belgium), the city's first musical citizen makes his home in the old-fashioned and palatial Fairmount Hotel on Nob Hill. (A daughter by an earlier marriage and her small son, Pierre-Jacques, who is said to look like his grandfather, live at the conductor's summer home in Maine.) Although a "jovial, easy-going guest," Monteux dislikes the dinner parties to which he is always being invited and would rather be found at the Blue Fox, a small French restaurant across the street from the city morgue. His geniality and friendliness are proverbial, and his discipline of his men, though likened to that of a "good-natured, grandfatherly, but absolute czar," is said to spring from affection rather than from intimidation. "He has never been known to break a baton or raise his voice in rehearsal," writes Alfred Frankenstein, and "he has a prodigious memory, [using] a score perhaps once a season." Dignity and authority mark him on the podium, notes Leonora Wood Armsby of San Francisco in *Musicians Talk*, but not in private life. "At the outer edge of his extremely bright dark eyes are small creases which show that laughter lies not only upon his lips but that it sparkes through the core of his being." After he left the Boston Symphony Orchestra in 1924, Monteux was made a Chevalier of the Legion of Honor. On March 2, 1942, he became an American citizen.

References

Time 43:58 Ap 3 '44
Victor Record R p9+ O '41 il por; p4+ S '44

Eaglefield-Hull, A. ed. A Dictionary of Modern Music and Musicians (1924)
Ewen, D. Dictators of the Baton (1943) por; ed. Living Musicians (1940) por
Grove's Dictionary of Music and Musicians Am suppl (1928); Suppl vol (1940)
Thompson, O. ed. International Cyclopedia of Music and Musicians (1943)
Who's Who in America, 1946-47

MOONEY, EDWARD, CARDINAL May 9, 1882- Roman Catholic prelate

Address: b. 1234 Washington Blvd., Detroit, Mich.; h. 1880 Wellesley Dr., Detroit, Mich.

"Few men in America are as profoundly informed on current world affairs," said the Detroit *Free Press* editorially of Edward Cardinal Mooney, Archbishop of Detroit, one of the four American Roman Catholic ecclesiastics elevated to the Sacred College by Pope Pius XII [41] in the Consistory at Rome in February 1946. A scholar, an administrator, and the first American in the Vatican's diplomatic service, His Eminence had served his Church on three continents. In Detroit, of which he became Archbishop in 1937, his role in industrial disputes was summarized by the *Free Press*: "His has been a quiet but withal powerful voice of amelioration in the turbulent conflicts of Detroit industry, seeking always to bring to both sides the light of understanding, to eliminate blind hates and passions."

Born in Mount Savage, Maryland, on May 9, 1882, to Thomas and Sara (Heneghan) Mooney, Edward Cardinal Mooney is of Irish descent. One of seven children, his boyhood was spent in Youngstown, Ohio, to which his parents moved when he was five. Thomas Mooney was a laborer in a tube mill. At the age of fifteen Edward decided to study for the priesthood, whereupon he began his classical

EDWARD CARDINAL MOONEY

studies at St. Charles College (Ellicott City, Maryland). He remained there for six years (1897-1903), after which two years in philosophical courses at St. Mary's Seminary in Baltimore won him a B.A. degree (1905). His scholastic record at these colleges admitted him to the North American College in Rome, from which he received a Ph.D. in 1907 and two years later the degree of Doctor of Divinity. After twelve years of study and preparation, "the solemn goal of ordination and the priesthood" were attained on April 10, 1909.

The young priest returned to the United States to accept a professorship in dogmatic theology at St. Mary's Seminary in Cleveland. After six years (1909-16), his next post, which he held until 1922, was that of head of the Cathedral Latin School. In August of that year he became pastor of St. Patrick's parish in Youngstown, his home town. His brilliant work as a student and the "deep spiritual insight" he had displayed in Rome were not forgotten: a year later he was appointed spiritual director of North American College. In 1925 the Pope made him a Monsignor, a title conferred upon distinguished clerics.

In January 1926, when he was forty-four, the future Cardinal was elected Titular Archbishop of Irenopolis and made apostolic delegate to India, the first American to be appointed to a diplomatic post in the Holy See. While serving as a delegate to India, Mooney established eleven new mission territories and three more sees were entrusted to the direction of native Indian bishops. After five years' residence in India, the apostolic delegate was ordered to Japan, where he served in the same capacity for two years.

His appointment in 1933 as Bishop of Rochester (New York) was the beginning of his work as an administrator in the United States. In 1934 he was elected a member of the administrative board of the National Cath-

MOONEY, EDWARD, CARDINAL—*Cont.*

olic Welfare Conference, the policy-making organization of the hierarchy in the United States. At the same time he acted as episcopal chairman of the conference's department of social action. The following year saw his election as board chairman of the organization, a post he continued to hold until November 1945. Upon the death of Bishop Michael J. Gallagher of Detroit in 1937, the Vatican announced that the Detroit diocese had been elevated to an archiepiscopal see with the entire state of Michigan as its province. Simultaneously came the announcement that Edward Mooney had been named its first archbishop—the spiritual leader of more than eight hundred thousand Roman Catholics.

Long a proponent of Catholic interest in the labor movement, the Archbishop in a public announcement—at the time of the sit-down strike in the automotive industry in 1937—stated, in refutation of numerous rumors, that the Church did not disapprove of the newly formed CIO and that Catholic workingmen should join labor unions (*Catholic News*). He guided the establishment of the Association of Catholic Trade Unionists in February of that year, and initiated courses for priests of the archdiocese in labor and social problems. Cardinal Mooney's liberalism in political and economic affairs, said the Detroit *Free Press*, subscribes neither to the doctrine of *laissez faire,* nor to Marxian socialism, but is of the "heart and soul!" His was a protest against a system which "handed over the workers, each alone and defenseless, to the inhumanity of employers and the unbridled greed of competitors." According to the *Free Press*, "he was applying the fundamental tenets of Christianity to the economic issues of the market place."

As Father Charles E. Coughlin's [40] superior, the Archbishop used his influence to curb the priest who had exercised his privileges as a private citizen and not as a representative of the Roman Catholic Church to express his opinions on political and economic questions both over the radio and in the publication *Social Justice. PM* reported in 1942 that three days after the Archbishop had announced that he had obtained the radio priest's "solemn promise that he would halt forever" the activities that brought investigation of *Social Justice* by the Post Office and Justice Departments for spreading sedition (from which Coughlin later was exonerated) the publication had gone "out of business." The Archbishop was quoted as saying: "My understanding with him is sufficiently broad and firm to exclude effectively the recurrence of any such unpleasant situation." Although Father Coughlin later returned to the radio, "his scripts are always read beforehand by officials of the archdiocese."

In 1943 the Archbishop, as board chairman of the National Catholic Welfare Conference, was one of the leading figures in the framing of the seven-point "declaration on World Peace," which was signed by 144 prominent individuals of the Catholic, Jewish, and Protestant faiths. This, the first American interfaith pronouncement on world order, was released by the Federal Council of Churches of Christ in America, the Social Action Department of the N.C.W.C., and the Synagogue Council of America. The summarized seven points of the declaration are as follows: "The moral law must govern world order; the rights of the individual must be assured; the rights of the oppressed, weak or colonial peoples be assured, and states must repudiate racial, religious, or other discrimination in violation of these rights; the rights of the oppressed, weak, or colonial peoples must be protected and the progress of undeveloped, colonial, or oppressed peoples toward political responsibility must be the object of international concern; the rights of minorities must be secured, to equal opportunity for educational and cultural development, and to political equality; international institutions to maintain peace through collective security must be organized; international economic cooperation must be developed; and a just social order within each state must be achieved."

The prelate's achievements as an administrator of his archdiocese have been considered successful. He established catechetical centers, some of which later developed into parishes, for the religious instruction of children attending nonparochial schools. Through refinancing, at a lower rate of interest, loans that had been made to the churches for building purposes in the 1920's, he improved the financial condition of churches of the archdiocese; he inaugurated in May 1943 the Archdiocesan Development Fund, a campaign conducted by a committee of laymen to provide for current and future needs. A total of seven hundred thousand dollars was realized for 1943, two hundred thousand dollars more than the goal set.

The announcement that Edward Mooney, together with thirty-one other Catholic prelates, had been named as Cardinal, was made by Pope Pius XII on Christmas Eve of 1945, in a radio broadcast on the subject "A True and Lasting Peace." The Pope announced that the creation of the thirty-two new Cardinals would bring the membership of the Sacred College of Cardinals (a council or senate of the sovereign Pontiff in the government of the Church) to its full complement of seventy members. Because of the length of time which had elapsed since the last Consistory (1940), the membership of the College at the time of the Pope's announcement, was only thirty-eight. For two centuries, however, the Sacred College had not had its full complement. This number had been established in 1586 by Pope Sixtus V, who at that time had observed "that in ancient times the Sacred College had been too small, and in more recent times, too numerous." Pope Pius XII stated that the Cardinals had been selected from a variety of nations "so that this creation may portray in a living manner the universality of the Church." This, he said, was especially significant now—"in a time of stress. . . .She [the Church] must now more than ever be supranational. . . .It is a question here of a spiritual factor, of having an accurate sense of the Church's supranationalism, and not measuring or determining it according to mathematical proportions." Heretofore, the membership of the Sacred College had been predominantly Italian. The new membership was now composed of twenty-six Italians and forty-four citizens of eighteen other countries. The comment of the Catholic periodical *Commonweal* on the College's composition was that the conclusion was not to be drawn that the next Pope would be a non-Italian, although the possibility of such a choice was greater than it had been in some centuries.

The *Christian Century*, an "undenominational journal of religion," published an editorial on the Pope's reconstitution of the College of Cardinals: "Once again the leadership of the Roman Catholic Church has risen to meet a crisis of first magnitude with a display of ecclesiastical statesmanship of the first order . . . a decisive step to insure that the Italian orientation of the church shall end . . . a new international outlook for days when only a truly international church can play a major part in a world of dissolving nationalisms and sweeping social revolutions." While looking with disfavor on the whole concept of "the hierarchical order" of the Roman Catholic Church, "culminating in the papacy and a College of Cardinals called 'princes of the church,'" the editorial concluded with: "But taking the Roman Church as an existent fact in the world, we cannot be otherwise than grateful when the head of this Church displays a true Christian statesmanship. This we believe the Pope has done in recognizing the supranational character of Christianity in the superior order of the hierarchy."

When interviewed, after the announcement of his appointment to the Sacred College, Archbishop Mooney said that he was deeply grateful to the Pope for "his token of confidence," and that the responsibility inspired a feeling of sincere humility. In the company of Archbishops Samuel Stritch [46] and John Joseph Glennon (who died in Ireland after his return from the Vatican), Cardinal-designate Mooney flew to Rome, to which Archbishop Francis Spellman [40] of New York had already come for his elevation. The conferring of the Cardinal's red hat on the thirty prelates (two were unable to be present because of illness) took place in Rome before the culmination of the five days (February 18-22) of ceremonies solemn and rich in the colorful tradition of the Catholic Church. The high regard of Pope Pius XII for the American representatives of the Church was shown when they were assigned the Palazzo della Cancellaria for the reception following the religious ceremonies. This famous building, traditionally the property of the reigning Pope, is five centuries old and is built of stone from the Colosseum. Santa Susanna was assigned to Cardinal Mooney as his titular church in Rome. Such an assignment is customary, dating back to the time when the members of the Sacred College were parish priests living in Rome. Upon his return to Detroit Edward Cardinal Mooney resumed his archiepiscopal duties. His duties as Cardinal include, besides the privilege of voting in the elections of the Popes, the discussion with the sovereign Pontiff of all ecclesiastical affairs of any importance.

Edward Cardinal Mooney was one of many Roman Catholic Church dignitaries who denounced, in October 1946, the trial of Archbishop Aloysius Stepinatz of Zagreb, Yugoslavia, as a "Communist purge" and an attempt to "terrorize" those opposed to "Communist tyranny." He questioned the official United States attitude toward the Yugoslav Government's indictment and conviction of Archbishop Stepinatz on charges of "aiding puppet Premier Ante Pavelić's [42] wartime Croat Ustashi regime, of provoking racial hatred and of forcibly converting Serbs to Catholicism." The Acting Secretary of State, Dean Acheson [41], also criticized the trial. Later in the same month Cardinal Mooney stated in an interview that there was no cause for alarm in the "increasing struggle between the Christian principles of the Western world and the atheism of the East." "Every crisis," he remarked, "is, in a sense, another opportunity to improve our civilization."

The Cardinal wore his biretta only once—when it was conferred in the last of the five-day ceremonies in Rome. However, if the Cardinal follows rules of etiquette in cardinalate matters his scarlet biretta will be seen on a tray just inside the door of his residence on days that His Eminence is at home. One of the Cardinal's recreations is golf. Of his personality the Detroit *Free Press* wrote: "He has never lost the common touch. . . .Detroit people . . . have found him gracious, gentle, self-effacing . . . with a glorious sense of quiet humor."

References

Cath N p6 D 29 '45
Detroit Free Press D 25 '45
International Who's Who, 1945-46
Morgan, T. B. Speaking of Cardinals (1946)
Who's Who in America, 1946-47

MOREELL, BEN (môr-ēl') Sept. 14, 1892-
Former United States naval officer and Government official; engineer
Address: b. c/o Turner Construction Co., 420 Lexington Ave., New York

When Admiral Ben Moreell retired from active duty in September 1946 to enter private industry, he brought to an end twenty-nine years of outstanding service in the United States Navy. A naval engineer and organizer of the Seabees, Admiral Moreell since October 1945 had been serving the United States Government in various capacities. At that time Moreell became officer-in-charge of the Naval Petroleum Plants Office, managing the petroleum plants seized under President Truman's order when a stalemate developed in the strikes between the CIO Oil Workers International Union and the oil operators. Moreell became Coal Mine Administrator in the bituminous coal mine dispute. As manager and mediator, Moreell was successful in effecting long-sought compromises in strikes involving these two industries.

Ben Moreell was born in Salt Lake City, Utah, September 14, 1892, the son of Samuel and Sophia (Sossnitz) Moreell. When he was

ADM. BEN MOREELL (RET.)

two years old, his family moved to New York City, but four years later they settled permanently in St. Louis, where Ben received his education. Upon completion of elementary school at the age of twelve, he went to work during the summer, a practice which he continued for years. The first summer, he found a job at a wage of three dollars a week in a shoe factory, and increased his earnings by selling newspapers every Sunday. Always ambitious to learn, and encouraged by his mother, an avid reader herself, he "devoured" all of Dickens' works as well as any mystery stories he could lay his hands on. In the company of his sister, he frequented secondhand bookstores to pick up copies of his favorite novels.

Although Moreell has always regarded hard work as the road to success and achievement, his career in high school and college was a "rare combination" of work and play, of study and athletics. In high school, despite the fact that his program of his own choice included more subjects than necessary and that he remained after school some days to study college algebra and Latin and played ball the remaining free afternoons, he received high grades in the majority of courses. He was graduated from Central High School at sixteen years, the first in his class, and secured the four-year honor scholarship to Washington University. While he worked at various jobs to supplement his scholarship and maintained his reputation as a brilliant student, he insisted on participating in sports, was chosen captain of the track team, and won much applause as fullback. He was graduated in 1913 with the Bachelor of Science degree in civil engineering.

Moreell immediately went to work as resident and designing engineer on construction projects for the department of sewers in St. Louis, a position he held until 1917. His first connection with the Navy came in June 1917, a few months after the United States entered World War I. Having passed a competitive exam-

ination for a commission, he was appointed to the Civil Engineer Corps of the Navy with the rank of lieutenant, junior grade. After he finished a short indoctrination course at the Naval Academy, he began his first assignment, that of assistant to the public works officer at the New York Navy Yard. Soon after, in January 1918, he became aide on the staff of the Commander, Azores Detachment of the Atlantic Fleet, and simultaneously, public works officer at the naval base, Ponta Delgada, at San Miguel in the Azores; his service in these capacities ended in May 1919. By this time Moreell had decided to remain in the Navy. A month later he was appointed civil engineer member of the Plant Board with headquarters at Quincy, Massachusetts, and also plant engineer of the destroyer plant at Squantum, Massachusetts.

The ability of the young officer as naval engineer did not pass unnoticed, so that Moreell, though not a product of Annapolis, steadily advanced through the grades. During the years 1920-24 he was the principal assistant and executive officer to the engineer in chief of the Department of Public Works in Haiti. Afterwards, in succession, Moreell saw duty as principal assistant and later as public works officer at the Norfolk Navy Yard, at Portsmouth, Virginia, from September 1924 until April 1926; and as assistant design manager of the Bureau of Yards and Docks, in the Navy Department, in Washington, from July 1926 to the middle of the year 1930.

Consistent with his belief in hard work is the remark Moreell once made to a friend: "If you can't find enough work to keep busy, you can always write a book." He followed his own advice. With some spare time on his hands in 1929, while occupied with his duties in the Bureau of Yards and Docks, he wrote *Standards of Design for Concrete,* which is praised in several articles as "one of the outstanding and most widely accepted treatises on concrete" and as being "favorably received throughout the engineering profession, both in this country and abroad." Assigned in June 1930 to service as public works officer of the Navy Yard in Puget Sound, and the Thirteenth Naval District, in Seattle, he completed in 1932, "a large emergency construction program with such splendid results" that he earned the commendation of the Navy Department.

In June 1932 Moreell (then a lieutenant commander) was sent to France to study European methods of engineering design and construction at the Ecole Nationale des Ponts et Chausées in Paris. His knowledge of French, acquired in Haiti, was very useful. Returning to the United States in June of the following year, he became assistant design manager with personal supervision of planning the ship Model Testing Basin at Carderock, Maryland. His earlier researches on engineering in concrete aided him in this undertaking; and the project at Carderock was hailed for its practicality and innovations. Project manager of shipbuilding and repair facilities of the storage and submarine base section (May 1935 through July 1937), and public works officer of the Navy Yard at Pearl Harbor, and of the Fourteenth

Naval District (August through December of 1937) were among his other assignments. By this time Moreell had attained the rank of commander. Then, in December 1937, at the age of forty-five, he became Chief of the Bureau of Yards and Docks and Chief of Civil Engineers of the Navy, and was promoted to rear-admiral, one of the youngest naval officers to hold that rank.

Six days after Admiral Moreell was sworn in to his second term of the office of Chief of the Bureau of Yards and Docks, the United States entered World War II when the Japanese attacked Pearl Harbor. (As early as 1937 Moreell had stressed the need for extension of docking and repair facilities on United States possessions in the Pacific. Admiral Moreell formulated a naval expansion program, according to the *Christian Science Monitor,* most of which Congress endorsed.) That same month saw the formation of the Naval Construction Battalions known as the Seabees, by Admiral Moreell. The Seabees, whom Moreell nicknamed the "Can-Do Boys," became famous for their Paul Bunyan-like exploits. Comprised of trained construction men and engineers, the Seabees not only preceded the main forces of assault by laying out roads, manning floating drydocks, and building advance bases, airfields, and barracks, but also took part in the actual fighting. In February 1944 Moreell was nominated by President Franklin D. Roosevelt for advancement to the rank of Vice-Admiral, an action which occasioned some controversy at the time. The point in dispute was whether, legally, a chief of a bureau serving mainly in an administrative capacity and not on sea duty could be appointed to that rank. The nomination was upheld by Rear-Admiral Thomas L. Gatch, Judge Advocate General, and later confirmed by the Senate. On November 23, 1945, for his success in directing the "construction of shore facilities, including outlying bases, for the support of the Fleet," Moreell received the Distinguished Service Medal, and, at about the same time was awarded the Legion of Merit for his assistance in "expediting the construction of aviation gasoline plants during the war."

Moreell was chosen by the Navy Department in October 1945 to direct the operation of fifty-four strikebound oil refineries and pipelines by naval officers when the Government took over the plants to insure needed output of oil for the Navy. A month later he was appointed Chief of the Material Division, Office of the Assistant Secretary of the Navy, to begin work in December 1945. From the very beginning Admiral Moreell's handling of the oil strike was considered unconventional. As mediator, he resolved that the issues dividing the CIO Oil Workers International Union and the operators would be concluded to everyone's satisfaction. An example of his methods is evident in the following account: Moreell ordered to Washington the labor relations director and the leader of the strikers of one oil plant, both uncompromising in their attitude, and told them to negotiate a settlement. The two men tried, not without bitterness and repeated threats that they would leave. With each threat, writes Jim G. Lucas in the New York *World-Tele-*

gram, "the Admiral [who was pretending to read his mail] would hoist his glasses to his forehead, assume an air of injured surprise, and inject a new idea. At the end of five and one-half hours, there was an agreement."

Both labor and management have lauded Moreell's objectivity in dealing with strike problems. When the Administration faced a similar deadlock in the soft coal dispute involving John L. Lewis' United Mine Workers, Secretary of the Interior Julius A. Krug [45] in May 1946 named Moreell Deputy Coal Mine Administrator in charge of operating the bituminous coal mines, and later gave him complete control. The bituminous mines were seized under the Smith-Connally Act which specifies that Government-confiscated properties must be returned to the private owners within sixty days. Krug and Moreell, representing the Government's interests, after discussions with both sides decided upon terms, signed the contract with the union (the miners were given, among other things, an 18½-cent-an-hour wage increase and a welfare and retirement fund "financed by a levy of five cents per ton of coal produced"), and attempted to effect a labor-management truce. Also in May of 1946 Moreell was designated a member, by Secretary of War Robert P. Patterson, of a board of engineers formed to propose methods of improving the Panama Canal in matters relevant to navigation and defense. One month later Moreell attained the temporary rank of full admiral.

Moreell meanwhile helped to draft a safety code for the soft coal industry; and in July he signed another agreement, following a National Labor Relations Board ruling, in which he recognized in several seized coal mines of the Jones and Laughlin Steel Corporation, a subsidiary U.M.W.A. union of foremen and other supervisors. Much objection was expressed by the operators to foreman unionization because it established a precedent in which supervisors and workers would be under the jurisdiction of the same union. Moreell invited the owners and U.M.W.A. officials to confer in September about a contract providing for the return of the mines to the operators. Negotiations on a modified basis of the May 1946 proviso were halted in September by a division between Northern and Southern coal operators, the U.M.W.A. being unwilling to accept conditions advanced by the Southern group. Moreell then announced that at the end of September he would resign from active duty and from the Coal Mines Administrator post, declaring that "his retirement had been under consideration for almost a year and that his personal plans made further delay impracticable." He had hoped, it is said, "to be able to turn the coal mines back to private ownership before leaving the Government service." The retired Admiral continued to act for a time as consultant to Captain Norman H. Collison, who succeeded him as Coal Mines Administrator.

In the meantime Moreell had in October 1946 become president and member of the board of the Turner Construction Company in New York, an organization which specializes in all

MOREELL, BEN—*Continued*

types of building projects. One month later in an address before the University Club (New York), Moreell, as reported in the New York *Herald Tribune* (November 26, 1946), was of the opinion that Government controls on building materials would be discarded shortly. He declared that the removal of controls "would release large supplies of necessary material which has either not been offered because sale at ceiling prices would have been unprofitable, or not produced for the same reason" and "would be followed by stabilization of the construction industry on a basis of definitely known costs and could be attended by a cut in construction rates from current levels of as much as 20 per cent."

In addition to having served as president of the Army and Navy Club (Washington), of the American Concrete Institute, and of the Society of American Military Engineers, Moreell is a member of the Washington Committee of the Newcomen Society of England, the American Society of Civil Engineers, and the Society of Naval Architects and Marine Engineers—to name a few. Elected to Tau Beta Pi and Sigma Xi, the Admiral has also had conferred upon him the honorary degrees of Doctor of Engineering by Washington University (1943) and the Illinois Institute of Technology (1944), and of Doctor of Naval Science by the Pennsylvania Military College (1945). He has been decorated by the British Government and twice by the Republic of Haiti, has received various military citations and honors from the United States Government, and is the recipient of the Wason Medal (1935) for his research paper, *Articulations for Concrete Structures,* the Henry C. Turner gold medal of the American Concrete Institute (1942), and the 1942 annual award of the Moles (in 1943).

Moreell, who is prouder of being the "King Bee of the Seabees" than of any other distinction, is a large man, six feet tall. He has brown hair and blue eyes, a ruddy complexion, and a deep voice. Known among his colleagues as a tireless worker, Moreell, when Admiral, was accustomed to arrive rather early at his office in the Navy Building and was said to keep his assistants and secretaries "on their toes." Ability as an impromptu speaker, humor, and friendliness are considered to be among his other characteristics. Moreell likes to relax from everyday duties by playing golf, his special pastime now, although he once excelled at tennis. His hobby other than "hard work of all kinds" is collecting famous quotations and autographed pictures of friends and celebrities, and decorating the walls of his office and his study at home with them. He was married to Clara Julia Klinksick of Toledo, Ohio, on October 23, 1923; the couple have two daughters, Marion and Patricia. The members of the Moreell family are described as "great pals."

References

Christian Sci Mon p5 O 2 '46 por
Civil Eng 13:50-1 Ja '43 por
N Y Times Mag p18 Ag 12 '45 por
Newsweek 27:37 Je 17 '46 por
Who's Who in America, 1946-47
Who's Who in Engineering, 1941

MORGAN, ANNE (TRACY) July 25, 1873- Philanthropist; social worker

Address: b. c/o American Relief for France, Inc., 457 Madison Ave., New York; h. 3 Sutton Pl., New York

A leading American volunteer worker in many types of public service, Anne Morgan has "had a controlling voice in no less than fifty patriotic and civic organizations" in forty-odd years. The causes that have engrossed her have been summed up as "France, preparedness, international good will, cooperation, opportunities for women." Her activities have ranged from leading ambulance units in two world wars to sponsoring a prize fight or helping to run a dance hall.

According to the *National Cyclopædia of American Biography,* Anne Tracy Morgan was born to Frances Louisa (Tracy) Morgan in New York City on July 25, 1873. Six years younger than her brother, the late J. P. Morgan, she is the youngest child of the fabulously rich and powerful international financier of the "robber baron" era, John Pierpont Morgan, ardent sportsman, noted philanthropist, renowned collector of art and rare books, and lay leader in the Episcopal Church.

Young Anne's upbringing was "superlatively conventional." For her education she was sent to private schools in New York and on European travels. Much of her girlhood was spent in the Morgans' rambling country house at Highland Falls, in upstate New York, and she early became fond of sports, especially golf, tennis, and yachting. "A shy girl who did not like society," wrote Margaret Leech in the *New Yorker,* Miss Morgan is said to have "made the prescribed round of parties in frocks ordered in wholesale lots from a famous Paris dressmaker," and to have been "active in church work, teaching sewing in the parish house to a class of little girls." She was nearly thirty before she emerged from her secluded life. "There was something pathetic about this splendid girl, full of vitality and eagerness, yet who, as the youngest of a large family, had never been allowed to grow up," Elisabeth Marbury wrote in her memoirs, *My Crystal Ball* (1923). Miss Marbury, seventeen years her friend's senior, was a member of New York society who had become a literary agent for French authors; and it was she who introduced Miss Morgan to artists, musicians, authors, actors, singers, decorators—the world of personal achievement and individualism.

With Miss Marbury, Mrs. J. Borden Harriman [40], and others, Miss Morgan was one of the founders and early officers of the Colony Club. Organized in December 1903, the Colony was the first social club for women in New York, and is still one of the most exclusive. Miss Morgan also became active in the National Civic Foundation, and her first important philanthropic work was done under the auspices of its Women's Department when she established a clubroom and restaurant in the Brooklyn Navy Yard where workers could get good food at cost. She was a volunteer factory inspector in New York and New Jersey, as a member of a committee investigating the industrial conditions of women. A believer in the then unpopular idea of trade unionism, Miss Morgan supported the girl shirtwaist makers in the famous strikes of December 1909 and January 1910.

In the latter year Miss Morgan was active in the Vacation Committee and Vacation Savings Fund of New York, which was formed to help working girls save for their vacations; this became the Working Girls' Vacation Association, headed by Mrs. August Belmont ⁴⁴, and later the American Woman's Association. The year 1915 saw the publication of Miss Morgan's *The American Girl: her Education, her Responsibility, her Recreation, her Future,* and in the same year the National Institute of Social Sciences awarded her a medal for "tireless endeavor to develop a sense of mutual understanding among members of the human race." The banker's daughter has also written a number of articles on the business and professional women of America.

Before and after World War I Miss Morgan spent every summer in Europe, where in 1907 she had been one of the few civilians invited to witness Wilbur Wright's first flight at Le Mans. In 1912 she added a wing to the Versailles villa of her friends Elisabeth Marbury and Elsie de Wolfe, the fashionable decorator. A few years later she and Miss de Wolfe jointly took over Miss Marbury's share of the Villa Trianon. In America the three friends were associated with Mrs. William K. Vanderbilt in establishing and operating "a respectable dance hall," serving only soft drinks and featuring a cafeteria—then a novelty—which was staffed by "volunteers of distinction." The experiment failed after the novelty wore off, however, and the owners sold out to a professional cabaret manager. According to Miss Marbury, the serious civic movements Miss Morgan fostered during these early years of her welfare activity were too many to enumerate.

When World War I broke out in August 1914 Miss Morgan and Miss Marbury were taking their annual cure at Brides-les-Bains. For three weeks they were marooned there, without funds. The banker's daughter returned to the United States that fall, but in early 1916 she was back in France as a leader of the American Fund for French Wounded. She and her friends established and supported a home for convalescents, close to their villa, which was staffed by Sisters of a nursing order. One month after the American declaration of war in April 1917, she, Anne Murray Dike, and others formed the American Committee for Devastated France, with headquarters in the château of Blerancourt, in the Aisne. Former Ambassador Myron Herrick was president of the organization, and Anne Morgan served as vice-president and chairman of the executive committee. To restore that part of France devas-

ANNE MORGAN

tated by enemy action and Allied guns, the committee built barracks for the homeless, provided agricultural implements, seeds, plants, trees, livestock, and loans; established dispensaries, resthouses, and traveling canteens for soldiers, and clinics for civilians. Miss Morgan's assistants fed and cared for the children of a hundred villages. The committee also provided training for the disabled, schools for both children and adults, libraries, and children's camps; and restored homes, shops, churches, and historical monuments.

After the war the committee raised more than five million dollars to continue its work. Miss Morgan, "perpetually remote and impersonal" though she was to all but her intimates, sought and obtained publicity for the cause. When she sponsored a benefit bout between the lightweight champion, Benny Leonard, and Ritchie Martin, the affair brought in almost twenty thousand dollars—and headlines cried, "Clergy Flay Anne Morgan." Before bringing the committee's work to an end, Miss Morgan established a museum of Franco-American cooperation at Blerancourt, and an organization, Les Amis de Musée de Blerancourt, which served as the nucleus of later expansion. (She was treasurer and headed various committees.) In 1917 Miss Morgan and Mrs. Dike had been awarded medals by the United States Department of Agriculture; in 1918, silver medals by the French Academy of Agriculture, and later that year, the Croix de Guerre with palm. Fourteen years later, in 1932, the French Government made Anne Morgan a Commander of the Legion of Honor: she is the only American woman to receive this decoration.

In 1924 the fifty-one-year-old philanthropist turned to New York, where she became chairman of a working committee of the American Woman's Association which was preparing to erect a twenty-seven-story residential clubhouse.

MORGAN, ANNE—*Continued*

Miss Morgan took an office in Wall Street, from which she directed the association's three-and-one-half-million-dollar stock-selling campaign. According to Margaret Leech, Anne Morgan personally secured well over a million dollars, although she never asked for a subscription over ten thousand dollars, and at the same time held meetings of two or three hundred clubwomen four nights a week in her Sutton Place home. In 1928 she was elected president of the A.W.A., a post she filled for fifteen years. (When she retired in May 1943 she was to remain as honorary president and member of the board of governors.) During those years, to quote the *Independent Woman,* "though steering other projects, any one of which would absorb an ordinary woman, Miss Morgan was continuously engaged in the multiple activities centering in the clubhouse, all aimed to help women create for themselves more gracious, purposeful lives." In 1932 the A.W.A. awarded its president the annual Anne W. Porter Memorial Medal for "cooperative and constructive contributions," and in 1943 presented her with the Award for Eminent Achievement. Russell Sage College also awarded the philanthropist an honorary Doctorate of Humane Letters in 1935.

Before the outbreak of World War II Miss Morgan conferred with General Maurice Gamelin [40], commander in chief of the French forces, who approved her plan for civilian relief. In June 1938 the sixty-four-year-old clubwoman applied for a license to organize the American Friends of France, known in France as the Comité Americain de Secours Civil, and when war came she and her corps of women volunteers were ready. "Concerned only with feeding and sheltering noncombatants," Miss Morgan's activities were described by *Cue* as combining "knowledge, practicality, and timeliness. She and her corps were there when the first wave of Belgian refugees began flooding the French highways; they were there when the refugees of occupied France crowded those same highways. . . .When the big break-through came they evacuated entire regions into unoccupied territory; on the second of November [1939], for example, they moved fifteen hundred people from Ardennes, in the Sedan vicinity, to the Vendée. The Meuse Valley evacuation was done under heavy bombardment—and with the railroads destroyed." "Miss Morgan is simply wonderful," reported one of her workers. "She is absolutely fearless, and she led us like a general."

Forced to leave Europe in late 1940, Miss Morgan was re-elected president of the A.F.F. in May 1941; at the end of 1940, its American branch had a cash balance of $110,008.23, after disbursements of $198,064.35. It joined with more than a dozen organizations to form the Coordinating Council of French Relief Societies, with Miss Morgan becoming chairman of the council's executive committee and of its subcommittee on prisoners of war. Later, the American Friends of France merged with Marion Dougherty's Fighting French Relief to form American Relief for France. In October 1945 Miss Morgan returned from France, where she had been surveying relief needs. She made a second trip in July 1946 for the same purpose.

At that time, when Miss Morgan was seventy-two, Mary Watts wrote, "She is as vigorous as ever, and her black eyes are as flashing and her smile is warmer than when I first interviewed her after World War I." The white-haired aristocrat, who has never married, is described as a handsome woman, tall and erect, with a full figure and an imperious manner. She is said to resemble Pierpont Morgan in her organizing ability, her energy, and "concentrated opinions," and in her impatience with opposition or delay. Like him she maintains a reserve about her private life, although she is gracious in granting interviews to promote a cause.

Miss Morgan is a member of the Society of Colonial Dames, the American Institute of Social Sciences, and the Pen and Brush, as well as of various philanthropic organizations. Her clubs include the Colony, Cosmopolitan, Town Hall, Whippoorwill Golf, Mt. Kisco Country, Women's National Republican, and Woman's City Club of New York. It is said she still likes to golf and fish, and enjoys the theater and movies. "Hers is not among the spectacular fortunes," Margaret Leech wrote back in 1927, "and she gives away much of her income. Her life has the simplicity enforced by long hours of work."

References

Ind Woman 19:161 Je '40 (por cover)
N Y Post p12 Jl 23 '43
New Yorker 3:21-2 O 22 '27 por
American Women, 1939-40
Marbury, E. My Crystal Ball (1923)
National Cyclopædia of American Biography Current vol E p333
Who's Who in America, 1946-47

MORGAN, SIR FREDERICK (EDGWORTH) Feb. 5, 1894-   British Army officer

Address: b. c/o British War Office, London; h. Newbury Rd., Northwood, Middlesex, England

A veteran of two world wars, Lieutenant General Sir Frederick Morgan was the chief planner of the Allied invasion of the European continent, which was launched on June 6, 1944. When General Eisenhower [42] took over the supreme command of the armies fighting the Nazis, Morgan became the American general's deputy chief of staff, in which capacity he continued to serve until the cessation of hostilities. His next appointment was as chief of the United Nations Relief and Rehabilitation Administration for Germany, a post entailing responsibility for more than a million displaced persons. In January 1946, after the publication of one of his press conference statements on the migration of Jews from Poland, he became the center of a controversy concerning Jewish displaced persons. Although at that time he was not removed from his post by Director-General Herbert H. Lehman [43], in August 1946 his charge that UNRRA activities were being used to cloak Russian undercover operations was followed by his release by Director-General Fiorello H. La Guardia '40. In December 1946 he was retired by the British Army with the honorary rank of lieutenant general.

Frederick Edgworth Morgan was born on February 5, 1894. At the age of nineteen, on July 18, 1913, a year before the outbreak of World War I, he was commissioned a second lieutenant in the Royal Artillery, a branch of the service in which he was to remain during most of his career. In November 1914 the young officer was sent to France, and in August of the next year he was appointed aide-de-camp to the Brigadier commanding the Royal Artillery in France. He served in this post until 1916, then as a staff captain until 1919. Twice during World War I he was mentioned in dispatches. Then, in August 1919 he was made adjutant, which post he held until 1922. During the succeeding nine years Morgan led a varied military life. First posted to regimental duties, he afterward attended the Staff College at Camberley in Surrey and in 1930 served as a brigade major at Quetta Staff College in British Baluchistan, a land of deserts and rugged mountains. His next assignments took him to India, first as staff officer, Royal Artillery, in the year 1931-32, then as major and General Staff Officer 2 from 1932 to 1935. (On January 1, 1934, he had been brevetted lieutenant-colonel—meaning he had the rank but not the pay.) In March 1936 Morgan was back in England, at the War Office, as General Staff Officer 2; he held this post until December 1937, when he was promoted to colonel and appointed deputy assistant military secretary in the War Office. From May 1938 to August 1939 the soldier served as General Staff Officer 1 in the Southern Command.

A month before the beginning of World War II Morgan was made a temporary brigadier and given command of the First Armored Support Group, in the First Armored Division. He went to France with the First Support Group in the spring of 1940 and there took part in operations south of the Somme. Later that year, when the troops under his command were called home to become part of the reorganized Home Forces, Morgan relinquished his command to become a brigadier on the General Staff. A few months later, given the rank of acting major general, he assumed command, first of the Devon and Cornwall District from February to October 1941, and then of the Fifty-fifth Division until May 1942. In that month he was promoted from the permanent rank of major general to the temporary rank of lieutenant general in the British Army and placed in charge of the First Corps, a post he occupied until April 1943. (Both the Fifty-fifth Division and the First Corps formed part of the Home Forces when they were under Morgan's command.)

In April 1943, by decision of the Combined Chiefs of Staff committee, General Morgan was ordered to survey and plan the European invasion project, which had been under advisement since the famous retreat from Dunkerque in June 1940. The blueprint for the landing in France was thus begun fourteen months before

British Official Photo.

LT. GEN. SIR FREDERICK MORGAN

D-Day (June 6, 1944). Morgan, with Brigadier General Ray W. Barker of the United States Army as his deputy and a small Anglo-American staff, worked in strictest secrecy in an office established above a well-known West End London store whose customers were ignorant of his existence above their heads. He even had a false address listed in *Who's Who.*

The British general surveyed the whole invasion project: every move had to be planned, every check foreseen and forestalled. All types of landing devices, old and new, were examined; orders were given for the necessary training of troops, while special exercises for the invasion were worked out and tested. When the plan had been completed, it was long enough to fill a book the size of a family Bible. During the last days of the planning Morgan and his staff worked a seven-day week. The chief often put in a twenty-four-hour day, and slept in a bed beside his desk. The plan was ready in time for Winston Churchill '42, then Prime Minister, to take to the Anglo-American conference at Quebec in August 1943. There the statesman submitted it to President Roosevelt '42 and the United States Army Chiefs of Staff, who agreed with the principles of General Morgan's strategy.

When General Eisenhower and his Chief of Staff, Lieutenant General W. Bedell Smith '44, arrived in London in December 1943, the Supreme Headquarters had already taken form around General Morgan. The British officer now became a deputy to General Smith. In recognition of his services with the Normandy invasion, in August 1944 Morgan was created Knight Commander of the Bath (K.C.B.). Sir Frederick was further honored by General Eisenhower, who made him a Commander of the American Legion of Merit. The citation commended Morgan for his "exceptionally

MORGAN, SIR FREDERICK—*Cont.*

meritorious conduct in laying the groundwork for the invasion of France."

Sir Frederick was appointed chief of the operations of the United Nations Relief and Rehabilitation Administration for Germany in September 1945. "It's good to have a constructive object after so much that has been destructive," said the UNRRA chief before he left for his headquarters at Hoescht, near Frankfort-on-the-Main. There he was responsible for one and a quarter million displaced persons. Two months later the General told a New York *Herald Tribune* correspondent, that he had found the problem of displaced persons in Germany the most complex he had ever encountered. His first step was to reorganize the UNRRA in his territory. He stated that even well-trained welfare workers found it difficult to cope with the problems in their joint relations with the army and the displaced persons in four to five hundred camps. As early as the summer of 1945 displaced persons repatriated from Germany had begun to return voluntarily to that country. By December the influx of migrants into Berlin had reached a rate of two hundred daily.

The situation came to a climax on January 2, 1946. In the course of a press conference, General Morgan stated that thousands of Polish Jews were coming into the United States UNRRA zone from the East. He described the trainloads of Jews arriving in Berlin from Lodz and other Polish centers as "well dressed, well fed, and rosy cheeked." He further maintained that the Jews had "a well-organized, positive plan to get out of Europe," and that the problem of Palestine was closely linked with the movement.

Sir Frederick's statement had far-reaching repercussions. The UNRRA chief was denounced by prominent leaders and his resignation demanded. His charges were pronounced "palpably anti-Semitic," "an outrageous libel," and as "savoring of Nazism." Robert Wagner [41], United States Senator from New York, accused the British Government of conducting an "insidious, world-wide" campaign against the Jews. Eddie Cantor [41] inserted a two-column advertisement in the New York *Times* headed, "I Thought that Hitler [42] Was Dead." New York's *PM* editorial writer said of Morgan, "The General laments the failure of Hitler to finish up his 'solution' of the Jewish problem." Simon H. Rifkind [46], United States District Court Judge and adviser on Jewish affairs to General Joseph T. McNarney [44], who commanded the American forces in the European zone, called the report of a Jewish conspiracy "poppycock." The British general was also blamed for inciting anti-Semitic demonstrations by Arabs in Palestine.

Morgan was defended by a number of writers. William H. Stringer, staff correspondent for the *Christian Science Monitor*, held that Morgan was exasperated by the burdens imposed on him by this new influx of displaced persons from Poland. Portions of what Sir Frederick had said were true, Stringer said, when the distortions had been removed: "He [Morgan] did not speak of a Jewish 'con-spiracy' but rather of a 'plan'" and his statements were "borne out by facts from other sources." In England Professor Samson Wright declared that the charges had been of the utmost value to Jewry. Wright pointed out that for the first time there was an official declaration that the Jews in Europe had views of their own. The *Zionist Review* was of the opinion that "Sir Frederick's review of the Jewish situation contained both true and untrue information; the result was half-truth, which was mischievous and harmful. It is true that a great many Jews are determined to leave Europe." Toward the end of the month a number of foreign correspondents and a report of the United States Third Army stated that a large part of the illegal infiltration of Polish Jews into the American zone of Germany was being financed by Zionist organizations.

Meanwhile, on January 4, Herbert H. Lehman, director of UNRRA, notified the general of his suspension from the post because his remarks had been outside the scope of his authority. Morgan refused to resign, however, pointing out that his remarks, made in an informal question-and-answer interview after the formal press conference, had been distorted. He appealed his dismissal, requesting a personal interview in New York, and on January 18 was temporarily reinstated pending Lehman's review of his case. Then, on January 29, after "several long and searching talks" with the general, the head of UNRRA announced to the press that he was restoring Morgan to duty in Germany. "I have given the most serious consideration to all the circumstances," Lehman stated in part, "including his personal representations to me. . . . I have concluded that I am justified in continuing to place confidence in him. I believe that he did not intend to impute sinister motives to individuals or organizations seeking to improve the sorry plight of groups of displaced persons, and that he does not hold religious prejudices; that when restored to duty he will treat all groups of displaced persons fairly and in accordance with their needs and UNRRA principles." In his letter of apology to Lehman, dated January 28, Morgan had written that he took full responsibility for his statements, that he regretted that he had unintentionally laid UNRRA open to charges of bias, and that he himself was neither anti-Semitic nor racially biased; nevertheless, he did not retract his original assertions.

Seven months after this incident, General Morgan's outspokenness resulted in his ouster by UNRRA's new director-general, Fiorello H. La Guardia. According to Edwin Hartrich, foreign correspondent of the New York *Herald Tribune,* on August 10, at a general press conference in Geneva, Morgan charged that UNRRA was an "umbrella under which Soviet spies are working." La Guardia challenged the statement and, after his talk with Morgan, the British War office recalled Morgan. It was said by some correspondents that General Morgan's charges were based on unreleased British and American intelligence reports. Those correspondents made the comment that, without a statement from Morgan (who was then unable to speak because he had been returned to active service with the British Army), the matter would be allowed to drop. At the end of the year the British War Office issued the following directive: "Major General Sir Frederick E. Morgan, G.C.B., retires on retired pay on December 29, 1946, and is granted honorary rank of lieutenant general."

Sir Frederick has been described as having the "tidiest mind" in the British Army, natural courtesy, and a sense of humor. He is a tall man with graying hair and blue eyes. He and Lady Morgan live in Newbury Road, Northwood, Middlesex. During World War II his address in *Who's Who* was wrongly given as a small village in Wiltshire. The mistake was intentional, a precaution taken to screen the General's presence in London while he was planning the assault on Normandy.

Reference

Who's Who, 1946

MORGAN, JOY ELMER Dec. 11, 1889-
Educator; magazine editor
Address: b. c/o Journal of the National Education Association, 1201 16th St., N.W., Washington, D.C.; h. 4109 17th St., N.W., Washington, D.C.

Through the *Journal of the National Education Association*, which reaches approximately four hundred thousand subscribers monthly, editor Joy Elmer Morgan has "tried to build up the teaching body and the public attitude toward teaching to the end that teachers may be well-rounded personalities, intelligent professional experts, and active citizens."

A sod house near the town of Callaway, Nebraska, on the border of the range country, was the birthplace of Joy Elmer Morgan. The son of Wesley and Jennie (Nelson) Morgan, he was born on December 11, 1889. When he was about four years old the boy's mother died, and he was sent to live with his grandparents on a farm in Upland, Nebraska. He remained with them until he reached his early teens, when he left home to support himself. He wandered about the Republican River Valley, working for farmers, sometimes for board and sometimes for a small wage, gaining what he now considers an important factor in his early education: "the opportunity of comparing different standards and points of view." He attended elementary school in Franklin County, and received his higher education at the Nebraska State Normal School (now Teachers College) in Peru, where he enrolled in 1906 for a combined preparatory and college course. He has since said that he owes much to exceptional teachers, among them Jennie Collins—who impressed him with the importance of education —and the Peru faculty, which "during those years furnished as many names to *Who's Who* in proportion to its enrollment as did Harvard or Yale." After graduation in 1910, Morgan went to Nebraska Wesleyan University for a while and then to the University of Nebraska, from which he received his B.A. in 1917.

While still studying for his degree, Morgan in 1911 had become superintendent of schools of Bloomington, Nebraska, where he remained until 1913, when he accepted a similar position in Guide Rock, in the same state. This he held for four years. While he was at Guide Rock, a new school building, still in use, was erected. It was a period of expansion among the Nebraska town schools, which were changing from eight-grade to twelve-grade institutions, and Morgan points out that both Bloomington and Guide Rock were at this time sending a large number of their graduates to the University of Nebraska. In 1917, resigning from his post, Morgan went to Camp MacArthur in Waco, Texas, where he spent a year in charge of the camp libraries. The next year he worked in Washington, D.C., as assistant to the acting director of the Library War Service, and in 1918 he went to the New York State Library School (now the School of Library Service of Columbia University) for his B.L.S. degree.

Although he had intended to become a librarian, the year he received his degree (1920) Morgan was persuaded by his friend and former teacher at Peru, J. W. Crabtree, to come to Washington to begin publication of the *Journal of the National Education Association*, and to become the director of publications of the National Education Association. The first issue of the *Journal* appeared in January 1921. At that time the NEA had a comparatively small membership and only thirty thousand copies of the magazine were printed. In the twenty-five years that followed the NEA has become the largest professional organization in the world, and the *Journal's* circulation has increased almost fourteen-fold. Morgan has attempted to make the publication an "expression of the best ideals and practices of our [the teaching] profession." In addition to his monthly editorials, he has contributed many articles on education to the magazine. During the prohibition years Morgan spoke for himself and the NEA when in the *Journal's* pages he attacked the movement to repeal the Eighteenth Amendment. In 1943 he published an editorial entitled "Old Enough To Fight: Old Enough To Vote," advocating passage of the Vandenberg [40] bill for the extension of suffrage to eighteen-year-olds. "The youth who have just finished high school," he wrote, "are among our most thoroughly informed citizens. They are well equipped to assume this new responsibility which their Mexican contemporaries already enjoy, as did the youth of ancient Athens." Also in 1943, he served as director of the War and Peace Fund Campaign of the National Education Association, which raised four hundred thousand dollars.

Morgan's work outside the Association has encompassed numerous other educational pursuits. From 1922 until 1927 he was a contributing editor of the *Child Welfare Magazine*. An active member of the National Congress of Parents and Teachers for more than ten years he was a member of its executive committee and served as director of its publications from 1927 to 1934. In 1930 he was "drafted" as chairman of the National Committee on Education by Radio, which was lobbying for legislation which would have provided that 15 per cent of the available radio channels in the United States be used exclusively for education. The new me-

JOY ELMER MORGAN

dium, Morgan felt, was "a million times more powerful than any other mechanism ever invented for reaching the human mind." But by 1930 commercial interests had discovered the airways, and their programs were, in Morgan's opinion, being used to drive out the college radio stations, which had heretofore broadcast educational programs. The advertisers, he wrote, "show no concern as to whether radio is to be used to inform or to dupe the public."

An admirer of Horace Mann, "founder of our public schools," Morgan served as director of the Horace Mann Centennial during 1936 and 1937. None of the earlier biographies of Mann was in print. Through the action of the centennial committees, however, hundreds of thousands of copies of a small book on Mann were distributed. The centennial was also the occasion for the formation of the Future Teachers of America, an organization of young people in schools and colleges interested in teaching as a profession. Of this Morgan became chairman. His work with it may in the long run, he believes, prove to be his most important achievement. In 1938, with the aid of his friend Hugh Taylor Birch, Morgan established the Hugh Birch-Horace Mann Fund of NEA to publish the "Personal Growth Leaflets," because he felt that "the right message at the right time may change the course of a life." Some of their titles are *Your Life in the Making, Your Mind in the Making, Your Personality in the Making, Future Teachers of America, Shall I Become a Teacher, Selections From Ralph Waldo Emerson, Selections From Abraham Lincoln.* By 1945 nearly two hundred titles, written or edited by Morgan, had been published, and had a circulation of over thirty-four million copies. They are in wide use among Boy and Girl Scout groups, in adult education, among guidance workers, at commencement exercises, and in schools, churches, and Sunday schools.

Morgan was awarded the honorary degree of D.Sc. in Education by Boston University in 1941. He is a life member of the National Education Association; a member of the Horace Mann League and of the American Library Association; and a trustee of American University (Washington, D.C.). The educator wrote the original draft of the Congressional resolution designating the third Sunday in May each year as "I Am an American Day." He has contributed articles on education to periodicals other than the *Journal,* such as *School and Society,* the *Journal of Home Economics,* and the *Wilson Library Bulletin,* and his testimony has appeared in the *Congressional Digest.* He is the editor of several book-length volumes on Horace Mann, among which are *Horace Mann, His Ideas and Ideals* (1936) and *Horace Mann at Antioch* (1938), a study in personality and higher education which includes some of Mann's addresses. In 1941 he edited the *American Citizen's Handbook,* which was published by the Hugh Birch-Horace Mann Fund for the Committee on New Voter Preparation and Recognition. At present he is engaged in preparing what he calls "some educational writings on Horace Mann."

Morgan was married in 1912 to Frances Willard Blake, who is the president of the National Women's Guild of the Methodist Episcopal Church. The brown-eyed, gray-haired educator is a member of Phi Sigma and Phi Delta Kappa, and is a Mason. His favorite form of relaxation is gardening.

References

Leaders in Education (1941)
Who's Who in America, 1946-47

MORGAN, THOMAS HUNT Sept. 25, 1866—Dec. 4, 1945 American biologist, called "the twentieth-century Mendel"; his theory of the gene is generally accepted; awarded the 1933 Nobel Prize in medicine, although not a physician; director of the Kerckhoff Laboratories of Biological Science of the California Institute of Technology from 1928 until retirement, then professor emeritus of biology; his books are classics in the literature of genetics.

Obituary

N Y Times p23 D 5 '45 por

MORINI, ERICA (mō-rē′-nē ě′rĭk-à) Jan. 5, 1908- Violinist

Address: b. c/o Columbia Concerts, Inc., 113 W. 57th St., New York; h. 1200 5th Ave., New York

For a long time cited by the reviewers as the greatest of present-day women violinists— an appellation for which she has an intense dislike—Erica Morini, the former child prodigy, is today generally considered the peer of the great male violin virtuosi, and the offending phrase now seldom appears.

Erika (now Erica) Morini, the daughter of an Italo-Austrian father of a family of professional musicians, Oscar Morini, and an Austrian mother, Amalia (Weissmann) Morini, was born in Vienna, the Austrian capital, whose very name suggests music. The date she gives as January 5, 1908. Her musical aptitude was evinced at the early age of three, when she used to sit playing with her dolls in the corner of a classroom in her father's music school. If any of the pupils hit a wrong note, she recounts, she would look up with a frown. Sometimes she would leave her toys to pick out the correct notes on the piano by ear—"my babe's senses were acute with harmony." Musical instruction was begun when she was four years old. Erica wanted to play the piano, but her father, himself a violinist, noting her perfect ear and flexible hands, started her lessons on the violin. At first rebellious therefore, the child would often lay aside her miniature instrument for the more fascinating keyboard, but gradually her own affinity for the violin reconciled her to it. She did, however, continue to work at the piano and was able to master that instrument without any formal instruction.

Until she was seven Erica studied with her father, who meanwhile tried several times to have her admitted to the Vienna Conservatory. The Conservatory, however, imbued with the prejudices of its day, was at that time admitting girls only to the piano classes, and the talented child was consistently turned away because of her sex. It was not until a friend persuaded the noted Czech violinist and teacher Otakar Sevčík to hear her and he took her under his wing that she was finally able to enter the renowned school. Her first few lessons, it is said, prompted Sevčík to remark, "She knows everything that cannot be taught." Within a year, though only eight years old, she had completed the master course at the Conservatory —taught by Sevčík by the same method, later set forth in four detailed volumes, which, musicians agree, had done so much to advance the talent of Sevčík's other famous pupils, Jan Kubelik, Jaroslav Kocián, and Marie Hall. On October 16, 1916, not yet nine years old, Erica Morini made her debut in Vienna. Her success was so great that another six appearances were scheduled for the same season, followed by her debut as orchestral soloist during a Beethoven Festival with the orchestra of the Leipzig Gewandhaus directed by Arthur Nikisch. At Nikisch's invitation she next appeared in Berlin, after which a recital tour took her throughout Germany and to Poland, Rumania, and Hungary.

Following the Armistice of 1918 Miss Morini reappeared on the concert platforms of Austria, and in 1920 she was singled out as the only solo artist to perform with the Vienna Philharmonic during its festival week. Her progress during the war had been marked by her winning of the public competition for the State Prize—but once more her sex had operated against her, this time to deprive her of much-needed lesson money, as the wording of the award specified "the man who. . ." On January 26, 1921, the young violinist made her American debut with the New York Philharmonic Society under Artur Bodanzky. Other appearances in New York and in other Ameri-

Halsman

ERICA MORINI

can cities followed. At the end of the year, the 1921 New International Year Book recorded: "Erika Morini . . . made a distinctly favorable impression at her debut. . . .She had a large, sympathetic tone, a brilliant and reliable technic and a remarkable feeling for style, even if her interpretation was not quite mature. But on her reappearance, in November, it was evident that she had made considerable strides forward in this latter respect." In 1922 and again in 1923 the New International Year Book listed Miss Morini among the eminent violinists of the season.

After three successful years in the United States, Erica Morini returned to Europe, where she won new laurels in Germany, Russia, and England, as well as in Australia. She toured the United States briefly in 1930; then not again until 1935, when Olin Downes wrote: "As a young girl, Miss Morini made herself known in this city as a performer of exceptional but uneven equipment. . . .It is evident that in five years' time Miss Morini has made a prodigious advance. . . .Everything . . . was done beautifully. Where the player's temperament might have run away with her, it was held in control, serving only to heighten the contagious spirit of the interpretation. Nothing was insignificant, and nothing was out of proportion."

In the ensuing years Erica Morini has proved her right to be considered not only the greatest contemporary woman violinist, but, in the words of Etude, "without any qualifications, among the few truly great present-day violinists." "Her tone," wrote Francis D. Perkins of the New York Herald Tribune in 1940, "once sometimes rather rough-hewn, is now remarkable for its consistent clarity and evenness of texture; it has become a laudable medium for fine expressive and dynamic shadings and interpretative sensitiveness." "Masterly

MORINI, ERICA—*Continued*

violin playing," wrote Olin Downes in the *Times* in 1941; "a notable exhibition of virtuosity and interpretative skill," said his colleague Noel Straus on another occasion; "a violin recital of rare refinement and consummate art," commented the *Sun*'s Oscar Thompson in 1945. Again from Francis D. Perkins, after a Town Hall recital: "One characteristic that particularly distinguishes Miss Morini's playing is its sense of style and atmosphere. . . .The Kreisler Praeludium was played with notable tonal breadth; the Allegro with energy and momentum. In the Mozart sonata, the performance was marked by lucidity, delicacy, and dynamic shading and distinctions of mood, and a sense of musical line. The lyric sobriety of this interpretation contrasted effectively with the memorable bravura and vividness of color which characterized the Paganini-Wilhelmj work. . . .The Brahms sonata had a meditative and expressive performance, with the artistic discernment in tonal volume and timbre which marked the recital as a whole."

March 5, 1946, found the reviewers even more appreciative. "Violin playing of the utmost distinction was vouchsafed by Erica Morini at her annual recital in Carnegie Hall last night," Jerome D. Bohm informed his *Herald Tribune* readers the next day. "While some exception might have been taken on stylistic grounds to the rhythmic liberties taken in the Kreisler Allegro, her work in the three principal offerings on her program . . . was of unsurpassable excellence from every point of view. Unsullied glowing transparency of tone and complete technical mastery pervaded her traversals of everything she undertook." "It is useless to talk about her brilliant technique or about her tone and the way she colored it," wrote Robert Bagar under the headline "Erica Morini Plays with True Artistry" in the *World-Telegram*. "These she has always had as prime possessions. But it was her imagination, the keen intellect, the spontaneous life she breathed into the works programmed that caught the mind and heart of the listener." "There were uneven moments last night," observed Olin Downes, "but this was always great playing, never small in scale, or cheap in sentiment; always characterized by intensity and beauty of tone and the virility of style which put her in a place of her own among present-day violinists." In the summer of 1946 she won more praises for her performance at the annual Berkshire Music Festival in August and earlier, in June, for her rendition of the Mendelssohn Violin Concerto at New York's Lewisohn Stadium.

Ordinarily cheerful and friendly, with a quick sense of humor, the Viennese artist becomes resentful when praised as "the greatest woman violinist," a judgment she considers patronizing to her sex. "What does it matter whether I am a woman or a man?" she demands. "Either I am a great violinist or I am not. It means nothing to me to be the greatest woman violinist." But she is optimistic: "I am convinced," she has written, "that our generation will witness the last vestige of prejudice against women musicians lifted, will see women eager to be judged not as women but as artists, and critics willing to consider them as such." But if she has had to struggle to gain recognition as an artist rather than as a woman, she has not been deprived of tangible evidence of her success. Her most prized possession is a white linen handkerchief, embroidered with coronet and crest, once the property of the famous Spanish violinist Sarasate and bequeathed by him to the Musical Society of Madrid "to be given to the violinist of a later generation whose playing best reflected the fire of his Spanish dances"—which she received in Madrid in 1933 and which now occupies a gold frame above her piano. Among her other mementos are a Rumanian peasant costume received from her friend and admirer, the late Queen Marie, and a large blond doll received after a command performance from the Archduke Karl, later last emperor of Austria. Although she now plays on a forty-five-thousand-dollar Stradivarius violin, Miss Morini once owned the Guadagnini of Maud Powell, famous American violinist, presented to her as the performer who best qualified as the "next great woman violinist" after her New York debut in 1921. This she gave up, however—to some deserving student who might otherwise be without an instrument—because it was too large for her. In addition, when, because of her Jewish heritage, she fled Austria at the time of the Anschluss, the violinist left behind her a substantial fortune resulting from her far-flung concert tours.

Of medium height (five feet four inches tall, weighing 135 pounds), with dark brown hair and black eyes, Miss Morini is characterized as a vital and well-rounded individual, athletic and domestic as well as artistic. Destiny made her a musician, she says, but she made herself a cook. She is also a horsewoman, hiker and mountain climber, an expert dancer—she once won a charity ball contest as the partner of the Austrian professional Harold Kreutzberg—and a collector of paintings. But because she must protect her hands, she may never ski or skate, nor may she use sharp kitchen knives. Other moments of leisure she spends with books, at the movies, or with friends, among whom her gift for story-telling is appreciated. On April 28, 1938, she was married to Felice Siracusano, a jewelry merchant. Their apartment overlooking Central Park reflects her Viennese tastes, but Erica Morini's dream home is a quiet mountain retreat.

References

Etude 60:383+ Je '42 por
N Y Times II p6 Jan 21 '40 por
Ewen, D. ed. Living Musicians (1940) por
Grove's Dictionary of Music and Musicians suppl. vol. (1940)
Macmillan Encyclopedia of Music and Musicians (1938)
Saleski, G. Famous Musicians of a Wandering Race (1927)
Thompson, O. ed. International Cyclopedia of Music and Musicians (1943)
Who Is Who in Music (1941) por
Who's Who, 1946

MORRIS, ROLAND SLETOR Mar. 11, 1874—Nov. 23, 1945 Attorney and former United States Ambassador to Japan (1917-21); credited with fostering good will between two nations, but in 1918 also warned against Japanese imperialism; active in Democratic politics in Pennsylvania; professor of international law at University of Pennsylvania from 1924 until death.

Obituary
N Y Times p19 N 24 '45 por

MOSCICKI, IGNACE (môsh-chēts'kĕ ēg-nä'tsĭ) 1867—Oct. 2, 1946 President of Poland from 1926 until the invasion of that country by the Nazis in World War II; chemist and inventor; in the nationalist movement, he fled to England in 1892; taught electrochemistry and electrophysics in Switzerland, 1897-1911, returned to Poland in 1912 to teach in the Polytechnic School of Lwów; governed the country while Marshal Pilsudski was dictator.

Obituary
N Y Times p27 O 3 '46 por

MOTHERWELL, HIRAM 1888(?)—Dec. 1, 1945 American writer, editor, lecturer; author of *The Theatre of Today* (1914), *The Imperial Dollar* (1929), and *The Peace We Fight For* (1943); European correspondent of Chicago *Daily News* (1919-27); one of the first to recognize the menace of fascism; frequent contributor to magazines; editor of *Stage* magazine (1928-35).

Obituary
N Y Times p21 D 3 '45 por

MOULTON, F(OREST) R(AY) Apr. 29, 1872- Astronomer
Address: b. c/o American Association for the Advancement of Science, Smithsonian Institution Bldg., Washington, D.C.

Considered one of the foremost contemporary American educators and scientists, F. R. Moulton, as co-editor with J. J. Schifferes of *The Autobiography of Science*, in 1945 presented the layman, in the words of book critic Harry Hansen '42, with a "crutch" to aid in understanding the atomic bomb. Now permanent secretary of the American Association for the Advancement of Science, Moulton was for thirty years a member of the University of Chicago's department of astronomy and at the turn of the century co-worker with Thomas Chrowder Chamberlin in the formulation of the planetesimal hypothesis of the origin of the earth.

Born on April 29, 1872, to Belah G. and Mary C. (Smith) Moulton, who were homesteading on a tract near Reed City (now Le Roy), Michigan, Forest Ray Moulton was reared with six brothers and a sister. His mother, a former teacher in a rural school, insisted that all of her children obtain an education despite their small means. As a consequence, three of the other Moulton boys have since achieved high places in the field of education and also in the field of business; a fourth son, Harold G. Moulton '44, is president of the Brookings Institution and author of a dozen books on economics. The perseverance of the Moultons in obtaining an education is exemplified by Mary, the only daughter, who continued her studies while teaching in various Michigan schools, received her B.A. in her late forties, and in 1945, when in her sixties, her M.A. from Wayne University. To celebrate the latter event, all seven of her brothers attended to see "the spry little teacher" march up in cap and gown to receive the hard-earned degree.

Forest Ray, eldest of the brothers, did not begin his secondary education until he was seventeen. By 1894, at the age of twenty-two, he had earned his B.A. at Albion College (Michigan), serving there meanwhile as an instructor from 1892 to 1894 and playing on the football team. In 1899 he obtained his Ph.D., *summa cum laude*, from the University of Chicago, where in 1896 he had begun his long career on the university's teaching staff. From 1896 to 1898 he was an assistant in astronomy; 1898 to 1900, an associate in astronomy; 1900 to 1903, an instructor; 1903 to 1908, an assistant professor; 1908 to 1912, an associate professor; and from 1912 to 1926, a full professor.

In 1898, although little more than a graduate student at the time, Moulton was invited by Thomas Chrowder Chamberlin, then chairman of the University of Chicago's geological department, to cooperate in an investigation of the earth's origin. Chamberlin had for some time suspected the validity of the nebular hypothesis of Laplace, reaching this conclusion through his work on glacial phenomena. Moulton likewise doubted the correctness of the theory, but on astronomical grounds. The ideas of the veteran scientist and the young instructor, relates William D. MacMillan in *The Journal of Geology,* were revealed to each of them by their students in class discussions. "Conferences were arranged, and there began an intimate friendship that was terminated only by [Chamberlin's] death" in 1928. Because Chamberlin was primarily a geologist and a naturalist, he sought a collaborator versed in astronomy and celestial mechanics, but he pointed out on one occasion: "Our relations have been so intimate and our exchange of ideas so free and so frequent that it is impossible to apportion the responsibility for the various methods adopted and the modes of carrying them out. The higher mathematical work is, however, to be credited to Dr. Moulton. It has perhaps been my function in the main to formulate problems and suggest general modes of attack, and Dr. Moulton's to devise methods of analysis and bring to bear the mathematical principles of dynamics, but this has not been uniformly so. Quite often we have proceeded by successive alternative steps, in which each was the parent of its successor."

The first tangible results of their cooperation were two papers written for the *Journal of Geology* (by Chamberlin) and the *Astrophysical Journal* (by Moulton) in 1900 to show that the Laplacian hypothesis failed to explain existent astronomical data. By 1904 a full discussion of the new theory had appeared in the

F. R. MOULTON

Year Book No. 3 of the Carnegie Institution of Washington. In 1905 the planetesimal hypothesis was discussed in Chamberlin and Salisbury's *Geology*, and in 1906, in Moulton's *Introduction to Astronomy.* According to the old nebular hypothesis, as briefly defined in *Webster's Unabridged Dictionary*, "the matter of the solar system. . .existed originally in the form of a vast, diffused, rotating nebula, which, gradually cooling and contracting, threw off, in obedience to physical laws, successive rings of matter, from which, by the same laws, were produced the several planets, satellites, and other bodies of the system." This theory, Chamberlin and Moulton had determined, was unable to account for such phenomena as the alternate periods of glaciation and warm temperatures throughout geological history, the peculiar formation of the land and sea areas on the earth's surface, and others. Study of the dynamics of the solar system then led them to postulate as the prime cause of the earth's origin a "dynamic encounter of the sun and a passing star," which had acted to disrupt the essentially fluid mass of the sun, forming huge tidal waves and giving rise to violent eruptions of the sun's molten material, which was then ejected with varying velocities from these tidal regions. Those masses not ejected beyond the sun's gravitational pull were drawn into elliptical orbits by the conflicting attraction of sun and star and, after the passing of the star, cooled and condensed into the planetesimals, small planet-like solid bodies in space. Nuclear attraction of the smaller planetesimals to the larger then built up the planets when planetesimal orbits crossed. This is the theory accepted today.

Moulton remained in the department of astronomy of the University of Chicago until 1926, a period of thirty years. In addition to his teaching, scientific investigation, and writing, he gave hundreds of public lectures on astronomy in leading American cities, and free lectures in Chicago at Hull House, the Hebrew Institute, and in churches, recreation centers, and museums. From 1907 to 1912 he was an associate editor of the *Transactions of the American Mathematical Society*; from 1908 to 1923, a research associate of the Carnegie Institution. From March 1918 to April 1919 he interrupted his teaching to take charge of artillery ballistics in the Ordnance Department of the American army, serving with the rank of major. (He is now a lieutenant colonel in the Reserves.) Returning to Chicago, at the end of this service, he was one of the founders of the Society for Visual Education, established in 1920, and with this group he pioneered in education by radio, giving the first radio address broadcast from the University of Chicago. About 1919 he also became a trustee and president of the board of Albion College, holding this position until 1923, and in 1920 he became a trustee and member of the Exposition Committee of Chicago's Century of Progress Exposition. (The latter post he held until 1936, being also director of the concessions from 1931 to 1933.) From 1925 to 1938 he was a director of the Utilities Power and Light Corporation.

Moulton became permanent secretary of the American Association for the Advancement of Science in 1936, and his work there for the next four years coincided with a series of weekly radio broadcasts on science which he was giving, first from Chicago (1935-37) and then from Washington (1938-40). "The most distinctive and important function" of the A.A.A.S., says its secretary, "is to serve as the integrating agency in the ever-increasing specialization in science. The mingling of men of somewhat different points of view is important because excessive specialization leads to sterility." The A.A.A.S., which was founded in 1848 and has a present membership of twenty-nine thousand, is composed of fifteen sections, includes one hundred ninety-six affiliated societies, and brings together at its semi-yearly meetings specialists from all fields of science in planned special and joint sessions. "If anyone," says Moulton, "overvalues his own subject in such an environment, he is likely to get his bias corrected."

Throughout his long career Moulton has not only written several important treatises on astronomical subjects, but has also been a frequent contributor to leading scientific periodicals and has edited more than twenty scientific volumes. His earliest work, *Introduction to Celestial Mechanics* (1902, 1914), has been translated into Russian and German. Others of his works are *Descriptive Astronomy* (1905, 1923), *Astronomy* (1906), *Periodic Orbits* (1920), *New Methods in Exterior Ballistics* (1906), *Differential Equations* (1930), *Introduction to Astronomy* (1931), and *Consider the Heavens* (1935). In 1937 and 1939 he was editor of and a contributor to *The World and Man As Science Sees Them*, of which the *Saturday Review of Literature* wrote: "This is not a book which can be read; it must be studied. . . .Yet, considering how expert all these men are in their various fields, they have done remarkably well in withholding, for the reader's benefit, nonessential bits of information." Moulton's chapter, "The Orderly Universe," in *A Treasury of Science* (1943), has been called "an astronomical education, in brief a bird's eye view of modern astronomy." *The Autobiography of Science* (1945, edited with J. J. Schifferes) is an anthology of key passages from scientists in all fields through the centuries, with each selection prefaced by a "vignette of the author, evaluating his work in its relation to the whole pattern of science." It was praised by the New York *Times* as a volume from which layman and scientist alike would profit.

In 1900 Moulton was elected to membership in Phi Beta Kappa by the chapter which had been established at the University of Chicago the year before. The astronomer's honorary degrees include a D.Sc. from Albion College (1922), an LL.D. from Drake University (1939), and a D.Sc. from the Case School of Applied Science (1940). He is a Fellow of the Royal Astronomical Society; a member of the National Academy of Sciences, American Academy of Arts and Sciences, American Philosophical Society, American Mathematical Society, American Astronomical Society, and some fifteen or more other scientific societies.

On March 25, 1897, Moulton was married to Estella Gillette. The Moultons, who now live in Washington, D.C., have four children: Gail, Vieva, Mary, and Merle. The critic Harry Hansen [42], a former pupil of the scientist, says that Moulton is an unassuming man and a patient teacher. "Until 1933," says the astronomer, "I played tennis and handball. Today I find relaxation in an occasional game of billiards, the opera, and other classical music. I am well acquainted with classical literature, fond of poetry and painting." He is five feet ten, weighs one hundred and seventy-five pounds, has dark brown eyes, and graying dark hair. Although he has written biographies of his associates on occasion, his reply to questions concerning himself is, "This is much too much."

References

Time 45:51 Je 18 '45 por
American Men of Science (1944)
International Who's Who, 1945-46
Who's Who in America, 1946-47

MYRDAL, (KARL) GUNNAR (mür'däl gŭn'nàr) Dec. 6, 1898- Swedish Government official; social economist
Address: b. c/o Ministry of Commerce, Stockholm

The "most talked-about man in Sweden," Gunnar Myrdal, has been Minister of Commerce in the Social Democratic Government since July 1945. Long an expert adviser to his Government and an active participant in public affairs, he is a continual analyst of the organization of Swedish industry and business. Myrdal is the author of many books on economic and sociological problems, several of which have directly influenced Swedish national

policy. According to the New York *Herald Tribune*, Myrdal is considered Sweden's leading authority on American affairs. *Time* magazine calls him "the No. 1 authority on United States Negroes," a title Myrdal won by directing the six-year study which culminated in his book, *An American Dilemma*.

Karl Gunnar Myrdal was born December 6, 1898, in Gustaf parish in Dalecarlia region, Sweden. His parents were Carl Adolf and Anna Sofia (Carlson) Myrdal. At twenty-one Myrdal entered the University of Stockholm, where he studied law, and began practice after his graduation in 1923. In 1927 Myrdal obtained a doctorate of laws in economics, publishing a book on the theory of prices, and was appointed docent in political economy at Stockholm University.

The young economist visited England, Germany, and France in the years from 1925 to 1929. During the academic year 1929-30 he traveled in the United States on a Rockefeller Fellowship, and in 1930-31 he was in Switzerland as associate professor in the Post-Graduate Institute of International Studies at Geneva. On his return to Stockholm University, Dr. Myrdal became an acting professor. In 1932 there appeared his study, in German translation, of the political element in classical economic theory, and in 1933 his book on the economic effects of financial policy and another on the cost of living in Sweden from 1830 to 1930. In 1933, thirty-four-year-old Gunnar Myrdal was appointed to the Lars Hierta chair of political economy and public finance at Stockholm University, succeeding the internationally known economist Gustav Cassel.

During the economic instability and distress of the thirties, Gunnar Myrdal was active in public affairs, trying what he calls "voluntarily redirecting and coordinating human and natural resources in order to increase the common good." Although denying either that Sweden has solved all her social problems, such as poverty and poor housing, or that there is anything "particularly Swedish" about the nation's economic system, Myrdal has written, "We investigate our shortcomings intensively, and use the technique of social engineering to plan for their removal. . . .Rationally induced change, and the planning of it, are," he feels, "the dynamics of a properly functioning democracy." The economist had a chance to put some of his ideas on economic and population policy into direct practice as a deputy member of the board of the National Bank of Sweden, and, in 1936-38, as a Social Democratic member of the Senate.

Myrdal, who had married sociologist Alva Reimer in October 1924, collaborated with her on studies of Sweden's decreasing population, which he saw as a part of the entire picture of social planning. Their *Crisis in the Population Question* (1934) aroused wide public interest, and directly influenced the social policies of the Scandinavian countries during the thirties. The problem, as the Myrdals saw it, was how to overcome the excessive decrease in the birth rate while maintaining the improved

Uggla, Stockholm

GUNNAR MYRDAL

standard of living associated with it. Gunnar Myrdal was appointed to the new Swedish housing and population commissions which, like both their Danish and Norwegian counterparts, were reported as following the Myrdals' general theories and specific suggestions very closely. In Myrdal's words, the population problem became in his country "a crowbar for social reforms," with the state recognizing as a proper function the care of children without regard to income: a family housing subsidy, for example, would be based on the number of children. "The quantitative population argument," Myrdal wrote, "is for a general equalization of the economic burden of bringing up children"; this implied "the horizontal redistribution of income among different types of families and the vertical redistribution among different income classes." One of the suggestions adopted by the commission was for a "comprehensive scheme of school and adult education in sexual matters in which information on rational methods of birth control should have due place." "We do not want to keep up the birth rate by causing the birth of unwanted children, who have to thank ignorance or bad luck for their existence," said Professor Myrdal. (The Swedish experiment in "democratic family and population policy" has been described by Alva Myrdal in her *Nation and Family* [1941].)

Professor Myrdal traveled to the United States in the spring of 1938, to give the Godkin lectures on socioeconomic problems at Harvard University, later collected as *Population: A Problem for Democracy* (1940). He also outlined his theory of a policy for economic recovery before a symposium of economists: Fiscal policy should, he felt, "serve its purpose, among other measures, to mitigate the fluctuations in business activity." The degree of "soundness" to be maintained in a system of public finance must, he said, be based upon an analysis of the effects of each possible choice, and must therefore be "established by a political decision. . . .We must change the political psychology and give the state plenty of resources in depressions but hold them back in booms . . . make room for deficit spending during depressions by securing the building up of corresponding surpluses in good years." (While at Harvard, Myrdal was awarded an honorary LL.D. by that university.)

In 1937 the Carnegie Corporation of New York, casting about for a scholar to direct a study of the American Negro "in a wholly objective and dispassionate way as a social phenomenon," had chosen Myrdal as a competent man from a country without a background of imperialism and preconceptions. After a few months in their native land, the Myrdals returned to the United States for this purpose in September 1938. While Gunnar Myrdal directed the research project, Alva Myrdal investigated social and educational problems, lectured, and wrote articles which were published in several periodicals. After the German invasion of Norway and Denmark in April 1940, Myrdal felt it his duty to return to his country, which remained neutral in the conflict. There he served on the commission which worked out a new budgetary system for the national Government, based on the premise that, in Sweden, "depressions are only temporary setbacks in a rising trend of production and national income." (The economist's *Monetary Equilibrium* had been published in 1939.) In Sweden the Myrdals wrote their best-selling *Contact With America.* Describing United States folkways and institutions, the book was written, Gunnar Myrdal commented, "in order to remind the Scandinavian nations in their days of ordeal of the great democratic power reserve of the then still neutral United States."

After much traveling back and forth, in October 1942 Professor Myrdal resumed his teaching at the University of Stockholm. In 1943-44 he toured the United States, as economic adviser to the Swedish legation, and concluded after investigation that, following postwar prosperity, there would be a great depression, once controls were removed, especially as "political development in America is likely to be away from planning, rather than toward it." This opinion was said to be shared by a number of economists. Part of his *Warning Against Optimism* was translated for publication by the National Planning Association. In 1944 the author was appointed chairman of the Swedish Postwar Economic Planning Commission.

In that year, too, the Carnegie Corporation published Myrdal's report and conclusion, *An American Dilemma; The Negro Problem and Modern Democracy,* which sociologist Robert Lynd called "the most penetrating and important book on our contemporary American civilization that has ever been written." (It won the author one of the two Anisfield-Wolf awards for the best book on race relations in the year 1944.) Describing in detail the situation of Negroes in the United States, Myrdal said that the American dilemma was the conflict between the moral creed of brotherhood, equality, and freedom which he considered the American genuinely desired to live by, and "the valuations on specific planes of individual and group living, where personal and local interests; economic, social, and sexual jealousies; considerations of community prestige and conformity; group prejudices against particular persons or types of peoples; and all sorts of miscellaneous wants, impulses, and habits dominate his outlook." In the author's view, the Negroes' problem was the sharpest focus point of this general moral problem, and therefore impossible to consider in isolation. His thesis that the injustices he details constitute "a moral lag in the development of the nation," has been attacked by psychologist Leo Crespi of Princeton, who considers that the solution lies not in individual change of heart but that "the remedies are social and economic planning which will remove the gain from prejudice"— a statement which the author considers "not in conflict" with his thesis.

With the end of the Swedish coalition Cabinet, Gunnar Myrdal became Minister of Commerce in the new Government of Per Albin Hansson [42] continuing his service in investigating the nation's economy. In August 1946 when trade negotiations were being conducted between his Government and that of the Soviet Union, it was reported in a New York *Herald Tribune* column that the Swedish offer of one billion kronor ($278,500,000) in commercial credit on the Soviet Union was the "baby" of Myrdal and Finance Minister Ernst Wigforss. "By tying in with Russia," wrote Homer Bigart, "Myrdal [who] has little confidence in America's ability to solve the postwar economic mess, thinks that . . . Sweden will cushion a future crash, since the totalitarian economy of her eastern neighbor is less subject to world depression."

When there was international as well as Swedish disagreement in opinion over this pact, Commerce Minister Myrdal declared: The nation "reserves full freedom to judge the propriety of the various steps it may take for the promotion of international cooperation in the economic field. . . .The Swedish Government is prepared to subscribe to any international agreement which will bring about freer trade and communications, but until such agreement is concluded we feel we must continue cooperation on a bilateral basis to get commerce started again." The Swedish-Soviet trade agreement, one of a number of similar bilateral agreements which the Scandinavian country had made with other European countries, was signed in later September.

An interviewer has described the Swedish official as "giving off sparks of brilliance . . . a dazzling conversationalist." Myrdal is six feet tall and has greenish eyes and light hair. His sociologist wife is the director of the Stockholm Training College for Nursery School Teachers, which she founded. For a time the Myrdals' son Jan Gunnar and their daughters, Sissila and Kaj, attended a progressive school affiliated with Columbia University.

References

Ann Am Acad 197:215 My '38
N Y Herald Tribune p1+ Ag 16 '46
International Who's Who, 1945-46

NASH, PAUL May 11, 1889—July 11, 1946 British painter and designer; official war artist in both world wars, serving the Air Ministry and the Ministry of Information in 1940-41.

Obituary

N Y Times p15 Jl 13 '46

NEILSON, WILLIAM ALLAN Mar. 28, 1869—Feb. 13, 1946 Scottish-born president of Smith College (1917-39), professor emeritus until death; editor, co-editor, or author of a number of scholarly works and articles; at Smith his administration was progressive, cultural rather than vocational, and financially successful; defended academic freedom and freedom of belief; introduced several innovations.

Obituary

N Y Times p25 F 14 '46 por

NERVO, LUIS PADILLA *See* Padilla, Nervo, L.

NEURATH, OTTO (noi'rät) 1882— Dec. 22, 1945 Exiled Austrian sociologist; invented (1923) isotypes, pictograph symbols now widely used to visualize statistics; professor at Oxford University; founder and director of the Social and Economic Museum in Vienna, and director of the Internation Institute for Visual Education in The Hague; editor in chief of *The International Encyclopedia of Unified Science*.

Obituary

N Y Times p20 D 27 '45 por

NEVINSON, CHRISTOPHER R(ICHARD) W(YNNE) Aug. 13, 1889—Oct. 7, 1946 British artist; official artist in World War I; has exhibited continuously since 1910 in England, France, and the United States; works were purchased by the Imperial War Museum and the Canadian War Memorials Fund; his autobiography, *Paint and Prejudice,* was published in the United States in 1938.

Obituary

N Y Times p23 O 8 '46 por

NOEL-BAKER, PHILIP J(OHN) Nov. 1889- British Government official; diplomat

Address: b. The Foreign Office, London; House of Commons, London; h. 16 S. Eaton Pl., London

Britain's representative on the United Nations Security Council, from the international group's first meeting until November 1946, was Philip J. Noel-Baker, a world authority on international law and an ardent worker for peace and international organization from his youth. His United Nations post stemmed from his portfolio in the Attlee [40] Government as Minister of State, and, therefore, as Foreign Secretary

British Official Photo.

PHILIP J. NOEL-BAKER

Bevin's [40] first assistant. In the fall of 1946 he was transferred from the Foreign Office and made the Secretary of State for Air, a position which made him a member of the Prime Minister's Cabinet. Noel-Baker, who had been vice-chairman of the British Labor Party, in October 1946 succeeded Harold Laski [41] as chairman.

Philip John Baker, who was to add his wife's surname of Noel to his own when he was nearly forty, was born in November 1889. One of the seven children of Canadian-born parents, Joseph Allen and Elizabeth B. (Moscrip) Baker, he was brought up in a Quaker household. J. Allen Baker had come to England to establish a branch of his father's engineering business, and had become prominent in streetcar expansion, highways, and work for international Christian fellowship. When Philip was six, his father became a member of the London County Council, where he served for eleven years, until elected to the House of Commons as a Liberal in 1905. His son was therefore surrounded by politics from his childhood. (Noel-Baker has collaborated on a book about his father, *J. Allen Baker, M.P., A Memoir.*)

Young Philip attended the Bootham School in York and King's College of Cambridge University. *Who's Who* states that he also attended an American institution, Haverford College in Pennsylvania. At Cambridge he was "a brilliant scholar, a brilliant athlete, and a brilliant speaker," passing the honors examinations (tripos) in history (1910) and economics (1913), becoming a University Whewall scholar (1911, continued in 1913), and emerging with his M.A. He headed the Cambridge Athletic Club for two years, ran in the first Olympic games at Stockholm in 1912 and in those at Antwerp, and won every race he ran against Oxford. He was also president of the debating society. Gradually he changed from a Liberal

to a moderate Socialist, and in 1914 he became vice-principal of Ruskin, the Labor College of Oxford University.

In World War I the young Quaker equipped an ambulance, and in August 1914 became the first commandant of the Friends' Ambulance Unit, which he led in the front lines in France until July 1915. He holds the Mons Star for Service in that great battle. Then, as an officer in the first British ambulance unit for Italy, he won the Silver Medal for Military Valor in 1917 and the Croce de Guerra in 1918. In 1915 Philip Baker was married to Irene, daughter of Frank Noel of Achmetaga, Greece. Her grandfather, a cousin of Lady Byron, had settled on the island of Euboea after a historical expedition to Greece. (Mrs. Noel-Baker now owns the Euboea estate.) "Noel" first appeared in Baker's *Who's Who* listing in 1926, as a third prename; in 1930, as an addition to his surname; and in 1943, in the hyphenated "Noel-Baker."

At the Paris Peace Conference, young Baker was one of two "tireless subordinates" to Lord Cecil of Chelwood and Lord Parmoor on the commission which drafted the League of Nations covenant. Then he joined the League secretariat, reportedly as a close associate of its first Secretary-General, Sir Eric Drummond. He remained at Geneva till 1922. Baker was captain of the British Olympic team at Paris in 1924, the first Olympics in which the British achievements were felt to be "worthy of her place in the history of sport." At this time, he was a fellow of King's College, Cambridge. The future Minister, then thirty-five years old, became Sir Ernest Cassel professor of international relations at the University of London in 1924, a post he held until 1929. He also contested the Handsworth division of strongly Conservative Birmingham for the Labor Party in 1924.

Noel-Baker was elected to Parliament from Coventry, serving in 1929-31, and became Parliamentary private secretary to Arthur Henderson, the Secretary of State for Foreign Affairs, in the Ramsay MacDonald Labor Government. This was during the period of attempts at disarmament, a subject upon which Professor Baker had written two books (published in 1926 and 1927). In 1929 and 1930 he was a member of the British delegation to the Tenth Assembly of the League of Nations, led by Undersecretary Hugh Dalton [45]. There he worked with Fridtjof Nansen who, he related, taught him that a difficult problem takes time to solve and the so-called "impossible" only takes a little more time. Negotiations for evacuating British and French troops from the Rhineland were conducted at this time. Like most other Labor M.P.'s, Noel-Baker found himself out of office after Prime Minister MacDonald left the Labor Party in 1931. However, in 1932-33, he was principal assistant to Arthur Henderson, who was presiding over the Disarmament Conference at Geneva.

The author of three books, many pamphlets and articles, and innumerable lectures on international law, Noel-Baker was in the New World as Dodge lecturer at Yale University in 1933-34. In the latter year, Yale awarded him the Howland Memorial prize for distinguished work in the sphere of government. According to Wilson Harris, himself a writer on the League of Nations, Noel-Baker "has probably addressed more popular audiences on that subject than any man in Britain except one or two professional lecturers, and addressed them with remarkable effect."

In 1936 the Laborite was returned to Parliament from the industrial city of Derby. Until 1942, when Winston Churchill [42] reorganized the Ministries of his Coalition Government, Noel-Baker remained in the Opposition. At that time he was made Parliamentary secretary to the Ministry of War Transport. The Minister of Transport, Baron Leathers [40], was in the House of Lords, so that Noel-Baker was "the spokesman and defender of the Ministry in Commons." (Another Transport P.P.S. was Sir Arthur Salter [44].) As such, he pointed out that citizens who were shocked at war casualties were indifferent to the higher toll of civilian wartime accidents (588,742 accidents to 387,996 war casualties). A linguist who speaks fluent German, French, Italian, and Greek (and "owns some acquaintance, thanks to Nansen, with Norwegian"), Noel-Baker exhorted transport workers in Axis territory to sabotage Hitler's [42] communication lines.

Noel-Baker was mentioned in American newspapers as "one of the well-known figures who won seats" at the General Election of July 1945. His only child, twenty-five-year-old Captain Francis Noel-Baker, became the youngest member from London at the same election. The first general election in ten years brought the first Labor victory in sixteen, an overwhelming one. Philip Noel-Baker was chosen Minister of State in the Attlee Government, under Ernest Bevin [40]. This was a non-Cabinet office, ranking next to the Foreign Secretary in handling foreign affairs, and Noel-Baker's appointment was widely approved. He also became a Right Honorable by being sworn on His Majesty's Privy Council.

The new Minister of State was given charge of most of the British preparatory work in connection with the United Nations organization and with UNRRA, the relief and rehabilitation administration. Beginning in August 1945 he headed the British delegation on the fourteen-nation executive committee of the U.N. preparatory commission. There he stated the Anglo-American view that the U.N. secretariat should be an "international civil service founded upon international loyalty to the interests of all governments who join in the work of the United Nations." In September he was named chairman of the subcommittee which prepared a tentative agenda for the Assembly. The Briton, who had written several books on the subject, announced that he hoped to press for early regulation of the arms traffic. Other views expressed by Noel-Baker were that freedom of the press was "as important as the delegates themselves" to the future of the U.N., and must be a prime requirement in choosing its permanent seat. On historical grounds, he also opposed blanket diplomatic immunity for the U.N. staff: "While I favor

freedom of action, I do not think organization should be free to commit murder."

In October 1945 Noel-Baker had to leave this executive session to attend the United Nations Food and Agriculture Organization meeting at Quebec, which would establish precedents for the success or failure of other U.N. groups to be set up. There he steered a middle course between those who thought the FAO should be essentially a research body, and those who thought it should put its recommendations into action. His view: "We can and we should choose both courses, provided we do not make our program as a whole too big," and should seek to improve the lot of both producer and consumer. The United Kingdom delegation, however, opposed such "pessimistic measures" as international commodity agreements or control agencies to handle world surpluses.

As United Kingdom delegate to the Economic and Social Council, he called for concerted economic action to abolish unemployment and poverty in a world of plenty. He also favored the American plan for the economic unification of the four Allied-occupied zones in Germany. To expedite interim handling of refugees, he recommended similar action to that taken by the League of Nations: the issuing of "Nansen passports" to be recognized by all nations and the establishment of distribution centers both in countries from which refugees were leaving and those to which these people would come. Shortly before the October 1946 General Assembly session, the British delegate asserted that his country supported the United States plan for atom control. At first in favor of placing the Russian proposal that U.N. members reveal effectives and bases in nonenemy countries on the disarmament agenda, Britain later suggested a resolution embodying the Soviet plan and adding the statement on forces at home and in the occupation zones. This was passed by the Political and Security Committee, which established January 1, 1947, as the date on which the reports would be due.

Noel-Baker's Parliamentary position gained importance because Foreign Secretary Bevin left the Monday question period to him and Under Secretary Hector McNeil [46], with the result that they made most of the statements of Foreign Office policy. At the United Nations conference, meanwhile, Noel-Baker, France's René Massigli, and Belgium's Paul-Henri Spaak [45] were leaders in the campaign to have the organization's permanent site in Geneva, or at least in a small European country, where "the true urgency of the problems of war and hunger and employment" would be felt. A "brilliant and powerful speech for Europe" by Noel-Baker was described (by correspondent Saville R. Davis) as "easily the most outstanding address of the U.N. sessions." After the vote in favor of the United States, however, he moved to make it unanimous. When the United Nations Assembly opened session in January 1946, Noel-Baker was a member of the British delegation, headed by Prime Minister Attlee, and including Bevin, Education Minister Ellen Wilkinson [41], Attorney General Sir Hartley

Shawcross [45], and Undersecretary for India
Arthur Henderson.

Concurrently, the Minister of State had Foreign Office duties. He sat in on the Prime
Minister's conferences with Dutch and Indo-
nesian leaders, where they tried to achieve some
settlement that would restore order in Java
and make it possible to withdraw the British
troops there. (The troops, commanded by Sir
Philip Christison [45], had been sent to the East
Indies in the capacity of Allied forces, to clean
up the remaining Japanese and release Allied
prisoners and internees.) Other diplomatic
problems facing the United Kingdom included
developments in long-disputed Palestine and
India, as well as Greece, Iran, Poland, and
other countries. In October 1946 Noel-Baker,
who, a few months before, had been elected
chairman of the Labor Party, was transferred
from the Foreign Office as a result of reported
disagreements with Prime Minister Clement
Attlee and Foreign Secretary Bevin on several
questions, among them the Government's policy
on Palestine. Hector McNeil became Minister of State. Noel-Baker, however, was named
to the office of Secretary of State for Air, a
Cabinet post.

Wiry, spectacled Philip Noel-Baker is described by Gault MacGowan [45] as a suave, diplomatic aristocrat. "Few men have been richer
in friendships," writes Wilson Harris, "and few
men have more personal charm to account for
them. . . .He is capable as few men are of
enlarging his vision from the national to the
international. . . .His enthusiasm—one of his
outstanding characteristics—rests on deep and
intellectually proved convictions." *Newsweek*
sees in him "an intense intellectual, almost as
ascetic in appearance as his fellow Laborite
Sir Stafford Cripps [40]," and who "still refuses
to hunt because he will not kill animals. To
the Right wing of the Labor Party, he brought
impeccable manners, a lofty mind, and a limited
sense of humor." The *Newsweek* writer considers that he lacks "the cold, hard balance
necessary in a Foreign Secretary." One of his
friends is quoted as saying, "Phil never really
believes that God can possibly be on the side
of big battalions. At heart he really prefers
lost causes and small countries."

References

Independent 113:112 Ag 16 '24; 113:140
    Ag 30 '24
N Y Sun p6 My 6 '44
Newsweek 27:36 Ja 14 '46 por
Who's Who, 1946

NOURSE, EDWIN G(RISWOLD) (nôrs)
May 20, 1883- Economist; United States Gov-
ernment official
Address: b. Executive Office of the President,
Washington, D.C.; h. 3802 Jocelyn St., N.W.,
Washington, D.C.

Dr. Edwin G. Nourse, the vice-president of
Brookings Institution, in July 1946 became
chairman of the Council of Economic Advisers
which was set up to study and plan Federal
action under the new Employment Act. Con-

gress had recognized the importance of the
council posts in voting Cabinet-size salaries of
fifteen thousand dollars for each of the three
members. "It will not be possible to keep business on an absolutely level keel," said Nourse,
but "by using rational methods now at our
disposal we should certainly keep down acute
extremes." Nourse, who calls himself a liberal
"with both feet on the ground," has expressed
his basic political viewpoint thus: "As an economic engineer, I have a deep-seated conviction
that . . . economic life can be carried on more
efficiently under private direction than under
public direction. . . .It [private enterprise] is
not on that plane of performance or even of
real intention today. Nor will it be until capital
management and labor management are willing
to sit down together as equals to formulate the
terms of a just partnership. . . .The orderly
conduct of complex modern business requires
considerable active participation on the part of
Government." Nourse recommends, however,
"as little Government management as possible
in business, and decentralization of the planning
function." He points out that "this implies
business management responsible for the welfare and responsive to the needs and capacities
of all its members."

Born in Lockport, New York, on May 20,
1883, Edwin Griswold Nourse is a year younger
than his well-known sister, novelist Alice
Tisdale Hobart. Another sister, Mary Augusta
Nourse, taught in a missionary school in China
for fifteen years. The family is descended
from colonial settlers; their ancestor Rebecca Nurse, was conspicuous among the victims
of the Salem witchcraft trials of 1692. Through
his mother, Harriet Augusta (Beaman) Nourse,
the economist is related to the Choate family of
Massachusetts. When he was one year old
the family moved to Chicago, where his father,
Edwin Henry Nourse, became supervisor of
singing in the public schools. Eight years later,
the family moved to a small farm in Downer's
Grove, Illinois, in the hope of restoring Mrs.
Nourse's failing health. She died when her son
was nine, and the strait-laced father reared
the three children until his own death when
Edwin was in his teens. The boy had hoped
to become a farmer, but gave up the plan, he
says now, for lack of money to buy a farm.

Upon his graduation from the Downer's
Grove High School in 1901, young Nourse
studied at the Lewis Institute in Chicago and
at Cornell University in New York State,
receiving his B.A. from Cornell in 1906. There
he had studied agricultural economics and had
been elected to the agricultural honor society,
Gamma Sigma Delta, as well as to Alpha Zeta
and the general honor society Phi Kappa Phi.
When a professor asked the new graduate what
he planned to do, Nourse answered, "Anything
but teach." "As a result," he later remarked
to an interviewer, "I was teaching the next fall,
and except for one year I've been teaching or
in research ever since." He began by teaching
school in Ogden, Utah.

At the age of twenty-six, the agricultural
economist was an instructor in finance at the
University of Pennsylvania's Wharton School

of Finance and Economics. From 1910 to 1912 he was at the University of South Dakota as professor and head of the department of economics and sociology; and in the years 1915-18, after earning his Ph.D. at the University of Chicago, Nourse served in a similar capacity at the University of Arkansas. The first of his seven books on farm economics came out in 1916, the second in 1918; and in the latter year Nourse joined the Iowa State College faculty as professor of agricultural economics and chief of that section of the Iowa Agricultural Experiment Station.

In 1923, when he was forty, Professor Nourse joined the fact-finding Institute of Economics in Washington, D.C., becoming chief of its agricultural division. (In 1924 he served as president of the American Farm Economic Association, and in 1925-26 edited the *Journal of Farm Economics*.) In 1929, two years after the Institute of Economics had joined two other Brookings-promoted research organizations to form the Brookings Institution, Edwin Nourse was appointed director of the Institute of Economics, a post he held for thirteen years under Harold G. Moulton '44, president of Brookings Institution.

In 1936, as in 1924, Nourse was a United State delegate to the International Institute of Agriculture's biennial assembly at Rome, and from 1935 he served as a member of the League of Nations Mixed Committee on the Relation of Nutrition to Health, Agriculture, and Economic Policy, which made its final report in August 1937. In an article on the economic aspects of nutrition in 1938, the Brookings Institution official set forth his view that business should accept the "responsibility for the welfare of the entire labor force during its productive period," but he also saw "a global responsibility of Government to underwrite a decent minimum standard of subsistence" for those not provided for: "It is simply good national housekeeping and thrifty prevention of future wastes and costs to insure good feeding and medical care of all the rising generation up to the point when they are ready to work."

With one major exception, until 1938 Nourse's writings were concerned with farm questions, including the cooperative movement, a particular interest of his. The exception is *America's Capacity To Produce* (1934), written with five associates, which he, the senior author, described as a study of the productive capacity of the United States in 1900-30, in terms of the capital goods and labor force then available and of the technology and the general pattern of organization then prevailing. The conclusion of this 608-page study was that "our productive system as a whole was operating at about 80 per cent of capacity in 1929," the year of highest production. "There was nearly 20 per cent of reasonably available labor which was not turned into the productive stream. Our economic system lacked almost 20 per cent of living up to its means." The question of why this came about was left to the three other volumes of the series "The Distribution of Income in Relation to Economic Progress," which study Nourse directed from May 1932 to May 1934, when it came under Moulton's personal direction.

Underwood & Underwood

EDWIN G. NOURSE

Reviewers called *America's Capacity To Produce* "one of the most significant and one of the most accessible and absorbing of its type", "useful from the scientific as well as the practical point of view." "More important than mere economic finding," wrote R. S. McBride in *Chemical and Metallurgical Engineering*, "is the economic method of analysis of industrial situations which this book presents. The technique used is sound and valuable." Next came two books about the AAA, in one of which Nourse took a middle position of qualified approval between those of his coauthors Joseph S. Davis and John D. Black. In 1938 Nourse's *Industrial Price Policies and Economic Progress*, written with Horace B. Drury, received mixed notices. The Springfield *Republican* praised its independence and intellectual integrity and added, "Everything that is said is of interest from some point of view, but the study exhibits a lack of coherence which is recognized by the authors." In 1942 Nourse became vice-president of the Brookings Institution, was elected president of the American Economic Association, and began three years as chairman of the Social Science Research Council. He returned to the discussion of pricing and economic policies in his 1944 *Price Making in a Democracy*.

Nourse and Drury had stated that "the price-making executive [in which category they include union leaders] takes over . . . as guide and regulator of the economic process in a considerable part of our business world. He takes upon himself the responsibility for the standard of living for an ever-higher proportion of our people. Much as he generally hates the phrase, he becomes in fact the economic planner of our society rather than merely the adapter of his personal affairs as best he can to a largely automatic price mechanism." Six years later, in *Price Making in a Democracy*, his

NOURSE, EDWIN G.—*Continued*

thesis is that only consistent, planful policy of constant technological improvement, passed on to the consumer by constant price reductions, can enable private business to fulfill the needs of the masses—a goal never yet attained—and can save the system of free enterprise.

Reviewers in general approved Nourse's theories, but doubted that they would be put into practice. Herbert von Beckerath wrote in *Social Forces* that this "excellent treatise for the general student . . . clearly and simply presented" had "a realism and a tinge of practical wisdom which makes it particularly useful." The *Journal of Political Economy* called *Price Making* "a book which cannot be ignored and which should have more than perfunctory reading . . . an open-minded, courteous, and tolerant book, even where the author adversely criticizes . . . shortcomings. . . .While there are difficult fundamental problems which in the reviewer's opinion have not been successfully disposed of, this book is beyond doubt one of the 'musts' of the present decade." J. J. O'Leary, who complained of the "often repetitious and wearisome" exposition, declared, nevertheless, "every business executive and labor leader in America should read Dr. Nourse's valuable book." Evidently some of them did, for in the General Motors wage negotiations of October 1945 both labor and management quoted *Price Making in a Democracy*, and United Auto Workers leader Walter Reuther[41] called the book "epoch-making."

The Employment Act of 1946, popularly miscalled the full employment act, was signed by President Truman in February 1946. Five months later, in July, he appointed Edwin G. Nourse chairman of the Economic Advisory Council set up under it. The sixty-three-year-old economist had "mapped further studies in his profession . . . calculated to occupy the remainder of his useful span of life," but laid these plans aside to accept chairmanship of the three-man council, on which his fellow members were Dean John D. Clark, an oil millionaire turned economist, and Leon H. Keyserling, forceful young New Deal lawyer-economist said to have helped write the Act. The appointment was hailed by the New York *Times* as "one of the finest made by Mr. Truman . . . bound to increase public confidence in the activities of the council." Nourse, the editorial continued, "has had to deal with a wide diversity of economic problems and be familiar with all types of economic research . . . which will be valuable in connection with the economic surveys the council will have to make."

The *United States News,* quoting Nourse to the effect that he was "a liberal conservative or a conservative liberal," wrote that he had always been considered a middle-of-the-road economist, and that he considered the Employment Act, as passed, a "very useful instrument for synthesizing the many economic studies made by Government agencies and others." Clark and Keyserling had been appointed a few days before him and, according to *Newsweek,* Nourse's high opinion of them was a factor in his decision to accept the post. A *Na-tion's Business* article said of the three advisers, "They have to deal with a problem that no other Government in the world has had the nerve to tackle"—that of forecasting the economic weather of a capitalistic private-enterprise society and recommending Federal action to help stabilize it, and they "must be right every time." Nourse, the writer added, had been planning a book on that very topic before his appointment.

Soon after taking the oath of office, Nourse issued a statement comparing the council to "a driving band which ties many important wheels together in a complex but powerful mechanism." "The immediate task in maintaining the economic health of the nation," he said, "is to hold inflationary forces down so that we do not get into a runaway boom." The council's first duty, after getting its staff and quarters organized, was to prepare recommendations, to submit to President Truman by December, for what its report termed the "very carefully considered complementary role" of Federal action in the light of its estimate of the future situation.

Gray-haired, brown-eyed Edwin Griswold Nourse weighs 195 pounds and stands an inch more than six feet. *Time*'s adjective for him is "distinguished-looking." The spectacled economist is described as a friendly man who speaks with a drawl. Since August 1910 he has been married to Ray Marie Tyler of Utah; they have one son, John Tyler, born in 1922. Nourse first became interested in clay modeling when he bought a modeling set for his son; eventually he studied clay sculpture at Washington's Corcoran Evening School and has "had a grand time" with it ever since. An old injury to Nourse's ankle prevents him from enjoying any sport except swimming, but he is interested in the radio and movies, likes to cook, and enjoys taking turns with his wife at reading aloud. His aloofness from politics is such that he says he has voted only twice in his life, once for a Democrat and once for a Republican. Ray Tyler Nourse, herself a civically active writer of books and articles for young people, has said of her husband and sisters-in-law, "Nothing has ever been impossible for Alice and Mary and Edwin Nourse, if they wanted to do it"—except to sing.

References

N Y Herald Tribune II p3 Ag 4 '46 por
N Y Post Mag p25 Ag 12 '46 por
U S News 21:50-1 D 27 '46 por

International Who's Who, 1945-46
Who's Who in America, 1946-47
Who's Who in the Nation's Capital, 1938-39

OENSLAGER, DONALD (MITCHELL) (ō'ĕn-slā"gĕr) Mar. 7, 1902- Stage designer

Address: b. Times Bldg., 1475 Broadway, New York; h. 1010 5th Ave., New York

The stage designer, Donald Oenslager, has contributed settings for more than one hundred and fifty productions—plays, musicals, operas, and ballets—since his first connection with the theater in 1925. His stage sets, described by a number of drama critics as being "delightful fantasies" and as possessing a "deft, imaginative, scholarly touch," have gained for the designer a reputation for artistic originality and adaptability.

Donald Mitchell Oenslager, who was born in Harrisburg, Pennsylvania, on March 7, 1902, is one of three children of John Oenslager, Jr., and Jane (Connely) Oenslager. In his childhood, when he was taken to see plays like *Rip Van Winkle, Peter Pan,* and *The Music Master,* which he tried to reproduce on a soap-box stage, Oenslager showed his first interest in the theater. At ten he constructed scenery for a drama of his own invention, *The Burning of Rome.* Young Oenslager attended day school at the Harrisburg Academy, and from the age of fifteen to seventeen (1917-19) was a student at Phillips Exeter Academy, in New Hampshire. There he acquired added experience in stage design by planning sets for school plays and constructing Elizabethan stage models.

With his preparatory school education completed in 1919, Oenslager entered Harvard University to specialize in the fine arts. There he had as one of his professors Dr. George Pierce Baker, founder of the famous Harvard "47 Workshop," whose notable contributions to the literary and technical study of the drama broke "puritan and academic prejudices and prepared the ground for the renascence of the American drama." Oenslager served for a few years as art director of the college dramatic club and designed settings for many of its productions. Vacations found the undergraduate teaching stage design at the summer sessions of Middlebury College in Vermont. Oenslager, who in his senior year was awarded the Sachs Fine Arts Traveling Fellowship, was graduated from Harvard in 1923 with the B.F.A. degree.

Financed by the fellowship, Oenslager spent a year abroad (1923-24) studying fine arts and methods of production and stage design in the important theaters of Europe and the Near East. Returning to the United States in September 1924, he established himself in New York City and became associated with the Provincetown Playhouse and the Greenwich Village Theatre. Both were directed by Kenneth Macgowan, Robert Edmond Jones, and Eugene O'Neill. Oenslager's training in stage design began at this period under the guidance of Jones, famous as one of the eminent American artists in his field. At the same time, Oenslager was engaged in costume research.

In March 1925 the designer made his debut with the settings for the ballet *Sooner and Later.* John Mason Brown, in an article reprinted in *The Literary Digest* for July 18, 1925, described Oenslager's *décor* for the prehistoric-modernistic theme of the ballet: *"Sooner and Later* was a fortunate beginning, providing opportunities for virtuoso work usually denied the young designer. . . .The spirit of the pantomime was happily suited to Oenslager's special gifts." The best of Oenslager's work, Brown believed, was evident in the beautiful and parodically effective costuming. Oen-

DONALD OENSLAGER

slager next designed scenery for his first New York dramatic venture, an Actors Theatre production of Galsworthy's *A Bit O' Love* (1925). By means of a skeleton set easily adapted to scene sequences, staging problems were surmounted and "tasteful and restrained" realism of effect resulted. Since 1925, when he was appointed a faculty member, Oenslager has been connected with the Yale University Department of Drama (established the same year by Dr. Baker), where he holds the position of associate professor of scenic design.

With his first two productions Oenslager established himself as a promising young designer of the "new movement" in American stage art, which sought to "invest the stage picture . . . with beauty of color, enveloping light and expressive design" as against the old artificiality of background settings. Other of Oenslager's early New York productions include *Morals* (1925), *Good News* (1927), the musicals *The New Moon* and *Follow Thru,* and the opera, *l'Histoire de soldat,* staged for the League of Composers (1928). The 1930 theatrical season saw Oenslager sets for *Overture* and the musical comedy *Girl Crazy,* followed in 1932 by *Whistling in the Dark,* and in 1933 by *Forsaking All Others,* and *Uncle Tom's Cabin.* In the comedy *Forsaking All Others,* Oenslager adopted a new and unconventional stage design technique. Contrary to "traditional color symbolism" for comedy—a light setting—Oenslager staged the play amidst walls of deep blue-violet. His colorful scenery for the successful Players' production of *Uncle Tom's Cabin* he surpassed in the play's short-lived reproduction three years later as *Sweet River.*

The designer, who later in his career was to express the hope that the term, "a typical Oenslager set," would never be applied to any of his productions, had by 1933 fulfilled in his settings all the promise of adeptness he

OENSLAGER, DONALD—*Continued*

had shown originally. Three dramas—*Brand* (1928), *The Emperor Jones* (1931), and *Venice Preserved* (1933)—which Oenslager staged at Yale, are regarded as added proof of his ability to cope with varied dramatic situations. *Brand,* to insure its atmosphere of wildness and doom, was played against a background of "exaggerated light and shade—only grays, varying all the way from black to white" with color added solely by costumes and lighting. By altering lights on the playing areas and by projecting forms onto the cyclorama, the designer made the simple settings of *The Emperor Jones* "literally to act, to be an ever-changing but ever-present embodiment of Brutus Jones's fears."

In 1934 Oenslager provided the "picturesque" *décor* for *The Farmer Takes a Wife*; stage sets for the musical *Anything Goes,* and for the operas *Tristan and Isolde* and *Der Rosenkavalier* (Philadelphia Orchestra) and *Salome* (Metropolitan Opera Association). *Tristan and Isolde*'s settings, in which "there was nothing . . . of Broadway realism nor yet of the heavy and tasteless romanticism of the traditional Wagnerian scenery," received marked praise. Oenslager discovered, however, that the setting he had designed for *Der Rosenkavalier,* though supporting the music, attracted undue attention because of its novelty. His long observation of audience reaction to theater design led Oenslager to remark in a San Francisco *Chronicle* article for January 24, 1942, that there was something inherently wrong with a set that did not remain solely a background fusing with the dramatic action but instead drew applause as soon as the curtain was raised.

Even when designing for plays which provide little opportunity for him to display the "distinctive stamp" of his talent, Oenslager has, in one critic's opinion, manifested his skill as a scrupulously careful, "well-trained craftsman." "Workmanlike, realistic settings serving unobtrusively the modest scenic needs" he devised for plays like *First Lady* (1935), *Stage Door* and *You Can't Take It With You* (1936). The 1936 production of Paul Green's controversial *Johnny Johnson,* "one of the best anti-war plays of the present century" contained Oenslager's "imaginative settings." During the same season, Oenslager's commissions comprised stage designs for *Ten Million Ghosts, Russet Mantle, Matrimony Preferred,* and *Red, Hot and Blue,* a musical. The designer, who has worked in varied types of stage productions, admitted (in *The Spur,* December 1936) no preferences in his theater assignments, remarking that he liked to work with musicals equally as well as with dramas.

In 1937, for the dramatic version of Steinbeck's novel, *Of Mice and Men,* wherein "realism rose to the heights of poetry," Oenslager created "three settings which through their dignity and strength gave visual expression to the play's high seriousness" and brooding quality. In the same year he designed scenery for the operas *Amelia Goes to the Ball* (Curtis Institute of Philadelphia), and *Otello* (Metropolitan

Opera Association), and for the musical *I'd Rather Be Right.* Other of his *décors* have been for *The Circle,* and *The Fabulous Invalid* (1938) ; in 1939, *The American Way* (his settings "provided varied acting levels and exciting backgrounds" for the patriotic spectacle's many scenes), *The Man Who Came to Dinner,* and *Skylark* ; in 1940, *My Sister Eileen,* and *The Old Foolishness*; in 1941, *The Doctor's Dilemma,* and *Claudia*; and the San Francisco production of Bernstein's *Rose Burke,* in 1942. Oenslager maintains that settings should "appear to be the creation of, or at least an expression of, the characters in the play," not the revelation of the designer's individualism. He has always preferred the drawing-room type set, at which he excels, finding it more stimulating.

"Donald Oenslager, one suspects, enjoys the theater most," wrote Norris Houghton in *Theatre Arts Monthly* (November 1936), "when he is dreaming dreams about it." Some of those ideas have yielded sketches—they are for projects most of them as yet unproduced—different in technique from that employed by the artist in his "practical" Broadway work. (Oenslager had studied painting with Maurice Sterne, but except for figure drawing, has done little in art other than his designing.) Among them are sketches for Aristophanes' *The Birds,* for which the designer utilizes a modern aviation motif, and Wagner's *Ring of the Nibelung,* in which a permanent stage construction is based on the designer's conception of the tree of existence of the Scandinavian sagas (described in *Theatre Arts Monthly,* January 1927). When Oenslager's designs—both for his earlier stage assignments and for his imaginary, unproduced "projects"—were exhibited at the Marie Sterner Galleries during the month of December 1936, most art critics were impressed by his ability to "paint with light," to work effectively in all varieties of moods and masses, and to retain his artistic freshness and inventiveness, unexhausted by "his constant contributions to the commercial theater." Other collections of his designs have been shown in a number of galleries in the United States and abroad.

Oenslager's book, *Scenery, Then and Now* (1936), presents his philosophy of stage design. Many of his sketches found their way into this "original" and "unpretentious" volume, commended by various reviewers for its "exquisite prose" and for its intellectual as well as artistic approach to the theater. Neither "a consecutive survey or review of theatrical art," nor a technical handbook, *Scenery, Then and Now* contains Oenslager's theories of modern stage design as applied to his interpretation of plays selected from all periods of the occidental drama. Four years later, in December 1940, Oenslager issued a little volume, *Theatre of Bali,* termed a collector's item. The designer is, in addition, the author of a number of articles on the theater and has lectured on a variety of subjects in the field at museums and art societies in New York, Boston, Philadelphia, and elsewhere.

Oenslager's active career as designer was interrupted when he was commissioned in May

1942 as a captain in the United States Army Air Corps. After more than three years' duty (he served some months in the South Pacific) in the Camouflage and Intelligence Divisions, Oenslager received his discharge in December 1945, having attained the rank of major, and was awarded the Bronze Star. Since Oenslager's return to civilian life, he devised early in 1946 the settings for *Born Yesterday, On Whitman Avenue, Pygmalion,* and the musical *Three To Make Ready,* in all of which his work once more was lauded for its high level of artistry. (Adverse criticism of Oenslager's work has been leveled at a few of his designs for operas, including *Otello.* Settings too hurriedly executed for some plays, *Two Hundred Were Chosen* (1936) among them, were also criticized as being inferior to Oenslager's usual standards.) For the Central City (Colorado) Opera Association's *La Traviata* and *The Abduction from the Seraglio,* he "wielded a mellow brush as he conceived the brilliant settings and costumes." The latter opera, with Oenslager's designs, was presented in English at the Metropolitan in December. Other of his stage sets in 1946 were for *Park Avenue, Present Laughter, Loco, The Fatal Weakness, Land's End,* and *Years Ago.* During the fall of the same year Oenslager was engaged in providing the *décor* also for *The Temporary Mrs. Smith, The Eagle Has Two Heads, The Greatest of These,* and *Washington Square.*

"Good scenic designing," wrote Oenslager in the introduction to *Scenery, Then and Now,* "is good thinking, supplemented by reasonable performance in execution." His designs for professional productions are the result of painstaking planning. The effects Oenslager desires to achieve in his work—aside from the primary effect of the architectural background—are often accomplished by his novel use of color and light. In this respect, the conventional color division into dark and light settings for tragedy and comedy, respectively, he has sometimes discarded (as in *Forsaking All Others* and in *Tristan and Isolde,* with Tristan's meeting death in an autumnal setting of "pale yellow, fading to brown") for a color scheme he considered more symbolic of the play's essential elements. Light he regards as vital to color design and he has used lighting as a device to provide changes in settings and to create the illusory atmosphere of the heroic or legendary. Stage furnishings, also part of the intended effect, according to Oenslager, must be somewhat exaggerated to assume their proper proportions on stage. The complex routine of "setting a play" involving the acquisition of stage properties and occasionally the costuming (Oenslager usually designs the costumes for a period play) is described as "Donald Oenslager's method."

The organizations of which Oenslager is a member include the Harvard, Players, and Century clubs, the United Scenic Artists of America, the American Institute of Decoration, and Municipal Art Committee. He serves on the advisory board of the Museum of Modern Art's theater department, and on the board of directors of the Chicago Institute of Design;

and in 1946 he was chosen president of the board of directors of the Neighborhood Playhouse. For his contributions in the field of design, Oenslager received the American School of Design Scroll of Honor. His only apparent mark of artistic temperament is the frequency with which he loses hats on the sets, which turn up later as stage props. A tall man, over six feet in height and weighing 180 pounds, Oenslager has brown eyes and graying brown hair. His religious affiliation is Episcopalian. Tennis and swimming are his recreations, and he and Mrs. Oenslager, the former Mary Osborne Polak, to whom the designer was married in March 1937, are fond of traveling in remote regions of the world.

References

High School Thespian p5+ F 8-15 '42
N Y Morning Telegraph Mr 8 '41
San Francisco Chronicle Ja 24 '42
Theatre Arts Mo 20:885+ N '36
Who's Who in America, 1946-47
Who's Who in American Art, 1940-41
Who's Who in New York, 1938
Who's Who in the Theatre (1939)

OLDFIELD, BARNEY Jan. 29, 1878— Oct. 4, 1946 Pioneer automobile racer in the United States; began racing in 1902, was clocked officially as the first to travel a mile a minute, June 15, 1903, in Henry Ford's racing car, the "999"; retired in 1918.

Obituary

N Y Times p17 O 5 '46

OLIVIER, LAURENCE (ō-lĭv´ĭ-ā) May 22, 1907- Actor; director; producer
Address: b. c/o Old Vic Company, New Theatre, London

"The present champion of the English theater," wrote Leslie Stokes in 1945, "is Laurence Olivier," who had been known to American audiences primarily for his performances in the films *Wuthering Heights* and *Rebecca,* and who was remembered in New York for a "painfully bad" production of *Romeo and Juliet* in 1940. Almost overnight he came to be recognized on both sides of the Atlantic as "potentially the most important figure that the English theater has produced for many generations." His acting with the Old Vic Company in New York in the spring of 1946 brought him the unqualified and unanimous acclaim of drama critics; his technicolor production of Shakespeare's *Henry V,* released in America at about the same time, is destined, it is generally agreed, to become a film classic.

Laurence Kerr Olivier is descended from Huguenots who fled to England in 1572 to escape religious persecution. He was born in Dorking, Surrey, on May 22, 1907, the son of the late Reverend Gerald Kerr Olivier, an Anglo-Catholic clergyman, and Agnes Louise (Crookenden) Olivier. Laurence's family hoped he would study for the ministry. His early years were spent in close contact with the ritual, literature, and music of the church. A

LAURENCE OLIVIER

nine-year-old with a fine voice, he was sent to
the Choir School of the Margaret Street All
Saints, an Anglo-Catholic church in London
noted for its music, where musical and histrionic talents were valued and trained. Laurence received his formal education at St.
Edward's School, Oxford. At fifteen he made
his first stage appearance, playing Katharine
in a boys' performance of *The Taming of The
Shrew*, given at Stratford-on-Avon in an
April 1922 Shakespeare festival. When young
Olivier realized that he wanted to be an actor,
his clergyman father gave his approval and
financial support. Laurence was thus enrolled
when he was seventeen at the Central School
of Dramatic Art (second only to London's
Royal Academy of Dramatic Art), and there
studied under the famous Elsie Fogerty.

While a student, Olivier was engaged by
Sybil Thorndike for a walk-on part in *Henry
VIII*. He "was not popular with the old boys
of the company," wrote Sewell Stokes in
Theatre Arts. "They thought him far too im-
petuous, and advised him . . . to damp down his
unusual display of virility. Advice that fortu-
nately he never took." In 1925 Olivier earned
his first salary as assistant stage manager and
general understudy in a small provincial town.
Before he was nineteen the young actor had
also toured in a sketch and had minor roles
in several plays. Then he began three years of
apprenticeship (1926-28) at the Birmingham
Repertory Theatre, where he met Ralph Richardson, an actor a few years older than himself. Richardson himself is said to have influenced considerably the development of the
younger man. While with the Birmingham
group, Olivier played the title role in *Uncle
Vanya* (he was nineteen at the time), and with
an acquired American accent opened as the lead
in Elmer Rice's *Adding Machine*.

After he left the Birmingham company,
Olivier was the first Stanhope in *Journey's End*,

appearing in the play's tryout in December
1928. But before *Journey's End* opened for its
regular run, Olivier had left the cast to take
the "most coveted part in town," that of Beau
Geste. *Beau Geste* ran four weeks, but *Journey's End* was a long-remembered hit. The next
year, after a succession of short-run plays in
New York and London, Olivier essayed motion
pictures, acting in a German "talkie" made in
Berlin. Then, in 1930 he appeared with Noel
Coward and Gertrude Lawrence in Coward's
Private Lives, and in January 1931, came with
that play to New York. Remaining in the
United States for about three years, he made
several undistinguished motion pictures, and
was seen on the stage in *The Rats of Norway*,
and as Julian Dulcimer in *The Green Bay Tree*
(October, 1933). After his return to England,
the actor appeared in half a dozen plays including *Biography* and *The Royal Family*, turned
producer-director-actor with *Golden Arrow*,
which lasted two and a half weeks, and in
October 1935 teamed with John Gielgud to do
Romeo and Juliet. The two actors alternately
played Romeo and Mercutio. "The panning
the critics gave Olivier was the most brutal in
years," wrote Kyle Crichton in *Collier's*. One
critic, however, was impressed. "Here at last,"
wrote St. John Irvine of the twenty-eight-year-
old Olivier, "is a young and gallant Romeo, a
manly Romeo, a lad to take a girl by storm,
and be taken so himself."

After the *Romeo and Juliet* venture, Olivier
and J. B. Priestley presented the latter's *Bees
on the Boat Deck*. That was in May 1936.
Olivier next acted with Vivien Leigh in the
motion picture *Fire Over England*, an occasion
which marked the beginning of a romance leading to their marriage in 1940. After that film
Olivier found himself professionally "at an
impasse." He knew that with some luck he
could stay in motion pictures, be a West End
leading man, and also a manager—"it would be
quite easy to combine all three. But my eyes
kept straying towards the rocky mountain
tops. . . .I decided to start life all over again."
Whereupon the actor joined England's famous
Old Vic repertory company. Beginning with
Hamlet in its "eternity" (the players' word for
"ent'rety"), he acted at Old Vic from January
to November 1937, and again from February
to April 1938, taking the parts of Hamlet,
King Henry V, Macbeth, Caius Marcius, and
Sir Toby Belch. That season the Old Vic
Company brought *Hamlet* to the "very spot" in
the courtyard of Denmark's Elsinore Castle,
with Olivier as Hamlet and Vivien Leigh '46 as
Ophelia.

To Olivier, movies at that time were just
a "dull means of making money between interesting stage roles." When he went to Hollywood again in 1938 to make *Wuthering Heights*
(his thirteenth picture) with the painstaking
director, William Wyler, he began to change
his mind, but only to decide that, whereas the
stage was an actor's medium, the movies were
a director's medium. In any case, it was later
commented: "His fine performance as Heath-
cliff in *Wuthering Heights* first suggested that
Olivier might be a great actor in the making."
The picture was extremely well received by

critics (it was voted among the ten best of 1939). He then left Hollywood for New York to appear with Katharine Cornell in *No Time For Comedy*. In the role of a garrulous playwright, he kept the talkiness from becoming monotonous by decorating the role with trick gestures, which so intrigued the editors of *Life* magazine that they ran three pages of photographs of Olivier in action. Next, in 1940 Olivier starred with Joan Fontaine in *Rebecca*, the dramatization of Daphne du Maurier's novel. David Selznick, who produced the picture, had immediately penciled Olivier's name in the margin of the book when he came across the author's description of her hero's face as "arresting, sensitive, medieval."

Olivier returned to the stage in May 1940 in his own production of *Romeo and Juliet* in New York, with Vivien Leigh as Juliet. The show closed after thirty-six performances. The only good thing the critics had to say for the play was that the beautiful Miss Leigh "looked the part" of Juliet; Olivier's Romeo was described as "singularly lacking in emotion and eloquence." He made three more pictures, *Conquest of the Air* (1935), *Pride and Prejudice* (1940), and with Miss Leigh, who was by that time his wife, *That Hamilton Woman* (1941). Of his performance as Lord Nelson in *That Hamilton Woman*, the magazine *Time* said, "Undemonstrative . . . Olivier mumbles his lines in his gullet or grimaces slightly."

When England went to war in 1939 the thirty-two-year-old actor, who was anxious to join his country's Air Force, was told by the British Government to remain in the United States to promote good will and raise funds until his age group was called. Between acting assignments in New York and Hollywood Olivier took instruction in flying, piling up two hundred hours of flying time. When he returned to England early in 1941 he became a lieutenant in the Fleet Air Arm, did "second-line flying," and served as an instructor. In 1943 the Royal Navy gave him leave to act the role of a Russian in the motion picture *Adventure for Two*, in the interests of Anglo-Russian friendship.

It was, Olivier said, "in the interests of Anglo-British relations," that the Royal Navy extended his leave so that he could produce, direct, and take the leading role in a technicolor motion picture version of *Henry V*. When *Henry V* was released in the United States in April 1946, *Time* Magazine, displaying Olivier on its cover, announced, "The movies have produced one of their rare great works of art." John Mason Brown of the *Saturday Review of Literature* wrote: "By all odds the finest movie I have ever seen, and one of the most enthralling and stirring Shakespearean performances I ever hope to see." Olivier was praised for the brilliant casting, a superb performance in the role of Henry, poetic ideas in cutting and transition, an "anti-naturalistic conception of the film" in the true Shakespeare tradition, and the development of a camera technique suited to Shakespeare. *Henry V* was voted the best picture of 1946 by the National Board of Review of Motion Pictures.

London, meanwhile, had even more reason to be aware that a "remarkable new artist had appeared." Olivier and Ralph Richardson, old friends and fellow fliers, were released from service by the British Admiralty so that, together with John Burrell, they might reorganize the Old Vic repertory theater company in time for the 1944 fall season. In the new Old Vic repertory, the first since the German blitz had destroyed the old theater, Olivier's performances, particularly as Richard III, were considered "magnificent." The company went to the Continent that season to perform for British and Allied troops. Toward the end of 1944 Olivier also directed a London production of Wilder's *The Skin Of Our Teeth*, with Miss Leigh playing the lead. Her performance was well received; Olivier, it was said, "produced the play with a constant fertility of happy invention."

In the spring of 1946 the Old Vic Company was engaged to play in New York for six weeks. There over ten thousand mail orders for tickets were received, and hundreds waited on line outside the theater's box office. The six weeks were a series of major triumphs for Old Vic, with most of the applause for Olivier. Of his Hotspur in *Henry IV, Part 1*, Stark Young (*New Republic*) wrote: Olivier plays Hotspur with a definite charm and poetic fatalism of mind as beautiful as it is rare." Wolcott Gibbs (*New Yorker*) found the performance characterized by "brilliant imaginativeness." "Since Mr. Olivier is handsomely endowed by nature for heroics," he said, "his Hotspur has the additional advantage of being romantic visually, and altogether it is one of the real triumphs of the recent theater." In Old Vic's second offering, *Henry IV, Part 2*, Olivier took the minor role of Justice Shallow and gave a "delightful" performance. He was Dr. Astrov in Chekhov's *Uncle Vanya*, in which the critics thought him "better than ever," though the play, as a whole, was not so well received as the others.

The performance which sent "bravo" shouts echoing through a Broadway theater for the first time in several seasons, was Olivier's Oedipus. On the same bill with *Oedipus* (W. B. Yeats's English version of the Sophocles tragedy) Old Vic presented Sheridan's *The Critic*, with Olivier as Mr. Puff. "Laurence Olivier," wrote Howard Barnes, "turning from the tragic character of the doomed Theban to the brittle clown of Sheridan's lampoon in the space of an intermission, serves notice that he is as fine and versatile an actor as one may look for in any theatrical capital." Lewis Nichols of the New York *Times* wrote: "Mr. Olivier rises to the highest tragic playing. . . How he changes mood while the audience has one cigarette is Mr. Olivier's business; sufficient that in the second incarnation he is as amusing as he is tragic in the first." For his New York performances, Olivier was voted the best actor in the 1945-46 Broadway season in a poll conducted by *Variety*. The American radio performance of *Richard III* (one of the two presented by the Columbia Broadcasting System through the Columbia Workshop while Old Vic was in the United States) received the

OLIVIER, LAURENCE—*Continued*

1946 radio award of the National Council of Teachers of English.

After Olivier's return to England in June 1946, Old Vic opened its 1946-47 season in London with *King Lear*. As the tragic king Olivier earned high praise from London critics, who called his performance "unfaltering, unflagging"; "he was never less than first-rate and again and again he touched the magnificent."

What newspapers called "the most idyllic of modern off-stage romances" was climaxed when Olivier and Vivien Leigh, famous as Scarlett in *Gone With the Wind*, were married in August 1940. Both were newly divorced, Olivier from actress Jill Esmond, to whom he had been married in 1930, and Miss Leigh from Herbert Leigh Holman. Miss Leigh has a daughter, Olivier a son, by their first marriages.

References

Christian Sci Mon Mag p10 D 15 '45 por
Collier's 103:15+ Je 10 '39 por
N Y Times Mag p22 My 12 '46 por
Theatre Arts 29:711-18 D '45 pors
This Month 2:18 Je '46
Time 47:56-60 Ap 8 '46 pors
International Motion Picture Almanac, 1943-44
Who's Who, 1946
Who's Who in the Theatre (1939)

O'NEAL, EDWARD A(SBURY, 3d) Oct. 26, 1875-   Agricultural leader; plantation owner

Address: b. c/o American Farm Bureau Federation, 58 E. Washington St., Chicago; h. 1242 N. Lake Shore Dr., Chicago; Florence, Alabama

"Quite the most spectacular farm leader in the United States," read a *Fortune* description of Edward A. O'Neal. Its term for the American Farm Bureau Federation, which he has headed since 1931, is "quite the best lobby in the business." One of four organizations which represent farm interests, it is regularly opposed only by the Farmers Educational and Cooperative Union, of which James G. Patton [45] is president. The Farm Bureau, which is composed of large and small farm-owners, has the unique advantage of a quasi-governmental connection with the Department of Agriculture's county-agent service.

Edward Asbury O'Neal, born on his grandfather's Alabama cotton plantation on October 26, 1875, is the third in line to bear that name. His paternal grandfather was a brigadier general in Robert E. Lee's Army who later was Governor of Alabama for two terms. The present O'Neal's father, who also served in the Confederate Army, became a lawyer, and an uncle, Emmett, also became the State's chief executive. Through his mother, Mary (Coffee) O'Neal, Edward 3d is descended from the Tennessee pioneer families of Donnellson and Coffee.

"Ed O'Neal was not reared as a 'dirt farmer' and despises the breed of farm politician that so describes itself," *Fortune* has written. After attending the State Normal College and Paxton's Collegiate Academy, both in near-by Florence, young O'Neal entered Washington and Lee University, where he took up natural sciences and law, joined the Phi Kappa Psi fraternity, and played on the football team in 1895-96. After his graduation in 1898 the Alabaman rounded off his education with foreign travel before returning to take up the management of his nineteen-hundred-acre plantation in 1899.

"Not being trained in scientific agricultural methods," a Farm Bureau release reports, O'Neal "early adopted the program and practices of the agricultural college at Auburn, Alabama, applying science to the rebuilding of the soil. . . .He put into practice the latest production methods in raising the great crop of the South, cotton, as well as developing legumes, livestock, and grain, as a necessary adjunct to successful cotton production." In 1921 he became a charter member and first president of the Lauderdale County Farm Bureau, and in that year attended the national agricultural conference called by President Harding. In 1922 O'Neal was elected vice-president of the Alabama Farm Bureau Federation and member of the national finance committee; the next year he became president of the State federation and member of the national executive committee and gave up the management of his own farm.

For seven successive years O'Neal was reelected to the presidency of the State federation, heading its credit corporation, cotton association, poultry association, and mutual supply association. From 1924 to 1931 he was also re-elected to the national vice-presidency. He served as a director, as chairman of the convention resolutions committees, and on the taxation and legislation committees. He had helped to form the original farm bloc in 1921. "Few Congressmen have spent so many hours in the Capitol as he," reported *Fortune*; "Ed long ago started keeping track of teller and standing votes to see how the farm members were lining up. He once created a sensation by calling Congressmen off the floor during a roll call, and getting enough of them to change their minds and their votes to win the day."

O'Neal worked for the McNary [40]-Haugen bill, twice passed and twice vetoed by President Calvin Coolidge, which proposed to raise farm prices by dumping surplus staples abroad and to compensate the losers by an equalization fee collected from the beneficiaries. In 1927 the Auburn *Progressive Farmer,* publication of the State Agricultural and Mechanical College, awarded O'Neal a special medal for "farm leadership" (six years later he was given an honorary doctorate by Alabama Polytechnic Institute). During the Hoover [43] Administration the Republican President appointed Southern Democrat O'Neal to the Muscle Shoals Commission (O'Neal's farm is near Muscle Shoals).

When aging Sam H. Thompson resigned from the presidency of the American Farm

Bureau Federation in 1931, fifty-five-year-old O'Neal was elected to succeed him. At the time, the bureau had four hundred and eight thousand members in forty States; in 1944 the number had risen to six hundred and ninety thousand families in forty-five States, with dues ranging from two dollars a year in Georgia to fifteen dollars a year in Illinois. Edward O'Neal was closely associated with Secretary of Agriculture Wallace '40 during the early days of the Franklin D. Roosevelt Administration, and was a key figure in the passage of the first AAA Act and in obtaining appropriations for its work. In O'Neal's view, the desideratum for agriculture was a system of "special legislative measures by which the traditional policy of *laissez faire*, or a system of open and free competition, is changed to one of administrative prices resulting from coordination or cooperation in the adjustment of production to demand." This he considered equivalent to the protection afforded industry by the tariff, patent, and corporation laws, and afforded labor by immigration restrictions and labor relations acts.

Appointed by Roosevelt to the Committee to Direct Works Relief Expenditures in 1935, he helped distribute a four-billion-dollar appropriation. When the Supreme Court ruled the AAA unconstitutional, O'Neal "helped Henry Wallace salvage what he could with the Soil Conservation Act." O'Neal and his organization are credited with assisting in the draft of the Pope-McGill bill of 1937, intended to prevent overproduction by setting permissible crop reserves low and penalizing those who produced more. Secretary Wallace preferred the "ever-normal granary" plan of large reserves. Although O'Neal lost out on this point, he was successful in the repassage of parity, an economic basis for computing farm product prices which required agricultural prices to be as high in terms of purchasing power as they were in 1909-14, their highest point. The Farm Bureau was alone among the leading farmers' organizations in this, as the conservatives called for *laissez faire*, and the Farmers Union sought fixed farm prices.

From about 1940, O'Neal's Federation officers desired legislation to give more power in shaping farm programs to the Department of Agriculture's Extension Service, which for historical reasons was closely affiliated with the Farm Bureau. Possibly as a move in this direction, O'Neal proposed in March 1941 that existing Federal agricultural agencies be consolidated, to eliminate "duplication of effort, waste, extravagance, and confusion," and that the entire program be coordinated by a nonpartisan five-man board. Later that year he lobbied for an amendment forbidding the Commodity Credit Corporation to buy or sell farm products at less than parity prices. Analyzing its implications, the *New Republic* declared, "Under the guise of protecting farm prices, O'Neal appears dangerously close to putting through a measure that will raise retail food prices still higher and at the same time will not achieve its stated objective of materially raising farm income." To prevent inflation, O'Neal urged

Allison-Lighthall

EDWARD A. O'NEAL

in 1941 that income tax exemptions be reduced by at least 50 per cent, that the excess-profits tax be increased, and that wages be kept down and the work week increased, but led the unsuccessful move for setting farm price ceilings no lower than 110 per cent of parity. In 1942 he began his continuing battle against production subsidies to keep prices down, and in 1943 he scored a success against the FSA, the only agency which made loans to small farmers, tenants, and sharecroppers. The Appropriations Committee followed his recommendations to the letter in abolishing it, to the distress of liberals, progressives, and the Left wing generally. "The American farmer," O'Neal commented meanwhile, "has been made the whipping boy to appease the unreasonable demands of organized labor."

Of production (in an April 1944 speech) O'Neal asserted, "We should figure out our future on the basis of human needs—of goods and services—and not on the basis of money. The old theory based on the assumption of scarcity must go." That fall the Farm Bureau undertook a campaign to get out the farm vote, although no official endorsement was to be given to any particular party or candidate. In November the President named O'Neal as one of three agriculture members on the War Mobilization Advisory Board, and in February 1945, he was one of twenty-five advisers to the United States delegation at the Inter-American Conference in Mexico City. That April O'Neal endorsed the Bretton Woods plan for a world bank and world fund, and signed a letter expressing willingness to share food with the people of liberated areas. In June he had an "explosive exchange" with Senator Robert Taft '40 on extension of the Reciprocal Trade Agreements Act. "Farmers can't be prosperous selling to the unemployed," said O'Neal. In July he went on record for the United Nations

O'NEAL, EDWARD A.—*Continued*

Charter, and in October for a "World Commodity Credit Corporation," when he was at Quebec as an adviser to the United Nations Food and Agriculture Organization conference.

Not long afterwards came one of the few occasions when the National Grange joined the Farmers Union in opposing the Farm Bureau: O'Neal demanded that any general wage increase be accompanied by a corresponding rise in farm prices. He also favored vigorous anti-strike measures, including the Hobbs "Anti-Racketeering Act" and the Case '46 or a similar labor disputes bill. Several months later, in April 1946, O'Neal, along with Albert S. Goss '45 of the National Grange and James G. Patton of the Farmers' Union, reported the New York *Times,* testified "that the House had gone too far in amending the price control extension bill." While the three "were also in accord on the necessity of a positive program of price decontrol," the Farmers' Union advocated continuation of the subsidy program "as long as may be necessary," but the Grange and the Federation endorsed the amendment for elimination of subsidies by the end of 1946.

Appearing before the three-member Price Decontrol Board on August 13, 1946, O'Neal protested against putting commodities under control. There had been a bumper crop that summer, and Mr. O'Neal said: "We believe that such controls are unworkable and cannot be enforced, that the best long-term interests of the nation will be served if controls are not reinstated . . . and if an opportunity is given for free markets in these products to adjust to a lower level." The following month he joined Goss and Patton again to serve on a general advisory unit of the Office of War Mobilization and Reconversion. At the end of September 1946 O'Neal, in collaboration with Goss and the president of the National Council of Farmer Cooperatives, issued a statement calling for revision of the parity formula, disposition of crop surpluses, price stabilization, and international agricultural cooperation. O'Neal supported a suggestion presented to the Senate Agriculture Committee in October by J. E. McDonald of Texas. MacDonald recommended that farmers withhold their cotton until they received at least forty cents a pound for it. (The bottom had dropped out of the cotton market the week before.) At the annual convention of the American Farm Bureau Federation in December 1946, O'Neal, its president, announced its current policy of insisting that "the ever-normal granary, commodity loans and all price-stabilizing features of the old farm program be continued, because they proved their value in peace as well as in war."

O'Neal had occupied various Government positions. Since September 1941 he has been an adviser to the Social Security Board, in October 1942 he was appointed by President Roosevelt to the Economic Stabilization Board, and in November he accepted WMC Chairman Paul McNutt's '40 invitation to join the management-labor policy committee. In March 1943 O'Neal became a director of the National War Fund, and that December served on the Congressionally approved National Agricultural Jefferson Bicentenary Committee. He became an adviser to a special House Committee on Marketing in May 1944, and in November he was appointed by the President to the advisory committee to the Office of War Mobilization and Reconversion; and in March 1945 O'Neal accepted membership on a citizens' committee to advise the Commissioner of Education. In July 1945 the Farm Bureau head joined the agricultural communities committee of the businessmen's Committee for Economic Development, of which Studebaker president Paul G. Hoffman '46 is chairman. An elder in the Presbyterian church of his home town, O'Neal is an incorporator and adviser of the American Red Cross and serves on the National Council of the Boy Scouts of America.

Since November 1904, when he was twenty-nine, Edward O'Neal has been married to Julia Camper of Florence. Their children are Edward Asbury 4th, Moncure Camper, and Amelia Browne (Mrs. Neussle). White-haired, six-foot O'Neal is a "wisecracking" speaker whose drawl not infrequently rises to a roar. *Fortune* said of him in 1944 that he can outtalk and outlaugh any group he joins.

References

Fortune 29:156 Je '44 por
Rotarian 48:56 Ap '36
Who's Who in America, 1946-47

O'NEAL, FREDERICK (DOUGLAS)
Aug. 27, 1905-　Actor; manager

Address: b. c/o American Negro Theater, 15 W. 126th St., New York; h. 41 Convent Ave., New York

The American Negro Theater, an experimental theater in New York, has been producing three plays each season, contributing new scripts and production ideas to the Broadway stage, among them the long-running *Anna Lucasta.* This play introduced, to the commercial theater, Frederick O'Neal, who had founded the group with the assistance of Abram Hill '45, and who in 1946 is manager of this company of both Negro and white members.

Frederick Douglas O'Neal (he was named for Frederick Douglass, nineteenth century Negro orator and journalist), the fifth of eight children, was born in Brooksville, Mississippi, on August 27, 1905. His father, Ransome James O'Neal, was a teacher, lecturer, merchant, and owned land in the town. Frederick's mother, Ninnie Bell (Thompson) O'Neal, was the daughter of a former slave. In Brooksville, where he attended elementary school, young O'Neal presented plays with his friends and at school. In 1920, two years after his father's death, the family moved to St. Louis, Missouri, where he was graduated from Summer High School in 1921. He worked as file clerk for a wholesale drug concern and in 1925 also took on a nighttime job, sorting mail in the St. Louis Post Office.

For about eleven years (1925-36) O'Neal, moving about the country, with frequent returns to St. Louis, was employed in a series of jobs and in his own enterprises. Using the money earned as a laborer, clerk, farmer, bellhop, houseman, blacksmith, cowpuncher, automobile salesman, or any other occupation which turned up, O'Neal would go to school, taking various courses. He also managed to act with stock companies in whichever part of the country he happened to be. In St. Louis in 1926, O'Neal and Roy Glover organized the Adco Advertising Company. Three years later he was the sole proprietor of the Arrow Parcel Delivery Service, which had the slogan, "Service to the Point." In 1935 he tried his third business enterprise, the Bootcraft Valet Service. Lack of capital doomed this venture, although in the six months that the service existed, O'Neal and his partner, Louis White, built up a large clientele. For a little more than a year (1936-37) O'Neal was executive secretary of the Negro Businessmen's League in St. Louis, a position he held until he went to New York.

Meanwhile, O'Neal still maintained his interest in the theater. In 1927 he had organized and become president of the Aldridge Players, named for Ira Aldridge, the first Negro to play Othello. (The Players, the second oldest Negro theater group in the United States—the Gilpin Players is the oldest—is still in existence in St. Louis.) The nucleus of the group was formed as the result of the annual plays given by the Urban League of St. Louis. Appearing in almost every one of these, from 1921 to 1937, O'Neal met a group of amateur actors who wanted to produce more than one play a year. These became the Aldridge Players, who presented known plays, and occasionally a new one. O'Neal himself was cast in these productions as a villain, a father, or a minister. A tall, heavy-set man, he has never been able to play juveniles. Acting in over fifty productions between 1927 and 1936, he appeared in such plays as *As You Like It, Abraham's Bosom, Run L'il Chillun, Kismet,* and *Black Majesty* (O'Neal played Henri Christophe in the last-named). Later he took the same role in a different play for the American Negro Theater.) A firm believer in sound training for the stage, O'Neal organized instruction for the players. At the time, however, the members found classroom work tedious and overruled him on that point. During this period, the actor directed the Young People's Sodality at the St. Elizabeth's Catholic Church in St. Louis.

In 1937 thirty-two-year-old Frederick O'Neal left St. Louis to go to New York. He had hoped to become attached to the Federal Theater, but found the quota for membership in that group had been filled. With his years as an employee of the drug concern as a background, he found a position as laboratory assistant at the Sterosol Ampule Corporation, where he worked from 1937 to 1942, studying theater at night and making plans for a Negro theater in New York. During two of these years (1937-39) O'Neal took courses in acting and related subjects at the New Theatre

Bloom

FREDERICK O'NEAL

School, winning a scholarship after his first semester there. Later, he studied acting with Komarsajefsky and Nadya Romanoff, voice with Doris Sorrell, and movement with Benjamin Zemach. He also became a member of the Rose McClendon Players, an experimental theater group, and of the Richard Huey Players, who spent a great part of their time studying plays.

Frederick O'Neal had long hoped to see established "a nation-wide system of Negro community houses with a Harlem nucleus." In 1939 he met Abram Hill and the first step toward fulfilling that ambition was taken. Hill, who had helped organize the Negro Playwrights Company, and O'Neal laid preliminary plans; and eight other men who were dissatisfied with the state of the Negro theater were invited to participate in the formation of the American Negro Theater. They felt, as Hill later wrote, that "Negro drama has not as yet been given a fair chance to stand on its feet without the crutch of . . . clichés (Negro characters drawn as comical, lazy, ignorant, carefree, docile, and not too bright). . . . There is a need in the theater for expressing in terms of entertainment the refined and disciplined emotional experience of America's 'problem' minority, who are, despite all odds, fitting in, and contributing to, the progress of American civilization." It was with this in mind that A.N.T. issued its first call for membership in June 1940, with Hill as executive director and O'Neal as assistant executive director. In July the A.N.T. raised its first curtain, with a variety show. The first major production was *On Striver's Row,* a comedy by Hill which had previously been produced by the Rose McClendon Players. It "opened on September 11, 1940, and closed on February 1, 1941, after more than fifty performances; the longest run of any non-professional produc-

O'NEAL, FREDERICK—*Continued*

tion in the history of the New York theater and perhaps the entire country." In 1941 the group produced a second variety show as well as the play, *Natural Man,* by Theodore Brown. The following year *Starlight,* by Curtis Cooksey, was the major production; *Three Is a Family* opened the 1943 season. O'Neal appeared in all of these productions. His theatrical activities were interrupted by World War II: for six months, from November 1942 to April 1943, O'Neal served as a private in the 93d Infantry Division of the United States Army stationed at Fort Huachucha, Arizona.

The work of the A.N.T. was comparatively unknown until its production of *Anna Lucasta* in June 1944. Directed by Harry Wagstaff Gribble '45, the Philip Yordan play was sold to John Wildberg and was produced on Broadway the following September. In this, "the longest-running Negro play in the history of the American theater," O'Neal's portrayal of the bullying brother-in-law, Frank, was hailed: "What a compelling actor that man O'Neal is!" wrote Ward Morehouse in the New York *Sun;* "Mr. O'Neal, too, is worth a trip to 47th Street," Wilella Waldorf told her New York *Post* readers. Adolphe Menjou in a letter to the actor, wrote, "Just a line to tell you how much I enjoyed the play and particularly your superb performance. This is one of the finest the theater has, in my opinion, ever seen. Congratulations." For the best supporting performance on Broadway, O'Neal received the Clarence Derwent Award for the 1944-45 season.

In the same season of the original production of *Anna Lucasta* A.N.T. presented *Garden of Time,* a production in which O'Neal did not appear. He planned to take part in the November 1944 performances of *Walk Hard* (a play by Hill produced on Broadway in March 1946), but his *Anna Lucasta* commitment forced him to leave the cast before the opening. In June 1945 O'Neal played the title role in A.N.T.'s production of *Henri Christophe* (he had obtained a three-month leave of absence from *Anna Lucasta*). He went to Chicago with *Anna Lucasta* in September 1945, remaining there with the cast until July 1946.

As company manager of A.N.T., O'Neal is concerned with personnel. Another of his projects has been realized in the three-year training program required of all prospective members. Chosen by audition, they study acting, voice, movement, choral singing, body training, stagecraft, and playwriting. They pay a small tuition, take part in A.N.T.'s productions as well as in their own student productions, and are under strict discipline, which provides for fines for lateness and absence. The full members of A.N.T., who may be of any race, work on a cooperative basis: there are no stars, and the net receipts, after the A.N.T. treasury receives half, are shared equally. At the outset the organization's members contributed 10 per cent of their earnings (most of them worked in the daytime and devoted nights to the project) to support A.N.T. In 1944-45 Rockefeller grants enabled

the group to become partially self-supporting. (After that the director and the secretarial staff were paid regular salaries.) Originally, productions were presented in the basement of the 135th Street Branch of the New York Public Library, but in 1945, the group leased a larger, if not ideal, building elsewhere in Harlem. One of A.N.T.'s goals is to purchase its own building where it can have classrooms and workshops in addition to an adequate theater. The company manager headed the cast of A.N.T.'s first production in the fall 1946 season, *The Peacemakers,* a farce-fantasy by Kurt Unkelbach.

At the end of the 1946 O'Neal had made plans to appear in two Broadway presentations, both to be produced by Gribble. *A Lady Passing Fair,* scheduled for an early 1947 opening, will be followed by production of *Romeo and Juliet,* utilizing a Negro and white cast. In this interpretation, suggested by O'Neal, the Capulets will be Moors (O'Neal will portray Juliet's father) and race hatred will be the reason for the feud. (In June 1946 O'Neal was elected chairman of the Negro Actors Guild, a welfare organization.)

Frederick O'Neal's two hundred and twenty-five pounds cover a frame more than six feet tall. Busy with his duties with the A.N.T., he is rarely able to play or watch his favorite sport, baseball. The actor was married to Charlotte Talbot Hainey on April 18, 1942. A Catholic, with no political affiliation, he classifies himself as "definitely a progressive—a little left of center." He has summed up his outlook on life: "Things aren't always the way you want them. . . .We must keep a level head through all this turmoil. These changes can't be made with clubs. You have to reason them out to make them lasting."

OPPENHEIM, E(DWARD) PHILLIPS 1866—Feb. 3, 1946 English author, "the world's most prolific and popular writer of thrillers"; wrote one hundred fifty novels of international intrigue, many short stories and plays, which were translated into almost every language; *The Great Impersonation* (1920) was perhaps the most popular; autobiography, *The Pool of Memory,* published in 1941.

Obituary

N Y Times p25 F 4 '46 por

ORR, SIR JOHN BOYD Sept. 23, 1880- United Nations official; scientist; educator

Address: b. Food and Agriculture Organization of the United Nations, 2000 Massachusetts Ave., N.W., Washington, D.C.; h. Wardenhill, Bucksburn, Aberdeenshire, Scotland

To head the Food and Agriculture Organization of the United Nations, delegates at its first meeting in October 1945 chose Sir John Boyd Orr, internationally known nutritionist, for almost thirty years director of the Rowett Research Institute in Scotland, and, during World War II, Government adviser on food policies in Great Britain. He is described by commentators as a "practical idealist."

One of several children of the late R. C. Orr of Kilmaurs, Scotland, John Boyd Orr was born in that Ayrshire village on September 23, 1880. Because the family was poor, as a young boy he had to earn the money for his education and, in addition, to help pay for the schooling of his brothers and sisters. After graduation from the University of Glasgow with an M.A., young Orr taught for a number of years, long enough to earn money for further study. He had enrolled first as a student of theology, but the revolutionary Darwinian theory had turned his investigations toward science in an effort to discover whether Darwin was right or wrong. Hence, when he completed his formal education, he had also taken both the M.D. and D.Sc. at Glasgow, and he had been a recipient of the Bellahouston Gold Medal and of a Barbour research scholarship. Then, in 1914, unknown except for a small volume entitled *History of the Scotch Church Crisis of 1904,* he took the "humble, poorly paid" position of Director of Animal Nutrition Research at Aberdeen University in the north of Scotland. His workshop at the time was only a meagerly equipped laboratory in the basement of the university's agricultural college building, but out of it was later to grow the world-famous Rowett Research Institute.

Between 1914 and 1919, however, Orr's work was interrupted by war service, first in the Royal Army Medical Corps, in 1917-18 in the Navy, and in 1918-19 again in the Army, when he did research in military dietetics. In 1919 the results of the latter period of investigation, during which he had worked with the noted Scotch physiologist Edward Provan Cathcart, were published under the title *Energy Expenditure of Infantry Recruit in Training.* Twice Orr had been decorated, with the Military Cross and with the Distinguished Service Order, and he had also been mentioned in dispatches.

On his release from military service in 1919, Orr returned to Aberdeen, where he built up the Rowett Institute into a research center and clearinghouse for information on nutrition, serving the entire British Empire. The first building devoted exclusively to the work of the Institute was opened in 1922. Expansion continued into the late twenties: the Walter Reid Library became the largest center for books on nutrition in the United Kingdom; the John Duthie Webster thousand-acre farm for experimental purposes was set up; and Strathcona House was erected to accommodate the scientists who began coming to the nutrition center from all parts of the world. In 1925 the first large-scale experiment, designed to determine the effect of additional milk in the diet of reasonably well-fed Scottish school children, was conducted—the results establishing that the additional nutriment was responsible for an increase in growth of as much as 20 per cent as well as for an obvious improvement in the children's general health. In 1929 Orr founded and assumed the direction of the Imperial Bureau of Animal Nutrition, with headquarters at Rowett. In 1930 he established and became editor in chief of *Nutrition Abstracts and Reviews.*

Apart from his administrative duties at Rowett during these years, the Scot was engaging in research in problems of protein and mineral metabolism in animal nutrition. Among the works which helped to establish his reputation in this field was *Minerals in Pastures and Their Relation to Animal Nutrition,* prepared with Helen Scherbatoff and published in 1928. An earlier work, which had run to several editions, was his *Essentials of Physiology for Veterinary Students,* written in collaboration with D. Noel Paton. Soon he was being regarded as an authority outside of the United Kingdom as well. In the mid-twenties he had been made a member of the Colonial Advisory Council of Agriculture and Animal Health. In 1929, at the invitation of the Canberra Government, he undertook a survey of pastural problems in Australia, and, before returning to Scotland, visited New Zealand and Canada. In addition, he conducted several large-scale investigations for the (British) Empire Marketing Board's research committee. One, a comparison between two East African tribes, the first a master group of meat eaters and blood drinkers and the second a slave people existing on milk and cereals, provided further data to support his theory that food habits affect human behavior to a considerable degree.

It was largely this African survey, together with the 1925 experiment with Scottish school children, which served to divert Orr's interest from animal to human nutrition. In 1934 he published a pamphlet entitled *The National Food Supply and Its Influence on Public Health.* Two years later his *Food, Health and Income*—the result of a dietary survey of six specified income groups made the preceding year, "in part an original inquiry and in part a compilation of already existing data on total food consumption, consumption by income groups, and the state of health of different income groups"—brought Britain to a shocked awareness of the plight of half her population. For it showed that the varied diet necessary for normal health was attainable only at a level of income which exceeded that of 50 per cent of Britons and that at least 10 per cent of the people were badly undernourished. "Simply and clearly argued," said the *Economist,* "its conclusions are all the more convincing for their conspicuously dispassionate moderation."

That the book made its influence felt was evidenced by the fact, reported by Ritchie Calder, science editor of the London *News Chronicle,* that by 1939 two thirds of the population were being adequately nourished while the remaining third was eating better than previously. "From the moment it was issued," wrote Marquis W. Childs in the New York *Post* in 1946, "the Orr report became a political document of the first importance. It was a challenge to the Conservatives. The Laborites used it as proof that far-reaching changes were necessary." And when World War II broke out, it was Sir John Orr's recommendations, based on the findings published in *Food,*

British Official Photo.

SIR JOHN BOYD ORR

Health and Income and on subsequent surveys by the Rowett Institute, which provided the basis for Great Britain's food rationing system.

The wartime measures employed by the Home Government to keep fighter and worker efficiency at maximum strength—a policy of intensive agricultural production and rationing according to physiological needs—for the first time put into practice Sir John's theories of full production and full consumption. In print and on the platform he had long condemned the restrictive agricultural policies which provided profits for the producers and distributors at the expense of the consumers and had advocated the coordination of the Government's agriculture and health programs in the consumers' interests. Specifically, he had proposed the nationalization of the Agricultural Marketing Boards and the establishment of a Government Food Department empowered to guarantee to the farmer prices high enough to stimulate the production necessary to feed the entire population on a health basis and to pay to the farmer or the distributor in the form of a subsidy the difference between those prices and the retail selling prices.

"The time has come," he wrote in 1939, "to consider the production and consumption of food as different aspects of the one problem. . . .The fact that the capacity of markets to absorb foodstuffs fluctuates with purchasing power . . . [suggests that] the only way to avoid unsalable surpluses is to adjust the retail price to the purchasing power of the poorest class, in which case there will be no restriction of consumption due to fall in purchasing power, and we should then be able to adjust the supply to the food requirements of the nation, which would be constant irrespective of trade booms and slumps." The result would be an increase in both agriculture and trade,

and such a "nutritional policy might well be the spearhead for a movement for economic prosperity based on the satisfaction of human needs and the promotion of human welfare."

During the war Orr was a member of the Churchill Cabinet's Scientific Committee on Food Policy, and, beginning in 1942, he took over, as an emergency measure, the headship of the North of Scotland College of Agriculture and the Chair of Agriculture at Aberdeen University in addition to his directorship of Rowett, of the Imperial Bureau of Animal Nutrition and of *Nutrition Abstracts and Reviews*. Sir John was not present at the United Nations Conference on Food and Agriculture at Hot Springs, Virginia, in May 1943; but in Quebec on October 27, 1945, at the close of the first session of the Food and Agriculture Organization of the United Nations, he was unanimously elected director-general for a two-year term ending December 31, 1947. (The termination date was agreed upon at his own insistence, it being the intention of the FAO that its directors-general shall serve for longer periods of time.) Between the two meetings he had retired from his Scottish scientific and educational posts, his resignation becoming effective in January 1945, and with a majority of some eleven thousand votes had been elected to Parliament as one of the three representatives of the Scottish universities (St. Andrews, Glasgow, Aberdeen, and Edinburgh, which combine to form one constituency) at a by-election in April 1945. A year and a half later, however, on October 3, 1946, it was announced in London that he had applied for appointment to the Chiltern Hundreds, thus taking the traditional method for getting out of Parliament, from which a member cannot resign, in order to devote his full time to the FAO.

As the head of the FAO views it, the task of the "first full-grown working agency" of the United Nations (established prior to, and admitting nations not members of, the United Nations organization) will be the achievement, through the application of scientific methods of agriculture in backward nations and the formulation of an over-all economic and trade program, of a healthy interaction of world food production, distribution, and consumption. For "a food policy based on human needs," he asserts, "is the first step towards building the new and better world." The FAO, however, is not to be a permanent relief agency, he points out, nor will it, on the other hand, have power to enforce its recommendations. Its work will be advisory and educational, since the FAO's charter gives it no powers beyond the investigation and correlation of data pertinent to the food situation and the recommendation of programs of action to such agencies as the International Trade Organization, the World Bank, the Economic and Social Council of the United Nations, or to individual governments. But, it has been predicted, Sir John will go out of his way to make the FAO's advice as compelling as possible, for he expects world peace, prosperity, and political maturity to follow the abolition of world hunger and its attendant cares; and he has gone on record as advocating an international "food bank" to stabilize future world supply and demand.

As its initial public action the FAO in May 1946 called a special meeting for consideration of food problems of immediate urgency, which recommended the formation of an International Emergency Food Council to supersede the Combined Food Board of Great Britain, the United States and Canada. On June 20, therefore, at a meeting attended by delegates of nineteen nations, the IEFC, representing an expansion rather than an alteration of the CFB, was brought into being and held its first session. Meanwhile, Orr was also preparing a blueprint for a more permanent solution to the food problem for presentation to the FAO's second annual convocation in Copenhagen in September, and this was made public by the FAO on August 7. Essentially, it adapted to international markets the "ever-normal granary" plan introduced by Henry A. Wallace'⁴⁰ into the United States economy during the thirties. It proposed a board with powers to set maximum and minimum world price levels of foods, to purchase during periods of abundance when the world price would be below the declared minimum and to sell from its stock, with preferential treatment for nations whose circumstances warranted it, during periods of scarcity when the world price would exceed the declared maximum. The board would thus act both as a price control and as an emergency food reserve agency.

Immediately upon publication the proposal met with objections. Commentators remembered the failure of similar plans in individual nations, expressed fear that the plan would jeopardize the extension of international free trade and reciprocal tariff agreements, and saw it as unworkable without Russian cooperation. Despite the objections, the plan was adopted in principle at Copenhagen, and a sixteen-nation preparatory commission was ordered to explore the possibilities for the plan's implementation or alternative measures. But when this preparatory commission met in Washington in October, first the United States and then Great Britain withdrew their support of the Orr proposal. At the end of the year, the preparatory commission was drafting a plan embodying Orr's proposals of the two-price system and reserves to meet serious shortages in modified form but replacing his executive World Food Board by an advisory World Food Council to act as liaison between the FAO and the ITO. The basis of the new plan, which originated with the United States delegates, was to be voluntary cooperation among nations. It was expected that it would find acceptance.

Although, it has been pointed out, the tenor of the scientist's thinking concerning food is socialistic, he is neither a Laborite nor a Socialist in general doctrine, and was elected to Parliament as an Independent. He has been since 1932 a Fellow of the Royal Society and was knighted for his services in the field of agriculture and nutrition in 1935. A member of numerous scientific bodies, he holds honorary doctorates of laws from Scotland's St. Andrews and Edinburgh universities and from

Princeton, is a Justice of the Peace, and in 1945 was elected to a three-year term as rector of his alma mater, Glasgow University, succeeding Sir Stafford Cripps'⁴⁰. He and the former Elizabeth Pearson are the parents of one son and two daughters. "In appearance," wrote Walter H. Waggoner of the New York *Times* in 1946, "this white-haired Scot is as shaggy as tweed. Thick, tangled white eyebrows shelter sober eyes grown tired after a lifetime of study, and a generous nose and pink cheeks hint slyly of the sharp winds and mild whisky of his native Scotland."

References

N Y Post p35 My 24 '46
N Y Times p14 O 28 '45; VI p18+
  My 19 '46
Nature 155:168 F 10 '45
International Who's Who, 1945-46
Who's Who, 1946

ORSBORN, ALBERT (WILLIAM THOMAS) Sept. 4, 1886- General of the Salvation Army

Address: b. c/o Salvation Army, 101 Queen Victoria St., London

As General of the Salvation Army, Albert Orsborn heads an organization which sounds its evangelistic call in ninety-seven countries of the world. Salvation Army workers have described their international leader as "a combination of the dreamer and the man of action," with the "executive ability to materialize his visions." His first pronouncement after being elected General in May 1946 urged his followers "not merely to dream about a road on which men may travel to the Kingdom of God" but "to do something to drive that road through the ruin and desolation of our shaken civilization."

The Salvation Army had its origin in London's slums in 1865, when William Booth, its founder, became convinced that a practical program of social service was necessary before cold and hungry people would be receptive to the spiritual message. Albert and Jennie (Minshall) Orsborn early became associates of Booth. Their son Albert William Thomas Orsborn, eldest of seven children, was born September 4, 1886, in Maidstone, Kent, and grew up under the austere discipline typical of the home life of those who vow to accept the Salvation Army's authority. For a time, while Albert was still an infant, the Orsborns were pioneer salvationists in Norway.

Albert Orsborn recalls that it was his mother's concept of God, "a God who understood small boys," that first led him into the Salvation Army's ranks. At fourteen he became a "soldier" (a lay member), having been a junior soldier before that; and not many years afterward, he was made a corps cadet. The boy attended school and added to the family's meager income his small earnings in an apothecary's shop. When they moved to London he was employed as a junior clerk in the Salvation Army's International Headquarters, where he served in various departments. There

ALBERT ORSBORN

he met Commissioner Booth-Tucker, who became interested in his early attempts at writing hymn verses and gave him criticism and instruction in the fundamental rules of versification.

It was during a week-end spent at a corps cadet camp at Hadleigh that young Orsborn felt the call to dedicate his life to the work of a Salvation Army officer. Then followed a period of training at the International Training Garrison at Clapton and years of work in a number of British corps. Orsborn was especially concerned with evangelism and youth activities. His first appointment as an officer was to Chelmsford, in Essex, where he is said to have stirred local salvationists by his "vigor and unusual methods." He was promoted to captain in 1906. As a brigade officer on the staff of the International Training College, Orsborn trained young men for Salvation Army officership. Then, as divisional commander, and secretary of the young people's group in Norfolk, he was responsible for the development of youth work. He later served as divisional commander of South East London. From 1925 to 1933 he was stationed again at the International Training College, where after four months in the position of assistant chief side officer for men, he became the chief side officer. In keeping with the Army's policy of favoring the international exchange of leaders, Orsborn then received the appointment of chief secretary of the Salvation Army movement in New Zealand. He remained there until 1936, when he returned to England to serve as territorial commander for the subterritory of Scotland and Ireland, one of the four units into which the British territory was divided at that time. His rank now became that of lieutenant commissioner.

In 1939 the exigencies of World War II brought about the re-establishment of the British territory as a single command, and Ors-

born was made the British commissioner as well as director of the Salvation Army Trustee Company and of the Salvation Army Assurance Society. During the next seven years, when bombs reportedly destroyed more than four hundred Salvation Army buildings in England including the international headquarters in London, and evacuation problems, blackouts, and other war conditions complicated the everyday life of the people, the Commissioner had to overcome many obstacles. He met these challenges admirably, it was observed, and effectively geared the Salvation Army program to meet emergency needs. (*Time* reported in 1942 that approximately six hundred and fifty huts and canteens were operated by the Salvation Army for British troops throughout the world.)

In May 1946, succeeding George L. Carpenter [43], Orsborn became the sixth General of the Salvation Army. He was elected by a two-thirds majority vote of the high council, a body having the sole function of selecting the Army's chief commander. The new international head announced that the organization's emphasis would be on evangelism. He wished the Army to become "the bulldozer of evangelistic work," a goal he felt was essential to the fostering of world peace. At the same time, declaring that the Salvation Army would not neglect its social work program, he planned to develop an international youth department. "Youth," he said, "is searching hard for a faith"; it will respond to "a positive Christian program," that is, "a Christian program related to life." The General praised Government social welfare programs but stressed that there was still "plenty of room for voluntary service . . . provided it kept pace in training and equipment."

Orsborn's visit to Germany, Holland, Denmark, and the other Scandinavian countries in 1946 made him all the more aware of the need for relief organizations there. Declaring that the Salvation Army would help all sufferers regardless of race or creed, he deplored the plight of Jewish war victims in Europe and emphasized the necessity of preventing "the morale of the German people from falling too low." In line with his program of acquainting himself firsthand with the many groups under his command, the General also visited the United States in the fall of 1946, bringing a message of the need for a "spiritual offensive . . . against unbelief, pure materialism, and the mechanistic theory of human life." His three-month itinerary included many United States cities as well as a tour of Canada and twelve Central and South American countries.

As international head of the Salvation Army Orsborn has supreme command of its operations in all parts of the world. He appoints the chief leaders in each country and has jurisdiction over the system of councils which governs the entire organization. Since General Booth's "autocratic reign," the power of that office has been limited to some extent: a general must retire at seventy-three and can no longer appoint his successor; Salvation Army property in Great Britain, of which he was once sole trustee, is now held by a trustee company, of which he is chairman. (He is also president of the assurance society.) Orsborn has formed a representative advisory council, which will advise him on matters of major policy. During the war, international headquarters lost direct contact with twenty countries, but the link has already been re-established with most of them. In Japan, for example, United States occupation authorities have permitted salvationists to resume their work.

In the course of his many years of service in the Salvation Army, Orsborn has also distinguished himself as a hymn writer. A baritone himself, he has written the verses of more than two hundred and fifty hymns and songs, which, set to familiar melodies like "Tipperary", "The Old Rustic Bridge," and "There's a Long, Long Trail," are sung at meetings. Among the hymns are "Let the Beauty of Jesus Be Seen in Me", "Except I Am Moved With Compassion," and "Fellowship With Thee." Music has been an important element in Salvation Army work since General Booth, said a *Time* article, found that "in the clamor of crowded slums, a drum or cornet carried farther than a human voice." Orsborn's hymns, songs, and poems as well as his articles have appeared in Salvation Army publications, in English as well as foreign languages.

Orsborn has been twice widowed. In 1909 he was married to a daughter of Colonel Barker, who helped establish the movement in Australia. Mrs. Orsborn died in 1942. Of their seven children—Albert, Marie, Karl, Howard, Kenneth, Dorothy, and David—three served in the RAF and one was a Wren; Howard Orsborn is a captain in the organization which his father heads. The General's second wife, Major Evelyn Berry, who held a post in a Salvation Army hospital at Wellington, New Zealand, died in 1945, the year after their marriage. Five feet eleven inches tall and weighing 200 pounds, Orsborn has the carriage of the soldier. The *War Cry* considers him an outstanding speaker—"he is particularly at home on the public platform." Outside of the Salvation Army he has no affiliations, and his chief recreation is reading. He received the Order of Commander of the British Empire in 1943.

References

N Y Herald Tribune p26 My 10 '46
N Y Times p21 My 10 '46
Newsweek p87 My 20 '46
War Cry p3 Je 1 '46; p3 O 12 '46
Who's Who, 1946

OWEN, A(RTHUR) DAVID K(EMP)

Nov. 26, 1904- United Nations official; sociologist

Address: b. c/o United Nations, New York

Codirector of the work of the United Nations Economic and Social Council is British sociologist A. David K. Owen, in 1946 appointed assistant secretary-general in charge of economic affairs by U.N. Secretary-General Trygve Lie '46. Previously Lie's executive assistant in the U.N. secretariat, Owen was also

British Official Photo.

A. DAVID K. OWEN

actively concerned in each of the organizational steps preliminary to the first United Nations convocation.

Of Welsh parentage, the son of Edward and Gertrude Louisa (Kemp) Owen, Arthur David Kemp Owen was born on November 26, 1904, in the coal and iron industrial center of Pontypool, Monmouthshire, England, a district English by technical decree but Welsh in its natural affinity. Although his father was a minister, his parents were mild and tolerant, he says, and he had "an extremely happy childhood." It was spent, however, primarily in Yorkshire in the north of England—with vacations near the Welsh border, which, he emphasizes, served to keep him Welsh. He received his grammar school education in the city of Leeds and subsequently matriculated at Leeds University, where he specialized in economics, obtaining his B.A. degree in 1926 and his M. Com. in 1929. It was also at Leeds that he first became interested in international affairs. "I was the founder and secretary of my university information society," he told an interviewer. "It had two objects—to study international problems and to make students from all parts of the world feel at home in England."

After a short period spent lecturing in economics in 1929, Owen that year was appointed director of the Sheffield Social Survey. For the next seven years he conducted a study of living conditions in that city, paying special attention to the utilization and efficiency of Sheffield's existing social services, and in 1932-33 his findings appeared as the reports of the Sheffield Social Survey committee. Then, in 1933 he became secretary of the civic division of P.E.P., Political and Economic Planning, a research organization in London. Three years later he was selected by the Pilgrim Trust of London as one of a board of three to inquire into conditions of prolonged unemployment in England and Wales. The results of a year's

OWEN, A. DAVID K.—*Continued*

sample investigations in six representative areas were published under the title *Men Without Work* in March 1938. "A sober, thorough investigation, in the best social workers' tradition," said the *New Republic*. "It will richly reward careful study," was the opinion of *Survey Graphic*, "not only by those closely connected with the administration of services to the unemployed, but by all students and laymen interested in a penetrating analysis of the motives and conditions which lie back of human behavior." At the time of the study's appearance in print, Owen was already teaching at the University of Glasgow, Scotland, as Stevenson Lecturer in Citizenship, the only post of its kind in the United Kingdom, and one which he held from 1937 to 1940. In 1939-40 he was, in addition, National Service Officer for Scotland.

Rejoining P.E.P. shortly after the outbreak of World War II, the Welshman became acting general secretary and director of a survey of postwar economic and social needs of Great Britain and the Continent. In late 1941, however, he again resigned, to enter the governmental office of the Lord Privy Seal. There he was made personal adviser on social reconstruction to Sir Stafford Cripps '40, and in this capacity accompanied Cripps on the latter's unsuccessful mission to India in March of that year. A period on the staff of the Ministry of Aircraft Production followed; and in 1944 Owen was transferred to the reconstruction department of the Foreign Office, with which he first came into official contact with plans for an international organization to keep the peace. In April and May 1944, as a Foreign Office observer, he attended the twenty-sixth annual International Labor Office conference held in Philadelphia, at which recommendations to insure postwar security and improved living conditions for the peoples of all nations were promulgated, with the intention of having them, in so far as possible, written into the projected charter for world peace. Beginning in August 1944, Owen was present at the next step in the mapping of the peace, the Dumbarton Oaks Security Conference held in Washington, which drew up the proposals acted upon at San Francisco. And in April and May 1945 he was a member of the British delegation to the San Francisco Conference, which wrote the United Nations charter.

By this time, it is pointed out, the new world organization had become the pivot of Owen's career. Returning from San Francisco, the Briton became deputy to Gladwyn Jebb, executive secretary of the United Nations Preparatory Commission, which had been created for the purpose of smoothing the path for the first United Nations meeting scheduled to begin in London in January 1946. Owen's task in this position, in the words of Gertrude Samuels of the New York *Times*, was to effect "a small-scale peace by welding together widely divergent nationalities into an administrative staff," and it was his efficient handling of this assignment, she reported, which made Trygve Lie, Secretary-General of the United Nations, choose Owen as his executive assistant. Owen himself merely commented, "We had a Secre-

tariat of more than five hundred people drawn from seventeen nationalities and it was one of the happiest and friendliest groups I've ever worked with."

The new position as Lie's aide made Owen, as one New York *Post* reporter described it, a "one-man coordinating council" for the eight chief divisions of the Secretariat, the departments of Security Council Affairs, Economic Affairs, Social Affairs, Trusteeship and Information from Non-Self-Governing Territories, Public Information, Legal Affairs, Conference and General Services, and Administrative and Financial Services.

"My task," said Trygve Lie's aide on one occasion, "is to see that the U.N. is itself as well organized and as efficient as possible." And on another: "The special angle of my job is to build a truly international civil service. Its experts will be drawn from over fifty different nationalities, from the foreign services, universities, private professional life. The test will be competence. Chauvinism will have to be parked outside the international lot. There can be only one loyalty—to the Organization. Of course, it's very difficult to get people of different backgrounds and nationalities together. Ideas, language, even filing systems are amazingly different. But judging from my experience in London . . . it can work." That it did work—and within a relatively few weeks—was attested by the smoothly functioning administration which received the United Nations Security Council at Hunter College in New York City in March 1946.

Then, that commission having been discharged to his satisfaction, Trygve Lie on April 3 elevated his executive assistant to the assistant secretary-generalship—the eighth and last such position to be filled—in charge of economic affairs. Together with Henri Laugier, the assistant secretary-general in charge of social affairs, Owen will supervise the work of the Economic and Social Council, which opened its first session in New York on May 25, 1946. The hope of both men is that the Economic and Social Council will eventually be able to supersede the Security Council in world affairs by eliminating the basic economic and social causes of international friction and war. "We live in a wicked world," Owen told reporters at a news conference late in April. "We have to accommodate ourselves to it, and try to make the best of it. We won't do it tomorrow. But give us ten years, and, assuming the political situation does not deteriorate, we should do a lot of underpinning for the economic stability of the world." One of the Council's foremost problems, he added, is to bring about cooperation between nations having divergent economic, social and political structures; namely, "to reconcile the basic economic views of Russia and the western democracies" —if not at the ideological level, then at least at the "level of practical expediency." Further goals are world-wide full employment and the development of resources and productivity in economically backward areas. As a preliminary step, Owen in late April recruited a corps of experts in problems of trade, transportation, raw materials, communications, fiscal matters, statistics, and other economic factors bearing on international relations.

The Welsh sociologist is also the author of numerous articles appearing in such periodicals as *Survey Graphic, Foreign Affairs,* the *Economic Journal, International Labour Review, Political Quarterly,* and *Sociological Review,* and of several pamphlets on social and economic matters, including four editions of *British Social Services* (the first in 1941, the fourth in 1946), *End Poverty and Insecurity* (1941), and, with Neil Little, *Labour Situation in Great Britain; a Survey; May-October 1940,* for the I.L.O. His conversation is apt to be on political matters, it is said, and often it will be spiced with little shafts of humor. He has a Welshman's deep love of poetry. Books he considers his chief extravagance, and mountaineering, in which he indulged extensively in England, Wales, and Switzerland before the war, one of the "great passions" of his life. "I like the combination of the sense of physical achievement and a certain esthetic satisfaction one gets from the natural scenery—also the comradeship which is derived from mountain endeavor and danger," he told a New York *Post* reporter. "I am very, very fond of congenial friendship. It is the thing I value most in the world. But I am not a mass person. Part of the reason why I enjoy mountaineering is that it takes a small group into lonely places."

A medium-sized, dark man with green eyes framed by black-rimmed spectacles and a "Lloyd George" haircut, Owen once replied to an interviewer's suggestion that he looked like Hollywood's conception of a Welshman with a grinning "You make me feel like something out of *The Corn is Green*." One of the many whose homes in London were destroyed by fire, he plans to bring his wife, the former Elizabeth Joyce Morgan (a school teacher whom he met at a conference on international affairs at which he was a speaker, and to whom he was married in 1933), and children, Roger and Gillian, to the United States as soon as he can find a home for them, preferably "out Westchester way." He expects, he says as though it were the most natural thing in the world, to remain in America with the United Nations for the rest of his life. Remarked an associate recently: "He is a terrific worker. Frightfully energetic. He can work all day and all night. . . .A. David K. Owen is important, but he doesn't take himself importantly."

References

N Y Herald Tribune p16 Apr 4 '46
N Y Post p49 Mr 29 '46
N Y Times VI p31 Apr 7 '46

OWEN, STEVE   Apr. 21, 1898-   Football coach

Address: b. c/o New York Giants, 11 W. 42d St., New York; h. 250 W. 100th St., New York

Steve Owen "is just about the only man in the National Football League who can beat you from the bench," sports columnist Al Laney has written of the veteran coach of the professional New York Football Giants, who has also directed many all-star exhibition games. "The variety of Owen's methods has been a fascinating study" since he was made head coach in 1931. According to his friend and rival, Coach Earle ("Greasy") Neale, Owen's teams are the hardest in the league to beat.

One of three sons of Welsh-descended James Rufus Owen and Irish-descended Isabella (Doak) Owen, Stephen Joseph Owen was born on their ranch in the old United States Indian Territory on April 21, 1898. (He was nine years old when the Territory became the State of Oklahoma.) As a boy, Owen played with neighboring Indians. After being graduated in 1916 from the high school at Aline, Oklahoma, the youth entered Phillips University at Enid as a member of the Student Army Training Corps. In addition to his year in the SATC, Owen majored in education and physical education in the class of 1922, so that he took part in intercollegiate athletics for five years. "Played all sports and lettered in all," is the way Owen has summed up his college playing career.

The youth reportedly had aspired to be a jockey, and had made a start in that direction. When his interest turned to football, he became an outstanding tackle and captain of the Phillips team. "For five years," said his old teammate Everett Shelton, "I played defensive half in back of him, and I never had to make a tackle. Big Steve took care of everything." As a tackle, however, Owen never got a chance to carry the ball, and Shelton added that Owen was one of three teammates who did not score a point in those five years. During this period, Owen began to compete as a professional wrestler, using the name Jack O'Brien to preserve his amateur standing as Steve Owen. "For a while," sports columnist Arthur Daley has written, "he was quite a sensation in the corn belt and a tremendous attraction in Kansas," where he wrestled with Strangler Lewis, Joe Stecher, Stanislaus Zbyszko, Dick Daviscourt, and others. "He won some and lost some, but always he put on a good show."

The heavy-set six-footer entered the new and relatively low-paid field of professional football and became a tackle on the Kansas City club, then of the major National Football League. Joe Williams of the New York *World-Telegram* has recalled that Owen "landed in New York with what practically amounted to a medicine-selling show, a bogus football team," meaning that the players affected rodeo-type costumes, complete with ten-gallon hats and spurs. At the end of the 1924 season, Owen went barnstorming instead of going home, as usual, to Oklahoma, and played a series of exhibition games in Florida, where he caught the eye of Dr. Harry A. March, "father of professional football." March persuaded his financial backer, ex-bookmaker Tim Mara, to buy the twenty-six-year-old tackle from Kansas City. In 1925 Owen became a New York Giant, and two years later he captained the Giants to the League championship and shared in the financial reward of football victory. (His younger brother Bill, who also

STEVE OWEN

became a Giant tackle, is in 1946 one of Steve's assistant coaches.)

The Oklahoman, who maintains that he still has a few bumps on his head from trying to tackle the fearsome Bronko Nagurski, is remembered by sportswriters as "one of the play-for-pay immortals." Columnist Daley has called him "one of the greatest linemen ever to wear cleats." In his first meeting with Curly Lambeau, later to oppose him as coach of the Green Bay Packers, Owen knocked Lambeau down twenty-one of the twenty-two times Lambeau attempted to make a forward pass. Owen had little or no coaching experience, however, when Mara surprised observers by making the thirty-three-year-old lineman head coach in midseason of 1931.

With the help of Mel Hein, generally considered the greatest of pro linemen, Owen soon justified Mara's faith in him, however. In the twelve years from 1932 to 1944, his Giants won 87 of their 146 games, lost 49, and tied 10, running up a total of 2071 points to their opponents' 1591. They won the Eastern Division title in 1933, 1934, 1935, 1938, 1939, 1941, 1944, tied for it in 1943, and went on to take the championship twice, in 1934 and 1938. "Owen has had some great football players, to be sure," wrote one newspaperman, "but Steve always managed to get the best out of them." According to New York Sun writer Frank C. True, Owen is far less of a taskmaster to his players than he was to himself: "Stephen himself has played when all of his bones weren't intact, but he doesn't believe in watching others do it."

Ability to improvise methods of meeting new situations has been a factor in Owen's success. The 1934 championship play-off with the Chicago Bears in New York was decided by the rubber-soled shoes Owen persuaded his players to wear instead of the standard cleated shoes.

Realizing that the condition of the playing field was such as to make cleats useless, Owen borrowed the sneakers from near-by Manhattan College before the game, and made football history by having his boys wear them in the second half. Of Owen's other strategic coups, Arthur Daley has written, "The better team invariably won—unless, of course, the Giants were involved. Then the cute Steve Owen would lean his 270 pounds against the applecart and upset it." Among successful pro coaches, Tom Meany of PM ranks Steve Owen second only to George Halas of the Chicago Bears, while Coach Neale of the Philadelphia Eagles has said, naming three playing stars: "When you play the Chicago Bears, you must beat Sid Luckman; when you play the Packers, you must beat Don Hutson; when you play the Washington Redskins, you must beat Sammy Baugh; but when you play the Giants, you must beat Steve Owen."

Owen was not immune to frustration, however. There was the game his Giants lost to the Philadelphia Eagles by 14-10: Twice the Giants charged down the field and into the end zone, twice Giant halfbacks plummeted over the goal line—and then discovered that they had left the ball on the ten-yard line, where the Eagles picked it up and made two easy ninety-yard runs to touchdown. The World War II Giants were a "pick-up team," and in 1943 Owen eliminated the shift in his team's offense, because, reportedly, the shift was confusing the Giants more than the opposition. In 1943, however, the Giants tied with the Redskins for the Eastern championship, losing the play-off.

In 1944 Owen directed what one writer called a "gosh-awful collection of has-beens and never-will-be athletes." His only blocking back broke a leg in the first practice scrimmage and was out of action all season. The Giants lost one pre-season exhibition game after another, yet when it counted Owen shepherded his rookies and veterans to a record of seven victories in the ten games, five of them shutouts in which the opposition failed to score even one point. They won the Eastern championship, afterward losing the national title to the well-rested Packers. To the accompaniment of jeers, Owen had brought Arnie Herber out of retirement to throw passes, and had taken a similar, and similarly successful, gamble on Ken Strong. At the end of the season, the Giant tailbacks Bill Paschal and Howie Livingston led the league in yardage gained and in passes intercepted, respectively; Ken Strong held the field-goal-kicking title; and Frank ("Icehouse") Cope was chosen all-league tackle. In a day when the forward pass was considered the necessary basis of a successful offense, the New Yorkers got there with a running game, combined with exceptional defense. The Giants succeeded on one occasion in bottling up the great Don Hutson and preventing him from scoring a point for the Packers—Owen says this was because the task was given to rookie Livingston, fresh from junior college, who had never heard of Hutson and did not know enough to be handicapped by awe of him. In preparation for this game,

Owen had studied films of the previous Giant-Packers tilt seventeen times.

The 1945 Giants were strengthed by players returning from the armed forces, although perhaps less quickly than some other teams. In the first game of the season Owen's boys scored three touchdowns in thirty-five seconds, but after that they ran into trouble and experienced their worst season. Nevertheless, the team drew a total attendance of 282,382 to their six home games, outdrawing all other teams in the league, including the champions.

Steve Owen, who had restored the offensive shift the previous season, was able to reconvert in 1946 to his two-team system, sending in entire units to play alternate quarters. He retained only fifteen players from 1945, while his squad gained luster by the addition of Frank Filchock of the Washington Redskins, and rookies from half-a-dozen colleges, including Jim White of Notre Dame and All-American De Witt ("Tex") Coulter. Coulter was delighted because Owen allowed him to punt in a real game, for West Point coach Blaik '40 had never permitted him to do so. For once Owen's personnel problem lay in cutting down his roster to the allowed maximum of thirty-three, as well as getting players of varied football backgrounds to work smoothly together to execute his strategy.

The Giants used six defenses against the Chicago Bears in October 1946 and won from them for the first time in seven years. The score was 14-0, the first shutout the Bears had been held to since 1939. "Steve Owen can't get away from . . . being tops as a defensive genius," commented Jesse Abramson. Later that season, however, Owen saw his Giants "stumble and fumble like Keystone Cops through every error Giant teams never commit," losing to the Eagles, 24-14 (they had their revenge, 45 to 17, the next week).

The 1946 Giants set an attendance record of 544,719 for twelve games. They also added to Coach Owen's reputation as a specialist in shut-outs—since 1936 his teams had held opponents of eleven different teams scoreless in twenty-one games, six more than the powerful Bears had done. The Giants' 24-14 defeat in the all-league championship playoff with the Bears on December 15, 1946, was considered a moral victory because of the extraordinary combination of handicaps under which they labored, including the late-minute revelation of bribery scandal which barred Owen's fullback from play. Ironically, despite "furious" and "gallant" play, the team lost by the very ten points which the gamblers had sought to ensure; but their coach came out of the game "bigger than ever," with newsmen making such comments as: "Most astonishing of all . . . was the fact that the Giants came roaring into the final quarter in a tie with the Bears while forced to perform with their junior varsity backfield." (Their losers' share of the receipts came to $1,295.57 per man, with this share voted to Owen.)

"Most football coaches are not happy even when they win games, but the large Mr. Owen is of a much more sanguine temperament than the average," wrote Al Laney. "When he wins he is a jolly man, and even in defeat he has never been known to give anyone the back of his neck." Blue-eyed, brown-haired Coach Owen is known to sports page readers as "Stout Steve," in recognition of the 265 pounds which hearty eating has distributed over his six-foot frame. He is said to be like one of the family to his employers, the Maras, and to take a paternal attitude toward his players. Owen refers to professional football as a steppingstone, rather than a career, and advises the players to save their money and continue their education. "I believe that most of my boys will eventually wind up as college coaches," he wrote in 1942.

Married in November 1935 to Miriam Virginia Sweeny, sister of the team physician, Owen makes his home in New York. During the six-month off season, the spectacled "southpaw" is often seen on golf courses with Coach Neale, and at racetracks; and he has appeared as an expert witness in several courts. In February 1945, for the R. J. Reynolds Tobacco Company, the cigar-smoking and tobacco-chewing coach testified that he never advised his players against smoking, "except in front of kids." Owen, who likes all sports and travels throughout the country by automobile, says that his hobby is trying to make good football players out of ordinary ones.

References

N Y Times III p2 My 13 '45; p17 S 11 '45; p22 Ja 3 '46
N Y World-Telegram p24 D 15 '44

PADILLA NERVO, LUIS (pä-*thē'*yä nār'vō lōō-ēs') Aug. 19, 1898- Mexican delegate to the United Nations Security Council

Address: b. c/o United Nations, New York; h. Plaza Rio de Janeiro 30, Mexico, D.F.

Mexico's permanent delegate to the United Nations, Luis Padilla Nervo, is a diplomat who has served his republic in five countries of Europe and in eight of North and South America. With the rank of Ambassador Extraordinary and Plenipotentiary he was in 1946 the Mexican representative on the U.N. Security Council and on the U.N. Atomic Energy Commission. During the 1946 New York session of the U.N. General Assembly, he served as deputy chairman of the thirteen-member Mexican delegation headed by Foreign Minister Francisco Castillo Nájera '46; later, in October, he became chairman when Castillo Nájera returned to Mexico.

Luis Padilla Nervo was born on August 19, 1898, in Zamora, Michoacán, a state in the southwest of Mexico. His father was Luis G. Padilla, his mother Angela Nervo. Young Luis was graduated from the Faculty of Law at the National University of Mexico, and later from the School of Law of George Washington University, in Washington, D.C. He also studied law and social sciences at the University of Buenos Aires and in England, at London University. The young lawyer wrote poetry, which he describes as "modern stuff with a philosophical flavor"; some of it was published. According to Frank Gervasi of

LUIS PADILLA NERVO

Collier's, Padilla Nervo might have pursued a literary career had it not been for his uncle, Amado Nervo, a famous and beloved Mexican poet who died while Ambassador to Argentina. "I found it very difficult to compete with my uncle's reputation," Padilla Nervo told Gervasi. "So, for a long time I have not written poetry." Instead Padilla Nervo turned to a Government career, entering the Mexican diplomatic service in 1920 when he was twenty-two years old.

The young Mexican became a protocol assistant in the Ministry of Foreign Affairs. For a time, too, he was under secretary of public education and fine arts, and then assistant secretary of labor and social prevision in the ministry of labor and social welfare. Going into foreign service, he advanced from assistant to full secretary of the Mexican Legation at Buenos Aires. At the Mexican Embassy in Washington, D.C., Padilla Nervo was at various times chargé d'affaires, legal counselor, and Minister. He was also sent to Europe, where he served as secretary of the Mexican legations in London and Madrid. In 1933 the thirty-five-year-old diplomat was named Envoy Extraordinary and Minister Plenipotentiary. In that capacity he represented his country in the United States, El Salvador, Costa Rica, Panama, Uruguay, Paraguay, Holland, Denmark, and Cuba.

Also active in international bodies, in 1938 Padilla Nervo served as Mexico's delegate to the International Labor Conference at Geneva, Switzerland. The same year he was his country's delegate to the General Assembly of the League of Nations, again in Geneva. Five years later, in May 1943, he was the Mexican delegate to the United Nations Conference on Food and Agriculture at Hot Springs, Virginia. At the Inter-American Conference held March 1945 in Chapultepec, Mexico City, to discuss problems of war and peace, he served as technical adviser to the Mexican delegation.

The following month, again as an adviser, Padilla Nervo accompanied the Mexican delegation to San Francisco for the United Nations Conference at which the U.N. Charter was prepared. He was in London in August 1945 as chief representative of Mexico on the executive committee of the Preparatory Commission of the United Nations; and in November and December he served in the same capacity on the fifty-one-nation Preparatory Commission itself, which arranged for the first sessions of the General Assembly, Security Council, and other U.N. bodies. He also represented Mexico at the Assembly of the United Nations Educational, Scientific, and Cultural Organization which met during November 1945, and became Mexico's representative on the executive committee of the preparatory commission of UNESCO.

The United Nations General Assembly met for the first part of its first session in January and February 1946. A delegate to that session, Padilla Nervo two months later journeyed to Geneva as chief Mexican delegate to the last General Assembly of the League of Nations. After that he served under Foreign Minister Castillo Nájera as Mexican representative on the U.N. Security Council, which met in London and later in New York. He took Castillo Nájera's place at the Council table when the latter was in Mexico City, in October becoming permanent chairman.

As Mexico's representative on the U.N. Atomic Energy Commission in August, Padilla Nervo made the suggestion which was adopted by the Commission—that the scientific and technical committee of the Commission be charged with examining the technical feasibility of atomic control and with outlining the manner in which international control might be effected. In October the Mexican diplomat presented an atomic energy control plan which, it was hoped, would settle the pivotal problem of inspection. He suggested that all key nuclear plants be placed in a closely guarded international zone; and that, unsupervised, individual nations be permitted to use "denatured fuel" in plants for peaceful purposes. This plan was not acted upon, however, after a statement from the chairman of the scientific and technical committee to the effect that it was not a scientific possibility.

"As the representative of a small nation, new to international politics however ancient its civilization," Gervasi wrote, "Nervo is critical of the big powers' tendency to place their own selfish interests above those of the world family of nations." The Mexican, however, sees hope for world peace in the new form of "open diplomacy" produced by the U.N. "An informed public," he told Gervasi, "that does not like what is happening can bring pressure to bear upon the Governments to set matters right. They can cause their politicians to behave as they, the people, wish. And because plain people everywhere have good instincts, the net, ultimate result of these new processes in international relations will be good." Said to be particularly outspoken and "unusually lucid" on the subject of the veto, Padilla Nervo envisions "implementing and regulating" additions to those articles of the U.N. Charter having to do with the veto rights of the Big Five.

Padilla Nervo is usually described as "stocky"; he is five feet eight inches tall, weighs 160 pounds. His hair is black, his mustache trimmed "à la George Brent." His wife is the former Cecilia Winston Wilcox, of New York, whom he met while he was studying at George Washington University. Married in 1931, they have one child, Luis Adrian. The diplomat "chain-smokes" cigarettes while conversing, and "picks his English words slowly, as though he were choosing only the good berries out of a bowl." His liking for active sport, which in his youth led him to play tennis, now hurries him to the golf course as early as 7:00 A.M. whenever possible. He admits, however, that he is "still a pretty bad player."

References

Collier's 118:58 S 7 '46

Who's Who in Latin America Part I, Mexico (1946)

PANDIT, MRS. RANJIT *See* **Pandit, V. L.**

PANDIT, VIJAYA LAKSHMI (păn'dĭt vĭ-jä'ă lŭksh'mĭ) Aug. 18, 1900- Indian Nationalist leader, author

Address: b. c/o John Day Co., 40 E. 49th St., New York; h. Anand Bhawan, Allahabad, India

India's demand for its release from British rule "is not the result of the work of any political party or any superimposed propaganda. It is the natural result of world conditions. Gandhi '⁴² did not create the desire for independence. . . .India's desire for independence is more than a matter of merely wishing to become a 'nation.' What is actually at stake is the whole question of freedom itself." So declared Vijaya Lakshmi Pandit, the Indian Nationalist leader, in an interview she gave shortly after her arrival in New York in December 1944. On more than one occasion this sister of Jawaharlal Nehru '⁴¹ has been arrested for her outspoken championship of her country's cause. Prison, in fact, has become a second home to practically every member of her family. Mrs. Pandit was the first Indian leader to come directly from her country to the United States after the beginning of World War II. During her sojourn in the United States she was an observer at the San Francisco United Nations Conference, and made an extensive lecture tour.

Anand Bhawan, the name Motilal Nehru chose for the new home he built to accommodate his wife and children as well as the numerous relatives who lived under his roof, means "a home of joy." Here in the city of Allahabad, India, on August 18, 1900, his second child, a daughter, was born to his wife Swarup Rani (Kaul) Nehru. At the age of five Swarup Kumari, as Mrs. Pandit was named, was taken by her parents to England. There a governess was engaged for her and taken back to the Indian home, where the girl

Shelburne Studios
VIJAYA LAKSHMI PANDIT

was educated. The Nehrus, a Brahman family, had their own swimming pool, a large garden, horses, dogs, carriages, and automobiles. In this atmosphere and amidst affectionate parents and relatives, Mrs. Pandit grew to womanhood.

A "thin almost starved-looking man . . . wearing a loincloth" revolutionized the pattern of life of the Nehru family. In 1921 Motilal Nehru gave a lavish party for the marriage of his older daughter, Swarup Kumari, to a young lawyer, Ranjit Pandit. (Upon her marriage, in accordance with Hindu custom, the young girl was adopted into the clan of her in-laws and renamed by them Vijaya Lakshmi, a name derived from the given name of her husband and from the territory in which he lived.) Among the hundreds of guests at her wedding were Mohandas Gandhi, with whom her father had already become associated in the Nationalist movement, and a number of the leading members of the Congress Working Committee, then meeting in Allahabad. Two years before this occasion Gandhi had launched his *Satyagraha* ("Civil Disobedience"), a movement to obtain India's freedom by nonviolent methods, and by 1921 it had made considerable headway. In fact, wrote Jawaharlal Nehru, "1921 was an extraordinary year for us. There was a strange mixture of nationalism and politics and religion and mysticism and fanaticism. Behind all this was agrarian trouble and, in the big cities, a rising working-class movement. . . .It was remarkable how Gandhi seemed to cast a spell on all classes and groups of people and drew them into one motley crowd struggling in one direction. . . .Even more remarkable was the fact that these desires and passions were relatively free from hatred of the alien rulers against whom they were directed. . . .Undoubtedly this was due to Gandhiji's insistence on the implications of nonviolence. It was also due to the feeling of

PANDIT, VIJAYA LAKSHMI—*Continued*
release and power that came to the whole
country with the inauguration of the movement
and the widespread belief in success in the
near future."

One by one the Nehru family was drawn into
Gandhi's movement. Both Mrs. Pandit's father
and husband gave up their lucrative law practices to devote their energies to the nationalist
struggle, and the latter for his efforts spent
considerable time in jail, sometimes in the company of his renowned brother-in-law. (Pandit
died in 1944 shortly after the British Government released him because of his ill health.)
A short while before Gandhi's famous march
to the sea at Dandi, the starting place for his
campaign to destroy the salt tax law, Mrs.
Pandit's father decided to turn over the family home to the Indian National Congress.
(It was renamed Swaraj Bhawan ["Freedom
House"], while the house he had built for his
only son became the new "home of Joy" of
the Nehrus.)

When she experienced her first imprisonment
in 1932 Mrs. Pandit was the mother of three
daughters, the youngest only three. She and
her younger sister, Krishna, had been arrested
for their defiance of the Crown ruling forbidding them to participate in the public observance of India Independence Day. (January 26 is the day India pays tribute to the
independence it hopes to win.) To the surprise of those who were present at her trial,
Mrs. Pandit received a year's sentence plus
a fine for her refusal to "refrain from taking
part in meetings and processions . . . for a
period of one month." Repeated jailings focused national and international attention upon
the Nehru family, which together with Gandhi
became the symbol of India's struggle for
freedom. Mrs. Pandit was chairman of the
Board of Education in her native city from
1935 to 1937. In 1937 she became a member
of the Legislative Assembly as well as Minister for Local Self-Government and Public
Health, positions she held for the next two
years. The first Congresswoman to become
a provincial minister, she recorded her impressions in a collection of addresses and essays,
So I Became a Minister, which was published
in India at the end of her term of office (1939).
From 1942 to 1944 she was president of the
All-India Women's Conference.

After her last release from prison in 1943
Mrs. Pandit plunged into the work of relieving
the famine-stricken inhabitants of Bengal. Appalled by the suffering she saw in that province, the Indian woman leader observed, "I
think the Government and its 'stooges'—more
interested in that they continue in power than
that the conditions be cured—were responsible."
Although the political activities of her husband and herself deprived her children of normal family life, they shared her sympathies
and joined her in her work. Her oldest daughter, Chandralekha, spent seven months in prison
before she came to the United States in the
autumn of 1944 to study under the first fellowship granted by the Mayling Soong (Madame Chiang Kai-shek [40]) Foundation for
students from the East. The two younger

daughters of Mrs. Pandit escaped imprisonment
because of their youth. Nayantara accompanied
her sister Chandralekha to Wellesley College
as a fellow student. Later Rita, the youngest
of the three children, followed her sisters to
the United States for study.

During her visit to her student daughters in
1944-45 Mrs. Pandit became familiar to Americans as an unofficial ambassador of the Indian
people. In January 1945 she participated in
the Pacific Relations Conference at Hot
Springs, Virginia. Two months later she took
the affirmative side in a Town Hall radio debate, "Are Colonial Empires a Threat to
World Peace?" in which she was upheld by
orientalist Owen Lattimore [45]. Despite her far
from sound health, Mrs. Pandit also made an
extensive lecture tour. In late October Representative Emanuel Celler, who was responsible for proposing in Congress a bill to grant
American naturalization rights to Indian nationals residing in the United States and an
immigration quota, introduced Mrs. Pandit to
President Truman [45] at the White House.

At the United Nations conference, in the
spring, which she attended as an observer, Mrs.
Pandit informed a crowded press conference
that the official Indian delegates had not "the
slightest representative capacity, no sanction or
mandate from any responsible groups in India,
and are merely the nominees of the British
Government." Since world peace was the purpose for which the representatives of the
United Nations had met, the sister of Nehru
remarked, it was necessary to bring to their
attention the fact that "India is the pivot of
the whole system of imperialism and colonial-
ism which always breeds war. India's freedom,
therefore, is an acid test of the principles for
which this war has been fought and the continued denial of India's freedom by Britain is
a negation of those principles and of the sacrifices that have been made to win victory."

Returning to the General Assembly in the
fall as chairman of the Indian delegation she
asserted, in the first address by a woman to
that body, "India holds that the independence
of all colonial peoples is the vital concern of
freedom-loving peoples everywhere." Mrs. Pandit also favored continuation of the veto, calling it "the necessary device for securing that
vital decisions by the great powers rest on
unanimity." Outspoken against South Africa
for its racial policies, in December the Indian
delegate won the two-third vote necessary to
pass a General Assembly resolution calling
upon both countries to work toward a reformation of the African discrimination against
Indians and other minorities. In addition to
serving her country in the United Nations,
Mrs. Pandit, after her unopposed election to
India's first Central Assembly, was named
Minister of Local Government in Health on
the Executive Council, which is acting as an
interim Government until a constitution is
drafted and approved.

At the time of Mrs. Pandit's visit to the
United States in the spring of 1946, she had
almost completed her autobiography, "Sunlight and Shadows." Between this and her
first book, *So I Became a Minister,* she had

written *My Prison Days.* Both her countrymen and Americans have remarked upon her beauty and eloquence. One reporter wrote: "What a delight she is proving to be. Small, she has all the vivacity of a daring robin that dashes in and steals the tidbit right from under the beak of some bigger, more ferocious bird. It is a joy to listen to her, to watch her snatch points from her platform opponents in debate. Seeing her in action one understands better the spirit that has upheld both herself and her distinguished brother."

References

Christian Sci Mon p10 F 2 '45
N Y Post Mag p25 D 19 '44 por
PM p6 Ap 27 '45 por

International Who's Who, 1945-46
Nehru, J. Toward Freedom (1941)
Nehru, K. With No Regrets (1945)
Shidharani, K. My India, My America (1941)

PARES, SIR BERNARD (pârz) Mar. 1, 1867- British historian, university professor
Address: b. c/o University of London, School of Slavonic Studies, London

For nearly half a century a British scholar has been trying to influence his countrymen to see Russia as he sees her, in the hope of promoting a better understanding between the Russian and the English people. While still a youth Sir Bernard Pares became interested in Russia because of the conflicting views on that country, which was considered the hereditary enemy of England. He reasoned that "if Russia was the enemy, it was all the more necessary to study her. She might be an enemy to be respected, and she might be an enemy who could be turned into a friend." Pares's lifelong absorption in Russia has been responsible for his varied career as journalist, editor, historian, and professor and authority on Slavonic studies. He is the author of several books on Russia, of which *Russia and the Peace* appeared in 1944 at the time Pares completed his second year of lecturing in American universities.

Bernard Pares was born in England on March 1, 1867. He calls his father, John Pares (the son of a country squire), the greatest influence in his life. The elder Pares was "an ardent follower of Mr. Gladstone [William Ewart Gladstone, four times Prime Minister of Great Britain]—in his liberalism, in his high-church culture and in his love for the classics." Like his father, Bernard was educated at Harrow and at Trinity College, Cambridge. Later he lectured at the universities of Oxford and Liverpool as well as those at London and Cambridge. Without receiving his degree, Pares left Cambridge to become a "free-lance" student of nineteenth century European history. He set himself to learn the various European languages as a preparation for his study, earning money meanwhile by teaching. Between 1894 and 1897 the itinerant student traveled and studied in France, Germany, and Italy. He also summered in Austria and Hungary in 1896, although these countries were not included in his survey. At the end of three years of intensive research Pares felt that he was ready to start out for that vast, obscure country, Russia.

In *My Russian Memoirs* (1931) Pares describes his early impressions of Russia as well as the numerous changes he observed in that country through the Revolution. (It is in *My Russian Memoirs* that some evidences of anti-Semitism are observed.) The Russia which Pares saw for the first time in 1898 was passing through a period of "depression and the sense of impotence and failure." The assassination of Alexander II in 1881 was followed by an era of blind reaction and widespread distrust, particularly of foreigners. This did not however prevent the young Englishman from being accepted as a paying guest in the home of a middle-class family in St. Petersburg. His host, a genial insurance broker, undertook to help him master the difficult Slavic tongue. Recalling those early years, Pares has reflected that "a Russian friend is always your friend. It is not a question of what you do; if he is your friend, he remains so." After familiarizing himself with Russia and its language, the youth attended lectures at the University of Moscow. In less than a year the Government closed the school because its students had demonstrated against the regime, and the young Englishman returned to his homeland. Between his first and second visits there was a lapse of five years, during which he was a traveling lecturer for the extension program of the University of Liverpool.

For the decade from 1904 until the outbreak of World War I in 1914, Pares went to Czarist Russia regularly every year on trips which generally lasted for three months. With keen interest he observed the people's attempt to obtain self-government, a movement which the Emperor Nicholas II first encouraged by decree and then hamstrung by police interference. When the first Duma, the national legislative body, convened in 1906 in St. Petersburg, Pares attended its sessions as foreign correspondent for the London *Spectator* and the *Westminster Gazette.* Although the Duma was soon dissolved and the second and third elected Dumas met with a similar fate, Pares was impressed by the talents of the principal figures in the struggle for political freedom. His first book, *Russia and Reform,* published in 1907, was the fruit of the copious notes he made on the scene at this time.

In behalf of Russian-English friendship, Pares was able to arrange exchange visits between the two countries. His intercession with the British Government made it possible for delegated members of the moribund Duma to visit England in 1909 as official guests. In 1912 he conducted an English party of leaders in Parliament, business, and religion, as well as top ranking Army and Navy men, on a Russian tour. The Czar gave a special reception in their honor, and Pares had an occasion to meet him.

Sir Bernard's lifelong devotion to his youthful pursuit has given his life a color that is rarely associated with the academic profession. He helped to organize the School of Russian Studies at the University of Liverpool and was its secretary from 1907 to 1917. In England he

British Official Photo.

SIR BERNARD PARES

was also responsible for the creation of a traveling fellowship which enabled students to visit Russia. Additional funds made it possible for him to launch the *Russian Review* in 1912. This magazine was established to foster intellectual intercourse between the two countries and continued until 1914. As a member of the Anglo-Russian Chamber of Commerce, Pares also participated in the work of keeping his countrymen informed of business opportunities in Russia. From 1908 to 1917 he was professor of Russian history, language, and literature at the University of Liverpool, and at the University of London from 1919 to 1936.

During World War I Pares offered his services to the British War Office. At his own request he was assigned to the Russian Third Army as observer, a post he held until the collapse of the Czar's regime in 1917. For his work with the army, Pares was awarded the Russian Soldier's Cross and Medal of St. George in 1916. Later, at a military dinner, he had his second meeting with the Czar. Despite Pares's liking for the Czar as a man, he thought him a bad ruler and received the news of Nicholas' abdication with satisfaction.

In less than a year Russia experienced two revolutions. Pares's sympathies were entirely with the Provisional Government which ruled from March to November 1917. After that regime came the Bolsheviki, for whom he then had an intense dislike because he was convinced that they intended to take their country out of the war. Such a move, he felt, would expose the Western front of the British and French armies to danger. While he could sympathize with the Russian Leftists who wished their country to continue as a belligerent, he considered Lenin, Trotsky, and their co-workers, Kamenev, Zinoviev, Radek, Lunacharski, and Krylenko, "agents" of the Germans.

Shortly after the February (pre-Bolshevik) Revolution Pares was able to resign his post

with the Russian Army, after which Sir George Buchanan, Ambassador to Russia, arranged with the British Foreign Office to have Pares work with him to win popular sympathy for the English cause. During the existence of the short-lived Provisional (Kerensky) Government Pares spent considerable time traveling through Russia, striving to wean as many people as possible away from the Bolshevik influence. News of the second revolution, the October Revolution, reached Pares in England. The Bolsheviki had ridden into power behind the slogans "Peace Without Annexation and Contributions", "Self-determination of Peoples", "All Land to the Peasants," and "All Power to the Soviets."

The third upheaval took the form of a civil war when the Bolsheviki and their mass followers resisted the attempts of their opponents, under the leadership of the former generals of the Czar, to destroy the effects of the October Revolution. The armed intervention of Russia's former allies, principally Britain, on the side of the counterrevolutionists added to the chaos of an already confused scene. Admitting frankly that his War Office "had its natural affinities with the officers of the Russian Army," Pares supported the assistance it gave to the enemies of the Bolsheviki and once again offered his services in this venture. In Siberia, where a separate regime under the dictatorship of Admiral Kolchak had been established, there was need of propagandists to win over the people of that area to his side. The British Government selected Pares to work with the Admiral in an "educational" capacity. In 1919, before he departed on this mission, he was knighted.

Despite the intervention, the Bolsheviki were victorious. Although Pares did not set foot inside Russia again until 1936, he kept a close watch on the constant changes in that country through contact with occasional visitors who were permitted inside the Soviet Union and with Russian émigrés. In England Pares was able to stimulate continued interest in Russia and the rest of the Slavic world through the establishment of the School of Slavonic and East European Studies, which he directed during the years 1922-39. He followed the struggle for power between the Right and Left wings of the Russian Communist (Bolshevik) Party, after the death of Lenin in 1924. Although Pares disapproved of the Bolsheviki, he maintains in *My Russian Memoirs* that whereas Lenin had "faith" in the Revolution and Trotsky was a man of courage, Stalin's strength "lay not in ideas but in organization and political maneuvering. Like Robespierre in his latest stage, he played on the fears and ambitions of those around him, and his dominance of the Control Committee of the party made him the master of all of them."

In 1936 Stalin's regime opened the door of the U.S.S.R. to Sir Bernard. Since this, his first post-revolutionary visit, his hostile attitude toward the Soviet Union has been replaced by one of friendliness because he feels that, since 1921, Russia has been "a country ruled by Communists who had ceased to practice communism." Writing in the *New Republic* (April 19, 1943, "On the Fear of Russia"), he quoted

Stalin as saying that "revolution is not for export; every country must make its own. We are quite ready for working relations with any foreign Government, even capitalist, which is friendly to the Soviet Union." With evident satisfaction Pares commented, "The country, Russia, has come back, and step by step drives the world revolution into a remoter corner."

With a record of more than twenty-one trips to Russia in over fifty years, Sir Bernard may well be considered the dean of that country's guests. Many years after he first set eyes on the land he mentioned that "in one way or other, in the end I traveled in forty out of the sixty provinces of European Russia, and also passed right through Siberia." Convinced that the ideas most Americans and Britons have about the Soviet Union have been "outdated" for the past twenty-five years, Sir Bernard attempted to bring them up to date during a ten weeks' lecture tour he made in Canada and the United States in 1943. Taking careful note of audience reactions, he was particularly disturbed by the frequent references to a third world war, even while the second was not yet over. In a *New Republic* article he wrote: "While in this country [the United States], I have sometimes heard loose talk of a third war against Russia. Do not expect us [England] to take any part in such criminal foolishness or throw away the friend whom Hitler[42] has so stupidly given us beyond the deserts of our past understanding." In the United States he also participated in several radio discussions. On *America's Town Meeting* he and Albert Rhys Williams took the affirmative in a debate on the subject "Should We Support Russia's Plan for Poland?" (The negative view was presented by Louis Fischer[40] and Bertram Wolfe.)

In *Russia and the Peace* (1944), Sir Bernard attempted to describe the role Russia would play in the postwar world. Most of the New York critics found the book absorbing reading even when they did not agree with the author's conclusions. Stewart Holbrook of the *Herald Tribune* wrote that "the lay reviewer is not competent to doubt or criticize the findings of a man of Sir Bernard's knowledge and experience in Russia. He can report, though, that this book . . . leaves the reader with a feeling that he has at last penetrated the fog perpetrated by both her friends and her enemies." Harry Hansen[42] of the *World-Telegram* noted that "Sir Bernard has decided that Papa Stalin knows best about the Western frontiers of Russia, and that if he needs more land he ought to have it. . . .His [Pares's] views on Russia and the peace, while not any more authoritative than ours, benefit by his knowledge of Russian affairs." The *New Yorker* found that "those who have kept up with Russian developments are not likely to come across anything new in these pages." Waldemar Gurian of *Commonweal* took the attitude that "Sir Bernard Pares is quite impressive in what he says, but does he say all that must be said? . . . Only complete frankness, not tactful silence about disagreeable facts, can help to win the right attitude toward Soviet Russia."

Sir Bernard's travels and research work have yielded nine books and numerous articles for British and American periodicals. He is the author of *Russia and Reform* (1907), *Day by Day With the Russian Army* (1915), *History of Russia* (1926, revised 1928 and 1937), *My Russian Memoirs* (1931), *Moscow Admits a Critic* (1936), *The Fall of the Russian Monarchy* (1939), *Russia and the Peace* (1944); he also translated *Krylov's Fables* into English verse (1926), and he edited the *Letters of the Tsaritsa to the Tsar* (1924). In (1901) he was married to Margaret Ellis Dixon. During his visit to the United States when he was asked how he spells his last name he replied, "Take the first letters of the names of my five children, Peter, Andrew, Richard, Elizabeth, Susan, and there you have it—Pares."

References

N Y Post p25 Je 29 '45
International Who's Who, 1945-46
Pares B. My Russian Memoirs (1931)
Who's Who, 1946

PARKER, HOMER CLING Sept. 25, 1885—June 22, 1946 United States Democratic Representative from Georgia, 1932-35; Controller General of Georgia, 1936-37, 1940-45.

Obituary

N Y Times p40 Je 23 '46

PARODI, ALEXANDRE (pä"rô"dē' ä"lĕk"säN'dr') June 1, 1901- French Government official

Address: b. c/o United Nations, New York

Alexandre Parodi, the leader in the French underground resistance movement known as "Monsieur X," became France's permanent delegate to the United Nations Security Council in April 1946. In the fall and winter of 1946 he was the French delegate to the U.N. General Assembly and to the Atomic Energy Commission as well as to the Security Council. Before World War II, a lawyer in the civil service, and after the liberation of France the Minister of Labor in President de Gaulle's[40] provisional Government, the French statesman came to New York for the U.N. meetings from Rome where he had been serving as his country's Ambassador since December 1945. Parodi is described as a "Socialist, but without marked party affiliation in French politics."

Ambassador Alexandre Parodi, who bears the name of his playwright grandfather, was born June 1, 1901, in Paris. He was one of the four children of Hélène (Vavin) Parodi, and Dominique Parodi, a distinguished philosopher, who was an inspector general of higher education and a member of the Academy of Moral and Political Sciences. After earning a degree in law and literature, young Parodi became a "Master of Appeals" in the Council of State, the highest administrative court in France, which the head of the French Government and his ministers consult on legislative and administrative problems. He also worked in the National Economic Council, becoming its assistant secretary, and then its secretary-general. Although he considered himself a Socialist, the young lawyer was not particularly active in politics.

French Press & Inf. Service

ALEXANDRE PARODI

When World War II broke out in Europe, Parodi was serving as director general of the French Ministry of Labor, a post to which he had been appointed in 1938. His appointment was revoked in September 1940 (France had fallen to the Nazis the preceding June) by René Belin, Minister of Labor in Marshal Petain's '40' Government. Parodi remained in the civil service, however, resuming his duties with the Council of State, which was then in session at Royat, not far from Vichy, in unoccupied France.

In the four years before France was liberated, Parodi rose to be one of the key men in the well-organized underground resistance movement. (The name Parodi had become known to French patriots early in the occupation when Alexandre's brother René, assistant prosecuting attorney in Paris, was arrested by the Nazis and murdered in his cell.) Alexandre Parodi, using the name "Quartus," in the summer of 1942 became a member of the "General Council of Experts" of the underground, which held its first secret meetings at Evian in southeastern France. He had a narrow escape in mid-1943 when the Gestapo, in a raid of Paris resistance headquarters, found his name on a telegram he had received secretly from De Gaulle. Thereafter he traveled on forged identification papers. In the fall of 1943 Parodi was appointed president of the underground press commission, which made plans for the reorganization of the French press after the liberation.

In March 1944 he was designated by General de Gaulle as his delegate general inside Nazi-occupied France. In July the De Gaulle French Provisional Government, then in Algiers, announced by radio the nomination of "Monsieur X," a new member of the Government, Minister of the occupied territories and resident in France. It was revealed after the liberation

that "Monsieur X," De Gaulle's liaison with resistance leaders, was Alexandre Parodi. Forced further into hiding by subsequent developments, Parodi assumed a new alias—"Cerat." As De Gaulle's personal representative he had controlling powers over civilian and military action of the resistance, and also headed the financial and social committee of the resistance. According to a New York *Herald Tribune* article, for a long time he raised more than sixty thousand dollars a month for the underground forces.

In August 1944 Parodi sanctioned and guided the Paris insurrection, although General de Gaulle had not ordered an uprising. As Harold Callender told the story in the New York *Times* some months afterwards, reports reached Parodi on August 14 that a resistance group within the Parisian police intended to call a strike and that in consequence the Germans were planning to disarm the entire force. To prevent the loss of weapons, Parodi agreed that all the resistance groups among the police strike at once. The policemen struck, and did more: wearing civilian clothes they attacked and on August 19 occupied the prefecture of police. "It was then that the National Council of Resistance and I decided on an insurrection in Paris even without orders from General de Gaulle," Parodi told Callender. "We had seen it coming and we should have been responsible had it failed. Our quick decision enabled us to remain masters of the situation."

French military men in Paris considered that insurrection by the inadequately armed F.F.I. was "the wildest folly." After bitter arguments in the council, and a plea from the Parisian Committee of Liberation that the battle go on, Parodi, who had arranged a thirty-six-hour truce because he feared the destruction of the city by German bombardment, decided to continue the fighting. Paris was relatively little damaged, but many French and Allied military men afterwards held that the uprising was a mistake, since "it involved the risk of the destruction of the city just when Allied forces were about to surround and liberate it by deft strategy." On the other hand, "M. Parodi's aim, and that of resistance leaders," Callender reported in the *Times*, "was to save it [Paris], but by its own effort and at some risk—to save its pride and self respect as well as its monuments."

After the liberation of Paris, Parodi was named one of the twenty-one ministers of the Provisional Government, which was being reconstituted by President de Gaulle to give representation to the "Resistance of the Interior." As Minister of Labor and Social Security from September 1944 to November 1945, Parodi reorganized the social security system, and instituted labor-management committees in factories —measures which gave the workers larger representation in industry and its welfare institutions. Charged with the problem of salary adjustments in industry, he permitted a general increase, but found it necessary "to act cautiously so as not to cause a dangerous rise in prices." In January 1945 Parodi met in London with the governing body of the International Labor Office. Welcomed by that active offshoot of the League of Nations as the first French official to appear at an I.L.O. meeting since the liberation of France, Parodi told the members that it would be a great pity if the I.L.O. were to be a minor cog in the new world peace machinery. Subsequently Parodi was unanimously elected president of the I.L.O.'s twenty-seventh conference, held in Paris in October of the same year.

Parodi was named French representative to the Quirinal with the rank and prerogatives of Ambassador in December 1945, and while in Rome he served as French delegate to the Allied Advisory Council for Italy. Then, in April 1946 Parodi was appointed France's permanent delegate to the Security Council of the United Nations; he came to New York in May to replace Henri Bonnet '45, Ambassador to the United States and temporary delegate. On May 17 he assumed the presidency of the Council, since by an alphabetical rotation system it was France's turn to take the chair. On the question of Franco '42 Spain, the French representative was particularly outspoken. France, Mexico, Poland, and Russia were the minority of the Council which voted to break diplomatic relations with Spain. When Russia vetoed less direct action, holding that it was not strong enough, Parodi said in a radio address, "We can't afford to let the Spanish issue drop, veto or no veto. We must not fail in our first attempt to deal with a Fascist threat or potential threat." Parodi feared the outbreak of a civil war in Spain which would lead to a new world war. "Until the Spanish question is solved and Spain is in the United Nations," Parodi said later, "we can never have complete security from the danger of uncontrolled atomic development. . . . But Franco or no Franco, unless we can get unity on control of the atom, the United Nations will not be worth ten francs as a force against war."

In July and August 1946 the French delegation, under Parodi, worked to reconcile the American plan of Bernard Baruch '41 and the Soviet proposals for control of atomic weapons. In the U.N. Atomic Energy Commission Parodi sought a modification of Baruch's "no veto" clause of the control plan, suggesting that the words "no legal right" (also in the Baruch plan) fully covered the situation. When the U.N. adopted a world disarmament resolution, Parodi remarked that an "overenthusiastic atmosphere" had caused the League of Nations to fail; he warned of a long, discouraging road ahead. "Maybe we can say that this Assembly which, I trust, will appear to the eyes of history as marking the beginning of a magnificent work of peace, does indeed give grounds for hope," Parodi concluded soberly.

Described by newsmen as efficient and brisk, Parodi was the first chairman of the United Nations Security Council to use the French language rather than English, of which he has only a limited command. His sister, Jacqueline Parodi, who assisted him in the resistance movement, serves as his secretary. The delegate was joined in New York by his wife, the former Anne Marie Vautier, and their two sons, Jacques and Jean.

References

Collier's 118:96 S 21 '46
N Y Herald Tribune p7 My 18 '46
N Y Sun p7 My 14 '46
N Y Times p8 N 3 '44

PARTCH, VIRGIL F(RANKLIN) Oct. 17, 1916-   Cartoonist

Address: b. c/o Panorama, Fort Ord, Calif.; h. Box 4, Toluca Lake P.O., North Hollywood, Calif.

"Vip," as he signs his cartoons, and as he is known to his family and friends, is Virgil Partch, since 1942 the creator of a form of "maniacal humor," which some say is suited to the tenor of modern times. His cartoons in *Collier's* and other publications "exhibit the human race as a very unbalanced end product of evolution." According to Kyle Crichton, "Virgil Partch is nuts . . . but nuts in the nice American way. . . . If anybody is to be compared to Partch, it could be S. J. Perelman, the writer, who makes no sense, just fun."

Virgil Franklin Partch was a Navy son, born October 17, 1916, on St. Paul Island, Alaska, where his father, Petty Officer Paul C. Partch, was stationed. After sojourns in Kodiak, Sitka, Puget Sound, and San Francisco, the elder Partch left the Navy and settled with his family in Tucson, Arizona, because both Virgil's younger brother and Mrs. Partch, the former Anna Pavloff, had contracted tuberculosis. Paul Partch, a bookish man, cooked the family meals—his dietary ideas, *Newsweek* has related, were "influenced by whatever he happened to be reading at the moment." When it was Roman history, "the family dined on tough fibered meats, rabbits, and a concoction made of rabbits' eyes. Vip claims that chicken feed was a regular on the breakfast menu. At any rate, the patients recovered." In Tucson, meanwhile, Virgil entered the University of Arizona, where he won his first fame with a "slightly off-color drawing of an admiral and a sailor" for the campus humor magazine, *Arizona Kitty Kat*. The cartoon subsequently turned up, according to *Newsweek*, as a comic post card and in magazines.

After one year at college Vip went to Los Angeles to enroll at the Chouinard Art Institute. In six months his "grammar-school dream" came true: he began working at the Walt Disney studios—only an office boy, it is true, but with prospects. The twenty-one-year-old artist secured the job in December 1937, and the following May was married to Helen Marie Aldridge. After four years with Disney, Partch—by that time an assistant animator earning forty-four dollars a week—participated in a strike at the studios; shortly afterward he was discharged. For six weeks unemployment payments of eighteen dollars a week supported the Partches and their infant son Nicholas. Partch, meanwhile, worked out a batch of cartoons, which he mailed to *Collier's* cartoon editor, Gurney Williams. The drawings sold. In August 1943, explaining that

Hurl A. Swartz

VIRGIL F. PARTCH

he had yet to meet his "twenty-six-year-old discovery" (Partch lived in North Hollywood, had never been east of Albuquerque), Williams wrote: "*Collier's* bought the first of Partch's gags on January 8, 1942, has stamped an okay on the best he has turned out since, and has patiently answered letters from readers demanding to know if Mr. Partch is unhinged and are we in our right minds. Our patience has been rewarded; we seldom hear any complaints these days."

Those who complained that Partch's work "revealed plain signs of a pathological condition" were persons, Kyle Crichton has insisted, "who were obviously on the verge of a breakdown and needed only a touch of Partch to close the deal." The "touch of Partch" began to appear in the *Saturday Evening Post, Liberty* and *This Week* as well as in *Collier's,* and became a feature of the crusading newspaper *PM*—this last despite the fact that Vip, according to Crichton, "has no more social conscousness than a llama and the possibility that he knows who is the present occupant of the White House is entirely remote." Vip also appeared in the advertising columns: General Mills, Incorporated, chose Partch to illustrate with wild fantasy the strength-building effects of their "Wheaties"; and the cartoonist does other advertisements for "Squirt," a drink-mixer. To the *New Yorker* he sells gags, which are illustrated by Arno, Addams, and others.

A Vip character sometimes wears an expression of dazed or wondering imbecility, but more often is glaring at some person or thing with fanatic intensity. Oddly rectangular, with horse teeth, flat-topped heads, and astonishing noses jutting out from between bushy eyebrows, his people are said to "have something in common with the tragic figures

of Picasso's Spanish War *Guernica*." When the impossible happens in the Vip cartoon world, the characters are only mildly surprised —like some elements in modern civilization they are inured to shock. One Partch admirer has said, "the cartoons are funny if you enjoy remembering your nightmares."

Partch's humor is sometimes based on the literal interpretation of a common metaphor: "Boy! if looks could kill, eh, Steve?" asks a Partch man as he turns his head to look at a woman who has just strolled past. Steve does not react; he is sprawled dead on the sidewalk. Or, "Tom's den!" says a housewife to her friend, indicating a jagged hole in the wall in which are seen a stone ax, and a scattering of bones on an earth floor. A variation of this literal thinking is seen in his cartoon of two soldiers at a bar staring at a drinker in "the altogether" to whom one soldier says, "We've been wondering why you're not in uniform." Some are fantastic, as the drawing of a man exercising in a gymnasium, rowing machine, who is startled to see shark fins cutting through the parquet floor; more whimsically, Partch will picture a smiling snow-shoer returning to an arctic outpost with an armful of toys: "I didn't find any food, fellows," he tells two unshaven men, "but I met Santa Claus!" Much of Vip's effect depends on the facial reactions of the people he draws, which make them "funny in almost any situation."

Of his first collection, *It's Hot in Here* (1944), a Chicago *Sun Book Week* reviewer wrote that the drawings were "most often entirely wacky, now and then filled with hilarious satire. . . .His cartoons are . . . not to be probed and examined for deep hidden meanings." Crichton considered Vip "a symbol of nothing but dementia. . . .It is hard to be tolerant of people who find meanings in Partch when obviously he is as much a monument to fantasy as Peter Pan." To the *Time* reviewer the eighty-page book was "ferocious, slapstick, sometimes disturbing . . . slam-bang, explosive, insane." A later collection, *Water on the Brain* (1945), brought similar appraisals, a reference to the "wild humor of [his] conceptions" and the comment that "Vip's people, most of whom look like missing links, are practically indescribable, and his humor has to be seen to be appreciated."

The cartoonist enlisted in the Army in September 1944, and in 1946 was still in uniform, a staff artist for the Fort Ord *Panorama* in California. An inch under six feet tall, he weighs 185 pounds, has blue eyes, brown hair. Shy and mild-mannered, he wears gold-rimmed spectacles, likes South Sea Island attire, and once described himself as a born beachcomber. According to *Time*, he became a cartoonist because "he wanted to make a living sitting down."

References

Collier's 112:68 Ag 21 '43
Newsweek 21:99 Je 14 '43 por
Time 44:46 Jl 3 '44

PASQUEL, JORGE (päs-kāl' hôr'hā)
1907(?)- Mexican baseball executive; businessman
Address: b. c/o Pasquel Hermanos, Calle de
Ramon Guzman 71, Mexico City

President and self-declared dictator of the
Mexican Baseball League is Jorge Pasquel,
owner of the two Mexico City baseball clubs.
Dynamic member of a multimillionaire family,
he has been described as one of Mexico's
shrewdest businessmen and most skillful show-
men. In 1946 his name appeared constantly on
North American sports pages as he and his
agents attracted one player after another from
"Organized Baseball" with "fabulous" offers.

Jorge Pasquel, one of eight children, the
eldest of five brothers, was born about 1907
in the Gulf city of Veracruz, Mexico. His
father, Francisco Pasquel, began his business
career as owner of a little cigar factory, became
a customhouse broker in the late nineties, and
rose to be a well-known but seldom seen leader
of Mexican industry. "My family is in everything," Jorge Pasquel once told an interviewer.
"We have banks, ranches, real estate, ships.
We are agents for General Motors. We are
customs brokers for the Mexican Government."

As a boy, Jorge played sand-lot baseball; as
a man, he determined to bring Mexican *beisbol*
up to North American standards and force Organized Baseball to recognize it. (The term
"Organized Baseball" designates the American
and National Leagues, as well as the hierarchy
of tributary minor leagues which they recognize, but excludes independent clubs and so-
called "outlaw" leagues.) An ardent sportsman
and a fiery executive of the Larry MacPhail '45
type, in 1940 Jorge Pasquel himself managed
his Mexico City baseball team, winning the
Mexican League championship. However, the
owner-president says that he lost a hundred
thousand dollars on baseball that season. His
other Mexico City team is called the Veracruz
Blues, after his birthplace; he also owns the
local playing field, Delta Park. When Pasquel
became president of the Mexican League, his
next eldest brother Bernardo became vice-
president. The five Pasquel brothers owned
stock in each of the other teams, of which the
major owners were inconspicuous men of wealth
and family.

Don Jorge has been known to say, "I am
the Mexican League." Under its syndicate system, he represents the entire league in hiring
players, sending each man to whatever team he
thinks would be most benefited by the addition.
There is no limit on the number of players to
a team—Pasquel may build up a weak team by
giving it more players than a strong one. All
receipts are pooled; 45 per cent is set aside for
a reserve fund, and the remaining profit is ap-
portioned equally. Pasquel has stated that he
expects to realize a profit on his family's investment—estimated at twenty million dollars—
and in 1946 offered to bet skeptics two million
American dollars that his newly aggressive
league would last the season. He is counting
heavily on a postwar boom in tourist trade.

North Americans first heard of the Mexican
League in 1944, when it acquired Rogers Horns-

JORGE PASQUEL

by, a baseball immortal reduced to managing in
the Texas League, as a player-manager.
(Hornsby returned to the United States because, he said, the Mexican club owner chided
him for running up too one-sided a score,
on the ground that it would decrease the next
game's box office.) In 1945, according to figures released by Pasquel's office, the league took
in eight hundred thousand dollars and made a
net profit of four hundred thousand, with a
payroll of three hundred thousand. The next
year Pasquel brought the payroll up to $425,000
by offering dazzling salaries to players from
Organized and Negro baseball. "Bah, what is
money?" said Pasquel. "I have forty, fifty,
sixty million dollars American money." (He was
referring to the Pasquel fortune; the league is
said to command a hundred million.) The first
step in Pasquel's expansion program had been
to organize two new clubs, Torreón and San
Luis Potosí, bringing the league up to a total
of eight teams. Besides Pasquel's own Mexico City and Veracruz, the circuit included
Monterrey, Puebla, Tampico, and Nuevo Laredo—the last-named just across the border
from Laredo, Texas, from which American
town Pasquel hoped to draw attendance.

Within two months the Pasquel brothers and
their agents had signed up eighteen major-
league players from New York, Cincinnati, and
Chicago, besides a number of minor-leaguers.
Most of them were Latin-Americans who had
filled out the depleted ranks of wartime baseball
but had receded into the background with the
return of American baseball stars from war
service, but one, Luis Olmo of the Brooklyn
Dodgers, an outfielder who had batted .313 the
preceding year, was considered a distinct loss
to the team. Organized Baseball's move was
to establish relations with the small rival Mexican National League, which Pasquel's league
had seriously menaced, and to order the suspension for five years of all players who took part

PASQUEL, JORGE—*Continued*

in a Mexican game. The Pasquels countered with an invitation to Baseball Commissioner A. B. "Happy" Chandler '[43] to come down and join their setup.

They also proceeded to sign up two first-string men, Vern Stephens of the St. Louis Browns and Dodger catcher Mickey Owen. After several well-publicized changes of heart on the part of each, Owen finally settled down in Mexico under a five-year playing-managing contract, while Stephens returned to St. Louis—where he was reinstated—complaining about the Mexican altitude, the language, the primitive ball parks, the casual wearing of firearms, and the low standard of play. (Sports writers agree that Mexican baseball is of minor-league quality by North American standards, although they differ as to whether it ranks as AA, A, or anything down to D grade.) Pasquel's offers to stars were said to include unprecedented salaries, huge bonuses, long-term contracts, housing, expenses, transportation for players and their families, and the assumption of all taxes. To help finance this program, by May 1946 Pasquel had raised the price of admission twice.

In May 1946 the New York Yankees (Larry MacPhail), the Brooklyn Dodgers (Branch Rickey '[45]), and the New York Giants all sought injunctions restraining the Pasquels and their alleged agents from inducing players to repudiate signed contracts. The Pasquels charged in reply that Organized Baseball contracts were monopolistic, holding the players who signed them "in peonage for life." While the cases were pending the Pasquels continued to sign well-known players, including Max Lanier, Fred Martin, and Lou Klein, all of the St. Louis Cardinals. Meanwhile, in July 1946 Don Jorge again returned to the manager's bench of the Veracruz club, substituting for Mickey Owen, and was snapped in uniform by Associated Press photographers while he held Owen's little son on his lap.

The following month Owen reappeared in Brownsville, Texas. He claimed that the Pasquels had violated their contract with him; shortly afterward, the Pasquels filed suit against him, to which he entered a counter-suit. Meanwhile, Commissioner Chandler ordered Owen to be suspended for five years. The baseball czar also fined the Saint Louis Cardinals' owner, Sam Breadon, $5,000 (later rescinded) for flying to Mexico and conferring with Pasquel. Reportedly, the "entente cordiale" established between Breadon and Pasquel on this visit was to be the forerunner of a peace agreement to be negotiated between the Mexican League and the American and National Leagues.

At the time of Babe Ruth's '[44] visit to Mexico in May 1946, the New York *Times* correspondent Milton Bracker reported that interest in Mexican League doings "far transcends the realm of the diamond. People here who don't know third base from the bullpen are talking of the Pasquels. . . .In fact it has even been said that not since the historic oil expropriation of March 1938 has any circumstance so delighted the Mexican national ego as that of 'St. George' tilting with the 'dragon' of American baseball. . . .As one Mexican put it aptly, 'Nobody really likes Jorge—but he's a national hero.'" The Pasquels' plans for the future included construction of a forty- or fifty-acre "baseball city" near Mexico City, at a cost of two million dollars, which would include living accommodations for the players. "We will build boulevards especially to come here," Bernardo Pasquel told a reporter. "We will put in buses to come here. If necessary we will build a streetcar line." The league owners' power was said to be such that Government cooperation was a foregone conclusion.

One attraction for Jorge Pasquel in buying a large transport plane was that he could use it for lion-hunting in Africa in the winter months. He is an ardent sportsman who has his daily gymnasium workout, plays golf in the low 80's, and is a crack shot. He does not drink or smoke, nor does he permit his brothers to smoke. None of the brothers is married; Jorge is divorced from a daughter of the late General Plutarco Elías Calles, President of the Republic in 1924-28, who was in exile from 1936 to 1941.

Pasquel is said to speak deliberate, concise English. Rud Rennie, New York *Herald Tribune* sportswriter who went to Mexico in April 1946 to do a series of articles on the Mexican League, described Don Jorge as "a restless fellow with a different idea every five minutes. . . .Of medium height, compactly built, he resembles [New York] Governor Thomas Dewey, but he is darker. . . .He wears an eight-carat blue-white diamond ring. His wrist watch is on a platinum bracelet. His tie clip is an arrow studded with diamonds." Rennie also mentioned Pasquel's fifteen automobiles, the stained-glass windows in his blue-tiled office, the solid silver hunting knife on his desk, the fifty gold-monogrammed rifles at his "magnificent" home, the .38 Colt automatic tucked into his waistband. "Jorge had to kill a man in self-defense not long ago," the writer explained. In his relationship with "name" ball-players, however, Rennie says this "strong man of Mexico" is "eager and trusting."

References

    N Y Herald Tribune p16 Ap 6 '46; p22
        Ap 8 '46; p27 Ap 9 '46
    N Y Times p29 Ap 5 '46

PATCH, ALEXANDER M(CCARRELL, JR.) Nov. 23, 1889—Nov. 21, 1945

Lieutenant general in United States Army; commander of the Seventh Army in Europe during World War II; saw action in the Pacific area as leader of the Americal Division (1942-43); commander of Fourth Army Headquarters in the United States from July 1945 until death. See *Current Biography* 1943 Yearbook.

Obituary

    N Y Times p1+ N 23 '45 pors

PATMAN, (JOHN WILLIAM) WRIGHT
Aug. 6, 1893-   United States Representative
from Texas

Address: b. House Office Bldg., Washington,
D.C.; Post Office Bldg., Texarkana, Tex.; h.
3500 14th St., N.W., Washington, D.C.; 1205
Main St., Texarkana, Tex.

A champion of small business in the United
States House of Representatives and chairman
of its Small Business Committee is Wright Patman of Texas, now in his ninth term. A Democrat, he is markedly more liberal and progressive
than many of his colleagues from the South.
His particular fields have been veterans' benefits
and antimonopoly acts, and he has supported
them vigorously, persistently, successfully, and
some say undiscriminately. In 1945 he was one
of the original sponsors of the Full Employment
Bill and a proponent of the Emergency Housing Bill.

The son of John N. and Emma (Spurlin)
Patman, John William Wright Patman was
born on August 6, 1893. His birthplace was a
three-room log cabin on his parents' cotton
farm, near Hughes Springs in Cass County,
Texas. The boy "learned his three R's in such
rare intervals as the boll weevil gave him leisure," comments George Creel '44. "Later on,
there was a muleback ride of six miles that he
took every day to obtain the advantages offered
by the high school at Hughes Springs, and by
way of filling in his spare time, he lit the fires
in the morning and swept the building clean at
night." Finishing high school in 1912, the nineteen-year-old boy studied law by himself and
raised cotton for two years to pay for his final
year at Cumberland University in Tennessee.
But a storm destroyed the Galveston warehouse
where his cotton was stored, Creel relates, and
"as a consequence, he and a fellow student lived
in a house so tumbled down that they had to
take turns staying awake at night for fear the
roof might fall in."

In 1916 Patman won his LL.B., and was admitted to the Texas bar. The ambitious young
lawyer got his start in politics as assistant to
the prosecuting attorney of his home county.
Then came the United States entrance into
World War I. Wright Patman was rejected by
an officers' training camp because of serious
heart trouble. Undaunted, he enlisted as a
private and rose to a first lieutenancy as a
machine gun officer. The biography Patman
prepared for the *Congressional Directory* adds:
"Member of the American Legion, the Disabled
American Veterans of the World War, and
although not privileged to serve overseas during
the war by reason of a service-connected disability, an honorary member of the Veterans of
Foreign Wars." In February 1919 the twenty-
five-year-old Lieutenant was married to Merle
Connor of Winnsboro, Texas.

Patman was elected to the Texas House of
Representatives, where he served from 1921
through 1924. For the last two years, he was
chairman of the House Committee on State
affairs. Next came five years as district attorney
for the Fifth Judicial District, Cass and Bowie
Counties—which means the part of the city of
Texarkana which lies in Texas. As district

attorney, says the Creel article, he proved his
honesty and courage by fighting vice and graft;
and when he decided to run for Congress in
1928, he risked his political future by denouncing
the Ku Klux Klan, which was still quite strong
in Texas. His Congressional district, the First
of Texas, had a 1935 population of 255,452, and
by that year less than two-thirds of 1 per cent
of his constituents had ever sent in an income
tax return. (The 1940 census figures show
306,803 residents of Patman's eleven counties.)

Elected to the Seventy-first Congress in 1928,
District Attorney Patman has been re-elected
biennially ever since. He is chairman of the
twenty-three-man Texas Congressional delegation, although his nine successive terms are few
besides the seventeen each of Speaker Ray-
burn '40 and Hatton W. Sumners, the fifteen of
Joseph J. Mansfield, the fourteen of Fritz G.
Lanham, and the twelve of Luther A. Johnson
—all as of 1945. His committee assignments include second rank on the standing Banking and
Currency Committee, and chairmanship of the
nine-man Select Committee to Investigate and
Study Problems of Small Business.

Representative Patman broke Congressional
precedent by "refusing to regard the House as
a morgue where new members must lie on a
marble slab for several sessions," accumulating
seniority. A few months after taking his seat
as a minority member in March 1929, he made
his first speech for immediate cash payment
to war veterans of the paid-up life insurance
("adjusted compensation") granted them in
1924. This would cost more than two billion
dollars. Patman continued to campaign for
this objective for six years. Because he planned
to have the Government issue new currency for
the purpose, his proposal was considered an inflationary one. It was backed by inflationists,
by the Hearst press, by Senator Huey Long,
and most notably by Father Charles E. Coughlin '40, who urged his listeners to wire their
Senators demanding its passage, and then demanded that the President sign the bill. Three
times after 1932 the House passed it, and three
times the Senate rejected it. Finally in May
1935, the upper chamber capitulated, 55-33,
and in 1936 Patman's bonus went into effect
unamended. He had even the American Legion
and the American Veterans Association against
him in his fight, but had pushed the bill
"through the House of Representatives session
after session against the furious opposition of
party leaders, committee chairmen, the press,
and even the President himself"—for Roosevelt '42 did not like the proposal any more than
Hoover '43 did. Patman's was, incidentally, selected from thirty-one bonus bills before the
House for passage.

During President Hoover's term, the Texan
also "opened up on the trusts. . . demanded
that the profits be taken out of war, strangled
Wall Street wolves with his bare hands," and
accused Secretary of the Treasury Andrew
Mellon of going so far as to create the national deficit "deliberately and wilfully, as an
argument against the payment of bonus money
in cash." In January 1932 Patman pressed for
Mellon's impeachment, charging that he had

WRIGHT PATMAN

used his official influence to negotiate concessions for a petroleum company; and the Democrat did not drop the charges until ten days after Mellon's appointment as Ambassador to Great Britain, which Patman termed a "Presidential pardon."

An ardent prohibitionist, Patman voted against repealing the Eighteenth Amendment after the Democrats came to power in 1933, but generally followed regular Democratic lines. He interested himself in banking legislation, working to cheapen or, as he put it, expand the currency. In 1935, after a committee investigation, he proposed an amendment to the Clayton Antitrust Act to end price differentials to chain stores. The result was the Robinson-Patman Act of 1936, known also as the Fair Trade Practices Act, the Anti-Price Discrimination Act, and the Anti-Chain Store Act. (Robinson was the Senate majority leader.) This act proved difficult to interpret—*Business Week* called it "probably the finest bit of legislative obscurantism to come out of Washington"—and it had some unexpected results. One surprised group of sponsors were the food brokers, who approved the ban on splitting brokerage fees with buyers—only to find that some big chains thereupon bought direct from the food producers, saving all brokerage fees. Enforcement of the Act was under the Federal Trade Commission, and it was continually in litigation over a period of years.

Representatives Patman and Binderup headed an unsuccessful drive in 1937-38 for legislation under which the Government would nationalize the quasi-public Federal Reserve Banks by buying all their stock, then held by the member banks of each district. This plan was opposed by the President and twenty-two members of the Economists' National Committee on Economic Policy. In 1938 Patman also introduced a "reflation" resolution, offered a commercial bribery bill, lauded a change in the gold sterilization policy, and charged that there was a deliberate policy of destroying small banks during the depression. In 1940 he, Senator Logan, and Representative Jerry Voorhis [41] of California offered a bill sponsored by the American Federation of Little Business, to establish regional intermediate credit banks. This plan would have the Reconstruction Finance Commission provide the capital and insurance; but, unlike the Administration-backed proposal offered by Senator Mead [44], it would not have Jesse Jones's [40] RFC administer the banks. The Mead bill was pressed for a time, but was dropped eventually. The Texan continued to advocate inflation, and in 1941 proposed to "retire the Federal debt by a new money issue." He has long been an opponent, also, of "paying interest to banks on Government bonds."

Meanwhile, the various Patman trade-practices bills and acts continued to arouse much controversy, with various national groups lining up for attack and defense. In 1938 Patman campaigned for legislation to prevent manufacturers from retailing and retailers from manufacturing, to bar exclusive retail sale contracts between non-competing manufacturers, and to prohibit "reciprocity sales." But the greatest furor was aroused by his chain-store-tax bill, introduced in February 1938. For nine years the chains had fought chain tax legislation in twenty-three states, losing only in one, Colorado; but this new attack was the most alarming of all. Patman claimed (in an address broadcast nationally, October 11, 1938) that no corporate chain would thereby be forced to go out of business: "Under the bill as proposed it will be possible for a concern to operate as many as five hundred stores in one state profitably." All other sources agreed, however, that the tax—graduated from fifty to a thousand dollars per store, and multiplied by the number of states in which the chain operated—would be confiscatory in effect. The Great Atlantic and Pacific Tea Company, with 11,752 stores, would, for instance, have to pay $428,328,000 annually, more than half of their 1937 gross sales. Moreover, Patman's defense of the tax was not on the ground of revenue, but objections to chain stores: absentee ownership, leading to concentration of "huge fortunes in the hands of rich childless brothers [the Hartfords of A & P] and Barbara Huttons"; "destruction of local communities," by "refusing to assume the duties and burdens of local citizenship"; tendency to short-weight; and monopoly. "The Federal Government was never called upon to aid the needy in local communities," Patman asserted, "until absentee-owned chains concentrated the money and credit of the country in New York City. . . .It is right that the invader should pay invasion taxes. . . .The interstate chain store must go."

The Patman bill was supported by groups of independent dealers competing with chain stores, and the chain-tax principle was thought to be generally approved by a high proportion of private citizens. It was opposed as economically unsound by Henry Wallace [40], by the American Farm Bureau Federation, by the Congress of American Industry, by the A.F. of L., by research groups like the Twentieth Century Fund and civic groups like the New York City Federation of Women's Clubs. A six-year, million-dollar investigation by the Federal Trade Commission had revealed that food and drug prices were 6 to 18½ per cent lower in chain stores, and concluded that "on the whole, the number of people adversely affected by such a tax would constitute a very substantial percentage in comparison with the number adversely affected by the present conditions." Other opponents said the same thing, pointing out that such taxes raise the cost of living and bear down especially hard on those with small incomes.

On foreign and large domestic issues, Patman was a firm supporter of the liberal Democratic Administration, showing a general tendency to vote for appropriations. (Those who dislike him have said this is because of the proportionately small amount of the cost borne by his own constituents.) He voted for nearly all of Roosevelt's important wartime and prewar legislation, opposing the Administration only on a few occasions: in June 1940 for the drastic Smith [41] restrictions on organized labor and in December 1940 for the Smith Antistrike Bill; in March 1942 for continuing the Dies [40] Committee. He failed to vote, that same month, for the appropriations for power developments which had been urged by all the war agencies. In April 1943 he voted for the antiunion Hobbs Anti-Racketeering Bill; in June for a bill regulating the political and financial activities of labor unions, and for overriding the President's veto of the Connally [43]-Harness-Smith Antistrike Act; and in December failed to vote on freezing the Social Security tax at an actuarially unsound 1 per cent. After Truman's [45] accession, in June 1945 Patman again broke his record of "party regularity" to vote against anti-poll tax legislation. Patman was one Southerner, however, who in February 1944 supported the Worley Federal Ballot Bill for servicemen and opposed the States-rights ballot bills.

The Texan sponsored and became chairman of a nine-man committee to investigate ways of aiding small business. In May 1942 his committee amended the Senate Smaller War Plants bill, doubling its hundred-billion-dollar loan fund, and making mandatory the award of a specific government procurement contract to a specific small business or group when the chairman of the War Production Board had certified the plant(s) as equipped to handle the job. (The loan fund was later reduced to $150,000,-000 by a conference committee.) Patman also introduced a bill under which new tires could be sold and old ones recapped only by independent dealers, not by tire manufacturers and mail order houses.

In May-June 1944 Patman exposed to the House what he called "one of the most powerful, one of the most effective, one of the most wealthy, and also the most sordid and most sinister lobby that has ever been organized in the history of the United States of America." This group, spearheaded by the American Taxpayers' Association and Frank Gannett's [45] Committee for Constitutional Government, was working for the "Millionaire's Amendment" to the Constitution. This would repeal the Six-teenth and provide that the Federal income, estate, and gift taxes be limited to a maximum of 25 per cent; the only permissible increases would be in wartime and last for only a year. Their program called for the petitioning of Congress, by state legislatures, for a Constitutional convention—they claimed that a decrease in Federal taxation would leave more revenue for the states; and by early 1945 seventeen of the necessary thirty-two states had done so. After Patman's campaign in the House and in correspondence with state legislators, Arkansas rescinded its approval, stating that "the purport of this resolution was misunderstood by various members of the Legislature," and several other states followed suit.

Patman's one-man fight was interrupted by his own campaign for re-election, a campaign into which the Gannett group contributed money to defeat him. (How much is not known, because treasurer Edward A. Rumely refused to give such information to a Congressional investigating committee.) The argument with which Patman convinced the legislators was that, under such an Amendment, the Federal Government's entire revenue would be required for interest charges on the public debt and minimum operating expenses, and it would be forced to abandon most of its services and to impose a heavy tax burden on the smaller-income group. Ability to pay would cease to be a criterion of taxes, big business would be able to use its excess profits to crush competition, and the states would lose all Federal aid. Other revelations by Patman concerned cartels; a personal experience led him to order an investigation which indicated that an American-Swedish cartel "pretty well controls" the match industry of the world. In 1945 Patman was especially concerned with housing and the problem of full employment.

His interest in housing was intensified by the long Congressional battle over his Emergency Housing Bill in 1946. When the bill was finally adopted in March 1946, both the Administration and its author protested that the deletion of two clauses—one setting ceiling prices on existing homes and the other providing a six-hundred-million-dollar subsidy fund—had rendered it ineffectual. Wilson Wyatt [46], then President Truman's housing expediter, said that the bill, as it stood, would not meet the expected goal of 2,700,000 homes in eighteen months. Other measures Patman supported in 1946 were those for the British loan and the continuance of price control.

Patman has made national lecture tours. In 1936 and 1937 he toured the country explaining the Robinson-Patman law to retail druggists under the auspices of McKesson and Robbins, and reportedly received some $18,000. (Later, when the firm was involved in a front-page scandal, he explained that he got the money from the Brady Speakers Bureau.) Representative and Mrs. Patman have three sons; a fourth is deceased. As their father proudly wrote in the *Congressional Directory,* Connor Wright, James Harold, and William Neff enlisted as World War II privates, the first-named rising to major.

(Continued next page)

PATMAN, WRIGHT—*Continued*

Wright Patman is described as a tall, rather stout, pink-cheeked man who wears metal-rimmed glasses and speaks in orotund tones. George Creel says of his round face, curly hair, short nose, and small mouth, "Frame him in scalloped paper, and he could be mailed as one of those old-fashioned valentines." A Missionary Baptist and a thirty-second degree Scottish Rite Mason, Patman is president of the Washington Texas Club. It was his distribution of match folders advertising Lone Star State glories that led to the discovery of the match cartel; the folders were made in another state, and the loyal Texan therefore tried to get a match factory for his home town.

References

Collier's 95:25+ My 18 '35 por
Cong Digest 10:96 Mr '31
PM p17 N 15 '45 por
Congressional Directory, (2d ed., 1945)
Who's Who in America, 1946-47

PATTERSON, JOSEPH M(EDILL) Jan. 6, 1879—May 26, 1946 American journalist; began his career on his father's paper, the Chicago *Tribune*, in 1901; served one term in Illinois legislature; was captain in the Rainbow Division in World War I; founded the first successful tabloid in this country, the New York *Daily News*, which had the largest circulation of any newspaper in the United States; became bitter critic of President Franklin D. Roosevelt. See *Current Biography* 1942 Yearbook.

Obituary

N Y Times p1+ My 27 '46 por

PATTERSON, RICHARD C(UNNINGHAM), JR. Jan. 31, 1886- Diplomat; corporation executive
Address: b. c/o American Embassy, Belgrade; 40 Wall St., New York; h. Piping Rock Rd., Locust Valley, N.Y.

A businessman who several times in his career left high posts in private enterprise to take administrative public offices, Richard C. Patterson, Jr., became American Ambassador to Yugoslavia in November 1944. He was appointed by President Franklin Roosevelt, in whose Administration he had worked for cooperation between industrial executives and the "idea men," or "brain trusters," of the New Deal. In 1945 and 1946 he figured in the strained relations between the United States and the Yugoslav Government of Premier Josip Broz (Marshal Tito '43).

The Ambassador was born in the West, in Omaha, Nebraska, on January 31, 1886, and named for his father, Richard Cunningham Patterson. His mother was the former Martha Belle Neiswanger. He spent a year at the University of Nebraska when he was nineteen, but took his degree of Engineer of Mines at Columbia University's School of Mines in 1912, when he was twenty-six. A member of the university swimming team, he was the 1909-10

president of the Intercollegiate Swimming Association. His early experience included work as a day laborer in the gold mines of South Dakota, and he is still a member of the Western Federation of Miners.

In 1916 Patterson joined the Pershing expedition to Mexico, serving as a private in the Cavalry. In the interim before the outbreak of World War I, he was secretary of the New York City Fire Department. With the AEF in France, Patterson served thirteen months as a captain and a major in the Engineers, later becoming a colonel in the Officers Reserve Corps. Colonel House, President Wilson's confidant, named him administrative officer of the American Commission to Negotiate Peace in 1918. Before he came home he also helped to organize the American Legion in Paris. Colonel Patterson returned to civilian life in 1920 as assistant to the president of the J. G. White Engineering Corporation. The next year he was employed as an engineer for E. I. duPont de Nemours and Company. Five years of business and mining ventures in China followed; he was later recognized as an authority on Chinese-American trade.

In August 1927, shortly after his return from a trip to China, Patterson was appointed Commissioner of Correction of the City of New York and a member of the Parole Board. The correction office was a fifteen-thousand-dollar-a-year position at the head of the city's eighteen prisons, including district prisons, reformatories, penal farms, a penitentiary, a workhouse, and the city prison (the Tombs). Commissioner Patterson promised to better conditions in the Tombs, appointed a committee to study drug addiction in the city, and set to work to develop new methods of prison administration. During his five years in office he sought to improve prisons so that they would cease to be, as he termed it, "crime colleges." On his resignation in October 1932 to become an executive vice-president of the National Broadcasting Company, the city's leading newspapers as well as the National Committee on Prisons and Prison Labor praised his work.

The next year Colonel Patterson was offered —and declined—the Fusion nomination for mayor of New York. He remained with NBC as executive vice-president until 1936. In the four years under Patterson's direction, it was said, the broadcasting company became "completely revitalized in its administrative functions." In 1938-39 Patterson was Assistant Secretary of Commerce and, in the absences of the then Secretary, Acting Secretary. He represented his department in the 1938 antitrust investigation, on a commission which included six members of Congress and nine men from administrative departments of the Government. The only businessman among the investigators, the Assistant Secretary worked for cooperation between industry and the Roosevelt Administration. "One of his big assets," reported *Business Week* in July 1938, "is Mrs. Patterson. Their home is the present scene of animated discussion between big business executives and 'brain trusters' who have conjured up frightening images of each other." He next (1939) became chairman of the board of Radio-Keith-Orpheum. Loaned to the Treasury Department by that corporation in July 1941, Patterson devoted his full time for two years to the organization and direction of the New York War Savings Staff as its chairman. In 1943, resigning because of business commitments, he continued to serve in an advisory capacity, at the request of Secretary of the Treasury Morgenthau '⁴⁰.

When, in November 1944, Patterson was appointed Ambassador to the Yugoslav Government of King Peter—then in exile in London—*Life* described him as "a socialite" with "a reputation for doing things well." Patterson proceeded to Belgrade when King Peter's Government gave place to that of Marshal Tito. In September 1945 the Ambassador let it be known that he had been instructed by the State Department "to insist" on the Yalta guarantees of free elections and a free press in Yugoslavia. He also said he had acquired "a great admiration for the Yugoslav people," predicted they would settle their political problems, but emphasized that in the meantime the country urgently needed economic help—"about 75 per cent of the rolling stock, farm equipment, and live stock was stolen by the Germans." He described Marshal Tito as "a great personality, easy to like," and asserted that America's interest in Yugoslavia was the establishment of peace and freedom for all the people, adding, "I think Tito would like to have that done."

It was not until April 1946 that the United States accorded full diplomatic recognition to the Tito Government, re-accrediting Patterson, who had been the "American political representative" in Belgrade, although with the personal rank of Ambassador. At the same time the State Department desired "it be understood that," (as phrased in the note dispatched to Tito the previous December when it first offered to accord his Government full recognition) "the establishment of diplomatic relations . . . should not be interpreted as implying approval of the policies of the regime, its methods of assuming control [in November 1945 a one party election had been held], or its failures to implement the guarantees of personal freedom promised its people."

With the Allied Council of Foreign Ministers discussing peace treaties in Paris in the spring of 1946, Patterson returned to Washington for consultations. The drafting of the Italo-Yugoslav border was among the knottiest of the peace problems, the question of the disposition of Trieste causing particular friction. Strained relations between the United States and Yugoslavia roused speculation as to whether Patterson would return to Belgrade. In August, however, he arrived at his post, bearing as a gift for Tito, who had confided to him that he would like to own one, a suitably engraved American tommy gun. The tommy gun was never delivered to Tito because a few days later an American C-47 transport, carrying crew and passengers on a Vienna-to-Rome flight, was fired on by two Yugoslav fighters and forced to crash-land. "I consider this a wicked, inexcusable, and deliberate attack on a friendly nation's plane, which was lost in a storm," Patterson declared, "and only by the

NBC Photo.

RICHARD C. PATTERSON, JR.

grace of God and the expertness of the pilot were they not all killed." Ten days later, on August 19, a second American plane which had strayed off the course on a regularly scheduled flight from Vienna to Italy was shot down; the five men on board were killed. The State Department dispatched four notes to Yugoslavia, the last a "stiff" ultimatum, demanding, among other things, the release of the men of the first transport, who had been interned. (They were released as soon as Tito heard that the ultimatum was on its way.)

Ambassador Patterson immediately arranged to confer with Tito, who had justified the two attacks on the ground that hundreds of unauthorized flights over Yugoslavia by American aircraft had taken place (this the American authorities denied), and that the flights were a deliberate attempt to intimidate his followers and lend encouragement to his opponents, and were also for reconnaissance purposes. The situation was further aggravated by the fact that American and Yugoslav army patrols had several times clashed along the Italian-Yugoslav border, and near Trieste. In a two-hour conference with Tito on August 22, Patterson received assurances, later repeated in a Yugoslav note to the State Department, that there would be no further attacks on foreign planes. Tito also complied with other American demands, such as those relating to military funerals for the dead airmen. Soon after this Patterson returned to the United States for an indefinite period; John Moors Cabot of Massachusetts was appointed counselor to the American Embassy in Belgrade to manage its affairs during the Ambassador's absence.

In January 1940, when Patterson's major job was that of a businessman, he had presented arguments in the New York *Times Magazine* "in favor of a change in the make-up and activities of the boards which guide the big

PATTERSON, RICHARD C., JR.—*Cont.*

business of America." He himself was chairman of the board of Radio-Keith-Orpheum Corporation from 1939 to 1945, and continues to be in 1946 a director of RKO Pictures, the New York Water Services Corporation, the General Cigar Company, the National Can Corporation, and Pathé News; he is chairman of the board of the Ogden Corporation and a trustee of the Provident Loan Society. Patterson decried the appointment of directors who merely rubber-stamp the proposals of a few men in management. It would strengthen the whole American system of economics, he maintained, if directors were chosen who were qualified to advise as specialists on labor relations, social and economic trends, international affairs, finance, or a particular phase of industry, "whose thinking would be done in the public interest as well as in the interests of stockholders and employees."

The Ambassador is a "graduate member" of the Business Advisory Council of the Department of Commerce, having served on the Council five years. Until he resigned because of his diplomatic duties, he was a director of both the Salvation Army and the YMCA. In 1937-38 he was chairman of the board of the Citizens Budget Commission and president of the Travelers Aid Society, and in 1938-39 a member of the Temporary National Economic Committee. The organizer and first president of the New York Young Democratic Club, he was also a delegate to the Democratic National Convention in 1936 and 1944, and an alternate delegate in 1928, 1932, and 1940. He has been decorated with Serbia's Royal Order of White Eagle with Swords, Panama's Medal of Solidarity, the French Legion of Honor, and China's Order of Jade; and he has been awarded the Conspicuous Service Cross of the State of New York, a medal for distinguished public service from Columbia University in 1932, and a similar medal from the University of Nebraska in 1940.

With the Ambassador in Belgrade was his wife, the former Shelley McCutchen Rodes of Bowling Green, Kentucky, to whom he was married in May 1924, and their daughter Alice Rodes Patterson. Their home is in Locust Valley, Long Island. Patterson is gray-haired, five feet seven and a half inches tall, and weighs 158 pounds. One of his recreations is golf. Newspaper pictures show that the Ambassador also likes hunting: he and Marshal Tito have been photographed on shooting trips together.

References

Life 17:44 N 13 '44 por
International Who's Who, 1945-46
Who's Who in America, 1946-47
Who's Who in the Nation's Capital, 1938-39

PATTERSON, W(ILLIAM) A(LLAN)

Oct. 1, 1899- Air line executive

Address: b. c/o United Air Lines, Inc., 5959 S. Cicero Ave., Chicago; h. R.F.D. #1, Northbrook, Ill.

W. A. Patterson became the chief executive of United Air Lines, Incorporated, in 1934, when smaller air transport companies serving separate sections of the country first merged to form United's transcontinental route. In 1946 United was one of the "Big Four" among American air lines, embracing a system of ninety-three hundred miles with landing fields at sixty cities in twenty States, the District of Columbia and a Canadian province, and with future service to Honolulu; its personnel numbered approximately ten thousand.

The son of William Allan Patterson, an overseer for an Hawaiian sugar company, and the former Mary Goulter, the junior William Allan Patterson was born in Honolulu on October 1, 1899. He was sent to public grammar and high schools in San Francisco, returning to Hawaii in 1911 to enter the Honolulu Military Academy. By 1914 young Patterson was back in San Francisco as an office boy in the Wells Fargo Bank. In 1919 a ride in a pusher-type flying machine at Crissey Field (San Francisco) put wings in Patterson's mind. When the Pacific Air Transport Company, which was later to become a division of United Air Lines, opened an account with Wells Fargo Bank, Patterson was placed in charge of the account. Utilizing the chance to learn more about airplanes and air lines, he flew in the company's open cockpit planes, talked with its officials and employees, and learned how its operations were conducted. Patterson remained in the employ of the bank for fifteen years, in the course of which he rose to be assistant to one of the vice-presidents.

In 1929 Patterson resigned from the bank, to become assistant to the president of the Boeing Airplane Company and the Boeing Air Transport Company at Seattle, Washington. Two or three years later he was elected president of Boeing Air Transport, which flew planes between Chicago and San Francisco, and became president also of three other air lines coordinated by the new management corporation, United Air Lines. The other lines were the National Air Transport Company, flying between Chicago and New York; the Pacific Air Transport Company, operating from Seattle to San Diego; and Varney Air Lines, Inc., between Portland (Oregon) and Salt Lake City. As president of each company from 1931 and as vice-president of the coordinating company from 1932, Patterson was instrumental in merging the four independent lines into United Air Lines, Incorporated, in 1934, and became president of the new organization.

Under Patterson's administration, United Air Lines' research and communications laboratory embarked on costly research programs to increase the safety of air travel. United was the first to install successful two-way air-ground telephony and lights for night flying, also leading in establishing weather report services and radio range facilities. Other devices on which United research workers have made notable contributions include the constant speed propeller, the automatic gyro-pilot, and the wing de-icer. In May 1936, after four years of work on the technique of landing by instruments, research man Ragnar T. Freng discovered the secret (letting the automatic pilot do it all) and phoned "Pat"—who immediately rushed to the airport, climbed into the copilot's seat, and flew with Freng as he demonstrated twenty-two perfect blind landings. (In 1946 United was the first air line to take steps toward the installation of an automatic landing system, which would make possible instrument approach to airports in foggy weather.)

In his relations with his employees, Patterson followed a policy of consulting them on personnel complaints as well as company problems. This policy dated back to 1933; at that time, when the pilots' union threatened the line with a strike, he was invited to Newark airport to hear the pilots' grievances and came away convinced that they were "90 per cent right." The company president spent the next two months traveling along his air line, asking pilots and copilots for their suggestions about operations. Pensions and insurance, wrote Wayne Parrish in *Liberty* in 1946, are among the benefits which United offers its employees.

As a new means of transportation which had to sell itself to a public not yet air-minded, the air lines showed little profit for some time. The rapid development of safer devices meant that the air transport lines were constantly having to replace their obsolete equipment. The rate of increase in traffic volume was not so rapid as the rate of equipment replacement. By 1936, however, United Air Lines began to show a margin of profit. Nine years later, its net income for the first half of 1945 amounted to $3,541,785, as compared with a net income of $2,924,837 for the same period during the preceding year. After World War II, United's business continued to expand; its New York business alone for April 1946 represented an increase of 175 per cent over that of the same month in 1945.

When the Civil Aeronautics Board was created in 1938 to regulate air transportation, Patterson welcomed it as a means of providing for greater airline efficiency and stability. He has not always welcomed the decisions of the Board, however. One such occasion arose when the Board, in line with its policy of favoring the smaller companies, awarded to Western Air Lines the Los Angeles-Denver route which United had coveted. Patterson maintained that such a move was not in the public interest because it would mean that passengers would need to leave their berths to change planes in the middle of the night—a charge which the Board countered by suggesting that crews be changed at such points.

When war came, the air lines continued civilian service while supplying planes and trained personnel and contributing their knowledge of air operations to the country's war effort. Under contract to the Air Transport Command, United flew men, munitions, food, doctors, nurses, blood plasma, and medical supplies to strategic points. Aviation officials saw a postwar air age, but Patterson's outlook was a conservative one. In addresses and magazine articles, he discussed the obstacles which would be encountered in the proposed expansion of freight transportation during peacetime, pointing out that while the cost element had been

United Air Lines

W. A. PATTERSON

secondary during the war emergency, it could not be discounted for ordinary operations. According to Patterson's calculations, it would take fifty-seven airplanes to do the job of one freight train and cost thirty-five times as much. Patterson was nevertheless optimistic about the future of the airways, and in 1946, with fifty four-engined Douglas planes, thirty-five twin-engined Martin 303's and seven 340-mile-per hour Boeing Stratocruisers already on order, he announced that United would spend about eighty-two million dollars on expansion. He believed that air lines would offer increasing competition to surface lines in carrying passengers and the types of cargo where the element of "business time" involved in delivery is more important than the cost of transportation. (According to figures released by the Air Transportation Association, passenger traffic for April 1946 was nearly double that of April 1945. After the first half of 1946, however, reported *Business Week*, the demand for flight reservations declined. The air transportation companies will be losing money by the summer of 1947, predicted Patterson, also suggesting that fares might have to be raised in order to meet increased operating costs.)

While his colleagues argued for free competition in the international field, Patterson was the only head of a domestic air line who, along with Juan Trippe [42] of Pan American Airways, advocated a "chosen instrument" policy. He believed that, for the United States to hold its own in competition with the Government-controlled air lines of other countries, it must present a united air front in which the "experience, ingenuity, and technological skills" of all American air lines would be pooled. One or more chosen companies backed by the resources of all the others should handle United States overseas flying operations; otherwise, he stated, chaos would result and private enterprise

PATTERSON, W. A.—*Continued*

would have to yield to Government control. Other air line heads looked with disfavor on such a monopoly. The Civilian Aeronautics Board policy has represented a compromise viewpoint, granting three companies Atlantic licenses for a seven-year test period. Although United has a controlling interest in the LAMSA air line in Mexico (Lineas Aeras Mexicanas) and has acquired a new route to Hawaii, it has been Patterson's policy to keep his company out of foreign operations. Economic studies have led him to the conclusion that there may be too many United States and foreign air lines competing for the relatively narrow market in transoceanic operations.

A grant by Patterson and his board of directors made possible a study on the social effects of aviation in America, which William F. Ogburn, professor of sociology at the University of Chicago, completed in 1946. The air line president is on the boards of the Chicago Association of Commerce, the Insurance Company of North America, the Chicago City National Bank and Trust Company, and the Stewart Warner Corporation. He is a director at large of the chambers of commerce of the United States and of Illinois, a trustee of Northwestern University, and of the Committee for Economic Development, and a member of the Advisory Board of the Institute of Aeronautical Sciences. A Mason, he belongs to the Chicago, Economic, Union League, Tavern, and Commercial clubs in Chicago, the Bohemian Club of San Francisco, and the Philadelphia branch of the Newcomen Society of England. Fond of golf, horseback riding, and fishing, he is a member of the Glen View golf club. In 1924 William Patterson was married to Vera A. Witt of Berkeley, California; they have two children, Patricia Ann and William Allan. "Quiet and slight of stature . . . youthful, energetic, and dynamic," is *Time*'s description of the air line executive.

References

Liberty 23:11+ S 28 '46
National Cyclopædia of American Biography Current vol E p300
Who's Who in America, 1946-47

PATTON, GEORGE S(MITH), JR. Nov. 11, 1885—Dec. 21, 1945 General of the United States Army; tank expert; one of the most colorful, brilliant, and most controversial military men of World War II; holder of D.S.C., D.S.M., from World War I; also Silver Star, Purple Heart, Congressional Medal of Honor; known as "Old Blood and Guts." See *Current Biography* 1943 Yearbook.

Obituary

N Y Times p1+ D 22 '45 por

PAULI, WOLFGANG (pou'lē vôlf'gäng) Apr. 25, 1900- Physicist

Address: b. Physikgebäude, Eidigenössische Technische Hochschule, Gloriastr. 35, Zürich, Switzerland

Late in 1945 the Swedish Academy of Sciences announced that it had awarded the year's Nobel Prize in physics to Wolfgang Pauli, professor of theoretical physics at the Eidgenössische Technische Hochschule in Zürich, Switzerland, and from 1940 to 1946 a member of the guest faculty of the Institute for Advanced Study in Princeton, New Jersey. His discovery of the exclusion principle, which bears his name, marked a fundamental advance in the history of atomic physics.

Born on April 25, 1900, in Vienna, Austria, Wolfgang Pauli is the son of Wolfgang Joseph Pauli, a physician who later became professor of biochemistry at the University of Vienna. His mother was Bertha (Schütz) Pauli. (Hertha Pauli, the author and former actress, is his younger sister.) His formal education Pauli received in the Viennese schools. At the same time, he was introduced to the world of science by his father who often, the scientist says, would discuss questions of physics with him. Then, not yet twenty years of age, he enrolled at the University of Munich, from which he received his Ph.D. in 1921, and where his scientific career must be said to have begun.

Pauli's mentor at this time was Arnold Sommerfeld; his tangible work largely in the sphere of relativity theory. Among the first papers he published were several dealing with a unified field theory of gravitation and electromagnetism advanced by Hermann Weyl in 1918. This theory, Weyl has recorded, "in truly Paulinean fashion . . . he dealt . . . a pernicious blow." And the measure of the young physicist's progress up to this time, Weyl has pointed out, can be taken from his article on relativity theory for the *Mathematical Encyclopaedia*. Written while Pauli was still a student at Munich, it is, Weyl says, "a mature and masterly work which shows the author in full command of both the mathematical and physical aspects of the subject."

The history of his discovery of the exclusion principle, Pauli has stated, must also be traced to his student days at the University of Munich. Whereas in Vienna he had received his preliminary training in classical physics and had also, it is true, come into initial contact with the then new Einstein [41] relativity theory, first presented in complete form in 1916, it was at Munich that he was introduced by Sommerfeld to atomic physics and the revolutionary quantum theory of the atom postulated by Niels Bohr [45]. At this time, Pauli says, two approaches to the problems inherent in the new ideas were being explored. On the one hand, Bohr was working toward the generalization which would reconcile the differences between the laws of quantum theory, applicable to atomic structure, and classical physics, applicable only to larger phenomena, now known as his Correspondence Principle. On the other, Sommerfeld was attempting to surmount the difficulties caused by the inapplicability of the latter by a direct interpretation of atomic phenomena in terms of integral numbers. "Both methods," Pauli has said, "which did not appear to me irreconcilable, influenced me."

Leaving Munich in 1921 Pauli went as an assistant in theoretical physics to the University of Göttingen, long famous as a center for mathematical and physical research, where Max Born and James Franck were teaching at the time and Bohr came in 1922 to deliver a series of guest lectures. Here it was that Pauli first came into personal contact with Bohr and that a new direction was given to his scientific thinking by Bohr's reports on his theoretical investigations in the periodic system of the elements. It made a strong impression on him, Pauli says, that Bohr was seeking a general explanation for the observed fact, inexplicable according to classical mechanics, that all the electrons in an atom in its ground state are not bound in the shell closest to the nucleus but are distributed in definite groups throughout the other shells of the atom's structure.

Later in 1922 Pauli went to Copenhagen to become Bohr's assistant in the editing of the Danish physicist's works for German publication. He was much surprised when the offer was made, Pauli says, but "after considering a little while I answered with that certainty of which only a young man is capable: 'I hardly think that the scientific demands which you will make on me will cause me any difficulty, but the learning of a foreign tongue like Danish far exceeds my abilities.'" As a matter of fact, he admits, the opposite proved to be true: he found that it was far easier for him, for instance, to understand the complicated system of half-multiples of 20 used to express such numerals as 50, 70, and 90 in Danish than to understand the half-integers employed as magnetic quantum numbers in Alfred Landé's explanation of the spectral phenomenon designated by physicists as the anomalous Zeeman effect.

As early as 1896 the Dutch physicist Pieter Zeeman had discovered that the application of a strong magnetic field to an atom emitting a line spectrum caused each spectrum line in its path to split. Normally, the splitting was into three lines, the result being called a triplet. But this was not always so, and while, says Pauli, "the anomalous type of splitting was on the one hand especially fruitful because its exhibited beautiful and simple laws, . . . on the other hand it was hardly understandable, since very general assumptions concerning the electron, using classical theory as well as quantum theory, always led to the simple triplet." Although by early 1923 he had succeeded in generalizing some of Landé's analyses, a matter "of decisive importance for the finding of the exclusion principle," Pauli says, the problem was still bothering him later that year when, upon Bohr's departure for the United States, he went to the University of Hamburg, first as an assistant in theoretical physics, and shortly thereafter as *Privatdozent,* or assistant professor.

His inaugural lecture as *Privatdozent* was given on the periodic system of the elements, but was, Pauli felt, highly unsatisfactory because neither the anomalous Zeeman effect nor the problem of the "closing" of the electron shells of the atom which had been troubling Bohr was thereby brought any nearer to solution. "The only thing that was clear," he says, "was that a closer relation of this problem to

WOLFGANG PAULI

the theory of multiplet structure must exist." Consequently, during the next few months he began a re-examination of the simplest case of anomalous splitting, finally arriving at the conclusion that the orthodox explanation of this case was incorrect. Early in 1925 the *Zeitschrift für Physik* published his argument that a new quantum theoretic property of the electron, which he called "a two-valuedness not describable classically," was indispensable to a full understanding of the problem. This, Weyl has noted, for the first time brought the characterization of the "state" of an electron according to quantum theory into conformity with observed fact; and later, when Goudsmit and Uhlenbeck identified this fourth quantum number with an angular momentum of the electron, it was again Pauli who accurately described the nature of this spin, which differs radically from that of a top as familiar to classical mechanics.

From this point it was only a short step to the exclusion principle, which Weyl has called "decisive for an understanding of the periodic system of the elements" and "a lasting achievement, which will hardly be affected by any future changes of our physical theories." A paper by the English physicist Edmund Clifton Stoner gave him the final clue, Pauli relates, and his general formulation of the exclusion principle was made in the spring of 1925 and published in the *Zeitschrift für Physik* soon afterwards. In layman's language it states simply that no two electrons can be in the same quantum state. "A free electron," explains J. A. Eldridge in *The Physical Basis of Things,* "has its state specified by its three momentum and position coordinates and its positive or negative spin. Two free electrons, similarly spinning, very close together in a gas must necessarily differ considerably in speed, enough to put them into different quantum states. We have been too spacially minded. We have seen that two particles could not oc-

PAULI, WOLFGANG—*Continued*

cupy exactly the same position. Before Pauli's time it was not recognized that two similarly charged particles could not have exactly the same velocity."

Pauli remained in Hamburg until 1928, when he became professor of theoretical physics at the Eidgenössische Technische Hochschule (or Federal Institute of Technology) in Zürich, Switzerland. With the exception of the year 1935-36, which he spent as visiting professor of theoretical physics at the Institute for Advanced Study in Princeton, New Jersey, Zürich remained his home for the next twelve years. In early 1940, however, when the invasion of Norway and Denmark stirred fears for the safety of other European neutrals, the Institute for Advanced Study began negotiations to bring both Bohr and Pauli to the United States. Unlike Bohr, who considered it his patriotic duty to remain in his native Denmark, Pauli accepted the invitation to join the institute's faculty as a temporary member. He did not return to Zürich until some time after the end of the war, in early 1946.

Among the Nobel Prize winner's accomplishments since 1925 have been the explanation of the paramagnetic properties of degenerate gases, a paper on the paramagnetism of metals which provided the groundwork for the quantum mechanical theory of electrons in metals; an investigation undertaken with Werner Heisenberg which raised wave mechanics from a theory dealing with a single particle to one dealing with the interaction of an indefinite number of particles, an explanation of the meson or mesotron, and the discovery of the neutrino, sometimes called Paulino. "Lately," reported *Time* in November 1945, "he has been working on the 'binding force,' the powerful short-range attraction which holds the nucleus of an atom together."

Pauli believes in "pure and free research irrespective of applications." At the dinner tendered in his honor by the Institute for Advanced Study on December 10, 1945, he concluded his address: "The essential advance of physics rests on the creative imagination of the experimental as well as the theoretical investigator, and, contrary to expensive applications of known principles, cannot be forced by planning on a grand scale. Therefore it is not possible to say beforehand where and when one can expect the further development of the basic principles of present-day physics. . . .We know, however, that this further development can take place only in the same atmosphere of free investigation and unhampered exchange of scientific results between nations that existed at the time of the disclosure of the exclusion principle."

Pauli is a member of the American Association for the Advancement of Science, of the American Physical Society, and of the Swiss Physical Society. Prior to the award of the Nobel Prize in physics for 1945, he received a Lorentz Medaille. Short and stocky, with brown eyes and black hair, he was married to Franciska Bertram in April 1934. He is a keen student of philosophy, especially of the Chinese sages.

References

N Y Times p21 N 16 '45 por
Sci N L 48:341 D 1 '45
Science 103:213-18 F 22 '46
American Men of Science (1944)
Who's Who in America, 1946-47

PAWLEY, EDWARD (JOEL) Mar. 16, 1901- Actor
Address: b. Columbia Broadcasting System, 485 Madison Ave., New York; h. Sickelton Rd., West Nyack, N.Y.

The role of Steve Wilson in *Big Town,* the weekly radio feature which by 1946 had held a prominent evening spot on CBS for nine years, has been played by Edward Pawley since 1942. The casting of Pawley, said one critic, is "a happy choice. He not only acts the role convincingly but in real life is physically and apparently temperamentally suited to the part." Beginning as a repertory actor in a canvas-top theater, Pawley progressed through small parts in road companies to romantic leads and stardom on Broadway. Then, following ten years in Hollywood, he returned to the stage and, three years ago, took over the lead in *Big Town,* played originally by Edward G. Robinson.

The first Pawley to come to America was the son of an English earl, who believed in the cause of the American Revolution, left England, and joined General Francis Marion's armies in the Carolina swamps. The actor's father, Howell Jether Pawley, migrated from Kentucky to Missouri when he was sixteen and eventually found himself driving cattle from Westport Landing (later Kansas City) over the old Santa Fé Trail. In his maturer years, Pawley became one of the leading citizens of Kansas City, a founder of its Board of Trade. Ed Pawley, born in Kansas City on March 16, 1901, is one of the Kansas pioneer's "second batch," as Howell Pawley called the children of his second marriage, to Nellie Elizabeth Crane, of Welsh and Irish extraction.

Thomas Lipton Pawley of the "first batch" had a great influence on young Ed. Several of the Pawley brothers are actors; and Thomas owned, directed, and acted in a repertory theater which traveled under canvas through Kansas, Colorado, and other Western states. Further inspiration for Ed's chosen career came from watching the performances of Lester Longeran's Kansas City stock company. "Longeran was one of the most gifted men in the American theater at that time," says Pawley. (Longeran later directed John Drinkwater's *Abraham Lincoln* [1918] and won distinction in the role of the venerable Chinese, Lo Sank Kee, in the Broadway hit, *East is West,* 1918.) After graduation from Manual Arts High School in Kansas City, where he had studied dramatics under Herbert L. Drake, young Ed was permitted to join his half-brother's tent-show theatrical company. "We played former Broadway hits—*Alias Jimmy Valentine, Forty-Five Minutes from Broadway,* and, of course, some of the old melodramas like *East Lynne* and *Way Down East.*" Playing under canvas in

Kansas was sometimes an adventuresome experience, says the actor. "When a cyclone came up during a performance every actor in the cast was called upon to 'man the ship.' Between snorters we resumed our roles to the accompaniment of the rain on our canvas top—and rain on canvas can never be described as a gentle patter." All of which, someone has said, may have helped develop those resonant tones in the Pawley voice.

It was Lester Longeran who gave Pawley his first role under Broadway management—the romantic lead in a road show of *East is West*. His success on the road won him a role in the New York production of Lula Vollmer's *Shame Woman* (1923). This play of North Carolina mountaineers achieved a run of 278 performances on Broadway and established Pawley as "one of the most promising juveniles in the theater." By 1928 he had become a leading man. His portrayal of Elmer Gantry in Patrick Kearney's dramatization of the famous novel by Sinclair Lewis was unanimously acclaimed by Broadway critics, despite the fact that the play was considered a caricature of the novel and ran for only six weeks. "He has the stature and personal appearance," wrote Stephen Rathbun of Pawley in the New York *Sun*, "that help to make an ideal characterization of the evangelist." The stage critic, Percy Hammond (New York *Herald Tribune*), after delivering an indictment of the production, said that Pawley had given a "thoughtful and imaginative interpretation" to the difficult role. "One touch of veracity in the whole production," announced the New York *World*, "was Pawley's performance," while *Theatre Arts Monthly* summed up his acting as "vigorous, impassioned, capable."

Stardom came to Pawley in the play *Two Seconds*, after he had won further praise and a year's run in the role of Whitney Borden in the mystery novelty *Subway Express* (1929). In *Two Seconds* (1931), a grim story of a young man who had committed murder during a drunken moment, the play opened with Pawley seated in an electric chair. During the two seconds elapsing between the time he has been strapped in and his execution, the condemned man mentally reviews those events which have brought him to the chair. Again the actor won applause from the press, while the play was condemned. Playing opposite Pauline Lord in Dan Totheroh's *Distant Drums* (1932), a tale of pioneers traveling over the Oregon Trail in 1848, Pawley again scored an artistic success. The play, cast and directed by Guthrie McClintic, was considered poignant drama with a poetic quality. Burns Mantle listed it among the interesting failures—a victim of the depression.

When Pawley left the stage for motion pictures, one stage commentator lamented, "The theater has lost one of its most talented young stars—a Maurice Barrymore both in romantic appearance and the colorful quality of his superb acting." Outstanding among the thirty-three action films Pawley made in Hollywood between 1932 and 1942 are *Treasure Island* (1935), *Tom Sawyer, Detective* (1938), *Each Dawn I Die* (1939), and *G-Men*, in which he

EDWARD PAWLEY

will be remembered as the actor who impersonated Dillinger. Pawley's favorite motion picture role is that of the father of Mickey Rooney in *The Hoosier School Boy* (1937), produced as a "B" picture by Columbia. The father is a shell-shocked soldier who fails to make the readjustment to civilian life, becomes the town "bum," but finally redeems himself at the cost of his life. "That deathbed reconciliation," said Pawley, "is the finest piece of work Rooney ever has done."

Returning to Broadway in John Patrick's *The Willow and I* (1942), Pawley again found himself in a play which failed despite the fact that the critics agreed that the cast (Martha Scott, Barbara O'Neil, and Gregory Peck) was "faultless" and the acting "extraordinary." Upon the closing of the play Pawley remained in the East to free-lance in radio. On the Pacific Coast he had substituted on several occasions for Edward G. Robinson in the Steve Wilson role. When Robinson withdrew from *Big Town*, Jerry McGill, writer and director of the program, sent for Pawley. That evening, Pawley and McGill, meeting by chance on a commuter's train, discovered that they were not only neighbors in Nyack, New York, but also that McGill and Pawley's wife were cousins. Edward Pawley in 1937 had married Helen Shipman, the well-known star of *Irene* and other musical hits.

McGill, who has been a newspaper reporter and syndicate writer, has, since he started the program in 1937, "striven to faithfully portray the vigilance of newspaper men in detecting graft, corruption, demagogy, and intolerance." For this reason, says Pawley, "my work in *Big Town* has interested me as much as anything I've ever done. Aside from supplying entertainment, we feel we are doing a satisfactory job in rousing the public conscience to its civic needs." The slogan of Steve Wilson's newspaper is, "The freedom of the press is a flam-

PAWLEY, EDWARD—*Continued*

ing sword. Use it justly. Hold it high. Guard it well." Proof that this sentiment is appreciated by young Americans, says Pawley, "are the many requests we receive from young editors to use it as a masthead on high school newspapers." *Big Town* is heard every Tuesday evening at eight, over the CBS national hookup. Sponsored by the makers of Ironized Yeast and Phillips' Milk of Magnesia, the program is regarded as among the more intelligent of radio serial features. *Variety* reports its weekly production cost as $2,500.

The Pawleys have a fifty-nine-acre farm in West Nyack with a two-hundred-year-old farmhouse. Experimental farming and collecting early American furniture are the actor's hobbies. Pawley is one inch short of six feet in height, and weighs 175 pounds; his hair is black, and his eyes are an intense blue. One writer has summed up his personality in the phrase, "a two-fisted idealist."

References

Film Daily Directory (1944)
International Motion Picture Almanac, 1943-44

PEALE, NORMAN VINCENT, REV.
(pēl) May 31, 1898- Clergyman
Address: b. Marble Collegiate Church, 1 W. 29th St., New York; h. 40 Fifth Ave., New York

The pastor of Marble Collegiate Church in New York, the Reverend Norman Vincent Peale, is "possibly the most highly publicized of metropolitan ministers." Occupying an important position in national church leadership, Dr. Peale is well known to the general public as well through his radio lectures, *Art of Living*, which have been heard on a national network for a decade. In the psychiatric clinic

Fabian Bachrach
REV. NORMAN VINCENT PEALE

which is held daily in his study, aided by a psychiatrist, he ministers to the spiritual needs of the troubled. The pastor is also interested in public affairs and is active in secular as well as clerical organizations.

The son of a pastor, Norman Vincent Peale was born to the Reverend Charles Clifford and Anna (DeLaney) Peale on May 31, 1898, in Bowersville, Ohio. While a student at the Bellefontaine (Ohio) High School in 1916, the youth worked in the town grocery store after classes and rode to church in "the surrey with the fringe on top." He attended Ohio Wesleyan University, earning his B.A. by 1920, and two years later he was ordained in the ministry of the Methodist Episcopal Church. But before he entered the ministry Peale was a reporter on the *Morning Republican* in Findlay, Ohio, and later on the Detroit *Journal*. He first took up the duties of his clerical calling in Berkeley, Rhode Island, at the same time continuing his theological studies at Boston University. Here he won his S.T.B. and M.A. in 1924. That year he became minister of the Kings Highway Methodist Episcopal Church in Brooklyn, New York, where during his three-year pastorate the congregation increased from forty to nine hundred. Peale next assumed the ministerial duties at the University Methodist Episcopal Church in Syracuse, New York, where he filled the pulpit until 1932. A year before he left, Syracuse University awarded him a D.D. degree. (He later received this degree from Ohio Wesleyan in 1936, and Duke University in 1938.)

In 1932 when the Reverend Dr. Peale delivered a guest sermon at Marble Collegiate Church in New York he was invited to take over the dwindling congregation. His acceptance gave him the leadership of the oldest chartered church in New York (1696), located in the heart of the metropolis, in the shadow of the Empire State Building. Peale has contributed much to its distinguished reputation in the years of his pastorate. Marble Collegiate, "where old-fashioned friendliness still survives," now attracts capacity audiences. (Only 30 percent of its members live permanently within a mile of the church.) In addition, it maintains a mailing list of more than four thousand persons to whom copies of the minister's "down-to-earth" sermons are sent. Dr. Peale's daily psychiatric clinic "clinches the nail he drives in with his sermon on Sunday." In cooperation with Dr. Smiley Blanton, a New York psychiatrist, he serves as consultant for the ill or troubled, each man handling the particular cases which fall within his province. Dr. Peale considers that Christian faith, in functioning as a science, operates with the science of psychiatry to aid the distressed.

The clergyman considers the church a laboratory where people may find "relief from tension." "The best cure for high blood pressure and high-strung emotional reactions," he says, "is to worship in the quietness and peace of a church, cathedral, or synagogue." In a sermon in May 1941 the minister warned of the Fifth Column of "materialism, paganism, lust, sin, and selfishness," and declared, "This country almost falters and fails now because of the desecration of its religious life." In 1945, deploring the rise of immorality, he warned that "failure to inculcate Christian morals is to imply their lack of importance. It serves to remove spiritual resistance to the pagan codes that threaten the moral life of our people."

Dr. Peale's book *The Art of Living* (1937) is a collection of short essays on the Christian way of life. According to the *Churchman*, "the book appeals for the serenity of life, with winsome and telling illustrations to back up the author's own hortatory text." *You Can Win* (1939) is a group of essays on successful living based on a vital personal relationship with God, the author's key to a happy life. To the critic for the Springfield *Republican*, "Dr. Peale's words are religious without being didactic, and full of soundly based hope, without being Pollyanna-like." With Dr. Blanton, Dr. Peale wrote *Faith Is the Answer* (1941) which, in the opinion of the *Churchman*'s reviewer, was "the very best of all the recent books which attempt to bring psychiatry and religion together in meeting human problems." A victory message, "Faith for Today," which appeared in the October 1945 issue of *Woman's Home Companion*, was contributed by Dr. Peale. In it he emphasized the need for a religious revival in America to satisfy "a widespread hunger for a deeper spiritual life." The churchman's name has appeared in other periodicals: he is contributing editor of *Religious Digest* and has selected the best religious books of the year for the "Lenten Book List," an annual feature in *Publishers' Weekly*. He is the editor of Guideposts Associates, Inc., which issues "personal spiritual letters" contributed by prominent clergymen and laymen.

Like many present-day pastors, Peale has frequently dealt with public affairs in his addresses. He has hailed the United Nations Charter, warned against totalitarianism either of the Right or Left, and condemned the pessimistic attitude toward the atomic bomb. His views on President Roosevelt[42], labor, and communism, and his affiliation with several secular bodies, have drawn forth sharp criticism from some quarters. Frank E. Gannett's[45] Committee for Constitutional Government, of which Peale was once acting chairman, has been described by its opponents as one of the strongest anti-Administration lobbies in the country.

In 1941 a group of Protestant clergymen chose Dr. Peale to act as technical adviser for the Warner Brothers[45] film *One Foot in Heaven*, which starred Fredric March[43] in the life story of a minister. While in Hollywood for the entire filming of the picture, Peale took the opportunity to visit churches on the West Coast. (He has also traveled extensively in other parts of America and in Europe).

A popular speaker, Dr. Peale is reported to combine "a great sense of humor, unusual dramatic ability, and a down-to-earth, business-like approach with a spiritual fervor which makes him particularly effective with an audience." Among the many organizations which he has addressed are the Rotary Club of New York, of which he is a member, the Advertising Club of New York, and the Sales Executives Club of that city, which described the speaker as "America's most sales-minded clergyman." Under the auspices of the Greater New York Federation of Churches, since 1940 Dr. Peale and Dr. John Sutherland Bonnell[45] have conducted during Lent, a weekly series of noon lectures, entitled in 1945 "Inner Strength for Wartime Living." His radio talks on NBC's *Art of Living* program have treated such topics as "Life Can Be Magnificent," and "How To Face the Loss of Loved Ones." Affiliated with several church organizations, the minister is a member of various commissions of the Federal Council of Churches of Christ in America and is vice-president of the International Society of Christian Endeavor. Dr. Peale is a Mason and belongs to the Ohio Society of New York, Quill, the Union League, and National Republican clubs. His fraternities are Alpha Delta, Chi Alpha, and Phi Gamma Delta.

The minister's wife is the former Ruth Stafford, to whom he was married on June 20, 1930. The Peale children are Margaret Ann, John Stafford, and Elizabeth Ruth. (In 1942 Mrs. Peale became the first woman to head the Home Missions Council of North America.) Dr. Peale, whose favorite recreation is golf, has been described by one interviewer as a "crisply genial man. . .a decidedly urban type of cleric, handsome and impressive."

References

N Y Sun p13 D 22 '42
New Yorker 17:15 O 25 '41

America's Young Men, 1938-39
Religious Leaders of America, 1941-42
Who's Who in America, 1946-47
Who's Who in New York, 1938

PELLEY, JOHN J(EREMIAH) May 1, 1878—Nov. 12, 1946 President of the Association of American Railroads from 1934 until his death; mobilized the nation's railways for war, receiving the Medal for Merit in March 1946, and citations from the War, Navy, and Treasury Departments; former president of the New York, New Haven and Hartford Railroad.

Obituary

N Y Times p28 N 13 '46 por

PERRY, ANTOINETTE June 27, 1888—June 28, 1946 Actress, director, producer; made debut as Dorothy in *Mrs. Temple's Telegram* (1905); among other roles played the daughter in *The Music Master* with David Warfield (1906); married Frank W. Frueauff in 1909, and two years after his death in 1924 resumed her career; in a succession of plays, mostly under Brock Pemberton's management; directed *Strictly Dishonorable* (1929), *Personal Appearance* (1934), *Janie* (1942), *Harvey* (1944), and many other hit plays; leader in American Theatre Wing and other welfare organizations.

Obituary

N Y Times p19 Je 29 '46 por

PETHICK-LAWRENCE (FREDERICK WILLIAM PETHICK-LAWRENCE, 1st) BARON Dec. 28, 1871- British Government official

Address: b. 11 Old Square, Lincoln's Inn, London; h. Fourways, Rad Lane, Gomshall, Surrey

The man largely responsible for the proposals in Britain's widely praised May 1946 White Paper on Indian independence is Lord Frederick William Pethick-Lawrence, Secretary of State for India in Prime Minister Attlee's [40] Cabinet. Seventy-four years old when assigned the difficult Indian question, Pethick-Lawrence has had a long career as crusader, first in the fight for women's suffrage in England in the 1900's, and then for many years as a Labor Party member of Parliament. He has stated his credo at the end of his autobiography *Fate Has Been Kind*, which was published in 1943: "I venture to assert that, unless an individual can transcend the limits of sex, class, age and creed, his personality remains of necessity to that extent incomplete."

Frederick William Lawrence, the son of Alfred Lawrence, became Pethick-Lawrence at his marriage in 1901: he added his wife's name to his own to indicate that they were to be equal. His grandfather William Lawrence was a Cornish carpenter from Plymouth who founded a successful firm of contractors in London, two of his uncles were Lord Mayors of London, and others in his family were members of the House of Commons. Frederick William was born December 28, 1871. Because Alfred Lawrence died in his son's infancy, an uncle "of notable mind and character" directed the child's care in a cultured home environment. "This uncle," the British author Mary Agnes Hamilton tells, "was, like all his clan, an ardent Unitarian; he may have developed the boy's conscience to excess; but he saw to it that he had an excellent schooling. Moreover, he had ample means, and his nephew, while remaining simple to austerity in his personal tastes, has always had enough money to travel widely, to map his course as he chose."

Although an Etonian (one of the two in Prime Minister Attlee's Labor Cabinet), Pethick-Lawrence is "by no means a typical product" of the famous public school. A hard worker by nature, in a school which in the 1880's was "inhospitable to work," he considered Eton "mainly absurd," and was something of a misfit there. He came into his own, however, at Trinity College, Cambridge, where he made many close friends, played tennis, billiards and football, and became president of the Union Debating Society. His academic work gained him a "double first" (first class honors in mathematics in 1894, and in natural science in 1895), and the Adam Smith prize in economics for a paper on local variations in wages. On the basis of the economics paper, he was made a Fellow of Trinity in 1897. After Cambridge he traveled for a year in India, the Far East, Australia, and the United States, and then came back to London to read law. Interested in social reform from the beginning, he went to live in London's East End, became the treasurer of Mansfield House, a nonconformist settlement house in Canning Town, and as a young barrister took the cases of the poor.

At the settlement house Lawrence met an evangelist "Sister," Emmeline Pethick, the belle of an exclusive social circle who had offered her services to the West London Mission. According to Miss Hamilton, "When he fell in love with her—on sight—he was a Conservative. An impassioned social reformer, she told him this was an insuperable bar. Her stand and the Boer War [his sympathy was with the Boers] . . . awoke all his deep latent idealism and swept inherited prepossessions aside; it was not long before he was in the Labor Party." The two were married in 1901 in a public hall; the guests included David Lloyd George, and fifty workhouse women, who were friends of the bride's. He was now swept "heart and soul" into the movement for women's suffrage. The Pethick-Lawrences became the "hero and heroine" of the suffragettes.

At the time Lawrence was married he owned a controlling interest in *The Echo*, a pioneer halfpenny evening paper in London. He edited the paper from 1902 to 1905, and when it failed paid staff and creditors out of his own pocket. From 1905 to 1907 he was editor of the *Labour Record and Review*. Meanwhile, the suffragettes were becoming increasingly militant. In 1905 Mrs. Emmeline Pankhurst organized the Women's Social and Political Union, with Pethick-Lawrence as the union's financial guarantor. From 1907 to 1914 he owned and jointly with his wife edited the weekly *Votes For Women*. The offices of the paper were a headquarters of "insurgent women," who smashed post-office windows, chained themselves to iron fence palings, went on hunger strikes in England's jails, and otherwise caused "disturbances," in a campaign for suffrage which lasted until the outbreak of World I. Pethick-Lawrence stood bail for at least a thousand women. Both he and his wife were sentenced to prison in 1912, and endured forcible feeding, the Government's method of dealing with hunger-strikers. When the Prime Minister "capitulated," Pethick-Lawrence's nine-month sentence was cut to one month, his wife was released, and forcible feeding was abolished. "From beginning to end," reported the London *Observer*, "he displayed a fidelity to principle, a quiet and unfailing courage, which have ensured for him an honored place in the annals of women's enfranchisement."

When World War I broke out Pethick-Lawrence was forty-two, "again a rebel, though, as usual, a constructive one," writes Miss Hamilton—he was Treasurer of the Union of Democratic Control, which was pledged to fight for "open covenants openly arrived at." In 1917, standing for Parliament as a "peace-by-negotiation" candidate in South Aberdeen, he received only a few votes, but made numerous loyal friends. He was an unsuccessful Labor candidate in 1918 and in 1922. Then, in 1923, defeating Winston Churchill, who was making his last stand as a Liberal, Pethick-Lawrence entered Parliament as the Labor member for West Leicester, the seat he held until the Labor crash in 1931. One of the few Labor members who could handle questions of finance and currency, he was Financial Secretary to the Treasury in the 1929-31 Government. In 1931 he was not re-elected, but East Edinburgh returned him to Parliament four years later, in 1935. The post of leader of the Labor Party in the House was his from 1940 until 1942, when he yielded it to Arthur Greenwood (who had at that time ceased to hold office in the national Government), and himself became vice-chairman of the party. In August 1945 Prime Minister Attlee, in choosing nineteen ministers from among the most experienced men in the Labor Party, named him Secretary of State for India. The seventy-three-year-old Secretary the same day was created a Baron to sit in the House of Lords.

The new Secretary's interest in India had begun several decades earlier. In 1926 Pethick-Lawrence, in India with his wife on a "silver honeymoon," was permitted to attend the Indian National Congress; he talked with Indian leaders of all factions, renewed old associations, and made new ones. "These relationships were kept open," Miss Hamilton reports. "Indians coming to London were always made welcome at the Pethick-Lawrences'." Returning to London after the 1926 tour, he advised a "clear declaration of principle and aim," and the calling of a Round Table Conference. In 1931 he was a member of the second Indian Round Table Conference.

In early 1946 a special mission of three senior Cabinet members (Secretary of State for India Lord Pethick-Lawrence, First Lord of the Admiralty A. V. Alexander '40, and president of the Board of Trade Sir Stafford Cripps '41) left for India intending, in the words of Attlee, to use "their utmost endeavors to help India to obtain freedom as fully and speedily as possible." The mission had sufficient power to negotiate an agreement with Indian leaders. Leaving England "without any specific proposal or plan," Lord Pethick-Lawrence "refused to envisage failure." For six weeks the mission attempted to bring to agreement on a constitution the leaders of India's two strongest groups, the Hindus and the Moslems, but were not successful. Determined to "push through a solution," they prepared a White Paper which proposed a Federated Union of India, with complete independence or dominion status. Its constitution would include provisions to safeguard the interests of the Moslems, but the Moslem League's demand for a separate Moslem state (Pakistan) in India was rejected. This White Paper was adopted as the official Labor Government policy on India, Attlee reading the proposals in the House of Commons on May 16, 1946.

World reaction to the plan was favorable, with praise for the British Government for presenting "not a weasel-worded promise nor a string-tied offer, but a concrete plan—for the government of an independent, unified India." Indian leader Gandhi considered the plan "the best document the British Government could have produced in the circumstances" and advised his countrymen to accept it. But from Winston Churchill, leader of the opposition in Parliament, came the comment that the paper was "an

LORD PETHICK-LAWRENCE

able but melancholy document"; that the "sincerity" and "zeal" of the ministers "would be natural were it to gain an empire, not to cast it away." Indian leaders began discussing the proposals. Meanwhile, Pethick-Lawrence told reporters: "What will happen if one person . . . or groups of people in some way tried to put spanners [monkey wrenches] in the wheels, I am not prepared at this stage precisely to say; but the intention is to get on with the job." On June 5 came the announcement that the Moslem League Council had accepted the British proposals, and on June 25, 1946, although it had rejected the British plan for an interim government, the Working Committee of the All-India Congress Party accepted the long-range plan. This agreement by both the major Indian parties was considered a "triumph of British statesmanship" by newspaper commentators. On July 29 the Moslem League reconsidered its decision, and, objecting to the way the Congress Party interpreted the proposals, rejected the British plan.

In Parliament it was held that the main task of the mission—the task of removing doubts in Indian thought of Britain's sincerity in wishing for a free India at the earliest possible moment — had been successful. Indian independence was not yet in sight, however, as religious and political factions continued to disagree over how the proposed new Government was to be constituted. After four days of conferences in London, the Hindus and the Moslems reached no agreement and the Constituent Assembly began in India without the Moslems, although the British Government stated that no constitution would be "forced" on any part of India unless both sides approved it. In the House of Lords, Pethick-Lawrence announced that the Constitution must follow the basic form recommended by the Cabinet mission, unless a departure "is agreed upon with the

PETHICK-LAWRENCE, BARON—*Cont.*

approval of the representatives of each major party."

In his early career as editor and crusador, as well as in his later years with the Government, Pethick-Lawrence wrote and published articles, pamphlets, and books on mathematics, free trade, women's suffrage, finance and economics. His early writings include: *Women's Fight For the Vote, The Man's Share, A Levy on Capital, Why Prices Rise and Fall, Unemployment, The National Debt,* and *The Heart of the Empire.* His book *This Gold Crisis* appeared in 1931. He also wrote the finance chapter for *Twelve Studies in U.S.S.R.* (1932), and *The Money Muddle and the Way Out* (1933).

The elderly British peer and statesman, called Pethick by his friends, has been described by Miss Hamilton: "Though he is very thin, and rather dried, and what little hair remains on his high domed head is, like his bristling eyebrows, absolutely white, his dark eyes are as bright as ever; he still plays a good game of tennis, walks tirelessly, with a curiously short, springy step, and plays almost as good a game of billiards as when he used to encounter professionals on their own ground."

References

Cur Lit 53:162-4 Ag '12 por
Who's Who, 1946

PETRY, ANN (pē'trĭ) Oct. 12, 1911- Author

Address: h. 2816 Bronx Park East, New York

With a "powerful" first novel about a Harlem mother trapped in a life of violence and frustration, Ann Petry, Negro newspaperwoman, won the 1945 Houghton Mifflin Literary Fellowship. When her novel, *The Street,* was pub-

Peter S. Kaufmann

ANN PETRY

lished, Mrs. Petry announced that she had tried to show Negroes as human beings rather than as "types" who fit into special categories in a "problem novel." Critics and reviewers agreed that she had succeeded in what she set out to do. They praised the uncommon realism in her treatment of Negro characters, and several were reminded of the novels of Richard Wright by her critical approach to Negro life.

Though her novel is distinguished for its graphic pictures of life in New York's Harlem, Ann Petry is not a native New Yorker. The daughter of Peter C. and Bertha James Lane, she was born in Old Saybrook, Connecticut, on October 12, 1911. Her grandfather was a chemist, and her father, an aunt, and an uncle are druggists.

True to the family tradition, she decided to study pharmacy: After her graduation from Old Saybrook High School in 1929 Miss Lane entered the College of Pharmacy of the University of Connecticut, from which she received her Doctor of Pharmacy degree in 1934. Her training completed, she worked as a registered pharmacist in the drugstores owned by her family in Old Saybrook, and in Lyme. During these years, too, she wrote short stories, but she had every intention of continuing her career as a pharmacist.

Ann Lane's marriage, on February 22, 1938, changed the course of her life. Her husband, George David Petry, took her to New York City to live, and in that metropolis she first sought jobs that would give her the opportunity to write. In 1939 she sold advertising space and wrote advertising copy for the Harlem *Amsterdam News.* By 1941, however, she was covering general news stories and editing the women's pages for the rival *People's Voice* in Harlem; she then rapidly acquired a knowledge of New York's Negro communities. Thus, while covering fires, political rallies, accidents, and murders, she became familiar with Harlem's daily tragedies, its evil housing, its dismal family life. She had the opportunity of seeing the effects of segregation on the minds of children when, for nine months, she worked on an experiment in education in New York's elementary schools. Mrs. Petry for a time also taught a course in clerking at the YWCA trade school. For a while, too, she was a member of the now famous American Negro Theatre, and she wrote children's plays and acted in amateur theatricals. Then she turned again to short stories. Her first published story appeared in the November 1943 issue of *The Crisis,* a magazine published monthly by the National Association for the Advancement of Colored People. The story was read by a Houghton Mifflin editor who wrote to Mrs. Petry to ask if she were at work on a novel.

By this time Ann Petry, after living and working in Harlem for six years, felt that she had a good deal to say. Harlem had been studied by sociologists for years, masses of statistics had been compiled, and the problems of life in Harlem had been discussed and analyzed by experts. But Mrs. Petry wanted to do something which she felt had never been done adequately—she wanted to show the inhabitants of Harlem "as people with the same capacity for love and hate, for tears and laughter, and the same instincts for survival possessed by all men."

A year after her short story had attracted the attention of the Houghton Mifflin editor, she submitted the first five chapters and a complete synopsis of *The Street,* and was awarded the twenty-four-hundred dollar Houghton Mifflin Literary Fellowship for 1945. Ten months later she took the finished novel to the publishers, and in February 1946 the book was published. "I wrote *The Street,*" she said at the time, "in an effort to show why the Negro has a high crime rate, a high death rate and little or no chance of keeping his family unit intact in large Northern cities. There are no statistics in *The Street,* though they are present in the background, not as columns of figures but in terms of what life is like for people who live in overcrowded tenements. I tried to write a story that moves swiftly so that it would hold the attention of people who might ordinarily shy away from a so-called problem novel."

The Street was well received by reviewers, who most frequently stressed the novel's realism and "smashing power." Writing in the New York *Times,* Charles Poore called it "a skillfully written and forceful first novel. . . .You won't forget that Harlem street." Arna Bontemps, in the *Herald Tribune*'s Sunday book review section, described Mrs. Petry as a fresh new talent who deserved thoughtful reading. And Harry Hansen of the New York *World-Telegram* said, "the place is Harlem, and the victims are Negroes, but the situation is universal. The author packs a powerful pen." Although several critics found the book to be overwritten and uneven in narrative interest, most reviewers expressed satisfaction that a novel dealing with an important social problem could exhibit the literary quality of *The Street.* In May 1946 the writer was among those honored by the Women's City Club for "exceptional contributions to the life of New York City." Several of her short stories were being included, in 1946, in well-known anthologies.

Mrs. Petry in 1946 was working on a new novel. Soon after her book was published, she said in a newspaper interview, "I have to write another book. You see, I have the feeling that there's just too much prejudice in this country. But it isn't all directed at Negroes; it goes to all minorities." The author is executive secretary of Negro Women Incorporated, an organization (it was established by the novelist in 1941) which watches local and national legislation in order to keep Negro citizens informed. Mrs. Petry has been active also in enlisting civic support for play schools. One of her relaxations is painting. She also plays the piano —she claims to be "the least promising pupil of a well-known composer and pianist."

References

N Y Herald Tribune II p5 Ap 14 '46
Opportunity 24:78+ Ap-Je '46
PM p4 Mr 3 '46

PHILLIPS, LENA MADESIN (măd'ĭ-s'n)
Lawyer; lecturer; writer

Address: b. c/o International Federation of Business and Professional Women, Biltmore Hotel, New York; h. Stonybrook Rr, Westport, Conn.

Lena Madesin Phillips has spent most of her life working for economic equality for women. As president of the International Federation of Business and Professional Women since 1930, she has spoken at numerous meetings in the United States and Europe, as well as on national and international broadcasts. During World War II she made two trips to Europe, and since the return of peace she has been occupied with the task of rebuilding the Federation's European branches which were disrupted by the war. A former associate editor of a women's magazine, she has contributed articles, short stories, and poems to periodicals in the United States.

The daughter of Alice (Shook) and William H. Phillips, Lena Madesin Phillips was born in Nicholasville, Kentucky, where she received her early schooling. After she was graduated in 1899 from the Jessamine Institute, she studied for four years in Baltimore at Goucher College. It was the girl's early ambition to be a concert pianist and to that end she attended the Peabody Conservatory of Music, also in Baltimore, when she had completed her college courses. However, on her return to her home she had to content herself with giving piano lessons to the neighbors because of an injury to a nerve in her arm. By organizing various little orchestras and musical groups, the young woman found an additional outlet for her energies. Later, having taken up the study of law at the University of Kentucky, she was in 1917 the second of her sex to receive an LL.B. degree there.

The young attorney of the YMCA was admitted to the bar in 1917. Shortly afterward she became secretary of the Women's War Work Council. Attracted by the excellent performance of her work, the National Board of the YWCA, in New York, offered her a position as field secretary, but she wired back, "I am not interested in being one of eleven field secretaries." Then followed an exchange of letters, after which the board offered her, instead, the post of business women's secretary. Miss Phillips promptly accepted and was entrusted with the task of supervising a survey of the country's business and professional women. Out of this survey grew the National Federation of Business and Professional Women's Clubs, with Miss Phillips as its executive secretary in 1919.

In order to be able to practice her legal profession Miss Phillips resigned from the Federation position in 1923, the year she received her LL.M. degree from New York University. She opened her office, and, according to the November 1928 *Ladies' Home Journal,* for six months "she sat while her earnings mounted to the huge sum of seventy-five dollars." Gradually her practice increased until she eventually became known as one of New York's leading women lawyers. But she did not sever connections with the organization for whose

Laure Albin Guillot
LENA MADESIN PHILLIPS

origin she was responsible. After serving, successively, as chairman of the membership and program committees, in 1926 she became president of the National Federation, an office she held for three years. The National Federation of Business and Professional Women's Clubs was associated for a time with the National Council of Women but is not now (1946) connected with it. From 1931 to 1935 Miss Phillips was president of the Council, which is affiliated with organizations of women in over thirty-five countries. Previously, in 1930, her organizational abilities won her the presidency of the organization she founded that year, the International Federation of Business and Professional Women.

Miss Phillips was the "prime mover" of the International Congress of Women held in 1933 at the Chicago Century of Progress Exposition. In the principal address she delivered to business and professional women representing thirty-one countries in Europe, Asia, and North America, she stated, "We have mastered production; we have not mastered distribution." In deploring the dislocations which this caused and the insecurity it brought to workers, she said: "We have not yet learned how to keep peace between individuals or between nations. And yet these problems can and must be solved. . . . To such endeavor we dedicate this Congress on our common cause—civilization."

Her activities as the president of the International Federation of Business and Professional Women took her to Paris a year later; there she broadcast from the grand amphitheater of the Sorbonne at a mass meeting of feminists who demanded the right to work. Miss Phillips has probably participated in more international broadcasts than any other nonprofessional American woman radiocaster. When the International Federation Congress met in Paris in 1936 she was a cospeaker with Frances Perkins, the then Secretary of Labor of the United

States. The globe-trotting lawyer has also addressed groups in twenty-two countries and been presiding officer at her organization's meetings in some of Europe's principal cities, among them Geneva, Brussels, Stockholm, Budapest, and Edinburgh. In addition, she has been a contributor, of short stories, poems, and of many articles of interest to her sex, to American magazines, and from 1935 to 1939 was associate editor of *Pictorial Review*. A few months before the outbreak of World War II, Lena Madesin Phillips was awarded the honorary degree of Doctor of Laws by the University of Kentucky.

In the midst of World War II Miss Phillips did not lose contact with the units of the International Federation. In an address to the Canadian Federation in British Columbia she said that she had been a pacifist for many years but had come to feel that while war might not settle all problems, "it sometimes destroyed the obstruction which lay in the path of human progress." In 1943 she spent five months observing conditions in England and Sweden for the Office of War Information. In Stockholm she had tea with the Crown Prince and Princess, luncheon with Prime Minister Hansson, and dined with the Russian Ambassador, Madame Kollantay at the Legation of the U.S.S.R. She also had an opportunity to meet Norwegian women members of the underground movement and to discuss with them the postwar problems they faced in their own country. As president of the International Federation, she addressed audiences in England, Wales, and Sweden, and was the recipient of a "sensitive gesture" from a Swedish hostess. While walking through one of the student clubhouses at the University of Uppsala, she heard the strains of "My Old Kentucky Home."

Speaking at a tea given by member clubs in New York on her return to the United States, Miss Phillips described as one of her strongest impressions "the yearning dependency of peoples abroad on American spiritual leadership in the war crisis." She added that if the United States failed to provide this leadership, the Soviet Union would take the dominant place in international affairs. Miss Phillips' trip to Europe in 1945 was for the purpose of helping to rebuild the branches of the International Federation. She visited England, France, and Italy and in her article, "New Spirit Abroad Among Europe's Women", reflected the feeling of optimism she sensed among the European women who, after helping to win the war, were "determined not to lose the peace." (Two of Miss Phillips' activities in the United States during the war were her memberships in the advisory committees of the women's division of the United States War Savings Drive and of the Civilian Defense Board of Westport, the Connecticut town in which she lives.)

Miss Phillips was also active in the discussion of the problems of the postwar world. On a nation-wide broadcast her organization sponsored in New York she contributed to a discussion, "Problems of the Peace Table," a consideration of the necessity for more intelligent economic planning. (Among the other speakers were the Russian journalist, Mrs. Nila

Magidoff, the Chinese official of Worldwide Press, Miss Pin Pin T'An, and the former United States Minister to Norway, Mrs. J. Borden Harriman.) In two successive years, 1943 and 1944, Miss Phillips was one of the speakers at a two-day forum on postwar problems at Christ Church Methodist in New York. In other speeches, interviews, and writings, the president of the International Federation of Business and Professional Women stressed the need for women's active participation in helping to solve the problems of world reconstruction. She feels that the United Nations organization offers an opportunity for such action because, according to its charter, one of its specific purposes is "to achieve international cooperation in . . . promoting and encouraging respect for human rights and for fundamental freedoms for all without distinction as to race, sex, language, or religion." The International Federation, she declared, ought to have a representative at all U.N. conferences dealing with the interests of business and professional women.

In May 1946, Miss Phillips, at a conference of the New York Federation of Women's Clubs, advocated "stronger national measures to assure food to the starving of Europe." Two months later, she flew to Brussels to be present at the meeting of the board of directors of the International Federation of Business and Professional Women. Among the subjects discussed were the renewal of "activities before the United Nations for the removal of discrimination against women" and the "exchange of business and professional women, similar to exchange of college students, long accepted between nations." During her brief sojourn in Europe, Miss Phillips was the recipient, at a conference of the British National Federation of the International Federation of Business and Professional Women in London, of a check for the sum of five thousand pounds to be employed to "restart business women's clubs in war-torn European countries." The International Federation had donated the money before the outbreak of the war for the organization of British clubs. Speaking in September at a World Faiths Conference in New York after her return from Europe, Miss Phillips declared that the Europeans' faith in peace had in the last year "been largely destroyed and replaced with a feeling of apathy and despair." "The peace of the world," she added, "depends on the United Nations. The leaders of the United Nations must return to the fundamentals of all great religions." They must "try to solve the world's problems in terms of the golden rule."

A member of the board of directors of the National Woman's Party, Miss Phillips is a strong advocate of an equal rights amendment to the Constitution. Unless such a measure is passed she believes that it will take women in the United States one hundred and fifty years to remove, through their State legislatures, the many laws which still discriminate against them. She has pressed for this amendment on the American Forum of the Air and in an address delivered on January 1943 at the Capitol in Washington. "America does not want its women penalized because of laws based upon a feudal tradition," she declared. Like Madame Chiang Kai-shek [40], she does not believe that sex was ever known to have brains. "Not until we have passed this amendment, as we shall, may we claim to be the equal of this Oriental woman in our understanding and appreciation of true democracy." At the eighth biennial convention of the National Federation of Business and Professional Women's Club early in July 1946, a resolution was recommended calling for the federation and its affiliated clubs to "continue to indorse and work for the election and appointment of qualified women" to local, state, and national offices. In the discussion which ensued, Miss Phillips stated that she would overlook party affiliation if a "qualified woman were nominated by another party," and that she would "choose a liberal man over a conservative woman."

Miss Phillips is honorary president of the New York League of Business and Professional Women, one of the member clubs of the National Federation of Business and Professional Women's Clubs. In 1943 the Federation's Midtown Club of New York City, having had its charter revoked by the New York State Federation for admitting two prominent Negro professional women to its membership, brought suit against the State body. Deeply disturbed by the situation, Miss Phillips replied to criticism in the *Nation* by pointing out that the National Federation had no provision in its constitution or bylaws which excluded Negro women; "In fact," she said, "it has had them as members. Clubs have long enjoyed complete autonomy within the framework of the organization."

The president of the International Federation is also honorary president of the National Council of Women, and of the National Federation of Business and Professional Women's Clubs. She is vice-president both of the National Kindergarten Association and of the International Council of Women, and holds membership in the Southern Women's Educational Alliance. A member of the Consumers Cooperative, she served on its advisory board during the NRA, and in 1939 was a member of the women's activities committee of the New York World's Fair. Among the other associations to which she belongs are the Chi Omega, the Phi Delta, and the Order of the Coif. Miss Phillips, who is tall and well built, is described as a "vibrant" person with keen gray eyes and a shock of gray hair. Her favorite relaxations are reading, gardening, and, above everything, travel.

References
  Ladies' H J 45:69 N '28
  International Who's Who, 1945-46
  Who's Who in America, 1946-47
  Who's Who in New York, 1938
  Women of Achievement (1940)

PICK, LEWIS ANDREW Nov. 18, 1890-
United States Army officer; civil engineer
Address: b. c/o War Department, Washington,
D.C.; h. 360 N. College St., Auburn, Ala.

Rivers and harbors, flood control and navigation, dams and bridges in the United States are
the responsibility of the Army Corps of Engineers. To Brigadier General Lewis Andrew
Pick, division engineer of the Missouri River
Division, goes the main responsibility for protecting from devastating floods and erosion an
area larger than France, Spain, and Italy combined. He is the author of the Army's Pick
Plan for the Missouri Basin, and builder of
the "incredible" Ledo section of the Stilwell
Road, which was cut through the jungle from
India to China at a reported cost of a million
dollars a mile.

Lewis Andrew Pick, son of George and
Annie (Crouch) Pick, was born November 18,
1890, in Brookneal, a village of Campbell
County, Virginia, with a turn-of-the-century
population of about three hundred. He attended
high school at Rustburg, a slightly larger
village a few miles away, and was graduated
from the Virginia Polytechnic Institute, in
Blacksburg, with his Civil Engineering degree
in 1914. For two years after his graduation,
Pick held the position of civil engineer with
the Southern Railway.

In August 1917, after attending officers' training camps in Georgia and Virginia, the twenty-
six-year-old engineer was appointed a first
lieutenant in the Engineer Reserve and went
on active duty in the World War I Army.
Assigned to the Office of the Chief of Engineers in Washington until November, Pick
joined the Twenty-third Engineers and went
overseas with them in March 1918. He served
in France and Russia, took part in the Meuse-
Argonne offensive, returned to the United
States in June 1919, and was honorably discharged at Camp Lee in September. On July
1, 1920, he joined the Regular Engineers, was
recommissioned and immediately promoted to
captain.

Captain Pick's first Regular Army assignment was to Ninth Corps Area headquarters
at the Presidio of San Francisco, for duty in
the office of the engineer corps. In January
1921 the Virginian was ordered to Fort Mills
in the Philippines. From September 1921 to
April 1923 he commanded a company of Philippine scouts in Rizal province of Luzon and
organized the first native engineer regiment,
the Fourteenth Engineers. Back in the United
States, Pick spent some time preparing engineer training regulations before entering the
officers' course of the Army Engineer School
at Fort Belvoir in his native state. Reserve Officers Training Corps service was followed by a year at Auburn, Alabama (where he
now has his home') as professor of military
science and tactics at Alabama Polytechnic
Institute.

From August 1925 until August 1928 Pick
served in the New Orleans Engineer District,
first as military assistant to the district engineer, then in 1927-28 as acting engineer, and
the last six months as district engineer. During

this period, in December 1925, the thirty-five-
year-old officer was married to Alice Cary.
(They now have one son, Lewis Andrew Pick,
2d.) From Louisiana Pick went to Texas
Agricultural and Mechanical College, where he
organized the first ROTC unit, and in August
1932 he entered the Command and General
Staff School in Fort Leavenworth, Kansas.
Captain Pick was graduated in June of 1934,
and he remained at the same school to teach
military tactics, was promoted to major in
August 1935, and detailed in August 1938 to
the Army War College in Washington, which
gives the service's highest training. After his
graduation in June 1939, Major Pick went to
Cincinnati as executive assistant to the division
engineer of the Ohio River Division.

Seventeen days after Pearl Harbor, the engineer was given a temporary promotion to
colonel, and in April 1942 he was sent to Nebraska as division engineer, Missouri River
Division. In his eighteen months there Pick
supervised more than one billion dollars' worth
of military construction in the vast Missouri
Basin, which is one-sixth of the total area of
the country. As many as ninety-three thousand
construction workers at one time were building
airfields, cantonments, hospitals, munitions
plants, relocation centers for Japanese evacuated from coastal areas, and other projects
under his command. Colonel Pick also directed
the battle against the Missouri spring floods in
1943, when the swollen waters of the "Big
Muddy" and its tributaries inundated more than
two million acres of the country's best farm-
land and damaged property to an estimated
value of sixty-five million dollars.

Protests from the people of the lower Missouri Valley caused the Congressional Flood
Control Committee to allow the Army Engineers to make a restudy of the flood situation in
the valley, a project Pick had advocated for
months. Utilizing and adding to data from
previous Army surveys, in less than three
months he submitted a report and recommendations to the Chief of Engineers, Major General
Eugene Reybold.[45] The Pick Plan, as it came
to be called, was "a comprehensive program for
over-all control and utilization of the full water
resources of the basin." It provided for construction of twenty-two reservoirs on the river
and its tributaries and a series of levees and
appurtenant works on both sides of the Missouri from Sioux City to the mouth of the
river. Ten of the dams in the Kansas-Missouri
area had already been authorized; Pick added
five above Sioux City, five in Nebraska, one
in Montana, and one in Wyoming. Twelve of
his dams were to be multiple-purpose projects
for "the maximum practicable development" of
irrigation, navigation, hydroelectric power, flood
control, and other desiderata.

Having mapped the plan, the Colonel "toured
the valley, talking it up," wrote Wesley Price.
"An outstanding engineer, he is also a great
handshaker, sanguine and persuasive." The
people of the lower, eastern end of the valley
were enthusiastic, as, reportedly, was Missouri
Senator Harry S. Truman; but the farmers of
the arid upper plains put their faith in the
irrigation projects of the Bureau of Reclama-

tion. (Pick's plan had allowed the bureau, builders of the famous Boulder, Shasta, and Grand Coulee dams, to construct tributary dams, but provided that all main-stem dams be built and operated by the Engineers.) In November 1943, when the author of the Pick Plan was in Burma, the two factions got together on a compromise Pick-Sloan Plan, enacted into law in December 1944; it was understood that Pick would return after the war to replace General R. C. Crawford as chairman of the Missouri Basin Inter-Agency Committee.

Around Burma campfires Colonel Pick would talk about the Missouri Valley and illustrate his thesis with diagrams drawn in the earth with his famous long rattan jungle stick—which had been worn short by the time he left the East. As commander of Advance Section Three of the Army Service Forces, the "Old Man With the Stick" was faced with a road-building problem which laymen and experts alike declared impossible to solve. The Ledo Road, needed to link with the Burma Road to carry supplies to China from India, was halted after almost a year of work in the rain-washed jungles of the steep Naga Hills, forty-five miles from the starting-point in Assam, India. Eighty per cent of the engineers were hospitalized with malaria. Pick's men had to lay a broad all-weather military highway across more than a hundred miles of densely jungled mountains, scores of miles of sweltering, disease-ridden swamp, ten major rivers and 155 secondary streams calling for a total of seven hundred bridges. In addition they had to build "combat trace" roads going off into whatever direction the enemy was, so their own troops could move up on the Japanese—and all without the aid of basic engineering data. Pick's quartermaster, at the end of the world's longest supply line, had to supply seven different rations to workers speaking more than a hundred tongues. Under Pick's command were twenty-eight thousand American soldiers (more than half of them Negroes), five thousand Chinese troops, and thirty thousand Indian and Burmese tribesmen.

Engineering surveys of the terrain were nonexistant, surveyors' transits were useless in the jungle, survey parties were hampered by the presence of enemy Japanese, and Pick frequently located the route from a plane by "engineering instinct." From his headquarters at the most advanced point, to quote General Stilwell [42], Pick "covered the road by foot, jeep, and liaison plane twenty-four hours a day. He knew every rock quarry, every mudhole and slide, every curve, every cutback and bridge. . . . He kept his construction right on the heels of his combat troops."

Through all-but-impassible terrain his men pushed the road a mile a day, utilizing every known type of bridge and inventing one or two new ones. Pick suffered from jungle infections and from two attacks of malaria; hospitalized for forty-eight hours, he directed activities by telephone. According to an *Atlantic Monthly* article by David L. Cohn, Pick's men worked around the clock for twelve days to

U.S. Army Signal Corps
BRIG. GEN. LEWIS ANDREW PICK

build an airfield for use by Merrill's [44] Marauders in the battle of Myitkyina.

When the first convoy started for China over "Pick's Pike" in January 1945, Brigadier General Pick was in the lead jeep. He had chosen the men for the convoy to represent each group who had worked on the road; the first work was done by Negro Engineers, and the first jeep was driven by one of them. Pick, who had been given his first star in February 1944, was made a major general (temporary) in March 1945, and in September he was back in Washington. The Ledo Road project had won him the Distinguished Service Medal and the Chinese order of the Banner and Cloud.

Assigned in October 1945 to the Office of the Chief of Engineers in Washington, Pick was one of three Southerners on a four-man board which conducted an official study of the Army's utilization of Negro manpower. Their recommendations were for limiting segregation to units no larger than the infantry regiment (larger units to be composite), stationing Negro troops "where community attitudes are most favorable," and selecting Negro Regular officers by the same standard as whites. "Courageous leadership in implementing the program is imperative," said the report. In November 1945 Pick returned to Omaha to resume his river duty, and five months later he was one of thirty-eight generals stepped down one grade in keeping with the Army's decreasing size.

The Missouri River public works projects of Pick's Army Corps of Engineers were little affected by an Administration order in 1946 to economize on all such constructions: the General's group "had allocated all of the funds available to it prior to receipt of the . . . economy order." The Department of the Interior's Bureau of Reclamation, however, did not allocate the funds appropriated for it and thus faced some delay in its development plans. In

PICK, LEWIS ANDREW—*Continued*

August 1946 the Army civil engineer, who will serve as chairman of the Missouri Basin Inter-Agency Committee until July 1947, was engaged in getting preliminary work on his part of the project done "to make way for the actual construction of a network of huge dams" in the following year. The problems which face the entire Missouri Valley Basin undertaking, however, include the question of all future appropriations, which many fear will be cut, and that of retaining the project under interagency control or of establishing a Missouri Valley Authority similar to the TVA. In 1946 the Governor of South Dakota chose Pickstown as the name of the Fort Randall dam townsite in recognition of General Pick's achievements.

General Pick's political affiliation is Democratic, his church is Presbyterian, and his favorite recreations are fishing, hunting, golfing, and reading biographies. He holds membership in the society of American Military Engineers and in Theta Chi. The brown-eyed, gray-haired engineer is described as a square-jawed, erect, sturdily built six-footer who speaks softly in a slow drawl, seldom laughs, but often smiles. Pick's patience, gentleness, and concern for his troops' welfare in the jungles were remarked upon by correspondents. David Cohn has written, "There is nothing about him to betray the fact that he is a man of relentless, driving energy and indomitable will. . . .Exacting but sympathetic, hard-driving but a lover of life, this man nonetheless has . . . that aloofness characteristic of those who, even while they are intent upon the task at hand, are dreaming of new worlds."

References

Atlan 176:86-9 Ag '45
N Y Times Mag p12+ F 11 '45 por
Scholastic 46:10 F 26 '45 por
Who's Who in America, 1946-47

PINCHOT, GIFFORD (pĭn'shō) Aug. 11, 1865—Oct. 4, 1946 Governor of Pennsylvania from 1923 to 1927 and from 1931 to 1935; first American to plan systematic forestry work; chief of the Forest Service, 1898-1910; president of the National Conservation Association from 1910 to 1925; professor of forestry at Yale from 1903 to 1936; author of books on forestry, including *Breaking New Ground* (1946).

Obituary

N Y Times p56 O 6 '46 por

PINERO, JESUS T(ORIBIO) (pē-nyā'rō hä-sōōs' tô-rē'byō) Apr. 16, 1897- Governor of Puerto Rico

Address: b. La Fortaleza, San Juan, Puerto Rico; h. Carolina, Puerto Rico

The new Governor of Puerto Rico, Jesús T. Piñero, has the distinction of being the first native of the Caribbean island to be appointed to that office. Since 1510 (Puerto Rico was discovered in November 1493 by Columbus), when Ponce de León first directed the admin-istration of the island, the governors have been appointed by Spain, and after 1898, by the United States. Piñero, who assumed the governorship on September 3, 1946, succeeding Rexford G. Tugwell [41], promised the Puerto Rican people that he would work to win for them the right to elect their chief executive.

Jesús Toribio Piñero, of Spanish extraction, was born on April 16, 1897, in Carolina, Puerto Rico. He is the son of Emilio and Josefa (Jiménez) Piñero. His father was a wealthy proprietor of a four-hundred-acre sugar cane and dairy farm. Young Piñero received his elementary school education in Carolina, at the Model School in Rio Piedras, to which city the Piñeros moved in 1905, and in the United States at the Colegio Janer in Baltimore, Maryland. He was graduated from Central High School in San Juan. At the age of seventeen, Piñero entered the College of Liberal Arts at the University of Puerto Rico at Rio Piedras, where he remained for two years (1914-16) before he left for the United States to pursue his technical education. He enrolled at the University of Pennsylvania School of Enengineering, which he attended from 1916 until 1918, when his studies in electrical engineering were terminated by his decision to return to his native island to join the World War I army. The Armistice prevented the realization of this plan.

Establishing his residence once more in Caroline, Piñero followed the profession of agriculture as well as that of engineering, occupations that were interrupted in 1923 and for several months during 1924 while Piñero, his sister María Josefina, and his father traveled in Europe. Jesús Piñero's "meteoric career" in Puerto Rican politics began in 1928 (his interest in politics dates from 1926—he then began to aid various political organizations to obtain benefits for the people) when he was elected chairman of the municipal assembly of his home town. At the time he and his brother, Emilio, were operating the large plantation which their father had left to them, Piñero becoming one of the leaders of the independent sugar growers. He gained his first political position on the Socialist Party ticket, accepting the nomination, it is said, "on the condition that he could act freely and in accordance with the dictates of his conscience." Among the accomplishments of his administration was the founding of a second unit (rural vocational) school bearing his name.

Piñero remained in his municipal assembly post until the year 1933, when he was chosen president of the Puerto Rico Sugar Cane Farmers Association. It was about a year after Piñero's promotion to the organization's presidency that the Puerto Rican sugar industry reached the highest point in its development. Although it has since declined, "sugar is still king." Since sugar plantations furnish the workers with only a six- to eight-month labor season, a large proportion of the populace in this United States possession must receive Government aid; and a high tariff wall has been established to protect the industry. Early in President Franklin D. Roosevelt's Administration, Piñero and Luis Muñoz Marín, a political leader, went to Washington to seek financial aid for insular relief and rehabilitation. Their mission a success, Puerto Rico was granted more than seventy million dollars for its relief program. He also protested in Washington in 1935 the passage, a year previous, of the Jones '43-Costigan Act (it amended the Agricultural Adjustment Act) which restricted insular sugar exports to the United States, necessitated sugar acreage reduction and a "readjustment of island industries dependent upon the sugar crop," and resulted in a sugar surplus. In the 1930's he made several other important missions to the United States. Since 1935 Piñero has been a member of the board of directors of the Puerto Rico Reconstruction Administration.

In 1936 Piñero was a Liberal Party candidate for the Insular Senate from the senatorial district of Humacao, which includes the city of Carolina. The Liberal Party (founded in 1931) was, however, defeated at the polls by a coalition of the island's Republican and Socialist parties. Shortly after his failure to gain the Senate seat, Piñero aided Muñoz Marín to organize the Popular Democratic Party, a slightly left-of-center faction, whose doctrine of social and economic reform was embodied in the motto *Pan, tierra, y libertad* ("Bread, land, and liberty"). The Popular Democratic Party came into full existence in 1938, and Piñero's political fortunes rose with the growing importance of the party. In the 1940 elections Piñero became a member of the Puerto Rican House of Repre- in the Insular Senate. He represented District Thirty-five. Four years later, in the 1944 voting, which gave his party an overwhelming majority in both houses of the Puerto Rican legislature, Piñero was elected Resident Commissioner of Puerto Rico.

As Resident Commissioner, with headquarters in Washington, Piñero, though entitled to sit in the United States House of Representatives and to discuss bills related to Puerto Rican affairs, had no vote. (The fact that the Resident Commissioner, Puerto Rico's sole political representative in the capital, can take little constructive part in making laws for the colony, has been a source of island discontent. Added to this is Puerto Rican dissatisfaction with their legislative system: the natives elect municipal officials and members of the legislature, "but acts of the legislature can be vetoed by the Governor, or if approved by the Governor, can be annulled" by the United States Congress. Nor can they vote in the United States national elections.) In his new position which he assumed in January 1945 Piñero was connected with the work of six committees: agriculture, labor, territories, insular, naval, and military affairs. He helped formulate the Tydings '45-Piñero bill. The bill was discussed in Congress in the spring of 1946, but no conclusion was reached on the issue of Puerto Rico's future form of government.

Rexford G. Tugwell, Governor of Puerto Rico since 1941, had attempted to obtain for Puerto Ricans "Congressional approval for the election of a native Governor." He was not

JESUS T. PINERO

successful. After Tugwell announced, late in 1945, his intended resignation, the Puerto Rican legislature, with his support, petitioned President Harry Truman to elevate to the Governorship "the highest Puerto Rican official elected at large by the people in their last election." Then in July 1946 Truman acceded to the Puerto Ricans' request by appointing Resident Commissioner Piñero to the position vacated by Tugwell late in June. Piñero's selection, ratified by the United States Senate, was called "concrete evidence of President Truman's belief that the Puerto Rican people are fully capable of administering their own governmental responsibilities." (This statement was made by Secretary of the Interior Julius Krug '44, whose office administers territorial affairs.) Some opponents of Piñero's appointment were those who objected to what they termed Muñoz Marín's "bossism" (Muñoz Marín, Piñero's friend, has been the President of the Insular Senate since 1940); other objectors were Democratic National Committee members who wished Francis Murphy, the ex-Governor of New Hampshire, to be given the ten-thousand-dollar-a-year office (*Time*, August 5, 1946).

After attending in the United States a number of celebrations in his honor during the month of August—for example, he was adopted as a "son of New York City"—Piñero flew to Puerto Rico for the inaugural ceremony held on September 3 at San Juan. At the installation, the forty-nine-year-old Puerto Rican Governor, in paying tribute to President Truman's Government for granting the office to a native, remarked: "The appointment of a Puerto Rican to the Governorship does not in itself fulfill the aspirations of our people, nor fully comply with the provisions of the Atlantic Charter. But it does constitute an extremely significant step forward. . . .I pledge myself to make my own term of office as short as possible, and to

PINERO, JESUS T.—*Continued*

strive to win for the Puerto Rican people the right to elect their own representative Governor, as soon as feasible, at the polls."

Part of Piñero's plans as Governor of this island (with an area less than half the size of Massachusetts and a population of two million) will be the continuation of the economic and social policies and reforms of his predecessor, which at times have been criticized in some American quarters. Among these policies are the programs of public ownership of public utilities and social control of the sugar industry through a Public Service Commission. Two bills pending in the United States Congress are also of interest to the Puerto Ricans: the Organic Act Reform bill, and the so-called Plebiscite bill, which, adopted, would permit the islanders to choose their Governor in the future and would give the colony an opportunity to decide its form of Government—complete independence, statehood, dominion status, or a man acceded to the Puerto Ricans' request by wider measure of self-government. The Popular Democratic Party platform favors the use of a plebiscite in this matter, but Governor Piñero and many insular political leaders believe that the "independence question should be postponed until the island's shaky economic condition has been improved," or until certain economic guarantees can be obtained from the United States. In October 1946 President Truman vetoed an insular legislature bill requiring the use of Spanish instead of English throughout Puerto Rican schools; the legislature had originally overridden the Governor's veto. As a means of bringing much-needed money into the country, Piñero favors the development of tourist trade, aided by American air line companies.

Piñero has been described as a short, sturdy man, with a gentle voice. Both in Washington and San Juan he has gained the reputation for "calm judgment and dependable strength." He does not like to deliver speeches. An amateur photographer, Piñero has traveled much on the island showing to the people motion pictures which he has taken in Puerto Rico and elsewhere. The Governor is also known as one of the radio pioneers in his country: "He established the first amateur station in Puerto Rico and was one of the first persons to tune in on programs broadcast from the United States." Astronomy is Piñero's other hobby. The Governor was married to Aurelia Bou in June 1931; their two children are Haydée and José Emilio, both of whom in 1946 were students at schools in the United States capital. In addition to his membership in economic and social organizations, Piñero is an executive board member of the Puerto Rico Council of the Boy Scouts of America.

References

N Y Herald Tribune p2 Jl 26 '46; p7 Ag 16 '46; II p9 S 15 '46 por
N Y Times p2 Jl 26 '46

Congressional Directory (2d ed., 1945)
Who's Who in America, 1946-47

PIPER, W(ILLIAM) T(HOMAS) Jan. 8, 1881-   Airplane manufacturer

Address: b. c/o Piper Aircraft Corp., Lock Haven, Pa.; h. Island Route, Lock Haven, Pa.

William Piper bought an airplane company when he was past fifty, and has been a pioneer of the aviation industry ever since. Often called the Henry Ford of aviation, he was the "Nation's No. 1 mass-producer of small, inexpensive planes" in 1945. According to the magazine *Life*, before World War II Piper built 60 per cent of all the light planes, and 48.6 per cent of the non-military planes in the United States. Seventy-five per cent of America's civilian fliers, and "countless Army pilots" learned to fly in Piper Cub trainers. Reports *Life*: "Long before Pearl Harbor the name 'Cub' had become a generic term, popularly but erroneously applied to all light planes. In the war the Cub became a legend." While Cubs made aviation history, Piper himself campaigned to convert the United States into a nation with a landing field in every town, a family flivver plane on every farm.

William Thomas Piper was born in Knapps Creek, New York, on January 8, 1881. His parents were Thomas and Sarah Elizabeth (Maltby) Piper. He attended the Bradford (Pennsylvania) high school, saw service in the Spanish-American war, and then took a degree in engineering (B.S. *cum laude*) at Harvard's Lawrence Scientific School in 1903. At college he was a star hammer-thrower on the track-and-field team, played football, and acquired a reputation as the campus "strong-man." When he had his degree he went west to Lorain, Ohio, to work for the United States Steel Corporation until 1905. After that, for nine years he held jobs as a construction engineer in various parts of the country, returning in 1914 to the oil town of Bradford, where he had lived when he was a boy. There he became, and still is, an operator of oil wells. In World War I he served as a captain in the Engineer Corps of the AEF. (Piper had served as private in the Pennsylvania Volunteer Infantry in the year 1898.) Thereafter, oil production held all his attention until C. G. Taylor moved his Rochester aircraft plant to Bradford in 1929. Taylor's company required refinancing, and Piper, thinking that the new industry would be beneficial to Bradford, invested in the failing firm.

In 1931 Piper, then fifty years old, bought the assets of the Taylor company at a bankruptcy sale. With C. G. Taylor retained as president and chief engineer, and Piper as treasurer, the company produced the first Cub, a low-priced, inexpensively operated monoplane. In that year, according to *Fortune* magazine, the company marketed twenty-four planes ($1,325 each), at a loss of $9,460. By 1933 the selling price was up to $1,470 but production was down to sixteen planes, and the company was still losing. A new time payment plan, made possible by the Aviation Funding Corporation, helped boost sales, beginning in 1934; but even in 1935, with 228 sales, the company lost $1,080. It began to look as if the Piper Cub would disappear from the American scene before it had a chance to make an impression. *Life* magazine has related that "Piper frequently met the company payroll by dipping into his oil earnings—a circumstance which led his wife to remark that aviation was a wonderful business so long as one had a few producing oil wells to maintain it."

After a disagreement over policies of design in 1936, Piper bought out Taylor's half interest, and became president himself. The first year Piper was on his own the company produced a new, improved Cub, cut the selling price to $1,270, and sold 523 planes. And for the first time the books showed a profit—$9,700 on a gross of $632,000. Suddenly fate took a hand. In March 1937, fire broke out in the plant's "dope room", where a mixture of cellulose acetate and a solvent is applied to plane fabrics. The Bradford plant, insured for only 5 per cent of its value, was completely destroyed. Piper, visiting Western airports, got the news in California by telephone, and said, "Well, at least we'll get some publicity." The fifty-six-year old manufacturer came east, set production going in a hangar, a barn, and a shed, and went looking for a new factory. On the Susquehanra River, in Lock Haven, Pennsylvania, he found an abandoned silk mill near the municipal airport. With loans from J. E. Swan and Company, a New York investment house, and from two Lock Haven banks, plus $15,500 of his own, Piper organized the Piper Aircraft Corporation. Despite the fire, the necessity for retooling and inventory replacement, and the time consumed in moving, Piper made 687 Cubs in 1937. The following year the Piper firm developed the first side-by-side seater, the Coupé, for private airplane owners. In 1939, the Piper Cruiser, a three-place enclosed monoplane for passenger-carrying and for pilot training, appeared, and in that year Piper could show a profit of $94,000 on 1,806 Cubs. Piper was selling more planes than all his competitors together.

W. C. Jamouneau, Piper's chief engineer, has stated: "Throughout the history of this company every attempt has been made in design to make it possible to produce and sell airplanes at a minimum price." Airplane production required more handwork than was needed on an automobile assembly line, but Piper was able to keep costs almost comparable to those in mass production because of the unique nature of the industry he was pioneering. He instituted an employment policy, which was, in effect, an apprentice system. *Fortune* has explained it: "He could tap an unlimited reservoir of smart, eager boys, so crazy about flying that they were willing to work for nothing if they could only start their days off by laying hands on a Cub wing. This eagerness was a godsend to a man who couldn't pay Detroit prices for machinists and hand workers." By 1940, according to *Fortune*, Piper had one thousand employees whose average age was twenty-three. He paid about forty-four cents an hour; the auto industry paid ninety-three. But anyone at Piper Aircraft could check out at any time and take flying lessons in the company's Cubs for the price of the gasoline and oil, $1.10 an hour.

Darr

W. T. PIPER

Piper, who had learned to fly at fifty, wanted to get everyone into a plane. His three sons became first-rate pilots, and almost all his employees flew or were learning to fly. The leading advertiser in the airplane industry in 1940, Piper told Americans: "For Only $333 Down You Can Buy A New Piper Cub And Learn To Fly Free!"

Shortly before Pearl Harbor, military authorities, concerned with national defense, advised Piper to take subcontracts from warplane manufacturers. But instead, making the army a gift of a dozen Cubs, Piper continued to produce light planes. The dozen Cubs were used for artillery observations in the Army's 1941 maneuvers in Louisiana. Army officers were impressed with their effectiveness, and ordered several, then several hundred. Before the end of the war Piper supplied the Air Corps and the Signal Corps with 7,000 L-4's, a modified version of the Cub trainer. Lincoln Barnett reported on the Cubs war record in *Life* magazine (October 29, 1945): "Piper Cubs were the eyes of the artillery, hovering over enemy lines, spotting hidden defenses and directing American fire via two-way radio. Officially designated L-4s, they were known to GIs as 'grasshoppers,' 'puddle jumpers,' 'flying jeeps' and 'putt-putts.' The Germans called them 'Hell Raisers' because their appearance in the skies invariably heralded a rain of steel from American guns. . . .In the Pacific, Cubs carried blood plasma, mail and supplies to units deep in impenetrable jungles. Rebuilt as ambulance planes, they fluttered down into tiny clearings and brought out wounded. . . .By virtue of their slow landing speed (38 mph) Cubs were able to fly in and out of places inaccessible to fast planes. . . .Slow, unarmed, thin-skinned, Cubs were the most vulnerable planes in the sky. Yet few were shot down. When attacked by enemy planes Cub pilots simply dived for

PIPER, W. T.—*Continued*

the ground and ducked around barns, between trees and into ravines."

After V-J Day warplane manufacturers turned to the peacetime market with new light planes designed for private ownership. Piper Aircraft faced tremendous competition for the first time, but to help him race his competitors Piper had an $11,000,000 backlog of orders, and several bold ideas. He contracted to sell his planes in department stores (John Wanamaker's in New York and Philadelphia, Mandel Brothers in Chicago). While other manufacturers concentrated on one plane, Piper produced two models—the Piper Cub Special (an improved J-3 Cub Trainer), and the three-place Piper Cub Super-Cruiser. Meanwhile, his experimental department worked on plans for a single-place "Skycycle"; a four-place, family model "Skysedan"; and a two-place "Skycoupe." By February of the year 1946 Piper was planning to multiply production five times over his best prewar year. In March the Piper corporation delivered the fourteen hundredth plane it had built since V-J Day in August 1945. The same week the New York *Times* announced: "While military plane manufacturers are contemplating putting factory space to other uses, Piper will within thirty days begin an addition to the [Lock Haven] plant here which will bring production to fifty units a day." In April 1946 Piper's corporation began to export Piper Cubs to the Union of South Africa. The planes were the first light civil aircraft to be sent there since the beginning of the war. The Piper company by September had acquired also a new assembly plant in Ponca City, Oklahoma.

So far as Piper is concerned, the air age will not have arrived until "the man of small income, everywhere," is flying instead of motoring. "Eventually," he predicts, "this country will need as many aircraft landing and servicing spots, as many airplane tourist camps, as the automobile now has super-filling stations and motor camps." Lincoln Barnett, writing in *Life,* related how Piper campaigns for landing areas in every community. ("Some of the nicest fields in the U.S. are nothing but grass, and you can level one off and stick up a windsock for as little as $1,000.") And how Piper scoffs at the idea that flying requires rare coordination, and special skill. ("The word [coordination] ought to be kicked out of the dictionary.") An enthusiastic pilot himself, Piper makes flights around the country, "exhibiting a disregard for weather that gives his friends the shakes." He steps out of his Cub after a long trip, to inform reporters that the farmers in Idaho and Nebraska are demanding light planes, that family travel of the future will require "tens of thousands" of airports, or that restrictions on private pilot licenses must be relaxed. He is a frequent contributor to aviation magazines, his favorite subject being airport locations. As he did during the company's early history, Piper still permits his employees to fly during working hours, if they make up the time, and maintains for them four instructors, and twelve training planes. Ever since his

brother Arthur Piper, a missionary, discovered the efficiency of the Cub in the Belgian Congo, Piper has offered free instruction to missionaries. In August 1946 Piper was among the speakers who addressed the World Congress on "air age education," which was devoted to discussions concerning the advances in aeronautical science and in air transportation and communication and their integration into school curriculums.

Piper was married to Marie Van de Water in July 1910. Mrs. Piper died in 1937, and Piper was married to Mrs. Clara Taber in December 1943. A Republican in politics, Piper is a "rugged individual" who believes "all of us are depending too much on the Government." He is a Methodist and a Rotarian. Besides being president of the Bradford Filling Station, Piper is a member of the firm of the Dallas and the Gridiron oil companies. The gray-haired airplane manufacturer is a square-jawed, heavy-set man, five feet ten inches tall; his weight is 220 pounds. At Lock Haven, "he hates desk work. . . .usually recoils from his neglected bales of correspondence and wanders off into the plant. . . .His suit is invariably rumpled, his shirt frayed and his hair mussed." Writer Barnett describes him as a "Spartan in tastes and habits", "a man of inflexible convictions. . . .He is a teetotaler and an anti-nicotine crusader and so violent on both counts that none of his three grown sons or two married daughters has ever ventured to drink a highball or smoke a cigarette in his presence." Piper reads food and health magazines, and experiments with unusual diets. "His health has remained excellent and his vitality immense."

References

Fortune 21:77+ Je '40
Life 19:67+ O 29 '45
Who's Who in America, 1946-47

POINDEXTER, MILES (poin'dĕks"tẽr) Apr. 22, 1868—Sept. 21, 1946 United States Republican Senator from Washington from 1911 to 1923, after one term as Representative; Ambassador to Peru, 1923-28; honored by the city of Lima; author of *Ayar-Incas* (1931), *Peruvian Pharaohs* (1938).

Obituary

N Y Times p63 S 22 '46 por

POLLOCK, CHANNING Mar. 4, 1880— Aug. 17, 1946 Author and playwright; wrote over thirty plays, most of which were produced; among his hit plays were *The Sign of the Door, The Fool,* and *The Enemy*; also wrote two books of essays, three novels, many songs, verses, and magazine articles; lectured widely on various aspects of the theater and on international topics.

Obituary

N Y Times p47 Ag 18 '46 por

POPENOE, PAUL (BOWMAN) (pŏp'ē-nō) Oct. 16, 1888- Biologist; author

Address: b. 607 S. Hill St., Los Angeles, Calif.; h. 2503 N. Marengo Ave., Altadena, Calif.

An author, lecturer, and research worker in biology, eugenics, heredity, social hygiene, and family relations, Paul Popenoe has been called "one of America's foremost authorities on marriage." He is founder and director of the American Institute of Family Relations, described by Emmet Crozier of *American Magazine* as "a human laboratory where marriage problems are classified, studied—and solved."

Paul Bowman Popenoe was born on October 16, 1888, in Topeka, Kansas, the son of Marion Amanda (Bowman) and Fred Oliver Popenoe, a businessman and newspaper publisher. The name was originally spelled Papineau by the family's French Huguenot ancestors, who came to the United States in 1696. The Popenoes had two younger children, one of whom is now horticulturist Dr. Wilson Popenoe, director of the Escuela Agricola Panamericana in Honduras; psychologist Dr. Herbert Popenoe is an educator in the Los Angeles school system. The boy Paul and his family moved from Kansas to California after his graduation from the Washburn Academy in Topeka in 1905. Interested in journalism and debating in high school, Popenoe entered Occidental College in Los Angeles as an English major, and remained there from 1905 until 1907. At Stanford University, where he studied the following year, he became acquainted with David Starr Jordan, the university's first president; a scientist, he influenced the youth's choice of lifework. After leaving college, Popenoe was a newspaperman in Pasadena and in Los Angeles from 1908 until 1911.

Popenoe's father had established the avocado industry in California, brother Wilson had done pioneer work in tropical pomology, and Paul Popenoe now became an agricultural explorer in fruit in 1911. His research expeditions took him to Algeria, northern India, eastern Arabia, Iraq, and twice to North Africa, by way of Europe. Returning to the United States with sixteen thousand date palm specimens, he wrote his first book, *Date Growing in the New and Old Worlds* (1913). Popenoe's interest in dates continued until 1935, with particular regard to cultivation of the fruit in California. From 1913 until 1917 the former newspaperman worked as editor of the *Journal of Heredity*, official organ of the American Genetics Association in Washington, D.C.

Early in World War I, in 1917 Popenoe assisted the medical section chief of the Council for National Defense before being drafted and commissioned on the staff of the surgeon general of the United States Army Sanitary Corps. As a lieutenant, in 1917-18 he was director of the control of infectious disease, and, as a captain, in 1918-19 was in charge of law enforcement for the control of vice and liquor around Army camps in the United States, a function of the War Department's committee on training camp activities. After the close of the war Popenoe joined the American Social Hygiene Association in New York as law enforcement secretary in 1919-20 and as executive secretary in 1920. He temporarily abandoned the field of his lifework to grow dates and other crops on his Coachella Valley ranch outside of Los Angeles from 1920 until 1926. Resuming his scientific career in 1926, he became secretary and director of research for the Human Betterment Foundation in Pasedena, which was devoted chiefly to the spread of eugenic principles. He remained with the organization for eleven years.

After two years of preparatory work, the American Institute of Family Relations at Los Angeles opened on February 3, 1930, founded by Paul Popenoe to serve as an educational center and information bureau in connection with the problems of marriage, heredity, and parenthood. This was the first attempt made in the United States to bring the resources of modern science to the promotion of successful marriages, although there had been pre- and postmarital clinics in Europe as early as 1922 (there were two hundred European marriage clinics in 1931). The nonprofit, philanthropic (fees are waived for charity cases) foundation was established, according to Popenoe, its secretary and general director, "not . . . to solve all the problems of mankind, but . . . to aid many applicants directly, and to refer others to sources of information."

During the first three years of operation, the institute took care of more than five thousand persons, and in the first eight years of its work, not one couple to which it gave premarital guidance was divorced. In addition to personal services, the institute carries on research and cooperates with State agencies concerned with mental hygiene, children, domestic relations, the law, and public welfare. Public education for marriage and family life in American schools and colleges is promoted through its lectures before institutional conferences and student organizations, articles in popular magazines, radio programs, and a monthly service bulletin, *Family Life,* of which Popenoe is editor.

In addition to his many pamphlets, Popenoe has written articles and research reports for magazines: for the *Scientific Monthly* and *Hygeia* (on personality types); for the *Scientific Monthly,* the *Journal of Social Hygiene, Parents,* and *Your Life* (on youth); for the *Journal of Home Economics, Public Health Nursing,* and *National Parent-Teacher* (on the family); for *Social Forces, Eugenics, Journal of Genetic Psychology, Mental Hygiene,* and *Survey* (on eugenics and heredity); and for the *American Sociological Review, Sociology and Social Research,* the *Journal of Social Psychology,* the *American Magazine,* and a 1942-43 series for the *Ladies' Home Journal* (on marriage). Popenoe has spoken on these topics, particularly marriage and sex education, as lecturer and visiting professor at more than one hundred fifty colleges and universities in the United States. From 1927 until 1932 he offered a summer course in modern marriage at Columbia University, and in 1932 became a

Vogue Studio

PAUL POPENOE

regular lecturer in biology at the University of Southern California.

Modern Marriage (1925, revised 1940) is one of Popenoe's principal nontechnical works. E. C. Thompson (in the American Library Association's *Booklist*) found it "enlightening, reassuring, full of common sense, as well as easy for the ordinary reader to understand." A number of Popenoe's pamphlets, collected in *Marriage, Before and After* (1942), express his belief that the three primary causes of marital unhappiness are the failure to adjust biologically, mismanagement of family finances, and malallocation of recreation. Believing the survival of western civilization to be dependent upon the institution of the family, he has also written *The Conservation of the Family* (1926). To check the growing divorce rate closely associated with urbanization, Popenoe looks to the schools, the community, the courts, and the existing families for extensive marital and family education. He notes, too, that mathematical probability of divorce decreases with the number of children born to a couple. This is one reason for advocating the selective or proportional family wage used successfully in France and Belgium, which was used by the United States Army for family allotments. Equal pay for equal work discriminates against the family man in favor of the bachelor, as parenthood reduces the real wage. To correct this, Popenoe would have each industry establish a fund for automatic salary increases to cover the expense of additions to the worker's family.

Applied Eugenics (1918, revised 1933, translated into Japanese), which is generally considered "a standard book in its field," was written by Popenoe in collaboration with Roswell Hill Johnson. The *American Journal of Sociology* printed reviews of the textbook: N. E. Himes agreed with most of Popenoe's and

Johnson's proposals, noting that "only rarely do the authors go beyond the evidence," while E. B. Reuter called their proposals "a highly uncritical piece of special pleading." H. M. Parshley (New York *Herald Tribune*) wrote: "*Applied Eugenics* is simply indispensable . . . [as a] complete, authoritative, up-to-date, and levelheaded compendium of the subject"; and N. M. Grier in the *Christian Century* recommended it "for all who wish to have a clearer viewpoint into the proposals of eugenics." Popenoe has also written *Problems of Human Reproduction* (1926), *The Child's Heredity* (1929, translated into German), and *The Practical Applications of Heredity* (1930). The Human Betterment Foundation published another of his books, *Sterilization for Human Betterment* (1929, translated into German and Japanese) upon which he worked with Ezra Seymour Gosney, summarizing the results of six thousand operations in California from 1919 to 1929. Popenoe has also brought out collected papers on eugenic sterilization in California. For his work in eugenics, Occidental College awarded him an honorary D.Sc. in 1929.

Dr. Popenoe is a member of the American Genetic Association, the Genetics Association of America, the American Eugenics Society (on the advisory council), the Eugenics Research Association, the International Federation of Eugenics Organization, the American Association for the Study of Human Heredity, the Population Association of America, the American Social Hygiene Association, and the American Association for the Advancement of Science. He is Republican in party affiliation; his club is the Cosmos in Washington, D.C. Popenoe and the former Betty Lee Stankowitch were married on August 23, 1920; their four sons are Paul, Jr., Oliver, John, and David. Blue-eyed and gray-haired, Popenoe stands five feet nine inches in height, weighs 175 pounds. His favorite recreation is gardening and his favorite addiction is reading newspapers. The scientist has a sense of humor which asserts itself in his personality, in his writing, and in his lectures: while delivering scholarly lectures, he is yet "scintillating, witty, and brilliant."

References

Am Mag 115:60+ Je '33 por
Bet Homes & Gard 18:34+ S '39 por
American Men of Science (1944)
Who's Who in America, 1946-47

POTEMKIN, VLADIMIR P(ETROVICH) 1878—Feb. 22(?), 1946 Soviet diplomat and educator; active in Russian Revolution; had brilliant diplomatic career from 1922 to 1937, in Turkey, Greece, Italy, France, Geneva; vice-commissar for foreign affairs 1937-40; commissar for education of Russian Federal Socialist Republic from 1940; member of the Supreme Soviet of the U.S.S.R.

Obituary

N Y Times p44 F 24 '46 por

POTOFSKY, JACOB S(AMUEL)   Nov. 16, 1894-   Trade union leader

Address: b. c/o Amalgamated Clothing Workers of America, 15 Union Sq., New York; h. 164-24 86th Rd., Jamaica Hills, N.Y.

Jacob S. Potofsky, lifelong associate and co-worker of Sidney Hillman [40], was elected unanimously on July 13, 1946, to succeed his late chief as general president of the Amalgamated Clothing Workers of America. Potofsky is credited with a major share of the responsibility for the steady growth of the A.C.W.A., the union which has pioneered in collective bargaining and voluntary arbitration, now conducted on an industry-wide basis, to promote industrial peace. The new head of Amalgamated —its three hundred fifty thousand members in United States and Canada have 96 per cent of the men's clothing industry under contract— pledged "a continuing Hillman policy and a continuing Hillman tradition."

Born in Radomisl, in the Russian Ukraine, on November 16, 1894, to Rebecca and Simon Potofsky, Jacob Samuel Potofsky was brought to the United States at the age of eleven. The family settled in Chicago, and, after three years, Jacob got his first job and began to attend night school. Starting as a three-dollar-a-week "floor boy" at the Hart, Schaffner, and Marx men's clothing factory, where his father, brother, and sister were also employed, in the course of a year he was earning five dollars as a loop-turner, and then seven dollars and twenty-one cents a week as an operator.

Young Potofsky became a member of Pantsmakers Local 144, and in October 1910 took part in the historic strike which Hillman led against the firm to protest the wage reductions and sweatshop conditions prevailing in the sharply competitive clothing industry. The agreement negotiated the following January provided for the establishment of a three-man arbitration board—"the first realistic step in collective bargaining in America." The "autocratic" officers of the national union, the United Garment Workers, had lost favor, however, for their "conservative tactics" in calling off the strike before the fought-for increase in wages and reduction of working hours were granted. Three years later, when a group of opposing delegates were not seated at the 1914 convention, they seceded and, with Hillman as president, set up the independent Amalgamated Clothing Workers of America.

Potofsky's thirty-six years' association with Hillman began with the 1910 strike. "My career has been to do whatever needed to be done in the union," Potofsky has said. "I was a soldier in the ranks. Hillman was the chief, and I followed his orders. I did clerical work, I wrote, I made speeches, I organized workers. I followed the demands of the hour." Immediately after the strike sixteen-year-old Potofsky became union secretary in his shop. Then, in 1913, after a year without pay as treasurer of his local, the youth was made the office manager of Locals 144 and 39. In 1914 he became secretary-treasurer of the seven-local Chicago joint board and, in 1916, with three years' experience as a full-time union executive, he went to New

JACOB S. POTOFSKY

York to help Hillman open the new national office.

There Potofsky was assistant general secretary-treasurer of the A.C.W.A. for the next eighteen years. He was concerned with the activities which caused Carroll R. Daugherty in *Labor Problems in American History* (1933) to take note of the organization as "the outstanding union in the country." "The Amalgamated Clothing Workers are avowedly revolutionary in the socialistic sense," wrote Daugherty, "but for years there has been no better example of business unionism than that afforded by the progressive leaders of this organization." Combining "social idealism with practical and constructive measures," Daugherty wrote, the union cooperated with employers to increase efficiency and output and to stabilize employment. It operated a joint employment agency for members and clothing employers, and, to relieve unavoidable idleness, helped to manage joint unemployment insurance funds with the large manufacturers. The union's two banks, the Amalgamated Bank of New York and the Trust and Savings Bank in Chicago, both of which had withstood the depression, were named by Daugherty as the two largest and most successful of the seven labor banks in operation in 1932. In New York City the union built cooperative apartment houses, financed largely through its own bank.

In the depths of the depression, after the first election of President Roosevelt [42] and the advent of the New Deal, Potofsky became the "inspiring leader and spark plug" of the successful Amalgamated drive to organize seventy-five thousand cotton garment workers. After a year of organizing in Pennsylvania, where the drive was concentrated, and in New Jersey, Connecticut, upstate New York, and the St. Louis area, he "cracked sweatshop rule" in the shirt industry. This organizing drive has

POTOFSKY, JACOB S.—*Continued*

been considered the union leader's greatest achievement. In October 1933 the independent Amalgamated joined the A.F. of L.; but, after two years, it affiliated with the newly founded Congress of Industrial Organizations. Potofsky, a member of the executive board of the CIO since its inception, has found occasion to praise the policy of the A.C.W.A., which has been in favor of unity between the A.F. of L. and CIO.

In 1934, when Hillman was being appointed to positions on New Deal industry and labor advisory boards, Potofsky received the official title of assistant president of Amalgamated. During the next six years he testified before the Minimum Wage boards created under the NRA, directed organizing activities, and conducted negotiations with employers. By the end of 1937 A.C.W.A. membership had grown to two hundred thousand, and the drives, which had aimed at a subsistence wage level for textile workers, resulted in contracts with 95 per cent of the men's garment industry. In 1940 Potofsky was elected general secretary-treasurer. In this office he had under his direction the plans for life insurance, sickness and hospitalization benefits in which membership is covered by the union's two insurance companies. (A new pension plan will be started in 1947.) Since 1940, also, Potofsky has been chairman of the CIO Latin-American Affairs Committee, the labor organization which works for improvement of living standards of workers in Latin America. In November 1946, upon the invitation of the Mexican Federation of Labor, Potofsky led the CIO delegation which attended the inaugural ceremonies of Miguel Alemán '46 as president of Mexico. Earlier that month, when the CIO declined an invitation from the Argentine Government to send representatives to observe labor conditions in that country, Potofsky declared, "There is no democratic functioning in labor circles of that country [Argentina] today."

The "order" to Potofsky was to "run the union" in 1940-41 while Hillman was serving in Washington as associate director of the Office for Production Management. At a meeting of the CIO executive board in July 1941, Potofsky, a "fierce fighter for the causes in which he believes," had an open break with John L. Lewis '42. Accusing him of "playing politics," Potofsky sharply criticized his anti-Roosevelt policies, policies which led to Lewis' resignation as president of the CIO. In answer to Lewis' attack on Administration labor policy, which the Amalgamated leader saw as an invitation to his union to quit the CIO, he pledged loyalty to the parent body. "There are sharp contrasts, in tradition, in tactics, in temperament," *PM* observed at the time, "between the Lewis wing of labor-leading and the Hillman school of which Potofsky is a veteran and skillful disciple." Potofsky believes that Roosevelt "captured the imagination and hopes of working people for material benefit." The New Deal, which Potofsky saw as the fulfillment of labor dreams, "expresses their higher aspirations as well," he commented. "Its social

legislation has enabled us to go forward. Despite all raving and criticism, the key fact is that we never before [1941] had eleven million workers organized."

On July 10, 1946, three days after the death of Sidney Hillman, Potofsky was unanimously elected general president of the A.C.W.A. Pledging to devote his energies "to the advancement of Amalgamated membership and to the cause of labor generally," Potofsky said that Amalgamated would continue its active participation in the CIO Political Action Committee, the American Labor Party in New York State, and the promotion of world peace through the World Federation of Trade Unions. Amalgamated is engaged in the fight for desired legislation in Washington and the State capitals and in the CIO campaign to organize the South. Like that of his predecessor, Potofsky's concern will be to equip the union with "young, able blood and all available experts from within and without." In his initial interview, the new president said that he would adhere to the principles of harmonious collective bargaining and arbitration that had made the men's clothing industry a model of peaceful labor relations during Hillman's lifetime. "The rest of the country," he said, "would do well to follow the example of the clothing industry and allied trades [which] have been leaders in promoting industrial peace." Both the union and the employer group, which is represented by the national bargaining committee of the Clothing Manufacturers Association of the United States, have, declaredly, found industry-wide bargaining and the closed shop, which the A.C.W.A. enforces, "of great benefit in stabilizing the clothing industry and ending cutthroat competition."

Potofsky, who voted the Socialist ticket prior to 1932, when he cast his vote for Roosevelt, joined no party before the formation of the American Labor Party. A participant in the first convention called by Labor's Non-Partisan League, he has been vice-chairman of the A.L.P. from its inception. He was also a founder of the CIO-PAC. The Amalgamated executive was active in war relief and civilian defense drives, including the CIO War Chest, the War and Victory Loan Drives, for which he was awarded the Treasury Silver Medal, and the American Red Cross, which gave him several citations. He has been a prominent worker for the United Jewish Appeal, and the Federation of Jewish Charities, of which he has been the speakers' bureau chairman. The union leader is a member of the Civic Center Board and an advocate of "more good music at low prices." He has joined the Citizens' Committee on Displaced Persons, which seeks modification of United States immigration laws, to permit that country to receive some four hundred thousand European refugees within the next few years.

Potofsky is a widower; with him live a daughter by his first marriage, Mrs. Delia Gottlieb, his son-in-law, and grandchild, and the children of his second marriage, Jacqueline and Bruce. An enthusiastic fisherman with little time for fishing, he likes his intermittent vegetable gardening at a New Jersey farm, chess playing, and reading "a biography or some poetry." Jacob Potofsky is known as a "disciplined" man, who speaks "slowly and thoughtfully," without raising his voice. He is six feet tall and has brown eyes and black hair. His goatee, which interviewers agree he does not require for dignity, he attributes to a European visit in 1921—"I thought I'd bring something back."

References

Advance 32:1 Ag 1 '46
N Y Herald Tribune p16 Jl 15 '46 por
N Y Post p12 Jl 15 '46; p31 Ag 23 '46 por
N Y Times p27+ Jl 15 '46 por
Newsweek 28:61 Jl 29 '46 por
PM p20 Jl 10 '41 por; p14 Jl 15 '46 por; p14 Jl 16 '46
Who's Who in Labor (1946)

PRATT, E(DWIN) J(OHN) Feb. 4, 1883-
Poet; college professor
Address: b. Victoria College, Toronto, Canada; h. 21 Cortleigh Blvd., Toronto, Canada

E. J. PRATT

E. J. Pratt, Canada's most famous contemporary poet, became more widely known as one of today's greatest writers of verse upon the publication in the United States of his *Collected Poems*. Pratt is the sea-loving, chiefly narrative poet who describes "icebergs, whales, prehistoric giants and ocean storms," and whose lighter verse, commentators declare, will assure him a "cordial welcome in Elysium from Aristophanes and his fellow craftsmen."

Born in the small fishing village of Western Bay, Newfoundland, on February 4, 1883, Edwin John Pratt spent the first twenty years of his life in the harbor towns of the island. The strong influence of the sea was supplemented by that of the books in the library of his parents, the Methodist minister Reverend John Pratt, and Fanny Pitts (Knight) Pratt. At fifteen young Pratt halted his education in local schools for a time, to become a clerk in a retail store. About five years later, in 1903, he was teaching in the elementary schools and had become a student-preacher in the churches of Newfoundland whaling and sealing villages, among them Moreton Harbour.

Meanwhile, having been graduated from St. John's Methodist College in Newfoundland, Pratt left his church and school positions in 1907 to attend Victoria College of the University of Toronto. While there he became interested in philosophy and psychology. Pratt received his B.A. degree in 1911, his M.A. in 1913, and his Ph.D. in 1917, offering as his thesis *Studies in Pauline Eschatology*. From 1913 until 1919 he lectured in psychology and philosophy at Toronto University, while writing much published and unpublished verse. In 1917 was published privately an imitative Newfoundland narrative, *Rachel*, done in the manner of Wordsworth's *Michael*. The poet then completed a long lyrical drama entitled *Clay*, which he recently described as "full of theories and reflections of theories about life . . . bald,

very bald generalizations—practically the whole cargo of the department of philosophy as it existed twenty years ago in the University of Toronto."

The "failure" of this book caused Pratt to become "disenchanted" with psychological and philosophical approaches to human experience, E. K. Brown, author of *On Canadian Poetry*, reports. In revolt, Pratt sought the emotional element through literature. He was aided in his search by his appointment, in 1920, to the English literature faculty of his alma mater, Victoria College. Now thirty-seven years old, Pratt had not been prepared to teach advanced English literature or language, nor had he printed more than a few distinguished short pieces locally. He was appointed, Brown says, entirely upon his "creative potentialities," and assigned to teach the Shakespearean period.

During the thirties, while the depression "sobered" the poet-professor's attitude, he toured the Dominion as a lecturer and taught in summer schools from Halifax to Vancouver, observing at the same time the political and sociological manifestations which later appeared in his allegorical *Fable of the Goats* (1937). From the earlier pessimistic, abstract subject matter, Pratt's poetry during World War II showed a change to the historical subjects and narrative method for which he has been most praised.

At forty, in 1923, Pratt bought out the first of the works he now lists among his publications. The lyrics, sonnets, and narratives in *A Book of Newfoundland Verse* are chiefly late romantic in mood, natural in theme, and experimental in structure. Very different from these is *The Witches' Brew* (1926), an extravaganza in verse "to be read and reread in delight," which celebrates the "effect of warm, supernatural intoxication . . . notably upon a remarkable electrified sea cat from Zanzibar."

PRATT, E, J.—*Continued*

Much to the author's amusement, the fable, exhibiting Pratt's interest in animal lore, his preference for scientific, rather than literary reference, his hearty sense of humor, and the earthy tradition of the supernatural, was variously interpreted in Great Britain as a mysterious, profound political treatise, as a liquor advertisement, and as a scathing condemnation of demon rum. In reality *The Witches' Brew* was written, Pratt revealed to William Rose Benét (who wrote the introduction to the American edition of the *Collected Poems*), "in celebration of my fifth wedding anniversary and dedicated to my wife." The poem, "if such it may be called," was a "straight 'let her go Gallagher' for a wedding feast."

Said to have established Pratt as the "preeminent figure in Canadian poetry" of the time, *The Titans* (1926) was hailed as the "work of a poet who has defined his personality and determined his form. In one of the two sea narratives comprising this volume, *The Cachalot*, a powerful story of a whale, Pratt employs a rhymed "racing tetrameter", "Byronic verve," and the skill he has for twisting the "big word into a humorous effect, while caressing it at the same time for its resonant beauty." *The Cachalot,* which Benét considers "the greatest whale poem in the language," and which others believe surpasses even *Moby Dick*, was written, Pratt says, before he read the Melville novel he was later to edit for use in Canadian secondary schools.

"The Iron Door" (1927), a "somber and eloquent" ode on the death of the poet's mother, was suggested to him in part by "The Man Against the Sky," a poem by Edwin Arlington Robinson, one of Pratt's earliest American admirers. Robinson, Henry W. Wells stated in the magazine *College English*, returned the compliment by imitating Pratt in parts of his own narrative, *Matthias at the Door.* For his next volume, *The Roosevelt and the Antinoe* (1930), based on the rescue of the crew of a British freighter by the American liner, *President Roosevelt*, Pratt received critical accolades for "one of the most brilliant and startlingly sincere of all English poems dealing with the sea and ships." That same year Pratt's *Verses of the Sea*, edited for use in Canadian high schools, was issued. The poet's 1933 collection was entitled *Many Moods*; his next work was *The Loss of The Titanic* (1935). The latter, "less epic" than many of Pratt's earlier poems, displayed the theme of *hubris*. Published two years later was *The Fable of the Goats* (1937), Pratt's pessimistic depression allegory of the "deep *malaise* in the communal heart of the world."

The long verse story of the martydom of the early North American Jesuit missionaries, *Brébeuf and His Brethren*, the first volume of Pratt's verse to appear in the United States, was issued there in 1943, four years after its Canadian appearance. It was hailed as the best Catholic poem of recent years: most American reviewers appreciated Protestant Pratt's use of Catholic religious values and pronounced the workmanship "respectable but not remarkable." A dramatic arrangement of the poem,

entitled *The Life and Death of Jean de Brébeuf*, with music by Healy Willan, was given its première by the Canadian Broadcasting Corporation on September 26, 1943, and in January of 1944 was presented as part of the golden anniversary season of Toronto's Massey Hall by the Toronto Symphony Orchestra and the Mendelssohn Choir.

Dunkirk (1941), a long poem based on the British evacuation from the French port, is considered outstanding for its accuracy, for its "intense portrayal of the sea," and for the heroic climax. With the publication of *Still Life and Other Verse* in 1943, Pratt's bibliography included twelve recognized volumes of poetry. His latest work is *They Are Returning*. In preparation are "Sea Poems on the Work of the Canadian Navy in the War," and a poem on the arctic explorer, Sir John Franklin, and his crew.

The *Collected Poems*, a large representative selection of Pratt's work, issued in Canada in 1944 and in the United States the following year, received high praise. The most obvious and outstanding quality, wrote L. A. Mackay in the *Canadian Forum*, "is the sheer natural vitality of the writing, all the more exciting at a time when so many poets offer us a choice between a natural anemia and a forced heartiness." Critics who admire his narratives compare them favorably to the best of Stephen Vincent Benét '43 and Archibald MacLeish '40, while those who do not care for his works compare them unfavorably with the weakest of John Masefield, whom all agree his work resembles. The shorter lyrics, said to resemble Hardy's and Robinson's, are thought to fall short of the longer verse, often through faulty rhyming, and perhaps because, as Brown says, "The microscopic is not congenial to his space- and size-loving nature." Some brief meditative poems and especially "Come Away, Death," are also highly praised. The distinctiveness of Pratt's approach is apparent from the author's poetic theory: "Poetry ought to be, at least in part, the expression of a grand binge, making for healthy physiological releases where the world for a time is seen backside-up, and the poet becomes gloriously emancipated from the thralldoms of day-by-day routine."

From its inception in 1936 until 1943, Pratt edited the *Canadian Poetry* magazine. The poet was awarded the Litt.D. degree in 1945, the Companion of St. Michael's and St. George in the Dominion Day Honours of 1946, the Governor-general's medal for *The Fable of the Goats* in 1937, and the Lorne Pierce Gold Medal of the Royal Society of Canada in 1941. He has been a Fellow of the Royal Society since 1930, a member of the Canadian Author's Association and of the Toronto Arts and Letters Club.

The poet was married to Viola Leone Whitney on August 20, 1918; they have one daughter, Mildred Claire. A member of the United Church of Canada, Pratt is an ordained minister. He is five feet ten inches tall, weighs 160 pounds, and has blue eyes and brown hair. William Rose Benét has described him as "delighting in both dreams and action," and as one of the youngest men of his acquaintance in "enthusiasm, generosity, and good fellowship." Pratt, who enjoys his dinner and "his Irish whisky," dedicated *The Titans* to the "boys of the stag parties," of which he is a frequent host. Of these gatherings Brown has written: "Pratt is never so much himself as when he sits at the head of his table with half a dozen men around him, a great fowl before him, and vigorous easy conversation in the air."

References

Col Engl 7:452+ My '46

Brown, E. K. On Canadian Poetry (1943)

Pratt, E. J. Collected Poems (1945)

PRIMROSE, WILLIAM Aug. 23, 1904-
Violist

Address: b. c/o Columbia Concerts, Inc., 113 W. 57th St., New York

Despite music critics' usual wide divergence of opinion, when contemporary violists are the topic of discussion they are in agreement that William Primrose is one of the greatest, as well as the man who has made the viola popular as a solo instrument. As expressed by *Newsweek*'s critic, "It has taken Primrose's musicianship and style to show this country that the viola can be an instrument of glowing, vibrant warmth."

William Primrose was born in Glasgow, Scotland, on August 23, 1904. He is the son of John Primrose, a musician proficient on both the violin and the viola, violist for a time of the Scottish Symphony Orchestra and later librarian of the London Philharmonic Orchestra under Sir Thomas Beecham '41. The boy's first instrument was the violin, on which he began taking lessons from his father at the age of four. At seven he was playing for Glasgow's citizens in a series of free concerts called "The Pleasant Sunday Afternoons." There is a story that a visitor to the Primrose home once attempted to tease the young violinist with the remark that he could play only scales— "whereupon the outraged youngster piped up with 'I play key of C key of G Jesus Loves Me and Home Sweet Home' all in one breath and then stalked out of the house." But whatever his repertoire then, at the age of ten, a pupil of Camille Ritter, he made his debut in the Mendelssohn Concerto in E Minor for violin and orchestra in Glasgow's largest concert hall under the baton of the late Henri Verbrugghen.

Six years later, in 1920, Landon Ronald, then in his last year as conductor of the Scottish Symphony, heard him play and, impressed, arranged for the Corporation of the City of London to finance the young Primrose's further musical education at the Guildhall School of Music in London, of which he was principal. Primrose studied at the Guildhall School for three years, making his official debut in 1923 as soloist in Edward Elgar's Concerto in B Minor for violin and orchestra with the Royal Albert Hall Orchestra, Sir Landon Ronald conducting. For the occasion a friend of his

father's lent him the famous Betts Stradivarius violin now in the Library of Congress.

Primrose points out, however, that all this time the instrument he was playing was not the one he most desired to play. His father owned a rare Amati viola with the mellow contralto tone of which, he says, he was "passionately in love." But this, which he had sometimes played after learning to pick the lock on the case, he was forbidden, because "at that time," he explains, "the viola was thought of as a sort of Cinderella of the strings—a harbor for disappointed fiddlers." It was not until he went to study with the world-renowned Belgian violinist Eugène Ysaÿe in 1925 that Primrose was finally able to substitute his beloved viola for the violin. The Belgian master's word was law in the Primrose household, as in many another musical household, and Ysaÿe, having heard the young man play the viola, advised him to make the change. Primrose studied both the violin and the viola with Ysaÿe and by 1930 had permanently decided upon the latter and acquired mastery of it.

That year, as he was about to return to England, Primrose received a cable from the London String Quartet: they were in the United States, heavily booked for engagements, but their violist was ill; could Primrose join them at once? From 1930 to 1935 with this famous chamber music ensemble he toured the United States, South America, and Europe. At intervals in South America he also appeared as a solo violist, his first recital, in Rio de Janeiro in 1931, eliciting from one critic the comment, "there has never existed a viola player with such phenomenal technique." But it was not until the quartet was disbanded in 1935 that he made a beginning toward the career as a solo performer which was eventually to popularize the viola as a virtuoso instrument. Then, returning to England, he made his London debut as a solo violist under Sir Thomas Beecham, and for the next two years toured Europe in recital and as solo violist with the major symphony orchestras.

In 1937 National Broadcasting Company officials, engaged in a talent hunt for virtuoso musicians to fill the posts of section leaders in the NBC Symphony Orchestra which they were forming for Arturo Toscanini '42, heard a recording of Primrose playing a Paganini caprice. Wondering if it could be a violinist like Heifetz '44 performing under an assumed name, they wired Primrose an offer of the first viola desk. Though still interested in a virtuoso career, the violist accepted, and this time he came to the United States to remain permanently. Primrose was Toscanini's first violist from the autumn of 1937 through 1942. At the same time he filled solo engagements with other orchestras and several times also appeared as soloist with the NBC Symphony. The first time was in 1938, when he introduced the William Walton '40 viola concerto, which had been especially written for him, under the baton of Sir Adrian Boult '46.

On April 3, 1938, over the NBC network Primrose inaugurated a series of radio programs featuring music for the viola and that

J. Abresch

WILLIAM PRIMROSE

same year founded the Primrose Quartet to give radio performances of great chamber music. When this quartet later made its concert debut, under the auspices of the New Friends of Music in Town Hall on November 5, 1939, the critic of the New York *Times* wrote: "The quartet . . . in the perfection of its ensemble and in the unity of its thought . . . blows to smithereens the traditional conception that no ensemble is fit for the public ear until it has played so long together that the response of its members to each other's playing is quite atrophied, and their playing becomes respectably cold-storaged. The fact is that New Yorkers have rarely—in recent seasons at least —heard such playing as the Primrose Quartet vouchsafed yesterday."

Primrose remained as first violist of the NBC Symphony until 1942, when he left the orchestra to devote all his time to what he had wanted to do ever since he was a small boy. Making as many as eighty appearances in a season, he toured the United States, Canada, and the Latin American countries and was featured as soloist with the Boston, Philadelphia, NBC, and other orchestras as well as in recital. Critics began to term him "the blue ribbon violist", "the world's foremost violist", "the finest violist of our time." Earlier, Ernest Newman, the English musicologist, had written of one of his London performances: "Playing so rich in subtleties and delicacies as his raises the critical listener's sensitiveness to its conceivable maximum of acuity. He treats us in abundance to the delicacy of shading and accentuation in which he specializes." Concerning a performance of Berlioz' *Harold in Italy* with the Boston Symphony under Serge Koussevitzky [40], Olin Downes [43] said: "Mr. Primrose played not only as a master but a poet and dramatist of his instrument . . . and gave such haunting beauty and intensity to his part that

this work alone would have made the occasion memorable."

Primrose, it is said, has done perhaps more than any other musician to persuade American music lovers that the viola ranks with the violin and the cello as a solo instrument. He is emphatic in pointing out that the viola, which is somewhat larger than the violin and has a tone a fifth deeper, "is *not* just an overgrown fiddle. . . .It poses its own particular problems, demands an entirely different treatment technically and tonally, and has its own distinct personality. . . .Always when I am playing the viola I feel a sense of oneness with the instrument that I never felt when I was playing the violin. I have heard a number of violinists who seemed to me more suited to the viola, and it has been interesting to discover that several of them did later make the change." He finds it gratifying to observe that students today are choosing the viola as a virtuoso rather than as a secondary instrument, thus rescuing it from its hitherto comparatively insignificant role in the orchestra or string quartet.

Primrose plays on one of two violas, the Amati, *circa* 1630, which was formerly his father's, and one, *circa* 1945, especially made for him by William Moennig, Jr., of Philadelphia, which, it is said, achieves the mellow roundness of tone of an Amati in combination with the greater brilliance of a Stradivarius through a judicious blending of the measurements of both. With the latter, which famous musicians have chosen in preference to his Amati, and which he has played at over forty concerts to establish his point, he has been able to disprove one of his pet aversions, that tenet of "musical snobbery" which holds that no modern instrument can equal in tone the product of the old masters.

Besides being extremely active as a concert and radio artist, Primrose teaches at the Curtis Institute of Music in Philadelphia. He has recorded a large repertoire of viola literature, and in this field was honored by Victor's release of *Harold in Italy* as its first album following the two-year Petrillo-imposed recording ban which was lifted at the end of 1944. Avocationally, he is equally active. In his student days, before his teachers interfered to protect his hands, he was an amateur boxer, and today the sport still forms one of his chief interests, as do cricket and golf, chess, and American history. Together with fellow members of New York's Lotos Club he is sometimes able to arrange scratch cricket games, and he proudly wears the specially striped ties of the Surrey, Yorkshire, and Middlesex cricket clubs of England, of which he is an honorary member. When he is in California he takes lessons in chess from Herman Steiner, international master, and at present, with Zino Francescatti, the French violinist, is playing a series of games by mail, with Columbia Concerts acting as the forwarding agent for the correspondence. And at any time, reported interviewer George Keaney of the New York *World-Telegram,* "he will discuss the Whiskey

Rebellion or the Missouri Compromise, instilling his listeners with his own unbounded enthusiasm for his adopted land."

References

N Y World-Telegram p9 Mr 14 '45 por
Newsweek 25:108+ Mr 26 '45 por
Time 34:56+ N 27 '39 por
Victor Record Review 7:3+ Mr '45 por
Ewen, D. ed. Living Musicians (1940) por
Thompson, O. ed International Cyclopedia of Music and Musicians (1943)
Who Is Who in Music, 1941

QUISLING, VIDKUN (ABRAHAM LAURITZ) (kvĭs'lĭng vĭd'kōōn) July 18, 1887-Oct. 24, 1945 Norwegian Army officer, diplomat, Cabinet member; as founder of the Nasjonal Samling (National Union) party he allied his party to the ideology of the Nazis; aided the Germans to invade Norway in April 1940; became head of the State Council as Norway's sole political leader during the occupation; found guilty by the Norwegian High Court of being a traitor and executed October 24, 1945. See *Current Biography* 1940 Yearbook.

Obituary

N Y Times p1 O 24 '45

QUO TAI-CHI (gwô'tī"chē) 1889- Chinese Government official; diplomat

Address: c/o United Nations, New York

Quo Tai-chi, China's permanent representative in the United Nations Security Council, was the chairman of the Council during the first month of the New York session in the spring of 1946. During his long years as what he calls "a good party diplomat" prior to his appointment in February 1946 by the Nationalist Government of Chiang Kai-shek '40, Quo Tai-chi had been foreign secretary, Minister, and Ambassador of the Chinese Republic; and many times was delegate to the League of Nations for the early Chinese Republic.

Quo Tai-chi was born in 1889 at Kwang-tsi, in the province of Hupeh, where he received his early education from his father, "well-known scholar and much respected teacher." Then, after a year of study at Wuchang in 1903-04, he won a Chinese Imperial Government scholarship to the United States. He attended Easthampton High School and Williston Seminary in Massachusetts, and in 1908 entered the University of Pennsylvania. Editor on *The Pennsylvanian* and for a time reporter for a Philadelphia paper, Quo is said to have been disappointed when the paper printed his articles exactly as he wrote them, because this spoiled his opportunity to learn how to write better English. He was elected to Phi Beta Kappa and graduated in 1911 with a B.S. in political science. But he did not follow his father into the teaching profession. "In China, a teacher is right up there in the place of honor," Quo once remarked. "I am like the black sheep of the family."

Shelburne Studios

QUO TAI-CHI

In March 1912, within a year after his graduation, Quo Tai-chi returned to China to become secretary to General Li Yuan-hung, the vice-president, and subsequently president, of the new Republic. He served concurrently, in 1916-17, as Foreign Office counselor. After five years with the Peiping Government, upon the Tuchun Rebellion in 1917, Quo left to join Dr. Sun Yat-Sen's revolutionary movement in the south. When President Yuan Shih-kai's attempt to found a new dynasty was defeated and the Constitutional Government was set up at Canton that year, Quo became secretary to President Sun. In 1918 Quo was again in the United States, this time sent by the Constitutional Government as a member of a special commission. The following year he was technical delegate to the Paris Peace Conference.

Throughout the next decade Quo Tai-chi served his Government in China. Attached to the president's office in 1921-22, he was counselor to Dr. Sun and chief of the publicity bureau. Through 1922 he served under the governorship of Dr. Wu Ting-fang, as head of the Political Department of the Kwangtung Provincial Government. Becoming active in the diplomatic sphere, he was in Canton in 1923-24 (later at Nanking) as Vice-Minister for Foreign Affairs; in Shanghai, in 1927-28, as Commissioner and Vice-Minister, and for a time Acting Minister, for Foreign Affairs. In 1932, as a member of the foreign relations commission and Political Vice-Minister for Foreign Affairs, he was chief delegate to the Shanghai armistice negotiations for the cessation of hostilities and withdrawal of the Japanese troops. But his activities had been varied in 1925-26, when he served as President of the National Wuchang Commercial University, and in 1928, when he became a member of the Legislative Yuan, in which capacity he contin-

QUO TAI-CHI—*Continued*

ued until 1930, having refused a ministerial appointment to Rome in 1929.

After resigning as Vice-Minister for Foreign Affairs in May 1932, Quo went to London as Minister to Great Britain. At the same time, as Chinese delegate to the Disarmament Conference and the World Economic and Monetary Conference of 1933 and to the thirteenth, fourteenth, and special Assemblies of the League of Nations, in 1932 and 1933, Minister Quo, declaring that China would never recognize the Japanese occupation of Manchuria, sought application of the League's principles to the Far East. Commentators reported that he "rose to a high level of world statesmanship" when he insisted at Geneva that "the democracies could not with safety suffer aggression against the least and the weakest among them—that their destiny would be . . . indivisible against the enemies of civilization." The Chinese minister warned in a 1934 conference with British Foreign Secretary Sir John Simon that Japanese claims for special privileges in China constituted a threat to the League's work for the rehabilitation of his country and a breach of the Nine Power Treaty of 1922, which guaranteed the territorial and administrative integrity of China and the "Open Door" principle of equal opportunity in China for the commerce and industry of all nations.

In 1934 the Chinese envoy to Great Britain was also a representative on the League of Nations Council and First Delegate to the fifteenth assembly. In 1935, still his nation's representative at the Court of St. James, he became China's first Ambassador to Great Britain when the Chinese Legation was raised to the status of an Embassy. And that same year he was a delegate, together with V. K. Wellington Koo [41] and Chien Tai, to the Brussels Nine Power Conference. During the years of the Sino-Japanese War, Ambassador Quo conferred frequently with British Foreign Minister Anthony Eden [40] and bent all his efforts in seeking for China the aid of Great Britain, the Soviet Union, and the United States. In April 1940 he urged that Britain and the United States cease shipping supplies to Japan; in July, in conference with Winston Churchill [42] and Lord Halifax [40], he objected to the British closing of the Burma Road. Then, in 1941, resigning from the ambassadorial post, Quo returned to China to become Minister of Foreign Affairs in the Nationalist Government. By this time, he noted, he had become "fully committed to the diplomatic life."

Quo's appointment as Foreign Minister in April 1941 was one of several involved in a shakeup of the Kuomintang, and was seen as a move to strengthen Chinese ties with Great Britain and the United States. En route from London to Chungking, capital of Free China ("in mid-passage between two bombed capitals," as Quo described it), the former Ambassador to Britain proposed a strategic and "spiritual" pooling of American, British, and Chinese economic and natural resources to fight the invader. "Do not give weapons to our enemies . . . who are . . . your enemies too. Do not give them the materials and the fuel to bomb

us," he warned, asking for raw materials, guns, and planes for the defense of China. When the war began its spread from Burma to Singapore in 1941, Quo, in conference with United States Secretary of State Cordell Hull [40], helped lay the groundwork for the "definite" relinquishment of American extraterritorial rights in China after the war. (These Hull-Quo agreements were interpreted by the *Christian Science Monitor* as an American pledge not only to give military aid to China but to "see to it" that she would be "internally free after the war.") Six days after the Nazi invasion of the Soviet Union, Foreign Minister Quo called for cooperation particularly among China, the United States, Britain, and Russia. On the fourth anniversary of the Sino-Japanese War Quo had asserted that his country was "prepared to fight for four or fourteen more years"; after the Japanese attack on Pearl Harbor in December 1941, the Foreign Minister announced his country's declaration of war against Germany and Italy two days before the Axis declaration of war on the United States.

After a year as Foreign Minister, Quo was appointed to the Supreme National Defense Council, on which he served as chairman of the foreign affairs committee. (Generalissimo Chiang Kai-shek is chairman of the Council.) Formed by the Fifth Kuomintang Central Executive Committee in 1939 to supersede the inactive Political Committee, this "highest organ of political direction" is empowered to direct all organs of high authority in the Government, and considers principles of legislation, Government administrative policies and programs, military and fiscal plans, and the selection of political and other officials.

In February 1946 Quo became the Chinese Nationalist Government's permanent representative to the Security Council of the United Nations, and during its opening session in the spring of 1946 at Hunter College in New York he served as first president from March 17 to April 17, when "by rote [since the chairmanship is monthly rotated alphabetically among the member nations] and with pleasure" he relinquished the position to Hafez Afifi Pasha, the Egyptian delegate. As president, Quo had been faced with the solution of procedural problems for which there was no precedent, and during the weeks between the opening meeting on March 25 and Quo's retirement on April 16, the Security Council agenda had included the Russo-Iranian dispute concerning the continued presence of Russian troops on Iranian soil in violation of a Russo-Iranian agreement and the hotly-debated issue of the status of Franco [42] Spain. On his last day as Council president the Chinese delegate joined the majority who opposed the request to remove the Russian-Iranian dispute from the Council agenda. (Secretary-General Trygve Lie [46] questioned the legality of the Council's action in keeping the Iranian question on the agenda when both Russia and Iran had requested its dismissal.) The New York *Herald Tribune* editorially described Quo's chairmanship as "close to perfection" and added that "while Dr. Quo would be an exceptional man in any country, as he is in China, he nonetheless is thoroughly Chinese." During his presidency the Chinese delegate's adventures in New York included a speech over the first permanent television network in America.

A member of the twelve-man U.N. Atomic Energy Commission, Quo favored the American plan to abolish the veto on questions on atomic power. In July Quo left for Paris as a member of his country's delegation to the Peace Conference, and upon his return in October he resumed his duties on the U.N. Security Council.

Quo Tai-chi's wife and two sons, now living in Santa Barbara, California, have been in the United States since 1939. One son, Mo-Lin, was attending the University of Southern California in 1946; the other, Mo-Ying, a "regular American bruiser," was in grade school. Dr. Quo was awarded honorary doctorates in 1938 and 1946 by Oxford University and the University of Pennsylvania, respectively. In the fall of 1946 he participated in the New York *Herald Tribune* Forum discussion "Atomic Power for Peace," and was one of the lecturers at the experimental Romford School in Connecticut, where short seminars were being conducted by international figures.

Quo is a slight, round-faced man with a ready smile, who speaks a "felicitous" English. "I used to know some very superior American slang . . . left over from my college days," he adds, but he found it a bit dated in 1946. His leisure-time interests include listening to music and playing "inexpert" golf, and he says, "I look forward to the days when I will pick up a newspaper and read about a happening and not have any idea who pulled what off, or, as I guess you would say, what is the real dope."

References

N Y Herald Tribune II p4 Mr 24 '46 por; II p3 Mr 17 '46 por
N Y Sun p17 Ap 28 '41; p22 Ap 4 '46
China Handbook, 1937-43
Who's Who in China (1936)

RAGLAND, RAGS 1905(?)—Aug. 20, 1946 Comedian; appeared in burlesque, musical comedy, and motion pictures; after a Broadway appearance in *Panama Hattie* in 1940, he went to Hollywood and played in *Whistling in the Dark;* among other films were *Meet the People* (1944), *Anchors Aweigh* (1945), and *The Hoodlum Saint* (1946).

Obituary

N Y Times p27 Ag 21 '46 por

RAIMU, JULES (rā-mü zhül) 1883(?)— Sept. 20, 1946 French stage and film comedian; established himself as the chief comic actor in the troupe of Théâtre de Paris; appeared for years at the Folies Bergère; first entered motion pictures in 1929; acclaimed for his roles in Marcel Pagnol's *Marius* and *Caesar;* recognized in the United States with the release of the film *The Baker's Wife* in 1940.

Obituary

N Y Times p15 S 21 '46 por

RAINEY, HOMER P(RICE) Jan. 19, 1896- College president
Address: b. c/o Stephens College, Columbia, Mo.

"For his efforts in behalf of academic freedom, Dr. [Homer P.] Rainey has earned the gratitude of our profession and of the friends of education throughout the country," the Council of the American Association of University Professors announced in June 1946. This was a year and a half after Rainey's clash with the Texas State Board of Regents had resulted in his dismissal from the presidency of the university. Rainey, a leading American educator since the late 1920's, unsuccessfully ran for Governor in the 1946 Democratic primaries in Texas. After two years' absence from the educational field, the educator accepted the post of president of Stephens College, in Missouri.

Born January 19, 1896, in Clarksville, a ranch town in Texas, Homer Price Rainey is the son of Jenny (Price) and Edward Rainey. Before the youth was nineteen, he was an ordained Baptist minister. By washing dishes, waiting on tables, singing in church choirs, and "sitting" at night with children, he was able to attend Austin College, in Sherman, Texas. At twenty-three, immediately upon receiving his B.A. degree, he began to play professional baseball, as the star pitcher of the Galveston team in the Texas League. That year (1919) he received an offer to pitch for the St. Louis Cardinals, but decided instead to become an instructor at Austin College. In the second of the four years he taught there (1919-22) he was married to Mildred Collins, a University of Texas graduate. She accompanied him when he went to the University of Chicago for graduate study in 1922, working in a Chicago department store while he earned his Master's degree. A fellowship enabled him to remain at Chicago a second year, at the end of which he received his Ph.D. degree. He then went to the University of Oregon as associate professor of education; two years later, in 1926, he was advanced to full professor. Two financial studies he made in that period were published as monographs: *A Study of School Finance in Oregon* (1925), and *The Distribution of School Funds in Oregon* (1926). A third monograph, *The Achievement of Elementary School Pupils in Oregon,* appeared in 1927.

In 1927 Franklin College, a small Baptist school in Indiana, appointed the thirty-one-year-old professor of education its president. "The core of a liberal education in our day must be the study of human relationships," Rainey wrote at the time. "Our great fields of study . . . are necessarily sociology, politics, government, psychology, and most of all religion." Under his four-year administration Franklin College revised completely its requirements for the Bachelor's degree. Mathematics and languages became optional, except for students requiring them for professions such as teaching and engineering. Also, a system of specially guided independent study for students of exceptional ability was introduced. Baptist Bucknell University in Lewisburg, Pennsylvania, "stole" the young Franklin College head in November 1931.

HOMER P. RAINEY

In four years as president of Bucknell, Rainey "made news," according to *Time*, "by scrambling the curriculum to make room for more creative work in art, music, literature."

A fourteen-member American Youth Commission, including Rainey, President Robert Maynard Hutchins '40 of Chicago University, novelist Dorothy Canfield Fisher, and Newton Diehl Baker, was appointed in 1935 by Dr. George Frederick Zook '46, the Director of the American Council on Education. The commission, which had at its disposal $800,000 from the Rockefeller-endowed General Education Board, was to make a survey of youth, recreation, and health programs in the country with a view to improving them. Elected its director by the commission, Rainey immediately resigned as Bucknell's president, and launched an investigation which was to include thousands of interviews with young people, and surveys to determine employment trends, the correlation between education and employment, the need and value of vocational and other guidance programs. "It must be understood," he wrote, "that any attempt to analyze the youth problem will be futile and meaningless apart from the total contemporary social scene."

In 1939 the wealthy and rapidly growing University of Texas, which had struck oil on its State-endowed lands in 1923 and had subsequently built a ten-million-dollar campus, "set out," as *Time* phrased it, "to make itself an important educational institution." At the death of the university president Harry Y. Benedict in 1937, the State Board of Regents began scouting for a "big name" for president. Rainey, by that time known as "a crack investigator, a liberal educator with a leaning toward the arts, an able administrator," was offered the post in his home State at an annual salary of seventeen thousand five hundred dollars. After a year as acting president, the Texan was formally inducted as head of the South's largest university in December 1939.

Within a year friction developed between Rainey and the nine-man Board of Regents. The board included Texas big businessmen who were appointed by Governor W. Lee ("Pappy") O'Daniel and his successor Governor Coke Stevenson. The first public notice of the "civil war" at the university occurred in 1942, when the American Association of University Professors "censured" the school for the dismissal by the regents of three economics professors after they had unsuccessfully attempted to speak to correct misstatements about the wage-hour law at a public rally. Rainey fought several other dismissals of so-called "radical" professors, book banning (John Dos Passos' *U.S.A.* was stricken from the sophomore reading list on the grounds of "obscenity"), and the refusal of the regents to appropriate funds for a school for social work and at various times for social science projects. In October 1944, when he had been requested by one of the regents to "stop making so many speeches," particularly before religious organizations, Rainey brought the situation to a head by reading before the faculty a sixteen-point statement outlining "restrictive measures actual and attempted." When he refused to retract the statement, the Texas Board of Regents responded by voting on November 1, 1944, to dismiss him.

The university's students backed Rainey. Six thousand marched to the State capitol bearing a crepe-draped coffin labeled "Academic Freedom." Listeners at rallies were saluted as "Fellow fighters of fascism," raised over six thousand dollars for a "spread-the-facts" fund, and let loose "a blizzard of free speech," pro-Rainey leaflets, reprints of pro-Rainey editorials, and mimeographed letters that were sent to students' parents and Congressmen. The faculty, unanimously behind the deposed president, commended the student body for its "maturity and restraint." All over the State, members of the Ex-Students Association of the university banded in committees to fight (unsuccessfully) for Rainey's reinstatement.

At a series of hearings held by a committee of the State Senate, Rainey charged that Governor O'Daniel's appointments to the Board of Regents had been part of "a deliberate program to put control of the State educational system in the hands of a small group of men with interlocking business interests and with similar educational and political views." He later said: "I made repeated attempts over a period of two or more years to dissuade [the regents] from courses which I knew could lead only to disaster. Eventually, I realized that I was sacrificing my own position with the university." Governor Stevenson commented, "I do not believe any fundamental issue is involved and there is no thought of throttling academic freedom. The differences are a culmination of little things, trifles." A year and a half later, after a final investigation the American Association of University Professors put Texas University on its list of "censured administrations" because of "attempts by a politically dominant group to impose its social and educational views upon the university."

Refusing offers of posts at other universities, Rainey remained in Texas to "fight it out." "If I left the State it would mean that I'd be doing nothing but taking a new job." Like most of his supporters, he considered the university affair a political issue, a pointing up of what Rainey called the "shackling" of Texas by "eastern and northern monopolies who control its natural resources, especially oil, gas and sulphur," as well as part of the continuing fight between the "Texas Regulars," who broke from the Democratic party to support Thomas Dewey[44] for president, and the New Deal Democrats. The educator therefore agreed in 1946 to run in the primaries for the Democratic nomination for Governor. In the campaign before the July 27 election, Rainey, seen as one of the major candidates heading the list of twelve, advocated taxing oil and gas interests to pay for a program of public health, welfare, and education. He proposed building a Negro University. Said to have the silent support of the CIO-PAC, Rainey was the object of a "whispering campaign" charging "communism" and "atheism." The *New Republic* reported "For Men Only" meetings which were run by Grover Sellars, one of the many candidates for Governor, "for the reading of 'lurid' passages from John Dos Passos' *U.S.A.*, which Dr. Rainey was accused of placing on the reading list at the university, but which many voters undoubtedly believed he wrote before the campaign was ended." Although campaign observers predicted his victory, Rainey was a poor second in the voting to Beauford H. Jester, the "middle-of-the-road" candidate, who interpreted Rainey's defeat as indicating that Texans wanted no part of "new-fangled theories of government." The general tenor of the opposition to Rainey had consisted of charges of "radicalism"; and Jester, former member of the State Railroad Commission and an oil attorney, had made the assertion that no new taxes were necessary to pay for the reforms comprising the educator's platform.

It was generally agreed at the time of his dispute with the regents that Rainey had no political ambitions. "I'd rather be president of the University of Texas than to hold any job in the world." He added, however, "It is more important to protect the principles of democracy and the integrity of these principles than to be president." Rainey had a large radio following in Texas built by his regularly scheduled program, *Religion in Life*.

In November 1946 Homer Rainey signified that he was returning to the field of education when he accepted the offer of the presidency of Stephens College for Women, in Columbia, Missouri. In an address at the college in December, he spoke of education's responsibility in advancing world cooperation. "The paradox of the situation [of democracy having repelled two attacks from without]," he said, "is that while we stand at the peak of our power and opportunity, unquestioned victors in the test of economic and military strength, we are still fearful and insecure. Is it because we have lost, in a measure, our early spiritual and uni-

fying faith in a liberal democracy? . . .Is it because of a creeping apathy, on the part of youth, with respect to our democratic institutions and traditions?" Rainey will formally succeed James Madison Wood as the head of Stephens College at the end of the 1946-47 academic year.

There are two daughters, Helen Collins and Lenore, in the educator's family; Mrs. Rainey is said to be a popular speaker before students' and women's groups.

References

Collier's 115:18+ Ja 6 '45 por
Look 17:51+ Ag 20 '46
N Y World-Telegram p21 N 21 '44; p21 N 22 '44
Nation 163:68+ Jl 20 '46
New Repub 3:740+ D 4 '44
Newsweek 13:40 Ja 9 '39; 24:84+ N 13 '44 por; 28:24+ Ag 5 '46 por
PM p10+ D 17 '44; p6 D 19 '44; p6 Jl 29 '46 por
Time 26:23 S 30 '35 por; 33:26 Ja 9 '39; 44:54+ N 13 '44 por; 48:26+ Ag 5 '46

Leaders in Education (1941)
Who's Who in America, 1946-47

RATHBONE, ELEANOR 1872—Jan. **2,** 1946 Independent member of British Parliament from combined universities since 1929; worked for feminism and social reforms; first woman member of the London County Council (1909-34); author of several books. See *Current Biography* 1943 Yearbook.

Obituary

N Y Times p20 Ja 3 '46

REA, GARDNER (rā) Aug. 12, 1892- Cartoonist
Address: Brook Haven, N. Y.

Cartoonist Gardner Rea is "a tiny man who has kept three generations of Americans laughing." Since 1908 Rea, who unlike most cartoonists is his own idea man, has been writing "gags" and illustrating them with his distinctive "wiggly" line drawings. Such publications as the *New Yorker* and *Collier's* have long considered him the top gag man in the country.

Three of Gardner Rea's grandparents were trained artists—"good ones," says Rea. One grandfather was a protegé of Eastman Johnson, the noted American genre and portrait painter, one of the family's frequent guests. Gardner Rea's maternal grandmother, a niece of Franz von Liszt, designed church vestments. That grandmother's brother formed, and conducted until his death, the Columbus (Ohio) Philharmonic Orchestra, while her other brother was the captain of a gun crew during the Battle of Mobile. His maternal grandmother's people fled to this country from Bavaria, a hundred or so years ago, at a time when European liberals were finding refuge here; his paternal ancestors came to America from Ipswich in 1630. Gardner was born into the family August 12, 1892, in Ironton, Ohio, the

GARDNER REA

son of Charles Oscar and Mary Elizabeth (Duffy) Rea. Young Rea attended East High School in Columbus, where schoolmates included Eddie Rickenbacker and Donald Ogden Stewart. Ted Lewis was one of his boyhood friends. With three artist grandparents influencing him, the boy intended to be a painter, and exhibited oil paintings at sixteen. But he had sold his first gag cartoons to the old *Life* magazine the year before, when he was fifteen. Later Rea stopped painting entirely, because, he says, he became more interested "in mentally suggesting color, than in smearing it on."

A member of the 1914 class of Ohio State University, Rea spent a lively four years there, which he likes to recall. "Every few minutes," Charles D. Rice wrote in an article on Rea for the magazine *This Week*, "he steers the conversation around to something that happened in the palmy days when he was editor of the college paper, and B.M.O.C. (Big Man On Campus)." Rea helped start, and later edited, the college humor magazine, *The Sundial*; helped edit the newspaper *The Lantern*; for three years served as art editor of the college yearbook *The Makio*; played on the college's first tennis team; and, although he never weighed more than ninety pounds, won three varsity letters. But he considers the triumph of his college career his winning of the annual prizes of both the Serious Poetry Committee and the Humorous Poetry Committee. "The pay-off," Charles Rice quotes Rea as chortling, "is that I submitted the exact same poem to both committees! Now there's a trick not everybody could do." As a result, *The Makio* suspended its competitive prizes for the following three years. The sonnet on Joseph Conrad's death, which Rea later wrote, is considered a classic. When graduated in 1914, Rea was a member of Alpha Sigma Phi, Sigma Delta Chi, and of Sphinx

and Toastmasters, the two senior honorary societies.

After graduation Rea came East. Based in Manhattan, for over a year he wrote drama criticism for the *Ohio State Journal*, and free-lanced, selling drawings, rhymes and essays. Much of his prose and verse appeared in the old humor magazines, *Life* and *Judge*. Then came World War I, and he found himself a private in the Chemical Warfare Service. With "lots of officers" working under him, Private Rea put out the service's book *Gaz Alèrte*. Upon his discharge from the army he began to free-lance again, but he "really settled down to work" after a visit from a young woman graduate of the Pratt art institute. The girl, Dorothy Julia Calkins, was sent to Rea for criticism of her drawings. He not only criticized her drawings, but in time proposed marriage, and in April, 1920, the two were married. "Haven't had a vacation since," Rea adds. After a few years in New York the two moved to Brook Haven, on Long Island, where they designed and built their own home. They are still there—"ducking people."

Rea was one of the small group which Harold Ross gathered around him to start the *New Yorker* in 1925. Of the first issues of the magazine, two of its chroniclers have written (*Harper's* April 1943): "In one way or another everyone connected with it was slightly mad." Rea, who was "mad" enough to turn out "sardonic and sophisticated gags" continued to work for the *New Yorker* "more or less regularly," depending on how busy he was elsewhere. He also contributed to *Collier's* and King Features, and to so many other publications he cannot list them. The *New Yorker*, *Life*, and *Judge* once ran covers by the artist during the same week.

The cartoonist writes about forty gags a week. Most of these he sells to editors who assign them to other cartoonists to draw. "I get more kick out of seeing these in print than I do my own cartoons," he says. "There's an element of surprise in how the artist works them out." Rea thinks he has published some ten thousand of his own wiggly-line cartoons (though Charles Rice puts the figure at twenty thousand). Somewhere in the picture there is always a small shape (a lady's hat, a necktie, the panes of a window) inked in flat black. He uses his pen line sparingly, eliminating sketchy detail. "I consider, as have most critics, that line is the highest, most difficult form of art," Rea has said. "And so long as the fundamental design is there, I can't see that it makes the slightest difference, technically speaking, if the subject matter is humorous." As for the characteristic "wiggle" of his line, he once laughed, "I'm sticking to it now so nobody will catch on when I get senile."

Gardner Rea's cartoons have to do with the follies "of his contemporaries everywhere—from cocktail lounges to rough army camps." But the artist himself is so much of a recluse that Ogden Nash once concluded that he lives in "a diving-bell at the bottom of Long Island Sound." Actually, Rea lives in his Brook Haven home with his wife and two daughters, Mary Elizabeth and Barbara Jane. Once a year, which he considers too often, he visits New York to see his editors. He finds it simple enough to account for his wide knowledge of the foibles of humanity: "When I read in the papers that some society lady is divorcing her husband because he takes a hostile attitude toward her pet guppies, I don't have to go out and interview the lady to discover it's a damnfool business. I have a quick mind and I can come to that conclusion right here in my arm chair."

The first collection of Rea cartoons, *The Gentleman Says It's Pixies*, selected from 250 issues of *Collier's*, appeared in 1944. His second collection, *Sideshow* (1945), which includes cartoons from the *New Yorker, Saturday Evening Post, Collier's,* and other publications, was dedicated: "To my beloved family—despite whose untiring efforts, this modest opus finally saw the light of day." Reviewers consider that his cartoons have "distinction of style and humor," and that they "repay study." Rea is in numerous cartoon anthologies, and was one of the contributors to *The Stag At Eve*. He did the cover for the book, a picture of the stag which has been called the "perfect portrait" of humorist Ogden Nash. The artist has exhibited cartoons in most of the important museums in the United States, South America, and in Europe, and has frequently been awarded money prizes.

Rea reads twelve languages, is interested in anthropology and psychology, likes to listen to chamber music, and occasionally plays tennis on the clay court in his backyard. The one-time drama critic has seen only three motion pictures in the last thirty years—"I saw a number as a youngster, when they were better." He has also avoided the theater. According to Rice, he has earned close to a million dollars as a cartoonist, spends a good deal of it on art treasures, which clutter his home, and anthropology books. Rea is five feet five inches tall, weighs ninety pounds. "You have the feeling he would fit nicely into a shoebox," Rice has written. A "smiling pixie of a man," the cartoonist has red hair and a small bristling mustache. His pipe is very large—"The size," he says, "is for my ego's sake. I like the feeling of being the master of something larger than I am."

Reference

This Week p13 Ap 7 '46 por

REECE, B(RAZILLA) CARROLL Dec. 22, 1889- Republican National Chairman

Address: b. Republican National Committee, 1337 Connecticut Ave., Washington, D.C.; h. Johnson City, Tenn.

After twenty-three years in Congress as a Republican representative from Tennessee, B. Carroll Reece was elected Republican National Chairman to succeed the retiring Herbert Brownell, Jr. [44] in April 1946. A Representative who introduced little legislation, the Southern Republican was backed for the party chairmanship by the most conservative wing of the Republican Party, including Senator Robert A. Taft of Ohio. Reece's election pointed up a

Fabian Bachrach

B. CARROLL REECE

party difference: Harold Stassen of Minnesota, leader of the progressive group in the party felt obliged to comment that he disapproved of Reece's attitudes (which had tended toward isolationism and "stand-pattism") on many issues. But since Reece would have the big responsibility of trying to lead the party to victory in the 1946 Congressional elections and in the 1948 Presidential race, even party members who disliked his voting record gave him support.

Brazilla Carroll Reece grew up on a farm in the Great Smoky Mountains of East Tennessee. Born in Butler, Tennessee, on December 22, 1889, one of the thirteen children of John Isaac and Sarah E. (Maples) Reece, he was named for an ancestor who fought in the War of 1812, Major General Brazilla Carroll McBride. "Brazilla," which has nothing to do with South America, is thought to have been derived from the Old Testament name "Barzillai," meaning "Man of Iron." Reece is also a direct descendant of Captain Jacob Brown, founder of Nollichucky, one of the first settlements in that section of the Great Smoky Mountains.

Young Reece attended Watauga Academy, and in 1914 took his B.A. degree at Carson and Newman College in Tennessee. At both his high school and college graduations he was class valedictorian. As a college undergraduate he was president of the student government organization and of the debating society, class president, and president of the college YMCA. An athlete as well as a student leader, he excelled in football and basketball. After he had received his degree in 1914 he was appointed principal of a high school. A year later he went East to New York University to study for a Master's degree in economics and finance, and from 1916, when he received the degree, until he enlisted in the army in May 1917, he

REECE, B. CARROLL—*Continued*
taught economics at N.Y.U. (He later furthered his studies at the University of London, in the winter of 1918-19, before returning from overseas service.)

A month after the United States entered World War I the twenty-seven-year-old instructor enlisted in the army. Entering as a private, Reece was commissioned a lieutenant in August 1917, and later commanded the Third Battalion of the 102d Infantry of the "Yankee Division" (26th Division, American Expeditionary Forces). He was cited for extraordinary heroism in action by Marshal Petain, Generals Pershing, Edwards, and Hale, and Colonel Lewis. The Distinguished Service Medal was awarded him because he had "brilliantly" led his company, and had later taken command of a badly disorganized battalion, and had molded it "into a good fighting unit." He also received the Distinguished Service Cross. "On several occasions," read the citation, "under heavy enemy machine gun fire he crawled far in advance of his front line and rescued wounded men, who had taken refuge in shell holes." His other decorations include the Purple Heart, and the Croix de Guerre with palm.

When Reece returned from Europe in 1919 he became director of the School of Commerce, Accounts and Finance, and instructor in economics, at New York University. But he took a leave of absence from the university after one term, in order to run for Congress in 1920 on the Republican ticket in the First District of Tennessee, one of the two (out of ten) Tennessee districts which have been traditionally Republican. In the 1920 election Reece, then thirty years old, won a seat in the House by a substantial margin, after a "hard-fought race." Taking law examinations after his election, he was admitted to the bar in Tennessee. (He had studied law at New York University). He also became a banker while in Congress. The House seat was his until he resigned in 1946, except for one term (1930-32) when he was defeated by an independent candidate. After 1934 Reece was unopposed in the primaries, and was never challenged in the elections by a Democrat.

"His voting record has been in line with the position of the party," the Republican National Committee has stated. During Roosevelt's presidency Reece consistently voted against Administration-sponsored legislation, with some exceptions—like most other Republicans, he voted for anti-poll tax measures and for Federal anti-lynching legislation. In his early years as Representative, he served on the Military Affairs Committee. Also, for fourteen years a member of the Interstate Foreign Commerce Committee, he was active in the formulation and passage of the Federal securities, stock exchange, Federal communications commission, and Federal power Acts, and the amendment to the interstate commerce Act which extended its jurisdiction to motor transportation. In 1938 he was on the fifteen-man Congressional commission instructed to investigate monopolies, and on the sub-committee which drafted its report. The same year, together with Representative Chapman of Kentucky, he developed and sponsored the Food, Drug, and Cosmetic Act of 1938.

During the nation's defense preparations, Reece's vote was isolationist. In November 1939, soon after the outbreak of war in Europe, he voted against supplying England with arms, and against modifying the Neutrality Act. In September 1940 he voted against the draft, and the next year he opposed extending it. In February 1941 he opposed Lend-Lease, and the following fall he objected to repealing the law which forbade the arming of American merchant ships. In November 1941, just before Pearl Harbor, he opposed lifting bans on American shipping to ports of belligerent nations. After the United States entered the war, he voted against the Fulbright [43] Resolution.

On bills of special interest to organized labor, his vote was in opposition to the Administration. In December 1941 he voted for the Smith [41] antistrike bill, and in 1943 he favored the amendment to the Smith-Connally [41] bill prohibiting labor contributions to political campaigns. He also voted to override President Roosevelt's veto of the Smith-Connally bill. In February 1946 he voted for the Case bill to limit union power. He voted against President Roosevelt's self-liquidating public-works bill (August 1939), and against additional appropriations to the National Youth Administration (March 1940). In the spring of 1943 he opposed giving incentive payments to farmers through the Department of Agriculture, voted against the bill which appropriated money to the Department of Agriculture for soil conservation, and opposed increasing appropriations for the Rural Electrification Program. He opposed the price-control act (1942) and the extension of price control in 1944 and 1945. He also opposed the 1944 soldier-vote bill, and in 1945 he voted for a permanent House Committee on Un-American Activities (to continue the work of the Dies [40] Committee).

In the months immediately preceding his election as Republican chairman, Reece went on record once again as being against Government action to control prices and rents. Convinced that private industry would provide housing for veterans, he vigorously opposed the Wilson Wyatt [46] housing program. During this time also, Reece introduced a bill which would call for judicial review of Federal Trade Commission rulings on fraudulent advertising, and which would limit FTC action in the case of product misrepresentation.

Reece had been elected National Committeeman for Tennessee in 1939, and had come to be regarded as the head of the Republican party in his State and in the South. He achieved national prominence in the party as chairman of the resolutions committee which was expected to bring accord between Congressional leaders and committee members at the 1944 Republican National Committee meeting. At the resignation of Chairman of the party Herbert Brownell, Jr., in April 1946, a clash of some bitterness ensued between the "Old Guard" Republicans and the progressive wing of the party. Reece was the candidate of the "Old Guard"; the core of his support came from the South. His nearest opponents were Senator John Danaher, and John W. Hanes, who, as one newspaperman stated, "represented an unacceptable Willkie-Stassen viewpoint." On the third ballot the Reece forces won. Reece's election as chairman was greeted as a victory for Senator Taft and his supporters. The new chairman declared, however, that he would foster no one's candidacy for the presidential nomination. His job was "to elect, and not select," he said. Though he gave up his Congressional seat to devote himself to his new post, he refused to accept a salary from the Party, explaining that he had private means. (He is president of three banks in his Tennessee district, and is a board member of the Farmers Bank at Blountville.)

A favorable reaction to Reece's election came from Colonel Robert R. McCormick, editor of the *Chicago Tribune,* who said that Reece's selection was "a victory for the real Republicans and a distinct setback for the Me-Too Republicans who would have the party continue a futile echoing of the New Deal." The New York *Herald Tribune* found Reece's record "disappointing": "The intention of the Reece supporters plainly was to initiate another stretch of stand-pat politics." Arthur Krock (New York *Times*) discovered a "striking unanimity" among editors, commentators and politicians of both the Republican and Democratic parties, in their reaction to the Reece election. These observers believed, said Krock, that "Mr. Reece was chosen by the conservatives in the Republican Party because they think he will be a standard chairman, who will not give committee encouragement to any newfangled ideas." Reece's supporters, added Krock, "are certain that Republican victories in 1946 and 1948 will be founded on negative thinking, on the votes of those who want a 'change', on simple and automatic reaction."

After Reece's first speech as party chairman, Republican Senator Wayne Morse '42 of Oregon said: "We listened to the same old clichés and reactionary nostrums . . . which have produced Republican defeats since 1932." Reece characterized Morse's comment as "just one man's opinion." To the critics who were disturbed because he was not a liberal, Reece replied that "the true liberal is the man who fights encroachment by the Federal Government upon the freedom of the citizens," that the Republican party was therefore the liberal party of the nation. He charged that the Political Action Committee of the Congress of Industrial Organizations (CIO) had tried to steal the name of "liberal," that the PAC was really "the spearhead of Red reactionism in the United States."

During the fall 1946 Congressional election campaign, which ended in the Republicans winning control of both the Senate and the House, Reece stumped the country. He described the election issues as "houses or blueprints, sound currency or inflation, government by majority or pampered minorities, abundances or shortages, balanced budgets or deficit spending, Americanism or communism, full production or restricted production, free economy or planned economy." After President Truman asked for the resignation of Secretary of Commerce Henry Wallace '40 in September 1946, Reece, who called foreign policy a central issue of the campaign, saw Truman as a "prisoner of a Democratic-Political Action Committee-Communist" alliance in American foreign policy. A Republican Congress, Reece asserted, would provide a "coherent foreign policy."

The new Republican Party chairman was married in 1923 to Louise Despard Goff, whom he met in Washington soon after he came to Congress. Mrs. Reece, who is the daughter of the late Senator Guy Despard Goff, always accompanies her husband on campaigns, and "if she has to do it can make a good political speech." Their daughter, Louise Despard Goff, in 1946 was a student at Stephens College in Missouri. Reece is a member of the board of regents of the Smithsonian Institute, the American Economic Association, American Statistical Association, American Academy of Political Science, Delta Sigma Pi, Newcomen Society, and of the American, Tennessee, and District of Columbia bar associations. He has steel-gray hair, gray eyes, and is of slight build—his height is five feet nine inches, his weight 155 pounds. He plays golf, likes bridge and books, does not smoke, and rarely drinks. Associates describe Chairman Reece as "very quiet, patient, and even-tempered in disposition."

References

National Cyclopædia of American Biography Current vol F p245
Who's Who in America, 1946-47

REID, IRA DE A(UGUSTINE) July 2, 1901- Sociologist; educator; author

Address: b. c/o Atlanta University, Atlanta, Ga.; h. 588 Beckwith St., S.W., Atlanta, Ga.

Sociologist and author, Southern-born Ira De A. Reid is the first Negro to be named to a full-time professorship at New York University. Reid, who is chairman of the sociology department of Atlanta University, and editor of *Phylon,* the university's quarterly review of race and culture, was appointed visiting professor of sociology at N.Y.U. for the academic year of 1946-47. His books and monographs on interracial problems, many prepared for Government offices, are highly regarded by sociologists, and at least two, *Sharecroppers All,* which he wrote with A. F. Raper, and *In a Minor Key,* have been considered by reviewers to be worth the attention of "everyone concerned with the future of our civilization."

Although he was born in Clifton Forge, Virginia—the date of his birth was July 2, 1901— Ira De Augustine Reid spent his early boyhood in Pennsylvania, in Harrisburg and Philadelphia. He attended public schools in Germantown, a suburb of Philadelphia, until his father, D. Augustine Reid, a Baptist minister, heard a "Macedonian cry" which led him to Savannah, Georgia, to preach. "The move was quite a lark for my brother and me, but for my mother [Willie Robertha (James) Reid] it was an arduous one," Reid recalls. There being no public high school for Negroes in Georgia at that time, Ira attended Morehouse Acad-

Leonid Skvirsky

IRA DE A. REID

emy, and at sixteen entered Morehouse College, Atlanta University's undergraduate school for men. That same year young Reid's father died, and the family moved to Mrs. Reid's home in West Virginia. With the entrance of the United States into World War I, Reid tried unsuccessfully to get into an officers' training camp. In West Virginia he was exempted from the draft, but he was conscripted for service in Georgia. "When the war was over I tried returning to college but was not in the mood for the work it took." Reid stayed out of school for a year and a half, later made up a half year, and was graduated with a B.A. in 1922. "By the time I finished college I was sick of the Deep South and its peculiar social structure and resolved to leave it forever." But "forever" turned out to be only a short time.

In September 1922 Reid went to Tyler, Texas, to instruct in the social sciences at Texas College. He spent the summer of 1923 studying at the University of Chicago, and then became an instructor (1923-24) at the Douglas High School in Huntington, West Virginia, where he discovered he had "neither the temperament nor the experience for high school teaching." Next, at the University of Pittsburgh, Reid earned his Master of Arts degree in 1925. He then went to New York to work as the industrial and research secretary of the New York Urban League for Social Work among Negroes. While on this first New York job (1925-28) Reid became interested in Harlem churches, made a study of them, and wrote an article entitled "Let Us Prey." He and his publisher were subsequently sued for fifteen thousand dollars, but "there was so much evidence against the plaintiff," according to Reid, "that the suit was withdrawn."

In 1928 Reid became Director of Research for the National Urban League. In that capa-

city, from 1928 to 1934, he made surveys of community racial problems in Albany and Troy (1928), in Denver (1929), in New Jersey (1930-31), in Pittsburgh (1932), and in Baltimore (1934), and undertook special studies for such groups as the National Commission on Law Observance and Enforcement, and the White House Conference on Child Care. Meanwhile, he pursued graduate studies in sociology at Columbia University. In 1934 he was appointed professor of sociology at Atlanta University. But in the New Deal years to come he was on leave from the university on Government assignments a good part of the time: in 1937 he directed a Federal survey of white collar and skilled workers, from 1937 to 1941 he was a consulting social scientist for the Social Security Board, and in 1941-42 the board's consultant on minorities. He was also, in 1942-43, consultant on minorities for the War Manpower Commission. Meanwhile, in 1942, Reid became director of People's College at Atlanta, an adult education school of the university, and in 1943 he was named chairman of the university's sociology department. Both of these last-named posts he still holds, while lecturing on Negro culture and education in 1946-47 at the New York University School of Education. He was also scheduled to teach three days a week at Haverford College (Haverford, Pennsylvania) as a visiting professor of sociology, a post to which he was named in September, 1946.

Awarded a Fellowship of the Julius Rosenwald Fund, Reid studied race and population problems at the London School of Economics in the 1939 Lent term. He also traveled in the West Indies and West Africa in 1938 and 1939. Then, late in 1939 his Ph.D. dissertation (the degree was conferred by Columbia University) was published as *The Negro Immigrant*, a book in which Reid dealt "objectively with the characteristics and social adjustment of the one hundred thousand foreign-born Negroes in the United States . . . who constitute our largest group of colored aliens." Reid's *In A Minor Key; Negro Youth in Story and Fact*, prepared for the American Youth Commission, was published in 1940. A survey of the status and problems of Negro youth, the book was recommended by the *American Sociological Review* as a vivid portrayal of "disgraceful and dangerous conditions." "He does not shout—but his facts do; he does not allow any virtue-and-vice words to mar the simple, straightforward—and terrible—stories he has to tell."

The sociologist's next book was the result of what he considers his most interesting study. Reid, who was concerned with the urban South, collaborated with Arthur Raper, a white teacher of sociology interested in the rural south, to write *Sharecroppers All*, (1941) using the term "sharecroppers" to include nonfarm Southern workers who "share in the risk without sharing in the control" in trade and industry. "We collaborated rather successfully on that job," Reid has written, "the folkways, mores, and conservatism of the region to the contrary, notwithstanding." Reviewers found it a "thoroughly stimulating work" which made "an electric, if sometimes startling, combination of views about life in the Southern regions." Though it had a "freshness of presentation" which made it good for popular consumption the book was also regarded as important and of real value by specialized sociological journals.

Others of Reid's books and monographs include: *The Negro Population of Denver, Colorado* (1929), *Social Conditions of the Negro in the Hill District of Pittsburgh, Pennsylvania* (1930), *Negro Membership in American Labor Unions* (1930), *The Negro's Relation to Work and Law Observance* (1931), *The Negro in New Jersey* (five volumes, 1932), *The Problem of Child Dependency Among Negroes* (1933), *The Negro Community of Baltimore* (1935), *Adult Education Among Negroes* (1936), *The Urban Negro Worker in the United States: 1925-1936* (1938), and the chapter "The Church and Education for Negroes" in Trevor Bowen's *Divine White Right* (1934). In addition to editing *Phylon,* the sociologist is a contributor to such journals as *Social Forces, The Virginia Quarterly, Opportunity, Nation,* and *Survey Graphic.* He is currently at work on two books, one "The Hidden South," and another, a textbook in urban sociology. His manuscript "Manners and Minorities" is scheduled for publication in 1946.

Associate director of the division of race relations of the American Missionary Association in 1943, and associate executive director of the Southern Regional Council in 1944-45, Reid holds membership in the American Sociological Society, and the Academy of Political and Social Science, as well as positions on the executive or directing boards of the Southern Sociological Society, the Southern Regional Council, the Southern Conference for Human Welfare, the Committee on Mass Education in Race Relations, and the National Sharecroppers Fund. "My life in Atlanta has been directed toward making the social sciences effective in community life," Reid has said. "This has been a full-time job but I have enjoyed every minute of it. It has meant that my writing has been neglected." The sociologist was married in October 1925 to Gladys Russell Scott. Before the 214-pound professor departed for New York he remarked to a *Time* magazine reporter, "There will be six feet four of the Negro problem standing up before the students. I do not need to discuss it separately."

References

N Y Times p23 Ap 25 '46
Time 47:90 My 6 '46

Who's Who in Colored America, 1941-44

REVES, EMERY (rēvs) Feb. 16, 1904-
Author; publisher

Address: b. c/o Cooperation Publishing Co., 30 Rockefeller Plaza, New York; h. Plaza Hotel, New York

Emery Reves, student of world affairs, is the author of *The Anatomy of Peace,* which Albert Einstein called "intelligent, brief, clear, and . . . dynamic on the topic of war and the need for world government." Reves intended his latest book, a best seller, to offer a solution to the problem of creating a successful world organization to maintain peace and control the use of atomic energy.

Emery Reves was born in the small village of Bacsfoldvar in southern Hungary on February 16, 1904. His father, Simon Reves, was connected with the lumber industry in that region. His mother, Gisele (Gross) Reves, died a victim of Hungarian Fascists in 1942. Fifteen years after his birth, Reves's native village became part of the Hungarian territory ceded to Yugoslavia after World War I. His early education he received in Novisad (Yugoslavia), his secondary school education in Budapest. During the year 1922-23 Reves was a student at the University of Berlin. He left Germany for the University of Paris, and, after a year of study there (1923-24), went to Switzerland. Reves was graduated from the University of Zurich in 1926, at the age of twenty-two, with the degree of Doctor of Political Economy. His doctoral dissertation *Walther Rathenau und sein wirtschaftliches Werk* was published in Dresden in 1927 as a trade book.

After a period of attempting unsuccessfully to establish himself in the field of political journalism, in 1930 Reves founded the Cooperation Press Service and Cooperation Publishing Company. He established main offices in Paris and London and branches in other important cities of Europe. Since its inception, Reves has been president and director of the firm. The program of his organization was to publish, all over the world, views of leading statesmen on international affairs. In time Reves acquired what amounted almost to a monopoly in handling exclusive world rights on the articles of men of divergent views such as Clement Attlee, Winston Churchill, Léon Blum, Anthony Eden, Edouard Herriot, Alfred Duff Cooper, Paul Reynaud, Count Carlo Sforza, and other European statesmen. The articles, released almost daily, were published in some four hundred newspapers (twenty-some independent American newspapers among them) in about seventy countries before the outbreak of World War II curtailed communications. (Reves's account of his experiences as syndicator and publisher is given in his introduction to Thyssen's *I Paid Hitler.*)

Since he has always been an active opponent of Nazism, Reves was adamant in his refusal to allow any spokesman for the Nazi system to utilize his syndicate for propaganda purposes. (In April 1933, Reves had fled just a few hours before Storm Troopers raided the Berlin offices of his service. He had two other narrow escapes from the Gestapo: when the Nazis entered Vienna and when they were nearing Paris.) His organization did accept, though rarely, articles contributed by the Fascist journalist, Virginio Gayda. This was permitted because Fascist newspapers in Italy occasionally printed other Cooperation Press Service articles. The interchange of views ended in 1935, however, when Reves placed

Carlyle Studios

EMERY REVES

an anti-Fascist article, written by Clement Attlee, in a Rome newspaper and had to leave the city shortly after the article's appearance.

For ten years Reves maintained contact with well-known political figures and attended all the important international conferences, so that his syndicate became a "rather unique observation tower." As the political crises mounted in Europe later in the 1930's, he urged all democratic countries to combat the insidious Nazi propaganda technique perfected by Josef Goebbels by means of a vigorous one of their own and advocated, now openly, opposition to totalitarian Italy. That these articles had influence and were anathema to the Nazis became evident to Reves when Hitler, in the first speech he delivered after the Munich agreement in 1938, "shouted hysterically that 'this propaganda by Churchill, Eden, and Duff Cooper must stop.'"

In the early and less intense phase of World War II Reves was engaged in the publication of memoirs and histories of German and Italian nationals antagonistic to Nazi and Fascist doctrines; their written testimonies, he believed, would serve as invaluable source material for democratic propaganda. The first book of this type to be published under the auspices of the Cooperation Publishing Company was Hermann Rauschning's conversations with Hitler which appeared first in Paris in 1939 under the title *Hitler m'a dit*. In the middle of June 1940, following his forced departure for Bordeaux, Reves was transported to England in a British cargo ship. Reves had lived intermittently in England since 1933 and in 1940 he became a naturalized British subject. Less than a year later, in February 1941, the publisher went to the United States and there established his organization in New York City. Reves's firm acted as agent in 1941 for the publication of the Thyssen memoirs as *I Paid Hitler,* and in

1942 for Prince Ernst Starhemberg's *Between Hitler and Mussolini,* which offered more documentary evidence of the dictators' designs on all free institutions.

Reves incorporated into his own book, *A Democratic Manifesto* (1942), his firsthand observation of the causes for the war and the collapse of so many European nations. The principal philosophy of Reves's *Manifesto* was that nationalism would have to be subordinated to international interdependence if wars were to be averted. Reves proposed that the administration of international law be delegated to a central authority having power to compel obedience by force. Various critics of Reves's tenets maintained that the author was not adequately aware of the conflicting forces in the world or "of the really radical changes in our domestic social orders which the adoption of his program of international relations would necessitate." Written from a practical rather than from a theoretical standpoint, *A Democratic Manifesto* made no claim to complete originality since much of its content had been suggested before by writers with similar viewpoints. What it had to offer, according to Charles A. Ferguson writing in *The Saturday Review of Literature*, was "focus and clarity." Reves's book, he decided, was "one of the most incisive books of our generation—a clear, simple, direct statement of the forces that brought on the present debacle." *A Democratic Manifesto* sold slowly at first. Soon, however, it received the notice of prominent men and finally of the general public. It was published in a number of foreign editions and was adopted as a textbook in several schools and universities in the United States.

The theses advanced by Reves in many of his previous writings were developed and elaborated in *The Anatomy of Peace,* published in June 1945, less than one month after Germany was defeated. Reves reasserted the need for a world government ("a legal order between men beyond and above the existing nation-state structure") to maintain democracy and preserve peace. Under nationalistic practices, Reves is convinced, there is a "trend toward ever-increasing nationalist state machinery and ever-growing pressure on the individual by control, regulation and infringement of his personal liberty." As a result, capitalism and socialism (both economic systems) tend to develop into fascism; the latter, Reves wrote, is a politico-social order encompassing the complete subjection of the individual to the will of the state, and can function under any economic system. Collective security pacts, treaties, and leagues of nations are useless in that they have no legal power or force to carry out their decrees, and, being disguises for power politics, lead inevitably to war.

Some commentators criticized Reves for being a perfectionist, a theorist with an objective but with no concrete plan, an idealist who, unwittingly, might help to bring about the failure of the United Nations organization. Most reviewers commented favorably on the author's "admirable force and clarity" and on "the semiscientific style of the book, and its logical method of development." Among the book's supporters was Clifton Fadiman, who suggested that Reves's work might "help to arrest our slow march to suicide," and a *Christian Science Monitor* critic who wrote: "Mr. Reves's book will be a big help to the thousands of puzzled men and women who are seeking to understand their way through the labyrinth that is this shrunken, chaotic, and numbed world of 1945." In October 1945, an open letter, urging Americans to read the book, was printed in the New York *Times* and signed by a group of well-known people led by Owen J. Roberts [?], former associate justice of the United States Supreme Court. Later a condensation of the book appeared in three issues of the *Reader's Digest.* Since June 1945 the book has been reprinted a number of times, and a postscript dealing with the implications of the atomic bomb was added. In May 1946, Pocket Books, Incorporated, published *The Anatomy of Peace* in their first "king-size" edition. The book is to be published in many countries of the world and will also be available in Braille.

After World War II, Reves devoted his efforts to working for a world federation. The work of the United Nations was of particular interest to him. Before this Reves had warned (in the *American Mercury*, March 1943, and the New York *Times Magazine*, April 23, 1944) that the adherence of the Atlantic Charter to the anachronistic doctrine of self-determination would only establish more nation-states whose rivalry would plunge the world into more wars. Since the U.N. approved self-determination rather than the merging of all nations into a world federation, Reves predicted in his books and elsewhere that it would have a disastrous end. The United Nations Charter, he stated, was "nothing more than 'a multilateral treaty without legal authority over individual nations'—a treaty which, like all treaties, is completely incapable of stopping nations from going to war." In October 1945, Reves attended the conference on world peace meeting in Dublin, New Hampshire, to consider methods of correcting the weaknesses in the U.N. Five months later, in March 1946, Reves was present at the Rollins College conference on world government at Winter Park, Florida, and signed the petition, drawn up at the conference, suggesting amendments to the U.N. charter so that the organization might be transformed "from a league of sovereign states into a government deriving its specific powers from the peoples of the world." Reves's other writings have dealt with such subjects as the progressive sales tax and the reformation of Nazi Germany. He has also made a number of radio appearances.

The "volatile" and "energetic" Reves, who is unmarried, is five feet six inches in height, weighs 160 pounds, and has brown hair and eyes. An interviewer for the New York *Herald Tribune* wrote of him: "His speech is fast, accented, positive. He answers questions in blocks of one hundred words or more, as though he were dictating to a stenographer, and he covers ground while doing it." Reves's controversial ideas have brought him more than four thousand letters; many of these, from men high in public life who have sanctioned his proposals, he cherishes.

References

> N Y Herald Tribune p 7 Mr 24 '46
> Thyssen, F. I Paid Hitler (1941)
> Who's Who in America, 1946-47

RHYS, ERNEST (rēs) 1859—May 25, 1946 English author, editor, and poet; creator and editor of *Everyman's Library*; wrote a dozen volumes of poetry and essays, his reminiscences of men of letters, *Everyman Remembers* (1931), *Rhymes for Everyman* (1933), *Letters from Limbo* (1936), *Song of the Sun* (1937), and his autobiography, *Wales England Wed* (1941).

Obituary

> N Y Times p32 My 26 '46 por

RIBBENTROP, JOACHIM VON (rĭb'ĕn-trōp jō'a̅-kĭm fŏn) Apr. 30, 1893—Oct. 16, 1946 Nazi Minister of Foreign Affairs from 1938; aided in the formation of Hitler's Government in 1933; served as Ambassador to Great Britain from 1936 to 1938; tried by the International Military Tribunal, judged "responsible for war crimes and crimes against humanity because of his activities with respect to occupied countries and Axis satellites"; condemned and hanged. See *Current Biography* 1941 Yearbook.

Obituary

> N Y Times p1+ O 16 '46

RICHARDSON, HENRIETTA *See* Richardson, H. H.

RICHARDSON, HENRY HANDEL 1880 (?)—Mar. 20, 1946 Henrietta Richardson, expatriate Australian author; her *Maurice Guest* (1908) is considered by many the greatest of first novels; also wrote *The Getting of Wisdom* (1910); *The Fortunes of Richard Mahony,* comprising *Australia Felix* (1917), *The Way Home* (1925), and *Ultima Thule* (1929); *Two Studies* (1931), *The End of a Childhood* (1934), *The Young Cosima* (1939).

Obituary

> N Y Times p25 Mr 21 '46 por

RIEVE, EMIL (rē'vē) June 8, 1892- Trade union official
Address: b. c/o Textile Workers Union of America, 15 Union Sq., New York

Emil Rieve, whom Victor Riesel of the New York *Post* described as "one of the nation's most highly respected, experienced labor leaders," is the general president of the Textile Workers Union of America. The fourth largest union in the CIO, it represents more than four hundred thousand workers in fifteen hundred and seventeen mills, or four-fifths of the organized employees in the textile industry. Also a vice-president of the CIO, Rieve is "an

RIEVE, EMIL—*Continued*

acknowledged leader of the anti-Communist elements in the CIO" and has been a sharp critic of Soviet policies in postwar world relations.

The union executive, son of a textile machinist, became familiar with sweatshop conditions at an early age. Born in the province of Zyradow, Poland, on June 8, 1892, to Fred and Pauline (Lange) Rieve, Emil Rieve came to America in 1904 and went to work in a Pennsylvania hosiery mill—his formal education did not go beyond elementary school. He had been a hosiery worker for a year when he joined the union. At twenty-two he became the vice-president of the American Federation of Hosiery Workers and, in 1929, after fourteen years in this capacity, he was made the president of the union.

In those days, the textile employees, among the lowest paid industrial workers in the nation, were without organization except for a few small unions: those of the hosiery workers and the A.F. of L. United Textile Workers, a weak group, according to Morris Markey (*Liberty*, February 9, 1946). Rieve, a member of the National Executive Board of the United Textile Workers, in 1934 was one of a committee of five who conducted the nation-wide strike of nearly five hundred thousand textile employees, from which little had been won. The job of effectively organizing the underpaid textile workers, many of whom were illiterate and resigned to substandard living conditions, was begun in 1937 by the late Sidney Hillman [40] of the CIO, a good friend of Rieve's. A preliminary committee, the CIO Textile Workers Organizing Committee, was formed with Rieve as its executive director. Aided by a treasury of about a million dollars, most of it contributed by Hillman's thriving Amalgamated Clothing Workers Union, the labor leaders set up children's nurseries and adult education projects and curbed the efforts of the mill owners to prevent unionism. In 1939, when the committee was ready to assume the status of a full-fledged union, Rieve left the American Federation of Hosiery Workers to become the president of the Textile Workers Union of America; in the same year he was also made a vice-president of the CIO. By 1941 the TWUA head was able to announce that pay increases ranging from 5 to 10 per cent had been secured for woolen, cotton, rayon and synthetic yarn workers through collective bargaining—there had been no strikes. The union also won paid vacations and secured life insurance benefits paid by the employer for more than one hundred thousand employees.

During World War II, wages in the vital textile industry were still substandard, and rising prices reduced their purchasing power even more. Nevertheless, Rieve, while condemning antistrike legislation, agreed that strikes had to be avoided and looked to the National War Labor Board, the machinery set up for peaceful solution of labor's grievances, to improve the living conditions of the employees whom he represented. An alternate labor member of the board, he urged it to abandon the Little Steel Formula, the wage-determining rule which had been adopted to help prevent inflation. Calling the formula "obsolete, unfair and unrealistic" and maintaining that "ten cents an hour in a worker's pocket [was] no more inflationary than fifteen million dollars in the company's pocket," Rieve asked for a minimum wage rate of sixty cents and for a general wage increase of ten cents an hour in the textile cases which came before the WLB. Although a critic of the board, he regarded it as "the one Governmental agency concerned with the prosecution of the war effort in which labor has participated as an equal in the determination of policy."

In February 1945, however, when be became convinced that the board had been stripped of its powers, he resigned and released one hundred thousand cotton and rayon workers from the no-strike pledge which organized labor had adopted in December 1941. Although the board had granted a compromise decision in the textile cases, setting fifty-five cents as the minimum wage and allowing a general increase of five cents, its voice was ineffective because Frederick M. Vinson [43], the stabilization director, had issued an order forbidding the WLB to order wage increases unless they were first approved by the OPA. Rieve had no quarrel with the board but felt that it was "being a collective yes-man for Mr. Vinson" and that "other agencies [had] in effect taken over its functions." The executive council of TWUA recommended that the CIO withdraw from the WLB entirely unless the board's powers were restored, but such a suggestion was turned down by the CIO's executive board. While the labor leader was criticized for breaking the no-strike pledge—CIO officials withheld comment on the measures which he had taken—Rieve's action was followed by steps that made effective the WLB decision to raise textile wages.

That was not the only time Rieve acted independently of his CIO colleagues. In the same year (1945) he opposed the extension of the Reciprocal Trade Agreements Act: in its stead, he advocated that the United States lead in the establishment of international labor standards by refusing to trade with a country unless it maintained fair wages and working conditions. However, the textile union head later changed his stand and joined the other CIO officials in support of the extension of reciprocal trade authority. (In an international peace program which he had outlined in 1943, he had suggested the elimination of "unreasonable" tariff barriers.)

In October 1945 Rieve was a member of a CIO delegation which visited Russia as guests of the Soviet trade union movement. (A delegation from the All-Union Central Council of Trade Unions of the U.S.S.R. had made an earlier visit to the United States as guests of the CIO). Rieve concurred in the delegation's report which praised the work of the Soviet unions in promoting the economic, social, and cultural welfare of the people and made particular note of their social insurance system. But his opinions of Russia were not all laudatory. He found that the country lacked freedom of the press; while conceding that Russia had many "legitimate" needs and rights, he condemned her policies in Iran and maintained that she had "no right to play poker with the seeds of war as chips." The New York *Times* believed that this criticism from the textile union head would widen the rift between Right- and Left-wing groups in the CIO over foreign policy. Rieve's attack on Russia, however, did not go so far as to advocate an anti-Soviet bloc among the Western powers: he censured Winston Churchill's '42 proposals and placed all emphasis on the United Nations as a means of maintaining harmonious relations between the U.S.S.R. and its allies. He urged that the United States prove its good faith by giving the United Nations responsibility for the atomic bomb, for Pacific bases, and for the solution of questions involving economic rivalry. While approving State Department policies on Iran, the union official did not favor its stand regarding Spain.

In April 1946, at TWUA's fourth biennial convention, Rieve was unanimously re-elected general president. (His salary had been raised from seven to ten thousand dollars.) Although the average wage in the textile industry had been increased at least 50 per cent since 1937 by this time, the union president, a firm advocate of an amendment pending in Congress in 1946 to increase the national minimum wage, announced that the TWUA would continue to fight for a wage increase which would put the textile employees on a par with workers in other manufacturing industries. The union, which has contracts with fifteen hundred and seventeen mills, would also seek health welfare insurance for its members but would not demand an annual wage because, according to Rieve, the textile industry was not yet ready for such a step. Of the more than one million textile workers in the nation, over half are still outside the union fold. Organization covers only 20 per cent of the cotton-mill hands in the South where, it is reported, textile wages have risen 106 per cent since TWUA first began to function. The textile union has sent organizers into the region and, in addition, has pledged a sum of one hundred twenty-five thousand dollars to the CIO to support the general organizing drive in the South. Regarding its financial status, TWUA has followed a policy of making its expenditures public. Its president believes "the public is entitled to a strict accounting of every penny taken in and spent by the unions." Rieve also maintained that unions should not have exclusive administration over health and welfare funds but agreed with other union leaders that employers should carry the complete financial responsibility for such funds.

In December 1946, the TWUA, without resort to striking or arbitration, won a ten-cent-an-hour wage increase (it had bargained for a fifteen-cent raise) for approximately ninety thousand cotton textile workers in New England and Middle Atlantic States, thereby raising their minimum hourly wage to eighty-three cents on hour. (The TWUA's contracts with many firms provide for arbitration in case of an impasse in collective bargaining negotiations.) Rieve announced that the union would now seek a fifteen-cent-an-hour increase for

Shelburne Studios

EMIL RIEVE

employees in Southern cotton mills. At the 1946 CIO convention, the textile union head, a leader of the Rightist group, was a member of a committee representing conflicting opinions within the CIO, which formulated a policy statement on communism. According to this statement, the CIO would "resent and reject" interference by "the Communist Party or other political parties and their adherents."

A delegate to the World Federation of Trade Unions since 1945, Rieve has already taken action on plans to form an organization which would seek international labor standards among the world's textile workers. He is an executive of the National Committee in the International Labor Office and is a member of the board of directors of the Foreign Policy Association and the American Arbitration Association. The labor leader believes in the use of only voluntary arbitration to settle labor disputes but is working for the day when "our economic order is so stabilized that compulsory arbitration is possible and desirable." In 1942 he was the American delegate to the Inter-American Conference on Social Security in Santiago, Chile. When the National Citizens Political Action Committee was formed in 1944 to work for the re-election of Roosevelt, Rieve was one of the committee's members, and in the same year he was one of the sponsors of the Council for a Democratic Germany. In 1946 when the CIO Political Action Committee was enlarged, he was among its new members. Also a member of the special committee on labor standards and social security of the Interdepartmental Committee on Postwar Economic Policy (United States Department of Labor), he warns those who see a postwar era of unprecedented prosperity in the nation, that "unless we sober up and stop drinking . . . we are going to have the same hangover we had in 1929."

(Continued next page)

RIEVE, EMIL—*Continued*

Rieve's family consists of his wife, the former Laura Wosnack, to whom he was married in 1919, and their son Harold. Five feet ten inches in height and weighing 180 pounds, the gray-eyed union executive, who belongs to the Lutheran church, has been characterized as "heavy-handed, cautious, and non-conformist." According to *Time,* he was once a Socialist.

References

Who's Who in America, 1946-47
Who's Who in Labor (1946)

RIFKIND, SIMON H(IRSCH) June 5, 1901- Federal judge; Government adviser

Address: b. United States Courthouse, New York; h. 415 Central Park West, New York

In October 1945, shortly after the publication of the Earl G. Harrison '43 report which severely criticized the treatment of Jews in occupied Germany, United States District Judge Simon H. Rifkind was assigned as temporary special adviser on Jewish affairs to General Dwight D. Eisenhower '42 in Europe. Considered by many especially fitted for the task of ascertaining the needs of Jewish displaced persons because of his background, Rifkind five months later filed a report with the War Department urging the immediate opening of Palestine to the Jews.

The son of Jacob and Celia (Bluestone) Rifkind, Simon Hirsch Rifkind was born in Meretz, Russia, June 5, 1901; at the age of nine he was taken to the United States. In New York he attended DeWitt Clinton High School and at twenty-one was graduated from the College of the City of New York, a member of Phi Beta Kappa, the national honorary fraternity. In 1925 Rifkind received his law degree from the Columbia Law School. He

Virginia F. Stern
SIMON H. RIFKIND

had become an American citizen the preceding year. In 1927 the young lawyer became secretary and legislative assistant to Senator Robert F. Wagner '41, who had been a justice of the New York Supreme Court before his election. For six years Rifkind retained this position; and like the new Senator he was a Democrat working for progressive measures under a Republican Administration. Meanwhile, in 1930 he had become a partner in the firm of Wagner, Quillinan, and Rifkind, although continuing as his partner's secretary until June 1933. During the following eight years he specialized in real estate and corporation cases, becoming well known in his field, and also served on the boards of many Jewish organizations.

At the age of thirty-nine, in April 1941 Rifkind was named by President Roosevelt to one of two newly created Federal judgeships in the Southern District of New York State. The New York *Times* recalled that he was the second of Wagner's law partners to be appointed to the Federal bench within recent years, the first being Judge Vincent Leibell. Newspapers remarked also that Rifkind's appointment, together with that of John Bright of Middletown, constituted a rebuff to the Tammany Hall Democratic organization and to Boss Ed Flynn of the Bronx, inasmuch as the machine candidates had been passed over in favor of Bright and Rifkind.

Judge Rifkind came to public attention in October 1945 when he took a leave of absence from the bench to accept appointment as General Eisenhower's adviser on Jewish affairs. The General, it was said by Secretary of War Robert P. Patterson, had requested an adviser on August 10 and had indorsed the nomination of Judge Rifkind. To Rifkind Secretary Patterson had written: "I am glad to join with General Eisenhower in inviting you to accept this position. Your broad knowledge of Jewish affairs and your high reputation and ability place you in a unique position to render invaluable service to our Government in discharging its responsibilities to these unfortunate people. General Eisenhower has estimated that your mission could be completed in about three months." In January 1946, at the request of General Joseph T. McNarney '44, who succeeded Eisenhower as theater commander, and of Secretary Patterson, Rifkind's term of service was extended for an additional two months. Thus, from mid-October 1945 to mid-March 1946 the jurist was in Europe inspecting and advising on food, fuel, housing, and morale in the camps for Jewish displaced persons, on the conditions of German Jews outside the camps, on resettlement and repatriation, and on Army relations with UNRRA and other agencies. "The only limitation on me is my own discretion," he had told reporters before sailing.

"Over a period of two months," Rifkind said in January 1946, "I have in their own language examined and cross-examined hundreds of infiltrees from Poland. I found them in Berlin, Vienna, Salzburg, Munich, Frankfurt, Nuremburg, and in most of the Jewish displaced-persons centers in the American zone in Germany and in the American zone in Austria."

The number included not only persons rescued from concentration camps, but men who had fought in the Polish Army and in the Partisan ranks and some who had managed to escape persecution during the German occupation. In many cases, the Judge said, these people fleeing their native Poland were leaving relatively comfortable economic circumstances for poverty and hardship. They were, or believed they were, he added, fleeing for their lives, which were being menaced, according to all indications, by the anti-Semitic acts of many of their fellow-countrymen. Despite the efforts of the Polish Government to end the persecutions, Rifkind reported there had been many instances of threats and violence. But the supposition that this "second exodus" of the Jews was being directed by some unknown worldwide Jewish organization, as stated by the local UNRRA chief, Lieutenant General Sir Frederick E. Morgan [46], the American dismissed as "poppycock." "No organization, secret or non-secret," he averred, "could bring out women and children, young and old, strong and weak, orthodox and non-religious, well-off and poor, such as I have seen."

The judge's final memorandum to General McNarney was made public in April 1946. Analyzing the position of the Jews remaining in Europe, Rifkind pointed out that almost all of them wished to leave that continent permanently, preferably for Palestine; that they felt that in the meantime they were entitled to German food, clothing and habitation as a matter of right in payment for their sufferings, and that they want these instead of American charity. "We must recognize," he wrote," that insofar as we fail to require the Germans to satisfy the needs of these Jews and satisfy them ourselves, we are discharging a portion of the debt owed by Germany. It would, it seems to me, be preferable, certainly from the moral point of view, to insist that Germany discharge that obligation in the first instance, though this cause some discomfort to the German population." Among the several Governmental agencies responsible in the American zone, he reported, only the Army had made "a substantial and noteworthy contribution" to the solution of the problem; UNRRA had refused to contribute supplies and had "failed to bring to its task the necessary initiative, administrative skill, and imagination." Improvement in all ways was still required, and his report specifically recommended the use of civilian-type housing instead of barracks, variation in diet, the introduction of rehabilitation and training projects, intensification of the educational and religious program, and provision of employment opportunities.

But, he concluded—pursuing a theme on which he had previously spoken at length before a closed session of the Anglo-American Committee of Inquiry on Palestine—, "I recognize that no matter how wise the policies formulated and no matter how sympathetic their implementation, they can only ameliorate the present conditions of life of the displaced Jews and prepare them more adequately for the future. They cannot solve the problem of the displaced Jews. . . .Rapid, mass resettlement is the only means of solving that problem; life in the displaced persons centers cannot, at its very best, begin to approach normal life and the inevitable consequence of a prolonged stay there is demoralization. Disintegration has already begun and may rapidly spread. . . .I believe their problem is insoluble without Palestine."

Blue-eyed and brown-haired, Judge Rifkind is a short man; he is five feet six inches tall, and weighs one hundred and forty pounds. "His comparative youthfulness," wrote one reporter, "is concealed somewhat by a generous mustache, spectacles, and a corncob pipe." In June 1927 he was married to Adele Singer; their two sons are Robert Singer and Richard Allen. Rifkind is a member of the Association of the Bar of the City of New York, the New York County Lawyers Association, and the New York Lawyers Club. He has been a member of the staff of the Council of Research in the Social Sciences, working in the field of legal economics, and he is the author of a study entitled *Money as a Device for Measuring Value*. On December 17, 1945, he was honored for his services by the award of the Medal of Freedom, a decoration created by President Truman for meritorious acts by civilians outside the United States since Pearl Harbor.

References

N Y Herald Tribune p6 O 3 '45

Who's Who in America, 1946-47

Who's Who in American Jewry, 1938-39

Who's Who in Law, 1937

RIOS, JUAN ANTONIO (rē′ōs hwän än-tōn′yō) Nov. 10, 1888—June 7, 1946 President of Chile from 1942 until his death; broke with the Axis in 1943 against the opposition of Chilean Nazis; visited the United States in October 1945 at the invitation of President Truman. See *Current Biography* 1942 Yearbook.

Obituary

N Y Times p21 Je 28 '46 por

ROBERTS, ALBERT H. July 4, 1868—June 25, 1946 Democratic Governor of Tennessee from 1919 to 1921; a leader in the fight for ratification of the woman suffrage amendment to the Federal Constitution.

Obituary

N Y Times p21 Je 27 '46

ROBERTSON, CONSTANCE Sept. 27, 1897- Author

Address: h. "Struan House," Kenwood, Oneida, N.Y.

Constance Robertson, wrote the critic of the New York *Times,* Nash K. Burger, "is a novelist who loves the time and place she has chosen for her fiction, and by now, with her fourth [historical] novel, she is in the way of being an authority on nineteenth century New

CONSTANCE ROBERTSON

York." Her latest book, *The Unterrified* (1946) is concerned with the antidraft riots and political dissensions in the North in 1863. Mrs. Robertson's fidelity to her sources, in this recreation of Civil War days, is complete, "even the colloquialisms in the dialogue and the figures of speech . . . smack of an earlier time." The book has also some "strangely modern overtones," according to Mr. Burger, who stated that the author is not unaware of the implications for our own era in some of her material.

Although Constance Pierrepont Noyes Robertson, daughter of Pierrepont Burt and Corinna Ackley (Kinsley) Noyes, was born in Niagara Falls, Ontario, Canada—September 27, 1897—she was brought up in New York State, where her family has been connected for several generations with the Oneida community, founded by her grandfather, John Humphrey Noyes, in 1847. Young Constance was graduated from Dana Hall, in Wellesley, Massachusetts, in 1916, and then spent two years at the University of Wisconsin. In 1918 marriage interrupted her college career, and for several years she traveled outside the United States with her husband, Miles E. Robertson. After living for a time in Sydney, Australia, the Robertsons spent a year in the Far East—China, Japan, the Philippines, Singapore, Java, Ceylon, India—and then went to London. Using the British capital as a base, they made frequent journeys about Europe, staying for a time in Coblenz, where Mrs. Robertson's father was the American High Commissioner of the Rhineland during the occupation after World War I. In 1921 they returned to the United States.

From the time that she was a small child with an insatiable appetite for reading, Con-

stance Robertson had known that she wanted to write, she says. Her first serious effort, a story based on an experience in China in 1920, sold at once. This initial success made the long interval when no work was accepted seem fairly painful, but she kept on writing short stories and articles, and from 1925 to 1930 edited a small privately published magazine, the *Community Quadrangle*. When it "expired for lack of an angel," she decided to try a novel. *Enchanted Avenue* came out in 1931, to the delight of the author, who wrote a second book on the same subject—the world of reality supplemented by the world of dreams. This work, however, was not published. Mrs. Robertson emerged from a subsequent period of inactivity with a detective story, *Five Fatal Letters,* which appeared in 1937 under the pseudonym "Dana Scott." It was awarded the novel prize at the Bread Loaf Writers' Conference, attended that year by the author.

Stimulated by her experience at Bread Loaf, Mrs. Robertson embarked upon her first historical novel, *Seek-No-Further* (1938), a "rich and revealing description" of American communal life. She refutes the assumption of some reviewers that this book was based on the Oneida community, "except in matters of physical detail." There followed a story of the Civil War with the ironic title, *Salute to the Hero* (1942), well received by the critics, who hailed "the wit and vigor and realism" of Mrs. Robertson's writing. The enormous amount of research required for this book turned up more material than could be used in a single volume. The surplus was developed into another novel of the same period, *Fire Bell in the Night* (1944), based on the Underground Railroad movement in upstate New York. G. W. Wakefield wrote in *Library Journal* that "none of the characters quite comes alive," but praised the "exciting picture of this great struggle for human liberty, filled with new meaning to a world in which the underground movement is again a living reality [1944]." GIs who also appreciated this picture sent Mrs. Robertson letters from most of the battle fronts, when *Fire Bell in the Night* was included in the Armed Services Editions.

Constance Robertson lives in Oneida, at "Struhan House," so called for one of the place names of the Roberston clan in Scotland. In these busy times she denies the existence of a hobby, but before the war she and her husband used to collect antiques "in the good old-fashioned way, driving over the countryside and buying from the original owners." Her true avocation, contends the brown-eyed, brown-haired author, is reading, but she does not name any favorite volumes—there are far too many. Now revising her new book, tentatively entitled *The Raid,* which will come out in 1947, Mrs. Robertson is already researching for two future novels, continuing her interpretation of American history in the last century. When conditions permit, she hopes to travel again, preferably on the two continents she knows least, Africa and South America.

ROGERS, BRUCE   May 14, 1870-   Book
designer
Address: h. New Fairfield, Conn.

"Bruce Rogers makes a page of type which
is so spaced and margined that it is as beautiful as a classic design . . . and in some way,
he gives it exactly the mood, the feeling, of
the author he is putting into print." Thus critic
Walter Prichard Eaton has expressed the apparently unanimous appreciation which printers
and booklovers have voiced of the more than
four hundred books Rogers has designed. A
"tramp printer" according to his own description, he is considered "a vital force in modern
typography," and has exercised an important
influence on the bookmaking art in both England and America.

Of English ancestry, Bruce Rogers was born
to George and Ann E. (Gish) Rogers on May
14, 1870, in the village of Linnwood, Indiana.
Some of his forebears had come West from
Virginia, risking the dangers of an overland
trip in the days of the Conestoga wagon.
Young "Bert," as he was then called, had a
gift for drawing which his father encouraged
him to develop; and upon entering Purdue
University at sixteen he was ready for the advanced courses in drafting and decorative design. One of the only two boys in coeducational Purdue's art department, he "mapped his
own course." His onetime professor, Ernest
Knaufft, recalls that "there was no worry as
to how he was spending his time" if he were
absent from a class. Not especially interested
in college sports, theatricals, or dances, Rogers
made drawings, illustrations, and covers for
the university's annuals and other publications.

After receiving his B.S. degree in 1890,
Rogers found a job as an illustrator for the
Indianapolis *News*. The noise and speed of
newspaper work, however, was not to his liking, and after a year he returned to Lafayette
to paint landscapes, which brought him little
income. The year 1892 found him working for
sixty dollars a month in a Parsons (Kansas)
railroad office managed by his brother, but by
the next year Rogers was back in Indianapolis,
this time as a general draftsman for the Indianapolis Illustrating Company. Then, in the
spring of 1895, at the suggestion of his friend
J. M. Bowles, he went to Boston to work for
fifty cents an hour as a designer for L. Prang
and Company. His hours were irregular and
only occasionally did he make the weekly ten
dollars he had been promised. But he was
never rushed, wrote Bowles in the *Colophon*,
and was able to "work for a few hours, then
. . . walk in the beautiful Massachusetts country for one, two, or three days." *Modern Art,*
which was edited by Bowles and published by
Prang, contained many of Rogers' contributions
at that time.

Bruce Rogers had made his first attempt at
book designing as early as 1885, when he produced a hand-lettered copy of William Cullen
Bryant's *Forest Hymn*, "illustrated with water
colors and imitations of etchings on which the
plate mark was pressed with a hot iron in the
family kitchen." But his ambition at the time,
the book designer has related, was to become

BRUCE ROGERS

a landscape painter and it was mainly through
Bowles that he was steered toward the composing room. "His whole interest in book
production became rationalized and intensified,"
wrote Frederic Warde in *Bruce Rogers, Designer of Books* (1926) when in 1893 Bowles,
who had given him commissions for making
book decorations, showed him some of the books
published by William Morris' Kelmscott Press
in England. In 1896 Rogers met George H.
Mifflin, who asked him to join the Houghton
Mifflin Company's well-known Riverside Press
at Cambridge, Massachusetts. For the next
four years the young artist gained valuable
technical training in the production of trade
editions under Mifflin's guidance.

With the opening of a special department
for the publication of fine limited editions at
Riverside in 1900, Rogers was able to experiment freely with his ideas on bookmaking. *The
Sonnets and Madrigals of Michelangelo Buon-
arroti* (1900), set in Caslon italic, was the first
of a twelve years' series in which Rogers, influenced by Updike of the Merrymount Press
according to one critic's analysis, sought to
give each book an individual typographic style.
Next came the *Rubáiyát of Omar Khayyám,*
printed in Brimmer, a type which had not been
used for many years. For *The Essays of
Montaigne* (1902-3-4), which a 1908 writer described as the "most obviously impressive" of
the Riverside Press editions, Rogers designed
the Montaigne, a type derived from the Jen-
son; it was cut only in the 16-point size and
had the "boldness and distinction" required for
the three-volume work. He also designed the
Riverside Caslon, a modification of the much-
used Caslon.

Most of the books on which Rogers worked
were of a bygone age. He regarded "each . . .
as a problem . . . to be undertaken only upon
a sympathetic basis of knowledge both of the
printing of its own period, the thought of its

ROGERS, BRUCE—*Continued*

author, and the relation of a cultivated contemporary audience to a similar audience in the present century." To create the proper typographic setting for *The Song of Roland* (1906), the designer suggested the elements of the period, when printing was new and "scribe and illuminator did their magnificent best to prove printing an unworthy substitute." Set in double columns of French Gothic type imported from Paris, with marginal notes in brown, capitals in blue, and rubricated folios for page headings, the book had hand-colored decorations modeled after the legend as pictured in one of the stained glass windows in the Chartres Cathedral. Rogers' experiments in the medieval style, however, which also included Chaucer's *Parlement of Foules* (1904) and the *History of Oliver and Arthur* (1903) were, in the opinion of Warde, not "so grateful to the eyes" as his designs for three classic works: Plutarch's *Consolatorie Letter or Discourse* (1905), the *Georgics of Virgil* (1904) and the *Idylls of Theocritus* (1906). In all Rogers designed more than one hundred Riverside Press editions—they were books which critics agree were "astonishing in their variety of style, their unfailing fitness and beauty, their demonstration of the capacity for superb printing resident in America."

In 1912 Rogers left Riverside and, after traveling abroad for a summer, decided to freelance. He received few commissions, however; for three years he did commercial work in New York, designing only four books in this period, one of which was *Franklin and his Press at Passy* (1914), an example of "reminiscent" printing. An important development in printing at this time was Rogers' Centaur type (a refinement of the Montaigne), hailed by printers as "a letter which in its surety of drawing and virile delicacy has not been equaled by any modern type designer." In 1915 Rogers was the first living typographer to be honored by the reading of a paper on his work (*The Work of Bruce Rogers, Printer*, by Alfred W. Pollard) before the Bibliographical Society.

Rogers now became associated with Carl P. Rollins at the Montague Press in Massachusetts, there designing three books, among them Maurice de Guérin's *The Centaur*, which marked the first use of the Centaur type in book publication. He then returned to New York and became an occasional adviser to the Metropolitan Museum of Art's Museum Press. Late in 1916 he sailed for England to work with Emery Walker, who was then establishing the Mall Press. After designing one book, a translation of Dürer's *On the Just Shaping of Letters*, he was asked to be the printing adviser to the Cambridge University Press. As a result of his efforts to improve the typography of university publications—efforts involving such details as standards of spacing and arrangement, page and margin proportions, the discarding of old and bad type—a high degree of excellence was achieved. During this period, which was spent mainly on trade editions, Rogers' edition of the volume of sixteenth century verse, *On Friendship* (1918), was an

example of the results of his experiments with printer's flowers (typographical ornaments) for book decoration. According to Warde, the designer's residence in England marked "the beginning of a new tendency in his work, namely the development of the resources of type and caste-type ornaments alone."

Upon returning to the United States in 1919, Rogers joined William Edwin Rudge, a printer at Mount Vernon, New York, and also became the printing adviser to the Harvard University Press (1920-34). The book designer, who "has somehow never gotten around to having a workshop of his own," has said that Rudge's was the only place where he had a really well-equipped studio for his work. Turning out about eighty books during his eight years there, he designed, among others, such privately printed editions as *Several Reasons,* by Increase Mather, and *Christmas Epithalamium,* by Hervey Allen. One of six printers invited by the Grolier Club in 1921 to design a book of his own choice, Rogers created what Warde has called "a triumph of whimsical humor over the mechanics of typesetting" with Ernest Dowson's *Pierrot of the Minute.*

Since the period from 1928 to 1931, when he was again an associate of Emery Walker in London, Rogers has worked independently. His "monumental" work in these later years was the Oxford Lectern Bible (1935) printed in England, of which Carl P. Rollins has said, "It is a mature and sophisticated publication, serene and masterly." (Rogers has written about the four years he spent on the edition in his *Account of the Making of the Oxford Lectern Bible.*) At the same time the designer was also occupied with other projects, among them Homer's *Odyssey* (1932), Thomas More's *Utopia* (1934), and the eighteen-volume *Private Papers of James Boswell from Malahide Castle* (1929-33), in which the recently revealed papers of Samuel Johnson's biographer reached print for the first time. "I want to be free of books for a while," Rogers said when the Lectern Bible was nearing completion. Relaxing from his serious labors, "B.R.," as he is known to his associates, produced *An unHoly BRible Story,* an "unauthorized perVersion of the Making of the New Oxford Lectern Bible." This was one of the numerous examples of the designer's flair for "typographic tomfoolery." (Rollins has written in detail of Rogers' humorous pieces in *B. R., America's Typographic Playboy.*) Since 1935 Rogers has worked on such projects as the twelve-volume autograph edition of the novels and stories of Willa Cather (1937-38) and the poems of Thomas Gray (1937), as well as a thirty-seven-volume edition of Shakespeare and an American folio Lectern Bible. (The publication of the latter was planned for the fall of 1947.)

"There has been too much praise written about my things and too little real criticism," Rogers told Paul Bennett in an interview in 1935. Pressed by Bennet to speak about his work, he revealed some of the principles and methods which have guided him. "I don't care for so-called 'originality' in books," Rogers said. "Little touches of the designer's personality are bound to creep in and books should primarily embody the quality of the text." To achieve the variety which has been one of his main aims, he has mixed types, at times even combining the capital letters of one face with the lower case of another. He believes that bookmaking does not demand an extreme finish —"a certain roughness within limits is . . . a sign of vigor and life in the work." Asked to comment on his style, he maintained that it could be described only as "a sort of eclecticism." In *Paragraphs on Printing,* which Rogers designed and wrote or "literally spoke" to a colleague, are contained the designer's ideas on bookmaking as well as specimen pages from his work.

Many honors have been bestowed upon Bruce Rogers. He is the only living bookmaker whose printer's emblem decorates a panel of a pair of bronze doors in the Library of Congress. It formerly appeared, also, on a stained glass window in the library of the American Type Founders Company in Jersey City, and is used for ornamentation at Baltimore's Enoch Pratt Free Library. The British Museum has collected a set of his works, and in 1938-39, his "prodigious output," including his sketches, bookplates, greeting cards, and miscellaneous pieces, as well as his books, was exhibited in New York for about two months by the American Institute of Graphic Arts and the Grolier Club. He has received several honorary degrees: an L.H.D. from Purdue in 1932, an M.A. from Yale in 1928 and one from Harvard in 1939. An honorary life member of the American Institute of Graphic Arts, Rogers lists honorary memberships in Odd Volumes, (Boston), Book Club of California, Society of Printers (Boston), Grolier (New York), the John Barnard Associates (Cambridge, Massachusetts), Caxton (Chicago), Quarto (New York), and Double Crown (London). He also is a member of the Century Club in New York.

A widower—he was married to Anne E. Baker in 1900—Rogers has a small country home in Connecticut, which he calls October House. He sketches for relaxation and has a passion for sailboats, owning a small one himself and occasionally building ship models. He has sailed on the Baltic in several Finnish barks and on the ship *Joseph Conrad,* for which he carved a figurehead of the English author. According to *Time,* the book designer likes bright clothing and Italian food. A late sleeper, he has said he intends to leave this note for Gabriel on judgment day—"Call me last."

References

Bookman 59 :708+ Ag '24
Colophon No. 11 p1+ 1932
Pub W 138 :334 Ag 3 '40
Time 42 :43 Jl 5 '43 por; 33 :61 Ap 3 '39 por
Bennett, P. A. Bruce Rogers of Indiana (1936)
Columbia Encyclopedia (1935)
Fryer, N. and Johnson, J. Bruce Rogers and the Figurehead of the Joseph Conrad (1938)
Warde, F. Bruce Rogers, Designer of Books (1926)
Who's Who in America, 1946-47
Work of Bruce Rogers; a Catalogue (1939)

ROOSEVELT, ELLIOTT Sept. 23, 1910- Radio executive; writer

Address: b. 14 Washington Sq., North, New York 11; h. Hyde Park, Dutchess County, N. Y.

"Elliott Roosevelt, stormy petrel of his family, has written a surprisingly good book about his father," wrote Sterling North in the New York *Post* shortly after the publication of Roosevelt's *As He Saw It,* a best seller at the end of 1946. In an issue of *Look* magazine, which contained a condensation of his book, the second son of the thirty-second President of the United States introduced himself as that Roosevelt who had been the subject of large-type headlines in the country's newspapers.

In the same year that Franklin Delano Roosevelt [42] was elected to the New York State Senate, their third child was born to the young lawyer and Anna Eleanor (Roosevelt) Roosevelt [40] on September 23, 1910. He was named Elliott after his maternal grandfather, who was the brother of President Theodore Roosevelt and also distantly related to Franklin Roosevelt. As his father had been, the boy was reared in New York City, his birthplace, in Hyde Park, the Roosevelt estate, and in Campobello, the family's Maine vacation home. In 1923 he was sent to Groton, his father's preparatory school, from which he was graduated in 1929. After spending an additional year at the Hun School in New Jersey, he was graduated from that school in 1930, first or second in his class. Breaking a family tradition, Elliott was "the Roosevelt who did not go to Harvard"; instead he went to work as an assistant account executive for Albert Frank and Company, a New York advertising agency. In 1931 he became vice-president of Kelly, Nason, and Roosevelt, Incorporated, and in 1932 account executive with Paul Cornell, Incorporated, both of them advertising firms. "The surpassing eagerness of companies to become his clients" had forced him to change, reported *Business Week.* In January 1932 the twenty-two-year-old executive had been married to Elizabeth Donner of Philadelphia. After their divorce in July 1933, he was married to Ruth Googins of Texas.

In another year Elliott Roosevelt joined the Los Angeles *Examiner* and other papers in the William Randolph Hearst chain as aviation editor. During the period of his association with the Hearst papers (1933-35) he had become an experienced pilot, and in 1934 he was unanimously elected vice-president of the Aeronautical Chamber of Commerce of America. When the Mead air mail bill was introduced in the House of Representatives in 1935, the twenty-four-year-old editor was accused of having participated in the air line lobbies, a charge he denied. In 1935 Roosevelt worked toward the establishment of United States-South America air races. As vice-president of the Young

ELLIOTT ROOSEVELT

Democrats of Texas (he was living on his 1500-acre Dutch Branch Ranch near Fort Worth), he was outspoken on political issues, at times expressing a Texas anti-New Deal point of view. A brief association with Anthony H. G. Fokker brought young Roosevelt into public notice in 1936. To the charge that he had been under contract to the airplane designer and industrialist to sell planes to a foreign Government at high prices he replied that the contract with Fokker, subsequently canceled, stipulated that he would not contact any Government's officials.

With the furor of adverse publicity making his association with the aviation industry unpleasant, Roosevelt turned to radio in 1936, when he became vice-president of Hearst Radio, Incorporated, in charge of four stations in the Southwest and president of the Hearst-owned KTSA and KNOW. (That same year he was a Texas delegate to the Democratic National Convention which nominated his father for a second term in the White House.) The following year the radio executive appeared before the Federal Communications Commission to receive a charter for the Frontier Broadcasting System, composed of several stations bought by himself and his second wife, Ruth (Googins) Roosevelt. Also in 1937, he became president and general manager of Hearst Radio, a position from which he resigned in 1939. In 1938 he was a commentator over the Texas State Network (which he had founded) and in 1939 for Emerson Radio and Phonograph, Incorporated, over the Mutual Broadcasting System. Continuing to operate his chain of twenty-three stations, he and a group of men laid plans for the formation of a national network, the Transcontinental Broadcasting System. His exact position with the organization was not defined since he invested no money in it, nor was he

to hold any office. In 1940 TBS went into receivership.

Elliott Roosevelt was the first member of his family to enter the armed forces. In September 1940 he was commissioned a captain in the Army Air Forces (again breaking a family tradition by not entering the Navy). He had enlisted without his father's knowledge and was given the rank because of his aviation and radio experience and his age. The publicity given to the President's son in an election year brought wide comment: "During the Presidential campaign of 1940 I got some thirty-five thousand letters and post cards from all over the country," the young Roosevelt reported, at the same time suggesting that they were not all friendly. Subsequently the Captain first tried to resign his commission and when this failed, he applied for an overseas assignment. At the end of 1940 he was being trained at Bolling Field, in Washington, D.C., as an intelligence officer. Next stationed in Newfoundland, he volunteered for a survey of the North Arctic area which was being made for the purpose of establishing an air ferry route across the North Atlantic.

Completing navigation training, which he had requested, and two months' service in the United States, the officer was ordered to the First Mapping Group and was sent to North Africa in the winter of 1942 to make pre-invasion maps by means of aerial photography. In March Roosevelt received his majority. After a few months' duty in the United States in the summer of 1942, he was ordered to England to command the Third Photographic Reconnaissance Group as a lieutenant colonel. His group entered North Africa with the invasion, which took place in November 1942. Early in 1943 his squadrons took air photographs of Sicily, also preparatory to the invasion, and in July 1943 Colonel Roosevelt (he had become a full colonel in March) returned to Washington to confer on the reorganization of reconnaissance operations. In September he returned to Tunis, then proceeded to Italy, and in 1944 to England, working under General Carl Spaatz [42] to reorganize and supervise the preinvasion reconnaisance work of the Eighth and Ninth Air Forces. During a brief visit to the United States, Roosevelt was married to Faye Emerson, motion picture actress, on December 3, 1944 (he had been divorced by his second wife earlier that year). Back in England, he helped to plan the details of bombing Germany in shuttle-flying between England and Russia, and on that assignment visited Moscow.

In February 1945 Elliott Roosevelt was promoted to the rank of brigadier general after some delay—his dog had "bumped" three servicemen from an Air Transport Command cargo plane, an incident that caused much public and Congressional indignation. Congress, however, finally approved the promotion on the basis of the thirty-five-year-old officer's war record. In the course of the war, Roosevelt won the United States Air Medal, the Legion of Merit, the Distinguished Flying Cross with an oak leaf cluster; he was also made a Commander of the Order of the British Empire, the third highest honor that can be awarded to those who are not citizens of Britain, the French Legion of Honor, and the Croix de Guerre with Palm. In June an attorney for John Hartford, president of the Great Atlantic and Pacific Tea Company, in claiming tax deduction for an unpaid debt, revealed that Elliott Roosevelt had borrowed $200,000 from the executive and had settled the debt for $4,000. The explanation by Roosevelt, which was confirmed by the House Ways and Means Committee and the Treasury Department, denied that the late President had been involved in the investment or the debt settlement. A month before the Hartford loan was revealed, the War Department had authorized the release of Roosevelt, who has applied for the discharge, which became effective in August.

After the war, Roosevelt renewed his activities in both the radio and airplane industries. For a few months he held the position of president of Empire Airlines, an intra-New York State air service, but resigned because of the pressure of other duties, one of which was the transcription of a series of interview radio programs with his wife. Roosevelt and his wife left for Russia in November 1946 to gather material and photographs for magazine articles. His interview with Marshal Stalin [42] was scheduled for January 1947 publication in Look. While in Russia, Roosevelt reportedly criticized the foreign policy of the United States (he called Newsweek's account "completely inaccurate"). Upon his return home at the end of the year he announced that he planned to take an active part in the 1948 Presidential campaign.

Elliott Roosevelt was present with his father at five major conferences, which, with the Yalta conference as reported by his sister, are the substance of his book, As He Saw It, published in October 1946. The book, dedicated "to all those who believed in my father," was written because, in the author's words, "the most articulate voice for integrity among nations and the peoples of the world was stilled." The late President's son records promises given and plans laid for future international cooperation, and asserts that many of these were broken. He pleads for the salvaging of world peace through adhering to the principles put forth by his father. Orville Prescott, writing for the New York Times, summarized Elliott Roosevelt's ideas as consisting "chiefly of distrust of Britain and admiration for Russia." In the same newspaper, Henry Steele Commager [46] reported that "it gives a great deal of valuable incidental information." "It is not always easy to have implicit confidence in the reporting of an observer who is capable of judgments so strange as those of Elliott Roosevelt," was Harold J. Laski's [41] opinion in the New Republic.

Critic Max Lerner [42] of PM saw the book as "chatty, engaging, dramatic—and very much a matter of surface rather than penetration or analysis." Pointing out that "Elliott Roosevelt may seem a boy engaged in a man's work," Jonathan Daniels wrote in the Saturday Review of Literature: "But Elliott is his father's boy. . . .There will be plenty to describe it as an indiscreet book. . . .But if the book seems indiscreet, it seems always history on its most intimate level. Nobody who starts it will fail to finish it." Gerald Johnson, the Herald Tribune reviewer, seemed to express general critical opinion when he called it "swift, terse, sparkling," and added that some readers "cannot accept the dedication if it involves believing the son also." A condensation of As He Saw It appeared serially in Look before the book was published. Prepublication sales exhausted the first printing, and by early December As He Saw It had reached third place among nonfiction best sellers. For this book, in the field of public affairs, Roosevelt received one of the twenty-eight Page One awards from the Newspaper Guild of New York.

Elliott Roosevelt has four children: William Donner, the son of his first wife, and Ruth Chandler, Elliott Jr., and David Boynton, born to his second wife. He is a Master Mason and a member of the Fort Worth and Rivercrest country clubs, both in Fort Worth. Blond, husky, and six feet three inches in height, he was described by Maxine Davis in Look as "a man who works hard and plays hard," and was characterized as "sometimes easygoing, sometimes bellicose." He calls himself a Democrat who "thinks independently."

References

America's Young Men (1938-39)
Roosevelt, E. As He Saw It (1946)
Who's Who in America, 1946-47

ROSE, ARNOLD JOSEF Oct. 24, 1863—Aug. 25, 1946 Austrian violinist, known for bringing to light much of the chamber music of Brahms; concertmaster of the Vienna Court Orchestra from 1881 until the Nazis entered Vienna in 1938; in 1882 he founded the Rosé Quartet, unrivaled in its interpretation of the classics, which introduced most of the string quartets from Dvořák to Schoenberg; died in England.

Obituary

N Y Times p23 Ag 26 '46

ROSENBACH, A(BRAHAM) S(IMON) W(OLF) July 22, 1876- Bibliophile; rare book dealer; author; bibliographer

Address: b. 1618 Locust St., Philadelphia; h. 2006 De Lancey St., Philadelphia; 15 E. 51st St., New York; Strathmere, Corson's Inlet, N.J.

"He can hardly enter an auction room without becoming news," it has been said of Dr. A. S. W. Rosenbach. The world's foremost dealer and collector of rare books and manu-

A. S. W. ROSENBACH

scripts, Rosenbach believes that the book germ must have entered his blood with his first vaccination, for he cannot remember a time when books were not a large part of his life. In 1946, on the occasion of his seventieth birthday, he was presented with a volume of scholarly essays in his honor—*To Doctor R.*—of which Lawrence C. Worth, writing in the New York *Herald Tribune,* said, "In this book we find a spontaneous expression of admiration or affection for him, not alone as dealer and collector but as man and friend, from those who have for many years been associates in the numerous fields of his interest and activity."

One of seven children, others of whom were also imbued with the collector's urge, Abraham Simon Wolf Rosenbach was born in Philadelphia on July 22, 1876. His father, Morris Rosenbach, was a cotton goods manufacturer of moderate income and good though not outstanding education. His more literary mother, the former Isabella Polock, was the sister of Moses Polock, whose combined bookshop and publishing house on Commerce Street in old Philadelphia had become a rendezvous for publishers, writers, and collectors. At an age when anything rather than books attracted his schoolmates, it likewise became the constant resort of her young son—whose delight it was to substitute in his imagination rare volumes for the Spanish doubloons of *Treasure Island.* Both parents were determined that their children should have the finest education obtainable, and the mother, marking not only her boy's desire for books but his unusual sensitivity to their physical characteristics and his care in handling them, encouraged his bent. In this she was aided by Uncle Moses, who made it his habit to remember birthdays and other occasions with the gift of a pretty little book, but reserved the choicest presents for young Abie and his sister Rebecca (who later was drawn to book collecting as a hobby).

It was in 1885, when he was only nine years old, the bibliophile writes, that he first became really "spellbound" by the "mystery and intangible beauty which becomes a part of the atmosphere wherever fine books are brought together." Whatever it was, this craving which some "glibly" dismiss as bibliomania, it entered his consciousness then, he adds, and "has grown out of all proportion ever since." At first Moses Polock was not too pleased to have the little boy poking around among the rare and semi-rare volumes in his bookshop, but when he had satisfied himself that his nephew's interest was indeed genuine, he expanded. In the years that followed, young Abie absorbed with relish his uncle's recitals of literary and bibliographical lore and listened with fascination while Polock and other bookmen argued heatedly about their favorite books and authors or made "bookish prophecies, most of which came true." And, he says too, he unwittingly developed his extraordinary memory when, hurrying home "in the twilight, the moon, just coming up, throwing long shadows across the white slab of Franklin's grave," he braved imaginary fears by cross-examining himself on dates and quotations from books and manuscripts through which he had "prowled" earlier in the day.

Young Rosenbach's first purchase at auction—an illustrated edition of *Reynard the Fox,* for which he paid twenty-four dollars—was made when he was only eleven, but out of enthusiasm rather than financial means; for at the conclusion of the sale he had to confess to the auctioneer, the famous Stan V. Henkels, that he had only ten dollars in his pocket. As he tells it in *Books and Bidders,* "at the same time I explained I was Moses Polock's nephew, instinctively feeling, I suppose, that such a relationship might account for any untoward action concerning books. . . .Henkels burst into a fit of laughing. . . .When he ceased . . . he looked down at me, a sombre little boy with a book under his shaking arm, and said, 'I've seen it start at an early age and run in families, but in all my experience this is the very first baby bibliomaniac to come my way!' With this admission he kindly consented to . . . trust me for further payments, which I was to make weekly from my school allowance. . . .I marched from the auction room," Rosenbach continues, "feeling for the first time in my life that swooning yet triumphant, that enervating and at the same time heroic combination of emotions the born bibliomaniac enjoys so intensely with the purchase of each rare book." (Although he did not know it then, this was also the beginning of a lifelong friendship.) Soon Moses Polock was trusting his nephew to act as his agent in the auction rooms. Though merely a schoolboy and at an age when he was not even expected to show an interest in such matters, young Rosenbach was gaining the knowledge and experience which were to enable him to achieve legendary fame as a bookman in his own lifetime.

When in 1894 the youth entered the University of Pennsylvania, the book fever was attacking him more virulently than ever. He attended sales at all hours, day or night, he relates. He neglected his studies for them. He bought books whether he could afford them or not, forgot to eat, and looked upon sleep as quite unnecessary. Books enthralled him "to a disastrous extent." Then, at the age of eighteen, while he was a sophomore, he made his first important discovery. Attracted to a pile of pamphlets in the corner of Henkel's auction room one night, he came upon a copy of Gray's *Odes*, a first edition and the initial work to have been issued from Horace Walpole's Strawberry Hill Press. This was an interesting item—but, bound with it, he recognized the long-lost first edition oᶠ the famous *Prologue* written by Samuel Johnson for David Garrick to recite at the reopening of the Drury Lane Theatre under Garrick's management in 1747. The youthful booklover leaned heavily against the wall to steady himself, he says, afraid some more practiced collector would realize what it was he held in his hand. With a caution born of experience in the auction rooms he bid it up ten cents at a time, and, when, after little opposition, it was finally sold to him for all of three dollars and sixty cents, he sat as one in a trance. Although at a later date, when he needed the money, Rosenbach was offered five thousand dollars for this find, it rests today in his private collection, one of the books which, once they cross his De Lancey Street threshold, are never sold. In 1902, four years after he had received his B.S. from the University of Pennsylvania, he published an edition of this *Prologue* in collaboration with Austin Dobson, the poet and eighteenth century scholar.

From 1898 to 1901 Rosenbach taught at the University of Pennsylvania as a fellow in English, at the same time studying for his Ph.D., which he received in the latter year. Then, concluding that the only way to obtain money to collect books was to buy and sell them, he gave up teaching to enter the rare book trade. Feeling half guilty as he made the change, he did not at that time appreciate, he recalls, "what a high adventure the business was to prove," what excitement as well as anxiety lay in the chase, but, above all, what far greater opportunity to uncover original literary and historical source materials—from the first he had been primarily interested in these—would be his outside the conventional halls of learning. A few months before his twenty-eighth birthday, on March 15, 1904, he issued his first catalogue from 1320 Walnut Street, the location he was to make famous over a span of forty years. Invaluable advice as to the choicest items on the market came from two bookloving friends whom Rosenbach credits with a large measure of his early success, Clarence S. Bement, a noted visitor of his uncle's and the owner of "a glorious collection over which he had spent years of constant study and search," and Joseph M. Fox, whose friendship had been gained over a sixteenth century missal which both had wanted and who for a time became his partner. They enabled him, points out Frederick M. Hopkins in *Publishers' Weekly*, "to begin at the top and to accomplish in five years more than many successful booksellers are able to do in a long life." In addition, the psychological insight into the habits of bookmen which he had acquired as a boy now stood him in good stead, while his excellent memory and wide knowledge of the idiosyncracies of his collector clients helped him to secure a large percentage of long-desired volumes.

Backed thus by an augmented reputation and a growing bank account, Rosenbach began to increase the amounts of his bids in the auction room until other dealers, reports Miss Avery Strakosch, "thought him mad and were angry that he insisted on pushing prices to ridiculous heights." But he attracted the attention of Henry E. Huntington, who, first amused, then impressed, commissioned him to help assemble the great library of English literature, Spanish-American history, Americana and incunabula which he was to give to the public at his death. Pierpont Morgan came to rely almost exclusively on his judgment in forming the magnificent Morgan library of rare books and illuminated manuscripts. Others, too, were quick to avail themselves of his aid. Commission followed commission until it became possible to say that Rosenbach had had a hand in forming all the great private collections in the United States. Meanwhile his bids continued to be described as "wild." In London he became known as the "Terror of the Auction Room"—which he interprets as "the highest bidder and therefore the greatest damn fool"—; in Paris, as "Le Napoleon des Livres"; in the United States, informally as "Dr. R."

The layman, notes Miss Strakosch, is prone to ask whether Rosenbach has ever regretted his rash buying, whether his shelves are not at times overstocked, but the answer is that no one has ever heard him complain about a lack of customers. When in 1925, for instance, he paid $106,000 for a copy of the Gutenberg Bible, up to that time the highest price ever commanded by a book at auction, he was enabled before the end of the year to see it in the library of Yale University, a gift from the purchaser, Mrs. E. S. Harkness. As to whether he became primarily a book collector or a book dealer, those who know him answer "both." Others point out that there are times when a book bought for resale finds its way into his private collection because he cannot bear to part with it. Such, they speculate, may be the destiny of the manuscript of Lewis Carroll's *Alice in Wonderland,* which in April 1946 was knocked down to Dr. R. at the Eldridge R. Johnson sale in New York exactly eighteen years after he had first purchased it in Sotheby's auction rooms in London from the original Alice, Alice Liddell, later Mrs. Pleasaunce Hargreaves. That time he sold it again almost immediately; this time, the bibliophile has said, he has formed no plans for its sale.

A love of fine books, a secure grasp of details, a retentive memory, keen intuitive appreciation of rare volumes, accuracy in judgment, swiftness in decision, courage in action, and the ability to keep friends and win the loyalty of subordinates—these are the traits which, writes Hopkins, have combined with Rosenbach's good fortune in living in a golden age of increasing demand and shrinking supply to place him at the summit of his profession. In

ROSENBACH, A. S. W.—*Continued*

addition, he has a scholar's knowledge not only of bibliographical matters, such as the number of editions of a work, their points, their whereabouts, and their possible market values, but of the volumes' contents as well. And this is matched by a business acumen which led the late A. Edward Newton, author of *The Amenities of Book-Collecting,* to call him "the most astute bandit out of Wall Street" and to note that when he moves toward a purchase it is almost impossible to follow him. According to Avery Strakosch, Rosenbach would rather be a bookman than anything else in the world. "Books are the final appeal," he wrote in 1927 from the vantage point of twenty-five years' experience in the trade. "When the collector is through with the things that decorate his house, he turns to the things that decorate his mind—and these last forever." For the book collector new experiences and the thrills of discovery are unlimited; he risks neither boredom nor satiation; each new auction sale "brings a delightful thrill never to be duplicated"; and the appeal of the first edition— "almost as much the original work of its author as the painting is of an artist."—and of the association copy remains ever new. But of one thing Rosenbach would warn: books are not valuable or desirable merely because of age; intrinsic worth or beauty should be the primary criterion, then rarity, then condition, and only lastly antiquity.

Many of his experiences as a book collector and dealer in the bibliophile has related with "gusto" and "charm" in three volumes, *The Unpublishable Memoirs, Books and Bidders,* and *A Book Hunter's Holiday,* published in 1917, 1927, and 1936, respectively. (Most of the essays in the latter two appeared originally in the *Saturday Evening Post,* as told to Avery Strakosch; some, in the *Atlantic Monthly* and *Publishers' Weekly.*) A member of the Historical Society of Pennsylvania, the New York Historical Society, the American Antiquarian Society, the American Philosophical Society, the Bibliographical Society of London, and president of the Shakespeare Association of America and the American Jewish Historical Society, Rosenbach has also published a number of monographs in American, Jewish, and theatrical bibliography and history. His *Early American Children's Books* (1933) is a description of an "avocational collection" which has grown out of a gift from his uncle in 1900. A trustee of the Philadelphia Museum of Art and an associate trustee and member of the Board of Graduate Education and Research of the University of Pennsylvania, he is an honorary member of Phi Beta Kappa, and was awarded an honorary doctorate in fine arts (D.A.E.) by Pennsylvania in 1927 and another honorary degree by Jewish Theological Seminary of America in 1945. In 1930 he established the Rosenbach Fellowship in Bibliography at the University of Pennsylvania. His clubs are the Philobiblon and the Grolier.

The bibliophile can be at home in either Philadelphia or New York. On Philadelphia's old-fashioned De Lancey Street he keeps bachelor quarters with his brother Philip, a connoisseur of and dealer in antique furniture, prints and paintings, and old silver. It is a house which "itself, with all its contents," wrote Emily Kimbrough, "should be considered as the collector's piece . . . . [for it] is a series of rooms, each treated separately, in a manner which will best set off the objects which it contains." But, she added, "the choice of the objects themselves is so much more influenced by the individuality of the two brothers than by the things' intrinsic worth, that the rooms, instead of being museum-like settings, are essentially drawn together as a unified house." Whatever is brought here is never again taken out to sell. Up to 1945, when it was moved to Locust Street, the main office of the Rosenbach Company in Philadelphia was at the familiar 1320 Walnut Street location. Bookish and elegant, and long considered without a peer, it had, however, been relegated to second place with the establishment in New York of the combination branch shop and home which is said to resemble a luxuriously furnished dwelling far more than it does a conventional place of business. And at Strathmere, Corson's Inlet, on the New Jersey shore of the Atlantic, Rosenbach maintains a summer home where he can indulge in his favorite recreation, fishing. The man himself is described as "medium-sized, stocky, and unpretentious," and his nickname "Rosy" is said to reflect his florid complexion, his "aura of subdued conviviality," and his smile. It is "the perfect description of his personality," says Avery Strakosch. "Roseate, yet tinged with nostalgia for another day— that of Shakespeare, preferably, with all the lusty qualities of Ben Jonson or Beaumont and Fletcher."

References

    Am Collector 4:6-7 Ag 8 '35
    New Yorker Ap 14 '28
    Pub W 123:1620-4 My 20 '33
    World Today 52:282-6 Ag '28

    International Who's Who, 1945-46
    Rosenbach, A. S. W. Books and Bidders
        (1927)
    Who's Who, 1946
    Who's Who in America, 1946-47
    Who's Who in American Jewry, 1938-39

ROSENBERG, ALFRED   Jan. 12, 1893— Oct. 16, 1946   Nazi Party ideologist; editor in chief of the *Völkischer Beobachter* from 1921; tried for war crimes by the International Military Tribunal, found guilty on all counts; judged "responsible for plunder throughout invaded countries"; condemned and hanged. See *Current Biography* 1941 Yearbook.

Obituary

    N Y Times p1+ O 16 '46

ROSENFELD, PAUL   1890—July 21, 1946 Music and art critic and author; champion of modern music; music critic of *The Dial,* 1920-27; author of *Men Seen* (1925); the novel *The Boy in the Sun* (1928); *By Way of Art*

(1928); and *Discoveries of a Music Critic* (1936).

Obituary

N Y Times p21 Jl 22 '46 por

ROSENTHAL, MORIZ (rō'zĕn-tôl mō'rĭts) Dec. 18, 1862—Sept. 3, 1946 Polish pianist; studied under Franz Liszt; made his American debut in 1888; called "a perfect pianist"; coauthored a treatise on piano technique and composed études and preludes for the piano.

Obituary

N Y Times p23 S 4 '46 por

ROSS, C(HARLES) BEN 1877(?)—Mar. 31, 1946 Political figure and farmer-stockraiser; Governor of Idaho three terms, 1930-37; mayor of Pocatello, 1922-30.

Obituary

N Y Times p27 Ap 1 '46

ROTH, ALMON E. July 31, 1886- Shipping association executive

Address: b. c/o National Federation of American Shipping, Inc., 1809 G St., N.W., Washington, D.C.; h. 2300 Ralston Ave., Burlingame, Calif.

Almon E. Roth is the president of the National Federation of American Shipping, which was organized in 1944 "to provide an 'authoritative' voice for American shipping interests" in the postwar period. As head of the San Francisco Employers Council, the first of the nation's "boss unions," and of the Waterfront Employers Association of the Pacific Coast, a forerunner of the council, he helped bring comparative peace to San Francisco's industrial front during the 1930's, thereby establishing a national reputation as an organizer of employers.

Born in Crandon, South Dakota, on July 31, 1886, the son of Edward Herman and Magdalena (Beckley) Roth, Almon E. Roth was taken to California at the age of four and grew up in Mendocino County, in the redwood country. After graduation from Ukiah High School he attended Stanford University, supporting himself by waiting on tables and operating stereopticon machines for lecture courses. Roth was active in campus extracurricular activities: he led in developing a system of student government, and in his senior year served as president of the student body. He was a member of the varsity track, relay, and football team; and he took part in the international rugby matches between the United States and Canada in 1909; the following year he played with the All American Rugby team in Australia and New Zealand. Upon obtaining his B.A. degree in 1909, Roth became Stanford's first dean of men. During the next three years, he was both administrator and law student at the university, from which he received his J.D. degree in 1912. He then practiced law in San Francisco until 1919, when he returned to Stanford as its business manager and comptroller.

Harris & Ewing

ALMON E. ROTH

Eighteen years later, in 1937, Roth, who had been taking a bystander's interest in the industrial strife that threatened to make San Francisco "a black spot on the business map," left Stanford's campus to become the president of the Waterfront Employers Association of the Pacific Coast. Into the new organization, which a few of the city's shipowners had decided to form, Roth, dubbed the "collegiate mariner," brought "one hundred and forty shipping firms operating 93 per cent of all Pacific Coast tonnage" and proceeded to meet with Harry Bridges [40], president of the West Coast International Longshoremen's Association. Roth also became the president of the Pacific American Shipowners Association, an office he held until 1939.

The united front among shippers was so successful in reducing strikes that employers in other fields began to see the merits of organizing. Under the direction of Roger D. Lapham, later mayor of San Francisco, the San Francisco Employers Council was organized in 1939, with Roth as its first president. During the first nineteen months of its existence, reported *Business Week*, the new organization effected amicable settlements in 262 management-labor disputes and negotiated 177 collective bargaining agreements. Membership, which included the owners of almost every type of business in San Francisco, from hotels to bowling alleys, grew from 1,102 to 1,700. In 1939, the council's first year, the city that had had as many as fifty strikes in a year had thirty-nine strikes, and during the first nine months of 1940, *Forbes* stated, there were no more than eleven strikes and five jurisdictional disputes. In four major strikes the men returned to their jobs under agreements which had been in effect previously. One factor which helped to reduce work-stoppages in San Francisco was the voluntary "cooling-off period"

ROTH, ALMON E.—*Continued*

before the calling of a strike. Neither the Central Labor Council of the A.F. of L. nor the Industrial Union Council of the CIO authorized strikes before attempting to settle the dispute with the Employers Council, which, at the same time, refrained from lockouts.

Much of Roth's success in carrying out the purpose of the council, which became a model for councils in other parts of the country, was attributed to his "sense of fair play" and "his insistence upon the sanctity of contracts." Although he was against strikes, he believed in labor's right to organize and fight injustices through collective bargaining. He did not approve of the trend toward bargaining on a nationwide scale, however, maintaining that for effective employer organization, it would be more practical to limit the industry bargaining group to a community or area where the fundamental conditions of operations and the cost of living are fairly uniform. While some contended that "boss unions" would lead to a lack of freedom for the individual employer, Roth insisted that they were necessary in order to maintain the balance of power in the "pressure game" of labor-management relations. "What else can the employer do," he wrote in 1941, "but organize to protect his business against local, state, and national organizations of employees operating . . . under the aegis of State and Federal legislation?"

Roth spoke on the subject of labor relations to many groups: to students at the Harvard School of Business Administration, at the University of Wisconsin, and numerous other universities; to radio listeners, on such programs as *America's Town Meeting of the Air,* and *Wake Up America* (he is on the advisory committee for both radio forums); to businessmen at many national conventions, among them the United States Chamber of Commerce and the National Association of Manufacturers. As president of the San Francisco Employers Council, he spoke before agricultural groups as well as business and civic clubs; this won for industry the support of farmers in San Francisco's back country, a factor which is said to have helped the council to win the 1939 ship clerks' strike, Harry Bridge's first major defeat since the successful general strike of 1934. At times Roth had to cope with the danger of desertions from the ranks of the employers' united front. During a dispute in which the owners of sixty-seven restaurants struck against the conditions imposed upon them by culinary unions, "strike benefits" were administered to some of the proprietors from the council's treasury. (The council successfully opposed unemployment benefits for the restaurant employees, according to a *Business Week* article.)

As one of the industry members of the National War Labor Board during World War II, Roth held fast to the Little Steel principle for limiting wage increases. In a case involving metal miners where the majority of the board felt a departure from the formula was warranted in order to lessen the shortage of miners in the West, who were migrating to higher paid jobs, the head of the San Francisco Employers Council dissented. He argued that such an exception would "open the door for a flood of exceptions which would soon become the rule and end in disastrous inflation without offering any relief for the acute labor shortages which the nation was facing."

In February 1944 Roth resigned from the national board and took a leave of absence from his position with the San Francisco Employers Council (he became chairman of the Council's board of directors) in order to head the new National Federation of American Shipping. The organization, representing virtually all United States shipowners, was to plan for the postwar American merchant marine. Roth announced that his first task would be to establish a basis for cooperation between the shipping industry and such Government agencies as the War Shipping Administration, the Maritime Commission and the State Department. His goal, he declared, would be a United States merchant fleet which would adequately provide for the country's legitimate trade interests, but which would not engage in destructive competition against the British or other maritime nations nor embark upon a program of extreme economic nationalism. (The United States shipping was said to comprise more than 50 per cent of the world's trading vessels in 1945.)

When, following the end of the war, Reconversion Director John Snyder [45] recommended that surplus ships be chartered to foreign nationals on "equal terms" with American operators, Roth charged that such a policy would amount to "selling the United States Merchant Marine down the river." By October 1946 the American trade fleet had declined from its wartime peak of forty-three million to twenty million deadweight tons, according to Roth, who predicted a further drop and criticized "the lack of any aggressive national policy" to promote the use of American vessals in foreign commerce. Although recognizing that foreign flagships could be operated at a lower cost, he argued that an adequate United States merchant marine was essential for the development and protection of the country's trade and for national defense purposes.

The N.F.A.S. president also assailed the Civil Aeronautics Board for prohibiting the operation of airplanes by shipping companies, a measure which he considered important in the future of American shipping. In addition he called for protection against competition from Government-owned vessels and urged the use of idle ships to fill the needs of domestic transportation instead of the costly building of freight trains, proposed by the Office of Defense Transportation. As later set forth in a brief submitted by the N.F.A.S. to a House commerce subcommittee, the American domestic shipping industry was "faced with the threat of complete destruction, with Government ownership and operation as the only alternative" during the postwar period of transition. Roth viewed destructive railroad competition as a basic cause of the shipping industry's difficulties and requested legislation to remedy a situation whereby railroads imposed rates (depressed before the war to meet water competition) which water carriers could not now afford to charge. Roth denied National Maritime Union charges that shipowners had "fleeced the Treasury of twenty-one billion dollars during World War II" as "fantastic falsehoods," and during the 1946 shipping strike declared "unreasonable labor demands . . . sheer folly." In 1946 he acted as adviser to the United States Government delegation to the United Maritime Authority meeting in London, and was a member of the United States delegation to the Amsterdam meeting of the Maritime Consultative Council.

Roth, who is a trustee of the Industrial Relations Counselors and of the World Trade Foundation, has advised a number of communities and employers on labor relations. His numerous articles on industrial relations and on shipping have appeared in such magazines as *Rotarian*, the New York *Journal of Commerce*, and the *Atlantic Monthly*. In 1931, as president of Rotary International (1930-31), he presided over the Vienna international convention and was awarded the Great Golden Cross by the Austrian Government. A former vice-president of the California State Chamber of Commerce, he is a member of the California Bar Association, of the council of the United States Associates in the International Chamber of Commerce; and in 1945 he participated in the President's Management-Labor Conference. The list of his club memberships includes Rotary, Commonwealth, Bohemian, Chevy Chase, and Phi Delta Phi. His religious affiliation is Methodist. In politcs, he is a Republican.

Roth and Mildred Mary Hayes were married in 1912, and reared a family of three children: William Edward, Mary Elizabeth, and Miriam Virginia. (All the children are married.) One hundred and ninety pounds in weight and five feet ten and a half inches in height, Roth retains the muscular physique of his football days, and likes to hunt and fish; in golf his score is in the upper seventies. Building is another of the "highly energized" executive's hobbies: working week ends and on holidays, he designed and himself built a log house near Santa Cruz. He also had an important part in planning and supervising the construction of a large number of Stanford University's buildings. (From 1940 to 1942 he was a trustee of the university.) The school's Frost Memorial Amphitheater, which has an outdoor seating capacity of ten thousand, was designed by him to resemble a glade in a natural forest.

References

Forbes p13-15+ F '41
Who's Who in America, 1946-47

ROTHERY, AGNES (EDWARDS) 1888-
Author

Address: b. c/o Dodd, Mead & Company, Inc., 432 4th Ave., New York; h. University Sta., Charlottesville, Va.

A most ingenious paradox, it has been said, is evident in the literary career of Agnes

Bassano

AGNES ROTHERY

Rothery: she has made a dual reputation as an inveterate world traveler and as an equally enthusiastic homemaker. She is the author of almost a score of travel books and of many articles on homemaking. A glance at the *Readers' Guide* shows her advising, in June 1946, to "Let Your House Speak for Itself." Her most recent work, a novel with a Cape Cod setting, *Balm of Gilead,* was published in 1946. This was the author's twenty-ninth book.

Agnes Edwards Rothery was born in 1888, in Brookline, Massachusetts, the daughter of John Jay Elmendorf and Rosamond Dale (Pentecost) Rothery. In *Family Album* (1942), Miss Rothery gives a lively account of an uninhibited New England girlhood. She and the four other children "were boisterous and argumentative, and permitted incredible freedom of speech, action, and opinion." "We swarmed and clamored all over the place, and brought hordes of people home to meals, to spend the night, and to visit indefinitely." After attending Wellesley High School and then Wellesley College, where she obtained her B.A. in 1909, Miss Rothery began her career with editorial work on the *Ladies' Home Journal.* In 1910 she took over the woman's page of the Boston *Herald,* soon becoming literary editor of the paper and contributing, until 1914, a daily column under the title of *Agnes Edwards' Morning Talks.* From 1912 to 1916 she also conducted a weekly column in the *Christian Science Monitor,* and was a contributing editor to *Youth's Companion* and *House Beautiful.* Her first published book, *Our Common Road,* appeared in 1913.

On September 24, 1917, Agnes Rothery was married to Harry Rogers Pratt, musician and actor, who had appeared with John Drew, the Ben Greet company, and the Coburn Players. The Pratts then began housekeeping in a one-room studio set in a backyard in the residential district of Hartford, Connecticut. Their

ROTHERY, AGNES—*Continued*

home was embellished with a carved Jacobean chest, some Quimper jugs, and a few first editions. The next move was to a gardener's cottage. After a trip to France, where Mrs. Pratt learned to make an acceptable omelet and acquired some more Quimper ware, her husband was appointed to a musical directorship at the Lake Placid Club, and the couple moved to a farmhouse on a hilltop near the lake.

In 1927, when Pratt became associate professor of music and dramatics at the University of Virginia, their new abode was a ramshackle cottage—former slave quarters—hidden behind Thomas Jefferson's famous serpentine wall on "The Lawn." Their present home, named "Recoleta," is placed on a hilltop outside Charlottesville, within sound of the university's famous bells. This home is "still building, in spite of shortages," writes Mrs. Pratt, "and when my husband recently asked me if he could give me some intimate personal present I said immediately, 'Yes, a cement mixer.'"

Agnes Rothery's travel books have been characterized as "stimulating reading, written with grace." The Pratts' three-month vacations have consistently been spent abroad, and have as regularly been recorded by Miss Rothery in such books as *Central America and the Spanish Main* (1929), *South America, West Coast and East* (1930), *Sweden, the Land and Its People* (1934). Her *Denmark, Kingdom of Reason*, published in 1937 in the United States, appeared in London the same year and has been translated into French. She has also written books on Virginia, Cape Cod, Guatemala, Finland, Norway, and British Columbia. The four "Roundabout" books, covering South America, Washington, D.C., Central America, and Scandinavia, were written for children. A fifth, on Maryland and Virginia, was in progress in 1946.

Miss Rothery has also written two autobiographical books, *Family Album* (1942), which Katherine Woods, in the New York *Times Book Review,* called a book of rare quality, pungent in flavor and delightful in style; and *A Fitting Habitation* (1944), a lively and detailed account of the succession of houses in which the author and her husband have lived. She has written three novels besides *Balm of Gilead*—*The House by the Windmill, The High Altar*, and *Into What Port?* (her favorite book)—and a play, *Miss Coolidge. Balm of Gilead*, a novel of the romantic and supernatural, is clearly designed, according to John Cournos of the New York *Sun* "to assuage the troubled and the perplexed."

On the first anniversary of the liberation of Denmark, His Majesty King Christian X's Medal of Liberation was bestowed on Agnes Rothery "as an appreciation of [her] contribution to Denmark's cause during the Nazi occupation." The author is of the Catholic faith. Five feet six inches in height, she has hazel eyes and brown hair "with gray coming." She says she has "never had a nervous breakdown or a divorce, so [is] quite out of

style." Miss Rothery "loves to cook," and can serve up dishes of many countries on their own native crockery, but she is glad she can "teach a maid to do the actual work." "If I had the muscles and backbone of our colored man," she adds, "I would ask nothing more of life."

References

> Rothery, A. A Fitting Habitation (1944); Family Album (1942)
> Who's Who in America, 1946-47

ROXAS (Y ACUNA), MANUEL (rô'häs ē ä-kōō'nyä mä-nwĕl') Jan. 1, 1892- President of the Philippines

Address: Malacañang Palace, Manila

In April of 1946 Manuel Roxas—orator, economist, lawyer, publisher, politician—was elected President of the new Philippine Republic, to come into being July 4, 1946, and also of the interim Commonwealth. Known as the idol of Filipinos educated under the American system, Roxas emerged from World War II with a controversial record and won election to pilot his country of seventeen million people and seven thousand islands through its first voyage alone. According to General Eisenhower, the Philippines had suffered the worst devastation of any country in the world.

Manuel Roxas y Acuña, whose ancestors were natives of the Philippine Islands, was born on January 1, 1892. His birthplace was Capiz, Panay, a small provincial capital in the Visayan Islands, central Philippines. By birth, therefore, he belongs to the largest ethnic group of Filipinos. His parents, Gerardo and Rosario (Acuña) Roxas, were ardent libertarians, and his father was one of the first Filipinos killed in the revolt against Spanish rule. After the Spanish-American War, as he was later to tell the United States Congress, six-year-old Manuel learned his first English at the knee of an American soldier. He attended the English-language public schools set up by the United States. "I am truly a product of the American system of education," says Roxas. "I would like to emphasize that."

Grade school in Manuel's home town was followed by high school in Manila, where his teachers recognized and encouraged his ambition to become a leader. At seventeen he entered the University of the Philippines College of Law, where he was a brilliant student, taking first honors. Here he earned money by digesting and simplifying complicated subject matter for fellow students. Graduating with his LL.B. in 1913, when he was twenty-one, Roxas reportedly studied for a time at St. Joseph's College in Hongkong to perfect his English. He worked, too, to master Spanish, the second official language of the Philippines, and he has a speech-making ability in at least one other native tongue, Tagalog. In 1915-16 young Roxas was a law professor at the National University, later returning to his native province to practice. In 1919 he ran for Governor against the local political machine, and won. When his term expired in 1921, Governor Roxas was elected from Capiz to the House of Representatives, which was fairly evenly

divided among three parties. Roxas was a
protegé of Senate President Manuel L. Quezon [41], who controlled the Nacionalista-Colec-
tivista combination. After an intense ten-day
struggle, the thirty-year-old first-termer from
Capiz was elected to the speakership, succeeding Sergio Osmeña [44], who had moved to the
Senate.

According to Joseph Ralston Hayden in *The
Philippines* (1942), "Mr. Roxas proved to be a
man of brilliant intellect and powerful personality. Fully utilizing the power and prestige
of the speakership, he eventually contributed
substantially to the establishment of the Quezon
leadership in the lower house" and became one
of the country's political "Big Three." The
first session over which Roxas presided was,
however, an embarrassingly undisciplined and
fruitless one, as a split between Quezon and
Osmeña had left the party system in a state of
confusion. Finally the friendly rivals were
brought together, their parties consolidated, and
a legislative majority won by making the most
of demands for immediate independence. Speaker Roxas' contribution to the cause included
organizing the Bagong Katipunan, a nonpartisan
patriotic society to "save the Philippines from
American imperialism." Apart from the question of political independence, however, Roxas
described himself as loyal to American institutions.

The Speaker of the House, who had been
a special envoy to Washington with independence delegations in 1923-24 and again
in 1929-30, had a similar mission in 1931-33.
The Ninth Independence Mission, like those
which preceded it, was composed of leaders
of both major parties. Headed by Senate
President Osmeña and Speaker Roxas, it
had been voted "entire freedom" in negotiation. Together with the two resident commissioners, the "Osrox Mission" spent nearly
two years in Washington, working with Congressional committees on what became the
Hare-Hawes-Cutting Act of 1932, passed
over President Hoover's veto. This set a
definite date for independence (July 4, 1946)
and permitted a high degree of autonomy in
the interim, but it also contained economic
provisions which threatened Philippine stability and made it unacceptable to President
Quezon. The dispute over the bill, which
Osmeña and Roxas considered imperfect but
the best obtainable, grew into a bitter contest for control of the party and thus of the
Government. Receiving a vote of confidence,
Quezon removed Osmeña and Roxas from
the Senate presidency and speakership, and
the latter, in turn, formed an opposition
party. In October 1933 the Philippine Legislature rejected the Act and Quezon went
off to Washington to get a better one. The
Tydings [45]-McDuffie Act he brought back
was almost identical with the rejected law,
but the Legislature accepted it, with Quezon
getting the credit for securing the Islands'
independence.

Despite this setback, Roxas was elected to
the Constitutional Convention of July 1934-
February 1935, where he was leader of the
anti-Quezon men. Roxas "probably exerted

MANUEL ROXAS

the greatest influence in shaping the new
constitution," which proved to embody
Quezon's views and accord with his desires
on all but one or two points later changed
by amendment. The ex-Speaker accompanied President Quezon to the United States
to get President Franklin D. Roosevelt's approval of it as in conformity with the Tyd-
ings-McDuffie Law; and on his return Roxas
was elected to the single-chamber National
Assembly of the new Commonwealth. Despite the combination of the Osmeña-Roxas
party with an old minority party and its
eventual consolidation into the new Na-
cionalista party, all factions were alike, said
Judge Juan Sumulong, in representing "the
intelligentsia and . . . the Philippine plutocracy" and not "the needy classes."

Soon afterward, Roxas retired to the practice of law and service on the University of
the Philippines board of regents. In 1937
he was appointed to the Joint Preparatory
Committee on Philippine Affairs, a research
group to recommend to the American Congress the steps that should be taken to lessen
the shock to Philippine economy of the loss
of American protection. On the completion
of fifteen months of work on this topic,
Roxas was appointed by Quezon chairman
of the National Economic Council of economists and industrialists. Later the President added to Roxas' duties that of chairman of the National Development Company,
a Government corporation working toward
national economic self-sufficiency. And in
November 1938 Manuel Roxas joined the
Quezon cabinet as Secretary of Finance. He
is described by David Boguslav in the *Christian Science Monitor* as "a first-rate, top-
flight economist." (As a lawyer, it is reported that Roxas has refused appointment to
the Supreme Court, and as a businessman
he owns three publications, the tabloid *Daily*

ROXAS, MANUEL A.—*Continued*

News, the bimonthly magazine *Light,* and the Tagalog-language weekly, *Ilang-Ilang.*) In a significant radio address in September 1940, Secretary Roxas asked for arms and defense equipment from the United States, and for "prolonging the economic adjustment period for at least ten years more and postponing the gradual imposition of quotas and tariff duties on Philippine exportations to the United States until four years after peace has been reestablished," but without altering the date of independence.

Shortly before Pearl Harbor, the forty-nine-year-old economist was elected to the Senate—a Senate that never really served, because of the Japanese attack. A lieutenant colonel in the Philippine Army Reserve, he was detailed as liaison officer and aide to United States General Douglas MacArthur on December 16, 1941. Roxas accompanied his admired general to Bataan after the fall of Manila on January 2. When MacArthur flew to Australia Roxas remained on Corregidor, but later escaped under fire from that besieged and indefensible rock to Mindanao, where he was taken prisoner by the Japanese. Most Filipinos of any importance were either prisoners of the Japanese or members of the Japanese-sponsored puppet Government of Supreme Court Justice José P. Laurel. Brigadier General Roxas was one of the latter group.

All reports agree that Roxas was a minister without portfolio in the Laurel Government, that he helped draft the constitution of the "independent" Philippines which declared war on the United States, and that he headed the Economic Planning Board and the Biba, the rice-purchase pool. Roxas himself, backed by MacArthur, says that he used these positions as a cloak under which to carry out espionage and to direct guerrilla activities, a claim challenged by certain guerrilla leaders. H. Ford Wilkins, who was a prisoner in the Philippines throughout the enemy occupation, took the position in a New York *Times* article that Roxas' statement is correct, that he escaped the duties of his posts in the puppet Government by losing weight and using drugs to convince his captors that he was ill, that he "could not resist helping to revise the document [the constitution] to conform more closely to his ideals of democracy," and that he was allowed to live in his usual style only under strict guard and after brutality had failed to break his spirit. President Quezon's posthumously published autobiography, *The Good Fight,* states that Roxas remained in the Philippines on Quezon's orders to mitigate the severity of Japanese occupation.

At any rate, when members of the Laurel cabinet turned themselves over to MacArthur after the fall of Baguio, the summer capital, in April 1945, Roxas was "rescued," while the others were "captured" and imprisoned. Unanimously elected president of the reconstituted Senate, many members of which had similar wartime records, General Roxas applied for inactive status. This enabled him to campaign for the Presidency against Sergio Osmeña,

who had succeeded Quezon on the latter's death in August 1944.

As candidate of the Liberal wing of the Nationalist party, Roxas carried on a vigorous campaign, while dignified, elderly President Osmeña rested on his record. The campaign issues included Osmeña's age and Roxas' relations with the Japanese occupation forces. On the latter question, the Communists and their sympathizers generally, although grudgingly, supported Osmeña. The Roxas supporters said: "We have no suspicions against American capital or businessmen," while the Osmeñists were less cordial and objected to the "interference" of United States High Commissioner McNutt. In general, however, the platforms were reported to be highly similar. In April 1946, the ballots were cast, and fifty-four-year-old Manuel Acuña Roxas was elected President of the Commonwealth of the Philippines and President-Elect of the Republic of the Philippines. In May he visited Washington, seeking a four-hundred-million-dollar loan, and was reported to have made an excellent impression on the Administration and Congress before returning to rubble-strewn Manila for his inauguration.

The period immediately following Roxas' inauguration on July 4, 1946, was marked by domestic and foreign problems. During the summer of 1946 a revolt of Hukbalahaps (remnants of guerrilla fighters) in the central Luzon provinces north of Manila rendered Roxas' program of agrarian reform infeasible. The guerrillas demanded at least 70 per cent of the 1946 crop for the tenant farmers. Acting on orders from their president, the military police arrested the leaders of the revolt, put them "in protective custody . . . without loss of civil rights," and forced the Hukbalahaps to give up their firearms. Roxas also ordered a commission on land tenure to investigate their grievances. A political crisis was precipitated by Roxas' espousal of the Bell Act (Philippine Trade Act), which gave American buyers a virtual monopoly of important Philippine exports for the next twenty-eight years. Since the Philippine constitution calls for all corporations dealing with resources and utilities to have at least a 60 per cent Filipino membership and capital, the Roxas Cabinet suspended licenses granted to Americans under terms of the Bell Act until the constitution could be amended by a plebiscite to be held in March 1947.

Meanwhile, President Roxas continued negotiations with the United States for defense bases on Filipino territory. The final settlement of the problem was contingent upon the instructions brought back to Manila from the United States by Ambassador Paul McNutt early in December 1946. Although a written agreement had not yet been signed by the middle of that month Roxas was able to announce, "We have an agreement with the United States permitting her to establish bases here for the mutual defense of our two countries." That same month, the United States presented President Roxas with a one-million-dollar check, the first installment of 620 million to be used for reconstruction of war-damaged public property in the Philippines. To determine the extent of damages and to survey postwar labor and agricultural conditions, the Philippine president spent most of the month of December 1946 touring the southern islands of his republic. He found that crop loans and UNRRA supplies had been misappropriated by certain rich planters and corrupt Government officials, which led him to promise an investigation and punishment of those responsible.

Described as "a slim, dark man whose face still bears the marks of three years of virtual captivity under the Japanese," Manuel Roxas is taller than the average Filipino. By all accounts he is a colorful, dynamic person and a fiery and convincing speaker. Since April of 1921 he has been married to the former Trinidad de León, (Mrs. Roxas, who says she prefers that title to "First Lady," impressed reporters with her poise, friendliness, and quick answers.) The Roxas' daughter, María Rosario, called Ruby, was in the United States to attend Vassar College at the time of her father's election; her brother Gerardo was studying law at the University of the Philippines. Roxas is a member of Los Tamaraos Polo Club, the Wack Wack Golf Club, and the Philippines Columbian, Baguio Country, and Filipino clubs. Like Quezon, and unlike most of his Catholic countrymen, he is a Mason and has passed the thirty-second degree.

References

N Y Herald Tribune II p3 Ap 21 '46 por
N Y Times Mag p20+ My 12 '46 por
Philippines 1:11 Ag '41
Who's Who in the Philippines, 1940-41

RUSK, HOWARD A(RCHIBALD) Apr. 9, 1901- Physician; journalist
Address: b. c/o New York Times, 220 W. 43d St., New York; c/o New York University, Washington Sq., New York; h. 50 Greenacres Ave., Scarsdale, N.Y.

Dr. Howard A. Rusk, author of a column on rehabilitation for the New York *Times*, who has the title of associate editor, is the Colonel Rusk who revolutionized the entire set-up of United States Army Air Forces hospitals. His theory is that "any program designed to give the patient maximum treatment and opportunity . . . must, to be successful: 1) treat the whole man, regardless of what his needs may be; 2) treat the patient as an individual; and 3) be early, continuous, and progressive from the earliest possible moment following acute illness or injury until maximum possible benefits have been received." In practice, it turned hospitals from places of quiet boredom to humming beehives of prescribed activity—activity ranging from bed exercises to competitive sports, from the study of reading and writing to foreign languages, from washing dishes to raising pigs. It proved itself in speeding up recovery, reducing readmissions, greatly increasing the patients' knowledge and skills, and tremendously improving their morale. When the Institute for Rehabilitation and Physical Medicine, part of the New York University-Bellevue Medical

HOWARD A. RUSK

Center, opens in 1947, Rusk, it was announced, will serve as director.

Howard Archibald Rusk was born in Brookfield, Missouri, on April 9, 1901. The names of his parents are Augusta Eastin (Shipp) and Michael Yost Rusk. After graduation from the Brookfield High School in 1919, young Howard attended the University of Missouri (B.A., 1923). He won his medical degree in two years at the University of Pennsylvania. In 1925 Dr. Rusk returned to Missouri to begin practice, and in October 1926 the twenty-five-year-old physician was married to Gladys Houx. During his seventeen years of practice in St. Louis, Rusk specialized in internal medicine and diagnostics. He feels, however, that he was able to escape the occupational failing of specialists, that of "being so busy treating the disease as to neglect treating the patient." He laid stress on caring for the whole man, taking into account the nonmedical factors of personality and circumstances.

Appointed to the Washington University faculty in 1929 as an instructor in medicine, Rusk also became associate chief of staff at St. Luke's hospital (St. Louis) six years later. Within a year after Pearl Harbor, Rusk, then forty-one, entered active Medical Corps duty with the rank of major, and in late 1942 was given charge of medical service in the two-thousand-bed Army Air Forces hospital at Jefferson Barracks, Missouri. Seeing patients lying in bed, bored and indifferent, during illness and convalescence, he began a program of teaching and activity for them. "At first Dr. Rusk hoped mostly to alleviate boredom," to quote an article by Albert Q. Maisel. "But once the program got under way, surprising things began to happen. The patients got well faster than they ever had before. And not nearly so many of them came back with relapses. The Air Surgeon, Major General David N. W. Grant, heard about the program and looked into it. Within

RUSK, HOWARD A.—*Continued*

two weeks thereafter he assigned Colonel Rusk to establish it in all Army Air Forces hospitals." This was done in December 1942 at the direction of AAF General H. H. Arnold.

From March 1943 until his discharge as a full colonel in October 1945, Howard Rusk's title was Chief of the Convalescent and Rehabilitation Branch, Professional Services Division, and Chief of the Convalescent Services Division, Office of the Air Surgeon. As such, he directed a program of training and therapy which began with simple exercises while a patient was still confined to bed. Military instruction went right on; training films, lectures, discussions, and constant study of plane identification, radio code, camouflage, and other basic studies, as well as cultural and vocational subjects, were prescribed, with medical and physical therapy. Men with limbs in casts played ball—and enjoyed it. Illiterates learned, in one day, to sign their names and serial numbers. Radio men sent messages from bed to bed in blinker code, and kept telegraph keys on their bedside tables. Hospitalized mechanics worked on assembling and disassembling carburetors, tachometers, altimeters, and other small parts, and sometimes worked on engine sections wheeled into the wards and sunrooms. The men were kept extremely busy—each had the need and purpose of each step in his program explained to him—and "the hospital was transformed into a combination gymnasium, schoolroom, machine shop, and New England Town Hall," with an adjoining victory garden.

Under Rusk's direction, hospitalization time was shortened, yet relapses became as much as 25 per cent fewer. Sick leave was eliminated in all but extraordinary cases, and morale improved immensely. Patients went back to duty in as good general condition as before, and in some cases, in better condition, with their military skills maintained or increased. In many cases patients had kept up with the work of their original units and were able to rejoin their friends after leaving the hospital.

Designed originally for precombat patients, Rusk's program was extended in September 1943 to special hospitals for men returning from overseas combat. As described by Rusk, "Each patient is assigned a personal physician who becomes his 'family doctor' for the period of his hospitalization. This personal physician . . . is the captain of the team of medical specialists, physical therapists, educators, athletic trainers, occupational therapists, social service workers, personal counselors, and vocational guidance experts, and, as such, integrates their efforts in the treatment of the whole man." The primary aim of this program was to return men to their original duties at the peak of their physical fitness. At second best, they were trained for another military occupational specialty which fitted in with their experience and physical condition. Disabled navigators and aerial photographers became air intelligence officers; others studied teaching practices, becoming instructors in their subjects.

For those whose disabilities dictated their return to civil life, the aim was to help them become socially and economically self-sufficient.

This included physical reconditioning, educational training, psychological readjustment, and resocialization ("the restoration of those attitudes, habits, values, and concepts accepted by American society"). Under a staff of vocational guidance and instructional workers, these men were given a chance to try working in various fields, ranging from academic and commercial subjects to photography, art, woodworking, metalsmithing, welding, machine-shop practice, and automotive repair. At several of the eight convalescent centers, there were farms where trainees raised food for the hospital kitchen. Emphasis was placed on practicality. Some centers had a room which reproduced a city street crossing, where men with crutches and artificial legs practiced crossing before the traffic light changed. Whenever feasible, the hospital staff was drawn from veterans of overseas combat, many of whom were first given intensive postgraduate courses at the Institute for the Crippled and Disabled in New York. By May 1945, Rusk reported, more than sixty million man-hours of physical and educational training had been given under the AAF program, in time which would otherwise have been wasted.

Although attention had been focused upon the veteran, Rusk noted that "the largest minority group in America—the twenty-three million physically handicapped," was composed mainly of civilians. Rusk would use civilian pensions as a means of rehabilitating the handicapped so that they might compete with physically normal workers. The hiring of disabled personnel because of sympathy, legislative compulsion, or arbitrarily defined quotas is rejected by Rusk. During the wartime manpower shortage, civilian "unemployables" filled jobs fitted to their disabilities with an efficiency equal to that of nonimpaired workers. Their absentee rate was seven times lower, their safety record and rate of labor turnover five times better than that of other employees. Rusk's civilian work in rehabilitation had begun with his appointment in September 1946 as head of the New York University teaching faculty of rehabilitation and physical medicine, the first department of its kind in the country. The university, in collaboration with the Bellevue Medical Center later set up the Institute for Rehabilitation and Physical Medicine, a $15,575,000 model rehabilitation center, of which Rusk was named director, to assume his post when the institution was scheduled to open early in 1947.

Colonel Rusk's work with convalescents brought him several distinctions. He was invited to speak at the 1944 *Herald Tribune* Forum, was given one of the American Design Awards for 1944 (one thousand dollars and a citation), and was cited also by the American Academy of Physical Education. He was chosen to edit the Medical Clinics of North America's special issue on rehabilitation (May 1945). In September his story was dramatized over NBC on *The Doctor Fights,* starring Walter Abel. He was appointed consultant on physical rehabilitation for the Baruch Committee on Physical Medicine. He conferred with President Truman. After his discharge from the

Army, he received the Distinguished Service Medal, joined the New York *Times* staff, and in December 1945 was appointed to the nine-man President's Committee for Study of Government Medical Services with a view to coordinating them. He was also asked to speak on radio forums and to address various gatherings, many of them under the auspices of the *Times*. Rusk's suggested plan of enlisting housing assistance for veterans through the churches was adopted by the President in February 1946.

Besides his weekly column on rehabilitation and innumerable speeches on the subject, Rusk has written a chapter for *Doctors At War* (1944), special articles, and frequent papers for scientific publications. A member of Phi Delta Theta and Nu Sigma Nu, the Missourian belongs to the American, Missouri State, St. Louis, and Southern medical associations. He is a fellow of the American College of Physicians and a member of the American Board of Internal Medicine. The physician serves the Veterans Administration as consultant in rehabilitation—some commentators think he should head the VA. He is also chairman of the New York Veterans Service Center advisory committee, and a member of the subcommittee on occupational therapy of the A.M.A. Council on Physical Medicine. He is on the advisory council of the National Arthritis Research Foundation.

Nearly six feet three inches tall, Howard Rusk weighs 195 pounds. The black-haired, hazel-eyed ex-Colonel is described as a good-looking man with "a great store of gentle persuasion." In religion Rusk is a Protestant. He and Mrs. Rusk, who now live within commuting distance of New York, have three children, Martha Eastin, Howard Archibald, and John Michael. Rusk's favorite recreation is riding.

Reference

Who's Who in America, 1946-47

SABATH, ADOLPH J(OACHIM) Apr. 4, 1866- United States Representative from Illinois

Address: b. House Office Bldg., Washington, D.C.; h. 1902 S. Ashland Ave., Chicago

Raising his voice in protest against the amendments passed by the House to weaken the OPA and speaking for such legislation as housing for veterans and the establishment of a permanent Fair Employment Practice Committee, eighty-year-old Adolph J. Sabath in 1946 continued to be active in the affairs of the nation. For twenty-one consecutive terms, a record surpassed by no other Representative, he has been elected by the fifth Congressional District of Illinois, a section of Chicago inhabited largely by Poles, Czechs, Lithuanians, Yugoslavs. Newspapermen agree that Sabath is a thoroughgoing New Dealer. "His whole record," wrote John R. Beal in his chapter on Sabath in *Public Men In and Out of Office* (1946), "reflects a sympathy for the underprivileged."

The poverty of his early surroundings made a lifelong impression on Adolph Joachim Sabath. One of eleven children born to Joachim and Barbara (Eissenschimmel) Sabath, he began life in Zabori, Bohemia (now in Czechoslovakia), on April 4, 1866. His father, a butcher, was the only Jew in the town of about four hundred people, which was the seat of the Catholic diocese. Together with his brothers and sisters, Adolph attended the parochial school. At thirteen he left for Horazdovic, a neighboring town where he worked as an apprentice-clerk in a dry-goods store. The stories he heard from his employer's brother-in-law, who had been to the United States, inspired the young boy to save his money and go to America. In 1881, when he was only fifteen, Adolph arrived alone in Baltimore, Maryland, with little more than enough money to take him to Chicago, where a cousin lived.

His first job in the New World was in a planing mill at three dollars a week. Discharged at the end of six weeks because he was too small to do the work, Adolph found another job in a shoe and house-furnishings store. By the time he was twenty-one, the age at which the young immigrant became a naturalized citizen, he had been manager of the store for three years. He then decided to go into real estate, a business which he felt would give him the chance to earn more money. At the same time that he was establishing himself financially and bringing his family to the United States, the future Congressman continued his education. After his graduation from Bryant and Stratton Business College in 1885, he attended the Chicago College of Law and then Lake Forest University, where he received his LL.B degree in 1891. Admitted to the bar that year, he began to practice law in 1893.

Sabath soon took an interest in Chicago's civic affairs. To fight the corrupt practices of a group of the city's aldermen, known as the "Gray Wolves," he joined an independent citizens' club which subsequently grew into a Democratic political organization. At about this time he was also a member of the Pilsen Sokol, an athletic club, and helped to organize several groups which became popular among Chicago's Bohemian immigrants—the Pilsen Youth Club, the Singing Club and the Czech-American Club. In 1895 he was made a justice of the peace, and two years later he was elected police magistrate, a post which he held for ten years. Sabath, who preferred the title "Judge" even after he became a Congressman, was instrumental in abolishing the fee system and establishing the juvenile court and the parole system for first offenders.

In 1906, in the Administration of Theodore Roosevelt, Sabath was elected to the United States House of Representatives. Aided by William Jennings Bryan, whom he had supported for the Presidential nomination, Sabath was assigned to the committees on Alcoholic Liquor Traffic and Immigration and Naturalization. Beginning with his first speech in the House, a speech in defense of a bill to enlarge the Philadelphia immigrant station, he opposed the laws which restricted immigration. Sabath introduced the first workmen's compensation legislation in the United States, a bill for railroad workers which won him the attention of

ADOLPH J. SABATH

Theodore Roosevelt. In 1909 he sponsored the first old-age pension resolution; he was also the first Congressman to recommend Federal aid for highways.

Sabath, who was chairman of the Cook County Democratic Central Committee for ten years and has been a delegate to Democratic National Conventions since 1896, was a member of the "Champ Clark-for-President" delegation from his State in 1912; a rival Illinois delegation for Woodrow Wilson, however, was seated by the credentials committee. At first, Sabath, who thought that Wilson was unfriendly to immigrants and labor and that he favored prohibition, was unwilling to support the Democratic candidate. After meeting him, however, the Illinois Congressman changed his opinion: he grew to be Wilson's admirer and friend.

In 1917 Sabath was among those who voted for the declaration of war and when the war ended he urged the President not to make a separate peace with Austria-Hungary, for such a peace treaty would have prevented Czechoslovakia, Poland, and the Baltic states from becoming independent nations. The legislator was also an active supporter of the movement for the independence of Eire. A member of the historic Committee on Foreign Affairs, Sabath was a confirmed internationalist. He backed the League of Nations and believed in the importance of establishing good will between the United States and Russia: he sponsored a Congressional resolution urging the recognition of Russia in 1920, and in Hoover's Administration he tried to cement commercial relations between the two countries.

In the bootlegging era of the twenties, Sabath ran for Congress as an anti-prohibition candidate. Fearful of a stock market crash long before it finally came, he advocated restrictions on short-selling practices and early in September 1929 recommended the closing of the stock market until legislation for the pro-

tection of investors "and the country as a whole" could be secured. He introduced the first bill to establish the Reconstruction Finance Corporation, but this measure to meet depression problems was not passed until January 1932. It was in the years of depression that Sabath persuaded the House to set up a committee to investigate an alleged racket in real estate bondholders reorganizations. The committee headed by Sabath recommended reform legislation, some of which was enacted, and attempted to recover funds for those who had invested some twenty billion dollars in defaulted real estate bonds. Sabath later maintained that at least half the value of the bonds was salvaged.

During Franklin D. Roosevelt's Administration Sabath was a stanch supporter of New Deal policies, both domestic and foreign. He worked for White House-backed labor and relief measures, principally the social security law and the Wagner Labor Relations Act. He also urged the creation of the Securities and Exchange Commission, and was a co-sponsor of the Federal Deposit Insurance Act. Perceiving the menace to peace in the rise of Hitler and in the formation of the Berlin-Rome-Tokyo axis, the Illinois Congressman shifted from an anti-militaristic stand to support conscription and enlargement of the Navy. He voted for the repeal of the arms embargo and of the ban on arming ships as well as for the much-disputed 1941 Lend-Lease bill. During the years that the United States was at war, Sabath urged the passage of a bill to establish a national lottery as a means of preventing a sales tax. He voted for the Ramspeck Federal pay bill designed to help Federal employees meet the higher cost of living, for the Worley Federal ballot bill, and for the extension of reciprocal trade authority. He supported the President's tax program, crop insurance, and the Home Owners Loan Corporation, but did not back a motion to increase funds for the Rural Electrification Administration.

In Franklin D. Roosevelt, Sabath found his idol. He urged the President to run for the third and fourth terms and he hailed Wallace's suggestion in 1943 to make Roosevelt permanent chairman of the peace conference after the war. Since Roosevelt's death Sabath has continued to fight for the same goals for which he feels the New Deal President would have continued to work. The last message that he received from the President asked him to do all he could to establish a permanent Fair Employment Practice Committee. As chairman of the House Committee on Rules since 1939, (he was a committee member for ten years prior to that) Sabath strove against the Republican-Southern Democrat majority of the committee to get the bill to the floor of the House. In June 1945 Congress passed a compromise measure extending the FEPC for one year.

In his position as chairman of the rules committee, which can block legislation, Sabath had to report, to the House, measures meeting with his disapproval. Such was the situation in the Case [46] Labor Disputes Act which he felt was "designed to wreck unions." (In 1943 he had voted against the Smith '41-Connally '41 antistrike bill.) While occasionally outmaneuvering the majority with whom he had to work in his committee, the chairman in many instances was shouted down. A measure to increase the minimum wage to sixty-five cents an hour died in the Rules Committee in 1946 despite his efforts to send it to the House floor. A bill providing for a State Department cultural relations program, which he favored, was blocked for six months before it was finally granted a rule and passed.

Alarmed by the signs of disunity among the countries that had fought in the war as allies, particularly the increasing suspicion in relations between the United States and the Soviet Union, the Congressman was one of the sponsors of the Win the Peace Conference, held in Washington in April 1946. When some of the Representatives who had originally sponsored the group began to withdraw because of charges that it was "Communist-inspired," Sabath decried the attempts made to discredit it. Nevertheless, for those Representatives who wanted to support the ideas of the conference but who did not wish to associate their names with that group, he formed the Congressional Committee to Win the Peace.

He was a severe critic of the 1946 bill for the $3,750,000,000 loan to Britain. Later, nevertheless, on the ground that its defeat would merely be a victory for British conservatives opposing the Labor Government in England, the legislator, to whom President Truman had appealed to support the measure, voted for the loan. Sabath subsequently charged that Britain was showing "no intention of maintaining the spirit of the loan" and also attacked the State Department for permitting United States foreign policy to "be tied to the kite of British colonial exploitation and oppression."

Sabath's protests against "Red-baiting" by the Committee on Un-American Activities, which he had voted to abolish in 1943 and 1945, and against some of John E. Rankin's '44 statements have made him one of the Southern Congressman's targets of attack on the floor of the House. Following Sabath's demand for an investigation of the barring of foreign medical school graduates from the Veterans Administration, the restrictions were eased. In his fight for the Administration's housing and price-control programs, the Representative in March 1946 introduced a resolution calling for a thorough House investigation of any lobby "which seeks to influence consideration of legislation by Congress." He also called for a Federal investigation "of collusion among meat packers" during the meat shortage in September 1946, a shortage described by industry spokesmen as "the worst meat famine in the country's history."

A number of Sabath's measures have benefited the city he represents. He was largely responsible for the passage of a bill which made possible lake-front construction in Chicago and the building of the Navy Pier. By persuading Congress to pass a bill allowing the Chicago Board of Education to borrow twenty-two million dollars he was instrumental in providing for the payment of back salaries to Chicago schoolteachers and other city employees. He also obtained a forty-two-million-dollar grant for the building of filtration plants for the metropolis. During the war he saw to it that the industrial plants of the Lake Michigan center received "a fair share of war contracts" and also succeeded in having some of the agencies in overcrowded Washington transferred there. In Chicago's April 1946 Democratic primary, in which Sabath ran for the twenty-first time, he had sharp competition from his opponent, but was renominated. In November 1946 he won election to the Eightieth Congress.

In 1917 Sabath was married to Mae Ruth Fuerst, daughter of a newspaperman who was impressed with his reform platform. The Illinois Congressman smokes cigars and a pipe, and likes an occasional "strong" drink. When he had the time, he used to enjoy pinochle and horse races. A New York *Post* writer described him as "a chubby, fussy" little man with gray hair and a "golden heart."

References

N Y Post p7 F 2 '46 por
P M Mag p 15 Mr 10 '46 por
Salter, J. T. ed. Public Men In and Out of Office (1946)
Who's Who in America, 1946-47

SAMAROFF, OLGA (sä-mä′rŏf) Aug. 8, 1882- Pianist; teacher of music
Address: h. 24 W. 55th St., New York

"She has made for herself a special and widely influential place in the musical life of this country," wrote the late Lawrence Gilman of Olga Samaroff, concert pianist, music critic, teacher, radio and platform lecturer, and adviser to important musical institutions. Aroused to American discrimination against non-European musicians, she established the Schubert Memorial, a foundation devoted to the sponsorship of exceptionally talented young Americans at the very outset of their careers; perceiving a "wonderful possibility in the development of active listeners," she founded the complementary Layman's Music Courses; sensitive to the economic reverses affecting instrumentalists, she became a cofounder of the Musicians' Emergency Fund. A professor of piano on the faculty of the Juilliard School of Music and of the Philadelphia Conservatory of Music, Mme. Samaroff is also the author of several books, among them her autobiography.

Olga Samaroff, the daughter of Jane (Loening) and Carlos Hickenlooper, was born in San Antonio, Texas, on August 8, 1882, and christened Lucie Mary Olga Agnes. Through her mother she is descended from a long line of New England Protestants, although her great-grandfather emigrated to a Louisiana plantation in the 1840's and her grandmother received a Catholic education. On her father's side she is of Dutch descent and a second cousin of the Northern Civil War general Andrew Hickenlooper—a circumstance which occasioned much dismay during her Southern girlhood.

OLGA SAMAROFF

She received her first schooling at the Ursuline Convent in Galveston, Texas, and at an early age began taking piano lessons from her maternal grandmother, Lucie Palmer, from whom she had inherited her talent and to whose realism she is indebted for her opportunity for a concert career. Lucie Palmer had early showed exceptional musical talent but because of social prejudices had never prepared for a professional career. Instead, she had married at the age of sixteen and when, as the penniless young widow of George Loening, she had returned from Germany to find the Palmer plantation ravaged by the Civil War, she had been forced to eke out a living for herself and her two children as a teacher of piano. Thus, when she discovered her young granddaughter's talent, Lucie Palmer determined that the girl would, if it became necessary, be able to fall back on a concert career.

In the family discussions of her granddaughter's future, Lucie Palmer convinced General Hickenlooper, then considered the head of the family, that counterpoint and fugue, French and German, would provide as good mental discipline as Latin and mathematics in college; and since auditions before Edward MacDowell, Vladimir de Pachmann, William Steinway, and others had brought the verdict "Send her to Europe," it was decided that young Lucie Hickenlooper should go, accompanied by her grandmother. In Paris a year's private study with Antoine Francois Marmontel and Ludovic Breitner prepared her to enter the scholarship competition at the Conservatoire de Musique, where in 1896, at the age of fourteen, she became the first American girl to win a scholarship as a piano pupil. She was placed in a class of twelve pupils, ten French, one Russian, under the "eccentric" master Elie M. Delaborde, who greeted her with the remark that Americans were not meant to be musicians, the prevailing opinion of the time. Later, however,

he was won over by her angry rendition of Schumann's G Minor Sonata and she became his favorite pupil. "In retrospect," writes Mme. Samaroff, "the chief advantage of studying music at the Conservatoire de Paris was the acquisition of artistic self-discipline in an atmosphere of intensive work." Her day, for instance, began at seven in the morning and ended at ten at night, with approximately seven hours devoted to musical studies and the remainder, except for meal hours and one hour spent "on a bicycle, racing along the lovely cycling paths of the Bois de Boulogne," to academic subjects at the Convent of the Holy Sacrament, where she and her grandmother were boarders.

After two years at the Conservatory, however, her grandmother, dissatisfied with Delaborde's teaching and the lack of theoretical work, took the young girl to Berlin. There she studied piano with Ernst Jedliczka and Ernest Hutcheson, organ with Hugo Riemann, composition with Otis Bardwell Boise, and ensemble with her grandmother and a group of string players whom she had brought together. "The number of good concerts and operatic performances available at low prices," says Mme. Samaroff, "the general atmosphere of hard work and the prevailing thoroughness, made music study in the Berlin of those days extremely valuable to all serious students, [and] the prevalent European approach to attendance at the opera and at concerts [with its emphasis on the music rather than the performers] was significant and salutary for the American students." But in 1900, instead of making her debut as a concert pianist, she married Boris Loutzky, a Russian civil engineer, and became, until her divorce and annulment of the marriage by the Pope, a subject of Czar Nicholas II and a resident of Petrograd as well as of Berlin.

During the period of this first marriage, the young musician had neglected her pianistic studies; hence, when she arrived in New York in the autumn of 1904 with little money and the knowledge that her family had lost nearly everything in the Galveston flood, she faced, like her grandmother before her, a choice between a concert career, despite inadequate preparation, and teaching. Determined to justify her parents' earlier sacrifices, she chose the former and became engaged, as she puts it, "in the hardest struggle a young musician can have, namely, to keep up with circumstances that always threatened to outstrip my possibilities. I did not have enough technique I did not have enough repertory, and I faced the terrible ordeal of playing things in public as fast as I learned them instead of having time to let them mature. Other difficulties in her path were her lack of European press notices, her sex, and an unsuitable name. But as Olga Samaroff (the name of a remote Slavic ancestor) she made her debut on January 18, 1905, in Carnegie Hall with Walter Damrosch's New York Symphony Orchestra—in a concert paid for by the remainder of her mother's and her grandmother's savings.

After that things became easier. A letter of introduction from Geraldine Farrar, who had shared her student days in Berlin, next brought the pianist a salon engagement at the home of a Miss Dehon who numbered among her intimate friends the outstanding musicians of the day, and this in turn led to other private engagements. In the late spring she made her London debut—as a public solo recitalist for the first time—before a small but select audience. Then a previous engagement as soloist with the Boston Symphony Quartet led to an appearance with the Boston Symphony Orchestra, and Mme. Samaroff was finally launched on the career which kept her busy, as soloist with all the major American orchestras, until her marriage to Leopold Stokowski '41 on April 24, 1911, shortly before the conductor assumed the leadership of the Philadelphia Orchestra. Prepared by close association with Wilhelm Gericke, conductor of the Boston Symphony Orchestra, and Mme. Gericke, for the duties of a conductor's wife, Mme. Samaroff spent much of the next two years in helping her husband overcome the opposition he at first met in Philadelphia. Upon her marriage she had decided to forsake the uncongenial life of a concert artist but gradually, after 1913, she drifted back to public appearances. Until two years after the dissolution of her marriage in 1923, however, she subordinated public to private life.

Then, one day in 1925, she was asked by Dr. Eugene Noble, secretary-manager of the Juilliard Foundation, to join the piano faculty of the Juilliard Graduate School of Music, in New York. Believing that if she hesitated she would never have the courage to sign the contract, Mme. Samaroff completed the arrangements that same afternoon, beginning an association which has continued to the present day. Early in 1928, after the death of Henrik Ezerman, director of the Philadelphia Conservatory of Music, she also took over Ezerman's piano classes at the Conservatory—for, as she then thought, only the remainder of the year. However, her intense interest in the work of the Conservatory, which, unlike the Juilliard School and the Curtis Institute of Philadelphia, is conducted for the benefit of the non-professional student and the potential teacher of music, still takes her to Philadelphia one day a week. In her teaching she has made it a rule never to play for her students unless absolutely necessary, lest imitation suppress their individuality, and never to criticize without adequate explanation. And because she believes that the truly great musician is in the last analysis a product not only of what he can do but of what he is, she has always concerned herself with the human development of her students. From the beginning she loved teaching, she says, but adds that it is doubtful whether she would have satisfied the needs of her gifted pupils had she not had the opportunity of watching Leopold Stokowski's orchestral technique in rehearsals. Among her pupils have been the acclaimed young artists Rosalyn Tureck, Eugene List, William Kapell, Joseph Battista, and Solveig Lunde.

Through 1925 Mme. Samaroff had continued to make concert appearances, but late that year an accident in which she tore a ligament in her arm forced her to cancel all engagements for the remainder of the season. When, therefore, Ernest Newman resigned as music critic of the New York *Evening Post,* she was free to accept the offered position. Although not known as a writer, she had the courage to do it because, she points out, she had been writing—plays, poems, essays, fiction—for her own pleasure all her life. Her first act was to write her "credo," in which she declared that her column would express not a final judgment but only the opinion of one individual. Possibly her second was to criticize the critics for reviewing what they had not heard, writing without the requisite knowledge, and sacrificing the artist for the sake of a witty remark. In 1927, however, she relinquished the position because the new editor, Julian Mason, vetoed her plans for a music department for the paper. But she did not return to the concert platform, preferring to devote her full time to the broader field of music education, in which her name is especially linked with the Schubert Memorial and the Layman's Music Courses.

The Schubert Memorial was incorporated in New York in October 1928; its aim was to provide the exceptionally talented but young and unknown American artist with an opportunity for a debut with orchestra such as Mme. Samaroff had been forced to pay for herself. Opposition from the New York critics developed with the first concerts, but generous cooperation elsewhere enabled the founders to organize Schubert Memorial committees and concerts throughout the United States; and within a few years a partnership with the National Federation of Music Clubs established the foundation on a sound basis. A system of state, district, and national contests organized by the Federation is now in operation, with the national winners competing for the Schubert Memorial award of an appearance with the Philadelphia Orchestra in Philadelphia and New York.

The Layman's Music Courses sprang from Mme. Samaroff's conviction that "it would be more constructive to work at an increase in audiences rather than to refuse education to gifted potential performers" on the premise that there were already too many. Unlike most musical education for the layman they teach not merely the history of music but music itself.

Today, having outgrown the facilities of the David Mannes Music School, which provided their first location, the New York classes are being given by Mme. Samaroff and her assistants at Town Hall, while other classes, many begun by enthusiastic graduates, are being conducted throughout the country. In addition, the needs of the layman students have occasioned the publication of three of Mme. Samaroff's books: *The Layman's Music Book* (1935), a basic textbook; *A Music Manual* (1936), which "contains things everyone might like to know and remember about music"; and *The Magic World of Music* (1936), an introduction to music in fairy tale form. Although she is still intensely interested in both projects and her "pen and tongue are always

SAMAROFF, OLGA—*Continued*

at their disposal," Mme. Samaroff is no longer so active a participant, having withdrawn from the former in order to obviate the stigma of favoritism which might have resulted had her own pupils been winners and largely from the over-all direction of the latter because there were enough younger enthusiasts to carry on.

In 1939 Mme. Samaroff published her autobiography, *An American Musician's Story,* which, said John Erskine, "radiates the creative force, the common sense, and the imagination of a great personality," and which Lawrence Gilman called a "book of exceptional interest, value, frankness and sagacity. . . memorably candid and illuminating." The following sentences from it may be said to crystallize her musical philosophy: "The function of *interpretation* is not only the sole *raison d'être* of the musical performer, but also his highest approach to music. It is relatively unimportant to the world what the individual performer experiences in the way of emotion, but it is enormously important if his emotional force can breathe life into a great musical masterpiece that only exists for the listener through re-creation in sound. This bringing to life of music is worth all the work a musician must do in order to accomplish it."

In addition to her teaching at Juilliard (where she also taught summer classes for the first time in 1946) and at the Philadelphia Conservatory, where she is head of the piano department, extracurricular activities, so to speak, have expanded Mme. Samaroff's program during recent years. In 1936 she was sent by the State Department in Washington to represent America at the International Music Education Congress in Prague. Two years later she was a delegate to the Concours Eugène Ysaÿe in Brussels, an undertaking, founded by Queen Elizabeth of Belgium, similar to the Schubert Memorial, its object "the finding of unusual talent and the encouragement of its possessor." She has been presenting the New York series of the Layman's Music Courses in the Town Hall Short Course Division since 1939, and during the summers of 1941 and 1942 she taught master classes at the Los Angeles Conservatory of Music and Chautauqua, respectively. In 1944 and 1945 she conducted a series of radio broadcasts for the Interstate Broadcasting Company patterned after her Layman's Music Courses, and in the winter of 1945-46 she began to apply these techniques at the Children's Concerts of the National Symphony Orchestra in Washington, D.C., with gratifying results. Mme. Samaroff, who in 1946 is preparing a new book on the problems of the listener, is an honorary member of Phi Beta Kappa, was awarded an honorary Doctor of Music degree by the University of Pennsylvania in 1931 and the Cincinnati Conservatory of Music in 1943, and received the Order of the Crown of Belgium in 1938.

A woman of lively temperament, with a keen sense of humor, not above many kinds of pranks in her younger days, the tall (five foot six), brown-eyed musician finds her recreation in reading, in the theater and motion pic-tures, in a collection of rare phonograph records, and in winter sports and mountain climbing. She is stating her own case when she says, "The human being . . . who can feel the great surging currents of human aspirations, or sense compassionately the needs on every side that render each service to humanity or to the arts and the sciences doubly valuable, can find a real meaning in life."

References

Etude 57:640 O '39
Musician 19:727-8 N '14 il por
Stokowski, O. S. An American Musician's Story (1939) il pors
Who Is Who in Music (1941)
Who's Who in America, 1946-47

SAUCKEL, FRITZ (zou'kĕl) Oct. 27, 1894—Oct. 16, 1946 Nazi commissioner general of manpower in occupied territories from 1942; tried by the International Military Tribunal; judged as having had "over-all responsibility for the slave labor program . . . aware of the ruthless methods . . . [used] to obtain laborers and vigorously supported" those methods; condemned and hanged.

Obituary

N Y Times p1+ O 16 '46

SAXON, LYLE Sept. 4, 1891—Apr. 9, 1946 American author, "chronicler of the South": newspaperman, 1912-27; books include *Father Mississippi* (1927), *Fabulous New Orleans* (1928), *Old Louisiana* (1929), *Lafitte, The Pirate* (1930), *Children of Strangers* (1937); Louisiana State director of WPA Federal Writers Projects.

Obituary

N Y Times p25 Ap 11 '46

SCHACHT, AL(EXANDER) Nov. 12, 1894- Baseball comedian; restaurateur

Address: b. Al Schacht's, 137 E. 52d St., New York; h. 711 Walton Ave., The Bronx, New York

"For thirty years," wrote Leonard Cohen in the New York *Post,* "Al Schacht has been a 'ham' on the [baseball] diamonds of America. Hardly a fan in the nation has not seen him on some major league field or in some far-away hamlet. Millions have howled with glee at his antics and pantomime." Unique in his field, Schacht is also a successful restaurateur and has two books to his credit. He entertained an estimated two million troops in World War II.

Al (short for Alexander) Schacht claims to have been born in the Yankee Stadium. The date was November 12, 1894, the Bronx was a suburb, and Al's birthplace was the approximate site of the as yet unbuilt stadium. It was to the New York Giants' Polo Grounds in Manhattan, just across the Harlem River from the Bronx, that little Al went to worship his baseball heroes and run errands for them in the time he had left from school, from the fifty-cent piano lessons his mother insisted on despite the family's poverty, and from selling newspapers. He became "special sandwich-bearer" to the great pitcher Christy Mathewson.

A pitcher himself, Alexander led the Public School No. 42 team to the New York City championship in 1908, and at the High School of Commerce afterwards the boy pitched for what has been called the greatest high school team ever assembled. In the summer he played "Borscht Circuit" baseball in the Catskill Mountains for room, board, and four dollars a week, of which he sent two dollars home. When the high school officials discovered this professionalism on the part of a student athlete, he was not only ordered out of athletics but expelled from school. This was in 1911.

After winning sixteen games in a row for the semi-professional Walton (New York) team, young Schacht was asked to report to the major league Cincinnati Reds. The teen-ager had made his 130-pound physique more impressive by wearing extra layers of clothes; but after an ecstatic week of rubbing shoulders with baseball idols and pitching for their batting practice, young Schacht was told to go home and fatten up. Instead he pitched independently for two different teams each Sunday, making enough to support himself, while working out each weekday with the New York Giants, then at the top of the league. Schacht had talked Manager John J. McGraw into letting him act as an unpaid batting-practice pitcher. Christy Mathewson still liked the eager, curly-haired youth, answered all his questions, and finally showed him how to throw the famous "fade-away" pitch for which Mathewson was noted.

After finishing out the 1911 season as home batting-practice pitcher for the Giants, young Schacht got his first professional contract, with the Cleveland Club of the new Federal League. Reporting in 1912, he was sent onto the mound for the first time in the fifth inning of a game with the bases loaded and the other team leading by nine runs. Schacht thereupon "set some kind of world's record by striking out the next eight batters on twenty-five pitched balls . . . and finished the game with a record of eleven strikeouts against the fifteen batters." He adds, however, "That was the last time I escaped unscathed with the bases loaded," and as it was, the Federal League dissolved a week later. In the interstices of his baseball career, according to a *Collier's* article by Bill Cunningham, Schacht always returned to New York, where he could make about seventy-five dollars a week playing independent ball with two different teams, as against the $120 or $130 a month pay in minor league baseball.

In 1913, however, the Bronx-born pitcher did sign with the Newark (New Jersey) club of the minor International League. Although serious about his business of baseball, he became known for his practical jokes—more or less in self-defense, as the eccentric manager, Harry Smith, had adopted Al Schacht as his favorite stooge. Schacht had less success amusing umpires; they usually fined him, or threw him out of the game when he tried one of his stunts. In the spring of 1916, when the combination of a sore arm, malaria, and ulcers caused Newark to suspend him, the brash young pitch-

AL SCHACHT

er somehow persuaded John McGraw to sign him for the New York Giants. Unable to pitch at all, Schacht was nevertheless retained for the following year, and McGraw sent him to an osteopath all winter. The next spring, however, the sore-armed ballplayer was demoted to the minor league Rochester (New York) Red Wings, who used him as a relief pitcher.

Inducted into the World War I army despite his partial deafness, Schacht spent his entire military career at Fort Slocum, New York, where he pitched on the baseball team, broke his toe on the football squad, and rose to the rank of corporal. Leaving the Army in 1919, he resumed his minor league career with the Jersey City Skeeters. The team ended the season in last place, having won only forty-five games; but Al Schacht had pitched twenty of those winners, including ten no-hit games, the all-time league record. This was his best year in baseball, and he took advantage of it by sending anonymous letters singing his own praises to Clark Griffith, manager of the Washington Senators. Eventually "Griff" gave in to this epistolary barrage and put Schacht under contract late in the 1919 season, thus placing him on the same team with his greatest idol, Walter Johnson.

From 1919 until 1934, with some interruptions, Schacht remained on the Washington payroll. The first interruption came in the 1922 season, after Schacht had won six games and lost two. A shoulder injury caused his release, after which Schacht signed with the minor-league Reading Club and later with the New Haven team. In 1924, after a knee injury had finally ended the Schacht career as a full-time pitcher, he returned to the Senators as assistant to the new manager, Bucky Harris. Club president Griffith provided the three hundred dollars Schacht needed to buy his release from New Haven, and the player remained as third-base

SCHACHT, AL—*Continued*

coach and clown until 1934. The team won pennants in 1924, 1925, and 1933, and the World Series in 1924. When Manager Joe Cronin left the Senators for the Boston Red Sox, he took Coach Schacht along with him. Bill Cunningham says that Al was considered one of the best third-base coaches in the business.

Not long after Schacht first joined the Washington club, he had teamed with another coach and amateur comedian, Nick Altrock, to entertain fans before the start of games. By 1921 they were well known enough to be offered a thousand dollars each to present their comedy act for the World Series audience. Altrock dropped out of the act in 1933, but Schacht has been engaged to clown at almost every World Series since 1921. While continuing as a coach, he accepted invitations to entertain also at other special baseball events, as well as an occasional off-season week on the vaudeville stage. Finally, having calculated that besides the two major leagues there were thirty-two minor leagues and seven thousand independent baseball clubs in the country, and having received an enthusiastic response to his inquiries, Schacht gave up coaching in 1937, assumed the title of "Clown Prince of Baseball," and set out on his travels as a one-man circus.

Having built up his repertoire to twenty pantomime burlesques, Schacht appeared at minor-league parks all over the country during the first two months on his own, breaking attendance records everywhere. And, as he tells in his autobiographical *Clowning Through Baseball*, he showed a faculty for unintentional adventure. By 1941, when the book was written, he had driven some two hundred thousand miles. In that year his earnings were thirty thousand dollars, five times his highest salary as a major leaguer.

Clowning Through Baseball was published in March 1941, with "Grammar and adjectives by Murray Goodman" on the title page. The autobiography gave author Schacht a chance, faithfully reported by John Kieran, to gloat over his close friend Moe Berg, lawyer, linguist, and former fellow-coach for the Washington team, who had not written a book. "We still prefer this funster in person," said the *Boston Transcript* reviewer, "but for rain-check days this may do." The book was also mentioned on several selected library lists.

In the off-season of 1941-42 (in Al's business the off-season is every month except July and August), he embarked on another venture: a restaurant on East Fifty-second Street in New York. Decorated and labeled like a ballpark, it soon became notably successful; although the place is comparatively small and open only for dinner, an average of five hundred patrons are served each night, and newspaper critics have remarked on the "simple food of the best quality" and on the "hearty eaters from Broadway, Hollywood, and the world of sports" who frequent Al Schacht's.

After Pearl Harbor, Schacht packed up the baseball uniform, battered silk hat, red-lapeled tail-coat, and five-foot baseball glove which constitute his clowning costumes, and went on USO tours. Despite the fear of heights which

he mentioned in his autobiography, he flew to Africa and Sicily for one tour (five shows a day) and to New Guinea, the Dutch East Indies and the Southwest Pacific for another, playing 159 stage shows, 72 hospitals and 230 wards spread over forty thousand miles, in eight weeks. He went to Japan and the Philippines for the 124 performances of his third tour, which he enjoyed especially because he was not under bombardment that time. "He put on his act whenever and wherever he could," wrote Jerry Mitchell. That included the front lines. Others added that at home "Schacht never misses a week without at least one hospital visit and averages about six appearances a month. . . . Often at a camp he will put on a quiz show, paying the prize money from his own pocket." Besides entertaining the servicemen, he played third base in their infield practice and answered their questions about the major leagues. Al Schacht's own story of his tours is told in *GI Had Fun* (1945; "Composition and spelling by Murray Goodman"). Sportswriter Joe Williams called it "surprisingly readable," and remarked on "the astonishingly fine quality of feeling, understanding, and sincerity which pervade the pages. In some off way," added Williams, "he almost manages to achieve the Ernie Pyle touch."

In January 1946 the New York chapter of the Baseball Writers of America unanimously voted Al Schacht the twentieth annual Bill Slocum Memorial Award for high contribution to baseball over a long period, "with stress on his work during the war." Sixteen days after the presentation, the clown prince opened in Chicago as star of a romantic farce comedy about baseball, *Second Guesser*. The Civic Opera House was decorated like a stadium for the occasion, the tickets included rain checks and a warning against gambling, and the reviewers followed through with baseball terminology. "No hit, no run, no error" was more or less the verdict. The audience seemed, however, "rather like a fond parent watching a favorite child perform—not good, maybe, but cute" and gave Schacht four curtain calls on the opening night.

Known as a tireless and ever-entertaining storyteller, Al Schacht looks quite different from the "scrawny kid" of his autobiography. The black-haired, black-eyed comedian weighs 185 pounds, is an inch less than six feet tall, and has what he calls a rudder-like profile. He is described as "lean and agile. . . .Some of the stunts he does would tie most younger men into rheumatic knots, but he's spry as a kitten." Two operations have made his deaf ear almost normal. Schacht lists his religion as Jewish, his politics as impartial, and his first love as baseball, and it is said that he never turns down an invitation to any sort of baseball gathering. The restaurateur, who has discovered that his business "gets on better without him," lives in his native borough with his mother, Mrs. Ida Schacht. Ford Frick, president of the National League, has given him a lifetime pass for all National League games, and his USO services have brought him a number of awards and citations. He is perhaps proudest of a watch with a wristband made from a Japanese Zero, presented to him by servicemen in the Pacific.

References

Collier's 100:24+ S 4 '37 pors
N Y Herald Tribune p31 Ja 22 '46
Schacht, A. Clowning Through Baseball (1941)

SCHLESINGER, ARTHUR M(EIER), JR. (shlā'zĭng-ẽr mī'ẽr) Oct. 15, 1917-
Writer; historian

Address: b. c/o Harvard University, Cambridge, Mass.; c/o Fortune, 815 15th St., Washington, D.C.; h. 4202 Curtis Rd., Chevy Chase, Md.

Arthur M. Schlesinger, Jr., is the author of *The Age of Jackson,* the 1945 Pulitzer Prize history, which became a best seller. It has been widely acclaimed for richness, brilliance, and "pioneering novelty." Bernard De Voto predicted it would "create a school." Other critics have commented that he wrote "with an eye on our time and on tomorrow," thus providing "valuable ammunition for radical progressives." Also the author of magazine articles, including a series for *Fortune,* Schlesinger has been called a "progressive liberal" on the one hand, and on the other has been condemned by the Communist newspaper, the *Daily Worker,* as "a younger generation Max Eastman."

Writing of the Arthur Meier Schlesingers, father and son, a book reviewer noted in September 1945: "There is no doubt that one of them stands in the shadow of a great name, and but yesterday the world would have agreed that it is Arthur Schlesinger, Jr. But today he publishes a book so good that a flicker of doubt appears." The elder Schlesinger, a noted American historian who had received all historical distinctions except the Pulitzer Prize itself, was a native Ohioan, the son of German immigrants. He had been teaching for two years at Ohio State University when in 1914 he was married to Elizabeth Bancroft. Arthur Meier, Jr., the first of their two sons, was born in Columbus on October 15, 1917. Two years later the family moved to the University of Iowa, where the senior Schlesinger taught, and wrote books on American history, always pressing the thesis that history is not "merely past politics" but should be "as inclusive as life itself." In 1924, when young Arthur was seven, his father went to Harvard as a professor of history. The boy was thus "surrounded by American history" and "read a great deal of it." He attended public schools in Cambridge, Massachusetts, but finished his secondary education with two years at Phillips Exeter Academy in New Hampshire. Graduated in 1933, during the next year (1933-34) he accompanied his parents and brother (who is now a newspaperman) on a trip around the world.

On his return young Schlesinger entered Harvard, and in 1935 won the LeBaron Russell Briggs Prize for submitting the best of six hundred and thirteen historical essays by freshmen. He "pretty much specialized" in history and in literature, with F. O. Matthiessen as his

ARTHUR M. SCHLESINGER, JR.

tutor one year and Perry Miller for two. His honors thesis was on Orestes Brownson, a Jacksonian and transcendentalist who became Catholic. Schlesinger considered him "an interesting character because he cut across so many intellectual currents of the first part of the nineteenth century." Graduated from Harvard in 1938 when he was not yet twenty-one, with a B.A. degree *summa cum laude* and membership in Phi Beta Kappa, Schlesinger spent the summer expanding his thesis into a book. That fall he left for England to attend the University of Cambridge in 1938-39 on a Henry Fellowship granted by an inter-university committee. While he was at Cambridge the book, *Orestes A. Brownson: A Pilgrim's Progress* (1939), was published. "His account of the social, political, financial, and theological struggles of a century ago," wrote Odell Shepard in a criticism in the *Saturday Review of Literature,* "is remarkably well informed and still more remarkably thoughtful. In the cogent and always significant marshaling of fact that his book everywhere shows one cannot fail to recognize the hand of a young master." Other reviewers mentioned Schlesinger's painstaking scholarship, his "admirable gift for portraiture."

Schlesinger returned to Harvard in 1939 as a Junior Fellow. This was a three-year appointment granted to young men who showed "promise of notable contribution to knowledge and thought," which enabled them to spend their whole time on scholarship free from academic prescriptions. It was as a fellow that he wrote *The Age of Jackson.* In the winter of 1941, when he had finished delivering a series of Lowell lectures on Jackson and his times, he found that he had done much of the work for a book. The next year, except for a half-year course on American intellectual history which he gave at Radcliffe College in Cambridge, he wrote steadily. "I worked on

SCHLESINGER, ARTHUR M., JR.—Cont.

the book with two small children tearing all over the place, wrote quite a lot with a year-old daughter sitting on my lap." (Schlesinger had been married in August 1940 to a writer and illustrator of children's books, Marian Cannon, the daughter of the late Walter B. Cannon, Harvard physiologist. Their son and daughter are twins.) In 1942 Schlesinger became a writer for the Office of War Information. Working in Washington, he spent the evenings and week ends of eighteen months revising the Jackson manuscript. Resigning from the OWI he joined the Office of Strategic Services in 1943. During 1944-45, while his wife and father did the "dirty work of seeing the book through the press," Schlesinger was overseas as a corporal. In England he got out a weekly magazine, restricted in circulation to American agencies and American Army headquarters, which reviewed political developments in Europe. In Paris and in Germany Corporal Schlesinger gathered political intelligence for SHAEF. He was discharged from service late in 1945.

The Age of Jackson, published in September 1945, was an "exhaustive inquiry, and a brilliant one," said the *New Yorker,* "into Jacksonian democracy as an intellectual as well as a political-philosophic movement." Full of "pungent comment and quotation," abounding in "brilliant sketches of actors on the national scene," the book was clearly a product of "detailed and intensive scholarship," but more importantly it presented a "clear-cut philosophy of history." Bernard De Voto commented: "Far from avoiding judgment, as the historian's guild does increasingly and obsessively, he runs out to meet it. . . .Finally he is heretical in that he believes we can learn something from history." As *Time* summed it up, Schlesinger had held that democracy is a condition of tension, "in which neither side has a permanent advantage." This theory of tension distinguishes . . . Schlesinger's from . . . Marx's theory of class struggle, which ends each bout in a sullen victory for one side or the other, or 'in the common ruin of the contending classes.'" Schlesinger had "reinterpreted" Jacksonian democracy, according to Allan Nevins, in the light of an immense body of facts previously ignored. Jackson's times were presented as a period of class conflict rather than sectional conflict; the era's permanently fruitful body of radical doctrine was held to have come from the Eastern working classes and not from the Western frontiersmen. The young historian denied that he had set out to write "an apologia for the New Deal" as several reviewers had indicated, but said that since he had written the intellectual history of a movement, intellectuals and writers would find in the book "all kinds of implications" for themselves.

In addition to the Pulitzer Prize for 1945, Schlesinger's best seller won for him a grant of one thousand dollars from the American Academy of Arts and Letters and the National Institute of Arts and Letters. He also received a Guggenheim Fellowship for 1946 for his next project, a book on the age of Franklin Delano Roosevelt, for which he planned to interview men and women who played influential roles in the Roosevelt Administration "before these guys die off. . . .And the new book will be no party work. It will be sympathetic, but the aim will be to get the facts. . . .What primarily interests me is the relationship, in the sphere of politics, between thought and action— the course that ideas take as they travel from the mind of the teacher, or perhaps the journalist, and make their way into the mind of the politician or the man of action and become powers modifying social conditions, laws on the statute books, accepted axioms for conduct and judgment."

One of the youngest men ever to be appointed an associate professor at Harvard, Schlesinger is to begin his teaching duties in 1947. In 1946 his by-line appeared with frequency in the book review sections of the New York *Times* and New York *Herald Tribune.* The *New Republic* serialized *The Age of Jackson* in a ten-installment condensation, for which Schlesinger provided additional interpretative material. *The Age of Jackson* sold forty thousand copies in its first year as well as fifty thousand distributed by the Book Find Club in May. He also wrote for *Fortune,* the *Atlantic Monthly,* and *Life.* In *Life* (July 29, 1946), Schlesinger analyzed and criticized the Communist Party as a danger to the American Left, which it succeeded "in dividing and neutralizing." The first of his *Fortune* articles discussed what he considered the failures of United States State Department policy in dealing with *Peronismo* and communism in Latin America.

Mrs. Schlesinger (the only person, according to her husband, who believed the *Age of Jackson* would be a best seller) is a writer herself —the author of a children's book called *Twins at Our House,* about their children, Stephen Cannon and Katharine Bancroft Schlesinger. The historian is brown-eyed and brown-haired, five feet ten inches in height, 165 pounds in weight, and "looks even younger than his years." Described as "very good company, alert and responsive to a rare degree," for recreation he plays tennis and squash, reads, and is "a great believer in the movies."

References

N Y Herald Tribune p1+ My 7 '46 por
N Y Times Book R p3 Mr 10 '46 por
Time 47:76 Ap 29 '46

SCHNEIDERMAN, ROSE (shnī'dĕr-mǎn) Apr. 6, 1884- Labor leader

Address: b. National Women's Trade Union League, 247 Lexington Ave., New York; h. 235 E. 22d St., New York

The president of the National Women's Trade Union League, Rose Schneiderman, has been re-elected at each annual membership meeting since 1928. The National WTUL, composed of fourteen local leagues in the United States and one in Canada, is considered by many the spokesman for American working women, and is devoted to improving their welfare through unionization, legislation, and education. Among the lecturers on its 1945-46 program (some of the courses are free, fees for others are not higher than·five dollars) was Eleanor Roosevelt ['40], an old friend and associate of Miss Schneiderman's. The League president is a former official of the NRA, reportedly a member of President Roosevelt's ['42] "brain trust," and until May 1944 was secretary of the New York State Department of Labor.

Rose Schneiderman was born April 6, 1884, in a small city in Russian Poland, the name of which she does not know. Her parents were Adolph Samuel and Dora (Rothman) Schneiderman. When she was six the family emigrated to America, where her father got work as a tailor in New York. The five of them (Rose had two younger brothers) lived in two rooms in the ghetto of the lower East Side for three years, until Adolph Schneiderman's death of brain fever. This was a month before the birth of his second daughter. Nine-year-old redheaded Rose had to leave school to cook and take care of the younger children, while her mother worked in a fur house for six and, later, eight dollars a week. "I was a serious child," Miss Schneiderman has said, "and cared little for children's play, and I knew nothing about the country, so it was not so bad for me as it might have been for another. Yet it was bad, though I did get some pleasure from reading, of which I was very fond; and now and then, as a change from the home, I took a walk in the crowded street." Finally the girl was able to go back to school; an aunt took the baby into her home, and the boys were sent to the Hebrew orphan asylum. One of those brothers is now a certified public accountant, and the other was, until his retirement, an official of the American Jewish Committee and editor of the *American Jewish Yearbook*.

After completing the sixth grade of public school, little Rose went to work as a cash girl in Hearn's department store. After three weeks she got a job at Ridley's instead, starting at two and a quarter dollars a week; later she was promoted to a sales job. When she left at the end of two and a half years her salary was two dollars and seventy-five cents a week. When a friend had told her that she could make more money stitching linings in caps, she found work in the Hein and Fox factory. In 1900 working hours were from eight to six, and the piecework rates yielded an average take-home pay of five dollars a week for steady workers. The actual earnings were a little higher, but money was taken out to pay for the sewing machines the workers used (forty-five dollars each), for the thread, and later for the electric power. When the building burned down all the girls' machines were destroyed, but they received no insurance or other compensation for them. Miss Schneiderman was fortunate in that she had paid only a few installments on her machine.

She became an assistant sample maker, and later a sample maker. This work had to be of higher quality but yielded no more money, because it was not quantity production. To make up for this, the foreman would give her more work during the slow season than the

ROSE SCHNEIDERMAN

other girls had. After the girl had been there three years the employers began to make small but constant reductions in the rates paid the women workers: the manufacturers were making up to themselves the increases won by their skilled male capmakers' union. Encouraged by another girl, Bessie Brout, Miss Schneiderman joined her and another sympathizer in asking the national executive board of the United Cloth Hat and Cap Makers to take the less-skilled women lining-stitchers into their union. They argued that otherwise the bosses would form a company union in order to use the union label.

Their arguments convinced the men, and the first dozen girls were organized into Local 23, with the teen-age worker as secretary and volunteer organizer. Within a few weeks all the girls in the factory were members. Then they struck for pay increases—a big strike, involving about a hundred girls, in five of the thirty cap factories in the city. The strike was successful, piece rates being increased by an average total of two dollars a week. This was in 1903.

While working steadily at her trade, Rose Schneiderman took a more and more active part in unionism, and was elected to the National Board of her own union. In December 1904 came a test of strength: the cap manufacturers joined together to break the union by declaring an open shop. Their intention, as the workers saw it, was to discharge all union members and replace them with "child labor and newcome foreigners who would work for next to nothing." The whole union went on strike, picketing from seven in the morning to six at night. "We did not believe in violence," Miss Schneiderman says, "and never employed it." Other unions aided them, for the open shop issue affected all labor, and the first strike against it (by tailors) had been a failure.

(Continued next page)

SCHNEIDERMAN, ROSE—*Continued*

After thirteen weeks the employers yielded. "The shops are open now for all union members, and for them only," Miss Schneiderman announced in an article she wrote for the *Independent* in March 1905; "and all nonunion people can join the union. In order to take in newcome foreigners we have for them cut the initiation fees down to one-half what we Americans have to pay, and we trust them till they get work and their wages." The magazine described her at this time as "a small, quiet, serious, good-looking young woman of twenty years . . . fast rising in the labor world." At about this time she joined the two-year-old Women's Trade Union League, which had helped with publicity during the strike.

In 1907 Miss Schneiderman was elected vice-president of the New York WTUL, and in 1908 it offered her a part-time job as organizer. She accepted because it paid as much as she earned working full time at her trade. (Miss Schneiderman is still a paid-up member of the present United Hatters, Cap and Millinery Workers' International Union, and is honorary vice-president.) She wanted to earn enough money to go to college, to achieve her ambition of becoming a teacher; but she had to give up the idea after a year because, when there were strikes to be handled, the part-time job expanded into a full-time, day-and-night job. The League was not only an organ of trade unions, but of men and women interested in the organization and education of women workers, including a number whose money and influence were of great help to the struggling labor movement.

Miss Schneiderman's and the League's part in a strike were illustrated by the famous strike of shirtwaist makers in November 1909-February 1910. About twenty-five thousand women walked out, although only about two hundred were organized. The League arranged for meeting halls and instructed the strikers about their rights as picketers. In this period union activities and strikers were looked upon as "radical movements of the foreign element" by law enforcement agencies and the public; as a result, picketers were assaulted, often with considerable violence, and were arrested on the slightest excuse and harshly dealt with. The League therefore obtained the services of some socially prominent women, such as Anne Morgan [46] and Mrs. O. H. P. Belmont, who walked with the picket line and appeared as witnesses for strikers brought into court. It arranged for legal defense, organizing a group of outstanding lawyers who would never in the ordinary course of events have practiced in the magistrates' courts. As only propertied persons were allowed to go bail, the League arranged to have sympathetic property owners deed real estate to persons who would then sit in day and night courts, going bail for strikers. Mrs. Henry Morgenthau, Sr., for instance, deeded a house to a bailer from the Henry Street Settlement.

The shirtwaist makers had no treasury, and the League raised all that was spent from other unions and from sympathizers. Rose Schneiderman covered the New England area, speaking before unions, parlor meetings, and college assemblies; and when the strike was settled she was placed on the shirtwaist makers' union executive board for a while, to help work out the settlement of grievances. She was similarly concerned with the 1913 general strike of the White Goods Workers' Union. The young leader did organization work as well, until each union was in a position to employ a business agent of its own. The WTUL always urged affiliation with existing unions whenever possible. Of Miss Schneiderman's work with the White Goods Union, Dr. Gladys Boone writes that she "nursed it from a small and weak organization until it was strong enough to call a general strike."

Miss Schneiderman left the League's employ in 1914 to become an organizer for the International Ladies' Garment Workers Union, which is now one of the best known and most successful unions in the country. Her work in the cloakmakers' strike of 1916 included organizing a medical service for the strikers and their families, obtaining medicine from pharmacists at cost, and providing milk for the children of strikers. The I.L.G.W.U. sent her to Cleveland, then to Chicago, Worcester, Springfield, and Boston—in each case to revive a union which had been more or less disastrously defeated. In Boston she was greatly disturbed over the workers' seeming coolness and lack of enthusiasm, and not until a mass meeting was packed to the doors did she realize that that was merely Bostonian reticence. Here she succeeded in getting the employers to make a closed-shop contract with the union president after only a three-day work stoppage. In 1917 she returned to the New York WTUL as its only organizer, and continued in this capacity after being elected president in 1918. In 1919 she was elected vice-president of the National WTUL, which is made up of local leagues.

Miss Schneiderman had taken out her citizenship papers in 1916; an active worker for woman suffrage since 1910, she foresaw its adoption and wanted to be ready to use her vote. Besides the matter of simple justice, she felt that the labor movement was hampered by being only half-enfranchised. Active in the 1915 campaign for the Nineteenth Amendment, she was an officer of the New York City industrial section of the National Woman's Suffrage Party in 1916-17, touring the state, speaking at street meetings, and handing out leaflets.

The League had formulated standards for American working women, and its president, Mrs. Robins, asked President Woodrow Wilson whether it would be advisable to send a small delegation to present their viewpoint to the Paris Peace Conference of 1920. The League's delegates, Mary Anderson [40] of the United States Department of Labor and vice-president Rose Schneiderman, were appointed to the Conference by the President. Their sailing was delayed some four weeks by a strike, however, so they were too late to influence the formation and charter of the International Labor Organization. Miss Schneiderman was also a League delegate to the International Conference of Working Women at Washington that year, which decided upon seeking legislative as well as trade union activity (the foreign unions were so poor at this time that the League had to pay the expenses of many of the foreign delegates); and she was sent to the International Federation of Trade Unions in Vienna in 1923. Toward the beginning of Miss Schneiderman's tenure as president, the League clubhouse in New York was cleared of debt; Eleanor Roosevelt and Mrs. Thomas W. Lamont raised thirty thousand dollars for the purpose and presented it to her.

Earlier, in 1920, she was a Farmer-Labor Party candidate for Senator. Miss Schneiderman says she did no work on the campaign, sought no contributions, and was amazed that she polled even twenty-six thousand votes. The party, which she had helped to organize, was dissolved the next year. Miss Schneiderman says she has never taken an active part in politics because she has no taste for name-calling and because she prefers the more direct tangible results of union work in improving wages and working conditions. She announced support of Governor Franklin D. Roosevelt for President in 1932, however, and headed the women's division of the American Labor Party in his 1936 campaign; and she once sued a man for libel for making accusations against the "brain trust," stating that the term referred to herself and others.

Rose Schneiderman was the only woman member of the Labor Advisory Board to the National Industrial Recovery Administration, serving as such from the summer of 1933 until NRA's end in June 1935. As president of the National WTUL, which she had been for seven years, she was considered the spokesman for women industrial workers and, serving as resident adviser in Washington, she was concerned mainly with the industries which employed many women workers. She continually urged that labor be represented on the authorities which set the fair practice codes for each industry. She worked hard to stop the setting of lower wages for women than for men doing the same work. "More than one story circulates in Washington," wrote Emily Newell Blair in *Good Housekeeping*, "of verbal wars behind closed doors where the diminutive 'Redhead' carried her point to the surprise and, doubtless, the dismay of seasoned industrial giants."

General Hugh Johnson[40], the NRA Administrator, sent her to Puerto Rico to work out its needle trade codes, and her ten weeks there were a distressing experience. She found the people living in indescribable poverty, and wage scales so incredibly low that the best possible codes were unsatisfactory to her. Employers objected to a three-dollar-a-week minimum for needle workers as too high.

In the spring of 1937 Miss Schneiderman was appointed secretary of the New York State Department of Labor, in the Democratic Lehman[43] administration. Besides the routine work of approving documents, signing checks,

maintaining liaison with other departments, and selling public documents, she and the three deputy commissioners formed Commissioner Frieda Miller's[45] policy council; thus she participated in all the important decisions. She organized drives for the Red Cross, for bonds, and other causes; and in the winter of 1943, when many of the workmen's compensation referees were ill, she took over some of the compensation hearings. In May 1944, with the election of Republican Governor Dewey[44], the sixty-year-old secretary resigned from her post.

The labor leader is a member of the Women's City Club of New York. Her activities have included directorships of Brookwood Labor College, the first resident school for working men and women, of the similar Bryn Mawr summer school for working women on a scholarship basis, and the Hudson Labor School which superseded it a decade later. Miss Schneiderman was largely responsible for persuading the Bryn Mawr president to admit Negroes to the school and to put the working staff on an eight-hour day, an innovation later extended to the winter session as well.

Rose Schneiderman is a small woman, less than five feet tall, with short, wavy, dark red hair. Her eyes are grayish-blue, under slanting light eyebrows, and she wears rimless spectacles. Her manner is friendly and direct. "My best hobby is books," says Miss Schneiderman, who prefers historical novels and biographies. "Next the theater, which I haven't the time for. I am fond of music, and very fond of the country. I always thought that I'd get myself a little house where I could putter around and grow flowers, but it never materialized."

References

Good H 102:166 (por p38) Ja '36
Independent 58:935 Ap 27 '05
Lit Digest 116:9 Ap 12 '33 por
Scholastic 30:20 Ap 17 '37
Boone, G. The Women's Trade Union Leagues in Great Britain and the United States of America (1942)
Who's Who in American Jewry, 1938
Who's Who in Labor (1946)

SCOTT, JOHN R. K. July 6, 1873—Dec. 9, 1945 Former United States Republican Representative from Pennsylvania (1914-18); served in Pennsylvania House of Representatives (1908-12); Senator in State Legislature (1936); criminal lawyer.

Obituary

N Y Times p21 D 10 '45

SCOTT, TOM May 28, 1912- Composer; ballad singer

Address: b. 53 W. 53d St., New York

Tom Scott, billed as "The American Troubadour" on his radio program, is a singer of folk songs who accompanies himself on the guitar, and a professional arranger of music. Although known for his interpretation of the songs of the people over the radio and in concert halls,

TOM SCOTT

theaters, and supper clubs, he considers himself primarily a composer.

A native of the central Kentucky of which he sings, Thomas Jefferson Scott was born on May 28, 1912, on the Campbellsburg tobacco plantation of his father, Charles Jefferson Scott. The boy's mother, the former Olive Arnold, had been a schoolteacher before her marriage. Scott remembers being told that his grandfather "sang by note." During his childhood in Kentucky, where in 1918 his family moved to La Grange, Tom learned spiritual and work songs while trailing after the Negroes on his father's farm, and they also taught him to play the harmonica. He attended high school in La Grange (1926-30), participating in athletics, the glee club, and orchestra, and leading his own dance band. In this period he won a State contest as clarinetist. After school hours he worked at odd farm jobs, and delivered coal and ice.

While Scott was a high school student, his interest in music was noticed and furthered by Reuben "Booky" Taylor, a former Rhodes scholar on whose farm Scott worked at times. At Taylor's suggestion Scott heard his first symphony concert, at Louisville, where the Cincinnati Symphony gave a performance. He writes of this experience: "It really opened my ears to the world of serious orchestral music . . . 'Booky' patiently went over my possibilities for a career. . . .While I had picked up for myself and learned to play (after a fashion) a number of instruments including piano, I had no formal training in any of them, and 'Booky' felt it might be full late to begin the technical training necessary to become a concert instrumentalist. . . .On learning that I was continually hearing music of my own, 'Booky' advised me to equip myself to write some of it down and consider the possibility of becoming a composer. I took this advice seriously." In 1930-34 Scott majored in music

at the University of Kentucky, in Lexington, where he then lived. Although illness compelled him to stop college study two months before graduation, he had managed, in the meantime, to play with the school band and symphony orchestra, to sing with the glee club, to cover a ten-mile newspaper route, and to commute (by hitchhiking) the more than fifty miles from Lexington to Louisville for special instruction in piano and theory under Dwight Anderson, now dean of the University of Louisville Music School.

At the age of twenty-four Tom Scott traveled to New York to seek a career in music. In order to pay for lessons in theory and in voice, he worked as a singing waiter; he was also a frequent winner of money prizes on amateur nights. "I sang in every burlesque house in New York," he says. "My repertoire was "Asleep in the Deep" with a very low note and "Old Man River." During 1936-38 he sang in the Broadway musicals *Two Bouquets* and *Virginia,* and with the San Carlo and the Russian opera companies. Soon after coming to New York Scott began to study theory and composition with Harrison Kerr, executive secretary of the American Composers' Alliance and recently appointed by the United States Government supervisor of music for occupied countries. In 1938, after having first appeared in assorted guest spots as a soloist, Scott was engaged for Fred Waring's '40 Glee Club. In 1941 and after, he utilized his knowledge of Negro spirituals, work songs, and ballads to prepare some selections for Fred Waring, for whom he became an arranger. The next summer Scott sang several of these native tunes at a Cape Cod benefit. On that occasion he was heard by ballet dancer Mona Montes who, later, while dancing at the Rockefeller Plaza Rainbow Room, asked Scott to sing some of the songs for the manager. This led, two weeks later, to his engagement as a featured soloist at the Rainbow Room. His career as a ballad singer was thus launched by accident in September 1942.

The Kentuckian has appeared at a number of New York supper clubs besides the Rainbow Room and the Village Vanguard. In addition to his broadcasts over the "highbrow" radio station WQXR (New York) and over national networks, he has had concert engagements at Town Hall, the Brooklyn Academy of Music, MacMillan Theatre of Columbia University, Times Hall, and Carnegie Hall. These recitals have gained for Scott a widespread public and largely favorable reviews. The New York *Herald Tribune* in October 1945 wrote that he "deserved much praise both for his quality of tone and the clarity of his diction, as well as for his realization of the spirit" of these folk tunes. The New York *Sun* noted Scott's "keen perception", "authentic manner" in delivering the songs, and added that he "has enough sophistication to realize that simplicity is necessary in the presentation of his material." Reviewers approved the "finish", "style", "reserve", and "man's way" Scott had with the songs and ballads, and the lack of "embarrassing artiness" in his delivery, qualities which had made the singer popular at the canteens and hospitals at which he has appeared. In November 1945 *Musical America* was of the opinion that his work had "seemed more effective a year ago," and less studied; but *Music Business* for February 1946 commented: "We have been most fortunate in . . . [the] interpretive artists who have brought . . . folk songs among us through various channels; among these . . . may be mentioned the Allisons, Burl Ives '46, Lead Belly, [Richard Dyer-] Bennet '44, Josh White '44, and Tom Scott, the latter being the most gifted both vocally and from an interpretative standpoint."

Scott's repertoire includes songs of the sea, the South Appalachian mountains (his largest collection), and the North woods; the songs of the Negro, the American Indian, the cowboy, the Creole, the Latin American; his songs come also from France and the Low Counties. All of these Scott has arranged, many he has collected, although he calls himself "an interpreter rather than collector." One critic wrote (*Program*, May 1945), "When he renders the superbly beautiful 'The Foggy, Foggy Dew,' you don't want him to ever stop." The reviewer for the Lexington (Kentucky) *Leader* liked Scott's rendition of the spiritual, "The Story of the Twelve," Scott's favorite folk song. Scott believes there is no more eloquent expression of the spirit of America than the native folk songs; he ascribes the neglect of them to "our comparative youth as a nation and our natural distrust of the cultural value of our own products." He feels, however, that the folk song has now reached a static point. "The conditions that produced great folk songs have, by and large, passed on," he says.

The singer, who has been associated with Waring as arranger since 1941, prepared a series of nineteen American folk songs for the 1941-42 season, and the same number of United Nations songs in 1942-43. He has published about one hundred choral arrangements of folk songs and has been folk music specialist for the publishers Words and Music, Incorporated. Among Scott's compositions are a symphony which was first performed in October 1946 under Howard Hanson '41 in Rochester, New York. "It's a good first symphony, full of vigorous life, honest, compelling, youthful music," wrote George Antheil in his *Bad Boy in Music*. Reviews in the Rochester papers found the work one of "strength, dignity, and originality." Scott also wrote "From the Sacred Harp," a short composition for the chamber orchestra. The piece was commissioned by Joseph Barone, and was premièred by him in the Carnegie Chamber Music Hall in February 1946. It was given two radio performances that October.

"Hornpipe and Chantey," based on American folk themes Scott found in Nantucket, was given its première by the Los Angeles Symphony Orchestra on July 21, 1946, in the Hollywood Bowl. (The conductor was Leopold Stokowski '41, an admirer of Scott.) The work was again performed, on the Columbia School of the Air under Bernard Herman. During the summer of 1946 Tom Scott directed, arranged, and composed the musical score for the Theatre

Guild production *Devil Take a Whittler*. He has been commissioned to write a piano concerto for Harry Kaufman, designed for a première with Hans Kindler '46 and the National Symphony Orchestra, and to compose an orchestral work based on an Appalachian folk tune for Joseph Barone and the New York Little Symphony. It was announced in December 1946 that Scott would be the choral director for *Brigadoon*, a musical to be produced by Cheryl Crawford '45. His collection of American ballad arrangements, the volume *Sing of America*, will appear sometime in 1947. Scott is also engaged in compiling three other books, in collaboration with his wife Joy (Pride) Scott, the artist-writer, to whom he was married in June 1938. The Scotts, who had met in New York for the first time after having lived two doors apart in Lexington for a year, have also collaborated on several plays. One, by Weldon Stone, for which Scott wrote the music and his wife the lyrics, was a Theatre Guild summer tryout in 1945. Joy Scott also writes her husband's radio script material.

Cue has described Tom Scott: "A tall, rangy, Gary Cooperish sort of fellow." It added that he sings in a voice "low and sonorous," with manner "slow and measured," and with convictions "as deep as his voice." Scott is one inch over six feet in height, weighs 170 pounds, and has dark hair and blue eyes. The Scotts live in a New York apartment, which is decorated with many of Joy Scott's abstract paintings. Scott is an amateur astronomer, plays tennis for exercise. George Antheil, the pianist, who is a musical adviser to the folk song interpreter, quotes a "very, very serious Scott" as saying, "Mahler bores me to death." The classical composers he likes are, in this order: Bach, Debussy, Brahms, Tschaikowsky, Beethoven, and Moussorgsky; and among the contemporaries, his favorites are Sibelius, Bartók, Shostakovich, Berg, and Hindemith. Scott belongs to the Baptist Church; he is a member of the Lambs Club, Kentuckians, American Composers' Alliance, Society for the Classical Guitar, Musicians Union, American Federation of Radio Artists, Chorus Equity, and American Guild of Variety Artists. Before he became a ballad specialist, Scott was variously considered a bass, a baritone, and a bass-baritone—the last is, perhaps, most accurate. "However," he has said, "the conception of singing ballads and folk songs is so different" that any such classification of his voice should not be made.

SEID, RUTH *See* Sinclair, J.

SERT, JOSE MARIA (sĕrt) Dec. 24, 1876 —Nov. 27, 1945 Internationally known Spanish muralist; painted a series of murals depicting "the pictorial epic of humanity's struggle" for the RCA Building in New York, and did murals for Sert Room of Waldorf-Astoria in same city; other works appear in France, Switzerland, and Spain; known also for his painting and illustrations.

Obituary

N Y Times p27 N 28 '45 por

SETON, ERNEST THOMPSON (sē't'n) Aug. 14, 1860—Oct. 23, 1946 Author and naturalist; a trained artist, he combined that skill with an intensive study of nature, writing and illustrating over forty books on wild life, woodcraft, and Indian lore; his best-known book is *Wild Animals I Have Known* (1898); he delivered more than three thousand lectures in twenty years; was chairman of the committee which established the Boy Scouts in the United States in 1910. See *Current Biography* 1943 Yearbook.

Obituary

N Y Times p27 O 24 '46 por

SEVITZKY, FABIEN (sĕ-vĭt'skē) Sept. 30, 1893- Conductor; composer

Address: b. Murat Theatre, Indianapolis; h. 1321 N. Meridian St., Indianapolis.

Among the younger men who have made their mark in American musical life is Fabien Sevitzky, former double-bass player and composer for that instrument, now musical director and conductor of the Indianapolis Symphony Orchestra and stanch champion of American composers. Said G. H. A. Clowes, nationally known art collector and music patron in 1941, four years after Sevitzky had assumed the orchestra's leadership: "To Mr. Sevitzky must be given the credit for building a musical organization of which the entire state of Indiana is justly proud and which has, we know, attracted more national attention for its accomplishments than any other major symphony orchestra in the first four years of its existence."

J. Abreschi

FABIEN SEVITZKY

Scion of a noted musical family, the son of Adolf Aleksandrovich and Raisa Nesterowna (Meshberg) Koussevitzky, Fabien Sevitzky (who shortened his name so that it would not be confused with that of his famous uncle Serge Koussevitzky [40]) was born in the Russian town of Vyshnii Volochek near Moscow on September 30, 1893. His musical education was begun while he was a schoolboy in St. Petersburg, where the family had moved. He originally contemplated study of either the violin or the piano when he would be ready to enter the St. Petersburg Conservatory. But when the time came he found only the César Cui scholarship for the double-bass (sometimes called the contrabass or bass viol, the largest and lowest-pitched of the viols) available at St. Petersburg. Familiarizing himself with the instrument in the short period of a few weeks, therefore, he won acceptance and enrolled at the conservatory for a general music course with special emphasis on that instrument. In this he was following the example of his uncle, who accepted a Moscow Philharmonic Conservatory scholarship for the double-bass because only that scholarship and two others—for horn and trombone—were open.

Attending the conservatory during non-school hours, Sevitzky studied the double-bass with Bech; theory, harmony and composition with Rimsky-Korsakov, Liadov, and Glazunov; and piano with Siloti. And in 1911, one year after he had completed his academic education at the St. Petersburg Gymnasium, he was graduated from the conservatory *magna cum laude*, the first recipient of a gold medal for the double-bass in the institution's history. After making his professional debut in St. Petersburg, Sevitzky during the next three or four years occupied a position in the orchestra of the Moscow Imperial Theatre. Early in 1915 he toured Russia as a contrabass virtuoso, giving approximately one hundred and fifty recitals in six months, and acquiring, in the words of David Ewen, "a reputation on his instrument second only to that formerly known by his uncle." Later that year, however, his musical career was interrupted by his induction into the czarist army, with which he served in the infantry as a dispatcher at the front, "a particularly perilous assignment," until the outbreak of the Russian Revolution in 1917.

Returning to Moscow, which he now made his home, Sevitzky again became a double-bass player in the orchestras of the city's state theaters, and at the same time began to study acting. "For a while," David Ewen has recorded, "he actually fulfilled a few important roles as an actor in the movies and acquired a considerable reputation as an interpreter of character parts." Then, in 1922, he was forced to flee Russia and finally, after harrowing experiences of which he does not care to talk, arrived in Poland. During eight months of the year that followed, he found employment in the orchestra of the State Opera and with the Warsaw Philharmonic; during the remainder of his stay in the country, "he knew the privations of cold and hunger." But it was while he was in Poland that he met the operatic soprano Maria Dormont, who became his wife on New Year's Day of 1923.

Shortly after their marriage, the Sevitzkys left Poland for South America and Mexico, where in the summer of 1923 they undertook an extensive joint concert tour, giving as many as five concerts in Mexico City alone. In the autumn the musician joined the Philadelphia Orchestra, then conducted by Leopold Stokowski [41], as a double-bass player. For two years he was content to be merely a member of the orchestra. Then, in 1925 he ventured into conducting, organizing the Philadelphia Chamber String Sinfonietta, with its eighteen performers drawn from the string section of the Philadelphia Orchestra. Unique as the "first permanent string orchestra in the world," under its young conductor's guidance the ensemble over a period of years became known throughout the United States for its "excellent" programs of seldom-played works, both old and new, including at least one work by an American composer on each bill. In 1927-28 he was called upon to conduct the Philadelphia Grand Opera Company; and from 1928 to 1930, the Pennsylvania Opera Company. In 1928 Sevitsky had become an American citizen.

By this time he knew that he wanted to be a conductor. Resigning as double-bass instrumentalist with the Philadelphia Orchestra, therefore, he left for Boston, which he was to make his headquarters for the next six years. In the Hub City between 1930 and 1936 he conducted first the symphony orchestra of the Metropolitan Theatre, of which he was also musical director, and later the Peoples' Symphony Orchestra, and he organized and conducted both the Young Musicians' Orchestra and the Sevitzky Vocal Ensemble. In addition, the musician made two European tours, the second as a result of his reception on the earlier, conducting among other orchestras the Paris Symphony, the Berlin Philharmonic, the Vienna Philharmonic, and the Warsaw Philharmonic; and when he returned to the United States he appeared as guest conductor with the Philadelphia Orchestra, the Los Angeles Philharmonic, and the National Symphony Orchestra of Washington, D.C. Then, in November 1936 he led the Indianapolis Symphony Orchestra in the one performance which resulted in his engagement as its permanent conductor on a three-year contract in 1937.

Within a year or two Fabien Sevitzky's "dynamic" leadership had raised the Indianapolis Symphony from a struggling local organization to a "position of commanding importance among the orchestras of America." In fact, continued David Ewen, "it is acknowledged that the history of the Indianapolis Symphony Orchestra as a major musical organization actually dates from the moment Sevitzky took command." "An indefatigable organizer, an able and zealous drillmaster, a penetrating interpreter," wrote James Q. Thrasher in the *Christian Science Monitor,* "he worked acknowledged wonders with a group of young and comparatively low-salaried musicians." From the beginning of his conductorship he took the orchestra on tour to the principal cities of Indiana, and then outside the State, finally arriving at New York's Carnegie Hall in December 1944. From the beginning, too, he secured radio engagements: in 1937-38, ten concerts over the Mutual network; in 1938-39, eighteen over the Columbia Broadcasting System. By 1943 he and the orchestra had given about seventy-five concerts over the three major radio networks.

Invariably, in planning his concerts, Sevitzky follows a rule which he laid down for himself when he organized the Philadelphia Chamber String Sinfonietta in 1925, that at least one American work be included on each of his programs. (When an all-Beethoven or an all-Brahms program makes this manifestly impossible, he is careful to schedule an all-American concert for a later date.) "Not even Koussevitzky, Stokowski, or Stock has sponsored American music more passionately than he," Ewen has observed. From the two hundred-odd American scores he receives each season the conductor makes his selection, choosing perhaps one hundred which he deems worth a reading in rehearsal, and from these he chooses the compositions—which in the average season 1940-41 totaled thirty-two works by twenty-five Americans—to be presented to the public on future occasions. Sevitzky plays this American music because he believes in it. "There is unlimited vitality, unlimited power and beauty in American music," he has said. "In modern American music there is much that is worthwhile, and some that is great. American composers have a right to a fair hearing by their compatriots, and I am doing my best to see that they get it." For his efforts he was in 1938 cited by the National Association for American Composers and Conductors and in 1941 was awarded an honorary Mus.D. by De Pauw University.

Although New York critics have at times called Fabien Sevitzky "a very excellent musician and a very brilliant conductor" and "a leader of force and refinement," these same New York critics have also expressed themselves as dissatisfied with his performances or have qualified their praise with criticism of his tempi, which they have found generally erratic, in his 1944 and 1945 appearances inclining to sluggishness, in 1946 to excessive speed. A typical comment is Mark A. Schubart's in the New York *Times* of July 20, 1945: "He [Sevitzky] obviously knows his orchestra and is able to draw from it fine, balanced sonorities and clean attacks. But, as in an earlier concert this season, his readings seem plagued by an unsteadiness of tempo which upsets the balance and cumulative emphasis of the work as a whole."

Other notices of the conductor's New York appearances between 1944 and 1946 ranged from harsh disapprobation to complete approval, his 1945 engagement at Lewisohn Stadium running the entire gamut—with Jerome D. Bohm writing in the *Herald Tribune* of July 17, 1945: "Mr. Sevitzky's interpretation of Brahms's First Symphony was highly mannered, unconscionably dragged tempi being juxtaposed with equally arbitrary bursts of speed. The result was that the work's architectonics were shattered and Brahms's ideas disaffectingly distorted"; and Olin Downes writing in the *Times* of July 26, 1945: "The performance of Beethoven's Ninth was prevailingly of high excellence . . . . it was clear that Mr. Sevitzky had a thorough grasp of the score and was well aware of its traditions in projecting the

SEVITZKY, FABIEN—*Continued*

music. Thus the tempo of the first movement, fortunate in the spaciousness it afforded the articulation of the great themes and the rugged as well as lyrical characteristics of the music. The slow movement was sung with real eloquence and without affectation or sentimentality. The architecture of the finale, which is no simple thing for any conductor to establish, was made significant and dramatic."

Fabien Sevitzky has been called by David Ewen "the answer to an orchestra's prayer" because he can be a friend of each of his men "without sacrificing his authority." Likable, gentle in manner, with a ready sense of humor, he is capable of deep affections and quick enthusiasms. By the "verve and passion" of his performances he is said to have raised the Indianapolis Symphony to "virtuoso caliber" and his compositions for the double-bass, said *Etude*, are characterized by "melodic" line and "rhythmic and dynamic sweep." An inveterate conversationalist, the conductor will talk volubly on topics of literary, artistic, political, or gastronomic interest. His chief avocations are two: skeet and trap shooting, for which he has won many medals, and collecting ties. He is said to have the second largest collection in the United States, many from foreign countries and some woven to his own designs. In keeping with this hobby, he habitually chooses his tie first, dressing to harmonize with it. In order to be both comfortable and well-groomed on the podium, the aim of many a less ingenious conductor, he has designed a special dress suit so cut and adjusted that he is able to execute the most violent movements without displacing the sartorial neatness of his tall form.

References

> Ewen, D. Dictators of the Baton (1943); ed. Living Musicians (1940)
> Macmillan Encyclopedia of Music and Musicians (1938)
> Pierre Key's Musical Who's Who (1931)
> Thompson, O. ed. International Cyclopedia of Music and Musicians (1943)
> Who Is Who in Music (1941)
> Who's Who in America, 1946-47

SEYSS-INQUART, ARTUR VON (zīs'ĭng'kvärt) July 2, 1892—Oct. 16. 1946 Austrian-born Nazi Deputy Governor of occupied German territory in Poland, 1939-1940; German High Commissioner of the Netherlands after 1940; tried by the International Military Tribunal, found guilty of "ruthless [application of] terrorism"; condemned and hanged. See *Current Biography* 1941 Yearbook.

Obituary

N Y Times p1+ O 16 '46

SHAVER, DOROTHY July 29, 1897- Business executive

Address: b. c/o Lord and Taylor, Fifth Ave., New York; h. 414 E. 52d St., New York

To her outstanding record in the merchandising field, Dorothy Shaver added her election to the presidency of Lord and Taylor, large New York department store, in December 1945. Probably the first woman to head a thirty-million-dollar corporation, Miss Shaver now directs the institution which she has served in an executive capacity for more than two decades. Her ideas and innovations in advertising and merchandising have been widely effective. She is credited with being largely responsible for securing recognition for American designing talent, and has discovered or developed more than seventy-five native designers in the field of fashion and decoration.

Dorothy Shaver was born in the small town of Mena, in Howard County, Arkansas, on July 29, 1897, to James D. and Sallie Hunter (Borden) Shaver. Descended from the Kentucky Bordens, she lists among her ancestors, her paternal grandfather, General Robert Glenn Shaver—"Fighting Bob" of Civil War fame. In her father's family there were lawyers; her mother's was a family of many artists. The girl was educated in her home state, where she attended the University of Arkansas. After World War I she went North for further study at the University of Chicago. In time, with her sister Elsie, she decided to "crash" the Big City, and the two ambitious Arkansas girls came to New York. There the future large-scale merchandiser, with her sister's help, soon made her initial success—in dolls. Elsie, an artist, chanced to design a modern doll for her own amusement, but shrewd Dorothy quickly saw its sales possibilities. This marked the beginning of "The Five Little Shavers," a prosperous doll business which brought Dorothy's merchandising talents to the attention of Lord and Taylor. In 1924 she joined the store's staff to reorganize the comparison shopping bureau. A year later she suggested the establishment of a bureau of fashion advisers and then proceeded to organize the first bureau of stylists in an American department store, now an essential part of this business.

In recognition of her ability, Miss Shaver was made a member of the board of directors of the company in 1927. She impressed the fashion world a year later when she staged the first comprehensive exhibit of modern decorative art. Featuring material which she had brought from Paris, the show displayed furniture, glass, screens, rugs, and paintings, and resulted in a surge of modern decoration all over the country. By 1931 Miss Shaver was a vice-president of the company, with an expanding influence in the retail sphere. Her long but rewarding fight on behalf of American designers has brought native talent to public attention. Among the many designers she encouraged are Clarepotter, Nettie Rosenstein, Lilly Daché [41], and Elizabeth Hawes [40]. From her sponsorship of American creative artists developed the four one-thousand-dollar awards made by Lord and Taylor annually to the industrial designers contributing the most important work of the year. Eager to promote America, and especially New York, as the world's fashion center, Miss Shaver challenged the traditional leadership of Parisian stylists. In 1940, after the fall of France, she said, "Of course our American designers must assume style leadership now that Paris has relinquished it. New York can't help becoming the center of fashions. We have everything here with which to work, including rich talent, and our own designers have been doing a great job for years, although they have lacked the attention they deserved." To reinforce her claim for American style leadership, Miss Shaver has pointed out that American women have always been considered the best-dressed in the world. Devoted to the cause of the allied arts, she has also promoted the artist-craftsmen —designers who have produced original American work in fabric designs, leather, and jewelry.

From 1937 until her promotion in 1945 the executive was first vice-president of Lord and Taylor, charged with handling the advertising, fashion promotion, public relations, and display programs of the store. In this capacity she worked with wardrobes for teen-agers, that large body of consumers in the awkward ten-to-sixteen age group for whom Miss Shaver had fashions especially designed. Under her touch the company's advertising "took on an elusive feminine quality." Her innovations in the store included the "Bird Cage" lunchroom and the Men's Soup Bar. In the matter of window displays her hand was apparent—the striking Christmas bell windows and the original blizzard windows. But she hesitates to take the credit for such accomplishments, declaring, "I often do nothing but recognize or organize the idea when it is presented to me." In discussing her work Miss Shaver has said, "My job, and a job I love, is to give inspiration, to bring a fresh point of view to selections, and to correlate all the ideas that are fed to me."

The executive applied her knowledge of merchandising to the war effort in her service as general consultant to the Office of the Quartermaster General. Appointed to this post by the War Department in May 1942, Miss Shaver was an advisory member of the research and development committee of the Military Planning Division. During this time, while Miss Shaver continued in her position with Lord and Taylor, she made frequent trips to the capital for conferences. Her other war activities included the vice-chairmanship of the committee on public information of the American Red Cross, membership on the War Writers' Board and the board of directors of the American Women's Volunteer Services. In late 1945, by her election to the presidency of Lord and Taylor, the career woman again established precedent. Believed to be the first woman to head a department store of this size, she succeeded Walter Hoving [46] at a significant time in the history of the New York store. The corporation has a broad postwar expansion plan— the erection of a new building on Fifth Avenue, and additional suburban branches. In May 1946 Miss Shaver was elected a director of the Associated Dry Goods Corporation, the parent organization with which Lord and Taylor is affiliated.

Miss Shaver has crossed the Atlantic often, establishing merchandising markets in Europe. She has been described as a woman "sizzling with ideas, not only about design, but about politics and the world in general." She has many interests besides her work and believes that outside interests are essential to the most efficient

DOROTHY SHAVER

functioning of the working woman. A devotee of the theater, she has the opportunity to indulge her feeling for the dramatic in staging fashion shows which, according to theatrical producer Brock Pemberton [45], are as good as anything Miss Shaver has admired on the stage. The merchandising authority is a member of the advisory council of the New York School of Applied Design for Women, the Cooper Union Art School; and a trustee of the Parsons School of Design. An honorary life Fellow of the Metropolitan Museum of Art, she was instrumental in assisting that institution in the establishment of a Fashion Institute in 1945. Miss Shaver is a member of the board of directors of the Advertising Federation of America and, as the hospitality subcommittee's expert on retail shopping, serves on the United Nations Committee of New York. She is also a member of the Menninger [45] Foundation for Psychiatric Education and Research, and of the National Committee for Mental Hygiene.

A dynamic personality, Dorothy Shaver is tall, slim, and attractive, with dark hair and large dark eyes. She is unmarried and lives with her sister. Isabella Taves has written that one of Miss Shaver's constant qualities is her "delight in the new and untried. She flew, when few people were interested in aviation. She took up mountain climbing, even when she had a secret conviction in her heart that she would hate it." Her adventurous spirit once led her to charter a boat and live on it for six months. And once, Miss Shaver says, "at the risk of life and limb, I learned to ski. Once I had mastered it, I came back to New York, put my skis on the shelf, and thanked heaven it was over. But I wouldn't stop until I had learned."

References

Fortune 12:86 S '35 por
N Y Herald Tribune p1+ D 19 '45 por
N Y Sun p31 Ap 26 '41; p11 Ag 2 '45
    por; p17 D 19 '45 por

(Continued next page)

SHAVER, DOROTHY—*Continued*
Newsweek 26:60 D 31 '45 por
Time 46:82 D 31 '45 por

Taves, I. Successful Women (1943)
Who's Who in America, 1946-47
Who's Who in Commerce and Industry
(1944)

**SHELDON, CHARLES M(ONROE),
REV.** Feb. 26, 1857—Feb. 24, 1946 American Congregational minister, religious author, and editor; wrote more than thirty books; a novel, *In His Steps* (1896), is said to have outsold every book except the Bible; edited the New York *Christian Herald* 1920-25, contributing editor from 1925; active Prohibitionist and advocate of world peace; called himself "a Christian Socialist."

Obituary

N Y Times p12 F 25 '46 por

SHELDON, EDWARD (BREWSTER)
Feb. 4, 1886—Apr. 1, 1946 American playwright, known for the "color, charm, elemental passion and extraordinary instinct for the theater" of his plays; greatest success with *Romance* (1913); his fourteen works include *Salvation Nell* (1908), and in collaboration, *Lulu Belle* (1926), *Dishonored Lady* (1930); while blind and partially paralyzed for more than twenty years was friend and adviser to important figures in the theater.

Obituary

N Y Times p7 Ap 2 '46 por

SHIDEHARA, KIJURO, BARON (shē'dĕ-hä"rä kē'jōō-rō) Aug. 11, 1872- Japanese Government official
Address: Tokyo

To guide the Japanese in the work of reconstruction during the first phase of the occupation after World War II, and particularly until a representative Diet could be duly elected, Emperor Hirohito in October 1945 recalled from his retirement to be Prime Minister the aging Baron Kijuro Shidehara, former Foreign Minister and one-time Japanese Ambassador to the United States. The appointment was regarded in some quarters with approval, in others with disapproval—"because he paid only lip service to democratic principles"—while the New York *Sun* reminded its readers that Shidehara was perhaps as liberal a Japanese as one could find and that in any case it was General MacArthur, and not either Hirohito or his Prime Minister, who was in control. Technically he held the office until April 22, 1946, twelve days after Japan's first free elections had resulted in no clear majority for any party. He then resigned, together with his Cabinet. Thereafter he was acting Premier until a new Government was formed by Shigeru Yoshida '46 on May 22, when he was retained as Vice-Premier.

Born in Osaka on August 11, 1872, Kijuro Shidehara was educated to be a lawyer, graduating from the Law College of Tokyo Imperial University in 1895. His interest in, and very healthy respect for, the United States—which early resulted in his becoming known as "a very good friend of the United States"—was, according to Delos Lovelace of the New York *Sun*, acquired at about the same time from Henry Denison, "an odd, able Vermont Yankee in our consular service." Shidehara served his government first in the Agriculture and Commerce Department. Then, in 1899 he entered the Japanese consular service with a post at Chemulpho in Korea, a Japanese treaty port and the port for Seoul, capital of the country. Later that year he was transferred to the Japanese London consulate, and in succeeding years to consulates in Antwerp and other cities. In 1911 he was secretary at the Head Office; in 1912, counselor to the Japanese Embassy in Washington; in early 1914, counselor to the Japanese Embassy in London; in 1914-15, Japanese Minister to the Netherlands.

Shidehara received his first high office in the Japanese home Government in 1915 when he was appointed Vice-Minister of Foreign Affairs in the Japanese Cabinet. In 1919 he was again in the diplomatic service, as Japanese Ambassador to the United States, a post which he continued to occupy for three years. By 1920 his services had earned him a baronetcy. As Ambassador to the United States he was a prominent member of the Japanese delegation to the Washington Naval Disarmament Conference (1921-22). That resulted in, among other treaties, a three-power pact guaranteeing the maintenance of the status quo in regard to naval bases and fortifications in the western Pacific and a nine-power pact guaranteeing the independence and territorial integrity of China, both of which were signed by Japan.

Between 1924 and 1931 Shidehara was Minister of Foreign Affairs in six of the seven Japanese governments; and in 1925 he was also a member of the House of Peers. He came to office in the coalition ministry of Viscount Takaaki Kato (Kenseikai party) on June 11, 1924, and subsequently retained his portfolio when a reorganization of the Cabinet replaced members of the Seiyukai party because of their opposition to Kato's financial program. With the formation of a new cabinet under Reijiro Wakatsuki in January 1926, Shidehara was reappointed to his post, and in June of that year he survived another Cabinet reorganization. In the spring of 1927, however, the Wakatsuki Cabinet's inability to cope with the financial crisis and the resulting panic induced by the failure of several large business houses and banks—including the Suzuki Company, Ltd., which, it was estimated, conducted approximately one quarter of the foreign trade of Japan—forced that ministry to resign, and Shidehara went out with it.

The Japanese statesman held no portfolio in the succeeding ministry of Baron Tanaka, but returned to the Foreign Affairs post in July 1929 in the Cabinet of Premier Yuko Hamaguchi, leader of the Minseito or Liberal party, who, records the *New International Year Book,* gave Japan its first real party ministry. Hamaguchi, whose administration was punctuated by controversy over ratification, which he supported, of the London Naval Treaty drafted at the London Conference of 1930, remained in office technically until April 14, 1931, when he yielded to opposition demands for his resignation. Having been severely wounded, however, on November 14, 1930, in an assassination attempt by a member of a reactionary patriotic society opposed to the London Naval Treaty, he had been replaced by Foreign Minister Shidehara as acting Prime Minister, and his resignation in April was the direct result of his inability to resume the reins of Government. Hamaguchi's resignation brought Baron Reijiro Wakatsuki once more to the head of a Minseito Government, with Shidehara again as his Minister of Foreign Affairs, during the period of increasing Sino-Japanese tension over Manchuria immediately preceding the second Sino-Japanese war.

Throughout the summer of 1931 Foreign Minister Shidehara continued negotiations to effect a peaceful settlement of the Japanese claims in Manchuria; but, "apparently without consulting the Tokyo Government," reports the *New International Year Book*, Japanese military leaders in Manchuria on September 19 "launched a carefully planned offensive covering the whole zone of the South Manchuria Railroad," the focus of dispute. The new Sino-Japanese crisis had been brewing for some years, fostered by a growing Chinese nationalist sentiment, nurtured in its turn by, and looking with suspicion upon, Japanese activities in Manchuria. These were a steady expansion of economic spheres and gradual acquisition by purchase and other methods of land within Japanese treaty jurisdiction. Along with other incidents in the summer of 1931, trouble arose over Chinese plans to construct new railways and ports which the Japanese feared would cut into their revenues from the lucrative South Manchuria Railroad, acquired from Russia by the Treaty of Portsmouth in 1905.

The Minseito or so-called "liberal" group (actually moderate rather than liberal in the Western sense), it is pointed out by students of Japanese history, were by no means opposed to this economic penetration of Chinese territory: they differed with the militarists only concerning the means, the use of force, to accomplish their purpose, Japanese expansion. Especially, it is said, was this true of Shidehara, whose name is frequently given to this policy of peaceful economic imperialism, and who, it is further pointed out, is married to a daughter of the house of Iwasaki, which controls the wide-spread Mitsubishi interests. Within a few months of the opening of hostilities all of Manchuria had been brought under Japanese control by the militarist forces, while in Tokyo the Government, in line with aroused Japanese feeling, felt itself obliged to condone the aggression which it could not curb. Nevertheless, observers say, when the Wakatsuki ministry finally fell on December 12, 1931, to be succeeded by a Government more sympathetic to militarist policies, it succumbed at least as much to internal political troubles as to repercussions from the Manchurian situation. The date marked the beginning of Shidehara's fourteen years of absence from the political

BARON KIJURO SHIDEHARA

scene, which he is said to have spent mostly with his law books and during much of which he seems to have been fearful of assassination by the militarists.

On October 6, 1945, Shidehara was summoned from his retirement by Emperor Hirohito to form an interim cabinet to succeed that of Prince Higashi-Kuni until the first postwar general elections could be held. The third choice for the position (a reorganized Higashi-Kuni or a Shigeru Yoshida Cabinet having been suggested), he was said to meet the need for a man with political and administrative ability, of liberal views, and with considerable acquaintance with the United States. Informed American observers, however, recalling his record as Foreign Minister, thought the appointment only a slight improvement; the newly liberated Japanese press soon became veiledly critical, the Russian press openly so. Shidehara's first conference with American newsmen upheld these judgments, when he set forth an eight-point reform program designed to establish a more democratic government in Japan, but at the same time dodged the issues of economic reorganization of the Zaibatsu and a constitutional convention, said he saw no reason for abolition of the Emperor as the divine head of the Japanese state, objected to the suppression of State Shintoism (the ideological basis for Japanese totalitarianism and imperialism), and traced the Pearl Harbor attack to United States pressure on Japan because of the Japanese penetration into China in and after 1931.

Until early January 1946 Shidehara more or less followed what the outspoken Japanese newspapers referred to as a "do-nothing" policy. Then, on January 4 a new MacArthur directive excluding ultra-nationalists from public office, which affected the majority of Shidehara's ministers, precipitated a Cabinet crisis. When the situation was finally resolved—after the min-

SHIDEHARA, KIJURO, BARON—*Cont.*

isters concerned had spent ten fruitless days maneuvering to retain their positions and General MacArthur had been forced to intervene to prevent Shidehara from resigning—a new spirit seemed to have taken hold of the reorganized Cabinet. On January 20 the Government announced severe penalties for farmers withholding their officially set grain quotas under the price-fixing program. On January 29, after three weeks of indecision, it decreed that candidates for the coming election would be screened by the Government. In February it inaugurated strong measures to halt the growing inflation and ordered the cessation of civilian employment discrimination against returning soldiers, who were barred from official positions. On March 6 it published the proposed revolutionary constitution, which had MacArthur's "full approval" and which, as summarized by *Facts on File,* "renounces war 'forever,' prohibits maintenance of an army, navy or air force, limits the Emperor's powers to those of a constitutional monarch, establishes a 'Bill of Rights,' substitutes an elective 'House of Councilors' for the House of Peers in a bicameral Diet, and creates a strong supreme court." Four days later, reported Lindesay Parrott to the New York *Times,* Shidehara, again "interpreting" the terms of the January 4 directive, "ordered a purge of Japanese intellectuals as well as businessmen in private life or public capacities who assisted the Empire's aggression or financed propaganda in its favor."

On April 10 the Japanese held their first postwar elections, returning 139 Liberals, 92 Social Democrats, 91 Progressives, 16 Cooperatives, 5 Communists, 84 independents, and 38 members of other minor parties for a slightly Right-of-center Diet. Since no party had obtained a majority, a period of political maneuvering, during which Shidehara and his supporters attempted to keep control of the Government, followed. But on April 22, having been unable to obtain sufficient support to remain as a coalition leader and criticized by almost all factions, Shidehara handed in his resignation. Until May 22, when the new Cabinet of Premier Shigeru Yoshida was finally installed, Shidehara then remained as acting Premier. In the Yoshida Cabinet he became Vice-Premier and was entrusted with the task of guiding the recently drafted constitution through the new legislature.

The gray-haired Vice-Premier is a slight man, no longer robust in health as he once was, "with full lips a little withered under a white mustache." Although reportedly a little unsure of himself in his latest role, Shidehara, says Delos Lovelace, "was long noted for his prompt and witty repartee, his ability to floor an opponent with a right upper-quip." He is one of the few Japanese who really know English well: it is said that when he was foreign minister, believing English a subtler language with more varied shades of meaning, he would prepare his formal speeches to the Diet in English, then recast them into Japanese.

References

N Y Herald Tribune p1,6 O 7 '45
N Y Sun p2 O 8 '45
Columbia Encyclopedia (1935)
International Who's Who, 1945-46
Japan Year Book, 1930
Japan-Manchukuo Year Book, 1938

SHONE, TERENCE ALLEN Sept. 4, 1894- British Government official

Address: c/o Foreign Office, London

Acting upon a decision taken in June 1945, the British Government on September 18, 1946, announced the appointment of the first High Commissioner to represent United Kingdom interests in India. The man chosen was career diplomat Terence Allen Shone, Britain's envoy to Syria and Lebanon, who earlier had served in the British legations in Cairo, Belgrade, and Berne. The appointment was received as another proof that Indian independence was near, "just at a time," wrote Peter Lyne, Parliamentary correspondent of the *Christian Science Monitor,* "when British 'imperialism' seems to be the cause of another of those periodic world stirrings-up."

When he went to take up his new post in India early in November 1946, Terence Allen Shone was returning to the country which he had left as a child of one year. He was born in Simla, in the foothills of the Himalayas, in northern India, on September 4, 1894, the only son of Janet (FitzGibbon) Shone and the late Lieutenant-General Sir William Shone of the Royal Engineers. On his mother's side he was a grandson of the Irish wit Lord Justice Gerald FitzGibbon. Shone was educated at the English public school of Winchester, where he was an exhibitioner, or scholarship student; and for a year he attended University College, Oxford. But World War I broke out in the middle of his university course, and in August 1914 he joined the Army's Hampshire Regiment, serving as a captain with the 10th Battalion at Gallipoli. There he was wounded in August 1915. Subsequently, he was transferred to the Intelligence Corps, with which he served in Belgium, Italy, and France. He had been mentioned in dispatches.

Following his discharge from the Army, Shone took the examination for the diplomatic service, and on September 8, 1919, was given the rank of third secretary. Twelve days later he received a civil service certificate and was appointed to the British Legation at Lisbon, Portugal. There he served for two years, during the second, from December 15, 1920, under the higher designation of second secretary. Then, on December 10, 1921, he was transferred to the Foreign Office in London, where he ranked as a second secretary for the next six years. Promoted to first secretary on December 4, 1927, on December 16 he was transferred to Oslo and served in the Norwegian capital until September 1928. Between September 1, 1928, and April 14, 1933, when he was again assigned to the Foreign Office, Shone was stationed in the British Embassy in Washington, as Head of Chancery under Ambassadors Sir

Esme (later Lord) Howard and Sir Ronald Lindsay, succeeding Sir Ronald Ian Campbell in this position.

From Washington the diplomat returned to London, to remain in the Foreign Office again until January 24, 1935, when he took up his assignment as chargé d'affaires in Berne. And from the Swiss capital he was transferred, two years later, on November 28, 1936, to Belgrade, Yugoslavia, where he remained until March 1940, serving as chargé d'affaires part of the time and in other capacities. These five years, immediately preceding, and including the first year of, World War II, were a trying period in the history of those two countries. In 1935 and 1936 Switzerland was wrestling with the problem of preserving her democratic institutions and her neutrality while in the grip of continued economic depression and in constant fear of the imminence of a war which would see Nazi Germany violating her territorial integrity to approach Paris from south of France's eastern frontier defenses. In 1937, 1938, and 1939, Yugoslavia was beset by one internal crisis after another, consequent upon the continuance until early 1939 of the minority dictatorship of Premier Milan Stoyadinovitch, the agitation of the Croatian peoples for autonomy, the primarily successful attempt of Hitler to gain a stranglehold on the Yugoslavian economy, and the British and French attempts to break that hold.

When on March 4, 1940, Shone was promoted to acting counselor (he had been given the personal rank of acting counselor on November 20, 1939, while still in Belgrade) and assigned as Minister Plenipotentiary to the Egyptian Government in Cairo, under Ambassador Sir Miles Lampson (now Lord Killearn), he found that it was an exchange of one location in the midst of unrest for another. For Egypt, predominantly anti-British but in the path of Italian armies in North Africa, was finding herself unable to come to a decision about declaring war against the Axis powers, and this proved a major complication in her internal affairs during the next four years. Pleading the ineffectualness of her resources and her people's overwhelming objection to involvement, however, she managed to resist the pressure brought by the British, merely ending relations with the Axis nations shortly after each declared war on the Allies. Not until February 24, 1945, did she take positive action. One indication of what Shone had to cope with while his Government's representative in Cairo was given by Joseph G. Harrison of the *Christian Science Monitor* in June 1944 when, discussing the proposed Arab union, he wrote: "Today Egypt manages to limp along with the help of vast sums of Allied money. Yet whenever the Government gets into trouble, its spokesmen immediately set up a terrific shout that it can do nothing because its hands are tied by a foreign power, meaning the British."

While still at Cairo, Shone, who had been promoted to the rank of counselor on March 4, 1942, had been called upon to handle the delicate situation arising from the assassination by terrorists in the streets of Cairo of Lord Moyne, British Resident Minister in the Mid-

British Official Photo.

TERENCE ALLEN SHONE

dle East, on November 6, 1944. When on December 22, 1944, Shone was made Envoy Extraordinary and Minister Plenipotentiary to the Governments of Syria and Lebanon, he was plunged into the crisis consequent upon Syrian-Lebanese attempts to gain independence from France. Syria and Lebanon, assigned as mandates to France by the League of Nations after World War I, had already been granted full recognition as independent states by Britain, the United States, and Russia. France, however, had refused to surrender such control as she considered necessary to protect her interests in the region, and this Syria and Lebanon regarded as an infringement of their sovereignty. In this situation Shone's predecessor, Major General Edward Spears, had sided with Beirut and Damascus against France, although without the full approval of the Foreign Office, and his replacement by Shone was said at the time to mark a modification in the British attitude toward France's claims.

Although, during the first few months of Shone's residence at the Legation, negotiations between France and the Levantine states had dragged on without serious incident, late in May 1945 the landing of additional French troops, regarded by Syria and Lebanon as a show of strength to enforce French demands, caused the Levantine states to break off the talks in progress. A general strike was followed in a few days by serious fighting, and on May 31, after other measures had failed, Prime Minister Churchill [42] instructed British troops to intervene to restore order while at the same time sending a sharp reprimand to General Charles de Gaulle [40] of France. Later this action nearly precipitated another crisis when France still refused to withdraw her troops and Britain insisted that hers had to remain to forestall any renewal of the trouble. But on December 13, 1945, Britain and France

SHONE, TERENCE ALLEN—*Continued*

signed a pact agreeing to the simultaneous regrouping and ultimate withdrawal of both their troops from the Levant and in March 1946, after Syria and Lebanon had appealed to the United Nations Security Council to speed the process, began to carry out their commitments. By April 30 British and French troops had completely evacuated Syria; by June 30 only a small contingent of French troops remained in Lebanon. For the remainder of his appointment Shone represented British interests in the independent nations of Syria and Lebanon, which had been accepted as members in the Arab League.

It was this background as well as the indication the appointment gave of the nearness of Indian independence which occasioned satisfaction in the British and American press when Shone was named Great Britain's first High Commissioner in India on September 18, 1946. The decision to appoint such a representative of the United Kingdom's interests, announced in Parliament on June 14, 1945, had resulted from the recognition that, as India worked her way toward self-government, the Viceroy might be placed in the embarrassing position of being concerned with Indian interests while at the same time being expected to represent the material interests of Great Britain. The new official's functions were described as analogous to those performed by the High Commissioners in the Dominions and as consisting primarily in the maintenance of economic and financial relations between the two countries. One of the most immediate of Shone's tasks, it was pointed out, was to negotiate the clearing of blocked sterling balances resulting from Britain's World War II debt to India. Commented the London *Daily Telegraph* at the time of the appointment: "Those who know Mr. Shone well believe that he will carry out his duties in India quite as successfully as did Sir John Maffey in neutral Dublin during the difficult war years."

Terence Allen Shone was made a Companion of the Order of St. Michael and St. George on January 1, 1943. He has been married to Sophie Marie Andreae since 1927, and the couple have one son, in 1946 a scholarship student at Trinity College, Oxford. The High Commissioner in India is described by the London *Daily Graphic* as "the beau ideal of the diplomat. Tall, dignified, with a touch of austerity in his bearing, his appearance set off by suitably distinguished tailoring, he is as impressive as any novelist or playwright, creating the part, would wish him to be."

References

International Who's Who, 1945-46
Who's Who, 1946

SHORT, WALTER C(AMPBELL) Mar. 30, 1880- Retired United States Army officer; business executive

Address: b. c/o Ford Motor Co., Dallas, Tex.

One of the important figures in perhaps the most controversial episode in American history is Major General Walter C. Short, retired, who was commanding general of the Hawaiian Department at the time of the Japanese attack on Hawaii. Just why the attackers were able to bring devastation at so low a cost to themselves has been under discussion ever since. A large segment of opinion placed the blame exclusively on the immediate commanders (Short and Admiral Husband E. Kimmel[42]). Others divided the blame among most or all of the higher Army and Navy officers concerned, at Pearl Harbor or in the Capital; former isolationists and certain old-line Republicans sought to prove the responsibility of the late President Roosevelt[42] for the disaster; and the blame was placed on the nation as a whole by President Truman[45]. The Roberts'[41] commission in 1942, the official Army investigating board in 1944, and the Congressional investigating committee in 1946 found Short directly responsible for the failure of his defenses; but the elderly general, who had an unblemished record of nearly forty years' service, declared that his conscience was clear and that when all the facts were known he would be vindicated.

Walter Campbell Short was born in Fillmore, Illinois, on March 30, 1880. His parents were Dr. Hiram Spait Short, a physician, and Sarah Minerva (Stokes) Short. Graduated from the University of Illinois with a B.A. in 1901, the doctor's son was appointed a second lieutenant of Infantry that February, but did not accept until March 1902, more than a year later. Reporting for duty in San Francisco that April, he served with the Twenty-fifth Infantry in the Southwest for five years; then, as a first lieutenant, he was ordered to Malabang in the Philippine Islands in the summer of 1907. In early 1908 Short returned to America and joined the Sixteenth Infantry, serving with that regiment in Nebraska and for two years in Alaska. In early 1913, after duty in California, Short became secretary of the School of Musketry (Fort Sill, Oklahoma), and commanded a detachment of the Twelfth Infantry. During this period, in November 1914, the thirty-four-year-old lieutenant was married to Isabel Dean of Oklahoma City, whose father was in the jewelry business. (The Shorts have one son, Walter Dean, an Army officer who served in World War II.)

Rejoining the Sixteenth Infantry in March 1916, Short participated in the punitive expedition against Villa's raiders and was promoted to captain in July 1916. After the United States entrance into World War I, Short had duty as a musketry officer and at an officers' training camp in Georgia, then sailed for France in June 1917. There he taught in the AEF First Division School for several months, and was then assigned to direct the First Corps' automatic weapons school. A few months of instructing at the AEF school was followed in turn by direction of the Second Corps' infantry weapons school. From April to November 1918 Lieutenant Colonel Short was a member of the General Staff training section and "rendered conspicuous service in inspecting and reporting upon front-line conditions pertaining to the work of this section. During the Saint Mihiel and Meuse-Argonne operations of the First Army Corps he efficiently directed the instruction and training of machine-gun units at every available opportunity during rest periods." Short also participated in the Aisne-Marne battle. Later he became assistant chief of staff in charge of the Third Army's training in Germany. There, to quote the citation for his Distinguished Service Medal, "he manifested the same assiduous devotion to duty in organizing schools, conducting necessary inspections, and carrying out the intensive training program."

Returning to the United States in July 1919, Colonel Short joined the faculty of the General Service Schools at Fort Leavenworth, Kansas. That August the thirty-nine-year-old Middle Westerner reverted to his permanent rank of captain, and in July 1920 he was promoted to major. While an instructor, Short himself was graduated from the School of the Line. In the early half of 1921 he served with the Sixth Division in Illinois as assistant chief of staff for operations and supply, and in July of that year he was ordered to Washington as a member of the War Department General Staff.

Short served three years with the Far Eastern Section of the Military Intelligence Division, winning advancement to lieutenant colonel in 1923. His *Employment of Machine Guns* came out in 1922. Next he attended the Army War College (the highest service training), and after graduation in July 1925 left for Puerto Rico to join the Sixty-fifth Infantry in San Juan. From August 1928 to September 1930, Short was again an instructor at the Command and General Staff school at Fort Leavenworth. Then came four years behind a desk as assistant to the chief of the Bureau of Insular Affairs, and in June 1934 Short, by then a colonel, was given a field command—the Sixth Infantry, at Jefferson Barracks, Missouri, which he held until June 1936.

Colonel Short's next orders were to go to the Infantry School (Georgia), as assistant commandant. While there, in December 1936, he was given the single star of a brigadier general. In February 1937 the fifty-six-year-old general was given command of the Second Infantry Brigade at Fort Ontario, New York, and in June 1938 he was transferred to the command of the First Infantry Brigade, at Fort Wadsworth. A month after the outbreak of war in Europe he was ordered to command the First Division, with headquarters at Fort Hamilton. In the vast expansion of 1940, which included selectees, Short was promoted to major general and sent to Columbia, South Carolina, to build up the First Corps. Four months later, on February 8, 1941, Walter Short assumed command of the Hawaiian Department, with the temporary rank of lieutenant general.

Exactly what happened from then until December 7 is clouded by controversy. After what is considered the greatest military disaster in United States history, Short and Admiral Husband E. Kimmel were recalled to Washington, where the former reverted to his permanent rank of major general on December 18. President Roosevelt appointed an investigating committee, headed by Supreme Court

U.S. Army Signal Corps

MAJ. GEN. WALTER C. SHORT (RET.)

Justice Owen J. Roberts, and its fifty-one-page report in January 1942 charged Short and Kimmel with "dereliction of duty" in failing to consult with each other on the imminence of hostilities and the appropriate measures of defense. Despite repeated warnings, said the report, "the Japanese attack was a complete surprise to the commanders and they failed to make suitable dispositions to meet such an attack. Each failed properly to evaluate the seriousness of the situation. These errors of judgment were the effective cause for the success of the attack." At the end of February, rounding out forty years of Army service, the sixty-one-year-old general was retired on three-quarters pay (six thousand dollars a year); and that September he became traffic manager for the Ford '44 Motor Company in Dallas, Texas. His retirement, like Kimmel's, was made on his own application and "without condonation of any offense or prejudice to any future disciplinary action."

From Pearl Harbor on, there were demands in Congress for a court-martial of the two commanders, and both waived the statute of limitations which would have prevented court-martial after a lapse of more than two years. In June 1944 Congress passed legislation calling for an official investigation by the Army and the Navy; Short and Kimmel were among the witnesses who testified at length before each of the two boards. The Army Board, made up of three distinguished generals at or near retirement age, devoted three months to its inquiry, which produced forty-one volumes of testimony and seventy exhibits; it had the help of the Department of Justice and the Truman Senate Committee Investigating the War Effort. Among the facts revealed was that General Short, arriving in Hawaii to command his forty-three thousand troops, had instructions from Chief of Staff George C.

SHORT, WALTER C.—*Continued*

Marshall '40 to end "old Army and Navy feuds"; but that, although his personal relations with Kimmel were cordial, they did not effect Army-Navy liaison. Although the board granted that General Short had faced shortages of personnel and equipment, the verdict was: "Had the equipment and material available been utilized, had there been in existence a detailed plan of operation of the staff and lower echelons, and had sound judgment been exercised in the selection of the alert, the disaster of Pearl Harbor undoubtedly would have been materially mitigated, if not wholly avoided."

The Army report states that Short leaned heavily on an inadequate chief of staff, and the administration of his General Staff was therefore marked by lack of harmony and decision; that he failed to hold periodic conferences with subordinate commanders or to take his second in command into his confidence; and that his relations with his G-2 (Intelligence) were "particularly inadequate in view of then existing tense situation." As was already known, his response to a war warning from General Marshall on November 27, 1941, was confined to an antisabotage alert which actually left the armed forces, particularly the air forces, in a weaker position to defend themselves than if there had been no alert; however, he reported the placing of his command under this alert, and the War Department failed to correct him. After a thorough review of the situation, the report concluded by placing blame on Marshall and War Plans chief Gerow '45 for not keeping Short fully informed and for not investigating the readiness of his command. As for Short, to condense the Board's finding, he failed in his duties to place his command in a state of readiness for war, to attempt or reach an agreement with the Navy leaders to implement joint plans then in existence, to inform himself of the long-distance scouting conducted by the Navy, and to replace inefficient staff officers. In an attached statement Secretary Stimson '40 declared that Short's "error of judgment" was his own, and not excused by circumstances, and that he had received adequate warning.

On November 15, 1945, another Congressional investigation of eight months' duration was begun. As his testimony before preceding groups had been delivered at close meetings, Short made his first public statement regarding the situation at Pearl Harbor before this committee. In his fifteen-hundred-word statement, Short stressed his lack of sufficient information and timely warning from the War Department; Navy officials at Hawaii had assured him they anticipated no surprise attack, while the shipment of unarmed bombers he received shortly before December 7 had seemed to indicate the Army was similarly inapprehensive. Since General Marshall had once before specified the exact type of alert required (an all-out alert called in 1940), Short believed that, in the event of a war crisis, Marshall would again order the type of alert necessary. Short maintained that his equipment would have been inadequate for protecting the fleet even when

properly alerted; the same lack of facilities would have prevented the adequate protection of his own planes as well. The majority report signed by eight of the ten Congressional committee members again placed overshadowing blame for the debacle upon the Army and Navy commands in the Pacific under Short and Kimmel, while both the War and Navy Departments in Washington were also criticized. The report made twenty-five recommendations for organizational reforms in the armed services providing for unity of command and the "scrapping of . . . military shibboleths" which prevent subordinate officers from pressing their views in an emergency.

Short was described by a columnist at the Congressional hearings in November 1945 as "a smallish gray-haired man with a good suntan and a first-class tailor." The retired general is an Officer of the Legion of Honor and a member of Phi Beta Kappa. He belongs to the Army and Navy Club and the Army and Navy Country Club in Washington. Politically, he is a Republican.

Reference

Who's Who in America, 1946-47

SHOULDERS, HARRISON H. Feb. 27, 1886- Physician; medical association official

Address: b. 508 Doctors Bldg., Nashville, Tenn.; h. Belle Meade Blvd., Nashville, Tenn.

The 1946-47 president of the American Medical Association, an organization which was founded in 1847 and which in July 1946 held its ninety-fifth annual convention, is Dr. Harrison H. Shoulders, a surgeon of Nashville, Tennessee. The doctor, in practice for more than thirty years, had served between 1928 and 1945 as member and as speaker of the house of delegates of the A.M.A., becoming president-elect in December 1945. As the A.M.A.'s president for a year, Dr. Shoulders pledged himself to campaigning for a system of private medical prepayment plans to prevent a system of Federal health insurance from being instituted.

Harrison H. Shoulders was born on February 27, 1886, in Whitleyville, Tennessee. He is one of five children (he has three brothers and one sister) of Leonard Hogg and Belle M. (Clark) Shoulders. Both his mother's and father's people had migrated to Tennessee from Virginia, at which time the Clarke branch of the family dropped the "e" from their name. Leonard Hogg Shoulders was a farmer and lumber dealer, and Harrison's early youth was spent on his father's Tennessee farm, situated in a "fine, rural community," where the Shoulders led an "industrious and frugal" existence. Cordell Hull, later Secretary of State, was the circuit judge of the district in which the Shoulders family lived.

The Tennessee-bred youth obtained his early education in a one-room, one-teacher schoolhouse. His teacher, Dr. Shoulders recalls, taught the pupils more than could be found in textbooks, particularly a philosophy of life. After attending a number of private schools, Shoulders, at the age of sixteen, became a student at Potter Bible College, in Bowling Green, Kentucky. He had always intended becoming a doctor despite the fact that he had to overcome many objections to this aim of his. After two years (1902-4) at the Potter Bible College, therefore, he transferred to the Medical College at Tennessee's University of Nashville. He was graduated with the M.D. degree (1909), his scholastic record placing him in the upper third of his class. While at the university he became a member of Kappa Psi, a medical fraternity.

In that year, 1909, Dr. Shoulders began his medical work as an interne in St. Thomas Hospital in Nashville. Except for a four-year period from 1917 to 1921, the physician has been established in this city. He left St. Thomas Hospital in January 1910 to become house surgeon at the Forts Infirmary, remaining in this post through a part of 1912. Then, for five years Dr. Shoulders served in a public capacity as assistant secretary and executive officer of the Tennessee Department of Health. When the United States entered World War I, the physician was commissioned a captain in the United States Army Medical Corps; and after duty overseas and in the United States Army of Occupation, he received his discharge late in August 1919. At this period in his career Dr. Shoulders returned to medical school for postgraduate study, first at Cornell University Medical College and next at the New York Post Graduate Hospital. Positions as resident surgeon at St. Luke's Hospital, and a year later as house surgeon at the Hospital for the Ruptured and Crippled, both in New York, followed. In the fall of 1921 Dr. Shoulders returned to Nashville.

While occupied with his surgical practice, Dr. Shoulders was engaged in activities related to his calling. In 1927 the surgeon was made president of the Nashville Academy of Medicine. The following year he became secretary of the Tennessee State Medical Association and editor of its *Journal*. In these posts he served until 1945. Besides writing numerous editorials for the Tennessee State Medical Association *Journal*, Dr. Shoulders has contributed a number of articles to periodicals such as the American Medical Association *Bulletin*, and the journals of the Kansas, Georgia, and Kentucky Medical Associations. He is the author, too, of the article, "A New Stitch for Uses in Partial Gastrectomy," which was published in the November 1944 issue of *Surgery, Gynecology, and Obstetrics,* an international magazine. Dr. Shoulders, in addition, has been connected with the Nashville General Hospital as chief of the surgical service and with the Vanderbilt University and Protestant hospitals as staff member. Medical education, too, is among the Southern doctor's activities: he is assistant clinical professor in the surgical department of Vanderbilt University. Dr. Shoulders belongs to the Southern Medical Association, is a fellow of the American Medical Association and of the American College of Surgeons, and is certified as a member of the founders group by the American Board of Surgery. In 1940 he served as president of the Nashville Surgical Society.

HARRISON H. SHOULDERS

Meanwhile, Dr. Shoulders participated, in administrative capacities, in the American Medical Association which represents one hundred and twenty-five thousand doctors throughout the United States. For ten years Dr. Shoulders was a member of the American Medical Association's house of delegates, and from 1938 to 1945 he acted as speaker of the house. Chosen president-elect, to take office at the A.M.A.'s next annual convention, Dr. Shoulders early in July 1946 assumed his new role in the association.

At the ninety-fifth annual convention of the American Medical Association held in San Francisco, over which Dr. Shoulders presided, most of the significant policy for the A.M.A. members was adopted at executive sessions. In the open sessions, however, the American Medical Association's board of trustees approved a reorganization of the association's central office. This reorganization includes provisions for the appointment by the board of trustees of an economist to head the bureau of medical economics, and for the selection of an executive assistant in the headquarters office to have charge of a division for coordinating and servicing the various councils and bureaus of the association in their relations with the medical profession and the public.

Confronting Dr. Shoulders and the delegates was the issue of health insurance. The American Medical Association sponsored the "associated medical care plans, a national nonprofit organization which includes all State and local nonprofit medical care plans it has approved for minimum standards of service." Designed to furnish medical care to all at a cost within each individual's ability to pay, this private, voluntary health plan would provide prepaid medical treatment, all medical costs and the physicians' fees being paid out of "health-insurance premiums." (Presumably, *Newsweek* stated, the economist of the association's bu-

SHOULDERS, HARRISON H.—*Continued*

reau of medical economics will direct the furthering of A.M.A.'s plan "for voluntary. . . medical care.") As competitor to A.M.A.'s program is the Government-sponsored compulsory health program as embodied in the Wagner[41]-Murray[44]-Dingell bill, which, if passed, would afford "medical, surgical, hospital, and dental care for . . . citizens, including dependents of wage earners, under the administration of the Surgeon General of the United States Public Health Service."

In his addresses to the convention delegates, Dr. Harrison H. Shoulders condemned Government participation in a health program as a violation of the fundamental principles of the medical profession. "Political crackpots, the yearners for political power, the enemies of freedom, and the importers of alien philosophies of government find favorable opportunities for their most strenuous activities" in reconstruction periods like the one through which the United States is passing, Dr. Shoulders asserted. Campaigns for socialized medicine, he believed, were the work of these individuals. The A.M.A. house of delegates did, however, adopt a resolution supporting the Veterans Administration program directed by Generals Omar N. Bradley[43] and Paul R. Hawley[46], and Dr. Shoulders admitted in an interview given to Albert Deutsch of *PM* (July 5, 1946) that the Veterans Administration medical and hospital program was free of political influence. But he remained opposed, he said, to other Government-operated medical programs, maintaining that the United States Public Health Service was "neglecting some of its public health duties" to take part in political activities.

The blue-eyed, gray-haired Nashville surgeon, who is known to be jolly and gregarious, is almost six feet in height and weighs 196 pounds. He raises Tennessee walking horses (they are like him, Dr. Shoulders has said, "slow-gaited and dependable"), and his favorite sport is riding them. He is an independent in politics, and a member of the Belle Meade Country Club (Nashville), and of the Masons (Knight Templar and Shriner). Some time ago Dr. Shoulders also served as president of the Exchange Club, a Nashville civic organization. The A.M.A. president and his wife, the former Virginia Swiggart, to whom he was married in December 1922, are the parents of a son and two daughters, Harrison H., Jr., Virginia Hale, and Mary Swiggart.

References

PM p16 Jl 5 '46
Directory of Medical Specialists, 1942
The Southerner, 1945
Who's Who in America, 1946-47

SHREVE, R(ICHMOND) H(AROLD) (shrēv) June 25, 1877—Sept. 10, 1946 Architect; senior member of the firm which designed the Empire State Building and many other commercial buildings, as well as housing projects and dormitories and academic buildings; president of the American Institute of Archi-

tects, 1941-43. See *Current Biography* 1945 Yearbook.

Obituary

N Y Times p7 S 11 '46 por

SIMON, CHARLIE MAY Aug. 17, 1897- Author

Address: b. c/o E. P. Dutton & Company, 286 4th Ave., New York; h. Johnswood, Route 5, Box 435, Little Rock, Ark.

Charlie May Simon, author of juvenile books which have had a warm reception from critics and librarians alike, writes for the most part of the Arkansas mountain country. Critics see nothing artificial about her regionalism: it is the product of her heritage and of working a homestead in the Ozarks, where the author was born and to which she later returned after living for many years in large cities. It was not until 1931 when Charlie May Simon returned to the Arkansas backwoods that she began to write, and since then she has published sixteen books, as of 1946.

Charlie May Hogue was born in Drew County, near Monticello, Arkansas, August 17, 1897. (She was meant to be a Junior, hence her name.) Her father, Charles Wayman Hogue, taught school in the lowlands of Arkansas and there met her mother, Mary Gill. Hogue is the author of *Back Yonder*, an account of his boyhood experiences in the mountains of Arkansas and in 1946, at the age of seventy-six, he completed another book. Of her family background, the author says: "My grandfather Hogue would tell you that I have no notable ancestors. He is right in the sense it is usually meant. All my people were farmers, living close to the land, until my father left Arkansas and moved to Memphis. The Hogues and Gills came when the country was new, and settled in Virginia, and with each generation . . . they pushed on farther West, carving out a home in the wilderness, doing their little bit to build a new country."

At the age of thirteen Charlie May Hogue essayed a long novel and "to her surprise" found it returned with a printed rejection slip. She burned the manuscript and for a long time imagined she was an artist instead of an author. After she had attended the Memphis public schools and had taken a course at the State Teachers College (then called the Normal School), she studied at the Art Institute in Chicago and later under Bourdell at the Grande Chaumière in Paris. There she met and was married to Howard Simon, the artist, in 1926. The marriage was terminated by divorce in 1935.

It was in the depression of the 1930's, when Charlie May Simon was thirty-three, that she began writing again—and met with an instantaneous success that "must have sponged out" the disappointment she had encountered twenty years earlier. This successful effort was made when she went back to the land for a physically blistering three-year struggle to create a home in virgin Ozark country. Squirrel, rabbit, an occasional possum was her fare when

Pinchot

CHARLIE MAY SIMON

she was lucky. She says, "I invented more ways to cook corn meal for our table than I thought possible" when the harsh winter came. Despite the primitiveness of much of the daily living, the ten-mile isolation from store and post office, Charlie May Simon sat down to her dinner of spoon bread and poke greens, wearing an old party dress, and drank her tea from a Limoges cup because, she tells, "We needed the feel of soft silk and thin china and linen, after a twenty-mile hike down hill and up again, with a load of thirty pounds on our backs the hardest half of the way."

During this homesteading, a bank failure consumed her rainy-day hoard, and it was to eat and clothe herself that she wrote an article in the log house at Rocky Crossing. It was accepted immediately by *Scribner's* and a short time later her first book, *Robin on the Mountain*, was published. The New York *Herald Tribune* thought the story "so fresh-spirited, lively and happy that one earnestly recommends it both to children and to their elders looking for illustrative material of life in lesser known parts of our country."

By 1946 Charlie May Simon had published thirteen juvenile books, among them *Teeny Gay* (1936), *Popo's Miracle* (1938), *Bright Morning* (1939), *Roundabout* (1941), and *Younger Brother* (1942). *Joe Mason, Apprentice to Audubon* (1946), her latest juvenile title is her favorite of all the books she has written. The author's art background is reflected in her book, *Art in the New Land: Stories of Some American Artists and Their Work* (1945), a companion volume to her *Lays of the New Land; Stories of Some American Poets and Their Work* (1943). Her homesteading experience is told in *Straw in the Sun* (1945), in 1946 in its third printing. Harry Hansen, reviewing this book in the New York *World-Telegram,* found that the author shared

her experiences with the reader in pages "lit with sunlight." A novel for adults is to be her next book.

John Gould Fletcher (poetry Pulitzer Prizewinner), to whom the author was married in January 1936, says of his wife's writing: "The Ozarks, and through them, the entire pioneering experience of backwoods America, came to her through inheritance—but also because of deliberate choice, after she had lived in many large cities, and even for a time, abroad." The new York *Times* reported: "As always, Mrs. Simon writes of people and places with a warm, true touch, bringing the wilderness alive in unforgettable little scenes." The *New Yorker's* opinion of this regional writer for children is that she is skillful and sympathetic. Librarians have praised her work for children for its realism, content, and style. They have paid her one of the highest compliments a children's author can receive by recommending her books to adult as well as juvenile readers, and as good "reading aloud"

At home, in Little Rock, Mrs. Fletcher can frequently reread Mary Webb and Jane Austen and "best of all," Thoreau's *Walden*. With her husband she pursues their hobbies of travel (just wishful in the war years) and gardening. Mrs. Fletcher says, "We live in a gray stone house overlooking the Arkansas river, with ten acres of pine woods. We have chosen to live where we have our roots."

References

Simon, C. M. Straw in the Sun (1945)
Who's Who in America, 1946-47

SINCLAIR, JO July 1, 1913- Author
Address: b. c/o Harper & Brothers, 49 E. 33d St., New York; h. 3513 Shannon Rd., Cleveland Heights, Cleveland, Ohio

Since 1922 the publishing house of Harper and Brothers has conducted a biennial prize contest for the novel which, in the opinion of the judges, offers the best study of some aspect of American life. The 1946 award of ten thousand dollars went to a young Cleveland woman, Jo Sinclair, for her first novel, *Wasteland*. One of seven hundred entrants, she had sent in her manuscript only a few days before the close of the competition. When she learned that her novel had been accepted for publication she felt that she had at last achieved the goal toward which she had been working for ten years.

Jo Sinclair is the pen name of Brooklynborn Ruth Seid. The fifth child and third daughter of Jewish immigrants, she was born July 1, 1913, a few years after her parents Ida (Kravetsky) and Nathan Seid had come from Russia to the United States. When she was three years old the family moved to Cleveland. But the poverty the Seids sought to escape in Brooklyn followed them to their new home. Although the girl knew she would have to become a breadwinner at an early age, she always knew she wanted to write. At the John Hay High School she studied shorthand and bookkeeping, but soon dropped both subjects. All she ever got out of the commercial course, she

Geoffrey Landesman

JO SINCLAIR

says, was typewriting. "I went straight for English and journalism," she told a reporter. She also edited the school newspaper and was valedictorian of her class.

In July 1930 the seventeen-year-old girl found her first job as a clerk-typist. Hating the work which seemed humdrum to her, she found a respite from it in a night course in playwriting at Cleveland College. The wave of unemployment which swept over the United States during the depression of the thirties forced the girl and her family to accept relief. Soon she was placed on a WPA project. The humiliation of this experience Jo Sinclair has described in an early writing. "I became gradually, in my own eyes, one of these same unemployables," as she called those on the projects. When she was in a room with people and the conversation turned to jobs she kept shamefacedly silent. "So run the fears, like little fierce wolves, from door to door of the heart. Fears get into you and sap the blood and weaken the tissue of independence." During the five years she spent on the WPA she did writing, editing, and historical research in the "past local glories" of Ohio. Later she became an editor of the Foreign Language Newspaper Digest project, which abstracted and recorded the history of Cleveland's many new immigrant groups. As employment came to many with America's preparation for war, a sixteen-dollar-a-week job in a bookbindery gave the girl a chance to get back into that world which, as she wrote, "for so desperately long a time, seemed to me mythical."

During the WPA years Jo Sinclair had been writing constantly in her spare time. With an affinity for those who suffer she wrote of human beings ground down by want, fear, and hate. Finally, in 1938, her first paid story appeared in the January issue of Esquire. The year 1938 was, in fact, a fortunate year for Jo Sinclair. Two of her articles and stories

appeared in the New Masses, a third in the magazine Ken, and a fourth in the Coronet. Between acceptances, however, rejection slips were plentiful. Then a Cleveland benefactor, learning of her talents, arranged to subsidize her for a year. Five of the ten dollars a week Miss Sinclair received she gave to her family, with whom she lived. Occasionally her sisters and brothers helped her, too, and friends supplied her with notebooks, cigarettes, stamps, and concert tickets. Miss Sinclair insists that she "didn't suffer a minute, culturally, physically, mentally or any other way." For twelve months she worked steadily on her first novel, and short stories which did not seem to sell. Dissatisfied with her own work she began a second novel with equally unsatisfactory results. At the end of the year she thanked her patron and apologized for her seeming lack of progress. "I'm sorry I don't have several books. I hope to some day." In 1941 she obtained a publicity job in the Cleveland office of the Red Cross. During the four years she remained there she extracted as much time as she could for her own work.

The 1941 spring issue of Common Ground published her "Red Necktie," a story the New York Post's Clip Boutell considers one of her best. Included in the anthology This Way to Unity, "Red Necktie" describes the anxiety of a lonely old immigrant who dreads the recurrence of the nightmare of beatings and pogroms. In that same year her description of the emotions of a former WPA worker now in private industry appeared in Harper's Magazine (1942). Crisis also published one of her writings. Later, Common Ground published two other articles by Miss Sinclair: "I, Too, Sing America" (1942) tells of the contributions made to the dance, music, art and the theatre by the American Negro under the auspices of the Karamu Settlement House in Cleveland; "Freedom's Blood" (1944) describes the blood bank established by the different minority groups at the Cleveland Chapter of the American Red Cross. She also contributed to the Chicago Jewish Forum (1945-46), and the Cleveland College Skyline. Her poetry and short stories have appeared in the Jewish Spectator (1942, 1946), Crossroad (1939-40), and the Villager (1946). A short play, Folk Song, America, was produced at Cleveland College in May 1940, and her series of four one-half hour plays was broadcast over a Cleveland radio station in 1942. Anthologies in which her writings have been included are Theme and Variation in the Short Story (1938), Of the People (1942), America in Literature (1944), and Cross Section (1946).

Wasteland, a novel dealing with the problems of second generation Americans of Russian Jewish origin, made its appearance in February 1946 and became the Book Find Club selection for June. Miss Sinclair believes the story of the protagonist, who is ashamed of his people, is the story of countless others who live in the wasteland of the mind. In general, the critics were responsive to the problem presented in Wasteland although some felt that its author had not entirely overcome her youthfulness as a writer. The consensus of opinion as indicated by Lewis Gannett of the New York *Herald Tribune* was: "*Wasteland* is not the most distinguished novel to win the Harper Prize, but it has a kind of good-apple soundness." The writer Richard Wright expressed the belief that the book "lifts itself easily above the current pious hopes and delusions that claim so much of our fiction. . . .In her refusal to be bound by the traditional lumber of novel-building, Miss Sinclair has demonstrated her independence as an artist." To this Thomas Sugrue of the *Herald Tribune Books* added: "Miss Sinclair chose difficult material and a tricky frame for her plot. She did more than well with both. *Wasteland* is not only a good novel, it is an important expedition into the great continent of American consciousness."

Evidence points to a strong physical resemblance between Jo Sinclair and Debby, the heroine of her novel. The author's features are full, and in repose her blue eyes are described as brooding and expressive of sympathetic understanding. Slightly under medium height, with blond hair cut severely short, she gives the impression of being able to "swing a mean golf stick." She is fond of tennis, the theater, and classical music. One interviewer mentioned that she blushes whenever she is singled out as a Harper Prize winner.

References

Harper 184:161-3 Ja '42
N Y Post p24 Ja 29 '46 por
PM p5 F 3 '46 por

SINCLAIR, MAY 1865(?)—Nov. 14, 1946 British novelist, first achieved success in 1904 with *The Divine Fire*; other works include *The Three Sisters* (1914) and *Anne Severn and the Fieldings* (1922); early contributed to the "stream of consciousness" school in *Mary Olivier* (1919); author of philosophical essays and books of poetry.

Obituary

N Y Times p23 N 15 '46 por

SKIDMORE, HUBERT STANDISH Apr. 11, 1909—Feb. 2, 1946 American novelist, Army lieutenant; his six novels deal with his native Blue Ridge countryside, the first, *I Will Lift Up Mine Eyes* winning the 1935 Avery Hopwood Prize.

Obituary

N Y Times p4 F 4 '46

SMALL, JOHN D(AVIS) Oct. 11, 1893- United States Government official; business executive

Address: b. Civilian Production Administration, Social Security Bldg., Washington, D.C.; Publicker Alcohol and Chemical Sales Corp., 105 W. Madison St., Chicago; h. 5 W. Blackthorn St., Chevy Chase, Md.

The task of guiding the reconversion of American industry from a wartime to a peacetime basis, as Civilian Production Administrator, was given by President Truman [45] to Commodore John D. Small in November 1945.

Although an agency which functioned for little more than a year, CPA had the residual powers of the potent War Production Board, which it superseded. In addition to the potential effect on national productivity and the standard of living, the policies of the Administrator may be of permanent importance in determining which of those residual powers will be eliminated from the frame of government and which retained by transference to permanent agencies.

John Davis Small was born in Palestine, Texas, on October 11, 1893. His parents were John Clay and Louise Moran (Lynch) Small. The boy attended Kemper Military Academy at Boonville, Missouri, then obtained an appointment to the United States Naval Academy. Graduated from Annapolis in 1915, Small began an eleven-year career as a naval officer, which brought him the eventual rank of lieutenant commander. In 1920 he received his M.S. from Columbia University in New York. Small served under future Fleet Admiral King [42] as engineer officer of Atlantic Fleet submarines, and later served in the same capacity with the Pacific Fleet. The young man also completed flight training and was given command of a squadron of the early VO-6 observation planes, attached to Atlantic Fleet battleships.

In 1926 Commander Small left the Navy to enter private industry, becoming executive vice-president of the Dry Ice Corporation of America; and in March 1928, at thirty-four, he was married to Gwendolyn Davis. Four years later Small joined Publicker, Inc., a Philadelphia concern, as its Western manager, with headquarters in Chicago. (Publicker is a distiller of industrial alcohol and dealer in chemicals.) A Naval Reserve officer, in 1942 Small was called to the Navy Department in Washington as deputy director of the Army and Navy Munitions Board. In 1943-44 he was Navy materials control officer and landing craft coordinator. According to a Government release, the fifty-year-old captain was the only senior officer with the first Allied troops to land on the Normandy beaches on D-Day in the first wave at zero hour.

Still a naval reservist on wartime active duty, Captain Small was assigned to the War Production Board with the title of executive officer in October 1944. In April 1945 he was appointed chief of staff to WPB chairman J. A. Krug [44]. Small headed the WPB Committee on Period One, which handled the "tooling up and tuning up for reconversion." The major points of policy decided upon included spreading the cutbacks in war production by industry, to free the most vitally needed production facilities first, and by area, to free manpower where it was most desperately needed. The committee also decided on giving small business "the best possible break on materials." Small and the WPB "chief of operations" also served as Krug's deputies.

Small's promotion to the newly revived rank of commodore went through on November 2, 1945, and on the next day he assumed command of the newly created Civilian Production Administration, which superseded the WPB.

JOHN D. SMALL

The functions of Small's agency were extended beyond the originally planned few months, when production was retarded early in 1946 as a result of strikes and shortages of raw materials. That year CPA undertook the job of using its powers to expand production of scarce items, while limiting use of scarce goods. On December 28, 1945, Small reported that the physical reconversion of industry was virtually complete, but that 1946 production would fall far short of demand. Two serious shortages were in clothing and housing, and Small announced steps to make as much as possible of both available to war veterans. Fabric quotas for the first quarter of the year were to be designated for the production of men's apparel; housing priorities were also to be set up to assure ex-soldiers, sailors, marines, and merchant mariners that half of all available building materials would be used for shelter for them. Much of the other 50 per cent was expected to be "channeled without priorities" to repair work and to essential construction of factories, veterans' hospitals, and school dormitories—provided that at least 60 per cent of the dormitory space was reserved for veterans.

Small guided the CPA through a crippling steel strike in December 1945 and January and February 1946 and a coal strike two months later, which, he estimated, set production back three months. He was criticized by labor when he proposed an emergency act curtailing strikes for six months and by groups interested in housing for his allowing some nonhousing construction to be carried on. In February 1946 he stated, "We stand at the threshold of the greatest prosperity the United States has ever known," and thereafter he maintained his optimism. In June, he was able

to announce that production was near capacity. Controls were lifted in November 1946, and in December, during a second coal strike which threatened to be devastating, Small resigned, leaving the few CPA tasks that remained to the Office of Temporary Controls, a liquidation agency which took over the remaining functions of all the control boards. In his letter of resignation, the administrator told Truman, "Production has been the highest in our peacetime history. For these reasons I believe the industrial transition from war to peace largely behind us." In his final report issued at the end of the year, Small announced that production had reached a new peacetime peak and that employment had topped the wartime level as well as those immediately preceding and following World War II.

Bespectacled Commodore Small is a square-faced man with gray eyes and straight brown hair. He is five feet seven inches tall and weighs one hundred and sixty pounds. He is of the Protestant Episcopal faith and is a member of the Democratic Party. The Texas-born executive has one married daughter, Mrs. Preston Marshall, and two other daughters, Joan and Storm.

Reference
Bsns W 819:8 My 12 '45 (por cover)

SMALL, JOHN HUMPHREY Aug. 29, 1858—July 13, 1946 United States Democratic Representative from North Carolina, 1899-1921; for many years was chairman of the Rivers and Harbors Committee.

Obituary
N Y Times p25 Jl 15 '46

SMITH, LOGAN PEARSALL Oct. 18, 1865—Mar. 2, 1946 American-born British essayist and critic; classicist, considered a foremost English stylist; books include *The Youth of Parnassus* (1895), *Songs and Sonnets* (1909), *The English Language* (1912), *Trivia* (1918), *More Trivia* (1921), *Words and Idioms* (1925), *On Reading Shakespeare* (1933), *Reperusals and Re-collections* (1936), *Unforgotten Years* (1938).

Obituary
N Y Times p45 Mr 3 '46

SNYDER, J(OHN) BUELL July 30, 1879 —Feb. 24, 1946 American legislator and educator; United States Representative from Pennsylvania from 1933; coauthor of Guffey-Snyder Bituminous Coal Act of 1935; known as "father of superhighways"; district manager, the Macmillan Company, 1912-32; founder of Pennsylvania Inter-High School Literary, Debate, and Music League.

Obituary
N Y Times p25 F 25 '46 por

SOCKMAN, RALPH W(ASHINGTON), REV. Oct. 1, 1889- Clergyman

Address: b. Christ Church, Park Ave. and 60th St., New York; h. 830 Park Ave., New York

The Reverend Dr. Ralph W. Sockman became the minister of Christ Church, Methodist, in New York, in 1917. He is the presiding minister as well for the *National Radio Pulpit* of the National Broadcasting Company. Also widely known for his books, essays, and magazine articles on the ethical and moral problems of our day, Dr. Sockman was named one of the six foremost clergymen of all denominations in the United States in a poll conducted by the *Christian Century* in 1941.

An Ohio farm boy, Ralph Washington Sockman was born October 1, 1889, in Mt. Vernon, Ohio, the son of Rigdon Potter and Harriet O. (Ash) Sockman. At twenty-two, with a B.A. degree (1911) from Ohio Wesleyan University, Ralph Sockman came to New York to take graduate work at Columbia University. While a Columbia student, from 1911 to 1913, he was an active member of New York's Madison Avenue Methodist Episcopal Church (now Christ Church), and served as intercollegiate secretary of the YMCA. During these two years of layman's service to his church in New York, Sockman was prompted to enter the ministry. After he received his M.A. degree from Columbia in 1913, he began studies at Union Theological Seminary, where among his instructors was Dr. Harry Emerson Fosdick [40], the minister long associated with the Riverside Church in New York, in whose "liberal footsteps" Sockman was to follow.

When he was graduated from the seminary in 1916, Ralph Sockman was also "graduated" from the congregation to the pulpit of the Madison Avenue Methodist Episcopal Church, becoming associate minister. He continued to study at Columbia, and received his Ph.D. in 1917, with the thesis *The Revival of the Conventual Life in the Church of England in the Nineteenth Century*. The same year that he received his doctorate he became minister of the church, and he has been reappointed by the official board of the church every year thereafter. (Methodist pastorates are assigned for only one year.) Sockman has the unique record of having served more than a quarter of a century in his first parish, the only minister with that distinction in the history of the Methodist church.

The minister early became known for his "tart, epigrammatic" sermons, which included pointed comments on topics of the day. His congregations were always large, and his books, lectures, and radio sermons introduced him to an ever-widening audience. In 1934, after seventeen years in the pulpit, Sockman moved with his congregation to a Byzantine-style church on Park Avenue. The church changed its name to Christ Church, eliminating the denominational Methodist title; its pews were no longer rented to members, but were made available to all visitors. The new church's ornate interior was said to be "a marked de-

REV. RALPH W. SOCKMAN

parture from the staid bareness and simplicity of the old-type Protestant church."

During World War II, Dr. Sockman, who had served since 1928 as chairman of the World Peace Commission of the Methodist Church, declared that the view of churches must "be enlarged by world outlooks and unified by interdenominational programs." One of the most successful of his own programs was the two-day, non-sectarian, non-partisan forum on world affairs held at Christ Church in September 1944. The general theme, "Building a Better World," was discussed at the forum by statesmen of the United States, Europe and Asia; President Franklin Roosevelt, in a letter to Dr. Sockman, praised the timeliness of the sessions. The following year a similar forum was held on the theme "Tomorrow's Challenge."

Dr. Sockman was one of the first to deliver a sermon over the radio. In June 1928, when the National Broadcasting Company was only two years old, he spoke on the *National Radio Forum* from the studios of WEAF. Sixteen other NBC stations also carried his talk. He was an NBC guest speaker until November 1, 1936, when he became the minister for the *National Radio Pulpit* series, on the death of Dr. S. Parkes Cadman, the program's founder. His sermons are now carried regularly from October to May every Sunday morning on fifty stations in the United States and Canada, and before wartime restrictions were transmitted abroad by short wave. By May 1946 Sockman had received almost one and a half million letters from his radio audiences. The letters are usually requests for sermons, but a good proportion have to do with the personal problems of his listeners. They come at the record rate of four thousand each week, *Time* has said, thus enabling the radio minister to get a good view of the current thinking in his nationwide parish.

(Continued next page)

562 CURRENT BIOGRAPHY 1946

SOCKMAN, RALPH W., REV.—*Continued*

The minister's gift for the witty phrase and the incisive comment became known to a reading as well as a listening audience. His earlier books were *Suburbs of Christianity and Other Sermons,* published in 1924, and *Men of the Mysteries* (1927). *Morals of Tomorrow,* which appeared in 1931, attracted considerable comment. Most of the reviewers spoke of the clergyman's "lucid and fascinating style," his "sparkling epigrams." The critic for *Bookman* wrote, "It is not deeply original, being in a good sense a popular presentation of contemporary ethical thought from a well-stocked file of notes." The *Literary Digest,* however, devoted over a page to a discussion of the book, pointing out that "companionate marriage, control of the birth rate, and the right to divorce, so sternly denounced in other quarters, find a strong advocate in [this] militant pastor." As his other books were published Sockman was applauded for his "extraordinary gift of apt illustration." *Parodoxes of Jesus* appeared in 1936, *Recoveries in Religion* in 1938, and *Live For Tomorrow,* a collection of lectures, sermons, and essays, in 1940. The 1940-41 Lyman Beecher lectures which Dr. Sockman delivered at the Yale Divinity School were published in 1942 as *Highway of God.* Of his book *Date With Destiny* (1944) a reviewer for the New York *Herald Tribune* wrote: "Dr. Sockman discusses modern man in the various personal, economic, political, and international aspects of his life. He says the things which one would expect him to say, but says them with exceptional vigor and beauty and with unfailing illumination." *Now To Live,* a compilation of Sockman's radio sermons, chosen on the basis of an evaluation of radio audience response, was published in 1946. *Christian Century* characterized the sermons contained in this book as having the "qualities of directness, moral urgency, clarity . . . and religious positiveness."

Dr. Sockman has lent his name and skill as a speaker for many causes of international importance. He was among the churchmen who appealed to the United States Congress and the President in April 1944 to take steps immediately toward forming an international organization. With other church leaders he led appeals for food for Europe, called for the early establishment of a permanent international office for education, and worked on the National Interfaith Committee of the American Society for Russian Relief. After the war he urged his congregation to work patiently for world cooperation, and warned against "being stampeded into exaggerated suspicions of former allies." Over the radio he preached sermons "in everyday terms" on subjects close to his listeners—among them, "Fears May Be Liars", "How Easy Is Evil?" and "Does It Pay to Be Good?" In July 1946, he visited Russia as one of a seven-member delegation sent by the American Society for Russian Relief to study the distribution of supplies sent to Russia by relief agencies.

The New York minister is a trustee of Drew University, and of Ohio Wesleyan University, a director of the Union Theological Seminary and of the New York Medical College. Since 1936 a member of the New York University Council, the university's governing board, he was named chaplain of N.Y.U. in March 1944. He was president of the Federation of Churches from 1927 to 1929, and president of the Ohio Society of New York from 1940 to 1943. He is a member of Phi Beta Kappa, Delta Sigma Rho, and Phi Delta Theta; and holds honorary degrees from many colleges and universities, among them the degree of L.H.D. from Rollins College and from Washington and Jefferson College, a Litt.D. from Florida Southern, and a D.D. from New York University. His clubs are the Century, Monday, Quill, and Sigma Chi. Dr. Sockman was married in 1916 to Zellah Widmer Endly. They have one daughter, Elizabeth Ash. "Well-groomed, gray-haired Dr. Sockman," reads a *Time* description, "looks like a successful lawyer and talks like the man next door. . . .For Dr. Sockman, radio religion is no substitute for church-going. Says he: 'Religion is like art, or music, or books. The more of it you get, the more you want.'"

References

Lit Digest 117:20 Mr 17 '34 por
Time 47:74+ Ja 21 '46 por
Who's Who in America, 1946-47

STACY, WALTER P(ARKER) Dec. 26, 1884- Judge; labor mediator

Address: b. c/o Supreme Court of North Carolina, Raleigh, N.C.; h. Wilmington, N.C.

Walter P. Stacy, the chief justice of the North Carolina Supreme Court and chairman of the Labor-Management Conference which met in November 1945, is "an old hand at labor relations." Since 1927 he has acted as "neutral arbitrator" in some of the most important labor disputes in the nation. Four Presidents, Coolidge, Hoover [43], Roosevelt [42], and Truman [45], have called upon him to allay industrial-labor friction. Long before he was called upon to officiate at the Washington parley, Stacy had been chosen to perform the role of peacemaker between employees and employers in the railway, steel, and textile industries and in the department store field. He was also appointed to the fact-finding board in the General Motors strike.

A native of North Carolina, Walter Parker Stacy was born the day after Christmas, 1884, to Rosa (Johnson) and the Reverend L. E. Stacy, a Methodist minister, in Ansonville. Young Stacy received both his B.A. (1908) and his law (1909) degrees from the University of North Carolina. Until 1927 his activities, though successful, were local in nature. He practiced law from 1910 to 1916 and served in the state legislature for a short period in 1915. During the summers from 1922 to 1925 he lectured in the Law School of his university, which conferred the degree of LL.D. upon him in 1923. When he was appointed to the vacant post of chief justice of the North Carolina Supreme Court in 1925, he was the youngest man ever to have attained that office. The next year he received the position through election and again in 1934 and in 1942.

The Railway Labor Act of 1926, which created the machinery for arbitrating "double-tracked rows," was indirectly responsible for giving the North Carolinian jurist his first assignment as mediator. As chairman of the United States Board of Mediation, he was called upon to settle a controversy between several Southern railroads and the Brotherhood of Locomotive Engineers. In 1927 President Coolidge appointed him a member of the emergency board set up under the Railway Labor Act to avert a strike of conductors and trainmen on lines west of the Mississippi.

In 1934 Stacy again was given a post as mediator when President Roosevelt appointed him chairman of the National Steel and Textile Relations Board, and during World War II Judge Stacy served in that role with the National Defense Mediation Board, the National Railroad Labor Panel, and the National War Labor Board. As one of a committee of three on a railroad emergency board, Judge Stacy in September 1943 helped to write the majority opinion which favored a four-cent-an-hour or thirty-two-cent-a-day increase in the salaries of some three hundred thousand transportation employees in train and engine service, instead of the 30 per cent or three-dollar-a-day raise they had demanded. In March 1943, as a representative of the public, he was one of a panel of three which unanimously recommended to the National War Labor Board that a union-security agreement be granted the CIO's United Retail and Wholesale Employees Union at four Montgomery Ward stores. The company's anti-union advertising in newspapers throughout the country was cited as a key factor in the decision thus reached.

The Labor-Management Conference of 1945 was called by the President for the purpose of helping the Government alleviate the tense situation which had become aggravated since the close of the war. Labor and management each sent eighteen delegates to the conference. The principal organizations represented were the A.F. of L., the CIO, the United Mine Workers, the railway brotherhoods, the National Association of Manufacturers, and the United States Chamber of Commerce. Representing the public but without power to vote were Secretary of Labor Lewis Schwellenbach '45, Secretary of Commerce Henry Wallace '40 and Judge Stacy as presiding chairman.

With keen interest the press observed the opening of the conference on November 5, 1945, and its actions during its sessions for the succeeding four weeks. According to the Scripps-Howard writer Charles T. Lucey, Judge Stacy opened the proceedings with a short, simple speech delivered "in utmost earnestness," without "fanfare or posies." He told the labor-management leaders, wrote the reporter, that "there comes a time in every man's life when he has an opportunity to rise above the stress of circumstances and take part in the universal opportunity. That time, he said, is now. He spoke of a foundering world and the relationship of this conference to it." The importance of the role Judge Stacy was

WALTER P. STACY

called upon to perform was pointed out by one correspondent in these words: "There are some who see the chairman's job at this conference as mere presiding, but it may be that his function as moderator-without-vote will have full weight as days of wearing sessions unwind."

The agenda of the Labor-Management Conference listed as problems needing settlement: collective bargaining; voluntary arbitration of disputes arising under contracts as well as of those occurring during extension of contracts; fact-finding in case of a disagreement between employees and employers; and the prerogatives of management. Management's proposal that in certain industrial quarrels there be a fifty-day "cooling off" period to enable a fact-finding board to investigate and make recommendations brought a unanimous rejection from the labor delegates. A committee formed by members of both sides at the parley recommended that "collective bargaining should be undertaken promptly in good faith; that conciliation should follow only after a genuine effort had been made to settle differences without a third party." Although it was expected that there would be sharp differences between the two participating factions, arguments occurred within the family of labor as well. John L. Lewis '42, head of the United Mine Workers, and Philip Murray '41, president of the CIO, did not see eye to eye on the matter of determining wage increases. The attitude of the management delegates on the other hand was that there could be no rise in pay unless price increases were permitted.

When the delegates to the conference adjourned on November 30 without having reached any understanding on the matter of wages, bargaining, and the handling of disputes, William Green '42 and Lewis congratulated their chairman for the way he guided the conference through the shoals of disagreement. Judge Stacy's concluding words to the departing

STACY, WALTER P.—*Continued*

conferees were, "Gentlemen, we have come to the close of a chapter of the industrial life of America." Commenting on this statement Mark Sullivan of the New York *Herald Tribune* intimated that Americans were witnessing not only a close of a chapter of their country's industrial life, but also of its entire political and social life as well. "Either Congress will write legislation which makes labor relations workable and thus permits the system of free enterprise and private ownership of industry to continue, or the present condition will continue, and by continuing grow more extreme, reaching finally a stage already beginning to show itself," that is a "paralysis of private industry" which "could have only one ultimate outcome, socialization of industry by an avowedly labor government, such as is now under way in Britain."

Most of the writers for the New York newspapers were frankly disappointed by the failure of the Labor-Management Conference to make a single contribution which would help to break the deadlock then existing between organized labor and industry. John T. Moutoux of *PM* observed that "the paradox of the present conference was that the labor and management delegates, after voting down each other's proposals on the important topics of the agenda, wound up the affair by sweet talk about how nice the other side had been." Joseph A. Loftus of the *Times* believed that the inability of the conference to "produce anything resembling a panacea for the immediate strike problem" could be expected to "give new impetus to demands in Congress for repressive labor legislation."

On December 12, 1945, shortly after the close of the conference, President Truman appointed Judge Stacy to serve on a three-man fact-finding board in the nationwide General Motors strike. The other two were Lloyd Garrison, head of the War Labor Board, and Milton Eisenhower [46], president of Kansas State College and a brother of General Dwight D. Eisenhower [42]. Through its officials the union assured the President of its "cooperation in getting all the facts in the dispute," but the spokesmen of General Motors in Detroit refused to make any comment. As the investigation of the automobile strike proceeded, General Motors made it known that it would refuse to present its case if the board decided that prices and profits were "pertinent issues" involved in the union's demand for a 30 per cent increase. The company did not plead an inability to pay, but rather that prices and profits were its own concern, whereas the union maintained that it was interested in the stabilization of the national economy and therefore deeply concerned about prices. Although observers in Washington had very little hope that the fact-finding committee would meet with success in its undertaking, they had no complaint to make about the men President Truman had chosen to untie the Gordian knot in the automobile industry.

Mrs. Stacy, who is now deceased, was the former Maude de Gran Graff, to whom the jurist was married in 1929. Charles Lucey has described the graying judge: "His suit is somber blue, his plain blue bow tie is not merely conservative but almost reactionary. . . .He chisels out his words carefully, slowly, in a deep voice. . .and handles a gavel with a kind of affection, as any good workman shows respect and fondness for the tools of his trade."

References

N Y Sun p14 N 6 '45
N Y World-Telegram p30 O 26 '45 por
Who's Who in America, 1946-47
Who's Who in Law, 1937

STARR, MARK　Apr. 27, 1894-　Trade union official; educator

Address: b. c/o International Ladies' Garment Workers Union, 1710 Broadway, New York; h. 3953 47th St., Long Island City, N.Y.

A man whose whole life has been "a struggle to learn and teach," Mark Starr, heads the educational department of the International Ladies' Garment Workers Union. He is nationally known among educators for his creative work in the field of adult education. "Few men have proved themselves so able to interest large numbers of citizens in study and discussion," the presidents of the four New York City colleges once said of him in a joint statement.

Mark Starr was born in Shoscombe, in Somersetshire, England, on April 27, 1894, the son of William and Susanna (Padfield) Starr. His father had begun to work at the age of seven, driving crows from a wheat field; Mark began work at thirteen. After he was graduated from St. Julian's National School in Shoscombe in 1907 he became a hod carrier, working 56½ hours a week for four shillings. One shilling was deducted from his first week's salary to pay for the shovel he used for filling the hod with mortar. In the evenings his mother would read aloud, usually from the Bible, to young Mark and to his three sisters and three brothers. Mark thus knew his Bible well enough to teach Sunday school in Shoscombe's United Free Methodist Church for three years. Later he went on to Ruskin, Carlyle, Huxley, and Marx, and always remained "a great one for bookreading."

After carrying hods for a year, fourteen-year-old Mark entered the coal mines in England, where he worked as powder monkey, carting boy, and hewer. For easier work at better pay he followed his brother to the mines at Ynysbwl, Wales. There he learned how to say in Welsh, "Is there work tomorrow?" and "some of the loveliest cuss words you ever heard." He attended night school in 1913 and 1914. Starr had been working in the mines seven years when, in 1915, the Rhondda district of the South Wales Miners' Federation awarded him a two-year scholarship to the Labor College in London. Before he returned to the mines he had written a book, *A Worker Looks at History*, published in 1917, when he was twenty-three. The scholarship was renewed for two years (1919 and 1920) after World War I.

Starr taught economics and social history to the miners of the South Wales Federation in 1920-21. Then he became divisional organizer and lecturer in the British National Council of Labor Colleges, a post he held for seven years. During this time he also taught Esperanto, which he had learned during World War I and about which he has always been enthusiastic—he has urged its use for the United Nations. While a Labor Council executive Starr wrote two more books, *Trade Unionism: Past, Present, and Future* (1923), and *A Worker Looks at Economics* (1925), which, together with his first book were widely used as textbooks in the teaching of labor history and labor problems. He also wrote articles for *The Plebs* and for other labor papers. Twice in these years he was the Labor Party candidate for Parliament from the Wimbledon district.

In 1928 Starr sailed for the United States to teach British labor history and economics at Brookwood Labor College in Katonah, New York. This school, founded in 1921, trained nearly five hundred persons for "responsible positions in labor and social movements" before it closed in 1937. John Dewey once said of it: "The college, more than most institutions of whatever sort, has been truly educational in living up to its efforts to lead students to think —which means, of course, to think for themselves." Starr returned to England in 1930, re-entered the United States on the quota in 1931, and went back to Brookwood. (He applied for citizenship, and in 1937 received his final papers.) Another teacher at Brookwood, Helen G. Norton, of Kansas, became Starr's wife in 1932. He instructed at Brookwood until 1933, and then was appointed its extension director. In addition, for two summers he taught economics, labor history, and economic geography at the Bryn Mawr Summer School for Women Workers.

Mark Starr left Brookwood in January 1935 to accept an appointment as director of the pioneering Educational Department of the International Ladies' Garment Workers Union. Since Starr has been director, I.L.G.W.U. has had over twenty thousand students in some six hundred classes every year. Studies include English, current events, labor history and problems, economics of the garment industry, and consumers' problems, as well as arts and crafts, music, dancing, and athletics. The classes are held in all parts of the United States and in Canada. "Set him down anywhere on a desert island, as Robinson Crusoe was set down," Max Lerner once wrote, "and in no time [Starr] will have persuaded Friday to enroll in an evening class for adult education." In his new post, Starr worked twelve to sixteen hours, six days a week. During the winter, he visited classes every weekday evening from six to eight. He turned out numerous pamphlets, magazine articles, editorials, and reviews, on workers' education and the subject of "teaching the truth about unions." "We measure our success," he said in 1941, "in the growing social awareness of our members and their desire to build up organizations which will help the workers to improve their conditions as consumers in cooperatives, as citizens in an independent political labor party, as well as in their day-to-day trade-union activities. . .[and] in the growing social intelligence of our rank-and-file members."

MARK STARR

Suddenly in April 1943 Mark Starr became the center of a storm of comment in New York. Mass meetings, protests by civic leaders, editorials in the city's major newspapers, and a special investigation ordered by the Mayor, resulted when I.L.G.W.U.'s education director was rejected by New York's Board of Education for a $7,500-a-year post as the city's first director of adult education. Starr was the only one of a hundred candidates to pass all the "grueling examinations" given by the board of superintendents in its two-year search for an adult education director. A college degree, or the equivalent, and graduate work, had originally been stipulated as requirements for the new position. But Starr, who had no degree, was nevertheless the only one recommended by the board of superintendents—it was explained that adult education was a new field in which few schoolmen were expert. The Board of Education, however, rejected Starr. The only explanation came from the board's president Ellsworth Buck who said that he had opposed Starr because of his "long record as a labor protagonist," and that he would have equally opposed a labor antagonist. Immediately prominent New York educators, national and local labor leaders, and civic leaders vigorously protested, and urged that the board reconsider Starr.

Mayor La Guardia's Commissioner of Investigation William B. Herlands reported that Starr was "exceptionally well qualified for the post." Starr himself replied to Buck's accusation that his writings tended "to create class hatred": "If I had not been a radical in the circumstances of my early youth I should have been a moron. I ask to be judged . . . by [the opinions] which I now hold. These are, in brief, that the union-management cooperation developed in wartime should be expanded and made the basis of orderly progress by intelli-

STARR, MARK—*Continued*

gent consent in the solution of our social problems. Further, I regard education as a never-ending process and believe that the schools should become real community centers for all age levels." Under strong public pressure, the board voted to reconsider Starr, but he was rejected by a one-vote majority. The board maintained that Starr did not meet the necessary educational requirements. The Public Education Association declared, "The reactionaries in education . . . are growing dangerously active. . . .To them, Mark Starr, the liberal, is a menace."

The same week that Starr's rejection caused a flurry of editorials, the Office of War Information and the British Ministry of Information invited the I.L.G.W.U. educational leader to visit England to lecture on the cultural and educational work of American labor unions, and to gather information on the development of workers' education in England. Starr was a wartime consultant for the OWI, wrote an OWI text for use in Europe, and was one of ten experts on "some phase of United States wartime living" chosen by OWI to lecture in Britain and answer questions of the people in the fall of 1943. Two years later, Starr again visited London as an adviser to the American delegation attending the United Nations Educational, Scientific and Cultural Organization conference (UNESCO). Returning from six weeks in Japan as labor education consultant to the Military Government, Starr commended General Douglas MacArthur for his recognition of trade unions. In the 1946 Congressional elections, Starr unsuccessfully ran as Liberal Party candidate for Representative from the Fourth District, Queens, of Greater New York.

Starr's other books include *Lies and Hate in Education* (1929), a study of national and class bias in European textbooks; and *Labor in America* (1944) which he wrote together with Harold U. Faulkner. The last-named is a nationally used textbook for fourth-year high school classes in problems of democracy. (It was the second text of its kind published in the United States.) Starr was also one of the authors of the 1941 yearbook of the John Dewey Society—*Workers' Education in the United States.* His articles have appeared in the *Saturday Review of Literature,* the *New Republic,* and in many labor and education publications. Among his many pamphlets are *Labor and Consumer Education, Training for Union Service, The Worker As A Consumer, Cap and Gown Meets Overalls,* and *Labor Looks At Education.*

As member for two years of the executive council of the American Federation of Teachers (A.F. of L.), Starr is said to have been instrumental in "dislodging alleged Communists" who held office in the union; he heads its Local 189. Starr is also president of the League for Industrial Democracy, and has been chairman of the Queens County Liberal Party since 1945. A trustee of Town Hall, and since 1920 active in the cooperative movement, his other affiliations include membership in the New York Adult Education Council (he serves on the executive board), in the American Adult Education Association, the American Labor Education Service, the Public Affairs Committee, and the Council for Democracy. He is a director of the Union for Democratic Action. In June 1946 Starr was one of thirty men and women appointed by President Truman to the National Commission on Higher Education, which was to "re-examine our system of higher education in terms of its objectives, methods and facilities, and in the light of the social role it has to play."

The author and critic John Chamberlain once called Starr "a canny soft-spoken person who has a deep respect for other people's rights to their opinion. His teaching method is Socratic; if he disagrees with you he merely commends to your attention some factors which he thinks you may have overlooked." The I.L.G.W.U. educational director is five feet ten, weighs 170 pounds, and his eyes are blue. He and his wife have one daughter, Emily (two other children died). The Starrs live in a two-family house in Queens. Starr's favorite "vices" are reading and clipping newspapers and labor publications, drinking tea, and singing in a loud voice somewhere between tenor and baritone.

References

N Y Herald Tribune p15 Mr 29 '43
N Y Post p35 Ap 12 '43
PM p2 Mr 28 '43
Who's Who in America, 1946-47
Who's Who in Labor (1946)

STEEL, KURT *See* Kagey, R.

STEIN, GERTRUDE (stīn) Feb. 3, 1874—July 27, 1946 American author; developed her own literary style, using words for their sound rather than for sense; lived in France after 1903, becoming the patron of Picasso, Matisse, and Bracque; her first book, *Three Lives* (1909), was followed by two autobiographies, *The Autobiography of Alice B. Toklas* (1933), and *Everybody's Autobiography* (1937); her opera libretto, *Four Saints in Three Acts,* was set to music by Virgil Thompson in 1934; *Wars I Have Seen* (1945) concerned her experiences in occupied France.

Obituary

N Y Times p39 Jl 28 '46 por

STELLA, JOSEPH (stĕl'á) June 13, 1880 —Nov. 5, 1946 Artist; came to the United States from Italy in 1896; began his career drawing for the *Outlook, Century,* and *Survey Graphic;* began painting as a realist, turned to abstractionism and then to "lyric fantasy"; *Brooklyn Bridge* and the huge canvas *Coney Island, Battle of the Lights, Mardi Gras* are two of his best-known paintings.

Obituary

N Y Times p23 N 6 '46 por

STELLE, JOHN (stĕl) Aug. 10, 1891-
Veterans' leader
Address: h. McLeansboro, Ill.

"A lawyer, soldier, statesman, farmer, and businessman" who is "as American as apple pie," said the American Legion's public relations department in introducing the 1946 national commander, John Stelle. Onetime Governor of Illinois, he has been an active member of the Legion since its formation in 1919, helping to build it up from a small group of World War I officers to the largest veterans' organization and one of the most influential lobbyist groups in the United States.

Born at McLeansboro, Hamilton County, Illinois, on August 10, 1891, John Stelle was brought up in the home that has belonged to his family for more than one hundred years. It is said that his mother was a woman of unusual kindliness, a characteristic which Stelle's friends and supporters say he inherited. His father was county judge of Hamilton County for many years. Stelle attended grammar school and high school in his home town, where he showed particular interest in athletics. Later he was enrolled as a student at the Western Military Academy in Alton, Illinois. For a few years after graduation he played professional baseball as second baseman on the Henderson, Kentucky, team of the old Kitty League. (Albert B. ["Happy"] Chandler[43], commissioner of baseball in 1946 and a friend of Stelle's, played on the Hopkinsville, Kentucky, team in the league at the same time.) In 1912 Stelle gave up baseball and returned to McLeansboro to study law. He completed his law course at Washington University, St. Louis, Missouri, in 1916 and passed the Illinois bar examination the same year.

Stelle went home with his new LL.B. degree, but his legal days were short-lived. On April 17, 1917, the day the United States entered World War I, the young lawyer enlisted in the Illinois State Guard. By August he had been promoted from private to sergeant and was selected for admittance to the officers' training school at Fort Sheridan. Three months later he was commissioned as a first lieutenant and was soon on his way to Europe with a machine gun battalion. In France he was gassed and wounded in action. Before the Armistice was signed he had become a captain. His last assignment was with the now famous Thirtieth ("Old Hickory") Division. At the end of the war he returned to the United States with Company B of the 115th Machine Gun Battalion.

Upon his arrival in McLeansboro, in 1919, Stelle resumed his law practice, but a year later went into business with the McLeansboro Creamery. He continued in politics, helping to organize the Democratic Service Men's Organization in 1926. Having been assistant State treasurer of Illinois from 1913 until 1931, he became assistant State auditor for 1933-34, and served as State treasurer from 1934 until 1936. In that year, as running mate of the Democratic candidate for governor, Henry Horner, Stelle was elected lieutenant governor. In Horner's subsequent term

in office, which was his second, he became ill and, in April 1940, Stelle attempted what *Newsweek* (December 30, 1940) called "a State House *Putsch*" when he named himself Governor of Illinois, but failed to win recognition of his claim; and in the primary elections he lost his party's nomination for that office. A few months later, when Governor Horner died on October 6, 1940, however, Stelle succeeded him in the State House. During his short term of office, which was to last only the hundred days remaining until the new Governor, Republican Dwight H. Green, was inaugurated, Stelle made some changes in the administrative offices. He dismissed most of Horner's "bedside cabinet," replacing them, opponents charged, with his personal and political friends. He also assigned a few contracts to other friends, these opponents added. Stelle answered his critics with: "All you can truly say about John Stelle is that he has changed a hell of a lot of positions and put his friends in. . . .If Dwight Green does not do the same thing, I will eat this desk at State and Madison Streets [the most important corner in downtown Chicago]."

After Stelle's short stay in the Illinois State House he directed his energies toward the development of his growing commercial enterprises. In addition to the McLeansboro Creamery he had acquired profitable oil interests, and in 1941 he became president and owner of the Arketex Ceramic Corporation at Brazil, Indiana, which made him the largest manufacturer of structural glazed tile in the United States. He is also president of the Evansville (Indiana) Coal Company, Incorporated, the McLeansboro Shale Products Company, and is the owner of Stelle Farm.

Stelle's unanimous election as national commander of the American Legion at the Chicago convention in November 1945 was not unexpected. He had not only been associated with the Legion since its formation, but he was the choice of the organization's "King-makers," the group of men who direct the Legion's national policies and pass on candidates for high office. Twenty-six years earlier, in 1919, when Stelle returned from overseas, he attended the St. Louis caucus at which the organization was perfected. The Legion had been formed a few months earlier in Paris by a small group of officers and businessmen who wished to combat what they felt was radicalism in the United States Army. Stelle became the leader of a movement within the Legion that advocated equal recognition for noncommissioned officers, and he helped to establish McLeansboro Post 106, of which he is still a member. During the years that followed he served several terms as district commander of the Twenty-fourth District of Illinois and as a member of the national executive committee. He attended state and national conventions regularly as a delegate or an alternate. Credited with being the framer of the GI Bill of Rights, Stelle was chairman of the special Legion committee which drafted the bill (officially known as the Servicemen's Readjustment Act of 1944) and successfully lobbied for its passage. He later appointed a "watchdog" committee to prevent

JOHN STELLE

"hamstringing" of the bill by dubious or illegal application.

In his acceptance speech the new commander stressed the Legion's current policy of welcoming World War II veterans into the organization and offering them an equal share of the responsibilities and benefits: "There is now in the making the greatest team ever developed in the peacetime history of the world—a team of veterans of World War I and World War II in the American Legion. As commander, it will be my objective to make this a winning team—an aggressive team—a team which has fought and won on the battlefields of war and which will continue to fight and win in the battles of peace in the interest of our country and of the veteran." The Legion's campaign for new members resulted in a mass induction of several thousand veterans at the convention.

At the convention Commander Stelle outlined the defense plan which the Legion had drawn up for 1946: "1) Twelve months of universal military training; 2) unified command of the armed forces, with the Army, Navy, and Air Force on an equal level; 3) retention of all secrets of the atomic bomb; 4) establishment of an independent secret foreign intelligence system; 5) retention of a Navy strong enough in ships, bases, guns, and men to maintain the honor and security of the United States; 6) maintenance of the National Guard at not less than 425,000 men plus necessary officer personnel; 7) continuation and strengthening of the ROTC, NROTC, and AROTC; 8) creation by Congress of a civilian board for the study of scientific development of the arms and material for modern warfare as well as for industrial development and for the planning of industrial mobilization for the effective production of war needs; 9) maintenance of adequate stockpiles of strategic materials; 10) preservation of the American Merchant Marine as a vital arm of American national defense." In later speeches Stelle urged that the United States, as a matter of foreign policy, avoid "the road to appeasement" in dealings with Soviet Russia and Yugoslavia.

As commander, Stelle originally endorsed the Wyatt '46 veterans' emergency housing program, but later withdrew his support. Shortly after taking office, Stelle made his first attack upon the Veterans Administration's director, General Omar N. Bradley '41, charging that the VA had suffered a "tragic breakdown." The Legion approved of Stelle's request for an investigation of the VA and began issuing monthly reports on VA activities. Stelle's recommendation that Bradley be removed from office, however, did not receive Legion approval. President Truman '45 and General Eisenhower '42 defended Bradley and newspapers and the public generally strongly criticized the Legion head's recommendation, following which Stelle withdrew his request for the ouster. The dispute was reopened when Stelle later charged that Bradley "broke faith" with the veterans by supporting a bill which provided time and salary limits for on-the-job training. In this the Legion supported Stelle, who was by that time retiring as commander. In October 1946 he was succeeded by Paul H. Griffith.

Stelle was married in 1912 to Wilma Wiseheart of Shawneetown, Illinois. The Stelles are the parents of two World War II veterans, both of whom were lieutenants. One of their sons, John Albert, was wounded in the breakthrough at St. Lô, and the other son, Russell, a pilot, saw action in Europe. John Stelle believes that the veterans of the two wars have in common "the care of our disabled comrades, and the preservation in peace of the American way of life which we both fought to save in war."

Reference

Newsweek 16:11 D 30 '40
Who's Who in America, 1946-47

STEPHENS, HUBERT D(URRETT) July 2, 1875—Mar. 14, 1946 American lawyer and legislator; district attorney 1907-10; United States Representative from Mississippi 1911-21; Senator from Mississippi 1923-35; director, Reconstruction Finance Corporation 1935-36.

Obituary

N Y Times p21 Mr 15 '46 por

STEVENSON, GEORGE S(ALVADORE) Oct. 5, 1892- Psychiatrist; neurologist
Address: b. c/o National Committee for Mental Hygiene, 1790 Broadway, New York; h. Everett Rd., Red Bank, N.J.

As medical director of the National Committee for Mental Hygiene Dr. George S. Stevenson works with that organization to raise the standards of psychiatric clinics and institutions. The psychiatrist and neurologist, whose particular province is the community clinic for children, is coauthor of *Child Guidance Clinics;*

a Quarter Century Development, described by Dr. James S. Plant as "an invaluable guide for those who venture into the field."

George Salvadore Stevenson was born in Philadelphia on October 5, 1892. His father, George Edward Stevenson, who was in the dry goods business, could trace his Quaker family back to the first Governor of New Jersey. His mother, Anna Ida (Musso) Stevenson, a daughter of the Sicilian, Salvator Musso, who had fought under Garibaldi before emigrating to Philadelphia, was part German in descent. The boy George had a brother (John, who died in 1926) and two half-brothers (Robert Edward and Wayne Jennings Stevenson). Reared in Vineland, New Jersey, George Stevenson lived in the town in which were the Training School for Mental Deficiency and the State Institution for Mentally Deficient Women. This accounted for his early interest in psychiatry—he became acquainted with the psychologist Henry Goddard, director of the research department at the School for Feeble Minded Children at Vineland from 1906 to 1918.

Following a great-uncle who had also been a physician, young Stevenson decided to study medicine after his graduation from the local high school in 1911. He took his premedical work at Bucknell University, where his extracurricular activities were track athletics, and work as a waiter and laundry agent. After earning his B.S. in 1915, he received his M.Sc. four years later (in 1940 the same institution awarded him an honorary D.Sc.). He earned his M.D. degree at John Hopkins University by 1919, and served his internship in psychiatry as resident house officer at Johns Hopkins Hospital in 1919-20. That year Stevenson received his New York license to practice medicine and in 1921 his license from New Jersey; he was accredited in psychiatry and neurology, the field in which he specialized almost exclusively.

From 1920 until 1922 Stevenson worked both as an assistant in neuropathology at the New York State Psychiatric Institute and Hospital, and as a clinical instructor in nervous and mental diseases at the Cornell University Medical School (he returned to Cornell in 1929 to teach there for another five years). In 1922 Stevenson became a research psychiatrist in the Training School at Vineland; this he left in 1924 to accept a fellowship at the Minnesota Child Guidance Clinic. There, from 1924 until 1926 he taught as assistant professor of nervous and mental diseases, and directed the psychopathic department at the State Clinic at the University of Minnesota. He was also attending neurologist and psychiatrist for half of the ward service at the Minneapolis General Hospital in 1925-26. Stevenson's association with the National Committee for Mental Hygiene began in 1926-27, when he worked as field consultant on the prevention of delinquency. For twelve years (1927-39) he directed the division on community clinics for child guidance work, particularly with the Commonwealth Fund clinics. Succeeding Dr. Clarence M. Hincks, Stevenson became medical director of the National Committee for Mental Hygiene in 1939.

Associated News, Inc.

GEORGE S. STEVENSON

The National Committee for Mental Hygiene was established in 1906 to improve conditions in mental hospitals; the founder, Clifford Beers, had been a patient in three such institutions and had seen and suffered much neglect, humiliation, and abuse. The committee gives support to institutional officials in the adoption and maintenance of standards set by the American Psychiatric Association, helps in the establishment of such institutions, and works for the promotion of better mental hygiene practices. This work is financed by grants from the various philanthropic foundations and from five thousand smaller contributors. During World War II the committee urged more careful examination of draftees, stressing the danger of taking psychological problem cases into the armed services; Stevenson also advocated camp mental hygiene units to deal with maladjustments that arose in the service. (For his work in this field, the doctor was awarded the Selective Service Medal and the Certificate of Merit in 1946.) Before the end of the war Stevenson proposed the training of needed psychiatrists through liberalization of the GI Bill of Rights to provide four additional years of study in medicine. Much of the on-the-job training (internship) would be in Government hospitals, and four more years would be devoted to veteran or other approved full-time community service. He later pointed out that, until medical shortages were remedied, the requiring of the Veterans Administration to help men and women with non-service disabilities would deprive service-disabled veterans of needed care.

Child Guidance Clinics; a Quarter Century of Development (1934), is the collaborative work of Stevenson and Geddes Smith. In it the authors note that emphasis now tends to go beyond delinquency and the court to the "more subtle" signs of maladjustment at school and

STEVENSON, GEORGE S.—*Continued*

in the home. Merrill E. Champion, writing in the *American Journal of Public Health,* judged the book "worth the reading by everyone interested in the progressive welfare movements of the day." Its appeal is widespread since, wrote Howard Yale McClusky in the *Elementary School Journal,* the book is "written with a minimum of technical language and deals with a situation which is essentially a problem for the community at large." Although he praised the style and skillful treatment of subject, Dr. James S. Plant in *Survey* scored what he considered an "unfortunate inability to distinguish between refined clinical psychiatry and mental hygiene," but added that the book "commands thoughtful reading." Stevenson has written many scientific articles for medical journals, among them "Organizing a Child Guidance Clinic" (1930), "The Training of Psychiatric Social Workers" (1938), and a chapter in the book *Mental Hygiene in Modern Education* (1939). He is also editor of *Mental Hygiene,* the National Committee for Mental Hygiene quarterly.

While working with children, Stevenson saw that it was the neurotic adults who "more or less crippled" the mental health of many children, and as such constituted a serious menace to youth. In a neurotic home, divorce often served to compound the difficulty. Stevenson explained that when a child (or anyone else) is forced to organize his behavior to live with a neurotic, he imposes personality "distortions" upon himself which cause him to "fit less comfortably with healthy persons." An authority in the field, Stevenson is a member of the maternal and child health advisory committee of the United States Children's Bureau and of the executive board of the Society for Research in Child Development. He is also a fellow of the American Medical Association and the American Orthopsychiatric Association, having served in the latter as secretary from 1927 to 1934, president in 1934-35, and treasurer for more than six years thereafter. (The association, founded in 1924 to aid scientific work in "social psychiatry," regards delinquency as a "deformity of behavior" requiring medicopsychological treatment.)

Stevenson is a member of the American Psychiatric Association, the American Association on Mental Deficiency, the American Board of Psychiatry and Neurology, the Central Neuro-psychiatric Association, the Minnesota Neurological Society, the New York City committee for mental hygiene of the State Charities Aid Association, and the Medical Society of New Jersey. Stevenson was married to Amy Llewelyn Patterson on September 2, 1920. Their children are William Chandler, Anne Elizabeth, and Amy Llewelyn. The brown-haired, brown-eyed doctor is five feet six and a half inches tall and weighs 136 pounds. He is a Republican, and his clubs are the Bison and the Bucknell.

References

Directory of Medical Specialists, 1942
Who's Who in America, 1946-47

STIEGLITZ, ALFRED (stēg'lĭts) Jan. 1, 1864—July 13, 1946 Photographer and editor; experimented in three-color work; was one of the early supporters of modern American and European art; editor of *American Amateur Photographer,* 1892-96; founder and editor of *Camera Notes,* 1897-1903; editor and publisher of *Camera Work,* 1903; photographs exhibited in most of the major museums of the United States. See *Current Biography* 1940 Yearbook.

Obituary

N Y Times p38 Jl 14 '46

STILWELL, JOSEPH W(ARREN) Mar. 19, 1883—Oct. 12, 1946 United States Army major general, commander of the Sixth Army; served with the AEF and Army of Occupation in World War I; spent thirteen years in China; with the outbreak of World War II he was made Chief of Staff of Generalissimo Chiang Kai-shek, and put in command of the Chinese armies in Burma as well as United States forces in China, Burma, and India; routed from Burma in 1942, he returned to defeat the Japanese there in 1944. See *Current Biography* 1942 Yearbook.

Obituary

N Y Times p1+ O 13 '46 pors

STIRNWEISS, GEORGE (HENRY) Oct. 26, 1919- Baseball player; athletic coach

Address: b. c/o New York Yankees, 745 5th Ave., New York; c/o University of North Carolina, Chapel Hill, N.C.

George ("Snuffy") Stirnweiss of the New York Yankees, voted the best baseball player of 1945 by the sports writers of the United States, was one of the few bright spots in the Yankees' dismal wartime years. "In fact," wrote John Lardner of *Newsweek,* "it is possible to imagine putting Stirnweiss on an all-star team in any year, so skillful and valuable has this young reformed football player become." Babe Ruth [44] said, "That sawed-off runt playing second base is the only ballplayer who could've gotten a uniform when the Yankees really had a ball club."

The son of a New York City policeman, Patrolman Andy Stirnweiss, George Henry Stirnweiss was born and reared in the Bronx borough of New York. His birth date was October 26, 1919. From the age of eight he was an ardent Yankee fan. He took part in Police Athletic League sandlot games before entering Fordham Preparatory School, the Jesuit institution in his native city, where he starred in baseball, football, and basketball. According to Stanley Frank, he also won championships in handball and tennis, without ever having played those games before. At sixteen, too, he played with the high-ranking semi-professional Bronx Giants, "doing a man's job at second base for three dollars a game." From Fordham Prep George went to Fordham University on an athletic scholarship, but left after four weeks: he preferred to accept a scholarship at the University of North Carolina, which he entered in September 1936. The six months in between he spent as a runner in the Wall Street brokerage firm of William Carmichael, who "made the necessary diplomatic arrangements" for his matriculation. The time George spent at Fordham barred him from freshman athletics, but after that he justified his athletic promise.

At Chapel Hill young Stirnweiss played second base in the spring and summer, and halfback in the fall and winter. "He was," says Arthur Daley, "a triple-threat back who could do everything phenomenally well." In his sophomore year, the Tarheel signals were called by "Snuffy" (nicknamed for his sinus trouble). He smoked cigars, chewed tobacco, and ate and drank with such abandon that in 1939, at the age of twenty, he was unable to play the entire football season because of the pain from gastric ulcers. A scout from the Yankee organization offered him a baseball contract, but he refused it because he wanted to continue with his football, and perhaps become an All-American star. After his graduation in 1940, however, Snuffy accepted the contract. His father was fatally ill (he died a few days later) and the twenty-one-year-old athlete had to support his mother and young brother. Among the offers he did not accept was one from the Chicago Football Cardinals, with a starting salary of four thousand dollars a year.

While keeping theoretically to a diet of eggs, milk, and cream (plus an unauthorized glass or two of beer), the stocky young second baseman played for the Yankees' wholly-owned Class B Piedmont League farm team at Norfolk. On the basis of his football record Stirnweiss was signed to coach the professional Norfolk Shamrocks of the Dixie Football League after the baseball season was over. In his second year as a professional (1942), the Yankee-in-training was ordered to report to Newark, a Class AA team and one of the Yankees' two top farms. There he batted only .268. Despite a ripped rib muscle, however, he attracted much attention by stealing seventy-three bases, a record unprecedented in his league and second only to the immortal Ty Cobb's ninety-six in one season. Unlike Cobb, Stirnweiss stole bases in a studied and unspectacular way, and was seldom caught. Fritz Maisel, holder of the International League base-stealing record which Stirnweiss had just topped by ten, congratulated him, adding, "You don't do it with your legs. You steal bases with your head." After that season, Stirnweiss was sold to the Yankees. He also acquired an off-season job as football and basketball coach at the Canterbury School in Connecticut, an exclusive Roman Catholic preparatory school for boys. He was now a married man.

Joining the Yankees in spring 1943, Stirnweiss was forced to play shortstop because the Yankees' second base was already covered by the star Joe Gordon, one of the three remaining members of the 1942 team. The reserved Yankee manager, Joe McCarthy, who is known for his refusal to discuss the merits of players or otherwise commit himself, astonished players and reporters by flatly stating that Stirn-

GEORGE STIRNWEISS

weiss would make a great shortstop. This, coming from a man who had managed the fabulous prewar Yankees, made Stirnweiss an object of interest to his teammates and opponents, as well as the reporters ("Everybody wants to see the kid Joe has gone overboard on"). But he proved a disappointment, and in late June McCarthy benched him for the season. Playing in a total of only eighty-three games, Stirnweiss ran up a dismal .219 batting average; he did, however, steal a crucial base in the World Series. And he was, perforce, enrolled in what *Look* calls, "Baseball's most exclusive school—the seat on the bench next to McCarthy," which had formerly been occupied by such respectable workmen as Gordon and Phil Rizzuto. And before the next season began (club president Larry MacPhail '45 later told reporters) Stirnweiss' eight-thousand-dollar salary was doubled, putting him among the four highest-salaried players on the team and giving him more than Frankie Crosetti and Billy Herman got at their peaks.

In 1944 Stirnweiss blossomed out. For one thing, he was no longer overweight (he suffered a six-week recurrence of illness during spring training); for another, Gordon had been called into service, and Stirnweiss was able to play his natural position, second base. In August, when McCarthy called him "the best second baseman in the game today," writers agreed that he deserved praise. He was said to have held the team together throughout the season. He was the only Yankee except Nick Etten to play in every game, and in every inning except a few he missed because of a bruised shoulder. He stole so many bases that McCarthy let him use his own judgment as to when to do so—and by the end of the season had run up the impressive record of fifty-five stolen bases to eleven times caught out. His shoulders "finally got rid of that tight feeling they had acquired

STIRNWEISS, GEORGE—*Continued*

with years of football," and as lead-off batter he averaged .319. His plays were often brilliant, and some writers called him "The Yankee of the Year"—not much of a distinction in that year, however.

Stirnweiss played in each of the 152 games on the teams's 1945 schedule. He led the American League in batting—a remarkable accomplishment for a lead-off hitter. His .309, the lowest League championship average in forty years, was actually ten points below the 1944 average which put him in fourth place. It included the League championships in triples (22), base hits (195), total bases (301), and runs scored (107). He led also with 33 stolen bases. Stirnweiss made 29 errors, but led the second basemen in putouts (432), total chances (953), and double plays (119), and was second in assists with 492. Two months before these figures were finally tabulated, the New Yorker had been honored with a "George Stirnweiss Day," arranged by the Bronx's State Senator Lazarus Joseph and a citizens' committee. Stirnweiss was presented with a scroll from the Police Athletic League (the game's receipts were earmarked for its sandlot baseball) and with gifts from the committee and from his teammates, including an order for a four-door Cadillac Sedan. (The baseball club management presented him with a share of the profits of exhibition games in New England.) "In typical manner," one reporter commented, "he upset the tradition which attaches a jinx to any 'day' for any ball player." In November Stirnweiss was voted the American League's third most valuable player; but in February 1946 the Baseball Writers of America, New York Chapter, gave him the Sid Mercer Memorial Award as "the player of 1945," an award which had previously been made to such luminaries as Lou Gehrig '40, Carl Hubbell, Dizzy Dean, Hank Greenberg, and Joe DiMaggio '41.

Snuffy Stirnweiss had given up his off-season job in October, but later that year he joined Carl Snavely's staff as assistant baseball and football coach at the University of North Carolina. "I always wanted to live in Chapel Hill," said the Bronx-born athlete. In 1946, after a month-long holdout, Stirnweiss won an unprecedented two-year contract and "one of the most remarkable financial promotions in the history of a club that has had its Ruth [$80,-000] and its DiMaggio [$42,500]": a salary reported by Dan Daniel as eighteen thousand dollars a year and by others as twenty thousand.

Stirnweiss' insufficiencies during the 1946 season led baseball observers to charge that he was a "wartime" player. His batting average declined fifty points below his 1945 game. Perhaps one cause of this was that Manager McCarthy transferred him to third base where, the player said, "I've had to readjust my throwing. At second base, I'd get rid of the ball the instant I got it. At third, it gets to you so quickly, you have to hold your throw and give the first baseman a chance to get over the bag." Stirnweiss, however, went errorless during the first forty-four games of the season.

A stocky, sandy-haired man of five feet eight inches, George Stirnweiss is described as resembling Frank Frisch in appearance and playing style. " 'Bounce' is the word which best describes it," says *PM*'s Tom Meany. "There is no grace in this type of speed, but sheer physical force." Observers think, too, that Joe McCarthy's extra fondness for him is based on the fact that "smart, hustling, quietly aggressive" Stirnweiss is exactly the sort of player McCarthy himself tried to be in his playing days. The manager says of Stirnweiss, "You cannot overlook his general hustle and competitive spirit. I've never known a player to take a defeat more to heart, especially after losing a tough one. A manager simply has to go all-out for a player like that." The New Yorker is said to be "enormously popular" with his teammates. He still suffers severe attacks of pain despite Mrs. Stirnweiss' supervision of his diet and banning of beer and chewing tobacco, and he was therefore draft-exempt. George and Jane Stirnweiss have two daughters, Susan and Barbara, and a son, George, Jr.

References

Collier's 112:30-1 Jl 17 '43 por
Liberty 23:22+ Mr 16 '46 por
Look 9:40+ My 29 '45 pors
N Y Times p18 Je 2 '45
Newsweek 24:78-9 Jl 3 '44

STODDARD, GEORGE D(INSMORE)
Oct. 8, 1897-   University president
Address: b. c/o University of Illinois, Urbana, Ill.

George D. Stoddard, educator and child psychologist, took office in July 1946 as the tenth president of the University of Illinois, succeeding Dr. Arthur Cutts Willard on the latter's retirement. Earlier in 1946 Stoddard, the former Commissioner of Education for the State of New York, was appointed chairman of a group of educators sent to Japan to aid the American occupation authorities in revising the Japanese system of education.

George Dinsmore Stoddard was born October 8, 1897, the son of Eugene Anson and Charlotte Temple (Dinsmore) Stoddard. He passed his childhood in his birthplace, Carbondale, Pennsylvania. After being graduated from Carbondale High School, Stoddard entered Pennsylvania State College. His studies were interrupted by World War I, during which he served in 1918 as second lieutenant in the Field Artillery Reserve Corps, holding his rank in the Reserves until 1923. As soon as his active duty terminated with the end of the war, the young man returned to Pennsylvania State College to complete his courses, receiving the B.A. degree in 1921. He then went to France for graduate work at the University of Paris and, in 1923, received its *diplôme d'études*. Two years later Stoddard completed his graduate studies at the University of Iowa and was granted the degree of Ph.D. The same year, 1925, saw the publication, by the University of Iowa, of his thesis, *Iowa Placement Examinations.*

Stoddard's career as an educator began at the University of Iowa with his appointment to the position of associate in psychology and education in 1925-26. Assistant professor from 1926 to 1928, he became associate professor of psychology in the year 1928-29. Added to his responsibilities as teacher were duties of administrator and research worker. During the years from 1929 to 1942, while the educator was professor of child psychology, he served as director of the Iowa Child Welfare Research Station at the university. He also held the posts of head of the department of psychology (1938-39) and of dean of the graduate college (1936-42). Aside from his professorial commitments, Stoddard numbered among his achievements the writing of books dealing with education and psychology. Those which were published during his years at Iowa were *Tests and Measurements in High School Instruction,* written in collaboration with G. M. Ruch (1927); *The General Shop,* with L. V. Newkirk (1928); *Study Manual in Elementary Statistics,* aided by E. F. Lindquist (1929); *Getting Ideas from the Movies,* with P. W. Holaday (1933); and *Child Psychology* (1933) and *Manual of Child Psychology* (1936), both in conjunction with B. L. Wellman.

At the age of forty-three Stoddard was chosen in September 1941 by a special committee of the Board of Regents of New York State to be president of the University of the State of New York and Commissioner of Education, succeeding Dr. Ernest E. Cole. By that time Stoddard had already established a reputation for himself as "one of the foremost authorities in the field of child development" in the United States; he had also become known as the author, in addition to his books, of about one hundred and fifty articles in the fields of tests and measurements, child psychology and development, and in childhood, parent, and higher education. He assumed his duties as the new commissioner on July 1, 1942.

As State Commissioner of Education Stoddard attempted, first, in August 1943, "to prevent a serious impairment of educational development of youth affected by industrial recruitment in war centers" by favoring, through the State Department of Education, legislation releasing nongraduates under eighteen for part-time work only. This program, differing from the prevailing system, required that all children up to the age of eighteen continue at school. In 1944, while serving on the Governor's committee on State aid, Stoddard "was instrumental in winning increased aid for schools and extending State aid to adult education programs and summer high schools." Under his direction, graduates of medical and dentistry schools not recognized by New York State were permitted to take examinations to practice in the State after they had fulfilled specific requirements. In October 1945, Stoddard, attempting to raise the declining prestige of New York State with respect to the provision of college opportunities for its youth, proposed that twelve thousand scholarships at $350 each year be instituted to replace the previous system of

GEORGE D. STODDARD

awarding seven hundred and fifty scholarships at $100 a year. He favored also the establishment of a State university (not to be confused with the University of the State of New York, which has, as one of its main duties, the setting of educational standards for all schools—elementary, secondary, colleges, and universities—in the State).

Two months later, in December 1945, Stoddard was requested by the New York State Board of Education to examine the report of Frank E. Karelsen, Jr., who had resigned in October as chairman of the Advisory Commission on Human Relations to the New York City Superintendant of Schools in protest against "chaos" and "administrative bankruptcy" in the municipal schools. After a month's study of Karelsen's charges and of the defense submitted by the City Board of Education, Stoddard concluded that a State investigation was unnecessary since he was "unable to discover issues which could not be met by local authorities." One of the remedies he suggested was a larger budget. Another action which Stoddard advocated that December was the substitution of Regents' examinations for high school students (he maintained that they discouraged pupils from remaining in school) with a comprehensive all-youth examination for individuals of high school age whether attending school or not. In April 1946 he criticized the releasing of children over fourteen from school for farm work, because of the danger of exploitation.

While Stoddard was occupied with his work as Commissioner of Education his *The Meaning of Intelligence* was published in 1943. According to its author, the book "brings into a focus various research findings on the broad question of intelligence" and "attempts to relate technical issues to certain problems in modern life." In his book Stoddard deals with the influence

STODDARD, GEORGE D.—*Continued*

of economic and social factors on the I.Q. Some of the findings, derived from the experiments of a number of psychologists, are that children of so-called inferior or feeble-minded parents are not necessarily so themselves, that the existing I.Q. tests and testing methods do not always offer valid proof of genius or feeblemindedness, and that environment does affect the I.Q., though often only slightly. Described in one review as "an able, well-organized, and in places sparkling exposition of the systematic view of the members of the rebellion in educational psychology," the book, in another review, was recommended to all who would learn "what the progressive educators will in all probability soon accept as another of their gospels." A certain paragraph dealing with superstition and dogma aroused a number of people to oppose Stoddard's becoming president of the University of Illinois, but his election was upheld by the university's board of trustees. In 1944 his *Tertiary Education* was published.

Early in 1942 Stoddard and other educators, faced with new problems brought on by World War II, formulated plans for the rehabilitation of war veterans and for education for brotherhood among nations. The necessity of "exporting" American methods of education to a Europe destroyed by war and temporarily bereft of the means of education was stressed by Stoddard at that time. In *School and Society* (September 19, 1942) Stoddard expressed faith in ultimate victory and discussed the importance of "guidance, chiefly under American auspices, of the youth of Germany, Italy, and Japan, at first with the consent and finally with the active support of their elders." Terming it "the greatest educational task in history," Stoddard added: "For such a price as we are paying, and are about to pay, anything less than a thorough regeneration of the nations that have attacked us would make the game not worth the candle. It is moreover the only means offered for extending economic and social aid to our present enemies."

Nor were Stoddard's activities in postwar educational planning confined to the United States alone. In October 1945 he was chosen as one of the American delegates to a conference of the United Nations Educational, Scientific, and Cultural Organization held in London, beginning in November 1945. The goals of the UNESCO—preservation of peace, prevention of international misunderstanding, promotion of democratic principles, and diffusion of culture—were presented by Stoddard in *New York State Education* for January 1946. In March 1946, a group of twenty-seven American educators, with Stoddard as chairman, was sent to Japan to help General Douglas MacArthur'[4i] revise the Japanese system of education. The commission a month later drew up a report emphasizing the need for such reforms as "lay education agencies" similar to American boards of education, compulsory free education for all through lower secondary schools or until the age of sixteen, elimination of imperial and mythological influences from textbooks, substitution of the Roman alphabet

for the Chinese-style characters, and greater provision for advanced education for the majority. Later in 1946 Stoddard remarked that a generation would be needed to re-educate the Japanese people to ideals of individual liberty. While in Japan, Stoddard was requested in an unprecedented move by Emperor Hirohito, to select an American woman as tutor for the Crown Prince. Mrs. Elizabeth Gray Vining, a former teacher and writer of juvenile books, whose appointment to the tutorship was announced by the State Department late in August, was one of the two women whom Stoddard had recommended for the post.

Stoddard became president of the University of Illinois in July 1946. When the educator was informed of his election to the presidency in May of the previous year, he is reported to have remarked that "he liked the university and its spirit" and "university life." Before he left the State commissionership of education for his Illinois position, Stoddard, in a statement printed in *New York State Education,* June 1946, paid tribute to the New York State Teachers Association and various other groups for their efforts to advance the cause of education. Stressing the importance of the fine arts and ethical values in education and the need for liberalism and freedom in the schoolroom and in school administration (as expressed in the report of the United States Mission to Japan), Stoddard commented: "The chief function of a school is not to pack the mind with unrelated facts or data, but to establish the structure of thought and to improve human relations." In July, the president of the university of Illinois became a member of the National Commission on Higher Education, appointed by President Truman, which will re-examine the "objectives, methods, and facilities" of higher education and study higher education's functions and performance of functions in the United States democracy. Two months later, Stoddard was made a member of the commission "which will advise the American delegation" to the UNESCO (Stoddard attended the meeting of the organization held in Paris in November 1946), and a member of the supervisory board of visitors of the Army Air Forces' new Air University at Maxwell Field, Alabama. The Air University's supervisory board helped to establish the school's higher education program and will make "periodic inspections of the various schools" and reports on the workings of the system.

Most of Stoddard's connections with professional organizations have been in executive or administrative capacities. He has served as a member of the board of directors of the National Society for the Study of Education, as former president of the National Association of Nursery Education, as secretary of the American Council on Education, and as fellow of the American Association for the Advancement of Science, and of the Society for Research in Child Development. A member as well of the American Psychological Association and of the University clubs of Albany and New York City, Stoddard also has been elected to such "letter" societies as Phi Beta Kappa,

Sigma Xi, and Kappa Delta Pi. Among the honorary degrees conferred upon him are the Litt.D., LL.D., and L.H.D.

The youthful-looking progressive educator, described as "tweedy," is almost six feet tall, and has blue eyes and brown hair. His favorite recreation is golf. He has called himself a liberal, but has no definite political affiliation. In his religious beliefs he is a Unitarian. Mrs. Stoddard, to whom he was married in December 1925, is the former Margaret Trautwein. Their family numbers three sons and two daughters—Philip Hendrick, Arthur Dinsmore, Eleanor, Caroline, and Alfred Eugene.

References

N Y State Ed 29:167 N '41 por; 33:73 O '45 por

Leaders in Education (1941)
Psychological Register (1932)
Who's Who in America, 1946-47
Who's Who in American Education, 1933-34

STOKOWSKI, OLGA SAMAROFF *See* Samaroff, O.

STONE, HARLAN FISKE Oct. 11, 1872 —Apr. 22, 1946 Jurist; twelfth Chief Justice of the United States, appointed by President Coolidge in 1924; "Great Dissenter", outspoken member of the liberal wing of the Court in the decisions on the constitutionality of New Deal measures; member of many national legal associations; held numerous honorary degrees. See *Current Biography* 1941 Yearbook.

Obituary

N Y Times p1+ Ap 23 '46 por

STOUT, REX (TODHUNTER) Dec. 1, 1886- Author; lecturer
Address: High Meadow, Brewster, N.Y.

With the cessation of hostilities at the end of World War II, militant Quaker Rex Stout, author, lecturer, and radio personality, turned his attention from the iniquities of the Axis to mobilizing public opinion against atomic warfare. He is also active in an organization formed to prevent World War III, for he seems to feel that this cannot be left entirely to the United Nations organization because, he says, "while UNO is good, it just isn't good enough."

Rex Todhunter Stout was born in Noblesville, Indiana, on December 1, 1886, the sixth of the nine children of John Wallace Stout and Lucetta Elizabeth (Todhunter) Stout, birthright Quakers. When Rex was still a small child, his parents moved to Wakarusa, Kansas, where his father had been appointed a superintendent of schools. The boy received his early education in a little country school in Shawnee County. At the age of thirteen he became the state spelling champion. Later he was graduated from the near-by Topeka High School as the class poet. A very short stay at the University of Kansas proved to be more than enough; and a period of "bumming" followed, which led eventually to the Navy. Attracted by a glowing Navy recruiting poster, Stout tried to enlist, but discovered that bad tonsils were an obstacle. When these had been rather crudely removed by a young medic who performed the necessary operation in a barbershop—accepting as his fee the two dollars which was all that his patient could offer—Stout found himself in the United States Navy. Assigned in 1906 as pay yeoman on President Theodore Roosevelt's yacht, the *Mayflower*, he was shortly promoted to warrant officer, in order, as Stout himself relates, to make an eighth officer in the wardroom, thus completing two tables for whist. After forty thousand miles at sea and two years of whist-playing, Stout purchased his discharge and proceeded to do his traveling on land.

From 1908 to 1912 he roamed over the United States. A short period studying law was followed by jobs such as cook, clerk, bellhop, motorman, plumber's assistant, and finally New York hotel manager. It was while Stout was holding his hotel job that President William Howard Taft made a trip to New York. Using the visit as a pretext, Stout offered to do an article on the palm prints of the President and of Senator Tom Loftin Johnson, who had accompanied him, for the Sunday editor of the old New York *World*—for two hundred dollars. Although he knew nothing about palmistry, Stout called upon the two notables, whose acquaintance he had made aboard the *Mayflower*, and as a stunt, induced the men to use an ink pad for impressions. When he had secured the palm prints, Stout bought a cheap book on palmistry and then wrote an article claiming that both men were "kind, capable, and good to their mothers." After this easy success, he decided to become a writer. At first he sold serious articles to magazines such as *Munsey's* and *Everybody's*, but before long he realized that he could turn out a ninety-thousand-word adventure story "in half the time for twice the money."

After six years of alternately writing and squandering the proceeds of writing (on symphony concerts, opera, the theater, and, as he says, "investigating the woman question"), Stout recognized the desirability of a more solid financial foundation. Accordingly, for the next ten years he devoted his time to business. Utilizing the mathematical aptitude that had become evident in his childhood, he invented a school banking system, the Educational Thrift Service, which he installed in four hundred towns and cities from coast to coast. When the United States entered World War I, Stout turned his accounting system over to the Government, for the sale of War Savings Stamps, and stayed on as manager. In 1927, having acquired a modest fortune, he withdrew from the business world and went to Paris to write.

Critics greeted with enthusiasm Rex Stout's first novel, *How Like a God* (1929). The New York *Times* found that "in spite of the lack of sequence in the narrative the author succeeds in building a complete picture of a life." This "picture" is conveyed to the reader in the space of time that the hero, gun in hand, mounts

W. Colston Leigh, Inc.

REX STOUT

two flights of steps on the way to destiny, at the apartment of his mistress. Employing the unusual device of having the narrative run through the mind of Sidney, the chief character, the author explored "the dark regions of sex psychoses" in a way that the New York *Herald Tribune* called "glowingly articulate." Three other psychological novels appeared— *Seed on the Wind* (1930), *Golden Remedy* (1931), and *Forest Fire* (1933), before Stout, caught in the market crash of the thirties, turned to a more lucrative form of expression.

Faced with the necessity of making money quickly, he abandoned the straight novel and entered the mystery field. In his first detective story, *Fer-de-Lance* (1934), Stout created a fabulous character, Nero Wolfe—a veritable mountain of flesh, referred to by Will Cuppy as "that Falstaff of detectives"—who, with the help of his agile assistant Archie Goodwin, solved his cases without leaving his desk. The success of this book resulted in ten other stories about Wolfe and his Archie. Outstanding are *Too Many Cooks* (1938), which for skill in presenting a specialized background has been compared to Dorothy Sayers' *The Nine Tailors*; *Some Buried Caesar* (1939); *Black Orchids* (1942); *Not Quite Dead Enough* (1944); and *The Silent Speaker* (1946). Howard Haycraft, in *Murder for Pleasure,* considers that Stout has "brought to the detective story not only its keenest wit, but also exceptional literary talent . . . his plots, detection, and narration are of the highest order."

After Nero Wolfe had become firmly established in the hearts of detective fans, Stout invented other sleuths: Tecumseh Fox, the hero of three books, of which *The Broken Vase* (1941) is perhaps the best; Dol Bonner, a female detective who appeared in *The Hand in the Glove* (1937); and *Alphabet Hicks* (1941), of whom Will Cuppy wrote in the New

York *Herald Tribune*, "Alphabet Hicks strikes us as a slick snoop, an entertaining fellow, and an all-round incentive to puzzling." Other critics, however, felt that this book did not compare with the Nero Wolfe tales, and summed up their feelings by saying, "We all want Archie back again." Stout's formula for writing his stories is, according to Robert van Gelder in the New York *Times Book Review,* very simple: he takes a setting that interests him, thinks of what might happen there, selects the most entertaining incident and asks himself, "Why should a murder occur under such circumstances?" The answer provides the plot— and Stout writes it out. It is, he says, a pleasure. Besides his mystery novels, the author has found time to write an occasional romance, short stories, and articles. In 1942 he edited a volume of propaganda, *The Illustrious Dunderheads,* a "record of what our isolationist Senators and Representatives said before Pearl Harbor." He has also edited, with Louis Greenfield, a volume of murder, mystery, and horror stories which had previously appeared in magazines, *Rue Morgue No. 1* (1946). Many of Stout's books have been translated into foreign languages; they have also been adapted for the radio and for motion pictures.

To Rex Stout, onetime contributor to the old *Masses,* and a founder and former director of the Vanguard Press, the rise of Hitler was anathema. In his early days, Stout had, according to Gilbert W. Gabriel, "often backed stormy causes, radical and humanitarian." After the crisis at Munich in 1938 he gave up most of his fiction-writing to conduct his own campaign against the Axis. He became connected with such organizations as Fight for Freedom, Inc., the Council for Democracy, the Committee to Defend America by Aiding the Allies, and the Associated Leagues for an Immediate Declaration of War. A guest appearance on the radio program *Information, Please* discovered Stout's talent for broadcasting. He subsequently became the master of ceremonies on the *Speaking of Liberty* program, sponsored by the Council for Democracy in 1941. After the United States entered World War II, Stout's was the "voice" that exposed fascist technique for the first six months of 1942, in *The Voice of Freedom,* under the auspices of Freedom House. Later that same year he appeared on a program for the Columbia Broadcasting System, *Our Secret Weapon,* in which he served as the "lie detector," debunking Nazi propaganda. More than five thousand copies of Stout's scripts were sent out each week to schools and colleges, Army camps, Naval stations, and Japanese relocation centers. The broadcasts were shortwaved to England and to the east and west coasts of South America.

The chairman of the Writers War Board (now the Writers Board), a director of Freedom House, and president of the Society for the Prevention of World War III, Stout was a frequent speaker at forums, Town Meetings, and rallies. The "deep and implacable resentment" he expressed toward the Germans for "their savage attack upon the rights and dignity of man" and his "contempt for their arrogant and insolent doctrine of the German master race" often brought him into conflict with public figures. When he urged a hard peace for Germany, in 1944, he encountered opposition from columnist Dorothy Thompson '40, who charged that Stout, Lord Vansittart '41, and other advocates of a harsh policy toward the Germans were aiding Goebbels' propaganda. When the author resigned from Freedom House in protest, Miss Thompson, the president of the organization, followed suit. However, after much publicity and acrimonious debate—in which Miss Thompson denied that she questioned Stout's patriotism and Stout admitted that there were a few "good" Germans—both protagonists were prevailed upon to resume their posts. Stout and his organization late in 1945 supported the separation of the Ruhr, to eradicate Germany's future war potentiality; they are currently concerned with the problems of the United Nations organization.

A man of medium height and weight, Stout has brown eyes and hair, a beard that is turning gray. He is a great traveler: in addition to trips abroad, including an aerial tour of the European theater of war as guest of the Army Air Forces in 1945, he has made four automobile journeys all over the United States and says that he is personally acquainted with more towns, rivers, valleys, mountains and back roads than anybody but the National Geographic Society. His first marriage, to Fay Kennedy of Topeka, Kansas, in 1916, terminated in divorce. In 1932 he was married to Pola Hoffman of Vienna, now a well known designer of textiles, fashions, and interior decorations. The Stouts, with their two daughters, Barbara and Rebecca, make their home at High Meadow, a farm near Brewster, New York, where they live in a fourteen-room house built by the author himself with the assistance of his farmer-neighbors. Stout's recreations include cabinetmaking, "arguing," and gardening; in prewar days he grew many varieties of roses and iris. Known as an epicure, he has been elected to the Society of Amateur Chefs. He is also a member and former president (1943-44) of the Authors' Guild, the editor of the Authors' League Bulletin, and a member of Mystery Writers of America, Inc. His most recent activity is the editorship of the Rex Stout Mystery Magazine.

References

Cue 10:34 N 1 '41
Look 7:42 F 23 '43
N Y Post p33 My 16 '45
N Y Times VI p2 S 21 '41
Sat R Lit 16:6-7 S 18 '37

Haycraft, H. Murder for Pleasure (1941)
Kunitz, S., and Haycraft, H. eds. Twentieth Century Authors (1942)
Who's Who in America, 1946-47

STRACHEY, (EVELYN) JOHN (ST. LOE (strā'chǐ ēv'lǐn sǐn-loō') Oct. 21, 1901- British Government official; economist

Address: b. 112 Regent's Pk. Rd., London; h. "Ewen Bridge Farm," Shalford, Braintree, Essex, England

In May 1946 John Strachey, author of the widely read Coming Struggle for Power and other political books, was appointed Great Britain's Minister of Food to succeed Sir Ben Smith '45. This position will make demands on all the powers of persuasiveness and eloquence he first exerted in his political career in the Labor Party and later in his writings expounding Marxian communism.

Born in Guildford, the capital of Surrey, on October 21, 1901, Evelyn John St. Loe Strachey is the oldest surviving son of the late John St. Loe Strachey, editor and publisher of the *Spectator* until his retirement in 1925, and a cousin of Lytton Strachey, the historian and biographer. The family was Conservative, and so young John Strachey remained during his years at Eton, where he was "chiefly engaged in games," he says, and until he went up to Magdalen College, Oxford. But at Oxford he came under the influence of Edmund D. Morel, and, as the London *Daily Herald* phrased it, "went Left, very Left." In 1923, still a student at Oxford, he joined the Independent Labor Party, always the radical element of the British Labor movement—having appeared with his sponsor, Arthur Ponsonby, in the offices of Archibald Fenner Brockway, general secretary of the I.L.P., to offer his services in the cause. "Mr. Brockway," related the London *Observer,* "thought the new recruit was sincere in his desire to help, but that he understood little about socialism."

It was not long before Strachey learned, however. Scarcely a year later, at the age of twenty-three, he was contesting the Parliamentary election from Aston division of Birmingham, and when defeated, continued to work actively for socialism as a journalist. He became editor of the *Socialist Review,* the official organ of the Independent Labor Party, and later, of The Miner, the publication of the Miners' Federation of Great Britain. In this latter capacity he was described as "a kind of public relations officer for the industrial side of Labor." It was he who, during the General Strike of 1926, popularized the miners' cause, and who, after listening for hours to A. J. Cook, the Federation's leader, regularly put into finished form the "flaming" editorial carried by The Miner under Cook's name. It was also during these early years of his socialist adherence that Strachey became a follower of Sir Oswald Mosley '40, who was then still the hope of those Laborites who were dissatisfied with the growing conservatism of the Labor Party's leaders, Ramsay MacDonald, Philip Snowden, and James Henry Thomas. In 1925 Strachey published his first book, Revolution by Reason, subtitled An Account of the Financial Proposals Submitted to the Labor Movement by Mr. Oswald Mosley. Its main title became Mosley's campaign slogan.

Four years later, in the Labor Party landslide, Strachey joined Mosley in Parliament,

British Official Photo.

JOHN STRACHEY

elected from the Aston division of Birmingham, and also became the latter's secretary and lieutenant. What happened after that—so that Mosley turned fascist and Strachey communist (in theory, though he insists he never joined the party)—has been described by the London *Observer*: "Mosley's proposals swept the Labor Conference of 1930, and the triumph went to his head. He carried the battle into Parliament, and when he lost, he lost also his faith in Parliament and the people." In February 1931 he resigned from the Labor Party and formed his own New Party—taking with him his still loyal lieutenant John Strachey. However, although Mosley was at this time not yet a fascist, his increasing arrogance and growing contempt for the ordinary man before very long began to alienate Strachey, who, while still in Parliament, had come under the influence of Aneurin Bevan's [43] passionate belief in democracy of the common people and government by legislative assembly. Before Mosley organized his British Union of Fascists in October 1932, Strachey had broken with him, and in his third book, *The Coming Struggle for Power*, published just one month later, Strachey was already an "ardent advocate of Marxian Communism."

The Coming Struggle for Power, an analysis of the origin and growth of capitalism, the causes of decay seen as inherent by the author, and its future, concluded, in the words of Max Lerner, with a "cocky assurance of the approaching triumph of the proletarians." From critics of all shades of political opinion it obtained a varied reception. The reviewer for *Forum and Century* wrote: "Mr. Strachey has an enormous range of knowledge, a considerable fund of wit, and a fine crusading eloquence. He has translated Marxism into clear, concrete terms suited to the Anglo-Saxon mind. Whether one tends to agree with him

or not, this is as stimulating and arresting a book as the current crisis has produced." Matthew Josephson of the *New Republic* felt that the volume was "the sanest, the most intelligent apologia for communism that has been written in many years by any Western thinker," and that to the testing of the Marxian tenet that "the economic crisis is the inevitable consequence of the essential features of capitalism" its author brought "a tenacious logic and its (necessitous) strategems that is still too seldom found in Communist writers." On the other hand, C. E. M. Joad wrote in the *New Statesman and Nation*: "Mr. Strachey's judgments are always intriguing; they would be more convincing were it not for the author's instinctive dependence on the ready-mades and hand-me-downs of the rag-shop in which Communist theory keeps its stock of dogmas to misfit all situations." And the *Saturday Review of Literature* summarized: "An able and brilliant but one-sided and often misleading argument."

Six months after the publication of *The Coming Struggle* Strachey reappeared in print with *The Menace of Fascism*, a full discussion of that political system's causes, method of development, and purposes, which the New York *Herald Tribune* reviewer found to be rather obviously a propagandist tract aimed at converting the British Labor Party to communism. This, although conceded by most critics to be a brilliant and forceful piece of writing, was generally condemned as "hysterical," only the *Christian Science Monitor* finding it calm and controlled. In the following years the young Marxian produced treatises expounding the Communist Party line in rapid succession. In *Literature and Dialectical Materialism* (1934), "in substance the lecture delivered . . . before the John Reed Club of New York," he analyzed many of the leading writers of the day and came to the conclusion that the "'bourgeois' writers have come to the end of their rope; only the Marxists are truly vital and creative." Wrote Malcolm Cowley in the *New Republic*: "This booklet . . . has more good sense in it than most critical essays five times its length." But in the *Saturday Review of Literature* Irwin Edman countered: "It can hardly be taken seriously as an examination of the present social function or social conditioning and certainly not of the present esthetic function of literature."

The Nature of Capitalist Crisis (1935) was, in the words of the New York *Post*, "an attempt to prove that capitalism will not work, no matter how modified, because it is based on unsound principles . . . [and] argued that the best course for intelligent people to pursue is to hasten the coming of communism." In *The Theory and Practice of Socialism* (1936) the aims of the working-class movement as a whole were set forth in historical perspective and socialist planning was held up as the ideal consummation. *What Are We to Do?* (1938), which took its title by analogy from Lenin's famous question of 1902, "What is to be done?" considered the development of labor movements in general, traced the ineptitude of the British labor movement to its abandonment of Marxian "scientific socialism" for Fabian "evolutionary socialism," and called for a united-front labor party. In general, criticism of all of these books ran a similar course. The reviewers agreed on the "clarity" and "vigor" of the presentation but disagreed as to whether the contents represented a truthful or a distorted and uncritical exposition of his theses. Strachey's books, however, sold well on both sides of the Atlantic, with *Publishers' Weekly* reporting in October 1938 that, all told, their American sales amounted to approximately a hundred thousand copies, including fifty thousand copies of *The Coming Struggle for Power* in a Modern Library "Giant" edition. (Part of the sale, it has been pointed out, was undoubtedly due to the publicity Strachey gained when on lecture tours in 1935 and 1938 he ran afoul of United States immigration authorities on charges of Communist Party membership.)

For a time during the years when he was writing to popularize the Moscow party line, Strachey worked on the old *New Leader* under H. N. Brailsford and together with Victor Gollancz and Harold Laski [41] organized the Left Book Club, which built up an entirely new public for this political literature. But when World War II broke out he rejected the anti-war attitude of the Communists and joined Gollancz and Laski in a "bitter denunciation" of his late comrades' "betrayal of the Left." His *A Programme for Progress* (1939) shows a modification of his views away from Communism with an admixture of the doctrines of John Maynard Keynes [41]. For the first year or so of the war Strachey served as an air raid warden in London, publishing some of his blitz experiences—related, as one critic said, with "fantastic British restraint,"—as *Post D* (in America, *Digging for Mrs. Miller*) in 1941. Also in 1941, he applied for service with the RAF, becoming, first, public relations officer and, later, the BBC commentator who, in order to forestall any British sympathy for the bombed German civilians, "expertly took the public mind off the receiving end of the bombing attacks and fixed it on the courage of the crews and the master plans behind the attacks." Then, in the general election of 1945, a wing commander, and once more a member of the Labor Party, he was returned to Commons by the Scottish constituency of Dundee and appointed Under-Secretary for Air, a position which he held until he succeeded Sir Ben Smith as Minister of Food on May 27, 1946, in the first ministerial change made by Prime Minister Attlee [40] in the Labor Government which took office in July 1945.

At the time of the appointment the press announced that it expected Strachey to show the same industry and acumen which, the London *Observer* noted, had won him the favor of the House of Commons when, because his superior, Viscount Stansgate, sat in the House of Lords, he handled Air Ministry matters in Commons. His first real test came when he proposed bread rationing in addition to the continued strict rationing of other foods which had occasioned so much criticism for his predecessor. It was necessary, Strachey maintained, because, as a result of the uncertainty concerning Britain's

own harvest and the fulfillment of United States commitments, the Government found itself with the possibility of having to reduce supplies for the British occupied zone of Germany below the thousand-calorie minimum considered essential if serious economic and political consequences were to be avoided. Not without heavy opposition, Strachey guided the measure through the House of Commons for a vote of 305 to 182. In November, during a food crisis in the British zone of Germany, the *Christian Science Monitor* reported: "Attlee Government spokesmen are giving themselves a pat on the back that Food Minister Strachey had the courage to take the unpopular decision to ration bread more than three months ago. As a result, Britain today still has a tight grip on its own bread consumption."

Strachey and the former Celia Simpson, his second wife (his marriage to Esther Murphy was dissolved in 1933), are the parents of a son and daughter, Charles and Elizabeth, to whom their father dedicated *A Faith to Fight For* (1940), a book in which he expressed his belief in England's ultimate victory in the battle between her truth and love on the one hand and Hitler's [42] lies and hate on the other. During his occasional free hours Strachey is certain to be found either on the cricket field or the tennis court. A striking figure, tall and heavy-set, the athletic Strachey has "black, crinkly hair, a broad brow and wide fat face, round brown eyes, projecting nose, and puffy lips" and a personality that is "mild, ample, effortless, abstractly inquisitive, placidly diverting all things with even interest into a mental drainpipe, with Olympian ends."

References

Nation 147:405-8 O 22 '38
Newsweek 27:45 Je 10 '46 por
Time 47:31-2 Je 10 '46 por
Wilson Lib Bul 9:400+ Ap '35 por
International Who's Who, 1945-46
Kunitz, S. J. and Haycraft, H. eds.
  Twentieth Century Authors (1942)
Who's Who, 1946
Who's Who in America, 1946-47

STREET, JAMES (HOWELL) Oct. 15, 1903- Author

Address: b. c/o Doubleday & Company, Inc., 14 W. 49th St., New York; h. Old Lyme, Conn.

James Street, author of *The Gauntlet*, has had a varied career as a minister, reporter, and novelist. He is known for his historical novels, *Oh Promised Land, Tap Roots,* and *By Valour and Arms,* and also for his dog stories. He has reported for the New York *World-Telegram*, the Hearst papers, and the Associated Press, and has covered such events as the Scottsboro trial, the career of Huey Long, and the Hauptmann kidnapping trial. At the age of nineteen, however, before either of his careers as reporter or novelist, James Street was ordained a Baptist minister. He spent two

JAMES STREET

years in the ministry and has used this experience as background for *The Gauntlet.*

James Howell Street was born October 15, 1903, in Lumberton, Mississippi, the son of John C. Street, a lawyer, and William (Scott) Street. (His maternal grandfather had no son and was determined that there should be a "Jr." in the family—thus Street's mother was christened William Thompson Scott, Jr.) James Street comes of stock that is American back to the seventeenth century; among his forebears were, evidently, a number of notables, but he knows little about them and cares less. What is important, he says, is this: "We have melted enough to have everything in us, except Chinese—and I could do with some of that."

Street went to the Laurel (Mississippi) High School and to the Massey Military School at Pulaski, Tennessee. Afterward he attended Southwestern Theological Seminary and Howard College, but he took no degrees. He became a writer at the age of fourteen, when he started reporting for the newspaper in Laurel, presumably the same paper that two years earlier had published a "very bad poem" he had sent in. When he was sixteen he went to another reporting job in Hattiesburg, Mississippi.

Three years later, disregarding friendly advice that he study law, Street left newspaper work to become the youngest Baptist minister in the United States. For some time he had felt compelled to speak out about the brotherhood of man and the democracy of Christ—particularly to "the lowly, mostly Negroes, to the 'terrible meek.'" In that same year, on January 20, 1923, he was married to Lucy Nash O'Briant. Street then took his wife with him to a Baptist seminary in Fort Worth, Texas, but he was not happy in his studies, largely

because he was unable to reconcile the idea of a democratic Christ with what he felt to be the superstitions of theology. He left the seminary for several reasons—he had "nothing ahead" economically and his wife was expecting a child. For the next two years he was a Baptist minister, holding three successive pastorates, in St. Charles, Missouri, in Lucedale, Mississippi, and in Boyles, Alabama. He himself contends that he was a bad preacher—he was never, he says, entirely certain that he knew what he was talking about, he confused religion with rules, and he tried to turn God into a "police judge." He also had what proved to be an unfortunate habit, that of stepping on the toes of important church members. His last sermon, "The First Million Years of Creation" (its theme: should Christ return today, he would be lynched as a radical, or "legally" executed), was preached in 1925.

Street now returned to the newspaper field when he became a reporter on the Pensacola (Florida) *Journal.* For the next thirteen years he remained in journalism, moving from paper to paper across the country. In 1933 he went to New York as a feature writer for Hearst. Four years later he was on the New York *World-Telegram* as assistant literary editor.

Since 1937 Street's stories and articles have appeared in numerous newspapers and magazines. "Nothing Sacred," his first short story, was sold to Hollywood, and the check for this gave him a backlog sufficiently large to let him turn to free lancing. He had already begun to write novels in 1935, and then years later had a half-dozen to his credit (*Look Away, Oh Promised Land, In My Father's House, The Biscuit Eater, Tap Roots, By Valour and Arms,* and *The Gauntlet*). *Look Away,* his first, was written during the month-long Hauptmann kidnapping trial, which he was covering for a Southern paper. *The Biscuit Eater,* published in 1941, had an unusual history. It was written originally as a short story, went into the films, was presented over the radio, and appeared last of all, in expanded form, as a novel. *Oh Promised Land* (1940), *Tap Roots* (1942), and *By Valour and Arms* (1944), historical novels of the South, have been praised for the author's feeling for their period and locale. "He writes," said Lewis Gannett in the New York *Herald Tribune,* "with a communicative sense of the country from the dry red hills of Georgia to the hot swamps of the Delta."

The Gauntlet, a Literary Guild selection, is the most recent of Street's novels. It was written, he says, because he had long wanted a Protestant minister "to get a square deal in a novel." He had mulled it over for several years, but it did not take proper form until 1945. He usually dictates his work, but he typed this last book himself, working until his "shoulders sagged"—principally because a last-minute change in the development of the book necessitated the writing of a new second half. Its working title, "Of Things Hoped For" (from Paul's Epistle to the Hebrews), was considered a "bit too flossy" and therefore was changed. The trials of the novel's unorthodox

Baptist minister, London Wingo, are not necessarily autobiographical—Street drew on several persons for them. The composite, says the author, is "a bit stuffy . . . and vain. . . . But he is a man of convictions, the kind of man I want on my side."

Street has two sons, James, Jr., and John Lee, both of whom served in the armed forces during the war, and a daughter, Lucy Ann. The family has moved nineteen times in twenty-two years, and has finally decided to settle down in Chapel Hill, North Carolina. Street has been described as "small, compact, gray-haired, restless; and he has a pleasant Southern softness in his speech." He likes to raise rare cacti, collect recordings of American ballads, or to work in his garden. "I am," he says, "because of my dog books and stories, supposed to be quite a hunter and dog fancier. I hate hunting and my only dog is a little Cairn terrier."

References

N Y Post Mag p41 N 29 '45
Wings p4-7 N '45
Who's Who in America, 1946-47

SAMUEL CARDINAL STRITCH

STREICHER, JULIUS (shtrī′ĸĕr) Feb. 12, 1885—Oct. 16, 1946 Nazi No. 1 Jewbaiter; took part in the Hitler *Putsch* in 1923; appointed chief of Franconia and general during World War II; tried by the International Military Tribunal, the verdict of which was: "His persecution of Jews was notorious. . . . As early as 1938 he began to call for the annihilation of the Jewish race"; condemned and hanged.

Obituary

N Y Times p1+ O 16 '46

STRITCH, SAMUEL (ALPHONSUS), CARDINAL (strĭch) Aug. 17, 1887- Roman Catholic prelate

Address: b. 719 N. Wabash Ave., Chicago; h. 1555 N. State St., Chicago

"As long as two pennies are ours, one of them belongs to the poor," once said Cardinal Stritch, Archbishop of Chicago, one of the four American prelates of the Roman Catholic Church elevated in February 1946 by Pope Pius XII [41] to the Sacred College of Cardinals. Noted for his work in Catholic charities, in the Catholic Youth movement, and in the cause of world peace, in 1940 Samuel Stritch, then Archbishop of Milwaukee, became head of the Chicago archdiocese, the See with the largest number of Catholics in the United States. Robert Flaherty wrote of the church dignitary in the Chicago *Daily News*: "The Cardinal exemplifies the ideal of a pastor in the spiritual sense—a man who gives paternal guidance to his congregation, who speaks always the highest spiritual aspirations, whose mien and voice give inspiration."

Born in Nashville, Tennessee, on August 17, 1887, Samuel Alphonsus Stritch is the son of Garrett Stritch, who had been a school teacher in his native County Kerry, Ireland, but who,

after coming to the United States, became a manufacturer. The Cardinal's mother, the former Catherine Malley, a Kentuckian, is also of Irish stock. In Nashville, young Samuel, one of eight children, attended St. Mary's parochial school and early displayed his religious leaning by serving as an altar boy. His unusual mental abilities were revealed when he finished grammar school at the age of ten, high school at fourteen. Having elected to enter the priesthood, the youth enrolled at St. Gregory's Preparatory Seminary, where in 1904, before he had reached his seventeenth birthday, he received the B.A. degree. His unusual intellectual and spiritual qualities prompted the Most Reverend Thomas Byrne, Bishop of Nashville, to select him for further study at Rome's North American College. There young Stritch continued his progress, obtaining his Ph.D. at the age of nineteen, and four years later that of S.T.D. (1910). His studies for his priestly career had been completed, but because of his youth (he was then not quite twenty-three years old), he was ordained by special dispensation. That ceremony took place in Rome on May 21, 1910, with Cardinal Respighi officiating.

Returning to the United States, the young priest was assigned as a curate at St. Patrick's Church, Memphis, and within a year he rose to the pastorate of that church. Then, in 1915 Father Stritch was chosen by Bishop Byrne as his private secretary and two years later was promoted to Chancellor of the Bishop's Nashville diocese. In 1921 Pope Benedict XV appointed the thirty-four-year-old priest a domestic prelate with the title of Right Reverend Monsignor, and in the same year he was made Bishop of Toledo, the youngest American to achieve that rank in the Catholic hierarchy. "For nine years he headed the Diocese of Toledo," reports the *Catholic News*, "and he brought to his episcopal task the profound learning, spiritual solicitude, and admin-

STRITCH, SAMUEL, CARDINAL—*Cont.*

istrative ability that have marked his work in each of the sees he has headed." During his regime there a new cathedral and a million-dollar Catholic high school were built—a Toledo banker is reported to have said of him, "He has a mind as swift as a hair trigger in matters of finance."

In 1930 the prelate was appointed Archbishop of Milwaukee. It was during the next nine years, in his administration of that archdiocese, that the ecclesiastic, in order to meet the unemployment problems of the thirties, began expanding Catholic charitable activities, particularly through the St. Vincent de Paul Society and the Catholic Social Welfare Bureau. He placed the youth of the diocese in charge of the Holy Name Societies and founded the local Catholic Youth Organization; by 1939 that organization was composed of 275 parish units with a total membership of 35,000. The Archbishop was also active in the Catholic Church Extension Society, of which he was appointed vice-chancellor by George Cardinal Mundelein, Archbishop of Chicago since 1915. Before his death in 1939, Cardinal Mundelein is said to have recommended Stritch as his successor in the Chicago archdiocese. Thus it was that Archbishop Stritch began the third chapter in his ecclesiastic career as Archbishop of Chicago in March 1940. From a small Indian mission established in 1674 by Père Marquette, what was to be the ecclesiastic jurisdiction of Archbishop Stritch had grown to include (in 1945) 350 parochial schools, and 400 churches with 1,652,578 parishioners.

During the constant participation in the war effort and in postwar guidance which marked his five years in Chicago, Archbishop Stritch reminded his people that military victory was a means toward establishing a peace of justice and charity. (In 1938 he had denounced the Nazis for "savagery and barbarism.") As treasurer of the Bishops' War Emergency and Relief Committee he supervised the collection and distribution of large sums to help the victims of war in Europe and Asia. In speech and action he protested against religious persecution in Poland and other European countries. Noted for the fluency of his speech, he was known to speak spontaneously before twenty groups in two weeks without referring to notes or repeating himself, and his utterances were often quoted. On V-J Day he said in a radio address: "Let it be written in human history that when attacked we were strong and resourceful in war, but that in our aspirations and in our actions we were Christian peacemakers." In endorsing the San Francisco Charter of the United Nations, he said: "We have broken with our past tradition of isolation and we have done so rightly. We are the most powerful nation, but by that very fact we have much to give the world and an obligation to do so." Later, in October 1946, he was to declare that although the U.N. Charter did not contain the "juridic", "ideal plan" for "peace in international communal living, it provided for a world organization that was better than none at all and for the perfection of the U.N. through amendment of the charter.

As chairman of the Bishops' Committee, appointed to prepare a statement for the Roman Catholic Church in America on the peace points of Pope Pius XII, Archbishop Stritch said in 1941 that the committee "without entering into the realm of statesmanship, will try to make clear the indispensable postulates for a just peace treaty. Its work is to try to help, as becomes churchmen, our Government in being the instrument of Almighty God for the setting up of a new era in which human rights, human dignity, human freedoms, and a sane human solidarity will offer to all peoples prosperity and a chance for the pursuit of happiness." It was also during his chairmanship of the Bishops' Committee that an 894-page volume containing the peace pronouncements of five Popes in the last sixty-five years was prepared and published under the title *Principles of Peace* (1943). The Chicago *Sun Book Week* considered the work "an integrated and completely authoritative program of political, social, and economic principles based on the natural law and Christian revelation so vitally basic to the cause of international peace." Among the Cardinal's other activities is his work with the National Catholic Welfare Conference. Elected a member of the administrative board in 1935 he has held various offices with the organization ever since and is in 1946 serving as board chairman. After receiving the scarlet hat of a Cardinal, one of His Eminence's first messages was an appeal made through the Welfare Conference for funds to alleviate suffering in Europe and Asia. For that purpose the campaign for the contribution of twenty million cans of food began on Mother's Day of 1946 in fifteen thousand Roman Catholic parishes in the United States. Shipment was made directly to the representatives of Catholic relief organizations working abroad with local authorities. In December of the same year the Cardinal, through the same organization, directed a relief drive to collect clothing for the war-stricken. On behalf of the National Catholic Community Service, of which he is president of trustees, he had accepted, a month previous, a special award from the War and Navy Departments for the services's wartime welfare work.

When Pope Pius XII announced that the thirty-two new members he had selected for the Sacred College of Cardinals were from nineteen countries in six continents and that this reorientation of his "privy council" had been made because the Church "must be now more than ever supranational," the announcement caused considerable editorial comment. "A tremendous gesture of spiritual empire . . . one of the most sweeping adaptations to circumstance in the Church's long history," observed *Time*, while another writer called the action "re-creation close upon the lines of the renewed philosophy of a united world." *Commonweal*, the Catholic weekly, regarded "the weight given to non-European Catholicism" of "paramount importance." For the first time since the sixteenth century there would not be an Italian majority in the College of Cardinals, a circumstance on which *Commonweal* said further: "We do not jump to the conclusion that the next Pope will therefore be a non-Italian, but this possibility is now certainly greater than it has been in recent centuries . . . the, Holy See has acted with great wisdom in a new world." The *Christian Century* called the Pope's action "a display of ecclesiastical statesmanship of the first order."

"It is indeed an honor to be close to our Holy Father in the Sacred College of Cardinals and be permitted to lend help to His Holiness in his blessed Apostolate for the salvation of souls," said Archbishop Stritch when told of his nomination. In the company of the Cardinal-designate from Detroit, Edward Mooney [46], he made the airplane trip to Rome, where the creation was to take place at a series of solemn ceremonies beginning with a private "assemblage of the cardinals in council around the Pope," the Consistory, called for February 18. At this first meeting the Pope announced the names of his appointees, which included Archbishop Francis Spellman [40] of New York. He then asked the incumbent Cardinals for their opinion, and they signified assent, according to the custom of this ancient ceremony, by removing their scarlet skullcaps. At the second Consistory, each of the new cardinals was presented with the sapphire ring and skullcap of office and given a titular church of deaconry. Cardinal Stritch was made protector of the Church of St. Agnes Outside-the-Walls. This church, an ancient edifice located in the north outskirts of Rome, was founded by Constantine over the tomb of St. Agnes and rebuilt by Pope Honorius in the seventh century.

Another innovation made by Pope Pius XII in his creation of the Cardinals was to open to the public the last ceremony—the conferring of the *Galero Cardinalizion,* or red hat, upon the new Cardinals. "For sheer pageantry," Herbert L. Matthews (New York *Times*), wrote of the scene in St. Peter's, "it was a breathtaking sight, but it was much more than a mere pageant. It was visible evidence for the 'prelates, dignitaries, and laity' of the power of the church now mobilized from all corners of the world, as the Pontiff said yesterday, to fight 'modern imperialism.' "

In addition to his appeals for contributions of food, money, and clothing for Europe's needy through Roman Catholic associations, Cardinal Stritch also urged that an organization be established to supersede UNRRA when the latter relief agency was dissolved at the end of 1946. The Chicago prelate has lauded the USO's services to veterans and hospitals and endorsed the USO campaign to raise more funds to carry on its work. He has, in various statements, warned of the dangers of materialistic concepts of totalitarianism to the Christian concept of life, deplored the "tragic delay by the victor nations in reaching decisions on which the reconstruction in many lands depends," and with other Roman Catholic dignitaries protested the trial and conviction by the Communists of Archbishop Aloysius Stepinatz of Zagreb, Yugoslavia, and of other Yugoslavian clerics. Earlier he had urged the United States to protest the action. He was, in November, one of the signers of the statement

made by Roman Catholic bishops charging that " 'Soviet totalitarianism' is abridging basic human freedoms in occupied lands" and warning "against any peace-conference compromise between Russia and the West." In 1946, the same year that he celebrated his twenty-fifth anniversary as a bishop, Cardinal Stritch received an honorary LL.D. degree from Notre Dame University.

Stritch's duties as a Cardinal call for consultation and advice with the Pope on ecclesiastical affairs of importance. Some of the "musts" of the office of a Cardinal are that the chambers of his apartment be severely furnished, and that he maintain a private chapel and a throne-room for audiences. He must dress in black, with no outward sign of his rank, he must avoid public meetings and festivities of every kind and dine in his own chambers exclusively, except when he is the guest at a dignified function, where his presence is helpful to a meritorious cause. "Chicago Catholics are proud," said the Chicago *Daily News* in its announcement of the Archbishop's nomination to the cardinalate dignity. "They have learned to know him well. They know him as a man of modest, quiet, friendly demeanor, a gray-haired man of medium height and medium build, who smiles easily. . . .An efficient administrator who can accept counsel as well as give it, and who wins the utmost in cooperative effort."

References

Cath N p6 D 29 '45
Chicago Daily N D 24 '45
Morgan, T. B. Speaking of Cardinals (1946)
Who's Who in America, 1946-47

STUART, J(OHN) LEIGHTON, REV.
June 24, 1876- Diplomat; missionary; educator
Address: b. American Embassy, Nanking, China; Yenching University, Peiping, China

The Reverend J. Leighton Stuart, whose twenty-five years in China as missionary-educator made him respected in the eyes of many Chinese, was appointed United States Ambassador to that country in July 1946.

The son of American missionaries, John Leighton Stuart was born in Hangchow on June 24, 1876, and spent his early years in the Celestial Kingdom. For his higher education he was sent across the sea to Hampden-Sydney College in Virginia, receiving both the B.A. and LL.B. degrees in 1896, when he was twenty. Nine years later, having studied at the Union Theological Seminary of Virginia and having been ordained in the Presbyterian ministry, Stuart returned to China, with his bride, as a missionary. From 1908 to 1919 he taught the New Testament at Nanking Theological Seminary. In 1915 Hampden-Sydney gave him the degree of D.D.

In 1919 the forty-three-year-old Reverend Dr. Stuart became president of the merged Peking University, an American Methodist school, and North China Union College, sup-

REV. J. LEIGHTON STUART

ported by the American Presbyterian and American and English Congregational churches. The new Yenching University's property consisted of land in the southeast corner of the city of Peking, on which were several old buildings. There were fewer than a hundred students, who attended on mission scholarships. The "first great encouragement" Dr. Stuart received, in his words, "was the affiliation of North China Union College for Women in the spring of 1920, which has enriched the institution in every aspect of its life."

About a year later, Dr. Stuart's university found a two-hundred-acre site, five miles outside the city walls, in the former summer garden of a Manchu prince, and within another five years the new plant was occupied. The formal dedication was postponed until September 1929 because of a "threatening political disturbance." By that time the campus had cost about two and one half million dollars, and there was an endowment of slightly greater size. Yenching was called an achievement "that compels the admiration of all who realize the vision, the faith, the almost superhuman effort involved." Columnist George Sokolsky [41] credits Stuart with "an astounding ability at fund raising." Contributors to the Yenching endowment include Princeton and Harvard universities and Wellesley College.

In Stuart's view, Yenching's purpose was to blend Eastern and Western culture in a manner symbolized by the university buildings, which were built in Chinese style of Western materials. Two thirds of the faculty members were Chinese, nearly all of whom had studied in Europe or America. The board of managers was headed by a three-term Prime Minister. When the new National Government of Chiang Kai-shek [40] decreed that every educational institution in China must be headed by a Chinese, the Vice-Minister of Education resigned his Government post to become chancellor and nominal "executive head" of the university.

During the Nanking Affair of March 1927, when the then-called revolutionary and Communistic Kuomintang was being established, Stuart had declined to move his faculty inside the Peking city walls and place them under the protection of the American Legation. In those days, Randall Gould wrote (*China In the Sun*), "to manifest any trust in the Chinese was regarded as equivalent to treason" in foreign circles. Stuart's "courageous, independent, sympathetically pro-Chinese attitude," as Gould was later to call it, was an important factor in his friendship with Chinese of all parties. The Kuomintang Government is one of the contributors to Yenching's endowment fund. Even after relations between the Nationalists and Communists had deteriorated from cooperation to strife, Dr. Stuart managed somehow to remain on good terms with Generalissimo Chiang and with Communist General Chou En-lai [46]. He was aided in this by the presence of Yenching graduates in both groups. On his travels throughout the country, the American missionary "met and endeared himself to Chinese of every stripe." Sokolsky said of him: "Dr. Stuart, in the nearly three decades that I have observed him in China, never adopted a positive stand on any issue requiring positiveness. . . .He is popular with all factions, as all are who have no positive position on anything."

On his visits to the United States in 1923, 1928, and 1930, Stuart warned of the dangers of Japanese aggression. During the years of Japanese occupation of North China, when all except one of the other schools fled to Free China, he was able to keep Yenching open and free, and was treated with respect by the invaders. In June 1938, when the local commander ordered him to mobilize the faculty and students into pro-Japanese demonstrations, Stuart refused; he also refused, with impunity, to fly the flag of the puppet regime and to obey other orders, and was able to "bail his Nationalist-minded students and faculty members out of Jap occupation headquarters." The Japanese found him useful to transmit peace feelers to and from the defending Chinese. "For a time," reported *Life* in February 1941, "some Chinese patriots suspected Yenching of 'appeasing' the conqueror. Today Chinese know better. For from Yenching campus, whose academic tranquillity President Stuart defends with endless labor and pain, go new hundreds of Chinese to lead the Chinese people."

By December 1941 Yenching housed more than eleven hundred students—in space originally intended for eight hundred. Then came Pearl Harbor. On December 8 the Japanese interned sixty-five-year-old Dr. Stuart in a private house in Peking, together with two officers of Peking Union Medical College. (Captured Yenching students and faculty members were not only imprisoned but "third-degreed," according to reports, and the university was looted of books, equipment, and every metal fixture.) Stuart says that he himself was not abused, although he was taken to Japanese headquarters four times and questioned for three hours at a time about his relations with

Chiang Kai-shek and about anti-Japanese activity by his Chinese colleagues and students. (He said that he was "quite ready" to die rather than compromise any Chinese.) Because a wealthy Chinese friend had paid the occupation authorities a large bribe, Dr. Stuart and his fellow prisoners were allowed to send their cook to market each day to get food and news; a group of their Swiss friends organized a committee to supply the educators with fresh foods. Dr. Stuart occupied himself by playing fifteen hundred games of anagrams and by writing a long Chinese commentary on the Apocalypse. (He has also written a Chinese text on New Testament Greek, a Greek-Chinese-English dictionary of the New Testament, and a number of English-language articles on Chinese problems.) During Stuart's imprisonment the Chinese were able to establish the university "in exile" in Chengtu.

After Stuart had been a prisoner forty-two months, the Japanese Foreign Office offered to release him to initiate peace negotiations with the Allies. The sixty-nine-year-old missionary-educator refused to consider being freed unless his friends were also released. With the end of the war, in September 1945 Dr. Stuart arrived in Chungking, a free man. Urged by remaining members of the Yenching staff to reopen the university at once, he assumed the task of rebuilding it. On Chinese Independence Day (October 10), while the Japanese armies in North China made their formal surrender, Yenching was reopened for freshmen and subfreshmen only. Plans were made for the return in autumn 1946 of the university-in-exile at Chengtu which had kept Yenching's name alive in Free China for three years. Meanwhile, in November of 1945 Stuart was flown in a Navy hospital plane to the United States, where he remained long enough to regain his health.

Upon the educator's return to Yenching in the spring of 1946, he became an unofficial adviser to General George C. Marshall '40, President Truman's special peacemaking envoy to China, and in July 1946 Truman nominated "Dr. J. Leighton Stuart of New York" as American Ambassador. Stuart said he was the most surprised man in China. Correspondent Ronald Stead of the *Christian Science Monitor* stated: "The reputation of this China-born university president is so high among Chinese and is of such long standing that both Government and Communists say a more suitable man could not have been selected." Other reports agreed; the *Christian Century* commented, "Dr. Stuart has long been one of the most valued of Marshal Chiang Kai-shek's American counselors. . . .The United States could ask for no abler or more distinguished representative at one of the most difficult diplomatic posts in the world."

Among the few dissenting voices was George Sokolsky, who wrote: "At this moment, the United States needs strength in China; it sends as Ambassador an excellent public relations counsel. . . .Dr. Stuart knows Chinese personalities, but it is doubtful if by training and habit of mind he is capable of understanding China's role in world affairs." The New York

Herald Tribune, editorially: "In many respects his qualifications hardly could be equaled—but . . . many of his close friends among the Chinese have been men who are now associated with reactionary elements in the Kuomintang Party. . . .Encouragement of this intransigent group would be a calamity not only for China but for the United States." Answering this charge, seminarian J. Spencer Kennaird, Jr., wrote to the editor: "No university president in China has a better record [than Dr. Stuart] for defending his professors and students against Generalissimo Chiang Kai-shek's Gestapo. To illustrate the comparative spirit of his university, Yenching: a few months ago, when the head of another institution with which I am personally connected agreed to a thirty-day holiday with full academic credit to all students who would be willing to organize a hate parade against the Soviet Union and Chinese Communists, the faculty and students of Yenching firmly refused to join in the mock demonstration. As a result, they paid for it by having their gate battered down and the beating up of one of their leading professors, besides other damage."

The septuagenarian Ambassador contracted a fever on the 250-mile trip from Nanking to Chiang's summer capital at Kuling by plane, gunboat, automobile, and sedan chair, which involved being carried thirty-five hundred feet up the mountains. He recovered under the care of Chiang's physician, and held "very detailed conferences" with the Generalissimo for several weeks, while Special Envoy Marshall was conferring with Communist negotiators. On August 10, 1946, the American diplomats issued an unprecedented joint public statement: that, after "exploring together every possibility of terminating the present growing conflict in China and for the initiation of preliminary steps in the development of a truly democratic form of government," they had concluded "it appears impossible for the two parties to reach a settlement of these issues which would permit a general order to be issued for the complete cessation of hostilities in all of China." The situation was further complicated by clashes between American marines and Chinese Communist troops, and by Chiang's reported resentment at the embargo UNRRA director F. H. La Guardia '40 had placed on further UNRRA shipments to China because of distribution scandals.

The educator's prestige was such, Royal Arch Gunnison reported in late September 1946, that high-ranking officers of both of China's parties "do not seem to mind Mr. Stuart's talking to them sternly, as a father to his children or as a professor to his students." Stuart himself denied that the problem was one of clashing ideologies, holding rather that it was a matter of clashing personalities and of "face." Despite some encouraging results of the Marshall-Stuart efforts, Kuomintang and Communists leaders seemed as far apart and hostile as ever, and warfare between their troops continued as the year 1946 ended.

The United States envoy to China was married to Aline Hardy Rodd in 1904; their one son is named after his father. The white-haired

STUART, J. LEIGHTON, REV.—*Cont.*
scholar has been awarded several honorary degrees, including an LL.D. from Princeton in 1930. A trustee of the China Foundation, which administers the Boxer Indemnity funds remitted by the United States for the education of Chinese students, Dr. Stuart has been decorated with the Special First Class Order of Merit of the Republic of China.

References

N Y Herald Tribune p1 Jl 10 '46
N Y Sun p 15 My 26 '42; p6 Jl 27 '46
N Y Times p4 Jl 10 '46 por
Scholastic 49:13 O 14 '46 por
Time 46:77 O 1 '45 por; 47:18 Jl 22 '46 por

Who's Who in America, 1946-47

STURZO, LUIGI (stōōr′tsō lōō-ē′jē) 1871- Italian priest and political leader; author

Don Luigi Sturzo, Italian Catholic priest, writer, and political leader, whose latest books, *Italy and the Coming World* and *Spiritual Problems of Our Times,* appeared in 1945, has been called the forgotten exile. The once prominent figure in Italian politics was forced to leave his native land because he denounced the Mussolini '42 regime and warned that it would bring desolation to Italy. He had lived in England from 1924 to 1940, when he came to the United States. The frail, scholarly priest, who is regarded as "the spiritual leader" of the Italian anti-Fascist movement, has contributed many articles on religion, politics, and world affairs to periodicals both in the United States and in Europe and is the author of at least seventeen books. During World War II he broadcast frequently to his countrymen from the United States under the sponsorship of the Office of War Information.

The youngest of five children (three girls and two boys), Luigi Sturzo was born in 1871 in Caltagirone, Sicily. According to the writer Malcolm Moos, "his full name is Don Luigi Sturzo, the practice of titling Sicilian priests 'Don' being a carry-over of Spanish dominion." For generations his ancestors had been large landowners in Sicily and Italy and were renowned in Florence at the time that Dante lived there. Young Sturzo studied for the priesthood at Caltagirone, where he was ordained in 1894. Later he went to Rome, took his Doctorate in Divinity at the Gregorian University, and received an equivalent diploma in Thomism at the Academy of Thomist Philosophy. At the beginning of his career Sturzo had hoped to become an instructor in philosophy in some Italian university. However, the social unrest in his country in the eighteen-nineties and the poverty of the workers in Rome's former ghetto caused him to enter politics. He was also influenced in taking this step by the modernist movement of that time, which sprang up from the need to "divorce the Church from its association with oligarchies and aristocrats and merge it with democracy."

The ruthless suppression of the uprisings of Sicilian peasants and workers in the sulphur mines of Sicily caused Sturzo to organize these people upon his return to his native Caltagirone. The founder of the newspaper *la Croce di Constantino,* he resisted the Government order disbanding Catholic and Socialist workers' associations. In 1905 the thirty-four-year-old priest was elected Mayor of Caltagirone on the Christian-Democrat ticket. During the fifteen years he was in office his administration was responsible for the construction of community homes for workers, the establishment of a municipal power plant, and the founding of a high school of technical studies. The priest-mayor managed to add to his duties the teaching of philosophy and sociology at the Seminary of Caltagirone. He was also a provincial councilor for Catania (in Sicily) for fifteen years and for twenty years a councilor and then vice-president of the Association of Italian Municipalities.

In the July 1945 *Catholic World* Malcom Moos wrote that, as a protest against the occupation of Rome, the Vatican in 1870 had issued the Non Expedit decree, which made it prohibitory for Catholics to vote or participate in any political activity. After the Armistice of World War I Sturzo succeeded in having this measure revoked, and in January 1919 he organized a national political party, the Italian Popular Party (known today as the Christian-Democratic Party). As *segretario politico* ("political secretary") of the new party, he saw it become, practically overnight, the second largest in Italy and a rival for leadership with the Socialist Party. Although Sturzo maintained that his party was "Christian in spirit and not at all sectarian," its following was mostly Catholic.

After his party had captured ninety-nine out of the 508 seats in the national Chamber of Deputies, he became a powerful influence in the country's politics; no cabinet could be formed until he had been consulted. However, not once during that period did he accept a post in the National Government. Years later, in exile, he came to the conclusion that his party leaders had shown a lack of courage in refusing to take office when the Democratic Liberals had shown themselves incapable of assuming the responsibilities of directing the Government of Italy. Sturzo's proposal in July 1922 for a coalition cabinet fell through because of the objection of the Socialist leader, Filippo Turati. Despite this important role, Sturzo preferred seclusion to social life. The "Sphinx of Italian politics" reproved one of the country's premiers because as he expressed it, "You statesmen dine too much, wine too much, trifle too much." He enjoined his followers to "be practical—that is the thing in life."

Moos, a great admirer of Sturzo, once expressed the belief that, although the clergyman "has always managed to reconcile the role of political leaders with his spiritual mission as a priest," his activities disturbed his opponents to the Right as well as to the Left. When he was mayor of Caltagirone there was a clamor for his excommunication after he had come out against the return of Rome to a Papal State. Pope Pius X refused to give in to the demand, but nevertheless warned Sturzo to "watch out for others who suspect you." Gaetano Salvemini [43] and George La Piana, authors of *What To Do With Italy* (1943) complained that "the able, honest, and well-intentioned Sicilian priest, Don Luigi Sturzo, was not radical enough to become a Socialist." Another Italian writer, Professor G. A. Borgese, criticized the priest because "Don Sturzo loves liberty above anything else, but his religion above his liberty."

As the Italian Fascist movement grew in strength after World War I, frequent clashes occurred between the radical members of Sturzo's Popular Party and the Black Shirts. Father Sturzo was opposed to having any Deputies from his party enter the cabinet formed by Mussolini after the march on Rome; and, undaunted by the fate of Matteotti the priest made a blistering attack on the dictator. Mussolini, in turn, "through obscure threats of reprisals," tried to have him "muzzled" by the Vatican.

Moos mentions that although Sturzo denied that the Pope had anything to do with his retiring for a short time in July 1923 to the Benedictine monastery at Monte Cassino, the feeling persisted among certain of his countrymen that his exile to England in 1924 was not entirely voluntary. As a footnote to his departure from Italy, the political party which Sturzo had founded in 1919 was dissolved by royal decree in 1926. During the next fifteen years he wrote numerous books, contributed to the press in many of the European countries, and traveled often to France, Germany, Belgium, Switzerland, Holland, and Spain in the cause of "the diffusion of the ideals of Christian democracy." In Paris he founded the International Secretariat of Political Parties of Christian Inspiration, and in London, the People and Freedom Group. He also founded the International Christian Democratic Union at the beginning of World War II. Another of Sturzo's activities during the war was the founding of an association to aid war orphans. In 1940 after seven bombs had burst around the London house in which he lived, his physician advised him to leave for the United States. He spent three years in a hospital at Jacksonville, Florida, then went to Brooklyn, New York, in April 1944, to live at the home of an old friend.

After more than twenty years of exile Sturzo's ideas remain essentially unchanged. In an article entitle "Politique et théologie morale" (Politics and Theological Morality"), which first appeared in the *Nouvelle Revue Théologique* in Paris in 1938, he said that the moral and social values should be defended "even though we must return to the catacombs." His book *Church and State* (1939), the fruit of seven years of labor, was written to help the reader "understand the Catholic outlook upon the social problems and the line of action to which the Catholic Church is committed by its tradition." In his book *The True Life* (1943) Sturzo reflected that "society, while obeying the basic laws of human life, has always its historical novelty, its aspects of revelation, its inward dynamism." One reviewer,

LUIGI STURZO

while warning that this book was not to be read in haste, found that it would restore hope for Italian Christianity to those who had lost it. Sturzo's *The Inner Laws of Society* (1944), another of his numerous books on politics and religion, contained the statement that "parallel with positivist sociology there has grown up a conception of society which we may call metaphysical." The critics found this work difficult reading but "another important book by one of the truly great men of our generation" and "a guide for the average man who is looking for a sound conception of society."

Spiritual Problems of Our Times and *Italy and the Coming World* were both published in the United States in 1945. The Chicago *Sun Book Week* found in the first work the "spiritual facets" of the author's beliefs, with "religion and morality on the one hand, democracy on the other." Through this work Father Sturzo expressed the belief that "all spiritual life is a search for God, who is Truth and Goodness." On the other hand, *Italy and the Coming World* presented his political credo and his undying faith in Italy and her survival. Although the *Christian Science Monitor* liked Sturzo's "realistic approach to the problem of clericalism in Spain and the actual character of the Franco [42] dictatorship," the *New Yorker* felt that the book had been written in a hurry and could have been better translated. The *Weekly Book Review* thought the priest's ideas interesting, but felt that his manner of presentation was "not such as to carry conviction or win new friends among American readers." The three hundred and three pages of *Italy and the Coming World* contain Sturzo's views on fascism, religion, democracy, the United Nations organization, as well as the difficulties Italy would face in its attempt to gain democracy after the overthrow of Mussolini. In an introduction to the book, which is dedicated to those "who never lost their confidence in a new, free, and

STURZO, LUIGI—*Continued*

democratic Italy," Sumner Welles [40] said it would "help to destroy the dangerous illusion which still persists in so many American minds that the regeneration of the Italian people requires the imposition upon them of our particular brand of democracy." His *Nationalism and Internationalism,* published in November 1946, called for a moderate nationalism, moderate liberalism, and moderate socialism. Among the dangers to peace, he lists Spanish fascism, Soviet communism, fascism within the democratic countries and British, Russian, and American imperialism.

Like many another exile, Father Sturzo planned to return to his native land after World War II. He had booked passage on the Swedish ship *Gripsholm,* but just before it sailed in October 1945, his ill health compelled him to cancel the trip and to remain behind in New York. It was not until August 1946 that the priest could end his twenty-two-year exile. When asked his views of the Italian monarchy, he told a reporter, "The majority of the Christian-Democratic Party is republican. Personally, so am I, but the King's future status must not be decided in a revolutionary way but by the will of the people at the Constituent Assembly, which should be convened at the earliest possible moment." During the height of his political influence in Italy, Sturzo was known for his Spartan habits. Few persons knew him intimately, and those who succeeded in visiting him were awed by his cassock, "his quick stride, and appearance of gliding across a room." The London *Times* described him as gracious in manner but "impassive and without any warmth, and as calm and rigid as any Anglo-Saxon." Today his snowy white hair has lent a softening note to his features, particularly his prominent nose "resembling an eagle's beak," which was once as frequently caricatured as Mussolini's chin.

References

Am Pol Sci R 39:269-92 Ap '45
Cath World 161:311-17 Jl '45
N Y Post Ja 28 '46 por
International Who's Who, 1945-46

SUMMERVILLE, SLIM 1895(?)—Jan. 5, 1946 Motion picture comedian since 1913; one of the original Keystone Cops, considered the screen's leading portrayer of "hick" roles; his pictures include *All Quiet on the Western Front* (1930), *Rebecca of Sunnybrook Farm* (1938), *Western Union,* and *Tobacco Road* (1941); directed some pictures.

Obituary

N Y Times p19 Ja 7 '46 por

SYDNEY, MRS. BASIL *See* Keane, D.

SZYK, ARTHUR (shǐk) June 3, 1894- Artist

Address: b. 45 E. 66th St., New York; h. Weed St., New Canaan, Conn.

One of the few manuscript illuminators of modern times is Arthur Szyk, a miniaturist of "consummate skill," whose work has been compared to that of the monks of the medieval cloisters. When, as a cartoonist, he "enlisted his brush" in World War II, Szyk declared, "The origin of all art is what we call propaganda. The art of Egypt, Greece, Rome, the Renaissance, was the propaganda of religion. I do not say that art is my aim; art is my means."

Born in Lodz, Russian Poland, on June 3, 1894, Arthur Szyk is the son of Alexander Solomon and Eugenia (Rogatzki) Szyk, and is, so far as he knows, the first artist in his family. "Father was a textile mill owner from a very ancient Jewish family of great scholars," Szyk says. The boy began painting at the age of four. His talent was discovered, it is said, by an examination of the flyleaves of his school textbooks, and was also seen in a series of drawings of the Boxer Rebellion which he made at the age of six. His first public exhibit was held while the young artist was still attending school.

Elementary school was followed by business college, but when Arthur was fifteen his father allowed him to go to Paris to study under Bachet and Royer at the Julian Academy. After two years the teen-age student decided that his field lay in the almost forgotten art of manuscript illumination, although he can assign no reason for this preference except a "born habit of always looking for the hard way to do things." After serving an apprenticeship under Axentovich at Cracow, in 1914 young Szyk traveled to the Middle East to study Oriental art, especially the work of the Moslem miniaturists.

Then came World War I. After six months as a private in the Russian Imperial Army, during which he saw front-line action against the Germans, Arthur Szyk was taken prisoner. The enemy confined him in his own home but permitted him to resume his work, and "from Hindenburg down" they became some of his best customers. (His major work of this period was the illustration of *The Song of Songs,* in 1917.) A few years later the young painter, now a married man, was back in uniform, fighting the Bolsheviks as an officer of the Polish forces under Pilsudski. Szyk, who had done cartoons and caricatures of the German leaders, became head of the Polish art propaganda under General Sikorski [40]. Their friendship was to last until the General's death in 1943, a death which Struthers Burt was to call "one of the severest blows liberalism suffered in central Europe." In that war Szyk won a decoration for bravery.

In 1921 the Szyks settled in Paris, where they lived for ten years. There the artist "steeped himself in the influences of the earlier masters," (to quote the *Connoisseur*), "grafting upon the Gothic traditions and style a fresh and original vision . . . avoiding archaisms and imitations." Szyk's major work continued for a number of years, however, to deal with biblical and medieval themes: the Book of Esther, Flaubert's *Temptation of St. Anthony,* Pierre Benoit's *Jacob's Well,* and *The Song of Roland.* Commissioned by the French Minister of Education in 1924 to go to Morocco to paint a miniature of El Glaoui, Pasha of Marakech, Szyk lived for six weeks in the Arabian Nights atmosphere of the Pasha's palace. When the portrait was finished, the Pasha presented Szyk with a signed photograph, saying, "Tell your master I am pleased." Evidently the French Government shared his sentiments, for it awarded the Polish artist the *Palmes académiques* of France.

Among the hundreds of miniatures in Szyk's richly colored, quasi-medieval style are some which hang in the Luxembourg Palace and the National Library in Paris. He also did a book of caricatures called *The Laughing Jew,* designed to "show that Jews are not entirely a melancholy race." Szyk's finest work in the field of illumination was thought to be *The Statute of Kalisz,* the Magna Charta of Polish Jews, which he executed in fifty-six pages of elaborately detailed Gothic lettering and illustrated with forty-six paintings. "The illustrative miniatures for this text, as well as the enrichment for the printed page, are close to the characteristics of medieval art," according to the *Art News,* and they won the painter Poland's Golden Cross of Merit.

America came to know Szyk's work through his illustrations for Ludwig Lewisohn's novel *The Last Days of Shylock* (1931). "The drawings of Arthur Szyk, loaded down as they are with intricate line work," said the New York *Times* reviewer, "match the archaic style which Lewisohn has adopted for this particular novel." In 1931 the League of Nations invited the expatriate artist to join the Polish delegation at an international conference on design. He also began the illumination of the League Covenant; the unfinished work was exhibited in the Museum of Art History at Geneva, and reserved for the National Library of Paris. During the twenties and thirties Szyk's works were exhibited in all the capitals of Europe.

The chronology of Szyk's work is sometimes difficult to establish; but the series of thirty-eight miniatures called *Washington and His Times,* which took two years to complete, was issued as a "monumental" portfolio for the Washington Bicentennial Celebration of 1932. (The widest street in Warsaw was named for George Washington as a bicentenary tribute, and special stamps were issued by Szyk's native country.) The *Art News* said of this Colonial series: "Although thoroughly a European and never having been a visitor to America, this Polish artist succeeded in capturing an uncanny representation of Revolutionary America." Shown in Paris at the International Exhibition of 1934, the series was purchased by President Mościcki of Poland as a gift for President Franklin D. Roosevelt, and hung in the White House until 1943 (it is now in the Roosevelt Museum at Hyde Park, New York). At the time of presentation, Szyk received the George Washington Medal, and a large exhibition of his works was held by the Library of Congress.

The artist, who took up residence in London in 1937, exhibited his paintings at the Fine Arts Society and the Royal Academy of Miniature Painters. Among the subjects he treated before World War II was *The Epic*

ARTHUR SZYK

of *Simón Bolívar.* Szyk worked four years to illustrate and illuminate the Hebrew text of *The Haggadah,* the service for the first two nights of Passover, which tells the story of Exodus; and the printer took three more years to assemble exquisite materials and publish it in 1940—perhaps the most costly new book in the world, which the London *Times* called the most beautiful book ever produced by human hands. Dedicated to King George VI, who owns the first copy, the edition was limited to 240 copies at a hundred guineas each (five hundred dollars). The *Studio* called this "a magnificent production . . . assured of a treasured place among the outstanding books of the world. The illustrations and Hebrew text are the work of the Polish artist Arthur Szyk, who shows himself a master of his craft." Six years later Roger Bourne Linscott commented that *The Haggadah* had made Szyk "probably the only illustrator, past or present, who has lived to see a book of his own sell at top collectors' prices. . . .Before the edition was exhausted, demand had pushed the price per book up to as high as three thousand dollars."

When the Germans invaded Poland, Szyk's immediate family and his wife's immediate family of eight persons were wiped out, except for one brother-in-law serving in the Russian Army. Arthur Szyk himself went "on duty" by devoting his time and effort to making war cartoons, while his only son, reared in France, fought in De Gaulle's forces. Six months after the German invasion of his native country, Szyk had produced enough meticulously drawn cartoons for an exhibition called "War and 'Kultur' in Poland." One of his anti-Nazi cartoons, showing Death in an SS uniform, was used by the Japanese later—dropped by the hundreds on the defenders of Bataan in an attempt to terrorize them. Szyk also drew some heroic war pictures; one of them, show-

SZYK, ARTHUR—*Continued*

ing a British Tommy as St. George slaying the Nazi dragon, is owned by Queen Mary and hangs in Windsor Castle. From July to December 1940 the artist was in Canada on a commission for the Canadian War Department, working on illustrations for the history of the Dominion; after this he took a New York apartment and continued his war cartooning.

"The change in [Arthur Szyk's] approach from art for art's sake to use of pen as a propaganda weapon is a striking one in which all the luxury of a highly refined art suddenly becomes a prop for the depiction of barbaric evil," wrote the *Art Digest.* "And a great part of the effectiveness of Szyk's satires is due, no doubt, to the fact that seldom before has brutal invective been leashed to such consummate craftsmanship and jeweled color." The *Connoisseur* added, "It is a satisfaction to note that public appreciation has manifested itself in a goodly number of sales. . . . [The caricatures] expose at once the savage vindictiveness of the enemy and depict with sympathy the cruel sufferings of the victims, thus arousing our compassion in a way rarely possible to the pencil of the artist." Of the eight illustrations to the *Rubáiyát of Omar Khayyám* (to be published by the Limited Editions Club of New York), the critic wrote, "They are executed with prodigious labor and skill in a mosaic of brilliant colors perfectly harmonized." Other Szyk works shown at the same time were the illuminated *President Roosevelt's Inaugural Prayer,* portraits of several historical figures, and a series, *Polish-American Patriots Who Have Figured in American History.*

Thirty-eight of Szyk's cartoons were reprinted as *The New Order* in July 1941. That September saw the first of his monthly contribution of six cartoons to the *American Mercury* ("a truly original form of cartoon art, distinguished by fine composition, lucidity, firmness, and brilliant characterizations," the magazine commented editorially). That November came the first of his covers for *Collier's* in the same vein, and in 1942 the War and Navy Departments and the USO began exhibiting a selection of Szyk cartoons to servicemen at hundreds of places throughout the country. Advertisers began to use Szyk drawings. Reviewers praised his "eloquent loathings" almost without exception, although in 1941 the *Commonweal* was "revolted after the first half-dozen specimens," and C. G. Spaulding of that magazine deplored in July 1942 what he called "these bitter, thin, cheap, and meticulously drawn cartoons. . . . The distortion is that of the comic strip. . . . It is very bad for us to see our enemies as they are drawn by Mr. Szyk. . . . In so doing, we are cheapening our war, and our war aims, and our soldiers."

Of the twenty-six portrait miniatures drawn by Szyk for a new version of *Canterbury Tales* in 1946, the director of the Heritage Press said, "To look at them is to drown the eye in an ocean of rainbow color . . . the vibrating reds and the electric blues." The *Time* reviewer's comment was that Szyk's pilgrims "seem a little tired and dusty in illustration, and strangely short in the legs. But Szyk's faintly medieval touch had caught some of the richness, if not much of the reality, of Chaucer's characters." The Heritage Press also had in preparation a collection of eighty of Szyk's pictures, many to be reproduced in six colors, for which the artist had chosen the title, "Ink and Blood." In the accompanying text, Struthers Burt explains that Szyk's cartoons, which reportedly caused Hitler to put a price on his head, never were aimed solely at the Germans, Japanese, and Italians, but at them as symbols of the evil they represented. Szyk's fight is a part of "the oldest quarrel there is," against all forms of "tyranny, of cruelty, of torture, of injustice, of intolerance, of rapine, of lust, of prejudice."

Szyk's other works include illustrated editions of Andersen's *Fairy Tales,* the Limited Editions Club version of the *Book of Job,* and Mortimer J. Cohen's *Pathways Through the Bible.* The United Nations series, in which he painted one historical figure to symbolize each country, called for as much work at research and at deciding upon the personage to be represented as on the actual painting. (This is true of a number of Szyk works.) Szyk, who has been the subject of a Universal Pictures *Person-Oddity,* is in 1946 at work on the Book of Ruth and *Arabian Nights,* and his name has appeared in a number of full-page advertisements as one of twelve vice-chairmen of the American League for a Free Palestine, the Zionist organization which claims 140,000 members under the presidency of ex-Senator Guy M. Gillette '46'. Szyk is a sponsor of American Relief for Greek Democracy, and is one of the thirty directors of the International League for the Rights of Man.

Blue-eyed Arthur Szyk is described as "a small, round, smiling, gentle man," who wears spectacles and uses a very long cigarette holder. He is five feet five inches tall, weighs 168 pounds. The artist rises regularly at six o'clock to begin work; on the hottest days he spends hours in a cold bath. For relaxation he goes to the movies. Szyk lives in New Canaan, Connecticut, with his wife, the former Julia Likerman, to whom he was married in September 1916. Their son Georges is (in 1946) an officer in the French Army, and their daughter Alexandra-Miriam is Mrs. Joseph Braciejowski, married to a Pole who lives in the United States. Arthur Szyk says that his little granddaughter's dictatorship is the only totalitarian regime he will ever accept. The artist, who began to learn English as a sixth language in 1937, moved to the United States because he felt that it was the inner bastion of democracy, and took out American citizenship as soon as he could.

References

Cue 11:15 Ag 8 '42
N Y Post p5 Je 3 '44 por
N Y World-Telegram p26 Jl 7 '42
New Yorker 17:12 Ag 2 '41
Newsweek 17:53 Je 9 '41

PM p45 My 25 '41
Time 18:63 S 9 '46
Szyk, A. The New Order (1941)
Who's Who in America, 1946-47

TARKINGTON, (NEWTON) BOOTH

July 29, 1869—May 19, 1946 Novelist and
playwright; became famous with the publication
of *The Gentleman From Indiana* in 1899;
author of *Penrod* (1914), *Seventeen* (1917);
twice received the Pulitzer Prize for Literature—in 1918 for *The Magnificent Ambersons*
and in 1921 for *Alice Adams*; many of his
writings were adapted for the screen and radio.

Obituary

N Y Times p23 My 20 '46 por

TAUSSIG, HELEN B(ROOKE) *See* Bla-
lock, A., and Taussig, H. B.

TAYLOR, HAROLD (ALEXANDER)

Sept. 28, 1914- College president

Address: b. c/o Sarah Lawrence College,
Bronxville, N.Y.; h. 7 Meadway, Bronxville,
N.Y.

Pach Bros.

HAROLD TAYLOR

The first man to head Sarah Lawrence College, the progressive school for women in
Bronxville, New York, is Harold Taylor. In
May 1945, when he was chosen for the presidency, Taylor was a thirty-year-old assistant
professor of philosophy at the University of
Wisconsin.

Canadian-born Harold Alexander Taylor
(who filed final application for United States
citizenship in 1946) is the son of Charles W.
and Elizabeth (Wilson) Taylor. He was born
on September 28, 1914, in Toronto, where he attended the public schools. In his high school
days the youth was captain of the football,
basketball, and track teams, edited the school
magazine, and conducted an orchestra. His interest in music (he played the clarinet), in
writing, and in athletics, continued when he entered the University of Toronto. There he
majored in philosophy and English literature,
intending to write novels when he graduated,
and played on the Victoria College football and
basketball teams. When he was awarded his
B.A. degree in 1935, he received the Moss
Scholarship to continue with graduate work,
awarded to him for being "the best all-round"
student in the university's graduating class.
Remaining at Toronto another year on the
scholarship, Taylor worked in philosophy and
literature, writing his thesis for the Master
of Arts degree on the relation between the two
fields. Upon receipt of his M.A. in 1936, he
went to England to attend Cambridge University on a fellowship. But, not finding what he
wanted at Cambridge, he transferred to the
University of London, and there worked for
his doctorate. Meanwhile, he earned his expenses by writing for London periodicals, editing a musicians' newspaper on modern jazz,
and leading an orchestra aboard the cruising
liner *Lancastria*.

In June 1938, twenty-four-year-old Taylor
completed the Ph.D. degree with a thesis
on eighteenth century philosophy and literature entitled *The Concept of Reason*. "While
I was studying I was particularly concerned
with Hume and William James, their emphasis
on human problems and their relation of philosophy to living society," Taylor once told a
PM interviewer. "I read a book by Max Otto,
head of the philosophy department at Wisconsin, and I thought 'Here is a man I'd like to
work with.' When I had completed my formal
education, I wrote to Otto and asked if I
could work with him." Otto agreed and Doctor
Taylor went to the University of Wisconsin
as research fellow and instructor in philosophy
in September 1939. He became a regular member of the philosophy faculty in 1941, and an
assistant professor in 1942. Meanwhile, in 1940
he had applied for United States citizenship,
and in November 1941 he was married to Grace
Muriel Thorne, an English girl he had met
eighteen months before on shipboard in the
Mediterranean. With his wife he "settled down
in a remodeled barn for what he thought was
a lifetime of philosophy and writing." He was
very happy, "grew to love teaching," and "felt
right" at Wisconsin—"we were working
towards a philosophy which could develop a
better life for all."

In 1943 Professor Taylor was Armed Forces
Representative at the University of Wisconsin.
From April 1944 to January 1945 he served as
a research associate in psychology on a war
project under the United States Office of Scientific Research and Development. Returning
to the classroom in January, Taylor resumed
the teaching of philosophy, and became coach
of the university tennis team. Early that
year, Helen Lynd, faculty member of Sarah
Lawrence College, visited Professor Taylor

TAYLOR, HAROLD—*Continued*

on a "president-hunt," Constance Warren, the president of Sarah Lawrence, having announced her retirement. Taylor later recalled, "We sat down and talked about education, the Sarah Lawrence kind of education especially."

Founded in 1928, Sarah Lawrence College was the first school to use principles of progressive education on a college level. There some three hundred young women paid high tuition fees (seventeen hundred dollars a year for resident students) for an educational program with no system of required courses. Instead, each student, with the guidance of a faculty "don," worked out her own study program. The college sought to develop the individual, with emphasis on social responsibility. A Sarah Lawrence education included "field work" in clinics, hospitals, and nursery schools; seminars, frequent round table discussions, and a close relation between student and teacher. The school had attracted a young and gifted faculty. Professor Taylor decided that "the college would never have to rub its eyes in surprise at a changed world; it would change and grow constantly by its very nature. This made sense to me." In May 1945, it was announced that the thirty-year-old philosophy teacher had accepted the appointment as president and trustee of Sarah Lawrence. He would be the first of his sex to be its president and one of the youngest college presidents in the country.

The faculty at Sarah Lawrence has an unusual share in determining policy. When Taylor took over his duties as president in August 1945, he said he wished to be considered a member of the faculty rather than an administrator; in fact, he would teach a class in philosophy. In his first talk to the student body he said: "If we can learn to look at the future as full of an infinite number of possibilities for the good of man, we may find that the lost generation has found itself in us." At his installation in October 1945, the young president spoke on education: "The test of a truly liberal education will become not the student's verbal acquaintance with college courses but the quality of the student's responsible thinking about man and nature."

President Taylor took office at a time when education in many American institutions (Yale and Harvard among them) was being questioned as to its effectiveness and reorganized in the direction of "compulsory classicism." Taylor considered the reform misdirected. Writing in the *Antioch Review* (Winter, 1945-46) he criticized the "genteel tradition" in liberal education—"a great number of sincere intellectuals who press for reform of liberal education do so in terms of an implicit class philosophy which seeks to educate individuals to occupy gracefully a place in a ruling leisure class. . . .For the cutting edge of an informed and critical understanding of contemporary society and human nature, liberal education substitutes the polished surface of respectable social virtue." Taylor saw no solution to the inadequacies of modern higher education in

compulsory courses: "As in the case of required courses in English literature and foreign languages . . . students will devise adequate means of meeting the curious examination requirements, and will reject the knowledge and the subject during the rest of their lives." He would substitute for the traditional educative process, a "program for individual development and social use . . . informal, honest, private discussion with teachers by students . . . adequate motivation for student learning . . . the organic unity of intellect and emotions in the educational process." The use of the source materials in the classical curriculum, he said, "must be in response to a need for historical or contemporary knowledge. . . .Before we can wring the greatest value from that material, we must be clear about what it is we want from it."

The various papers by Taylor in philosophical journals include: "Hume's Theory of Imagination," (*University of Toronto Quarterly*, January, 1943); "Further Reflections on the History of Ideas," (*Journal of Philosophy*, July 1943); "The Philosopher in Society," (*Antioch Review*, Spring 1944); "The Genteel Tradition in Liberal Education," (*Antioch Review*, Winter 1945-46). In 1946 he was at work on "Santayana as a Reactionary", "Freedom for Education," and "David Hume and William James."

Taylor is as "informal and curious as the liveliest of his students," a constant pipe-smoker, and, according to *Life* magazine, "easily one of the best-looking college presidents in the country." The president takes Thursdays off—"I simply disappear and write." The Taylors' daughter Mary attends the college's nursery school; her father says that both Mary and the family's English sheep dog Ben "prefer the company of the students to ours." *Time* quotes Sarah Lawrence students as saying: "You can tell him anything."

References

Life 19:95+ S 24 '45 pors
PM Mag p2 O 14 '45
Time 46:92 N 5 '45 por

TAYLOR, MAXWELL D(AVENPORT)

Aug. 26, 1901-   United States Army officer

Address: b. c/o War Department, Washington, D.C.; United States Military Academy, West Point, N.Y.

Commander of the famous 101st Air-borne Division in some of the fiercest fighting in Europe during World War II, Major General Maxwell D. Taylor became superintendent of the United States Military Academy at West Point in September 1945. As the first superintendent to be appointed after the close of the war, General Taylor was to direct a reorganized curriculum at the academy—a balanced four-year course in the arts and sciences —which would be followed by training in military tactics at the Army's special schools.

Maxwell Davenport Taylor was born August 26, 1901, the son of John Earle Maxwell and Pearle (Davenport) Taylor, in Keytesville, the county seat of Chariton County in north-central Missouri. His father was an attorney for the Missouri-Kansas-Texas Railroad Company in Oklahoma. The boy was graduated from Northeast High School in Kansas City when he was fifteen, and, wrote Delos W. Lovelace in the New York *Sun*, "he might have bettered that if he had not had to help with the family laundry, although his mother says he studied even while helping in that." After attending the Kansas City Polytechnic Institute for one year, Taylor entered the United States Military Academy, where he received his B.S. in June, 1922, when Douglas MacArthur was superintendent. On the same day Taylor was commissioned a second lieutenant in the Engineer Corps; he was graduated fourth highest in his class after receiving the honor of appointment as cadet captain. (He had served as captain of the tennis team for two years.) In the undergraduate publication, the *Howitzer*, he was called, "Without doubt one of the most learned members of the class."

Before going on duty in the field, the twenty-year-old second lieutenant was assigned to Fort Humphreys, Virginia, where he studied at the Student Engineer School in 1922-23. Upon completion of this course in March 1923, young Taylor joined the Seventeenth Engineers at Camp Meade, Maryland. His first overseas order, to Schofield Barracks, Hawaii, came in May 1923, when he was assigned to the Third Engineers. Appointed aide to the commanding general in July 1925, he held that post until his return to the United States in June 1926, when he was stationed with the Sixth Engineers at Camp Lewis, Washington. One month later he was transferred to the Field Artillery; he served with the Tenth Field Artillery until July 1927, then went to Paris to take a summer course in French at the University of Paris. (He had been promoted to the rank of first lieutenant on February 2, 1927.)

Lieutenant Taylor returned to the United States in September 1927, when he was ordered to West Point to teach French and Spanish. (During his instructorship he won the officers' squash racquets championship and the Biff Jones trophy.) Again he left the Academy to go to school, this time enrolling in August 1932 in the Field Artillery School at Fort Sill, Oklahoma. One year later he went on to the Fort Leavenworth, Kansas, Command and General Staff School. Shortly after his graduation in 1935 he sailed for Japan; there he was promoted to the rank of captain and stationed with the American Embassy at Tokyo as a student of the Japanese language. Captain Taylor left his Tokyo post in September 1937 for three months to serve as assistant military attaché at Peiping. Upon his return to the United States in June 1939, for one year he attended the Army War College in Washington, D.C., which gives the service's highest training. Next Taylor proceeded on a special mission to the Latin American countries, and was promoted to major on July 1, 1940. Subsequently assigned to Fort Sam Houston, Texas, in December 1940 thirty-nine-year-old Major Taylor commanded the Twelfth Field Artillery Battalion. This was followed by duty as assistant secretary to the War Department General Staff for one year, beginning in July 1941, and promotion to the temporary rank of lieutenant colonel seventeen days after Pearl Harbor.

Taylor was ordered to Camp Claiborne, Louisiana, in July 1942 as chief of staff of the Eighty-second Infantry Division. He assisted in organizing the first air-borne divisions of the Army when he trained these infantrymen to attack from the air. Taylor received the temporary grade of brigadier general on December 4, 1942, and was sent overseas in March 1943 as division artillery commander. The Eighty-second Air-borne, called the "best in the best Army in the world," took part in the Sicilian and Italian landings, spearheading or reinforcing the invasion of American forces. In September 1943 Brigadier General Taylor volunteered for a mission in enemy Italy. With an air intelligence officer he left Allied headquarters in Palermo, Sicily, for Rome, to prepare for the air-borne landing of American soldiers scheduled to invade the Italian mainland forty-eight hours later. The Italian-Allied armistice had been signed four days earlier (September 3, 1943), but it was not to be announced publicly until the following day. When the two officers arrived in Rome they found that the strength of the Germans in that area had increased so much in the preceding few days that the Italian garrisons "were virtually disarmed and immobilized"; Premier Badoglio sent a message to General Eisenhower that not only was he unable to safeguard the airfields for Allied paratroops, but that the surrender must wait. The paratroop attack was canceled, but the armistice was announced as planned. Taylor was awarded the Silver Star for volunteering for the mission "with complete disregard of the imminent danger involved and without thought of personal safety." When Badoglio and King Victor Emmanuel fled from Rome, an Allied Control Commission was established to provide liaison with, and control of, the Badoglio Government. General Taylor was senior United States member of the commission which obtained, among other things, Italy's declaration of war against Germany.

In England in March 1944, Taylor became commanding general of the 101st Air-borne Division in the European theater of operations; the last day of May he was temporarily appointed major general. On D-Day, June 6, 1944, Taylor, with his men, was the first general to land in Normandy. He was awarded the Distinguished Service Cross and British Distinguished Service Order for his part in the invasion: he led a successful assault on a river causeway, clearing the way for advancing sea-borne units. After thirty-three days of fighting in Normandy, the 101st Division went back to England, and on August 10, 1944, became a part of the First Allied Air-borne Army. They liberated the first Dutch city, Eindhoven, after landing in Holland on September 17, 1944. General Taylor was wounded in the seventy-three-day fighting while inspecting a forward post of Nijmegen, and spent two weeks away from active duty. He was awarded an oak

U.S. Military Academy
MAJ. GEN. MAXWELL D. TAYLOR

leaf cluster to his Silver Star during the invasion.

At the end of their hard fighting in Holland the division was sent back of the front lines to rest, and Taylor went to Washington on a special mission. The morning of December 16 saw the Germans advance with tremendous force, and the 101st was hurried 300 miles to the front in trucks. The "Screaming Eagle" paratroops and glidermen jumped from their trucks to set up a defense of Bastogne, the intersection of seven roads and a railroad and a major German objective. Surrounded by elements of eight German divisions and outnumbered four to one, the men at Bastogne reported their position to headquarters as "the hole in the doughnut," but General Anthony MacAuliffe, then in command, refused to surrender. Taylor, who had flown back from Washington on Christmas Eve, joined his men when the Fourth Armored Division established a relief corridor to Bastogne. Its Mayor gave the General the flag of the city, and the entire 101st Division received the Presidential citation on March 15, 1945, the first time in American history that an entire division had been cited. They also received the Belgian Croix de Guerre with palms in November.

After the Battle of the Bulge, General Taylor led his men through central Germany to Berchtesgaden, Hitler's mountain retreat. There he directed its operation as a resort for GI tourists and sponsored an exhibition of art masterpieces from the collection of Herman Göring. His men rounded up Julius Streicher, Minister of Labor Robert Ley, Colonel General Heinz Guderian the leading German tank expert, and lesser Nazis, including Hitler's chauffeur.

In September 1945 General Taylor took office as thirty-seventh superintendent of the United States Military Academy at West Point,

succeeding Major General Francis B. Wilby '45. At forty-four he was the youngest head of that institution since Douglas MacArthur, who assumed charge at thirty-nine in 1919. Paralleling General MacArthur's action after World War I, Taylor announced the revision of the academy's curriculum some months after his appointment. He planned to institute the reforms recommended by a board appointed by the Secretary of War with Dr. Karl T. Compton, president of Massachusetts Institute of Technology, as chairman. The reforms included return to a four-year course, additions to the faculty, and enlargement of its physical equipment. A balanced and liberal education in the arts and sciences was the aim of the reorganization: one-third of the cadets' time was allotted to the study of economics, government, and history, and a new department of physics and chemistry was organized. It was decided that the academy should continue to stress character building and training in leadership, and that training in military tactics would be given in specialized courses at various schools of the Army. The board repeated the recommendation of a similar group in 1942 that the academy itself select cadets from a list of nominations made by members of Congress. Such a change was expected to "decrease the loss of time and money expended at present on inferior cadets" appointed by the legislators. Taylor made the statement, "The cadets should not live in a mental cloister; their interests must be catholic, avoiding the small horizons sometimes attributed to the military mind."

The General also favored a full athletic program for the men, observing, "A brilliant mind is of little value in war if it is not housed in a vigorous body." He charged in the fall of 1946 that colleges, offering "fantastic" sums, had attempted to bribe Army football stars to leave the military institution. This was his reply to a statement made by the coach of Mississippi State College that a former Mississippi halfback had been unable to resign from the academy. While athletic directors and football coaches denied the General's charge, the New York Sun's comment was that "the recruiting of athletes for collegiate football teams is rapidly becoming a national scandal." In December Taylor spoke at the convention of the Eastern Collegiate Athletic Conference, urging college presidents to take full responsibility for their athletic programs. He also proposed the certification of athletes as genuine students and regular examination of the financial statements of college athletic departments.

Shortly after this speech General Taylor announced jointly with the president of Notre Dame that the classic football rivalry between the two colleges would cease after 1947. Ticket speculation and the growth of gambling in college football were held to be the reasons for the decision, which also heralded the end of "big-time" football at the Academy. "It was a distracting influence," Taylor said, "which pulled us away from our major objective."

The General's rows of ribbons include those indicating the Distinguished Service Medal, Legion of Merit, Bronze Star, Purple Heart, British Companion of the Bath, French Officer of the Legion of Honor (with rosette) and Croix de Guerre with palms, Belgian Grand Officer of the Order of the Crown with palm, ETO Ribbon with six campaign stars and arrow head, American Defense Ribbon, World War I and II Victory Ribbons, and the American Theatre Ribbon. Given the permanent grade of lieutenant colonel on June 13, 1945, after his return to the United States the temporary Major General received the honorary degree of Doctor of Engineering from New York University in 1946.

Maxwell Taylor was married on January 26, 1925, to Lydia Gardner Happer; they have two sons, John Maxwell and Thomas Happer. His church affiliation is Protestant. The General is lean, fast-moving—his sports are tennis, handball, squash, and hiking. Blue-eyed, six feet tall, weighing 180 pounds, a "vibrant speaker," in military circles he has earned by his aggressiveness the nickname of "Mr. Attack."

References

Harper 189:462+ O '44
N Y Herald Tribune p14 Ag 25 '46 por
N Y Sun p26 Ag 28 '46
N Y Times p4 O 11 '44; p20 Ag 28 '46 por
Sunday News (N Y) p38 Mr 10 '46
Time 46:24 S 3 '45
Shugg, R. W. and DeWeerd, H. A. World War II (1946)
Who's Who in America, 1946-47

TENER, JOHN KINLEY July 25, 1863—May 19, 1946 Republican Governor of Pennsylvania, 1910-15; president of the National Baseball League, 1913-18; attained success as a pitcher for the Chicago Cubs.

Obituary

N Y Times p23 My 20 '46 por

THOMPSON, ROY L(ELAND) Jan. 10, 1891- United States Government official; land bank president

Address: b. c/o Price Decontrol Board, 20th St. & Constitution Ave., N.W., Washington, D.C.; c/o Federal Land Bank of New Orleans, 860 St. Charles St., New Orleans, La.

The chairman of the three-man Price Decontrol Board, created by the June 1946 Office of Price Administration Extension Act, is Roy L. Thompson. As president of the Federal Land Bank of New Orleans and a former professor of economics at Louisiana State University, Thompson, in the opinion of the New York *World-Telegram*, is "an excellent balance of the practical and the theoretical." He is the board's expert on agricultural affairs.

Roy Leland Thompson, the son of John Wilkes and Emma Gertrude (Tate) Thompson, was born in Gilsburg, Mississippi, on January 10, 1891. After his graduation from Ches-

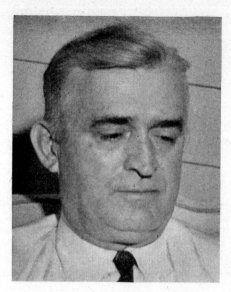

ROY L. THOMPSON

brough High School in June 1914, Thompson began his teaching career as principal of the high school in Spring Creek, Louisiana, where he remained from 1915 until 1917. During World War I, he served as a private in the United States Army in 1917-18. Upon his return to civilian life he resumed his work as principal in rural high schools: he was at Chesbrough in 1918-19 and Centerville in 1922-23. Thompson received his B.S. from Louisiana State University in 1922, where he later taught as a professor of economics from 1923 until 1932 and served as chairman of the department of economics in 1932-33. In those years he had also received his M.Sc. from the University of Wisconsin (1924) and his Ph.D. from the University of Minnesota (1929).

After a short interval of additional graduate study, Thompson left the academic world in 1933 to enter banking. He worked first as a field organizer for the production credit division of the Farm Credit Administration and later as a regional director, before serving with the FCA's division of program planning in Washington, D.C., from October 1933 to July 1934. Returning to Louisiana as deputy general agent for the FCA of New Orleans, he served in that capacity in 1934-5 and then as general agent until 1941. In 1938 Thompson became president of the Federal Land Bank of New Orleans, of which he was still chief executive in 1946. The bank is one of twelve such institutions under the jurisdiction of the FCA designed to make loans to farmers and agricultural corporations for the purchase of land and equipment. Thompson is also a member of the Louisiana State Land Use Planning Committee and of the State Committee of State and Federal Agencies.

When President Truman appointed the bank president to the chairmanship of the three-member Price Decontrol Board on July 27, 1946, it was, according to Thompson, "no doubt

THOMPSON, ROY L.—*Continued*

the most outstanding recognition" he had ever received. The President, true to his promise to provide an "unpacked jury" on the board, chose three men previously unconnected with the Office of Price Administration to form "a court of last resort" for determining which commodities were to be subject to regulation. Chairman Thompson is considered a spokesman for agriculture, while the two remaining members, former civil service career man Daniel W. Bell '46 and paper manufacturer George H. Mead '46, are regarded as representing the public and industry, respectively.

The Price Decontrol Board was created as part of the OPA Extension Act of June 1946 when, said the New York *Sun,* "Congress, unable or unwilling to decide whether ceilings should be restored on articles decontrolled, passed the buck to these three men." As an independent agency in the executive branch of the Government, the board is all-powerful in itself and can overrule the OPA, the Department of Agriculture, and the advisory committees of any industry regarding the release or re-ceiling of commodity prices. The board's primary function is that of decontrol; the burden of proof lies with those who favor regulation. Chairman Thompson, who, according to *Time,* is "no crusader for Government controls," says that he intended first "to remove controls speedily from commodities which are produced in such quantities that normal competition can keep prices stable; second, to make sure that all commodities which are important to living costs or business costs are kept under price control as long as necessary."

Thompson's first task as chairman of the Price Decontrol Board was to bring his group to a decision by August 20, 1946, upon whether grains, meat, milk, poultry, eggs, soybeans, and cottonseed should remain exempt from price ceilings. In preparation for this, the board received reports from various agencies and heard the testimony of interested groups and individuals at its legally prescribed open meetings begun on August 12. Weighing the considerations of industrial, consumer, and labor needs, "the three Solomons" worked in closed conference for twelve hours on Sunday, August 18, fifteen hours the following day, and were able to release their decision on the August 20 deadline.

In his special nationwide broadcast, from which were deleted the sharp words Thompson had originally addressed to opportunists among the industrial, consumer, and labor groups, the chairman delivered the board's report to the country. In accordance with Thompson's expectation that "we are going to hear plenty of criticism," the board's decision to put meat and seed oil products under OPA control met with disapproval from many quarters: some thought it too narrow in scope, others found it too extensive. Those who found it too sweeping were able to take heart at the abandonment of virtually all controls in October 1946, at which time the Price Decontrol Board began preparations to disband. (Of the last remaining controls, on sugar, rice, and

rent, only the first two were within the jurisdiction of the board.)

Thompson, a member of the American Farm Economic Association, is the author of a number of agricultural papers, including studies of farm credit, cooperative markets, and the Louisiana tax situation. He has also lectured before press clubs and other groups. Among his fraternity and club affiliations are Alpha Zeta, Delta Sigma Pi, Phi Kappa Phi, Omicron Delta Kappa, and the Boston Club, in New Orleans. Thompson is a Baptist, a Mason, and has been elected to the Rotary International.

Eunice Holland Pierce and Thompson were married in May 1916. After her death Thompson was married to Douglas May Green, on August 1, 1935. Their children are Sue Ann, John Clifton, and Wilsie Leland. Hazel-eyed, gray-haired Thompson weighs about 185 pounds and is five feet eleven inches tall. Hunting, fishing, and camping are his hobbies. Since his teaching days, a number of the official's ideas have undergone revision: "A lot of things have happened that don't seem to jibe with any doctrine. At one time I felt I had a good grasp of economic theory, but I'll concede some things have been done that I never believed could work." Thompson, a Democrat who rarely discusses his partisan views, told one reporter: "I don't believe even my family always knows how I vote."

References

N Y Post p53 S 19 '46 por
Time 48:22 Ag 5 '46 por
Who's Who in America, 1946-47

THOREZ, MAURICE (tô"rĕz' mô"rēs') Apr. 28, 1900- French Government official
Address: b. c/o Communist Party Headquarters, Paris

"With a million members, five million voters, six ministers in the Cabinet, the French is the first Communist Party in any nation to make a serious bid to win a majority through democratic processes," said *Time* in its June 3, 1946 issue. The "French Stalin" is Maurice Thorez, elected secretary-general of the party in July 1930 and first elected to the Chamber of Deputies in 1932. In June 1946 he became one of France's vice-premiers.

Maurice Thorez was born April 28, 1900, in Noyelles-Godault, a small village in the Channel coast Department of Pas-de-Calais. Son and grandson of coal miners, his earliest memory is of a mining accident in which hundreds were killed. He remembers, too, a miners' hunger march when he was ten in which his mother represented the women of Noyelles. At twelve Maurice went to work in the pits at Dourges; then, in 1914, when the Germans occupied Pas-de-Calais, the boy was sent to Creuse in central France. When the war was over Thorez returned to the mines but, according to Andrey Siedykh, having already acquired a reputation as an agitator, he was not accepted at his old job and therefore turned to construction work. Thorez seems to look upon himself as a miner, however.

After his brief schooling, Thorez continued his education by himself; an unusual memory helped him to become what *Newsweek* calls "a man of considerable culture . . . [with] a great knowledge of classic literature as well as Marxist dialectic." A militant unionist, Maurice joined the Socialist Party while in his teens. At the time of the Third Communist International twenty-year-old Maurice Thorez was one of the two-thirds majority of the Socialist Congress of 1920 which voted for Marcel Cachin's motion to form itself into the French Communist Party. From 1923 on, the young organizer held party offices: as secretary of the Communist Federation of Pas-de-Calais, then secretary of the Nord region, member of the central committee, member of the political cabinet; and in July 1930 he became secretary-general of the Communist Party in France, its leader and chief strategist.

During this period Thorez was "in and out of jail, in and out of Russia." His agitation against the Moroccan war caused his imprisonment in the Santé, with Cachin and Jacques Duclos '46. Thorez did not become known to the public, however, until his thirty-second year, when the working-class Paris suburb of Ivry-sur-Seine elected him to the Chamber of Deputies. "At first," one Paris newspaper recalled in 1937, "nobody in the Chamber paid any attention to this stocky, blond, always smiling Deputy. From time to time he would mount the rostrum to make a speech which he had carefully written down. According to custom, all the parliamentary reporters would promptly retire to the corridors, since everybody knew in advance exactly what charges . . . Communist speakers would hurl against the Government." Thorez, one of the party's best propagandists, is described as speaking logically and without the flowery eloquence characteristic of French politicians.

In 1936 Thorez became leader of the Communist delegates. As such, he expressed the party's platform, adopted two years earlier, of a united front against the Nazi-Fascist menace. The next election brought the Communist membership up to seventy-three from twelve, and from that time Maurice Thorez was recognized as "one of the rulers of France's destiny." With the Communists supporting Socialist Léon Blum's '40 Popular Front Cabinet, Thorez was considered by some Rightists to be the "real" Minister of the Interior. "After having been an incendiary all his life," said one commentator of Thorez' new governmental responsibilities, "he finds himself compelled to be a fireman." Until the signing of the Russo-German pact the French Communists laid stress on rearmament. Not wanting to hamper the defense program, they worked against strikes; and in order to maintain the Popular Front they did not retaliate when Blum refused to aid Loyalist Spain against the rebels because he feared to offend Germany and Italy. Thorez, however, did advocate graduated income taxes to "make the rich pay . . . for a free, strong, and happy France," sending out invitations to foreign correspondents for the press conference at which he announced his views. Correcting a widespread impression, Thorez points

French Press & Inf. Service
MAURICE THOREZ

out that in September 1939, after the signature of the Nazi-Soviet pact, the French Communists voted for the ninety-million-franc credit asked for national defense.

At the age of thirty-nine, Deputy Thorez was conscripted into the World War II Army. After receiving a twenty-four-hour pass he disappeared. Court-martialed *in absentia*, he was sentenced to a six-year prison term for desertion, and was deprived of citizenship in February 1940, while his whereabouts was the subject of many rumors later denied. By 1943 Thorez was known to be living in Moscow with French Deputy Jeannette Vermeersch and their sons, but when and how he reached the U.S.S.R. is a matter of dispute. André Le Troquer, a Socialist who fought in the resistance movement and whose position as Minister of the Interior in postwar France gave him access to the nation's archives and secret dossiers, publicly stated as his opinion that Thorez had fled through Switzerland to Germany, perhaps under a Spanish passport, and thence to Russia. French Communists, on the other hand, maintain that Thorez fled the Army only under orders from the party's central committee to save him from Premier Daladier's roundup of Communist leaders during the Soviet-Nazi non-aggression pact, and that he directed fighting against the Germans from a hiding-place near Paris. According to Randolph Churchill's syndicated column, Thorez himself said that he had moved through Europe, organizing underground resistance to the Germans, and went to Russia only in the spring of 1943. The method by which the Frenchman made his way to Moscow remains a mystery.

While in Russia, Thorez busied himself with writing for future publication. (His published works include books, articles, and pamphlets.) He "set up a clamor" to be permitted entrance to the first liberated French territory. When

THOREZ, MAURICE—*Continued*

the French Committee of National Liberation was formed in Algiers, General de Gaulle [40] denied his appeal, and refused again when the Provisional Government was established in Paris. As soon as France was liberated, the Communists began to agitate for Thorez' return. Finally, in November 1944, the absent leader was elected to the Consultative Assembly, and an amnesty was ordered for "any French citizens sentenced for desertion whose subsequent activities were connected with resistance to the enemies of the French nation." Thorez reportedly refused the pardon as an admission of guilt, but obtained an entrance visa nonetheless. As De Gaulle flew to Moscow to work out the Franco-Soviet accord in late 1944, his plane passed one carrying Maurice Thorez back to Paris. A poll by the French Institute of Public Opinion (the French "Gallup Poll") showed 63 per cent opposition to his return. "Don't have Thorez placed under arrest too quickly," Stalin [42] is reported to have told De Gaulle. "You may find him useful."

On his return, Thorez called for "a national union at the side of our allies to win the war and to reconstruct France," while attacking "great employers who now as in 1936 paralyze the economic life of the country so as to subdue the people, and who have accomplices in the national administration." In January 1945 he reversed the former Communist position of November 1944 by agreeing to disarmament of the Patriotic Militia resistance groups; he departed once from the Communists' policy of supporting the Government to defend France's exclusion from the Big Three conference at Yalta in February 1945. Expounding this idea in a four-hour speech to the first party congress since 1937, in June 1945 Thorez declared, "We badly need our friends, the Allies, and we need to have more modesty and less talk about France's greatness. . . .One must not be deceived: the greatness of France must be recreated."

Thorez à Pouvoir ("Thorez to Power") was the slogan under which the Communists campaigned in the 1945 elections for the Constituent Assembly, which was charged with writing a new constitution for the Fourth Republic. All the Communist leaders were elected, and the party made the most impressive showing of any, winning 152 of the 555 seats (the Socialists won 142, and the Left-wing Catholic resistance fighters, the MRP, won 142). But Thorez did not become president. De Gaulle, who did, soon found himself in conflict with the Communists: maintaining that they were not truly members of a French political party but held allegiance to a foreign Government, De Gaulle refused their demands for one of the key ministries and was upheld by the Assembly in a vote of 400 to 163. The Communists joined the Socialists, the General Confederation of Labor, and the League for the Rights of Men, in the Delegation of the Left, which laid down a legislative and constitutional program. Under the plan agreed upon, owners of all nationalized property would be fully compensated by life pensions. The constitutional demands included a single-chamber assembly elected by universal proportional representation, subject to recall at any time, and possessed of direct and complete control over the executive. General administrative posts and judgeships were also to be elective. It was this constitution which caused De Gaulle's resignation in January 1946 and his succession by Socialist Félix Gouin [46], who chose Thorez as a minister without portfolio.

By February 1946 observers were remarking on the Communists' parliamentary "respectability." "Maurice Thorez has been a reserved and modest-behaving Minister of State," commented Volney D. Hurd in the *Christian Science Monitor*. "The Communists have jumped in and worked out three-party compromises at every turn." Thorez spoke of the need to reduce civil and military expenditures and simplify the "overabundant" Government structure; he called for reparations from Germany and Italy, including a third of the Italian fleet, for the internationalization of Germany's industrial Ruhr Valley, for a prolonged occupation of the Rhineland, and for ceding the Saar coalfields to France. Then came May 5, the referendum on the Communist-supported constitution—rejected by a 6 per cent margin—and at the June elections to the new Constituent Assembly, Thorez' followers lost about ten seats, with the MRP replacing the Communists as the largest single party. Communists lost strength in Paris and gained votes in the country. Again proposing election of a Socialist president, the Communists abstained from voting when MRP Foreign Minister Georges Bidault [45] was chosen. On June 24, having come to an agreement with Bidault on permitting a general wage increase, Thorez accepted appointment as one of four vice-premiers.

At the November 1946 elections, there were twenty-six additional Assembly seats to be contested. The Communists won a total of 183, making them the largest single party, the Socialists lost seats, the MRP failed to gain, and the Rightist parties made a gain. In a post-election interview, Thorez said that the Communists wished to create a French workers' party by fusion with the Socialists (who had emerged as the party of the center); that they would open their ranks to Roman Catholic workers ("religion is a private affair"); and that "there should be no war against religion, but an absolute neutrality of education with regard to religion." Neither he nor anyone else was able to command a majority of the Assembly votes to form a new Cabinet, leaving France in what correspondents called a classical Cabinet crisis, finally solved by the formation of a temporary emergency Cabinet under the venerable Socialist Blum. The issue was thus postponed until the presidential elections of January 1947.

A solidly-built, brush-haired, blue-eyed man of five feet ten inches, fond of playing the flute, Thorez is described by *Time* as "one of the few Marxists who laugh. . . .In lectures and debates at the Sorbonne, in meetings of legal and philosophical societies, he shines—a grinning, grown-up Quiz Kid with a cowlick over his forehead." *Newsweek* reports that

Thorez' fellow-workers speak of him by his first name in "half-awe, half-affection. . . .He is as much a legend as a leader." "It is known," the magazine added in December 1945, "that he has a son of twenty who is in technical preparatory school studying mining . . . but no one seems to know who the boy's mother was or where she is now. It is known that he has two younger sons, nine-year-old Jean and five-year-old Paul, by his 'companion,' the brilliant young blond Communist Deputy Jeannette Vermeersch. But it is not known whether or not they are married." According to American newsmen, Thorez' home and party headquarters in Clichy, a crowded industrial suburb of Paris, is known to those outside his circle as an "inaccessible citadel." There he lives a quiet, hard-working life with Mme. Vermeersch, their children, and her mother and sister. Bland-mannered Thorez is said to be "totally indifferent to wine, food, and purposeless argument."

References

Collier's 118:18+ Jl 20 '46 pors
Free France 8:257 Nov-Dec '45 por
Liv Age 352:52+ Mr '37
N Y Sun p30 D 7 '45; p30 D 12 '46
Newsweek 26:48+ D 3 '45 por
Time 47:29+ Je 3 '46 por
International Who's Who, 1945-46

THORKELSON, JACOB (tôr′kĕl-sŭn) Sept. 24, 1876—Nov. 20, 1945 Former United States Republican Representative from Montana (1939-41); noted isolationist; turned from life as ship's navigator and captain to become physician and surgeon.

Obituary

N Y Times p21 N 21 '45

TIEN, THOMAS, CARDINAL (tyĕn) Roman Catholic prelate Oct. 28, 1890-
Address: Fujen, Peiping, China

The first Chinese cardinal of the Roman Catholic Church is Thomas Cardinal Tien, a priest of the missionary Society of the Divine Word. He was elevated to the College of Cardinals in the history-making consistories of February 1946, which gave the Sacred College a representative from each continent and ended the centuries-long majority held in it by Italian prelates. As head of the Church in China, which by a decree in April 1946 was elevated from missionary status to a hierarchy, Cardinal Tien has a flock of more than three million. In the newly decreed hierarchy, Cardinal Tien is the first Archbishop of Peking.

Tien Tung-Lai was the name first given to Thomas Tien. He was born to Catholic converts, Peter and Mary Tien, on October 28, 1890, in Changtsiu, Yenchowfu. His father was so pious and learned in Catholicism that the local vicar asked him to teach in the seminary at Puoly in South Shantung. There the elder Tien put such effort into his work that he died from overstrain at the age of forty-seven.

Despite the dangers which menaced Christians in China—persecution of Christians and

THOMAS CARDINAL TIEN

hostility to all foreign elements were at their height during the Boxer Rebellion—little Tung-Lai was determined to follow his parents' example and become a Catholic. After two years as a catechumen, at the age of eleven he was baptized, choosing as his Christian name Thomas, the name of one of the Twelve Apostles. When he was fourteen, Thomas was admitted to the seminary at Yenchowfu. While his decision to become a priest was not opposed by his mother, who suppressed the desire of a Chinese matriarch to see an only son married and continuing the family name, his uncle raised loud protests—he offered to send him to the Middle School in Tsining and to consolidate the properties of the two families, a step which would have given Tien considerable wealth. But the boy was deaf to all such suggestions and went on with his studies at the seminary.

Ill health interfered with the theological student's work, however; he was compelled to suspend his studies to rest three times. When he developed tuberculosis, the threat of dismissal hung over him. Pointing out that the seminary was not a hospital, the rector, Monsignor George Weig, told him, only two months before Tien would become subdeacon, that illness was a sign he was not fitted for the priesthood. Grief-stricken, Tien sought the advice of other churchmen; all urged him to remain at the seminary. On June 9, 1918, Father Tien was ordained at the Church of the Holy Ghost in Yenchowfu. There, two days later, on the Feast of Saint Barnabas, he said his first Solemn Mass. Years of missionary work followed. He went from Shanhsien to Kuyeh and to Chucheng, where he was principal of a primary school for boys; then back to Kuyeh, and on to Fanhsien, devoting his efforts to helping the people and converting them to his faith.

In 1929, while at Yutai, Father Tien entered the Society of the Divine Word, the German-founded missionary organization. (Priests of

TIEN, THOMAS, CARDINAL—*Continued*

this Society had been his guides as a student and his colleagues as a missionary.) After his novitiate and first vows Tien continued working as a missionary at Kiasiang, Yuncheng, and Yutai. Early in 1934 he took the final vows as a member of the Divine Word Society. Soon afterward, in February, the Vatican appointed him Prefect Apostolic of Yangku in Shantung. In his new capacity, Father Tien continued his efforts to convert the Chinese and also helped to promote Catholic Action, the movement to strengthen Catholicism by social, cultural, and recreational means.

After being elevated to the post of Vicar Apostolic of Yangku in July 1939, only a few months passed before Monsignor Tien became Bishop Tien. At this time of unrest in China his trip to Rome to be consecrated by Pope Pius [41] was beset by many difficulties. When he returned to China, Bishop Tien continued at Yangku for three years; during his vicarship there the Catholic population was increased by about ten thousand converts. Then, in 1942 the Bishop was transferred to Tsingtao to succeed the same Bishop Weig who had once told him to give up the idea of becoming a priest.

His new vicariate presented problems. Aside from having to adjust himself to administering to a large urban population which included many foreigners—in the Yangku Mission, there had been "simple country folk"—Bishop Tien had to contend with the conditions brought about by Japanese occupation. The Japanese had closed the Marist Brothers' School for boys as well as Saint Joseph's Middle School for girls and had imprisoned the brothers, nuns, and priests. Although other vicars wanted to close the Yenchowfu seminary, which was attended by students from all the vicariates in the Divine Word territory, Bishop Tien insisted that greater sacrifices be made to keep the school functioning. The seminary remained open.

The landing of the Sixth Marine Division in October 1945 to disarm the Japanese forces and accept their official surrender was a time of rejoicing in Tsingtao. Priests, nuns, and brothers were freed, schools were reopened, and activities resumed. To many of the American marines Tsingtao was a happy landing place, the Catholics among them flocking to the Cathedral and finding a friend in the Bishop. At the Solemn Pontifical Mass of thanksgiving Bishop Tien was able to speak to them in their own language. Aided by Sergeant Louis J. Maloof, who later wrote a biography of the prelate, he had diligently practiced English for the occasion.

Two days before the end of 1945 Bishop Tien received a cable from the Vatican announcing that the Pope had named him Cardinal-designate. That this honor should be bestowed upon him, the humble Bishop could hardly believe. This time Tien crossed the Pacific to the United States on an American troopship and flew to Rome in an American Army bomber with Cardinals-designate Spellman [40] of New York and Glennon of St. Louis. And on February 18, 1946, he was one of the twenty-eight prelates inducted into the Sacred College, re-

ceiving the papal embrace and the red hat which made him Thomas Cardinal Tien and the head of the Catholic Church in China. Before returning to his native country, the Cardinal traveled in Germany, France, Holland, and in the United States. During interviews in New York, Tien stated that the methods of bringing Catholicism to his people must be modernized to take account of the psychology of the people, that the native clergy, who work close to the people, must be increased and given a better and more modern education. The Cardinal also spoke of plans for improving the education of the people along vocational and industrial lines.

Three United States colleges conferred upon Cardinal Tien the honorary degree of Doctor of Laws in 1946—Manhattan College, in New York; Creighton University, in Omaha, Nebraska; and Loyola University, in Los Angeles. The Chinese prelate is of medium height and gray-haired. His smile is described as "frequent and thoroughly jovial." The general comment of American reporters on the Cardinal's personality was: "A kind man—simple, humble, courteous, and cordial."

References

China Mo 7:128-9 Ap '46
N Y Post p41 F 15 '46

Maloof, L. J. Adveniat Regnum Tuum: the Story of China's First Cardinal (1946)

TOBIN, MAURICE J(OSEPH) May 22, 1901- Governor of Massachusetts
Address: b. State House, Boston; h. 30 Hopkins Rd., Jamaica Plain, Boston

In January 1945 the forty-three-year-old mayor of Boston, Maurice J. Tobin, moved three blocks up Beacon Hill into the State House to become Governor of the Commonwealth of Massachusetts. A New Deal Democrat, he sponsored the Bay State's anti-discrimination-in-employment act, one of the first to be passed by any State. Tobin had achieved the Boston mayoralty against a veteran political boss, after one term of service in the State legislature and six years on the elected Boston School Committee. He held the gubernatorial office for one term, until the end of 1946.

The son of Irish immigrants Margaret M. (Daly) and James J. Tobin has found his blood and faith to be political assets in strongly Irish Catholic Boston. Born in Roxbury, South Boston, on May 22, 1901, little Maurice Joseph earned his first money selling newspapers. After the High School of Commerce and a prelegal course, he studied at the Boston College School of Law, but did not complete the requirements for a degree. (He has since been given honorary doctorates from Boston University and from Portia Law School, a Boston institution for women.) Tobin's other studies include a Knights of Columbus course in public speaking.

The future Governor's first full-time job was as a sorter for the Conway Leather Company. In 1922 the young man went to work for the New England Telephone and Telegraph Company, and while in their employ was elected to the Massachusetts House of Representatives, which meets biennially in odd-numbered years. Tobin held this $2,000-a-session post for the two-year term of 1927-28; in the latter year he was promoted to unit traffic manager for his company. In 1931 the businessman was elected to a four-year term on the Boston School Committee, a "proving ground for the politically ambitious," which directs some five thousand employees; and in 1935 Tobin was re-elected to the five-man board. At this time he was division traffic supervisor for the telephone company, a position he held until 1937.

Committeeman Tobin's "boyish frankness," engaging smile, and ability as a speaker caused Mayor James M. Curley to predict in 1932 that "perhaps he will be the next mayor of Boston." Not until 1936 did Tobin justify this prediction, when he defeated Curley, who had become Governor, for the mayor's office. The nonpartisan election law, which had no provision for primary elections to determine party candidates, enabled the Republican minority to cast the deciding votes between evenly matched Democrats; and Tobin, who was running on a platform of reform and economy, received Republican votes on that account. The final tally showed 105,212 votes for Tobin, and 80,376 for Curley, his nearest rival.

Assuming office in early 1938, Tobin began to carry out his economy pledges, and the 1938 tax rate reportedly set a record. (In 1946, according to a *Saturday Evening Post* article by George Sessions Perry, Boston still had "the highest per capita cost of government of any large American city—more than twice that of St. Louis, for instance.") To solve one of the city's problems, in 1939 Mayor Tobin advocated construction by private capital of municipal garages underneath Boston Common and the Public Gardens—a change which had been advocated ten years earlier, and which Tobin, as Governor, finally signed into law in 1946.

The United States entry into World War II brought Tobin all the problems of a mayor in an industrial seaport metropolis. In June 1941 he was appointed Federal director of civilian defense for the Boston area, and in 1942, after re-election, he was named to the Civilian Defense Board. Tobin's problems during these years included dealing with the fuel shortage (he was never able to carry out his plan to dramatize it by giving Solid Fuels Administrator Ickes an unheated hotel room) and with a police department scandal in 1943. During Tobin's second term charges of "do-nothingism" were leveled against him for alleged failure to take action to prevent scattered anti-Jewish violence.

Another problem was the condition of the schools, in a section and a city that had long prided themselves on having the highest educational level in the country. In 1944 the Mayor and city councilmen appropriated $75,000 for a survey by Dr. George D. Strayer and thirty other noted educators, who found "obsolete and inefficient" conditions. The most important suggestion, as summarized by a *Look* article called "Bungling In Boston," was for nonpolitical choice of the School Committee; but, as this recommendation struck at one of Boston's old-

est traditions and one cherished by politicians, nothing was done about it. The Massachusetts Mayor delivered a speech at a New York Police Department Communion breakfast in April 1943, on "a problem affecting the entire white race": foreseeing "another struggle in the next generation" and "possible international complications" with India and China, he urged a high birth rate to make available "a sizable backlog of children." A high birth rate in 1929-35 would have gone far toward solving the depression, he declared: the increased number of children would have consumed the farm surplus, and the farmers, in turn, would have been able to purchase industrial goods.

In November 1944 Tobin was a candidate for the governorship to be vacated by popular Leverett Saltonstall'[44], who won election to the United States Senate; and the Boston Mayor was elected to the higher office, which paid a lower salary than he had been receiving. In his last few months as Mayor, Tobin was said by a New York *Times* Boston correspondent to have "established a record for 'lame duckery' by salary increases and appointments." Then, in January 1945, Maurice Tobin resigned from the mayoralty and went to the State House, where Saltonstall gave him the key to the Governor's office (the usual nineteen-gun salute was omitted to save gunpowder). "In his inaugural address"—to quote *Newsweek*—"he presented a liberal social program to the predominantly Republican legislature." The State surplus at the time was expected to exceed fourteen million dollars.

One of Governor Tobin's first actions was to suggest that the Civil Aeronautics Board certify Boston, rather than New York, as the sole transatlantic air terminal, asserting that choosing the Bay City "would preserve the greatest possible volume of business for domestic carriers." Another recommendation, that suitable quarters for child wards of the State be established, was made after the new Governor, on an inspection tour, found eleven children herded into a sub-basement of the State House. When black market operations had virtually stripped Massachusetts of poultry supplies, Tobin conferred with Federal, State, Army, trade, and consumer representatives; then, in late March, he requested a law granting him extraordinary powers to seize poultry for emergency use by State institutions and hospitals—a request granted by the legislature within three hours. Less success attended his proposed fair employment law, which was rejected in June 1945. One of the bills Tobin had signed, incidentally, was aimed at ending the much-criticized unofficial literary censorship by criminal action against the bookseller; in its place, the new act substituted action against the book in question after adjudication by the State Supreme Court.

In June 1945 Tobin signed a bill dissolving a railroad holding company, which, it was charged, was unduly influenced by its stockholder, the New York, New Haven and Hartford Railroad, to the detriment of the port of Boston. In July Tobin was one of five Democrats who joined eight Republicans at the Governors Conference in calling for the appointment of one Federal agency to assume

MAURICE J. TOBIN

responsibility for the nation's entire food program; he also delivered a statement to the effect that the Federal Government had taken over fields of taxation which had formerly been considered the province of State and local governments. Later that year the Massachusetts Governor used his wartime emergency powers to seize the Eastern Massachusetts Street Railway, on which a strike of about two thousand employees had halted transportation of more than five hundred thousand persons in seventy communities. This was, he said, probably the first such seizure in the history of the Commonwealth. In late November 1945, Tobin flew to London to present the case for a permanent U.N. site in Massachusetts. He was armed with films, slides, and literature, and accompanied by a distinguished committee, including M.I.T. president Karl T. Compton '41, *Christian Science Monitor* editor Erwin D. Canham '45, a banker, and the head of the Harvard University department of regional planning. Tobin told the site-finding committee that the State was prepared to use its power of eminent domain to provide the international organization with all necessary land, buildings, and living accommodations. (The trip cost Tobin a pair of shoes, which he presented to a shoeless Englishman who wore his size.) When the committee arrived in Massachusetts some time later, the Governor conducted them on a tour of the proposed areas, which were, however, rejected for reasons of population and temperature.

When the new legislature (known in Massachusetts as the General Court) convened in January 1946, Tobin presented a legislative program which some observers thought might set the pattern for the entire New England area. It embraced housing, veterans' benefits, unemployment aid, construction of highways, air facilities, and public structures. The vet-

erans' program, wrote William H. Blair in the New York *Times*, promised to shape up as a real trial. "It is said," he wrote, "that even some administration Democrats are dissatisfied with the Governor's handling of the problem. The Governor promised to make other recommendations to aid veterans during the session but there are many persons who [would] like to see promises already made carried out now in addition to the hundred-dollar bonus being paid." Among the 1945 items Tobin resubmitted was the bill outlawing discrimination in hiring or promoting employees on the grounds of race, creed, color, or national origin. Almost identical with the New York State Ives-Quinn law, the measure passed, making Massachusetts the second or third State to have such legislation (depending on how one rated the not entirely similar New Jersey commission). By the terms of the act, anyone who "violates its final orders or willfully files a false complaint" is guilty of a misdemeanor.

At the May 1946 Governors Conference Tobin reportedly sought action against strikes "threatening the health or welfare of the nation"; he has said, however, that he has never heard of a labor racket in Boston in his political life. On the problem of housing, he had in 1945 appealed to commercial builders to halt non-residential use of materials for construction and repair; and in June 1946, when the OPA was not extended, he announced that he would use his emergency powers to freeze all residential rents at their current ceilings.

Tobin was renominated with a 133,000 majority at the primary elections of June 1946. He came into the national news also as a sponsor of the Albert Einstein '41 Foundation for Higher Learning; as he suggested, the nonsectarian Jewish liberal arts university to be endowed by the Foundation was named after Justice Louis D. Brandeis. In September the Bay State executive took action to relieve the meat shortage after appealing to the Federal Government: Tobin ordered five State officials to ascertain the amount of meat in every slaughterhouse, warehouse, and freezing plant in Massachusetts and determine whether such meat was being "deliberately withheld from the consuming public." On the first day of this unprecedented search, six million pounds of dressed meat were discovered in one plant, two million being Army property.

Governor Tobin's campaign for re-election was hampered by an open break with popular Mayor Curley, whom he had twice defeated for office, and who refused to stump for the Democratic ticket. In the nationwide Republican landslide of November 1946, Tobin was defeated, receiving 741,882 votes to 893,523 for Lieutenant Governor Robert F. Bradford, a direct descendant of the second Governor of the Massachusetts Bay Colony.

Maurice Tobin is a brown-haired, blue-eyed man of striking good looks, over six feet tall and weighing 180 pounds. Married to Helen Noonan in November 1932, Tobin has two daughters, Helen Louise and Carol Ann, and a son, Maurice Joseph, Jr. Fond of reading, swimming, fishing, golf, and baseball, Tobin, Sr., is the author of articles on various phases of State and municipal affairs. The Mayor is a "joiner," in the tradition of American political figures, belonging to various Catholic, social, business, and civic groups, and to the Commonwealth Country Club. Among his memberships are the Clover Club, the Tipperary Association, Charitable Irish Society, Lions, Automobile Club, S.P.C.A., National Aeronautic Association, and Advertising Club, and he is a fourth-degree Knight of Columbus. One reporter at the May 1946 Governors' Conference summed up his impression of Governor Tobin with the adjective "precise."

References

N Y Sun p22 Ja 24 '46
Who's Who in America, 1946-47

TOCH, MAXIMILIAN (tŏk) July 17, 1864—May 28, 1946 Chemist, art expert; lecturer at the University of Peking and the National Institute of Technology in China; developed the battleship-gray formula; called America's first camoufleur; in 1931 told a meeting of the New York Microscopical Society that all except one of the thirty-odd Rembrandt paintings in the Metropolitan Museum of Art were not genuine; explained his procedure and findings in *Paint, Paintings and Restoration* (1931); another book was *Materials for Permanent Painting* (1911).

Obituary

N Y Times p23 My 31 '46

TRAIN, ARTHUR (CHENEY) Sept. 6, 1875—Dec. 22, 1945 American lawyer, novelist, and short story writer; created "Mr. Ephraim Tutt," the legendary lawyer, in the novels *Mr. Tutt's Case Book* (1935), *Mr. Tutt Comes Home* (1941), *Mr. Tutt Finds a Way* (1945), and eleven other books; served as assistant district attorney of New York County (1901-08); president of the National Institute of Arts and Letters from 1941 until his death.

Obituary

N Y Times p18 D 23 '45 por

TSALDARIS, CONSTANTIN (tsäl-*thä*'rēs kŏn'stăn-tĭn) 1884- Greek Government official

Address: Ministry of Foreign Affairs, Athens

Constantin Tsaldaris, on becoming Premier of Greece in April 1946, directed his major efforts towards a restoration of the monarchy and to maintaining Greece's position as the only Balkan country outside the Soviet sphere of influence. Despite diplomatic pressure exerted by Greece's neighbors, Albania, Bulgaria, and Yugoslavia, and opposition from the minority parties in Greece, Tsaldaris effected the return of King George II in September.

The son of Stavros Tsaldaris, a merchant, and his wife Chrysantina, Constantin Tsaldaris was born in Alexandria, Egypt, in 1884. He belongs to a prominent Greek family of Corinth, of which the late Panagis Tsaldaris, a former Premier of Greece and sometime leader

Kagkides

CONSTANTIN TSALDARIS

of the Populist Party, was also a member. Tsaldaris was graduated from the law school of the University of Athens and continued his studies, both in law and political science, between 1904 and 1910 at universities in England, France, and Germany. Upon his return to Greece, Tsaldaris practiced his profession for a short time, until he was elected a representative to the Greek parliament.

Tsaldaris was prefect (chief administrative officer) at Patras and Corfu for a year (1916-17). A few years later, from 1920 to 1922, he served as a minister for the Greek royal Government in Crete. For his activities in a counterrevolution against the Greek republic, which had been established in 1924, Tsaldaris was sentenced to prison in 1926, but was released after he had served only seven months of his three-year term. He was elected to represent Athens in the Greek parliament in 1932, and re-elected in 1933 and 1935. In the Cabinet formed in 1934 by his relative, Panagis Tsaldaris, Constantin Tsaldaris held the post of Under Secretary of Communications. Within another year, when General Metaxas assumed the premiership in 1936, Tsaldaris entered his Government as Under Secretary of State.

During part of the German occupation Tsaldaris remained in Greece. Then, because of his activities in the national underground movement, he was forced to flee to Egypt to escape the Gestapo. Since he disagreed with the Greek Government-in-exile on its conciliatory policy towards the Communists and EAM groups, he refused to cooperate with its representatives. Back in Greece after the close of the war, he persuaded the Populist Party to adopt a pro-Royalist policy. An election of members to the national legislature, in which the Communist-dominated EAM Party refrained from voting, was held in March 1946 under the scrutiny

TSALDARIS, CONSTANTIN—*Continued*
of several hundred British and American observers. When the Populist Party emerged
triumphant, Panayotis Poulitsas, a coalition
leader, was chosen temporary Premier. During the two-week existence of the Poulitsas
Government, Tsaldaris held five ministries in
the Cabinet; subsequently, upon the resignation
of Poulitsas and three National Bloc leaders,
he formed a new Cabinet. The new Premier
decided to retain the three coalition spokesmen
as ministers without portfolio and to send them
as delegates to the Conference of Foreign Ministers in Paris. At the beginning of July,
Tsaldaris himself went to Paris to present the
Greek claims to Northern Epirus, the Dodecanese Islands, and the demands for the rectification of the Bulgarian frontier. After
stipulating that the islands be demilitarized of
their Italian-constructed fortifications, the Big
Four agreed to return the Dodecanese to
Greece.

In an attempt to secure financial credits from
the British on the basis of new trade agreements, Tsaldaris visited London in the summer
of 1946. Since there had been no stabilization
of the Greek Governmental budget nor any attempt to establish price controls, the British,
who had granted a ten-million-pound loan to
the Greek Government at the beginning of the
year, refused further aid. Tsaldaris returned
to Greece empty-handed to find that guerrilla
activities against his Government had increased
in the northern provinces. Shortly afterward
the Government closed the offices of the Federation of Labor and placed its executives under arrest, and martial law was proclaimed in
the provinces of Thessaly, Macedonia, and
Epirus.

On his return to Paris in August, Tsaldaris
once again presented Greece's counterclaims to
Bulgaria's demand for the Greek province of
Western Thrace and to Albania's for Northern
Epirus. The Greek Premier brought out that
Albania and Bulgaria had engaged in the war
as Axis partners and cited a record of their
aggressive actions towards Greece. Support
of the Bulgarian resolution was furnished by
Dmitri Manuilsky, the Ukrainian delegate, who
charged that the cession of Thrace to Greece
in 1919 had deprived Bulgaria of an outlet to
the Aegean and declared himself "categorically
opposed" to Greek demands for rectification of
the Rhodope mountain border. The following
week Tsaldaris and the Albanian delegate, General Hoxha, entered upon an "intemperate debate." Hoxha, who characterized the Greek
policy as one of "imperialistic expansion in the
Balkans," sought to demolish the Greek claim
to Northern Epirus.

Although Allied observers had recommended
a revision of Greek voters' registration lists,
Tsaldaris urged that the plebiscite to determine whether or not King George II [43] would
return be held on September 1, in which stand
he was supported by the predominantly Populist
parliament. (This was the first parliament to
have been held in ten years, since the King, in
fear of a Communist uprising, had allowed
General Metaxas to set up a dictatorship in

August 1936.) Disaffection throughout Greece
had grown since the Populist Government's
suspension of civil liberties (habeas corpus
and search warrants) in June 1946. The September 1 plebiscite was preceded by the departure of the Soviet Ambassador and the arrival of an American task force in Aegean
waters. On the eve of the election, the Leftist
EAM Party and the Royalists accused each
other of acts of terrorism. According to Government figures, the plebiscite authorized the
return of King George by a majority vote of
from 69 to 72 per cent. (The EAM claimed
that the proper tally was only 20 per cent.)
A week after the voting, martial law was proclaimed throughout Greece.

With the return of the King, both Liberals
and Leftists feared a resumption of the type
of dictatorship that had marked the last years
before he went into exile. (A few days before his return, the deportation of thirty-three
officers of the ELAS, Army of Liberation, provoked indignation; Argyris reported that there
were thousands in concentration camps awaiting
deportation.) When the King arrived on September 27, 1946, the country was in a chaotic
economic state, and fighting in the border provinces had reached the magnitude of "war,"
according to the Premier. Foreign observers
said, however, that it was a "harassing campaign on the part of the Government's opposition." Tsaldaris charged that the "freedom
fighters"—who were called Communists (a
term referring to Communists as well as to
democrats opposing the King) by the Government, were receiving armed assistance from
Yugoslavia and Bulgaria. In reply, the Greek
Communist Party issued demands for the withdrawal of British troops from Greece and inclusion of their party in the Government; upon
rejection of these demands the Communists
declared, "The people will continue their resistance, which will assume a more general
character." Tsaldaris, whose appointment as
Premier was re-affirmed by the King, was unsuccessful in his attempts to form a coalition
Cabinet in September 1946. The Cabinet thus
remained predominantly royalist.

Leaders of the other parties represented in
parliament accompanied Tsaldaris when he returned to Paris in the middle of October 1946.
There Greece's major claims—to Northern
Epirus, the Bulgarian frontier rectification, and
Italian reparations—were refused. Analyzing
the failure of Tsaldaris' diplomacy, Argyris
was of the opinion that "the internal policy of
the Greek Government rendered it inevitable,
in the Opposition view, that miscalculations on
foreign policy should finally come to be dearly
paid." All through October 1946, rumors circulated to the effect that the Tsaldaris Cabinet
had resigned. At the end of the month, several
of the Cabinet members corrected the report,
saying they had offered to present their portfolios to the Premier if his new negotiations
toward a coalition Cabinet were successful.
The revised Cabinet list, however, did not contain ay major party changes.

Agitation for the broadening of the Greek
Government continued and the Premier was
urged to include moderate and Leftist elements

in his Cabinet as a safeguard against increased internal dissension. The Greek Government gathered evidence of the alleged infiltration of foreign-trained guerrilla bands into the northern provinces which the Greek Army was unable to combat. Premier Tsaldaris brought a brief of the Greek charges against her neighbors to New York in December 1946 for presentation to the United Nations General Assembly and urged the Assembly to send an investigating committee to Northern Greece to study conditions on both sides of the border.

Two objectives were gained by the Greek Premier on his visit to the United States: the U.N. appointed an eleven-nation commission of inquiry which was to visit Greece and her neighbors at the end of January 1947, while the United States Government promised to contribute food and other supplies to Greece after the cessation of UNRRA shipments. With the assurance that the frontier political problem would be adjudged by impartial observers (among whom was Mark Ethridge '46, who had previously visited the Balkans on a special mission for Secretary of State Byrnes), the Greek Premier was able to return to his country late in December and devote himself to preparing liberalizing reforms, upon which both United States and British aid was contingent.

For his services to the Greek Government, Tsaldaris has been awarded the War Medal and the Cross of Saint Crysostom. He is the author of a number of articles on parliamentary questions. Now married to the former Nadine Schliemann, by his first marriage the Greek statesman has one son, Athanasios.

References

Newsweek 28:47, 76 O 7 '46
Time 48:31 Jl 8 '46; 48:33 O 7 '46

TUCK, WILLIAM M(UNFORD) Sept. 28, 1896- Governor of Virginia
Address: b. State Capitol, Richmond, Va.; h. Governor's Mansion, Richmond, Va.

Virginia's Governor William M. Tuck, elected in November 1945, is a Southern Democrat in the tradition of States' rights Senator Harry F. Byrd '42. Beginning his career as a country lawyer, Tuck progressed steadily from membership in the Virginia House of Delegates and the State Senate to become lieutenant governor, and, at forty-nine, Governor.

William Munford Tuck, the son of Robert James and Virginia Susan (Fitts) Tuck, was born in Halifax County, Virginia, on September 28, 1896, in the farmhouse built by his grandfather, who served during the Civil War as a company commander in the Confederate army. A tobacco grower, his father was a member of the Virginia House of Delegates and served on the Halifax County school board for thirty years. William attended local public schools and Hargrave Military Academy. Later he studied at William and Mary College (1915-17) prior to serving in World War I as a private with the United States Marines in 1918-19. Resuming his education in the

Colonial Studios

WILLIAM M. TUCK

latter year. he entered Washington and Lee University, from which he received his LL.B. in 1921, the same year he was admitted to the Virginia bar.

In August 1921 Tuck began the practice of law in South Boston, Virginia. Two years later, at twenty-eight, the lawyer became the youngest member of the Virginia House of Delegates, where he served eight years. A member of State leader Byrd's Democratic machine, Tuck's 1931 election to the State's upper legislative chamber, where he was the next youngest member, was, according to New York *Sun* commentator Delos W. Lovelace, "pretty good proof that his growing constituency thought well of him, along with Senator Byrd, whose feathers he may have ruffled once or twice in spurts of individualism which evidently didn't trip him." At this time, too, Tuck was Halifax County chairman of the Democratic Party and also a member of the law firm of Martin and Tuck. After ten years in the State Senate, over which he was presiding officer for a time, Tuck received the Democratic nomination for the lieutenant governorship in 1941, defeating Moss Plunkett, leader of the Virginia Electoral Reform League, by a wide margin.

In nominating Tuck for Governor of Virginia in August 1945, the "Byrd wing . . . scored again," commented Lovelace. Elected for a four-year term, Tuck won by "almost a rock slide." The inaugural address which he delivered on January 19, 1946, was given the title "Improvement and Preservation of State and Local Self-Government" when reprinted in *Vital Speeches* (March 15, 1946). "There are a multitude of bills calling for huge additional grants to States now pending in Congress," Tuck declared. "If this policy of expansion of Federal activities into State fields continues it will result in the virtual abolition of the

TUCK, WILLIAM M.—*Continued*

States. . . .There have been . . . regulations of domestic affairs adopted under the guise of war measures which had no real purpose of aiding the war effort." Pointing to the Fair Employment Practice Committee as an example of such regulation and opposing the Congressional bill for a permanent FEPC, Tuck declared, "One does not have to be a constitutional lawyer to perceive that this invasion of a private individual's rights to select his own employees on the basis of efficiency, or for any other reason, or such an individual's right to be so selected, is but the first step in the complete destruction of all his personal liberties."

Governor Tuck attacked Federal grants to States in the same address. He believes that Virginians themselves are willing to finance an improvement in their educational, agricultural, and health standards through State and local taxation. Grants from a national Government already deeply in debt, stated the Governor, were not a gift, for they could come only from the State taxpayers themselves. In addition Virginia taxpayers would be burdened with the operating costs and other expenses incurred in the handling of such grants, thus having to pay for them twofold. Because of Federal supervision of their use, Governor Tuck opposed Congressional grants for most highways, and asked the abolition and State reimposition of the Federal gasoline and some other taxes.

The Governor's March 1946 order drafting approximately sixteen hundred essential production and maintenance workers of the Virginia Electric and Power Company into the State's "unorganized militia" to avert a strike, was called "unprecedented." Under the order, the men became subject to martial law, and would have been compelled to remain on the job if the American Federation of Labor International Brotherhood of Electrical Workers had called its scheduled strike. The official action, which A.F. of L. President William Green[42] declared involved "involuntary servitude," and which Governor Tuck termed "a Virginia matter," was carried out under a combination of laws, one of them, an old Virginia statute authorizing the Governor to draft any able-bodied male citizen between the ages of sixteen and fifty-five into an "unorganized militia." Tuck ordered the draft after union-management negotiations had been stalemated by a dispute over the amount of retroactive wages to be paid to the workers, and a strike seemed imminent. Deeming it "improper for a public official to negotiate . . . with those who threaten to do violence to the public interest," he had refused to use the power of his office to effect a settlement unless the union first withdrew its strike order.

On March 30, 1946, the day after the draft order was put into effect, when the company and the union agreed to submit to arbitration the question of fair retroactive pay, Governor Tuck granted the militarized workers "honorable discharges." "My sole purpose," said Tuck of the affair which received both favorable and unfavorable comment, "was to see that the public safety and welfare were protected. This I believe to be the responsibility of every Governor, of every legislator, of every public official." While maintaining that public utility employees have no right to strike, he affirmed labor's right to strike in nonessential industries. To insure fair treatment for the public utility workers he contemplated the establishment of machinery through which grievances could be heard.

Later policy has shown the Governor, along with twelve other Democratic and eighteen Republican chief State executives, to favor a balanced Federal budget. On April 21, 1946, Tuck was one of these leaders to sign and endorse statements prepared by the nation's taxpayers associations advising budget economy. After the death of Senator Carter Glass, Tuck on May 31 nominated Representative Thomas Granville Burch, Virginia Democrat, to fill the vacancy. In July 1946 the Governor took steps to find facilities for 1,141 Virginia veterans in State colleges and universities, a number that included some Negroes. On the occasion of the dedication of a monument to James A. Bland, Negro author of "Carry Me Back to Old Virginny," Tuck took the opportunity to declare that the event "served to refute the malicious charge against . . . [Virginia] . . . and against other of the Southern States that there is no mutuality of understanding, no tolerance, no cooperation, and no love between the members of the white and Negro races below the Mason and Dixon Line."

Although provoking opposition, the Governor's entire legislative program was passed by the General Assembly in 1946. Said to be one of the first programs to receive complete acceptance by the General Assembly in recent decades, its passage was attributed mainly to Tuck's knowledge of legislative procedure. One phase of his recommendations provided for raising the salaries of State employees but at the same time prohibited the unionization of such employees. In line with Tuck's "campaign to get the farmers out of the mud," a one-cent increase in the gasoline tax was levied to provide funds for improving "farm-to-market roads"; the State Highway Department was also permitted to construct roads to farmhouses with the provision that expenses would be paid by owners. Other measures recommended by the Governor abolished flogging as a form of punishment, eliminated the supposedly useless office of Examiner of Records, and provided for the "periodic examination of school children and the treatment of their ills," as well as for "a bipartisan commission to study and recommend reorganization of State Government."

At the close of 1946 Tuck called the General Assembly for a special session in January 1947 to enact measures which would increase teachers' pay rates, outlaw the closed shop and strikes in public utilities, and provide for State rent controls upon the expiration of Federal controls. Mindful of Virginians' recreational needs, Tuck was also in favor of a State subsidy for drama, and according to Gerard Tetley (New York *Times,* December 15, 1946), liberal legislators were preparing a bill to apportion funds for this purpose.

Since 1935 Governor Tuck has been director of the Citizens Bank of South Boston, Virginia, and on February 18, 1946, he was elected to the board of governors of the Thomas Jefferson Memorial Foundation, which owns and operates Monticello as a national shrine. He belongs to Sigma Phi Epsilon and Phi Delta Phi fraternities, is a Mason (Shriner), an Elk, a member of Woodmen of the World, and has been associated with the Kiwanis. He also holds memberships in the American and Virginia Bar associations and in the Richmond, Virginia, Commonwealth Club. He lists his religious affiliation as Baptist.

"Genial Big Bill Tuck" as the full-faced, 225-pound, five-feet-ten-inch Governor was called during his campaign, likes to have people around him. The dining room of Virginia's executive mansion, where he now resides with his wife, the former Eva M. Lovelace Dillard (they were married in 1928) and his stepson Lester L. Dillard, has been described as "the breakfast club of Capitol Hill." Tuck, whose income is supplemented from the sales of the flue-cured tobacco grown on his farm, is a moderate smoker. He likes to relax on his big four-poster bed with a long-stemmed clay pipe while reading history or listening to records of the "Red River Valley" and similar tunes. According to one description, he is "gifted with a sense of humor and a knack for telling stories."

References

N Y Sun p22 Ja 28 '46

America's Young Men, 1936-37

Who's Who in America, 1946-47

Who's Who in Government (1932)

TUTTLE, (HENRY) EMERSON Dec. 10, 1890—Mar. 8, 1946 American artist and educator; master of Davenport College and curator of prints, Yale University from 1930; head of the English department at Groton School 1918-29; his prints are in the British Museum, Chicago Art Institute, Library of Congress, Bibliothèque Nationale.

Obituary

N Y Times p13 Mr 9 '46 por

UBICO (CASTANEDA), JORGE (ōō-bē'kō käs'tä-nyä'thä hôr'hä) Nov. 10, 1878—June 14, 1946 President of Guatemala, 1931-44; made brigadier general in 1919; suspended rights of public assembly and freedom of speech and of the press in the summer of 1944; resigned in the midst of his third term after a general strike; policies strongly favored the United States. See *Current Biography* 1942 Yearbook.

Obituary

N Y Times p40 Je 16 '46

UNDERHILL, CHARLES L. 1867—Jan. 28, 1946 American legislator; United States Republican Representative from Massachusetts

(1923-1933); formerly member of the Massachusetts Legislature.

Obituary

N Y Times p25 Ja 29 '46

UTLEY, GEORGE B(URWELL) Dec. 3, 1876—Oct. 4, 1946 Librarian of the Newberry Library in Chicago from 1920 until his retirement in 1942, when he was appointed librarian emeritus; secretary, executive officer, and member of various committees of the American Library Association from 1911 to 1920; during World War I served as executive secretary of the Library War Service of the A.L.A.; wrote the *Life and Times of Thomas John Claggett* (1913), *Fifty Years of the American Library Association* (1926).

Obituary

N Y Times p17 O 6 '46

VALENTINA May 1, 1904- Fashion designer; dressmaker

Address: b. c/o Valentina Gowns, Inc., 21 E. 67th St., New York; h. 114 E. 78th St., New York

One of America's leading couturières and costume designers is Mme. Valentina, of whose stage costumes Brooks Atkinson once wrote, "Valentina has designed clothes that act before a line is spoken." Valentina, who looks upon herself as an architect of dress—she says that her basic inspiration is derived from Grecian architecture—handles fabrics in such a way that the shadows and highlights of the color of a dress help to create the effect desired: Color, she feels, "should never be obvious, static, or flat." By "subtle combination of unusual colors," a fashion magazine said in 1941, the designer "achieves dramatic effects without resorting to extreme cut."

Mme. Valentina, whose full name is Valentina Nicholaevna Sanina Schlee, was born Valentina Sanina, the daughter of Nicholas Sanin, a member of a wealthy family of Kiev. Her birth date is May 1, 1904. At fourteen Valentina was in Kharkov to escape the World War I battles in Kiev, and while there persuaded her parents to let her enter the school of dramatic arts. Her training for the stage was interrupted by the Russian Revolution in 1917, in which her mother and brother were killed; and at fifteen she fled alone to the Crimean peninsula, carrying only the family jewels.

In Sevastopol Valentina Sanina met George Matthias Schlee, to whom she was married at seventeen. His family, refugees from St. Petersburg, had originated in the Crimea and owned large estates there. In the Crimea young Schlee had founded and endowed a free people's university and published the only newspaper to remain in embattled Sevastopol. When the White Army collapsed in 1920, the Schlee family and Valentina fled to Athens, where they attempted various business enterprises. As Mme. Valentina puts it, they ate their diamonds

VALENTINA

for a year before leaving to avoid ruin in the Greek inflation.

Taking up residence in Paris after a sojourn in Italy, Valentina Schlee was encouraged by her friend Leon Bakst and by other artists to continue designing her own clothes to suit her personality, without following the fashion; it was Bakst who discovered that she had exceptional talent in the field and who helped develop her color consciousness. Her ambitions for an acting career approached fulfillment in a theatrical company which her husband organized to "express . . . a new and modern approach to the stage," and which furnished them a comfortable living for eight months. When the Schlees moved across the Atlantic to New York in 1923, however, success did not follow them. "The idea was too modern and new," they now say.

In New York the clothes of young Mrs. Schlee began to attract attention. In a day when every woman wore loose, low-waisted dresses with tubular skirts which ended at the knee, Mrs. Schlee appeared at opening nights, smart cafes, and parties in high-necked, long-sleeved, floor-length gowns with natural waistlines, such as were to become the fashion seven years later. Mrs. Schlee continued to defy the mode, and gradually a circle of admirers of her clothes began to emerge. After two years a socially prominent woman approached her and offered to back her in a dressmaking establishment. At first fearful of the responsibility, Valentina was persuaded to go into the business in 1925 in partnership with the "angel" and her own mother-in-law, who lived with the Schlees. The business proved fairly profitable—until the backer disappeared with the funds. After a period of other business problems, in 1928 George Schlee went into partnership with his wife in their own establishment, Valentina Gowns, Incorporated.

When Valentina Gowns opened a small shop the Schlees took fourteen hundred dollars' worth of orders the first hour, and Valentina sold thirteen dresses from her own wardrobe. The first year's sales totaled ninety thousand dollars. As soon as she was financially able to do so Valentina returned to Paris to study the technical aspect of dressmaking. At that time, when practically all American fashion was copied from the Parisian *haute couture,* the woman who bought an "original creation" in Paris was likely to find it duplicated on every hand when she returned to America. Valentina concluded that her opportunity lay in creating designs independently for women who were prepared to pay for individuality. Since then, Valentina gowns have been difficult to make and all but impossible to copy, because of their intricacy of cut and because, like Vionnet, she often shapes and places her seams in ways which make both cutting and fitting long and expensive processes.

On Mme. Valentina's return to New York the theatrical and musical worlds were the first to rediscover her. In 1933 came her "first big job," Judith Anderson's costumes for *Come of Age.* Although the play ran less than a month (January-February, 1934), Miss Anderson's costumes attracted much attention, and Valentina's reputation as a stage costume designer was established. By 1936, when she did Lynn Fontanne's clothes for the role of a White Russian pseudo-countess in *Idiot's Delight,* the designer was well-known enough for columnists to recognize and duly record the fact that Miss Fontanne had copied her dressmaker's speech and mannerisms for the part—"the fluent torso, the expressive shoulders . . . the Slavic hauteur . . . the waving cigarette holder . . . the musical Slavic drawl . . . and nobody was more entranced than Valentina."

Valentina has also done stage costumes for Helen Hayes, Mary Martin, Zorina, and Clifton Webb (dressing gowns and pajamas for *The Man Who Came to Dinner*). In the musical field Valentina's following includes Grace Moore, Jarmila Novotna, Lily Pons, Gladys Swarthout. After Miss Swarthout had worn a Valentina wardrobe to Hollywood, the moving picture colony became interested in her clothes, and Valentina's customers came to include Norma Shearer, Rosalind Russell, Paulette Goddard, and Greta Garbo, friend of the Schlees. The names Astor, Vanderbilt, Mellon, and McCormick are also to be found in Valentina's appointment book.

"On-stage or off," Valentina has written, "it is essential to know a woman's physical and psychological equipment as well as—and often better than—she knows it herself, in order to create a dress that will have meaning in relation to her as a woman, or to her in relation to the character she portrays. . . .Every dress should identify a personal style through the elements of personality which it accentuates. . . . [Otherwise] it cannot be called a work of art." For this reason, she has several times broken away from the conventions of costuming a particular character, especially of opera; for this reason, too, her *Carmen* costumes for Rosa Ponselle were entirely different from those she designed for Gladys Swarthout to wear in the same role. "Each new costume brought a gasp of delight," said *Newsweek* of Miss Ponselle's. Her feminine version of the matador's costume was pictured in the French *Vogue* in 1935; and the bolero which formed a part of it appeared in several Paris designers' collections the following spring, was copied universally, and remained in favor for years. Similarly, Valentina claims credit for the vogue of hoods and snoods, large fur hats, dolman sleeves, pleated skirts and blouses, aprons for decorative purposes, and scarf handkerchiefs.

Valentina has designed the costumes for several entire stage productions. Of her costumes for the Lunt-Fontanne *Amphitryon 38*, which included Jupiter's comment-provoking beard of golden corkscrew curls, John Mason Brown [42] wrote, "Valentina's costumes are a sheer joy . . . rise to the rarest sort of distinction. . . . Their lines are beautiful . . . their contribution to the evening truly creative." Winsor French called her costumes for Katharine Cornell's *Herod and Mariamne* (1938) "entirely breathtaking," and Valentina's gowns for Katharine Hepburn to wear in *The Philadelphia Story* (1939) were said to have "changed a rangy tomboy into a Philadelphia Main Line doll."

By October 1938 *Collier's* called Valentina "the most talked-about dressmaker in New York" and "America's most glamorous dressmaker," and quoted her ideas—including that, in choosing clothes, "what women want is nearly always wrong." Dramatically posed photographs of Valentina in her own creations appear often in fashion magazines, and articles under her signature are to be found in the February 1941 *Theatre Arts* and the February 1945 *McCall's*. In the fall of 1940 the Schlees purchased the four-story building off Fifth Avenue which now houses Valentina Gowns' staff of sixty-five. A strict taskmistress, Mme. Valentina supervises fittings whenever possible, as well as acting as the establishment's one model and one *vendeuse*. She designs all her own clothes and accessories, except for shoes (of which at one time she had several hundred pairs, all low-heeled), and each of her public appearances is followed by a number of requests for copies of whatever outfit she wore. Some of the two thousand women who buy Valentina dresses have annual accounts with her running to thirty thousand dollars; others save on all their other clothes to be able to buy one Valentina dress a year, paying two hundred and fifty dollars or more.

A tall, slender blonde, Mme. Valentina is said to be an excellent mime. She fits the popular definition of the word "exotic," even to the high cheekbones, prominent arched brows, inscrutable expression, very long fingernails, and an accent which is not always easy to understand. Her favorite jewel, a Maltese cross of diamonds and emeralds, forms a part of nearly every costume she wears. The Schlees are "seen everywhere," and hers are often the most dramatic entrances at first nights and other glittering affairs. (At the opening of the 1946 Metropolitan Opera season, for which she had designed Lily Pons's *Lakmé* costumes, Valentina was "the most stunning woman in

the house," wrote one reporter.) At home in their brownstone house in one of the most fashionable sections of New York, the Schlees give "fabulous" parties, the most lavish being the Russian Easter celebration.

References

Collier's 102:18+ O 8 '38 pors
Cosmopolitan 110:84 My '41 por
Life 16:98+ Ja 31 '44 por
Who 1:10 Ap '41 por

Taves, I. Successful Women and How They Attained Success (1943)

VALENTINE, LEWIS J(OSEPH) Mar. 19, 1882——Dec. 16, 1946 Police expert

Bulletin: Lewis J. Valentine died on December 16, 1946.

From June 1946 issue:

A reform Mayor of New York announced in 1934 that he had selected "an honest cop" as his police commissioner. The man who won that appellation, Lewis J. Valentine, retired in 1945 after forty-two years as a "policeman," eleven of them at the head of the world's largest police department. Then, in 1946 General Douglas MacArthur [41] asked him to help reorganize the Japanese police force, which had for decades been an instrument of totalitarian rule. This Valentine did, taking leave for a time from a new career as narrator on the *Gangbusters* radio program of the American Broadcasting Company network.

The police expert was born in Brooklyn's Williamsburg section on March 19, 1882. His parents, John and Elizabeth (Daly) Valentine, gave him the names Lewis Joseph. He attended Brooklyn's Manual Training High School from 1896 to 1898, left to take a job as a delivery boy for the Abraham and Strauss department store, and before he was twenty-one had advanced to become the store's Greenpoint

Cosmo-Sileo

LEWIS J. VALENTINE

VALENTINE, LEWIS J.—*Continued*

agent. Realizing, however, that business bored him, Valentine took examinations for both the police and fire departments. When the appointment as an eight-hundred-dollar-a-year probationary patrolman came through first, in 1903 a twenty-one-year-old rookie, he began patrolling Manhattan and Flatbush.

Promotions came to him slowly and erratically, while almost as frequent were demotions and "exile" to remote districts of Greater New York. Serving a city in the control of a powerful and unscrupulous political machine, Valentine time after time refused to compromise his integrity, while promotions passed him by and less able men rose in rank. It was ten years before he became a sergeant. As a sergeant, and lieutenant, he supervised the work of "Honest Dan" Costigan's "shoofly"—or confidential—squad, charged with keeping the department "clean." Valentine routed out grafters among his fellow policemen and rapidly acquired a reputation as a "straight cop" who could not be "fixed." He also made political enemies among the Tammany powers.

Though the promotions were due him, Valentine did not reach the rank of captain until 1926, when a new police commissioner, George V. McLaughlin, was appointed. In the same year McLaughlin made him a deputy inspector and told him to drive out New York's gamblers. Records show that Valentine was relentlessly thorough, not even overlooking the "big-time" gambling in political clubhouses. In 1928 Grover Whalen became commissioner. One of his first acts was to demote the deputy inspector to captain and to send him to a "quiet precinct across the river where he could ruminate on his Manhattan activities." Meanwhile, a New York State committee had appointed Judge Samuel Seabury to investigate alleged corruption in the city's government, an investigation which led to the ousting of Mayor James Walker and the downfall of the Tammany political machine. Called before the investigating committee in 1931, Valentine gave a startling account of political intrigue. Then, in 1933, on a reform ticket Fiorello La Guardia [40] was swept into the office of Mayor. Promising to exclude politics, the Mayor appointed his new administrative force, naming John F. O'Ryan as his Police Commissioner and, as chief inspector, Valentine, who hated dishonest police as bitterly as he hated thugs and racketeers. Before the year was out O'Ryan resigned, and in September La Guardia pinned the commissioner's badge on Valentine.

While to reporters he was "as taciturn and inaccessible as the Dalai Lama," to his men Valentine opened his office door. "If they had any gripes they could tell me directly. They found that pull no longer counted and that a district leader asking a favor was not welcomed at headquarters." Valentine declared: "Known criminals can be driven from a community if they are never permitted to rest. . . .Treat them rough. . . .Arrest them on sight for anything. . . .If gambling games, disorderly districts and other large-scale black spots exist in any city, it's due to the fact that the politicians and not the police are doing business." Though he disliked the sensational, Valentine often made colorful news. A story frequently retold is that of his encounter with a manicured, elegantly dressed thug on the police line-up: to the two hundred assembled detectives Valentine growled, "Blood should be smeared all over [his] velvet collar." He went on to warn his men against the coddling of gangsters and "muscle men," ordered the detectives to "mark 'em up and muss 'em up." Many police chiefs throughout the country, reported *Newsweek* in 1934, believed that Valentine's plan would lead to "unwarranted police brutality," but Denver's new chief declared the plan "dead right."

In his eleven years in office Valentine was on call twenty-four hours a day—"tied to the telephone and radio." To the problems of crime were added those of New York's tremendous traffic flow, and holiday and special-event crowds, which required extraordinary police precaution. During the war the Commissioner was particularly concerned with New York's juvenile delinquents: "We have men and women of the force at all railroad stations, bus terminals and ferry houses, as well as in all other places where crowds congregate. They are not only on the lookout for known criminals but are trying to save youngsters." Valentine's "philosophy of the policeman's vocation" was: "The cop on the crossing near a public school is a friend of the kids he sees every morning. He is an example and a teacher. He stands for what they learned in the classroom. . . . Members of the force . . . at times must act as lawyers, arbitrators, and doctors. Often they are the confidants of family secrets. The police must, above all else, be human. . . .They must be intelligent citizens, ready to protect, direct and advise the rest of the community." He has also said, "No police department in any part of the world can be sincere or honest unless it has security, permanence of tenure and adequate wages."

Valentine is credited with regenerating New York's eighteen-thousand-man police force. Under him the racketeer and the professional gambler were driven out of the city or under cover. New Yorkers, *Time* magazine has reported, "boasted for the first time in memory of the most honest police force in the land." In his first six years in office, *Time* has estimated, Commissioner Valentine "fired some three hundred men, officially rebuked three thousand, fined eight thousand," and was "even harder on the crooks." The Commissioner held his post for eleven years, longer than any other man in New York's history (the second longest term was seven years). Then, in September 1945, at sixty-three, he announced his resignation and his acceptance of an offer from radio producer Phillips Lord. Valentine was to be narrator-commentator on the weekly radio show *Gangbusters*, a dramatization of true crime investigations. Fiorello La Guardia, then completing his last term as Mayor of New York, told his former partner-in-reform: "Busting gangs on the microphone, Lew, is going to be real easy. . . .Give them the works."

In January 1946 General MacArthur [41] asked Valentine to come to Japan to reorganize the police, fire and prison systems of that "police state," where, as the New York *Times* put it, "the supposed guardians of the law . . . were really the gangsters." The retired "gangbuster" considered MacArthur's request "a call from Uncle Sam" and in March he left for the Far East by plane with seven other police experts. Valentine felt that the big job was "to help democratize Japan, to remove fascist, Nazi and imperialist influences, and eliminate terrorism and Gestapo methods." The Japanese police, he said, "must realize they are not public enemies but public friends." The New York *Times* editorial comment was: "If he develops a police force there as competent and trustworthy as he built up in this city, Japan will at last see something new under the rising sun."

In May Valentine presented his two hundred and eighty-three page report to MacArthur, who found it "sound and comprehensive." Valentine's three major points were proposals that local democratic control over the police replace national direction; that, to attract better men, there be an improvement in the policeman's working conditions, including shorter hours and a sufficient increase in pay to remove incentive to dishonesty; and that the police be stripped of non-police functions—"policemen are hardly qualified to combat epidemics, distribute charity or build sanitary facilities." Valentine also recommended that young police candidates be sent to the United States for indoctrination and training. The former police commissioner celebrated his sixty-fourth birthday in Tokyo, with a cake which he cut with a samurai sword. But he considered Japan "a good place to get away from. . . .I sure was glad to see those beautiful Brooklyn cops when I got back. . . . There you got cops!" To a *New Yorker* reporter he summed up Japan's police difficulties: "Jap cops have no idea of being public servants. They used to go around assaulting people without having them tried. Before MacArthur dismissed them, there were Thought Police, who could torture anyone suspected of 'thinking against the Government and Emperor.' The Japs have twenty-six hundred years of brutality behind them. They got to teach the cops to be patient and help old ladies and little children across the street instead of jailing kids because they're orphans."

The retired commissioner was guaranteed fifty thousand dollars a year for his radio work, which included the weekly appearance on *Gangbusters* and occasional guest appearances on other programs—although, after a recent exchange of comic lines with Hildegarde '44, Valentine is said to have muttered, "They're trying to make a comedian out of me but they'll never do it." In 1946 he was also signed to appear in a series of movie shorts on crime, to write his autobiography, to review crime stories for a publishing house, and to serve on the editorial board of *True Police Cases,* a new magazine. Another appointment came to him in October 1946, when he accepted the nonsalaried position of chief investigator for New York State's Election Frauds Bureau, which, for the first time, was to function throughout the year.

The former "Boss of New York's Finest" is granite-jawed, thin-lipped, with "cold, steely blue eyes." Many have discovered a sentimental streak in the "tough cop." Called a "flawless family man," he has four married daughters (a son is deceased), and nine grandchildren. His first wife, the former Elizabeth J. Donohue, died in 1910, and he was married a second time four years later, to Teresa A. Donohue. "It's nice to stay home all day with the family once in a while," he has said, although he welcomes his radio, moving picture, and writing routine. "I lived so long at the end of a telephone, I would have gone crazy without something to do."

References

    Lit Digest 117:9 F 10 '34 por
    N Y Times Mag p16+ N 19 '44 por
    N Y World-Telegram p3 S 24 '43 pors
    New Yorker 21:20-1 S 29 '45; 22:15-16
        Je 29 '46
    Newsweek 4:5-6 D 8 '34
    St. Louis Post-Dispatch O 17 '45
    Time 46:72 S 17 '45 por

    Who's Who in America, 1946-47

VAN PELT, JOHN V(REDENBURGH)
Feb. 24, 1874- Architect
Address: b. 45 W. 45th St., New York; h. Roe Blvd. West, Patchoque, N.Y.

For almost half a century, John V. Van Pelt has practiced, taught, and written about architecture. Designer of many churches, rectories, convents, schools, sanatoriums, and other structures, he was dean of Cornell University's College of Architecture and has also been professor of design at the universities of Columbia and Pennsylvania.

The Van Pelts were among the early American settlers. The architect's great-great-grandfather, Teunis Jansen Lanen Van Pelt, left his native Holland and settled at what later became New Utrecht, Long Island, in March 1663. Another of his ancestors was the Reverend James Caldwell, the "fighting parson of the Revolution." Thus, of Dutch and also of English and French descent, John Vredenburgh Van Pelt was born in New Orleans, Louisiana, on February 24, 1874, to John Vredenburgh and Emma Louisa (Fields) Van Pelt. When he was only about ten months old he developed hip disease as the result of an accident. "Until I was six, my life was not a good risk," Van Pelt recalls. He used crutches for about seventeen years until one time, finding himself without them, he discovered that he could manage with a cane.

A good part of John's childhood was spent in Germantown, near Philadelphia, where his aunt had a girls' school and his mother taught French. The boy attended the private school of William Heins, there receiving his first lessons in mechanical drawing. His father, who had been fatally poisoned as the result of a young doctor's mistake when John was very young, had been a civil engineer, and John too wished to pursue this career. But Mrs. Van Pelt, feeling that her son was not strong enough for it, encouraged him to think of

JOHN V. VAN PELT

architecture as his profession. Following the suggestion of some friends she decided to take him to Paris to study at the Ecole des Beaux Arts. Van Pelt was only fourteen when he sailed for Europe.

In Paris, while his mother managed a pension young Van Pelt attended the Ecole des Arts Décoratifs and the Atelier Droillard-Thierry-Deglane. He passed the examinations for the Ecole des Beaux Arts at the age of sixteen, there studying architecture for five years and also painting in his free time. The first American to obtain the credit for a diploma, he received the title Architecte Diplômé par le Gouvernement in 1895. The plan he presented for his thesis was for a tuberculosis sanatorium, and was afterward published as *An Ideal Sanatorium for Tuberculosis,* in a thesis by the physician Dr. S. A. Knopf, who provided the student architect with much of the necessary technical advice. In 1895-96 Van Pelt exhibited his work in the section on architecture at the Paris Salon. During 1896 and 1897 he continued his studies at Beaux Arts, taking postgraduate courses and winning honors. Both years he was laureate of the Société des Architects Diplômés par le Gouvernement, in 1896-97 receiving the grand medal of the Société for obtaining the greatest number of medals after graduation. His awards include the grand medal of the Société Centrale des Architectes for 1897, a first medal and two second medals in plan, two medals in *esquisse* (1896 and 1903) as well as first and second mentions, and a medal for modeling. In 1904 he received from Beaux Arts the Prix St. Agnan Boucher of one thousand francs for holding the greatest number of values of all graduates.

Upon returning to the United States in 1897, the twenty-three-year-old Van Pelt became assistant professor of architecture in charge of design at Cornell University. Working with A. B. Trowbridge, then the dean of Cornell's College of Architecture, he instituted a system of instruction whereby student designs were judged in competition. In 1900 he went abroad again for two years of travel in Germany, Italy, Sicily, and England. Back at Cornell in 1902, he was full professor and dean of the College of Architecture until 1904, when he resigned to become director of the Hastings Atelier at Columbia University. In the meantime he had written the *Discussion of Composition,* published in 1902 (revised in 1913 as *Essentials of Composition as Applied to Art*). Of it Ralph E. Winslow, head of the department of architecture at Rensselaer Polytechnic Institute, wrote to Van Pelt some twenty-three years later: "Although the spirit of the times has changed, the principles of decorative composition expressed in your little book are as sound today as they were when it was published."

After nine years at Columbia, Van Pelt became professor of design at the University of Pennsylvania, where he remained from 1914 to 1917; and from 1918 to 1921 he was at the Cooper Union Women's Art School. For the next six years he was again at Columbia University, this time in charge of the extension studios in architecture. Later, from 1929 to 1935, he was a lecturer on architectural composition and planning at Columbia.

During all these years of teaching, Van Pelt, a critic of American architectural training who firmly believed that the director of a school of architecture should be "a practicing architect of recognized ability," was also privately engaged in his profession. From 1904 to 1912 he was the architect of the Otisville Sanatorium (New York), a municipal institution for the treatment of tuberculosis, and in 1917-18 he designed two buildings for the Loomis (tuberculosis) Sanatorium at Liberty, New York. Between 1917 and 1945 he was in charge of four operations for the Union Health Center of the I.L.G.W.U. Dressmakers Union, for which he is now the consulting architect. (He is at present also engaged in the same capacity for Local 22 of the I.L.G.W.U.)

In the Gennadeion Library of the American School of Classical Studies in Athens, Greece, which he planned in collaboration with W. S. Thompson, Van Pelt produced a modern version of ancient Grecian grandeur. While the building is "in no sense a copy of the temple form" and was not intended to be "an archaeological essay," Van Pelt has written, it was "my prime motive . . . to so gauge the scale and feeling of the building that it would be in entire harmony with the Greek architecture of 440 B.C., the architecture that still plays such an important role in controlling the artistic expression of Athens."

A designer of churches, Van Pelt protested against the idea that the "Gothic is the only style that can architecturally express religious emotion" and proclaimed the Romanesque as "equally beautiful" and to his mind "even more inspired." He also disagreed with those who, in championing progress and the development of an American art, advocated a complete break with the past. "In progress I believe," he wrote, "—progress that utilizes new methods and materials as well as old ones, whichever is most applicable, most indigenous to the locality." The Church of St. John of Nepomuk and the Church of the Guardian Angels, both in New York, are two of the many churches of which Van Pelt is the architect. He also designed the pedestal and setting of the Joan of Arc Monument on Riverside Drive.

Among the municipal buildings designed by Van Pelt are the Patchogue (New York) Post Office, the Patchogue Library, and the Brookhaven Town Hall. With F. L. Ackerman and Joshua Lowenfish, he also designed the Contemporary Arts Building of the New York World's Fair. The homes Van Pelt has designed have ranged in price from eighteen hundred and fifty to one hundred fifty thousand dollars. His work in the field of landscape architecture includes the Cornell alumni athletic fields (executed in collaboration with Warren Manning of Boston and Charles Lowrie of New York) as well as the tunnel entrance and two bridges across the stream at Watkins Glen, a New York State park. During World War I he was employed by the United States Housing Corporation, a Government agency responsible for the housing of those working in certain war plants. He was chairman of the investigation committee charged with deciding upon the selection of housing projects and was then placed in charge of the preparation of the budget. While the New York State Fine Arts Commission was functioning, Van Pelt was its secretary, and for about fourteen years he was also secretary of the New York Fine Arts Federation. A life member of the Museum of the City of New York, he is the chairman of its committee on architecture and for several years was a member of its board of trustees. For about nine years he was secretary of the Chamber of Commerce in Patchogue, the town where he resides.

Member emeritus of the Beaux Arts Society, Van Pelt is also a fellow and member emeritus of the American Institute of Architects and a life member of the Société des Architectes Diplômés. He has held membership in the New York Architectural League, the National Arts Club, the Cornell University Club of New York, the Cosmos Club of Washington, D.C., the Century Association, the Sons of the Revolution, and several other groups. A Presbyterian, he was at one time elder of the Park Avenue Presbyterian Church. He registers as a Republican. In addition to being the author of *Essentials of Composition,* Van Pelt has written four other books (one is the *Monograph of the W. K. Vanderbilt House*) and numerous magazine articles. He has been married to the former Betsey A. Southworth since 1902. An exhibitor in the section on oil paintings in the Paris Salon in 1898, the architect finds painting in oils and watercolors a favorite pastime.

References

Am Inst Arch J 3:107+ Mr '45; 5: 208+ Ap '46
Who's Who in America, 1946-47

VICKERY, H(OWARD) L(EROY) Apr. 20, 1892—Mar. 21, 1946 American naval officer; served as international technical adviser and during World War II as vice-chairman of the Maritime Commission; called "the miracle man of the war." See *Current Biography* 1943 Yearbook.

Obituary

N Y Times p21 Mr 22 '46 por

VON GALEN, CLEMENS AUGUST, CARDINAL, COUNT *See* Galen, C. A., Cardinal, Count von

VON RIBBENTROP, JOACHIM *See* Ribbentrop, J. von

VON SEYSS-INQUART, ARTUR *See* Seyss-Inquart, A. von

VON TILZER, HARRY 1873—Jan. 10, 1946 American song writer and publisher; his two thousand published songs include "Wait Till the Sun Shines, Nellie", "A Bird in a Gilded Cage", "On a Sunday Afternoon", "In the Sweet Bye-and-Bye", "Down on The Farm", "I Want a Girl Just Like the Girl That Married Dear Old Dad"; made several fortunes from his songs and lost them financing musical productions; began as a vaudeville singer-pianist-dancer.

Obituary

N Y Times p3 Ja 11 '46 por

WAESCHE, RUSSELL R(ANDOLPH) (wä′chē) Jan. 6, 1886—Oct. 17, 1946 Commandant of the United States Coast Guard from 1936 to 1945; was in large part responsible for the development of that branch of the armed forces before and during World War II; after his retirement in 1945 was named by President Truman to a ten-man military body for national defense. See *Current Biography* 1945 Yearbook.

Obituary

N Y Times p23 O 18 '46 por

WAKEMAN, FREDERIC Dec. 26, 1909- Author
Address: b. c/o Rinehart and Co., Inc., 232 Madison Ave.; New York; h. 1035 5th Ave., New York

"Nothing succeeds like young Mr. Wakeman," George Mayberry wrote in the *New Republic* of Frederic Wakeman. "A successful account executive before the war, he went into the Navy, from which he emerged with *Shore Leave,* a critically and popularly successful first novel. Back for a stretch in radio advertising . . . at 'a presidential salary,' he comes up with a Book-of-the-Month Club selection, *The Hucksters,* a satirical onslaught on the advertising agency, the radio, and Hollywood," of which more than seven hundred and fifty thousand copies were in print by August 1946.

(Continued next page)

FREDERIC WAKEMAN

Frederic Wakeman was born the day after Christmas, in 1909. His native town, Scranton, Kansas, which then had a population of 538, was twenty miles south of Topeka and "well within the orbit of the late William Allen White." At the time of Frederic's birth, his father, Don Conklin Wakeman, was a newspaper man; later the elder Wakeman went into politics, and still later, into Government service. Frederic's mother was the former Myrtle Evans. After finishing high school the boy spent what John Selby calls "a *wanderjahr*, in the course of which he trouped with a Santa Fe telegraph gang and worked in the railway mail terminal in Kansas City." Then he entered Park College, a small coeducational Presbyterian institution in Missouri, near Kansas City. Young Wakeman edited the Park College paper and literary magazine. During the summer vacations he "bummed around," working on newspapers, harvesting wheat, and, when he got east to Long Island, delivering ice and caddying.

Upon graduation with his B.A. in 1933, twenty-three-year-old Frederic Wakeman began writing for the Kansas City *Journal-Post,* and did some free-lance work for Midwestern radio stations. In 1934, the year of his marriage, he entered advertising—for department stores first, and then for an agency—at the same time continuing his radio writing. Moving to New York in 1937, he joined the large Lord and Thomas advertising agency, becoming copy chief. From that job he went into radio advertising and became account executive for organizations like Westinghouse Corporation, Aluminum Corporation of America, American Can Company, and Ford Motor Company.

In February 1942 the thirty-two-year-old advertising man enlisted in the Navy. He served as an air combat intelligence lieutenant, junior grade, on active duty in World War II. "I was in the Pacific for a short and undistinguished

period," Wakeman insists, "and I won't stand for any of this hero-veteran stuff whatever, because it isn't true." At any rate, Lieutenant Wakeman spent five months in a naval hospital on the West Coast before receiving his medical discharge and rejoining his agency (renamed Foote, Cone, and Belding) in 1943. In six weeks there he wrote a novel based on his Navy experiences and observations. Published as *Shore Leave* in March 1944, it was reportedly selling a thousand copies a week two years later.

Of *Shore Leave* John Chamberlain of the New York *Times* wrote: "It is a scary document. For what it does is to take four Navy aviators . . . and show how war has unfitted them for peace. . . . Just as war has oversimplified the characters of *Shore Leave,* so it has simplified Mr. Wakeman's problem of characterization. The deeper, more subtle aspects of personality have been buried . . . for the duration. . . . *Shore Leave* is not a finished work of art. But it has a rough vitality and it boldly tackles all the taboo subjects." R. L. Nathan in the *Saturday Review of Literature* summarized general literary opinion when he wrote, "This is the whole story, done in an open-eyed narrative style, not creative writing but good reporting." Front-line correspondent Robert Sherrod [44] declared that the psychology of *Shore Leave* "is solid as a rock, particularly as it applies to fliers." And, according to Lieutenant Oliver O. Jensen's [45] history of the sea-air war in the Pacific, the originals of Wakeman's leading characters became so well known in the Navy by the names under which Wakeman had portrayed them that they even signed those fictional names on flight lists.

The author felt that the dramatic adaptation of *Shore Leave,* called *Kiss Them For Me,* went further in analytical treatment of the problems described in the novel. (While handling such advertising accounts as Campbell's Soup, RKO pictures, and Lucky Strike cigarettes, Wakeman had advised Luther Davis in the dramatization.) New York reviews agreed that *Kiss Them For Me* had a strong first act, but lost momentum after that; the play ran for 125 performances, however, aided by some good performances from the starless cast.

Meanwhile, in July 1945, Wakeman resigned from his agency position to accept an optionless contract to write scripts for MGM. For reasons of health, however, Wakeman went to Cuernavaca, Mexico, instead of Hollywood, taking his family with him and remaining until the spring of 1946. In two months, "without a touch of the trembles which usually attack the author of a really successful first novel when it is time to write a second," he wrote *The Hucksters,* which did for radio advertising what *Shore Leave* had done for—or to—the Navy Air Force.

The Hucksters also became a best seller. Russell Maloney called it "a story that should be read by every literate adult who has ever suffered through a radio 'commercial announcement.' . . . The only other novelist who could have done justice to Evan Llewelyn Evans and his soap business," he added, "is Charles Dickens." All reviewers praised the satire: "Pity and terror are what you get in *The Hucksters* . . . and a lot of fascinating dope about the radio end of the advertising business. The pity and terror are heaped up and running over, in a measure generous enough to satisfy Aristotle himself, and the dope is apparently so accurate that *Variety* has gone so far as to announce that this is a *roman à clef* (though naturally not in those precise words). . . .As a matter of fact, Wakeman's Hogarthian realism is in danger of being dismissed by the general public as sheer fantasy, which would be a great pity." Reviewers were also unanimous in their disapproval of the love story, with adjectives ranging from "naive" to "revolting," and several suggested that Wakeman shared his hero's delusion that the sordid intrigue was a tragic romance. The author has insisted, however, that he intended to show "how a person like that would retrogress into juvenility. When a cynic like Vic falls in love, he is a mooncalf. I've seen it happen."

Reputed resemblance of characters to actual persons (one has often been compared to George Washington Hill '46, whose Lucky Strike account Wakeman had formerly handled), aroused so much interest in advertising circles that advance copies were reportedly "bootlegged" at a hundred dollars apiece. The very advertising practices which the author had held up to ridicule were followed to promote *The Hucksters*; his fictional soap slogan was changed to "Love That Book!" and the singing commercials were adapted therefrom—all of which resulted in valuable word-of-mouth publicity.

"Whatever the nation may be reading," remarked a New York *Herald Tribune* columnist in June 1946, "every other person you meet along Broadway is carrying with him a copy of . . . *The Hucksters*." Billy Rose '40 devoted one of his columns to it. MGM had already leased the screen rights for seven years for two hundred thousand dollars, with an additional option, and Wakeman was negotiating with would-be producers of a stage version, and also had an application for permission to produce the play on file with the Dramatists' Guild. In June 1946 *The Hucksters* was a selection of the Book-of-the-Month Club and was rising to the top of the list of best sellers. A condensed version appeared in the September issue of *Reader's Digest*, and the screen rights were purchased by MGM. Asked by *Broadcasting* magazine for suggestions on how radio might be "unhuckstered," Wakeman replied, "Apply the publishing technique to radio, by throwing the program responsibility back to the stations and networks, taking all of same away from the agencies and sponsors and talent agencies. Then advertising time is sold next to 'editorial and program matter' just as it is done in our newspapers and magazines."

Like the narrator of *Shore Leave,* to whom he bears other resemblances, Wakeman has two children: Frederic, Jr., born in 1938, and Sue, born in 1941. His wife is the former Margaret Keys, whom he met at college. Politically, Wakeman believes in individualism. and feels that "mass movements of any kind

trample on writers." In his two published novels Wakeman has written very fast and, he says, has "tried to keep everything on a level of action—an illusion like that of the theater—no introspection, no beautiful periodic sentences." John Selby has described Wakeman in the *Book-of-the-Month Club News.* "He will answer questions directly, and he always knows why he wrote a given scene a given way. He will stand like a granite grave marker on this scene if he really believes he's right, and if he doesn't, he will rewrite it before your eyes with no self-consciousness whatever, and with quite remarkable skill. . . .He sees his books as a succession of scenes acted out by people, and not as 'messages.' " Of the tall, brown-haired author's personality, Selby said, "He is difficult to know intimately and difficult to understand fully. But it is quite impossible not to like him. . . .He gives himself no airs, wears no startling clothes, does not infest night clubs, is sure of his own mind without being opinionated, has few close friends and no enemies at all. He is reserved, a little shy, slow to move toward intimacy. Yet he inspires loyalty."

References

Book-of-the-Month Club N My '46 por
PM Mag p13+ Ag 25 '46 pors

WAKSMAN, SELMAN A(BRAHAM)
July 2, 1888- Scientist

Address: b. New Jersey Agricultural Experiment Station, New Brunswick, N.J,; Rutgers University, New Brunswick, N.J.; h. 35 Walter Ave., Highland Park, N.J.

Unlike that of penicillin, the discovery of streptomycin, which promises to become one of man's most powerful weapons against his microbe enemies, was not a dramatic accident. It took years of directed, methodical research for Dr. Selman A. Waksman, microbiologist, and his small group of assistants to unearth this new antibiotic which is found in the soil.

A trace of a Russian accent may still be detected in the speech of Selman Abraham Waksman. The son of Jacob and Fradia (London) Waksman, he was born in Priluka, Kiev, Russia, on July 2, 1888, and received his secondary education at the Fifth Gymnasium in Odessa. At the age of twenty-two he came to the United States, and a year later entered Rutgers University. In 1915, the same year in which he became a naturalized citizen, Waksman received his B.S. degree. It was also in that year that, as research assistant at the New Jersey Agricultural Experiment Station, he began his career in the field of science. After attaining his M.Sc. degree at Rutgers in 1916, he attended the University of California as a research fellow, receiving his Ph.D. degree from there in 1918. Along with his school studies, the young scientist continued to get practical training as a biochemist at the Cutter Laboratories.

In 1918 Waksman was back at Rutgers, this time to give lectures on soil microbiology. At the same time he worked as a bacteriologist at the Takamine Laboratories for two years. In

SELMAN A. WAKSMAN

1925 he became associate professor of soil microbiology at Rutgers and six years later he was promoted to a full professorship in that department. This post he maintained until 1943 when he was made professor of microbiology. In addition to teaching, Waksman carried out his duties as microbiologist at the New Jersey Agricultural Experiment Station, a post which he assumed in 1921. Continuing his study of the microbial inhabitants of the soil, he related his research to the important problem of soil conservation.

As the years went by Waksman's research projects developed, taking in other phases of microbiology. Included were such subjects as the role of bacteria in the oxidation of sulphur in the soil (1921-23); methods for studying the biochemical processes in the soil (1923-28); the decomposition of plant materials in composts and in soil (1923-36); the chemical nature and origin of peat (1929-39); and the formation and nature of soil humus (1929-39). Beginning in 1931, his summers as microbiologist at Woods Hole Oceanographic Institute enabled him to study the microbiological population of the sea. In connection with his research work, Waksman wrote some three hundred papers which were published in scientific journals in the United States and other countries. He was also the author of books, among them, *Enzymes* (1926), whose authorship he shared with W. C. Davison of Johns Hopkins University; *The Soil and the Microbe* (1931) written in collaboration with R. L. Starkey of Rutgers University; and *Humus* (1936, 1938). His *Principles of Soil Microbiology* (1927, 1932), one thousand pages long, was called "the most exhaustive work on the subject in any language."

Waksman's work in the field of chemotherapy, which was to carry his name to popular publications outside the scientific world, was begun in about 1939. (As defined in Webster, chemotherapy is "the treatment of internal disease by chemical reagents that have a specific and immediate toxic effect upon the microorganism that causes the disease, without seriously poisoning the patient.") Thirty-nine years of studying the microbial inhabitants of the soil particularly fitted the New Jersey microbiologist to search for the antibiotics in the soil. Having observed throughout his bacteriological studies that actinomycetes won out against other soil microbes in the struggle to survive under adverse conditions, he thought they might also destroy the germs in man and decided to center his investigations on the huge family of actinomycetes. For four years Waksman and his associates experimented with thousands of strains, trying to find an antibiotic which would destroy the germs surviving penicillin's attack (the "gram-negative" bacteria) but which at the same time would not have a harmful effect on animal bodies. Once when it seemed as if the scientists had finally reached success, they observed that the animals which at first suffered no ill effects from injections later gave evidence of poisoning. At last in 1943 the microbiologist and his staff found the substance which fulfilled all requirements. In January 1944, when rigorous tests had proved that it had no delayed ill-effects on animal bodies, Waksman and his assistants Albert Schatz and Elizabeth Bugie announced the discovery of streptomycin.

The limited amounts of streptomycin available narrowed the extent of clinical research. Although experience in the production of penicillin had made the job of producing streptomycin an easier one, and some fifteen companies were beginning to manufacture it, not until December 1946 was the new drug produced on a scale large enough to make it available on the general market. The hopes held out for streptomycin have ranged all the way from the expectation that, together with penicillin, it would subdue almost all diseases, to the warning by Dr. Hans Molitor of the Merck Institute for Therapeutic Research that there is great danger that many strains of bacteria resistant to both drugs will develop in from five to ten years. Already, wrote *Fortune* in July, 1946, "doctors throughout the country have uncovered more and more evidence that, despite the brilliant successes of penicillin, streptomycin, and other new drugs, many common germs are beginning to fight back."

Jane Stafford, Science Service medical writer, in an article published in March 1946, summed up results in clinical experimentation as follows: "Although its value is not established in all of the following diseases, streptomycin appears at this time to be the antibiotic agent of greatest promise for treatment of typhoid fever, brucellosis, tularemia, sulfonamide and penicillin-resistant urinary tract infections, Klebsiella and hemophilus infections, bacteriemias due to some penicillin-resistant organisms, and tuberculosis. There is hope that it may eventually prove to be of value in bacillary dysentery, cholera and bubonic plague."

Probably the greatest excitement caused by streptomycin's discovery came with the announcement that it might exert an effect in arresting the progress of tuberculosis. Much more time and study, however, will be required to determine its value in fighting this disease. Waksman has cautioned that streptomycin may not prove to be a cure for tuberculosis and that it may take many years before an effective remedy is found; however, he firmly believes that "a derivative of streptomycin or some other antibiotic" will eventually be discovered to help tuberculars. Meanwhile he and his staff of twelve concentrate further on the study of antibiotic substances and their relation to the control of disease. Since the discovery of streptomycin they have found two other antibiotics, but neither appears to be very promising. Of value to other interested scientists is a book entitled *Microbial Antagonisms and Antibiotic Substances,* which Waksman has written about his work on the subject of antibiosis.

While research in the field of commercial products has been backed by the laboratory resources of American industry, research in the field with which Waksman is concerned has had little financial support. The proposed bill for a National Science Foundation to administer Federal aid to research would remedy this to some extent. One of the many scientists who have expressed themselves in favor of the measure, Waksman has appeared at a hearing before the Joint Senate Subcommittee on the bill and was also among the six scientists whom Senator Claude Pepper '41 questioned in a survey on the proposed legislation.

While carrying on his research projects and writing about them, Waksman continued to teach. Most of his students were graduates, many of them from foreign countries. He has lectured on the subject of microbiology outside of the classroom too, his activities taking him not only to various institutions in the United States but also to countries in Europe, where honors have been conferred upon him. He is a corresponding member of the French Academy of Sciences, the Swedish Academy of Agriculture, the Indian Chemical Society, the Leningrad Microbiological Society, and others. In the summer of 1946, at the invitation of the Soviet Academy of Science, Waksman visited Moscow, where he gave several lectures and consulted with Russian scientists on developments in antibiotics and allied fields. He hoped to help cement friendly relations between American and Soviet scientists. He was also to visit other European countries, including Belgium, where at the University of Liége, he was to receive an honorary Doctor's degree for his work in antibiotics.

A member of the National Academy of Sciences and of the National Research Council, Waksman served during World War II on the National Defense Research Council. He belongs to numerous other scientific societies in the United States; among them are the Society of American Bacteriologists, of which he was president in 1942, the Soil Science Society of America, the American Chemical Society, the Society of Experimental Biology and Medicine, and the American Society of Agronomy, of which he was vice-president during 1930-34 and from which he received the Nitrate of Soda Research Award in 1930. In 1942, Rut-

gers University honored him with the title, Doctor of Science.

Helping the busy microbiologist and teacher with his work, even though she is not a scientist, is his wife Bertha D. Mitnik, whom he calls "Bobili." Married on August 5, 1916, they have one son, Byron, who in 1946 was captain in the Medical Corps. Waksman is described as "a fatherly, wise little man." In his small, crowded laboratories, "enthusiasm is the keynote." Though he now finds very little time for leisure reading, Anatole France, Pushkin, Byron, and Poe find a place on the shelves of his library. On the rare evenings when he can get away, his wife and he enjoy the New York theater and concert hall.

References

PM p14 Jl 22 '46

Who's Who in America, 1946-47

WALSH, J(OHN) RAYMOND   1901-
Economist; lecturer; author

Address: b. c/o Radio Station WMCA, 1657 Broadway, New York

Nationally known lecturer and radio commentator J. Raymond Walsh is an economist who has taught at Harvard University and served on the National Labor Relations Board. He has directed the CIO's research and publicity, and is the author of *CIO—Industrial Unionism in Action,* (1937), the first study made of that organization.

John Raymond Walsh was born in Beloit, Wisconsin, in 1901. When he was twelve, his lawyer uncle, Senator Thomas J. Walsh, began twenty-four years of service in the United States Congress, where he was in charge of the investigation which uncovered the great Teapot Dome scandal in 1923. Young Walsh attended Beloit College, earning his B.A. and his membership in Phi Beta Kappa in 1921.

J. RAYMOND WALSH

WALSH, J. RAYMOND—*Continued*

Following his uncle's example, Walsh was a high school teacher and principal from 1923 to 1926. However, he wished to become a singer, and accordingly obtained a Mus. B. from the Chicago Musical College. This was followed by a short engagement with a Middle Western opera company. But the low salaries of the troupe turned his interest from music to the economics of labor, and in 1928-29 Walsh resumed teaching in the Wisconsin secondary schools.

Walsh received his Ph.D. at Harvard, and was appointed to that university's department of economics in 1930. After seven years, he and Dr. Alan R. Sweezy, despite recommendation by the economics department that their instructorships be continued, were given "terminating" appointments of two years each by the university as a result of new budget policy. The two economists later resigned, Walsh leaving in the fall. An investigating committee appointed by the administration reported that "Drs. Sweezy and Walsh were recognized by faculty and students alike as outstanding tutors and teachers. They occupied a special position because of the unorthodox direction of their outlook on economic problems and because of their leadership in the work of the Cambridge Union of University Teachers, an affiliate of the American Federation of Labor." The report concluded, however, that there was, in the university's rejecting the recommendations for renewal of the instructorships, "no departure whatsoever from Harvard's tradition of tolerance and of untrammelled scientific inquiry." A year after this case "attracted an uneasy national attention," the New York *Herald Tribune* editorialized, "Harvard lost two brilliant classroom teachers under circumstances tending to confirm their colleagues in the notion that, at Harvard, research is everything, and it is 'dangerous' to have great teaching abilities."

After leaving Harvard Walsh served in 1937-38 as an examiner for the National Labor Relations Board. Then he became chairman of the economics department and director of citizenship at Hobart and William Smith Colleges in Geneva, New York. Walsh resigned, over student protest, in February 1941, along with the president of the affiliated colleges and two other faculty members. The report in the New York *Times* was that "the faculty was unwilling to support the present four-year citizenship requirements unless the general faculty has a voice in shaping the program and a share in the selection of the future teaching staff." Walsh then accepted a professorship of economics at Williams College, in Williamstown, Massachusetts.

In 1942 Professor Walsh was chosen director of research and education for the Congress of Industrial Organizations and for its Political Action Committee. In his *CIO—Industrial Unionism in Action*, Walsh had written, in 1937, that the organization's publicity and research means were inadequate. He cited the ineffective attempts of existing understaffed offices to dispense accurate labor information which could counteract distorted accounts; and

he outlined a plan for a national research and publicity bureau which could do the job successfully, "fortifying" future CIO economic, social, and political activities.

Walsh's new bureau was designed to fill this need. The newspaper *PM* called him, in 1943, "the man who has succeeded quickly in bridging the gap between campus and union hall while sticking to his own role as a man who does paper work." Walsh had, by this time, built up a large CIO library, and had gathered study material on the OPA and postwar planning, among other problems. Since 1945, when Walsh became New York chairman of the Citizens' Political Action Committee, his comments on the news have been broadcast on Monday through Friday evenings over New York radio station WMCA and twenty-three other outlets. Walsh's first sponsors were a department store, the *Encyclopædia* Britannica, and a bank.

In his broadcasts Walsh defended the Spanish Republicans as "our allies," denounced Petrillo[46] as a "despot" in his ruling which closed the National Music Camp at Interlochen, Michigan, and opposed the hostile A.F. of L. attitude toward Russia for its "immaturity and lack of realism." In March 1945 Walsh made known his contempt for opponents of the Bretton Woods monetary agreement. He termed President Truman's[45] appointment of Bennett Champ Clark[41] as associate justice of the United States Court of Appeals for the District of Columbia a "scandal," scoring Clark's Senate record as "one of the half-dozen bitter isolationists." In October 1945, when President Truman refused to reveal the secrets of atomic-bomb manufacture, Walsh said, "This seems to me the extreme in irresponsible diplomacy. It reveals no comprehension on the President's part of the state of world feeling. . . .There is widespread fear in the world of the United States—not so much of American power, the bomb, our finances, and so on, but fear of the way we will use that power. President Truman contributed to that fear yesterday."

The New York *Post* quoted Walsh's report that the 1945 London foreign ministers' conference "was a fiasco . . . because 'the United States has won for itself a reputation for failing to keep its promises made at Potsdam..., not, as [Secretary of State] Byrnes[41] has been trying to tell us, because the Russians wouldn't agree with him.'" Opposing "repression of freedom" in Palestine, Walsh said, "Every moral [and political] consideration argues for decisive political action by the British and Americans on behalf of the Jews."

Late in 1945 Walsh's name appeared among the list of the six commentators whose scripts were requested for review by the Wood-Rankin[44] House Committee on Un-American Activities, for unstated reasons and over public protest. Walsh's commentaries continued on the air uninterrupted. In addition to his nightly commentary, Walsh has presided over radio quiz programs, and appeared as guest on the forums *Wake Up America, People's Platform, Author Meets the Critics,* and *America's Town Meeting of the Air.*

As a member of the board of Freedom House, in early 1945 he cast the only vote opposing refusal of a five-thousand-dollar donation to the Willkie [40] Memorial Fund from the Communist Political Association. In April 1946 he was named by Secretary of the Navy James V. Forrestal [42] to serve on the Navy's Civilian Advisory Committee to study ways of making naval service a more attractive career. Walsh was chosen as the "keynote" speaker at the State Convention of the American Labor Party, held in September 1946. He represented those organizations "supporting what is expected to be the joint Democratic-Labor-Liberal party State ticket," according to the New York Times. When the National Citizens Political Action Committee merged with the Independent Citizens Committee of the Arts, Sciences, and Professions at the end of December 1946, Walsh was chosen one of thirty vice-chairmen in the new organization, which was named the Progressive Citizens of America. The new political group, according to PM, laid "open the way for the formation of a third national party for the 1948 Presidential election."

The economist's writings include The Capital Value of Man and an essay, "A Labor Movement for the United States," in Explorations in Economics (1936), the F. W. Taussig tribute collection. CIO—Industrial Unionism in Action, published twenty months after the formation of the organization, Samuel Yellen in the Nation called "an excellent . . . summary," having among its "many virtues . . . simplicity and clarity—the ability to pick the salient happenings out of the current turmoil and to cast them in direct, non-academic American language." The Christian Century reviewer said, "Professor Walsh's informed but sympathetic study of the CIO . . . deals only with the rise of the CIO, and is severe in its strictures on the A.F. of L." David Ramsey wrote in the New Republic, "Dr. Walsh has not sufficiently digested the experiences of the CIO or the A.F. of L."; Professor Paul H. Douglas in the Saturday Review of Literature found the volume "a timely and an interesting book." Walsh's articles have been published in magazines, among them Survey Graphic and the New Republic. Some of his reviews of political and economic volumes have appeared in the New York Herald Tribune, PM, and the New Republic.

A member of the executive board of the National Bureau of Economic Research, Walsh is also affiliated with the Urban League of Greater New York, the Independent Citizen's Committee of Arts, Sciences, and Professions, the American Economic Association and the Royal Economic Society.

Over the radio Walsh may be recognized by a deep, well-modulated voice, the characteristic of the trained singer. Still a devotee of serious music, Walsh plays the violoncello. He is pleased that he draws as many letters as the station's leading "disc jockeys"; he has immense faith in his listeners, numbering among them some who first wrote to him when, as a speaker on a sedate forum, he called the remarks of a fellow speaker "unadulterated drivel." Walsh says, Harriet Van Horne reported, that the letters he receives "reflect the growing interest of the public in international politics—a healthy omen for missionaries of world democracy." The commentator agrees with the late Raymond Clapper that one must "never overestimate the knowledge of the people; never underestimate their intelligence."

References

N Y World-Telegram p26 S 25 '45
PM p3 O 30 '46
Sch & Soc 47:758+, 771 Je 11 '38; 47: 800+ Je 18 '38
Who's Who in Labor (1946)

WALSH, JOSEPH Dec. 16, 1875—Jan. 13, 1946 American lawyer, judge, legislator; United States Republican Representative from Massachusetts (1915-1923); justice, Superior Court of Massachusetts, 1922 to death.

Obituary

N Y Times p19 Ja 14 '46

WAMBAUGH, SARAH (wäm'bô) Mar. 6, 1882- Author; lecturer; consultant on international affairs

Address: h. 22 Berkeley St., Cambridge, Mass.

Sarah Wambaugh, a world authority on plebiscites, was in March 1946 technical adviser to the six hundred Americans designated to observe the Greek elections. After experience on the League of Nations secretariat, Miss Wambaugh served as expert adviser to the Peruvian Government for the Tacna-Arica plebiscite of 1925-26, and as technical adviser and member of the Saar Plebiscite Commission in 1934-35. She has taught history and government in the Netherlands and Switzerland, as well as in her own country, and has presented her views on the maintenance of peace through articles and lectures.

A descendant of Flemish and Scotch pioneers who settled in New Jersey, Virginia, and Ohio, Sarah Wambaugh is the daughter of Eugene and Anna S. (Hemphill) Wambaugh. She was born on March 6, 1882, in Cincinnati, where her father had his law practice. When she was ten, her father, a specialist in constitutional and international law, was appointed to the Harvard Law School faculty, and Sarah was brought up in the academic atmosphere of Cambridge, where she still lives. Graduated from Radcliffe College in 1902, she remained there as an assistant in history and government until 1906, and received her Master's degree in international law and political science, also from Radcliffe, in 1917. (She has been an honorary research fellow since 1926.)

After World War I there were some minor plebiscites held for the inhabitants of disputed border territories. Consulting the Harvard library catalogue for books on the subject of plebiscites, Miss Wambaugh found only one thin, paper-bound French book; dating from the turn of the century, it had been written by an Alsatian who hoped that his province might vote on whether to belong to Germany

SARAH WAMBAUGH

or to France. In 1920, after Sarah Wambaugh had begun a year's graduate study at the London University School of Economics and at Oxford, her *Monograph on Plebiscites* was published by the Oxford University Press. Written for the Carnegie Endowment for International Peace, the monograph was an exhaustive study of all the plebiscites on exchanges of sovereignty from their beginning with the French Revolution up to World War I. It was described (by the November 1923 *Century*) as "the standard work on the subject . . . well known and liked in the various foreign offices abroad."

While studying in England, Miss Wambaugh was asked to substitute temporarily for an American member of the League of Nations secretariat serving on the Administrative Commissions and Minorities Section. She did so in July 1920, when the League was still housed in London, and went with it to Geneva, where she remained through the first Assembly. In an article on the subject, Miss Wambaugh lists some two dozen documents placed on her desk in the course of a single day, in addition to a world press review, and mentions that one day's work included "a talk with a Spaniard about printing documents . . . then a talk with a Greek from Smyrna regarding the Greco-Bulgarian treaty, later a Drafting Committee where an Englishman, a Frenchman, a Serbian and a Dane . . . went over the French and English translations of a German document for distribution to the Council. Greek, Serb, Dane, Briton, Spaniard, so they were," she adds, "but I had forgotten it until I came to write it down. For in a few weeks they had become to me just so many interesting, courteous, and friendly men and women, working unselfconsciously together with a common purpose for a common cause."

Miss Wambaugh's work on the secretariat ended in January 1921. For one semester she was an instructor in history at Wellesley College, then in May 1922 sailed for Europe to study the postwar plebiscites. A month in Geneva examining the documents on the Upper Silesian plebiscite was followed by three months in the affected areas of Austria, Poland, Denmark, Belgium, and Germany, in the course of which the investigator crossed international borders thirty-two times. She again returned to Geneva to observe subsequent four-week Assemblies of the League. "To the student of politics," she wrote in 1924, "there can be no more fascinating occupation than to watch at Geneva the effort to banish the old diplomacy, with its basis of partisanship and emotion, and to put in its place a wholly new technique which shall turn politics into a science." Miss Wambaugh was involved in this effort as an expert adviser on questions regarding the administration of the Saar Basin and the Free City of Danzig.

Sarah Wambaugh was an expert adviser to the Peruvian Government in the Tacna-Arica plebiscite, held in 1925-26 to settle a dispute between Peru and Chile. General John J. Pershing was the arbitrator accepted by both countries. For two months, Miss Wambaugh worked in the Foreign Office at Lima, where her office was the Viceroy's private dining room in the old Torre Tagle palace. When the Peruvian delegation arrived at the scene of the dispute, where they spent ten months, they were forced for their own safety to live on a transport anchored a mile offshore. In 1927, after her work in Peru and Washington, Miss Wambaugh became a professor of the French-language Academy of International Law at the Netherlands capital. Her *La pratique des plébiscites internationaux* was published in 1928, and her *Plebiscites Since the World War* in 1933. Her most recent book is *The Saar Plebiscite* (1940). Her articles appear in *Current History*, the *Atlantic Monthly*, and other periodicals.

In 1934 the League appointed Sarah Wambaugh, together with a high court judge from Italy and one from the Netherlands, to draft the regulations for the Saar Plebiscite. Held in January 1935, it settled the vexing question of whether the rich industrial valley was to belong to France or Germany. As a technical adviser and deputy member of the Saar Plebiscite Commission, the American woman lived for seven months in the Saar, "on top of Europe's bonfire." Later in 1935 Miss Wambaugh lectured at the Institute for Advanced International Studies in Geneva. "Miss Wambaugh, the brilliant historian, has become one of the great artisans of peace," said the citation accompanying the University of Geneva's award of an honorary doctorate in social sciences. "It is thanks to the cooperation of the one who represents the greatest technical competence in this field, that the organization of the Saar plebiscite was a model of precision." This degree was conferred upon Miss Wambaugh in November 1935. Earlier, in June she had within one week received LL.D.'s from Ohio State and Western Reserve Universities and an L.H.D. from Tufts; and she has been further honored by LL.D.'s from

Columbia (1936) and Russell Sage College (1938).

Miss Wambaugh is described as a handsome woman with brown eyes and soft brown hair. "She talks slowly and calmly, depending on understatement to emphasize her points and showing every indication of being a skillful public speaker," writes Harold B. Hinton. "She dresses carefully, in the best of taste." A bright accent to her costume is the ribbon bar which indicates the four decorations she has received: Knight Cross, 1st Class, of the Austrian Order of Merit (1935), Officer of the Peruvian Order of the Sun (1937), Heraldic Order of Christopher Columbus of the Dominican Republic (1940), and the Gold Decoration of the City of Arequipa (1926). Among Miss Wambaugh's memberships are the American Society of International Law, the American Political Science Association (her father once edited its journal), the Grotius Society of London, and the Sociedad Geográfica de Lima (honorary).

References

    Century 107:vi-vii N '23
    Lit Digest 119:12 F 23 '35 por
    N Y Times VI p21 F 17 '46 por
    Scholastic 25:27 Ja 12 '35 por
    American Women, 1939-40
    Who's Who in America, 1946-47

WANAMAKER, PEARL A(NDERSON)
Jan. 18, 1899- Educator
Address: b. c/o State Office of Public Instruction, Olympia, Wash.; h. Coupeville, Wash.

In electing Pearl A, Wanamaker, superintendent of schools in the State of Washington, to its presidency, the National Education Association chose a woman whom Washingtonians have long regarded as "an inspiration to the professional organizations" in their State, and who believes that if given guidance in the right direction parents, teachers, and legislators "will go far in maintaining the integrity of the public schools." After visiting Japan as a member of the United States Education Mission in 1946, Mrs. Wanamaker was convinced that the schools must remain free of political control and that "the responsibility of leadership, even on a world-wide scale, rests largely upon the teaching profession."

Pearl Wanamaker, née Anderson, was born on January 18, 1899, the daughter of Nils and Johanna (Hellman) Anderson. Her birthplace is the town of Mabana on Camano Island, the smaller of the two Puget Sound islands comprising Island County of the State of Washington; and it was on Camano Beach that, as a child, she "hunted for agates, dug for clams, and raced with the wind." As she grew older her father began to foster her interest in political activity as one means toward insuring good government, taking her to meetings so that she might become familiar with political procedures. In his lumber camps she acquired the practical knowledge which was later to be of value to her as custodian of Washington's

PEARL A. WANAMAKER

school-owned timberlands. In 1917, after her graduation from high school, eighteen-year-old Pearl Anderson began her pedagogical career as mistress of a one-room country school. As she advanced from this position to that of teacher in a graded elementary school and then to principal of another elementary school between 1917 and 1921, she combined her work with the completion of her formal education, in 1919 studying at Bellingham Normal School and later attending the University of Washington, from which she received her B.A. in 1922.

Following her graduation from the University of Washington, the young educator taught in a small rural high school in Montana. At the end of a year she accepted her first administrative position, that of Island County's superintendent of schools, a post which she held for four years before again entering the classroom as a high school teacher in 1928. One year earlier, in 1927, she had been married to Lemuel A. Wanamaker, a civil engineer. (They have three children, Robert Allison, Helen Joanna, and James Niles.) In 1929, the *Christian Science Monitor* has recorded, "when the citizens of Whidbey Island [the larger section of Island County] were campaigning for a bridge to connect them with the mainland across Deception Pass and needed someone to push the matter in the legislature," they sent Mrs. Wanamaker to Olympia as their representative. Released from her classroom activities for the duration of the legislative session, Mrs. Wanamaker succeeded in obtaining authorization for the bridge (in 1933) and won re-election to the State House of Representatives in 1933 and 1935. In 1937 and 1939 she was elected to the State Senate.

Her chief concern during the biennial sixty-day periods of lawmaking was the schools, and it has been pointed out that the majority of the improvements made in the educational pro-

WANAMAKER, PEARL A.—*Continued*

gram of the State of Washington between 1933 and 1941 were due largely to her "dynamic" leadership. In 1933-34, when teachers' salaries throughout the state still averaged only twelve hundred dollars a year, with some as low as eight hundred, she led the fight for State aid for the schools which made the first salary increases possible; and thereafter, she was instrumental in obtaining the successive increases which by 1941 had resulted in an average annual salary of seventeen hundred dollars, with a statutory minimum of twelve hundred. Mrs. Wanamaker was coauthor, in 1937, of the Yantis-Wanamaker Equalization Law, which, by sanctioning special State assistance to tax-poor districts, equated school support in all areas of the state. To illustrate concretely her arguments in favor of this bill it is recalled that she used kindergarten blocks, and statistics show that, with subsequent improvements, it has given Washington the highest standard of compensation for rural teachers in the United States. Also under her superintendence, the legislature enacted a State-wide joint contributory teacher-retirement law, said to be Washington's "first actuarially sound" plan, to replace the multitude of local programs then in effect. On another front, she was chairman of the Senate Labor and Labor Statistics Committee for two sessions, she sponsored civil service legislation, and in January 1935 served on the Governor's Arbitration Board in the Puget Sound ferry strike.

Then, in 1940 Pearl Wanamaker ended her connection with the State legislature and the high school where she had been teaching in order to take office as Superintendent of Public Instruction of the State of Washington on January 1, 1941. At once she found herself in charge of Washington's newly launched school district consolidation program, which in the interests of economy and efficiency reduced the number of organizational units from twenty-seven hundred to eight hundred. At the same time she lent "effective leadership" to the organized teacher groups engaged in contesting exploitation of the State's large acreage of school-owned lands and forests, thereby securing the passage of legislation which gave the schools a much stronger voice in their disposition. Believing that the profession is best served by the healthy, happy individual, Superintendent Wanamaker worked also for further salary adjustments and through the Contract Relations Law, which she sponsored with the Washington Education Association, instituted standardized contracts and improved tenure and sick-leave conditions. State-wide curriculum improvement, carried out with the cooperation of classroom teachers, state-wide in-service training, a code of ethics for school board-teacher relations, and state aid for school plant construction and rehabilitation were other goals she accomplished.

As elsewhere, the outbreak of World War II brought to the State of Washington the problems of teacher shortages, mothers in industry, nursery schools, the adjustment of the curriculum to war needs, and a manpower shortage which turned the eyes of industry and agriculture to the potential labor market in schools. These problems Mrs. Wanamaker is considered to have met successfully. Insisting that youth must not forego education entirely for the necessity of the moment, the Superintendent effected a compromise—shorter school hours and more intensive industrial training in the schools, combined with part-time work in the factories and on the farms. During the harvesting emergency, for instance, she refused to allow the schools to be closed until nonessential establishments had sent their employees to help out. The schools would give their support to the war effort, she told a conference of military, industrial, and agricultural leaders, but they in turn had to be "protected in their function of education."

Early in 1946, as one of twenty-three men and four women, Pearl Wanamaker served on the commission appointed, at the request of General MacArthur [41], to advise on the democratization of the educational system of conquered Japan. On July 5, 1946, she was elected to the presidency of the National Education Association. Said an N.E.A. spokesman: "As president of the National Education Association, Mrs. Wanamaker will bring to our national organization the same dynamic leadership which has been so successful in Washington. She stands for a united and progressive profession, improved working conditions for all teachers, and adequate educational opportunities for every child."

In addition to being Washington State Superintendent of Schools, the N.E.A. president is chairman of the State Board of Education, the State Board of Vocational Education, the State Library Commission, the State Council of National Citizenship Education, and the Northwest Council of the National Council on School Building Problems. Vice-president of the National Council of Chief State School Officers for 1943, Pearl Wanamaker is now, in 1946, a member of the Washington Education Association and the American Association of School Administrators. She is also active in a number of other organizations, among them the Joint Canada-United States Committee on Education, of which she is a member, and the Educational Policies Commission, on whose board of directors she is serving her second three-year term in 1946.

References

Christian Sci Mon p5 Jl 6 '46
Who's Who in America, 1946-47

WARD, MARY JANE Aug. 27, 1905-
Author
Address: h. R.F.D. #2, Box 290, Elgin, Ill.

Mary Jane Ward "so excellently fashioned" the story of a mental hospital patient in *The Snake Pit*, both an imaginative work of fiction and a social document, that it was purchased for a motion picture, made a dual selection for April by the Book-of-the-Month Club, reprinted in part in that month's *Harper's Bazaar*, and condensed in *Reader's Digest* for

May. In addition, rights were sold for its publication abroad. "I really hope it does some good," is Miss Ward's comment on her "first real success."

Born in Fairmount, Indiana, August 27, 1905, Mary Jane Ward is the daughter of Claude Arthur Ward and the former Marion Lockridge. As a child she showed a talent for the piano and drawing, and many were the five-cent notebooks she filled with stories. Seven-year-old Mary Jane described the Wabash River flood of 1913 in Peru, Indiana. It was a frightening, yet droll, spectacle: the boat taking her aunt out of the bedroom window just as the new piano floated out of the front door, elephants from a circus farm thrashing through the water, and monkeys weeping in the tree-tops. When she was ten years old the family moved to Evanston, Illinois.

Until Mary Jane was fourteen she showed an interest in music as a career. In a piano recital at the Lyon and Healy Hall in Chicago she played a program, half of Grieg and Schumann, and half her own composition. But after her graduation from Evanston Township High School in 1923, English assumed a major importance in her studies. For two years she attended Northwestern University, following this with one year at the Lyceum of Arts Conservatory. Miss Ward next had an assortment of jobs: selling dresses and china, writing mail-order advertising, designing and decorating glass novelties, and teaching art at a summer camp.

On March 7, 1928, Miss Ward was married to Edward Quayle, a statistician who wrote plays and painted. She then began her career as a writer, setting herself the task of writing a hundred short stories—"she would make money, perhaps a great deal of money." Her first sale was to the Chicago *Daily News* mid-week magazine. Of the many other short stories she wrote, a half dozen or so were sold to national magazines. But somewhere before the hundredth she lost sight of that goal and began a novel which was never published. Money continued to be a problem. "For years we lived on pork and spaghetti," Miss Ward once said, "and for a while our home was on top of a garage where we didn't have to pay rent." A ten-dollar award in a newspaper contest for a meat loaf recipe was a windfall in the years of discouragement. In 1937 the author reviewed books and edited a short story feature for the Evanston *News-Index*. Sometimes she covered concerts and lectures as well.

Miss Ward's second novel, *The Tree Has Roots*, was accepted, reaching publication in 1937. And a year later her third, *The Wax Apple*, appeared. These books met with limited literary and financial success. *The Tree Has Roots* depicted life in a university community, dealing with a handy man, waitresses, and stenographers, not with students or faculty. The New York *Times* reviewer called the work "unusually even" and "very moving," but added, "To repeat, however, that her book is solely a portfolio of first rate portraits is to praise and to damn it at the same time." Miss Ward's **characterizations** in her second published novel

MARY JANE WARD

were praised with similar qualifications. Wrote the *Times* reviewer of *The Wax Apple*: "Miss Ward has an astonishingly sure insight into the lives of humble people. . . .Her characters . . . are touching, amusing, vivid. . . . it is a pity that *The Wax Apple* is to some extent marred by its eccentricities of style."

The Quayles moved to New York in 1939, getting rooms in Greenwich Village and hoping for the best in a locality where other writers had succeeded. For three years they wrote persistently without profit and frequented the topmost seats in theaters. In 1941 Miss Ward suffered a nervous breakdown and spent nine months in a mental hospital.

Miss Ward's latest novel, *The Snake Pit*, was published in March, 1946. "My agent bounced the book, said nobody would buy it," she told Sally MacDougall in an interview for the New York *World-Telegram*. While she wanted to put the book away, her husband found a publisher for it. The theme of abnormal psychology is indicated in the title. In medieval times insane persons were lowered into snake pits; it was thought that the same fright that would drive a sane person out of his wits might shock an insane person back into sanity. The story is so true to life that Miss Ward has found it necessary to state that both characters and setting are fictitious. Although the author acknowledges that "the novel was based on personal experience and observation," she insists it is not autobiographical: "There was no attempt to write any sort of factual report. . . .Juniper Hill, from tubs to tunnel, was built and peopled by a mind that was on vacation."

Literary and medical men agreed in their praises of Miss Ward's work. The *New Yorker* reviewer wrote: "Charm and humor are strange words to describe a novel of life in an insane asylum, but they apply to this

WARD, MARY JANE—*Continued*

record of the year spent by a patient in a state hospital. A young wife who has suffered a mental blackout carries with her into this institution the most engaging gentleness, good manners, and, when she is at all conscious of her whereabouts and her identity, a gift for ironic observation." Dr. Frederic Wertham, psychiatrist and president of the Association for the Advancement of Psychotherapy, vouched for the authenticity of conditions described in the mental hospital. "Juniper Hill, the hospital, is far above the average. That makes this novel as a document even more telling. Here is the smell, the monotony, the nobody-to-listen, the diet, the shortage of personnel and supplies ('there wasn't enough of anything but patients'), the strait jacket and its variants . . . the treatment—terrifying at the brief moments when it comes and in the endless stretches when it is completely absent." The nurses' chief concern with the women patients was to keep them quiet—thinking patients might disturb the peace, might draw up petitions and demand rights. "There simply were not enough nurses to handle thinkers." Instead, a nurse shouted mechanically, "Cafeterialadies," and the patients raced down a watery tunnel to bolt their food. Or a patient came out of mental darkness to find herself in wet packs in a tub of running water. "Miss Ward's ability to make the plight of a patient in an insane asylum seem not just horrible or pitiful, but natural and understandable, is remarkable," wrote Orville Prescott. Jack Conroy remarked in *Book World*, "You somehow identify yourself intimately with the demented girl's bafflement and frustration, share her joy when the dark outside doors of Juniper Hill open to free her and she steps forth into the sunlight." All of the descriptions are so realistic that more than one reader has become concerned over his own mental state. "When Virginia Cunningham tried to dig out her memory it seemed to be swathed in a kind of wet, gray chiffon that stuck to the very part she wanted most to examine. . . . Miss Ward tells her story entirely as from within the bewildered mind of Virginia Cunningham," Lewis Gannett wrote in the New York *Herald Tribune*, "and I have seldom read a story so consistently convincing. This is Virginia, and, but for the grace of God, it might be you or I."

The author wrote *The Snake Pit* in thirteen months by taking four hours each day from her housework. The first trade edition consisted of fifty thousand copies. After the Book-of-the-Month Club printed four hundred twenty-five thousand more in its April distribution of the book, the publisher brought out a second printing of twenty-five thousand copies. The book earned over one hundred thousand dollars in its first month, partly from these sales and partly from its reprinting in *Harper's Bazaar* for April 1946 and *Reader's Digest* for May of the same year. Foreign rights cover editions in English, Dutch, French, Swedish, Danish, and Spanish. The motion picture of Miss Ward's novel is to star Joan Fontaine and be directed by Anatole Litvak.

In the spring of 1946 Miss Ward and her husband bought a dairy farm thirty miles west of Chicago. "My husband manages the farm, which is operated by an experienced dairyman. My activities here are about the same as they were in town—writing and housekeeping. . . . The novel I am working on now is somewhere in third or fourth draft and may not be finished until the end of the year [1946]." Miss Ward is five feet five inches tall and weighs 130 pounds. A friend has described her: "Magnificent thick dark auburn hair and the quickest, most oddly penetrating, yet friendly, brown eyes in the world . . . a lovely, low-pitched voice." The author's favorite means of recreation are riding, cooking, and gardening.

References

Book-of-the-Month Club N Mr '46
Chicago Sun Book Week Ap 7 '46
N Y Times p23 Ap 5 '46
New Repub Ap 8 '46
New Yorker Ap 6 '46

WASON, ROBERT R(OSS) (wä'sŭn) May 1, 1888- Business executive
Address: b. c/o Manning, Maxwell & Moore, Inc., 405 Lexington Ave., New York; h. 1 Gracie Sq., New York

In succeeding Ira Mosher [45] as president of the National Association of Manufacturers for 1946, Robert R. Wason assumed control of the influential industrial body in a crucial period for labor-management-Government relationships. Long a member of the NAM, Wason was elected chairman of the board of the NAM after his year as president expired. He is president of the New York engineering firm of Manning, Maxwell and Moore, Inc.

A Midwesterner, Robert Ross Wason was born in Ashtabula, Ohio, on May Day, 1888. His parents, Samuel and Anna Ross (Wallace) Wason, had both come from Northern Ireland to the United States and had met and married in Ohio. Samuel Wason was a builder, but his family of seven children lived in what his son describes as "biting poverty." At the age of eleven Robert got his first job, as a grocer's boy, and he continued to work throughout his school years. He entered Harbor High School in his native city in 1901, working during the summer vacations as deckhand on a Lake Erie ore boat. By the time he was seventeen he had been janitor of both the church and the high school. After graduation from high school in 1905, he worked on the ore docks for a time, earning forty-five dollars a month. Then followed a period in which he worked as longshoreman, structural steel helper, and blacksmith's helper; and when he was twenty he was running a hoist on the docks. Finally, in 1910 he decided to give up seasonal dock work for journalism and began as a reporter on the newly launched Ashtabula *Independent*. After some months he switched to the advertising angle of the business for a three-dollar raise, which brought his weekly salary to eighteen dollars. But two and a half years later the paper was sold to its competitor and Wason's newspaper work ended.

About this time Wason was offered a chance to invest in the manufacturing end of one of the early electric washing machines. The project failed, however, and with it went Wason's money. At the age of twenty-five he thereupon set out to find new opportunities in Cleveland. Through the help-wanted advertisements, he found a job selling advertising; later a position in an advertising agency. Gaining recognition for his novel ideas on merchandising, he was soon traveling through the country selling the products of this agency's clients. Not drafted for service in World War I, he was able to continue with his advertising work, later joining Lees Advertising Agency, where he wrote copy for important national accounts. After another two years he moved to Cincinnati, where in 1920 he became a vice-president and director of merchandising of the Proctor and Collier advertising agency. In this period he lectured at the University of Cincinnati on marketing and merchandising and wrote *Cincinnati, Possibilities and Opportunities* (1923), reported to have won business support and thereby to have led to the installation of a form of city management government in Cincinnati. From 1923 to 1925 the Ohioan was sales manager of A. S. Boyle Company in the same city, but in 1925 he returned to Proctor and Collier. Here his accounts grew, and by 1928 he was earning more than twenty thousand dollars a year. Then, in 1929 Wason accepted an invitation to come to New York City as president of the Clarke Lighter Company, an insolvent firm which perished in the depression despite Wason's efforts to keep it going.

In 1931 forty-three-year-old Wason accepted the offer of the presidency of Manning, Maxwell and Moore, Inc., an engineering firm among whose present products are listed showbox cranes and hoists, consolidated safety valves, ashcroft gauges, industrial recording instruments, apparatus for jet propulsion planes, and other equipment for heavy industry. At that time the company was "long on engineering and short on merchandising," and a man of Wason's experience was needed to correct the situation. Charles A. Moore, chairman of the board, points out that Wason quickly became familiar with all aspects of the business and that he established a school for the salesmen to give them an understanding of the equipment which they were selling. Between 1932 and 1942, it is reported, "the shipments of Manning, Maxwell and Moore, Inc., increased seventeen-fold. An analysis showed 75 per cent of the engineering goods shipped had not been in existence ten years earlier; 19 per cent had been modernized; 6 per cent were more than ten years old. A completely new business had been progressively created. And it was done without bringing in any new capital funds." In 1945 the company employed more than three thousand men in its four plants—in Bridgeport (Connecticut), Boston, Muskegon (Michigan), and Tulsa (Oklahoma). Wason deals with the men through the plant managers and in terms of local conditions. "No one has a greater appreciation of labor's position than I," he says, "because all my life I have been one of those who always labored." *Business Week* reported that Wason, once a

ROBERT R. WASON

union member in good standing himself, believes in unions as a means of protecting the worker.

An active member of the National Association of Manufacturers, the executive served as chairman of its Economic Principles Commission from 1942 to 1945 and directed this group of academic and business economists in the preparation of a textbook "to present the modern free enterprise system in this country." In August 1945 he became chairman of the NAM Reconversion Council. In this capacity he has been coordinating and presenting to the public the Association's ideas on reconversion. Shortly after V-J Day the NAM spokesman called for immediate reversal of OPA price policies, declaring that "large volume production with consequent large volume of employment can only be obtained under fair prices which yield incentive profits—unrealistic low prices will discourage production." Since that time the NAM has been carrying on a steady campaign against the OPA. In November Wason appeared before the special House committee on Post-War Economic Policy and Planning as a member of a three-man NAM group to present the organization's views. Wason submitted to the Congressional group a ten-point program which had resulted from the NAM's three-year reconversion study. The main point was removal of all OPA controls by February 15, 1946. Other measures which would have wide effect were the elimination of wage and salary stabilization, discontinuance of wartime subsidies, and a 20 per cent income tax reduction for corporations and individuals. Wason was of the opinion that only rent controls should remain. He also denied the charge that manufacturers had been deliberately holding up sales until termination of the excess profits tax with the new year.

(Continued next page)

WASON, ROBERT R.—*Continued*

At the NAM's golden anniversary convention in New York in December 1945 Wason was elected president for 1946. The organization's objectives and program for the coming year, he declared, would include "genuine security that should begin at once with a good job at fair pay; resistance to inflation that we have up to now and the danger of more inflation that impends; and an offer of cooperation to President Truman [45] and to Congress, which we earnestly hope will be accepted." After his election Wason reiterated his demand for the abolition of price control. (Previously the convention had heard a plea for continued price control by OPA Administrator Chester Bowles [43], who warned that sudden abandonment of the Government's anti-inflation program would produce "national disaster.")

Wason later charged that the Administration's wage increase policy was a dangerous source of inflation; the "lack of equality between labor and management," he said, favored labor, and constituted a "roadblock to prosperity." After the price-control program was virtually abandoned in November 1946, Wason predicted price decreases only if costs were not increased "by another round of wage demands." He urged complete removal of rent ceilings by 1947. These and other ideas were expressed by Wason in 145 formal addresses, two appearances before Congressional committees, forty radio broadcasts, sixty-one press conferences, and many NAM regional meetings. (The statistics are *Time*'s.) At the New York convention in December 1946 Wason was succeeded in the presidency by Earl Bunting, and became chairman of the NAM board. Wason, one of six business executives to tour Germany in June 1946 as guests of the Military Government, urged that control of that occupied country's market be relaxed "to get the German economy moving" as well as to stimulate foreign trade. He also attended the council meeting of the International Chamber of Commerce held in Paris.

Wason's business career, it is said, has been characterized by "steady progress rather than high-pressure methods." He is reported to be a patient listener, respected as an organizer and manager. From 1935 to 1939 he was also president of the Zonite Corporation of New York, which he has since served as director and executive committeeman. According to *Business Week*, "Wason has the advertising man's knack of putting his convictions into striking phrase and ringing slogan." Several of the industrialist's addresses to organizations have been published in booklet form by his company. Among these are three speeches delivered in 1944, entitled *Man-made Miracle— American Enterprise, How Long Should We Be Faced With Government Controls?*, and *Let Freedom Ring!* Wason belongs to the Ohio Society of New York.

The NAM leader is five feet ten, weighs about one hundred eighty-five pounds, and has grayish hair and hazel eyes. His wife is the former Hilda Bradford of Falmouth, Kentucky, to whom he was married on August 28, 1922. For recreation Wason attends the theater and enjoys reading books on politics and economics.

References

Who's Who in America, 1946-47
Who's Who in Commerce and Industry (1944)

WATERS, JAMES R. (?)—Nov. 20, 1945 Hungarian-born American radio, vaudeville, and theatrical comedian; used stage name in private life; noted for his interpretation of Yiddish characters; appeared as Jake in the radio serial *The Goldbergs* from 1929 until retirement in 1944; starred on the road in *Potash and Perlmutter* and *Abie's Irish Rose*; his Broadway plays include *Wonder Boy* (1931), *Excursion* (1937), and *All in Favor* (1942).

Obituary

N Y Times p21 N 21 '45 por

WATSON, MARK S(KINNER) June 24, 1887- Journalist

Address: b. c/o The Baltimore Sun, Baltimore, Md.; h. 1 Merryman Ct., Baltimore, Md.

Mark S. Watson, associated with the Baltimore *Sun* for more than twenty years and by 1946 its military correspondent for five years, is a newspaper man who has had much experience in the reporting of world affairs. In addition to covering and editing the news of various sections of the United States and foreign countries, Watson was a correspondent in World War II—his distinguished telegraphic reporting of international events in the war won for him the Pulitzer Prize in 1945.

The son of Winslow Charles and Ella (Barnes) Watson, Mark Skinner Watson was born in Plattsburg, New York, on June 24, 1887. His family was of early American stock; one of his great-grandfathers, an outstanding agriculturist, introduced county fairs and "more serious farming innovations" to the western region of New York State. Young Mark's advanced education was obtained at Union College in Schenectady, New York. An honor student in history and philosophy and a recipient of prizes for his high scholarship, Watson was graduated from that college in 1908 with a B.A. degree. Twenty-five years later, in 1933, Watson's college conferred upon him an honorary M.A. degree for his journalistic achievements.

Watson's newspaper career began during his college vacations when he worked on his hometown Plattsburg *Press,* as, according to his description, a "reporter, editor, and typesetter-when-all-the-printers-were-tight." For one year after graduation (1908-09) Watson remained with the *Press,* then left to take a job as reporter and traveling correspondent for the Chicago *Tribune.* At this Watson worked from 1909 to 1917, taking leave from the Chicago newspaper for some months during 1914-15 to accept the post of publicity director for the San Diego (California) Exposition. During the journalist's latter years with the *Tribune* he was sent to cover the complicated political situation in Mexico. The Government of Venustiano Carranza, a revolutionary Mexican president recognized by the United States in 1915, was under attack by Francisco Villa. The insurgent's raids across the border into the State of New Mexico to protest United States recognition of his opponent provoked a punitive expedition into Mexico in 1916 under General Pershing. Carranza in turn eventually grew suspicious of the presence of United States troops on his country's soil. Watson, while this tense relationship existed between the two nations, managed to get the first interview with Carranza. Other of his assignments in this period included a Canadian trip for a "Dominion-at-war survey," work at the Washington and New York bureaus of the *Tribune,* and editorial writing.

The same day that the United States entered World War I against the Central Powers— April 6, 1917—Watson enlisted in the Illinois Field Artillery of the United States Army. Soon after, he was sent to the Fort Sheridan officers' training camp, where he was commissioned a second lieutenant. As a member of the American Expeditionary Forces, he was sent overseas in September, later to be stationed at the United States general headquarters in Chaumont, France. There, until assigned to field duty in October 1918, he served in the intelligence division. When the Armistice was declared in November 1918, the journalist was relieved of his field duty and was transferred once more to general headquarters. Within a week, he became officer-in-charge of the Army publication *Stars and Stripes.* His work on the soldiers' newspaper was primarily supervisory and was not "conspicuously easy . . . for his was a high-spirited, if talented, staff" containing "Harold Ross, now editor of the *New Yorker,* Alex Woollcott, John T. Winterich, *et al.*" Remarked Watson: "While I had been stationed at GHQ one of my numerous functions was to work at long distance to keep that whole staff out of the angry clutches of infuriated general officers and outraged military police. As officer-in-charge this was still my function, but I also now had to keep some of the personnel from cutting the throats of the other personnel."

In July 1919 Watson received his discharge from the Army, meanwhile having been promoted to the rank of major. His being attached to general headquarters, it is said, "was to prove invaluable experience when he became a war correspondent twenty-five years later" for the Baltimore *Sun.* Watson's friendships with officers with whom he had daily contact he retained through the years. Both at headquarters and on field service, the journalist had been able to view "a great Army as a whole, and to place each of its component parts in its proper perspective." A frequent visitor to American divisional areas, to British headquarters, and to all sections of the war front, Watson had occasion to conduct on one of these short tours the late Franklin D. Roosevelt, then Assistant Secretary of the Navy. In France,

MARK S. WATSON

too, Watson had learned "the value of tiresome, patient planning as well as of sudden, exciting fighting." He was cited for his meritorious service abroad.

A brief period as managing editor of *The Ladies' Home Journal* in 1920 followed for the veteran, who in the same year went to work for the Baltimore *Sun* as assistant managing editor. This editorship Watson retained for seven years until he was appointed Sunday editor of the Baltimore newspaper (1927). In this capacity, late in 1939 Watson first turned his attention to "extended writing" about World War II: he submitted "two lengthy series of articles on the state of American defenses, which he found to be dismal." Discussing in detail the inadequacies of existing military and naval installations, Watson in his numerous articles urged that speedy protective measures be undertaken by the American Government because of the international crisis and pointed out that "fully eighteen months would be needed to equip even a small army of one million men for a purely defensive war" on United States soil. Two years later the Sunday editor became the journal's military writer (1941). In June 1943, Watson, who for some months had been acting editor of the *Sun,* left the United States for Great Britain, in order to take, as he had planned, a six weeks' vacation trip. The fifty-six-year-old journalist remained overseas, however, to report from the European front. For the duration Watson's duties kept him traveling between the United States and the European and African battle sectors.

Watson covered the war from England for a short period, then toured the North African war zone. In July 1943 the correspondent, a firsthand observer of the Allied landings in Sicily and of a good deal of the front-line action thenceforth, accompanied the American Fifth Army invasion forces when they debarked at Salerno in Italy. At one point in

WATSON, MARK S(KINNER)—*Cont.*

the ensuing campaign, during September, Watson, three reporters, and two officers, found themselves in advance of Fifth Army columns and "captured" a small Italian town. He entered Naples in October 1943.

Before he returned to the United States in December 1943 for a rest, Watson was one of three correspondents (Herbert L. Matthews of the New York *Times* and Gerald Norman of the London *Times* were the other two writers) permitted to interview Marshal Pietro Badoglio, who assumed the administration of the Italian Government in the wake of the Fascist debacle. The meeting took place "somewhere in southern Italy" in the middle of October. Watson's report, "distributed in behalf of the combined American press," expressed, among other things, the hope that the Italian people would support the "patently honest" Badoglio in his attempts to reconstruct his wartorn nation. The activities of the Allied Control Commission in Italy were discussed, too, in the *Sun* correspondent's dispatches. Once again in the United States, Watson, from Washington, concentrated on aircraft carrier training and operations in his military writings.

Mark S. Watson was in England when the Allies invaded Normandy on D-Day, June 6, 1944. Two weeks later the *Sun* correspondent joined the American First Army, going with it to Cherbourg and St. Lô. Watson was drafted to "guide" the first American troops into Paris—none of them could speak French or German—and to "explain our peaceful purposes to any inquisitive citizens." When he and the contingent of soldiers finally entered Paris on August 25, they were greeted by a French band playing the Union Civil War song, "Marching Through Georgia," a circumstance which Watson was reluctant to divulge to his Southern readers. After accompanying the ground forces sent to support the American air-borne troops which landed in Nijmegen, Holland, and after sojourning with the Eighty-Second and 101st United States Air-borne divisions and paying a brief visit to the Aachen sector early in December 1944 where events were still "quiet," he decided to examine the "forgotten" front in the Loire river valley (thus he missed the large-scale German counter-offensive in the Ardennes) where the French Forces of the Interior had large numbers of the Nazis surrounded.

In May 1945, three months after he resumed writing military analyses from Washington, Watson was awarded one of the Pulitzer prizes for his outstanding wartime reporting. His knowledge of the "complex panorama" of war gained from his varied experiences at the battlefronts and behind the lines and his writing skill had enabled him to write "movingly of the effect of war on noncombatant civilian populations and knowingly of its destruction of the great works of art and architecture of old Europe." After the war in Europe ended (May 1945), the Pulitzer Prize-winning journalist, who has been described as the "professional soldier's war correspondent," went to China to get material for a series of military and political articles "designed to give a more balanced appraisal of the obscure situation in the China of 1945 than had been available up to then." From China he continued through the United States' Pacific bases for the last of his wartime dispatches. The following year (1946) Watson was one of the large group covering the tests of the atomic bomb at Bikini. An observer, in addition, of political and social forces in America, Watson has contributed articles on these subjects to the periodicals *Forum* and the *Saturday Review of Literature*.

The Baltimore *Sun* writer was married to Susan Elizabeth Owens in September 1921; the couple have two daughters—Ellen Brashears and Susan Barnes. A Presbyterian in his church affiliation, Watson is a member of Sigma Phi, the Masons, and the National Press Club of Washington, D.C. For his work he has been honored, too, by France, in the Officier d'Academie citation.

References

N Y Times p16 My 8 '45 por
Who's Who in America, 1946-47
Who's Who in Journalism, 1928

WATTS, LYLE F(ORD) Nov. 18, 1890- United States Government official

Address: b. c/o Department of Agriculture, Washington, D.C.; h. 1911 R St. N.W., Washington, D.C.

As chief of the United States Forest Service, Lyle F. Watts supervises the administration of one hundred and fifty-eight national forests covering more than one hundred seventy-eight million acres. "A scholar in the woods" for thirty-three years, his foremost concern is to perpetuate timber growth for future generations while meeting present needs. On the conservation of the woodlands depends the supply of lumber, water, and of much of the nation's food requirements.

Lyle Ford Watts was born in Cerro Gordo County, Iowa, to James A. and Mary Jane (Liggett) Watts on November 18, 1890. At the age of twenty-two he obtained his B.S. degree from Iowa State College in 1913 and began his lifework as a forest assistant in the United States Forest Service. His first assignment was to the Intermountain Region, which has its headquarters at Ogden, Utah. He operated tree nurseries, patrolled the ranges, cruised and mapped timber stands, and guarded the woods against fire, its most dangerous enemy. At Ogden he met Nell Bowman, who became his wife in 1915.

In 1917 Watts was promoted to forest examiner and a year later he became assistant forest supervisor; in 1920 he was assigned as supervisor of the Weiser National Forest, and after two years he was transferred to the Idaho National Forest. Another promotion came in 1926 when he was made forest inspector, again at Ogden. In 1928, the same year he received the degree of Master of Forestry from Iowa State College, he left the Forest Service to organize the School of Forestry at the Utah State Agricultural College.

After one year in the educational field, however, he returned to the Forest Service as senior silviculturist of the Intermountain Forest and Range Experiment Station. The five years from 1931 to 1936 were spent in further research—he was director of the Northern Rocky Mountain Forest and Range Experiment Station with headquarters at Missoula, Montana, during this period. He then became regional forester of the North Central Region, a position in which he supervised the administration of wooded areas in Indiana, Illinois, Iowa, Michigan, Minnesota, Missouri, North Dakota, Ohio, and Wisconsin. From 1939 to 1942 he was regional forester of the North Pacific Region, which included Washington and Oregon.

Because of his experience in handling both skilled and unskilled workers, his contacts with construction crews, livestock men, and the general public, Watts in the fall of 1942 was called to assist Secretary Claude Wickard in the work of the Department of Agriculture on wartime problems of farm labor. In the early part of the following year Wickard, expressing confidence in Watts's ability to meet requirements of the wartime emergency as well as the nation's long range timber needs, appointed him to fill the vacant position of Forest Service chief. During the war years Watts's organization conducted a training program, for conscientious objectors, for fighting forest fires. They were taught to make hazardous parachute jumps while carrying shovels, portable pumps, and other equipment. (A plane can drop parachute jumpers within ten or fifteen minutes after a blaze has been sighted.)

Heavy drain on the timberlands in the war emergency period, when wood products were in great demand for military needs, increased Watts's concern for forest conservation. According to the Forest Service Chief the nation's total stand of saw timber had been reduced more than 40 per cent in a little over thirty years, and now 50 per cent more than the amount of saw timber grown was cut or destroyed each year. In articles and speeches he warned the public against the publicity of lumber industrialists which he said was intended to create the belief that the wood supply was plentiful. Although not overlooking the examples of private operators who carefully followed conservation policies, he claimed that 80 per cent of the cutting under private management (the public owns less than a third of the United States forest lands) was done without planning for the future. He recommended stronger Federal regulation "aimed to encourage private forest enterprise in every legitimate way" but "requiring timberland operators to recognize the public interest," and also proposed increased Government ownership of wooded areas "unsuited for private management, or where the public interest cannot otherwise be protected." The secretary-manager of the National Lumber Manufacturers Association, on the other hand, contradicted Watts's statements and attributed his stand to a traditional "gloomy approach to the whole forest

U.S. Forest Service
LYLE F. WATTS

conservation program" by the Forest Service and "the logical approach to a program of intended domination of a great industry by a Federal bureau."

In 1946, when there were further demands on the nation's forests to meet postwar housing and other peacetime needs, Watts urged the adoption of a more adequate conservation program. This would provide measures to encourage selective logging, more intensive fire protection, the saving of young timber and a sufficient number of trees for reseeding, the prevention of logging methods harmful to uncut trees, and above all, the development of a conservation-conscious American public. Addressing the American Forest Congress in October 1946, the Forest Service Chief and Secretary of Agriculture Clinton P. Anderson [45] as well as representatives of the CIO recommended Government control aimed at curbing destructive practices in privately owned timberlands.

A contributor to scientific journals and Department of Agriculture reports, Watts is a member of the Society of American Foresters, the American Forestry Association, and the American Association for the Advancement of Science. His other affiliations are the Izaak Walton League, Alpha Zeta, Phi Kappa Phi, the Cosmos Club, and the Masons. He is of the Presbyterian faith and says that his political affiliations are dictated only by his conscience. The Wattses' son, Gordon Lyle, is also a forester, while their daughter, Arline June, is married to a woods worker in Oregon. The chief forester is five feet ten and a half inches tall, weighs 160 pounds.

References

This Week p8 Ag 11 '46
Who's Who in America, 1946-47

WEBB, JAMES E(DWIN) Oct. 7, 1906-
United States Government official
Address: b. c/o Bureau of the Budget, Washington, D.C.

As Director of the United States Budget, James E. Webb, lawyer and former Marine Corps flier, is "the business manager for the Government." Virtually unknown in Government circles before President Truman named him for the post in July 1946, he had been personnel director, secretary-treasurer and vice-president of the Sperry Gyroscope Company. Under Secretary of the Treasury, O. Max Gardner, has described Webb as a believer in "the homely virtues of living within an income except in times of emergency . . . a disciple of the balanced budget."

JAMES E. WEBB

One of five children, James Edwin Webb was born October 7, 1906, in Oxford, Granville County, North Carolina, to John Frederick and Sarah (Gorham) Webb. His father was the county superintendent of schools for twenty-six years. While attending Oxford High School, James spent his afternoons and Saturdays in the employ of local five-and-ten-cent stores and grocery stores. In 1923 he enrolled at the University of North Carolina. To help pay his expenses there, he took whatever part-time jobs were available, but the money he earned was not sufficient; he thus borrowed funds to complete his freshman year. During the following year he worked in the accounting department of R. G. Lassiter and Company, contractors, at Raleigh, North Carolina, in order to repay his debt. In his spare time he attended Kings Business College, where he learned typewriting and shorthand and subsequently was made secretary to the president of the company.

The nineteen-year-old Webb re-entered the University of North Carolina in 1925 and received his B.A. degree three years later. A

Phi Beta Kappa student carrying a full program of study, he continued to earn his expenses during this period by working in the university's School of Education as secretary of the Bureau of Educational Research. There he received valuable business experience in the performance of duties which involved the handling of funds and account books, the preparation of budgets and of statistical records, and other functions. After graduation, Webb became full-time secretary of the bureau, but in 1929 he accepted a position as law clerk and stenographer for Parham and Lassiter, attorneys at Oxford, his home town, and there studied law for a year. During 1930 and 1931 he learned to fly as a private (first class) in the United States Marine Corps Reserve at the Naval Air Station in Pensacola, Florida. When the training was completed, he was commissioned a second lieutenant in the Fleet Marine Corps Reserve and spent one year on active flying duty as a naval aviator with the aircraft squadrons of the East Coast Expeditionary Force, United States Marine Corps, Quantico, Virginia.

Webb returned to a desk job in 1932. As secretary to Edward W. Pou, Representative from North Carolina and chairman of the House Rules Committee, he managed the office and committee staff, attended all meetings of the committee, handled official and personal correspondence, and represented Pou in a number of official matters for two years. At the same time (1933), he began to attend night classes at the George Washington University Law School. The combination of his law and flying training proved valuable when, in 1934, he was employed by O. Max Gardner, attorney at law and ex-Governor of North Carolina, who was then general counsel to the Aeronautical Chamber of Commerce of America. Webb assisted on the legal phases of the aviation industry program prepared for the Federal Aviation Commission and acted for Gardner on many occasions. During this period he also supervised the training of Marine Reserve Aviation personnel at Anacostia, District of Columbia, and continued to attend night law school.

In 1936, the year he was admitted to the District of Columbia bar, Webb went to Brooklyn, New York, to become the personnel director and assistant to the president (Thomas Morgan of North Carolina) of the Sperry Gyroscope Company, Incorporated. In this capacity he worked for five years, handling the staff work on major management problems referred to the president, recommending industrial relations policies, negotiating with labor unions, and supervising the administration of wages, workmen's compensation, and other matters connected with personnel. Webb's activities were not confined to Sperry Gyroscope: besides serving as operations officer for the Marine Reserve Aviation Squadron at Floyd Bennet Field (Brooklyn, New York) at various times, he held a commercial pilot's license and was a member of many aeronautical organizations, among them the National Aeronautic Association, of which he was a director and executive committee member and president of its Greater New York chapter. In connection with the exhibitions at the New York World's Fair in 1939, he was on the Aviation Advisory Committee and was also the secretary-treasurer and a member of the board of directors of the United States Aviation Exhibit, Incorporated. In the field of labor relations he was a member of the advisory panel of the Public Contracts Administrator on formulation of minimum wage determination for the scientific and laboratory instruments industries, United States Department of Labor, and was one of the faculty for the Princeton University summer seminar course in industrial relations. At the third inauguration of President Roosevelt, he was executive vice-chairman of the committee on reception to Governors of States.

The year that the United States entered World War II, in 1941, Webb was made secretary and treasurer of Sperry Gyroscope Company. Its manufacture of gyroscopes, bombsights, gunsights, control apparatus, and other devices needed in aerial, land, and sea battles made it a vital part of the nation's wartime industrial system—from less than three thousand, the number of its employees increased to more than thirty-three thousand. The future director of the United States Budget was responsible for the organization of all phases of budgetary control and management procedure at the company and supervised the work of the general controller.

In 1943 Webb became vice-president of the Sperry Gyroscope Company and assistant secretary-treasurer of the Sperry Corporation, the parent company which owned the Ford Instrument Company in Long Island City, Vickers, Incorporated (in Detroit), the Sperry Gyroscope Company, and several smaller companies. The following year, however, he left for active duty with the Ninth Marine Aircraft Wing with the rank of major. The commanding officer of the First Marine Air Warning Group, which included five squadrons, he trained aviation men in radar and electronics, in the techniques of aircraft control, and in military organization and administration.

When Webb returned to civilian life in 1945 he worked as an attorney with the firm of Gardner (O. Max), Morrison, and Rogers in Washington, D. C. In March of 1946 he was appointed to his first Government post. As executive assistant to the Under Secretary of the Treasury, O. Max Gardner, he was Gardner's day-to-day adviser on the over-all policies, objectives, programs, and operations of the Treasury Department. Four months later, the thirty-nine-year-old Webb, who was considered Gardner's protégé, was made the Director of the United States Budget. His appointment, which came at a time when the House Republican Tax Study Committee was demanding a reduction in Government spending and in taxation, followed the selection of several other North Carolinians for important fiscal positions in the Federal Government. The President's designation of the former Sperry Gyroscope Company vice-president, wrote *United States News,* "brought to light the fact . . . that one of the big influences within the Truman Administration is O. Max Gardner,

an old-line North Carolina politician of conservative bent."

The appointment was also considered significant because it would bring about a more direct relationship between the Treasury and the Budget Bureau (the bureau is an independent agency) and consequently better coordination between tax policies and expenditures. In his position as head of the bureau, Webb would assist the President in the preparation of the budget, advise him on legislative enactments, and keep him informed on the activities of the various Government agencies in order to coordinate their work programs and make their operations as efficient and economic as possible. It would also be Webb's job to "supervise and control the administration of the budget," to aid in the preparation, consideration, and clearance of executive orders, to promote the improvement of Federal and other statistical agencies and to recommend better administrative practices to the executive departments and agencies of the Government. One of his first acts, in carrying out the provisions of the Federal Employees Pay Act of 1946, was to order a reduction of 104,400 in the number of Federal civil service personnel by November 16, 1946. A delay in sending the Budget Bureau's analysis of railroad wartime "profiteering" to the Department of Justice caused Senator Glen Taylor to accuse Webb of an "extreme solicitude" for the railroads. According to the legislator, the budget director had stated in a letter that the payment of reparations for having charged the Government excessive freight rates would "seriously affect the financial condition of the carriers."

In the interest of budget economy and greater efficiency Webb ordered a further cut of 144,833 in Government personnel ceilings and firmly advocated the proposed unification of the armed services. While supporting Federal aid for education, Webb maintained that a permanent universal military training program would receive consideration before aid-to-education legislation. After study of the Federal public works program by the Budget Director and Reconversion Director John R. Steelman '[41], President Truman announced that spending for construction projects during the 1947 fiscal year would be increased. It was expected that the President's 1947 budget message, drafted in close collaboration with Webb, would recommend a budget for the 1948 fiscal year (beginning July 1947) balanced at approximately thirty-seven billion dollars and allowing for moderate tax reduction and debt retirement. This was at variance with estimates by Republican Congressmen who deemed it possible to cut expenditures to about thirty-two billion dollars and to reduce personal income taxes 20 per cent.

In November 1946 Webb was elected by the Administrative and Budgetary Committee of the United Nations General Assembly to a three-year term on the committee on contributions. The executive has been married to the former Patsy A. Douglas since 1938; they have one daughter, Sarah Gorham, born in 1945. Among the societies to which Webb belongs are

WEBB, JAMES E.—*Continued*

the American and the District of Columbia bar associations, the North Carolina Business Foundation, the University Club (New York and Washington), the Institute of the Aeronautical Sciences (New York), and the Marine Corps Reserve Officers Association. He is a member of the Central Presbyterian Church in New York. Of medium height and broad-shouldered, he is described by a United States *News* writer as having "a round-faced, boyish handsomeness."

References

N Y Herald Tribune p2 Jl 26 '46
N Y Times p1+ Jl 26 '46
U S News p36 Ag 2 '46 por; p76 D 6 '46 por

WEIGLE, LUTHER ALLAN (wĭg'l) Sept. 11, 1880- University dean

Address: b. Yale University Divinity School, New Haven, Conn; h. 142 Cold Spring Street, New Haven, Conn.

The dean of the Yale University Divinity School, the Reverend Doctor Luther Allan Weigle is known to churchmen for his numerous activities in the field of religious instruction. The graduate interdenominational school Dean Weigle directs provides training for missionary service and prepares ministers for urban and rural churches. It also instructs those who aspire to religious leadership in colleges and universities as well as those who plan to teach or do research in religion. In many countries, Weigle's books, essays, and published addresses have been of value to Sunday-school teachers and clergymen. As the chairman of the Standard Bible Committee of the International Council of Religious Education he collaborated on the American revision of the Bible. A project sponsored by forty-four Protestant denominations, the first half of the completed work, the Revised Standard Version of the New Testament, made its appearance early in 1946.

The son of Hannah Maria (Bream) and Elias Daniel Weigle, Luther Allan Weigle was born in Littlestown, Pennsylvania on September 11, 1880. In an autobiographical article, "The Religious Education of A Protestant" (in *Contemporary American Theology*), he reports that his father, a minister, belonged to the least conservative of the Lutheran bodies, the General Synod. He tells, too, that while the spirit and practice of religion pervaded the home, his boyhood was normal and happy. Seeing his eagerness to help him in his work, his father gave him a typewriter on which he copied the Sunday sermons. Of his relationship with his father, Weigle says "there was remarkable freedom. He let me enter with him into the realm where reality and truth lay for him, then encouraged me to do my own thinking and to make my own decisions." This the boy tried to do both at the Dickinson School in Carlisle (Pennsylvania) where he received his preparatory education and later at Gettysburg College in the same state.

As an undergraduate young Weigle studied logic, and through his pursuit of ancient Greek received his introduction to the *Dialogues* of Plato. In his course in geology he came in contact with the theory of evolution. After he was graduated with honors from Gettysburg College in 1900, he spent two years as a student at the neighboring Lutheran Theological Seminary of whose board of directors his father was president. While studying systematic theology, the New Testament, and church history, Weigle wrestled with the meaning and method of revelation and inspiration. "In what sense is the Bible the Word of God?" he wondered. Toward the close of this period at the seminary he decided to become a college instructor. This did not imply that he was abandoning his original ambition to become a Lutheran pastor inasmuch as teaching was a recognized part of ministerial service.

Before entering the Graduate school of Yale University as a student in 1902 he spent a summer preaching at Messiah Church in Harrisburg, having been licensed to do so by the East Pennsylvania Synod. On the occasion of his ordination in the summer of 1903 it was his father who delivered the sermon. During the second of the three years he spent at Yale, Weigle served half of each week as pastor at a Bridgeport church, but resigned so that the pulpit might be filled by a full-time minister. The theistic philosopher, Professor Ladd, then engaged in writing his *Philosophy of Religion*, was one of the Yale instructors who had an enduring influence upon Weigle. Particularly enjoyable to the graduate student were the two years he devoted to the study of Immanuel Kant's philosophy, the subject of his doctorate's thesis. Recalling those years he spent at Yale, Weigle has declared: "Though we did not know it at the time, we were looking from afar at the early stage of the movement which was destined to issue in the new physics and Einstein's theory of relativity." Since Weigle preferred religion to mathematical physics, he confined his readings to the philosophers. From sometime in 1904 until the twenty-five-year-old theological student received his doctorate in 1905, he was an assistant in psychology at the university.

From 1905 to 1916 Weigle was professor of philosophy at Carleton College in Northfield, Minnesota, and for the latter five years of this period he was dean of the college. Among the contributions he made to this school of only three hundred students at the time of his arrival was the founding of a department of education. He was also responsible for the training and placing of four hundred graduates as high school teachers. In his spare time, at the request of the Lutheran Board of Publication he worked on a textbook for the training of Sunday-school teachers, *The Pupil and Teacher*, published in 1911. The reading of this book by a former teacher, Professor Sneath, led to the selection of Weigle in 1916 as Horace Bushnell Professor of Christian Nurture in Yale Divinity School. In 1924 he gave up this chair after he was newly appointed Sterling Professor of Religious Education. In 1928 he succeeded Charles R. Brown as Dean of the Divinity School at Yale.

It was Luther Allan Weigle's work on the revision of the Bible, a task he was charged to undertake as chairman of the American Standard Bible Committee, organized by the churches through their educational boards associated in the International Council of Religious Education, which brought him to the attention of the lay public. When the first half of the undertaking, the New Testament, was published in February 1946, Weigle in a joint statement of purpose with his fellow collaborators explained that it is his feeling that "the Word of God is needed by men in our time and hereafter as never before. And the Word of God must not be disguised in phrases no longer clear or hidden under words that have changed or lost their meaning." According to Weigle the King James Version of the Bible of 1611 was also a revision based on the Bishops' Bible of 1568, itself a revision of the Greek Bible of 1539. The King James Bible had been used for more than two and a half centuries as the English Bible; however, archaeological discoveries after 1881, such as the unearthing of Greek papyri in the tombs of Egypt and new-found manuscripts, had revealed information not previously available. An earlier American revision had been published in 1901 but it was based on the English Revision of the New Testament, of 1885, when the scholars did not have the benefit of later research. While the members of the American Standard Bible Committee admired the beauty of the King James Version, they felt that a revised edition should be closer to the idiom of the people while it retained the "power to stir the hearts of men anew and convey God's Spirit to them."

Pointing out the timeliness of the Revised Standard Version of the New Testament, Donald Fraser Forrester of the New York *Times* said, "Modern English . . . has its own strength and beauty, and the new version has succeeded admirably in capturing those qualities." In his review in the New York *Herald Tribune*, the Rev. John Haynes Holmes wrote: "The miracle wrought by the King James translation is not here repeated, but it is at least suggested. . . . This is as near a reproduction of the New Testament from Greek into English as we perhaps shall ever see." Remarking that the greatest gains in clarification had been made in the test chapters—I Corinthians 13, and Romans 12 —Holmes praised the entire work as a "triumph of modern Biblical knowledge."

Among the principal writings of Luther Allan Weigle are *Talks to Sunday School Teachers* (1920), *Training Children in a Christian Family* (1921), *We Are Able* (1937), *Jesus and the Educational Method* (1939). In collaboration with H. H. Tweedy he wrote *Training the Devotional Life* (1919), and he contributed to *Education for Service in the Christian Church in China* (edited by Chester A. Miao, 1935). He also edited Horace Bushnell's *Christian Nuture,* and has contributed to the *Dictionary of American Biography* and the *Encyclopædia Britannica.* In 1928, his book, *American Idealism* appeared as volume ten of *The Pageant of America.*

LUTHER ALLAN WEIGLE

In retrospect, Weigle has observed: "The years have brought increased responsibilities and multiplied contacts, and have opened to me many increased opportunities for cooperative and interdenominational service." While he was still teaching at Carleton College he attended the Congregational church because there was no English Lutheran church in Northfield. After he moved to New Haven he transferred his ministerial standing to the New Haven West Association of Congregational Churches and Ministers. He has been a member of the International Sunday School Lesson Committee since 1915 and was its chairman for one year (1922-23), director of the Congregational Education Society and the Congregational Publishing Society (1917-36), and a member of the executive committee of the International Council of Religious Education since 1920.

Chairman of the joint advisory committee for Sunday School Lessons in Foreign Lands from 1923 to 1932, he has also been a member of the executive committee of the World's Sunday School Association since 1924 and its chairman since 1928. He was chairman of the committee on Christian education of the Federal Council of Churches of Christ in America from 1924 to 1929, when he became chairman for four years of the Council's administrative committee. From 1927 to 1936 he was also director and vice-president of the Congregational Home Board. He has been chairman of the Committee on Closer Co-operation of Interdenominational Agencies since 1941, and chairman of the Co-ordinating Committee for Wartime Service of the Churches since 1942. Since 1929 Weigle has been chairman of the Interseminary Committee for Training for the Rural Ministry, and he was president of the Connecticut Council of Churches from 1931 to 1933. He has been president of the Federal Council of Churches (1940-42), and in 1913 Weigle headed the Minnesota Education Association.

WEIGLE, LUTHER ALLAN—*Continued*

The dean of the Yale University Divinity School holds memberships in the American Philosophical and the American Psychological Associations. He is a member of the Phi Delta Kappa and the Alpha Tau Omega fraternities, of the Yale Book and Bond, and of Phi Beta Kappa. One of the board of founders of the Nanking Theological Seminary, he is a trustee of the Northfield Schools and of Monson Academy, both in Massachusetts, and since 1931, of the Hazen Foundation.

Weigle has derived "enriching experience" from the travel his work has occasionally required, as in 1928, when he was a delegate to the meeting of the International Missionary Council in Jerusalem. Again in 1932 he presided over the World's Sunday School Convention in Rio de Janeiro. From February to September of 1935 he was in China at the invitation of the National Christian Council to conduct a survey of the education of ministers in that country. In 1938 he was a delegate to the meeting in Utrecht, Holland, to devise a constitution for the World Council of Churches.

Among the various educational institutions the dean of the Yale Divinity School has visited are Duke University as Avera lecturer (1926), the Lutheran Theological Seminary in Gettysburg as Holman lecturer on the Augsburg Confession (1921), the Union Theological Seminary in Richmond (Virginia) as Sprunt lecturer (1925 and 1938), and the Hebrew Union College in Cincinnati (1942). He has also been a Pond lecturer at the Bangor Theological Seminary (1937); a Duncan lecturer at the Presbyterian Theological Seminary (1926) and a Norton lecturer at the Southern Baptist Theological Seminary (1928), both in Louisville, Kentucky.

The recipient of honorary degrees which include a Doctor of Letters from Muhlenberg College (1925), a Doctor of Laws from Dickinson College (1933), a Doctor of Divinity from Queens University in Canada (1941), Dean Weigle received special recognition from his fellow alumni of Gettysburg College in March 1941 when they awarded him a plaque inscribed, "He Earned his 'G' in Life." This was given to him in honor "of his pre-eminent service and achievement to the general welfare of the people of college and country." In 1934 Ohio University conferred upon him the degree of Doctor of Sacred Theology, and in 1939 Boston University honored him with the degree of Doctor of Canon and Civil Laws.

Luther Allan Weigle was married to Clara R. Boxrud in 1909. They have two sons, Richard Daniel and Luther Allan, Jr.; and two daughters, Margaret Hannah (Mrs. W. F. Quillan, Jr.) and Ruth Alice (Mrs. Arthur F. Guyton). The dean of Yale's Divinity School tells that he is five feet ten inches tall, weighs one hundred and eighty-two pounds, and has brown eyes and gray-brown hair. His earlier hobby of tennis has been superseded in later years by wood-cutting at his summer home in New Hampshire.

References

Ferm, V. ed. Contemporary American Theology (1933)
National Cyclopædia of American Biography Current vol F p142
Who's Who in America, 1946-47

WELLS, GABRIEL Jan. 24, 1861—Nov. 6, 1946 Dealer in rare books and manuscripts; chiefly known for his sale of Balzac material and single pages of a defective Gutenberg Bible; saved the Balzac house from being torn down, made many gifts to institutions in Europe and the United States.

Obituary

N Y Times p31 N 7 '46 por

WELLS, H(ERBERT) G(EORGE) Sept. 21, 1866—Aug. 13, 1946 British novelist, historian, and scientific writer; his pseudo-scientific romances are *The Time Machine* (1895), *The Invisible Man* (1897), *The Shape of Things to Come* (1933); influenced the younger generation with his realistic novels *Tono-Bungay* (1909), *Marriage* (1912), *Mr. Britling Sees It Through* (1916); traced the ages from Genesis to the future in *The Outline of History* (1920); *The Science of Life* (1929); despaired of man in *Mind at the End of Its Tether* (1945).

Obituary

N Y Times p1+ Ag 14 '46 por

WEYERHAEUSER, RUDOLPH M(I-CHAEL) (wī′ĕr-hou″zēr) Mar. 11, 1868—July 12, 1946 Lumberman; director of Weyerhaeuser timber empire and sales companies; president and chairman of the board of forest and paper interests; director of a bank and railway.

N Y Times p15 Jl 13 '46
Obituary

WHERRY, KENNETH S(PICER) (hwâr′rĭ spī′sĕr) Feb. 28, 1892- United States Senator from Nebraska

Address: Senate Office Bldg., Washington, D.C.; h. 444 Argyle Dr., Alexandria, Va.; Pawnee City, Neb.

Republican party discipline in the United States Senate is partly the responsibility of Senator Kenneth S. Wherry of Nebraska, who calls himself a thorough party man. Elected to the Senate in 1942, Wherry defeated the distinguished fifth-term Senator George W. Norris, and was still a Senate freshman when the caucus of February 1944 elected him minority whip, filling a post which had been vacant several years. In private life, Senator Wherry has been a businessman with many interests, and a farmer and stockman. A New York *Herald Tribune* dispatch by Samuel Bell said, in October 1946, that Wherry was "acknowledged to be the most practical rough-and-tumble politician of the Republicans in the Senate."

Kenneth Spicer Wherry takes pride in the name of his birthplace, Liberty, Nebraska. Born February 28, 1892, he lived there only six months, however. His parents, Jessie (Comstock) and David Emery Wherry, moved to Pawnee City, a banking-post village on Turkey Creek with a turn-of-the-century population of 1,969. There David Wherry established himself as a merchant in Wherry Brothers Company. He was, and is, active in farming and cattle-raising also, and has served five terms as mayor of Pawnee City.

One of four brothers descended from Welsh settlers of Pennsylvania, Ken Wherry spent his Saturdays working in the family furniture store while attending the public grade and high schools of Pawnee City. While at the University of Nebraska (B.A., 1914) he sold pianos, starred in intercollegiate debates, and won election to the presidency of his senior class. The Nebraskan went East to study law and business administration at Harvard University in 1915-16. In 1915, at twenty-three, he became a partner in his father's business. He later took the Wherry Ford Agency, practiced law, sold automobiles, farm implements, furniture, livestock, and farms, conducted auctions, and opened branch offices in other towns. When war was declared in April 1917, "Lightning Ken" Wherry took a civilian post buying mules for the Army's remount division. Later he enlisted in the Naval Flying Corps and served in Chicago, Pensacola, and other parts of the United States. After his return, in September 1920 Wherry was married to Marjorie Colwell, daughter of a Pawnee City druggist.

In addition to his sales activities, Wherry was licensed as an embalmer and funeral director in Nebraska, Kansas, Iowa, and Missouri; he maintained two offices in Nebraska and one in Kansas. Since 1927, Wherry has been president of the Pawnee City Agricultural Society, and in that year he was elected to the City Council. The enterprising young businessman had been active in Republican politics—he says he was Pawnee County chairman in 1918—and in 1929 he went from the City Council to the Mayor's chair, serving until 1931. As president of the County Fair Association, Mayor Wherry was exasperated with the muddy roads which kept farmers away from the fair, and won election to the State Senate concurrently in order to do something about road improvement. He served in two regular and two special legislative sessions.

According to a *Collier's* article by Milton Lehman, Kenneth Wherry "quickly became known as the most radical Republican in the State capital. . . .As State Senator, he not only was known as 'Senator Norris' errand boy' for backing Nebraska's great progressive, but he also supported the program of the State's Democratic Governor." It was after his two political defeats, when Wherry had retired temporarily to private life to enlarge his business and farm holdings, that he broke with Norris, who had once expressed the hope that Wherry would succeed him in the Senate.

KENNETH S. WHERRY

Wherry's State legislative term expired in 1932, and the next year he ran unsuccessfully for the Governor's office. In 1936 the businessman-lawyer-farmer was the Republican candidate for United States Senator, and in 1938 he returned to local office as mayor. President of the State Founders' Day in 1938, a member of the Republican State Central Committee in 1938-42, Wherry has been Republican State Chairman since December 1939. "Utilizing the experience he gained in promoting Pawnee County fairs," said an Associated Press report, "Mr. Wherry organized caravans of candidates that traveled all over the State. He bored into party organization work, strengthening every county unit." The Republican success in Nebraska in 1940 brought Mayor Wherry to the attention of the Republican National Committee and of Chairman Joseph W. Martin, Jr. [40]. Martin appointed Wherry its western director to supervise party activities in twenty-two States, a post he filled in 1941-42. He was still president of the Pawnee County Fair, a post in which he revealed showmanship.

In the three-cornered 1942 Senate race, Wherry received 186,207 votes to Norris' 108,-899. Upon his election Wherry said of his defeated opponent, "Norris has been a great statesman, there is no doubt of that. He has lent respectability to the New Deal."

The real work of Congress is done in committee, and at his party caucus Wherry was given a place on five standing committees—those on Appropriations, Claims, Judiciary, Public Buildings and Grounds, and the Committee to Audit and Control the Contingent Expenses of the Senate. He was also appointed to the special Small Business group. Among the investigations in which the "Cornhusker" took a prominent part were those the Small Business Committee conducted on the paper shortage in the spring of 1944 and of the aluminum situation in 1945. Four days be-

WHERRY, KENNETH S.—*Continued*

fore his fifty-second birthday, in 1944, Wherry was elected minority whip. The duties are defined in Smith and Zurcher's *Dictionary of American Politics*: "to remind members of his party to be present when important votes are to be taken; to arrange pairs for members unavoidably absent; to conciliate members who are dissatisfied with the party program; and to keep his party leaders informed as to the attitude of members toward public questions."

A party-line Republican, Wherry was a particular enemy of the Office of Price Administration, especially in relation to meat. In June 1943 he voted against the Bankhead [40] Amendment to raise agricultural price ceilings, but all or most of his other votes on the issue were anti-Administration, and Wherry introduced many bills to defeat the OPA program, aiming especially to increase the prices of meat, farm products, automobiles, and farm equipment. For weeks at a time (reported the New York *Times*) Wherry made a daily speech in the Senate, prefaced by the full text of the Chicago livestock market reports.

On foreign policy Wherry followed the general Old Guard Midwestern line, and consistently opposed the Reciprocal Trade Agreements Act. In April 1943 he went on record as opposed to postwar participation in an international police force to preserve the peace, and in February 1944 he was one of seven Republican and seven Democratic Senators to say no to the UNRRA appropriation. In November Wherry voted against incorporating the Atlantic Charter provisions in the resolution of postwar policy. April 1945 saw Wherry voting to make the termination of Lend-Lease automatic with the end of the war; and eight days later the Nebraskan was one of ten Senators opposing the Mexican Water Treaty. Having tried without success to postpone from July to November 1945 a vote on American participation in the World Bank and World Fund agreed upon at Bretton Woods, he cast his own ballot against the international agreement. Nine days later, however, he voted with the overwhelming majority to ratify the United Nations Charter.

Earlier, in January 1944, the Senator had included Bretton Woods with Dumbarton Oaks and the Trade Agreements Acts as "schemes" in which "lies the end of self-government in the United States" and the beginning of a form "combining the worst features of all known social systems." The Crimea Conference of Roosevelt, Churchill, and Stalin, Wherry called "a step forward in American participation in European power politics." In April-May 1945 Wherry was one of the bipartisan group of twelve Congressmen flown to Europe on General Eisenhower's invitation to inspect Nazi German slave labor and concentration camps. The group report described the ghastly conditions imposed on prisoners of the Nazis and stated that they saw "no evidence that the people of Germany as a whole were suffering from any lack of sufficient food or clothing." In a one-man minority report, Wherry warned "we mustn't judge [the Germans] too hastily."

Later in 1945 he and Bilbo [43] were the two Senators who expressed opposition to continuing some wartime restrictions in the United States if this were necessary to enable the United States to aid in the rehabilitation of the liberated countries.

In January 1946 Senator Wherry accused the American Government of participating in "the crime of mass starvation" by not restoring mail and package service from America to Germany. The starvation of Germans was denied by the American administrator, General Lucius Clay [45], and by correspondents, who pointed out that conditions in the American zone of the Reich were much better than in the areas which had been invaded by the Nazis. Wherry was active among opponents of the loan to Britain. A speech of Wherry's in March 1946 called on the Administration to halt its "abject policies of appeasement of imperialism of all our allies."

In the month before V-J Day Wherry had made public the text of a peace offer which an unnamed authority had submitted to the President, declaring "we do not regard military occupation of Japan proper as necessary." He defended General MacArthur, the field commander, against what he called the "blackening of his name" by the official disavowal of MacArthur's modest estimate of the forces needed, inserted into the *Congressional Record* in September a laudatory Chicago *Tribune* editorial on the General, and attempted to block the confirmation of Dean Acheson [41] as Undersecretary of State for "rebuking" MacArthur.

On domestic issues, Wherry's record includes votes against a hundred-million-dollar appropriation for soil conservation in June 1943, and against continuing the Farm Security Administration's power to make loans to small farmers. He was for the McKellar [46] anti-TVA "ripper bill" and "patronage-grab," for blanket deferment of farm labor from military service, for the modified Ruml [43] Plan, for the Smith [43]-Connally [41] antistrike bill, for requiring tax-exempt, nonprofit labor unions and farm cooperatives to file financial reports. He voted against increasing the Social Security Tax, giving the Federal ballot to service personnel, and building the St. Lawrence Seaway. On the other hand, his votes coincided with Administration aims in a few matters: he voted against killing the Marcantonio Poll Tax Repeal Bill in the Judiciary Committee in November 1943, and then voted against reporting out the O'Mahoney [45] Anti-Poll Tax Amendment, which was a delaying alternative. Later, however, Wherry introduced a bill for an almost identical amendment. Wherry voted for the FEPC and for the George [43] Reconversion Bill, providing for over-all planning. One bill he introduced was to prohibit any Government agency from imposing a penalty on individuals refusing to comply with orders of another Government agency; another would apply the proposed 1946 increase in excess-profits-tax exemption to 1945 income also. In October 1945 Wherry asked Congress to declare the war emergency at an end, thus ending the Executive's wartime powers. In April 1946 he and Eastland of Mississippi proposed to forbid the "making available" to any foreign Government or person any radar or electronic equipment or information.

Earlier, Senator Wherry had charged in a public speech that the postwar confusion in Washington was "a confusion planned by those in high places, who mean that it shall produce a state of mental futility on the part of our people so that regimented chaos can eventuate." This would enable them to "seize power, take over the Government, and liquidate those who opposed them." In line with this view, he and Senator Styles Bridges demanded the discharge of a list of alleged Communists in the State Department.

After the 1946 Republican landslide had assured him of being one of the "big four" in the 1947 Senate, Wherry took an unofficial three-week fact-finding trip to Europe. He returned to repeat his charges that UNRRA food in Russian-occupied or -influenced countries was being diverted to Soviet use, and again declared that the United States Army could do a better job at relief distribution than UNRRA had.

Ebullient Kenneth S. Wherry's resemblance to Styles Bridges of New Hampshire has caused them to be dubbed "the Senate twins." Vice-President Truman, when presiding over the Senate, was known to mistake one for the other. Wherry, of average height (five feet nine inches), has blue eyes and receding brown hair. His manner is described as blunt, direct, often heated; his speech, as loud, rapid, and emphatic; and he has never felt the awe which usually hampers first-term Senators. Wherry is a Mason (Shriner), a member of Beta Theta Pi, a trustee of Nebraska Wesleyan University, and belongs to the Nebraska State and American Bar Associations, the American Legion, the Lions, Kiwanis, and the Public Service and Round Table Clubs. Senator and Mrs. Wherry have two children, Marilyn, and David Colwell, who in 1946 was a midshipman at the Naval Academy at Annapolis.

Milton Lehman has given a description of Senator Wherry at work: "The husky Senator bustles at his desk, dictating speeches to two secretaries at once. . . .Recently the Capitol Hill secretaries, polled on their favorite Congressmen, voted him the jolliest Senator." A former teacher in a Presbyterian Sunday school, Wherry never drinks or smokes, and in November 1945 succeeded in having the noun "damn" deleted from a speech by Tom Connally, as "beneath the dignity of the Senate."

References

Christian Sci Mon p3 D 1 '42 por
Collier's 118:56+ D 14 '41 por
N Y Post p12 Ja 24 '45
N Y Sun p6 Ag 5 '44; p34 D 5 '45
N Y Times VI p10 D 29 '46 por
Congressional Directory (2d ed., 1945)
Who's Who in America, 1946-47

WHITE, S(EBASTIAN) HARRISON
Dec. 24, 1864—Dec. 21, 1945 Lawyer, former United States Representative from Colorado,

elected on Democratic ticket in 1927 to fill the unexpired term of William Vaile; District Attorney of the tenth Judicial District of Colorado (1904-08); Justice in the Supreme Court of Colorado from 1909 to 1919.

Obituary

N Y Times p18 D 23 '45

WHITE, STEWART EDWARD Mar. 12, 1873—Sept. 18, 1946 Author; experiences of his life in the West, the Yukon, and Africa interpreted in his many historical novels and books of adventure; the most successful was *The Blazed Trail* (1902); among others were *Ranchero* (1933) and *Stampede* (1942); *The Unobstructed Universe* (1940) is a record of spiritualistic communications.

Obituary

N Y Times p31 S 19 '46

WHITNEY, A(LEXANDER) F(ELL)
Apr. 12, 1873- Labor leader
Address: b. 1370 Ontario Street, Cleveland, Ohio

A. F. Whitney, president of the Brotherhood of Railroad Trainmen since 1928, is recognized by both official Washington and the American press as the key railroad labor spokesman in the country. He represents more than two hundred thousand union men. He has also written numerous articles for labor periodicals in the United States. The veteran labor leader is fond of quoting his favorite American economist Henry George, founder of the single tax movement, to the effect that "a great wrong dies hard. And the great wrong which in every civilized country condemns the masses of the men to poverty and want will not die without a bitter struggle." In May 1946 Whitney was a central figure in the two-day railroad strike.

Alexander Fell Whitney was born on April 12, 1873 at Cedar Falls, Iowa, to the Canadian-born Reverend Joseph Leonard Whitney and Martha Wallin (Batcheller) Whitney. The father, a circuit-riding minister, struggled with the temporal problem of raising a family in the western backwoods area of the 1870's. From him young Whitney inherited a fierce hatred for all those who oppressed and exploited their fellow men. It was not long before he had an opportunity to obtain a firsthand knowledge of the conditions under which the average breadwinner worked in those days. As a boy he worked as a farmhand from early morning until late at night. At the age of fifteen, with some high school education behind him, he set out to become a news agent. Having invested his entire capital of two dollars in a basket of fruit and candy, he boarded an eastbound train at Cherokee, Iowa. When the conductor demanded his ticket he replied angrily, "What ticket? I'm the news butcher." The concessionaire at Dubuque, impressed by the ingenuity of the boy, offered him his first steady job. At the end of a year of hawking on trains, the boy's aplomb helped him to get a job as a railroad brakeman. Although the

Ben Strauss

A. F. WHITNEY

trainmaster of the Illinois Central Railroad at Cherokee knew the young applicant was considerably under the twenty-one years he claimed for himself, he admired the boy's self-assurance and hired him.

In the 1880's the railroad companies had perfected a system of "hire, fire and rehire," which enabled them to avoid paying the brakemen the extra twenty-seven cents they had agreed to add after three months to the $1.73-a-day salary. After three months they would discharge the brakemen and then rehire them at the original rate. In this way, Whitney, who was hired and fired three times during the first year he worked, successively, with the Illinois Central, the Fremont, Elkhorn and Missouri, and the Union Pacific railroads, never reached the $2.00-a-day rate. Realizing that singlehandedly he could not get redress for such wrongs, Whitney in 1896 became a member of the G. E. Boynton Lodge 138 of the Brotherhood of Railroad Trainmen at Eagle Grove, Iowa. The "Big Four" of the railroad labor unions (the Brotherhood of Locomotive Engineers, the Brotherhood of Railroad Trainmen, the Order of Railroad Conductors and the Brotherhood of Locomotive Firemen and Enginemen) began not as labor unions but as fraternal brotherhoods, similar to the Moose and the Elks.

By 1900 the policy of the officials of the Railroad Trainmen was still one of appeasement towards the management at the expense of the workers; they concentrated instead on securing mutual benefits and insurance. Early in his career Whitney's belief in the principles of unions took on the fervor of a religious conversion. His fellow workers found his enenthusiasm contagious and elected him master of his lodge and chairman of the local grievance committee.

The entrenched union officials eyed him suspiciously as a threat to the established order of the brotherhood. At the biennial meeting of

the central grievance committee in Chicago in 1901, the general chairman accused him of "creating friction with management and stirring ill-will against the organization." The chairman also condemned the new delegate for carrying appeals in wage disputes over the heads of the division superintendents to the executive officers of the railway system. Whitney countered with the argument that "what happens to the just complaint of one of my members is all that counts. We're fighting for a principle and if you accept defeat at the hand of a division superintendent when your demands are fair, you can expect to get other defeats on other matters of principle." As a result of his militancy, Whitney was elected the new chairman of the general grievance committee. While serving in this capacity he was elected vice-president of the Western Association of General Committees of the Order of Railway Conductors and Brotherhood of Railroad Trainmen when it was first organized in June 1902, and a year later was elected secretary-treasurer of the organization. At the Atlanta Convention of the Brotherhood of Railroad Trainmen in 1905, Whitney was elected a member of the board of Grand Trustees, and at a convention held two years later, he was elected vice Grand Master. He served in that office (later called vice-president) until February 1, 1928, when he assumed the office of general secretary and treasurer of the Brotherhood following his election in January by the Board of Directors. These posts he held until July of the same year. His present position as president of the Brotherhood of Railroad Trainmen dates from 1928, when he was elected to that office at the June convention.

The crash of 1929 and the unsettled conditions which it brought in its wake caused labor to lose many of the gains it had made. Whitney showed how the railroads through labor-saving machinery were handling fifteen times the tonnage of a quarter of a century before and at the same time, despite the increasing productivity, were unable to provide all their employees with jobs. "I do not believe," he said, "that the inventor of labor-saving machinery should reap all the returns from his invention, but only a share, so that the employer and employee, especially the latter, who has been hardest hit, may share in the increased production through higher wages and shorter working hours." A six-hour day with no overtime, he felt, would solve the unemployment problem. During the winter of 1931, however, the railroad owners demanded a reduction in the wages of their employees. At a national conference held in Chicago in January 1932, twenty organizations, members of the Railway Labor Executives' Association headed by D. B. Robertson, president of the Brotherhood of Locomotive Firemen and Enginemen, accepted a 10 per cent pay roll deduction. The only dissenting voice came from the Brotherhood of Railway Trainmen. Its president and his general committee adamantly rejected the idea of any wage decrease. Although he argued that this reduction would curtail the purchasing power of the millions of railroad workers and thereby lessen the chances of a return to prosperity, he was forced to yield to the decision of the leaders of the other unions. The continued downward trend in the per capita income of the nation was regarded later as proof of the soundness of his thinking, and in August 1932 he was elected chairman of the Railway Labor Executives Association. This new office, which he held for two years, made him the spokesman for millions of railway employees in the twenty-one labor organizations.

When, in 1933, the railroad management sought to obtain a further wage cut of 12½ per cent, thus cutting the workers' wages by a total of 22½ per cent, Whitney insisted that "the railroads have no more chance of getting a wage reduction than they have of riding on the tail of Halley's comet!" Armed with thousands of statistical reports and "mountains" of economic data, he countered the railroads' argument with a proposal for a restoration of the wage cut of 1932, and won his point. On several occasions Whitney was suggested as a possible choice for United States Secretary of Labor in President Roosevelt's '42 Cabinet. Although nothing came of it the President did select him as a delegate to the Inter-American Conference for the Maintenance of Peace, held in Buenos Aires in December 1936.

On the four successive occasions Franklin Delano Roosevelt ran for President of the United States, Whitney not only supported him but influenced the entire Brotherhood to throw its political weight behind the Democratic candidate. After Roosevelt entered office Whitney took advantage of the Administration's support of labor to work for legislative improvements for the railway workers. Through his efforts the Railroad Retirement Act was passed in 1935; and under his guidance the Brotherhood obtained further benefits through the safety provisions written into the Omnibus Transportation Act of 1940, known as the "Harrington Amendment." Whitney helped to launch the National Citizens Political Action Committee, which worked for the re-election of President Roosevelt in 1944.

Not unreservedly a supporter of Roosevelt, Whitney was incensed by the "failure of the Government to recognize the worker's interest in price stabilization" during World War II. He fought for labor representation on many boards of the Office of Price Administration and in the policy-forming committee in Washington. When he appeared before the Emergency Board of the National Railway Panel on June 19, 1943, which was conducting hearings in Washington on the 30 per cent increase demanded by the railroad workers, he is reputed to have said that there had been "no serious attempt" by the OPA to control rising living costs or to curb inflation since the spring of the previous year. At the same time he severely criticized the railroad industry which he judged "the most powerful monopoly the American people have had to contend with," a monopoly that was projecting its power "under the pretext of promoting the American war effort." Angered by the board's decision to award the railroad workers only a thirty-two-cent raise, Whitney telegraphed the New York Times that "the board might just as well have availed itself of easily obtainable statistics as to have gone through the farce of holding extensive public hearings."

In December 1944 a threatened railroad strike was averted, when, through the mediation of President Roosevelt, the railroad workers received a five-cent increase above the four-cent-an-hour raise recommended by an emergency board, and an annual paid vacation of one week. In January 1946, with the wartime "no strike" pledge no longer in force, the twenty unions involved in the railroad industry demanded an increase. Invoking the Railway Labor Act which provides for a thirty-day mediation period and another thirty days in which to take action on the findings of the mediators, President Truman ordered a delay in the strike plans of Whitney's Brotherhood of Railroad Trainmen and Alvanley Johnston's[46] Brotherhood of Locomotive Engineers, the two railroad unions which did not arbitrate. At the end of the sixty-day period, Whitney and Johnston refused to accept the compromise offered by a Presidential Emergency Board and set May 18, 1946, as the date for the first railway tie-up since 1922. A five-day postponement, in which the railroads were taken over by the Government, brought no change in the situation, and on May 23 members of the Brotherhood of Railroad Trainmen and of Locomotive Engineers left work for a two-day period in which no rail service was provided except for milk, troop, and hospital trains. An offer from the unions of an eighteen-and-a-half-cent-an-hour increase and the rule changes recommended by the Emergency Board was made, but on May 26, Whitney and Johnston were forced to call off the strike; they accepted the increase without any rule changes. This action was announced by the President in an address to Congress on that date in which he asked for drastic emergency measures to curb labor. Whitney strongly criticized the President for the manner in which he handled the dispute, and announced that he would work against Truman in future elections.

Outstanding among Whitney's writings is his pamphlet, *Wartime Wages and Railroad Labor*, which appeared in 1944. He is also the author of *Main Street, Not Wall Street* (1938), in which he presented the "cold facts of the labor claims" and "the abuses practiced by the railroads as the result of financial chicanery of their big-money control." His pessimistic answers to a series of questions *Look* magazine put to him appeared in the January 8, 1946, issue. He believes that the Government will not succeed in keeping the cost of living down "because Congress has never been sympathetic to price control and will sabotage it in 1946." He looked forward to a further tax reduction by the end of that year but hoped that this time it would be in the interest of the lower income groups, not the corporations. Whitney predicted that the Democrats would lose control of Congress in the 1946 elections and said, in fact, it had "already passed to a coalition of Southern poll tax Democrats and reactionary Republicans." In the 1946 convention of the Brotherhood of Railroad Trainmen, which re-elected

WHITNEY, A. F.—*Continued*

Whitney as president, the union decided to remain independent of both the CIO and the A.F. of L.

A. F. Whitney's activities have not been confined to the management of his union. In 1936 he was chairman of the Good Neighbor League of Northern Ohio. Appointed by President Roosevelt, he served on the Committee on Unemployment Census in September 1937. He has consistently urged the members of the Brotherhood to participate in public activities and in the civic affairs of their own communities. During World War II the Labor Committee of which he was a member received an Army-Navy E Award for its work in recruiting blood donors for the Blood Donor Service of the American Red Cross. The Brotherhood of Railroad Trainmen supported the War Bond Drives, the Grand Lodge alone purchasing more than sixteen million dollars' worth of bonds of the United States and Canada. For the funds it raised for an airplane the Brotherhood was awarded the "Iron Eagle."

In 1893 Whitney was married to Grace Elizabeth Marshman, who died in March 1923. Their three children are Joseph Lafeton, Everett Alexander, and Lydia Marie (Mrs. Richard J. Olson). With his present wife, the former Dorothy May Rowley, to whom Whitney was married in 1927, Whitney resides in Ohio. The President of the Brotherhood of Railroad Trainmen is known as an omnivorous reader, particularly of literature concerning labor. Years ago he discovered that "the best way to meet the press attacks against labor was by meeting rumor with fact." The Education and Research Bureau, which he established at the headquarters of the Brotherhood, keeps him supplied with the necessary data on working conditions, cost of living, and hours of employment. Whitney is a member of the Presbyterian Church and belongs to a Masonic lodge. He has white hair, wears glasses, and is generally dressed in a pin-striped suit, with a conservative tie.

References

Lit Digest 101:15 Ap 20 '29 por
Newsweek 1:20 Je 24 '33 por
Who's Who in America, 1946-47
Who's Who in Labor (1946)

WILLIAMS, FRANCIS Mar. 10, 1903-
British Government official; author

Address: b. 3 Essex Court Middle Temple, London; h. Cammocks, Hinxworth, nr. Baldock, Herts, England

Francis Williams, the man whose position in the British official family parallels that of Charles G. Ross [45] in Washington, is regarded by many observers as the Labor's Party's most promising young statesman. Before becoming public relations adviser to Prime Minister Attlee, he had been, in turn, a free-lance newspaperman, financial editor and editor of the Laborite *Herald*, and head of the Ministry of Information's wartime press relations and censorship division. A man of strong democratic convictions, he has written several books setting forth his views.

The eldest son of J. E. Williams, a Shropshire farmer whose ancestors had tilled the land for five hundred years, Francis Williams was born March 10, 1903, in the village of St. Martins. His formative years, however, were spent in Lancashire, where he attended the Queen Elizabeth Grammar School of Middleton until he was seventeen. As a schoolboy he had indulged a youthful flair for writing poetry—some of which was accepted for publication by the editor of the old *Saturday Review*—and when he became a cub reporter on the Bootle (a town close to Liverpool) *Times* in 1920, he persuaded the editor to let him write a weekly rhymed column satirizing local government officials, a procedure which he continued despite protests from the Bootle town hall. In addition, like all apprentices, he was assigned other tasks of every description.

Williams's second job was with the Liverpool *Daily Courier*, but at the age of nineteen an urge to study English living conditions at first hand, and a bequest of twenty-five pounds from a great-uncle, started the future Labor journalist on a tour of the country in a horse-drawn van and made a free-lance writer of him. The articles he wrote at this time, describing his observations and experiences, appeared in the *Daily Herald*, the national Labor newspaper which he was later to edit (then edited by the late George Lansbury), and netted him thirty shillings each. For some years Williams continued as a free-lance newspaperman in Fleet Street. Then a feature article he wrote about the sculptor Jacob Epstein [45] for the *Sunday Express* attracted the attention of Lord Beaverbrook, who, for some reason known only to himself, decided that its author would make a good finance writer and asked Williams to take over the City column of the *Evening Standard*.

Undaunted by his ignorance of the subject, Williams accepted the position and soon became one of the most talked about men in financial journalism. In 1929 his reputation led to his appointment as financial editor of the Laborite *Daily Herald*, and he at once proceeded to turn that paper's purely informational financial columns into a medium for the discussion of economic and social conditions. In 1931 he attracted wide attention with his prediction of the economic collapse of Germany (which was to enable Hitler to rise to power in 1933) and his anticipation of Britain's abandonment of the gold standard during the international economic crisis of that year. Four years later he achieved even wider prominence with his publication of the first full information on the extent to which Hitler was rearming Germany, revelations which were quoted by Winston Churchill [42] in the House of Commons in an effort to warn Prime Minster Stanley Baldwin of the impending danger of Nazism. Also in 1935, he wrote *Plan for Peace* (published in 1936) in which he analyzed the circumstances tending to promote a state of aggression in Germany, Italy, and Japan. Together with his newspaper articles, this treatise caused his writings to be banned in Germany and Italy.

In 1936 Williams succeeded to the vacant editorial chair of his paper, and under his guidance during the next few years the *Herald* played an influential role in the education of British public opinion to the dangers of Nazism, attaining wide circulation among progressive Conservatives as well as Laborites. "His acute understanding of policy and his deep fidelity to the cause of democratic socialism," said the London *Observer* in 1945, "gave the *Herald* distinctive character. His treatment of politics was always large-minded and adult, and he adhered rigidly to his conviction that newspaper readers were more intelligent than the commercial upholders of journalism suppose." Williams remained as editor of the *Herald* until early 1940 when, refusing an offer to remain as political and economic adviser of the *Herald* without executive duties, he handed in his resignation after "a period of acute controversy between myself and the management of the paper, Messrs. Odhams, as to the functions and responsibilities of a Socialist paper during wartime." "I held, and still hold," he wrote in an explanatory letter to the *New Statesman and Nation* which summarized his editorial policies, "that since socialism is both a political creed and a social philosophy, and since the future shape of society for many years will be determined by this war, a Labor paper has certain very specific duties to perform during it. These duties are not confined to a legalistic adherence to the line of party policy. . . .It seems to me it is the responsibility of the official Labor paper to keep its readers informed on the serious problems which have been created by the war and are likely to be created by the peace, when it comes, and to put before them a responsible, intelligent, and reasoned discussion of these problems in leaders and special articles."

Shortly after his resignation as editor of the *Herald*, Williams brought out his second book, *War by Revolution*, in which he reaffirmed his belief in the principles of democracy and urged that Britain sponsor a democratic revolutionary movement in the occupied nations of Europe backed by British pledges of food, economic security, and political freedom in a federated Europe after the war. The *New Republic* called it "a short and hastily written but persuasive book." The *Saturday Review of Literature* commented: "This little book has one great virtue; it is not content with analyzing the past and distributing blame. It knows that it is the future that really matters. At the same time it shows unusual realism and detachment regarding the war and peace situation." In 1941 the author of *War by Revolution* was appointed Controller of Press and Censorship in the Ministry of Information, a position which he held until the close of the war. "By general consent of pressmen and politicians," records the *Observer*, "he did outstanding work. His crowning achievement was at San Francisco, where he took charge of the information service of the British delegation," with a deftness which one American editor called "a beautiful job to watch, an object

British Official Photo.

FRANCIS WILLIAMS

lesson in public relations to all the other nations."

Then, on October 8, 1945, Williams began work as the Government's public relations adviser, a post intended by Prime Minister Clement Attlee [40] to remedy what he had quickly found to be a central flaw in his administration, the inability of the new Labor Government to "project itself sufficiently on the public mind." The new appointment was hailed by the *Observer*: "It is to the Prime Minister's credit that he quickly detected this weakness. And his choice of Mr. Francis Williams to put it right is likely to prove admirable. For Mr. Williams not only knows what newspapers want. He has a real flair for sensing what the public wants to know, a flair sharpened by a lifetime's work as a journalist. He brings to his job a cool mind, understands the outlook of ordinary people, believes profoundly in the methods of democratic discussion, hates absence of reason, and has considerable technical competence. His primary interest is in information and explanation, not in propaganda. He will not be found pulling strings or out on 'fixing' expeditions for the purpose of stopping criticism of the Government. He will rather regard himself as an outpost of the public, looking at everything in Downing Street and Whitehall from their point of view, putting their questions to Ministers, and aiming all the time at giving full facts and clear explanations so that the newspapers and the public can arrive at informed but independent opinions." In November 1945, in his new capacity, Williams accompanied Prime Minister Attlee on his first visit to Washington. In January 1946 he headed a committee studying recommendations for the U.N. information service to be organized under one of the assistant secretaries-general. (Williams' own name had been suggested for the post of assistant secretary-

WILLIAMS, FRANCIS—*Continued*

general in charge of information but Attlee's reluctance to part with his aide made it necessary to appoint another.)

Since 1940 the journalist has also written three additional books. In *Ten Angels Swearing* (1941) he suggested methods for a wartime election and considered political trends of the future. In *Democracy's Last Battle* he traced causes of Nazism, fascism, and communism to their origins and then continued with a frank criticism of Britain's democracy, economic system, schools, press, and pulpit. "For . . . those who have both hope and confidence in the capacity of democracy to fight for its own survival with weapons as revolutionary as those with which it started," wrote Joseph Barnes in the New York *Herald Tribune*, "this is a heartening book. . . .Mr. Williams uses simple writing, plain enough to be disliked by those who confuse democracy with privilege and to be used by those who don't." In *Press, Parliament and People* Williams argued for "less secrecy and more positive information" in international diplomacy as a contribution to the proper functioning of democracy. May Lamberton Becker wrote of it in the New York *Herald Tribune*: "It goes straight to the center of Britain at this hour in history. For the facts that first impress an American visitor in this season of postwar crises and confusions are the freedom with which the British criticize their leaders and the extent to which they trust them. He soon finds that one depends on the other, and how this works the book shows. The British public trusts because it has been informed. . . .And this public is convinced that to keep any Government up to the mark . . . it must be made aware, by free criticism and controversy, that its actions are under constant scrutiny."

Williams and the former Jessie M. Hopkin, to whom he was married in 1926, are the parents of one son and one daughter. The ex-newspaperman has been described by one writer as "a chunky youngish fellow who stuffs the pockets of his ill-fitting clothes with papers and documents, rumples his hair, and looks somewhere between Winnie-the-Pooh and an American courthouse reporter." "Plumpish, genial, warm-hearted, modest" are some of the adjectives applied to him. He lists his recreations in *Who's Who* as "talking, walking, and doing nothing."

References

N Y Sun p18 N 21 '45
Newsweek 26:93 N 19 '45

International Who's Who, 1945-46
Who's Who, 1946

WILLIAMS, GLUYAS (glōō-yàs) July 23, 1888- Cartoonist

Address: b. c/o Bell Syndicate, 247 W. 43d St., New York; h. 14 Sylvan Ave., West Newton, Mass.

As of 1946, an estimated five million people see Gluyas Williams' newspaper cartoons in seventy-odd newspapers throughout the English-speaking world. They are published in newspapers from Boston to California, in South Africa, Bermuda, Canada, Nova Scotia, and in London, where the *Evening Standard* once devoted more than two columns on its editorial page to praise of his drawings. Many know his work from its appearances in the *New Yorker* and from his illustrations for all of Robert Benchley's [41] books. Williams' drawings have been printed in foreign-language publications, even though all his characters and situations are drawn from middle-class American suburbia. *Life* sees the reason for his universality in his "fine, clean line" and ability to make "every gesture and face a masterpiece."

The son born to Robert Neil and Virginia (Gluyas) Williams on July 23, 1888, was given his mother's Cornish maiden name of Gluyas. From San Francisco his parents sent Gluyas across the country to Harvard University, in the hope that he would absorb some of Harvard's dignity. A member of the class of 1911, which twenty-five years later was to vote him its outstanding graduate, young Williams joined the Harvard *Lampoon* staff and became art editor. In this capacity he advised another undergraduate, one Bob Benchley, to give up art and stick to writing.

After graduation Williams went to Paris to study art, for six months drawing from life in Colrossi's studio. Returning to the United States, he spent three months with the old Boston *Journal* doing a comic strip. Afterward he worked in the editorial department of the *Youth's Companion*. Before long, however, the cartoonist was transferred to the art department, of which he became head. During his ten years there, Williams continued drawing cartoons with moderate success. Finally Frank Casey of *Collier's* bought a Williams cartoon which had been rejected by the humorous weeklies *Puck* and *Life*, used it as a cover, and began to buy cartoons regularly from this "discovery." When Charles Dana Gibson bought *Life* in 1918 and installed Casey as art editor, Gluyas Williams became a regular contributor.

In 1920, when he was thirty-two, Gluyas Williams gave up his position on the *Youth's Companion* to free-lance, doing caricatures for the staid Boston *Transcript*. Meanwhile, realizing the limitations of the comic strip, the artist originated his one-panel drawings of suburban life, and in 1924 he signed a contract with the Bell Syndicate for a daily newspaper cartoon. With titles which varied with the subject (*Suburban Heights, The World At Its Worst, The Neighborhood League, The Moment That Seems A Year*) the drawings showed middle-class suburban Americans—businessmen, housewives, and their offspring—in minor crises or every-day situations. "Two things I strive for in my cartoons," Williams has said: "to bring the reader to smile at himself in the past or to make it easier for him when the incident happens in the future."

Gluyas Williams cartoons, drawn with economy of line but often portraying dozens of persons and objects, specialize in small children and in adults over thirty-five; seldom does he include a character of the age most interesting to poets. Some of his favorite series are

Industrial Crises, portraying the havoc that ensues when the California and Florida fruit salesmen arrive simultaneously at a shop known for its choice viands, when a director of the Diamond Match Company absent-mindedly lights his cigar with an automatic lighter, or when a sundial company gets an order for an instrument showing daylight-saving time. Another Williams series is *Literary Renegades*: the Albert Payson Terhune collie which failed to stop a runaway, the Kathleen Norris heroine who didn't wait for the right man, the Zane Grey hero whose shots went wild, the Booth Tarkington boy who won all the prizes at school. Still other favorite titles of the cartoonist's include *The Inner Man, Club Life in America*, and *Raconteurs*, the latter varying from a well-intentioned matron boring her friends' children with a long nature story to an old lady holding visitors spellbound with embarrassing facts about the family's ancestors.

Williams has illustrated all of the late Robert Benchley's books—one reviewer called him Benchley's "illuminator." The first of more than a dozen was *Of All Things* (1921), followed by *The Early Worm* (1927), *The Treasurer's Report* (1930), and others. Reviewing *From Bed to Worse* (1934), Robert Van Gelder gave "a round of loud applause" for the "very funny" illustrations. Of *After 1903—What?* (1938), the *New Republic* reviewer held that "the best of it is Gluyas Williams' generous work of illustration." Others called his drawings discerning and amusing. More Williams illustrations are found in Ed Streeter's *Daily Except Sunday* (1938), in which he portrayed the ways of commuters; Laurence McKinney's *People of Note* (1940), verse about "symphony faces"; and William Freeman's *Hear! Hear!* (1941), in which, said the Springfield *Republican* critic, "Gluyas Williams' amusing illustrations accurately reveal the agonies of amateur speakers who fail to heed such simple rules. Audiences have seen and heard these labored unfortunates many times, but it remained for Mr. Williams to immortalize them." In June 1946 the Boston Museum of Fine Arts exhibited one hundred Williams cartoon originals.

Two collections of Gluyas Williams cartoons have been published by Doubleday, Doran and Company. *The Gluyas Williams Book*, with an introduction by Charles Dana Gibson and a preface by Benchley, came out in 1929. Benchley wrote the introduction for his friend's *Fellow Citizens* eleven years later, a collection which one reviewer called "a treasury of intelligent fun." Prefacer Benchley said, "One of the remarkable things about Gluyas Williams' work is that he not only keeps it funny but, through the exercise of some sort of necromancy, he has managed to keep drawing as well as he did twenty years ago. This is nothing short of bourgeois respectability in an age when many artists take great pride in drawing worse and worse each year. . . .Now the fact that Gluyas Williams still draws feet that look like feet does not mean that he is insensitive to present-day social problems. He lives in a neck of the woods . . . where a man is considered a Communist if he reads the *New Republic* and where they are still proud of having got Sacco and

Fabian Bachrach

GLUYAS WILLIAMS

Vanzetti out of the way whether they were guilty or not. I happen to know that Gluyas, in a quiet way, burns with a slow, steady fire at being considered a pariah for even countenancing 'that fellow in the White House.'"

Williams' neck of the woods is West Newton, the suburb from which he commutes to his Boston studio. (His summer home is on Deer Isle, Maine.) The artist reportedly arrives at 8:30 A.M. and leaves before 1 P.M., four days a week of this routine being enough to furnish his weekly quota of work done. "His syndicate keeps pestering him to do a Sunday page," according to a 1937 article by Willis Birchman, "and how he evades the issue is probably what a few rivals would like to know." Of Williams' methods, Birchman says, "His work is carefully penciled but inked in with a rapid stroke. He knows how to use one line where other artists need a dozen lines to get the same effect." Williams works on many drawings at once, and is unique in keeping about twelve weeks ahead of his schedule, which means always having a backlog of seventy-some unpublished cartoons. In March 1933 he had cause to regret this: when the banks closed under President Roosevelt's orders, only feverish efforts on his part enabled the cartoonist to get into his bank, under guard, to remove a supply of drawings from his safe deposit vault for use.

The green-eyed, almost bald cartoonist has been married to Margaret Kempton since May 1915. Their children are Margaret and David Gluyas. Shy, stooped, spectacled Gluyas Williams is six feet tall and weighs 155 pounds. He is fond of cabinetmaking, sailing, billiards, detective stories, and bridge; but golf—and cartoons on that sport—have no attraction for him. Like the singer Lawrence Tibbett [45], Mary Margaret McBride [41], and many others, Williams is a volunteer "dining detective" for the where-to-eat expert Duncan Hines [46]. "He

WILLIAMS, GLUYAS—*Continued*

is a good artist and a good guy," Benchley wrote of Williams in 1940. "And, oddly enough, you never hear anyone say anything different."

References

Christian Sci Mon p7+ D 21 '40
Look 4:18 D 31 '40 por
Birchman, W. Faces and Facts (1937)
Who's Who in America, 1946-47
Who's Who in American Art, 1940-41

WILLIAMS, TENNESSEE 1914- Playwright

Address: b. c/o Eddie Dowling, 246 W. 44th St., New York

Hailed as an extraordinarily sensitive playwright, Tennessee Williams won high praise with his first Broadway venture, *The Glass Menagerie,* New York Drama Critics' Circle award play of the 1945 season. No literary novice, the young writer was recognized only after a number of years during which he earned his living doing various odd jobs while writing. Those writings—many unproduced or unpublished—include eight full-length plays, a number of one-acters, and many short stories; some of his poems appeared in *Five Young American Poets,* published in 1945. He came within reach of Broadway five years earlier when the Theatre Guild produced his *Battle of Angels,* which, however, closed after a Boston tryout. In late 1945 he had two plays running simultaneously on Broadway, *The Glass Menagerie* and *You Touched Me,* a romantic comedy written in collaboration with Donald Windham.

The parents of Tennessee Williams gave him the first names of Thomas Lanier. He was born in Columbus, Mississippi, in 1914, of pioneer Tennessee stock. (He took the name Tennessee himself.) Since his father was a traveling salesman the family lived with his mother's parents. "My grandfather was an Episcopalian minister. We were brought up in an atmosphere of Southern Puritanism," Williams says, observing, "it's like Northern Puritanism, except that it's more fractious. Also more old-fashioned." In the small Mississippi town where the Williamses lived, the boy played in the family backyard with his older sister, another brother being too young to join in the games. "Life was pleasant—gracious, full of imaginings," he says. When he was about thirteen the family moved to St. Louis where the father had found a job in a shoe company. There for the first time they were forced to live in crowded tenement apartments. To make his sister's dark little room livable, Williams helped her to paint the walls and furniture white and to install her collection of glass animals, "making a place of white and crystal in the midst of squalor." This collection of tiny glass creatures affected the young man deeply—"By poetic association they came to represent in my memory all the softest emotions that belong to recollections of things past. They stood for all the tender things that relieve the austere pattern of life and make it

endurable to the sensitive." This experience provided the material and title for his first successful play.

Upon graduation from high school Williams entered the University of Missouri, where during the first year he spent so much time at outside writing that his grades were very poor. His father therefore insisted that he go to work in the shoe company. For two years the youth worked at different jobs in the firm, but, he remarks, "I was a miracle of incompetence." During this period he stayed up at night to write, until the day-and-night schedule brought on a collapse. When told that he would not need to return to the shoe company, he quickly recovered. Returning to his studies, he worked his way through the University of Iowa by waiting at table at the Iowa State Hospital. After he received his degree he studied for a while at the University of Washington before setting out on his roving writing career. He traveled all over the country, working as a bellhop, elevator operator, usher, teletyper, warehouse handyman, and waiter and reciter of verses in a Greenwich Village night club. "I lived carefully," Williams says, "and whenever I'd saved enough to go some place else, I'd get a bus ticket and go."

The writer gradually became known in theatrical circles, and his plays were presented by Little Theatre and community groups in different parts of the country. In 1939 he won a Group Theatre prize of one hundred dollars for four one-act plays entitled, *American Blues.* About that time the Theatre Guild showed an interest in his work and in 1940 bought his *Battle of Angels.* Directed by Margaret Webster '40 and starring Miriam Hopkins, the play was a failure at its Boston opening. "I never heard of an audience getting so infuriated," says the author, adding by way of explanatory note, "The thing is, you can't mix up sex and religion, as I did in *Battle of Angels.*" (The play was banned by Boston's Watch and Ward Society.) Since 1940 Williams' work has appeared annually in Margaret Mayorga's *Best One-Act Plays.* Through the efforts of his agent, Audrey Wood, he was awarded two Rockefeller Fellowships to enable him to continue his writing, and in 1943 he won a thousand-dollar grant from the Institute of Arts and Letters. About that time he tried another literary medium by becoming a script writer for MGM in Hollywood. After things went wrong with his first assignment—a picture for Lana Turner '43—he was assigned to do a scenario for little Margaret O'Brien. According to the *New Yorker,* "when he had finished telling MGM what he thought of child actors, they barred him from the studio." Williams therefore spent the duration of his contract on the beach at Santa Monica, where he started work on *The Glass Menagerie.*

Co-directed by Eddie Dowling '46 and Margo Jones, *The Glass Menagerie* enjoyed a "sensational" run in Chicago before its New York opening on March 31, 1945, the deadline for consideration by the judges of the New York Drama Critics' Circle. The first-night audience applauded the play so enthusiastically that the author was called to the stage, the only playwright so honored that season. Its reception by the critics was equally enthusiastic, transforming Williams from a little-known writer into a popular, successful playwright. Described as a "memory play," *The Glass Menagerie* is a study of frustration, a story told through a son's recollections of his family. With a cast of only four characters, the mother, son, daughter, and the Gentleman Caller, Williams had created a poignant family portrait. Owing much to the author's St. Louis period, the play is set in a slum apartment in that city, where the crippled daughter lives in a dream world with her collection of glass animals. Eddie Dowling appears in the dual role of son and narrator and Laurette Taylor [45] plays the mother, a former Southern belle, at once heroic and pitiful, a performance which received much applause.

Unanimously agreed that Williams showed great promise, the critics brought out their superlatives to describe his first play. Described as eloquent, touching, heart-warming, and unforgettable, it was also called "a successful violation of Broadway convention," for it has no plot in the traditional sense; it is a mood play, a poetic comedy-drama. In the words of John Mason Brown [42] "Although it follows trails blazed by Thornton Wilder [43] and William Saroyan [40], it manages to walk down them with a gait of its own." This critic further declared that Williams "writes about his characters warmly, with a sympathy that is constant yet probing." In agreement, Stark Young wrote, "The mother's characterization is both appalling and human, cold and loving. No role could be more realistically written than this, but it has the variety, suddenness, passion and freedom, almost unconscious freedom perhaps, of true realism." Several critics spoke of an unevenness in the play and Lewis Nichols pointed out some flowery writing. Joseph Wood Krutch stated that *The Glass Menagerie* "is a remarkable play and its author a man of extraordinary talent. But there is no use failing to mention that his weaknesses are as patent as his gifts, or that very good writing and very bad writing have seldom been as conspicuous in the script of one play. It has a hard substantial core of shrewd observation and deft, economical characterization. But this hard core is enveloped in a fuzzy haze of pretentious, sentimental, pseudo-poetic verbiage." Similarly, Louis Kronenberger [44], while describing the play as "more than a little Chekhovian," found that it is "fancied up with otiose and imitating stage tricks, and its good writing is offset by its bad." Some reviewers thought the narrator unnecessary to the play.

About two weeks after its première the play won the New York Drama Critics' Circle award as the best American play of the season. For the first time in its ten-year history the Circle named the prize play on the first ballot, choosing Williams' work for its "sensitive understanding of four troubled human beings." The playwright candidly stated that, in his opinion, another play should have won. He also indicated that the critics might not like his future plays as much. "In this play I said all the nice things I have to say about

TENNESSEE WILLIAMS

people," he remarked. "The future things will be harsher." Subsequently the play brought added laurels to Williams by winning the fourth annual award of the Catholic monthly, the *Sign,* and the Sidney Howard Memorial Award of fifteen hundred dollars, presented by the Playwrights Company. In June the play set a new record for advance sales when mail orders were being taken for the end of the year. In August producers Dowling and Louis J. Singer announced plans for the organization of a London company with Laurence Olivier in the Dowling role. Published in book form that summer, the play again evoked differing opinions. While Lewis Nichols found that in the reading it lacked "the steady moving and human quality it submits from the stage," Sterling North [43] compared the playwright's artistry with that of the great glass craftsmen: "The lines are fluid, the substance transparent, but the surfaces are cool, hard, and unblemished." Early in August 1946, after 563 performances, *The Glass Menagerie* closed in New York. Two road companies, one with members of the original company, toured with the play in the fall of 1946. Toward the end of the same year motion picture rights to the play were purchased by a Hollywood agent.

Williams' next play grew out of his interest in the life and work of the English writer, D. H. Lawrence, whose real importance, according to Williams, lies "in his affirmation of the fullness of life. In an age of very negative and cynical attitudes, he was one of the few who felt the great richness and glory of being alive." In 1939 the playwright had visited Frieda Lawrence, the novelist's widow, on her ranch in Taos, New Mexico, and had expressed his hope to write eventually a play on Lawrence's life. Thereafter he was unable to pursue this interest until he joined Donald Windham in creating a play out of a Lawrence *ocurring*

WILLIAMS, TENNESSEE—*Continued*

story, *You Touched Me*. First performed at the Cleveland Playhouse and then at the Pasadena Playhouse, the comedy opened in New York on September 25, about six months after the playwright's Broadway debut. The play had received good notices in Boston, but the New York reviewers were less generous. In general, they found the play a disappointment, coming, as it did, in the wake of *The Glass Menagerie*. Directed by Guthrie McClintic '43, *You Touched Me* is described by its co-author as "an allegory of the closed and open attitude toward life." Briefly, it is the story of how boy rescues girl from a "neurotic spinsterhood" imposed by an old maiden aunt, while the girl's seafaring, drinking father supports youth. On the credit side, Howard Barnes found in the play "good acting, eloquence, and a modicum of meaning"; Stark Young pronounced it "fresh, speakable, and civilized"; and Burton Rascoe called it "first-rate comedy."

Less enthusiastic, Joseph Wood Krutch, while pointing out some genuinely moving scenes, declared that the worst scenes are those "in which the attempt is made to give this personal drama some significance both political and cosmic." Woolcott Gibbs wrote in his *New Yorker* review: "Reduced to its simplest terms, what they have written is an elaborate and intensely literary variation of *Snow White*." In his column in the New York *Sun*, Ward Morehouse described *You Touched Me* as "a tenuous and fragmentary comedy," and Wilella Waldorf in her *Post* review remarked on the play's "confusion of tongues and strange medley of dramatic styles." Definitely on the debit side was *Time* magazine, which commented that the authors are "so busy extolling Life that they do little to create it." *You Touched Me* appeared as a book in the latter part of 1946.

Overnight fame and fortune did not change Williams, who, despite his reported thousand-dollar-a-week income, is not attracted to luxurious living. He planned to finish two plays he was writing, then see his *Battle of Angels* go into production again in about a year. His new play, *Stairs to the Roof*, had a test performance at Pasadena's Playbox, and *Stage Pictorial* in Autumn 1945 wrote that it might soon be produced professionally. Late in 1945 Williams was working on another new play, *Fiddler's Green*, set in the Mississippi Delta region. In 1946 eleven of Williams' one-act plays (there are about twenty of them) were published with the title, *27 Wagons Full of Cotton*, the book taking its name from the first play. The collection was received with mixed reactions on the part of the reviewers. Williams' poetry has also been included in *New Directions* (Number Nine), which was published in the same year. He also has collaborated with Paul Bowles in providing words and music for several "Blue Mountain Ballads."

Deeply concerned with the present and future of the American theater, Williams has written and spoken for the establishment of noncommercial theaters. He favors national theaters, "not run primarily for profit but to give con-

tinuous work to creative artists." "The theater should be financed like parks and schools. Great theater is the highest and purest form of religion and should be fostered and respected, because it is concerned with truth." In June 1945 Williams was elected to the board of trustees of the Dallas Civic Repertory Theater, newly established on the plan he advocates. Discussing his theatrical ideas in the "Production Notes" in *The Glass Menagerie*, Williams wrote: "They have to do with a conception of a new, plastic theater which must take the place of the exhausted theater of realistic conventions if the theater is to resume vitality as a part of our culture." Williams also reveals his liberal ideas in praising Henry Wallace's '40 book, *Sixty Million Jobs*, for the New Dealer's social ideas and ideals. In November 1946 Williams was one of thirty-three members of the Dramatists' Guild to agree that they would present their plays in Washington, D.C., only if no race segregation or discrimination were "practiced on either side of the footlights."

The playwright, who is small, blue-eyed, and whose smile is boyish, impressed one interviewer as an "amiable and adaptable young man," and another with the "disarming honesty" of his answers. Laurette Taylor has described him as "a very gentle fellow," and revealed that one day, during rehearsals of the play, he mildly criticized her Southern accent. With his permission she thereafter used his speech, thus giving Amanda the Southern accent of the character's creator. Williams talks eagerly and seriously about his work; he has said, "The one dominant theme in most of my writings, the most magnificent thing in all human nature, is valor—and endurance."

References

    Christian Sci Mon p21 S 21 '45
    N Y Herald Tribune p19 Ap 4 '45 por
    New Yorker 21:18-19 Ap 14 '45
    PM Mag p6+ My 6 '45 por
    Stage Pict 2:18+ Autumn '45 por
    Theatre Arts 30:85+ F '46
    Time 45:88 Ap 23 '45 por

WILLIAMS, TOM   Mar. 18, 1888- British Government official

Address: b. c/o Ministry of Agriculture and Fisheries, 55 Whitehall, London; h. Town Moor Ave., Doncaster, England

The desperate post-World War II food shortage, as it affects the United Kingdom, is the immediate problem of Food Minister Sir Ben Smith '45 and Minister of Agriculture Tom Williams. Like Smith, Williams has supported himself since he was eleven, came to Parliament from the trade-union movement, and had served in the junior ministry before elevation to ministerial rank in the Attlee '40 Labor Party Government of 1945.

The seventh son of a Derbyshire farmer, Tom Williams was one of fourteen children. Born March 18, 1888, he went to work in the coalpits when he was eleven, one or two years younger than the average beginning miner. At the age of nineteen, the ambitious miner enrolled in a correspondence course in general education; he says he never signed his name with greater profit. The excellent command of English with which he is credited probably helped Williams in his rise to prominence in trade union activities. By 1911 he was a union leader.

In 1916 Williams became a checkweigher at Barnborough Main Colliery in Yorkshire, a job he held until 1922. Elected to Parliament from the Don Valley Division of Yorkshire in that year, when he was thirty-four, Williams has served in Commons ever since. He was appointed Parliamentary private secretary to the Minister of Agriculture in the first Labor Party Government (1924). When Ramsay MacDonald formed the second Labor Government in 1929, Tom Williams was made Parliamentary private secretary to the Minister of Labor. He retained his Commons seat in the Conservative landslide of 1931 which followed MacDonald's abandonment of his party. While on a visit to the United States during the twenties, incidentally, Williams had been given the honor of addressing Congress on the subject of world peace.

Seven years after his assignment to the Ministry of Agriculture, Tom Williams took up farming and became keenly interested in it, continuing until 1935. In May, 1940, when Conservative leader Winston Churchill '42 formed his Coalition Government, Williams was Parliamentary Secretary to the Ministry of Agriculture. After the overwhelming Labor Party victory of July 1945—at the first general election in ten years—he became a full-fledged Minister, one of several former miners in the Attlee Government. Williams, at fifty-seven, was several years below the average age of the members named to important Ministries.

With the end of the war in August 1945, it was hoped that the British farmers, who had greatly increased their cereal production at the expense of livestock and other products, would be able to revert to the mixed farming which was less exhausting to the soil. In line with this hope, the Government halved the Wheatland subsidy, abandoned other means of stimulating wheat production, and promised an increase of animal-feeding stuffs. But in early 1946 Agriculture Minister Williams and Food Minister Smith had to tell the public that the years of scrimping and sacrifice were not over; that the world food shortage was far more desperate than had been foreseen; that meat, eggs, fats, and sugar were still in the distant future; and that farmers who had started to increase livestock were caught in an unfortunate situation. Staples like butter and cheese were even scarcer than during the war.

Williams was faced also with labor problems, the solution of which was to employ many prisoners of war, to expedite the release of agricultural workers from the armed forces, and to raise the enlistment period of the Women's Land Army to two years. In March 1946 Williams announced a scale of higher prices for wheat, milk, fat stock, and eggs for a year ahead, and guaranteed minimum prices for livestock for four years ahead. Too late to affect the 1946 harvest, these

British Official Photo.

TOM WILLIAMS

price incentives were to be backed up by the reimposition of compulsory cropping directions to obtain planting of two-and-a-half-million acres of wheat (during the war, three million acres were planted). The acreage for 1946 was, Williams said, as large as for 1945, when Britain was the only country in the world to show an increase over 1938 production. In March 1946 he broadcast a nation-wide appeal, not only for Women's Land Army recruits, but for a hundred thousand city dwellers and fifty thousand children to spend their vacations in helping gather the harvest, as they had done during the war.

A bad situation grew worse. In June 1946 Williams announced what he termed "a very tragic, almost disastrous" cut in stock feed from October 1946 to April 1947, because it had come to a choice between human and animal consumption of an insufficient grain supply. Stating that there was money to buy grain if any had been found by the various missions sent to Argentina, Africa, the United States, and the Far East, he ordered from 25 to 60 per cent in stock feed. Nine days later the forty-fifth annual Labor Party conference at Bournemouth passed a resolution criticizing the Government's agricultural policies; but when the question came to a vote five days after that, the House of Commons upheld its leadership by 284 to 187.

At the same time that Williams was wrestling with current problems, he was one of the Ministers concerned with economic affairs who formed the "high command" of the Labor Government's experiment in "the planning of the nation's entire economy, internal and external, on a long-range basis." *World Report* commented in September 1946, "On the ability of the new Economic High Command to deal effectively with these . . . complex matters depends Britain's ultimate chance for success

WILLIAMS, TOM—*Continued*

in creating an economic order that combines socialism and capitalism."

The Right Honorable Tom Williams, P.C., M.P., is described as "a tall, gaunt, good-looking character with a pleasant voice, a fine presence, and an excellent command of English." Some think he looks "like Lincoln, but handsome." The Minister, whose home is in Doncaster, became a Right Honorable in 1941 by being sworn on His Majesty's Privy Council. Williams has one son, who is married to the only daughter of Herbert Morrison [40], leader of the Labor Party in the House of Commons and Lord President of the Privy Council.

References

N Y Sun p18 Ag 28 '45
Who's Who, 1946

WILLISON, GEORGE F(INDLAY) July 24, 1896- Author

Address: h. 2100 19th St., N.W., Washington, D.C.

George F. Willison, historian and former teacher and public relations consultant, is the author of *Saints and Strangers* (1945). This book, the result of nine years of study and research, Willison has described as "a group portrait of the Pilgrims and their families, aimed at dispelling the almost universal misconception of them as pale plaster saints, hollow and bloodless. They were not anemic Victorians. On the contrary, they were virile Elizabethans and reflected most of the qualities of that amazing age."

Born on July 24, 1896, in Denver, George Findlay Willison is the son of Robert and Ann (Brunton) Willison. His boyhood was spent in Denver, which in the early forties has

GEORGE F. WILLISON

given the literary world two other authors of distinction: Gene Fowler '44 and Mary Chase '45. After attending the East Denver High School, young Willison entered the University of Colorado, where he majored in Greek and was graduated *magna cum laude* with a B.A. degree in 1918. A member of Phi Beta Kappa, Willison also was active on debating teams between the years 1915 and 1918, was a member of the college dramatic club and vice-president of the student body (1917-18).

World War I interrupted young Willison's studies. Entering the United States Army Machine Gun Corps in 1918, he rose to a second lieutenant but was not sent overseas. After the Armistice his outstanding work at the University of Colorado won him a Rhodes Scholarship at Oxford in 1920. There he studied literature, economics, and political science, and after three years was given a diploma in the two last-named subjects. A year in literature and history at the University of Paris followed. During his student days abroad Willison also gave more than a tourist's attention to England, France, Scotland, Germany, and Italy. Returning to the United States in 1925, Willison devoted three years to writing. Not finding this highly profitable, he entered the teaching profession as head of the classics department at St. John's College, in Annapolis. A year later he joined the teaching staff of the progressive Hessian Hills School at Croton on Hudson. In 1930 he was made a member of the school's board of trustees and in the 1934-35 term, its acting director.

While with the Hessian Hills School, Willison published his first book. *Here They Dug the Gold* (1931), concerning gold discoveries and frontier life in Colorado, was considered "a spirited piece of work picturing a time and society by tracing the history of one of Colorado's notorious and notable figures," the picturesque H. A. W. Tabor, who succeeded while others suffered hardship and deprivation with little or no reward. "The people are real," commented C. J. Finger in the Pittsburgh (Missouri) *Bulletin,* "and the life of the mining camp and town is rendered with fidelity." (This "lively frontier chronicle" was reprinted in 1936, and a revision of it was published in the summer of 1946.)

Upon his retirement from teaching in the spring of 1935, Willison wrote *Why Wars Are Declared,* a study of war as a socioeconomic phenomenon. It was published in "Basic Books" the following year and distributed by Random House. In that year, 1936, Willison joined the Provincetown, Massachusetts, branch of the Federal Writers' Project, a WPA program. He was assigned to the "American Guide Series," a project of studies designed to present the history of, and other valuable information on, the states of the Union. From writer, Willison rose rapidly to the position of editor and then to the post of editor in chief, with offices in Washington. Although the writers engaged in the project were paid out of Federal and State funds, each of the books written as a result of the project had to win publication on its own merits from private publishing firms. Almost without exception the "Guides" were highly praised by reviewers. Among those for which Willison personally acted as supervisory editor was *Colorado, a Guide to the Highest State.* It was while he was engaged in research for the New England guide books in 1936 that he became interested in the history of the Pilgrims.

"Like most Americans," he says, "I assumed I knew everything about the Pilgrims from school texts." But his research into records made him realize that he knew "literally nothing." "The general impression of the Pilgrims," he wrote, "was false in almost every particular, both as a matter of fact and as a matter of interpretation. Soon a book about them, with emphasis upon their qualities as distinct and often as clashing personalities, took shape in my mind." Nine years later *Saints and Strangers* was published, the outcome of intermittent work between his duties in several important posts. "The book is a sheer joy to read," said the New York *Times* reviewer, "because the vast work that went into assembling the facts has been so completely digested. Much of the earlier digging into the old records has been done by men who could neither digest nor write, each adding one little piece more to the picture. Mr. Willison has put these pieces together, created the whole picture and filled it with convincing life." After pointing out that the discovery of elementary facts about the Pilgrims has been going on for a hundred years or more—beginning in 1841 when Reverend Alexander Young produced *The Chronicles of the Pilgrim Fathers—the Saturday Review of Literature* said that Willison had accomplished "the commendable task of combining accurate scholarship, critical and unconventional in tone, with a lively and picturesque presentation; the task, in short, of furnishing a good popular history of Plymouth Colony from its English origins to the end of its separate existence in 1691."

While the book was in preparation, Willison had worked with the Federal Writers' Project (1936-41), as a writer and public relations consultant for the Civil Aeronautics Administration (1942-43), and as a writer and assistant to the publicity director of the Democratic National Committee (1944-45). His resignation from the last-named post took effect on January 1, 1946. "I intend to devote myself entirely to my own writings," says the author. "My next project, already under way, is a story of the first century of the Puritan settlements in and around Boston."

In addition to contributing articles to the *Nation, New Yorker, Mademoiselle, Current History,* and *Reader's Digest,* Willison has edited *Let's Make a Play: Twelve Plays by Children,* which was published in 1940. In 1928 the author was married to Florence ("Toni") Hauser. The Willisons have one son, Malcolm. In recent years they have made their home in Washington, but Willison's future plans include a place on the Maine coast or Cape Cod. "There he would like to fish, play the piano, take long afternoon naps, play tennis, pull corks with congenial friends, do some carpentering, paint, bake on the beach, toss

parties which end up in the kitchen with everybody singing." Between these relaxations he says he will manage a few hours of writing. His favorite authors are Aristophanes, Rabelais, Gibbon, Auden, Joyce, and Howard Fast [43]; he recommends the reading of Francis Steegmuller's *Flaubert and Madame Bovary* and Katharine Hathaway Butler's *The Little Locksmith.* His favorite character in history is the late Franklin D. Roosevelt [42]; his favorite actor, Victor Moore; and he likes Rita Hayworth. He also enjoys the New York Philharmonic, *Information Please,* and what the Pilgrims called "strong waters." Willison is five feet ten, weighs one hundred and forty pounds, has blue eyes and gray hair.

Reference

Philadelphia Record O 17 '45

WILSON, FRANK J(OHN) May 19, 1888· United States Government official

Address: b. United States Secret Service, Treasury Bldg., Washington, D.C.; h. 2910 Tennyson St., N.W., Washington, D.C.

Frank J. Wilson, who became the head of the United States Secret Service in 1938, had previously distinguished himself on the Capone and Lindbergh [41] cases as a member of the Treasury Department Intelligence Unit. The few hundred operatives he directed until his retirement on the last day of 1946 constitute one of the Treasury's seven law enforcement agencies, the others being Foreign Funds Control, Alcohol Tax Unit, Intelligence Unit, Customs Agency Service, Internal Revenue, and Narcotics. Secret Service activities, although confined to a few fields, are international: "When . . . Orizaba or Lisbon counterfeiters . . . are ultimately apprehended," wrote Laurence Dwight Smith in *Counterfeiting,* "nine times out of ten the United States Secret Service . . . possibly the most efficient investigating organization that has ever existed . . . has broken the case."

Frank John Wilson, one of a family of two brothers and a sister, was born in Buffalo, New York, on May 19, 1888. His parents, John Frank and Mary Ann (McGreevy) Wilson, had come from different small towns of the State to Buffalo, where his father was a police officer. Wilson has told interviewer John J. Floherty that, as a young boy, he might have become a delinquent—he belonged to a neighborhood gang which seemed to be tending toward lawbreaking. Before the boys' mischief developed into serious trouble, however, Frank's father solved the problem by diverting their interest to a gymnasium he installed in the Wilson barn. Later Frank and three other "husky, healthy, happy lads" managed to save twenty-five dollars and purchased an old twenty-eight-foot schooner which they put into sailing condition.

Young Frank entered Lafayette High School at thirteen and was graduated in 1904. The next year he entered the real estate business, while studying at the Buffalo Business Institute until 1906, and remained in real estate and contracting until 1917. Wilson, then twenty-nine

FRANK J. WILSON

years of age, saw World War I Army service at Fort Niagara, New York, in September-October 1917, and immediately upon discharge became chief New York State investigator for the United States Food Administration. In July-December 1919 he managed the surplus army food sale in his native city, and also attended classes at the University of Buffalo.

The first six months of 1920 found Frank Wilson working for the Federal Department of Justice Fair Price Commission. Later that year he joined the Treasury Department Intelligence Unit, which had been started the year before with a personnel of six agents. For the next thirteen years Wilson was in and out of the capital, serving as a special agent in Chicago, San Francisco, Baltimore, and New Orleans. From 1933 to 1935 he was special agent in charge of the Cleveland Intelligence Unit.

In *The Giant Killers* (1945), author Alan Hynd fills in some of the details of investigations in which Wilson and other Intelligence Unit of the Treasury men "almost single-handed broke the back of organized crime in the United States during the twenties and the thirties," using the technical weapon of failure to pay taxes on illicit income. When President Hoover ordered an investigation of Al Capone's underworld empire, and a year of spadework had built up cases only against "small fry," Frank Wilson was one of the four agents whom Intelligence Unit head Elmer L. Irey called upon in 1930 to help formulate a plan of operations. One of the four was agent-in-charge Madden of the Chicago office, and the other two were agents assigned to infiltrate the Capone mob. Wilson's task was to be liaison with the undercover men, to make further investigation, and to correlate the evidence secured to pass on to Irey in Washington and Madden in Chicago.

Special agent Wilson spent sixteen to twenty hours a day studying the volumes of accounts

of Capone enterprises which had fallen into Government hands, examining more than a million checks cleared by Capone henchmen, looking for a trail to the racketeer. Two days before Christmas one of the planted agents warned Wilson of a plan to murder him the next day. The New Yorker managed to elude the gangsters but refused to leave the city, merely checking in at another hotel and continuing his work. On a tip from the other agent, Wilson searched through stacks of old records to find an all-revealing ledger for 1924-26 which had escaped attention through being mislabeled. To confer with his chief and colleagues on this discovery, he had to go to a rendezvous in Gary, Indiana, switching taxis four times on the way to the bus to escape any pursuers.

Next Wilson was sent to Miami to follow up a lead to one of the bookkeepers and incidentally to help restore his own health, which had suffered. Having found the man, Wilson got him out of town under the noses of the Capone organization, which had orders to shoot him on sight. Besides ordering his mob to "get" Wilson and both bookkeepers at all costs, Capone enlisted the aid of gangsters in other cities, putting a price of $25,000 on Wilson's head. Finally, in October 1931, Alphonse Capone was indicted for failure to pay $215,030.48 in back taxes; his offer to settle out of court for one and one-half million dollars was refused and he was convicted and sentenced to prison. His leading henchmen met similiar fates, as did smaller criminals. The prosecution was handled for the Government by a thirty-five-year-old lawyer named Dwight H. Green, who was to become Governor of Illinois.

Frank Wilson worked also on the Lindbergh kidnapping case, beginning two months before Attorney General Mitchell offered the services of the Department of Justice to the New Jersey State authorities in May 1932. Wilson is credited with responsibility for having the serial numbers of the ransom money properly recorded, a task on which fourteen clerks spent eight hours and through which the case was finally broken and the kidnapper arrested in September 1934. Meanwhile, however, Wilson and others were examining New York City directories published in the preceding thirty-three years for clues to the identity of a certain suspect. It was Wilson, also, who suggested checking on the fifty thousand persons who had been pupils of Dr. "Jafsie" Condon, on the chance that the kidnapper had gained his knowledge of Condon in that way—an investigation carried out by the New York, New Jersey, and FBI identification bureaus.

In July 1935 Wilson refused appointment as chief investigator for special prosecutor Thomas E. Dewey [44], who had begun his racket-busting career two years earlier by using complex Intelligence Unit data to convict mobster Waxey Gordon. About a year after his conference with Dewey, the investigator became acting chief of another Treasury agency, the Secret Service, and on New Year's Day 1937 he succeeded Chief W. H. Moran. As head of the Secret Service, Wilson was concerned with two main duties: protecting the President, his family, residence, and guests, and the President-elect, "in all cases whatsoever"; and protecting United States currency, securities, and property. The first-named duty was more or less public in nature; the second had always been kept a mystery.

With the backing of Treasury Secretary Henry Morgenthau, Jr.,[40] Wilson decided to reverse the policy of secrecy about counterfeiting. Setting aside that portion of the criminal code which forbade any printed, photographed, or engraved reproductions of currency or Government securities, the new chief determined to give the widest possible publicity to characteristics of good and bad money in a great campaign of public education. This was tried first in Brooklyn in 1937, where an unprecedentedly large number of counterfeits were in circulation. A score of Wilson's agents covered the area for months, explaining to merchants and cash handlers how to detect counterfeits, and leaving printed instruction cards. "It is as astonishing," wrote Laurence Dwight Smith in *Counterfeiting, Crime Against the People* (1944), "as if twenty lawyers suddenly descended upon a district and began to teach the public, gratis, how to draw a will. . . . Like all professional men, criminal investigators treasure the lore gained by years of hard work, and they are more than loath to reveal secrets that might some time—they feel, rightly or wrongly—aid a malefactor."

The next step in the "Know Your Money" campaign was to give public lectures and exhibits for civic clubs, trade associations, and meetings of merchants. "At this point," Wilson has said, "there was a surprising reaction from the criminal world. Counterfeiters began dropping in on our lectures and seeing our movies. A few, deciding the racket was getting too hot, pulled out of it then and there." To speed up this decrease, and to arm the country against a possible flooding with counterfeits by some hostile nation, Wilson moved the campaign into the high schools in 1940, and by May 1945 it had been brought to all except nine thousand of the public secondary schools in the country. His aim was to get all the high schools to incorporate this information into the course of study, whether as art, economics, civics, or other subject. Students were particularly important to inform, because they taught their families and because children were favorite "passers" for counterfeiters. By 1943 annual losses from counterfeits had dropped 97 per cent from the 1933-36 level and, as Secret Service men recalled with particular satisfaction, juvenile violations of counterfeiting laws had dropped 60 per cent—in a time of generally increasing juvenile delinquency.

Wilson had new problems to handle, however. The advent of wartime rationing and price control brought false ration stamps and coupons, as well as black-market activities; the state of war added greatly to the necessity for vigilance in protecting Federal workers and property. The flood of service dependency checks was an invitation to what Chief Wilson called "the meanest racket in the world"—that of the check thief and forger. This cost businessmen alone hundreds of thousands of dollars a year in loss

on fraudulently cashed checks. To counteract these "check pirates," the Secret Service launched another publicity campaign of warning to the public, and articles on the subject appeared in national magazines under the signature of Frank J. Wilson. In September 1946 the Treasury announced the planned retirement of Chief Wilson. He was to be succeeded by James J. Maloney, another upstate New Yorker.

Wilson likes to race sailboats, has been a member of the Buffalo Yacht Club since 1906 (in 1920 he was its vice-commodore). A Catholic, he joined the Knights of Columbus; as a writer of pamphlets and articles in his field, he joined the National Press Club. A member of the executive committee of the International Association of Chiefs of Police since 1940, the Secret Service chief has honorary life memberships in the Chief Constables Association of Canada, the Maryland Police Association, and the Washington Numismatic Society. Since October 1926, when he was thirty-eight, he has been married to Judith Mary Barbaux, a native of the capital.

A stocky five feet eight and a half inches tall, "ham-handed, sharp-nosed" Frank John Wilson weighs 180 pounds, and has sparse black hair. "Nobody was ever more unlike the bearded secret service agent of haymow literature than is Mr. Wilson," wrote one observer. "He is a quiet, professorial, scholarly, persistent, nearsighted citizen with pale brown eyes and tight lips," fond of smoking five-cent cigars. As head of the Secret Service, Wilson established a reputation as a man of few words; in 1939 the press release in which he announced the organization's seventy-fifth anniversary read, in full, "The Service is seventy-five years old this year." Six years later, however, Wilson granted an interview to John Floherty without "fuss or formality," and enlarged upon his confidence in the young people of the nation, saying, "Despite the deplorable increase of crime in the teen-age bracket . . . never has youth risen to heights of accomplishment and ideals as it has during the demoralizing days of war. Perhaps the relentless passing of the years has caught parents, educators, and the rest of us adults a little out of step while youth marches on, its eyes fixed on a better world than we gave them."

References

N Y Sun p13 Ag 21 '41; p24 O 25 '46
Floherty, J. J. Men Against Crime (1946) pp138-44
Who's Who in America, 1946-47
Who's Who in the Nation's Capital, 1938-39

WINSOR, KATHLEEN Oct. 16, 1919-
Author

Address: b. c/o Macmillan Company, 60 5th Ave., New York

The 972-page best seller *Forever Amber,* which was being produced as a film in the fall of 1946, has brought fame and wealth to its author, Kathleen Winsor. Since its publication

Brockway Studios, Inc.
KATHLEEN WINSOR

in October 1944, more than a million copies of the novel have been printed.

Kathleen Winsor's English ancestors are said to have migrated to America as early as 1630. Born in Olivia, Minnesota, on October 16, 1919, to Harold Lee and Myrtle (Crowder) Winsor, she grew up in Berkeley, California, where her father dealt in real estate. She received her B.A. degree from the University of California in 1938, two years after she had been married to Robert John Herwig, a star player on the university's football team. While he helped score a record of straight victories for California in 1937, his wife sat in the stadium press boxes, observing that the football field has taken the place of the ancient Roman amphitheater. Her writing at this time consisted of pieces on football "from the woman's point of view" for the Oakland Tribune. Herwig remained at California as a football coach after his graduation, and in the meantime Miss Winsor worked as a receptionist for the Tribune, hoping that it might lead to a job as a reporter. When this did not materialize after six months, she left.

It was a class paper which her husband had to write on the death of Charles II that, according to the publishers, the Macmillan Company, brought about the writing of Forever Amber. Browsing through one of the books Herwig was using, Miss Winsor became fascinated by England's Restoration period and recognized the potentialities which the dramatic events of the Merry Monarch's reign held for a historical novel. After leaving the Oakland Tribune she began the intensive research task she felt was necessary to present a picture of life during Restoration years. While following her husband from camp to camp after he became a marine in World War II, and then while he fought as an officer in the Pacific with the Sixth Marine Division, the young writer reportedly read some three hundred and fifty-

six books on her subject and wrote a total of six drafts of her novel. Then, in December 1943 she sent what is supposed to have been the only manuscript she possessed to the Macmillan publishing house in New York. "I can't say that I was surprised when it was accepted," she has stated. "It seemed only justice after five years of effort."

Before the publication of Forever Amber (it was originally entitled Wings of the Morning) Macmillan launched a promotion campaign which, according to "talk in publishing circles," was intended to make the book another Gone with the Wind. In the September 9, 1944, issue of Publishers' Weekly, which carried a photograph of the attractive Miss Winsor on its cover, Macmillan announced that an initial sum of twenty thousand dollars would be used for the promotion of the book throughout the country. Five days before the publication date, a story in the New York World-Telegram stated that a spokesman for the Hays office (the Motion Picture Producers and Distributors of America) had "admitted in effect that bidding for Miss Winsor's book by film companies had been discouraged." On October 16, the day the book first appeared in bookstores, Miss Winsor spoke at the opening session of the Boston Book Fair. This was followed by her appearance on several radio programs and also at luncheons and autographing parties in such cities as Cleveland, Chicago, Nashville, Atlanta, and Detroit. Soon after its publication the New England Watch and Ward Society saw to it that Forever Amber was removed from Boston's bookstore shelves. (In the summer of 1946, an interlocutory decree was issued prohibiting its sale in Massachusetts. The case, expected to reach the courts in January 1947, was to constitute the first test of a new Massachusetts censorship law.)

It was such factors, wrote PM, that made Forever Amber "a best seller in spite of itself," for the critics were in general agreement that, while the 972-page account of a courtesan's adventures in Charles II's England might be historically authentic, it lacked literary merit. "The story shows considerable narrative skill," wrote Harry Hansen of the New York World-Telegram, agreeing with several other reviewers who praised its "pace and action," but he added, it shows no skill "whatever in characterization." Nevertheless Kathleen Winsor had "hit the bull's-eye." "If [the novel] is three times as long as it has much excuse for being, and if it is in all essentials a vulgar and trivial book," said the New York Times Orville Prescott, "it still is moderately entertaining. Forever Amber has what it takes for commercial success." From the advance sales alone the author was reported to have earned fifty thousand dollars. The novel, which was translated into at least ten foreign languages including Finnish and Bulgarian, continued to be a best seller: during 1945 the demand for it exceeded that of all others, the bookstores selling 868,630 copies, according to Publishers' Weekly.

In November 1944, hardly a month after its publication, Twentieth Century-Fox purchased the screen rights to Forever Amber for two hundred thousand dollars, a price said to be four times that which had been paid for *Gone with the Wind.* Later Miss Winsor signed a contract with the motion picture studio "calling for writing, technical advice, and acting," and for a time it was rumored that she might appear in the role of the heroine which she had created. In May 1945, however, she was reported to have given up her plans for acting and more than a year later, when the film was going into production for a second time (a first attempt involving three hundred thousand dollars of footage had been abandoned), she was not working on any aspect of the filming. The book was adapted for the screen with the theme of "crime doesn't pay," reported Frank Nugent in the New York *Times Magazine.*

The fame and wealth which Miss Winsor has acquired from the writing of *Forever Amber* have been her admitted goal. "When I was eighteen," she told a *PM* reporter, "I wrote a list of things I was going to do with my life. One of them was that I was going to write a best seller." She describes herself as a realist and maintains that the ambition of all authors is not different from hers. "If most writers were really honest with themselves," she has said, "they'd admit that the only reason they are writing books is in the hope that they'll have a best seller. . . .That's what every writer really wants—to make money." In 1946 Miss Winsor was reportedly working on another novel. She participated in war bond tours during the war, has made guest appearances on radio programs, and helped promote a perfume named "Forever Amber." After her husband returned from overseas (three times wounded, he was the recipient of the Navy Cross and the Silver Star), she traveled in South America with him for about six months. In 1946 they were divorced, and Miss Winsor was subsequently married to band leader Artie Shaw.

A tall, striking brunette, Miss Winsor wears hats styled by Lilly Daché and dresses by Hattie Carnegie. Art Cohn, her onetime sports editor on the Oakland *Tribune,* in an article called "Forever Winsor" has written that she has an "incisive sense of humor and is the first to tell a joke on herself". The author does not like jokes about *Forever Amber,* however. Bennett Cerf has called "the literary glamour girl . . . sensitive and unbelievably shy." Reportedly an excellent swimmer, she enjoys a good play, does a little water-color painting and likes to design some of her clothes.

References

Liberty 22:19 Ja 13 '45
Life 17:41+ O 30 '44
PM Mag p2+ Ja 14 '45
Who's Who in America, 1946-47

WINSTER, (REGINALD THOMAS HERBERT FLETCHER, 1st) BARON
Mar. 27, 1885- British Government official; journalist

Address: b. Government House, Cyprus; House of Lords, London; h. 27 Palace St., London; Fivewents Way, Crowborough, Sussex, England

As Minister of Civil Aviation in the Attlee Labor Government, Baron Winster had the task of nationalizing all air transport service in the United Kingdom and of building it up to a position of leadership. (He was relieved of this post and appointed colonial Governor of Cyprus in October 1946.) The former Lieutenant Commander Fletcher is himself one of the "favored few" who broke with class and family tradition by entering the socialist Labor Party. In Lords as in Commons, he had remained one of the most energetic and sharp-tongued members since his elevation to the peerage in 1942.

British Official Photo.

BARON WINSTER

Lord Winster was born Reginald Thomas Herbert Fletcher on March 27, 1885. The only son of Nicholas and Dinah Fletcher, of Rampholme, Windermere, in Westmorland county, he comes of an old North Country family. One of his ancestors, a Crockermouth merchant, is said to have presented Mary, Queen of Scots, with a gift of crimson velvet when she was fleeing from Scotland to England. The Fletchers planned to have their son become a barrister, but, as the London *Observer* tells it, "his sister married a sailor, and the uniform so dazzled and fascinated the youthful Rex Fletcher that there was no other aim in his young life than to join the Navy too. So, from a prep school in Blackheath he went to H.M.S. *Britannia,* and through the mill." Rex was fourteen when he became a naval cadet. "The switch from parental plans for a career to that of his own choice was, in itself, evidence of a forceful character," the *Observer* writer adds. "Victorian parents were less flexible in these matters than the parents of today."

The officer served on destroyers and light cruisers in World War I, with the Grand

WINSTER, BARON—*Continued*

Fleet and in the Channel Patrol. Later he spent some years at an Admiralty desk as head of the Near Eastern section of the Intelligence Division. In 1922 he left the sea after more than two decades of service to enter politics, and that September he was promoted to the rank of lieutenant commander. Fletcher's family was Conservative, but he became a Liberal. A free-lance journalist, he contested the Basingstoke division of Hampshire in 1922. Sent to Parliament the next year, he served from December 1923 to October 1924, and then lost his seat in the 1924 general elections. Next Fletcher fought the Tavistock by-election of 1928, losing by a narrow margin. The next year the Commander joined the Labor Party. "I felt," he explains, "that if one wanted to bring reforms one should belong to a party likely to come to power."

In 1935 Fletcher was returned as a Labor member from the Nuneaton division of Warwickshire, and continued to fill this seat until his entrance into the House of Lords in 1942. As a back-bench (new) member of the Opposition, he was known as one of the most pertinacious questioners in Commons. A vigorous debater, he said some particularly "wounding" things about the British Broadcasting Company, of which he strongly disapproves. In January 1938 the Commander urged a reorganization of the Air Ministry; his ideas have been expressed also in two books on which he collaborated, *The Air Defences of Britain* and *The War on Our Doorstep*. He has carried on an energetic campaign to improve the pay and conditions of enlisted sailors and Merchant Navy men. Then, in July 1939, fifty-four-year-old reserve Lieutenant Commander Fletcher was recalled to active duty, being forced during this period to refrain from political activity. Posted at the London docks, he "worked all hours of day and night" supervising the fitting of guns onto merchant ships. After that he was chief staff officer at the Grimsby naval base, looking after East Coast convoys.

When Conservative Winston Churchill '42 formed his Coalition Government in May 1940, the Laborite was called back into politics as Parliamentary private secretary to A. V. Alexander '40, First Lord of the Admiralty. A London *Observer* article describes Fletcher striding into the Admiralty in his lieutenant commander's uniform, "sweeping aside doorkeepers and admirals of the fleet with the same genially imperious air. And, quite soon, he was taking a leading part in the running of the King's Navee." In December 1941, however, Fletcher stormed out, resigned his post, and pointedly corrected those who addressed him as Commander by insisting that he was now "plain Mr. Fletcher."

But in February 1942 "Mr. Fletcher" became "My lord." He and three other Labor M.P.'s were raised to the peerage, according to the official account, "as a special measure of state policy . . . to strengthen the Labor Party in the Upper House, where its representation was disproportionate at a time when a Coalition Government of three parties was charged with the direction of affairs." Created a baron, Fletcher chose as his title Winster of Witherslack in the county of Westmorland (Winster is the name of a river dividing Westmorland from Lancashire). As such, his presence "much increased Labor's debating strength in the House of Lords." In his first year there the new Lord Winster made seventy-four speeches, entering the discussion of one out of two subjects, and became the most frequent unofficial speaker in the Lords, one of the few clearly audible. One of his early crusades, growing perhaps out of his experience with convoys, was for building more aircraft carriers and escort vessels instead of battleships. In 1943 Winster campaigned in the Lords and in the press for intensified anti-U-boat warfare and for publication of the figures on shipping losses, which he claimed would stimulate production in shipyards but would tell the enemy little he could not figure out for himself. He held further that British shipbuilding should be dovetailed with the American program to eliminate waste. The Lord continued "fighting the cause of the lower deck and the noncommissioned ranks," and he urged close cooperation with the United States on postwar shipbuilding and trade problems. Another of his appeals was for "safeguarding the rights of one-man businesses."

The first Labor Government in sixteen years came into power in July 1945, with Clement Attlee as Prime Minister. "I seem to have been left out of the Government," Winster confided to friends an hour before the news of his appointment as Minister of Civil Aviation was made public. "To him," says the *Observer*, "this was a legitimate device to keep the secret." Lord Winster's Ministry was a new one, and he was uniquely fortunate, the London *Daily Herald* pointed out, in not inheriting "many Tory mistakes. The structure which has to be continued can be of his designing. The importance of the Ministry needs no underline. On it depends the place of Britain in future air transport." Winster's first problem was enlarging his own inadequate staff and quarters for the task. To get some firsthand knowledge of the British Overseas Airways operations and bases, Winster flew to America and Newfoundland; nearly seven thousand of the seventy-six hundred miles he covered in less than four days were as an ordinary passenger. That, comments the *Observer* writer, is characteristic. "He does not take kindly to official reports, preferring his own eyes. . . . It would be a fairly safe wager that the Minister knows (by sight, at any rate) every part of every aeroplane with which he is concerned, and that he is prepared to argue with every expert in the Ministry about the performance and general suitability of each aircraft."

On the first of November 1945 Winster surprised the public by announcing that all British air services, including all airports used for scheduled flights and all meteorological and traffic control services, were to be state-owned and state-operated, with the former owners receiving fair compensation. He said that the Government intended, in consultation with the Dominions, to build up "an air-travel system which will fit easily into a future world civil aviation organization," and to work through one domestic and two overseas national corporations. This Labor Government plan was denounced by Winster's Tory predecessor, Lord Swinton, as "the most disappointing and damning proposal put forward in this house"; and he charged Prime Minister Attlee with thereby plunging air travel into party politics and political theory.

A few weeks later, it was reported that the British aircraft industry then employed nine hundred thousand workmen, more than six times as many as its American equivalent, and that orders already given for more than ten thousand military planes were double the number projected in the American Army-Navy procurement program through mid-1948. Four days before Christmas 1945 Lord Winster announced the signing in Bermuda of an agreement to share transatlantic air services between Britain and Canada on an equal basis, each country to operate through a "chosen instrument"—British Overseas Airways Corporation and Transcanada Airlines. Another result of this Bermuda conference was that Newfoundland received sovereign rights over commercial air traffic. A White Paper, written for introduction in the House of Commons in January of 1946, set forth the Aviation Ministry's arrangements for Dominion and colony airlines parallel with United Kingdom lines over British Empire routes, expressed willingness to formulate joint undertakings with foreign governments over routes of mutual interest, and proposed to seek elimination of airline subsidies by international agreement, except where necessary to maintain essential but unremunerative services. It also stated as general policy "to require the use of British aircraft types"; but British civil aircraft not being immediately available, the Ministry purchased prewar German transports for domestic use, and five American Constellations to fly the New York-London route.

Previous British policy was almost completely reversed by the Anglo-American air agreement signed in February 1946, after four weeks of negotiation. In return for United States participation in an international rate-fixing body, Britain made a number of concessions, including complete freedom for each nation to establish the frequency of scheduled operations of its own air lines, and no interference with "fifth freedom traffic" (meaning the carrying of passengers from one country to another by planes from a third country) except to deal with obvious abuses. A permanent liaison setup was arranged. At the end of March Lord Winster himself returned from a visit to Australia and New Zealand to announce formation, also, of a permanent agency to coordinate the development of British and Commonwealth air routes in the Pacific through the British Commonwealth Pacific Air Lines. That October, when Prime Minister Attlee announced plans for Cabinet changes, bringing in younger Laborites, and for a sweeping re-

organization of the military establishment, Lord Winster was announced for the Governorship of Cyprus. He was succeeded at the Civil Aviation Ministry by Lord Nathan.

Reginald Thomas Herbert Fletcher, first Baron Winster, is described as a gray-haired man, young for his years, of "small stature, firm views, and strong mind." Despite his wish not to be called a bluff old sailor, Winster's "bluntness of speech and knack of ignoring irrelevant detail" are usually summed up as "the bluff manner of the quarter-deck." He has written numerous articles on naval strategy and other matters, and formerly contributed a London letter to an American daily newspaper. Winster is considered a first-rank broadcaster, although his voice has been called rasping and his speech drawling. The Labor peer is further described as a likeable, "clubable" man, a good host, and an expert story-teller. His writings and speeches, however, are described as caustic and unsparing, and in argument or debate he is marked by "grim purposefulness." Since 1909 Rex Winster has been married to Elspeth, daughter of the Reverend H. J. Lomax of Abbotswood, Buxted, Sussex. The Baron's particular pride and hobby is the garden of their Sussex home. (He is, incidentally, a justice of the peace in Surrey County.) In raising him to the peerage, the Labor Party followed its usual custom of choosing men without children, as it does not believe in perpetuating the system of inherited titles.

References

London Daily Herald O 3 '45
London Observer D 16 '45
N Y Sun p16 My 4 '44
Who's Who, 1946

WINTER, ELLA Mar. 17, 1898- Author
Address: c/o Little, Brown & Co., 34 Beacon St., Boston, Mass.

Ella Winter, journalist, and interpreter of the new Russia, was born in Melbourne, Australia, on March 17, 1898, the daughter of Adolph and Frieda (Lust) Winter. She was educated in England, where she studied at the North London Collegiate School for Girls, and then was graduated with first-class honors from the London School of Economics and Political Science. After a year at the school as lecturer and assistant professor, she received a research fellowship for the Cambridge Psychological Laboratory. A university organizer for the British Labor Party, she was sent to the Peace Conference in Paris in 1918 as assistant to Dr. Felix Frankfurter. She was secretary of the London University Labor Party from 1920 to 1922; member of the Foreign Affairs Committee of the Parliamentary Labor Party from 1920 to 1923; and in 1924 manager of H. G. Wells's campaign for Parliament.

While at the Conference in Paris she met Lincoln Steffens, American journalist, who—attracted by her "joyous" youth and "wonder and working interest in life"—followed her to

ELLA WINTER

London. The difference in their ages, however, seemed an obstacle to anything but friendship. Steffens left England, but conducted a voluminous correspondence with Ella Winter during the next four years. In the fall of 1923 he returned to London. Several months later Steffens and Miss Winter went to Paris; they were married there in February 1924.

Ella Winter's life with Lincoln Steffens was a varied pattern of travel, intimate contact with a wide circle of friends, and work. After the birth of their son, Pete Stanley, in November 1924, they spent much of their time on the Italian Riviera, where their villa at Alassio was a stopping point for many artists and writers, among them the Sinclair Lewises, the Hemingways, H. G. Wells, Max Eastman. Later, they lived for a while at Bêcheron, an old French *manoir* in Touraine belonging to their friend Jo Davidson, the sculptor. And always there were frequent trips to London, Paris, Rome, Berlin, Switzerland. In 1917 Ella Winter and her husband came to the United States and settled in Carmel, California, where in 1929 Miss Winter became a naturalized citizen. Encouraged by her husband, she began to write and contributed to such publications as the *New Masses,* the *Nation, Collier's,* the Manchester *Guardian,* and the London *Daily News.* She also edited the *Carmelite* (1928-30) and the *Pacific Weekly* (1934-36).

Deeply interested in social reforms, Ella Winter went to Russia in the summer of 1930, and again in the spring of 1931, to observe the Five Year Plan in operation. These visits resulted in a book, *Red Virtue* (1933). Although she was familiar with the writings of Marx and Engels and Lenin and could understand the objectives of the Soviet state, Miss Winter did not dwell to any extent upon Russian ideology, but rather concerned herself with human values and relationships. Some reviewers felt that her approach was not sufficiently critical, but most of them agreed that she had presented a vivid picture of Soviet life. *Red Virtue* was awarded the medal of the Commonwealth Club of San Francisco.

In 1944, Ella Winter went to Russia again, as a "roving" correspondent for the New York *Post.* She crossed the Atlantic "on top of dynamite" in a Norwegian freighter, part of a one-hundred-ship convoy that took four weeks to reach Egypt. For the next six months she traveled extensively in the Soviets. Out of her experiences came *I Saw the Russian People* (1945). "Absorbing as a novel, clear as a documentary film," according to Louise R. Miller in *Library Journal,* this book reveals the Russian "home" front. Lilian T. Mowrer, in the *Saturday Review of Literature,* considered the work 'an interesting companion piece to W. L. White's *Report on the Russians"* (1945). Miss Winter, writes Mrs. Mowrer, "notes many of the defects that so disturbed Mr. White, but over and above this understands and appreciates the indomitable spirit that sustains these people through their grim existence, and from which they draw a feeling of exaltation if not personal happiness."

In addition to her books on Russia, Miss Winter has translated from the German *The Diary and Letters of Otto Braun* (1924) and Kohler's *The Mentality of Apes* (1926). In 1936 she edited *Lincoln Steffens Speaking,* and two years later *The Letters of Lincoln Steffens.* She has also lectured extensively: in England on postwar conditions in Central Europe; and throughout the United States on social problems. In 1946 she was at work on a novel and a musical comedy.

According to a premarital agreement, the marriage of Ella Winter and Lincoln Steffens was terminated by divorce at the end of five years, in 1929. They remained, however, on friendly terms until Steffens' death in 1936. Three years later Miss Winter was married to Donald Ogden Stewart, the writer. The dark-eyed, dark-haired author enjoys such outdoor pursuits as tennis and walking. She is a member of the Authors League of America and of the 1917 Club of London.

References

Steffens, L. The Autobiography of Lincoln Steffens (1931); The Letters of Lincoln Steffens (1938)

WIRTZ, W(ILLIAM) WILLARD Mar. 14, 1912-　United States Government official
Address: b. Department of Labor Bldg., Washington, D.C.; h. 838 Locust St., Winnetka, Ill.

Early in 1946 a thirty-four-year-old assistant professor of law was assigned one of the reconversion tasks confronting the United States—that of guiding wage stabilization. W. Willard Wirtz, whose record on the War Labor Board qualified him for the position as chairman of the newly created National Wage Stabilization Board, inherited most of the problems of the outgoing body. Heading a tripartite group, he faced a period that posed a number of weighty and unforeseen situations, one of which resulted in a nation-wide strike.

Born in DeKalb, Illinois, on March 14, 1912, William Willard Wirtz is the son of William Wilbur and Alpha Belle (White) Wirtz. Reared in DeKalb with his brother and two sisters, young Wirtz attended the city's high school, participating in debates, dramatics, football, and basketball. From 1928 to 1930 he was a student at the Northern Illinois State Teachers College in his home town, and in 1930-31 he attended the University of California at Berkeley. He received his Bachelor of Arts degree with a major in sociology from Beloit College in Beloit, Wisconsin, in 1933. In Beloit he had continued his activities in forensics, winning various prizes for his achievements in argumentation. He was also a member of the dramatic group and the football team. Elected president of the student body, he also won academic honors, including membership in Phi Beta Kappa, Delta Sigma Rho, and Beta Theta Pi. From 1933 to 1934 the young man taught at the Kewanee (Illinois) High School, and in 1934 he entered Harvard Law School, where he became editor of the Harvard *Law Review*. After receiving his LL.B. in 1937 he was appointed an instructor in law at the University of Iowa. In 1939 he received an assistant professorship at the School of Law of Northwestern University.

It was Wirtz's appointment in 1942 as assistant general counsel to the Board of Economic Warfare that first prepared him for his later responsibility. This board was created in December 1941 to replace the Economic Defense Board. Under the leadership of Henry Wallace [40], the board's functions included the obtaining and distribution of supplies for the United States and her allies and keeping all supplies, whether needed in United States or not, from reaching the Axis. In 1942 Wirtz was appointed chairman of the appeals committee of the National War Labor Board. Set up in January 1942 to settle labor disputes which might interfere with the war effort and to "stabilize wages so far as practicable . . . on the basis which existed on September 15, 1942," this body had four members representing the public, four representing industry, and four representing labor (two from the American Federation of Labor and two from the Congress of Industrial Organizations) ; and it had regional counterparts. Once the national board had agreed to accept a case for decision, it might transfer the dispute to one of the regional boards. Either party could appeal to Washington, and it was the job of the appeals committee to recommend to the national board the action to be taken on the issues. The *Monthly Labor Review* reported that about one third of all the 1944 cases decided by the Regional Boards were appealed. In 1945 Wirtz was sent to Kansas City to "clear up a tangled situation." He accomplished his mission so ably that both labor and industry members protested his transfer to Washington in June as counsel to the WLB. In October, shortly before the WLB was terminated by executive order, Wirtz was **appointed a public member.**

At the end of World War II in 1945 the War Labor Board had announced that it would accept for decision only labor disputes in which both parties had agreed to accept the arbitration of the board. When this group was replaced by the National Wage Stabilization Board on January 1, 1946, all jurisdiction over labor disputes was removed. The organization of the new WSB was patterned after that of its predecessor, with twelve regional sub-boards and a tripartite nature (but each group in WSB had only two representatives and two alternates). Its duties were to make wage adjustments, including the approval of wage reductions, and to determine whether wage increases might be used as a basis for a request by the employer for higher prices. The board was also to act only in cases where agreements between the employer and the employee had already been reached. Wirtz, who had directed a similiar stabilization program for WLB, was chosen as a public member and chairman. At the time of its formation, WSB had eight to ten thousand cases of violations pending. Its national staff numbered seven to nine hundred persons. (WLB at its peak had a staff of twenty-six hundred).

In February President Truman announced a new wage-price policy. Matching as far as possible the estimated 33 per cent which Economic Stabilization Director John C. Collet [46] ruled had been the increase in the cost of living from January 1941 to September 1945, a general pattern for wage increases was to be established by the Wage Stabilization Board. In this pattern was to be considered, but not necessarily included, the increases allowed as the result of strikes in the automobile and other industries a few months before. Higher prices might be allowed by Paul Porter's [45] Price Control Board; but in considering requests for price increases, the PCB would recognize only wage increases approved by WSB. Under this ruling, a firm could give an "unapproved" raise (one not approved by WSB) but it could not point to this additional labor cost as an excuse for a price increase. "The Wage Stabilization Board," the *United States News* commented, "consequently had taken on an importance not foreseen when it was created." Having given the President factual data on the attitudes of labor and industry, Wirtz had played an important part in the formulation of the new wage-price policy. The chairman pointed out that "neither side got what it wanted and the consumer paid a big bill, but a certain balance was achieved."

The Wage Stabilization Board, in making decisions, rejected the idea that any "single pattern of increases" prevailed throughout all industry. In delivering an opinion on a case before the board, Wirtz pointed out that "these reconversion 'patterns' are not set by the Wage Stabilization Board. They are the definite patterns which developed during the August 1945-February 1946 period in private collective bargaining and through the awards and recommendations of arbitration and fact-finding panels." The price-control act was to expire on June 30 and with it, wage controls would also become defunct. Wirtz, in a release sent out by WSB,

W. WILLARD WIRTZ

presented his case for continued wage and price control. "It is the theory behind the proposed price amendments, apparently, that free prices will get full production and that full production will mean low prices. That theory disregards one basic factor. That factor is that American labor does not believe this theory and that it will probably reject an experiment which nearly destroyed it once in 1921 and again in 1930." He also declared, "Those disputes (arising in the six months before July 1946) were not labor's 'fault' and they were not industry's 'fault.' They were the inevitable consequence of the transition from a war period, characterized by patriotic sacrifice of special interests, to a period in which those self-interests have on 'both sides' re-emerged." In condemning "jack-in-the-box price amendments," he stated: "Labor cannot be expected to pay decontrolled prices with controlled wages."

With the return of price control at the end of July 1946, WSB faced more trouble. When the board refused to approve a wage increase for members of the Seafarers International Union (A.F. of L.) serving on ships operated by steamship companies for the Government because such a raise would be higher than one granted shortly before to members of the National Maritime Union (CIO) doing similar work, it precipitated a strike that tied up the nation's seaports. A contract for higher wages had already been negotiated between the companies and the union, subject to WSB's approval. The S.I.U. and the Sailors Union of the Pacific (also A.F. of L.), called a strike for September 5, 1946, declaring that they would not go back to work until WSB approved their wage demands. Despite the fact that the CIO unions did not cross A.F. of L. picket lines and asserted that they would demand the same increases that S.I.U. and S.U.P. received, WSB stood by its decision. Eight days after the strike began, John Steelman, Administra-

tor of the Office of Economic Stabilization, announced that Government agencies would be permitted to grant the same pay increase as that already absorbed by most of the private companies.

When wage and price controls were removed in November 1946, the Wage Stabilization Board still had a few functions assigned to it which postponed its termination. Under the War Labor Disputes Act, WSB had jurisdiction over changes in conditions of employment in plants in possession of the Government. The board was also supervising the work of two tripartite commissions who were planning the elimination of intra-plant wage rate inequities in the meat-packing and steel industries. Announcing that the staff of WSB had been considerably reduced, Wirtz expressed belief that the two remaining functions would be transferred to another agency to allow final liquidation of the wage board. The regional boards were given a January 15, 1947, deadline to settle all cases pending or to refer them to another Governmental agency.

Wirtz, who is a member of the American and Illinois bar associations, had hoped to resume his duties at Northwestern in the fall of 1946, but the pressure of work kept him at his desk with the Wage Stabilization Board. Married in September 1936 to Mary Jane Quisenberry, the tall, brown-haired official has one son, Richard Stanley. He is affiliated with no political organization. In Washington W. Willard Wirtz has gained a reputation for clear thinking and an ability to present facts without bias.

Reference

Who's Who in America, 1946-47

WITTE, EDWIN E(MIL) (wĭt'ē) Jan. 4, 1887- Economist; college professor; United States Governmental official

Address: b. c/o University of Wisconsin, Madison, Wis.; h. 1609 Madison St., Madison, Wis.

Serving during World War II as an active member of the National War Labor Board, "trouble shooter" Edwin E. Witte has been studying labor disputes for the past thirty-two years. Professor of economics at the University of Wisconsin since 1933, Witte has frequently been called upon to leave the classroom to solve practical problems, such as steering the formulation of the Social Security Act of 1935, and later, serving as chairman of the fact-finding board appointed to settle the packing-house workers' strike in 1946.

A native of Jefferson County, Wisconsin, Edwin Emil Witte was born January 4, 1887, the son of Emil and Anna (Yaeck) Witte. The farm boy "early formed the ambition to become a distinguished scholar," and upon his graduation from the Watertown High School entered the University of Wisconsin in 1905. He received the B.A. degree in 1909, winning as well membership in Phi Beta Kappa, Delta Sigma Rho, and Artus (an honorary scholastic economics fraternity), and immediately began his graduate work. In June 1912 he interrupted his studies to assume the position of senior statistician to the Wisconsin Industrial Commission. Shortly afterward young Witte became secretary to Congressman John M. Nelson, and in 1914 special investigator of the United States Commission on Industrial Relations. The following year he returned to the university as instructor, and completed the work toward his doctorate in 1916. The Wisconsin Industrial Commission again called for his services, and from 1917 to 1922 he served on its staff as secretary. It was in 1920 that he began part-time lecturing on economics and related social sciences at his alma mater.

Although lacking the technical training of the librarian, in 1922 Witte was placed in charge of the Wisconsin Legislative Reference Library, the pioneer in the field of legislative reference. He remained there for eleven years. During this period he served as secretary of the Wisconsin Committee on a Retirement System for State Employees (1929-31); and he began the writing of his numerous articles for legal and other periodicals, mainly on the subjects of trade union law, social insurance, and labor legislation. In 1932 his treatise *The Government in Labor Disputes* appeared; said to be the first book which covered the entire field, it dealt with every aspect of Governmental intervention in labor disputes and the social, economic, and legal phases of industrial troubles. It was during his librarianship, too, that Witte made an intensive study of the use and effect of injunctions in labor disputes. This report was in part responsible for the passage of the Norris-La Guardia '40 Anti-Injunction Act in 1932, which ruled that "yellow-dog" contracts were not enforceable in the Federal courts and limited the power of those courts to issue injunctions in labor disputes.

Then, while a member of the Wisconsin Interim Commission on Taxation (1933-34), the economist was appointed full professor at the university to teach courses not only in economics, but in political science, sociology, and law. His favorite subject is the relations of Government to business. Although Witte prefers to teach, he likes to feel, he says, that he has a "part in solving practical problems and shaping practical developments." Thus time and again he has left the university and served the Government as mediator and arbitrator, administrator, and member of a considerable number of advisory and policy-making boards. "In finding workable solutions of labor difficulties and in advising and assisting public officials with concrete problems in my fields of competence," Witte has written, "I am interested above all else in trying to help employers and employees to get along with each other in this day and age of organization and collective bargaining and to . . . minimize the conflicts between Government and business."

Witte considers his most important work his part in the formulation of the Federal Social Security Act of 1935, of which he is often called the author. After more than twenty years had elapsed since the first proposal for compulsory unemployment insurance had been made, on June 29, 1934, President Roosevelt created the Committee on Economic Security to study and report to him on methods of carrying

Harris & Ewing

EDWIN E. WITTE

out the Administration's plans for "the security of the men, women, and children of the nation." Witte was named secretary and executive director of the committee, of which other members were Secretary of Labor Perkins '40, Secretary of the Treasury Morgenthau '40, Attorney-General Cummings, Secretary of Agriculture Wallace '40, and Federal Emergency Relief Administrator Hopkins '41. The following January, President Roosevelt forwarded the committee's full report to Congress, which on August 14, 1935, finally passed a bill known as the Social Security Act of 1935, to provide for old-age insurance and unemployment compensation, as well as health, welfare, and rehabilitation services to the States.

The economist's next Washington posts were as staff member of the President's Committee on Administration Management (1936-37), and then as member of the United States Social Security Advisory Council (1937-38). Witte was meanwhile serving in his home State on the Wisconsin State Planning Board (1935-38), the Wisconsin Citizens' Committee on Public Welfare (1936-37), and on the Wisconsin Labor Relations Board (1937-39). In addition to these activities and his teaching duties, Witte completed the writing of *The Preparation of Proposed Legislative Measures by Administrative Departments* (1937).

In 1941 Witte accepted membership on the Federal Advisory Council for Unemployment Security and also became special agent of the National Defense Mediation Board. The National War Labor Board named the Professor chairman of the Regional War Labor Board for Detroit in January 1943. The knotty problems of the biggest war plants in the nation came under Witte's jurisdiction here, until his appointment as public member of the National War Labor Board (1944-45). In January 1946 Witte was appointed by Labor Secretary

WITTE, EDWIN E.—*Continued*

Schwellenbach[45] to head a three-man fact-finding panel to hasten settlement of the dispute of the two hundred and fifty thousand striking employees of the meat-packing companies, during which the nation's output was reduced about 75 per cent. Calling the industry "a low-wage industry in which the straight-time hourly wage rates are substantially below the average for all manufacturing industries," the board on February 7 recommended a 16-cent hourly increase for the workers. Back at the Wisconsin university, after devoting the war years to the adjustment of labor disputes, Witte in 1946 was working on a comprehensive history of social security in the United States, as well as on textbooks on social insurance and on the relations of Government and business.

The specialist in labor relations has long been a member of the Council of the American Economics Association, the Council of the American Association for Labor Legislation, and of the American Association for Social Security. In September 1916 Witte was married to Florence E. Rimsnider; the couple have a son and two daughters. Of average height, Witte weighs 180 pounds, and his black hair is thinning. He lists his religion as Methodist, and his favorite hobby as gardening. Witte gives the credit for his concepts in the labor field to his college teachers and to the contacts and experiences of his Government assignments. He belongs to no political party and seldom casts a straight party vote: "I have had appointments from politicians of all political faiths and have gotten along well with them," he has said of himself. "In my entire life I have never been an applicant for any job and have turned down most of the jobs offered me. . . .I am a hard-working man, but not a flashy or brilliant fellow."

References

Library J 58:491 Je 1 '33 por
Who's Who in America, 1946-47

WOODS, MARK Dec. 27, 1901- Radio executive

Address: b. c/o American Broadcasting Company, 30 Rockefeller Plaza, New York; h. Forest Dr., Short Hills, N.J.

Mark Woods, president of the American Broadcasting Company, in 1946 could claim the distinction of having been active in the broadcasting industry for approximately half his life. It was in 1922, when the industry was newborn and he had just come of age, that the American Telephone and Telegraph Company established a radio department and called upon him to set up its accounting system. He has thus had a part in developing many of the industry's important policies.

Mark Woods was born in Louisville, Kentucky, on December 27, 1901, to Michael and Johanna (Schroder) Woods. His school days were lived in Jacksonville, Florida, where he also acquired his first schooling in business during summer vacations as a clerk, assisting his father, who was custodian of the American

Naval Stores Company. In Florida the boy gained a knowledge of other things nautical, such as fishing, swimming, and sailing. At the outbreak of World War I he tried to enter the Navy, but was rejected because of his youth. He then found work in a Florida shipyard, as foreman of a pneumatic tool crew. A year later he became employment manager of the construction firm, which built concrete freighters for war service. According to *Who's Who in America,* Woods also worked in the personnel department of A. Wilson and Company in 1917-18. However, the young man was determined to go to sea, although he was not yet seventeen years old. As a member of the United States Naval Reserve he succeeded in joining the crew of a United States Shipping Board vessel. There he went through the experience of a near-shipwreck when his ship's engine and radio apparatus broke down, and the craft floated around the North Atlantic for twenty-six days before it was rescued. It has been said that this is the only time during his life that the radio pioneer has been adrift—his career has been outstanding for "purpose, perception, and plugging."

After the war, young Woods went north and became superintendent of machine tools at F. W. King and Company in 1918-19. Deciding he preferred a business career, in the latter year the Southerner got a job with the Thomas A. Edison Company in West Orange, New Jersey, as a salesman, later becoming a shipping clerk and bookkeeper. After a transfer, from 1920 to 1922 he was a bookkeeper, contract clerk, and finally methods man in the New York Telephone Company's revenue accounting division, and in 1922-26 he was successively accountant, office manager, and bookkeeping supervisor at the American Telephone and Telegraph Company. During this period he was studying at the Walton School of Accounting (1922-24), the New York Telephone Company Accounting School (1922-26), and taking extension courses at New York University (1922-28).

The A. T. & T. then owned Radio Station WEAF, and Woods established many of the early commercial policies of network broadcasting. By 1926 he was assistant treasurer, assistant secretary, and office manager of the Broadcasting Company of America, an A. T. & T. subsidiary set up to operate WEAF. Then, on November 1 of that year the broadcasting operations of A. T. & T. were taken over by the National Broadcasting Company, and Woods became treasurer in charge of finances while continuing in his other positions with the organization. In 1934 he became assistant executive vice-president and administrative officer of NBC, and two years later was made vice-president and treasurer.

In all this work, as well as in his task of establishing many of the branch offices for NBC, Woods was concerned with the necessity for maintaining a balance between the entertainment and business departments of the industry. His success is described as notable, not only in the solution of many of these problems, but in negotiations with labor unions, which were among his other assignments at NBC. He is reputed to be fair in his dealings, and the unions are said to have respect for his ability.

In May 1941 the Federal Communications Commission issued an antimonopoly regulation ordering NBC to dispose of one of its two networks, the Blue and the Red. NBC itself was a Radio Corporation of America subsidiary, and in January 1942 NBC-Blue also became a separate, wholly-owned RCA subsidiary, comprising stations WJZ in New York, WENR in Chicago, and KGO in San Francisco, while it continued to furnish program service on a contract basis to nearly two hundred independently owned but affiliated radio stations throughout the country. Woods, who was elected president of the new Blue network organization, stated: "The formation of a separate company comes at a time when radio is playing a vital role in the life of our country at war. The heavy responsibilities which rest today upon all broadcasters provide the highest incentive to the management and personnel of the Blue network to maintain and, if possible, to improve the standard of public service which has endeared this network to the radio listeners of America."

Early in the following month Woods provided evidence of his interpretation of this policy, when he acknowledged that censorship had been applied to the broadcasts of two popular and commercially-sponsored commentators— Walter Winchell and Drew Pearson. He explained that the rules adopted by the National Association of Broadcasters forbade discussion of controversial subjects on commercial programs, so that a financially stronger party to a dispute could not acquire more time on the air than the party who could not afford it. Thus Woods became involved in one of the most controversial issues in broadcasting—that of freedom of speech on the air. Although the Blue network has been the target of criticism for such action, the New York *Times* has pointed out that "it carries more commentators engaged in sundry controversies than any other network," and that "it is no secret in the radio industry that one chain flatly refused to carry, censored or otherwise, one of the Blue's present commentators." The newspaper also quoted a statement of Woods, that "preservation of the freedom of the air can be achieved only through broadcasting a full amount of criticism that is completely fair. It is through protection of that freedom that commentator, network, and listener can insure the larger liberties for which the nation as a whole is fighting." Woods also stressed the fact that, in national political campaigns, it is a FCC rule that both parties receive equal time, and that this rule has also come to apply to other subjects of major national concern.

After a year of independent operation the Blue ceased to be a stepchild and showed its first profits. Then, in July 1943, the network was purchased by Edward J. Noble '44 for eight million dollars, and the FCC granted him the authority to change the name to the American Broadcasting Company. Since the network thus lost the right to participate in the RCA-NBC work, it was faced with the necessity of developing its own experimental work in television and frequency modulation. Woods, as

MARK WOODS

president and later part-owner of the new organization, therefore became especially concerned with these problems. Another problem of the new network (Woods this brought out when he appeared before the Federal Communications Commission in April 1946) was the paucity of clear channels available to ABC; Woods urged that some of the channels—especially those used by CBS and NBC in rural areas—be reallocated to ABC and to Mutual. *Variety* pointed out that he thinks that the major networks will have to carry the experimental load for three or four years, and that it will not be until 1949 or 1950 that commercial television is a reality, because of the time required to get some fifteen million television receiving sets into the homes of the United States. The article continued, "Woods has some interesting thoughts on the future of motion pictures in television. Travelogues, newsreels and cartoons are particularly appealing. Also, there are many feature films which the public hasn't seen or would like to re-review in the leisure of their homes."

For his "enterprising leadership in network broadcasting and outstanding contribution to the welfare of the American public," Woods received the 1944 citation of merit awarded by the Poor Richard Club, one of the oldest advertising clubs in the United States. The executive is a director of the National Better Business Bureau, of the Council for Democracy, and of the United Service Organization Camp Shows; he is a member of the Masonic order and of the United States Junior Naval Reserve Force. His church affiliation is Presbyterian, and in politics he is Republican. His clubs include the Baltusrol Golf, Pine Valley Golf, Madison Square Garden, Wings, Metropolitan, Rockefeller Center Luncheon, and the Circus Saints and Sinners. Mrs. Woods is the former Edythe Carolyn Dittrich, to whom he was married in June 1926; and their children

WOODS, MARK—*Continued*

are Patricia Walton and Albert Edward. Woods is five feet eight inches tall, weighs one hundred and sixty-four pounds, and has blue eyes and straight light hair and a mustache. Golf is his chief recreation, although he continues to enjoy the water sports of his boyhood.

References

Who's Who in America, 1946-47
Who's Who in Commerce and Industry, 1940-41

WRIGHT, ORVILLE Aug. 19, 1871- Inventor

Address: b. Wright Aeronautical Laboratory, 15 N. Broadway, Dayton, Ohio; h. Park & Harmon Aves., Dayton, Ohio

Pioneer and, in many ways, guiding genius of an industry which grew from two young inventors' dream into an accepted scientific reality of unlimited scope in less than forty years is Orville Wright. Together with his brother Wilbur he invented the first practical airplane and, what is not so well known, worked out the basic laws of aerodynamics and invented many of the aeronautical devices which have made the subsequent strides in aviation possible.

Orville Wright was born in Dayton, Ohio, on August 19, 1871, a descendant of Puritan English, Dutch, and German-Swiss pioneers. His father, the Reverend Milton Wright, of the United Brethren in Christ, was keenly interested in science as well as in art, possessed a library of about two thousand volumes, and invented a crude typewriter. Orville Wright's mother was Virginia-born Susan Catherine (Koerner) Wright, the daughter of a German immigrant wagonmaker. One of the few college women of her day, she excelled in mathematics, and she shared her husband's interest in the little-known field of mechanics. She not only helped her four boys when they made their own playthings, but herself constructed some; and she encouraged Orville's use of her kitchen as a laboratory for experiments. (Mrs. Wright died when her son Orville was eighteen, after which the boys' sister Katharine became the family's housekeeper.)

The calling of Milton Wright, who became a bishop when Orville was six, made it necessary for the family to move frequently, and the boy therefore attended public schools in Cedar Rapids (Iowa), Richmond (Indiana), and Dayton. With Wilbur, his elder by four years, he earned spending money by collecting bones and junk and selling their homemade toys to playmates. Orville's exceptionally close "partnership" with Wilbur and younger Katharine was to continue until their deaths.

The first major device which the Wright brothers built was a practical eight-foot turning lathe, powered by a foot treadle and made entirely of wood and scrap. At sixteen the schoolboy worked on Saturdays folding copies of the religious weekly which his father and a brother managed. Following Wilbur's design he again ransacked the woodpile and the junk heap to build a treadle-operated folding machine which enabled one boy to fold as many papers as four or five boys could do by hand.

Orville spent two summers working sixty hours a week in a Dayton printing establishment. In 1888, when the youngest Wright boy was sixteen or seventeen, he and his brother built in a few months a large printing press which turned out up to fifteen hundred copies an hour, considerably more than the presses then in use could produce. Seventeen-year-old Orville then rented business space and in March 1889 published the first copy of a four-page weekly, the *West Side News,* which soon became fairly profitable. "Not [an] ordinary neighborhood sheet," wrote Mark Sullivan, the paper included intellectual abstractions and articles on machines. At about this time Orville Wright, who had had several years of high school education, continued to attend an hour or so each day for another year as a special student in Latin, but was never graduated. (He and Wilbur were the only members of the family who did not go to college.) In April 1890 Wilbur Wright joined Orville in plans to convert the *West Side News* into the daily *Evening Item.* This was discontinued after four months, and, apart from a two-page weekly of opinion called *Snapshots,* which they issued in 1894, the brothers confined their presses to more profitable job printing.

A bicyclist who won occasional prizes in YMCA races, Orville Wright, with his brother, had opened a bicycle salesroom and repair shop in December 1892, and in a few years they sold their printing plant. The shop prospered, was moved several times to larger quarters, and in 1895 the Wrights began assembling their own bicycles out of purchased parts, with a few improvements of their own—including a coaster brake and a wheel hub which had a reserve set of bearings. They made three models, one unusually low-priced, and sold several hundred locally. The brothers made all their own tools, to save expense and to make sure the tools would be perfectly dependable. In 1895 Orville made a new kind of calculating machine which not only added but multiplied, and he also worked on a simplified typewriter.

The Wright brothers had followed the gliding experiments of Otto Lilienthal with interest, and became so absorbed in discussing the cause of his accidental death in 1896 that they wrote to the Smithsonian Institution for a bibliography on flying and read the five volumes and the pamphlets which constituted the meager literature in the field. Impatient at "the wasteful extravagance of mounting delicate and costly machinery on wings which no one knew how to manage," they were drawn to sailing through the air on fixed wings, using the wind itself, rather than an engine for motive power. The period between 1885 and 1900 was one of much activity in aeronautics, but the efforts of eminent scientists in various parts of the world had ended in failure or "utter disrepute." Wilbur and Orville Wright concluded that the reason the experimenters had failed was that they had attacked the problem of balance incorrectly. Instead of trying to design a machine so that it could right itself when its balance was disturbed, why not have it as inert as possible, and let the operator balance it? After three years of study Orville suggested that the operator could vary the angles of the wing tips to restore balance. This idea became the basic claim of the original Wright patent, and is now incorporated in the aileron controls of every plane. The balance was effected by twisting or warping the wings, a method proposed by Wilbur, which is now obsolete.

This is one of the few occasions in the Wright brothers' work for which credit can be given to a particular one. As Archibald Henderson wrote in *Contemporary Immortals,* "never before in the history of the world have two individuals so completely merged themselves into one thinking organism for the achievement of an epochal invention." In their frequent differences of opinion, they impressed observers as "one man making up his mind." Sometimes each converted the other to his viewpoint and the argument went on with changed sides, after which (to quote General B. D. Foulois), they would "pick up the ends and parts and reassociate them as though there had been no difference of opinion whatever. Both knew instinctively what parts contributed to gaining their ultimate end." (Even when offered a drink or a smoke, either brother would refuse for both.)

The Wrights' first laboratory camping trip to the North Carolina sand-bar village of Kitty Hawk in 1900 showed them that their wing-warping was better than any earlier method of balancing, and that their operable front rudder or elevator successfully directed the glider up and down. But this experience and that of the next year's trial forced them to the conclusion that all the accepted aerodynamic data were useless: "Truth and error were everywhere so intimately mixed as to be undistinguishable." The task of working out correct tables of air pressure and drift was one for trained mathematicians and physicists—not for bicycle mechanics who had to run a business. That they did not abandon their attempts was due largely to encouragement by Octave Chanute, the glider experimenter who had written *Progress in Flying Machines,* and with whom they had been corresponding since May 1900. Wilbur Wright's September 1901 speech before the Western Society of Engineers, at President Chanute's invitation, made aviation history, for in it he made the first revelation of serious errors in the best air-pressure figures obtainable. Orville persuaded him to soften the printed version of his speech—but even the modified version was widely reprinted, quoted, and discussed.

To make sure of his brother's ground, Orville took an eighteen-inch starch box, put in a hastily constructed apparatus on the order of a weather vane, and through a glass top proceeded to measure the angles to the wind at which a curved surface and a plane surface produced equal pressures. This, the first wind tunnel, was soon replaced by a larger and more exact one, built of materials they already had. With this equipment, the brothers tested more than two hundred types of wing surfaces in late 1901. In those two months the amateur physicists had compiled the data necessary for me-

James N. Keen
Courtesy Aviation News

ORVILLE WRIGHT

chanical flight. "Even today," wrote Fred C. Kelly in 1943, "the refinements obtained over the Wrights' figures for the same shapes of surfaces are surprisingly small." To overcome tailspins, Orville Wright suggested, on their 1902 vacation, that the vertical tail be made movable, a principle generally used today. This suggestion was incorporated in the March 1903 application for the patent they received in May 1906.

One observer reported of the Wrights' self-instruction in flying: "In case of accident a round ball . . . of hands, arms, and legs . . . would roll neatly along the ground, and when it stopped Orville Wright would stand up, scratched and bruised, but always calm, dignified, and unemotional." Now, in 1903, the Wrights had worked out on paper exactly how much power would be needed to lift their plane into the air and how much weight could be carried. The engine they finally constructed is considered a great advancement in mechanical engineering. The Wrights had planned to use the formulas for marine propellers and adapt them to air conditions; but they discovered that, although ships had been propeller-driven for sixty-five years, there were no theoretical calculations to guide designers and all were worked out by trial and error. The brothers' one point of pride was said to be their mastery of this complex problem and the development of the first formulas for propellers. Their first airscrew, designed and built in a few months, was about one-third more efficient than the best propellers then in use.

On December 17, 1903, just nine days after Professor Langley's much publicized plane had failed, thirty-two-year-old Orville Wright made the first self-powered machine flight in history, against a twenty-seven-mile wind. To achieve this flight the inventors had spent a total of

WRIGHT, ORVILLE—*Continued*

about a thousand dollars, inclusive of their railroad fares.

Now they began to think of the airplane in terms of usefulness and resolved to devote more time to their experiments. They completed the unfinished bicycles in their shop but made no more, turned most of the management of their shop over to their chief mechanic, obtained the use of a cow pasture eight miles from Dayton for flying practice, and began intensive experimentation with new planes and new engines. Soon they devised the first catapult for launching from their monorail track.

By 1905 the Wright plane had been brought to the point where the inventors could offer it to the United States War Department. That Department showed no interest, but the British and French Governments did, the latter opening negotiations with the Wrights. While the flying machine met with disbelief or indifference in the United States, Europe became interested through the "missionary work" of Octave Chanute, and imitators began to appear. In mid-1907 Orville joined Wilbur Wright in Paris for fruitless negotiations with the French Government, and on their return the Wrights submitted a bid to the Signal Corps, which had drawn up specifications for a plane to carry two men for one hour, fly at an average of forty miles an hour for ten miles, carry fuel enough for 125 miles, and be demountable. The New York *Globe* expressed general opinion when it cast editorial doubt upon the "possibility that such an airship is within measurable distance of perfection." The Wrights' $25,000 bid to the Signal Corps was accepted in February 1908, and three weeks later they sold the French rights for cash, a block of stock, and royalties.

In September 1908, while his brother was in France, Orville Wright began the official Army tests of the Wright machine—and several "hard-boiled" newspapermen wept with emotion at witnessing the miracle. The thirteenth flight ended in a crash; the passenger, Lieutenant Selfridge, was fatally injured, and Wright broke a leg and several ribs. As a result of his injuries he developed a permanent slight limp and later severe neuritis, which made any vibration extremely painful and forced him after 1918 to give up flying.

After a seven-week convalescence Orville and Katharine Wright joined Wilbur in Europe, where they were received with homage and where they closed a contract for the German Wright Company. (Orville went back later that year to teach its first pilots). To the honors and acclaim of the Continent those of the United States were added on their return in 1909, including presentation of medals by President Taft at the White House. Orville finished the Army tests successfully in July 1909, and in November the Wright Company was incorporated, the brothers receiving stock, cash, and 10 per cent royalties. The younger Wright then began to train contract pilots in Dayton for exhibitions, forming the first Wright Exhibition Team in June 1910, after a month's arduous training. Every plane which took part in any exhibition was either owned or licensed by the Wright Company. According to Orville's secretary, who formerly worked in the Exhibition Department, that branch brought in "something like a hundred thousand dollars a year," which included trophies and prizes. The Wrights never sold airplane rides, although wealthy persons frequently offered large sums to fly with them for a few minutes. Orville continued, however to give flying lessons until 1915.

Orville Wright also supervised engineering at the Wright factories, and personally tested every new device used on the planes. After Wilbur's death from typhoid fever in 1912, Orville became president of the Wright Company and took up work in the successful patent suit against Glenn H. Curtiss and others, won in January 1914. He was also board chairman of the British Wright Company, formed in 1913. Later in 1914, as a preliminary to freeing himself for research, Orville Wright bought out all except one of the Wright Company stockholders and in October 1915 sold his entire interest in the company for an unannounced sum exceeding five hundred thousand dollars. After this he became a consulting engineer, did laboratory research, and for a short time was connected with the Wright Martin Company.

When the United States entered World War I, forty-five-year-old Orville Wright was commissioned a major in the Signal Corps Aviation Service and was consulted on many technical problems which arose at near-by McCook Field. In 1920-21 the pioneer airman developed the split wing flap, patented in 1924, which was much used in World War II dive bombers. Since 1916 he has kept regular working hours in his aeronautical laboratory, performing unpublicized experiments and perfecting various devices. Wright's shyness has declined with the years to the point where he often accepts invitations to public functions, at which he is recognized as "Dayton's leading citizen."

For many years bachelor Orville Wright has lived alone with two servants, having survived the other members of his family. Everywhere in his home and his summer camp in Canada one finds what he calls "some crazy contrivance" which he has never bothered to patent: self-opening doors and movable roofs in Canada, a simple automatic record-changer which preceded any on the market. At Kitty Hawk he devised a practical toaster; he once constructed a nine-key adding machine which did all the work of more complex calculators. During the thirties Wright designed for his manufacturer brother Lorin a line of mechanical toys "amazing for their simplicity as well as for their ingenuity." His horn-rimmed reading glasses have a frame, designed by their wearer, which requires only one temple piece; his reading chair is permanently tilted at his favorite angle. Wright has served on several aeronautical committees and in organization posts, and is chairman of the advisory committee to the Daniel Guggenheim School of Aeronautics of New York University. He is a member of seven professional societies and an honorary member of dozens throughout the world.

Scores of honors have been heaped upon Wright by Governments, universities, and other bodies; and he has seen many memorials erected to him and his brother, including the national park at Kitty Hawk. Yet it was not until September 1942, thirty-nine years after his first power flight, that full credit for designing the first practical airplane was granted the Wright brothers by the Smithsonian Institution, which then retracted its previous claim that Secretary Langley's 1903 machine was capable of flight. So long and tenaciously had the institution held to that faulty claim, however, that the impression had become general that the Wright brothers' plane was only a final development based on earlier experiments of others, as is true of most successful modern inventions. Authorities agree, however, that Wilbur and Orville Wright owe only the biplane form to their predecessors, all of whom worked on erroneous theories.

At seventy-two, white-haired, mustached Orville Wright was described as "a little stouter but . . . still in excellent physical condition . . . his gray-blue eyes sparkle as he discusses aeronautical theories or research in which he is presently engaged." He keeps himself informed on foreign and domestic affairs, and discussed the international situation in a seventy-fifth birthday interview with a Dayton *Daily News* reporter in August 1946. At that time he expressed his social views: "I am not a Communist and I have never cast a vote for socialism, but I do believe there are some good things in socialism which should be given serious consideration." He asserted that "the average price of an article sold in the open market is five times what was paid to the workman who produced it. . . .This is mostly due to unrestricted competition which . . . has become the most serious defect in our national economy. This condition must be corrected." Sixteen years earlier another interviewer had mentioned that Orville Wright was "not sure it's quite decent" to live, as he does, on the income from securities.

References

Coronet 20:120-27 Ag '46 por
Harper 1073:473-84 O '39
New Yorker 6:29-32 D 13 '30 por
World's Work 20:3303-15 Ag '10 pors; 56:52-7 S '28 pors
Charnley, M. V. The Boys' Life of the Wright Brothers (1928)
Fraser, C. C. Famous American Flyers (1941)
Kelly, F. C. The Wright Brothers (1943)
McMahon, J. R. The Wright Brothers, Pioneers of Flight (1928)
Who's Who in America, 1946-47

WURSTER, WILLIAM WILSON (wŭr'-stēr) Oct. 20, 1895- Architect; university dean

Address: b. c/o Massachusetts Institute of Technology, Cambridge, Mass.; Wurster, Bernardi, and Emmons, 402 Jackson St., San Francisco, Calif.; h. 14 Farwell Pl., Cambridge, Mass.

William Wilson Wurster, whom *Architectural Forum* has called "the founder of a school of regional architecture which is easily the best the contemporary movement in this country has produced to date," succeeded Walter McCornack as dean of the School of Architecture and Planning at the Massachusetts Institute of Technology in 1944. Under Wurster's guidance, the country's oldest architectural school has inaugurated an experimental housing program which will eventually cover ten acres along the Charles River, provide homes for veteran students, and act as a proving ground for architectural innovations.

William Wilson Wurster was born in Stockton, California, on October 20, 1895, to Frederick W. Wurster and Maine-bred Maude (Wilson) Wurster, who was the daughter of a Civil War veteran. Wurster's paternal grandfather, a German immigrant, came to California over the Isthmus of Panama and his grandmother around Cape Horn. Wurster attended the grade schools in Stockton, often being taught by the same teachers his parents had had. In 1913 he was graduated from Stockton High School. His parents believed in encouraging their child's natural inclinations, so that his interest in construction was fostered by family walks every Sunday. (Between 1900 and 1913, there was a great deal of building to be observed in Stockton since the town was doubling in size.) On bank holidays, Wurster's father, a bank employee, spent half the day showing his son how a small city works by taking him to the city and county offices and to various other enterprises, such as the newspaper plant, the iron works, the harvester works, and the planing mill. During school vacations, Wurster worked as an office boy for E. B. Brown, an architect with advanced ideas, who designed buildings adapted to the climate and which therefore seemed indigenously Californian.

Immediately after his graduation from high school at the age of seventeen, Wurster entered the University of California, where he studied under John Galen Howard, a former pupil of architect Henry Hobson Richardson (the creator of Richardson Romanesque). After a year and a half, Wurster's studies were interrupted by a serious illness, and it was necessary for him to spend the following year working out of doors for a surveyor in order to regain his health. At the outbreak of World War I, Wurster, then finishing his third year at the university, attempted to join the Navy, but was rejected. Consequently he decided to study naval architecture and marine engineering, and, on completion of the course, shipped to sea as an engineer. His transPacific trips made him familiar with Hawaii and the Philippines. Returning to California in 1919, he was able to complete his senior year and was graduated with honors. While in college he had been elected to Tau Beta Phi, an honorary engineering society.

In 1920 Wurster joined the staff of the architectural firm of John Reid, Jr., who was

WILLIAM WILSON WURSTER

at that time designing a group of buildings for the San Francisco school system. This experience was followed by two years of work in Sacramento under the direction of Charles Dean, architect, and Charles Gilman Hyde, sanitary engineer, in the office of the filtration division of the city. While in Sacramento, Wurster was assigned drawing, specification writing, and field inspection. The latter task required close collaboration between architects and engineers. Wurster's license to practice architecture in the State of California was granted in 1922.

At twenty-six the architect, with three years of varied experience behind him, was financially able to fulfill a desire to see the East Coast and Europe. He traveled for a year, studying architecture in France, Italy, and Spain. During 1923 and 1924, Wurster was employed in the New York offices of Delano and Aldrich, where William Adams Delano took an interest in his work and helped to formulate his maturing philosophy. Later Wurster was to express his credo in this manner: "I believe things should be done from the positive side, never doing so-called modern merely to be against what has been, keeping the tempo sympathetic with the life and with the size and expenditure." Over week ends, he visited Washington, Baltimore, Philadelphia, New Haven, and Boston, so that he might study Eastern regional architecture.

Wurster returned to California in 1924 to design a filtration plant for the East Bay Water Company. When this commission was completed in 1926, he opened his own office in San Francisco. At first work came in slowly, and it was only in 1934 that there were commissions enough to employ three draftsmen. *Architectural Forum* quoted him as saying that his staff that he ran his office as a group of teams composed "of a junior and a senior draftsman. . . .I always tried to have one or

both of this team present at every conference with a client."

Between 1926 and 1934 Wurster worked on from fifty to eighty small houses a year, several notable country houses (some were constructed of redwood and were equipped with ramps instead of stairs), and the development of the Pasatiempo Country Club estates near Santa Cruz. He was awarded a number of prizes in the *House Beautiful* annual competitions and honorable mentions in the northern California exhibitions of the American Institute of Architects. In 1937 Wurster went to Europe to study modern English housing projects and the work of outstanding Scandinavian architects. In Finland he visited Alvar Aalto and formed a friendship which was renewed when Aalto came to California in 1939. From Helsinki, Wurster went to Germany to study the Frankfurt housing projects and thence to the Paris Exposition.

Wurster claims that he has been encouraged by the "liberal attitude towards architecture in the San Francisco region." This stress upon regionalism and indigenous design is evident in the Yerba Buena Club (built for the San Francisco Fair, 1939), the Valencia Gardens housing project (in association with Harry Thomson, Jr., 1939), and the girls' dormitory at the University of California (in association with Corbett and MacMurray). In 1941 Wurster planned housing for defense workers, including the Carquinez Heights project at Vallejo, and the Parker Houses at Sacramento, California. (*Time* called the Vallejo project "hivelike" and an "eyesore", to which Wurster replied that "standardized, prefabricated houses on a bare piece of ground cannot and should not look like a country club suburb.") In that same year (1941), Wurster designed a country office building for the Shuckl Company. After the completion of the housing projects—in all, five thousand houses—Wurster was able to devote his time to postwar architectural problems and to research on urbanism and planning. Harvard University invited him to carry on his research as a fellow in the Graduate School of Design, where he studied under John Gaus, Alvin Hansen, and Joseph Hudnut, dean of the faculty of design. Except for a thesis, that study, together with a course Wurster took at M.I.T., completed the work necessary for a Harvard doctorate in regional planning. To broaden his knowledge, Wurster then accepted the position of coordinator of design in the Architectural School at Yale University for a term.

The architect was appointed dean of the School of Architecture and Planning at the Massachusetts Institute of Technology on July 1, 1944. During the fall of 1946, authorities at the institute announced that they planned to build one hundred prefabricated houses for married veteran students and their families. This will constitute what M.I.T. experts describe "as the largest educationally sponsored housing research laboratory in the United States." Dean Wurster has remarked, "There is no telling where our initial housing effort in behalf of war veterans may lead us." He pointed out also that the nation needed more information about prefabricated housing than the building industry could provide. In the

M.I.T. project, he added, "research will be conducted in single phases of housing needs such as insulation, solar radiation, radiant heating, air conditioning, and the uses of structural and decorative glass."

Appraising Wurster's work, an article in *Pencil Points* once stated, "The quality of humble materials used straightforwardly is something that Wurster recognizes more than most architects. Time and again he brings out the beauty that others have passed over and does it so naturally that one is set to wondering why it hasn't been done before." Wurster himself has said, "I like to work on direct, honest solutions avoiding exotic materials, using indigenous things so that there is no affectation and the best is obtained for the money."

In 1940 Wurster was married to Catherine Bauer, author of *Modern Housing* and *A Citizen's Guide to Housing*, who was at that time Rosenberg lecturer at the University of California, and in 1946 the teacher of a seminar on housing at Harvard University. They have one child, Sarah Louise. The architect is two inches over six feet tall, has brown eyes and hair. Since becoming dean at M.I.T., Wurster frequently goes to San Francisco, where he is an active member of the firm of Wurster, Bernardi, and Emmons. In politics he is a liberal.

Reference

Who's Who in America, 1946-47

WYATT, WILSON W(ATKINS) (wī'ăt)
Nov. 21, 1905- Lawyer; former United States Government official

Address: b. c/o Wyatt & Grafton, 312 S. 4th St., Louisville, Ky.; h. Alta Vista Rd., Louisville, Ky.

Wilson W. Wyatt was appointed National Housing Administrator by President Truman in December 1945, to solve the critical housing shortage, which had its genesis in the twenties, was aggravated by the depression of the thirties, and became acute during the wartime years of the forties. Despite Wyatt's comparative youth (he was forty at the time) and his newness in public office, he had in one brief term as the mayor of Louisville established himself as "certainly one of the three or four most important political figures to emerge in American political life in the last few years." His record of civic reform had won applause from such dissimilar publications as *Fortune* and the *New Republic*.

Born in Louisville, Kentucky, on November 21, 1905, the son of Richard H. and Mary (Watkins) Wyatt was given the alliterative name of Wilson Watkins. Although his father urged him to become a dentist, Wilson held to his decision to take up the law. He would have liked to attend Harvard, but could afford only one year at the University of Louisville, in 1922-23. He then left day school and got a job as a clerk for a shipper's bureau. This was followed by a better position with the Louisville and Nashville Railroad, which employed him at $180 a month. After work Wyatt attended night classes at the Jefferson School of Law, and in 1927 he received his LL.B., as

valedictorian. (He had also been valedictorian of his class when he was graduated from Louisville's Male High School at the age of sixteen.) Admittted to the bar, he began practice in Louisville with the firm of Garnett and Van Winkle.

As first president of the Young Democratic Club of Louisville and Jefferson County, Wyatt began to take an active role in politics. In the 1928 campaign, he marched with Al Smith and Senator Alben Barkley, thereby incurring the wrath of his future mother-in-law, who was a prohibitionist; in 1932, he campaigned for Franklin Roosevelt and in 1934 managed Emmett O'Neal's successful campaign for election to the House of Representatives. Wyatt joined the Jefferson School faculty in 1929, teaching there until 1935. (In June 1930 the twenty-four-year-old lawyer was married to Anne Kinnaird Duncan, daughter of a Louisville surgeon.) For four years Wyatt was secretary of the Kentucky Bar Association, in 1930-34. He established an individual practice in 1933, was trial attorney for the City of Louisville in 1934, and became a member of Peter, Heyburn, Marshall, and Wyatt in 1935. From then until he became mayor in 1941, Wyatt, a successful corporation lawyer, held various directorships—he was concurrently on the boards of the First National Bank of Louisville, the Kentucky Title Trust Company, the Kentucky Title Company, the First Kentucky Company, the First Kentucky Fire Insurance Company, and, from 1939, the Courier-Journal and Louisville Times Company, which publishes Mark Ethridge's [46] papers. He was a member of the Sinking Fund Commission in 1936-38, of the Louisville Committee on Foreign Relations, and was chairman of the latter in 1940-41. He was said also to control Democratic politics in his section of Kentucky.

The first time Wyatt was asked to run for mayor was in 1937. He refused. Back of his refusal was a growing family, which he felt he could not support on a five-thousand-dollar salary, and also his belief that he was not yet prepared to serve as mayor. When he felt himself ready in 1941, Wyatt gave up a private law practice which brought him a reported income of thirty-five to forty thousand dollars a year: the seriousness of world events made him want to serve his country. He thought of joining the army or taking a Federal post, but to his mind, "local government is where democracy begins"; in December 1941 he took office as mayor of Louisville, which ranks twenty-fifth in population among the cities of the United States.

The city's government was still in the pattern of 1893. There was a lack of clear-cut organization among the city departments; functions of the city government overlapped functions of the county government. To make things more complicated, no changes could be made without approval by the state government. The war brought additional problems: Louisville became a crowded defense center; the sixty thousand men in the nearby army camps at Fort Knox and Bowman Field increased the congestion and caused other social

WILSON W. WYATT

problems. Still another problem was the condition of city finances. Wyatt discovered others by acting as a one-man investigation squad; according to *Life,* he once made a midnight house-to-house survey checking on a dust plague created by an acetylene plant.

Not deterred by the lack of home rule, Mayor Wyatt worked hard to win the support of state senators and representatives, as well as of the Governor, before the opening session of the legislature; and on the first day of the session, he was there in person to remind them. The result was that his entire program, including the extension of planning and zoning authority and a merger of the city and county health departments, was passed. With like aggressiveness, Wyatt tackled the financial problem. In spite of the antagonism aroused, back taxes were collected and business property owned by churches and charitable organizations was taxed. He fought for municipal purchase of the Louisville Gas and Electric Company, which he had represented as a lawyer, because it meant an additional three to four millions in revenue for the city treasury. As mayor, Wyatt tried to help the Negro citizens. He appointed Negroes as members of city boards, doubled the quota allowed to serve on the police force, and worked successfully against wage discrimination; he saw to it that more hospital beds were given to Negro tuberculars and tried to get them their proportionate share of Government-built houses. (When he later became the National Housing Expediter, he also attempted to carry out a policy which would assure minority groups a fair proportion of housing.)

A valuable contribution was the mayor's organization of a city-planning group, the Louisville Area Development Association. Bruce Bliven of the *New Republic* particularly noted the tact which Wyatt used in order to steer clear of the hostility between businessmen and planners, which usually causes the failure of city-planning programs. The Mayor enlisted the cooperation of business from the start by asking businessmen to participate in the association along with trade-union men. In committees they took up such matters as hospitals, parks, flood control, playgrounds and slum clearance.

In order to carry out his program for the city, Wyatt went directly to the people. He made wide use of the radio and the platform to inform them on city affairs. A poll made by Elmo Roper for *Fortune* showed a high popularity rating for the mayor. As chairman of the Louisville Metropolitan Area Defense Council, he was twice awarded the Citation of Merit. He was serving also as president of the American Society of Planning Officials, and of the Kentucky Municipal League. He was vice-president, a trustee, and chairman of the postwar planning committee of the American Municipal Association, and on the advisory board of the United States Conference of Mayors. In addition, he was a special representative of the Board of Economic Warfare in North Africa from March to May 1943, his only Federal experience up to that time. According to Lowell Mellett, his work on this economic survey made such an impression on Washington that he was offered "a number of hard jobs, including one that would have put him in charge of the Army's whole Service of Supply, with the necessary number of stars decorating his shoulders"; but he preferred to continue his program of reform in Louisville.

When his term ended (Louisville law forbids a mayor to succeed himself), Wyatt planned to resume his private practice. But President Truman saw the need for one man to formulate a centralized program from the uncoordinated efforts which were being made to resolve the housing crisis. In December 1945 he persuaded the ex-mayor to become the nation's housing expediter—Wyatt refused to be called a coordinator—and in January 1946 Wyatt was appointed Administrator of the National Housing Agency, which embraces all the urban housing activities of the Federal Government. His orders from the President were to "make no little plans." With the exception of his experience with housing problems in Louisville when it became a crowded defense center, Wyatt knew very little about the housing problem when he arrived at the capital. By working late into the night, studying statistical charts and conferring with all groups connected with housing—veterans, manufacturers of building materials, labor representatives, local officials—he educated himself on the subject and within five weeks prepared a program which was approved by Truman without a change. Chester Bowles [43] termed it "courageous and realistic"; the New York *Herald Tribune* described it as "inspiring."

The program called for the building of 2,700,000 housing units within the next two years, 1,200,000 in 1946 and 1,500,000 in 1947; this goal was more than double the previous one, for only a maximum of 500,000 dwelling units had been thought possible for 1946. Wyatt emphasized that housing facilities must be built to sell at low cost to bring them within the means of veterans. A survey had shown that 84 per cent of the veterans could afford to pay no more than six thousand dollars per home and not more than fifty dollars rental per month. In order to stimulate the vast production which Wyatt believed possible, his program provided that the Government make "premium payments," that is, pay subsidies to manufacturers who increased their levels of production, and that the country insure the market for manufacturers of prefabricated homes and subsidize private research in new building methods and materials. The Administrator called for a million and a half new workers in the building trades to fill the labor shortage.

The program was received with much praise but not without opposition. Many denounced it as "socialistic" and "revolutionary" while other observers of various political shades emphasized the dire need for it. Most of the opposition centered on the issue of price control and subsidies. The National Association of Real Estate Boards, while praising the plan in general, could not see why price control on houses was necessary; the New York *Times* said higher prices, not subsidies, were needed to stimulate manufacturers.

With his plan formulated, Wyatt sought the cooperation which was required to carry out the program—cooperation from Congress, by passing the necessary legislation; from labor unions, by accepting new workers and new building codes; from local governments, by altering building codes; from the building industry, by producing to its utmost; and from other administrative agencies. In response to Wyatt's call, Mayor's Emergency Housing Committees were set up in many cities to work with the local housing expediter, the representative of the Federal Government, in solving problems on a community basis. William Green promised that union rules would be relaxed in order to help reach the housing goals. The housing bill introduced by Representative Wright Patman [46] was amended to include most of Wyatt's proposals; however, Congress did not pass the measure until after months of controversy (May 1946) and then, with provision for only four hundred million dollars for production subsidies instead of the six hundred million Wyatt had stipulated, and without his request for ceilings on the sales price of existing houses.

The legislation gave veterans preference in buying or renting houses, and through the control of building priorities the housing expediter attempted to channel materials into lower cost residential projects. (A maximum selling price of ten thousand dollars and a maximum monthly rental of eighty dollars were established for new houses and apartments.) But proportionately few veterans found their housing problems solved: a shortage of building materials, black market practices, a skilled labor shortage, strikes, the weakening of OPA controls, the death of the Wagner [41]-Ellender [46]-Taft [40] housing bill in the House Banking and Currency Committee all combined to retard Wyatt's veterans' emergency housing program. Despite such setbacks Wyatt, whose removal builders demanded, remained confident that 2,700,000 homes would be started before the end of 1947.

Although an order described as "sweeping" had been issued in April 1946 to curtail nonresidential construction, there were complaints that "race tracks, office buildings, bars and gas stations" instead of the necessary homes were being built. Late in August, after a disagreement with John D. Small [46], head of the Civilian Production Administration, who was said to believe that additional restriction of commercial and industrial construction would interfere with orderly reconversion, Wyatt ordered a further reduction of non-housing construction by 27 per cent and added twenty-seven materials to the thirty already on the high priority list. (From Government figures covering the first eleven months of the year, it was estimated that one million new dwelling units, of which 665,000 were completed, were started in 1946.) In the removal of price ceilings on building materials, a part of President Truman's sweeping decontrol order on November 9, 1946, the housing expediter saw a serious blow to the goals he had set. His program received a further setback when RFC director George E. Allen [46] opposed large-scale loans to producers of prefabricated houses. Finally, on December 4, 1946, after his recommendations for dealing with the housing crisis had been rejected by the President in favor of a policy of relaxing housing control, Wyatt resigned and returned to his law practice in Louisville.

In 1945 the Kentucky lawyer received an honorary LL.D. degree from Knox College. Besides his membership in the Kentucky, Louisville, and American Bar associations, and the other above-mentioned groups, he belongs to the American Academy of Political and Social Sciences. He is a member of Pendennis, Louisville Country, Wynn Stay, 235, Louisville Salmagundi, and Arts clubs. The Salmagundi Club is a discussion group, and the Arts Club, of which he was president in 1935-36, presents amateur productions, in which Wyatt has appeared as Huckleberry Finn and a number of Shakespearean characters. He is a Presbyterian. The Wyatts have three children: Mary Anne, Nancy Kinnaird, and Wilson Watkins, Jr.

Wilson Wyatt is a lanky Kentuckian, just under six feet tall, with a high forehead, a long, pointed nose, "jug-handle" ears, and a preference for loud shirts. He is described as looking like "a serious-minded leprechaun," as being intensely hard-working, energetic, and articulate, yet unpompous and possessed of a saving sense of humor. "He sells his brand of good government to the people the way a dignified lawyer sells an argument to a court, by full knowledge of the facts and patient explanation," says the *Fortune* commentator, who also credits him with "the requisite tough courage to advance his ideas against pressure groups, backroom political opinion, and public indiffer-

WYATT, WILSON W.—*Continued*

ence." Wyatt "works on nerve alone," wrote Peter Edson. "He smokes a lot of cigarettes, but doesn't exercise, doesn't drink much coffee or suck sugar lozenges, although he has averaged three hours sleep a night since coming to Washington. . . . His staff is beginning to show a little wear and tear, but 'His Honor the Mayor' bobs up serene, blue-eyed and smiling, every day."

References

Collier's 117:26+ Ap 20 '46
Fortune 30:138+ N '44 por
Housing Progress p14+ Winter '46
N Y Post Mag p7 Mr. 16 '46
N Y Sun p26 Ja 23 '46 por
New Repub 113:250+ Ag 27 '45
Read Digest 44:103+ F '44
U S News 19:74 D 21 '45

Who's Who in America, 1946-47

YEN, Y(ANG-) C(H'U) JAMES (yĕn' yäng' chōō') 1894 (?)- Educator; Chinese Government official

Address: b. c/o National College of Rural Reconstruction, Chungking, Szechwan, China

"An almost incredible cultural revolution" is what *Time* calls the Mass Education Movement founded and headed by Y. C. James Yen. Jimmy Yen, as he is known to many, devised the "Thousand Character" system of learning Chinese by which about fifty million illiterate peasants have been taught to read and write. With his co-workers, he led these new literates in a vast campaign of rural reconstruction against what he considers China's four main problems—ignorance, poverty, disease, and misgovernment. He won the interest and support of Generalissimo Chiang Kai-shek '40, and became one of Chiang's advisers and a member of China's wartime parliament.

Yen Yang-ch'u, who was later to add James to his name, was born in Southwest China. The year has been most often given as 1894. His native province is Szechwan, the then remote region of mountains and plateau, bordering on Tibet, in which Chungking is located. For a hundred generations Yen's ancestors had belonged to the Chinese aristocracy of scholars and officials. The boy was brought up in the Confucian tradition and attended the classical schools in which he memorized the Four Books and the Five Classics by the age of ten. Next Yen's father sent him to the China Inland Mission School of Western Learning at Pao-ning. Despite his homesickness, the child reportedly begged the principal not to send him back because he was too young to be away from his home. Here he studied the Christian religion and became a Christian at the age of twelve. He took first prize in the examinations for a Hong Kong University scholarship, but was not eligible because he was not a British subject.

Instead, Yen went to the United States to enter Yale University, where he supplemented a scholarship by his earnings as a choir singer. According to missionary-writer Sherwood Eddy,

he became the "natural leader" of the several thousand Chinese students then in America. While at Yale he assumed the prename James, which is inserted either before or after the initials "Y. C.," as Chinese custom permits great flexibility in the adoption and use of prenames and surnames. He took the name in memory of his friend James Stuart, a young missionary killed on a European battlefield in January 1916. Yen had taught for a year and had been assistant warden of a Szechwan hostel and primary school, when Stuart was warden, and had taught the American to speak Chinese.

Graduated with his B.A. in 1918, young James Yen sailed for France to serve as volunteer YMCA secretary among the twenty thousand coolies in the Chinese Labor Corps. He was assigned to run the canteen and interpret for five thousand laborers at Boulogne, and soon found himself writing letters home for them each day and translating the news for them each night. The peasants, who constituted the bulk of China's vast population, had always been illiterate and superstitious; but in France the scholar discovered that these humble countrymen of his were teachable and worth teaching. "Analyzing the coolies' letters," Yen recalls, "I found that a basic Chinese vocabulary of about a thousand characters [actually closer to 1,300] was sufficient for their simple needs. I called a mass meeting and told them I was going to teach them how to write. Of course they didn't believe me." But at last forty coolies accepted his offer. Yen taught them for ninety-six hours—an hour each night for four months—and at the end each pupil wrote a letter home and read a news bulletin Yen had prepared. The next group was a little larger. Finally the entire camp signed up; and eventually Major Cole, head of the YMCA work, asked Yen to teach his method to the eighty Chinese university men doing welfare work in the other Chinese labor camps. Then he had to create reading matter in the Thousand Characters. The result was the publication of the one-centime *Chinese Laborers Weekly,* which explained what was happening at the Paris Peace Conference.

"Now I knew I must dedicate my life to teaching my people," Yen recalls. But first he studied at Princeton University, receiving his M.A. in 1920. In 1923 he began operations at Changsha in Central China. "He has a great sense of the dramatic," writes J. P. McEvoy, "and he organized his campaign with all the skill of a community chest drive and the hurrah of an Elks' convention. . . .Stores, private homes, pleasure pavilions, and temples were turned into People's Schools. . . .He divided the city into sections, the students into recruiting teams, and he trained all those who could read and write into such fanatic teachers that, out of 1400 peasants in the first class, 965 passed the examinations. They mastered their first reader so quickly that Yen was caught flat-footed halfway through writing their second one."

Then Yen and his newly trained assistants ran similar drives—"all wildly successful"—in other cities, building up provincial Mass Education Societies. In the fall of 1924 the National Association for the Advancement of Mass Education was founded in Peking with secretary-general, or executive director, James Yen assisted by a part-time clerk and a part-time servant. It received much help from Mme. Hsiung, wife of a Premier of the Republic, who paid the first two years' expenses of ninety-six hundred Chinese dollars (about three thousand American dollars) and raised funds until her death in 1930. An important part in the movement was played also by Dean Hu Shih '42 of the Peking National University, "Father of the Chinese Literary Renaissance," who wrote historical, dramatic, and narrative texts and edited a reformist weekly.

By 1928 Yen won an honorary M.A. from Yale—and while in America to receive it, he managed to get half a million dollars from Henry Ford '44 and other businessmen, obtained grants from several funds, and attracted some volunteer American co-workers. To discover what was really possible, Yen now determined to choose one county or *hsien,* typical of the nineteen hundred in China, as a "social or human laboratory." After invitations and investigations his choice fell on Tinghsien, Hopei Province, in the cotton country of North China, about six hours' train ride from his Peking headquarters. When the local gentry offered to give twelve hundred *mou* (two hundred acres) of land for experimental purposes, plus a famous old examination hall for headquarters, Yen made the decision to give up all his work in the cities and concentrate on rural education in Tinghsien.

To this remote agricultural county of four hundred square miles and four hundred thousand population came sixty or seventy scholars and scientists—educators, economists, agriculturists, officials, businessmen, some of great distinction, most of them with foreign degrees, who had resigned their comfortable university positions for this unprecedented experiment. There they lodged in the farmers' mud huts, and immediately punched holes in the windowless walls. About one-third of the original staff later returned to Peking, because of the primitive living conditions or because they could not cope with problems so different from any with which they had ever come in contact. Jimmy Yen's main work was one of coordination: of getting individualistic scholars to work together and to express their ideas in terms easily grasped by the uneducated.

The basic teaching in the experiment was literacy, or the Thousand Characters. At the two experimental schools and then the eight demonstration schools, peasants of all ages studied before dawn or after dark in the summer; and for longer hours in winter. Those who learned most quickly were elected by their fellows as guiding students or pupil teachers, and when they had finished they were given training in teaching technique, handed a manual, and sent out to establish new classes. Finally each of the 472 villages in the county had its own People's School, taught on a volunteer basis and supported by the village. Proud of their new learning, the graduates organized themselves into the Fellow-Scholar Association for the double purpose of con-

Y. C. JAMES YEN

tinuing their studies and improving their communities. Learning became the entire community's preoccupation—and in this atmosphere, the Fellow-Scholar Association began publishing the first farm newspaper in all Chinese history, a weekly, began daily broadcasts over a new county network, organized theatrical troupes to go from village to village giving educational plays, and established reading clubs and traveling libraries.

From reading and writing the movement branched out into fighting poverty, disease, and misgovernment. "If it is the season for cotton we teach cotton, if it is the right time to tackle smallpox we teach vaccination," said James Yen. "In each village the whole school curriculum is related to the whole reconstruction program and everybody is learning and everybody is doing what he learns." When improved methods of farming had raised output, the farmers lost the benefit by being poor businessmen and paying 40 per cent interest rates to money lenders. So the movement organized Self Help Societies or credit and marketing cooperatives, and worked out a simple accounting system for them. As a result, Yen reported, the income of the Tinghsien farmers was nearly doubled. (Another result was opposition by the vested interests, landlords, politicians, and the moneylenders who were forced to go out of business. According to Sherwood Eddy, Yen was confronted by seventy-five lawsuits that sought to stop his work.) To combat disease, Dr. C. C. Chen, a graduate of Harvard Medical School and Johns Hopkins, worked out the "pyramid" health system, by which picked volunteer fellow scholars were trained to keep vital statistics, maintain sanitary wells, administer vaccinations and injections, and treat common ailments with safe, simple drugs. Cases they could not handle were turned over to the sub-county health doctor, and those beyond his

YEN, Y. C. JAMES—*Continued*

ability were referred to the well-staffed County Health Center. This system, which wiped out trachoma, smallpox, and a number of other diseases in Tinghsien within two years at a total annual cost of ten cents per person, was adopted for all China by the National Government in 1935.

Attacking China's fourth problem, misgovernment, proved more difficult. It took a year and a half (until 1933) to persuade the National Government to pass a law giving the Mass Education Movement control of the Ting County Government. Then Yen's best men became magistrates and bureau heads, and set about reorganizing the county Government to include the new functions of education, agriculture, cooperatives and public health. By 1936, the Tinghsien experiment having attracted the attention of students from all over China and the backing of Chiang Kai-shek, more than eight hundred similar "rural reconstruction centers" were started.

Then came the Japanese invasion, which prevented the first democratic local elections in all Chinese history. Meanwhile Yen served from 1936 to 1938 as vice-president of the Szechwan Province Planning Commission and became in 1938 a member of China's wartime parliament, the People's Political Council. He and his associates were reconstructing the invasion-menaced "rice bowl province" of Hunan, Central China, where Governor-General Chang had called them to help mobilize the people for resistance. They organized seventy-five county governments, retraining the five thousand higher officials and thirty thousand village heads of the province. The people of Hopei, Szechwan, and Hunan provinces put up such gallant resistance to the invaders that in 1939 Chiang had the new county Government system adopted by all Free China. He also encouraged James Yen in establishing the National College of Rural Reconstruction near Chungking, to train administrative and technical personnel for the movement (Yen is president). The Generalissimo contributed the equivalent of a' million American dollars, promising to give more when better times came. When the college was opened, between bombings, in November 1940, each of the impoverished provincial governments of Free China sent contributions.

In May 1943, "Dr." James Y. C. Yen was listed with Einstein '41, Henry Ford '44, and Orville Wright '46 as one of ten modern pioneer scientists receiving citations at the Copernican quadricentennial program. Yen "had been selected unanimously by the committee," reports J. P. McEvoy, "but no one knew where he was until ten days before the celebration, when he turned up in Washington on a global mission to study at firsthand the postwar reconstruction plans for the world." While on this tour of several years' duration, Yen delivered many speeches and wrote some articles. (He had already published half a dozen papers and books on his project, the first in 1923).

James Yen, who has several children, is one of the few Chinese of any class whose marriage was not arranged for them by their families. He married one of the four Huie sisters, American by birth and half American by blood, whose father was a Chinese Christian missionary to New York's Chinatown. Yen himself is described as physically slight, erect and graceful, with the grave courtesy and dignity of the Chinese. To this description Pearl S. Buck added, "I found in him a deep and simple humility. . . . His work had been his life, and now everything else was burned out of him." And *Time* reported, "When Jimmy Yen speaks [on his subject] he is the essence of will, exploding off his seat, talking even to a one-man audience like an evangelist under a big top."

References

Life 17:62 Jl 10 '44 por
Read Dig p38-44 N '43 por
Time 42:54-6 N 22 '43 por
Buck, P. S. Tell the People—Mass Education in China (1945)
China Handbook, 1937-43
Eddy, S. Pathfinders of the Missionary Crusade (1940)
International Who's Who, 1945-46
Who's Who in China (1936)

YERBY, FRANK (GARVIN) (yĕr'bē)
Sept. 5, 1916- Author
Address: b. c/o William Morris Agency, Inc., 1270 6th Ave., New York; h. Valley Stream, N.Y.

Twenty-nine-year-old Frank Yerby, whose "Health Card" won the O. Henry Memorial Award Committee special prize for a first published short story in 1944, made the best-seller lists with his first novel two years later. *The Foxes of Harrow,* written while Yerby was working twelve hours a day in a war plant, is unique among the writings of American Negroes in that it is a frankly romantic period novel and in no sense a work of propaganda.

The son of Rufus Garvin and Willie Ethlyn (Smythe) Yerby, Frank Garvin Yerby was born in Augusta, Georgia, on September 5, 1916. Of his childhood he says, "I was fat, shy, would rather read than eat. . . .Boyhood was dull." Yerby reports that his interest in writing was generated at seventeen, while he was attending secondary school at Haines Institute in Augusta. "The late James Weldon Johnson approved some verses of mine shown to him by my sister, then a student at Fisk University."

After having received his high school diploma in 1933, Yerby entered Paine College, also in Augusta, where he majored in English and languages, receiving his B.A. degree in 1937. Graduate work leading to an M.A. degree followed at Fisk University in Nashville, Tennessee. Yerby studied further in the department of education at the University of Chicago in 1939. While in that city the writer worked on the Federal Writers' Project of the WPA in the Ethnics Group for nine months, joining a semi-Mohammedan religious cult in order to obtain certain data he needed. Yerby considers the training he received through his work the best he has had.

Twenty-two-year-old Frank Yerby left Chicago in June 1939 to teach at the Florida Agricultural and Mechanical College in Tallahassee. He was a member of the English department there until May 1940, when he went to Louisiana to teach at Southern University in Scotlandville until October 1941. After several months of travel, Yerby, now a married man, settled in Detroit in June 1942, and began war work for the Ford Motor Company at Dearborn. Moving again, to New York, he worked for the Ranger Aircraft Company in Jamaica, Long Island, from June 1944 until the end of the war in August 1945.

Yerby gives his profession as "writer, as of V-J Day," but some of his early verse had appeared in "little magazines" during his high school and college years. A short story, "The Thunder of God," is in the 1939 New Anvil. "Health Card," Yerby's first nationally published story, was printed in Harper's in May 1944, when Yerby was twenty-seven, and was later chosen an O. Henry Memorial Prize Award story to be reprinted in the O. Henry collection for that year. "Health Card" is written in a purely objective style, exposing, solely through dialogue and action, an injustice visited upon a Negro couple by military police. Harry Hansen, reviewing the collection in the New York World-Telegram, mentioned the "punch" of Yerby's story. "White Magnolias," another short story, appeared in the summer 1944 issue of Atlanta University's Phylon Magazine. "My Brother Went to College" was published in Tomorrow (January 1946); and "Roads Going Down," and "The Home Coming," two "sensitive tales," were in Common Ground (Summer 1945 and Spring 1946 issues, respectively). In these stories as in others, Yerby has written sensitively of people and places he knows—the Negro people of Georgia and of neighboring states.

In sharp contrast to Frank Yerby's earlier work is his 534-page The Foxes of Harrow, published in February 1946, which was written "quite frankly for popular sales." Reviewers chorused that Yerby had used all the stock characters and situations of Southern romantic fiction, including a dashing, unscrupulous, but sensitive adventurer who has unfailing social, financial, and sexual success; several beautiful women, one cold and queenly, the others warm and passionate; politics, gambling, war and duels with sword and pistol; moonlight, magnolias, a pillared forty-room mansion in Louisiana, and final devastation. No social significance was visible to reviewers excepting Richard Match, who observed (in the New York Times) "some sympathetic evidences of the Negro's deep resentment against slavery"; and Hansen, who considered that Yerby "who understands the history of his race from careful study, picks up the familiar apparatus of romance for his own purposes in The Foxes of Harrow. . . .Toward the end Mr. Yerby gives more attention to the Negroes."

Several critics predicted great popular success for the book—Sterling North, who thought that "in two hundred thousand words of galloping prose there is never a dull moment or

FRANK YERBY

a really distinguished sentence," added that the author would "soon be richer than the Foxes of Harrow." The New Yorker's Edmund Wilson dismissed the novel with, "Mr. Yerby has packed everything in—passion, politics, Creole society, sex, the clash of races, and war—but he never captures the faintest flutter of the breath of life"; but the Christian Science Monitor reviewer saw "a breathless but lucid rapidity in the action . . . intimate knowledge of the locale and a study of the times . . . imagination, the ability to create clearly defined characters, a lush, full-bodied style and, quite naturally, considering Stephen Fox, more than a touch of melodrama." Yerby "can do a scene that crackles, when he sets his mind to it," (critic H. T. Kane in the New York Herald Tribune). "One difficulty is that he has crammed in so much plot that he seems never able to do a real development of his people or his theme. . . .This first novel indicates that Mr. Yerby has talent, a way with words. He needs, primarily, restraint—a firmer hand on the reins, or at least an editor with decision and a ready blue pencil for the overflamboyant."

In mid-April 1946, two months after publication, Time reported that at least six hundred thousand copies of The Foxes of Harrow had been printed; by the end of the year, well over a million copies of the novel had been sold. Besides these copies, reprints appeared in the Negro Digest, Omnibook, and Liberty; and screen rights were purchased by Twentieth Century-Fox. At this time the author was well into another novel, "Ignoble Victory" (retitled "The Vixens" by the publishers), about conflicts of the Reconstruction period in Louisiana. Two other books, one with a steel-mill background and the other a historical tale in the Caribbean, were in "the research stage."

The turning point of his life, Yerby says, had come with his marriage in New Orleans,

YERBY, FRANK—*Continued*

on March 1, 1941, to "tiny, intense Flora Helen Claire Williams, who supplied the drive hitherto lacking. Her belief in me, her endless attacks upon my monumental laziness," he continues, "finally resulted in the novel whose success continues to amaze us both." The Yerbys have three children, a son Jacques Loring, and two daughters Nikki Ethlyn and Faune Ellena. Yerby writes, "The person to whom, next to my wife, I am most profoundly indebted is Miss Muriel Fuller [editor of children's books, who assisted in editing the 1944 O. Henry collection]. . . .She had enough faith in my abilities, revealed to her through the medium of what was probably the world's worst attempt at a novel, to make for me the contacts that ultimately launched me upon my career."

Tennis is the favorite sport of the five-foot-seven-inch, 145-pound author. His hobbies are photography, painting, and chess, "which I play badly." "I attend the Catholic church," he writes, "on the rare occasions that I go to church, but I am a member of no specific sect, although I consider myself a Christian in a vague sort of way. I belong to no political party. I vote for the man and the issue, regardless of party lines."

YOSHIDA, SHIGERU (yō-shē-dä shē-gĕ-rōō) Sept. 22, 1878- Prime Minister of Japan

Address: 17 Nagata-cho 1-chome, Kojimachi-ku, Tokyo

A diplomat who had served his country "long but colorlessly" in foreign capitals, in May 1946 unwillingly accepted the post of Prime Minister of Japan, retaining as well the portfolio of Foreign Minister. Sixty-seven years old when he took office, Shigeru Yoshida, who described himself as an "amateur Prime Minister," was faced with a food crisis, nation-wide labor difficulties, and the enmity of leading newspapers, Social Democrats, Communists and labor leaders. He was supported by a coalition of the Liberal and Progressive parties. To the new Japanese Diet (elected April 1945) he presented a new constitution (purportedly prepared at Allied headquarters) for consideration. "His ultra-conservatism was well known," commented the New York *Herald Tribune* upon his election; it added the prediction that "the social unrest seething in Japan would find a foe in Yoshida."

Shigeru Yoshida was born in Tokyo on September 22, 1878, the fifth son of Tsuna Takeuchi, a prominent member of the Diet. As is not uncommon in Japan, he was adopted by an acquaintance of his father's, Kenzo Yoshida, who wanted a promising youth to carry on the Yoshida name. The young man made a "brilliant" record at Tokyo Imperial University, at twenty-eight was graduated from the Law College, and in the same year (1906) entered the diplomatic service. As a vice-consul he served in Tientsin, China, in 1906, and in Mukden, capital of Manchuria, in 1907. Japan had acquired railways and mining privileges in Southern Manchuria by the terms of the treaty

which concluded the 1904-5 Russo-Japanese War. Thus, when Yoshida was a young official his country was embarking on the program which eventually led to Japanese control of Manchuria. Having been married to the eldest daughter of Count Nobuaki Makino, one of the Emperor's closest advisers, Yoshida had access to inner court circles, and gained friends among the nobility, capitalists, and elder statesmen.

From 1908 to 1912 Yoshida served in Occidental capitals: he was a vice-consul in London in 1908, and after 1909 a third secretary of the Japanese Embassy in Rome. His three years in Italy were followed by four years in Manchuria (1912-16) where he served as consul in the port city of Antung. Assigned to the United States, Yoshida was a second secretary of the Embassy in Washington, when the 1917 Lansing-Ishii agreement was signed, in which the United States, over Chinese protests, recognized that Japan had "special interests" in China, but expressed faith that the Open Door and China's "territorial integrity" would be respected. In 1918 the forty-year-old diplomat was again sent to China as consul in Tsinan, capital of Shantung. He attended the Paris Peace Conference after World War I, served briefly in Tokyo in 1919 as secretary in the Foreign Office, and from 1920 to 1922 was first secretary of Japan's Embassy in London.

Again returning to the Orient, Yoshida was consul general in Tientsin from 1922 to 1925, and in Mukden from 1925 to 1928. The last post was in the nature of an ambassadorship, since the Japanese were entrenching themselves in Manchuria and seeking to detach that province from China. Yoshida's duties in Mukden were outlined in A. Morgan Young's book *Imperial Japan* (William Morrow and Company, 1938; copyright by the author). The consul general, Young wrote, faced with the unwillingness of the Chinese in Manchuria to lease land to the Japanese, "gave something like an ultimatum to Marshal Chang Tso-lin [warlord of Manchuria] that if leases could not be obtained, then ownership must be the alternative." He also told the civil governor "that anti-Japanese movements such as the collection of duties under the new Chinese tariff . . . must cease forthwith," and "prohibited the construction of railways which . . . would compete with the [Japanese] South Manchuria railway." According to *World Report* (June 13, 1946), Yoshida "spearheaded Japan's political and economic penetration of Manchuria. He intrigued among Manchuria's war lords, financed an anti-Government newspaper."

Advanced to the rank of Minister after his activity in Manchuria, Yoshida went to Sweden, where he served during 1928. From 1928 to 1930 he was Vice-Minister for Foreign Affairs in Tokyo. (Later the Communist Party of a defeated Japan accused Yoshida of having helped to formulate the Asiatic expansion program while he held that office.) His next assignment took him to Italy as Ambassador from 1930 to 1932. In the 1930's Ambassador Yoshida allied himself with a group of elder statesmen, members of the great capitalist families, and some aristocrats and politicians, who, although they did not oppose the conquest of Manchuria and North China, resisted the efforts of the militarists to take over complete control of the Government. Militarists assassinated key antimilitarists in 1936; the Army leadership also vetoed Yoshida's appointment as Foreign Minister in a new Cabinet. However, he was appointed Ambassador to Great Britain in April 1936. Returning to Tokyo after three years in London, Yoshida became president of the Japan-Britain Society, and began a movement for Anglo-Japanese amity. Six months later World War II began in Europe, and the sixty-one-year-old former envoy went into virtual retirement. After Pearl Harbor he smuggled a letter expressing regret over the war to the then interned American Ambassador, Joseph C. Grew '41.

Yoshida was next heard of in June 1945, when he was arrested by the Japanese Government, charged with advocating negotiations for peace through British channels. He was released, after three months in prison, at the time of the Japanese surrender in August 1945. In September, with American troops on Japanese soil, Yoshida was appointed Foreign Minister in the Japanese Government. The *Nippon Times* hailed the new Foreign Minister as "an outstanding symbol of heroic martyrdom in the cause of peace," and Yoshida himself recalled his "continued opposition to militarists" and to Japan's program of aggression. One of the few prewar political figures still eligible for office after General MacArthur's '41 "purge" of the warmakers, in May 1946 Foreign Minister Yoshida received an imperial command to form a new Government, the fifth since the surrender, to represent a coalition of the Liberal and Progressive parties.

It was only after five critical days that Yoshida could form a Cabinet acceptable both to Allied headquarters and to the Japanese political parties. Of the 466 Diet members, 143 were members of the Liberal Party, of which Yoshida accepted the presidency, and 94 were of the equally conservative Progressive Party, headed by Yoshida's good friend Baron Kijuro Shidehara '46, the outgoing Premier; thus the coalition of relatively conservative forces had only a small majority in the Japanese Parliament. Before the new Government was established, thirty Leftists and labor leaders, staging a "sit-down strike" in Yoshida's home, and threatening to remain until he resigned, had to be dispersed by Tokyo police acting on General MacArthur's orders. The Supreme Allied Commander had previously warned against intimidation by Leftists, after a demonstration before the Emperor's palace by two hundred thousand people brandishing "Down With Yoshida" banners, and shouting for more food and a "Democratic Front" regime. Commenting on Yoshida's acts in the opening weeks of his premiership, *Time* saw him as "stuffy" and "blundering."

Unwilling from the first to take the "thankless job" of Premier, Yoshida, according to NBC's Tokyo correspondent George Thomas Folster, was kept from resigning by conservative leaders because "he is the last key figure

SHIGERU YOSHIDA

in this bureaucratic crowd who can hold the feudalistic clique together." There was "no general rejoicing about the selection," wrote Marcus Duffield in the New York *Herald Tribune*. "One of Tokyo's leading newspapers said flatly that he represented the same old prewar ruling clique—the powerful shadowy figures around the imperial throne, and the family industrial monopolies known as the *Zaibatsu*." "Perhaps the most important of . . . [Yoshida's shortcomings] in this crisis," Mark Gayn reported to *PM* and the Chicago *Sun*, "is his belief that social unrest can be checked with force and his outspoken championship of the 'old' *Zaibatsu*. . . .Equally significant is his dependence upon the invisible Government, perhaps a dozen old-timers who pull the Government wires today as they did in the unfortunate thirties." However, a report from General MacArthur in May insisted that the prolonged negotiations among the parties had been for the first time in Japanese history conducted openly, thus creating an important precedent for the future. "The Cabinet represents the more conservative forces still active in Japanese political life (the extreme reactionaries, militarists and their sympathizers have been eliminated for all practical purposes)," the General's report stated. "It thus correctly reflects the present balance of political forces in the lower house as established by popular vote in the April election."

According to *World Report,* the headquarters of General MacArthur wanted to keep the "unpopular Cabinet" in office until the new constitution was approved, and consequently permitted the Japanese Government to "curtail the activities of Japan's labor unions." Adopted by the Diet in October 1946, the constitution provided that the Premier must be a member of the Diet, which meant that Yoshida, if still in office, would need to resign when the con-

YOSHIDA, SHIGERU—*Continued*

stitution became effective six months after promulgation.

One of Yoshida's four children was educated at Cambridge University. The diplomat's wife, Yukiko, died in 1940, but his father-in-law is said to be still a member of the "invisible Government" in the palace; Yoshida himself "ardently" supports the Emperor system. The Prime Minister wears pince-nez, smokes cigars, and spends his leisure hours reading history and politics. Short and stocky, he dresses "dapperly" in European clothes at the office, wears Japanese dress at home.

References

N Y Herald Tribune p13 My 17 '46 por
N Y Sun p26 My 24 '46 por
N Y Times p6 S 19 '45 por
Newsweek 27:45 My 27 '46
PM p6 My 17 '46
Time 47:36 Je 3 '46
World Report 1:34 Je 13 '46
International Who's Who, 1945-46
Who's Who in Japan (1937)

YOST, FIELDING HARRIS Apr. 30, 1871—Aug. 20, 1946 Athletic director; coached the University of Michigan's "point-a-minute" football teams from 1901 to 1927; his squads won 164 games, lost 29 and tied 10 in his coaching career; appointed director of athletics at the university in 1921, he expanded its athletic facilities to meet his ideal of "sports for all."

Obituary

N Y Times p27 Ag 21 '46 por

YOUMANS, VINCENT Sept. 27, 1898—Apr. 5, 1946 American songwriter and musical comedy producer; internationally popular songs included "Tea for Two", "Hallelujah", "Sometimes I'm Happy", "Without a Song", "Carioca", "I Want to Be Happy"; best-known scores were *No, No, Nanette* (1925), *Hit The Deck* (1927), *Flying Down to Rio* (1933). See *Current Biography* 1944 Yearbook.

Obituary

N Y Times p17 Ap 6 '46 por

ZIFF, WILLIAM B(ERNARD) Aug. 1, 1898- Publisher; author

Address: b. c/o Ziff-Davis Publishing Co., 185 N. Wabash Ave., Chicago; 1319 F St., N.W., Washington, D.C.

The chairman of the board of the Ziff-Davis Publishing Company, William B. Ziff, is the author of a number of controversial books that became best sellers and attracted international attention. As of 1946, these numbered four: *The Rape of Palestine, The Coming Battle of Germany, The Gentlemen Talk of Peace,* and *Two Worlds.* The publisher-author is also known for his syndicated articles and the part he has taken in numerous radio debates.

William Bernard Ziff was born in Chicago on August 1, 1898. His mother, Libby Mary (Semco) Ziff, had come to America from the Baltic city of Memel; his father, David Ziff, a farmer descended from Spanish Jews, had come from East Prussia. Young Ziff attended the Crane Technical High School, where he was class artist, an office in which he was followed by Walt Disney. In 1915-17 he studied at the Chicago Art Institute, intending to become a portrait painter. To earn money he "shoveled coal out of boxcars, washed dishes in restaurants, and sold everything from flatirons to shoes."

At seventeen Ziff set himself up as a commercial artist and also joined the Chicago *Daily News* staff as a cartoonist. In World War I he served with the Army's 202d Aero Observation Squadron. By 1920 the young veteran had opened his own business, the W. B. Ziff Company, "newspaper representatives," which, in the course of some years showed substantial earnings, and is still in existence. Subsequently he became president of the publishing house, the E. C. Auld Company, with which he remained as head for nine years.

Ziff's Magazine, a humorous periodical, was his first venture in the field of magazine publishing. It drew heavily on his drawing and writing abilities—he alone is supposed to have written and illustrated it. Its title was later changed to *America's Humor,* which Ziff edited in 1928-30. From 1931 to 1933 he was editor of *Aeronautics,* a magazine in which were published many of General Billy Mitchell's articles calling for a unified air force and a re-formed American air policy. Ziff is a strong believer in Mitchell's doctrines and has written much on aviation. (In 1941 he was to be honored by the Ligue Internationale des Aviateurs for his dissemination of aviation knowledge.) For some years during this period (1928-31) Ziff served as chairman of the Interracial Society, an organization of publishers and editors in the Chicago area, including between thirty and forty publications in foreign languages.

Two other interests claimed Ziff's attention for a time in the early 1930's: In 1932 he was an unsuccessful candidate for Congress on the Republican ticket, and in 1933 he was a member of an expedition searching for the lost city of Pueblo Blanco in Honduras, at the time unsettled conditions prevailed in that country. For the duration of his stay there Ziff was made an officer in the Honduran army.

William Ziff founded the Popular Aviation Corporation in 1933, the firm which became the Ziff-Davis Publishing Company two years later. (Bernard G. Davis, who had come from college to a job as Ziff's assistant in 1928, is now the president.) Ten years after its organization, according to Amos Stote (*Magazine World,* May 1946), Ziff-Davis had enlarged thirty-two times its original size.

Besides the *Little Technical Library* reference series, which Ziff-Davis house launched in 1933, and the trade (non-technical) and juvenile books it began publishing in 1942, the firm publishes a dozen magazines, as of 1946. The number includes the "slick," semi-technical *Flying, Plastics, Radio News,* and *Popular Photography,* and a group of highly successful "pulps"—

Amazing Stories, Air Adventures, Fantastic Adventures, Mammoth Detective, Mammoth Mystery, Mammoth Western. Of the latter, it is said: "This big Chicago house does its stuff with a certainty of hitting the mark that is almost uncanny." (Two periodicals the company dropped from its list are *Popular Pets* and *South Sea Stories.*) In addition, the book division of this house issues about sixty new titles annually.

William Ziff's first book was *The Rape of Palestine* (1938), which deals with the history of the Zionist resettlement and British treatment of the Jews. H. L. Mencken, who selected the volume as one of the three best books of the year, devoted five columns to his discussion of it in the Baltimore *Sun.* Mencken and other reviewers (writing in the *Annals of the American Academy of Political and Social Science* and the *Free Methodist*) spoke of its importance as an historical work, "a thoroughly documented revelation of violent discrimination against the Jews in Palestine." In a review of the book's new edition (published in 1946), Sterling North pointed out that it had been used as a textbook by the Mandates Commission of the League of Nations and had been praised by fair-minded Englishmen and the Anglo-American Commission on Palestine. The book was issued in Spanish and British editions and reprinted in digests in newspapers and magazines.

In 1942 the British Air Ministry flew the publisher-author to England in a bomber. In the course of a three-month inspection trip of that bombed island, Ziff was granted the opportunity to discuss with the leading figures the broad strategy of air war. This was reflected in part in his next book, *The Coming Battle of Germany* (1942), which saw air power as the determining factor in victory. While Ziff himself looked upon his book as a military work (it was required reading in military staff schools and was described as influencing the air strategy of the United States), it became a popular best seller in a few weeks, was reprinted in foreign editions and as a Pocket Book, was serialized in about fifty American newspapers and digested in several magazines.

The Coming Battle of Germany received praise in William Mead Earle's *Makers of Modern Strategy* (1943), was acclaimed by Major Alexander P. De Seversky, Captain Eddie Rickenbacker, and General William E. Gillmore. Gillmore's judgment was: "The noted civilian authority on aviation has at last put down for the permanent and public record the things he has been telling the experts, both military and civilian. . . .It is dynamite, and by that I mean that it is dynamite of the kind that is needed to win this war." W. R. Deuel found it "one of the best informed, most mercilessly logical, angriest, and hardest-hitting books that have come out of the war." Fletcher Pratt, who criticized the book adversely, considered it "hastily written, without checking facts." The year after its publication Ziff became a special consultant on the subject to the Department of Justice's Economic Warfare

WILLIAM B. ZIFF

Division, and was called upon several times to testify as an expert before the Military and Foreign Affairs Committees of the House and Senate.

In *The Gentlemen Talk of Peace* (1944) Ziff set forth what he considered to be a logical development of present trends in international problems. In this compendium of economic, military, and political facts, he maintains that the day of the small sovereign state has passed: "The little nation of today is an anachronism. . . .The world must be regrouped into large federations capable of meeting the needs of a modern manufacturing and distributing economy." "These aggregates," continues Ziff, would make international collaboration possible "in a world run by scientists, engineers, and executives, rather than by career diplomats. . . .There is room for all nations on the earth to exist on a high standard of comfort and nutrition without cutting each other's throats to achieve it." In his support of democratic systems, Ziff says: "The mere fact that free government has difficulty in dealing with authoritarian competition does not remove the desirable features of democratic rule." *The Gentlemen Talk of Peace* provoked wide discussion—controversial, brilliant, hard-hitting, cynical, realistic, prophetic were some of the adjectives applied to it—and it was a Literary Guild book dividend selection.

Ziff extended his thesis in *Two Worlds* (1946): 'The whole of history can be summed up in the progressive integration of human families, tribes, feudal provinces, nations, and finally, federations of nations. . . .To bring a totally unrelated group of states under the roof of a single government is illogical . . . [and] skips one necessary step in the sequence." Further: "If we wish to avert eventual defeat for this country, we must recognize that the U.S.S.R. and the United States must reorganize the world along federal principles.

ZIFF, WILLIAM B.—*Continued*

This is a responsibility we must share with the Soviet Union. . . .We have yet to make a proposition to the Russians based on a bold global-sized plan of settlement, which would embrace an acceptable conclusion to the future of the Orient, as well as what remains of Europe."

On its jacket *Two Worlds* bore the recommendations of six Senators of differing political orientations, from the ultraconservative Republican whip, Kenneth S. Wherry '46 of South Dakota, to Democratic Senator James M. Tunnell of Delaware. Alfred B. Lindsay, writing in the *Library Journal*, called Ziff's book "a sane study of political, social, and economic forces molding our future" and mentioned the author's "keen perception . . . delicate perspective . . . delicate balance." The sociologist R. M. MacIver warned, in the *Saturday Review of Literature*, "Lest we be carried away by the urgent impressiveness of Mr. Ziff, it may be well to raise some questions. . . Mr. Ziff tends to identify military strength with economic advantage. . . .To reach his conclusion Mr. Ziff expends much zeal, much virtuosity, much ingenuity, and a remarkable array of forceful words. Perhaps part of the trouble is that his words are too forceful." A condensation of *Two Worlds* appeared in the *Catholic Digest.*

Though he disbelieves completely in the future of small nations, William Ziff has been prominent in the fight to establish a free Hebrew Palestine, where the plight of the homeless and displaced Jews could be permanently settled. Such a free Hebrew state, he believes, would become part of an ultimate modern, industrialized federation of the Near and Middle Eastern peoples, whose destinies would be linked permanently with the free West. The essence of his view on this problem was given in a speech at the National Conference on Palestine, held at the Statler Hotel in Washington, D. C., on March 9, 1944. 'The question," he said, "is one that strikes deep at the future of the world. It is one of the fundamental issues which will determine what kind of world we are to inhabit, whether it is to be a world of compassion, freedom and decency in which universal ethics are to prevail; or whether the entire globe is to become a dark, treacherous jungle in which the only law will be brute force, and the only worship, the cult of expediency."

Ziff is the originator of the Romford Plan of education, designed to "bring the world into the classroom," to dissolve as much as possible the "disadvantages of the cloistered college." Chief among its aims is the development of leaders of democracy by giving young men an understanding of the social, political, economic, and technological problems of the age. The lecturers, in part, are prominent leaders in education, science, business, and politics, who by intimate association with students on the campus for periods of one or two weeks, give the boys the advantage of dealing with able and varied minds in all fields of achievement.

William B. Ziff is described as "jet-propelled, yet easygoing," a casually dressed man, six feet in height. He has brown eyes and thinning hair; his smile is broad, his voice deep, his speech drawling. He has lived for a number of years in Washington with his family: the former Amelia Morton, to whom he has been married since April 1929, their children, William Bernard, Jr., Priscilla Rae, and David Morton. (He has another daughter, Sylvia Antoinette Brady, by an earlier marriage, to Denea Fischer.) Their summers are spent on a sixteen-hundred-acre Maryland farm which once belonged to the first president of the Continental Congress. Ziff's sheep and geese have won prizes, and for a time he had a herd of sixty registered Herefords.

Among Ziff's many interests are writing poetry, painting and sketching (he plans to give a one-man show some day), cooking (although he has no sympathy with people who make "a doggone to-do about eating"), psychology (he has plans for a novel and a learned tome on the correlation of psychological with physical characteristics), and books (he has five thousand rare volumes in his five-room duplex studio). Other Ziff hobbies are hunting, fishing, woodcraft, and collecting weapons, canes, and perfume bottles. He reads extraordinarily fast, and has the ability to get along with only a few hours of sleep. The author-publisher is said to have a passion for exactitude, but can never balance his checkbook.

References

Mag World 22:8+ My '46 por
N Y Post p39 Je 30 '43 pors; p25 N 20 '44 pors; p12 Je 4 '46

Britannica Book of the Year, 1945
International Who's Who, 1945-46
Who's Who in America, 1946-47
Who's Who in Commerce and Industry (1944)

ZOOK, GEORGE F(REDERICK) (zōōk) Apr. 22, 1885- Educator

Address: b. American Council on Education, 744 Jackson Pl., N.W., Washington, D.C.; h. 4500 Klingle St., N.W., Washington, D.C.

A lifelong exponent of academic freedom, George F. Zook, president of the American Council on Education, is in the forefront of postwar discussions of, and plans for, education. The best protection for academic freedom among educators, he holds, is "to make ourselves worthy of the profession to which we have dedicated ourselves." To an uncommon extent, his own career is seen as combining a scholarly background and a practical understanding of the field of education, both public and private.

Born April 22, 1885, in Fort Scott, Kansas, George Frederick Zook is the son of Douglas and Helen (Follenius) Zook. After his graduation from Fort Scott High School, he attended the University of Kansas, where he received his B.A. in 1906 and his M.A. in 1907. From 1907 to 1909 he was assistant in European history at Cornell University. The two following years were spent as instructor in modern European history at Pennsylvania State College. Cornell awarded him a traveling fellowship in 1911 which enabled him to study European history abroad, and in 1913 he received his Ph.D. from the university. Appointed assistant professor of modern European history at Pennsylvania State College in 1912, Zook became associate professor in 1914, and full professor in 1916, continuing this association until 1920. In 1918 he was also a staff member of the Committee on Public Information in Washington, D.C., and the author of a series of illustrated lectures, *America at War*, issued by the committee. The following year Zook was associate director of the Savings Division of the United States Treasury Department, and published his first book, *The Royal Adventurers Trading Into Africa*. Cited as "a clear, straightforward account of the company's activities and relationships," the material in the book first appeared in the *Journal of Negro History* as a contribution to the history of the slave trade.

In 1920 Zook resigned from his college post to become chief of the Division of Higher Education in the United States Bureau (now Office) of Education. During the five years he held this position his reputation was established as "a careful, scholarly investigator." In 1925 he returned to the university work when he became president of the University of Akron. Commenting on the purposes of this municipal university in an article for the National Education Association *Journal,* Zook pointed out that such institutions are in the current of two main trends in higher education—the growing popularity of publicly supported institutions as well as of the "urban institution." "The keynote of an institution of this type," he declared, "is the direct correlation of the educational program of the institution with the needs of the city. Inasmuch as these needs, both cultural and technical, are at our very doors, they are easily identified and we can make our plans accordingly." Zook also emphasized the value of such institutions in meeting the demand for part-time study by the large proportion of adults beyond normal college age. "Anyone interested in higher education," he stated, "cannot help but be thrilled by buildings aglow with light at night and throngs of serious-minded students passing from one classroom to another. In Akron we say that the second shift of students is at work." Stressing his belief in the civic value of these public institutions, Zook concluded that "a positive community program of cultural education will, in the long run, draw more people away from crime and low pleasures than all the law and police combined."

The educator was president of the University of Akron for eight years, while, in the words of the *Educational Record*, "to a background of historical scholarship and mastery of the problems of higher education he added a growing interest in and understanding of the entire range of education." From 1926 to 1931 he was also secretary of the Commission on Higher Institutions of the North Central Association of Colleges and Secondary Schools. From 1929 to 1931, as a member of the National Advisory Committee on Education (appointed by President Hoover '43 to study the policies and activities of the Federal Government with regard to the education of the American people), Zook was credited with having made "a distinct and important contribution to the work of the committee." He participated, as well, in various state educational surveys, and was the author of survey reports on higher educational institutions in Arkansas, Oklahoma, Kansas, Massachusetts, North Carolina, and other states. He was a member of the California Committee in 1931-32 and of the Iowa Financial Survey made by the Division of Education in 1933.

In the latter year, when President Roosevelt '42 asked Zook to succeed William John Cooper upon the latter's resignation as United States Commissioner of Education, leaders in all branches of education were unanimous in their approval of the selection. *The Journal of Education* cited his understanding of the promotional nature of the office, while the new commissioner defined his task as twofold: 1) to keep educators and citizens informed of the implications which the Federal Emergency Relief Administration program and other recovery agencies had for schools; and 2) to cooperate with the various emergency projects, while directing as much "of our resuscitating power as possible to the schools." Throughout his year in office, Zook concentrated on smoothing the way for the recovery programs, especially as they affected the education of youth as well as adults. In a farewell review of his work, published in *School Life* in May 1934, when he relinquished his duties to assume his present position as president of the American Council on Education, Zook declared, "Our provision for education, in its broadest sense, is the greatest assurance to the American people of an opportunity for an abundant life." And at the National Education Association Convention in Washington in July, Zook spoke of the huge sums appropriated for building roads, while he warned of the need for improvement in the "245,241 one-room rural schools, a large proportion of which are a disgrace to the level of civilization which we claim to have attained."

Upon the retirement of Charles R. Mann in 1934 as director of the American Council on Education, Zook was elected to the office. Thus he became the third director of this educational organization, which was founded in 1918, as the Emergency Council on Education, by a number of prominent educators who had gathered in Washington to discuss the possible contribution of the schools and colleges in the national crisis brought on by the war. In Zook's first year as director his title was changed to president, and the council issued the first of its series of annual reports on the functions of the organization. In a foreword Zook described how the council, through conferences and investigations, "seeks to clarify educational issues of national significance, to define problems, and to enlist appropriate agencies for their solution."

The studies of the council have been intensified during the years of Zook's leadership. In May 1935 the president announced a grant of five hundred thousand dollars from the General Education Board of the Rockefeller Foundation for the expenses of a commission, called the

GEORGE F. ZOOK

American Youth Commission, to study the problems relative to the care and education of American youth. The first meeting of this group was held in Washington in September 1935, at a time when there were millions of unemployed young people in the United States. After six years of study on the part of leaders in education, business, government, and social work, a published report of the commission's activities carried a comprehensive program of action for homes, schools, churches, and private and governmental youth-serving agencies, "at the national, state, and local levels." Discussing this program in an interview for *Parents' Magazine* shortly after the United States entered the war, Zook said, "A new plan of education which might have stirred the whole country with its proposals for far-reaching changes in our educational system now stands in danger of being overlooked."

In his public addresses, as well as in numerous published articles, the educator has urged programs for giving youth an understanding of America's place in the world scene. His activities also include the writing (with M. E. Haggerty in 1936) of a book, *Principles of Accrediting Higher Institutions.* He has emphasized the importance of religious teaching in schools, and hailed the growth in the use of educational films as "potentially the most revolutionary modern instrument in education." In February 1944 Zook announced the formation of a board of noted educators, financed by major film companies, to study educational needs for motion picture material and to plan for production of new films for courses of study. Early in 1944 the council also issued a comprehensive report of a survey undertaken in 1942, under sponsorship of the Office of Coordinator of Inter-American Affairs, which had provided $37,500 for the study and preparation of a program designed to eliminate errors in books and other

teaching materials dealing with Latin America. Zook declared that this report might be considered a milestone in adjustment of educational work to international intellectual cooperation "as the solid rock on which the new world edifice must be built."

Throughout the war emergency the council has frequently represented the colleges in their work with the Army and Navy. In July 1945 Zook announced that, through a grant of one hundred and fifty thousand dollars from the Carnegie Corporation of New York and the General Education Board, the council would conduct a two-year study of what civilian schools and colleges could learn from Army-Navy wartime educational techniques. In September the council called a meeting of educators in Washington to present the attitude toward the proposed international education office. The group included representatives of the State Department, the Carnegie Endowment for International Peace, the Institute of International Education, the American Library Association, and the American Council of Learned Societies. The majority of these leaders expressed overwhelming approval of the United Nations educational organization as a possible means of assuring lasting peace by strengthening the power of the United Nations organization. Zook, who was consultant to the American delegation at the United Nations Conference, said that adoption of the San Francisco Charter was a true beginning toward a better society based on world-wide understanding.

Zook has endorsed proposed legislation for establishment of a National Science Foundation to develop the country's scientific manpower depleted by war. At a Senate committee hearing in November 1945 he observed that the United States had lost almost one college generation of young scientists in the chemical and technological fields as a result of the Selective Service system. In November he also appeared before the House Military Affairs Committee on universal military training legislation, and offered the council's substitute plan, which would defer action on such legislation pending the report of a proposed representative commission to be appointed by Congress and the President, to study every aspect of total defense.

In dealing with other problems of postwar education, Zook has continued to stress the need of Federal aid to schools and colleges, while warning against "legislation poaching on academic freedom." But he would turn the distribution of Federal grants over to the states, to avoid any possible destruction of "prohibitions in State constitutions." In the Inglis Lecture delivered at Harvard University in March 1945, he also urged Federal appropriations of five hundred million dollars per year for the support of education. A limited amount of this money should be available to assist needy talented students.

In July 1946, President Truman '45 appointed Zook chairman of a thirty-member commission on higher education, in charge of investigating the ability of American colleges to absorb the unprecedented number of applicants and to expand facilities for instruction in technological and professional fields. Zook's future educational plans are not wholly domestic, however. He is an advocate of internationalized education and, under his guidance, the American Council on Education supplied film strips on American life to Latin American schools, helped to rehabilitate Chinese schools with the aid of a $75,000 fund, and arranged for better teaching of American history in Canadian schools (and vice versa). As a member of a ten-man mission on education which surveyed schools in the American zone in Germany during September 1946, the educator found German schooling conducive to the development of a caste system and reported that no full democratization of Germany would be possible until its educational system is radically changed.

Zook has received a Litt.D. from Boston University (1934), LL.D. degrees from Ohio Wesleyan University (1931), University of Michigan, Duquesne University, Wayne University, Mt. Union College (all in 1934), and from University of Southern California (1935). In 1937 he was a member and vice-chairman of the President's Advisory Committee on Education. The educator was elected to the board of trustees of the Committee for Economic Development and to the board of trustees of the Institute of International Education in late 1946. He is a Methodist, a member of Phi Beta Kappa, Phi Kappa Phi, Omicron Delta Kappa, Kappa Delta Pi, and Phi Delta Kappa, as well as of the Cosmos Club in Washington. He was married to Susie Gant in 1911.

References

International Who's Who, 1945-46
Leaders in Education (1941)
Who's Who in America, 1946-47
Who's Who in the Nation's Capital, 1938-39

BIOGRAPHICAL REFERENCES CONSULTED

The publication dates listed are those of volumes in CURRENT BIOGRAPHY's reference collection.

American Catholic Who's Who, 1942-43

American Medical Directory, 1942

American Men of Science (1944)

American Women, 1939-40

America's Young Men, 1938-39

Baker's Biographical Dictionary of Musicians (1940)

Baseball Register (1945)

Biographic Register of the Department of State, Sep 1, 1944

Blue Book of American Aviation, 1940

Burke, J. B. Genealogical and Heraldic History of the Peerage and Baronetage, the Privy Council and Knightage (1936) (Burke's Peerage)

Catholic Who's Who, 1941

Chavez, A. V. Contemporary Mexican Artists (1937)

Chemical Who's Who, 1937

Cheney, M. C. Modern Art in America (1939)

Chi è?, (1936)

China Handbook, 1937-1943

Congressional Directory (2d ed., 1945)

Dictionary of the American Hierarchy (1940)

Dictionnaire National des Contemporains (1936)

Directory of Medical Specialists, 1942

Ewen, D. ed. Composers of Today (1936)

Ewen, D. Dictators of the Baton (1943)

Ewen, D. ed. Living Musicians (1940)

Grove, G. Dictionary of Music and Musicians (1927-28)

International Motion Picture Almanac, 1943-44

International Press Who's Who; New Zealand, 1938

International Who's Who, 1945-46

Japan-Manchoukuo Year Book, 1940

Key, P. Pierre Key's Musical Who's Who (1931)

Kunitz. S. J. and Haycraft, H. eds. Junior Book of Authors (1934)

Kunitz, S. J. and Haycraft, H. eds. Twentieth Century Authors (1942)

Leaders in Education (1941)

Mantle, B. Contemporary American Playwrights (1938)

Millett, F. B. Contemporary American Authors (1940)

National Cyclopædia of American Biography Current Volumes A-F (1924-42)

New Standard Encyclopedia of Art (1939)

Parkhurst, W. and De Bekker, L. J. eds. The Encyclopedia of Music and Musicians (1937)

Psychological Register (1932)

Religious Leaders of America, 1941-42

Sobel, B. ed. Theatre Handbook (1940)

Southerner, 1944

Streyckmans, F. B. Today's Young Men (1940)

Texian Who's Who (1937)

Thompson, O. ed. International Cyclopedia of Music and Musicians (1943)

Variety Radio Directory, 1940-41

Vodarsky-Shiraeff, A. comp. Russian Composers and Musicians (1940)

Webster's Biographical Dictionary (1943)

Wer ist Wer (1937)

Wer ist's? (1935)

Who is Who in Music, 1941

Who's Who, 1946

Who's Who Among North American Authors (1939)

Who's Who Among Physicians and Surgeons, 1938

Who's Who in America, 1946-47

Who's Who in American Art, 1940-41

Who's Who in American Education (1941-42)

Who's Who in American Jewry, 1938-39

Who's Who in Australia (1938)

Who's Who in Aviation, 1942-43

Who's Who in Canada, 1936-37

Who's Who in Central and East-Europe, 1935-36

Who's Who in China (1936)

Who's Who in Colored America, 1941-44

Who's Who in Commerce and Industry (1944)

Who's Who in Government, 1932-33

Who's Who in Engineering, 1941

Who's Who in Japan, 1937

Who's Who in Labor (1946)

Who's Who in Latin America (1946)

Who's Who in Law, 1937

Who's Who in Library Service (1943)

Who's Who in New York, 1938

Who's Who in Polish America (1940)

Who's Who in Railroading, 1946

Who's Who in the Clergy, 1935-36

Who's Who in the Nation's Capital, 1938-39

Who's Who in the Theatre (1939)

Who's Who of the Allied Governments, 1943

Wier, A. E. ed. Macmillan Encyclopedia of Music and Musicians (1938)

Women of Achievement (1940)

PERIODICALS AND NEWSPAPERS CONSULTED

A. L. A. Bul—American Library Association Bulletin single copy 25c; free to members. American Library Assn, 520 N Michigan Ave, Chicago 11

Adult Ed J—Adult Education Journal $2. American Association for Adult Education, 525 W 120th St, New York 27
Formerly Journal of Adult Education

Adv & Selling—Advertising and Selling $3. Robbins Pub Co, Inc, 9 E 38th St, New York 16

Am Artist—American Artist $3. Watson-Guptill Publications, Inc, 330 W 42d St, New York 18
Formerly Art Instruction

Am Assn Univ Women J—Journal of the American Association of University Women $1. American Assn of University Women, 1634 I St, N W, Washington 6, D.C.

Am Collector—American Collector $3. Collectors Pub Co, Inc, 432 Fourth Ave, New York 16

Am Federationist—American Federationist $2. American Federation of Labor, 901 Massachusetts Ave, Washington 1, D.C.

Am Hist R—American Historical Review $5; free to members of the American Historical Assn. Macmillan Co, 60 Fifth Ave, New York 11

Am Home—American Home $1.50. American Home Magazine Corp, 55 Fifth Ave, New York 3

Am Mag—American Magazine $3.00. Crowell-Collier Pub Co, 250 Park Ave, New York 17

Am Mercury—American Mercury $3. American Mercury, Inc, 570 Lexington Ave, New York 22

Am Phot—American Photography $2.50. American Photographic Pub Co, 353 Newbury St, Boston 15

Am Pol Sci R—American Political Science Review $5; free to members of the American Political Science Assn, 209 South Hall, Madison 6

Am Scand R—American Scandinavian Review $2; free to members. American Scandinavian Foundation, 116 E 64th St, New York 21

Am Scholar—American Scholar $2.50. United Chapter of Phi Beta Kappa, 5 E 44th St, New York 17

Am Sociol R—American Sociological Review $4 (to libraries $3: to students $2.50). American Sociological Society, C. Taeuber, ed. U.S. Department of Agriculture, Washington 25, D.C.

Amerasia—Amerasia $2.50. Amerasia, 225 Fifth Ave, New York 10

Ann Am Acad—Annals of the American Academy of Political and Social Science $5; free to members. 3457 Walnut St, Philadelphia 4

Apollo—Apollo 35s. Field Press, Ltd, Field House, Bream's Bldgs, Chancery Lane, London. EC 4 ($7.50. 18 E 48th St, New York 17)

Arch Forum—Architectural Forum $4. Time, Inc, 330 E 22d St, Chicago 16

Arch Rec—Architectural Record $3. F. W. Dodge Corp, 119 W 40th St, New York 18

Art Bul—Art Bulletin $10. College Art Assn, Inc, 625 Madison Ave, New York 22

Art Digest—Art Digest $3. Art Digest, Inc, 116 E 59th St, New York 22

Art N—Art News $5.50. Art Foundation, Inc, 136 E 57th St, New York 22

Arts & Arch—Arts and Architecture $3.50. John D. Entenza, 3305 Wilshire Blvd, Los Angeles 5

Asia—Asia and the Americas $4. Asia Press, Inc, 40 E 49th St, New York 17

Asiatic R—Asiatic Review £1. East and West, Ltd. 3 Victoria St, London, SW 1

Atlan—Atlantic Monthly $5. Atlantic Monthly Co, 8 Arlington St, Boston 16

Automotive Industries—Automotive and Aviation Industries $1. Chilton Co, 56th & Chestnut Sts, Philadelphia 39

Baltimore Sun Mag—Baltimore Sun Magazine $5.20. A. S. Abell Co, Baltimore & Charles Sts, Baltimore 3

Bet Hom & Gard—Better Homes & Gardens $1.50. Meredith Pub Co, 1714 Locust St, Des Moines 3, Iowa

Book-of-the-Month Club N—Book-of-the-Month Club News Free to members. Book-of-the Month Club, Inc, 385 Madison Ave, New York 17

Books (N Y Herald Tribune) See N Y Herald Tribune Books

Books (N Y Times) See N Y Times Book R

Books Abroad—Books Abroad $2. University of Oklahoma Press, Norman, Okla.

Brooklyn Eagle—Eagle $8. F. D. Schroth, 24 Johnson St, Brooklyn 1

Bul Bibliog—Bulletin of Bibliography and Dramatic Index $3. F. W. Faxon Co, 83 Francis St, Boston 15

Bul Museum Modern Art See New York City. Museum of Modern Art Bul

Bul Pan Am Union—Bulletin of the Pan American Union $1.50. Pan American Union, 17th St and Constitution Ave, N W, Washington 6, D.C.

Bsns W—Business Week $5. McGraw-Hill Pub Co, Inc, 330 W 42d St, New York 18

Calif Arts & Arch—California Arts & Architecture. See Arts and Architecture

Canad Forum—Canadian Forum $2. Canadian Forum, Ltd, 16 Huntley St, Toronto 5, Canada

Canad Hist R—Canadian Historical Review $2. University of Toronto Press, Toronto 5

Cath Lib World—Catholic Library World $5; free to members. Catholic Library Assn, P.O. Box 631, Scranton, Pa.

Cath N—Catholic News $2.50. C. H. Ridder, 22 N William St, New York 7

Cath School J—Catholic School Journal $2.50. Bruce Pub Co, 540 N Milwaukee St, Milwaukee 2, Wis.

Cath World—Catholic World $4. Missionary Society of St Paul the Apostle, 401 W 59th St, New York 19

Chicago Daily N—News $13.20. Chicago Daily News, Inc, 400 W Madison St, Chicago 6

Christian Cent—Christian Century $5. Christian Century Press, 407 S Dearborn St, Chicago 5

Christian Sci Mon—Christian Science Monitor (Atlantic edition) $12. Christian Science Pub Soc, 1 Norway St, Boston 15

Christian Sci Mon Mag—Christian Science Monitor Weekly Magazine Section $2.60. Christian Science Pub Soc, 1 Norway St, Boston 15

Civil Eng—Civil Engineering $5. American Society of Civil Engineers, 33 W 39 St, New York 18

Col Engl—College English $3. University of Chicago Press, 5750 Ellis Ave, Chicago

Collier's—Collier's $3. Crowell-Collier Pub Co, Springfield, Ohio

Commonweal—Commonweal $5. Commonweal Pub Co, Inc, 386 Fourth Ave, New York 16

Cong Digest—Congressional Digest $5. Congressional Digest, 726 Jackson Pl, N W, Washington 6, D.C.

Connoisseur—Connoisseur 43s. Connoisseur, Ltd, 28 & 30 Grosvenor Gardens, London, SW 1 ($7.50. Connoisseur and International Studio, 572 Madison Ave, New York 22)
Published quarterly after September 1941

Contemp—Contemporary Review $9.50. British Periodicals Ltd, 46-47 Chancery Lane, London, WC 2

Coronet—Coronet $3. D. A. Smart, 919 N Michigan Ave, Chicago 11
Cosmopolitan—Cosmopolitan $3.50. Hearst Magazines, Inc, 57th St & Eighth Ave, New York 19
Cue (Manhattan edition) $3. Cue Publishing Co, Inc, 6 E 39th St, New York 16
Cur Hist ns—Current History $3. Events Pub Co, Inc, 2030 Upland Way, Philadelphia 31
Cur Opinion—Current Opinion (discontinued)

Design—Design $3. Design Pub Co, 131 E State St, Columbus 15, Ohio
Detroit Free Press—Free Press $15.60. Knight Newspapers, Inc, 321 Lafayette Blvd, Detroit 31
Dram Mir—Dramatic Mirror (discontinued)
Dublin R—Dublin Review 15s. Burns Oates & Washbourne, Ltd, 28 Ashley Pl, London, SW 1 ($4 International News Co, 131 Varick St, New York 13)

Eccl R—Ecclesiastical Review $4. American Ecclesiastical Review, Catholic University of America, Washington, D.C.
Educa—Education $4. Palmer Co, 370 Atlantic Ave, Boston 10
El Engl R—Elementary English Review $2.50. National Council of Teachers of English, 211 W 68th St, Chicago 21
Engl J—English Journal $3. University of Chicago Press, 5750 Ellis Ave, Chicago 37
Engl J (H S ed) See Engl J
Esquire—Esquire $5. Esquire, Inc, 919 N Michigan Ave, Chicago 11
Etude—Etude $2.50. Theodore Presser Co, 1712 Chestnut St, Philadelphia 1

Facts on File—Facts on File $25. Person's Index, Facts on File, Inc, 516 Fifth Ave, New York 9
Flying—Flying $4. Ziff-Davis Pub Co, 185 N Wabash Ave, Chicago 1
For Affairs—Foreign Affairs $5. Council on Foreign Relations, Inc, 58 E 68th St, New York 21
For Policy Rep—Foreign Policy Reports $5. (to libraries subscription includes Foreign Policy Bulletins and 6 headline books); $3 to F. P. A. members. Foreign Policy Assn, Inc, 22 E 38th St, New York 16
Forbes—Forbes $4. B. C. Forbes & Sons Pub Co, Inc, 120 Fifth Ave, New York 11
Fortnightly—Fortnightly $8.50. Fortnightly Review, 4, 5, & 6 Soho Sq, London, W 1
Fortune—Fortune $10. Time, Inc, 330 E 22d St, Chicago 16
Forum—Forum $3. Events Pub Co, Inc, 2030 Upland Way, Philadelphia 31
Forum combined with Current History from May 30, 1940, to August 31, 1945; resumed publication as an independent magazine in September of 1945.
Free World—Free World $4. Free World, Inc, 144 Bleecker St, New York 12

Good H—Good Housekeeping $3.50. Hearst Magazines, Inc, 57th St. & Eighth Ave, New York 19

Harper—Harper's Magazine $4. Harper & Bros, 49 E 33d St, New York 16
Harper's Bazaar—Harper's Bazaar $5. Hearst Magazines, Inc. 572 Madison Ave, New York 22
Home & F See House B
Horn Bk—Horn Book $2.50. Horn Book, Inc, 248 Boylston St, Boston 16
House & Gard—House and Garden $4. Condé Nast Publications, Inc, Graybar Bldg, 420 Lexington Ave, New York 17
House B—House Beautiful $4. Hearst Magazines, Inc, 572 Madison Ave, New York 22

Illus Lond N—Illustrated London News £4 9s 6d. 1 New Oxford St, London, WC 1 (American edition $16. British edition $18. International News Co, 131 Varick St, New York 13)
Ind Woman—Independent Woman $1.50. National Federation of Business and Professional Women's Clubs, Inc, 1819 Broadway, New York 23
Independent—Independent $1. The Independent, Hotel Astor, Times Sq, New York 19
Inland Printer—Inland Printer $4. Maclean-Hunter Pub Corp, 309 W Jackson Blvd, Chicago 6
Inter-American—Inter-American $3. J. I. B. McCulloch, 415 Lexington Ave, New York 17

J Home Econ—Journal of Home Economics $3. American Home Economics Assn, 620 Mills Bldg, Washington 6, D.C.
J Negro Hist—Journal of Negro History $4. Association for the Study of Negro Life and History, 1538 Ninth St, N W, Washington 1, D.C.

Knickerbocker W—Knickerbocker Weekly. The Netherlands Pub Co, 30 Rockefeller Plaza, New York 20

Ladies' Home J—Ladies' Home Journal $3. Curtis Pub Co, Independence Sq, Philadelphia 5
Liberty—Liberty $3.50. Liberty Magazine, Inc, 37 W 57th St, New York 19
Library J—Library Journal $5. R. R. Bowker Co, 62 W 45th St, New York 19
Life—Life $4.50. Time, Inc, 330 E 22d St, Chicago 16
Life & Letters To-day—Life and Letters To-day 14s. 430 Strand, London WC 2 ($3.50 International News Co, 131 Varick St, New York 13)
Lon Studio. See Studio
Look—Look $2.50. Cowles Magazines, Inc, 511 Fifth Ave, New York 17

Mademoiselle—Mademoiselle $3. Street & Smith Publications, Inc, 122 E 42d St, New York 17
Mag Art—Magazine of Art $5; free to members. American Federation of Arts. Barr Bldg, Farragut Sq, Washington 6, D.C.
Mag of Wall Street—Magazine of Wall Street $10. C. G. Wyckoff, 90 Broad St, New York 4
Mag World—Magazine World $4. Magazine World, Inc, 40 E 49th St, New York 17
Mo Labor R—Monthly Labor Review $3.50. Supt. of Documents, Washington 25, D.C.
Motion Pict Classic—Motion Picture Classic (discontinued)
Movie Classic—Movie Classic (discontinued)
Mus Am—Musical America $4. Musical America Corp, 113 W 57th St, New York 19
Mus Courier—Musical Courier $3. Music Periodicals Corp, 119 W 57th St, New York 19
Mus Q—Musical Quarterly $3 G. Schirmer, Inc, 3 E 43d St, New York 17
Musician—Musician $3. AMF Artists Service, Inc, 139 E 47th St, New York 17

N Y Dram—New York Dramatic Mirror (discontinued)
N Y Herald Tribune—New York Herald Tribune $17, including Sunday edition. New York Tribune, Inc, 230 W 41st St, New York 18
N Y Herald Tribune Books—New York Herald Tribune Books $1. New York Tribune, Inc, 230 W 41st St, New York 18
N Y Post—New York Post $16.50, including Saturday edition. New York Post, Inc, 75 West St, New York 6
N Y State Ed—New York State Education $2. New York State Teachers Assn, 152 Washington Ave, Albany 6

N Y Sun—New York Sun $12. New York Sun, Inc, 280 Broadway, New York 7

N Y Times—New York Times $17, including Sunday edition. The New York Times Co, 229 W 43d St, New York 18

N Y Times Book R—New York Times Book Review $2. The New York Times Co, 229 W 43d St, New York 18

N Y Times Mag—New York Times Magazine $6. (Complete Sunday edition; not sold separately) New York Times Co, Times Sq, New York 18

N Y World-Telegram—New York World-Telegram $12. New York World-Telegram Corp, 125 Barclay St, New York 7

Nashville Banner—Banner $13. J. G. Stahlman, 11th Ave & Broadway, Nashville, Tenn.

Nat Ed Assn J—Journal of the National Education Association $3; free to members. National Education Assn, 1201 16th St, N W, Washington 6, D.C.

Nat Geog Mag—National Geographic Magazine $4. National Geographic Soc, 1146 16th St, N W, Washington 6, D.C.

Nat R—National Review 36s. Rolls House, 2 Bream's Bldgs, London, EC 4 ($8.50 International News Co, 131 Varick St, New York 13)

Nation—The Nation $5. The Nation Associates, Inc, 20 Vesey St, New York 7

Nation's Bsns—Nation's Busniess $12 (3 years). Chamber of Commerce of the United States, 1615 H St, N W, Washington 6, D.C.

Natur Hist—Natural History $4. American Museum of Natural History, 79th St and Central Park West, New York 24

Nature—Nature £4 10s; single numbers 1s 6d. Macmillan & Co, Ltd, St Martin's St, London, WC 2 ·($22.50; single numbers 50c. Macmillan Co, 60 Fifth Av, New York 11)

Nature Mag—Nature Magazine $3. American Nature Assn, 1214 16th St, N W, Washington 6, D.C.

New Eng Q—New England Quarterly $4. New England Quarterly, 200 Stevens Hall, Orono, Me.

New Repub—New Republic $5. Editorial Publications, Inc, 40 E 49th St, New York 17

New Statesm & Nation—New Statesman and Nation—Week-end Review 32s 6d. 10 Great Turnstile, London, WC 1 ($7 International News Co, 131 Varick St, New York 13)

New York City. Museum of Modern Art Bul—Bulletin of the Museum of Modern Art. 10c a copy; free to members. Museum of Modern Art, 11 W 53d St, New York 19

New Yorker—New Yorker $6. F-R. Pub Corp, 25 W 43d St, New York 18

Newsweek—Newsweek $5. Weekly Publications, Inc, Newsweek Bldg, 152 W 42d St, New York 18

19th Cent—Nineteenth Century and After $8.75. Constable & Co, Ltd, 10 Orange St, London, WC 2

Opera N—Opera News $3; free to members. Metropolitan Opera Guild, Inc, 654 Madison Ave, New York 21

Parnassus—Parnassus (discontinued)

Pathfinder—Pathfinder $1. Farm Journal, Inc, Washington Sq, Philadelphia 5

Pencil P—Pencil Points Progressive Architecture $3. Reinhold Pub Corp, 330 W 42d St, New York 18

Philadelphia Record—Philadelphia Record $9.36. Philadelphia Record Co, Broad & Wood Sts, Philadelphia 1

Photoplay—Photoplay $3.60 (two years). Macfadden Publications, Inc, 205 E 42d St, New York 17
   Combined with Movie Mirror

PM—PM $15.50, including Sunday edition. Harry C. Holden, Subscription Manager, P.O. Box 81, Times Square Station, New York 18; The Newspaper PM, Inc, 164 Duane St, New York 13

Poetry—Poetry $3. 232 E Erie St, Chicago 11

Pol Sci Q—Political Science Quarterly $5; free to members. Academy of Political Science, Columbia University, New York 27

Pop Mech—Popular Mechanics Magazine $2.50. Popular Mechanics Co, 200 E Ontario St, Chicago 11

Pop Sci—Popular Science Monthly $2.50. Popular Science Pub Co, Inc, 353 Fourth Ave, New York 10

Progress Educ—Progressive Education $3. American Education Fellowship, 289 Fourth Ave, New York 10

Prométhée—Prométhée L'Amour de l'Art (discontinued)

Pub W—Publishers' Weekly $5. R. R. Bowker Co, 62 W 45th St, New York 19

Q R—Quarterly Review 31s 4d. J. Murray, 50 Albemarle St, London, W 1. ($6.50 International News Co, 131 Varick St, New York 13)

Queen's Q—Queen's Quarterly $2. Queen's University, Kingston, Canada

Railway Conductor—Railway Conductor $1.50. Order of Railway Conductors, Cedar Rapids, Iowa

Read Digest—Reader's Digest $3. Reader's Digest Assn, Inc, Pleasantville, N.Y.

Ref Shelf—Reference Shelf $6 per volume of ten bound numbers, published irregularly. H. W. Wilson Co, 950-972 University Ave, New York 52

Rensselaer Polytechnic—Renssalaer Polytechnic $1.50 Renssalaer Polytechnic Institute, Drawer 958, Troy, New York

Rotarian—Rotarian $1.50. Rotary International, 35 E Wacker Drive, Chicago 1

Roy Inst Brit Arch J—Journal of the Royal Institute of British Architects £1 16s postpaid. The Institute, 66 Portland Pl, London, W 1

St Louis Post-Dispatch—Post-Dispatch $15. Pulitzer Pub Co, 1111 Olive St, St. Louis 1, Mo.

Sales Management—Sales Management $5. Sales Management, Inc, 386 Fourth Ave, New York 16

San Francisco Chronicle—Chronicle $21. Chronicle Pub Co, 901 Mission St, San Francisco 19

Sat Eve Post—Saturday Evening Post $5. The Curtis Pub Co, Independence Sq, Philadelphia 5

Sat R Lit—Saturday Review of Literature $5. Saturday Review Associates, Inc, 25 W 45th St, New York 19

Sch & Soc—School and Society $5; free to members of the Society for the Advancement of Education, Inc, 15 Amsterdam Ave, New York 23

Sch Arts—School Arts $4. School Arts, Printers Bldg, 44 Portland St, Worcester 8, Mass.

Sch R—School Review $2.50. University of Chicago Press, 5750 Ellis Ave, Chicago 37

Scholastic—Senior Scholastic (High School Teacher edition) $2.25 (teacher ed. only); school group rate (two or more subscriptions to one address) $1 for special eds, $1.30 for combined ed. Scholastic Corp, 220 E 42d St, New York 17

Sci Am—Scientific American $4. Munn & Co, Inc, 24 W 40th St, New York 18

Sci Mo—Scientific Monthly $5. American Assn for the Advancement of Science, Smithsonian Institution Bldg, Washington 25, D.C.

Sci N L—Science News Letter $5. Science Service, Inc, 1719 N St, N W, Washington 6, D.C.

Science—Science $6. Science Pr, American University, Massachusetts & Nebraska Aves, Washington 16, D.C.

Science ns—Science (new series) $6. Science Press, Lancaster, Pa.

Scrib Mag—Scribner's Magazine (discontinued)

So Atlan Q—South Atlantic Quarterly $3. Duke University Press, Durham, N.C.

Spec—Spectator 30s. 99 Gower St, London, WC 1 ($7 International News Co, 131 Varick St, New York 13)

Stage Pict—Stage Pictorial $2.50. Stage Pictorial Pub Co, 1501 Broadway, New York 18

Studio—Studio $6. Studio Publication, Inc, 381 Fourth Ave, New York 16 (30s; The Studio, Ltd, 66 Chandos Pl, London, WC 2)

Sunday News—News $2.50. News Syndicate Co, Inc, 220 E 42d St, New York 17

Sunset Mag—Sunset Magazine $1.50. Lane Pub Co, 576 Sacramento St, San Francisco 11

Survey—Survey Midmonthly $3. Survey Associates, Inc, 112 E 19th St, New York 3

Survey G—Survey Graphic $3. Survey Associates, Inc, 112 E 19th St, New York 3

Theatre Arts—Theatre Arts $5. Theatre Arts, Inc, 130 W 56th St, New York 19

This Month—This Month Magazine $3. Association for the Promotion of International Understanding, Inc, 247 Park Ave, New York 17

This Week Mag—This Week Magazine. Distributed each Sunday with different newspapers. United Newspapers Magazine Corp, 420 Lexington Ave, New York 17

Time—Time $5. Time, Inc, 330 E 22d St, Chicago 16

Town and Country—Town and Country $5. Hearst Magazines, Inc, 572 Madison Ave, New York 22

Travel—Travel $4. Robert M. McBride & Co, Inc, 116 E 16th St, New York 3

U S Bur Labor. See Mo Labor R

U S Bur Labor Bul—United States Bureau of Labor Statistics. Bulletins. Free to libraries. Bureau of Labor Statistics, Washington, D.C. Purchase orders, Supt. of Documents, Washington 25, D.C.

U S News—United States News $4. United States News Pub Corp, 24th & N Sts, N W, Washington 7, D.C.

U S Office Educ Bul—United States Office of Education. Bulletins. Free to libraries. Office of Education, Washington, D.C. Purchase orders, Supt. of Documents, Washington 25, D.C.

Va Q R—Virginia Quarterly Review $3. University of Virginia, 1 West Range, Charlottesville, Va.

Variety—Variety $10. Variety, Inc, 154 W 46th St, New York 19

Victor Record R—Victor Record Review 60c. RCA Victor div of Radio Corp of America, Camden, N.J.

Vital Speeches—Vital Speeches of the Day $3.50. City News Pub Co, 33 W 42d St, New York 18

Vogue—Vogue (Incorporating Vanity Fair) $6. Condé Nast Publications Inc, Greenwich, Conn.

War Cry—War Cry $3.50. The Salvation Army, 120 W 14th St, New York 11

Wilson Lib Bul—Wilson Library Bulletin $1. H. W. Wilson Co, 950-972 University Ave, New York 52

Woman's Home C—Woman's Home Companion $1.50. Crowell-Collier Pub Co, Springfield, Ohio

World Report—World Report $4. United States News Pub Corp, 24th & N Sts, Washington 7, D.C.

Writer—The Writer $3. The Writer, Inc, 8 Arlington St, Boston 16

Yale R ns—Yale Review $3. 143 Elm St, New Haven 7, Conn.

Young Wings—Young Wings Free to members. Junior Literary Guild, Garden City, N.Y.

NECROLOGY—1946

This is an index to notices of deaths which occurred between November 15, 1945, and December 31, 1946. Deaths which occurred in late 1946 are recorded in early 1947 issues of CURRENT BIOGRAPHY; references to those issues are included in this index. See 1940-1945 Yearbooks for the necrologies of those six years.

Adams, Joseph Quincy
Alekhine, Alexander
Ananda Mahidol
Andrews, Charles O(scar)
Antonescu, Ion (biog 1940)
Arliss, George
Arthur, Sir George (Compton Archibald)
Aston, Francis William
Atwill, Lionel
Ayres, Leonard Porter (biog 1940)

Bagley, William Chandler
Bailey, Josiah W(illiam) See Jan 47 (biog 1945)
Bailey, Thomas L.
Baker, Ray Stannard (biog 1940)
Bankhead, John H(ollis) (biog 1943)
Bantock, Sir Granville
Barclay, McClelland (biog 1940)
Barry, William Bernard
Bartlett, Robert A(bram)
Benchley, Robert (Charles) (biog 1941)
Boardman, Mabel (Thorp) biog 1944)
Bowes, Edward (biog 1941)
Bragon, Claude (Fayette)
Browne, Edward E(verts)
Browne, George Elmer
Bruce, William Cabell
Buell, Raymond Leslie
Burgin, William O(lin)
Butterworth, Charles (Edward)

Carr, Alexander
Cartier (de Marchienne, Emile de), Baron
Cartotto, Ercole
Case, Frank
Castañeda, Jorge Ubico See Ubico Castañeda, J. (biog 1942)
Chalmers, Philip O(wen)
Chapman, Frank M(ichler)
Cheatham, Kitty
Cullen, Countee
Curry, John Steuart. (biog 1941)

Daluege, Kurt
Dandy, Walter E(dward)
Davey, Martin L(uther)
De Cartier (de Marchienne, Emile), Baron See Cartier de M., E. de, Baron

De Casseres, Benjamin
De Falla, Manuel See Falla, M. de
Dixon, Thomas
Donahey, (Alvin) Vic(tor)
Donald, W(illiam) H(enry) (biog 1946)
Dreiser, Theodore

Erickson, John Edward

Fairchild, Benjamin Lewis
Fairfax, Beatrice (biog 1944)
Falk, Maurice
Falla, Manuel de
Ferguson, (George) Howard
Flexner, Simon
Frank, Hans (biog 1941)
Frick, Wilhelm (biog 1942)

Gág, Wanda
Galen, Clemens August, Cardinal, Count von
Gallagher, William J.
Garnsey, Elmer Ellsworth
Gasch, Marie Manning See Fairfax, B. (biog 1944)
Gaumont, Léon Ernest
Glasgow, Ellen (Anderson Gholson)
Glass, Carter (biog 1941)
Glennon, John, Cardinal
Glintenkamp, H(endrik)
Goldsborough, Phillips Lee
Göring, Hermann Wilhelm (biog 1941)
Gort, (John Standish Surtees Prendergast Vereker, 6th) Viscount (biog 1940)
Gould, Arthur R(obinson)
Grayson, David See Baker, R. S. (biog 1940)
Groves, Ernest R(utherford) (biog 1943)
Gullion, Allen W(yant) (biog 1943)

Hamilton, Clayton (Meeker)
Hansson, Per Albin (biog 1942)
Harris, William, Jr.
Hart, William S.
Hauptmann, Gerhart
Haushofer, Karl (Ernst Nikolaus) (biog 1942)

Henry, Mellinger Edward
Hertzler, Arthur E(manuel)
Hill, George Washington (biog 1946)
Hill, Patty Smith
Hillman, Sidney (biog 1940)
Holaday, William Perry
Honjo, Shigeru, Baron
Hopkins, Harry L(loyd) (biog 1941)
Houston, Robert Griffith
Hunter, Glenn
Hurley, Charles F(rancis)

Inglis, John J.

James, Alexander R.
James, W. Frank
Jeans, Sir James (Hopwood) (biog 1941)
Jodl, Alfred
Johnson, Jack
Judd, Charles Hubbard

Kagey, Rudolf
Kalinin, Mikhail Ivanovich (biog 1942)
Kaltenbrunner, Ernst (biog 1943)
Keane, Doris
Keitel, Wilhelm (biog 1940)
Kemmerer, E(dwin) W(alter) (biog 1941)
Keynes, (John Maynard Keynes, 1st) Baron (biog 1941)
Keyserling, Hermann (Alexander), Count
Konoye, Fumimaro, Prince (biog 1940)
Kunz, Stanley H(enry)

Lang, Cosmo Gordon, 1st Baron Lang of Lambeth See Lang of Lambeth, C.G.L., 1st Baron (biog 1941)
Lang of Lambeth, Cosmo Gordon Lang, 1st Baron (biog 1941)
Lanvin, Jeanne
Largo Caballero, Francisco
La Rocque, François de
Lazzeri, Tony
Lea, Luke
Lewis, Ethelreda
Li Lieh-Chun

Liggett, Louis Kroh
Long, Andrew Theodore
Luce, Robert

MacAlarney, Robert E(mmet)
MacDonald, William J(osiah)
McGovern, Francis Edward
Machado (Hernandez), Alfredo
McReynolds, James Clark
Magner, Thomas F(rancis)
Marburg, Theodore
Marion, George
Martin, Charles H(enry)
Matsui, Keishiro, Baron
Matsuoka, Yosuke (biog 1941)
Maxton, James
Mechau, Frank, Jr.
Mechem, Merritt Cramer
Merivale, Philip
Merritt, Matthew J.
Mikhailovitch, Draja (biog 1942)
Morgan, Thomas Hunt
Morris, Roland Sletor
Moscicki, Ignace
Motherwell, Hiram

Nash, Paul
Neilson, William Allan
Neurath, Otto
Nevinson, Christopher R(ichard) W(ynne)

Oldfield, Barney
Oppenheim, E(dward) Phillips

Parker, Homer Cling
Patch, Alexander M(cCarrell, Jr.) (biog 1943)
Patterson, Joseph M(edill) (biog 1942)
Patton, George S(mith), Jr. (biog 1943)
Pelley, John J(eremiah)
Perry, Antoinette
Pinchot, Gifford
Poindexter, Miles
Pollock, Channing
Potemkin, Vladimir P(etrovich)

Quisling, Vidkun (Abraham Lauritz) (biog 1940)

Ragland, Rags
Raimu, Jules
Rathbone, Eleanor (biog 1943)
Rhys, Ernest
Ribbentrop, Joachim von (biog 1941)
Richardson, Henrietta See Richardson, H. H.
Richardson, Henry Handel
Rios, Juan Antonio (biog 1942)
Roberts, Albert H.
Rosé, Arnold Josef
Rosenberg, Alfred (biog 1941)
Rosenfeld, Paul
Rosenthal, Moriz
Ross, C(harles) Ben
Rowe, L(eo) S(tanton) See Jan 47 (biog 1945)
Runyon, Damon See Jan 47 (biog 1942)

Sauckel, Fritz
Saxon, Lyle
Scott, John R. K.
Sert, José Maria
Seton, Ernest Thompson (biog 1943)
Seyss-Inquart, Artur von (biog 1941)
Sheldon, Charles M(onroe), Rev.
Sheldon, Edward (Brewster)
Shreve, R(ichmond) H(arold) (biog 1945)
Sinclair, May
Skidmore, Hubert Standish
Small, John Humphrey
Smith, Logan Pearsall
Snyder, J(ohn) Buell
Steel, Kurt See Kagey, R.
Stein, Gertrude
Stella, Joseph
Stephens, Hubert D(urrett)
Stieglitz, Alfred (biog 1940)
Stilwell, Joseph W(arren) (biog 1942)

Stone, Harlan Fiske (biog 1941)
Streicher, Julius
Summerville, Slim
Sydney, Mrs. Basil See Keane, D.

Talmadge, Eugene See Feb 47 (biog 1941)
Tarkington, (Newton) Booth
Taylor, Laurette See Jan 47 (biog 1945)
Tener, John Kinley
Thorkelson, Jacob
Toch, Maximilian
Train, Arthur (Cheney)
Tuttle, (Henry) Emerson

Ubico, (Castañeda), Jorge (biog 1942)
Underhill, Charles L.
Utley, George B(urwell)

Valentine, Lewis J(oseph) See Feb 47 (biog 1946)
Vickery, H(oward) L(eroy) (biog 1943)
Von Galen, Clemens August, Cardinal, Count See Galen, C. A., Cardinal, Count von
Von Ribbentrop, Joachim See Ribbentrop, J. von (biog 1941)
Von Seyss-Inquart, Artur See Seyss-Inquart, A. von (biog 1941)
Von Tilzer, Harry

Waesche, Russell R(andolph) (biog 1945)
Walsh, Joseph
Waters, James R.
Wells, Gabriel
Wells, H(erbert) G(eorge)
Weyerhaeuser, Rudolph M(ichael)
White, S(ebastian) Harrison
White, Stewart Edward

Yost, Fielding Harris
Youmans, Vincent (biog 1944)

CLASSIFICATION BY PROFESSION—1946

Agriculture

Bennett, Hugh H(ammond)
Capper, Arthur
Eisenhower, Milton S(tover)
O'Neal, Edward A(sbury, 3d)
Orr, Sir John Boyd
Pinchot, Gifford obit
Ross, C(harles) Ben obit
Thompson, Roy L(eland)
Watts, Lyle F(ord)
Williams, Tom

Architecture

Abercrombie, Sir (Leslie) Patrick
Bragdon, Claude (Fayette) obit
Mechau, Frank, Jr. obit
Shreve, R(ichmond) H(arold) obit
Van Pelt, John V(redenburgh)
Wurster, William Wilson

Art

Barclay, McClelland obit
Browne, George Elmer obit
Calder, Alexander
Cartotto, Ercole obit
Curry, John Steuart obit
Du Bois, Guy Pène
Gág, Wanda obit
Garnsey, Elmer Ellsworth obit
Gaumont, Léon Ernest obit
Glintenkamp, H(endrik) obit
Inglis, John J. obit
Irene
James, Alexander R. obit
Jones, Robert Edmond
Lanvin, Jeanne obit
Mechau, Frank, Jr. obit
Mielziner, Jo
Nash, Paul obit
Nevinson, Christopher R(ich-ard) W(ynne) obit
Oenslager, Donald (Mitchell)
Partch, Virgil F(ranklin)
Rea, Gardner
Rogers, Bruce
Rosenfeld, Paul obit
Sert, José Maria obit
Seton, Ernest Thompson obit
Stella, Joseph obit
Stieglitz, Alfred obit
Szyk, Arthur
Toch, Maximilian obit
Tuttle, (Henry) Emerson obit
Williams, Gluyas

Aviation

Göring, Hermann Wilhelm obit

Patterson, W(illiam) A(llan)
Piper, W(illiam) T(homas)
Roosevelt, Elliott
Winster, (Reginald Thomas Herbert Fletcher, 1st) Baron
Wright, Orville

Business

Allen, George E(dward)
Baillie, Hugh
Balaban, Barney
Billingsley, (John) Sherman
Birdseye, Clarence
Birdwell, Russell (Juarez)
Bowes, Edward obit
Bullis, Harry A(mos)
Burgin, William O(lin) obit
Capper, Arthur
Case, Frank obit
Chalmers, Philip O(wen) obit
Dart, Justin W(hitlock)
Davey, Martin L(uther) obit
Donahey, (Alvin) Vic(tor) obit
DuMont, Allen B(alcom)
Emery, DeWitt (McKinley)
Fairchild, Benjamin Lewis obit
Ferguson, (George) Howard obit
Hill, George Washington biog and obit
Hoffman, Paul G(ray)
Houston, Robert Griffith obit
Hoving, Walter
Hurley, Charles F(rancis) obit
Jackson, William K(enneth)
Korda, Sir Alexander
Lasser, J(acob) K(ay)
Liggett, Louis Kroh obit
Lincoln, Leroy A(lton)
Luce, Robert obit
Mack, Walter S(taunton), Jr.
Mead, George H(ouk)
Pasquel, Jorge
Patterson, W(illiam) A(llan)
Piper, W(illiam) T(homas)
Reece, B(razilla) Carroll
Rosenbach, A(braham) S(imon) W(olf)
Schacht, Al(exander)
Shaver, Dorothy
Short, Walter C(ampbell)
Small, John D(avis)
Stelle, John
Valentina
Wakeman, Frederic
Wells, Gabriel obit
Weyerhaeuser, Rudolph M(i-chael) obit
Wherry, Kenneth S(picer)
Woods, Mark
Wyatt, Wilson W(atkins)
Ziff, William B(ernard)

Dance

Dolin, Anton
Laing, Hugh

Diplomacy

Atcheson, George, Jr.
Cartier (de Marchienne, Emile de), Baron obit
Castillo Nájera, Francisco
Chalmers, Philip O(wen) obit
Fletcher, Sir Angus (Somer-ville)
Gavrilovic, Stoyan
Harriman, W(illiam) Averell
Hodgson, W(illiam) R(oy)
Hopkins, Harry L(loyd) obit
Johnson, Herschel V.
Leao Velloso, P(edro)
Lie, Trygve (Halvdan)
Machado (Hernandez), Alfredo obit
Marburg, Theodore obit
Matsui, Keishiro, Baron obit
Matsuoka, Yôsuke obit
Morris, Roland Sletor obit
Noel-Baker, Philip J(ohn)
Padilla Nervo, Luis
Parodi, Alexandre
Patterson, Richard C(unning-ham), Jr.
Poindexter, Miles obit
Potemkin, Vladimir P(etrovich) obit
Quo Tai-chi
Ribbentrop, Joachim von obit
Shidehara, Kijuro, Baron
Shone, Terence Allen
Yoshida, Shigeru

Education

Adair, Frank E(arl)
Adams, Joseph Quincy obit
Ayres, Leonard Porter obit
Baden-Powell, Lady (Olave St. Clair)
Bagley, William Chandler obit
Bantock, Sir Granville obit
Blanding, Sarah Gibson
Blunt, Katharine
Buell, Raymond Leslie obit
Carmichael, Oliver C(romwell)
Chapman, Frank M(ichler) obit
Cheatham, Kitty obit
Clement, Rufus E(arly)
Commager, Henry Steele
Condon, E(dward) U(hler)
Cullen, Countee obit
Dandy, Walter E(dward) obit
Day, Edmund Ezra
Ede, J(ames) Chuter

Eisenhower, Milton S(tover)
Flexner, Simon obit
Giral (y Pereira), José
Glintenkamp, H(endrik) obit
Goodspeed, Edgar J(ohnson)
Grosvenor, Gilbert (Hovey)
Groves, Ernest R(utherford)
  obit
Guérard, Albert J(oseph)
Haushofer, Karl (Ernst Nikolaus)
  obit
Haynes, George Edmund
Henry, Mellinger Edward obit
Hill, Patty Smith obit
Hovde, Bryn(jolf) J(acob)
Johnson, Charles Spurgeon
Judd, Charles Hubbard obit
Kagey, Rudolf obit
Kemmerer, E(dwin) W(alter)
  obit
Laird, Donald A(nderson)
Lamont, Corliss
Lange, Oscar (Richard)
Lasser, J(acob) K(ay)
Littledale, Clara Savage
Lynch, J(ohn) Joseph, Rev.
MacAlarney, Robert E(mmet)
  obit
Maddy, Joseph E(dgar)
Mechau, Frank, Jr. obit
Mistral, Gabriela
Morgan, Joy Elmer
Morris, Roland Sletor obit
Moscicki, Ignace obit
Moulton, F(orest) R(ay)
Myrdal, (Karl) Gunnar
Neilson, William Allan obit
Neurath, Otto obit
Nourse, Edwin G(riswold)
Orr, Sir John Boyd
Pares, Sir Bernard
Pauli, Wolfgang
Popenoe, Paul (Bowman)
Potemkin, Vladimir P(etrovich)
  obit
Pratt, E(dwin) J(ohn)
Rainey, Homer P(rice)
Reid, Ira De A(ugustine)
Samaroff, Olga
Schlesinger, Arthur M(eier), Jr.
Snyder, J(ohn) Buell obit
Sockman, Ralph W(ashington),
  Rev.
Starr, Mark
Stoddard, George D(insmore)
Stuart, J(ohn) Leighton, Rev.
Taylor, Harold (Alexander)
Toch, Maximilian obit
Tuttle, (Henry) Emerson obit
Utley, George B(urwell) obit
Van Pelt, John V(redenburgh)
Waksman, Selman A(braham)
Wanamaker, Pearl A(nderson)
Weigle, Luther Allan
Witte, Edwin E(mil)
Wurster, William Wilson
Yen, Y(ang-) C(h'u) James
Zook, George F(rederick)

Engineering

Clement, M(artin) W(ithing-
  ton)
Jewett, Frank B(aldwin)
Moreell, Ben
Patterson, Richard C(unning-
  ham), Jr.
Pick, Lewis Andrew

Finance

Altmeyer, Arthur J(oseph)
Ayres, Leonard Porter obit
Bell, Daniel W(afena)
Burgin, William O(lin) obit
Harriman, W(illiam) Averell
Kemmerer, E(dwin) W(alter)
  obit
Keynes, (John Maynard Keynes,
  1st) Baron obit
Reece, B(razilla) Carroll
Thompson, Roy L(eland)
Webb, James E(dwin)

Government—
Foreign

Aga Khan, The (Aga Sultan
  Sir Mahomed Shah)
Alemán, Miguel
Ananda Mahidol obit
Antonescu, Ion obit
Begtrup, Bodil
Cartier (de Marchienne, Emile
  de), Baron obit
Castillo Nájera, Francisco
Charles, Prince of Belgium
Chou En-lai
Corbett, Jim
Cunningham, Sir Alan (Gor-
  don)
Daluege, Kurt obit
Donald, W(illiam) H(enry)
  biog and obit
Duclos, Jacques
Dutra, Eurico Gaspar
Ede, J(ames) Chuter
Ferguson, (George) Howard
  obit
Fletcher, Sir Angus (Somer-
  ville)
Frank, Hans obit
Frick, Wilhelm obit
Gasperi, Alcide de
Gavrilovic, Stoyan
Giral (y Pereira), José
Göring, Hermann Wilhelm obit
Gort, (John Standish Surtees
  Prendergast Vereker, 6th)
  Viscount obit
Gouin, Félix
Hansson, Per Albin obit
Hasluck, Paul
Herriot, Edouard
Hodgson, W(illiam) R(oy)
Jodl, Alfred obit

Joliot-Curie, Frédéric
Kalinin, Mikhail Ivanovich obit
Kaltenbrunner, Ernst obit
Keitel, Wilhelm obit
Keynes, (John Maynard Keynes,
  1st) Baron obit
Konoye, Fumimaro, Prince obit
Kravchenko, Victor A(ndreye-
  vich)
Lange, Oscar (Richard)
Largo Caballero, Francisco
  obit
Lawrence, Sir Geoffrey
Leao Velloso, P(edro)
Lee, Jennie
Li Lieh-Chun obit
Lie, Trygve (Halvdan)
Machado (Hernandez), Alfredo
  obit
McNeil, Hector
Makin, Norman J(ohn)
  O(swald)
Matsui, Keishiro, Baron obit
Matsuoka, Yôsuke obit
Maxton, James obit
Mikhailovitch, Draja obit
Mistral, Gabriela
Morgan, Sir Frederick (Edg-
  worth)
Moscicki, Ignace obit
Myrdal, (Karl) Gunnar
Noel-Baker, Philip J(ohn)
Orr, Sir John Boyd
Owen, A(rthur) David K(emp)
Padilla Nervo, Luis
Pandit, Vijaya Lakshmi
Parodi, Alexandre
Pethick-Lawrence (Frederick
  William Pethick-Lawrence,
  1st) Baron
Potemkin, Vladimir P(etrovich)
  obit
Quisling, Vidkun (Abraham
  Lauritz) obit
Quo Tai-chi
Rathbone, Eleanor obit
Ribbentrop, Joachim von obit
Rios, Juan Antonio obit
Rosenberg, Alfred obit
Roxas (y Acuña), Manuel
Sauckel, Fritz obit
Seyss-Inquart, Artur von obit
Shidehara, Kijuro, Baron
Shone, Terence Allen
Strachey, (Evelyn) John (St.
  Loe)
Streicher, Julius obit
Thorez, Maurice
Tsaldaris, Constantin
Ubico (Castañeda), Jorge obit
Wambaugh, Sarah
Williams, Francis
Williams, Tom
Winster, (Reginald Thomas
  Herbert Fletcher, 1st) Baron
Yen, Y(ang-) C(h'u) James
Yoshida, Shigeru

Government— United States

Allen, George E(dward)
Altmeyer, Arthur J(oseph)
Andrews, Charles O(scar) obit
Atcheson, George, Jr.
Bailey, Thomas L. obit
Baldwin, Raymond E(arl)
Bankhead, John H(ollis) obit
Barry, William Bernard obit
Bell, Daniel W(afena)
Bennett, Hugh H(ammond)
Berge, Wendell
Biffle, Leslie L.
Boardman, Mabel (Thorp) obit
Browne, Edward E(verts) obit
Bruce, William Cabell obit
Buell, Raymond Leslie obit
Burgin, William O(lin) obit
Butler, Sally
Capper, Arthur
Case, Francis (Higbee)
Chalmers, Philip O(wen) obit
Chavez, Dennis
Coffee, John M(ain)
Collet, John C(askie)
Condon, E(dward) U(hler)
Davey, Martin L(uther) obit
Deupree, Richard R(edwood)
Dixon, Thomas obit
Donahey, (Alvin) Vic(tor) obit
Eisenhower, Milton S(tover)
Ellender, Allen J(oseph)
Erickson, John Edward obit
Erskine, G(raves) B(lanchard)
Ethridge, Mark (Foster)
Fairchild, Benjamin Lewis obit
Feller, A(braham) H(oward)
Gallagher, William J. obit
Gillette, Guy M(ark)
Glass, Carter obit
Goldsborough, Phillips Lee obit
Goldstein, Israel, Rabbi
Gould, Arthur R(obinson) obit
Gross, Charles P(hilip)
Gruening, Ernest (Henry)
Gullion, Allen W(yant) obit
Harriman, W(illiam) Averell
Hawley, Paul R(amsey)
Hillman, Sidney obit
Holaday, William Perry obit
Hopkins, Harry L(loyd) obit
Houston, Robert Griffith obit
Hurley, Charles F(rancis) obit
James, W. Frank obit
Johnson, Ed(win Carl)
Johnson, Herschel V.
Keenan, Joseph B(erry)
Kunz, Stanley H(enry) obit
Lausche, Frank J(ohn)
Lea, Clarence F(rederick)
Lea, Luke obit
Littlejohn, Robert McG(owan)
Luce, Robert obit
MacDonald, William J(osiah) obit
McGovern, Francis Edward obit
McKellar, K(enneth) D(ouglas)
McReynolds, James Clark obit

Magner, Thomas F(rancis) obit
Mankin, Helen Douglas
Martin, Charles H(enry) obit
Mead, George H(ouk)
Mechem, Merritt Cramer obit
Merck, George W(ilhelm)
Merritt, Matthew J. obit
Moreell, Ben
Morris, Roland Sletor obit
Nourse, Edwin G(riswold)
O'Neal, Edward A(sbury, 3d)
Parker, Homer Cling obit
Patman, (John William) Wright
Patterson, Richard C(unningham), Jr.
Pelley, John J(eremiah) obit
Pinchot, Gifford obit
Piñero, Jesús T(oribio)
Poindexter, Miles obit
Reece, B(razilla) Carroll
Reid, Ira De A(ugustine)
Rieve, Emil
Rifkind, Simon H(irsch)
Roberts, Albert H. obit
Ross, C(harles) Ben obit
Sabath, Adolph J(oachim)
Saxon, Lyle obit
Scott, John R. K. obit
Small, John D(avis)
Small, John Humphrey obit
Snyder, J(ohn) Buell obit
Starr, Mark
Stephens, Hubert D(urrett) obit
Stoddard, George D(insmore)
Stone, Harlan Fiske obit
Stuart, J(ohn) Leighton, Rev.
Tener, John Kinley obit
Thompson, Roy L(eland)
Thorkelson, Jacob obit
Tobin, Maurice J(oseph)
Tuck, William M(unford)
Underhill, Charles L. obit
Valentine, Lewis J(oseph)
Vickery, H(oward) L(eroy) obit
Walsh, Joseph obit
Watts, Lyle F(ord)
Webb, James E(dwin)
Wherry, Kenneth S(picer)
White, S(ebastian) Harrison obit
Wilson, Frank J(ohn)
Wirtz, W(illiam) Willard
Witte, Edwin E(mil)
Wyatt, Wilson W(atkins)

Industry

Bullis, Harry A(mos)
Clement, M(artin) W(ithington)
Deupree, Richard R(edwood)
Falk, Maurice obit
Ford, Henry, 2d
Frazer, Joseph W(ashington)
Gould, Arthur R(obinson) obit
Harriman, W(illiam) Averell
Hill, George Washington biog and obit

Hoffman, Paul G(ray)
Hormel, Jay C(atherwood)
Jackson, William K(enneth)
Mead, George H(ouk)
Merck, George W(ilhelm)
Metzman, G(ustav)
Patterson, Richard C(unningham), Jr.
Pelley, John J(eremiah) obit
Piper, W(illiam) T(homas)
Roth, Almon E.
Wason, Robert R(oss)
Weyerhaeuser, Rudolph M(ichael) obit

Journalism

Baillie, Hugh
Benchley, Robert (Charles) obit
Birdwell, Russell (Juarez)
Boutell, Clarence B(urley)
Bromley, Dorothy Dunbar
Buckmaster, Henrietta
Buell, Raymond Leslie obit
Carter, (William) Hodding, Jr.
Daly, Maureen (Patricia)
De Casseres, Benjamin obit
Donald, W(illiam) H(enry) biog and obit
Dunbar, Rudolph
Ethridge, Mark (Foster)
Fairfax, Beatrice obit
Gallico, Paul (William)
Gruening, Ernest (Henry)
Hansenne, Marcel (Fernand)
Hargrove, Marion (Lawton, Jr.)
Hasluck, Paul
Hibbs, Ben
Kuhn, Irene
Long, Tania
MacAlarney, Robert E(mmet) obit
McNeil, Hector
Motherwell, Hiram obit
Patterson, Joseph M(edill) obit
Phillips, Lena Madesin
Reves, Emery
Rosenberg, Alfred obit
Rusk, Howard A(rchibald)
Sauckel, Fritz obit
Saxon, Lyle obit
Streicher, Julius obit
Watson, Mark S(kinner)
Williams, Francis
Winster, (Reginald Thomas Herbert Fletcher, 1st) Baron

Labor

Beirne, J(oseph) A.
Hillman, Sidney obit
Johnston, Alvanley
Kroll, Jack
Largo Caballero, Francisco obit
Lee, Jennie
Maxton, James obit

Mooney, Edward, Cardinal
Potofsky, Jacob S(amuel)
Rieve, Emil
Sauckel, Fritz obit
Schneiderman, Rose
Stacy, Walter P(arker)
Starr, Mark
Thorez, Maurice
Walsh, J(ohn) Raymond
Whitney, A(lexander) F(ell)

Law

Alemán, Miguel
Baldwin, Raymond E(arl)
Barry, William Bernard obit
Berge, Wendell
Butler, Sally
Chavez, Dennis
Collet, John C(askie)
Ellender, Allen J(oseph)
Erickson, John Edward obit
Feller, A(braham) H(oward)
Ferguson, (George) Howard
  obit
Frank, Hans obit
Gullion, Allen W(yant) obit
Holaday, William Perry obit
Houston, Robert Griffith obit
Jackson, William K(enneth)
Keenan, Joseph B(erry)
Lawrence, Sir Geoffrey
Lea, Clarence F(rederick)
Luce, Robert obit
MacDonald, William J(osiah)
  obit
McKellar, K(enneth) D(ouglas)
McReynolds, James Clark obit
Magner, Thomas F(rancis) obit
Mankin, Helen Douglas
Mechem, Merritt Cramer obit
Mitchell, William D(e Witt)
Morris, Roland Sletor obit
Parodi, Alexandre
Pethick-Lawrence   (Frederick
  William   Pethick-Lawrence,
  1st) Baron
Phillips, Lena Madesin
Rifkind, Simon H(irsch)
Stacy, Walter P(arker)
Stephens,   Hubert   D(urrett)
  obit
Stone, Harlan Fiske obit
Train, Arthur (Cheney) obit
Walsh, Joseph obit
Webb, James E(dwin)
White,   S(ebastian)   Harrison
  obit
Wirtz, W(illiam) Willard

Literature

Adams, Joseph Quincy obit
Armstrong, Charlotte
Arthur, Sir George (Compton
  Archibald) obit
Baker, Ray Stannard obit
Benchley,   Robert   (Charles)
  obit

Bontemps, Arna (Wendell)
Bothwell, Jean
Boutell, Clarence B(urley)
Bragdon, Claude (Fayette) obit
Brink, Carol (Ryrie)
Bruce, William Cabell obit
Buckmaster, Henrietta
Bulosan, Carlos
Carter, (William) Hodding, Jr.
Case, Frank obit
Chandler, Raymond
Clapper, Olive Ewing
Cook, Fannie
Corbett, Jim
Cullen, Countee obit
Daly, Maureen (Patricia)
De Casseres, Benjamin obit
Dixon, Thomas obit
Dodd, Martha
Dreiser, Theodore obit
Du Bois, Guy Pène
Eberle, Irmengarde
Estes, Eleanor
Fairfax, Beatrice obit
Gág, Wanda obit
Gallico, Paul (William)
Glasgow,   Ellen   (Anderson
  Gholson) obit
Goodspeed, Edgar J(ohnson)
Graham, Shirley
Guérard, Albert J(oseph)
Hargrove, Marion (Lawton, Jr.)
Hauptmann, Gerhart obit
Henry, Mellinger Edward obit
Irwin, Margaret
Jeans, Sir James (Hopwood)
  obit
Kagey, Rudolf obit
Kendrick, Baynard (Hardwick)
Keyserling,   Hermann   (Alex-
  ander), Count obit
Kravchenko,   Victor A(ndreye-
  vich)
Lamont, Corliss
Laxness, Halldór (Kiljan)
Lewis, Ethelreda obit
MacDonald, Betty
MacLennan, (John) Hugh
Marburg, Theodore obit
Millar, Margaret
Mistral, Gabriela
Oppenheim, E(dward) Phillips
  obit
Petry, Ann
Pollock, Channing obit
Pratt, E(dwin) J(ohn)
Reves, Emery
Rhys, Ernest obit
Richardson, Henry Handel obit
Robertson, Constance
Rogers, Bruce
Roosevelt, Elliott
Rosenbach,   A(braham)   S(i-
  mon) W(olf)
Rosenfeld, Paul obit
Rothery, Agnes (Edwards)
Saxon, Lyle obit
Schlesinger, Arthur M(eier), Jr.
Seton, Ernest Thompson obit

Sheldon,   Charles   M(onroe),
  Rev. obit
Simon, Charlie May
Sinclair, Jo
Sinclair, May obit
Skidmore, Hubert Standish obit
Smith, Logan Pearsall obit
Stein, Gertrude obit
Stieglitz, Alfred obit
Stout, Rex (Todhunter)
Street, James (Howell)
Tarkington,   (Newton)   Booth
  obit
Train, Arthur (Cheney) obit
Wakeman, Frederic
Ward, Mary Jane
Wells,   H(erbert)   G(eorge)
  obit
White, Stewart Edward obit
Williams, Tennessee
Willison, George F(indlay)
Winsor, Kathleen
Winter, Ella
Yerby, Frank (Garvin)
Ziff, William B(ernard)

Medicine

Adair, Frank E(arl)
Blalock, Alfred
Castillo Nájera, Francisco
Dandy, Walter E(dward) obit
Flexner, Simon obit
Gruening, Ernest (Henry)
Hamilton, Alice
Hawley, Paul R(amsey)
Hertzler,   Arthur   E(manuel)
  obit
Rusk, Howard A(rchibald)
Shoulders, Harrison H.
Stevenson, George S(alvadore)
Taussig, Helen B(rooke)
Thorkelson, Jacob obit

Military

Arthur, Sir George (Compton
  Archibald) obit
Chou En-lai
Cunningham, Sir Alan (Gor-
  don)
Daluege, Kurt obit
Dutra, Eurico Gaspar
Göring, Hermann Wilhelm obit
Gort, (John Standish Surtees
  Prendergast   Vereker,   6th)
  Viscount obit
Gross, Charles P(hilip)
Gullion, Allen W(yant) obit
Harmon, Ernest N(ason)
Hawley, Paul R(amsey)
Hodgson, W(illiam) R(oy)
Honjo, Shigeru, Baron obit
Jodl, Alfred obit
Keitel, Wilhelm obit
La Rocque, François de obit
Li Lieh-Chun obit
Littlejohn, Robert McG(owan)
Martin, Charles (Henry) obit
Mikhailovitch, Draja obit

Morgan, Sir Frederick (Edgworth)
Patch, Alexander M(cCarrell, Jr.) obit
Patton, George S(mith), Jr. obit
Pick, Lewis Andrew
Roxas (y Acuña), Manuel
Short, Walter C(ampbell)
Skidmore, Hubert Standish obit
Stelle, John
Stilwell, Joseph W(arren) obit
Taylor, Maxwell D(avenport)
Ubico (Castañeda), Jorge obit

Motion Pictures

Arliss, George obit
Atwill, Lionel obit
Baker, Phil
Balaban, Barney
Benchley, Robert (Charles) obit
Borge, Victor
Borzage, Frank
Brice, Fanny
Butterworth, Charles (Edward) obit
Carr, Alexander obit
Chandler, Raymond
Crawford, Joan
Dixon, Thomas obit
Durante, Jimmy
Eisenstein, Sergei (Mikhailovich)
Gaumont, Léon Ernest obit
Hart, William S. obit
Horton, Edward Everett
Hunter, Glenn obit
Irene
Ives, Burl
Korda, Sir Alexander
Leigh, Vivien
McCarey, (Thomas) Leo
Marion, George obit
Massey, Raymond
Merivale, Philip obit
Milland, Ray
Olivier, Laurence
Ragland, Rags obit
Raimu, Jules obit
Summerville, Slim obit
Tarkington, (Newton) Booth obit
Youmans, Vincent obit

Music

Albanese, Licia
Baker, Phil
Bantock, Sir Granville obit
Borge, Victor
Boult, Sir Adrian (Cedric)
Branzell, Karin
Busch, Fritz
Cheatham, Kitty obit
Dunbar, Rudolph
Falla, Manuel de obit
Graham, Shirley

Henry, Mellinger Edward obit
Ives, Burl
Kindler, Hans
Kurtz, Efrem
Lombardo, Guy (Albert)
Maddy, Joseph E(dgar)
Monteux, Pierre
Morini, Erica
Primrose, William
Rosé, Arnold Josef obit
Rosenfeld, Paul obit
Rosenthal, Moriz obit
Samaroff, Olga
Scott, Tom
Sevitzky, Fabien
Von Tilzer, Harry obit
Youmans, Vincent obit

Naval

Bisset, Sir James G(ordon) P(artridge)
Erskine, G(raves) B(lanchard)
Long, Andrew Theodore obit
Momsen, C(harles) B(owers)
Moreell, Ben
Vickery, H(oward) L(eroy) obit
Waesche, Russell R(andolph) obit

Politics

Alemán, Miguel
Andrews, Charles O(scar) obit
Bailey, Thomas L. obit
Baldwin, Raymond E(arl)
Bankhead, John H(ollis) obit
Barry, William Bernard obit
Browne, Edward E(verts) obit
Bruce, William Cabell obit
Burgin, William O(lin) obit
Capper, Arthur
Case, Francis (Higbee)
Castillo Nájera, Francisco
Chavez, Dennis
Chou En-lai
Coffee, John M(ain)
Davey, Martin L(uther) obit
Donahey, (Alvin) Vic(tor) obit
Duclos, Jacques
Dutra, Eurico Gaspar
Ede, J(ames) Chuter
Ellender, Allen J(oseph)
Erickson, John Edward obit
Fairchild, Benjamin Lewis obit
Frick, Wilhelm obit
Gallagher, William J. obit
Gasperi, Alcide de
Gillette, Guy M(ark)
Giral (y Pereira), José
Glass, Carter obit
Goldsborough, Phillips Lee obit
Göring, Hermann Wilhelm obit
Gouin, Félix
Gould, Arthur R(obinson) obit
Hansson, Per Albin obit
Haushofer, Karl (Ernst Nikolaus) obit

Herriot, Edouard
Hillman, Sidney obit
Holaday, William Perry obit
Houston, Robert Griffith obit
Hurley, Charles F(rancis) obit
James, W. Frank obit
Johnson, Ed(win Carl)
Kaltenbrunner, Ernst obit
Kroll, Jack
Kunz, Stanley H(enry) obit
Lausche, Frank J(ohn)
Lea, Clarence F(rederick)
Lea, Luke obit
Liggett, Louis Kroh obit
Luce, Robert obit
MacDonald, William J(osiah) obit
McGovern, Francis Edward obit
McKellar, K(enneth) D(ouglas)
McNeil, Hector
Magner, Thomas F(rancis) obit
Makin, Norman J(ohn) O(swald)
Mankin, Helen Douglas
Martin, Charles H(enry) obit
Mechem, Merritt Cramer obit
Merritt, Matthew J. obit
Morris, Roland Sletor obit
Pandit, Vijaya Lakshmi
Parker, Homer Cling obit
Parodi, Alexandre
Patman, (John William) Wright
Patterson, Joseph M(edill) obit
Pinchot, Gifford obit
Piñero, Jesús T(oribio)
Poindexter, Miles obit
Rainey, Homer P(rice)
Reece, B(razilla) Carroll
Roberts, Albert H. obit
Ross, C(harles) Ben obit
Roxas (y Acuña), Manuel
Sabath, Adolph J(oachim)
Scott, John R. K. obit
Seyss-Inquart, Artur von obit
Small, John Humphrey obit
Starr, Mark
Stephens, Hubert D(urrett) obit
Strachey, (Evelyn) John (St. Loe)
Streicher, Julius obit
Sturzo, Luigi
Tener, John Kinley obit
Thorez, Maurice
Thorkelson, Jacob obit
Tobin, Maurice J(oseph)
Tsaldaris, Constantin
Tuck, William M(unford)
Underhill, Charles L. obit
Walsh, Joseph obit
Wherry, Kenneth S(picer)
White, S(ebastian) Harrison obit
Wyatt, Wilson W(atkins)

Publishing

Capper, Arthur
Carter, (William) Hodding, Jr.
Case, Francis (Higbee)

Phillips, Lena Madesin
Reid, Ira De A(ugustine)
Schneiderman, Rose
Stelle, John
Stevenson, George S(alvadore)
Stritch, Samuel (Alphonsus),
  Cardinal
Witte, Edwin E(mil)
Wyatt, Wilson W(atkins)
Yen, Y(ang-) C(h'u) James

Sports

Aga Khan, The (Aga Sultan
  Sir Mahomed Shah)
Blanchard, Felix A(nthony)
Davis, Glenn
Hansenne, Marcel (Fernand)
Johnson, Jack obit
Lazzeri, Tony obit
MacMitchell, (Thomas) Leslie
Oldfield, Barney obit
Owen, Steve
Pasquel, Jorge
Schacht, Al(exander)
Stirnweiss, George (Henry)
Tener, John Kinley obit
Yost, Fielding Harris obit

Technology

DuMont, Allen B(alcom)
Gaumont, Léon Ernest obit
Jewett, Frank B(aldwin)
Momsen, C(harles) B(owers)
Stieglitz, Alfred obit
Wright, Orville

Theater

Arliss, George obit
Atwill, Lionel obit
Baker, Phil
Brice, Fanny
Butterworth, Charles (Edward)
  obit
Carr, Alexander obit
Dixon, Thomas obit
Dowling, Eddie
Durante, Jimmy
Eisenstein, Sergei (Mikhailo-
  vich)
Graham, Shirley
Hamilton, Clayton (Meeker)
  obit
Harris, William, Jr. obit
Hart, William S. obit
Hauptmann, Gerhart obit
Horton, Edward Everett
Hunter, Glenn obit
Ives, Burl

Jones, Robert Edmond
Keane, Doris obit
Laing, Hugh
Leigh, Vivien
Marion, George obit
Massey, Raymond
Merivale, Philip obit
Mielziner, Jo
Motherwell, Hiram obit
Oenslager, Donald (Mitchell)
Olivier, Laurence
O'Neal, Frederick (Douglas)
Pawley, Edward (Joel)
Perry, Antoinette obit
Pollock, Channing obit
Ragland, Rags obit
Raimu, Jules obit
Schacht, Al(exander)
Sheldon, Edward (Brewster)
  obit
Stein, Gertrude obit
Tarkington, (Newton) Booth
  obit
Valentina
Waters, James R. obit
Williams, Tennessee
Youmans, Vincent obit

Other Classifications

Alekhine, Alexander obit

CUMULATED INDEX—1940 - 1946

This is a seven-year cumulation of all names which have appeared in CURRENT BIOGRAPHY from 1940 through 1946. The date following each name indicates the monthly issue as well as the annual volume in which a biography or obituary is included. Please note that three of the 1940 references are not to monthly issues of CURRENT BIOGRAPHY: "Jan-Feb" refers to the combined number which covered the first two months of that year; and since the June and December numbers were not published in monthly form, "Jan-Jun" refers to June material contained in that six-month cumulation, and "Yrbk 40" refers to December material included in that Yearbook.

Baker, Dorothy Dec 43
Baker, George Nov 44
Baker, Phil Nov 46
Baker, Ray Stannard biog Jan-Jun 40 obit Sep 46
Baker, S(ara) Josephine obit Apr 45
Balaban, Barney Oct 46
Balanchine, Geoge Nov 42
Balbo, Italo obit Aug 40
Baldomir, Alfredo Jun 42
Baldwin, C(alvin) B(enham) Nov 43
Baldwin, Hanson W(eightman) Aug 42
Baldwin, Raymond E(arl) Jul 46
Baldwin, Roger Nash Jan-Feb 40
Baldwin, William H(enry) Nov 45
Ball, Joseph H(urst) Oct 43
Ballantine, Stuart obit Jun 44
Bampton, Rose Mar 40
Bankhead, John H(ollis) biog May 43 obit Jul 46
Bankhead, Tallulah (Brockman) Jul 41
Bankhead, William Brockman biog Oct 40 obit Nov 40
Banning, Kendall obit Feb 45
Banning, Margaret Culkin May 40
Banting, Sir Frederick Grant obit Apr 41
Bantock, Sir Granville obit Dec 46
Barber, Mary I(sabel) Jul 41
Barber, Red Jul 43
Barber, Samuel Sep 44
Barber, Walter Lanier See Barber, R. Jul 43
Barbey, Daniel E(dward) Jan 45
Barbier, George W. obit Aug 45
Barbirolli, John Yrbk 40
Barbour, Henry Gray obit Nov 43
Barbour, Ralph Henry obit Apr 44
Barbour, W. Warren obit Jan 44
Barclay, McClelland biog Sep 40 obit Yrbk 46
Barker, Lewellys Franklin obit Sep 43
Barkley, Alben W(illiam) May 41
Barlow, Howard Jan-Feb 40
Barlow, Reginald obit Aug 43
Barnard, Chester I(rving) Mar 45
Barnard, Elinor M. obit Apr 42
Barnard, James Lynn obit Oct 41
Barnes, Albert C(oombs) Mar 45
Barnes, Clifford W(ebster) obit Nov 44
Barnes, William R. obit Mar 45
Barnett, Eugene E(pperson) May 41
Barney, Samuel E. obit Mar 40
Barnouw, Erik Nov 40

Barr, Frank Stringfellow Aug 40
Barr, Norman B., Rev. obit May 43
Barratt, Sir Arthur Sheridan Jan 41
Barrère, Camille Eugène Pierre obit Yrbk 40
Barrère, Georges obit Aug 44
Barrett, Wilton Agnew obit Mar 40
Barringer, Emily Dunning Mar 40
Barringer, Paul Brandon obit Mar 41
Barrow, Joseph Louis See Louis, J. Oct 40
Barry, Patrick Frank, Bishop obit Sep 40
Barry, William Bernard obit Dec 46
Barrymore, Ethel Mar 41
Barrymore, John obit Jul 42
Barrymore, Lionel Jul 43
Barthé, Richmond Jul 40
Bartlett, Robert A(bram) obit Jun 46
Bartók, Béla biog Sep 40 obit Oct 45
Bartol, William Cyrus obit Yrbk 40
Barton, George obit Apr 40
Barton, William H(enry), Jr. obit Aug 44
Baruch, Bernard M(annes) Aug 41
Basie, Count Jun 42
Basie, William See Basie, C. Jun 42
Bates, Blanche obit Feb 42
Bates, Ernest Sutherland obit Jan-Feb 40
Bates, Granville obit Sep 40
Bates, H(erbert) E(rnest) Sep 44
Batista Y Zaldivar, Fulgencio Sep 40
Batt, William L(oren) Feb 42
Baudrillart, Henri Marie Alfred, Cardinal obit Jul 42
Baur, Bertha obit Nov 40
Baur, Harry obit May 43
Bausch, Edward obit Sep 44
Bausch, William obit Dec 44
Bax, Sir Arnold (Edward Trevor) Sep 43
Bayard, Thomas F(rancis) obit Sep 42
Beach, Amy Marcy See Beach, Mrs. H. H. A. obit Feb 45
Beach, Mrs. H(enry) H(arris) A(ubrey) obit Feb 45
Beals, Carleton Jun 41
Beard, Charles A(ustin), and Beard, Mary Mar 41
Beard, Daniel Carter obit Aug 41
Beard, James Thom obit Yrbk 42
Beard, Mary See Beard, C. A. and Beard, M. Mar 41
Bearden, Bessye J. obit Nov 43

Beaton, Cecil (Walter Hardy) Oct 44
Beatrice Marie Victoria Feodora, Princess of England obit Dec 44
Beatty, Arthur obit Apr 43
Beatty, Bessie Jan 44
Beauchamp, Mary Annette See Russell, M. A. R., Countess obit Mar 41
Beaux, Cecilia obit Nov 42
Beaverbrook, William Maxwell Aitken, 1st Baron Jul 40
Beck, Jozef obit Jul 44
Beck, Martin obit Jan 41
Becker, May Lamberton May 41
Becker, William Dee obit Sep 43
Bedaux, Charles E(ugene) obit Apr 44
Bede, J(ames) Adam obit Jun 42
Bedford, Herbrand Arthur Russell, 11th Duke of obit Oct 40
Beebe, Lucius Sep 40
Beebe, William Jul 41
Beecham, Sir Thomas, 2nd Baronet Dec 41
Beeding, Francis See Saunders, H. A. St. G. Jun 43
Beer, Thomas obit May 40
Beers, Clifford W(hittingham) obit Aug 43
Begg, Alexander Swanson obit Nov 40
Begg, Colin Luke obit Mar 41
Begtrup, Bodil Sep 46
Behrman, S(amuel) N(athaniel) Feb 43
Bei Tsung-hsi See Li Tsung-jen and Pai Tsung-hsi Nov 42
Beirne, J(oseph), A. Mar 46
Bekessy, Jean See Habe, H. Feb 43
Bel Geddes, Norman See Geddes, N. B. May 40
Bell, Daniel W(afena) Oct 46
Bell, Edward Price obit Nov 43
Bell, Lawrence D(ale) Jul 42
Bell, Thomas M(ontgomery) obit May 41
Bellamann, Henry biog Sep 42 obit Jul 45
Belmont, Mrs. August Jul 44
Belmont, Eleanor (Elise) Robson See Belmont, Mrs. A. Jul 44
Belmore, Alice obit Sep 43
Bemelmans, Ludwig Apr 41
Benavides, Oscar (Raimundo) obit Aug 45
Benchley, Belle Jennings Oct 40
Benchley, Robert (Charles) biog Sep 41 obit Jan 46
Bendix, Vincent obit May 45
Benedict, Ruth May 41
Beneš, Eduard Jan 42
Benét, Stephen Vincent obit Apr 43
Benjamin, William Evarts obit Mar 40
Bennett, Henry Gordon Mar 42

Cripps, Charles Alfred, 1st Baron Parmoor See Parmoor, C. A. C., 1st Baron obit Aug 41

Cripps, Sir Stafford Jul 40

Crist, William E(arl) Nov 45

Croce, Benedetto Jan 44

Crompton, Rookes Evelyn Bell obit Mar 40

Cromwell, James H. R. Mar 40

Cronin, A(rchibald) J(oseph) Jul 42

Crosby, Bing Sep 41

Cross, Milton John Jan-Feb 40

Cross, Ronald H(ibbert), 1st Baronet Jun 41

Crossley, Archibald M(addock) Dec 41

Crouse, Russel Jun 41

Crow, Carl biog Oct 41 obit Jul 45

Crowell, T(homas) Irving obit Mar 42

Crowley, John J., Father obit Apr 40

Crowley, Leo T(homas) Jun 43

Crownfield, Gertrude obit Jul 45

Crumit, Frank obit Oct 43

Cruze, James obit Sep 42

Csáky, István, Count See Csáky, S., Count obit Mar 41

Csáky, Stephen, Count obit Mar 41

Cubberley, Ellwood P(atterson) obit Nov 41

Cudahy, John C(larence) obit Oct 43

Cugat, Xavier May 42

Cukor, George Apr 43

Culbertson, Ely May 40

Culkin, Francis D. obit Sep 43

Cullen, Countee obit Mar 46

Cullen, Glenn Ernest obit May 40

Cullen, Thomas H. obit Apr 44

Cullis, Winifred C(lara) Nov 43

Culver, Essae Martha Sep 40

Cunningham, Sir Alan (Gordon) Jun 46

Cunningham, Sir Andrew Browne May 41

Cunningham, William Francis obit Jan 41

Curie, Eve Mar 40

Curie, Irène See Joliot-Curie, I. Apr 40

Curran, Charles C(ourtney) obit Jan 43

Curran, Joseph E(dwin) Apr 45

Curran, Pearl Gildersleeve obit Jun 41

Currie, Lauchlin (Bernard) May 41

Curry, John Steuart biog Apr 41 obit Oct 46

Curtin, John biog July 41 obit Aug 45

Curtis, Ann Jun 45

Curtis, George Vaughan obit Oct 43

Curtis, Heber D(oust) obit Mar 42

Cushing, Charles C(yprian) S(trong) obit Apr 41

Cushing, Tom See Cushing, C. C. S. obit Apr 41

Czettel, Ladislas Mar 41

Daché, Lilly Jul 41

Dafoe, Allan (Roy) obit Jul 43

Dafoe, John Wesley obit Feb 44

Daladier, Edouard Apr 40

Dale, Benjamin J(ames) obit Sep 43

Dali, Salvador Sep 40

Dallin, Cyrus Edwin obit Jan 45

Dalton, Charles obit Aug 42

Dalton, Hugh Aug 45

Daluege, Kurt obit Dec 46

Daly, Maureen (Patricia) Jan 46

Daly, Thomas A., Father obit Mar 41

Damaskinos, Archbishop Nov 45

Damerel, Donna obit Apr 41

Damon, Lindsay Todd obit Jan-Jun 40

Damrosch, Walter (Johannes) Mar 44

Dandurand, Raoul obit Apr 42

Dandy, Walter E(dward) obit May 46

Danforth, William obit Jun 41

Daniell, (Francis) Raymond Mar 44

Daniels, Arthur Hill obit Apr 40

Daniels, Charles N. obit Mar 43

Daniels, Jonathan (Worth) Apr 42

Daniels, Josephus Oct 44

Dannay, Frederic See Queen, E. Jul 40

Danner, Louise Rutledge obit Nov 43

Dantchenko, Vladimir (Ivano-vich), Nemirovich- obit Jun 43

Danvin, Mme. Charles See Radzi-will, C., Princess obit Jul 41

Dardel, Nils von obit Jul 43

Dargan, E(dwin) Preston obit Feb 41

Darlan, Jean (Louis Xavier François) biog Mar 41 obit Feb 43

Darling, Jay Norwood Jul 42

Darré, R(ichard) Walther (Oskar) Nov 41

D'Arsonval, Jacques Arsène See Arsonval, J. A. d' obit Feb 41

Dart, Justin W(hitlock) Nov 46

Darwell, Jane Jun 41

Darwin, Leonard obit May 43

Dashiell, Willard obit Jun 43

Dashwood, Mrs. Edmée Elizabeth Monica (de la Pasture) See Delafield, E. M. obit Jan 44

Daudet, Léon obit Aug 42

Daugherty, Harry M(icajah) obit Dec 41

Daugherty, James Henry Jul 40

D'Aulaire, Ingri, and D'Aulaire, Edgar Parin See Aulaire, I. d' and Aulaire, E. P. d' Aug 40

Dauser, Sue S(ophia) Aug 44

Davenport, Charles B(enedict) obit Apr 44

Davenport, Eugene obit May 41

Davenport, Marcia Jan 44

Davenport, Russell W(heeler) Jan 44

Davey, Martin L(uther) obit May 46

Davidovitch, Ljuba obit Mar 40

Davidson, Jo Apr 45

Davies, Sir (Henry) Walford obit May 41

Davies, Joseph E(dward) Apr 42

Davies, William Henry obit Nov 40

Davis, Benjamin O(liver) Dec 42

Davis, Bette Oct 41

Davis, Chester Charles Jul 40

Davis, Elmer May 40

Davis, Glenn Dec 46

Davis, Herbert John Jan-Feb 40

Davis, J. Frank obit May 42

Davis, James Francis See Davis, J. Frank obit May 42

Davis, Joan Jun 45

Davis, Jonathan M(cMillan) obit Aug 43

Davis, Norman H(ezekiah) biog Jan-Feb 40 obit Aug 44

Davis, Robert C(ourtney) obit Oct 44

Davis, Robert H(obart) obit Dec 42

Davis, Stuart Aug 40

Davis, Watson Dec 45

Davis, Westmoreland obit Oct 42

Davis, William Ellsworth Apr 40

Davis, William H(ammatt) Jun 41

Davis, William Rhodes biog Mar 41 obit Sep 41

Davison, F(rederick) Trubee Dec 45

Dawes, Rufus Cutler obit Jan-Feb 40

Dawson, Bertrand, 1st Viscount Dawson of Penn See Dawson of Penn, B. D., 1st Viscount obit Apr 45

Dawson, William Apr 41

Dawson, William L(evi) Apr 45

Dawson of Penn, Bertrand Dawson, 1st Viscount obit Apr 45

Day, Edmund Ezra Sep 46

Day-Lewis, Cecil Jan-Feb 40

De Alvear, Marcelo T. obit May 42

Dean, Vera Micheles May 43

Deane, Martha See McBride, M. M. Apr 41

Deane, Sidney N(orton) obit Jun 43

Grant, Elihu obit Dec 42
Grant, Ethel Watts Mumford See Mumford, E. W. obit Jan-Jun 40
Grant, Heber J. obit Jun 45
Grant, Robert obit Jul 40
Grantley, John Richard Brinsley Norton, 5th Baron obit Sep 43
Graser, Earle W. obit Jun 41
Grau, San Martin, Ramón Oct 44
Grauer, Ben(nett Franklin) Feb 41
Graves, Bibb obit May 42
Graves, Frederick Rogers, Bishop obit Jul 40
Graves, William Sidney obit Mar 40
Gray, Elizabeth Janet Sep 43
Gray, George (Edward), Kruger-See Kruger-Gray, G. E. obit Jun 43
Grayson, David See Baker, R. S. biog Jan-Jun 40 obit Sep 46
Graziani, Rodolfo Apr 41
Green, Adolph See Comden, B. and Green, A. Mar 45
Green, Florence Topping obit Jun 45
Green, Mrs. Howard See Green, F. T. obit Jun 45
Green, Julian Jan-Feb 40
Green, William Mar 42
Greenbie, Sydney Sep 41
Greene, Frank Russell obit Jan-Feb 40
Greenfield, Abraham Lincoln obit Sep 41
Greenough, Carroll obit Oct 41
Greenstreet, Sydney (Hughes) May 43
Greenway, Walter Burton, Rev. obit Feb 41
Greenwood, Allen obit Dec 42
Greenwood, Arthur Oct 40
Gregory, Edmund B(ristol) Sep 45
Gregory, Menas S(arkis) obit Jan 42
Grenfell, Sir Wilfred Thomason obit Yrbk 40
Gresley, Sir (Herbert) Nigel obit May 41
Grew, Joseph Clark Feb 41
Grey, Clifford obit Nov 41
Gribble, Harry Wagstaff (Graham-) Sep 45
Grieff, Joseph Nicholas, Mgr. obit Aug 41
Griffin, Bernard (William), Cardinal Oct 46
Griffis, Stanton Oct 44
Griffith, J(ohn) P(rice) Crozer obit Sep 41
Grigg, Sir James Apr 42
Grigg, Sir Percy James See Grigg, Sir J. Apr 42
Grimshaw, Robert obit Jun 41

Griswold, Augustus H. obit Mar 40
Griswold, Oscar W(oolverton) Sep 43
Grizodubova, Valentina (Stepanovna) Dec 41
Groenman, Frans Eyso Henricus obit Aug 43
Grofé, Ferde Jul 40
Gromyko, Andrei A. Oct 43
Groninger, Homer M. Aug 45
Groot, Adriaan M(artin) de obit Mar 42
Gropius, Walter (Adolf Georg) Nov 41
Gropper, William Mar 40
Gros, Edmund L(ouis) obit Dec 42
Gross, Chaim Nov 41
Gross, Charles P(hilip) Mar 46
Grosvenor, Gilbert (Hovey) Dec 46
Grosvenor, Graham Bethune obit Dec 43
Grosz, George Apr 42
Groth, John (August) Feb 43
Groves, Ernest R(utherford) biog Jun 43 obit Oct 46
Groves, Gladys Hoagland See Groves, E. R. and Groves, G. H. biog Jun 43
Groves, Leslie R(ichard) Aug 45
Gruber, Frank Nov 41
Gruber, L(evi) Franklin, Rev. obit Feb 42
Gruenberg, Sidonie Matsner May 40
Gruening, Ernest (Henry) Dec 46
Grumman, Leroy R(andle) Aug 45
Gruppe, Charles Paul obit Nov 40
Guardia, Rafael Ángel Calderón See Calderón Guardia, R. Á. Jun 42
Guardia, Ricardo Adolfo de la See De La Guardia, R. A. May 42
Gubelman, Minei Izrailevich See Yaroslavsky, E. obit Jan 44
Guedalla, Philip obit Feb 45
Guérard, Albert J(oseph) Yrbk 46
Guertner, Franz obit Mar 41
Guest, Edgar A(lbert) Sep 41
Guffey, Joseph F. Mar 44
Guggenheim, Mrs. Daniel obit Jul 44
Guggenheim, Florence (Shloss) See Guggenheim, Mrs. D. obit Jul 44
Guillaumat, Marie Louis Adolphe obit Jul 40
Guiñazú, Enrique Ruiz See Ruiz Guiñazú, E. Apr 42
Guinness, Walter Edward, 1st Baron Moyne See Moyne, W. E. G., 1st Baron obit Dec 44

Guise, Jean Pierre Clément Marie, Duc de obit Oct 40
Guiterman, Arthur obit Mar 43
Gulick, Luther (Halsey) Jun 45
Gullion, Allen W(yant) biog Feb 43 obit Jul 46
Gunn, Selskar Michael obit Sep 44
Gunter, Julius Caldeen obit Yrbk 40
Gunther, Franklin Mott obit Feb 42
Gunther, John Nov 41
Gustav V, King of Sweden Sep 42
Guthrie, Charles Ellsworth, Rev. obit Sep 40
Guthrie, William Buck obit Yrbk 40
Guyer, Ulysses Samuel obit Jul 43
Gwathmey, James T(ayloe) obit Apr 44
Gwathmey, Robert Dec 43
Gwenn, Edmund Sep 43

Haakon VII, King of Norway May 40
Haas, Arthur E(rich) obit Apr 41
Haas, Francis J(oseph), Bishop Aug 43
Habe, Hans Feb 43
Hácha, Emil biog Dec 42 obit Sep 45
Hackett, Charles obit Feb 42
Hackett, Horatio B(alch) obit Nov 41
Hackett, Walter obit Mar 44
Haddon, Alfred Cort obit May 40
Hadfield, Sir Robert Abbott, 1st Baronet obit Nov 40
Hagen, Uta See Ferrer, J. and Hagen, U. May 44
Hagen, Victor Wolfgang von See Von Hagen, V. W. Mar 42
Haggard, William David obit Mar 40
Hahn, Emily Jul 42
Haile Selassie I, Emperor of Ethiopia Apr 41
Hainisch, Michael obit Mar 40
Haldane, John Burdon Sanderson Nov 40
Hale, Arthur, Rev. obit Mar 40
Hale, Richard W(alden) obit Apr 43
Halifax, Edward Frederick Lindley Wood, 3rd Viscount Sep 40
Hall, Florence (Louise) Aug 43
Hall, Frank O(liver), Rev. obit Dec 41
Hall, George A(lbert) obit Nov 41
Hall, George W(ashington) obit Dec 41
Hall, James obit Jul 40

Herring, Clyde L(a Verne) obit Nov 45

Herriot, Edouard Feb 46

Hersey, John (Richard) Feb 44

Hershey, Lewis B(laine) Jun 41

Hershey, Milton S(navely) obit Nov 45

Hersholt, Jean Dec 44

Hertz, Alfred obit Jun 42

Hertz, Emanuel obit Jul 40

Hertzler, Arthur E(manuel) obit Oct 46

Hertzog, James Barry Munnik obit Jan 43

Herzog, Paul M(ax) Jul 45

Hess, Myra Sep 43

Hess, Rudolf Mar 41

Hesselgren, Kerstin Jan 41

Heward, Leslie H(ays) obit Jun 43

Hewart, Gordon, 1st Viscount Hewart of Bury obit Jun 43

Hewart of Bury, Gordon Hewart, 1st Viscount See Hewart, G., 1st Viscount Hewart of Bury obit Jun 43

Hewitt, Henry K(ent) Apr 43

Hewlett, J(ames) Monroe obit Dec 41

Heydrich, Reinhard biog Jul 42 obit Yrbk 42

Heydt, Herman A(ugust) obit Oct 41

Heym, Stefan Mar 43

Heymann, Lida Gustava obit Sep 43

Heyward, Du Bose obit Jul 40

Hibbard, Edna obit Feb 43

Hibbard, Frederick P(omeroy) obit Oct 43

Hibbard, Henry D. obit Dec 42

Hibbs, Ben Jul 46

Hickey, Margaret A. Dec 44

Hickey, Thomas F., Archbishop obit Feb 41

Hickman, Emily (Gregory) Jun 45

Hicks, Clarence J(ohn) obit Feb 45

Hicks, Granville May 42

Higgins, Andrew J(ackson) May 43

Higgins, Frederick Robert obit Mar 41

Higginson, William obit Sep 43

Hildegarde Nov 44

Hill, Abram Aug 45

Hill, Billy obit Feb 41

Hill, Edwin C. Sep 40

Hill, Frank Pierce obit Oct 41

Hill, George Washington biog Jun 46 obit Oct 46

Hill, Helen obit May 42

Hill, Howard Copeland obit Aug 40

Hill, J(ohn) B(oynton) P(hilip) Clayton obit Jul 41

Hill, Justina Hamilton Apr 41

Hill, Lister Oct 43

Hill, Patty Smith obit Jun 46

Hill, Robert (Thomas) obit Sep 41

Hill, William Joseph See Hill, B. obit Feb 41

Hiller, Wendy Oct 41

Hillman, Sidney biog Jul 40 obit Jul 46

Hillyer, Robert Silliman Jul 40

Hilton, James Sep 42

Himmler, Heinrich biog Jun 41 obit Jun 45

Hinckley, Robert obit Jul 41

Hindemith, Paul Oct 41

Hines, Duncan May 46

Hines, Frank T(homas) Apr 44

Hingson, Robert A(ndrew), Edwards, Waldo B(erry), and Southworth, James L(arry) Jun 43

Hinrichs, Gustav obit May 42

Hinsley, Arthur Cardinal obit Apr 43

Hirohito, Emperor of Japan Jan 42

Hirsch I(saac) Seth obit May 42

Hirshfield, Morris Sep 43

Hirst, Hugo Hirst, 1st Baron biog Nov 41 obit Mar 43

Hitchcock, Alfred (Joseph) Mar 41

Hitchcock, Thomas obit Jun 44

Hitler, Adolf Mar 42

Hitz, Ralph obit Jan-Feb 40

Ho Ying-chin Oct 42

Hoare, Sir Samuel John Gurney, 2nd Baronet Oct 40

Hobby, Oveta Culp Jul 42

Hobson, John Atkinson obit Apr 40

Hodge, John R(eed) Jun 45

Hodges, Courtney H. May 41

Hodgson, Joseph V(ernon) Jun 45

Hodgson, W(illiam) R(oy) May 46

Hodson, William obit Mar 43

Hodza, Milan obit Aug 44

Hoellering, Franz Oct 40

Hoffman, Malvina Yrbk 40

Hoffman, Paul G(ray) Feb 46

Hogben, Lancelot (Thomas) Dec 41

Hohenlohe-Waldenburg, Stefanie Richter, Princess Jan-Feb 40

Hohenzollern, Friedrich Wilhelm Victor Albert See Wilhelm II, Former German Kaiser obit Jul 41

Holaday, William Perry obit Mar 46

Holcomb, Thomas Jul 42

Holden, Louis Edward obit Jun 42

Holland, Charles Thurstan obit Mar 41

Hollander, Jacob Harry obit Sep 40

Holm, Celeste Apr 44

Holmes, (Elias) Burton May 44

Holmes, Jesse Herman obit Jul 42

Holmes, John Haynes, Rev. Jan 41

Holmes, Julius Cecil Feb 45

Holmes, Phillips obit Oct 42

Holsti, (Eino) Rudolf (Woldemar) obit Sep 45

Holt, Arthur E(rastus) obit Mar 42

Holt, Rackham Apr 44

Honegger, Arthur Apr 41

Honeywell, Harry E. obit Jan-Feb 40

Honjo, Shigeru, Baron obit Jan 46

Hooper, Franklin Henry obit Oct 40

Hooton, Earnest Albert Yrbk 40

Hoover, Herbert (Clark) Mar 43

Hoover, Mrs. Herbert obit Feb 44

Hoover, J. Edgar Jan-Feb 40

Hoover, Lou Henry See Hoover, Mrs. H. obit Feb 44

Hope, Bob Jun 41

Hope, Victor Alexander John, 2nd Marquess of Linlithgow See Linlithgow, V. A. J. H., 2nd Marquess of Jan 42

Hopkins, Alfred obit Jul 41

Hopkins, Ernest Martin Oct 44

Hopkins, Harry L(loyd) biog Feb 41 obit Mar 46

Hopkins, Louis Bertram obit Sep 40

Hopkins, Nevil Monroe obit May 45

Hoppenot, Henri Etienne Mar 44

Hopper, Hedda Nov 42

Horder, Thomas J(eeves), 1st Baron Jul 44

Hore-Belisha, Leslie Jul 41

Horgan, Stephen H(enry) obit Oct 41

Horlick, William, Jr. obit Apr 40

Hormel, Jay C(atherwood) Jul 46

Hornblow, Arthur, Sr. obit Jun 42

Horne, Charles F(rancis) obit Nov 42

Horne, Lena Jun 44

Horner, Henry obit Nov 40

Horney, Karen Aug 41

Horowitz, Vladimir Sep 43

Horrocks, B(rian) G(wynne) Jan 45

Horsfall, Frank L(appin), Jr. Mar 41

Horthy, Stephen obit Oct 42

Horthy de Nagybánya, Nicholas Oct 40

Horton, Edward Everett Dec 46

Horwood, Sir William T(homas) F(rancis) obit Feb 44

Hoshino, Naoki Nov 40

Jenkins, MacGregor obit Apr 40

Jenks, Leon E. obit Mar 40

Jensen, Oliver O(rmerod) May 45

Jessel, George (Albert) Mar 43

Jewett, Frank B(aldwin) Dec 46

Jewett, James R(ichard) obit May 43

Jinnah, Mohammed Ali May 42

Jodl, Alfred obit Nov 46

Joesten, Joachim (Franz) Jun 42

John, Augustus (Edwin) Oct 41

Johnson, Alexander obit Jul 41

Johnson, Alvin (Saunders) Aug 42

Johnson, Amy obit Feb 41

Johnson, Arthur Newhall obit Sep 40

Johnson, Charles Spurgeon Nov 46

Johnson, Clifton obit Jan-Feb 40

Johnson, Crockett Dec 43

Johnson, Douglas Wilson obit Apr 44

Johnson, Edward Mar 43

Johnson, Ed(win Carl) Dec 46

Johnson, Hall Jan 45

Johnson, Harold Ogden See Olsen, J. S. and Johnson, H. O. Sep 40

Johnson, Herschel V. Jul 46

Johnson, Hewlett, Rev. Dean of Canterbury May 43

Johnson, Hiram (Warren) biog Feb 41 obit Sep 45

Johnson, Howard E. obit Jun 41

Johnson, Hugh S(amuel) biog Sep 40 obit Jun 42

Johnson, Jack obit Jul 46

Johnson, J(ohn) Monroe Feb 45

Johnson, Loren (Bascom Taber) obit Feb 42

Johnson, Louis (Arthur) Jun 42

Johnson, Mordecai Wyatt Apr 41

Johnson, Nelson Trusler Jan-Feb 40

Johnson, Nunnally Aug 41

Johnson, Osa Apr 40

Johnson, Paul B(urney) obit Feb 44

Johnson, Philip G(ustav) obit Nov 44

Johnson, Robert Wood Nov 43

Johnson, Van Jul 45

Johnson, William E(ugene) obit Mar 45

Johnston, Alvanley Jun 46

Johnston, Eric A(llen) Apr 43

Joliot-Curie, Frédéric Oct 46

Joliot-Curie, Irène Apr 40

Jolson, Al Nov 40

Jónasson, Hermann Aug 41

Jones, Billy Jan 41

Jones, Buck obit Jan 43

Jones, Chester Lloyd obit Mar 41

Jones, E. Stanley, Rev. May 40

Jones, Grover obit Nov 40

Jones, Jack See Jones, J. J. biog Nov 40 obit Jan 42

Jones, Jennifer May 44

Jones, Jesse Holman Oct 40

Jones, Joe Oct 40

Jones, John Daniel, Rev. obit Jun 42

Jones, John Joseph biog Nov 40 obit Jan 42

Jones, Marvin, Aug 43

Jones, Norman L. obit Jan 41

Jones, Robert Edmond Nov 46

Jones, Rufus M(atthew) Oct 41

Jones, Sam Houston Mar 40

Jordan, Frank C(raig) obit Apr 41

Jordan, James Edward See Mc-Gee, F. and McGee, M. Nov 41

Jordan, Marian See McGee, F. and McGee, M. Nov 41

Jordana (y Souza), Francisco Gómez biog Mar 44 obit Sep 44

Joseph, Sister Mary Dec 42

Josephson, Walter S. obit Mar 40

Jowitt, Sir William Allen Aug 41

Joyce, James obit Mar 41

Judd, Charles Hubbard obit Sep 46

Judson, Arthur (Leon) Aug 45

Juin, Alphonse (Pierre) Aug 43

Jules-Bois, H. A. obit Aug 43

Juliana, Crown Princess of the Netherlands Sep 44

Jung, Carl Gustav Apr 43

Justo, Agustin P. obit Mar 43

Kaempffert, Waldemar (Bernhard) Sep 43

Kaganovitch, Lazar (Moiseyevitch) Apr 42

Kagawa, Toyohiko Sep 41

Kagey, Rudolf obit Jun 46

Kahal, Irving obit Apr 42

Kahn, Albert biog Sep 42 obit Jan 43

Kahn, Ely Jacques Aug 45

Kahn Gus(tav Gerson) obit Dec 41

Kaiser, Henry J. Oct 42

Kaiser, John B(oynton) May 43

Kaiser Wilhelm II See Wilhelm II, Former German Kaiser obit Jul 41

Kai-shek, Chiang See Chiang Kai-shek Jan-Jun 40

Kalinin, Mikhail Ivanovitch biog Jun 42 obit Jul 46

Kállay, Nicolas von See Kállay de Nagy Kálló, M. Jun 42

Kállay de Nagy Kálló, Miklos Jun 42

Kallio, Kyösti obit Feb 41

Kaltenborn, Hans von Aug 40

Kaltenbrunner, Ernst biog Apr 43 obit Nov 46

Kander, Lizzie Black obit Sep 40

Kandinsky, Wassily obit Feb 45

Kanin, Garson Jan 41

Kan-in, Prince Kotohito obit Jun 45

Kanzler, Ernest C(arlton) Apr 42

Karelitz, George B(oris) obit Mar 43

Karloff, Boris Mar 41

Karno, Fred obit Nov 41

Karsner, David obit Apr 41

Kasner, Edward Nov 43

Kašpar, Karl, Cardinal obit Jun 41

Kast, Ludwig W. obit Oct 41

Kaufman, George S. Aug 41

Kaup, Felix F., Father obit Apr 40

Kay, Beatrice Dec 42

Kay-Scott, C(yril) See Wellman, F. C. Feb 44

Kaye, Danny Dec 41

Keane, Doris obit Jan 46

Keck, George Fred Sep 45

Keenan, Joseph B(erry) Sep 46

Keenan, Walter Francis, Jr. obit Apr 40

Keitel, Wilhelm biog Sep 40 obit Nov 46

Keith, Dora Wheeler obit Feb 41

Kelberine, Alexander obit Mar 40

Kellas, Eliza obit May 43

Keller, Helen (Adams) Dec 42

Kelley, Edgar Stillman obit Jan 45

Kellogg, John Harvey obit Feb 44

Kelly, Florence Finch obit Jan-Feb 40

Kelly, Gene Dec 45

Kelly, Howard A(twood) obit Mar 43

Kelly, Joe Jun 45

Kelly, Joseph William See Kelly, J. Jun 45

Kelly, Judith Oct 41

Kemmerer, E(dwin) W(alter) biog Oct 41 obit Feb 46

Kemp, Hal obit Feb 41

Kemper, James S(cott) Apr 41

Kempner, Robert M(aximilian) W(asilii) May 43

Kendall, William Mitchell obit Oct 41

Kendrick, Baynard (Hardwick) Feb 46

Kennedy, John B(right) Feb 44

Kennedy, Joseph Patrick Nov 40

Kenney, George C(hurchill) Jan 43

Kenny, Elizabeth Oct 42

Kent, George Edward Alexander Edmund, Duke of obit Oct 42

Kent, Raymond A(sa) obit Apr 43

Kent, Rockwell Nov 42

McBride, Mary Margaret Apr 41

McCain, John S(idney) biog Oct 43 obit Oct 45

MacCallum, William George obit Mar 44

McCarey, (Thomas) Leo Jul 46

McCarl, John Raymond obit Sep 40

McCarrens, John S. obit Sep 43

McCarthy, Clem Oct 41

McCarthy, Frank Sep 45

McCarthy, Leighton (Goldie) Oct 42

McClintic, Guthrie May 43

McCloskey, John Robert See McCloskey, R. Sep 42

McCloskey, Robert Sep 42

McCormack, Arthur Thomas obit Sep 43

McCormack, John obit Oct 45

McCormack, John W. Jun 43

McCormick, Anne O'Hare Mar 40

MacCormick, Austin H. May 40

McCormick, Jay (William) Apr 43

McCormick, Robert R(utherford) Aug 42

McCormick, William Patrick Glyn, Rev. obit Yrbk 40

McCoy, Frank R(oss) Nov 45

MacCracken, Henry Noble Sep 40

McCracken, Joan Jun 45

McCreery, Sir Richard L(oudon) May 45

McCullers, Carson Sep 40

McCune, Charles Andrew obit Yrbk 40

McCune, George S(hannon), Rev. obit Feb 42

McCurdy, William Albert, Rev. obit Feb 42

McDaniel, Hattie Sep 40

MacDonald, Betty Feb 46

MacDonald, Cordelia Howard obit Oct 41

MacDonald, Duncan Black, Rev. obit Oct 43

MacDonald, Sir George obit Sep 40

MacDonald, Pirie obit Jun 42

MacDonald, William J(osiah) obit May 46

MacEwen, Walter obit May 43

MacFarlane, F(rank) N(oel) Mason Feb 43

McGarry, William J(ames), Rev. obit Nov 41

McGeachy, Mary (Agnes) Craig Apr 44

McGee, Fibber, and McGee, Molly Nov 41

McGee, Molly See McGee, F. and McGee, M. Nov 41

McGillicuddy, Cornelius See Mack, C. Jun 44

McGinley, Phyllis Feb 41

McGovern, Francis Edward obit Jun 46

MacGowan, Gault Jan 45

McGroarty, John Steven obit Sep 44

McGuire, Dorothy Sep 41

McGuire, William Anthony obit Nov 40

Machado, Bernardino (Luiz) obit Jun 44

Machado (Hernandez), Alfredo obit Sep 46

McIntire, Ross T. Oct 45

McIntyre, Marvin H(unter) obit Feb 44

Mack, Connie Jun 44

Mack, Julian W(illiam) obit Oct 43

Mack, Walter S(taunton), Jr. Feb 46

Mackay, Sir Iven Giffard Apr 41

McKeever, Ed(ward Clark) Nov 45

McKellar, K(enneth) D(ouglas) Jan 46

McKenna, Reginald obit Oct 43

McKenney, Eileen See West, N. obit Feb 41

McKenney, Ruth Aug 42

Mackenzie, Clinton obit Mar 40

McKenzie, Roderick Duncan obit Jan-Jun 40

McKenzie, William P. obit Oct 42

MacKenzie, William Warrender, 1st Baron Amulree of Strathbraan See Amulree, W. W. M., 1st Baron of Strathbraan obit Jun 42

McKittrick, Thomas H(arrington) Jul 44

McLean, Alice T(hrockmorton) Jul 45

McLean, Evalyn Walsh May 43

MacLean, Malcolm Shaw Jul 40

MacLeish, Archibald Oct 40

MacLennan, (John) Hugh Yrbk 46

McMahon, (James O')Brien Dec 45

McManamy, Frank obit Nov 44

McMeekin, Clark See McMeekin, I. M. Sep 42

McMeekin, Isabel McLennan Sep 42

McMein, Neysa Feb 41

Macmillan, Harold Mar 43

Macmillan, Maurice Harold See Macmillan, H. Mar 43

MacMitchell (Thomas) Leslie Apr 46

McMurtrie, Douglas C(rawford) biog Jul 44 obit Nov 44

McNair, Lesley J(ames) biog Nov 42 obit Sep 44

McNamara, James Barnabas obit Apr 41

McNamee, Graham obit Jul 42

McNarney, Joseph T(aggart) Nov 44

McNary, Charles L(inza) biog Aug 40 obit Ap 44

McNaughton, Andrew (George Latta) Nov 42

McNeil, Hector Dec 46

MacNeil, Neil May 40

McNutt, Paul Vories Jan-Feb 40

MacPhail, Larry Mar 45

MacPhail, Leland Stanford See MacPhail, L. Mar '45

McPharlin, Paul Nov 45

McPherson, Aimee Semple obit Nov 44

Macrae, John obit Apr 44

McReynolds, James Clark obit Oct 46

MacRossie, Allan, Rev. obit Mar 40

MacVeagh, Lincoln Nov 41

McWilliams, Carey Oct 43

Maddy, Joseph E(dgar) Apr 46

Madeleva, Sister Mary Feb 42

Magee, James C(arre) May 43

Maglione, Luigi, Cardinal obit Oct 44

Magner, Thomas F(rancis) obit Feb 46

Magnuson, Warren G(rant) Oct 45

Magoffin, Ralph Van Deman obit Jul 42

Maher, Ahmed, Pasha obit Apr 45

Mailhouse, Max obit Dec 41

Maillol, Aristide (Joseph Bonaventure) biog May 42 obit Nov 44

Main, Charles Thomas obit Apr 43

Mainbocher Feb 42

Maisky, Ivan (Mikhailovich) Sep 41

Makemson, Maud W(orcester) Jun 41

Makin, Norman J(ohn) O(swald) Mar 46

Malinovsky, Rodion Y(akovlevich) Mar 44

Malinowski, Bronislaw (Kasper) biog Jun 41 obit Jul 42

Mallory, F(rank) B(urr) obit Nov 41

Maloney, Francis T. obit Mar 45

Maltz, Albert Jan-Feb 40

Mamlok, Hans J. obit Yrbk 40

Mandel, Georges Yrbk 40

Mangione, Jerre Mar 43

Mankin, Helen Douglas Apr 46

Manly, John Matthews obit May 40

Mann, Erika Yrbk 40

Mann, Klaus Yrbk 40

Mann, Thomas May 42

Mann, Tom obit May 41

Mannerheim, Carl Gustaf Emil, Baron von Apr 40

Manning, Marie See Fairfax, B. Aug 44

Manning, William Thomas, Bishop Apr 40

Mannstein, Fritz Erich von See Manstein, F. E. von Oct 42

Mansbridge, Albert Jun 42

Manship, Paul May 40

Manson, John T(homas) obit Apr 44

Manstein, Fritz Erich von Oct 42

Mantle, (Robert) Burns Nov 44

Mao Tse-tung Feb 43

Mapes, Victor obit Jan 44

Marble, Alice Nov 40

Marburg, Theodore obit Apr 46

March, Charles Hoyt obit Sep 45

March, Fredric, and Eldridge, Florence Mar 43

Marchal, Léon Sep 43

Marcial-Dorado, Carolina obit Sep 41

Marett, Robert R(anulph) obit Apr 43

Marge See Damerel, D. obit Apr 41

Margesson, David Feb 41

Margoliouth, David Samuel obit Apr 40

Margueritte, Victor obit May 42

Maria Theresa, Archduchess of Austria obit Apr 44

Marion, George obit Jan 46

Maritain, Jacques May 42

Marius, Emilie Alexander obit Apr 40

Mark, Louis obit May 42

Markham, Beryl Nov 42

Markham, Edwin obit Mar 40

Markova, Alicia Sep 43

Marquand, J(ohn) P(hillips) Apr 42

Marquardt, Alexandria obit Jun 43

Marquis, Albert Nelson obit Feb 44

Marquis, Frederick James, 1st Baron Woolton See Woolton, F. J. M., 1st Baron Oct 40

Marriott, Sir John (Arthur Ransome) obit Jul 45

Marsh, Reginald Sep 41

Marshall, George Catlett Oct 40

Marshall, Rosamond Van der Zee Aug 42

Marshall, Tully obit Apr 43

Marshall, Verne Feb 41

Martel, Giffard Le Quesne Jul 43

Martin, Charles H(enry) obit Nov 46

Martin, Collier Ford obit May 41

Martin, Edgar Stanley, Jr. obit Sep 40

Martin, Edward Oct 45

Martin, Frank L(ee) obit Sep 41

Martin, George Brown obit Dec 45

Martin, Glenn L(uther) Feb 43

Martin, Helen See Rood, H. M. obit Mar 43

Martin, Jackie Apr 43

Martin, Joseph William, Jr. Oct 40

Martin, Lillien J(ane) biog Apr 42 obit My 43

Martin, Mary Jan 44

Martin, Percy Alvin obit Apr 42

Martinelli, Giovanni Jan 45

Martínez, Maximiliano Hernández See Hernández Martínez, M. Jun 42

Martinů, Bohuslav Nov 44

Martland, Harrison Stanford Nov 40

Marvin, Charles F(rederick) obit Jul 43

Marvin, Dwight Edwards, Rev. obit Mar 40

Marvin, Harry obit Jan-Feb 40

Mary Joseph Butler, Mother obit Jan-Jun 40

Masaryk, Jan (Garrigue) May 44

Mascagni, Pietro obit Sep 45

Masliansky, Zvei Hirsch, Rev. obit Mar 43

Mason, Joseph Warren Teets obit Jul 41

Massee, W(illiam) Wellington obit Oct 42

Massey, Raymond Feb 46

Massine, Léonide Apr 40

Matheson, Samuel Pritchard, Archbishop obit Jul 42

Mathews, Shailer, Rev. obit Dec 41

Matisse, Henri May 43

Matsui, Keishiro, Baron obit Jul 46

Matsuoka, Yôsuke biog Mar 41 obit Jul 46

Matthews, H(arrison) Freeman Mar 45

Matthews, Herbert L(ionel) Nov 43

Matthews, J(oseph) B(rown) May 43

Mauldin, Bill May 45

Mauldin, William Henry See Mauldin, B. May 45

Maurier, Daphne du See Du Maurier, D. May 40

Maverick, Maury Mar 44

Max, Adolphe obit Jan-Feb 40

Maxon, Lou R(ussell) Aug 43

Maxton, James obit Sep 46

Maxtone Graham, Joyce Jan 41

Maxwell, Elsa Mar 43

Maxwell, Russell L(amonte) Nov 42

May, Andrew Jackson Apr 41

May, Charles H(enry) obit Jan 44

May, Henry John obit Jan-Feb 40

Mayer, Louis B(urt) Jun 43

Maynard, John A(lbert) F(onsegrive), Rev. Oct 43

Mayne, Ethel C(olburn) obit Jun 41

Maynor, Dorothy Jan-Feb 40

Mayo, Charles W(illiam) Nov 41

Mayo, Katherine obit Yrbk 40

Mays, Benjamin E(lijah) May 45

Mead, Charles Larew, Bishop obit Jul 41

Mead, George H(ouk) Oct 46

Mead, James M(ichael) Jul 44

Mead, Kate Campbell obit Feb 41

Mead, Margaret Nov 40

Means, Mrs. Alan Hay Jan 46

Means, Helen Hotchkin See Means, Mrs. A. H. Jan 46

Meany, George Jan 42

Mearns, Hughes Jan-Feb 40

Mears, Helen Mar 43

Mechau, Frank, Jr. obit Apr 46

Mechem, Merritt Cramer obit Jun 46

Medina Angarita, Isaías Mar 42

Meehan, Thomas F(rancis) obit Sep 42

Mei Lan-Fang obit Sep 43

Meitner, Lise Sep 45

Melcher, Frederic G(ershom) Jul 45

Melchior, Lauritz (Lebrecht Hommel) Jan 41

Mellett, Lowell May 42

Mello Franco, Afranio de obit Feb 43

Mellor, Walter obit Jan-Feb 40

Meloney, Mrs. William Brown obit Aug 43

Melton, James Sept 45

Melzer, Roman F. obit Jun 43

Mendenhall, Harlan George, Rev. obit Jul 40

Menninger, William Claire Sep 45

Menocal, Mario Garcia obit Oct 41

Menthon, François de Mar 44

Menuhin, Yehudi Feb 41

Menzies, Robert G(ordon) Feb 41

Merck, George W(ilhelm) Dec 46

Meredith, Burgess Jul 40

Merivale, Philip obit Apr 46

Merle-Smith, Van Santvoord obit Dec 43

Merman, Ethel Oct 1941

Merriam, C(linton) Hart obit May 42

Merriam, George Ernest, Rev. obit May 41

Merriam, John Campbell obit Dec 45

Merrill, Frank (Dow) Jul 44

Merrill, John Douglas obit Jan-Feb 40

Merritt, Matthew J. obit Nov 46

Messerschmitt, Willy Apr 40

Messersmith, George S(trausser) Oct 42

Meštrović, Ivan Oct 40

Metaxas, John biog Oct 40 obit Mar 41

Metcalf, Jesse H(oughton) obit Dec 42

O'Connor, James Francis obit Mar 45

O'Day, Caroline Goodwin obit Feb 43

Odell, George C(linton) D(ensmore) Dec 44

Odets, Clifford Nov 41

Odlum, Floyd B(ostwick) Nov 41

O'Donnell, Edwin P. obit Jun 43

O'Dwyer, William Sep 41

Oechsner, Frederick C(able) Mar 43

Oenslager, Donald (Mitchell) Sep 46

O'Flanagan, Michael, Rev. obit Sep 42

Ogden, C(harles) K(ay) Jan 44

O'Gorman, James A. obit Jul 43

O'Gorman, Patrick F., Father obit Apr 40

O'Hara, John (Henry) Feb 41

O'Hara, Mary Jan 44

O'Keeffe, Georgia Jun 41

Oldfield, Barney obit Nov 46

O'Leary, James A. obit May 44

Oliveira Salazar, Antonio de See Salazar, A. de O. May 41

Oliver, Edna May obit Jan 43

Olivier, Laurence Jun 46

Olmstead, Albert Ten Eyck obit May 45

Olsen, John Sigvard, and Johnson, Harold Ogden Sep 40

O'Mahoney, Joseph C(hristopher) Oct 45

O'Melveny, Henry W(illiam) obit Jun 41

O'Neal, Edward A(sbury, 3d) Sep 46

O'Neal, Frederick (Douglas) Nov 46

O'Neil, George obit Jul 40

Oppenheim, E(dward) Phillips obit Mar 46

Oppenheimer, Franz obit Nov 43

Oppenheimer, J. Robert Nov 45

Orlando, Vittorio Emanuele Feb 44

Orlebar, Augustus H. obit Sep 43

Orlemanski, Stanislaus, Rev. Jun 44

Ormandy, Eugene Jan 41

Orozco, José Clemente Sep 40

Orr, H(iram) Winnett Oct 41

Orr, Sir John Boyd Jun 46

Orsborn, Albert (William Thomas) Nov 46

Ortiz, Roberto M. obit Sep 42

Orton, Helen Fuller Jan 41

Osato, Sono Oct 45

Osborn, Frederick (Henry) Nov 41

Osborne, Oliver Thomas obit Yrbk 40

Osborne, William Hamilton obit Feb 43

O'Shea, William F(rancis), Bishop obit Apr 45

Osmeña, Sergio Sep 44

Osumi, Mineo Osumi, Baron obit Apr 41

Otero, Miguel Antonio obit Sep 44

Ott, Mel(vin Thomas) Jul 41

Ottinger, Nathan obit Jan 41

Ottley, Roi (Vincent) Oct 43

Otto of Austria, Archduke Jun 41

Oumansky, Constantine (Alexandrovitch) biog Feb 41 obit Mar 45

Oursler, Charles Fulton See Oursler, F. Oct 42

Oursler, Fulton Oct 42

Overman, Lynne obit Apr 43

Owen, A(rthur) David K(emp) May 46

Owen, Ruth Bryan Dec 44

Owen, Steve Dec 46

Owens, Clarence Julian obit Apr 41

Owens, Robert Bowie obit Yrbk 40

Oxenham, John obit Mar 41

Oxford and Asquith, Margot (Tennant) Asquith, Countess of obit Sep 45

Oxnam, G(arfield) Bromley, Bishop Nov 44

Paasikivi, Juho Kusti May 44

Pacciardi, Randolfo Mar 44

Pace, Charles Ashford obit Feb 41

Pacelli, Eugenio See Pius XII, Pope Apr 41

Packard, Eleanor Apr 41

Packard, Frank L(ucius) obit Apr 42

Packard, Winthrop obit May 43

Paddock, Charles W(illiam) obit Sep 43

Paddon, Harry Locke obit Jan-Feb 40

Paderewski, Ignace Jan obit Aug 41

Padilla, Ezequiel Jul 42

Padilla Nervo, Luis Dec 46

Page, Marie Danforth obit Mar 40

Pagnanelli, George See Carlson, J. R. Oct 43

Pai Tsung-hsi See Li Tsung-jen and Pai Tsung-hsi Nov 42

Palencia, Isabel de May 41

Paléologue, (Georges) Maurice obit Jan 45

Paley, William Samuel Oct 40

Palmer, Albert deForest obit Jan-Feb 40

Palmer, James Lynwood obit Aug 41

Palmer, John Leslie obit Sep 44

Pandit, Mrs. Ranjit See Pandit, V. L. Jan 46

Pandit, Vijaya Lakshmi Jan 46

Papandreou, George (Andreas) Dec 44

Papashvily, George, and Papashvily, Helen (Waite) Mar 45

Papashvily, Helen (Waite) See Papashvily, G. and Papashvily, H. W. Mar 45

Pape, William Jamieson Jan-Jun 40

Papen, Franz von Jun 41

Papi, Gennaro obit Jan 42

Paradise, N(athaniel) Burton obit Jun 42

Pardee, George C(ooper) obit Oct 41

Peres, Sir Bernard Jan 46

Parke, William obit Sep 41

Parker, Barnett obit Oct 41

Parker, Homer Cling obit Jul 46

Parker, Louis N(apoleon) obit Nov 44

Parma, V. Valta obit Nov 41

Parmoor, Charles Alfred Cripps, 1st Baron obit Aug 41

Parodi, Alexandre Jun 46

Parr, A(lbert) E(ide) Jul 42

Parran, Thomas Aug 40

Parri, Ferruccio Nov 45

Parseval, August von obit Apr 42

Parsons, Elsie Worthington obit Feb 42

Parsons, Herbert Collins obit Jul 41

Parsons, Louella Oct 40

Partch, Virgil F(ranklin) Jul 46

Partridge, Sir Bernard obit Sep 45

Partridge, Frank C(harles) obit Apr 43

Pascal, Gabriel Jan 42

Pasquel, Jorge Jul 46

Passos, John Dos See Dos Passos, J. Aug 40

Pasternack, Josef Alexander obit Jan-Jun 40

Pasvolsky, Leo May 45

Patch, Alexander M(cCarrell, Jr.) biog May 43 obit Jan 46

Patiño, Simón I(turi) Oct 42

Patman, (John William) Wright Feb 46

Paton, Stewart obit Mar 42

Patri, Angelo Nov 40

Patrick, Mary Mills obit Mar 40

Patrick, Mason Mathews obit Mar 42

Pattee, Alida Frances obit May 42

Patten, Gilbert obit Mar 45

Patterson, Eleanor Medill Nov 40

Patterson, Joseph M(edill) biog Jan 42 obit Jun 46

Patterson, Richard C(unningham), Jr. Oct 46

Patterson, Robert P(orter) Oct 41

Ruffing, Charles H(erbert) Nov 41

Rugg, Harold (Ordway) May 41

Ruiz Guiñazú, Enrique Apr 42

Rukeyser, Muriel Mar 43

Ruml, Beardsley May 43

Rumpler, Edmund obit Oct 40

Rundstedt, Gerd von See Rundstedt, K. R. G., von Nov 41

Rundstedt, Karl (Rudolf Gerd) von Nov 41

Runkle, Erwin W(illiam) obit Apr 41

Runyon, Alfred Damon See Runyon, D. Nov 42

Runyon, Damon Nov 42

Rupertus, William H(enry) obit May 45

Rusby, Henry H(urd) obit Jan 41

Rüshdi, Tevfik, Bey See Aras, T. R. Jun 42

Rushmore, David Barker obit Jul 40

Rusk, Howard A(rchibald) Mar 46

Russell, Bertrand Arthur William, 3rd Earl Apr 40

Russell, Charles (Edward) obit Jun 41

Russell, Charles Ellsworth See Russell, P. W. Aug 44

Russell, Herbrand Arthur, 11th Duke of Bedford See Bedford, H. A. R., 11th Duke of obit Oct 40

Russell, James Earl obit Dec 45

Russell, Mary Annette Russell, Countess obit Mar 41

Russell, Pee Wee Aug 44

Russell, Rosalind Jan 43

Rust, Bernhard Jul 42

Rutenberg, Pinhas obit Mar 42

Ruth, Babe Aug 44

Ruth, George Herman See Ruth, B. Aug 44

Rutherford, Joseph Franklin biog Nov 40 obit Mar 42

Rutledge, Brett See Paul, E. Jan-Feb 40

Rutledge, Wiley (Blount), Jr. May 43

Ryan, John (Augustine), Msgr. obit Oct 45

Ryan, T(ubal) Claude Jan 43

Ryti, Risto (Heikkie) Feb 41

Saarinen, Eliel Oct 42

Sabath, Adolph J(oachim) Jul 46

Sabatier, Paul obit Oct 41

Sabin, Florence R(ena) Apr 45

Sabry, Hassan, Pasha obit Yrbk 40

Sachs, Bernard obit Mar 44

Sachs, Curt Aug 44

Sackett, Frederic M(oseley), Jr. obit Jul 41

Sadler, Sir Michael (Ernest) obit Dec 43

Saerchinger, César Apr 40

Sage, Dean obit Aug 43

Saint Exupéry, Antoine de biog Jan-Feb 40 obit May 45

Saint-Gaudens, Homer (Schiff) Oct 41

St. George, Thomas R(ichard) Jan 44

St. John, Robert Jun 42

Saionji, Kimmochi, Prince obit Jan 41

Sakel, Manfred Jan 41

Salazar, Antonio de Oliveira May 41

Salten, Felix obit Nov 45

Salter, Alfred obit Sep 45

Salter, Andrew May 44

Salter, Sir (James) Arthur Mar 44

Saltonstall, Leverett Jun 44

Salvemini, Gaetano Dec 43

Samaroff, Olga Mar 46

Sanborn, (John) Pitts obit Apr 41

Sandburg, Carl Jan-Jun 40

Sandefer, Jefferson Davis obit Apr 40

Sanders, George Jun 43

Sanders, Jared Young obit May 44

Sanger, Margaret (Higgins) Aug 44

San Martín, Ramón Grau See Grau San Martín, R. Oct 44

Santayana, George Apr 44

Saposs, David Nov 40

Saracoglu, Sükrü Jun 42

Sarajoglu Shukri, Bey See Saracoglu, S. Jun 42

Sarg, Tony obit Apr 42

Sargent, (Harold) Malcolm (Watts) Dec 45

Sargent, Porter (Edward) Jul 41

Sarnoff, David Nov 40

Sarojini, Nayadu See Naidu, S. May 43

Saroyan, William Jul 40

Sarton, George (Alfred Léon) Jul 42

Sauckel, Fritz obit Nov 46

Sauer, Emil von obit Jun 42

Saunders, Hilary A(idan) St. George Jun 43

Saunders, John Monk obit Apr 40

Savage, Augusta (Christine) Jan 41

Savage, John Lucian Apr 43

Savage, Michael Joseph obit Apr 40

Saxon, Lyle obit May 46

Saxton, Alexander (Plaisted) Nov 43

Sayao, Bidu Feb 42

Sayles, R(obert) W(ilcox) obit Dec 42

Sayre, Francis Bowes Jan-Feb 40

Schacht, Al(exander) May 46

Schacht, Hjalmar (Horace Greeley) Oct 44

Schain, Josephine Jul 45

Schechter, A(bel) A(lan) May 41

Scheiberling, Edward N(icholas) Dec 44

Schelling, Ernest Henry obit Jan-Feb 40

Scherer, Paul (Ehrman), Rev. May 41

Schereschewsky, Joseph Williams obit Sep 40

Scherman, Harry Sep 43

Schertzinger, Victor obit Dec 41

Schiaparelli, Elsa Jan-Feb 40

Schick, Béla Jul 44

Schilder, Paul Ferdinand obit Jan 41

Schillinger, Joseph obit May 43

Schlauch, Margaret Dec 42

Schleich, Michel, Rev. obit Jun 45

Schlesinger, Arthur M(eier), Jr. Oct 46

Schlesinger, Frank obit Aug 43

Schlink, Frederick John Mar 41

Schlosser, Alex L. obit Mar 43

Schmelkes, Franz C(arl) obit Feb 43

Schmidt, Fritz obit Aug 43

Schmitt, Bernadotte E(verly) Dec 42

Schmitt, Gladys (Leonore) Mar 43

Schnabel, Artur Jul 42

Schneider, Eugene obit Jan 43

Schneider, Hannes Mar 41

Schneiderman, Rose Feb 46

Schoen-René, Anna Eugéne obit Jan 43

Schoenberg, Arnold Apr 42

Schoff, Hannah Kent obit Feb 41

Schofield, Frank H(erman) obit Apr 42

Schönberg, Arnold See Schoenberg, A. Apr 42

Schoonmaker, Edwin Davies obit Jan-Jun 40

Schorr, Friedrich Jul 42

Schram, Emil Oct 41

Schratt, Katharina obit May 40

Schreiber, Georges May 43

Schrembs, Archbishop Joseph obit Dec 45

Schroeder, R(udolph) W(illiam) Jul 41

Schuchert, Charles obit Jan 43

Schulberg, Budd (Wilson) Jun 41

Schuller, Mary Craig McGeachy See McGeachy, M.A.C. Apr 44

Schulte, Karl Joseph, Cardinal obit May 41

Schulthess, Edmund obit Jun 44

Schultz, Sigrid (Lillian) Apr 44

Schulz, Leo obit Oct 44

Schuman, William (Howard) Jun 42

Schurman, Jacob G(ould) obit Oct 42

Schuster, Max Lincoln See Simon, R. L. and Schuster, M. L. Jul 41

Schwellenbach, Lewis B(axter) Jun 45

Schwidetzky, Oscar (Otto Rudolf) Dec 43

Scobie, Ronald M(acKenzie) Feb 45

Scott, Arthur Carroll obit Yrbk 40

Scott, C(yril) Kay- See Wellman, F. C. Feb 44

Scott, Hazel (Dorothy) Aug 43

Scott, James B(rown) obit Aug 43

Scott, John R. K. obit Feb 46

Scott, Raymond Jul 41

Scott, Robert L(ee), Jr. Oct 43

Scott, Tom Nov 46

Scrugham, James Graves obit Jul 45

Scudder, Janet obit Jul 40

Seabrook, William B(euhler) biog Nov 40 obit Oct 45

Seabury, David Sep 41

Seagrave, Gordon S(tifler) Nov 43

Searing, Annie E(liza) P(idgeon) obit Jun 42

Sears, William Joseph, Sr. obit May 44

Seger, George N. obit Oct 40

Seghers, Anna Dec 42

Seibert, Florence B(arbara) Nov 42

Seibold, Louis obit Jun 45

Seid, Ruth See Sinclair, J. Mar 46

Seitz, George B. obit Aug 44

Selassie, Haile, I See Haile Selassie I, Emperor of Ethiopia Apr 41

Seldes, George Feb 41

Self, Sir Henry (Albert) Oct 42

Selfridge, H(arry) Gordon Mar 41

Sélincourt, Ernest de See De Sélincourt, E. obit Jul 43

Sell, Hildegarde Loretta See Hildegarde Nov 44

Selwyn, Edgar obit Apr 44

Selznick, David O(liver) Jun 41

Selznick, Myron obit May 44

Semon, Waldo Lonsbury Yrbk 40

Senarens, Luis Philip obit Jan-Feb 40

Seredy, Kate May 40

Sergio, Lisa Jun 44

Sergius, Metropolitan obit Jul 44

Serkin, Rudolf Jul 40

Serlin, Oscar Mar 43

Serrano Suñer, Ramón Nov 40

Sert, José Maria obit Jan 46

Seton, Ernest Thompson biog May 43 obit Dec 46

Sevareid, Arnold Eric See Sevareid, E. Jul 42

Sevareid, Eric Jul 42

Severance, H(arold) Craig obit Nov 41

Seversky, Alexander Procofieff de See De Seversky, A. P. Feb 41

Sevier, Henry Hulme obit Mar 40

Sevitzky, Fabien Jul 46

Sewell, James Luther See Sewell, L. Nov 44

Sewell, Luke Nov 44

Sexton, W(alton) R(oswell) obit Oct 43

Seymour, Charles May 41

Seymour, Flora Warren Jun 42

Seymour, Harriet Ayer obit Sep 44

Seyss-Inquart, Artur von biog May 41 obit Nov 46

Sforza, Carlo, Count Jun 42

Shambaugh, Benjamin Franklin obit May 40

Shang Chen Jul 44

Shannon, Peggy obit Jul 41

Shapiro, Karl (Jay) Oct 44

Shapley, Harlow Jan 41

Shaposhnikov, Boris M(ikhailovitch) biog Mar 42 obit May 45

Sharp, Harry Clay obit Yrbk 40

Shaver, Dorothy Jan 46

Shaver, Mary (Mumpere) obit Mar 42

Shaw, Artie May 41

Shaw, (George) Bernard Jun 44

Shaw, Henry (Larned Keith) obit May 41

Shaw, Irwin Oct 42

Shaw, Lau Oct 45

Shaw, Lloyd Sep 43

Shaw, Louis Agassiz obit Oct 40

Shawcross, Sir Hartley (William) Dec 45

Shawkey, Morris Purdy obit Apr 41

Shear, T(heodore) Leslie obit Aug 45

Shearer, Augustus H(unt) obit Jul 41

Sheckell, Thomas O. obit Apr 43

Sheean, Vincent Aug 41

Sheehan, Winfield R. obit Aug 45

Sheen, Fulton J(ohn), Mgr. Nov 41

Sheldon, Charles M(onroe), Rev. obit Apr 46

Sheldon, Edward (Brewster) obit May 46

Shellabarger, Samuel May 45

Sheppard, Morris obit Jun 41

Sherard, Robert Harborough obit Mar 43

Sherley, Swager obit Apr 41

Sherman, Frederic Fairchild obit Yrbk 40

Sherrod, Robert (Lee) Jun 44

Sherwood, Robert Jan-Jun 40

Shiber, Etta Dec 43

Shidehara, Kijuro, Baron Apr 46

Shifrin, Aleksandr Mikhailovich See Werner, M. Dec 43

Shigemitsu, Mamoru Jun 43

Shih, Hu See Hu Shih Feb 42

Shimazaki, Tôson obit Oct 43

Shine, F(rancis) W(ayles) obit Nov 41

Shinn, Florence Scovel obit Yrbk 40

Shinn, Milicent Washburn obit Oct 40

Shinwell, Emanuel Jan 43

Shiras, George obit May 42

Shirer, William L(awrence) Jul 41

Sholokhov, Mikhail (Aleksandrovitch) Jan 42

Shone, Terence Allen Nov 46

Shore, Dinah Jun 42

Short, Walter C(ampbell) Jan 46

Shostakovich, Dmitri May 41

Shotwell, James T(homson) Oct 44

Shoulders, Harrison H. Nov 46

Shoup, Oliver Henry obit Nov 40

Shreeve, Herbert Edward obit Jun 42

Shreve, R(ichmond) H(arold) biog Nov 45 obit Oct 46

Shridharani, Krishnalal (Jethalal) Jan 42

Shu, Ch'ing-ch'un See Shaw, L. Oct 45

Shumlin, Herman (Elliott) Mar 41

Shuster, George N(auman) Jan 41

Shute, Nevil Jul 42

Sickert, Walter Richard obit Mar 42

Sigerist, Henry Ernest Sep 40

Sikorski, Wladyslaw biog Jan-Feb 40 obit Aug 43

Sikorsky, Igor Ivan Oct 40

Siles, Hernando obit Jan 43

Sillanpää, Frans Eemil Jan-Feb 40

Silver, Abba Hillel, Rabbi Dec 41

Silzer, George Sebastian obit Yrbk 40

Simkhovitch, Mary (Melinda) K(ingsbury) Mar 43

Simmons, Furnifold McLendell obit Jan-Jun 40

Simms, Hilda Nov 44

Simms, Ruth Hanna McCormick obit Feb 45

Simon, Charlie May Yrbk 46

Simon, John Allsebrook, 1st Viscount Jul 40

Simon, Richard L(eo), and Schuster, M(ax) Lincoln Jul 41

Simonds, Frederic W(illiam) obit May 41

Simonds, G(uy) G. Oct 43
Simpson, Helen de Guerry obit Yrbk 40
Simpson, Kenneth F(arrand) obit Mar 41
Simpson, William H(ood) Feb 45
Sinatra, Frank Jun 43
Sinclair, Sir Archibald, 4th Baronet Sep 40
Sinclair, Jo Mar 46
Sinclair, May obit Dec 46
Sinclair-Cowan, Bertha Muzzy See Bower, B .M. obit Sep 40
Sinding, Christian obit Jan 42
Singer, Israel J(oshua) obit Mar 44
Singer, Richard obit Mar 40
Sitgreaves, Beverley obit Sep 43
Skidmore, Hubert Standish obit Mar 46
Skilton, Charles Sanford obit May 41
Skinner, Cornelia Otis Jan 42
Skinner, Otis obit Feb 42
Skouras, Spyros P(anagiotes) Jun 43
Slaughter, Frank G(ill) Oct 42
Slim, Sir William Joseph Jun 45
Sloan, Alfred Pritchard, Jr. Nov 40
Sloan, Samuel obit May 45
Slye, Maud Yrbk 40
Small, John D(avis) Feb 46
Small, John Humphrey obit Sep 46
Smart, David A. Jun 44
Smedley, Agnes Jan 44
Smedley, Constance obit Apr 41
Smetona, Antanas obit Feb 44
Smith, Albert W(illiam) obit Oct 42
Smith, Alfred E(manuel) biog Sep 44 obit Nov 44
Smith, Sir Ben Oct 45
Smith, Betty (Wehner) Nov 43
Smith, (Sir) C(harles) Aubrey Sep 44
Smith, Clara E(liza) obit Jul 43
Smith, Clyde Harold obit May 40
Smith, C(yrus) R(owlett) Sep 45
Smith, Lady Eleanor (Furneaux) obit Nov 45
Smith, E(llison) DuRant obit Jan 45
Smith, Ernest Bramah See Bramah, E. obit Sep 42
Smith, Sir George Adam, Rev. obit Apr 42
Smith, Gerald L(yman) K(enneth) Aug 43
Smith, Harold D(ewey) Jul 43
Smith, H(arry) Allen May 42
Smith, Holland M(cTyeire) Apr 45

Smith, Howard K(ingsbury) Mar 43
Smith, Howard W(orth) Feb 41
Smith, Ida B. Wise Feb 43
Smith, Kate Yrbk 40
Smith, Lillian (Eugenia) May 44
Smith, Logan Pearsall obit Apr 46
Smith, Margaret Chase Feb 45
Smith, Paul C(lifford) Apr 43
Smith, Rex Jan 42
Smith, Roy Burnett obit Feb 41
Smith, Thomas R(obert) obit Jun 42
Smith, Walter Bedell Apr 44
Smith, Wilbur Fisk obit Sep 40
Smoot, Reed obit Mar 41
Smuts, Jan Christiaan Aug 41
Smyth, Dame Ethel Mary obit Jun 44
Snell, Foster Dee Jan 43
Snell, Henry Bayley obit Mar 43
Snell, Henry Snell, 1st Baron May 41
Snook, H(omer) Clyde obit Nov 42
Snow, Edgar (Parks) Jun 41
Snyder, Alice D(orothea) obit Ap 43
Snyder, J(ohn) Buell obit Apr 46
Snyder, John W(esley) Jul 45
Sockman, Ralph W(ashington), Rev. Jun 46
Sodero, Cesare Mar 43
Soglow, Otto Sep 40
Soheily, Ali Sep 43
Sokolsky, George E(phraim) May 41
Somervell, Brehon (Burke) Aug 42
Somerville, Sir James (Fownes) Apr 43
Somoza, Anastasio Jun 42
Soong, Chingling See Sun Yatsen, Mme. Apr 44
Soong, T. V. Mar 41
Sorokin, Pitirim A(lexandrovitch) Jul 42
Soukup, Frantisek obit Yrbk 40
Soule, George (Henry, Jr.) Dec 45
Southworth, Billy Nov 44
Southworth, James L(arry) See Hingson, R. A., Edwards, W. B., and Southworth, J. L. Jun 43
Southworth, William H. See Southworth, B. Nov 44
Soyer, Isaac; Soyer, Moses; and Soyer, Raphael Mar 41
Spaak, Paul-Henri May 45
Spaatz, Carl Sep 42
Spaeth, Sigmund Jul 42
Spalding, Albert Jan 44
Spangler, Harrison E(arl) Aug 43
Spaulding, Rolland H(arty) obit May 42
Speaks, John Charles obit Dec 45

Spearman, Charles E. obit Oct 45
Spellman, Francis Joseph, Archbishop Apr 40
Spence, Hartzell Oct 42
Spence, John Hartzell See Spence, H. Oct 42
Spender, J. Alfred obit Aug 42
Spender, Stephen Jan-Feb 40
Sperry, Armstrong Oct 41
Sperti, George Speri Jan-Feb 40
Spiller, William Gibson obit Apr 40
Spitalny, Phil Oct 40
Spottswood, James obit Yrbk 40
Sprague, Embert Hiram obit Mar 40
Spring, Howard Jan 41
Sproul, Robert Gordon Jul 45
Spruance, Raymond Ames Apr 44
Spry, Constance May 40
Spurgeon, Caroline F(rances) E(leanor) obit Dec 42
Squires, Richard Anderson obit May 40
Stachouwer, Alidius Warmoldus Lambertus Tjarda Van Starkenborgh See Starkenborgh Stachouwer, A. W. L. T. van Feb 42
Stacy, Walter P(arker) Jan 46
Stagg, (Amos) Alonzo Mar 44
Stalin, Joseph Mar 42
Stamp, Josiah Charles Stamp, 1st Baron obit Jun 41
Standish, Burt L. See Patten, G. obit Mar 45
Standley, W(illiam) H(arrison) May 42
Stanfield, Robert Nelson obit Jun 45
Stanley, Freelan O. obit Nov 40
Stanley, Oliver (Frederick George) Apr 43
Stanley, Winifred (C.) Jun 43
Stanton, Frank Nov 45
Stark, Harold Raynsford May 40
Stark, Louis Jun 45
Starkenborgh Stachouwer A(lidius) W(armoldus) L(ambertus) Tjarda van Feb 42
Starr, Mark Jul 46
Stassen, Harold Edward May 40
Stauning, Thorvald obit Jun 42
Stauss, Emil George von obit Feb 43
Steagall, Henry Bascom obit Jan 44
Stearns, Harold E(dmund) obit Oct 43
Stebbins, George Coles obit Nov 45
Steber, Eleanor Mar 43
Steel, Johannes Jun 41
Steel, Kurt See Kagey, R. obit Jun 46
Steele, Frederick Dorr obit Aug 44

Vincent, Leon H(enry) obit Apr 41

Vinson, Carl Apr 42

Vinson, Fred(erick) M(oore) Aug 43

Vishinsky, Andrei Y(anuarievich) May 44

Voice of Experience See Taylor, M. S. obit Mar 42

Volterra, Vito obit Yrbk 40

Von Arco, Georg Wilhelm Alexander Hans, Graf See Arco, G. W. A. H., Graf von obit Jan-Jun 40

Von Bock, Fedor See Bock, F. von biog Oct 42 obit Jun 45

Von Brauchitsch, Heinrich Alfred Hermann Walther See Brauchitsch, H. A. H. W. von Mar 40

Von Dardel, Nils See Dardel, N. von obit Jul 43

Von Galen, Clemens August, Cardinal, Count See Galen, C. A., Cardinal, Count von obit Apr 46

Von Hagen, Victor Wolfgang Mar 42

Von Hammerstein-Equord, Kurt See Hammerstein-Equord, K. von obit Jun 43

Von Heidenstam, Karl Gustaf Verner See Heidenstam, V. von obit Jul 40

Von Kállay, Nicolas See Kállay de Nagy Kálló, M. Jun 42

Von Keitel, Wilhelm See Keitel, W. von biog Sep 40 obit Nov 46

Von Kleist, Paul Ludwig Ewald See Kleist, P. L. E. von Jul 43

Von Klenze, Camillo See Klenze, C. von obit Apr 43

Von Mannerheim, Carl Gustaf Emil, Baron See Mannerheim, C. G. E., Baron von Apr 40

Von Manstein, Fritz Erich See Manstein, F. E. von Oct 42

Von Paassen, Pierre See Van Paassen, P. Oct 42

Von Papen, Franz See Papen, F. von Jun 41

Von Parseval, August See Parseval, A. von obit Apr 42

Von Reichenau, Walter See Reichenau, W. von obit Mar 42

Von Ribbentrop, Joachim See Ribbentrop, J. von biog May 41 obit Nov 46

Von Rundstedt, Gerd See Rundstedt, K. R. G. von Nov 41

Von Rundstedt, Karl Rudolf Gerd See Rundstedt, K. R. G. von Nov 41

Von Sauer, Emil See Sauer, E. von obit Jun 42

Von Seyss-Inquart Artur See Seyss-Inquart A. von biog May 41 obit Nov 46

Von Stauss, Emil Georg See Stauss, E. G. von obit Feb 43

Von Tempski, Armine See Tempski, Armine von obit Jan 44

Von Tilzer, Harry obit Mar 46

Von Wagner-Jauregg, Julius See Wagner-Jauregg, J. von obit Nov 40

Von Zell, Harry Jun 44

Von Zemlinsky, Alexander See Zemlinsky, A. von obit May 42

Voorhis, Horace Jerry See Voorhis, J. Aug 41

Voorhis, Jerry Aug 41

Voronoff, Serge Jan 41

Voroshilov, Klementii (Efremovich) Mar 41

Wadhams, Robert Pelton obit Feb 41

Wadiyar, Sri Krishnaraja, Bahadur Maharaja of Mysore obit Sep 40

Wadsworth, James W(olcott) Jul 43

Waesche, Russell R(andolph) biog Mar 45 obit Dec 46

Wagner, Robert F(erdinand) May 41

Wagner-Jauregg, Julius von obit Nov 40

Wainwright, Jonathan M(ayhew) May 42

Waite, Alice Vinton obit May 43

Waite, Henry Matson obit Oct 44

Wakasugi, Kename obit Jan 44

Wakefield, Charles Cheers Wakefield, 1st Viscount obit Mar 41

Wakeman, Frederic Sep 46

Wake-Walker, Sir William Frederick obit Oct 45

Waksman, Selman A(braham) May 46

Wald, Lillian D. obit Oct 40

Walden, Percy Talbot obit May 43

Wales, George Canning obit May 40

Walker, Frank Comerford Oct 40

Walker, Margaret (Abigail) Nov 43

Walker, Stanley Nov 44

Walker, Stuart obit May 41

Wall, Evander Berry obit Jan-Jun 40

Wallace, (David) Euan obit Apr 41

Wallace, DeWitt Apr 44

Wallace, Henry Agard Aug 40

Wallace, Thomas W. obit Sep 43

Wallenstein, Alfred May 40

Waller, Fats biog Apr 42 obit Feb 44

Waller, Thomas Wright See Waller, F. biog Apr 42 obit Feb 44

Waln, Nora Jan-Feb 40

Walpole, Sir Hugh (Seymour) obit Jul 41

Walsh, George Ethelbert obit Apr 41

Walsh, James J(oseph) obit Apr 42

Walsh, J(ohn) Raymond Nov 46

Walsh, Joseph obit Mar 46

Walsh, William Henry obit May 41

Walsh, William Thomas Jul 41

Walter, Bruno Nov 42

Walter, Eugene obit Nov 41

Walter, Wilmer obit Oct 41

Walton, William Turner Mar 40

Wambaugh, Eugene obit Sep 40

Wambaugh, Sarah Apr 46

Wanamaker, Pearl A(nderson) Sep 46

Wang Ching-wei biog May 40 obit Jan 45

Wang Shih-chieh Sep 45

Wank, Roland (Anthony) Dec 43

Ward, Christopher L(ongstreth) obit Apr 43

Ward, Lem obit Jan 43

Ward, Mary Jane Jun 46

Waring, Fred Sep 40

Waring, George J., Mgr. obit Apr 43

Waring, Roane Dec 43

Warner, Albert Jan 45

Warner, Harry M(orris) Jan 45

Warner, Jack L. Jan 45

Warner, Milo J(oseph) Nov 41

Warren, Althea (Hester) Feb 42

Warren, Earl Jan 44

Warren, Harry Jun 43

Warren, Harry Marsh, Rev. obit Feb 41

Warren, Whitney obit Mar 43

Wash, Carlyle H(ilton) obit Mar 43

Wasilewska, Wanda Jul 44

Wason, Betty Aug 43

Wason, Edward H(ill) obit Apr 41

Wason, Robert R(oss) Jan 46

Waste, William Harrison obit Jul 40

Waterlow, Sir Sydney P(hilip) obit Jan 45

Waters, Ethel Apr 41

Waters, James R. obit Jan 46

Watrous, George Dutton obit Yrbk 40

Watrous, Harry Willson obit Jan-Jun 40

Watson, Clarence Wayland obit Jul 40

Watson, Edwin M(artin) obit Apr 45

Watson, John B(roadus) Oct 42

Watson, Mark S(kinner) Nov 46

Watson, Samuel Newell, Rev. obit May 42

Watson, Thomas John Nov 40

Watson-Watt, Sir Robert (Alexander) Sep 45

Watt, Robert J. Mar 45

Watts, Lyle F(ord) Oct 46

Waugh, Frederick Judd obit Oct 40

Wavell, Sir Archibald (Percival) Mar 41

Weagant, Roy A(lexander) obit Oct 42

Weaver, Affie obit Jan 41

Weaver, Arthur J. obit Nov 45

Weaver, Walter Reed obit Dec 44

Webb, Beatrice obit Jun 43

Webb, Clifton Mar 43

Webb, James E(dwin) Oct 46

Webb, Walter Loring obit Mar 41

Weber, Joseph M. obit Jul 42

Weber, Louis Lawrence obit Mar 40

Weber, Max Jun 41

Webster, H(arold) T(ucker) Mar 45

Webster, Margaret May 40

Wecter, Dixon Nov 44

Wedemeyer, Albert C(oady) Jan 45

Wedgwood, Josiah C(lement), 1st Baron Wedgwood of Barlaston biog Apr 42 obit Sep 43

Wedgwood of Barlaston, Josiah Clement Wedgwood, 1st Baron See Wedgwood, J. C., 1st Baron Wedgwood of Barlaston biog Apr 42 obit Sep 43

Wei Tao-ming Dec 42

Weidman, Charles See Humphrey, D. and Weidman, C. Apr 42

Weidman, Jerome Aug 42

Weigle, Luther Allan Mar 46

Weill, Kurt Dec 41

Weingartner, Felix obit Jun 42

Weir, Ernest T(ener) Jun 41

Weiss, Soma obit Mar 42

Weisse, Faneuil Suydam obit Mar 40

Weitzenkorn, Louis obit Mar 43

Weizmann, Chaim Nov 42

Welch, William A(ddams) obit Jun 41

Weld, John May 40

Welles, Orson May 41

Welles, Sumner Mar 40

Wellman, Frederick Creighton Feb 44

Wells, Carolyn obit May 42

Wells, Gabriel obit Dec 46

Wells, H(arry) Gideon obit Jun 43

Wells, H(erbert) G(eorge) obit Sep 46

Wells, Peter Aug 42

Welsh, Herbert obit Sep 41

Welty, Eudora Jan 42

Wenckebach, Karel Friedrich obit Yrbk 40

Wendt, Gerald Louis Mar 40

Wenner-Gren, Axel (Leonard) Oct 42

Werfel, Franz biog Yrbk 40 obit Sep 45

Werne, Isaac, Rabbi obit Mar 40

Werner, Max Dec 43

Werntz, Carl N. obit Dec 44

Werth, Alexander Apr 43

Wertheimer, Max obit Dec 43

Wesley, Charles H(arris) Mar 44

West, Annie Blythe obit May 41

West, Claudine obit May 43

West, Nathanael obit Feb 41

Westcott, John Howell obit Jul 42

Westley, Helen obit Feb 43

Westminster, Archbishop of See Hinsley, A., Cardinal obit Apr 43

Westmore, Perc Oct 45

Wetter, Ernst Feb 42

Weyerhaeuser, Frederick E(dward) obit Nov 45

Weyerhaeuser, Rudolph M(ichael) obit Sep 46

Weygand, Maxime Jan-June 40

Weymouth, Frank E(lwin) obit Sep 41

Whalen, Grover A(loysius) Sep 44

Wheat, Alfred Adams obit Apr 43

Wheat, William Howard obit Apr 44

Wheaton, Elizabeth Lee Jan 42

Wheeler, Burton Kendall Aug 40

Wheelock, Warren Mar 40

Wheelwright, John B. obit Nov 40

Wherry, Kenneth S(picer) Apr 46

Whipple, Maurine Mar 41

Whipple, Wayne obit Dec 42

White, Frank obit May 40

White, Harry D(exter) Sep 44

White, Helen C(onstance) Jul 45

White, Josh Aug 44

White, Margaret Bourke Jan-Feb 40

White, Paul W. Mar 40

White, Portia Mar 45

White, S(ebastian) Harrison obit Feb 46

White, Stewart Edward obit Nov 46

White, Trumbull obit Feb 42

White, Walter (Francis) Apr 42

White, Wilbert Webster, Rev. obit Oct 44

White, William Allen biog Nov 40 obit Apr 44

White, William L(indsay) Jan 43

Whitehouse, Sir Harold Beckwith obit Sep 43

Whiteman, Paul Aug 45

Whiteman, Wilberforce James obit Jan-Feb 40

Whitford, Harry Nichols obit Jul 41

Whitney, Gertrude (Vanderbilt) biog Jul 41 obit Yrbk 42

Whitney, A(lexander) F(ell) Feb 46

Whitney, John Hay Dec 45

Whittle, Frank Jan 45

Whittlesey, Charles F. obit Feb 41

Whitty, Dame May Dec 45

Wiart, Adrian Carton de See Carton de Wiart, A. May 40

Wick, Frances G(ertrude) obit Aug 41

Wickard, Claude Raymond Oct 40

Wicker, Ireene Apr 43

Wickware, Francis Graham obit Yrbk 40

Wiedoeft, Rudy obit Mar 40

Wiggam, Albert Edward Jul 42

Wilbur, Bernice M(arion) Sep 43

Wilby, Francis B(owditch) Aug 45

Wilcox, Herbert See Neagle, A. and Wilcox, H. Nov 45

Wilcox, J(ohn) W(alter), Jr. obit May 42

Wilder, Thornton (Niven) Aug 43

Wile, Frederic William obit Jun 41

Wile, Ira S(olomon) obit Nov 43

Wiley, William Foust obit Oct 44

Wilgus, Sidney Dean obit Mar 40

Wilhelm II, Former German Kaiser obit Jul 41

Wilhelmina, Queen of The Netherlands Jan-Jun 40

Wilkins, T(homas) Russell obit Feb 41

Wilkinson, Ellen (Cicely) Jul 41

Willard, John obit Nov 42

Willet, Anne Lee obit Mar 43

William II, Emperor See Wilhelm II, Former German Kaiser obit Jul 41

Williams, Alford Joseph, Jr. Oct 40

Williams, Aubrey May 40

Williams, Emlyn Feb 41

Williams, Francis Mar 46

Williams, Gluyas Jun 46

Williams, John D. obit May 41

Williams, Joseph John, Father obit Yrbk 40

Williams, Paul R. Mar 41

Williams, Ralph E. obit Jul 40

Williams, Tennessee Jan 46

Williams, Thomas Sutler obit May 40

Williams, Tom Apr 46

Williams, William Robert obit Jan 41

Williams, Wythe Oct 43

Willingdon, Freeman Freeman-Thomas, 1st Marquess of obit Oct 41

Willison, George F(indlay) Jan 46

Willkie, Wendell L(ewis) biog Jan-Feb 40 obit Nov 44

Willoughby, Charles C(lark) obit Jun 43

Wills, C. Harold obit Feb 41

Willson, Beckles obit Nov 42